Revenue Law—
principles and practice

Revenue Law— principles and practice

Ninth edition

Chris Whitehouse
BA, BCL, Barrister

Elizabeth Stuart-Buttle
LLB, Solicitor

Butterworths
London, Dublin, Edinburgh
1991

United Kingdom	Butterworth & Co (Publishers) Ltd, 88 Kingsway, LONDON WC2B 6AB and 4 Hill Street, EDINBURGH EH2 3JZ
Australia	Butterworths Pty Ltd, SYDNEY, MELBOURNE, BRISBANE, ADELAIDE, PERTH, CANBERRA and HOBART
Canada	Butterworths Canada Ltd, TORONTO and VANCOUVER
Ireland	Butterworth (Ireland) Ltd, DUBLIN
Malaysia	Malayan Law Journal Sdn Bhd, KUALA LUMPUR
New Zealand	Butterworths of New Zealand Ltd, WELLINGTON and AUCKLAND
Puerto Rico	Equity de Puerto Rico, Inc, HATO REY
Singapore	Malayan Law Journal Pte Ltd, SINGAPORE
USA	Butterworth Legal Publishers, AUSTIN, TEXAS; BOSTON, MASSACHUSETTS; CLEARWATER, FLORIDA (D & S Publishers); ORFORD, NEW HAMPSHIRE (Equity Publishing); ST PAUL, MINNESOTA; and SEATTLE, Washington

A CIP Catalogue record for this book is available from the British Library.

ISBN 0 406 00179 0

Acknowledgment
The cartoons in this book are reproduced by kind permission of *Punch, Daily Telegraph*, Mel Calman, and *The Times*.
    The cartoon on the cover of the ninth edition is reproduced by kind permission of © The Daily Telegraph plc, 1991.

Typeset by Kerrypress Ltd, Luton, Beds.
Printed and bound in Great Britain by Billings Book Plan, Hylton Rd, Worcester.

Preface to the ninth edition

Butterworths Tax Books Department, models of forbearance and tolerance throughout the past decade, are due particular thanks for the production of this ninth edition. The manuscript was produced in an erratic and arbitrary fashion even by earlier high standards and the fact that the pieces have all been slotted into their correct places (assuming that they have!) is a minor miracle. Gloria Day, predictably, coped with both incomprehensible writing and garbled dictation; Robert Geary of Auld & Co revised the commercial sections whilst Gareth Reed of Boodle Hatfield took charge of an unlikely combination in EEIGs and charities.

Undoubtedly the most encouraging feature of the past 12 months has been Chancellor Lamont's willingness to turn his own personal dislikes into legislative enactment. Few (if any) can deny the pernicious influence of the mobile telephone: indeed, telephones in general would surely be a fit subject for retribution in future Finance Acts. Stanley Spencer, the Cookham eccentric, commented (wisely) that such instruments were useful for ringing up people you wanted to talk to but otherwise should be ignored. All of which prompts the thought that other scourges of modern life might yet get their fiscal come-uppance. Deserving candidates include the executive box and hospitality package (do real people still go to Wimbledon, Henley and Covent Garden?); the corporate Range Rover or its Japanese derivative (especially useful for London driving); and watches that make alien noises during those key moments of life. You too will undoubtedly have your own list of dislikes: write early to Mr Lamont (or his successor) if you want your own pet hate included in next year's fiscal package . . ..

The law is stated as at 3 August 1991.

CJW
Boodle Hatfield

Preface to the first edition

Dr Johnson considered that 'the only end of writing is to enable readers better to enjoy life or better to endure it'. Our hope is at least to achieve this latter result since there is much to be endured and often little to be enjoyed in the subject of taxation. Yet it is also a subject rich in character and absurdities as one would expect of a wholly man-made system. It has a homogeneity all of its own and is a fascinating study of man's ingenuity both in devising a tax and avoiding it. To a few people then, a study of Revenue law may even prove enjoyable.

In writing this book we have tried to explain the principles and practical application of the tax system in simple language and have followed our belief that Revenue law can be made more comprehensible and human by the use of numerous examples. No advantage is gained from a mere recitation or paraphrase of statutory material. However, the course that we have adopted, necessarily, in places, involves the expression of opinions on provisions whose obscurity may yet try the intellects of the House of Lords.

We have been helped enormously by John Wells, Peter Stuart-Buttle and Linda Hapgood, who have read most of the manuscript, and by Bernard Sims, Bryan Lenygon, Charles Fielding and Barry McCutcheon, who have read portions of it. Denise Stock typed the bulk of the material and our thanks also go for their help in various ways to Sylvia Mead and at the College of Law to Barbara, Cathy and Madelane.

Finally, we must thank Butterworths and especially the taxbooks department, for their kindness and patience.

For the inevitable errors and omissions that remain, the responsibility is ours, although in the long tradition of joint authors we will probably argue that where they exist they are in the sections written by the other!

CJW
ES-B
College of Law
Chancery Lane

Contents

Table of statutes

References in this Table to *Statutes* are to Halsbury's Statutes of England (Fourth Edition) showing the volume and page at which the annotated text of an Act may be found.

Paragraph numbers preceded by a Roman numeral are to Appendices.

Table of cases

References and abbreviations

All statutory references are given in the text.
The standard abbreviations are as follows:

ACT	Advance corporation tax
CGT	Capital gains tax
CGTA 1979	Capital Gains Tax Act 1979
CTT	Capital transfer tax
DLT	Development land tax
DLTA 1976	Development Land Tax Act 1976
ESC	Extra statutory concession
FA (year)	Finance Act (year)
FII	Franked investment income
FYA	First year allowance
IA	Initial allowance
IHT	Inheritance tax
IHTA 1984	Inheritance Tax Act 1984
IRC	Inland Revenue Commissioners
LPA 1925	Law of Property Act 1925
LS Gaz	Law Society Gazette
MIRAS	Mortgage Interest Relief at Source
MCT	Mainstream corporation tax
PAYE	Pay As You Earn
PR	Personal representative
PYB	Preceding year basis
SA 1891	Stamp Act 1891
SAYE	Save As You Earn
SI	Statutory Instrument
SP	Statement of Practice
STI	Simon's Tax Intelligence
TA 1970	Income and Corporation Taxes 1970
TA 1988	Income and Corporation Taxes Act 1988
TMA 1970	Taxes Management Act 1970
VAT	Value added tax
WDA	Writing down allowance

Any other abbreviations in the text are defined there.

PART A PRINCIPLES

Section 1 Introduction

Chapters

1 UK taxation—structure and philosophy

'*Singleton J*—Your appeal must be dismissed. I will pass you back your documents. If I might add a word to you, it is that I hope you will not trouble your head further with tax matters, because you seem to have spent a lot of time in going through these various Acts, and if you go on spending your time on Finance Acts, and the like, it will drive you silly.
Mrs Briggenshaw—I will appeal to the higher court.
Singleton J—I cannot stop you, if I would. The advice which I gave you was for your own good, I thought. That is all.' (*Briggenshaw v Crabb* (1948) 30 TC 331.   [**1.1**]

I THE UK TAX PICTURE

1 Taxes in general

Taxes imposed in the UK may be classified in various ways. A tripartite division might be adopted into taxes on income, on capital and on expenditure. Alternatively, and arguably more satisfactorily, the classification might be into direct and indirect taxes. This book is concerned only with the following direct taxes:

> income tax (Chapters 3–13)
> capital gains tax (CGT) (Chapters 14–20)
> inheritance tax (IHT) (Chapters 21–27)
> corporation tax (Chapter 28)
> stamp duty (Chapter 30)

It, therefore, omits indirect taxes such as VAT, car tax and customs and excise duties, as well as such direct taxes as petroleum revenue tax and the community charge. In principle, the distinction between direct and indirect taxes is that a direct tax is borne by the taxpayer and is not passed on to any other person, whereas an indirect tax is passed on by the payer so that the burden of the tax is ultimately borne by another, eg VAT which although paid by the businessman, is passed on to the customer.   [**1.2**]

2 What is a tax?

The basic features of a tax may be simply stated. First, it is a compulsory levy. Secondly, it should be imposed by government or, in the case of rates, by a local authority. Finally, the money raised should be used either for public purposes or, if the purpose of the tax is not to raise money, it should encourage social justice within the community (CGT, for instance, was specifically intended to have that effect). So to describe the main features of a tax is not, however, to define the concept. Taxes shade off into criminal fines and into levies imposed for other purposes; water rates, for instance, are probably not taxes since they are paid to the water authority and are not used for general public purposes. So far as the distinction between fines and taxes is concerned, the line is often blurred. H L A Hart in the *Concept of Law* (Oxford, 1975) commented that:

> 'Taxes may be imposed not for revenue purposes but to discourage the activities taxed, though the law gives no express indications that these are to be abandoned as it does when it "makes them criminal". Conversely the fines payable for some criminal offence may, because of the depreciation of money, become so small that they are cheerfully paid. They are then perhaps felt to be "mere taxes", and "offences" are frequent, precisely because in these circumstances the sense is lost that the rule is, like the bulk of the criminal law, meant to be taken seriously as a standard of behaviour.'   [**1.3**]

3   **The purpose of taxation**

The primary object of taxation is, and always has been, to raise money for government expenditure. The twentieth century has witnessed increasing expenditure on social welfare whilst the use of taxation both as an economic regulator and for the promotion of the public good (or to discourage certain forms of conduct) may also be discerned in the legislation of this century. Thus, alterations to the rate of VAT can affect the level of economic life in the community as much as adjustments to the money supply and credit regulation. The various tax incentives afforded for gifts to charities may be seen as the promotion of public good and altruism; whilst the duties levied on tobacco and alcohol may be seen as bordering on moral control.

Finally, there is the vexed question of who should pay the bill. Apportioning the burden of taxation fairly amongst the community can turn into the more radical contention that tax should operate as a method for effecting a redistribution of wealth or even the confiscation of wealth above a certain level. One striking feature of the statistics of direct taxation is that the vast proportion of the total yield is from income tax: in 1989-90 receipts of income tax amounted to 64% of the total sum raised by direct taxes; corporation tax 28% and CGT (including the defunct Development Land Tax) 2.5%. Ten years earlier the comparable figures were 78% (income tax); 16% (corporation tax); and 1.5% CGT. The rise in the corporation tax yield is from a total (including ACT) of £8,341m in 1984/85 to £21,495m in 1989-90. In the Finance Act 1984, the Chancellor fixed corporation tax at the rate of 50% for 1983, 45% for 1984, 40% for 1985, and 35% for 1986. Increased yield has therefore gone hand in hand with falling tax rates although it may also be noted that 1984 saw the phasing out of 100% first year capital allowances. Statistics for the period reveal that the outstanding capital allowances of companies declined from a peak of £30,440m in 1984 to £18,740m in 1986.

Inheritance tax (including its now defunct predecessors, estate duty and capital transfer tax) accounts for 1.5% of the total tax raised: the same percentage as in 1978-79. In fact receipts have more than doubled in the period from 1982-83 to 1989-90 and a continued rise is likely as surviving spouses die so that estates exempt on death of the first spouse fall into the charge to tax. Receipts from lifetime transfers have fallen from a peak of £33.9m in 1986-87 to £15.4m in 1988-89: this coinciding with the cutback in the tax base which has resulted (generally) in only those lifetime transfers made within seven years of the transferor's death being taxed.

If one compares tax yield with collection costs, for each £1 raised in tax the collection costs of the Revenue were 1.9p (CGT), 2.9p (IHT), 1p (SD), 0.01p (oil taxes), 1.6p (income tax—employment), and 5.2p (income tax—the rest). DLT (now repealed) required collection costs of 6.3p and was a striking illustration of a tax of great complexity but disappointing yield.

Traditionally, the Conservative party has favoured indirect taxation and the provision of incentives to business and to the higher rate taxpayer. The Labour party has inclined towards direct taxation and to increased social welfare. There is little statistical evidence to suggest that taxation is or has been used as an engine to achieve a dramatic shift in the ownership of wealth. **[1.4]-[1.20]**

II FEATURES OF THE SYSTEM

1 **Legislation**

Fiscal legislation is complex and detailed. In part this is inevitable since, above all, tax legislation should be certain: persons should know whether they are or are not subject to tax or duty on a particular transaction or sum of money. It has always been held to be a cardinal principle that in a taxation matter the burden lies upon the Crown to show that tax is chargeable in the particular case. In a famous passage, Rowlatt J in *Cape Brandy Syndicate v IRC* (1921) expressed this rule as follows:

'...It is urged ... that in a taxing Act clear words are necessary in order to tax the subject. Too wide and fanciful a construction is often sought to be given to that maxim, which does not mean that words are to be unduly restricted against the Crown, or that there is to be any discrimination against the Crown in those Acts. It simply means that in a taxing Act one has to look merely at what is clearly said. There is no room for any intendment. There is no equity about a tax. There is no presumption as to a tax. Nothing is to be read in, nothing is to be implied. One can only look fairly at the language used...'

It follows that where the meaning of the statute is clearly expressed, the court will not consider any contrary intention or belief of Parliament or, indeed, any contrary indication by the Revenue. Recent illustrations of provisions being used against the expressed wishes of their authors include *Page v Lowther* (1983) in which an anti-avoidance section (now TA 1988 s 776) appears to have been used as a charging provision (see Chapter 8) and *Leedale v Lewis* (1982) where a provision that was intended to give relief was held not to do so (see Chapter 20).

Much of the complexity of recent legislation has been prompted by the growth of the tax avoidance industry. Whilst tax evasion is unlawful, the avoidance of tax is both lawful, and, on a relatively minor scale, widely practised. The growth of larger scale schemes, often devoid of all commercial reality, has inevitably prompted legislation. Hence, the Finance Bill of 1960 was the most technical in the history of income tax with its wide ranging provisions aimed at bond washing and dividend stripping (see Chapter 31). **[1.21]**

2 **Role of the courts—the 'new approach'**

Avoidance schemes have also affected judicial interpretation of the tax statutes with certain judges being prepared to look beyond the words to the underlying purpose and beyond the form of the transaction to its substance. The 1970's saw the development of a flourishing tax avoidance industry with many of the schemes marketed being wholly divorced from reality but obtaining a tax advantage because of the precise wording of the relevant legislation. Seeking to take away this advantage in the old way, for instance by relying upon the canons of statutory construction and the use of limited anti-avoidance legislation, was felt by some to be inadequate and there were those who felt that the Revenue should have new weapons at their disposal. Hence the development of 'the new approach' to tax avoidance schemes in the House of Lords and, in particular, in the speeches of the Law Lords in *Furniss v Dawson* (1984). Apart from illustrating that in certain circumstances it is the substance of the transaction which determines whether or not tax is chargeable, the case also showed an acceptance by the House of Lords that the courts can and should bolster up taxing statutes with judge-made law. Lord Scarman stated that:

> 'I am aware, and the legal profession (and others) must understand, that the law in this area is in an early stage of development. Speeches in your Lordships' House and judgments in the appellate courts are concerned more to chart a way forward between principles accepted and not to be rejected, than to attempt anything so ambitious as to determine finally the limit beyond which the safe channel of acceptable tax avoidance shelves into the dangerous shallows of unacceptable tax evasion. The law will develop from case to case. Lord Wilberforce in *Ramsay's* case referred to "the emerging principle" of the law. What has been established is that the determination of what does, and what does not constitute unacceptable tax evasion is a subject suited to development by judicial process. Difficult though the task may be for judges, it is one which is beyond the power of the blunt instrument of legislation.'

His approach marked a radical departure from established tradition and contrasted strikingly with the views of Rowlatt J quoted above.

Since 1984 there has been something of a reaction against this 'new approach'. Quite apart from doubts over the constitutional legality of judge-made fiscal legislation, many objected to the uncertainty generated by cases such as *Furniss v Dawson*. A discernible swing back towards more traditional views may now be observed in later cases and notably in the speeches of the House of Lords in *Craven v White* (1988). In that case Lord Oliver, for instance, first played down the symbolical aspects of the *Dawson* case as follows:

> 'It has been urged, in the course of the argument, that in *Dawson* this House crossed the Rubicon and that your Lordships should not be astute to confine the bridgehead thus created. That event, of course, constituted a declaration of war upon the Republic of Italy and I confess that I do not find the analogy drawn from so partisan an exercise an altogether happy one. I do not, however, quarrel with the general proposition, but before embarking even upon a reconnaissance into Republican territory it is at least desirable to test what the bridge will support by an analysis of the means by which the crossing was effected.'

and then concluded that:

> 'It has been said in the course of argument on the present appeals that *Dawson* is "judge made law". So it is, but judges are not legislators and if the result of a judicial decision is to contradict the express statutory consequences which have been declared by Parliament to attach to a particular transaction which has been found as a fact to have taken place, that can be justified only because, as a matter of construction of the statute, the court has ascertained that that which has taken place is not, within the meaning of the statute, the transaction to which those consequences attach.'

Taking the *Dawson* case back into the realm of statutory interpretation undoubtedly flies in the face of what was said in the case but can be seen as an attempt to reassert traditional values. **[1.22]**

3 Practice

Given the volume of legislation, it is not surprising that some provisions may impose hardship and cause unforeseen results in individual cases. As a result the Revenue operate a system of extra-statutory concessions (ESC) and publish Statements of Practice (SP). (For the difference between the two, see the replacement of SP 1/85 by an extra-statutory concession: [1987] STI 805.) The current ESCs are set out in the booklet IRI (1988) together with supplements and comprise over 170 concessions, the effect of which is that tax is not charged despite the case falling within the provisions of a taxing statute. Take for instance the ESC that permits miners to enjoy free coal or, alternatively, an allowance in lieu (ESC A6). The coal or cash allowance would undoubtedly be charged as emoluments under the rules of Schedule E were it not for the concession. More recently, the Revenue have stated that if an employee is occasionally required to work late, and either public transport has ceased or it would not be reasonable to expect the employee to use it, he will not be subject to income tax on the benefit that he receives if his employer sends him home by private transport, eg by taxi (see [1987] STI 724). It needs to be remembered that the published concessions are prefaced by a warning that 'a concession will not be given in any case where an attempt is made to use it for tax avoidance'. Thus in *R v IRC, ex p Fulford Dobson* (1987) an attempt to take advantage of a CGT concession, which, in certain cases, excluded from charge gains realised by a non-resident from the date of his departure from the UK, failed since the relevant asset had been transferred to the non-resident by his spouse with the sole object of benefiting from that concession.

The fairness of concessions is open to question as is their constitutional legality. In a pungent judgment Walton J expressed the objection to ESCs as follows:

'I, in company with many other judges before me, am totally unable to understand upon what basis the Inland Revenue Commissioners are entitled to make extra-statutory concessions. To take a very simple example (since example is clearly called for), upon what basis have the commissioners taken it upon themselves to provide that income tax is not to be charged upon a miner's free coal and allowances in lieu thereof? That this should be the law is doubtless quite correct: I am not arguing the merits, or even suggesting that some other result, as a matter of equity, should be reached. But this, surely, ought to be a matter for Parliament, and not the commissioners. If this kind of concession can be made, where does it stop: and why are some groups favoured against others? . . .
. . . This is not a simple matter of tax law. What is happening is that, in effect, despite the words of Maitland, commenting on the Bill of Rights, "This is the last of the dispensing power", the Crown is now claiming just such a power . . .' (*Vestey (No 2) v IRC* (1979).

By contrast, in the *Fulford Dobson* case mentioned above, the judge (McNeill J) accepted the existence and indeed the necessity for extra-statutory concessions, concluding that they fell 'within the concept of good management or of administrative common sense' and that they could fairly be said to be made 'within the proper exercise of managerial discretion'.

SPs set out the view that the Revenue take of a particular provision and should be treated with caution since they may not accurately state the law.

Thus, the CGT consequences that ensue when trustees exercise a dispositive power have been set out in a series of Revenue Statements. The first (SP 7/78) was withdrawn as a result of *Roome v Edwards* (1981); its successor (SP 9/81) suffered a similar fate after *Bond v Pickford* (1983); and current Revenue thinking is found in SP 7/84 (issued in October 1984).

There is an argument against inviting the Revenue to express views upon the meaning to be given to particular provisions since in cases where they indicate that tax is chargeable, it places professional advisers in a difficult position. Do they advise their clients that the Revenue are wrong and that the House of Lords are bound to accept the taxpayer's arguments or do they advise prudence in the face of the risk of protracted and expensive litigation? [**1.23**]–[**1.40**]

III   CONCLUSIONS

Tax is often seen as an ephemeral area: as a part of law devoid of principle and subject to the whims of politicians. In part this view is true; the annual (sometimes biannual) Finance Act often effects considerable changes. The underlying principles do, however, remain and it is usually only the surface landscape that is altered. The bedrock of income tax, for instance, can be traced back to 1803, whilst although the tax on gifts (now IHT, formerly CTT) is of more recent origin, it is based upon a relatively simple conceptual structure. In understanding tax law the golden rule must be to ignore the form in favour of the substance. Given that the whole edifice is man-made and is designed to achieve practical ends, it should also follow that it is fully comprehensible. There is nothing here of the divine and, in the last resort, one should follow the approach of Lord Reid in the House of Lords in *Fleming v Associated Newspapers Ltd* (1972):

> 'On reading it [now TA 1988 s 577(10)] my first impression was that it is obscure to the point of unintelligibility and that impression has been confirmed by the able and prolonged arguments which were submitted to us . . . I have suggested what may be a possible meaning, but if I am wrong about that I would not shrink from holding that the subsection is so obscure that no meaning can be given to it. I would rather do that than seek by twisting and contorting the words to give to the subsection an improbable meaning. Draftsmen as well as Homer can nod, and Parliament is so accustomed to obscure drafting in Finance Bills that no one may have noticed the defects in this subsection.'   [**1.41**]

2 Administrative machinery

I   GENERAL STRUCTURE

The government departments responsible for administering UK taxes are the Inland Revenue and Customs and Excise. All the taxes that are dealt with in this book, namely, income tax, corporation tax, CGT, IHT and stamp duty, are under the 'care and control' of the Inland Revenue, which is headed by a small number of higher civil servants known as the Commissioners of Inland Revenue ('the Board'). The commissioners answer to the Treasury and, therefore, to the Chancellor of the Exchequer.

The country is divided into tax districts headed in each case by an inspector of taxes who first assesses the taxpayer's tax liability; the tax that is due is then collected by a collector of taxes. Both the inspectors and collectors of taxes are full-time civil servants appointed by the Revenue.

Any appeal by a taxpayer against an assessment is first heard by the General or the Special Commissioners. Both bodies are appointed by the Lord Chancellor (TMA 1970 ss 2, 4). The General Commissioners are part-time unpaid laymen appointed locally for a district, like lay magistrates, and are assisted by a clerk who is usually a solicitor (TMA 1970 s 3). The Special Commissioners, who are 'overseen' by a Presiding Special Commissioner chosen by the Lord Chancellor, must be barristers, advocates or solicitors of at least seven years' standing (TMA 1970 s 4). To some extent the taxpayer can appeal to whichever of the two bodies he prefers: however complicated appeals involving technical questions of law will usually be heard by the Special Commissioners with the more routine appeals coming before the General Commissioners.

In practice, the different taxes are not all administered together. Income tax, corporation tax and CGT are administered from the Revenue's head office in the Strand (although delegated to districts) under TMA 1970. IHT is administered on a daily basis by the Capital Taxes Office in London, Edinburgh and Belfast (IHTA 1984). Stamp duty, which requires little administration, is under the supervision of the Controller of Stamps (Stamp Duties Management Act 1891). This chapter considers the administration of income tax, corporation tax and CGT; the procedures for IHT which are similar, and for stamp duty, are dealt with in the appropriate chapters on those taxes.   [**2.1**]–[**2.20**]

II   RETURNS, INFORMATION AND ASSESSMENTS

1   **Returns**

Every person (including a company) liable to tax in a tax year should inform the Revenue of this fact by the end of the following tax year (TMA 1970 ss 7, 10, 11A, 12 as amended by FA 1988). In practice, the Revenue send out tax returns requiring the taxpayer to give details of income or capital gains for the tax year and inviting him to claim any personal allowances (TMA 1970 ss 8, 11, 12). In the case of a partnership, the precedent partner is responsible for returning details of the partnership's profits and gains (TMA 1970 s 9). TMA 1970 ss 8 and 9, which are the basic provisions requiring individuals and partners to deliver a return of income, were re-drafted with effect from 6 April 1990. The wording has been widened so that instead of simply requiring details of income alone the taxpayer must now reveal 'such information as may be required' for the purpose of assessing him to income tax. The introduction of independent taxation for spouses prompted the Revenue to obtain these wider powers.

If no return is made, the Revenue can impose sanctions such as withholding personal allowances and levying penalties (TMA 1970 ss 93, 98 and charge interest on overdue tax: see SP 3/88). As from 6 April 1990 a penalty of up to 100% of the tax evaded may be imposed.

The Revenue accept facsimiles and copies as substitutes for the officially produced printed tax forms. This is to enable taxpayers (and their professional advisers) to take advantage of recent developments in information technology. So far as computer produced returns are concerned, a number of criteria must be satisfied before such facsimiles will be acceptable. Obviously, the same information must be produced as on the official return and the correct reference number must be inserted. In addition, prior approval is required. Photocopied returns may be submitted subject to the safeguard that the pages must be presented in numerical order and show the correct reference number. Not surprisingly, tax returns produced on a large scale for commercial gain are subject to a copyright fee! (See SP 5/87.)   [**2.21**]

2   **Information**

The Revenue can obtain information about a person's income from sources other than the taxpayer, eg from an employer the names of employees and details of payments to them (TMA 1970 s 15); from traders (and certain others) details of payments made for services to persons other than their employees, eg commissions and 'backhanders' (TMA 1970 s 16); from banks, names of customers to whom they have paid interest exceeding £15 in the tax year on a deposit account (TMA 1970 s 17); from persons paying interest gross (eg the Director of National Savings) the names of recipients of the interest and the amounts paid (TMA 1970 s 18); from government departments and other public authorities details of payments for services and the payment of grants and subsidies; finally, from lessees and other occupiers of land details of rent and other payments made for the use of the land (TMA 1970 s 19).

In addition, the Revenue have wide powers to obtain information about a person whose affairs are under enquiry. For instance, under TMA 1970 s 20, that person, or a third party, can be required to produce relevant documents. This provision has been modified by FA 1989 as a result of recommendations made by the Keith Committee. Accordingly, it is now possible, in addition to requiring the delivery of relevant documents, to require the taxpayer to give written answers to questions. This change is obviously sensible when the information is within the actual knowledge of the relevant taxpayer (written particulars cannot be demanded of a third party) and is likely to save the Revenue considerable time and trouble when the alternative would be to sift through a mountain of documents. A second modernisation of this section was to extend the definition of a 'third party' who could be compelled to furnish documents from only limited categories of person (broadly businesses and relatives of the taxpayer) to *any* person. Before the tax inspector can make a formal order requiring either the taxpayer or third party to provide the appropriate documents, he must first make an informal request for that information and, secondly, obtain the consent of a General or Special Commissioner for a formal order to be given. The exercise of the power is thus limited by the requirement for independent supervision (for a discussion of the role of the inspector and his duty to lay all relevant information before the Commissioner, see *R v IRC, ex p T C Coombs & Co* (1991)).

A 'tax accountant' (see TMA 1970 s 20A) who has been convicted of a tax offence or been subject to a penalty for making or assisting in making an incorrect tax return, can be required with the consent of a circuit judge or, in certain circumstances, the Board's authority, to produce any documents in his possession or under his authority regarding the tax affairs of any client past or present.

The power to demand information from third parties is limited in situations where the information is 'privileged'. Legal professional privilege may, for instance, be available for documents in the possession of a barrister, advocate or solicitor (TMA s 20B(8) and see *R v Inland Revenue Board, ex p Goldberg* (1989): note however that the claim of privilege is not available in relation to notices issued to a legal adviser *in his capacity as taxpayer*, see *R v IRC, ex p Taylor (No 2)* (1990)) and accountants are protected from disclosing audit papers and tax advice although the Revenue remain entitled to the facts essential to an understanding of the taxpayer's return and accounts (see SP 5/90). Personal records which are excluded from police search powers and journalistic material are likewise protected.

In cases where there are reasonable grounds for suspecting that an offence involving 'serious fraud' has been, is being, or is about to be committed, a tax inspector may request a circuit judge for a warrant to enter private premises (if necessary by force) to search for and remove documents which he reasonably believes to be evidence of such fraud (other than privileged documents; TMA 1970 s 20C as amended by FA 1989 and see *R v Inland Revenue Board, ex p Goldberg* (1989)). This power is extremely wide. No particular offence need be specified in the warrant other than 'serious fraud' (for an illustration of this power see *IRC v Rossminster Ltd* (1980)). Further, the occupier of the premises has no right to be informed of the precise grounds for which the warrant was issued although he is entitled to a list of the items removed and must be allowed reasonable access to them whilst they are in the possession of the Revenue.

One informal method available to the Revenue to compel the production of information in the absence of a return, or where a return is suspect, is to make a 'best of judgment' assessment on the basis of an estimate, often exaggerated, of the taxpayer's true liability. Such estimated assessments can be made in the case of overseas income; income from furnished lettings; and certain payments of interest (all of which are taxed on the current year basis) during the year in which the income arises (TMA 1970 s 29(1)(c)).

The taxpayer, if he appeals, can be compelled to produce all relevant documents on pain of losing that appeal.   [**2.22**]

3   Assessments

Assessments are usually made by inspectors, but sometimes by the Board (TMA 1970 s 29(1)). An assessment is the process from inspecting returns (if any) to determining the amount due from the taxpayer. If the taxpayer has not submitted a return or the inspector is not satisfied with the information produced, he may make an estimated ('best of judgment') assessment as a means of extracting correct or more complete information at an appeal (see above).

Where tax is deducted at source assessments are unnecessary if the Revenue have collected the correct amount of tax. Under the PAYE machinery of Schedule E, for instance, they receive the tax by automatic deduction from the employee's current year emoluments on the basis of the facts known to them in the previous year. Accordingly, only if the facts change (eg if the employee acquires another source of income) need an assessment be made and an appropriate adjustment made to the tax bill (TA 1988 s 205).

By contrast, direct assessments under Schedule D Cases I and II and for corporation tax are extremely important and are usually made on the basis that the Revenue and the taxpayer have already agreed the relevant accounts.

The assessment of the taxpayer's liability is conclusive unless he appeals against it or makes an agreement with the Revenue pending appeal. However, the making of an assessment does not preclude the Revenue from revising their own calculation if they 'discover' some grounds for an additional assessment (TMA 1970 s 29(3)). This 'discovery' need not be of new facts; it can be simply a discovery that the wrong conclusion was drawn from the same facts (*Cenlon Finance Co Ltd v Ellwood* (1962)) or that they had made an arithmetical error (*Vickerman v Mason's Personal Representatives* (1984)).

After a taxpayer has given notice of appeal against an assessment he may come to an agreement with the inspector that the original assessment was after all correct or that it be varied. Such agreement has the same effect as if the commissioners had so determined the appeal (TMA 1970 s 54 and see *Tod v South Essex Motors (Basildon) Ltd* (1988)). The precise relationship between this provision and the power to raise an extra assessment to give effect to a 'discovery' was considered by the House of Lords in *Scorer v Olin Energy Systems Ltd* (1985). The case involved the making of an additional assessment, after a s 54 agreement had been reached, because loss relief had been given erroneously to the taxpayer. In rejecting the extra assessment, the court held that, as the accounts submitted on behalf of the taxpayer set out all the facts relevant to the claim for loss relief, the Revenue were bound by the agreement entered into:

> 'The situation must be viewed objectively, from the point of view of whether the inspector's agreement to the relevant computation, having regard to the surrounding circumstances including all the material known to be in his possession, was such as to lead a reasonable man to the conclusion that he had decided to admit the claim which had been made.' (Lord Keith).

It should be stressed that, apart from s 54, the Revenue are not legally bound by an agreement (eg compromise) made with the taxpayer and nor can estoppel be raised against them (for an illustration, see *R v IRC, ex p Preston* (1985), where full disclosure of all relevant facts was not made). Accordingly, a taxpayer who is concerned to ensure that his case will not be re-opened should appeal against an assessment and provided he produces all the material facts to the Revenue, any subsequent agreement under s 54 will be binding.

The normal time limit within which to raise or revise an assessment is six years from the end of the tax year to which it relates (TMA 1970 s 34), although this is extended in cases of fraudulent or negligent conduct (post). Thus, in the tax year 1991–92 an assessment cannot normally be made for any year earlier than 1985–86. **[2.23]**

4 Postponement of tax pending appeal

Where a taxpayer disagrees with an assessment, he must inform the inspector within 30 days of his intention to appeal and within the same period of the amount of tax he considers excessive. If he fails to do so the whole amount becomes payable as if there were no appeal (TMA 1970 s 55). This provision prevents a taxpayer from postponing his payment of tax by instituting an appeal which he then abandons before the hearing. If the taxpayer and inspector are unable to agree on the amount of tax which is at issue on the appeal, the commissioners decide the matter (TMA 1970 s 55(5)). Only the amount of tax which depends on the outcome of the appeal is postponed until the appeal is heard. In the meantime the collector of taxes is not entitled to seek payment of the amount postponed under s 55(5), but only of the balance which is payable within 30 days of the agreement or the commissioners' decision under s 55(5) (see *Parikh v Back* (1985)).

On a further appeal to the High Court, the amount of tax as determined by the commissioners remains payable. If the court's decision results in an increased tax liability, this additional tax becomes due in accordance with a revised notice of assessment issued after the hearing. **[2.24]**

5 Interest on overdue tax (TMA 1970 s 86)

Interest on overdue tax is charged from a 'reckonable date' irrespective of whether the assessment had been agreed at that date (if the interest does not exceed £30 it has hitherto been remitted—as part of the computerisation process, however, this *de minimis* limit is to be abolished). The rate of interest is fixed by statutory instrument, and in recent years changes in the rate have occurred regularly in an attempt to keep it in line with commercial rates. FA 1989 s 178 (and see SI 1989/1297) introduced a streamlined procedure under which interest rates change automatically in line with the market.

Generally the 'reckonable date' under s 86 is the same as the date on which tax is due and payable although if the notice of assessment is made after these dates the due date then becomes 30 days after that notice. Income tax is payable on or before 1 January in the tax year (although for an assessment under Schedule D Cases I and II the tax is paid in two equal instalments—the first on or before 1 January and the second on or before the following 1 July). Corporation tax is normally payable nine months after the end of the company's accounting period and capital gains tax on or before 1 December following the tax year.

In cases where there has been an appeal against the assessment and all or part of the tax has been postponed under s 55, the due and reckonable date for interest purposes is usually six months from the date when the tax was due thereby ensuring that the taxpayer obtains no advantage (in terms of a delay in paying tax) from making an appeal against an assessment.

The taxpayer should be further dissuaded from a frivolous appeal by s 86(3) which provides that where the result of an appeal is that additional tax becomes due, interest shall be charged on that sum as if it were postponed tax contained in the original notice of assessment (ie the reckonable date is six months from the date when the original tax was due).   **[2.25]**

6 Repayment supplement

The Revenue will repay overpaid tax (eg where the taxpayer's appeal succeeds) together with interest at the current rate in certain (limited) circumstances. Hitherto repayments have not been made unless the tax overpaid exceeds £25: with the computerisation of interest charges this *de minimis* figure is to be abolished. (See SP1/80 for Revenue practice in this area.) Interest is only payable in respect of the period from the end of the tax year following the one for which the tax was paid to the end of the tax month (the 5th day of the month) when the repayment was ordered. Where the tax was itself paid more than 12 months after the relevant tax year, interest runs only from the end of the tax year in which it was paid (TA 1988 s 824). This repayment supplement is not itself taxable!
[2.26]-[2.40]

EXAMPLE 2.1

A taxpayer's appeal in respect of tax paid in 1989-90 is heard on 8 May 1991 and is successful. He will be entitled to interest on a repayment of tax for the period from 6 April 1991 to 5 June 1991.

III APPEALS

1 Structure of appeals

At the first level, an appeal is heard either by a panel of General Commissioners or by a single Special Commissioner unless the Presiding Special Commissioner directs otherwise (TMA 1970 s 45). From the decision of the commissioners, either the taxpayer or the inspector may appeal on a point of law to the High Court although certain appeals from decisions of the Special Commissioners may be referred direct to the Court of Appeal (TMA 1970 ss 56, 56A). For either party to appeal he must express immediate dissatisfaction with the commissioners' decision, and within 30 days thereof formally require the commissioners to state a case, ie to prepare a summary of their findings and the reasons for their decision. Within 30 days of receiving the case stated the appellant must transmit it to the High Court (TMA 1970 s 56(4)). This requirement is mandatory so that any breach of its requirements renders the appeal invalid (*Valleybright v Richardson* (1985)). By contrast, the two requirements, first, that an appellant must express immediate dissatisfaction with the commissioners' decision (TMA 1970 s 56(1)), and secondly that as soon as the case stated is transmitted to the High Court the appellant must inform the other party of that fact and furnish him with a copy (TMA 1970 s 56(5)) are directory only. Accordingly, failure to comply with either requirement will not necessarily deprive the defaulting party of the right to appeal (*Hughes v Viner* (1985)).

The difficult borderline between points of law and questions of fact and the role of the appellate courts was discussed by Lord Radcliffe in *Edwards v Bairstow & Harrison* [1956] AC 14 at 35:

'I think that the true position of the court in all these cases can be shortly stated. If a party to a hearing before commissioners expresses dissatisfaction with their determination as being erroneous in point of law, it is for them to state a case and in the body of it to set out the facts that they have found as well as their determination. I do not think that inferences drawn from other facts are incapable of being themselves findings of fact, although there is value in the distinction between primary facts and inferences drawn from them. When the case comes before the court, it is its duty to examine the determination having regard to its knowledge of the relevant law. If the case contains anything *ex facie* which is bad law and which bears upon the determination, it is, obviously, erroneous in point of law. But, without any such misconception appearing *ex facie*, it may be that the facts found are such that no person acting judicially and properly instructed as to the relevant law could have come to the determination under appeal. In those circumstances, too, the court must intervene. It has no option but to assume that there has been some misconception of the law and that this has been responsible for the determination. So there, too, there has been error in point of law. I do not think that it much matters whether this state of affairs is described as one in which there is no evidence to support the determination or as one in which the evidence is inconsistent with and contradictory to the determination or as one in which the true and only reasonable conclusion contradicts the determination. Rightly understood each phrase propounds the same test.' (The difficult borderline between questions of fact and law has been considered by the courts in the *Ramsay* line of cases: see, for instance, the judgment of Vinelott J in *Countess Fitzwilliam v IRC* (1990).)

It follows that a decision of the commissioners will not be reversed simply because an appeal court would have come to a different conclusion on the particular facts. The Schedule E case of *Glantre Engineering Ltd v Goodhand* (1983) illustrates the importance of the commissioners' finding of fact. Once they had concluded that the payment in question was an emolument (a finding of fact), the taxpayer was left with the burden of showing that such a finding was inconsistent with the only reasonable conclusion to be drawn from the evidence. When a rehearing before the commissioners is ordered, fresh evidence may not be adduced unless there are special circumstances. In *Brady v Group Lotus Car Companies plc* (1987), for instance, such evidence was allowed because the taxpayer had deliberately misled the commissioners in a material matter and that deception might have affected their decision.

Unless the appeal is referred directly to the Court of Appeal under s 56A there is a right of appeal from the High Court to the Court of Appeal and, with leave, to the House of Lords. Alternatively, use may be made of the 'leapfrog' procedure under the Administration of Justice Act 1969 to appeal directly to the House of Lords. **[2.41]**

2 Procedure before the commissioners

In general, the taxpayer can appeal to either the General or Special Commissioners although the latter will not hear 'delay' cases: ie those which lack the information necessary to settle the appeal. The distinction between delay cases and contentious appeals was the subject of an Inland Revenue Press Release dated 22 February 1990 (see (1990) STI 170). The Revenue may only insist on a case being referred to General Commissioners under TMA s 31(5)—thereby ignoring the taxpayer's election to have the matter heard by the Special Commissioners—in delay cases. In certain other cases, eg from an assessment by the Board, the taxpayer has no choice and the appeal must be to the Special Commissioners. Where the appeal involves difficult questions of law the taxpayer often chooses the Special Commissioners. In back duty cases, he may be better off with the General Commissioners whose business experience and local knowledge may help him.

The taxpayer must make his appeal to the commissioners within 30 days after his notice of assessment (TMA 1970 s 31) and in Schedule D cases he must specify the grounds of appeal.

Where the taxpayer elects for the Special Commissioners, this election may be disregarded at any time before the determination of the appeal by agreement between the parties or, failing agreement, by a non-appealable direction of the General Commissioners given after hearing the parties (TMA 1970 s 31(5A)).

Once started, an appeal cannot be withdrawn except with the agreement in writing of the inspector (TMA 1970 s 54 and see *Beach v Willesden General Comrs* (1982)). However, an appeal which is started before the General Commissioners may, on agreement with the Special Commissioners, be transferred to them (TMA 1970 s 44(3A)). The general principles of court procedures apply to the hearing at which the Crown is usually represented by the inspector and the taxpayer may appear in person or be represented by a barrister, solicitor or accountant. If the taxpayer does not appear in person, he has no legal right to conduct his case in writing except through a barrister or solicitor (TMA 1970 s 50(5); *Banin v Mackinley* (1985)).

The commissioners can call before them and examine on oath any person other than the taxpayer himself. However, costs are not awarded, and legal aid is not available. Under TMA 1970 s 57B the Lord Chancellor has the power to make procedural rules for the Special Commissioners and it has been suggested that such power might be exercised to permit the attendance at hearings of members of the Council on Tribunals and the publication of the Special Commissioners' decisions. To date, no such rules have been made.

The onus of proof is generally on the taxpayer to disprove an assessment, but, if the Crown alleges fraudulent or negligent conduct, it must prove it. The commissioners may discharge, reduce or increase the assessment (TMA 1970 s 50(6)(7)).   [**2.42**]

3   **Procedural changes for certain income tax appeals**

The majority of income tax appeals are the result of 'best of judgment' assessments raised simply because of the taxpayer's delay in returning his income, particularly his business profits ('delay appeals'). In an attempt to reduce the large number of delay appeals (estimated at 900,000 each year in England and Wales) and the consequently huge administrative costs, the Revenue introduced a procedural approach for income tax appeals (excluding Schedule E) against assessments made where the amount of tax paid on account under TMA 1970 s 55 is thought to be reasonable, the source of the income is continuing, and the tax charged is £10,000 or less. Appeals are not listed for a hearing until two years' accounts are outstanding whereupon all the 'two year appeals' will be listed at the same time after the June following the second year (IR Press Release 25 January 1983).   [**2.43**]-[**2.60**]

IV COLLECTION OF TAX

Once an assessment becomes final the collectors of taxes have wide powers to collect the tax. If the taxpayer fails to pay they can levy distress (TMA 1970 ss 61, 62) or, if he is an employee, arrange for the tax to be deducted at source under PAYE. Alternatively, the tax charged can be recovered in the magistrates' court, in the county court or in the High Court depending on the sum involved (TMA 1970 ss 65–67).

The insolvency of the taxpayer is no bar to the Revenue pursuing the debt, although, under the Insolvency Act 1986, their former preference is abolished, so that they rank as unsecured creditors, except where their claim is for 'quasi-trustee debts' (ie for arrears of PAYE and VAT where the taxpayer acts as collector for the Revenue). In the case of such quasi-trustee debts the preference is limited, in the case of PAYE, to sums owed in the twelve months, and, for VAT, in the six months, prior to the insolvency.

[**2.61**]–[**2.80**]

V BACK DUTY

A back duty case arises when the Revenue discover that a taxpayer has evaded tax, usually by not disclosing his true income, by supplying inaccurate or incomplete information, or by claiming reliefs and allowances to which he is not entitled. They often discover this from 'tip-offs' that they receive about the taxpayer, or by a 'confession' from the taxpayer himself. On discovering a back duty case the Revenue can commence criminal proceedings, and/or make assessments for the lost tax plus interest and/ or claim penalties. What the Revenue choose to do in any case depends largely on the degree of co-operation of the taxpayer. Criminal proceedings are rarely taken (the odds are roughly one in fifteen hundred); and the Revenue generally prefer to reach some settlement with the taxpayer. Their wide discretion in this area is aided by TMA 1970 s 105 which enables the Revenue to tell the taxpayer that they may accept a pecuniary settlement and that they are influenced by a full confession. Despite these inducements, statements made by the taxpayer are admissible in evidence, and any settlement creates a contractual debt for which the Revenue can sue (see *IRC v Nuttall* (1990)).

"I didn't think you people could re-open a case after a five year period."

Small back duty cases are dealt with by local inspectors who have the power to agree settlements. In larger cases the approval of the head office is required before any settlement can be reached. When arriving at a settlement, the factors that the Revenue consider include the amount of tax lost, interest payable, penalties available, the co-operation of the taxpayer and, most importantly, the need for uniformity in cases of a similar nature.   **[2.81]**

1   Criminal proceedings

Prosecutions can be brought against the taxpayer under the Perjury Act 1911; for forgery; for conspiracy to defraud; or under the Theft Act 1978 for evasion of a liability by deception or false accounting. Company officers can be made liable for such offences if committed by the company.   **[2.82]**

2   Assessments for lost tax plus interest

The normal time limit for making an assessment to tax is six years from the end of the relevant tax year (TMA 1970 s 34(1)). Formerly, this limit did not apply to assessments based upon fraud or wilful default by the taxpayer (which could be carried back to any year from 1936–37) and the normal time limit was further extended when assessments were based upon the taxpayer's neglect. As a result of proposals made by the Keith Committee designed to achieve a uniform time limit in the case of default assessments (and therefore to bring direct taxes into line with VAT), these provisions were replaced by a new time limit of 20 years for assessments to recover tax lost through fraudulent or negligent conduct (TMA 1970 s 36 as substituted by FA 1989). Leave of a Special or General Commissioner to make such an assessment is, however, no longer necessary. The 20 year period runs from the end of the year of assessment or accounting period to which the fraud or negligent conduct relates and, in cases where the defaulting taxpayer had carried on a business in partnership, there may be an extra assessment on the other individuals who were at that time his partners. A taxpayer assessed on the basis of fraudulent or negligent conduct is entitled to his full allowances and reliefs for the year in question even though the time limit for claiming them has expired.

A number of cases (pre-dating the 1989 legislative changes) illustrate the operation of back duty assessments. In *Kovak v Morris* (1985), for instance, persistent failure by the taxpayer to supply tax returns was held to amount to 'wilful default': today it would amount to negligent conduct. A particularly graphic illustration of what was then wilful default and today would be classified as negligent conduct, was afforded by the case of *Pleasance v Atkinson* (1987) in which the taxpayer's accountants purported to deduct, in arriving at the profits of his trade as a property developer, money which was actually expended on his private residence. The commissioners were entitled on these facts to conclude that, although the taxpayer was himself innocent of wilful default, his agent (the firm of accountants) was guilty and furthermore it was not necessary to prove any additional requirement, such as personal enrichment, in order to explain that breach of duty. Accordingly, in this case the taxpayer was assessed in 1981 on profits under-declared for the year 1972–73 (see TMA 1970 s 36(1) which refers to the conduct of a person 'acting on his (ie the taxpayer's) behalf').

For a back duty assessment to be made on a deceased taxpayer's PRs it must be made within three tax years of the year of death for fraudulent or negligent conduct by the deceased in any of the six years up to and including the year of his death (TMA 1970 s 40). Thus, if the deceased dies in the tax year 1991-92, the Revenue have until 5 April 1995 in which to assess his PRs for loss of tax because of his fraudulent or negligent conduct in the years from 1985-86 to 1991-92. An assessment is 'made' for these purposes when the certificate of assessment is signed in the assessment book and not when the notice of assessment is received by the taxpayer (TMA 1970 s 40 and *Honig v Sarsfield* (1986)).

In *Baylis v Gregory* (1987) the Court of Appeal had to consider the position when a taxpayer was assessed to CGT, but, because of a typing error, that assessment was stated to be for 1974-75 whereas it should have related to 1975-76. This error went unnoticed until the time limit for making an assessment for 1975-76 had passed. When it was noticed by the inspector he made a note in his records that the assessment for 1974-75 was vacated. On these facts, the court decided, *first*, that the 1974-75 assessment had not been properly cancelled since notice had not been given to the taxpayer, but, *secondly*, that it could not be treated as referring to 1975-76. The correct procedure was for a proper assessment to be made for that year but as the relevant time limit had passed the taxpayer in the particular case could not be taxed on gains realised in 1975-76.

Interest in back duty cases is charged from the date when the tax should have been paid. [**2.83**]

3 **Penalties** (TMA 1970 ss 93-107)

Tax offences may attract monetary penalties. Such a penalty is, of course, in addition to the tax itself and any interest thereon. A radical reform of penalties was advocated by the Keith Committee but implemented only in part in 1989.

In general, most penalties will now be imposed by a notice of determination made by the Revenue without the need for taking penalty proceedings before the Commissioners (TMA 1970 s 100). The legislation generally provides for a maximum penalty which can then be mitigated in the discretion of the Revenue: in practice, penalties are frequently agreed between the parties. The most controversial aspect of the Keith Report in this area was for the introduction of a series of automatic penalties graded according to the seriousness of the offence. This provoked generally adverse comments and the proposal was accordingly dropped: FA 1989 merely up-dated and streamlined the existing penalty system.

First, there is a penalty for failure to make an income tax or capital gains tax return. The initial penalty is £300 and the daily penalty £60 running from the date when that initial penalty is imposed. Should the failure not be remedied by the end of the year of assessment following that in which the notice was served, the taxpayer additionally becomes liable to a penalty equal to 100% of the tax unpaid because of the delay. *Secondly*, the penalty for submitting an incorrect return, declaration, statement or account for income tax or capital gains tax is 100% of the tax (ie the difference between the amount of tax payable and the lesser amount which would have been payable on the return or accounts as submitted). *Finally*, the maximum penalty for fraudulently or negligently supplying incorrect information or documents in response to a requirement under specified statutory provisions, is now £3,000 and a similar penalty may be imposed on a person who assists in or induces the preparation or delivery of an incorrect return or accounts.

The time limit for commencing penalty proceedings is generally six years from the date when the offence was committed except for penalties linked to the amount of tax lost (eg those levied for incorrect returns) where proceedings can be commenced at any time within three years of the final determination of the amount of tax in question. A person who has assisted in the preparation of an incorrect return may be subject to penalty proceedings at any time in the following 20 years (see generally TMA 1970 s 103).

The bankruptcy of the taxpayer does not preclude the Revenue from claiming maximum penalties (see *Re Hurren, ex p Trustee v IRC* (1982)).

In a change of previous practice the Revenue will seek monetary penalties for any offence which the taxpayer may have committed but which has not been brought before the criminal courts, and they may now seek penalties where the taxpayer has been negligent even though acquitted of any criminal intent. The Board will not, however, take steps to recover civil monetary penalties on the basis of fraud in respect of an offence which has been brought before the criminal courts (SP 2/88).   **[2.84]–[2.100]**

EXAMPLE 2.2

Tax was underpaid because of the taxpayer's fraud in 1974–75. If the assessment only becomes final in May 1990, the Revenue have until May 1994 to raise penalties, even though the offence was committed more than six years from the date of the assessment.

VI   REFORM OF THE ENFORCEMENT POWERS ENJOYED BY REVENUE DEPARTMENTS: THE KEITH REPORT

A committee under the chairmanship of Lord Keith of Kinkel was set up in 1980 to carry out an extensive review of the enforcement powers enjoyed by the Revenue departments which affect both the individual rights of the citizen and the ability of the Revenue to apply and enforce the law.

The committee published three substantial volumes in 1983 running collectively to 1056 pages (Cmnd 8822 and 9120) dealing with all the direct taxes and VAT. The fourth (and final) volume of the Report, dealing with customs, excise duties, and car tax was published in 1985 (Cmnd 9440). The Report contains a mine of detailed information and recommendations and the proposals in response to the recommendations in volumes 1 and 2 were published in a Consultative Document 'The Inland Revenue and the Taxpayer' in December 1986. This document contained 46 draft clauses and two schedules and F(No 2)A 1987 included clauses dealing with the 'pay and file' system for the administration of corporation tax although the provisions will not come into force before 1993 (see p 509). Further proposals dealing with penalties for failure to notify a liability to tax; the supply of information by certain persons and bodies to the Revenue; and the levying of interest on unpaid PAYE were implemented in FA 1988. Finally, a Consultative Paper, 'Keith: Further Proposals' was published in July 1988 and resulted in the changes to interest and monetary penalties for tax offences and the modification of the information and search powers of the Revenue carried through by FA 1989. The implementation of the proposals on income tax, capital gains tax and corporation tax has now been completed with the exception of the recommendations relating to the administration and conduct of appeals. On these proposals there will be a future Consultative Document or Consultative Documents.   **[2.101]**

Section 2   Income tax

Chapters

3 General principles

I   History   [**3.2**]
II   Statutory basis of the tax   [**3.21**]
III The Schedules   [**3.41**]

'... No one has ever been able to define income in terms sufficiently concrete to be of value for taxation purposes ... where it has to be ascertained whether a gain is to be classified as an income gain or a capital gain, the determination of that question must depend in large measure upon the particular facts of the particular case.' (Abbott J in *Oxford Motors Ltd v Minister of National Revenue* (1959) 18 DLR (2d) 712.)

'In principle, there is little economic difference between income and capital gains, and many people effectively have the option of choosing to a significant extent which to receive. And, insofar as there is a difference, it is by no means clear why one should be taxed more heavily than the other. Taxing them at different rates distorts investment decisions and inevitably creates a major tax avoidance industry.' (Nigel Lawson, Budget Speech, 15.3.1988.)   [**3.1**]

I HISTORY

Income tax is sometimes referred to as the 'tax which beat Napoleon'. Such claims amount to a gross exaggeration although it is true that the tax was first introduced in 1799 by Pitt the Younger as a wartime measure. Pitt's tax was not wholly innovatory; there had always been a tradition of direct taxation even if that taxation had been applied spasmodically. The origins of income tax may be seen in the land tax and in the Triple Assessment of 1798.

Early yields were disappointing; estimates predicted a yield of £10m in the first year, but under £6m was actually raised. Although the tax was repealed when peace with France was concluded in 1802, it was reintroduced by Addington when hostilities recommenced in the following year. Addington included two basic changes which have survived more or less intact: first, a requirement that returns should be of income from particular sources and not just a lump sum; and secondly, provisions for deduction of tax at source.

The final cessation of hostilities in 1816 led to the repeal of the tax with the resulting financial deficit being made good by increased yields from customs and excise. Income tax was brought back, this time for good, by Peel in 1842. It was not revived because of its own inherent merits, but as a way to simplify and reduce the tariff, as a first step towards the repeal of the Corn Laws in 1846.

By the end of the century, the tax, although an accepted part of the fiscal landscape, raised less than either customs or excise. The twentieth century with the extraordinary demands of war and welfare transformed the picture. By the end of the 1914–18 war, the income tax yield was some £585m as compared with the pre-war figure of £34m and the complexity of the modern tax had been established with earned income relief, supertax, a range of personal allowances, and a primitive system of capital allowances. The process was accelerated by the 1939-45 War with the yield rising from £371m in 1938 to £1,426m in 1945. PAYE was improved in 1943 and the tax avoidance industry maintained a steady growth.

Today, the flood of income tax legislation shows little sign of diminution; the statutory material was consolidated in 1952, again in 1970, and such is the output of Parliament that a further consolidation Act (TA 1988) came into effect on 6 April 1988.   **[3.2-3.20]**

II   STATUTORY BASIS OF THE TAX

1   The statutes and case law

The authority for imposing taxation is Act of Parliament and, in the case of income tax, the statutory basis is TA 1988 as amended by later Finance Acts. TMA 1970 deals with the administration of the tax. The legislation on capital allowances (see Chapter 7) which has been in a state of chaos for some years was reconsolidated in the Capital Allowances Act 1990 which came into effect for chargeable periods ending after 5 April 1990.

The meaning of the statute is primarily a question for a judiciary which ranges from commissioners to the House of Lords. Many concepts are not defined by statute (eg what is a trade? what is an income receipt/expense?), many provisions are obscure, and it is the role of the judiciary to resolve such difficulties and of case law to fill the gaps. It may even be the job of the courts to create judge-made law to deal with sophisticated avoidance schemes (see *Furniss v Dawson* (1984)).   **[3.21]**

2   Years and rates

The tax needs annual renewal by Parliament. The annual Finance Act normally receives the Royal Assent in late July or early August. By virtue of the Provisional Collection of Taxes Act 1968, however, the budget resolutions (such as the rates of tax) are given limited statutory force until the passage of the Act.

The income tax year runs from 6 April to the following 5 April and is termed the 'year of assessment' or simply the 'tax year'. It is referred to by reference to both the calendar years that it straddles—hence, the year of assessment beginning on 6 April 1991 is referred to as the tax year 1991-92. The curious starting date for the year (6 April) is explicable, as is so much of income tax, on historical grounds. 5 April was adopted as the terminal date because it was one of the old quarter days which marked the end of a period of account: (1985) BTR 56.   **[3.22]-[3.40]**

III   THE SCHEDULES

1   The source doctrine

Income tax is levied according to the source of the income and the five Schedules (see table below) exhaustively list the various sources. (Schedule B which imposed a charge on commercial woodlands was abolished as from 6 April 1988.) Each Schedule has its own rules for determining the amount

The Schedules

Schedule	Source	Basis of assessment
A	Rents and other receipts from land in UK	Rents receivable less outgoings of the current year of assessment
C	Public revenue	Income of the current year of assessment
D Case I	Profits of a trade in UK	Usually, the income of the preceding accounting year (Cases I and II) or preceding tax year (Cases III, IV and V)
Case II	Profits of a profession or vocation in UK	
Case III	Interest, annuities and other annual payments	
Case IV	Securities out of the UK not charged under Sch C	
Case V	Possessions out of the UK not charged under Sch C (but excluding foreign employment)	
Case VI	Annual profits or gains not falling under Cases I–V and not charged by virtue of any other Schedule; and certain income directed to be so charged	Income of the current year of assessment or, at the Revenue's option, average income of any period not exceedingone year
E Cases I, II and III	Offices, employments and pensions (both 'home' and foreign). Also, chargeable benefits under the social security legislation	Income in the year of receipt
F	Dividends and certain other distributions by companies	Income of the current year of assessment

of income and the available deductions (if any). Schedule A, for instance, taxes income from land. The charge is on rents and other receipts which arise as a result of the ownership of land (or of an interest therein) but the landlord may deduct expenses such as repairs and rates on the property. In arriving at the income of a taxpayer it is, therefore, necessary to discover what sources of income he possesses and then, by applying the rules of the relevant Schedules, to calculate the income arising under each. It follows, as a general principle, that tax is charged only so long as a taxpayer possesses the source of the income. Tax avoidance opportunities that would thereby exist are, however, generally prevented by the legislation. For instance, although the sale of trading stock after the permanent cessation of the relevant trade would not on general principles fall within Case I (because the source— the trade—had ceased when the sale occurred), there is express provision which brings into the tax net the value of stock unsold at the date of the discontinuance. Any loss of revenue is thereby prevented. *Example 3.1*, below, illustrates a second situation where the source doctrine left a gap in the tax net which has now been closed, in this case by FA 1989.   [**3.41**]

EXAMPLE 3.1

B, having been employed by G Ltd for 20 years, is transferred together with all the other employees to the employment of G Ltd's parent company in the tax year 1988-89. The trustees of a fund for the benefit of employees of G Ltd including B accordingly brought that trust to an end and made distributions to B in the following tax year (ie in 1989-90). Although that distribution may be an emolument (see Chapter 5) because it was paid after B's employment had ceased and could not be attributed to any year of that employment, there was no source of income in the year of receipt and therefore no liability to income tax (see *Bray v Best* (1988)). In the course of changing the charge to tax under Schedule E to the receipts basis, FA 1989 also widened the tax net to include emoluments received *after* an employment had ceased. Accordingly, payments of the type received in *Bray v Best* will now be 'treated as emoluments for the last year of assessment in which the employment was held' (TA 1988 s 19(1) para 4A: inserted by FA 1989).

2   The mutually exclusive rule

The Schedules are mutually exclusive with the result that the Revenue cannot assess income to tax under any Schedule other than the one to which that income is properly attributable (*Fry v Salisbury House Estate Ltd* (1930)). The same principle applies to the taxpayer who may not deduct expenses attributable to a different Schedule nor opt to have his income taxed under a different Schedule (*Mitchell and Edon v Ross* (1962)). So far as Schedule D is concerned there is some authority for the view that the Revenue can choose between the different Cases in the rare situations when an overlap between them exists (*Liverpool and London and Globe Insurance Co v Bennett* (1913)).   [**3.42**]

EXAMPLE 3.2

(1) Roger lets several properties to university students and works full time in the management of the properties. Tax must be charged under Schedule A (which applies to rent and other receipts from land), not under Schedule D Case I, because (except for furnished holiday lettings) there cannot be a trade of letting properties (see *Griffiths v Jackson* (1983) discussed in Chapter 8).

(2) A firm of solicitors acted as secretaries for a number of companies. The profits from the profession of solicitors are assessed under Schedule D Case II; remuneration from the office of company secretary is, however, charged under Schedule E (*IRC v Brander and Cruickshank* (1971) see Chapter 5).

3 What is income?

Income is not defined in the legislation. Furthermore, any definition is a matter for acute debate by both economists and philosophers. How, therefore, does the tax operate if the subject matter of the tax (income) is not defined? The answer is that income for this purpose means all the sums calculated under the five Schedules. Hence, a sum of money falling under one of the Schedules is subject to tax (and is, therefore, 'income'), whilst a sum which escapes the Schedules is untaxed (and may, therefore, be termed 'capital'). This approach results in 'income' and 'capital' being given artificial meanings; certain capital sums (notably premiums under Schedule A and golden handshakes and restrictive covenant payments under Schedule E) are deemed to be income for the purposes of the tax. It is likewise odd to refer to certain sums excluded from charge (such as student grants and Christmas presents) as 'capital'.

EXAMPLE 3.3

Augustus gives Oxfam £100 every Christmas. Despite the regular nature of the payment it is not income in Oxfam's hands because it does not fall within any of the Schedules. Were he to covenant the sum each year, however, it would become income because it is an annual payment falling within Schedule D Case III. (Note: just because the sum is income it does not follow that Augustus is worse off. Indeed, there are tax advantages from payments to charity by deed of covenant; see Chapter 10.)

Although the lack of a definition of income does not generally cause problems, difficulties do arise when the Schedule prescribes that only income receipts are subject to tax or only income expenses can be deducted (as under Schedules A and D Cases I and II where the tax is levied on the profits that remain after income deductions have been taken from income receipts). The meaning of 'income' has accordingly been debated all too frequently before the courts and the various tests that have been suggested for resolving the problem are considered in Chapter 6.

As a final curiosity, it may be noted that when capital sums are deemed to be income for the purposes of the income tax legislation, eg when premiums are treated as rent under TA 1988 s 34 the result is a divergence between those income tax rules and ordinary principles of trust law which identify what sums are income. Take, for instance, TA 1988 s 686 which imposes a surcharge on income received by discretionary or accumulation trusts: see generally [11.21]. Because the section is limited to 'income arising to the trustees' it does not catch profits which are of a capital nature under general trust law (eg lease premiums). [3.43]

4 Computation—charges, allowances and rates

I INTRODUCTION: STAGES OF THE INCOME TAX CALCULATION

Only income as defined by the Schedules is subject to income tax. The tax is levied at two rates; a basic rate of 25% and a single higher rate of 40%. It may be collected either by direct assessment, or by deduction at source. The following steps are involved in calculating the taxpayer's income and in working out his tax bill for the year:

Step 1 Calculate the individual's 'statutory income', ie the income which is taxable under the rules of the various Schedules and Cases.

Step 2 Calculate the taxpayer's charges on income, ie certain payments which the taxpayer is bound to make, such as certain interest payments.

Step 3 Deduct charges on income from statutory income to obtain 'total income' (TA 1988 s 835).

Step 4 Deduct personal reliefs from total income to obtain 'taxable income'.

Step 5 Calculate income tax at the basic and higher rate on the taxable income.

Step 6 From the total tax calculated in *Step 5* deduct any income tax which has been collected at source.

Step 7 Calculate basic rate tax on any charges on income from which the individual has deducted tax when making the payment.

The result of *Step 6* plus *Step 7* is the final amount of tax payable. All these steps involve terms requiring explanation, and the various stages in the income tax calculation will now be considered in detail.   **[4.1]**-**[4.20]**

II STATUTORY INCOME *(Step 1)*

1 General

Statutory income consists of the taxpayer's income from all sources calculated according to the rules of the particular Schedule or Case under which it arises and after deducting expenses appropriate to the particular Schedule or Case. Since the income tax year runs from 6 April to 5 April following, the income tax assessment (the 'basis of assessment') should logically be on the statutory income of an individual for that period (ie on a current year basis). This is so for income arising under all the Schedules except for Schedule D, which operates according to a preceding year basis. Hence, the taxable profits of a trade assessable under Schedule D Case I are deemed to be the profits of the accounts which ended in the previous tax year (the preceding year basis).   **[4.21]**

EXAMPLE 4.1

Mack, a trader (Schedule D Case I), makes up his accounts to 30 June 1990 showing receipts of £12,000. Certain deductions may be made (for instance, £2,000 paid by Mack in salaries to employees). As a result, Mack will include £10,000 of Schedule D Case I income in his statutory income for the year of assessment 1991–92.

2 Income received after deduction of tax

Some income is received and enters the statutory income calculation gross: ie without having suffered any tax. The tax on that income is collected by direct assessment. For certain types of income, however, tax is deducted at source. In such cases, the payer of the income is obliged to act as a tax collector by deducting from the payment an amount of tax (usually at basic rate) and handing it to the Revenue. If the recipient is not liable to income tax, he will obtain a repayment from the Revenue of the tax deducted. If, however, he is liable to higher rate tax, a further assessment will be necessary.

Accordingly, any sum received after deduction of tax must be grossed up to discover the original sum from which the tax was deducted. The resulting (gross) figure must be entered in the recipient taxpayer's calculation of statutory income to discover his tax liability. The tax that has already been paid on this income is credited against his tax bill.

EXAMPLE 4.2

Austin (with other statutory income of £10,000) receives a dividend (Schedule F) of £750 from which basic rate (25%) tax has (in the form of ACT) been deducted and handed to the Revenue by the paying company. Austin must include the 'grossed-up' amount of the dividend in his statutory income calculation for the year to work out whether the tax deducted is correct.

To gross up multiply the dividend received by $\dfrac{100}{100 - R}$ where R is the rate at which tax was deducted ie

$$750 \times \frac{100}{100 - 25} = 750 \times \frac{100}{75}$$
$$= £1,000 \text{ (gross dividend—therefore tax paid is £250)}$$

Austin's statutory income is

Other sources	£10,000
Schedule F	£ 1,000
Statutory income	£11,000

When the tax due on this income is calculated, Austin can deduct the £250 tax deducted at source by the company. If his liability to tax is for less than £250, he can reclaim from the Revenue the amount for which he is not liable.

The main examples of income received after deduction of tax at source are:
(1) Dividends and other distributions from companies, assessable under Schedule F (received with a credit for basic rate tax).
(2) Trust income received by a beneficiary after deduction (normally) of basic rate tax.
(3) Emoluments assessable under Schedule E from which tax (at the appropriate rate) is deducted under the PAYE system.
(4) Annuities and certain other annual payments, assessed under Schedule D Case III, from which basic rate tax is deducted, eg maintenance payments made under obligations entered into before 15 March 1988.
(5) Income arising from deposit accounts which is treated as received after deduction of basic rate tax (see 3 below).   **[4.22]**

3   Interest paid by building societies and banks

Building societies and other deposit-takers (notably banks) were, prior to 1991-92, subject to income tax at a special rate (the 'composite' rate, which for 1990-91 was 22%) and the interest paid to depositors was treated as having suffered basic rate income tax (TA 1988 s 476). Accordingly, the investor had to gross up the sum received in order to calculate his income tax bill and, depending upon his personal circumstances, the interest could be taxed at the higher rate of tax. Where, however, the investor was not subject to income tax (eg because an infant with unused personal allowances), he was unable to obtain a refund from the Revenue for the basic rate tax credited as paid.

EXAMPLE 4.3

In 1990-91 Zia received £75 interest from the Wailshire Building Society. This was treated as received by her after deduction of basic rate income tax. She had, therefore, to gross up the receipt to £100 for the purpose of her income tax calculation. She received a tax credit for the £25 basic rate tax, which was treated as having been paid, although she was not be entitled to any refund of that tax. Only the net income (£75) was available to cover any charges on Zia's income.

Largely to ensure that the average married woman with small savings was not over-taxed and doubtless to prevent wealthier married women from investing in offshore deposit accounts where interest is paid gross, the Chancellor announced in his 1990 Budget the abolition of the composite rate scheme with effect from 6 April 1991. The current system involves interest being paid net of basic rate income tax and non-taxpayers then being entitled to obtain a recovery of this tax on submitting the appropriate claim. To avoid the necessity for a multiplicity of such claims, there are arrangements whereby non-taxpayers are able to complete a certificate to that effect and then receive interest gross.

Deduction of tax at source must be applied in respect of 'relevant deposits' by any deposit-taker who falls within the statutory list. The list includes any recognised bank, the National Giro Bank, any trustee savings bank, any local authority and specified credit and finance companies (see eg SI 1987/1224 and 1987/2127). Notice that the National Savings Bank is not included. 'Relevant deposits' are widely defined to include deposits which are held by any person for the benefit of UK resident individuals or deposits where the person entitled to the interest receives it in the capacity of personal representative. Whether the deposit is maintained for private or business purposes is irrelevant; it may, therefore, be held for a partnership of individuals. Excluded from the definition of relevant deposits are those held for companies, associations, charities, and discretionary and accumulation trusts where no one individual is beneficially entitled to the trust fund or a part thereof. In addition, there are specific exclusions for 'qualifying time deposits' with a nominal value never falling below £50,000 and, more significantly, for all cases where the interest is payable to a person ordinarily resident outside the UK (so long as that person submits a declaration of non-residence to his bank). A deposit denominated in a foreign currency can constitute a relevant deposit. **[4.23]**

4 Taxation of husband and wife: independent taxation

Independent taxation of husband and wife came into effect on 6 April 1990 and resulted in a married couple being taxed as two separate individuals. In earlier tax years the income of a married woman living with her husband was generally taxed as his income for all purposes. This was the only situation where the income of different persons was aggregated: minor children, for instance, have been taxed independently of their parents for many years. An election for separate assessment under TA 1988 s 283 was possible but did not affect the total tax bill, merely apportioning that bill between the couple. More important therefore was the election for separate taxation of the wife's earnings under TA 1988 s 287 but this only provided for earned income to be taxed separately as her own. **[4.24]**

5 Earned and investment income

With the abolition (as from 1984–85) of the surcharge on investment income above a certain limit, the distinction between earned and investment income is relevant only in relatively few situations.

Under TA 1988 s 833 'earned income' falls into two main categories:
(a) All income chargeable under Schedule E which is derived from an office or employment including income from pensions (see Chapter 5).
(b) 'any income which is charged under Schedule D and is *immediately derived* by the individual from the carrying on or exercise by him of his trade, profession or vocation, either as an individual or, in the case of a partnership, as a partner personally acting therein.'

The borderline between earned and unearned income is not always easy to draw. The phrase 'immediately derived' has been strictly construed by the courts (see, for instance, *Northend v White, Leonard and Corbin Greener* (1975) and *Bucks v Bowers* (1970)). Generally, income under Schedule D Cases I and II is earned income, whereas that assessable under Schedule A (rent), Schedule D Case III (such as interest and trust income), Schedule D Case IV (foreign securities, such as dividends), Schedule F (dividends from UK companies), Schedule C (such as interest on government stock), and Schedule

D Case VI will be investment income. Note, however, that rent from 'furnished holiday lettings' is specifically treated as earned income (see Chapter 8). **[4.25]–[4.40]**

EXAMPLE 4.4

Winnie owns a honey shop and is chargeable for 1991–92 on £20,000 profit. He also receives rent of £300 from letting a garage.

Calculation of statutory income for 1991–92:

	Investment		*Earned*
	£		*£*
Profits from shop (Schedule D Case I)			20,000
Rent (Schedule A)	300		
Statutory income	£300	+	£20,000

Winnie's statutory income for the year is £20,300 from which various deductions will be made before tax is chargeable.

III   CHARGES ON INCOME *(Step 2)*

1   **General**

Charges on income are described in TMA 1970 s 8(8) as 'amounts which fall to be deducted in computing total income'. Thus, they are deductible from the individual's statutory income and technically may be deducted from investment income first. The 'amounts which fall to be deducted' are not defined, but consist of certain transfers of income which the taxpayer is obliged to make. The theory is that such income ceases to be that of the payer and becomes the income of the payee so that the payer should not be taxed on it. Charges are, therefore, deducted before personal reliefs because the latter cannot be deducted from income which is not the taxpayer's.

Charges on income comprise: annuities; certain other annual payments; and certain interest payments (see generally Chapter 10). In addition, a special deduction equal to the lower of maintenance payments made to a former spouse and (for 1991–92) £1,720 is available to the person who is taxed on such maintenance payments. As explained in Chapter 35, this will be the payee in the case of existing obligations and the payer in the case of new arrangements.

Finally, from 1990–91 income tax relief has been given for premiums paid by an individual under an 'eligible' private medical insurance contract. Contracts are only eligible if the person or persons insured are aged 60 or over when the payment is made and UK residents or, alternatively, are a married couple both UK residents with at least one of them being 60 or over. If the contract is eligible, tax relief is then given to *whoever* makes the payments. Accordingly, a wealthy son, for instance, can obtain the relief on insurance taken out for his elderly parents. The actual mechanics of giving the tax relief are that the payer obtains relief at the basic rate level by handing over reduced premiums to the insurer (as is the case with MIRAS payments, discussed below): at the higher rate relief is given on the appropriate claim being made (see further FA 1989 ss 54–57 and SI 1989/2389). **[4.41]**

EXAMPLE 4.5

In 1991-92 Viola has income from her employment (Schedule E) and from trading (Schedule D Case I) amounting in all to £27,500. From this sum she can deduct premiums paid on an eligible medical insurance contract which has been taken out for the benefit of her elderly parents. Assuming that gross premiums payable amount to £100 per month a total of £1,200 can be deducted by Viola giving her total income for tax purposes of £26,300.

(*Note*: In this example Viola's income is such that she is a higher rate taxpayer and accordingly relief is obtained by deducting the gross premium. Basic rate relief is obtained by handing over a net premium to the insurance company (ie by deducting 25% from the gross premium)).

2 Annual payments

The meaning of an annual payment is discussed in Chapter 10. As a result of FA 1988 only certain annual payments now qualify as charges on income. In such cases they are treated for tax purposes as part of the income of the person (the payee) to whom they are paid. Typical examples are:

(a) payments under a deed of covenant to a charity for four or more years, and

(b) annuities, certain royalties and certain maintenance payments made under an obligation entered into before 15 March 1988.

Although the above annual payments constitute a charge on the payer's income and, accordingly, are free of tax in his hands, the payer is used as an agent to collect basic rate tax on the amount paid (see TA 1988 ss 3, 348, 349). The annual payment is, therefore, added back to the payer's income for this purpose. To recompense himself, he is allowed to deduct and retain from the payment a sum equal to tax at basic rate on that payment.   [**4.42**]

EXAMPLE 4.6

Viola has statutory income of £26,300 (see *Example 4.5*). She has covenanted to pay the NSPCC (a registered charity) the sum of £1,000 pa (an annual payment). Under TA 1988 s 348 Viola may deduct from the gross payment of £1,000 a sum equivalent to basic rate tax on that figure (ie £250). She, therefore, pays £750 and retains £250.

The income on which she is subject to tax (before deducting personal reliefs) is:

	£
Statutory income	26,300
Less: charge on income (gross)	1,000
Total income	£25,300

From this Viola may deduct her personal allowance and she will be taxed on the balance. In addition, however, she must pay tax at 25% on the covenanted payment.

Notice that the charity receives the sum of £750 after deduction of basic rate income tax at source with a tax credit for the £250 deducted by Viola. As charities are not generally subject to income tax, the NSPCC can reclaim this £250 from the Revenue. (The tax reliefs available to charities are discussed in Appendix IX.)

3   **Certain interest payments**

An individual obtains income tax relief for certain interest payments by deducting them from his statutory income as a charge. Certain other interest payments are deductible in computing income from a particular source only (eg, interest payments made for the purposes of a trade are deductible in computing the profits of that trade under Schedule D Case I). Most interest payments, however, receive no tax relief at all. The ordinary bank overdraft, credit card interest, and hire purchase interest payments, to take three typical instances, receive no tax relief.

The rules governing the deductibility of interest are complex (the provisions are contained in TA 1988 ss 353–366). The interest must be payable on a loan made for one of the qualifying purposes dealt with below. Further, it must be either annual interest chargeable as the payee's income under Schedule D Case III, or must be payable in the UK on a loan from a bank, or from a person *bona fide* carrying on business as a member of a UK Stock Exchange or as a UK discount house (TA 1988 s 353). As a general rule, interest that is eligible for tax relief is paid gross and is deductible from the payer's statutory income as a charge. For exceptional cases where basic rate income tax must be deducted at source by the payer of the interest see [**10.81**].   [**4.43**]

Loans to acquire an interest in a close company (TA 1988 ss 360, 361, 363)   An individual may obtain income tax relief for the interest paid on a loan to acquire ordinary share capital in close trading companies and on a loan raised to lend money to such a company so long as it is used wholly and exclusively for the business of the company (or of an associated company which is likewise a qualifying close company). To qualify for relief, the borrower has to show *either* that he is a shareholder and works for the greater part of his time in the management or conduct of the company *or* that he controls more than 5% (a 'material interest') of the ordinary share capital (in the latter case the borrower need not work for the company).

To calculate whether the individual has the necessary material interest, shares of associates must generally be aggregated with his own shares. 'Associates' include an individual's relatives, partners, trustees of a settlement which he created, and trustees of a settlement holding shares for the benefit of that individual. However, unappropriated shares held by trustees under an approved profit sharing scheme and shares in which the individual has an interest only under an employee benefit trust are not included in deciding whether he has a material interest in the company (see generally TA 1988 s 360A).

To the extent that the borrower recovers any capital from the company during that time (eg by repayment of ordinary share capital), he is treated as having repaid the loan and the amount of interest available for relief is reduced accordingly. Relief is not withdrawn if the company subsequently ceases to be close (see SP 3/78). It is not possible to obtain double tax relief by using the loan to purchase shares qualifying for relief under BES (see [**4.83**]).   [**4.44**]

EXAMPLE 4.7

Gatty Ltd is the family trading company of the Gatty family. Sam Freebie, a full-time working director owning no shares in the company, borrows £5,000 from his bank to subscribe for ordinary shares. He will own a 4% shareholding and tax relief is available on the interest he pays. If, however, Jack Floor, the caretaker of the company's factory, were to subscribe for a similar number of shares no relief will be available because he is not concerned in the management or conduct of the company.

Loan to acquire an interest in a partnership (TA 1988 s 362)   Interest relief is available to an individual on a loan used to purchase a share in a partnership or to contribute capital or make a loan to the partnership, if it is used wholly and exclusively for the business purposes of the partnership. Relief is available only if, from the application of the loan to the payment of interest, the individual has been a member of the partnership (otherwise than as a limited partner) and has not recovered any capital from the partnership. Where the partnership is subsequently incorporated into a close company and the loan remains outstanding, relief continues to be available so long as relief would be available under the close company provisions considered above if the loan were a new loan taken out on incorporation.   **[4.45]**

Loan to acquire an interest in a co-operative (TA 1988 s 361)   Relief is available for interest payments made on a loan to acquire an interest in a co-operative, or to be used wholly and exclusively for the business of that body or a subsidiary. A co-operative is defined as a common ownership enterprise or a co-operative enterprise within the meaning of the Industrial Common Ownership Act 1976 s 2. Relief is available only if the individual shows that from the application of the loan to the payment of the interest he has worked for the greater part of his time as an employee in that co-operative or in a subsidiary thereof.   **[4.46]**

Loan to invest in an employee-controlled company (TA 1988 s 361)   Relief is available for interest payments on a loan taken out by an individual to acquire ordinary shares in an employee-controlled company (which must be a UK resident unquoted trading company). An employee-controlled company is one where full-time employees own more than 50% of the ordinary share capital and voting power of the company. When an employee owns more than 10% of the issued share capital, the excess is treated as not being owned by a full-time employee. Other conditions for relief are that the shares must be acquired within 12 months of the company becoming employee-controlled and that the taxpayer or his spouse must be full-time employees of the company from the time when the loan is applied to the date when interest is paid. Furthermore, in the year of assessment in which the interest is paid the company must either first become employee-controlled or be such a company for at least nine months. Accordingly, interest relief will be withdrawn when the company ceases to be employee-controlled. To the extent that the individual recovers any capital from the company, the same rule operates as for close companies and partnerships (see above).   **[4.47]**

Loan to purchase plant or machinery (TA 1988 s 359)   Where a partner or a Schedule E employee borrows money to purchase a car or other items of machinery or plant for which capital allowances are available, he can claim interest relief on that loan for up to three years after the end of the tax year when the debt was incurred. (Note that for a sole trader interest on such loans is a deductible business expense.)   **[4.48]**

Loans used to purchase land occupied for business purposes by a partnership or company (SP 4/85)   Where an individual takes out a loan to purchase land occupied by a partnership (of which he is a partner) or a company (of which he is a director) relief for interest paid on that loan may be available, depending upon the precise arrangements entered into. The SP considers various permutations and its conclusions are discussed in the following four situations. *Case 1*:   Felix purchases land with the aid of a loan and allows his partnership to use the land for business purposes. Felix is paid a rent for the use of the land which is sufficient to cover his interest payments. Felix will obtain tax relief by setting the interest payments against the rent received under TA 1988 s 355; see further [**8.18**]. The rent paid by the partnership is a deductible business expense.

Case 2:   as in *Case 1* save that the interest payments are made by the partnership and no rent is paid to Felix. The interest payments will be deemed to be rent for the use of the land and, as such, will be a deductible business expense of the partnership. Felix, however, will not be taxed on that sum because he may deduct the interest for which he is liable (TA 1988 s 355). In *R v Inspector of Taxes, ex p Brumfield* (1989) a partnership borrowed money which in turn it allowed one of the partners to use, interest free, towards the purchase of a plot of land. That land, which was acquired in the name of the individual partner, was then used rent free by the partnership. On these facts the court held that the statement of practice was inapplicable: the interest was not a deductible business expense of the partnership and the loan had not been taken out in the name of the individual partner as required in *Case 2*.

Case 3:   assume that Felix allows the land to be used by a company (Felix Ltd) of which he is a director. If a rent is paid to Felix it will be a deductible expense of the company and Felix will be able to set the interest that he pays against that rent (ie as in *Case 1* above). If the interest payments are made by the company, however, those sums will be taxed as part of Felix's remuneration under Schedule E and may be a deductible expense of the company. No question of interest relief will, therefore, arise.

Case 4:   Felix borrows money to purchase land which is used by either a company or partnership as in *Cases 1–3*. Felix pays interest on the loan and no rent is paid for the use of the land. No interest relief is available.

Given these permutations the following conclusions are suggested. First, *Case 4* leaves Felix in the disadvantageous position of paying interest without qualifying for tax relief thereon. Secondly, when the company discharges the interest payments Felix may be taxed on those sums without any set-off for the interest which he is liable to pay. Were the company to pay him the same sum as rent, the deduction of interest ensures that Felix will pay no income tax on that sum. Finally, Felix's possible entitlement to retirement relief in each case should be carefully considered. To the extent that a rent is paid (or, in the above cases, deemed to be paid) his retirement relief on the ultimate disposal of the land will be restricted (see further [**16.97**]).   [**4.49**]

Loan to pay inheritance tax (TA 1988 s 364)   PRs are eligible for interest relief on a loan used by them to pay IHT attributable to personal property situated in the UK to which the deceased was beneficially entitled and which has vested in them (see further Chapter 12). The relief is limited to a twelve month period.   [**4.50**]

Loan to purchase a life annuity (TA 1988 s 365)   Interest relief is available (as from 1991–92 at the basic rate only) on a loan not exceeding £30,000 to a person aged 65 or over to purchase an annuity on his life provided that at least nine-tenths of the loan proceeds are used to buy the annuity and that the annuity is secured on land in the UK (or Republic of Ireland) in which he has an interest and uses as his only or main residence at the time when the interest is paid (see below). [**4.51**]

4 Loans for the purchase of land and the MIRAS scheme (TA 1988 ss 354–358 and 367–378)

Prior to changes in FA 1988, interest relief was available in three circumstances: first, on a loan to acquire a main residence or develop land for use as a main residence; secondly, on a loan to improve a main residence; and thirdly, on a loan to purchase a main residence for use by one or more dependent relatives. In the first situation FA 1988 made important changes in the allocation of relief when more than one purchaser is involved but in the second and third situations it withdrew the relief altogether. Accordingly, this section will begin by considering the availability of relief when a main residence is purchased or land developed for use as such and will then look briefly at the other situations where relief has now been withdrawn. [**4.52**]

a) *Conditions for relief on a loan to purchase a main residence*

Interest is eligible for tax relief if it is paid on a loan by the owner of an estate or interest in land in the UK or the Republic of Ireland for the purpose of acquiring or developing the land for use as his only or main residence. Land includes a large caravan or houseboat. Expenditure on purchase includes the cost of any legal fees and stamp duty attributable to the purchase. Land is developed for these purposes if a new building, which is not part of an existing residence, is erected on land which immediately before that development began had no building on it (TA 1988 s 355(2B)). The following conditions must be satisfied for a borrower to qualify: [**4.53**]

Ownership The interest payments must be made by the person owning the interest in the land and not, for instance, by his rich mother-in-law. If the borrower dies, his PRs are not generally entitled to claim the relief against estate income (for exceptional circumstances where relief may continue to be available on a transitional basis see below). [**4.54**]

Qualifying purpose The loan must be used for the 'qualifying purpose' (*viz* the acquisition or development of land) either when it is obtained or within a reasonable time thereafter. [**4.55**]

EXAMPLE 4.8

Fred takes out a loan of £20,000 in October to build a modern bungalow for use as his main residence on land which he owns in Norfolk. However, the work cannot be started until the spring and in the meantime Fred invests the money in shares. The interest on this loan will not be eligible for tax relief. Fred should, therefore, repay the loan out of the sale proceeds of the shares and take out a new loan to be used for the building work.

Only or main residence The land must be used as the only or main residence of the borrower. Whether land is used as a person's 'only or main residence' is a question of fact and degree and, if the borrower has more than one residence, he cannot choose which is to be treated for income tax purposes as the main residence (compare the CGT exemption; [**16.61**]). The amount of time spent in the residence is only one of the facts to be taken into account.

In *Frost v Feltham* (1981) the taxpayer was the tenant and licensee of a public house in Essex which he was required by the terms of his employment to occupy (to some extent the actual decision in this case has been overtaken by the rules on job-related accommodation introduced after the case was decided and which are considered below). He bought a house in Wales with the aid of a mortgage on which he successfully claimed interest relief even though he only visited the house irregularly; the deciding factor was his intention to use the house as his main residence.

'If someone lives in two houses the question which does he use as the principal or more important one cannot be determined solely by reference to the way in which he divides his time between the two. I can test that by reference to an example far removed from the facts of this case and the conditions of our own times. In his "Lives of the Lord Chancellors", Lord Campbell tells how Lord Eldon was often prevented by the burdens of his office from visiting his estate in Encombe in Dorset for long periods at a time. Sometimes he was only able to get down there for three weeks or so in the year, for the partridge shooting in September. True it was that Lord Eldon also had a good house in Hamilton Place, but it could not really have been suggested that he did not use Encombe as his principal or more important residence.' (Nourse J in *Frost v Feltham.*)

In practice, the Revenue take the view that the accommodation should be furnished and more or less in a state of readiness for permanent occupation if relief is to be available. Temporary absences of up to one year are ignored. So too is an absence of up to four years caused by the borrower having to move elsewhere in the UK or abroad because of his job. In practice, he can string together several four year periods provided that he returns for a period of three months between each. (ESC A27.)

Where the taxpayer is required by his employment to live in job-related accommodation, he can claim relief for interest paid on another property, even though it is not his main residence, provided that at the time of the payment it is used by the borrower as a residence (for instance at weekends); or he intends to use it in due course as his only or main residence, for instance after the job ends: TA 1988 s 356. The accommodation is job-related if it fulfills the conditions laid down in TA 1988 s 145 (see p 69). This relaxation of the residence rule for job-related accommodation also applies to interest paid by the self-employed taxpayer or his spouse who is bound, under a contract made at arm's length, to carry on his business on the land of another and to occupy property provided by that person except where the accommodation is provided either by a company in which he or his spouse has a material interest or by his or his spouse's firm (TA 1988 s 356(3), (5)). [4.56]

£30,000 limit When a main residence is purchased by a single taxpayer relief is available to him for interest on a qualifying loan of up to £30,000. Hence, in so far as the loan exceeds £30,000 the interest on the excess is disallowed. If the borrower has more than one qualifying loan, they are aggregated for the purpose of the £30,000 limit and interest on earlier loans is relieved before interest on later ones. ('Top ups' involving a higher rate of interest should be signed first, therefore, although, if it is part of a single contract to purchase, the Revenue would treat both loans as made on the same day.)

EXAMPLE 4.9

Balthazar has two loans subject to different interest rates—loan 1 is for £25,000 at 12.5% pa and loan 2 (taken out after the first loan) is for £10,000 at 15% pa.
 Balthazar's interest relief in a full tax year would be:

$$£25,000 \text{ at } 12.5\% \qquad\qquad = \overset{£}{3,125}$$

$$£10,000 \text{ at } 15\% \times \frac{30,000 - 25,000}{10,000} \qquad = \underline{750}$$

Total interest relief $\qquad\qquad\qquad\qquad \underline{\underline{£3,875}}$

If the two loans were replaced by a single loan, or if both loans were taken out on the same day, the higher interest rate charged on the second loan would be spread evenly thereby enhancing the relief available: ie:

(a) *Total interest paid* $\qquad\qquad\qquad\qquad £$
£25,000 at 12.5% $\qquad\qquad\qquad = 3,125$
£10,000 at 15% $\qquad\qquad\qquad\quad = \underline{1,500}$
$\qquad\qquad\qquad\qquad\qquad\qquad\quad \underline{\underline{£4,625}}$

(b) *Total interest relief*
$£4,625 \times \dfrac{30,000}{35,000} \qquad\qquad\qquad = \underline{\underline{£3,964}}$

In the case of bridging loans, to which TA 1988 s 354 applies, each residence is treated separately for determining the £30,000 ceiling (see b) below).
 Finally, TA 1988 s 355(5) prevents relief in the case of artificial transactions; in particular, where the vendor and purchaser are husband and wife, or where the loan to improve the property is from a connected person and exceeds the value of that work. **[4.57]**

The residence basis For loans taken out before 1 August 1988 to purchase the borrower's main residence, the £30,000 limit applied to each borrower although spouses were treated as one person for these purposes and therefore only entitled to a single relief. As a result unmarried couples could obtain twice as much interest relief as a married couple and accordingly for loans taken out on or after that date (see TA 1988 s 356C(3) for when a loan is made for these purposes) the £30,000 limit on relief is given *per residence* irrespective of the number of borrowers (the 'residence basis'). The available relief must now be divided between the various borrowers as illustrated in the following examples:

EXAMPLE 4.10

Cain and Abel have qualifying loans on their main residence of £30,000 and £50,000 respectively. On the assumption that the loans were taken out:

(i) *Pre 1 August 1988:* Cain and Abel will both be entitled to interest relief on a loan up to £30,000 so that Cain will obtain full relief for the interest that he pays whilst Abel will be left with no relief on £20,000 of his loan.

(ii) *On or after 1 August 1988:* the £30,000 limit is shared equally between Cain and Abel so that both will get relief on a loan of up to £15,000. Accordingly, Cain will be left with no relief on a loan of £15,000 and Abel with no relief on a loan of £35,000.

Dividing up the £30,000 qualifying amount equally, as in *Example 4.10*, may result in a borrower being allocated an amount which exceeds his loan. In such cases the excess is re-divided between the other borrowers whose loans exceeded their original allocation.

EXAMPLE 4.11

Sing, Sang and Song have jointly purchased a main residence so that, *prima facie*, each is entitled to interest relief on a loan of £10,000. Assume, however, that Sing's loan was £6,000, Sang's loan £22,000, and Song's loan £18,000.

Sing can therefore only use £6,000 of his allocated £10,000 whilst Sang and Song will receive no relief on loans of £12,000 and £8,000 respectively. Accordingly, the unused portion of Sing's allocation (£4,000) will be transferred to the others so that Sang gets an extra relief of £2,400 (ie $\frac{12,000}{20,000} \times £4,000$) while Song gets an extra £1,600 ($\frac{8,000}{20,000} \times £4,000$).

If a husband and wife jointly purchase property with other borrowers they are treated as separate persons for the purposes of calculating each borrower's share of the £30,000 limit and once this computation is made the normal rules for allocating interest relief between spouses, discussed in Chapter 35, apply.   [**4.58**]

b) *Exceptions where relief is given despite non-occupation of the property*

In the cases considered below interest relief is available despite the fact that the property is not used as the only or main residence when the loan is acquired.

First, when the property becomes the main residence within 12 months after acquiring the loan (TA 1988 s 355(1)). This caters for property that requires substantial improvement before it can be occupied.

Secondly, where the taxpayer has obtained bridging finance, he will continue to receive interest relief on the loan on his old property for 12 months after acquiring a 'new loan' on the new property which he occupies as his main residence, provided that the new loan is acquired for a qualifying purpose and that he intends to sell the old property (TA 1988 ss 354(5), 357). Notice that the 'new loan' will not itself qualify for relief unless the new property is actually used as the individual's only or main residence; an intention to do so does not suffice (see *Hughes v Viner* (1985)). The 12 month period may, by concession, be extended if the taxpayer can show that he has been unable to sell the old property. In this situation, the loans are not aggregated and each loan is considered separately in applying the £30,000 ceiling. The relief for delay in occupying a new house and for bridging finance will often be useful when a couple get married.

Special rules apply to exempt from tax the benefit where an employee has to move house because of his employment and receives a bridging loan or a reimbursement of net loan interest from his employer (ESC A5: [**5.70**]). In this case the reimbursement will not be taxed but, of course, the employee will not be allowed to deduct the interest from his taxable income!   [**4.59**]

EXAMPLE 4.12

In the following cases Hugh and Wilma (H and W) are newly-weds. Assume that the loans referred to are for a qualifying purpose and do not (individually) exceed £30,000.

Case A H pays interest on loan 1 on a house which before marriage was his main residence. After marriage, it becomes the matrimonial home. H continues to receive interest relief.

Case B As in *Case A* above, except that H and W take out a new loan, loan 2, to purchase a house which becomes the matrimonial home. H continues to receive interest relief on loan 1 (as well as on loan 2) for 12 months from obtaining loan 2 so long as he intends to sell his original house.

Case C H and W both have loans (1 and 2) on houses acquired before their marriage. They take out another loan, loan 3, on a house which becomes the matrimonial home. By concession they will continue to receive interest relief on loans 1 and 2 (as well as on loan 3) for 12 months from taking out loan 3.

Case D As in *Case C* above except that H and W do not acquire a new house, but occupy W's existing house as the matrimonial home. TA 1988 s 354(5) cannot apply to this situation because H and W have not taken out a 'new' loan. However by ESC A35 they continue to receive relief on loans 1 and 2 provided that the property which is not the matrimonial home is sold within 12 months of H ceasing to live there.

Case E As in *Case C* above except that H and W occupy another property as their matrimonial home without taking out a new loan. H and W lose interest relief on loans 1 and 2 once they cease to occupy those properties. Neither para 6, the concession, nor ESC A35 apply to these facts.

c) *Method of obtaining tax relief—the MIRAS scheme* (TA 1988 ss 369–379)

Tax relief for interest payments at the basic rate is generally given under the so-called MIRAS scheme (Mortgage Interest Relief At Source). Prior to 6 April 1991 relief was also available against income tax at the higher rate and this was given by permitting the taxpayer to deduct the gross interest payment as a charge on his income. As from that date, however, higher rate relief was abolished. In the majority of cases today full tax relief is therefore given under the MIRAS scheme with the result that the interest payments can be ignored in computing the taxpayer's income tax liability.

MIRAS will cover the majority of mortgage interest payments because it applies whenever:
(a) a 'qualifying borrower' (basically all individuals);
(b) makes a payment of relevant loan interest, which is defined as interest paid in the UK after 5 April 1983 on a loan made for a qualifying purpose; and
(c) the payment is to a 'qualifying lender'. This term covers all bodies who normally make such loans (eg building societies, local authorities and housing associations).

Formerly, if the loan exceeded £30,000, MIRAS applied to so much of it as was within the limit only if the lender gave notice to the Revenue that he was prepared to accept the deduction in respect of all loans above £30,000 made by him. However, as from 6 April 1987, lenders are obliged to apply MIRAS to new loans which exceed £30,000 so that basic rate relief at source can therefore be given on that part of the loan which is within the limit (TA 1988 s 373).

The practical application of tax relief can be illustrated by the following two cases. The first is where the payer is a basic rate taxpayer who will receive all his tax relief within the scheme. The second is where the taxpayer is outside the scheme (eg because his loan is pre-April 1987, exceeds £30,000 and the lender has not elected for MIRAS to apply to it).   **[4.60]**

Case A—basic rate taxpayer   Basic rate tax on the interest payments is collected from the taxpayer along with his other income tax. Hence, his income is not reduced by the interest payments. To compensate the payer, he is entitled to deduct from the interest payment a sum equivalent to basic rate tax on the gross figure.   **[4.61]**

EXAMPLE 4.13

Sebastian, who has taxable income of £13,400, pays £200 relevant loan interest to the Dodgy Building Society each month. He satisfies his obligation to the building society by paying them each month:

	£
Gross payment	200
Less sum equivalent to basic rate tax	50
Payment to building society	£150

   The building society recover the amount deducted by Sebastian (ie £50) from the Revenue (s 369(6)). Sebastian's income tax liability for the year is 25% of his taxable income of £13,400 ie £3,350. Because Sebastian has deducted the equivalent of basic rate tax from his payments over the year (£600), the interest payments are effectively free of tax in his hands.

Case B—taxpayer outside MIRAS   Where the taxpayer is outside the scheme the interest payments are paid gross and are deductible as charges from the taxpayer's income for all tax purposes.

EXAMPLE 4.14

As in *Example 4.13*, except that Sebastian's payments are not within MIRAS. Accordingly, he pays £200 to the Dodgy Building Society each month. His income tax calculation is (ignoring personal reliefs):

	£
Statutory income	29,600
Less interest payments (gross)	2,400
	£27,200

	£
Tax on £23,700 at 25%	5,925
Plus tax on £3,500 at 40%	1,400
Tax due	£7,325

   The operation of MIRAS does not increase the cost of mortgages since, instead of tax relief, the borrower obtains a reduction in the interest payments made. However, there is a timing difference, in that the payer will pay less to his lender each month, thereby increasing his cash flow. (For the particular advantages on matrimonial breakdown, see Chapter 35.) MIRAS is positively advantageous to the taxpayer in the (unlikely) circumstances where his personal allowances exceed his income left after deducting the interest payments. Before the introduction of MIRAS the result would have been a loss of personal allowances, but now unused allowances can effectively be set against the interest payments on which the taxpayer is subject to basic rate income tax (see TA 1988 s 369(4), which was designed to compensate for the abolition of the mortgage option scheme).

EXAMPLE 4.15

Bertrand, a single man, has income for 1991-92 of £3,000 and pays relevant loan interest of £3,000 for the year. Therefore, he pays the lender £2,250 and retains £750 (being equivalent to basic rate tax).

But he has unused allowances of £3,005 so that by s 369(4):

	£
Sum assessed under s 369(3)	3,000
Less unused allowance	3,295
Sum taxed	Nil

ie the 3000 loan interest is not deducted thus leaving the income to be reduced by P.A

This may be contrasted with the position of Bertrand in 1982-83 (ie before the introduction of MIRAS) when, assuming the same figures, he would have paid no income tax since his interest payments (£3,000) would have been deducted from his income (£3,000). His personal reliefs for the year would have been wasted. In 1982-83 Bertrand would have made gross payments to the lender of £3,000 instead of £2,250 under MIRAS. As a result, Bertrand is better off under the MIRAS scheme by £750.

3000 Income
3000 Interest
NIL .·. personal allowances lost.

A taxpayer is not subject to UK income tax if he is working wholly abroad so that his emoluments from the employment are subject to the 100% foreign income deduction (TA 1988 s 193(1); see [**13.35**]). Nevertheless, the MIRAS scheme can still apply to interest payments made by such a taxpayer, provided that the loan is for a 'qualifying purpose'; this will be the case where, for example, the borrower is required by his job to be absent from the UK for up to four years because such absence does not prevent the property from being his only or main residence for the purpose of claiming income tax relief (see ESC A27). [**4.62**]

EXAMPLE 4.16

(1) Adam is an engineer. He has bought a house in the UK with the aid of a mortgage for £35,000 from the Roxy Building Society who (as it is a pre-April 1987 loan) have not elected to have MIRAS applied to that loan.

   (i) *whilst he is working in the UK:* interest is paid gross and Adam obtains relief in his PAYE coding or assessment.

   (ii) *he is absent from the UK on a two year contract in the Middle East:* Adam satisfies the requirements of ESC A27 so that the property remains his main residence. However, his earnings in the Middle East attract no UK income tax because of the 100% deduction (above) and Adam has no other UK income. Accordingly, he must continue to pay the interest gross and will obtain no tax relief thereon.

(2) Take the same facts as in (1) but assume that the Roxy Building Society have opted to bring loans over £30,000 within MIRAS. As long as the loan remains outstanding, Adam will pay interest on the relevant portion net (ie after deduction of basic rate tax). Thus he will continue to receive relief whilst he works abroad even though he has no UK taxable income.

d)   *Loans for home improvements*

Interest on loans taken out before 6 April 1988 qualified for relief if the
loan was used for the improvement of the main residence of the borrower,
his dependent relative, or his former or separated spouse. An improvement
involved expenditure of a capital nature rather than mere maintenance or
repair and the relief was only given if the loan was so used within a reasonable
time of being made. In practice, over 85% of such loans were taken out
for improvements which did not involve any extension to the property (most
were for the installation of double glazing or central heating). FA 1988 s 43
ended this relief for interest paid in such circumstances on loans taken out
after 5 April 1988. Relief will, however, continue to be given for interest
paid on qualifying loans taken out on or before that date although it will
not be available in the case of a replacement loan taken out
subsequently.   [**4.63**]

e)   *Dependent relatives*

Interest paid on loans taken out before 6 April 1988 for the purchase of
property used as the main residence of a dependent relative or former or
separated spouse of the borrower qualified for tax relief. Although the relief
was not limited to the provision of a single house for all dependent relatives
(so that theoretically so long as the borrower had enough dependent relatives
a number of houses could be purchased) in practice, the £30,000 ceiling
on relief, which applied per borrower, meant that it was unlikely that more
than one such residence would attract relief. Interest relief in such cases
was also withdrawn for interest paid after 5 April 1988 subject, however,
to continuation of relief where the relevant loan was made before 6 April
1988. Generally this transitional relief will continue to be available so long
as the property remains occupied by the same dependent relative or spouse
who was in occupation on 6 April 1988.

Relief had also been available for interest paid by personal representatives
of a deceased borrower when the relevant property had been used by the
deceased as his main residence at the date of death if, at the time when
the personal representatives paid the interest, it was occupied as the main
residence of a dependent relative of the deceased. With effect from 6 April
1988, relief ceased in this case as well unless the deceased had died before
6 April 1988 and the property concerned was occupied by the relative as
his main residence before that date.   [**4.64**]

5   **Vocational training** (FA 1991 ss 32–3)

With effect from 6 April 1992 the costs incurred by an individual in respect
of a qualifying course of vocational training qualify for tax relief at basic
and higher rate. Basic rate relief will be given by deduction from the study
and examination fees paid (in the same way as MIRAS relief) whilst tax
relief at the higher rate will be given on a claim being submitted to the
individual's tax office. Tax relief is given whether or not the individual obtains
the qualification! Detailed administrative arrangements are to be set out
in Statutory Instruments and the qualifying courses will be those leading
to National Vocational Qualifications at levels 1–4 (these qualifications being
accredited by two Government supported bodies: the National Council for
Vocational Qualifications in England, Wales and Northern Ireland and the
Scottish Vocational Education Council). It may be noted that because of
the way in which relief is given (at source by deduction from the fees) it

will be available even for the trainee with no taxable income: hence unemployed people retraining with a view to returning to work will be able to obtain some benefit from the new relief. **[4.65]**

6 Class 4 national insurance contributions

One-half of the class 4 national insurance contributions paid by a self-employed person each year are deductible in arriving at his total income for that year (TA 1988 s 617(5)). Hence, although not strictly a charge on income, this sum is deducted at this stage of the income tax calculation. It should be noted that the permitted deduction is for half of the class 4 contribution only (levied at the current rate of 6.30% subject to a lower earnings limit of £5,900 and an upper limit of £20,200) and not for the class 2 flat rate weekly contribution of £5.15 (where earnings exceed £2,900 pa).

Although an employer cannot deduct the national insurance contributions that he makes for his employees in arriving at his total income, these sums will be an allowable expense of the business (see **[6.122]**). An employee's contributions do not qualify for any relief from income tax.   **[4.66]–[4.80]**

IV TOTAL INCOME *(Step 3)*

Charges are deducted from income before any other deductions and the resultant sum is 'total income'. In so far as charges exceed statutory income, the unabsorbed charge receives no tax relief and cannot be carried forward to a future year. After charges, the individual deducts personal reliefs from total income to arrive at his taxable income. However, certain other deductions may be available and will be deducted before personal reliefs. Notice that it is the total income figure before further deductions are made that is used to calculate (where applicable) the age allowance and (where available) the $1/6$th for life assurance premium relief (see **[4.141]**).   **[4.81]**

1 Loss relief (TA 1988 ss 380–381)

Sometimes losses arising under a particular Schedule are deductible only in computing profits from the same source. Such losses, therefore, affect the calculation of the individual's statutory income by reducing income from that source.

EXAMPLE 4.17

Anita receives a salary as a lecturer (Schedule E) of £14,000 pa. She also owns a house in Chelsea which she rents to nurses from the Chelsea Hospital. In the current tax year her allowable expenses on the property under Schedule A exceeded her Schedule A rental income by £1,000. Her statutory income for the current year is:

	£
Schedule E	14,000
Schedule A (loss £1,000)	Nil
Statutory income	£14,000

Anita cannot deduct her £1,000 Schedule A loss from income from any other source. All she can do is carry the loss forward to a subsequent year and deduct it from Schedule A profits of that year. Thus, if in the following year her rental income exceeds her allowable expenses under Schedule A by £2,000, Anita's statutory income is:

	£	£
Schedule E		14,000
Schedule A: profit	2,000	
Less loss c/f	1,000	
		1,000
Statutory income		£15,000

Where the individual makes a loss in his trade, profession or vocation, however, he may choose to deduct that loss from his total income before deducting personal reliefs (see TA 1988 ss 380–381 and Chapter 7). The danger with claiming this loss relief is that it may so reduce total income that personal allowances are unused. **[4.82]**

EXAMPLE 4.18

Andrew is a barrister (Schedule D Case II) and a part-time lecturer (Schedule E) with a salary for the current year of £14,000 pa. He pays £1,000 pa to charity by deed of covenant. In the current tax year he makes a loss in his first year at the bar of £5,000 which he chooses under TA 1988 s 380 to deduct from his total income. His income tax calculation (in part) for the current tax year is as follows:

	£
Schedule E	14,000
Schedule D (loss £5,000)	Nil
Statutory income	14,000
Less charge on income	1,000
Total income	13,000
Less loss (TA 1988 s 380)	5,000
	£8,000

Andrew has £8,000 income from which he can deduct his personal reliefs.

2   **The business expansion scheme** (TA 1988 Part VII Chapter III as amended)

The scheme seeks to encourage investment in the ordinary share capital of trading companies. Investment may be by direct subscription or through an approved fund.

Subject to the conditions below being satisfied, a 'qualifying individual' can claim a deduction from his total income for the amount invested in 'eligible shares' in a 'qualifying company'. The maximum sum for which relief may be claimed each year is £40,000 and the minimum investment in any one company £500 (there is no prescribed minimum when the investment is through an approved fund, but in practice all funds set their own minimum investment which is usually greater than £500!).

The maximum investment eligible for relief in any one company over a specified period is restricted to £750,000 except for companies raising money for ship chartering or for private rented housing (see below) where the limit is £5 million. This specified period is the longer of the period of six months ending with the date of the issue of the shares or the period beginning with the preceding 6 April and ending with the date of the issue.

EXAMPLE 4.19

Croesus is subject to income tax at 40%. He invests £40,000 under the scheme in 1991–92.

	£
Total investment	40,000
Less income tax relief at 40%	16,000
Net cost of shares	£24,000

Note: The attraction of BES relief has been substantially reduced for 1988–89 and subsequent years with the abolition of the higher rates of income tax above 40%. Had Croesus made the same investment in 1987–88, for instance, when he was a 60% taxpayer, the net cost of the shares would have been only £16,000.

Interest paid on loans raised to acquire shares in a close company may qualify for income tax relief (as discussed at [**4.44**]) and it was formerly possible for a taxpayer to obtain double tax relief if the shares purchased also qualified for BES relief. Not surprisingly, FA 1989 closed this loophole by removing interest relief when the loan was used to acquire shares in a close company which qualified for BES relief.

In an attempt to prevent investment being concentrated in the last quarter of a tax year, where an individual invests under the scheme in shares issued after 5 April and before 6 October in any tax year, he can elect to carry back one-half of the sum invested (up to a maximum of £5,000) against his total income for the preceding tax year subject, however, to the overriding maximum of £40,000 per tax year. With the introduction of independent taxation, husbands and wives are both subject to the minimum (£500) and maximum (£40,000) limits for relief. However, neither can get relief on the other's subscriptions. [**4.83**]

EXAMPLE 4.20

Argent makes the following investments under the scheme:

				Sum invested	Tax year
				£	
9 Dec	1990	X	Ltd	35,000	1990/91
9 June	1991	A	Ltd	3,000	1991/92
9 Aug	1991	B	Ltd	5,000	1991/92
9 Oct	1991	C	Ltd	4,000	1991/92
9 Feb	1992	D	Ltd	34,000	1991/92

1   Tax year 1990–91
Argent can elect to carry back £1,500 of the investment in A Ltd and £2,500 of that in B Ltd in order to obtain relief against his total income in 1990–91 since this does not cause the total BES relief in that year to exceed the maximum of £40,000. Although a further £1,000 of his investment in C Ltd could be carried back without exceeding that maximum limit of £40,000 and the maximum carry-back of £5,000, this investment is not eligible for carry-back as it was made after 5 October 1990. 5 October 1991 : £ qualifying investment made before 6 October can be carried back to previous year.

2   Tax year 1991–92
Argent can, in effect, claim relief of more than £40,000 for shares issued in this tax year: ie of his total investment of £46,000 Argent claims relief for £40,000 in this tax year and carry-back relief to 1990–91 for £4,000.

The following conditions have to be satisfied for the relief to operate:

Investment by a qualifying individual   The relief is only available to an individual (not, therefore, to a trustee or company) who is resident and ordinarily resident in the UK throughout the tax year when the shares are issued and who is not connected with the company in either the two years preceding the issue (or from the date of incorporation, if later) or within the five years after the issue.

Broadly, an individual is connected with the company if he, or an associate of his, is an employee or paid director of the company; or a partner or a director of a company which is a partner with the company; or a tenant of a dwelling house of which the company is the landlord; or if he and his associates possess more than 30% of the capital (including loan capital) or voting power in the company. For these purposes an associate excludes brothers and sisters, but otherwise has the close company meaning (see [**28.124**]) whilst a director is not debarred from the relief if the only payments that he receives from the company are for travelling and other tax-deductible expenses. It follows that the obvious investors in small companies (working directors, employees and their relations) do not qualify and that the relief will not be available in management or employee buy-outs.   [**4.84**]

Investment in a qualifying trading company   Two conditions must be satisfied by the company.

First, it must have been incorporated in the UK and be UK-resident at the time of the share issue and for three years thereafter; all its share capital must be fully paid up; its shares must not be quoted on The Stock Exchange or dealt in on the Unlisted Securities Market; it must not be a subsidiary of, or be controlled by, any other company; and any subsidiaries that it has must be at least 90% owned.

Secondly, except for companies engaged in letting private rented housing (see below), the company must exist either for the purpose of trading 'wholly or mainly' in the UK (see SP 7/83 and SP 7/86) or to hold shares in subsidiaries which carry on qualifying trades. Notice, however, that the scheme extends to companies engaged in research and development from which it is intended that the company will carry on a qualifying trade and also to companies engaged in film production or distribution (TA 1988 s 289). Certain trades do not qualify, eg dealing in land, shares and commodities; leasing and letting assets; banking, insurance and other financial services (TA 1988 s 297). Changes in the definition of a qualifying trade may be made by statutory instrument.

The stated intention of the scheme is to encourage investment in unquoted trading companies carrying out more risky activities. Relief is therefore not given for wholesalers or retailers dealing in goods of a kind which are collected or held as an investment (eg, fine wines and antiques), if such goods are held 'for longer than would reasonably be expected . . . while endeavouring to dispose of them at their market value'. Similarly the scheme is not intended for concerns with a very secure asset backing. Relief is therefore not available if at any time before the end of the qualifying period (three years after the share issue or, if later, the commencement of trade) the net value of the company's land and buildings exceeds one half of the net value of the company's assets after deducting its liabilities (TA 1988 s 294). To prevent genuine trading ventures from being caught by this provision in the event of their property values rising sharply they can choose to value assets on the basis of land values at the date when the shares were issued. Farming and property development (where the developer company has an interest in the land being developed) will be caught by this limitation but even such companies may raise £50,000 annually under the scheme. **[4.85]**

Private rented housing   In an attempt to stimulate the rented property market, FA 1988 s 50 and Sch 4 extended BES relief to investment in shares issued before 1 January 1994 by unquoted companies which specialised in the 'qualifying activity' of letting residential property on the new style assured tenancy arrangements under the Housing Act 1988 over at least four years from the date of the share issue. The usual BES rules apply but subject to various modifications. Notably, the general restriction on the proportion of a company's assets which can be land does not apply to this investment. Broadly, the relevant company which may have 90% owned subsidiaries or may itself be a 90% owned subsidiary, may build new properties or use or acquire existing ones so long as they are employed for the qualifying activities and are unlet when acquired. To exclude expensive properties from relief, detailed valuation rules provide that the market value of each letting at the date when the shares are issued or the interest is acquired (if later) must not exceed £125,000 in Greater London or £85,000 elsewhere. The normal provisions denying relief to connected persons apply and, in addition, the investor or his associates must not have owned the property previously nor have been a tenant of such property let by the company. **[4.86]**

Subscription for eligible shares   Relief is given only for investment in new ordinary shares. The shares may carry different voting rights but otherwise they must not have any advantage over other shares, either in respect of dividends, a right to a company's assets on a winding-up or a present or future right to be redeemed.

If the conditions relating to the company cease to be satisfied within three years of the investment being made, the relief is withdrawn. It is also wholly or partly withdrawn if the individual receives value from the company (in the form, inter alia, of a redemption of his shares, a loan or the provision of a benefit) or disposes of his shares within five years of their purchase. When advantage has been taken of the carry-back facility, the relief given in the earlier tax year is withdrawn first. Withdrawal of relief involves reopening the income tax assessment for the year in which relief was given. In addition to the revised assessment, interest may be charged on the extra tax payable.

Claims for relief can be made when the qualifying trade or activity has been carried on for at least four months and must be made within two years of that date or, if later, two years from the end of the year of assessment in which the shares were issued. Further, the company must begin its qualifying trade or activity within two years of the share issue. A claim is made on a Revenue form completed by the company and on which it certifies that it has complied with the necessary conditions: the company can appeal against a refusal of approval in accordance with the procedure laid down in TMA 1970 s 42. When investment is made through an approved fund, relief is given by reference to the closing date for that fund's subscriptions rather than the date when the fund invested in the relevant companies.

If a taxpayer, who acquired shares under the BES, makes a subsequent disposal of those shares, CGT is not charged on any gain realised. For this CGT exemption to apply BES relief must not have been withdrawn from the taxpayer and the shares must have been issued after 18 March 1986. For shares issued on or before that date normal CGT rules apply so that the full acquisition cost can be deducted from the sale proceeds (see *Example 4.21(1)*). If that sale were for less than the taxpayer's acquisition costs, however,

BES relief cannot be used to create a CGT loss (see *Example 4.21(2)*). **[4.87]-[4.100]**

EXAMPLE 4.21

(1) Assume that Croesus sold BES shares (purchased for £40,000 in 1985-86) for £70,000 some six years later. His gain for CGT purposes would be £30,000 (ignoring indexation and other incidental expenses) so that after deducting his annual exemption (currently £5,500) the tax would be £9,800 (40% × £24,500). His profit on investment would be:

	£	£
Sale proceeds		70,000
Less total investment after tax relief at 60% in 1985-86 $(40,000 \times 60\%)$		
(£40,000 — £24,000)	16,000	
CGT	9,800	
		25,800
		£44,200

$$\text{Return on capital} = \frac{£44,200}{£16,000} \times 100 = 276.25\%$$

(2) Alternatively, if Croesus were to sell the shares for £30,000, his acquisition cost (£40,000) must be reduced by £10,000 of the relief given (£24,000) so as to produce neither gain nor loss on disposal. If the shares become valueless, eg on the company becoming insolvent, Croesus would have an allowable loss of £16,000 (£40,000 less relief of £24,000). That loss may be eligible for income tax relief under TA 1988 s 574 (see **[7.153]**).

V   PERSONAL RELIEFS (TA 1988 s 256) *(Step 4)*

1   General

Individuals resident in the UK can deduct personal reliefs from their total income. The availability of the reliefs depends not on the type of income involved, but on the taxpayer's personal circumstances. He must claim his reliefs each year by completing the section headed 'Allowances' in the income tax return. If personal allowances exceed the total income of the taxpayer, the surplus is unused and cannot be carried forward for use in future years. The position of a taxpayer who makes interest payments falling within the MIRAS scheme and who has surplus allowances has already been discussed at p 43.

A summary of the personal reliefs available for 1991-92 is set out below. It should be noted that since 1982-83, certain reliefs (marked with an asterisk) are linked to increases in the Retail Prices Index between December preceding the year of assessment and the previous December.

* Personal allowance: £3,295
* Personal allowance (age 65-74)†   £4,020
* Personal allowance (age 75 and over)†   £4,180
* Married couple's allowance   £1,720
* Married couple's allowance (age 65-74)†   £2,355
* Married couple's allowance (age 75 and over)†   £2,395
* Additional personal allowance (for a single person who has responsibility for a child)   £1,720

Widow's bereavement allowance	£1,720
Blind person's relief	£1,080
Income limit for age-related allowances	£13,500

†These allowances are reduced if the taxpayer's income exceeds the income limit.

A limited category of non-UK residents (as set out in TA 1988 s 278) may claim personal reliefs in respect of their UK income (see [13.61]). [4.101]

2 The reliefs

Personal allowance (TA 1988 s 257(1)) The personal allowance (for 1991–92, £3,295) is available to all taxpayers resident in the United Kingdom including minor children. The allowance can be set against any form of income but any surplus is wasted since it cannot be used in any other tax year nor transferred to any other taxpayer. The special rules which applied to husband and wife prior to 6 April 1990 are mentioned in Chapter 35. [4.102]

The married couples allowance (TA 1988 s 257A) This relief (£1,720 for 1991–92) can be claimed by a man who is married and living with his wife for *any part* of the tax year and is added to his personal allowance. In the event of this income being insufficient to utilise this allowance in whole or in part then *he* can elect for the surplus to be transferred to his wife to be set against her income. For these purposes a couple are treated as living together unless they are separated under a court order, written deed, or are in fact separated in such circumstances that the separation is likely to be permanent. Accordingly this allowance cannot be claimed by a husband who though separated from his wife continues to maintain her. (The utilisation of this allowance is considered in greater detail in Chapter 35.

The availability of the higher married allowance in a case where the man had two wives was confirmed in *Nabi v Heaton* (1983) but in *Rignell v Andrews* (1990) a taxpayer who had lived with the same woman for 11 years and who treated her as his common law wife was considered not to be married and therefore not entitled to a higher allowance. [4.103]

Additional personal allowance (TA 1988 s 259) This is also known as the single parent family allowance, which as the name suggests is intended to alleviate the financial position of the 'one-parent' family. Relief is £1,720 for 1991–92 and is available to a woman who is not *throughout* the tax year married and living with her husband and to a man who is either not married or not living with his wife throughout the tax year. To qualify for the relief the taxpayer must have a 'qualifying child' living with him for the whole or part of the year of assessment. A *qualifying child* is one who is:
(a) born in that tax year; or
(b) under the age of 16 at the start of the tax year; or
(c) over 16, but attending a full-time educational course or undergoing vocational training with an employer for at least two years;
and who is:
(a) the taxpayer's own natural legitimate or legitimated issue (including a stepchild and adopted child under 18 at the date of adoption); or
(b) any other child born in, or under 18 at the beginning of the year and maintained at the taxpayer's expense for the whole or part of the year (legal custody is not required).

Only one allowance is available to any one taxpayer, regardless of the number of qualifying children that he may have. When more than one person is entitled to the allowance (for instance, because they each maintain the child for a part of the year) the one allowance is apportioned between them, but not more than £1,720 can be received in total.

A claimant need not be living alone to receive the allowance provided that the above conditions are fulfilled. Cohabitees, who have produced more than one offspring, were formerly both entitled to a full allowance in respect of one child, provided that they could convince the Revenue that they were each separately responsible for the maintenance of one child. However, as part of the attempt to remove the tax disincentives of marriage, as from 1989-90 cohabitees are restricted to only one such allowance which will be given in respect of the youngest child.

A married man entitled to the married couple's allowance may claim the additional personal allowance if his wife was totally incapacitated mentally or physically throughout the tax year and there are qualifying children. There is no equivalent increase in allowances where the husband is similarly incapacitated.   [**4.104**]

Age allowance (TA 1988 s 257(2))   Personal allowances increase with the age of the taxpayer:
(a) *Up to 65* the personal allowance and (if appropriate) the married couple's allowance are available;
(b) *Between 65 and 75* a higher allowance is available and for taxpayers aged over 75 the allowances are further increased.

The higher allowances are given by reference to the tax year in which the 65th or 75th birthday falls—curiously they are available even if the taxpayer dies before that birthday!

The personal allowance depends solely on the age of the relevant taxpayer. From £3,295 it increased to £4,020 (for taxpayers aged 65-74 in the tax year) and then to £4,180 (for those aged 75 and over in the tax year).

By contrast the level of the married couple's allowance depends on the age of the *elder spouse* in the relevant tax year. The allowance rises from £1,720 to £2,355 (where the elder spouse is aged 65-74) and finally to £2,395 (elder spouse 75 and over).

These higher allowances for taxpayers aged 65 and over are subject to an income limit: this limit (currently £13,500) is the same for all taxpayers, male and female, married and single. Provided that the taxpayer's total income (see [**4.81**]) is below this figure *full allowances are due*. However, if total income exceeds £13,500 then the age-related allowances are reduced by half the difference between the taxpayer's total income and the limit (ie the reduction is £1 of allowance for every £2 of income above £13,500). At worst, this reduction will wipe out the higher allowances: no taxpayer, however, will have his personal allowance reduced below the level for those aged under 65 (ie £3,295 for the current year). So far as the married couple's allowance is concerned, the reduction is calculated solely by reference to the husband's total income and the allowance will only be reduced *after* the husband's higher personal allowance has been wiped out. At worst, the reduction will leave the husband with the basic married couple allowance of £1,720. Note, finally, that married couples cannot transfer any unused part of their income limits to each other.   [**4.105**]

EXAMPLE 4.22

(1) Fred is 50; his wife, Wilma, is 73. Fred has income of £8,000 pa; Wilma £13,800.

    (a) Fred is entitled to a personal allowance of £3,295. Wilma, because of her age, will qualify for an allowance of £4,020 but this will be reduced as follows:

        Wilma's income above £13,500: £300
        One half of the excess above £13,500: £150.
        Reduce full allowance by £150 = £3,870.

    (b) The married couple's allowance will be calculated by reference to Wilma's age and so will be £2,355. Despite Wilma's income, this allowance will not be reduced since Fred's income is below the £13,500 limit.

(2) Robert is aged 78 with an income of £15,440; his wife, Alison, is aged 68 with an income of £3,000.

    (a) Alison will be entitled to a personal allowance of £4,020 of which £1,020 will be wasted.

    (b) Robert's personal allowance of £4,180 will be reduced to the basic allowance of £3,295 because his income exceeds the £13,500 threshold by more than £1,770. The married couple's allowance (given by reference to Robert's age) of £2,395 will also be reduced—in this case by £85 to £2,310 because Robert's surplus total income after reducing his personal allowance exceeds the threshold by £170 (ie total income of £15,440 will have been reduced by £1,770 thereby reducing Robert's personal allowance and leaving an excess of £170 to reduce the married couple's allowance).

Widow's bereavement allowance (TA 1988 s 262)   Where a married man dies in a year of assessment in which he was living with his wife, his widow is entitled to an additional allowance both in the year of his death and in the following year provided she has not remarried before then. This allowance is £1,720 for 1991–92 and widows with dependent children are also entitled to the single parent allowance (see above).   **[4.106]**

Blind person's allowance (TA 1988 s 265(1), (2))   A taxpayer who is a registered blind person for the whole or part of the year of assessment receives an additional relief (for 1991–92) of £1,080. If a husband and wife are both registered blind they can each claim the blind person's allowance and if they are living together either can transfer any surplus allowance to the other.   **[4.107]**

Child benefit   As from April 1979, the mother (usually) has received tax-free child benefit for each child who is under 16, or under 19 and receiving full-time education at a recognised educational establishment. There are no child tax allowances.   **[4.108]–[4.120]**

VI   METHOD OF CHARGING TAXABLE INCOME *(Step 5)*

1   Rates of tax

Income tax is charged on an individual's taxable income for 1991–92 at the following rates:

	Income band
On the first £23,700 at 25% (basic rate)	£1–£23,700
on the remainder at 40% (higher rate)	Excess over £23,700

Since 1982-83 increases in the rate bands have been linked to the increase in the Retail Prices Index between the December before the year of assessment and the previous December. The indexed rises are, however, subject to a negative resolution of Parliament (ie they occur 'unless Parliament otherwise determines'; TA 1988 s 1(4)). The simple structure of the tax with only two rates (the basic 25% and the higher 40%) was introduced from 1988-89. Before that year there was more than one higher rate band: eg in 1987-88 there were five such bands and a top rate of tax of 60%.

It should be remembered that where payments are made by the taxpayer under deduction of tax at source (eg annual payments to charity and certain interest payments) those payments are added back to the taxpayer's taxable income for basic rate tax purposes, thereby effectively increasing the figure chargeable to basic rate tax above £23,700.* When payments are received by the taxpayer after deduction at source, the tax due from the payee will be reduced by the basic rate tax already paid on his behalf by the payer.   **[4.121]**

ie 23700 + 3000 @ 25%.

EXAMPLE 4.23

Brian has a statutory income for 1991-92 of £40,000. He makes covenanted payments to charity of £3,000 pa and is entitled to a personal allowance (including a married couple's allowance) of £5,015. His income tax calculation is as follows:

	£
Statutory income	40,000
Less charge on income	3,000
Total income	37,000
Less personal reliefs	5,015
Taxable income for basic and higher rates	£31,985

	£
Tax payable:	
First £23,700 at 25%	5,925
Balance of £8,285 at 40%	3,314
Add back for basic rate tax only payment	
to charity £3,000 × 25%	750
	£9,989

2   Dates for payment of tax

Tax is collected either by direct assessment or by deduction at source. Tax collected by direct assessment is generally due on 1 January in the year of assessment or within 30 days of a notice of assessment (if later). Tax under Schedule D Cases I and II, however, is payable in two equal instalments on 1 January in the year of assessment and 1 July following (subject to a later notice of assessment as above: see TA 1988 s 5).

Where income is received after deduction of basic rate tax, eg dividends, the recipient taxpayer is assessed to higher rate tax on 1 December following the year of assessment.

Tax is collected under the PAYE system of Schedule E at basic and higher rates on a current year basis (TA 1988 s 203). If the taxpayer's only source of income is from Schedule E, the correct amount of tax can be collected under this system necessitating no further adjustment. Otherwise, where the taxpayer has other sources of income, either too much or too little tax may be deducted, thereby necessitating an adjustment.   **[4.122]**

3   Specimen income tax calculation

Applying the steps listed at **[4.1]** it is now possible to calculate an individual's income tax liability for a tax year.   **[4.123]–[4.140]**

EXAMPLE 4.24

Benjamin has the following income for 1991–92:

(i) Lecturer (Schedule E)	£12,000
(ii) Author (Schedule D Case II)	£3,000
(iii) Part-time barman (Schedule E)	£9,000
(iv) Rents from houses (Schedule A)	£11,000
(v) Dividends (Schedule F) from Tenko Ltd (gross—including tax credit of £500)	£2,000

Benjamin is married to Bertha. He is liable to make interest payments of £3,000 pa to the Wonky Building Society and £1,000 pa to the RSPCA (a registered charity).

Schedule E (12000 + 9000)		£ 21,000
Schedule D Case II		3,000
Schedule A		11,000
Schedule F		2,000
Step 1: Statutory income from all sources		37,000
Step 2: Deduct charges on income:		
Annual payment		1,000
Step 3: Total income		36,000
Step 4: Deduct personal reliefs:		
Personal allowance	£3,295	
Additional allowance	£1,720	5,015
Step 5: Taxable income for basic and higher rates		£30,985
Tax chargeable at *Step 5:*		£
First £23,700 at 25%		5,295
Balance of £7,285 at 40%		2,914
Tax on £30,985 at basic and higher rate		8,839
Step 6: Give credit for tax deducted at source, ie from		
the dividends		500
		8,339
Step 7: *Add back for basic rate tax only sums paid to the RSPCA:		
ie £1,000 at 25% *ie Ben paid £750 to RSPCA*		250
Total tax due *and retained £250 ∴ has to pay this*		£8,589
also as tax.		

Notes: (1) Tax would have been deducted at source under the PAYE system in respect of the employment. Credit would be given for this tax in *Step 6*, thereby affecting the actual tax due from Benjamin by direct assessment. Nevertheless, Benjamin is actually liable (howsoever it is collected) for tax of £8,339 in 1991–92.

(2) The interest paid to the Wonky Building Society falls within the MIRAS scheme. With the restriction of tax relief to basic rate only the result is that, because Benjamin's payments to the building society are net of basic rate tax, he has obtained full tax relief. Accordingly these payments can be ignored in

the tax computation. Contrast the position in 1990–91 and in earlier years when relief was also available at higher rate(s).

VII   MISCELLANEOUS MATTERS (not affecting the income tax calculation)

1   **Life assurance premium relief** (TA 1988 ss 266, 267, 273, 274)

Tax relief is available for premiums paid by a UK resident on a 'qualifying' life assurance policy made *before* 14 March 1984 (TA 1988 ss 266–67). The relief is given by allowing the policyholder to deduct and retain 12½% of the premium, provided that the total annual premiums payable do not exceed the greater of £1,500 and ¹/₆th of his total income. The insurer reclaims the deduction from the Inland Revenue.

The relief is not available for policies made after 13 March 1984, nor to those made before that date where the holder subsequently alters the policy to increase the benefits secured or to extend the term. In such cases premiums will be paid without the 12½% deduction. The proceeds of a qualifying policy are not normally subject to income tax.

Premiums on *non-qualifying policies* however, and typically the single premium insurance bond, receive no tax relief. Any gain realised by the policyholder, net of premiums paid, which he obtains on encashment (eg on surrender or death) may be subject to income tax at higher rate (but not basic rate) subject to top slicing relief. He can make annual tax-free withdrawals. These withdrawals are allowed up to the value of the original investment so long as they do not exceed 5% of the premium paid for each year of the policy (ie the tax-free withdrawals cease after 20 years). Single premium bonds therefore provide shelter for income in the case of higher rate taxpayers.

From 1 January 1990 the rate of corporation tax on the relevant profits (both income and capital) of a life assurance company was reduced to the basic rate of income tax (25% in 1991–92). The policyholder is not charged on those accumulating profits.   **[4.141]**

2   **Exemptions from income tax**

There are a number of exemptions from income tax including the following. It should also be noted that a number of items are exempted from tax by virtue of Revenue Extra-Statutory Concessions (see generally pamphlet IRI (1988) and supplements).   **[4.142]**

a)   *Exempt organisations*

Certain organisations are exempt. In particular, the Crown is not within the tax legislation at all, whilst charities are generally (see Appendix IX) exempt from income tax in respect of:
(a) income from land and investment income provided that it is applied for charitable purposes only; and
(b) trading profits applied purely for charitable purposes where either the trade is part of the main purpose of the charity, or the work is carried out mainly by the beneficiaries (for instance Christmas cards made by the handicapped and sold for their benefit: TA 1988 s 505).

Foreign diplomats and members of overseas armed forces stationed in the UK are exempt (TA 1988 ss 322–3).   **[4.143]**

b) *Exempt income*

Some of the more important items that are exempt from income tax include:
(a) scholarship income in the hands of the scholar (TA 1988 s 331);
(b) certain social security benefits, namely: income support payments (other than those taxable under TA 1988 s 151); family credit; housing benefit; child benefit (TA 1988 s 617(2)). In addition, certain benefits are excepted from the Schedule E charge including: maternity allowance; widow's payments; invalidity benefit; and attendance and mobility allowances (TA 1988 s 617(1)). Notice, however, that maternity pay, statutory sick pay and unemployment benefit, are all taxable under Schedule E (TA 1988 s 150);
(c) interest on National Savings Certificates and schemes (TA 1988 s 326);
(d) the first £70 of interest each year from ordinary accounts at the National Savings Bank;
(e) interest on damages for personal injuries or death (TA 1988 s 329).
(f) dividends paid in a Personal Equity Plan ('PEP'): see [**37.7**];
(g) interest earned in a Tax Exempt Special Savings Account ('TESSA'); see [**37.8**]. [**4.144**]

5 Schedule E—offices and employments

I INTRODUCTORY

The emoluments derived from an 'office or employment', after deducting any allowable expenditure, are charged to income tax under one of the three Cases of Schedule E (TA 1988 s 19(1)). Tax is levied on a receipts basis and is usually collected at source under the PAYE system. In so far as the Cases of Schedule E involve a foreign element, the matter is considered in Chapter 13. This chapter will be limited to the charge under Case I which applies when the person holding the office or employment is resident or ordinarily resident in the UK.

Schedule E is of crucial significance in the income tax system since it raises, mainly through PAYE, some 75% of total income tax per annum. High rates of tax led to the proliferation of fringe benefits designed to minimise, or avoid the PAYE net. Accordingly a characteristic feature of the Schedule has been regular legislation seeking to close loopholes in its operation. It is now an area where detail has come to swamp principle.

Another important development that has affected this area in recent years was the substantial increase in 1985 in employer's national insurance contributions charged in respect of higher paid employees (see [**32.43**] for details). This change has provided a further incentive to employers to reward their employees not by wage increases (which will attract an increased national insurance contribution), but, instead, by fringe benefits which are not subject to the contribution. It may also encourage certain taxpayers to argue that they are self-employed (and, hence, subject to lower contributions) rather than employees. As the Revenue have sought to broaden the Schedule E net in recent years to catch workers who had traditionally been taxed as self-employed such attempts will be met with fierce opposition (see further the Inland Revenue booklet IR 56; for an illustration where the basis of assessment of a part-time lecturer was changed from Schedule D to Schedule E see *Sidey v Phillips* (1986) and note the controversy over the treatment of actors: see, for instance, *Taxation*, 29 March 1990).   [**5.1**]–[**5.20**]

II 'OFFICE OR EMPLOYMENT'

1 Meaning of 'office' and 'employment'

The term 'office' is not statutorily defined, but it has been described by Rowlatt J in *Great Western Rly Co v Bater* (1920) as 'a subsisting, permanent, substantive position which has an existence independent of the person who fills it, and which is filled in succession by successive holders . . .'. Although this dictum has been approved in cases over the years, in *Edwards v Clinch* (1981) the emphasis on permanence and continuity was played down in favour of the requirement of some continuity and of a position with an existence independent of the individual holding it. In that case a civil engineer who received *ad hoc* appointments as a planning inspector was held not to be an office holder because the position had no independent existence, but lapsed when the particular assignment was completed.

Typical examples of office holders include trustees, PRs, company secretaries and auditors. It is generally assumed that a company director, whether full-time and salaried or part-time and in receipt of fees, is an office holder under Schedule E (*McMillan v Guest* (1942)). Often the directorship will continue regardless of the person who occupies it; but it may still be an office, it appears, even if it is created for a particular person (see *Taylor v Provan* (1974) cp *Edwards v Clinch* (1981)). The employment law case of *Parsons v Parsons* (1979) is sometimes considered to cast a disturbing light on the status of a director in the small family company (the 'quasi-partnership'). In that case Denning MR held that a full-time director was not an employee for the purposes of claiming compensation for unfair dismissal since he and his fellow directors had regarded themselves as self-employed; there was no written or implied contract of service, and his remuneration had been paid without deduction of tax under PAYE. The court was not, however, directly concerned with the director's tax position and the case is not therefore authority for the proposition that such directors are self-employed.

Difficulties arise when a taxpayer acquires an office by reason of his particular profession; eg solicitor partners (taxable under Schedule D Case II) often acquire trusteeships. Each office will be separately assessed under Schedule E and not taxed under Schedule D, unless that office is acquired as an integral part of the trade or profession (see *IRC v Brander and Cruickshank* (1971)). In practice, the Revenue allow partnerships which receive directors' fees to enter those fees in their Schedule D Case II assessment so long as the directorship is a normal incident of the profession and of the particular practice; the fees form only a small part of total profits; and under the partnership agreement the fees are pooled for division amongst the partners (see ESC A37).

The term 'employment' is not statutorily defined. It connotes a job or a post: a position where there is a written or implied contract of service. If the taxpayer works for more than one person, the difficulty is to know whether he holds a number of separate employments (taxable under Schedule E) or is making a series of engagements carried out as part of a profession or vocation. The basic division is between a contract of service (Schedule E) and a contract for services (Schedule D) and each case depends on all its circumstances (the relevant factors that will be considered are discussed by Cooke J in *Market Investigations Ltd v Minister of Social Security* (1969)). In *Davies v Braithwaite* (1931), for instance, an actress who entered into a series of separate engagements to appear on film, stage and radio was held to be taxable under Schedule D. Rowlatt J looked at her total commitments during the year and, as the number was considerable, decided that each was a mere engagement in the course of exercising her profession. Compare *Fall v Hitchen* (1973) where the taxpayer was employed as a professional ballet dancer by Sadlers Wells under a contract which only allowed him to take other work with their consent (which was not to be unreasonably withheld). Pennycuick V-C looked at the characteristics of the contract in isolation and held that the taxpayer was taxable under Schedule E; undoubtedly one reason for the decision was that the taxpayer had only one contract which provided for a first call on his time. (For the Revenue's view of the considerations to be taken into account in deciding whether an individual is an employee or self-employed see booklet IR 56.)   [**5.21**]

2   **Taxing a partner/consultant**

An equity partner in a firm is self-employed and, therefore, assessable under Schedule D Case I or II. Difficulties may arise, however, as to the status of a salaried partner. Whether he is an employee or is self-employed does not depend upon the labels used or whether his salary is taxed at source under PAYE. Instead, all the facts and in particular the terms of the agreement between the parties must be considered. Thus, in *Stekel v Ellice* (1973), although the agreement referred to 'salaried partner' and a 'fixed salary', it was, in substance, a partnership agreement rather than a contract of employment. However, provided that the partnership determines the new partner's status in advance and drafts the agreement accordingly, its terms will be conclusive unless there is strong factual evidence to the contrary (*BSM (1257) Ltd v Secretary of State for Social Services* (1978)). If the partners are in any doubt on the matter, they should seek confirmation of status from the Revenue.

Similarly, whether a consultant is an employee or self-employed is largely a matter of arrangement. If the firm provides for him to receive annual remuneration and to work fixed hours, this points to a Schedule E assessment, whereas if he is to receive fees for *ad hoc* consultations an assessment under Schedule D Case II will be more likely. In practice, the Revenue look particularly at the direction and control of the taxpayer; at his freedom to choose his own methods of working, and at his ability to subcontract the work.   [**5.22**]–[**5.40**]

III   THE TAX IS ON EMOLUMENTS

1   **The statutory definition**

'Emoluments' are partially defined in TA 1988 s 131 as including 'all salaries, fees, wages, perquisites and profits whatsoever'. Although an emolument will usually be a payment made in return for services past, present or future, the term is not so limited and is wide enough to catch any payment which arises from the office or employment. Hence, in *Hamblett v Godfrey* (1987) a payment of £1,000 to each employee who relinquished his right to join a trade union, although not paid in return for services, was considered by the Court of Appeal to be so intimately connected to the taxpayer's employment as to constitute an emolument. Similarly, in *Bray v Best* (1989) the payment from the employee trust was an emolument although it could not be referred to any particular services.

'In my judgment the totality of the authorities lead to this conclusion. In order for an emolument to fall within the words of [TA 1988 s 131] as being "from" employment, it is not essential that the payment is received by way of reward or remuneration for services past, present or future. However the receipt of such a payment by way of reward for services is the paradigm of a taxable receipt: such a case provides valuable guidance to the meaning of the statutory words. The essence of a payment which is a reward for services is that it relates to the performance of the contract by the rendering of services, not merely to the existence of the contract of employment. *Hamblett v Godfrey* shows that other types of payment made by an employer to an employee may equally refer to the performance of the contract of employment. But this represents no departure from the essential characteristic required to make such payments an emolument "from" the employment, namely that they are referable to the performance of the services under the relevant contract of employment and nothing else. ... the payment is assessable if it has been paid to the taxpayer for acting as or being an employee ...' (Sir Nicholas Browne-Wilkinson in *Shilton v Wilmshurst* (1990).)

Basic pay or salary is clearly an emolument. Additional cash payments (bonuses, for instance) will generally be emoluments, although in exceptional circumstances a gift of cash from an employer may escape tax if it can be shown to be for the personal qualities of the employee rather than for any services which he performs (see [**5.92**]). Major problems are, however, caused by benefits in kind (or fringe benefits); this term encompasses all non-cash benefits received by an employee in connection with his job. To the extent that the benefit is provided gratuitously by the employer the benefit in kind rules and the gift rules interlink.   [**5.41**]

2 Third party payments

Tips will normally form part of an employee's taxable emoluments and in some businesses form a substantial part of take-home pay. In such cases the payment is made by a third party rather than by the employer. In *Shilton v Wilmshurst* (1991) the House of Lords decided that such payments could amount to emoluments even though the third party did not have an interest in the performance of the employment contract. The case concerned Peter Shilton, the England goalkeeper, who on his transfer from Nottingham Forest to Southampton received a payment of £75,000 from Nottingham Forest. Deciding that this sum was an emolument Lord Templeman stressed that:

'an emolument "from employment" means an emolument "from being or becoming an employee". ... there is nothing in [the section] or the authorities to justify the inference that an "emolument from employment" only applies to an emolument provided by a person who has an interest in the performance by the employee of the services which he becomes bound to perform when he enters into the contract of employment ... so far as the taxpayer is concerned, both the emoluments of £80,000 from Southampton and £75,000 from Nottingham Forest were paid to him for the same purpose and had the same effect, namely, as an inducement to him to agree to become an employee of Southampton.'   [**5.42**]

3 The *O'Leary* case

David O'Leary, like Shilton, was a professional footballer. He was domiciled in Eire and entered into an arrangement, designed to avoid income tax, with his employers, Arsenal FC. An offshore trust was established with

O'Leary as life tenant and the sum of £266,000 was loaned interest free and repayable on demand to that trust by Arsenal. The income produced by this sum (£28,985 pa) was then payable to O'Leary but, so it was argued, because the sum fell to be taxed under Schedule D Case V and because O'Leary was non-UK domiciled tax would not arise unless and until that sum was remitted to the UK (see [13.24]). Once O'Leary ceased to be employed by Arsenal the loan would be repaid. Vinelott J decided, contrary to the taxpayer's submissions, that the annual interest was correctly assessed as an emolument. He commented as follows:

'The fallacy which I think underlines Counsel for the taxpayer's submission can be shortly stated. If an employer lends money to an employee free of interest or at a favourable rate of interest and if the employee is free to exploit the money in any manner he chooses his employment cannot be said to have been the source of the income derived from the exploitation; the employer is the source of the money and the taxpayer is assessable to tax under Schedule E on the benefit to him of obtaining the loan on the terms on which the loan was made; but if the loan is repayable on demand that benefit cannot be quantified and form the basis of an assessment under Schedule E [but see [5.70]]. By contrast if an employee were to lend money to a bank on terms that interest was paid to the employee until further order the interest paid to him while he remains an employee would almost inevitably be taxable as an emolument of his employment . . . (*O'Leary v McKinlay* (1991)).   [5.43]

4   Sick pay

Sick pay (defined under the Social Security and Housing Benefits Act 1982 s 1) is a taxable emolument for all employees whether paid by the employer, a Friendly Society, an insurance company or a third person if it is paid as a result of arrangements entered into by the employer (TA 1988 s 150). Where an employer runs an insured sick pay scheme to which both employer and employee contribute, the employee is taxed under Schedule E on sums paid to him or his family due to his absence from work because of disability or sickness (TA 1988 s 149) except (by concession) to the extent that the sums reflect contributions made by the employee (these sums will be taxed under Schedule D Case III unless exempted under ESC A26 which excludes from charge payments in the first 12 months of sickness). Notice that maternity payments are also a taxable benefit.   [5.44]

5   Work training provided by employer

If an employer pays for certain costs in training his employee in skills relating to the current or prospective duties of his job, any benefit which would otherwise be chargeable to tax under Schedule E is not treated as an emolument (SP 4/86). This statement does not apply to the cost of training for a new employment, but TA 1988 s 588 provides that, where an employer meets the cost of a qualifying training course undertaken by his employee or former employee to retrain the latter in skills needed for a new job or self-employment, that cost will not be treated as an emolument of the employee. The employee must leave that employment within two years of completing the course and must not be re-employed by that employer within the two years thereafter.   [5.45]-[5.60]

IV   BENEFITS IN KIND

1   **General principles**

The legislature has steadily widened the Schedule E net to tax fringe benefits by introducing numerous intricate provisions, the details of which are beyond the scope of this book. All that this section attempts is a summary of the general principles and of the more important provisions. Employee incentives, in the shape of share options, employee trusts, and profit related pay are considered separately in Chapter 34.

The income tax legislation distinguishes between two categories of employee:

(a) lower-paid employees, and

(b) employees earning £8,500 or more per year and (most) directors.

There are also certain benefits in kind where the rules apply to both categories of employee. Some benefits are specifically excluded from Schedule E by Revenue concession. The best known examples are probably luncheon vouchers of up to 15p per working day (ESC A2); free coal provided for mineworkers (ESC A6; a cash allowance in lieu of free coal is also untaxed); and removal and relocation expenses (ESC A5; A67 and 1988 STI 800).   [**5.61**]

2   **Lower-paid employees**

Lower-paid employees are those whose total emoluments do not exceed £8,500 pa and who are not directors. In theory, the rules that follow apply to all employees. In practice, however, the special code that applies to employees earning £8,500 and above per annum (see [**5.65**]) will normally supersede these rules save in exceptional cases.   [**5.62**]

a) Basic principles

There are two basic principles. *First*, a benefit in kind is taxable in the hands of the employee if it is convertible into money; it need not be saleable. In the case of *Tennant v Smith* (1892) the House of Lords held that the benefit of a house which the employee was required by his employment to occupy but which he could not assign or sublet did not constitute an emolument since it was not convertible into money (for the other *ratio* of the case see [**5.75**]). The test is whether the benefit *could* be converted; it is irrelevant whether the employee actually converts it into money. Consider, for instance, a British Rail season ticket which cannot be sold because it is non-assignable, but which can be converted into cash by surrender.

Secondly, if the benefit is convertible into money, tax is levied on the value of the benefit to the employee: ie on the secondhand value. In *Wilkins v Rogerson* (1961), the company arranged with Montague Burton that each employee would be permitted to obtain clothes of up to £15 in value. The contract provided for payment directly by the company. When the Revenue sought to tax an employee on a suit costing £14.50 the court held that the benefit was convertible into money, because the taxpayer could sell the suit, but that he could only be taxed on the secondhand value estimated at £5 (see also *Jenkins v Horn* (1979), where this test operated to the taxpayer's disadvantage).

The practical application of these two principles can cause problems. For instance, the provision of a non-convertible benefit, such as the free use of a car, is not chargeable whereas the provision of money to enable the employee to purchase such a benefit is an emolument (see *Bird v Martland* (1982)). A further problem is that it may be difficult to decide whether particular facts involve the rules on benefits in kind or not. This is illustrated by the case of *Heaton v Bell* (1970) where a company operated a voluntary car loan scheme for its employees who were offered the use of fully insured company cars. If they accepted the offer they thereupon received slightly reduced wages. An employee could withdraw from the scheme on giving 14 days' notice whereupon he would revert to his original wage. The House of Lords by a majority of four to one decided that the case did not involve the benefit in kind rules (but see Lord Reid's dissenting judgment). Instead they concluded that an employee who joined the scheme was entitled to his original unamended wage and that he had merely chosen to spend a portion of that wage on the hire of a car. Thus tax was charged on the full wage since what the taxpayer chooses to spend his wages on is not tax deductible!

EXAMPLE 5.1

Simon is employed as a butler at a wage of £10 pw. He is required to 'live in' and 50p is deducted per week for board and lodging. Simon is assessed to tax on £10 pw (see *Machon v McLoughlin* (1926)). Compare the case of Rosie who is employed as a housemaid and is paid a weekly wage of £9.50. She is required to live in but is not charged for board and lodging. She is taxed on £9.50; the board and lodging is a non-convertible benefit in kind which, therefore, escapes tax.

Difficulties may also arise when the employer discharges debts incurred by his employee. In *Nicoll v Austin* (1935) a managing director told his employer company that he would have to sell his imposing house, where he entertained potential customers, because he could no longer afford to pay for its upkeep. To prevent the sale, the company paid the outgoings on the house and the employee was taxed on this sum as if he had been given the money to pay the bills himself. See also *Richardson v Worrall* (1985) where payment for petrol using an employer's credit card was held taxable since it discharged the taxpayer's liability to the garage.   [**5.63**]

EXAMPLE 5.2

(1) Employees are given £14.50 to buy clothes to wear to work. The sum is an emolument (cp *Wilkins v Rogerson* (1961)).
(2) Employees choose clothes and they send the bills to the employer for payment. As the debt has been incurred by the employee tax will be charged in accordance with *Nicoll v Austin* (1935).

b) *Expenses*

If a lower-paid employee receives an 'expense allowance' it will be presumed to be a reimbursement of expenditure unless the Revenue can show it to be an emolument. Where an employee incurs expenses which the employer reimburses, those reimbursements will not be taxed as emoluments provided that the employee could have deducted those sums from his Schedule E income as an expense of the employment (see TA 1988 s 198 and [**5.111**] for a discussion of what expenditure is deductible). In such cases it can be said that the employee has derived no personal profit from the reimbursement (in the sense that he is no better off) and, in addition, no practical purpose would be served by deciding that the reimbursement is an emolument but then permitting the employee to reduce that emolument to nil by setting off an equivalent expense.

In *Pook v Owen* (1970) a doctor holding a part-time hospital appointment who had to attend the hospital several times a week was reimbursed two-thirds of his travelling expenses. It was held that the reimbursements were not emoluments because he was no 'better off' as a result of them. They were (partial) repayments of actual expenditure which was deductible in arriving at the emoluments of the taxpayer.

In other cases, however, reimbursements have been held not to be emoluments even though the relevant expenditure would not have been deductible by the employee under s 198. Thus, in *Donnelly v Williamson* (1982), a teacher, who was reimbursed for travelling expenses incurred in attending out-of-school functions, was not taxable on the reimbursements. The court held that they were not emoluments because they were not derived from her employment (she attended the functions voluntarily) and that they were a genuine attempt to compensate her for actual expenditure. Compare *Perrons v Spackman* (1981) where a mileage allowance paid by the council to one of its rent officers was held to be an emolument because it contained a profit element.

Exactly what expenses may be reimbursed is not entirely clear if it is accepted that there is no correlation between the reimbursement rules and the test for deductibility of expenditure under Schedule E. Presumably, the expense must be directly connected with the employment (see *Hochstrasser v Mayes* (1960) discussed at [**5.93**]) since the reimbursement of, eg, the employee's private gas bill will be taxed as an emolument (*Nicoll v Austin*, above). [**5.64**]

EXAMPLE 5.3

Justinian, a law lecturer, attends a legal conference and his University employers refund the cost of the conference which he had paid. The reimbursements are not emoluments. If the University had instead paid for the conference so that he had received a benefit in kind Justinian would be taxed on it if it was convertible. If Justinian had borne the expenses himself he would have been unable to deduct them from his emoluments under TA 1988 s 198 (see [**5.111**]).

3 Employees earning at least £8,500 pa and directors (TA 1988 ss 153–168)

a) *Who is caught by these rules?*

The relatively lenient rules applicable to lower-paid employees will not be applied to employees falling within TA 1988 ss 153–168 which catch any employee with emoluments of at least £8,500 pa. The origin of the special legislation taxing directors and employees earning above an income threshold goes back to 1948 when, because of the then threshold, the rules only applied to very senior employees. When the legislation was redrafted in 1976, they were referred to as 'higher paid employees'. However, the threshold of £8,500 has not been raised since 1979 and the idea that these rules only apply to senior employees has become increasingly absurd since £8,500 is well below the national average of full-time earnings. In fact, the provisions now apply to the great majority of employees. Not surprisingly, therefore, FA 1989 deleted all reference to 'higher paid employees' and the government accepts the general principle that '*all* employees should pay income tax on the whole of their earnings whether received in cash or in kind'. Given such a categorical statement, it remains something of a mystery why these special rules remain confined to employees with earnings of £8,500 and above!

To determine whether the employee has emoluments of £8,500, it is assumed that the employee is within the special rules which are therefore applied in valuing the benefits and only if the resultant figure for emoluments is below £8,500 is he taxed as lower-paid.

EXAMPLE 5.4

Aziz receives a salary of £8,100 pa and an expense allowance of £400 (which is taxed as an emolument for a higher-paid employee). He is treated as receiving emoluments of £8,500 pa and is, therefore, within the special rules.

Sections 153–168 also apply to a director whose emoluments are less than £8,500 pa unless he has no material interest in the company (ie he does not control more than 5% of the ordinary share capital) and either works full-time for the company, or the company is non-profit making or a charity (TA 1988 s 167(5)).   [**5.65**]

b) *The purpose of the special rules*

The object of the general charging provision of TA 1988 s 154 is to tax all benefits (other than those specifically excluded or charged elsewhere) provided by reason of the employment by any person (not just the employer) to the employee or his family *and whether or not convertible into cash*. Generally, the cost incurred by the employer in providing the benefit is treated as an emolument, subject to a deduction for any payment made by the employee (TA 1988 s 156). In *Rendell v Went* (1964) the managing director of a company had a car accident and was prosecuted at the Old Bailey for dangerous driving. The company paid for the best available legal services for him and he was acquitted. He was taxed on the cost to the company of providing the legal services (a non-convertible benefit in kind) although he did not request the benefit and could have found cheaper services elsewhere. [**5.66**]

c) *The cost of providing the benefit*

TA 1988 s 156 provides as follows:

'(1) The cash equivalent of any benefit chargeable to tax under section 154 is an amount equal to the cost of the benefit, less so much (if any) of it as is made good by the employee to those providing the benefit.
(2) Subject to the following subsections, the cost of a benefit is the amount of any expense incurred in or in connection with its provision, and (here and in those subsections) includes a proper proportion of any expense relating partly to the benefit and partly to other matters.'

In *Pepper v Hart* (1990) the taxpayers were assistant masters at Malvern School and they each had one or more sons in attendance at the school under a concessionary fees scheme. Payments equal to 20% of the normal school fees were paid and it was accepted that these more than covered any *direct additional expense* resulting from the boys' presence in the school. The Court of Appeal decided, however, that s 156 was not solely concerned with 'additional direct expenses' but also involved a rateable proportion of the expenses incurred in providing the school facilities that were enjoyed generally by all the boys. The taxpayer's argument, that these indirect expenses would have been the same even if the sons of staff had not attended the school and were not increased because of their attendance at the school, was therefore rejected.

EXAMPLE 5.5

Chislehurst School (for the sons of gentlefolk) runs at a loss. Ninety-nine boys pay fees of £2,000 per annum each whereas the total running costs amount to some £300,000. Matron sends her son to the school under a concessionary arrangement whereby she pays £500 pa. Under the *Pepper v Hart* test she has received a benefit of £3,000 (£3,000 divided by 100) on which—after deducting the sum which she pays (£500)—she will be taxed.   [**5.67**]

d) Operation of the special rules

When the benefit consists of the use of an asset owned by the employer, the cash equivalent included in the employee's emoluments is the higher of the actual cost to the employer in providing the asset (eg the cost of hiring it) and the 'annual value' of the use of the asset. In the case of land, its annual value is the rent that it might be expected to fetch on a yearly letting and will usually be the rateable value (see TA 1988 s 837). For any other asset, the annual value is 20% of its market (capital) value when it is first put at the employee's disposal (TA 1988 s 156(6)). If assets are given to an employee, the cash equivalent is the market value of the asset at the date of transfer less any sum paid by the employee (TA 1988 s 156(3)). If, however, the employee had previously had the use of the asset, he is taxed on its market value at the date when he first used it less the sum of the annual value(s) on which he has already been taxed (TA 1988 s 156(4)).

EXAMPLE 5.6

On 6 April 1989, Mr C Rash was given by his employer the use of a hi-fi system costing £2,000. In October 1991 the employer transferred the system to Mr Rash free of charge when its market value was £800.

Market value at the date when first used by Mr Rash, ie cost	£2,000
*Benefit in kind in 1989–90: 20% × £2,000	£ 400
*Benefit in kind in 1990–91: 20 × £2,000	£ 400
Benefit in kind in 1991–92: £2,000 — £800 (£400 + £400)	£1,200

*If the employer had rented the system at £500 pa, this higher figure would be taxed as an emolument.

If the employee receives an expense allowance he is taxed on it in full as an emolument unless he can claim any allowable expenses under TA 1988 s 198 (see [**5.111**]). This forces the employee to justify his expenses.   [**5.68**]

EXAMPLE 5.7

Andy has a salary of £9,000 pa and an expense allowance of £4,000 pa. He is taxed on emoluments of £13,000 pa unless he can deduct any expenses under s 198.

d) *Exemptions from the charge*

Certain benefits are exempted from charge under TA 1988 s 154 namely:

(1) The provision of accommodation, supplies or services used by the employee purely in performing his work; for instance, the provision of an office or secretarial services (TA 1988 s 155(2)).

(2) The provision of a pension (or similar benefit) for the employee's family or dependants on his death or retirement (TA 1988 s 155(4)).

(3) The provision of meals in any canteen in which meals are provided for employees generally (TA 1988 s 155(5)). In practice, this provision is generously construed to enable different categories of staff to enjoy separate dining rooms (hence, 'two tier' canteens) and it may be possible to use outside restaurants as a 'canteen' in the absence of 'in-house' facilities.

(4) The provision of medical treatment, or insurance against the cost of such treatment, outside the UK where the need for the treatment arises because the employee is performing his job outside the UK (TA 1988 s 155(6)). The cost of providing medical insurance within the UK is a taxable benefit for higher paid employees and directors under TA 1988 s 154.

(5) The provision of nursery facilities ceased to be a taxable emolument from 6 April 1990. The facilities may be provided either at the work place or elsewhere by the employer and either alone or jointly with other persons. Neither is there are any charge when similar provisions are available for older children after school. Relief from the charge is not, however, available if the employer provides cash to enable his

employee to pay for nursery facilities nor, indeed, if the employer directly pays nursery fees to a third party. Similar costs incurred by a self-employed taxpayer do not qualify as deductible expenditure nor can an individual employee deduct the costs of a nanny or child help in the home! [**5.69**]

f) *Specific benefits*

Cars (TA 1988 s 157): These provisions tax employees and directors on the benefit that they derive from a firm or company car which is available for their private use. Tax is not, therefore, charged if the employee can prove that he was forbidden to use the car for private use and did not so use it (*Gilbert v Hemsley* (1981)). A lower-paid employee will not be taxed on this benefit because it is not convertible into cash.

The legislation distinguishes between two categories of car: the pooled car and all others. A pooled car is one which is made available to various employees; is garaged overnight at the employer's premises; and any private use is purely incidental to its business use (TA 1988 s 159). The benefits of using such cars are not taxable.

If a non-pooled car is available for the private use of an employee or his family, he is taxed on a cash equivalent of the car as fixed by statute (TA 1988 s 157 and see the Tables in TA 1988 Sch 6, as amended by statutory instrument). These rates were traditionally increased by 10% each year but for 1988-89 they were doubled; for 1989-90 increased by one-third, and in 1990-91 and 1991-2 increased by 20%. The cash equivalent depends upon the original market value of the car, its cylinder capacity and its age at the end of the year of assessment.

The tax charge varies according to the degree of business use. If the business use does not exceed 2,500 miles in the relevant year, the cash equivalent is increased by 50%; if the business use exceeds 18,000 miles in the relevant year, the cash equivalent is reduced by 50%.

There is a separate scale charge on the provision of petrol for private use in an employer's car (TA 1988 s 158). The provision of a personal chauffeur for an employee is a taxable benefit under TA 1988 s 154 but the employee is not taxed on any other benefits provided in connection with the car such as insurance, road fund tax and a car parking space provided by the employer (TA 1988 s 155).

In his 1988 Budget Speech the then Chancellor (Nigel Lawson) recognised that the company car was 'substantially undertaxed'. He concluded that 'this discrepancy is too great to allow to continue . . . but the scale of under taxation is so great that it cannot be put right in a single year'. The substantial increases in the table rates for the following years may be seen as the process of putting right that under-taxation and it may be that the position has now been reached where in many cases the provision of company cars is no longer tax efficient (see *Tax Journal*, 27 June 1991, p 10)   [**5.70**]

Mobile telephones (TA 1988 s 159A) From 1991-1992 employees have been subject to tax on *every* mobile telephone provided by their employer. The tax benefit is currently fixed at £200 per telephone but this level of charge will be kept under review and may be increased by Statutory Instrument. There is no charge in cases where there is no private use of the telephone by the employee nor where the employee is required to reimburse the employer for the whole cost of any private use (and does so!). Introducing this charge in the 1991 Budget Speech Norman Lamont commented as follows:

'I turn now to one of the great scourges of modern life: the mobile telephone. I propose to bring the benefit of car phones into income tax and simplify the tax treatment of mobile phones by introducing a standard charge on the private use of such phones provided by an employer ... I hope that as a result of this measure, restaurants will be quieter and roads will be safer.'   [5.71]

Beneficial loan arrangements (TA 1988 ss 160-1)   Interest-free (or cheap) loans to employees are not caught under TA 1988 s 154, because the actual cost to the employer in providing the loan is usually nil. Accordingly, s 160 provides that where a relevant employee or director obtains a loan by reason of his employment, either interest-free or at a low rate of interest, he is taxed on the cash equivalent of that loan. This is defined as the difference between interest for the year calculated at the 'official rate' and any interest actually paid by the employee. Prior to changes introduced in the 1991 Budget, the 'official rate' was set at average bank base rate plus 1.5%. This had led by 1991 to an official rate in excess of typical mortgage interest rates. As a result SI 1991/1120 reduced the official rate to 12.75% pa (from 1 July 1991 reduced further to 12.25% pa) and it is intended that this level will be kept under review and changed if necessary . Broadly, it will be kept in line with typical mortgage rates but will not generally change in response to movements of less than $1/2\%$ in such rates. The section applies whenever a benefit is obtained because of an interest free loan and it is not necessary to show that the employee derived a personal benefit therefrom (*Williams v Todd* (1988)).

EXAMPLE 5.8

Day, a consultant with Digday Ltd, borrows £25,000 in order to purchase a suite of Italian furniture. He pays interest at 2% pa and the capital is to be repaid on demand. For 1991–92 Day has received an emolument equal to:

	£
Interest at official rate (say) 12.25% of £25,000	3,062.50
Less: interest paid at 2% pa	500
Taxable emolument	£2,562.50

A loan to a relative of the employee is also taxed under TA 1988 s 160 unless the employee can show that he derived no benefit from it.

If a loan to a relevant employee or director is released or written off, he is treated as receiving an emolument equivalent to that amount, even if the release is made on the termination of his employment (unless the termination is due to his death). 'Golden handshakes' given in the form of the release of a loan will not have the benefit of the £30,000 exemption under TA 1988 s 148 (see [**5.96**]) and should, therefore, be avoided. Any sums advanced by the employer to cover expenses that will be necessarily incurred in the employment will not be taxed under these rules provided that the sum advanced is less than £1,000 and that the advance is spent within six months (SP 7/79).

There is no charge to tax where the cash equivalent of a loan is £300 or less, a *de minimis* level designed to ensure that the most common loan in practice (for an annual travel ticket) is outside the tax net.

Prior to 6 April 1991 loans for the qualifying purpose of acquiring a main residence were excluded from the charge under s 160. The intention behind this exclusion was to ensure that the same tax liability would result as between an employee whose remuneration included a home loan provided by his employer and one paid in cash only who then took out a mortgage on which tax relief was available. The following illustration, provided by the Inland Revenue, shows how this operated for periods up to 6 April.

ILLUSTRATION 1

(Commercial mortgage rates, and the 'official rate', are both assumed to be 13.75%.)

A and B both have total remuneration from their jobs of £34,125. Both have £30,000 home loans.

A's loan is provided interest-free by his employer, so the annual value of the benefit, based on the 'official rate', is £4,125 (£30,000 × 13.75%).

B has his loan on commercial terms from a building society and pays annual interest of £4,125.

A's cash salary is £30,000 and B's £34,125.

A is taxed on £30,000. No account is taken of the employer-provided loan since if interest had been paid it would have qualified for mortgage interest relief.

B is taxed on salary £34,125 less mortgage interest relief £4,125 = £30,000

So the income tax position of each taxpayer is the same.

With the restriction of tax relief on mortgage interest to the basic rate it became necessary to amend these rules in order to ensure that, in appropriate cases, tax will be charged at the difference between basic rate and higher rate (40 − 25 = 15%) on the benefit of an employer's loan.

ILLUSTRATION 2

Assume A and B in *Illustration 1* are higher rate taxpayers.

For A, the annual value of the beneficial loans (£4,125) will, in future, not be entirely exempt. It will be taxed at 15%, giving a liability of £618.75.

For B, the value of the mortgage interest relief received will in future be reduced from £4,125 at 40% (£1,650) to £4,125 at 25% (£1,031.25) as relief will only be given at the basic rate. So the tax paid also increases by £618.75, and equality of treatment is preserved.

ESC A5 exempts from tax the benefit of a cheap or interest-free bridging loan provided when an employee has to move house because of his job. The employee cannot obtain double tax relief, however, on a loan to purchase a dwelling house.   [5.72]

EXAMPLE 5.9

Dan, an employee earning in excess of £8,500 pa, is loaned £25,000 (interest-free) by his employer to enable him to buy a house. He borrows a further £25,000 from the building society to finance the purchase.

TA 1988 Sch 7 deems the loans to be made in the order (1) building society loan, (2) employer's loan, thereby ensuring that Dan is taxed at the 'official rate' of interest on £20,000 of the loan under TA 1988 s 160.

Shares (TA 1988 s 162) If shares are issued to a director or higher paid employee for less than their market value at that date, the difference between that value and any consideration paid is a taxable emolument. Furthermore, if shares are acquired and the consideration to be paid by the director or employee is left outstanding as a debt, s 160 may apply to that loan. However, if shares are issued at market value but only part of that price is payable on issue (so that the shares are issued partly paid), the resultant benefit to the director or employee does not fall within either of the foregoing situations and accordingly has to be dealt with by the special provisions of s 162. Broadly, this section applies when a person acquires shares at an undervalue as a result of a right or opportunity made available because of his employment: undervalue is defined as the difference between the market value of fully paid shares of the same class and the amount (if any) actually paid at the time of issue. If the section applies there is deemed to be an interest free loan equal to that difference.

EXAMPLE 5.10

Sandy, the buying manager of Cosifabrics Ltd, is allotted 10,000 £1 shares in the company in 1989. The market value of the shares is £2.25 each, but Sandy pays only 50p per share. Accordingly, the shares are issued partly paid. In 1991 he pays a further 50p per share to the company. The tax position is as follows:
(i) *From 1989 to 1991:* the notional loan per share is £2.25 − 50p = £1.75. This amounts to £17,500 so that interest on that sum at the official rate is treated as an emolument each year.
(ii) *After 1991:* the payment of a further 50p per share reduces the notional loan by £5,000 to £12,500. Henceforth, the official rate of interest on that figure is treated as an emolument.

Generally, the deemed loan remains outstanding until either the employee dies (IHT may then be charged on the shares as part of his estate on death); until the 'loan' is repaid (when liability to income tax will cease); or until the 'loan' is released or the beneficial interest in the shares is transferred (when tax is charged as if the 'loan' were written off). The section does not apply to the extent that the acquisition of the shares is already taxed as an emolument under other provisions. [**5.73**]
Scholarships Scholarship income is exempt from tax (TA 1988 s 331). However, scholarships awarded to the children of higher paid employees and directors are taxed as emoluments of the parents unless not more than 25% of the total payments from the fund are to children of employees (whether or not higher paid or directors) and the award is fortuitous, ie not resulting from the employment (TA 1988 s 165: see further 1984 STI 62). [**5.74**]

g) *Returns*

Employers are required to make an annual return in respect of each higher paid employee and director on IR Form P11D detailing all benefits, including expense allowances, and payments made to that employee. The employe can, however, apply for a blanket dispensation from having to include routin items such as travelling, hotel expenses and any other type of expense (other than round sum allowances) which need not then be included in Form P11D, nor in the employee's income tax return (TA 1988 s 166 and IR 69). [**5.75**]

4 Special cases—for all employees

The following benefits, which are not convertible into cash or which would have a low convertible value, are specifically taxed as emoluments under Schedule E for *all* employees. [**5.76**]

a) *Living accommodation* (TA 1988 s 145)

If an employer provides his employee with living accommodation, the employee is taxed under TA 1988 s 145 on the value to him of that accommodation less any sum that he actually pays for its use. In *Stones v Hall* (1989) the court concluded that the provision of services in return for accommodation was neither the payment of rent nor the making good of the cost to the company of providing that accommodation. Accordingly, the taxpayer was charged on the value of the accommodation. The value is the higher of the annual value of the premises (defined in TA 1988 s 837 as the rateable value) and the rent paid by the employer for that accommodation (TA 1988 s 145(2)). As a result, tax under s 145 is frequently on a nominal sum since the annual value bears little relationship to the rent that would be received if the property were actually let, and, if the employer owns the premises, the alternative charge cannot apply. The impact of the introduction of the Community Charge on this method of valuation was considered in an Inland Revenue Press Release of 19 April 1990. For properties on existing rating lists there will be no change: in the case of new properties estimated values will be used. Because domestic rating lists will become increasingly out-dated, the Government has announced that it is reviewing the long-term basis of this tax charge with a view to introducing new rules in the future.

Special rules apply in cases where the cost of providing the accommodation exceeds £75,000. Broadly, the employee will in such circumstances be charged to tax on an additional emolument calculated by applying the official rate of interest (as under beneficial loans; see TA 1988 s 160; [**5.70**]) to the excess by which the actual cost of providing the accommodation exceeds £75,000. That actual cost will usually be the cost of acquiring the property.

EXAMPLE 5.11

Giles, the managing director of Clam Ltd, sells to the company his house in Chelsea for its market value of £150,000. He is granted an option to buy the property back in ten years' time for its present value. The annual value of the house is £750 and Giles continues to live in the property. Giles is assessed to tax under Schedule E on an emolument of £750 pa plus (say) 12.25% of £75,000 (£150,000 — £75,000) ie £9,187.5 pa.

The charge under TA 1988 s 145 does not catch the provision of ancillary services such as cleaning, repairs and furniture but if the employee is higher paid or a director tax is charged on the cost to the employer of providing the services under TA 1988 s 154 (but limited to a maximum of 10% of the emoluments of the employment when the employee is in representative occupation: TA 1988 s 163) less any amount paid by the employee for those services.

No charge arises under TA 1988 s 145 for 'representative occupation'. This is defined as occupation which is:

(1) necessary for the proper performance of the employee's duties (eg a caretaker and see *Tennant v Smith* (1892) at [**5.63**]); or

(2) customary for the better performance of the employee's duties (eg a policeman who occupies a police house adjacent to the police station); or

(3) where there is a special threat to his security and special security

arrangements are in force as a result of which he resides in that accommodation.

It should be noted that a director who falls within the provisions of TA 1988 ss 153–168 cannot be a representative occupier under (1) or (2) above.

In *Vertigan v Brady* (1988) the owner of a nursery site near Norwich provided his 'right-hand man' with a rent free bungalow some three miles from the nursery. That employee was in direct charge of the plants and their propagation and was on standby at all hours during the week and on two out of three weekends to make adjustments to the heating and ventilation of the greenhouses. He was able to reach the nursery within five minutes of leaving the bungalow. There was evidence that he had been unable to obtain council accommodation in the area when he took up the job and he could not afford to buy a house in the vicinity. The court decided that on these facts the benefit of the rent free accommodation constituted a taxable emolument since the exception from charge for accommodation which was customarily provided ((2) above) did not apply. What was customary depended upon three main factors: statistical evidence (how common was the practice?); how long had the practice existed (a custom does not grow up overnight!); and whether the relevant employer accepted the customary practice. In this case although statistical evidence showed that approximately two thirds of all key nursery workers were provided with rent free accommodation, there was insufficient evidence to show that the practice had become so normal as to be an established custom.   **[5.77]**

b) Vouchers (non-cash and cash) and credit tokens (TA 1988 ss 141–144)

An employee (or his family) who receives a benefit in the form of a voucher or credit token may be charged to tax thereon.

Where he receives a non-cash voucher (ie a voucher or similar document, which can be exchanged for goods or services) he is taxed on the cost to the employer of providing the voucher rather than on its exchange value (except that meal vouchers which are non-transferable, used for meals only and the value of which does not exceed 15p for each working day are not taxed: ESC A2). The same rule applies to a transport voucher (such as season tickets and rail passes) except for lower-paid employees of transport undertakings who are exempted from the charge. Cheque vouchers (ie a cheque provided for an employee to be used by him to obtain goods or services) are similarly charged as emoluments.

Where the employee receives a cash voucher, ie a voucher which can be exchanged for a sum of money not substantially less than the cost to the person providing it, he is taxed on its exchange value.

Where the employee receives a credit token (including a credit card) he is taxed on the cost to the employer in providing the goods, money and services obtained by the use of that credit token (TA 1988 s 142).   **[5.78]**

5   Conclusions on the treatment of benefits in kind

The present system is neither logical nor fair and presents a bewildering range of alternatives. Consider, for instance, the following example.

                                                                    [5.79]–[5.90]

EXAMPLE 5.12

Rod wants his computer operator, Julie, to work overtime two evenings per week. Her salary is £4,500 pa. He plans to provide her with meals or a meal allowance on those two evenings. So far as Rod is concerned, the sum that he expends will be a deductible business expense, but for Julie taxation under Schedule E depends upon how the provision is made:

(1) If Rod, the employer, pays a cash allowance, that sum is an emolument.

(2) If Rod pays the bill incurred by Julie, that sum is an emolument (*Nicoll v Austin* (1935)).

(3) If Rod gives Julie a voucher exchangeable at a restaurant, the cost incurred by Rod in providing the voucher is an emolument.

(4) If Julie buys the food herself and is reimbursed, it may be that there is no charge (see *Donnelly v Williamson* (1982)).

(5) If the employer has an arrangement with the restaurant so that food is provided and the expense is directly met by the employer there is no charge (see *Wilkins v Rogerson* (1961)).

V PROBLEM CASES

The fact that a payment made to an employee is connected in some way with his employment does not automatically render it an emolument taxable under Schedule E. To be chargeable, it must be a reward for services or arise from the employment: see [**5.41**]). Three types of payment cause particular problems: gifts; contractual benefits unconnected with the services performed; and payments made on or after the termination of the employment. In all cases, whether the payment is chargeable must be considered from the position of the recipient regardless of whether it is tax-deductible by the payer. [**5.91**]

1 Gifts

There is a basic distinction between a payment which is a reward for services and which is, therefore, taxable and one which is made in appreciation of an individual's personal qualities, which is not taxable.

Various factors are relevant in drawing this distinction.

First, whether the payment is made once only or whether it is recurring (in the former case it is more likely to escape tax).

Secondly, whether it is made to only one employee or to a whole class of employees. In *Laidler v Perry* (1966), for instance, all the employees received a £10 voucher at Christmas instead of the turkey that they had received in previous years. The employees were taxed on the cash value of the voucher.

Thirdly, if the payment is by the employer there is a strong presumption that it is an emolument, whereas if it is from a third party, it is easier to show that it is a gift for personal qualities. However, tips are generally regarded as being in return for services and so taxable, even though made voluntarily by someone other than the employer. In *Calvert v Wainwright* (1947), a taxi driver was taxable on tips received from customers although the court suggested that a particularly generous tip from a special customer (eg at Christmas) might escape tax (see also *Blakiston v Cooper* (1909)).

Fourthly, a payment to which the employee is entitled under the terms of his contract of employment will be taxable as a part of his emoluments.

EXAMPLE 5.13

(1) Ham has played cricket for Gloucestershire for many years. At the end of his distinguished career the county grants him a benefit match (ie he is entitled to all the receipts from a particular game). The benefit is a tax-free testimonial paid for Ham's personal qualities (see *Seymour v Reed* (1927)). Compare:

(2) Mercenary plays as a professional in the Lancashire League and under the terms of his contract is entitled to have the 'hat passed round' (ie a collection taken) every time he scores 50 runs or takes 5 wickets in an innings. The sums that he receives will be taxed as emoluments because he is entitled to them in his contract of employment (see *Moorhouse v Dooland* (1955)).

Finally, it should be noted that the gift rules overlap with the benefit in kind rules. In deciding whether tax is chargeable under Schedule E, the gift rules should be applied first and then the benefit in kind rules.   **[5.92]**

EXAMPLE 5.14

Free Range Ltd gives all its employees a 25lb turkey at Christmas. In deciding whether tax is charged, (i) apply the gift rules (ie is the turkey given in return for services or is it for personal qualities?); then (ii) apply the benefit in kind rules (ie is the turkey convertible into money, in the case of lower-paid employees, or caught by TA 1988 ss 153–168, in the case of other employees and directors). If it is decided that the benefit is a gift, no tax is charged. If it is decided that it is in return for services, tax may be charged in accordance with the benefit in kind rules. It is likely in this example that tax would be chargeable.

2   Signing-on fees and the reimbursement of expenditure or losses

Payments made to compensate the taxpayer for some sacrifice that he has made by taking up an employment are generally not taxable because they are not in return for services. In *Jarrold v Boustead* (1964) an international rugby union player was not taxable on a £3,000 signing-on fee paid to him when he turned professional. The payment was not an emolument, but was to compensate him for permanent loss of his amateur status.

The same principle was applied in *Pritchard v Arundale* (1971) where a chartered accountant was not taxed on a large shareholding transferred to him in return for signing a service contract as managing director of the company. The benefit was held to accrue to him, not for future services as managing director which were to be adequately rewarded, but as compensation for loss of his professional status as a chartered accountant. It may also be noted that the shares were to be transferred in return for the taxpayer's signing the service contract. Hence, even if he had died without performing any services for the company, the shares would have been transferable to his estate. Further, they were given by a third party not by the new employer (see also *Vaughan-Neil v IRC* (1979) below).

Two features of these cases are, first, that the payment was compensation for a permanent loss to the taxpayer; if the loss is merely restricted to the period of the contract the payment is likely to be viewed as advance remuneration. Secondly, the taxpayer was fully rewarded for his services under the contract. Therefore, the payments in the following example would be taxable.

EXAMPLE 5.15

(1) Josh, who has been unemployed for 10 years, agrees to work for Workplan Ltd and is paid a £10,000 'signing-on fee' for giving up his life of leisure on the dole.

(2) Jason agrees to work for Workplan Ltd for 5 years at a salary of £100 pa but with a 'signing-on' fee of £60,000.

In *Glantre Engineering Ltd v Goodhand* (1983) an inducement payment made to a chartered accountant was held to be an emolument as the taxpayer failed to show that he had provided consideration in return for the payment since he was merely moving from one Schedule E employment to another. Once the taxpayer fails to show that he has been permanently deprived of something akin to amateur status or the status of being a partner, it must follow that the payment is a reward for future services in the new employment (hence the recent spate of 'golden hellos' in the City of London would appear to be taxable).

With the switch to the receipts basis of assessment in FA 1989, para 4A was inserted into TA 1988 s 19(1). This provides that if an emolument is received in a year when the employment has never been held, it is treated as an emolument of the first tax year of that employment. It is not thought that this change affects the basic principles outlined above since it is only relevant to payments which are classified as 'emoluments'.

The rule that compensation for loss caused to the employee escapes tax is not limited to signing-on fees. In *Hochstrasser v Mayes* (1960), ICI paid compensation to married (lower-paid) employees who suffered a loss on having to move house because of a relocation of their jobs. The compensation was not taxable as a reward for services (see further ESC A5; A67 and 1988 STI 800). It may be that compensation paid for a personal loss suffered by an employee will be non-taxable: **[5.93]**

EXAMPLE 5.16

Num Ltd pays its employee, Sid, £1,000 to compensate him for the anguish he suffers as a result of his wife running off with the milkman. The company may argue that the payment is necessary and, therefore, a deductible expense of the company, because otherwise Sid may suffer a mental and physical collapse. Further, the payment may be non-taxable in Sid's hands as compensation for his suffering rather than a reward for services.

3 Payments for entering into restrictive covenants (TA 1988 s 313)

The tax treatment of restrictive covenant payments made to former employees has undergone substantial revision over the years. Formerly, the sum paid escaped tax in the hands of the employee since it was thought to be neither a reward for the services which he had performed under his contract and nor was it provided for under the contract itself (*Beak v Robson* (1943)). For the employer, the sum would usually be non-deductible in arriving at his profits since it would be of a capital nature (*Associated Portland Cement Manufacturers Ltd v Kerr* (1946): see **[6.112]**). However, there were cases where it was accepted that if the restriction imposed on the employee was for a relatively short period, then the payment by the employer was tax deductible.

Legislation was then introduced (now TA 1988 s 313) which left the employer's position unchanged but which provided that in the hands of the employee income tax would be charged, at the higher rate only, on the sum which the employee received grossed up at the basic rate! This remarkable sounding process is illustrated in the following example.

EXAMPLE 5.17

On 1 June 1988, Ararat Ltd pays an employee, Thomas, £15,000 which is caught by the restrictive covenant rules. Thomas must gross up the £15,000 to £20,000 (ie £15,000100/75) and add it to his total income for the year of receipt. He must pay any higher rate tax due on that sum (treated as the top slice of his income) but receives a credit for the basic rate, ie £5,000 (£20,000 − £15,000).

This position, however, proved to be unsatisfactory since certain employers managed to use these rules in order to obtain substantial advantages. Broadly, instead of rewarding employees with salary increases, payments in return for restrictive undertakings were made and, because these undertakings only lasted for a comparatively short period, the employer was able to deduct the payments. The employee only suffered income tax at the higher rate on the sums received. Hence changes were made to s 313 in TA 1988 as a result of which *all restrictive covenant payments are now fully taxed in the hands of the employee and always deductible by the employer in arriving at his profits.*

The limitations on the ambit of s 313 are illustrated by *Vaughan-Neil v IRC* (1979) which involved the payment of £40,000 to a barrister to induce him to leave the planning bar and work for a company. This sum was not taxed. It was not a reward for services, being in effect a compensation payment (see *Pritchard v Arundale*, above), nor was it caught by s 313 because the barrister had given no undertaking to the company not to practise at the bar. His inability to do so was not caused by accepting the particular terms of employment, but rather by accepting the employment itself; the payment was merely recognition that the job would prevent his practising at the bar.   [**5.94**]

4   **Payments after the termination of employment**

a) *General*

Certain lump sum payments made to the holder of an office or employment after its termination are taxable in full under Schedule E as a reward for services past, present or future. For instance, a deferred payment for services is spread back and taxed as the emoluments of the years when it was earned. In *Heasman v Jordan* (1954) a non-contractual bonus payment at the end of the Second World War for overtime during the war was spread back over the years of work. As a result of the FA 1989 changes, emoluments are now taxed in the year of receipt unless paid after the employment has ceased when they are treated as emoluments for the last year of assessment in which the employment was held.

A sum paid for the variation of a continuing contract of employment is *prima facie* taxable as a payment in anticipation of future services under the varied contract. In *Cameron v Prendergast* (1940), a payment of £45,000 made to a director to persuade him not to retire, but to continue working on reduced hours and for a reduced salary was held to be advance remuneration. (See also *Holland v Geoghegan* (1972): compensation for dustmen's loss of totting rights taxed as advance remuneration; and to like effect *McGregor v Randall* (1984): compensation for loss of entitlement to profit commission.)

Any payment made under a contractual obligation will be taxed in full, even though it is paid because the termination of the employment. In *Dale v de Soissons* (1950) (followed in *Williams v Simmonds* (1981)), a director's service agreement provided for him to be paid £10,000 if it should be prematurely terminated. The taxpayer argued that the payment was not in return for services. It was held, however, that, as the payment was one to which he was contractually entitled, it was an emolument. In view of the generous taxation of non-contractual payments on a termination of employment (below), it is advisable to omit such compensation clauses from contracts of employment. In the case of payments in lieu of notice, the position is that if the sum is provided for in the contract of employment it will be fully taxed as an emolument whereas if there is no such contractual stipulation it will be payable in breach of contract and will therefore be subject to tax under s 148. [**5.95**]

b) *Compensation for loss of office* (TA 1988 ss 148, 188)

Lump sum payments, not falling within the above categories, formerly escaped tax as the sum was not a reward for services (the payment was often called a 'golden handshake').

TA 1988 s 148, however, applies a special scheme of taxation to 'any payment (not otherwise chargeable to tax) in connection with the termination of the holding of an office or employment or any change in its functions or emoluments'. This wide section includes payments made by a person other than the employer to someone other than the employee (eg to his spouse or PRs).

In general terms s 148 catches golden handshakes, compensation and damages for wrongful dismissal and redundancy payments. It also catches payments in kind, eg, the receipt by a dismissed employee of a company car as compensation. Crucially, the first £30,000 of any payment within s 148 is exempt from tax (see s 188(4)).

Redundancy payments can only be taxed under s 148 and not under the usual Schedule E rules (TA 1988 s 580(3)), although, in the majority of cases, tax is unlikely to arise because the payments will usually come within the exempt £30,000 limit. The Revenue have issued a Statement of Practice indicating what they regard as a genuine redundancy payment which qualifies for the £30,000 exemption (see SP 1/81).

Section 148 does not apply (TA 1988 s 188 and Sch 11) to:
(a) payments otherwise chargeable to tax under Schedule E (hence to payments caught by Dale v de Soissons);
(b) payments charged to tax under TA 1988 s 313;
(c) benefits received under approved retirement pension schemes (or unapproved schemes, if the employee was taxed on his contributions);
(d) payments because of death or disability; and
(e) certain payments for foreign service.

Major changes in the tax treatment of golden handshakes caught by s 148 were made by FA 1988. Before that date the first £25,000 of such payments was exempt from income tax and thereafter a system of 'top slicing' relief operated which provided that where a payment exceeded £25,000, tax on the slice between £25,000 and £50,000 was reduced by one half and tax on the slice between £50,000 and £75,000 was reduced by one quarter: that part of any lump sum which exceeded £75,000 was then taxable in full. From 6 April 1988 the exempt amount of such payments increased to £30,000 but the system of top slicing relief was removed. Accordingly, that part of any payment which exceeds the £30,000 exempt slice is now taxed in full. Two or more payments made in respect of the same office or employment or made by the same or associated employers are aggregated for this purpose.

EXAMPLE 5.18

During the year 1991–92, A (a married man) has the following income:

Earnings from employment	£25,000.00
Other income	nil
Lump sum on termination of employment	£80,000.00
Personal allowances	£5,015.00

Tax payable disregarding the terminal payment:

Taxable income:	£25,000.00
Less	£5,015.00
	£19,985.00
Tax payable: £19,985 at 25%	4,996.25

Tax payable including the terminal payment:

(1)   Calculate taxable slice: £80,000 − £30,000 exempt = £50,000

(2)   Calculate tax at marginal rate on £50,000 as follows:

	£
first £3,715 at 25% =	928.75
remaining £46,285 at 40% =	£18,514.00
	£19,442.75

Final liability is £4,996.25 + £19,442.75 = £24,439

Terminal payments caught by TA 1988 s 148 are treated as earned income from which tax must be deducted under PAYE on the sum above £30,000 in the year when the job is lost (not the year when the money is paid in cases when the two are different). If the payment is made before delivery of Form P45, the deduction should be in accordance with the employee's code for the relevant period. If made after delivery of Form P45, tax should be deducted at the basic rate. If the PAYE rules would result in the deduction of an excessive amount of tax it is possible to agree with the inspector of taxes that a lesser sum be paid or, alternatively, if the tax has already been deducted, that an interim repayment be made. For the relationship between s 148 and the '*Gourley* principle', see Appendix I.

Problems may arise when the employee is also a substantial shareholder in the employer company and the payments are made on the change of ownership of that company. In such cases, a payment, ostensibly for termination of his service contract, may be challenged on the grounds that it represents partial consideration for the shares transferred. To the extent that the challenge is successful the payment will not be deductible as a business expense of the company and will not qualify for the £30,000 terminal payment exemption (see *James Snook & Co Ltd v Blasdale* (1952)). To avoid this danger it is desirable to separate, so far as possible, arrangements for the share sale from the question of compensation for loss of office.

[5.96]–[5.110]

VI DEDUCTIBLE EXPENSES (TA 1988 s 198)

Tax under Schedule E is charged on emoluments after deducting allowable expenditure. Allowable expenditure is defined in TA 1988 s 198 which draws a distinction between travelling and other expenses.　　　　　**[5.111]**

1 Expenses other than travelling expenses

Expenses will be deductible only if incurred '. . . wholly exclusively and necessarily in the performance of the said duties . . .'. These provisions may be contrasted with the more generous expenditure rules of Schedule D Cases I and II (see Chapter 6).

Three requirements must be satisfied if an expense is to be deductible: first, it must be incurred 'in performing' the duties. No deduction is allowed for expenses which enable the employee to prepare for his duties or to be better equipped to carry them out. In *Shortt v McIlgorm* (1945), for instance, the taxpayer could not deduct the fee that he paid to an employment agency. (Contrast TA 1988 s 201A allowing agents fees paid by actors and other theatrical artists taxed under Schedule E to be deducted.) In *Simpson v Tate* (1952) a medical officer could not deduct the cost of joining learned societies which would enable him to perform his duties better (note the partial reversal of this decision by TA 1988 s 201). Secondly, the expense must be 'necessarily' incurred in the performance of the duties. This is an objective test; therefore, to satisfy it, every employee in the particular job would need to incur the expenditure. Nor is it sufficient that the employer requires the expenditure; the nature of the duties must require it.

In *Brown v Bullock* (1961) a bank manager was required by his employer to join a London club. He could not deduct his subscription because it was not necessary for the performance of his duties. It seems odd that the employer is not allowed to decide what is necessary to the particular office or employment!

The third requirement is that the expense should be incurred 'wholly and exclusively' in the performance of the duties. This same requirement is found in Schedule D Cases I and II and the meaning of these words is discussed in Chapter 6.

Few expenses will satisfy all three conditions. However, the harshness of TA 1988 s 198 is, in practice, mitigated in relation to various employments by a number of Revenue concessions (for instance, the flat rate allowance for the cost of tools and special clothing, ESC A1, and the deduction of fees for joining certain professional bodies and learned societies: [1991] STI 91).

An innovation, designed to encourage charitable giving, was the introduction in 1987 of the so called 'payroll deduction scheme'. So long as a recognised scheme is operated by their employer, employees can make donations to the charity of their choice up to a maximum amount of £600 per annum. These sums are deductible expenses for the employee and, as a novel feature, are paid gross to an approved charitable agent which then distributes the sums to the charity of the employee's choice (TA 1988 s 202).　　　　　**[5.112]**

2 Travelling expenses

If travelling expenses are to be deductible they must be 'necessarily' incurred 'in the performance' of the duties (or be 'expenses of keeping or maintaining a horse to perform the same . . .'). There is no 'wholly and exclusively' requirement. The expense of travelling to work is not, therefore, deductible because it is incurred before, rather than in the performance of the duties. In contrast, travelling between places of work is deductible.

EXAMPLE 5.19

(1) Sally is employed as a lecturer by the Midtech Poly and gives seminars at both the branches of the Poly which are two miles apart. Her travelling costs between both branches are deductible.

(2) Jim works as a postman and as a barman in a local pub. The cost of travelling between the sorting office and the pub is not deductible since Jim has two different jobs and is not therefore travelling between centres of work in the course of a single employment.

The requirement that travelling expenditure be 'necessarily incurred' has been considered in three House of Lords cases. In *Ricketts v Colquhoun* (1926) the travelling expenses of a barrister to and from Portsmouth where he had been appointed Recorder were not deductible. In *Pook v Owen* (1970), a general medical practitioner was allowed to deduct the expenses of travelling to a hospital where he held a part-time appointment, because some of the functions of that post were performed at his home so that he was travelling between two centres of work. Finally, in *Taylor v Provan* (1974) a Canadian director of Bass Charrington was allowed to deduct his travelling expenses to the UK, again, because he performed part of his duties at places outside the UK. What emerges from these cases is that travelling expenses for getting to work will not be deductible. Further, a job will not be treated as having two centres just because the taxpayer chooses to perform some of its functions at his home. Just how far an employment can be tailored to the particular personal circumstances of the employee is slightly unclear after *Taylor v Provan*, although it should be stressed that the qualities of that particular taxpayer were quite unique!

Travelling expenses raise two further problems. First, allowable expenditure has to be reasonable. In *Marsden v IRC* (1965) an Inland Revenue investigator could not deduct the full cost of travelling by car to perform his duties because he could have used a cheaper form of transport. This is not to say that the cheapest form must always be used, since the matter is one of fact and degree and allowance must be made for the inconvenience of certain forms of transport and for the dignity of the employee or office holder. Presumably, a company director will not be consigned to the local bus service! Secondly, the relationship between the rules for deductibility of expenditure and the taxation of reimbursements should be carefully noted (see [**5.64**]). In the case of higher paid employees and directors such reimbursements are automatically treated as emoluments (TA 1988 s 153).

Finally, it may be that the recent decision of the House of Lords in the employment law case of *Smith v Stages* (1989) will mark a relaxation in the courts' view of when an employee will be travelling in the course of performing the duties of his employment. In the case the Law Lords held that an employee who was travelling back home from a place of work to which he had been temporarily assigned, was still acting 'in the course of his employment' so as to render his employer vicariously liable for the employee's negligence. Were this decision to be applied in the context of deductible expenditure under Schedule E, it would suggest that if an employee has several places of work not only would expenditure on travel between those places be deductible, but so also would the cost of travelling from home to the first place of work, provided that it is not the employee's regular or normal place of work. [5.113]-[5.130]

VII BASIS OF ASSESSMENT AND PAYE

Prior to 1989-90 tax was charged under Schedule E on a current year basis and was levied on emoluments when earned. Accordingly the date of payment was strictly irrelevant to the tax charge. Inevitably this led to problems of referring back payments in the case eg of directors who are frequently voted bonuses long after the relevant tax year for which they performed the services. To tidy this area up and to correct certain other defects in the Schedule E legislation, FA 1989 altered the basis of assessment under Schedule E from the earnings to the *receipts basis*. [5.131]

1 General principle

Emoluments are subject to charge when they are received rather than when they are earned and, not surprisingly, this rule is backed-up by a detailed definition of when a payment is received for these purposes. In the case of directors, for instance, payment is made when the sum is credited in the company's accounts or records—hence crediting the director's account with that sum will constitute a payment for these purposes. [5.132]

2 Position of employer

Inevitably, if the employee is to be assessed on the receipts basis rather than the earnings basis, the question which then arises is how the employer should be treated. To permit him to deduct emoluments when they are earned even though he has not yet paid them would lead to an imbalance between the deductibility rules under Schedule D Cases I and II as compared with the emolument rules under Schedule E.

Accordingly, it is provided that an employer can only deduct the sum in question from his accounts if that sum is actually paid either *during* the period of account (the same definition of payment as above) or *within nine months* thereafter.

Sums earned, but not paid until more than nine months after the end of a period of account, will therefore be deducted not in that period but in the following accounting period when paid. [5.133]

EXAMPLE 5.20

Jason, a self-employed builder, makes up his accounts to 31 December each year. He employs Lumpy as his bricklayer. In 1990 he pays Lumpy £20,000 and at the end of the year (because of cash-flow problems) owes him £15,000. £7,000 of this sum he pays in June 1991 and the balance in October. He submits his accounts to the Revenue (showing £35,000 as a deductible expense) in April 1991.

(i) The £20,000 paid to Lumpy is a deductible expense in 1990.

(ii) The £15,000 unpaid when the accounts are submitted will be presumed not to be paid within nine months of the end of the accounting period and will therefore be *disallowed* in 1990: however the £7,000 subsequently paid within that period will result in an adjustment to the 1990 accounts if a claim is made.

(iii) The remaining £8,000 will be deducted in the 1991 accounts.
(iv) Lumpy will be assessed on the £15,000 in 1991-92 (year of receipt).

3   The source doctrine

One of the hallowed principles of income tax (discussed in Chapter 3) is that a charge can only be made if the source of the income is continuing. This principle has, of course, been much modified by statute. Thus, the old possibility of a barrister ceasing to practise and at some time during his peaceful retirement receiving arrears of fees which, because the source of the fees had ceased, escaped tax, has long since gone under the post cessation receipts rules. More recently, the case of *Bray v Best* discussed at [**3.41**], revealed an unsuspected gap in the Schedule E legislation on this matter.

This gap has now been closed and if an emolument is paid to an employee before his employment commences, it will be treated as an emolument of the first year of that employment: if paid after the employment has ceased it will be related back to the last year of employment. Accordingly, should the facts of *Bray v Best* recur in the future, the distribution payment will be related back to the last year of the employment. Note however that this charge merely extends the source doctrine to catch the payment: the tax itself will still remain charged in the year of receipt.

The principle that tax is charged in the year of receipt but that the source of the income must be determined in the year when it is earned, applies in the facts of the following example.   [**5.134**]

EXAMPLE 5.21

(1)   In 1990-91 Bert is resident and ordinarily resident in the UK. His job ceases and in 1991-92 he becomes non-resident (taking a job as a Eurocrat in Brussels). A bonus paid in 1991-92 in relation to the UK job is taxed under Schedule E Case I and is *taxed in year of receipt*.

(2)   Take the opposite case: ie in 1990-91 Henri is non-UK resident; his job ceases; he comes to the UK in 1991-92 when he receives a bonus in respect of 1990-91. He is not subject to UK tax since he was outside the tax net when the money was earned.

4   Directors

Finally, as already noted, a major purpose of the new rules was to deal more satisfactorily with the tax treatment of directors' emoluments. In this connection the term 'director' is widely defined to include 'shadow directors' and the Revenue generally take the view today that all directors fall to be taxed under Schedule E. Former practice which enabled certain directors to be self-employed under Schedule D will no longer be followed.   [**5.135**]

5   The collection machinery in PAYE

Tax is collected by a sophisticated method of deduction at source operated by the employer and known as the PAYE system. The system generally applies to all income assessable under Schedule E except where the employer is non-resident, when the Revenue assess the employee directly. It must be applied by any employer who pays an employee more than £63.40 per week (single person) or £96.50 (married man).

For directors and employees earning at least £8,500 pa, the employer must also complete Form P11D giving details of benefits in kind and payments by way of expenses (save, in the latter case, those for which a dispensation has been granted, see explanatory leaflet IR 69).

Before 1975, workers supplied through agencies who were self-employed could escape tax on earnings on a particular assignment by disappearing once it was completed. Accordingly, TA 1988 s 134 (originally introduced in that year), provides that where a worker receives remuneration under a contract with an agency to render personal services under supervision to a client he is taxable under Schedule E with the agency operating PAYE (*Brady v Hart* (1985) and, on the supervision requirement, see *Bhadra v Ellam* (1988)).

Certain workers (such as entertainers) are excluded from the operation of the section and special rules also apply to self-employed persons working in the construction industry. Tax must be deducted by the contractor unless the sub-contractor has a tax exemption certificate (see IR 40), otherwise the contractor will become liable to interest on such amount as he fails to deduct.

PAYE is an effective tax collector which reduces the opportunity and incentive for tax evasion. It can also be used to collect underpayments of tax in previous years by reducing or withholding completely allowances in the current year. An employer may be liable to interest on tax paid late where he has failed to apply PAYE correctly at the right time. This charge will begin to run fourteen days after the tax year to which the tax relates (TA 1988 s 203). In the event of an overpayment of tax in a previous year, this will be corrected either by direct repayment or by set-off against other tax liabilities of that year.

In an attempt to ensure that remuneration paid to directors is subject to deduction of tax at source, TA 1988 s 164 deals with the situation where a gross sum is paid to the director and the tax thereon is accounted for to the Revenue by a person other than the director. In such cases, unless the director makes good the sum overpaid, he will be treated as receiving a further emolument equal to the amount of tax that has been accounted for to the Revenue. This provision applies to directors falling within the provisions of TA 1988 ss 153–168.

Under the PAYE system the liability of the employer to deduct and account for the correct amount of tax is usually exclusive so that the Revenue cannot assess an employee for unpaid tax. The one exception is provided for by Reg 26(4) of the Income Tax (Employment) Regs 1973 (SI 1973/334) which applies when an employee receives the emolument knowing that the employer has wilfully failed to deduct the proper amount of tax. A heavy burden is placed on the Revenue if Reg 26(4) is to be satisfied since not only is actual knowledge on the part of the employee required but also an element of blameworthiness on the part of the employer must be shown. This burden was satisfied in the cases of *R v IRC, ex p Keys and ex p Cook* (1987) where the employees in question were the controlling directors of the employer company which had failed over a number of years to operate PAYE in respect of their salaries. **[5.136]**

6 Schedule D—trades and professions

> '. . . take a gang of burglars. Are they engaged in trade or an adventure in the nature of trade? They have an organisation. They spend money on equipment. They acquire goods by their efforts. They sell the goods. They make a profit. What detail is lacking in their adventure? You may say it lacks legality, but it has been held that legality is not an essential characteristic of a trade. You cannot point to any detail that it lacks. But still it is not a trade, nor an adventure in the nature of trade. And how does it help to ask the question: If it is not a trade, what is it? It is burglary and that is all there is to say about it.' (Lord Denning in *Griffiths v Harrison* (1963) but contrast the profits of prostitution which are derived from a trade: see *IRC v Aken* (1990).) **[6.1]**

I INTRODUCTION

Tax is charged under Schedule D Case I on the annual profits or gains arising to a UK resident from a trade carried on in the UK or elsewhere and under Case II from a profession or vocation (TA 1988 s 18). These Cases, therefore, charge the self-employed and apply equally to sole traders, trading partnerships, sole practitioners, and professional partnerships. (For partnerships see Chapter 29.) Generally, the same principles operate under both Case I and Case II so that the two Cases may be treated together. The following differences should, however, be noted:

(1) An isolated transaction may be a trade (under Case I), but it can never be the exercise of a profession or vocation (under Case II), and so may attract income tax only under Schedule D Case VI (Chapter 9).

(2) Certain capital allowances are available only to traders (see Chapter 7).

(3) The rule in *Sharkey v Wernher* ([**6.95**]) applies only to traders.

(4) Damages or compensation obtained for any wrong or injury suffered by an individual in his profession or vocation are not chargeable gains (CGTA 1979 s 19(5)).

In most cases it will be clear whether the taxpayer is self-employed or whether he is an employee holding a post or office under Schedule E (but see [**5.21**]). **[6.2]-[6.20]**

II WHAT IS A TRADE?

1 The problems involved

'Trade' is not defined. According to TA 1988 s 832(1) it 'includes every trade, manufacture, adventure, or concern in the nature of a trade'. This provision, although unhelpful, indicates that a single adventure may constitute a trade (see eg *Martin v Lowry* (1927) below). In *Ransom v Higgs* (1974) Lord Wilberforce considered that a trading transaction would usually exhibit the following features:

'Trade normally involves the exchange of goods or services for reward . . . there must be something which the trade offers to provide by way of business. Trade moreover presupposes a customer.' (1974 3 All ER at 964)

In the absence of a satisfactory statutory definition the meaning of trade must be sought from the voluminous case law in this area. The Final Report of the Royal Commission on the Taxation of Profits and Income (1955: Cmd 9474) concluded that there could be no single test but suggested certain objective tests ('the badges of trade').

Before considering these 'badges of trade', two general matters should be noted in connection with the case law. First, when the case is concerned with whether a taxpayer carried on a trade or not, caution needs to be exercised in citing it as precedent since the findings of the commissioners are decisions of fact which will rarely be overturned on appeal (see *Edwards v Bairstow and Harrison* (1956): [**2.41**]). The appeal court is often and reluctantly forced to conclude that facts exist to justify the findings of the commissioners. Secondly, before the introduction of CGT in 1965, the question whether or not a person had engaged in a trade was of fundamental significance. If he had, any profit was charged under Case I; if not income tax was inapplicable so that the resultant (capital) profit escaped tax altogether. Since 1965 the choice is not between a charge under Case I and no tax, but, normally, is between paying income tax and CGT or, for companies, corporation tax on their income and capital profits. The imposition of CGT at income tax rates from 6 April 1988 has further blurred the importance of the distinction between capital gains and income profits.   [**6.21**]

2 The 'badges of trade'

The Royal Commission identified six 'badges' designed to determine whether or not the purchase and resale of property is a trading transaction.   [**6.22**]

The subject matter of the transaction   Property which neither yields an income nor gives personal enjoyment to its owner is likely to form the subject matter of a trading transaction. Other property (typically land, works of art, and shares) may be acquired for the income and/or enjoyment which it provides.

In *Rutledge v IRC* (1929), the taxpayer was a businessman connected with the film industry. Whilst in Berlin he purchased one million toilet rolls for £1,000 which he resold in the UK at a profit of approximately £11,000. The Court of Session held that the taxpayer had engaged in an adventure in the nature of a trade so that the profits were assessable under Case I. They stressed that such a quantity of goods must have been intended for resale. Similarly, in *Martin v Lowry* (1927), the gigantic speculation involved in purchasing and reselling 44 million yards of government surplus aeroplane linen, at a profit of £1,600,000, amounted to a trade largely because of the nature of the subject matter and the commercial methods employed to sell it.

The purchase and resale of land inevitably causes more difficulty since owning land in quantity does not raise a presumption that trading is intended. In *IRC v Reinhold* (1953), for instance, despite the taxpayer having bought four houses over two years, admittedly for sale, the Court of Session concluded that 'heritable property is not an uncommon subject of investment' and that the taxpayer was not trading.

Similar difficulties arose in *Taylor v Good* (1974) where the taxpayer was held not to be trading when he resold at a vast profit, because of planning permission, a house which he had purchased with the original intention of living there. The Court of Appeal took the view that a person intending to resell property is entitled to take steps to ensure that he obtains the best possible price for it! (Today that profit would be subject to CGT.) In particular, the court decided that the house did not become his trading stock merely because he had applied for planning permission before the sale:

> 'If you find a trade in the purchase and sale of land, it may not be difficult to find that properties originally owned (for example) by inheritance, or bought for investment only, have been brought into the stock in trade of that trade. But where, as here, there is no question at all of absorption into a trade of dealing in land or lands previously acquired with no thought of dealing, there is no ground at all for holding that activities such as those in the present case, designed only to enhance the value of the land in the market, are to be taken as pointing to, still less as establishing, an adventure in the nature of trade.' (Russell LJ 1974 STC 148 at 155.)

The definition of a trade has been further limited in this area as a result of the decision in *Marson v Morton* (1986). In that case the taxpayer was a potato merchant and on advice from an estate agent friend, he purchased (in July 1977) land suitable for development. He paid £65,000: £35,000 out of his own resources and £30,000 on a mortgage arranged by the estate agent. At the time of the purchase the taxpayer said that he intended to make a medium to long term investment in the land. However, in September 1977, and on advice from that same estate agent, the land was sold for £100,000. Both the commissioners and Sir Nicholas Browne-Wilkinson VC held that the taxpayer was not trading and that land could be held as an investment even though it produced no income. The following passage from the judgment is especially worthy of note:

> 'In 1986 it is not any longer self evident that unless land is producing income it cannot be an investment. The legal principle, of course, cannot change with the passage of time: but life does. Since the arrival of inflation and high rates of tax on income, new approaches to investment have emerged putting the emphasis in investment on the making of capital profit at the expense of income yield. For example, the purchase of short dated stocks giving capital yield on redemption but no income has become commonplace. Similarly, split level investment trusts have been invented which produce capital profits on one type of share and income on another. Again, institutions now purchase works of art by way of investment. In my judgment those are plainly not trading deals; yet no income is produced from them. I can see no reason why land should be any different and the mere fact that land is not income producing should not be decisive or even virtually decisive on the question whether it was bought as an investment.'   [**6.23**]

Length of ownership   This is a weak 'badge' because the presumption that, if property is sold within a short time of acquisition, the taxpayer has traded will often be rebutted on the facts.   [**6.24**]

Frequency of similar transactions   Repeated transactions in the same subject matter point to a trade. Since a single adventure may amount to a trade this 'badge' will be applicable only in circumstances where that would not otherwise be the case. In *Pickford v Quirke* (1927) the court held that although a single purchase and resale by a syndicate of four cotton mills did not amount to trading, the series viewed as a whole did. Hence, subsequent transactions may trigger a Case I liability on earlier transactions (see also Leach v Pogson (1962) in which the founding and subsequent sale of 30 driving schools consecutively, was held to be trading). **[6.25]**

Work done on the property When work is done to the property in order to make it more marketable, or when an organisation is set up to sell the asset, there is some evidence of trading (see *Martin v Lowry* (1927): compare *Taylor v Good* (1974)). In *Cape Brandy Syndicate v IRC* (1921) three individuals engaged in the wine trade who formed a syndicate and purchased some 3,000 casks of Cape brandy which they blended (with French brandy), recasked, and sold in lots over an 18 month period were held to be trading. **[6.26]**

Circumstances responsible for the realisation A forced sale to raise cash for an emergency raises a presumption that the transaction is not a trade. Sales by executors in the course of winding up the deceased's estate and by liquidators and receivers in the administration of an insolvent company will often fall into this category (see *Cohan's Executors v IRC* (1924) and *IRC v The 'Old Bushmills' Distillery Co Ltd* (1927) and see 4, below). **[6.27]**

Motive If the transaction was undertaken in order to realise a profit, that is some evidence of trading. The absence of a profit motive does not prevent a commercial operation from amounting to a trade, however (see, for instance, dividend stripping; Chapter 31 and for the effect of fiscal motives, see *Ensign Tankers (Leasing) Ltd v Stokes* (1991)) and, conversely, the mere fact that an asset is purchased with the intention of ultimate resale at a profit will not of itself lead to a finding of trading. Often the subject matter involved will be decisive. In *Wisdom v Chamberlain* (1968) the taxpayer (a comedian) who bought £200,000 of silver bullion as a 'hedge' against an expected devaluation of sterling and three months later sold it realising a profit of £50,000 was held to be trading. His claim that he had made no profit, but rather that the pound had fallen in value, was rejected. **[6.28]**

3 Mutual trading

No man can trade with himself (but see the rule in *Sharkey v Wernher* **[6.95]**). Thus, when persons join together in an association and jointly contribute to a common fund for their mutual benefit, any surplus received by the members on a division of that fund is tax-free (*New York Life Insurance Co v Styles* (1889)). If the association trades with non-members, however, the profits attributable to that activity are taxable. In *Carlisle and Silloth Golf Club v Smith* (1913), fees paid by visitors for the use of the club facilities were held to be trading receipts. TA 1988 s 491 prevents the mutual trading doctrine from being used to avoid tax, by imposing a charge on the return of surplus assets in circumstances when the original contributions were tax deductible. **[6.29]**

4 Trading after a discontinuance

The mere realisation of assets after the permanent discontinuance of the business is not trading. Hence, in *IRC v Nelson* (1938) income tax under Case I was not charged when a whisky broker, who because of ill health had closed his business, sold the entire business including the stock-in-trade.

By contrast, a sale of stock with a view to the cessation of trading (a 'closing-down sale') is chargeable because the trade is still continuing (see *J & R O'Kane & Co Ltd v IRC* (1922)). Special rules operate for the valuation of trading stock held at the date of cessation of a business (TA 1988 s 100, see [**6.92**]).   [**6.30**]–[**6.40**]

III MEANING OF 'PROFESSION' AND 'VOCATION'

In common with 'trade', neither 'profession' nor 'vocation' are statutorily defined. 'Profession' has been judicially described as involving 'the idea of an occupation requiring either purely intellectual skill or manual skill controlled by the intellectual skill of the operator' (see Scrutton LJ in *IRC v Maxse* (1919)). This definition can be misleading, because a person exercising an occupation in those terms (such as a solicitor) may, as a question of fact, be an employee assessable under Schedule E (see Chapter 5). As already mentioned, a profession is unlike a trade in that it involves an element of continuity. Hence, casual profits and fees arising from an isolated transaction are taxed under Schedule D Case VI.

'Vocation' has been judicially defined by Denman J in *Partridge v Mallandaine* (1886) as '. . . the way in which a man passes his life'. This definition is somewhat unhelpful, but the term embraces self-employed bookmakers, jockeys, authors and photographers.   [**6.41**]–[**6.60**]

IV   COMPUTATION OF PROFITS

1   The accounts

Tax under Cases I and II is on the 'annual profits of the trade, profession or vocation' (TA 1988 s 18). 'Annual' in this context means of an income, as opposed to of a recurring nature (*Martin v Lowry* (1927)). From the profit and loss account income profits are calculated as income receipts less income expenditure. For instance, a trader whose income receipts are £40,000 and income expenses £25,000 has income profits of £15,000 (£40,000—£25,000).

The taxpayer's profits as shown in his accounts must be agreed for tax purposes with the inspector of taxes. Accounts prepared for commercial purposes and according to standard accountancy practice will rarely show the taxable profits. Some items which have been deducted in the accounts may not be deductible for income tax purposes (such as entertainment expenses: see [**6.114**]). Other items are treated differently for taxation purposes: expenditure on a capital asset, for instance, is written off annually over the life of the asset as depreciation under standard accounting practice but is deductible for income tax purposes only if it falls within the system of capital allowances (see Chapter 7). As a result the taxpayer's accounts must be adjusted by adding back deductions which are not allowable and, where appropriate, by making permitted deductions (such as capital allowances).   [**6.61**]

2   The different bases

In drawing up accounts for taxation purposes, the taxpayer must use one of three bases: the earnings; the cash; or the bills delivered (the cash and bills delivered bases are known as the 'conventional' bases).   [**6.62**]

a) *The earnings basis*

Profits are calculated by deducting the expenses incurred during the accounting period from the income earned during that period. It is irrelevant whether the expenses have been paid or the income received. If accounts are rendered on this basis stock-in-trade and work-in-progress must be valued (for the rules governing the valuation of trading stock see [**6.90**]).

EXAMPLE 6.1

Jasper runs a bookshop in Covent Garden. He makes up his accounts each year to 31 December. For the year ending in 1991 his sales of books amount to £25,000, although he has not received payment from a valued customer, Leo, for a set of Dickens (sold for £5,000); nor from the Astery Gallery for a set of art books sold for £3,500. His expenditure incurred during the year includes rent and rates on the bookshop of £3,000; staff wages, heating and lighting of £6,000; and expenditure on books (trading stock) of £13,000. Out of this incurred expenditure, Jasper owes rates of £1,000 and an electricity bill of £250. He further owes some £2,500 on the books purchased. He estimates that he owns stock at the end of the year which cost him £6,000. His opening stock was valued at £4,000. Jasper's accounts, computed on an earnings basis, will be:

	£	£
Total sales		25,000
+ closing stock		6,000
		31,000
Less total of:		
Opening stock	4,000	
Rent/rates	3,000	
Stock bought	13,000	
Wages, lighting etc	6,000	
	26,000	
Jasper's taxable profit		£5,000

Note: In drawing up the account it is irrelevant that £3,750 of the incurred expenditure is unpaid and that customers owe £8,500.

A sum cannot be treated as earned, or an expense as incurred, until all the conditions precedent to earning or incurring it have been fulfilled (see *J P Hall & Co Ltd v IRC* (1925)). This does not mean, however, that the legal date for payment must have arisen. Thus, where goods are supplied or services rendered in year 1 which are not to be paid for until year 2, the price (even if it has to be estimated) must be included in the accounts for year 1. If the figure proves to be inaccurate, the assessment for year 1 generally must be reopened (*IRC v Gardner, Mountain and D'Ambrumenil Ltd* (1947)).

This doctrine of relating back gives rise to two difficulties; first, if the goods or services are never paid for the bad debt cannot be related back to the year when the goods were supplied, but is deductible only in the year when it is shown to be bad (see [**6.119**]); and secondly, if the estimated payment was agreed between the Revenue and the taxpayer at the time as being correctly stated, the accounts cannot subsequently be adjusted if the amount proves inaccurate. Any adjustment will have to be made in a subsequent account when the error is discovered. [**6.63**]

EXAMPLE 6.2

Gazza installs central heating equipment and enters into long-term maintenance contracts. In return for a fixed annual sum he maintains the equipment for seven years. Most of the maintenance work is undertaken in the final two years and as a matter of accountancy practice the business defers part of the annual payment until these later years. *For tax purposes*, however, the payments are taxed in the year of receipt and may therefore only be reduced by the maintenance expenses *incurred in that year*.

b) *The cash basis*

Profits are calculated by deducting payments actually made from sums actually received during the accounting period ('cash in minus cash out'). This basis presents a misleading picture of the state of the business when the taxpayer gives and receives credit, and carries trading stock. Further, it can be manipulated by the taxpayer to reduce his taxable profits.   [**6.64**]

EXAMPLE 6.3

Justinian, a barrister, makes up his accounts to 31 December each year. For 1991 he received fees of £12,000 and is owed a further £50,000; and he has paid bills of £5,000, but owes a further £4,000. On a cash basis his accounts show a profit of £7,000 (£12,000—£5,000), but that profit would be reduced to £3,000 were he to pay off all his outstanding liabilities on 31 December.

c) *The bills delivered basis*

Profit is calculated on this basis by deducting bills received from bills sent out during the accounting period. Unlike the earnings basis, this does not involve the taxpayer in valuing work-in-progress and is, therefore, particularly appropriate for solicitors and accountants.   [**6.65**]

d) *Choice of basis*

Although there is no statutory authority stating whether the Revenue or the taxpayer can insist on using a particular basis, in practice the basis has to be agreed with the Revenue. As a general principle, the accounts should be drawn up on the basis which presents an accurate picture of the state of the business during the year. Most self-employed persons render accounts on the earnings basis, although solicitors, for instance, are usually allowed to change to the bills delivered basis after their first three years provided that they agree to bill clients regularly. The Revenue are reluctant to accept the cash basis except, eg, for authors whose royalties are earned only when received and for barristers, who cannot sue for their fees. Once the Revenue have assessed the taxpayer on one basis, they cannot supplement that assessment by an assessment on an alternative basis (see *Rankine v IRC* (1952)).

The taxpayer may, however, change his basis for a later period. On a change from the earnings (or bills delivered basis) to the cash basis, the taxpayer may suffer the penalty of a double charge to tax, because in year 1 he is taxed on the earnings basis on sums owed (or on sums billed) and in year 2 (on the cash basis) he is taxed on that same money when received. Although there is no relief against this double charge, the taxpayer may as a corollary obtain a benefit because the same expenses may be deducted in years 1 and 2.

On a change from the cash to the earnings or bills delivered basis, the taxpayer could profit, because in year 1 (on the cash basis) he is taxed only on receipts, whereas in year 2 (on the earnings basis) he is taxed on sums earned. Earnings not received in year 1, therefore, formerly escaped tax altogether; they are now taxed as post-cessation receipts under TA 1988 s 104. **[6.66]**

3 Post-cessation receipts

TA 1988 s 103 provides that where profits were calculated on the earnings basis, sums received in respect of the trade, profession or vocation after its discontinuance, which would not otherwise be charged to income tax because the source of the income no longer exists, are taxed under Schedule D Case VI. For this purpose, a debt released after a discontinuance is treated as a receipt (TA 1988 s 103(4)). Certain sums are excluded; in particular, receipts on the transfer of stock or work-in-progress in order to avoid an overlap with TA 1988 ss 100 and 102 (see TA 1988 s 103(3) and **[6.92]**).

Where profits were assessed on the cash basis, TA 1988 s 104 imposes a similar charge to tax on post-cessation receipts, except that sums received for the transfer of work-in-progress after a discontinuance are brought within the charge. Section 104 also catches receipts that would otherwise escape tax on a change from the cash to the earnings basis.

Receipts charged under ss 103 or 104 are taxed as earned income under Schedule D Case VI, generally in the year of receipt or, if the taxpayer elects, in the year of discontinuance so long as that discontinuance has not occurred more than six years before the receipt. **[6.67]–[6.80]**

V TRADING RECEIPTS

To be a 'trading receipt' a sum must possess two characteristics. **[6.81]**

1 The sum must be derived from the trade

If the payment is in return for services or goods the payment is a trading receipt, whereas if it is made voluntarily in recognition of some personal quality of the taxpayer it is not (compare the rules for Schedule E: **[5.92]**). In *Murray v Goodhews* (1976), for instance, Watneys took back tied tenancies (mainly pubs) from their tenant traders as they fell vacant and made *ex gratia* lump sum payments to the traders which were held not to be trading receipts; they were paid voluntarily, by Watneys to acknowledge the good relationship with the traders and to maintain their good name. (As to whether the payments were deductible expenditure of the payer, Watneys, see **[6.112]**.) As a contrast, in *McGowan v Brown and Cousins* (1977) the taxpayer, an estate agent, found sites for a company for which he was paid a low fee because it was expected that he would handle the subsequent lettings for the company. The company, however, found another agent to do the letting and 'paid off¹a' the taxpayer with £2,500. This was held to be a trading receipt: it was a reward for services even though paid in pursuance of a moral rather than a legal obligation.

In *Higgs v Olivier* (1952) Laurence Olivier starred in the film of *Henry V* which did not achieve instant commercial success. As a result, the film company paid him £15,000 not to be involved in any film for 18 months.

The payment was held not to be a receipt of his profession but compensation for not exercising that profession and, therefore, escaped tax. It might today attract a CGT charge as a part disposal of goodwill: see [**14.7**].

A payment which is not in return for services or goods may be, nevertheless, a trading receipt if it is designed to be used in the taxpayer's business. Thus, in *Poulter v Gayjon Processes Ltd* (1985), government subsidies paid to encourage a shoe manufacturer to retain persons in employment was held to be a taxable trading receipt (see also *Ryan v Crabtree Denims Ltd* (1987)). In *Donald Fisher (Ealing) Ltd v Spencer* (1989), compensation paid by an agent whose negligence had resulted in the taxpayer becoming liable to pay substantially increased rent on its business premises was held to be a trading receipt. In the course of his judgment, subsequently upheld in the Court of Appeal, Walton J stated that:

> 'If compensation is received which is in substance payable in respect of either the non-receipt of what ought to have been received or the extra expense which would not have been incurred if all had gone properly, it seems to me that the principle is exactly the same.' [**6.82**]

2   The sum must be income not capital

The difficulty of determining whether payments are income receipts (taxable under Case I or II) or capital receipts (when the only possible liability is to CGT) was forcibly expressed by Greene MR in *IRC v British Salmson Aero Engines* (1938):

> '. . . in many cases it is almost true to say that the spin of a coin would decide the matter almost as satisfactorily as an attempt to find reasons'.

A number of tests have been suggested. The classical test is the distinction between a sale of the fixed capital of the business and of its circulating capital. Sale of the circulating capital produces income receipts. The defect with this test is that the classification of the asset (is it fixed or circulating?) depends upon the particular trade.

EXAMPLE 6:4

(1) Koob, a bookseller, owns a freehold bookshop in Covent Garden. The books are his circulating capital (his stock-in-trade) so that the sale proceeds are trade receipts. The bookshop is his fixed capital, the sale of which would give rise to a CGT liability.

(2) Seisin buys vacant premises in Covent Garden which he renovates and sells as bookshops. He is trading in the sale of bookshops which are his circulating capital so that the receipts are income receipts.

Other tests are but variations on the original theme and contain the same defect. For example, whether the expenditure brings into existence an enduring asset for the benefit of the trade (capital) or not, and the 'trees and fruit' test (the tree is the capital producing the fruit which is income).

The case law in this area is considerable and characterised by subtle distinctions. Many cases involve compensation receipts where the question is, usually, whether the receipt is for the loss of a permanent asset (capital), or is in lieu of trading profits (income). In *London and Thames Haven Oil Wharves Ltd v Attwooll* (1967), the taxpayer owned jetties used by oil tankers.

A tanker crashed into and badly damaged a jetty. The taxpayer received compensation of £100,000, £80,000 to rebuild the jetty (capital) and £20,000 to compensate him for lost tanker fees (income). In *Lang v Rice* (1984) the taxpayer ran two clubs in Belfast until they were destroyed by bombings. He did not resume trading thereafter and received compensation from the Northern Ireland Office for, inter alia, 'consequential loss'. The Revenue argued that the payment was a once and for all capital payment to compensate the taxpayer for the permanent loss of his business (in effect, therefore, a payment for goodwill). The Northern Ireland Court of Appeal held, however, that the payment was designed to compensate the taxpayer for loss of profit during the period that would elapse before business could be resumed. Accordingly, the fact that business did not recommence had no effect on the nature of the payment. An air of some unreality pervades this decision since, as the premises had been totally destroyed and the taxpayer held only a short lease, there was never any question of the business being resumed. **[6.83]**

The decided cases will be considered under six headings:

Restrictions on activity If, as part of his trading arrangements, the taxpayer agrees to restrict his activities in return for payments made to him, the payments are trade receipts. In *Thompson v Magnesium Elektron Ltd* (1944), the taxpayers manufactured magnesium which required chlorine, a by-product of which is caustic soda. ICI agreed to supply the chlorine at below market value and paid the taxpayers a lump sum to prevent them from making their own chlorine and caustic soda, sales of which would compete with those of ICI. The sum was a taxable receipt paid as compensation for profits that the taxpayers would have made on the sale of caustic soda. In *IRC v Biggar* (1982), a payment to a farmer, under EEC regulations, to compensate him for changing from milk to meat farming was a trade receipt (it was compensation for lost profits). **[6.84]**

Sterilisation of an asset A payment for the permanent restriction on the use of an asset is capital even though the sum is computed by reference to loss of profits. In *Glenboig Union Fireclay Co Ltd v IRC* (1922), fireclay manufacturers who received compensation for the permanent loss of their right to work fireclay under neighbouring land were held to have received a capital sum. If the compensation is for the temporary loss of an asset, however, it is a trade receipt. Hence, in *Burmah Steamship Co Ltd v IRC* (1931), repairers of a vessel over-ran the contractual date for completion of the work and paid compensation for the lost profits of the owners. The payments were held to be trade receipts. **[6.85]**

EXAMPLE 6.5

Hercules arranges to have his new cargo ship built in a Liverpool shipyard by 31 December 1990. The agreed price is £2m, but this is to be reduced by £10,000 per day if the ship is not ready on time. The ship is delivered ten days late, so that the price is reduced by £100,000. Although this reduction is calculated on the basis of Hercules' lost profits, it would seem that he has not received a sum in lieu of trading receipts.

Cancellation of a business contract or connection When a taxpayer receives compensation for the cancellation of a contract, the nature of the receipt depends upon the significance of the cancelled contract to the business. If it relates to the whole structure of the profit-making apparatus, the compensation is capital. Thus in *Van den Berghs Ltd v Clark* (1935) a Dutch and an English company (both manufacturing margarine) had contracted to trade in different areas so as to avoid competition. The Dutch company cancelled the contract, which had 13 years to run, and paid £450,000 in compensation. It was held to be a capital receipt because the contract had provided the means whereby profits were produced; the English company had, therefore, lost the equivalent of a fixed asset of the business (see also *Whitehead v Tubbs Elastics Ltd* (1984)).

If, however, the contract is merely one of many and of short duration, the compensation received is income. In *Kelsall Parsons & Co v IRC* (1938) the taxpayer was a manufacturers' agent who had contracts with different manufacturers and received commission on a sale of their products. One such contract was terminated a year early and the manufacturer paid £15,000 compensation. It was held to be a trade receipt. The contract was the source of profits and the compensation equalled the estimated profit that the taxpayer would have made. Likewise in *Rolfe v Nagel* (1982) a payment to compensate a diamond broker for a client transferring his business elsewhere was taxable as a payment in lieu of profits. **[6.86]**

Appropriation of unclaimed deposits and advances   Sums are often received from customers as deposits to be used later in part payment towards the price of goods supplied. If they can be forfeited, because of the customer's failure to take delivery of the goods, they are trade receipts in the year of payment (*Elson v Price's Tailors Ltd* (1962)). If at the time of receipt, a deposit is not a trade receipt, however, it does not later become one by appropriation, unless its nature has been changed by statute. Thus in *Morley v Tattersall* (1938), deposits taken by auctioneers remained clients' money and were not trading receipts even though unclaimed and appropriated by the auctioneers. Contrast *Jays the Jewellers Ltd v IRC* (1947) where pawnbrokers' pledges, although originally customers' money, became trading receipts when rendered irrecoverable by statute. **[6.87]**

Sale of information ('know-how')   TA 1988 ss 530–1 provide that where a trader disposes of know-how but continues to trade, any receipt is a trading receipt (TA 1988 s 531(1)), but that, where he disposes of know-how as one of the assets of his business which he is selling as an entity, it is treated as a sale of goodwill. In the latter case liability will be to CGT, unless the trader elects to treat the sum as a trading receipt (TA 1988 s 531(2), (3)). Any sum received as consideration for a restriction on the vendor's freedom of activity (following a sale of know-how) is .reated as a payment for know-how (TA 1988 s 531(8)). **[6.88]**

Release of debts   A debt owed by the trader which has been deducted as a trade expense and which is later released, becomes a trade receipt in the year of its release (TA 1988 s 94). **[6.89]**

EXAMPLE 6.6

Bill, a greengrocer, obtains lettuces from his brother Ben who runs a market garden. In 1990-91 he incurs debts of £3,000 to Ben which on the earnings basis is a trading expense. In 1991–92 Ben agrees to forgo the debt because of the critical state of Bill's business, so that the £3,000 will be a trading receipt in the 1991–92 accounts.

3 Valuation of trading stock

a) *Why value stock (work-in-progress)?*

When the taxpayer calculates his profits on the earnings basis, he must value his unsold stock at the end of the accounting period, otherwise he could spend all his receipts on the purchase of new stock, thereby increasing his deductible expenses and reducing his taxable profits to nil. The same principle applies to unbilled work-in-progress.

EXAMPLE 6.7

In year 1 Zac, a trader, buys 10,000 units of stock at £1 each. During the year he sells 5,000 units at £2 each.

	£
Receipts (sales)	10,000
Less Expenses (purchases)	10,000
Profit	£ Nil

The trader appears to have made no profit whereas, in fact, his profit is £5,000. Therefore, at the end of the accounting year, his unsold (closing) stock must be treated as a receipt of the trade (ie it is treated as if he had sold it). Hence, the account becomes:

	£
Sales	10,000
Plus Value of closing stock	5,000
	15,000
Less Purchases	10,000
Profit	£5,000

At the start of the next accounting period the stock-in-hand (opening stock) or work-in-progress, must be entered into the accounts for that year at the same figure (ie £5,000 from *Example 6.7*) as an expense in order to avoid the stock being taxed twice. **[6.90]**

EXAMPLE 6.8

Continuing *Example 6.7*, in year 2, Zac has opening stock of 5,000 units valued at £1 each. His purchases during the year are 15,000 units of stock at £1 each and he sells 10,000 units at £2 each.

	£
Sales	20,000
Plus Closing stock	10,000
	30,000
Less Purchase	15,000
Profit	£15,000

Failure to value opening stock as an expense produces too much profit (£15,000): his true profit is only £10,000:

	£	£
Sales		20,000
Plus Closing stock		10,000
		30,000
Less Opening stock	5,000	
Purchases	15,000	20,000
Profit		£10,000

b) *Method of valuation*

Each item of unsold stock must be valued at the lower of its cost price and market value. This follows from *IRC v Cock Russell & Co Ltd* (1949) which, in effect, allows losses but not profits to be anticipated: ie the trader can apply 'cost' to items that have increased in value and 'market value' to items that have fallen in value. 'Cost' is the original acquisition price; 'market value' means the best price obtainable in the market in which the trader sells—for instance, a retailer in the retail and a wholesaler in the wholesale market (*BSC Footwear v Ridgway* (1972)).

'Cost' is more difficult to calculate where the price of stock has altered during the accounting period so that it is necessary to identify which stock is left. The only method acceptable to the Revenue is for the trader to treat the stock sold as the stock first bought ('first in first out' ie 'FIFO'). This rule is applied despite evidence that goods were sold on the basis of last in first out ('LIFO').

Unlike stock, work-in-progress cannot be valued as individual items. Instead, it is usually valued by adding to 'direct costs' (such as labour) a proportion of indirect overhead expenses (the 'on-cost' method). However, the taxpayer is allowed to value work-in-progress at direct cost only (see *Duple Motor Bodies v Ostime* (1961)). Because of the difficulty of valuing work-in-progress, professional persons often prefer to draw up their accounts on the bills delivered basis.   [6.91]

c) *Valuation on a discontinuance*

On discontinuance of a trade (which includes a deemed discontinuance under TA 1988 ss 113 and 337) the rule in *IRC v Cock Russell* does not apply and trading stock unsold must be entered into the final accounts at market value (TA 1988 s 100 and see *Moore v R J Mackenzie & Sons Ltd* (1972)). A similar rule applies to work-in-progress. This provision is designed to prevent tax avoidance by the taxpayer discontinuing his business, entering his unsold stock at cost in the final accounts and then selling it privately at a tax-free profit.

Section 100 does not apply:

(1) where the stock is sold to another UK trader for valuable consideration so that it will appear in his accounts for tax purposes anyway; and

(2) where the trade is discontinued because of the death of the single individual who carried it on. **[6.92]**

4 Gifts and dispositions for less than market value

A trader has no duty to make the maximum profit and normally tax is assessed according to the actual sum received on a disposal of his stock. There are, however, certain exceptions to this rule. **[6.93]**

Transfer pricing (TA 1988 s 770) TA 1988 s 770 is aimed at transfer-pricing arrangements entered into by multi-national corporations. It provides that on a sale between 'associated' bodies, the Revenue can substitute market value for the sale price if the sale is at an undervalue (TA 1988 s 770(1)). This provision aims to prevent the vendor company realising a tax deductible loss and the buyer company a profit which might be free from tax or charged at a lower rate than that applicable to the vendor. It, therefore, does not apply if the buyer is a resident UK trader.

For similar reasons, market value can be substituted where a sale is at an over-value, unless the seller is a UK resident trader (TA 1988 s 770(2)).

Bodies are associated for this purpose if one controls the other or both are controlled by a third party (for the definition of 'control' see TA 1988 s 840).

In cases where the exception applies (ie where the seller is a UK resident trader and the sale is at an over-value, or the buyer is a UK resident trader and the sale is an undervalue), the transaction may fall within the rule in *Sharkey v Wernher* (1956).

It should be noted that, in addition to sales, the section also applies to 'lettings and hirings of property; grants and transfers of rights, interests or licences and the giving of business facilities' (TA 1988 s 773(4)). **[6.94]**

Rule in Sharkey v Wernher (1956) If an item of trading stock is disposed of otherwise than in the ordinary course of the taxpayer's trade, it must be brought into account as a trading receipt at its market value at the date of the disposal. In *Sharkey v Wernher* (1956) the taxpayer carried on the trade of a stud farm. She also raced horses for pleasure and she transferred five horses from the stud farm to the racing stable. The House of Lords held that the market value as opposed to the cost price of the horses at the date when they left the stud farm must be entered in the accounts of the trade as a receipt.

EXAMPLE 6.9

(1) Rex is a diamond merchant and on the occasion of his daughter's wedding he gives her his choicest diamond which cost him £80,000 and has a market value of £110,000. As the disposal is not a trading transaction, the market value (£110,000) is a trading receipt. The result is that Rex is treated as making a taxable profit of £30,000 on the stone. (There is no distinction between the trader using the goods himself and giving them away to a friend or relative: see *Petrotim Securities Ltd v Ayres* (1964).)

(2) Company A sells securities for which it had paid £400,000 to an associated UK trading company (company B) for £200,000. The securities then had a market value of £800,000. The following points should be noted:

 (a) TA 1988 s 770 is inapplicable since the purchaser company is a UK resident trading company.

(b) The sale will be caught by the rule in *Sharkey v Wernher* which applies to both gifts of trading stock and to sales at undervalue (see *Petrotim v Ayres* (1964)).

(c) The recipient of trading stock caught by the rule in *Sharkey v Wernher* is treated as receiving the goods for their market value. Hence, company B is treated as having paid £800,000 for the securities (see *Ridge Securities Ltd v IRC* (1964)).

(d) In extreme cases both the purchase and the resale may be expunged from the accounts of the trader if neither constitutes a genuine trading transaction (see the Y transaction in *Petrotim v Ayres* (1964)).

The market value rule is subject to two major qualifications. First, it is only appropriate when the disposal of stock is not a genuine trading transaction. So long as the disposal can be justified on commercial grounds the general principle remains that a trader is free to charge what he likes for his goods.

EXAMPLE 6.10

Cutthroat runs a hi-fi business. In an attempt to encourage custom he gives away a cassette player (market value £40) to any customer who purchases goods costing more than £250. The gift is a commercial disposition and outside the scope of *Sharkey v Wernher*. Accordingly, Cutthroat is not required to enter the market value of the player as a trading receipt.

Secondly, the rule does not apply to professional persons (Case II taxpayers). In *Mason v Innes* (1967), Hammond Innes, the novelist, began writing The Doomed Oasis in 1958 and incurred deductible travelling expenses in obtaining background material. When the manuscript was completed in 1960 he assigned it to his father in consideration of natural love and affection when it had a market value of about £15,000. Innes was taxed under Case II and rendered accounts on the cash basis. When the Revenue sought to tax the market value of the copyright as a receipt of his profession the Court of Appeal held that the market value rule was limited to traders and to dispositions of trading stock. The fact that Innes was assessed on the cash basis was a further, but not the decisive reason, for excluding the rule. In rejecting the Revenue's argument, Lord Denning MR said:

'Suppose an artist paints a picture of his mother and gives it to her. He does not receive a penny for it. Is he to pay tax on the value of it? It is unthinkable. Suppose he paints a picture which he does not like when he has finished it and destroys it. Is he liable to pay tax on the value of it? Clearly not. These instances ... show that ... *Sharkey v Wernher* does not apply to professional men.'   **[6.95–6.110]**

EXAMPLE 6.11

Lex is a partner in the solicitors' firm of Lex, Lax & Lazy and he purchases a house in Chelsea. All the conveyancing work is done by his firm free of charge. The rule in *Sharkey v Wernher* does not apply.

VI DEDUCTIBLE EXPENSES

1 **Basic principles**

An expense will be deductible in arriving at the taxpayers profits under Cases I and II only if:

(a) It is an income and not a capital expense.

(b) fIt is incurred wholly and exclusively for the purpose of the trade, profession or vocation.

(c) Its deduction is not prohibited by statute (see generally TA 1988 s 74).

Deductible expenses are allowed under Schedule D only by implication from the charging section which imposes tax on 'profits' and from TA 1988 s 74 which contains a list of prohibited deductions. Generally, the rules for deductible expenditure under Schedule D are more generous than under Schedule E (see TA 1988 s 198 and Chapter 5).

Notice that a distinction is drawn between expenses incurred in earning the profits (which may be deductible) and expenses incurred after the profits have been earned, which are not deductible. For example, the payment of income tax is an application of profit which has been earned and is, therefore, not deductible (*Ashton Gas Co v A-G* (1906)). Other taxes, however, such as rates and stamp duty, may be paid in the course of earning the profits and so may be deductible.

The professional costs involved in drawing up the trader's accounts and fees paid for tax advice are, in practice, deductible, but expenses involved in contesting a tax assessment are not. In *Smith's Potato Estates Ltd v Bolland* (1948), Viscount Simonds stated that:

> '... His the trader's profit is no more affected by the exigibility to tax than a man's temperature altered by the purchase of a thermometer, even though he starts by haggling about the price of it.'   **[6.111]**

2 **The expense must be income not capital**

Similar tests are applied in classifying expenditure as income or capital as in deciding whether a receipt is income or capital (see **[6.83]**). Hence, a distinction is drawn between the fixed and the circulating capital of the business. A payment is therefore capital if it is made to bring into existence an asset for the enduring advantage of the trade (see *British Insulated and Helsby Cables v Atherton* (1926)). The asset may be intangible as in *Walker v Joint Credit Card Co Ltd* (1982) where a payment by a credit card company to preserve its goodwill was held to be a capital payment.

A once and for all payment, even though it brings no enduring asset into existence, is more likely to be of a capital nature than a recurring expense. In *Watney Combe Reid & Co Ltd v Pike* (1982), ex gratia payments made by Watneys (the brewers) to tenants of tied houses to compensate them for the termination of their tenancies were held to be capital, because their purpose was to render capital assets (the premises) more valuable.

Payments to employees are generally deductible in computing the profits of the employer, so long as they are paid in the interests of the business. In *Mitchell v B W Noble Ltd* (1927), a company deducted the sum of £19,500 paid to a director to induce him to resign. It was held to be in the interests of the company to get rid of him and to avoid undesirable publicity by encouraging him to 'go quietly'. Problems may arise when the payments in question are linked to the cessation of the business; in particular, such

"I hardly think it's worth claiming for your work clothes, Mabel."

payments may not satisfy the 'wholly and exclusively' test (discussed below). In *O'Keeffe v Southport Printers Ltd* (1984), however, payments made to employees in lieu of notice were deductible by the employer since they were incurred as part of the orderly conduct of the business prior to its termination.

In *Heather v PE Consulting Group* (1978) payments made by a company to a trust created in order to acquire shares in that company for the benefit of employees and to prevent outside interference in the affairs of the company were deductible expenses because, inter alia, they encouraged the recruitment of well-qualified staff (see also *Jeffs v Ringtons Ltd* (1985)). Not all payments to employee trusts will be deductible, however, and it was partly to deal with this uncertainty that FA 1989 introduced special provisions for ESOPs (employee share ownership plans). If such a trust is established all payments by the company to the trustees will be deductible business expenditure. These payments may then be used by the trustees to repay both interest and capital on external borrowings (see further [**34.27**]). Contrast, however, *Associated Portland Cement Manufacturers Ltd v Kerr* (1946), where payments to two retiring directors in return for covenants that they would not compete with the company for the rest of their lives were held not to be deductible. It was a capital expense being a payment to enhance the company's goodwill. The tie was for life in the *Kerr* case: had the covenant been for a shorter period the expenditure might have been of an income nature (and therefore deductible). To prevent the making of restrictive covenant payments instead of salary increases (which could result in the deduction of the payment by the employer even though it was not fully taxed in the hands of the employee), TA 1988 s 313 was amended to provide, inter alia, that such payments are now tax deductible by the employer in all cases (see [**5.94**]).

Although capital expenditure is not generally deductible, tax relief may be given in accordance with the rules governing capital allowances (see

Chapter 7). When there was a first year allowance for plant and machinery of 100% it was often a matter of indifference to the taxpayer whether a particular item of expenditure was of an income or of a capital nature. If income, it could be deducted in arriving at the profits of the business; if capital, then, so long as the item in question constituted plant or machinery, the system of capital allowances produced much the same result. As only a writing-down allowance (of 25%) is now available, however, the taxpayer will be concerned to argue, wherever possible, that the expense is of an income nature so that it can immediately be deducted in full. Hence, the awkward borderline between receipts and expenses of an income and capital nature has assumed a new importance. **[6.112]**

3 Expense must have been incurred 'wholly and exclusively' for business purposes (TA 1988 s 74(a))

The courts have generally interpreted the requirement strictly, so that the sole reason for the expenditure must be a business purpose. In *Bentleys, Stokes & Lowless v Beeson* (1952), Romer LJ explained the requirements that have to be satisfied for an expense to be deductible as follows:

> '... it is quite clear that the purpose must be the sole purpose. The paragraph says so in clear terms. If the activity be undertaken with the object both of promoting business and also with some other purpose, for example, with the object of indulging an independent wish of entertaining a friend or stranger or of supporting a charitable or benevolent object, then the paragraph is not satisfied though in the mind of the actor the business motive may predominate. For the statute so prescribes. Per contra, if, in truth, the sole object is business promotion, the expenditure is not disqualified because the nature of the activity necessarily involves some other result, or the attainment or furtherance of some other objective, since the latter result or objective is necessarily inherent in the act.'

Therefore dual purpose expenditure is not deductible and there are numerous cases where this rule has been strictly applied. In *Caillebotte v Quinn* (1975) a self-employed carpenter worked on sites 40 miles from home. He ate lunch at a nearby café which cost him 40p per day instead of the usual 10p which it cost him at home. His claim to deduct the extra 30p per day as an expense was disallowed on the grounds that he ate to live as well as to work so that the expenditure was incurred for dual purposes. Similarly, in *Prince v Mapp* (1970) a guitarist in a pop group could not deduct the cost of an operation on his little finger because he played the guitar partly for business, but partly for pleasure. In *Mallalieu v Drummond* (1983) the House of Lords held that expenditure on clothing to be worn in court by a female barrister was not deductible. Although she only wore the clothes for business purposes and that was her sole conscious purpose when she purchased the garments, Lord Brightman concluded that 'she needed the clothes to travel to work and clothes to wear at work ... it is inescapable that one object though not a conscious motive, was the provision of the clothing that she needed as a human being'. (In practice the cost of protective clothing is deductible and the Revenue have concluded 'clothing and tool allowances' with a number of trade unions.)

In general, the same test for deductible expenditure is applied whether the business is run as a sole trade or partnership. In a recent appeal, *MacKinlay v Arthur Young McClelland Moores & Co* (1990), the Court of Appeal had allowed a partnership to deduct removal costs paid to encourage two partners to move house: in one case from London to Southampton, in the other from Newcastle to Bristol. In both cases the move was desirable from the point of view of the firm's business and neither partner would have agreed to move had his relocation expenses not been borne by the firm. This decision was not easy to reconcile with earlier authorities and its reversal by the House of Lords was scarcely surprising. Their Lordships restated the principles underlying the rules governing deductible expenditure and stressed that the same rules applied to individuals and to unincorporated partnerships (see further Chapter 29).

The 'dual purpose' cases show that it is not possible to split a purpose: ie if the taxpayer incurs the expenditure for two purposes, one business and the other personal, none of the expenditure is deductible. It may, however, be possible to split a payment into a portion which is incurred for business purposes and a portion which is not. This approach was apparent in *Copeman v Flood* (1941) where the son and daughter of the managing director of a small private company were employed as directors at salaries of £2,600 each pa. The son was aged 24 and had some business experience, but the daughter was only 17 and incompetent. Although both performed duties for the company, the Revenue successfully claimed that the entire salary was not an expense incurred by the company 'wholly and exclusively' for business purposes. Lawrence J remitted the case to the commissioners for them to decide, as a question of fact, to what extent the payments were deductible expenses of the trade. He accepted that the expenditure could be apportioned into allowable and non-allowable parts.

In practice, payments are regularly split in this fashion when a car is used both for business and private use and when a business is run from the taxpayer's home and he claims to deduct a proportion of the overheads of the house.   [6.113]

4   Deduction of the expense must not be prohibited by statute

The deduction of expenses under Cases I and II is permitted by implication because TA 1988 s 74 contains a list of expenses which are stated not to be deductible. For instance, under s 74(l) no deduction is allowed for any sum 'recoverable under an insurance or contract of indemnity' whilst expenditure incurred for private as opposed to business purposes is made non-deductible by s 74(b). The deduction of business gifts and entertainment expenses is severely curtailed by TA 1988 s 577 which is drafted widely enough to catch hospitality of any kind (TA 1988 s 577(5)). A number of exceptions are permitted; the entertainment of *bona fide* members of staff is permitted (TA 1988 s 577(5); and it does not even have to be reasonable!); small gifts carrying conspicuous advertisements are permissible (TA 1988 s 577(8)), whilst there is an exception for the provision of that which it is in the ordinary course of the taxpayer's trade to provide (TA 1988 s 577(10) and see *Fleming v Associated Newspapers Ltd* (1972) where the House of Lords struggled to make sense of this all but incomprehensible provision).   [6.114]

5   Illustrations of deductible expenditure

Expenditure in heating and lighting business premises, rates on those premises and the wages paid to employees are obvious examples of allowable expenditure. Other expenditure may be more problematic, as the examples considered below show. [6.115]

Rent paid for business premises TA 1988 s 74(c) accepts that rent is deductible and it may be apportioned if part of the premises is used for non-business activities. An individual's private house may, of course, be used in part for business purposes and a portion of the overheads may be claimed as allowable expenditure. So long as no part of the house is used exclusively for business purposes the full CGT main residence exemption will still be available (see Chapter 16).

When the taxpayer pays a premium in return for the grant of a lease, a portion of the premium (corresponding to the portion that is taxed under Schedule A; see Chapter 8) may be deducted as an expense (TA 1988 s 87).

Specific provisions have been enacted to deal with the problems caused by sale and leaseback, and surrender and leaseback arrangements. The attraction of such schemes stemmed from booming land values which encouraged the owner of the land (or of an interest therein) to sell (or surrender) it, thereby realising a capital sum, and immediately to take a lease-back of the same property. TA 1988 s 779 prohibits the deduction of rent in excess of a commercial level and in certain circumstances TA 1988 s 780 imposes a charge to income tax on a capital sum received in return for surrendering a lease which has less than 50 years to run, when a lease-back for a term not exceeding 15 years is taken. [6.116]

EXAMPLE 6.12

Jake runs a pub on leasehold premises in Covent Garden. The lease has 30 years to run and property values have recently boomed in that area. The landlord offers Jake £50,000 to surrender the existing lease and agrees to grant him a new seven year lease at a dramatically increased rent:
(i)   The new rent will be deductible save for any excess above a commercial rent.
(ii) A portion of the capital sum received by Jake will be subject to income tax and the balance may be subject to CGT (Jake has disposed of a chargeable asset).

Repairs and improvements Sums expended on the repair of business assets are deductible (TA 1988 s 74(d)). The cost of improvement is not, however, allow-able being seen as capital expenditure (TA 1988 s 74(g)). The borderline between the two is a difficult factual question which depends upon the nature of the asset and the importance of the work in relation to it (see *Lurcott v Wakely and Wheeler* (1911) on the duty to repair and *O'Grady v Markham Main Colliery Ltd* (1932)).

The cost incurred on initial repairs carried out to a business asset may cause difficulties. In *Law Shipping Co Ltd v IRC* (1924), a vessel purchased for £97,000 was in such a state of disrepair that a further £51,000 had to be spent before it could obtain its Lloyd's Certificate. The Court of Session disallowed most of the subsequent expenditure; as Lord Cullen stated:

'It is in substance the equivalent of an addition to the price. If the ship had not been in need of the repairs in question when bought, the appellants would have had to pay a correspondingly larger price.'

By way of contrast, in *Odeon Associated Theatres Ltd v Jones* (1972) subsequent repair work on a cinema which had been purchased in a run-down condition after the war, was allowed. There are three points of distinction from the *Law Shipping* case: first, the cinema was a profit-earning asset when purchased despite its disrepair; secondly, the purchase price was not reduced because of that disrepair; and thirdly, the Court of Appeal accepted that the expenses were deductible in accordance with the principles of proper commercial accounting. (For the precise significance of the evidence of accountants see *Heather v PE Consulting Group* (1978).)   [**6.117**]

Pre-trading expenditure   Under TA 1988 s 401 income expenditure incurred in the five years before a trade, profession or vocation commences is treated as a loss (which therefore qualifies for tax relief) sustained by the business in its first year of assessment. The problem of identifying when a business commences trading is considered at [**6.146**].   [**6.118**]

Damages, losses, and bad debts   Damages and losses are deductible if 'connected with and arising out of the trade' (TA 1988 s 74(e)). Bad debts are deducted when shown to be bad (TA 1988 s 74(j)); if later paid they are treated as a trading receipt for that later year. In *Strong & Co of Romsey Ltd v Woodifield* (1906) damages paid to an hotel guest injured by the fall of a chimney from the building were not deductible. Lord Loreburn, somewhat unsympathetically, observed that 'the loss sustained by the appellants . . . fell upon them [sic] in their character not of traders but of householders' whilst Lord Davey rejected the claim because 'the expense must be incurred for the purpose of earning the profits'. Had the guest suffered food poisoning from the hotel restaurant any compensation would have been deductible! In practice, the *Strong v Woodifield* case will be avoided by the trader carrying insurance to cover compensation claims; further, the premiums that he pays for such insurance will be deductible.

Theft by employees causes particular difficulties. Petty theft by subordinates, so that money never finds its way into the till, will result in reduced profits for tax purposes, but defalcations by directors will not be similarly allowable (*Curtis v Oldfield* (1933); *Bamford v ATA Advertising* (1972)).   [**6.119**]

Work training   The costs of training an employee in skills relating to present or future duties of his job are deductible. In addition, the costs of retraining an employee or former employee for a new job with another employer (or for self-employment) are in certain circumstances deductible (see further [**5.43**]: TA 1988 ss 588-9). Training costs incurred by a self-employed person are deductible in computing his profits, provided the costs are incurred wholly and exclusively for the purposes of his trade or profession (TA 1988 s 74).   [**6.120**]

Travelling expenses   The cases establish two general propositions. First, that the cost of travelling to the place of business is not deductible; and secondly, that the cost of travelling in the course of the business is deductible. In *Horton v Young* (1971), for instance, a labour-only sub-contractor who operated from his home was entitled to deduct expenses incurred in collecting his team of bricklayers and travelling to the building site.   [**6.121**]

EXAMPLE 6.13

Wig is a barrister who travels into chambers each day from his home in Isleworth. He also travels from chambers to courts in the London area.

(1)   The cost of travelling from Isleworth to chambers is not deductible because chambers is his base. It does not matter that he does a substantial amount

of work at home and that he claims a deduction for a portion of the expenses of the house (see *Newsom v Robertson* (1953)).

(2) Expenses in travelling from chambers to court are deductible (contrast *Horton v Young* (1971): travelling between two centres of work).

(3) If he were regularly to go from Isleworth to a case at Bow Street Magistrates' Court and then on to chambers could he deduct all the travelling expenses? The difficult case of *Sargent v Barnes* (1978) in which a dental surgeon was unable to deduct travelling expenses to collect false teeth from a laboratory on his way to work, suggests that the answer is no, although it should be noted that the laboratory was not a place of work whereas the court is. A claim for travelling from the court to chambers might, therefore, succeed.

National insurance contributions Contributions paid by an employer on behalf of his employees are a deductible business expense. The employer cannot, however, deduct his own contributions, although TA 1988 s 617(5) affords a measure of relief by enabling one-half of the Class 4 contributions to be deducted in arriving at the total income of the self-employed taxpayer (see further [**4.66**]). [**6.122**]-[**6.140**]

VII   THE BASIS OF ASSESSMENT

1   The normal basis

A taxpayer can commence or cease his business at any time, but he should normally draw up his accounts over a 12 month period known as the 'accounting year' which need not coincide with the tax year (6 April to 5 April). This gives rise to two difficulties:

(1) The actual profits made in each year of assessment can only be arrived at by splitting two accounting years and taking the proportions which fall into the assessment year.

(2) The calculation of the taxpayer's liability has to await the completion and agreement of the accounts with the inspector of taxes.

Because of these problems and as an incentive to business, tax is assessed under Schedule D Cases I and II on the 'preceding year basis': ie in any year of assessment tax is charged on the profits of the 12 month accounting period which ended in the previous year of assessment (TA 1988 s 60(1)). This is the *normal basis*.

EXAMPLE 6.14

Ernest's accounting year runs from 6 October to 5 October following. He has made the following profits in recent years:

Accounting year ending	Profits
5 October 1988	£ 5,000
5 October 1989	£ 8,000
5 October 1990	£10,000

In the year of assessment 1991-92 Ernest will be assessed on the profits of the 12 month accounting period ending in the preceding year of assessment (ie ending between 6 April 1990 and 5 April 1991). This will be the accounting year to 5 October 1990 which shows £10,000 profit. Assessments on Ernest for the earlier years would be:

Year of assessment	Assessment
1990-91	£8,000
1989-90	£5,000

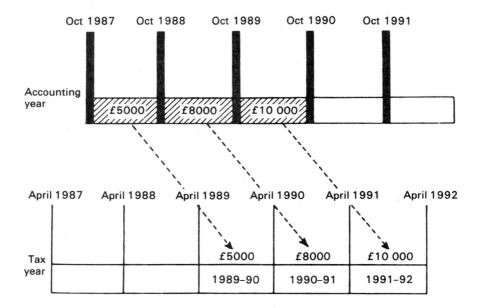

The taxpayer's duty to produce annual accounts is imposed indirectly. No time limit is provided in the legislation for making up accounts. However, if the taxpayer has not made up accounts in the three years preceding the relevant year of assessment, the Revenue take his accounting period to be the previous tax year (ie 6 April to 5 April) and make an estimated assessment (TA 1988 s 60(4)). The only way for the taxpayer to appeal successfully against such an assessment will be by rendering accurate accounts. Further, the taxpayer should render accounts over a 12 month period; if he produces accounts which relate to a period other than 12 months, the Revenue can assess him to tax on the profits of any 12 month period ending in the previous year of assessment (TA 1988 s 60(4)). This provision does not apply to the first or second years of a business (see below).

Tax is assessed directly on the taxpayer under Schedule D Cases I and II and, as a general rule, is payable in two equal instalments on 1 January in the year of assessment and on 1 July following (TA 1988 s 5(2)). The preceding year basis makes possible an assessment raised on the basis of accounts agreed before 1 December in that tax year. If, however, the assessment is not made until after 1 December, but before 1 June following, the first instalment of tax is due 30 days after the assessment and the second instalment on 1 July following; if the assessment is not made until after 1 June in the following year of assessment, all the tax is payable 30 days after the assessment (for details of appeals and related matters see Chapter 2).

To maximise the delay in paying tax, a taxpayer should choose his accounting period carefully. If that period coincides with the tax year, it will form the basis of charge for the tax year immediately following so that there will be a delay of only 9 and 15 months between the end of the accounting period and the payment of tax. If he chooses an accounting period which runs from 7 April to 6 April following, however, the maximum possible delay of 21 and 27 months will apply. Delay in paying tax is especially attractive when the profits of the business are rising. Not only will the taxpayer have the use of the tax for a considerable period of time but, additionally, he will be able to avoid immediate taxation on the current (higher) profits. If profits are constant the advantage is much reduced whilst, if they are falling, a large tax bill will have to be met out of current (smaller) profits.

Corporations are subject to current year assessment (see [**28.21**]) and the Revenue have been considering the introduction of an alternative basis of assessment for the unincorporated business for a number of years. The imminent publication of a Consultative Document (*A Simpler System for Taxing the Self-Employed*) was announced in the 1991 Budget. In the event, delays have occurred and it is now expected that the document will not be published before the late autumn of 1991. [**6.141**]

2 Exceptions to the normal basis

It is impossible to apply the normal basis in the opening years of the business and where the taxpayer changes his accounting date. In the closing years of the business, although it would be possible to use the normal basis, an exceptional basis is applied to prevent the closure being manipulated to avoid tax. [**6.142**]

a) *The opening years* (TA 1988 ss 61, 62)

For the year of assessment in which the business commences, the taxpayer is charged on his actual profits from the date of commencement to the end of the tax year (TA 1988 s 61(1)). If his accounting period straddles the end of the tax year, the profits are apportioned on a time (straight-line) basis.

In the second year of assessment the taxpayer is taxed on the profits of his first 12 months trading.

In the third and subsequent years of assessment, the normal basis of assessment under TA 1988 s 60 applies so he is taxed on the profits of the accounting period ending in the previous year of assessment.

EXAMPLE 6.15

Popeye begins trading on 6 October 1988 and makes the following profits:

Accounting period	Profit
6 October 1988–5 October 1989	£ 3,000
6 October 1989–5 October 1990	£ 9,000
6 October 1990–5 October 1991	£12,000

His first year of assessment is 1988–89 in which he is taxed on his actual profits from 6 October 1988 to 5 April 1989

ie $\frac{6}{12} \times £3,000 = £1,500$

In his second year (1989–90) Popeye is taxed on his first 12 months of trading: ie on profits from 6 October 1988 to 5 October 1989 = £3,000.

In his third year (1990–91) Popeye is taxed on the preceding year basis on the profits from 6 October 1988–5 October 1989 = £3,000 (again).

In 1991–92 he is taxed on £9,000.

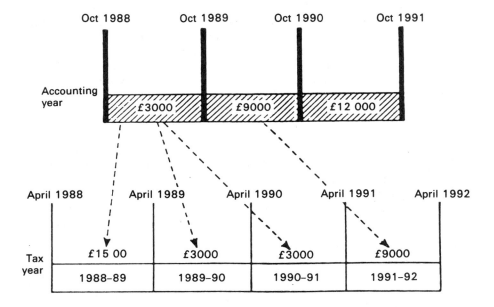

If the taxpayer's first accounting period is longer or shorter than 12 months (which may well be the case) this will not affect the assessment of his first and second years. However, in the third year, the normal basis cannot be applied, because there is not a 12 month accounting period ending in the previous year of assessment. The Revenue can, therefore, take any period of 12 months ending in the previous year of assessment. In practice, they will take the 12 months ending on the taxpayer's chosen accounting date.

EXAMPLE 6.16

Pluto begins trading on 6 August 1989 and makes up his first accounts to 5 October 1990 (14 months). The accounts show a profit of £14,000.

In 1989-90 (first year) Pluto will be assessed on his actual profits for the 8 month period ending 5 April 1990 ie £8,000. In 1990-91 (second year), Pluto will be assessed on his profit of the first 12 months of trading to 5 August 1990 ie £12,000.

In 1991-92 (third year), as Pluto intends to make up accounts to 5 October each year, the assessment will be on the 12 month period ending 5 October 1990, ie £12,000.

The effect of TA 1988 s 61 (the opening year rule) is to use the profits of the first 12 months of trading as the basis for the tax assessment in each of the first three years of assessment. This is not, however, double (or even triple) taxation because those profits are *deemed* to be the profits of the years of assessment. The taxpayer will be content with this duplication where the profits are low in relation to current profits, but not where the first year profits are higher than current profits. TA 1988 s 62 therefore allows him to elect to have the assessments of the second and third years made on the basis of *actual* profits earned in those years. The election must cover both years and be made within seven years of the end of the second year of assessment. It can be withdrawn within that period to cover the case where the taxpayer makes low profits in year two, elects for the actual basis, but then discovers that because of high profits in the third year, the election has made him worse off. **[6.143]**

EXAMPLE 6.17

Olive begins trading on 6 October 1989 and makes up accounts to 5 October each year. Her profits are (see diagram on following page)

Accounting period	Profits
6 October 1989–5 October 1990	£12,000
6 October 1990–5 October 1991	£ 4,000
6 October 1991–5 October 1992	£ 2,000

Assessment under TA 1988 s 61 produces profits of £30,000:

Tax year	Basic period	Profits £
Year 1 1989–90	Actual: 6 October 1989–5 April 1990	
	$\frac{6}{12} \times £12,000 =$	6,000
Year 2 1990–91	12 months to 5 October 1990	12,000
Year 2 1991–92	Preceding year to 5 October 1990	12,000
		£30,000

An election under TA 1988 s 62 products profits of £17,000:

Tax year	Basis period	£	Profits £
Year 1 1989–90	Actual: (no charge)		6,000
Year 2 1990–91	Actual: 6 April 1990–5 April 1991		
	ie $\frac{6}{12} \times £12,000 =$	6,000	
	Plus $\frac{6}{12} \times £4,000 =$	2,000	
			8,000
Year 3 1991–92	Actual: 6 April 1991–5 April 1992		
	ie $\frac{6}{12} \times £4,000 =$	2,000	
	Plus $\frac{6}{12} \times £2,000 =$	1,000	
			3,000
			£17,000

Olive should make a s 62 election. Whenever profits are falling the election should be made. When the trend is upwards it should be ignored.

b) *Change of accounting date*

If the taxpayer decides to change his accounting date, there will be at least one year which does not fit the normal assessment basis since he must make up a set of accounts for one period of less or more than 12 months in order to effect that change.

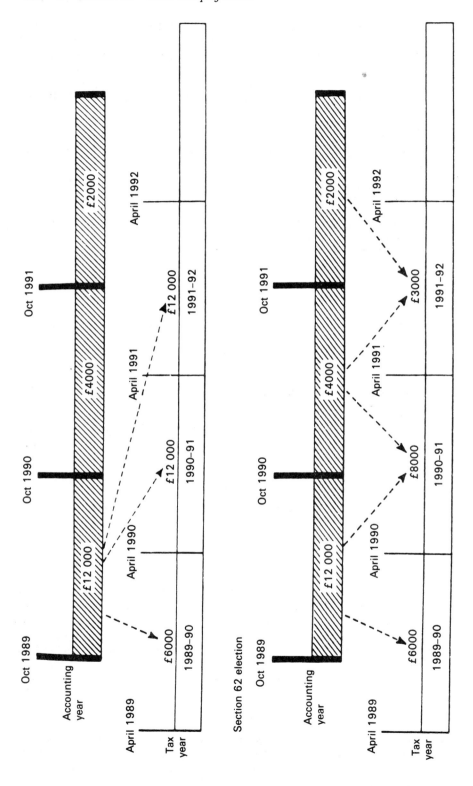

In this case, the Revenue may take 'any period of 12 months ending in the preceding year of assessment' as the basis period *and* if they think that the year before that should be dealt with on the same basis they have the power to do so (TA 1988 s 60(4), (5)). As a matter of practice, the Revenue normally take as a basis the period of 12 months ending on the date in the preceding year which the taxpayer has chosen as his new year-end date.

EXAMPLE 6.18

Unlucky changes his accounting date from 5 October to 31 December. His profits are:

Accounting period	Profits £
Year ended 5 October 1987	20,000
Year ended 5 October 1988	6,000
14 months ended 31 December 1989	21,000
Year ended 31 December 1990	10,000

Assessments		Profits £
1988–89	(Normal Basis) Year ended 5 October 1987	20,000
*1989–90	(Normal Basis) Year ended 5 October 1988	6,000
1990–91	(No Normal Basis) Revenue will take 12 months to 31 December 1989 ie $\frac{12}{14} \times £21,000 =$	18,000
1991–92	(Normal Basis) Year ended 31 December 1990	10,000

The Revenue can revise the last normal assessment before the change (1989–90) to an assessment based on the new accounting date which results in tax on additional profits of £2,000:

		£
1989–90	Twelve months to 31 December 1988 ie $\frac{10}{12} \times £6,000$	5,000
	Plus $\frac{2}{14} \times £21,000$	3,000
		£8,000

The taxpayer may appeal against the revised assessment under TA 1988 s 60(6). The principles on which the commissioners should act in considering such appeals were considered in *IRC v Helical Bar Ltd* (1972). Any appeal will not succeed merely because the Revenue are assessing profits of the same period twice since that is the effect of the legislation. In practice, the Revenue operate an 'averaging procedure' (see IR 26) which affects the revision year only (ie 1989–90 in *Example 6.18*) and aims to be fair to both parties.   **[6.144]**

c) *Closing year rules* (TA 1988 s 63(1))

In the year of assessment in which the business terminates, the taxpayer is assessed on his actual profits from the beginning of that tax year (6 April) to the date of discontinuance. This normally involves apportioning the profits of an accounting period on a time basis (TA 1988 s 72). The two years of assessment preceding the final year (penultimate and pre-penultimate years of assessment) are taxed on the normal basis. However, the Revenue can elect under TA 1988 s 63 to assess the taxpayer on his actual profits of those years. The election is needed since under the preceding year basis the actual profits of those years would never be charged, so that taxpayers could ensure that large profits were channelled into that period (on the Revenue's election, see *Baylis v Roberts* (1989)).

EXAMPLE 6.19 *(see diagram following)*

B ceased to trade on 5 July 1991. His profits for years ended 31 December were:

$$
\begin{array}{c}
£\ 9,000 \text{ for } 1987 \\
£15,000 \text{ for } 1988 \\
£12,000 \text{ for } 1989 \\
£18,000 \text{ for } 1990 \\
\text{and } £6,000 \text{ to } 5 \text{ July } 1991
\end{array}
$$

Tax year	Basic period	£	Profits £
1991–92 *Final*	Actual: 6 April 1991–5 July 1992		
	ie $= \dfrac{3}{6} \times £6,000$		3,000
1990–91 *Penultimate*	Preceding year: year ended 31 December 1989		12,000
1989–90 *Pre-penultimate*	Preceding year: year ended 31 December 1988		15,000
1988–89	Preceding year: year ended 31 December 1987		9,000
			£39,000

TA 1988 s 63 Revenue election:

		£	£
1991–92 *Final*	Actual: (as above)		3,000
1990–91 *Penultimate*	Actual: 6 April 1990–5 April 1991		
	ie $= \dfrac{3}{6} \times £6,000$	3,000	
	Plus $= \dfrac{9}{12} \times £18,000$	13,500	16,500
1989–90 *Pre-penultimate*	Actual: 6 April 1989–5 April 1990		
	ie $= \dfrac{3}{12} \times £18,000$	4,500	
	Plus $= \dfrac{6}{12} \times £2,000$	9,000	
			13,500
1988–89	Preceding year (as above)		9,000
			£42,000

The Revenue would exercise their option to amend the assessments of 1989–90 and 1990–91 to an actual basis. Otherwise, the higher profits of the period from 1 January 1990 to 5 April 1991 escape tax completely.

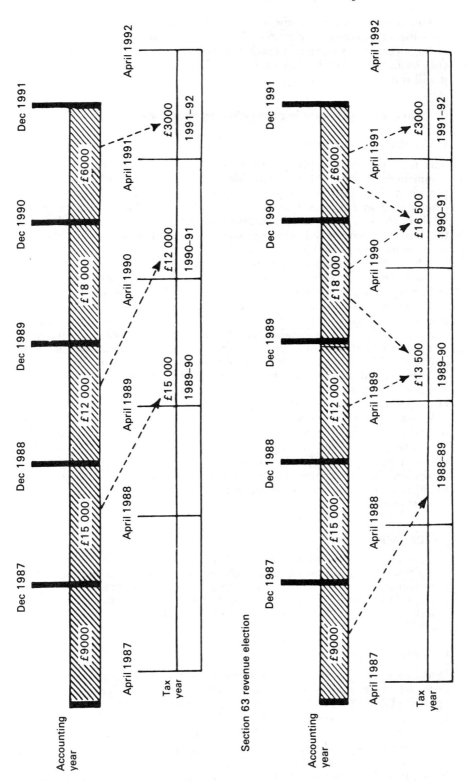

Section 63 revenue election

The Revenue must exercise their election for both years. Therefore (as with the s 62 taxpayer's election), it will only be made if the total profits of both years on an actual basis is higher than the total on the preceding year basis. Generally, if profits are rising the election will be made, if falling it will not.   **[6.145]**

3   **When to apply opening and closing year rules**

a) *Commencement of a business*

The taxpayer must apply the opening year rules from the date that he commences business. *Napier v Griffiths* (1989) illustrates the importance of precise dating. Had the taxpayer succeeded in arguing that his business commenced in May 1980 the sum of £1,296 would have been taxed (in total) in the first three tax years. However, because the court decided that the business commenced one year later the actual sum taxed in the first three years became £30,024!

When a business commences is a question of fact and acts preparatory to carrying on the business do not constitute commencement. For example, in *Birmingham and District Cattle By-Products Co Ltd v IRC* (1919) the construction of a factory, the purchase of machinery, and the making of contracts to purchase raw materials were preparatory acts. Business only commenced once the machinery was installed and the raw materials received. In practice, it is thought that renting premises, engaging staff, opening a bank account, and advertising are all evidence that a business has begun. Expenditure is normally only deductible after that date, although expenses incurred in the five years before the business starts are treated as a loss of the year of commencement (TA 1988 s 401).

When the taxpayer who already runs an existing business takes up new business activities, it is a question of fact whether he is merely extending his existing business or starting a new one (see *Seldon v Croom-Johnson* (1932) where a barrister who took silk was held to be continuing his existing profession). In the former case, the normal preceding year basis continues to apply to all activities. In the latter case, he must apply the opening year rules to the new business.   **[6.146]**

> **EXAMPLE 6.20**
>
> Lenny owns a health food shop which he extends to serve morning coffee (decaffeinated) and brown sugar (only) doughnuts. This is an extension of his existing business and he continues to be assessed on the normal basis.
>
> If Lenny turns his health food shop into a restaurant specialising in French cuisine, however, he must apply the closing year rules to the health food shop and the opening year rules to the restaurant business.

b) *Change of ownership*

When an existing business is transferred (including the incorporation of the business) the change of ownership results in the closing year rules being applied (TA 1988 s 113(1)). There are certain exceptions to this rule. First, where a business is transferred by a sole trader to a partnership in which he is a partner, or there is a change in the composition of an existing partnership (but with at least one continuing partner), all the persons concerned in the business before and after the change can elect for the business to be treated as continuing (TA 1988 s 113(2) and Chapter 29). Secondly, by concession, a change of ownership due to the death of the owner where the business passes to his spouse is not a discontinuance, unless claimed by that surviving spouse (ESC A7).

If the purchaser of the business is already running an existing business, he will have acquired either an entirely new business or assets to be used in the (expanded) old business (see also a) above). If the former, the opening year rules will apply to that enterprise but, at the end of the first three years of account, the businesses can normally be merged unless they are of a totally different nature. A mere purchase of assets does not trigger the opening year rules and the enlarged business continues on the normal basis. The question is one of fact. If a business and not just assets is transferred there will be a transfer of, inter alia, custom, staff and goodwill. (Compare *Reynolds Sons & Co Ltd v Ogston* (1930) and *Thomson and Balfour v Le Page* (1923).) There cannot be a succession to part of a trade; or through the accidental acquisition of another trader's custom; or to a trade which ceased before the new owner took over (typically the purchase of a trader's assets on his bankruptcy).   **[6.147]**

c) *Discontinuance of a business*

It is a question of fact whether the particular change results in a discontinuance. A trade which is in abeyance or quiescent has not necessarily ceased: 'Business is not confined to being busy; in many businesses long intervals of inactivity occur' (see Lord Sumner in *IRC v South Behar Rly Co Ltd* (1925)). One test is whether it still generates expenditure and loss. (Compare *Kirk and Randall Ltd v Dunn* (1924) with *Ingram & Son Ltd v Callaghan* (1969) and see *Watts v Hart* (1984).)

If a business is discontinued within two to five years of its commencement so that the opening and closing year rules overlap, the closing year rules prevail (TA 1988 s 63(1)).   **[6.148]**

4   Relief for fluctuating profits

The profits earned from certain businesses are so irregular that it would be unfair to tax them all in the year of receipt. Instead, they are deemed to have been received over a longer period ('averaged').   **[6.149]**

Farmers and market gardeners   TA 1988 s 96 allows farmers and market gardeners to compare the profits of two consecutive years of assessment and, if the profits of either year are nil or one is less than 70% of the other, the profits of both years are equalised. ('Profit' means profit before deducting loss relief and capital allowances.) The relief is tapered where the profits in one year are between 70% and 75% of the other. The trader must claim the relief within two years of the end of the second year of assessment and he may not claim it for his opening or closing years.   **[6.150]**

EXAMPLE 6.21

A farmer's profits in Year 1 are £600 and in Year 2 £16,000. £600 is less than 70% of £16,000. Therefore profits are equalised and in years 1 and 2 he is taxed on profits of £8,300 (£16,600 ÷ 2).

Authors and artists   Two provisions afford relief to authors who receive lump sums for copyright or royalties. TA 1988 s 534 provides that lump sums received for royalties within two years of the work's first publication, or for the assignment of copyright or in respect of non-returnable advances, may be spread back and taxed over either two or three years depending upon the length of time spent by the author on producing the work. This relief applies in respect of literary, dramatic, musical and artistic works.

By TA 1988 s 535, any sum received for the assignment of a copyright more than ten years after publication can be spread forward and taxed over a maximum of six years depending on the duration of the assignment. Special provisions apply where the author dies or retires within that six year period. Commissions, fees and similar payments received by a painter, sculptor or other artist for a sale of his work can be spread back over two or three years (TA 1988 s 538).   **[6.151]**

Inventors   Similar provisions apply to lump sums received by inventors for the exploitation of their patents. By TA 1988 s 524, a sum received in return for patent rights is spread over the year of receipt and the next five years. By TA 1988 s 527, sums received for the use of a patent for a period of at least six years may be spread back over six years.   **[6.152]**

7 Capital allowances and loss relief

'. . . there is little evidence that these incentives capital allowances have strengthened the economy or improved the quality of investment. Quite the contrary . . . Too much investment has been made because the tax allowances make it look profitable . . . We need investment decisions based on future markets . . . not future tax assessments.' (The Rt Hon Nigel Lawson MP, Chancellor of the Exchequer, Budget Statement 13 March 1984.)   **[7.1]**

I CAPITAL ALLOWANCES—INTRODUCTION

The cost of fixed assets and the depreciation of those assets due to gradual wear and tear are not allowable deductions from profits for income tax purposes although such expenditure is an unavoidable cost of a business and is incurred in earning its profits. A limited and controlled rate of depreciation for *certain* types of fixed assets is, however, given in the form of capital allowances which are deductible in arriving at taxable profits. The allowances may have the effect of replacing a trading profit with an allowable loss for which the taxpayer will be entitled to loss relief (see **[7.91]**). The mere fact that capital expenditure has been incurred does not, however, mean that a capital allowance is available. Allowances are given only for items of expenditure prescribed by statute, the most important allowances being given for plant and machinery and industrial buildings.

The relevant legislation was consolidated in the Capital Allowances Act 1990 which has effect in respect of allowances and charges falling to be made for chargeable periods ending after 5 April 1990. The system generally provides for a writing-down allowance which affords relief for capital depreciation. First year allowances were formerly available and were intended to encourage new capital investment but these allowances were withdrawn in stages over the period from 1984 to 1986 (see the remarks of Nigel Lawson quoted above) and are not considered further.   **[7.2]–[7.20]**

II PLANT AND MACHINERY

1 Definition

The terms 'plant' and 'machinery' are not defined in the legislation and are to be given their ordinary meaning. The plethora of cases in this area indicates, however, that the meaning is not always obvious! Recent cases, although adopting a more robust view of what constitutes plant and machinery, emphasise that the answer in each case must depend on the particular facts.

When considering the meaning of these terms, the usual starting point is the oft-quoted dictum of Lindley LJ in *Yarmouth v France* (1887):

> 'There is no definition of plant in the Act: but in its original sense, it includes whatever apparatus is used by a businessman for carrying on his business, not his stock-in-trade which he buys or makes for sale; but all goods and chattels, fixed or moveable, live or dead, which he keeps for permanent employment in his business.'

Accordingly, the following items are not plant (see the analysis of Hoffmann J in *Wimpy International Ltd v Warland* (1988) whose conclusions were subsequently confirmed by the Court of Appeal). First, anything which is not used for carrying on the business. Secondly, stock-in-trade which is both expressly excluded in the above quotation and, in any event, lacks permanence. Expenditure on assets which are quickly consumed or worn out in the course of a few operations is not of a capital nature and in practice, articles with a working life of less than two years are not treated by the Revenue as plant. In *Hinton v Maden & Ireland Ltd* (1959), for instance, knives and lasts used by a shoe manufacturer, with a useful life of only three years, were considered to be plant but in *McVeigh v Arthur Sanderson & Sons Ltd* (1969) designs used by wallpaper manufacturers lacked 'materiality' and were therefore of a revenue (income) nature and not plant. Thirdly, the item of expenditure must be incurred in the provision of apparatus: ie in providing 'goods and chattels, fixed or movable, live or dead, which (are) kept for permanent employment in his business'. Accordingly, the premises or place upon which the business is conducted is excluded from the definition (the 'premises test').

It remains to decide what precisely is meant by premises in this context and the courts have accepted that 'a building or a structure could be plant if it was more appropriate to describe it as apparatus for carrying on the business or employed in the business than as the premises or place in or upon which the business was conducted'. Accordingly, everything turns on the facts of the individual case and a particular item may be both premises and plant. Thus in *IRC v Barclay Curle & Co Ltd* (1969), the majority of the House of Lords held that a dry dock was correctly described as plant since it could be seen as apparatus for carrying on the business of a ship repairer rather than as merely the premises in which that business was conducted. Similarly, in *Cooke v Beach Station Caravans Ltd* (1974), a swimming pool constructed by a caravan owning and operating company for use in connection with a caravan park was plant. Contrast, however, *Benson v Yard Arm Club Ltd* (1979) where the taxpayer's argument that a ship used as a floating restaurant was plant because it attracted customers was rejected by the courts who held that it was merely the place in which the business was conducted. In *Brown v Burnley Football & Athletic Club Ltd* (1980), the football stadium was held not to be plant but the place where the business was conducted.

The three distinctions considered above and derived from *Yarmouth v France* are subtly different from each other as Hoffmann J explained in the *Wimpy* case:

'If the item is neither stock in trade nor the premises upon which the business is conducted, the only question is whether it is used for carrying on the business. I shall call this the "business use" test. However, under the second distinction, an article which passes the "business use" test is excluded if such use is as stock in trade. And under the third distinction, an item used in carrying on the business is excluded if such use is as the premises or place upon which the business is conducted.'

He further concluded that the distinction that had been drawn in earlier cases between expenditure incurred on the setting in which a business is carried on and on the apparatus used in that business is unhelpful since it was capable of blurring the distinction between the business use test on the one hand and the premises test on the other. Thus in *IRC v Scottish and Newcastle Breweries* (1982), the items in dispute were wall decor, plaques, tapestries and murals (which were detachable), pictures and metal sculptures used to decorate hotels. All of these were held to be chattels and not integral parts of the premises so that the premises test was irrelevant. The Revenue's argument, that they formed part of the setting of the business and so were not plant, was accordingly dismissed by the House of Lords because the chattels satisfied the business use test as they were used to please and attract customers and were therefore for the promotion of the trade. The facts in the *Wimpy* case were similar and again involved the question of whether the premises test should be applied to items which had been added to an original building by way of subsequent improvement. The items consisted mainly of tiling on floors and walls, glass shop fronts, raised and mezzanine floors, staircases and false ceilings. Hoffmann J, in deciding that such expenditure did not qualify for capital allowances, distinguished the *Scottish and Newcastle* case on the basis that the items in that case were plainly not part of the premises. By contrast, the disputed items in *Wimpy* had, save for one exception, all become comprised in the premises. The one exception was for the expenditure on light fittings which did qualify for a capital allowance. There is authority that such fittings are chattel fixtures and not integral parts of the building (see *J Lyons & Co Ltd v A-G* (1944)) so that the premises test is satisfied and the business use test is relevant. In applying this test the light fittings in the *Wimpy* case were not simply installed to provide general illumination but were specific to the particular trade since the volume of light was considered by Wimpy to be important in a fast food chain (contrast *Cole Bros Ltd v Phillips* (1982)).   [**7.21**]

2   **Who can claim the capital allowance?**

The capital allowance is available for taxpayers as follows:
(a) under Schedule D Cases I or II for companies, sole traders and partnerships; extended to furnished holiday lettings under Schedule D Case VI;
(b) funder Schedule E where an employee purchases plant or machinery 'necessarily provided for use in the performance of the duties' (CAA 1990 s 27(2)(a)). The difficulty of satisfying this test is illustrated in *White v Higginbottom* (1983) where a vicar was unable to claim an allowance for a slide projector used in parish work since Vinelott J applying the test in TA 1988 s 198 [**5.111**] concluded that, as another vicar could manage without a projector, the expenditure had not been 'necessarily' incurred for the performance of his duties. FA 1990 s 87 removed the requirement for the expenses to be incurred 'necessarily' but only for

cars provided by employees when the running costs are deductible under the normal Schedule E rules;

(c)   under Schedule A or Schedule D Case VI to a landlord who provides plant and machinery for use in the repair, maintenance or management of the property (TA 1988 s 32).   **[7.22]**

3   When may an allowance be claimed?

In the case of an individual subject to income tax under Schedule D Case I or II the allowance is first deductible from profits of the accounting period in which expenditure on the asset was incurred, provided that the asset belonged to the taxpayer at some time during that period (see *Ensign Tankers (Leasing) Ltd v Stokes* (1991)). Accordingly, under the preceding year rules, which generally operate, the relief will reduce the taxable profits of the following tax year.

EXAMPLE 7.1

A & Co, solicitors, make up their accounts to 31 December 1990. They show income profits of £15,000. During that year they purchased assets for which they are entitled to capital allowances of £2,000. The Schedule D Case II assessment for 1991–92 will be £15,000 – £2,000 = £13,000.

Under the opening year rules an accounting period may be used as the basis of assessment for more than one year of assessment. In that event any allowable capital expenditure is allocated to the earlier tax year. In the case of companies assessed on a current year basis the allowance will reduce profits of the current accounting period.

The date on which expenditure is incurred is usually the date on which the obligation to pay for the asset becomes unconditional (when title will normally pass) even though the agreement may provide a credit period for payment. Where, however, any such credit period exceeds four months from the date when the contract becomes unconditional, the expenditure is incurred only on the latest date by which the payment must be made (CAA 1990 s 159(5)). Furthermore, as an anti-avoidance measure, if the obligation to pay arises earlier than normal commercial usage for that trade would dictate, and the only or main benefit that results is the bringing forward of capital allowances to an earlier accounting period, the expenditure will be deemed to be incurred on the later date by or on which payment must actually be made.   **[7.23]**

EXAMPLE 7.2

On 1 February 1992 a solicitor buys five separate types of computer for his practice on the following terms:

	Title passes	Date payment due under normal terms of relevant trade	Date payment made	Date expenditure incurred for capital allowance purposes
Machine 1	1 Feb 1992	28 Feb 1992	14 Feb 1992	1 Feb 1992
Machine 2	1 Feb 1992	28 Feb 1992	10 March 1992	1 Feb 1992
Machine 3	1 Feb 1992	30 June 1992	16 April 1992	30 June 1992
Machine 4	1 Feb 1992	30 June 1992	16 May 1992	30 June 1992
Machine 5	1 Feb 1992	31 July 1992	12 June 1992	30 June 1992

4 How are the allowances used?

The allowances are deductible from taxable profits in the relevant tax year. If the allowance exceeds those profits or if there were no profits, the unused allowance can be carried forward and set against future profits. Alternatively, the taxpayer may elect to treat the surplus as a loss and deduct it from his other income under TA 1988 s 383, or carry it back under TA 1988 s 381 if appropriate (loss relief is discussed on at [**7.91**]ff). For companies, the effect of TA 1988 s 393(4) is broadly similar to s 383 save that it enables the allowance to be carried back for a period of three years to obtain a refund of tax. In cases other than trades, the allowance is deducted from the appropriate income (eg rent under Schedule A. In phasing out the first-year allowance the government sought to encourage genuine investment only and to prevent the taxpayer from manipulating his taxable profits by purchasing items of plant and machinery in a year of high profit simply to reduce that profit, and often in the case of small companies to take them out of the marginal corporation tax rate. **[7.24]**

5 The writing-down allowance

Capital allowances on plant and machinery (new or secondhand) purchased after 26 October 1970 and before 1 April 1986 consisted of a first-year allowance (FYA) which was available in the year the expenditure was incurred together with a writing-down allowance (WDA) for subsequent years until the cost of the asset was written off. FYAs are not available for expenditure incurred after 31 March 1986. **[7.25]**

a) *The basic allowance*

The WDA is a depreciation allowance of 25% of the 'qualifying expenditure' attributable to the asset. 'Qualifying expenditure' is defined as the original cost of the asset less any allowances already given. The allowance becomes available when expenditure is incurred even though the asset has not been brought into use in the business in that period provided that the expenditure was incurred wholly and exclusively for the purposes of the trade (CAA 1990 s 159: the position when the asset is bought *partly* for trade purposes is discussed below). The WDA may be *claimed* in whole or in part by individuals: in the case of companies, the allowance is given automatically unless *disclaimed* in whole or in part (although note that the position of companies will be brought into line with that of individuals as from the introduction of the Pay and File Scheme (CAA 1990 s 145A and Sch A1, inserted by FA 1990)). One attraction of not claiming a full allowance is to maintain a higher pool of qualifying expenditure (see below), thereby reducing the likelihood of a balancing charge. **[7.26]**

EXAMPLE 7.3

Alexis, an entrepreneur, makes up her accounts to 31 December each year. In July 1990 she purchased a computer wholly and exclusively for use in her business at a cost of £20,000. She claims WDAs as follows:

Assessment year 1991–92	£
Machine bought for	20,000
Less: 25% WDA	5,000
Qualifying expenditure	£15,000

Assessment year 1992-93

Qualifying expenditure b/f	15,000
Less: WDA (25% of £15,000)	3,750
Qualifying expenditure (c/f to 1993-94 *et seq*)	£11,250

b) *Pooling*

For ease of explanation the system of WDAs has so far been considered by reference to a taxpayer who acquires a single item of plant or machinery. In practice, however, it is more usual for a number of such items to be acquired and all the items are then treated for the purpose of the WDA as falling into a 'pool' of machinery and plant (save where a contrary election is made in the case of certain assets acquired after 31 March 1986: see d) below). The value of the pool (termed 'qualifying expenditure') is written down by 25% (or less) each year (see *Example 7.4(1)*). Certain items, however, such as cars, are never pooled (see [**7.31**]).

When an item of plant or machinery is disposed of, the disposal value of that item must be brought into account to ensure that the allowances given are exactly equal to the actual cost of the item to the business. A disposal occurs for these purposes whenever the asset ceases to belong to the trader (eg on sale); ceases to be in his possession (eg by theft); ceases to exist (eg by destruction) or to be used wholly and exclusively for the purposes of the trade; or where the trade is permanently discontinued (see CAA 1990 s 24(6)). The disposal value will usually be the sale price or insurance moneys or in other cases the open market value of the item. If the disposal is of a pooled asset, the qualifying expenditure in the pool is reduced by the disposal value of the item. This reduction is known as a balancing adjustment (see *Example 7.4(2)*).

EXAMPLE 7.4

(1) Albert, a trader, makes up his accounts to 31 December and purchases:

20 December 1990: machine A for £600
31 August 1991: machine B for £800
30 June 1992: machine C for £1,000

	First year £	Pool £
Assessment year 1991-92		
Purchase machine A on 20 December 1990	600	
WDA at 25%	150	
Qualifying expenditure carried forward	450	
Transfer A to pool		450
Assessment year 1992-93		
Qualifying expenditure brought forward		450
Purchase machine B on 31 August 1991	800	
Transfer B to pool		800
WDA at 25% on pool (£450 + £800)		312.50
Qualifying expenditure c/f		£937.50

Assessment year 1993–94

Qualifying expenditure brought forward		937.50
Purchase machine C on 30 June 1992	1,000	
Qualifying expenditure transferred to pool		1,000
		1,937.50
WDA on pool at 25%		484.37
Qualifying expenditure carried forward		£1,453.13

(2) Continuing (1) above, on 1 June 1993 Albert sells machine A for £453.13.

	Pool
Assessment year 1994–95	*£*
Qualifying expenditure brought forward	1,453.13
Sale of machine A on 1 June 1993	453.13
	1,000
WDA on pool at 25%	250
Qualifying expenditure carried forward	£750

So long as the business continues, it is unlikely that a balancing adjustment will exceed the qualifying expenditure in the pool, so as to give rise to a balancing charge (below). If the sale proceeds of an item of plant or machinery exceed its cost price the excess is charged not to income tax but to CGT (see Chapter 14). Thus, in *Example 7.4(1)*, if machine A had been sold for £700, the qualifying expenditure in the pool for the WDA would be £853.13 (£1,453.13—£600) with a chargeable gain of £100 (£700—£600): see further for the CGT rules [**14.53**]). [**7.27**]

c) *Balancing allowances and charges*

In the year when a business terminates there is no WDA; instead the proceeds received on the sale of the plant and machinery are deducted from the qualifying expenditure in the pool. If they are less than the value in the pool, the taxpayer receives a 'balancing allowance' for the difference which is deductible from his profits for the basis period. If the proceeds of sale are greater than the value left in the pool, however, the excess is a 'balancing charge' and is taxed as a receipt of the business (this is called the 'claw-back' of capital allowances). This procedure, which also applies to a disposal of a single item of plant and machinery which is not in a pool, ensures that allowances exactly equal the cost of the items to the business.

EXAMPLE 7.5

A trader sells his computer business for £50,000 of which £10,000 is paid for the plant and machinery. At the time of sale the qualifying expenditure in the pool of plant and machinery is £12,000. A, therefore, has a balancing allowance of £2,000 (£12,000—£10,000) which he can deduct from his final trading profits.

If A had instead received £14,000 for the plant and machinery his trading profits would be increased by a balancing charge of £2,000 (£14,000—£12,000). The purchaser will claim capital allowances on the £14,000 paid for the (secondhand) plant and machinery.

The amount of the purchase money attributed to the plant and machinery on the sale of a business is a matter for hard bargaining between the parties with the vendor wanting a low figure (to reduce the risk of a balancing charge) and the purchaser a high figure for the purpose of WDA. In practice, the Revenue will normally accept the figure that the parties agree, since they cannot lose!

The balancing adjustments on the termination of a business may be prevented in two cases where the taxpayer continues to be involved in the running of that business. First, on a change of partners in a firm (eg when C joins the firm of AB and Co as a partner) there is a deemed discontinuance (under TA 1988 s 113) of the old firm (AB and Co). Accordingly balancing allowances and charges will be calculated as if the assets were sold for their market value at that time. If, however, there is an election to treat the business as continuing, capital allowances continue as if the new owners had carried on the business throughout. Secondly, when the transferor and the transferee are connected persons they can elect not to treat the business as discontinued so that the transferee can take over the allowances of the transferor. This election will normally be used when a business is incorporated. Elections must be made within two years of the date of succession (CAA 1990 ss 77-8).   [**7.28**]

EXAMPLE 7.6

A, who has carried on a trade for many years, owns plant and machinery on which the qualifying expenditure at the end of 1990-91 is. On 1 June 1991, he transfers the business to A Ltd, a company controlled by him. A and A Ltd may elect for A Ltd to receive the allowances as if there had been no discontinuance. Hence, in financial year 1991, A Ltd receives a WDA on plant and machinery of 25% × £5,000 = £1,250.

d) *Short-life assets (see also SP 1/86)*

In the case of assets acquired after 31 March 1986, the taxpayer may irrevocably elect within two years after the end of the year of acquisition for that asset not to be pooled ('short life assets'): ie for the WDAs on each short life asset to be calculated separately from WDAs on the pool of qualifying expenditure (CAA 1990 s 37). The election is not available for items such as ships, cars, certain leased items and television sets and is intended for (although not specifically limited to) assets with a working life of less than five years. These 'depooling' provisions provided some compensation for the abolition of the FYA by ensu ring that the cost of such an asset can be written off for tax over the same period that it, in fact, depreciates. Thus if a 'short life' asset is disposed of within five years after the end of the year of acquisition, the disposal proceeds will trigger an immediate balancing allowance or charge for the trader, instead of effecting only a reduction in the overall qualifying expenditure in the pool.

If the asset is not disposed of within that five year period, the written down value must then be transferred to the pool.

EXAMPLE 7.7

Continuing *Example 7.4(1)* above, on 31 July 1992 Albert acquires Machine D for £1,200 for which he makes a depooling election by 31 December 1994. His capital allowances are calculated as follows, assuming that he retains the machine for five years:

Year ended	*Assessment year*		£
31 December 1992	1993-94	Cost of Machine D	1,200
		Less WDA at 25%	300

31 December 1993	1994–95	Written down value	b/f	900
		less WDA at 25%		225
31 December 1994	1995–96	Written down value	b/f	675
		less WDA at 25%		169
31 December 1995	1996–97	Written down value	b/f	506
		less WDA at 25%		127
31 December 1996	1997–98	Written down value	b/f	379
		less WDA at 25%		95
Qualifying expenditure transferred to general pool				£284

At the end of five years £284 is therefore transferred to Albert's pool of qualifying expenditure for tax year 1998–99. Consider, however, other possibilities:

If the machine is sold on 12 September 1995 for £400, Albert will have a balancing allowance of £106 (£506–£400) deductible from his 1996–97 profits.

If it were sold instead for £600, there would be a balancing charge of £94 (£600–£506) taxed as a receipt of his business in 1996–97.

To prevent the short life election from being abused by a sale to a connected person within the five year period, CAA 1990 s 37(8) provides that the purchaser in such a case will be deemed to have made the same election and, therefore, must transfer the asset into his general pool on the same date as the vendor would otherwise have done. The connected vendor and purchaser may, however, elect within two years of the year of sale for the asset to be transferred at its written down rather than market value, so that the vendor avoids a balancing allowance or charge (CAA 1990 s 37(8)). **[7.29]**

EXAMPLE 7.8

Assume an asset was bought by Adolph for £2,000 in July 1990 and he makes a short life asset election. In 1992 he sells the asset to his brother Benito for its book value of £1,200. A and B (1) do not make (2) make a joint election to transfer the asset at its written down value.

	£	£
A's position 1990: asset cost	2,000	
less WDA (25%)	500	
	1,500	
A's position 1991		
less WDA (25%)	375	
	£1,125	

	No election	*Election*
B's position 1992: cost	1,200	1,125
less WDA	300	281
	900	844
1993 *less* WDA	225	211
	675	633
1994 *less* WDA	169	158
Transfer to general pool	£506	£475

Notice that if no joint election is made Adolph has a balancing charge of £75; but if an election is made he suffers no balancing charge.

e) *Use for purposes other than trade* (CAA 1990 s 79)

Where expenditure is incurred on an asset not used wholly and exclusively for the purposes of the trade, the asset is kept outside the taxpayer's general pool: it is treated as used in a separate 'notional' trade. Further, if a pooled asset ceases to be used wholly and exclusively for trade purposes, this is treated as a disposal of the asset. Thus, its disposal value reduces the qualifying expenditure in the pool. In these cases WDAs are given on such portion of the expenditure on the asset (or, when it has come out of a pool, its disposal value) as may be just and reasonable having regard in particular to the extent to which the asset is used for business purposes.

If the asset is disposed of (which includes ceasing to use it for the purposes of the trade at all) its disposal value will give rise to a balancing allowance or charge.   **[7.30]**

6   Motor cars

The allowance for motor cars is restricted because they can (and usually will) be used for private as well as business purposes (CAA 1990 ss 34-6). Full WDAs are given on motor vehicles used for business purposes only. The vehicle must, therefore, be designed to carry goods (eg lorries); or unsuitable for use as a private car (eg taxis and buses); or a hire vehicle which is not hired to any one person for more than 30 consecutive days nor for more than 90 days in any period of 12 months.

Other vehicles qualify for 25% WDA subject to a maximum allowance calculated on the basis that the original cost was £8,000. Because of this restriction on the WDA for non-business vehicles, they are not pooled but are written down individually so increasing the likelihood of a balancing charge or allowance.

To prevent businesses leasing expensive cars (ie which cost at least £8,000) and circumventing the allowance restriction by claiming to deduct the entire rental as a business expense, it is provided that a deduction under TA 1988 s 74 shall be limited to the proportion that £8,000 plus one-half of the excess above £8,000 bears to the total original cost.   **[7.31]**

EXAMPLE 7.9

Footsore hires a car, which cost £12,000, for business use at a rent of £1,020 for one year. The hire charge that he can treat as a business expense is limited to:

$$\frac{£8,000 + \frac{1}{2}\ (£12,000 - £8,000)}{£12,000} \times £1,020 = £850$$

7   Leasing plant and machinery

CAA 1990 Part II Chapter V contains restrictions on, and sets out the conditions for, the availability of capital allowances to the lessor where plant and machinery is bought in order to be leased. WDAs are restricted unless the asset is used for a 'qualifying purpose'. Some of the attractions of purchasing assets for leasing have been reduced by the withdrawal of FYAs. When a lessor incurs capital expenditure on plant or machinery which he leases otherwise than in the course of a trade (eg where it is leased as part of the premises) he is entitled to capital allowances under CAA 1990 s 61 (see further Chapter 8).

EXAMPLE 7.10

L, a freeholder, installs a lift in his building and then grants a lease of those premises to a tenant. L has incurred capital expenditure on the provision of plant and machinery (the lift) which belongs to him. However, he is not carrying on a trade and therefore his entitlement to a capital allowance depends on s 61(1) which deems such expenditure to have been incurred for a trade carried on by L separate from any other trade which he may be carrying on at the commencement of the letting. Notice that it is irrelevant whether or not the item is used by the lessee in a trade which he carries on.

Care should be taken to ensure that a company does not both sell and lease the same plant and machinery. If the two activities are carried on in the same company *Gloucester Railway Carriage and Wagon Co Ltd v IRC* (1925) suggests that the expenditure on the leased assets is not subject to any capital allowance but that those assets form part of the general trading stock of the company. Accordingly, it may be desirable to separate into two companies the leasing and selling activities in order to ensure that in the former case a claim to allowances may be made.   **[7.32]**

8 Expenditure on plant or machinery which becomes a fixture

a) *Position before 12 July 1984*

Where a lessee of trade premises incurs expenditure on the installation of plant and machinery for use in his trade, he can claim allowances only for the items which 'belong' to him. This will be the case if they are tenant's fixtures (ie removable by him at the end of the lease). Where, however, they are landlord's fixtures (eg lifts), before FA 1985, they were treated for capital allowances as belonging to the tenant only if he was required by the terms of his lease to incur the expenditure (CAA 1990 s 61(4)(a)). In such a case, on the termination of the lease any balancing adjustment was levied on the landlord in recognition of the fact that the asset really belonged to him. In *Stokes v Costain Property Investments Ltd* (1984) a lessee who incurred massive expenditure on the installation of lifts and central heating under a separate agreement to develop the site *before* the commencement of his lease, could not claim allowances in respect of them as they did not 'belong' to him and neither could the landlord claim the allowances as he had not incurred the expenditure. This restrictive interpretation of the subsection represented a departure from the former Revenue practice which had permitted the tenant to claim the allowance in such cases. Accordingly FA 1985 introduced a new code to determine the entitlement to capital allowances whenever expenditure is incurred after 11 July 1984 on the provision of machinery or plant which becomes a fixture. The intention is to ensure that someone will be entitled to a capital allowance even though as a matter of property law the machinery or plant may not belong to him. In the case of expenditure incurred before 12 July 1984 or after that date but pursuant to a contractual or leasehold obligation arising before that date the position remains governed by the old law and *Stokes v Costain* (above).   **[7.33]**

b) *Tenant's fixtures*

Entitlement to allowances in respect of expenditure on installing 'tenant's fixtures' (ie plant and machinery which may be removed by the tenant at the end of his lease and which remains therefore a chattel) is governed by general property law and the amended s 61(4). Generally these assets will 'belong' to the tenant for capital allowance purposes even though he is required under the terms of his lease to incur the expenditure. When expenditure is incurred on plant and machinery which becomes a fixture however and which under general property law belongs to the fee simple owner of the land the question of to whom the fixtures 'belong' for the purpose of claiming allowances is governed exclusively by the provisions of s 61(4).   **[7.34]**

c) *The basic rule under the revised s 61(4)*

Fixtures will be treated as belonging to the person who incurred the expenditure of installing the item either for the purposes of his trade, or for leasing other than in the course of a trade, provided that at the time when the asset becomes a fixture such person has an interest in the (relevant) land. An 'interest in land' for these purposes includes a fee simple estate or a contract for its purchase; a lease or an agreement for a lease; an easement or agreement for an easement; a mortgagor's equity of redemption; and a licence to occupy land. As this rule may result in the fixture 'belonging' to two or more persons with different interests in the land at the same time, CAA 1990 s 52 lays down an order for priority of entitlement whereby the asset can belong to only one person at a time; generally to the person with the most subordinate interest.   **[7.35]**

EXAMPLE 7.11

(1)   T is a tenant of L and incurs capital expenditure on the provision of machinery which becomes a fixture. He grants a sublease of the property to ST. T will be entitled to capital allowances since (i) he has incurred capital expenditure; (ii) on an item of machinery; (iii) the expenditure is incurred for leasing otherwise than in the course of a trade under s 61(1), and (iv) he has an interest in the land.

(2)   A, B, C, D and E are all traders and they share the capital expenditure after 11 July 1984 of installing for the purpose of their respective trades a lift in the building. They each have an interest in the land serviced by the lift as follows:

(a)   A owns the fee simple estate, subject to a mortgage
(b)   B has a 99 year lease
(c)   C has an agreement for a 16 year lease
(d)   D has a licence to occupy part of the premises
(e)   E has a right to use the lift for transporting goods (from his adjacent premises (an easement)).

Although the fixture 'belongs' to each of A, B, C, D and E, the order of entitlement for claiming allowances in respect of their individual expenditure is E, D, C, B, A. Hence only E's expenditure qualifies for the allowance.

NB (i) a 'contributor' to the cost of the asset may be entitled to an allowance; (ii) an 'equipment lessor' may be entitled to the allowance.

d) *Modifications to the basic rule*

In a number of cases the basic rule is modified. For instance where a person buys an existing interest in land and the purchase price is partly referable to plant and machinery which is a fixture, the purchaser can claim capital allowances in respect of the portion of the price paid for the fixture provided that no one else is entitled to claim the allowances (eg on the sale of the fee simple with vacant possession) or that the person who was so entitled is required to bring the disposal proceeds into account under CAA 1990 s 24 (eg on the sale of a lease where the assignor ceases to use those fixtures in his trade).

Where a lessee purchases a new lease from a lessor who would be entitled to capital allowances for fixtures installed by him and all or part of the purchase price represents payment for such fixtures, the lessor and lessee can elect within two years from the end of that chargeable period for entitlement to the allowances to be transferred to the lessee unless the lessor and lessee are connected persons or the main purpose of the arrangement is to obtain a tax advantage. [7.36]

e) *Termination of entitlement to allowances*

Where a person who is claiming allowances because of his interest in the land ceases to own that interest for any reason, the fixture ceases to belong to him at that date and will 'belong' to whoever is otherwise entitled according to the order of entitlement considered above. Thus on the termination of a lease the fixture ceases to belong to the lessee and for capital allowance purposes now belongs to the lessor. Notice however that an interest in land does not cease for these purposes where, for instance, a lease is granted pursuant to an agreement for a lease, or the lessee acquires a new lease of the same premises, or 'holds over' after the termination of his current lease; or a lessee acquqires the interest of his landlord so that both interests merge.

A person will, however, cease to be entitled to allowances if, on the fixture being severed from the land so as to become a chattel again, the item in question does not 'belong' to him under general property law. [7.37]

f) *Balancing charges*

All the normal rules of CAA 1990 s 24 operate to determine when a person who is claiming allowances must bring disposal proceeds into account and what the value of those proceeds is. [7.38]

9 **Hire purchase**

The acquisition of plant or machinery on hire purchase is treated as an outright purchase so that capital allowances are granted to the hirer on the capital element of the purchase price as soon as the asset is brought into use in the business. The interest element is a deductible business expense in the year it is paid. [7.39]–[7.50]

III INDUSTRIAL BUILDINGS

Capital allowances are available under the Capital Allowances Act 1990 Part I for the construction (and purrchase) of an industrial building or structure used for manufacturing (not distributive) trades. [7.51]

1 **Definition**

Unlike plant and machinery, an industrial building is defined at length in the legislation. It includes a mill, factory or similar premises and a building used for the storage of manufactured goods or raw materials (see *Copol Clothing Co Ltd v Hindmarch* (1984) and generally the CAA 1990 s 18). This definition includes a workers' canteen but not normally a retail shop, house, showroom or office. Expenditure on acquiring the land itself is not allowed except for costs of tunnelling, preparing and levelling. Subsequent expenditure on improvements to the industrial building is allowable (CAA 1990 s 12). From 5 April 1991 the allowance has been extended to include the construction of toll roads (CAA 1990 s 18(1)(aa): inserted by FA 1991).

If part of an industrial building is used for a non-industrial purpose, the full allowance is still available so long as expenditure on that part does not exceed 25% of the expenditure on the whole building.   **[7.52]**

2   Form of the allowance

a) *A writing-down allowance*

An initial allowance was formerly available but, like the FYA on plant and machinery, it has been phased out and is not generally given on expenditure incurred after 31 March 1986. Accordingly the only allowance is a WDA at 4% of the original cost of construction (or of the purchase price) of an industrial building (CAA 1990 s 3(2)). The allowance continues for every year during which the taxpayer uses the building until after 25 years the entire expenditure is written off. It is also available to a landlord where the building is let, provided that he is the owner or where it is occupied by licensees. In these cases the allowances are deducted from any rent (or like payment) that the owner receives. Any balancing charge that arises is taxed under Schedule D Case VI.   **[7.53]**

b) *Balancing allowances or charges (CAA 1990 s 4)*

When the building is disposed of, the qualifying expenditure left on the building is compared with the disposal consideration and at balancing allowance or charge is made. A balancing charge can never recover more than the allowances given, so that if the disposal value exceeds the original cost of the building, the excess represents a capital gain chargeable to CGT.

The building is regarded as having been written down to nil value after 25 years (4% × 25 = 100% of cost). As a result, no WDA is available after 25 years (maximum), nor will a disposal after 25 years give rise to a balancing charge or allowance.   **[7.54]**

c) *Purchase of a secondhand industrial building*

A WDA is available to a purchaser whose use of a secondhand building qualifies as industrial. The WDA is calculated by spreading the 'residue of expenditure' over the balance remaining of the 25 year life of the building. The residue of expenditure is the written down value of the vendor plus any balancing charge (or less any balancing allowance).   **[7.55]**

EXAMPLE 7.12

Arkwright builds a jute spinning mill at a cost of £100,000 in 1986. In 1997 he sells the mill to Hargreaves for £87,000. Hargreaves continues the jute spinning business.

(i) *Position of Arkwright* he will qualify for allowances from 1986 to 1996 at a rate of 4% pa on £100,000. Accordingly, in 1997 (at the time of sale) he will have received WDAs totalling £40,000 and his remaining qualifying expenditure is £60,000.

(ii) On the sale to Hargreaves, Arkwright will suffer a balancing charge of £27,000 (£87,000–£60,000).

(iii) *Position of Hargreaves* he will qualify for WDA for the next 15 years on the residue of expenditure (£87,000) assuming that he continues to use the mill during that period. This sum is spread evenly over the 15 year period and is not tied to a 4% figure.

3 Miscellaneous

Hotel buildings (CAA 1990 s 7)   Expenditure on the construction or improvement of hotel buildings where the hotel has at least ten letting bedrooms, offers breakfast and an evening meal (see SP 9/87), and is open for at least four months between April and October, qualifies for an annual WDA of 4% of the cost.   **[7.56]**

Enterprise zones (CAA 1990 s 1)   To stimulate development in deprived areas, the Secretary of State has designated a small number of enterprise zones wherein expenditure on certain industrial buildings, hotels and commercial buildings (including shops and offices) qualifies for 100% Initial Allowance ('IA'). By ESC B 31 expenditure on machinery or plant which becomes an integral part of such a building may be treated by the taxpayer as part of the construction costs thereby qualifying for the 100% allowance. A WDA of 25% of the cost is also available where less than the full IA is claimed.   **[7.57]–[7.70]**

IV   OTHER CATEGORIES OF EXPENDITURE ELIGIBLE FOR CAPITAL ALLOWANCES

Agricultural or forestry buildings (CAA 1990 Part V)   Allowances are available for capital expenditure by the owner or tenant of agricultural or forestry land used for the sole purposes of husbandry and forestry. The expenditure must be incurred on the 'construction' of, inter alia, farm or forestry buildings including farmhouses (for which only one-third of the cost is allowed); farm cottages; fences and walls; and drainage and sewerage works.

The allowance comprises a WDA of 4% calculated on a straight line basis. At the option of the taxpayer a balancing adjustment may be made when an agricultural building etc is demolished, destroyed or sold. This election enables the allowance to be brought into line with actual depreciation.   **[7.71]**

Assured tenancies (CAA 1990 Part III)   Capital allowances for expenditure on the construction of property for letting on assured tenancies under the Housing Act 1980 were introduced in 1982 for approved bodies for an initial period of five years which was subsequently extended to 31 March 1992. With the replacement of the relevant portion of the 1980 Act by the 1988 Housing Act, this system of allowances has come to an end. Transitional arrangements ensure that allowances already given will not be withdrawn and that qualifying expenditure incurred before 15 March 1988 or incurred under a contract entered into before that date will continue to qualify for an allowance. (CAA 1990 s 84.) [**7.72**]

Scientific research (CAA 1990 Part VII)   Capital expenditure on scientific research continues to carry a 100% allowance. Scientific research is widely defined. However, as from 1 April 1985, the cost of land and houses ceased to be eligible for the allowance and there are stricter rules for the recovery of the allowance where an asset is sold. [**7.73**]

Patents and 'know-how'   The cost of purchasing a patent for use in a business is relieved by an annual WDA of 25% on a reducing balance basis calculated in respect of a separate pool for all patent expenditure. When the final patent in the pool is sold (or it expires) any balance then remaining in the pool will give rise to a balancing allowance (see TA 1988 s 528).
   The cost of acquiring 'know-how' comprises a separate pool for which an annual WDA of 25% is given on a reducing balance basis. [**7.74**]

Residual   Capital allowances are also available for mines and oil wells and mineral rights and for cemeteries and crematoria. There is an annual WDA on dredging at 4% of cost. [**7.75**]–[**7.90**]

V   LOSSES IN TRADES, PROFESSIONS OR VOCATIONS—THE MAIN RELIEFS

1   Introductory

Whenever an individual or partnership makes a loss, ie where allowable expenses in an accounting period exceed taxable income, there are two repercussions. *First*, any year of assessment using as its basis period one in which the loss was incurred will have a nil tax assessment. *Secondly*, the loss is, in tax terms, an asset which may be used to cancel out or relieve tax assessments of that or other years, so that the taxpayer will either pay less tax or be able to reclaim tax which he has previously paid.
   Where the loss is made by a trading company, it is not available for use by individual shareholders (even in a 'one man' company). Hence, where it is proposed to start a business, and early losses are anticipated, the advantages of income tax relief must be weighed against the protection of limited liability (see Chapter 32).
   When seeking to apply the reliefs it is important to realise that a loss may be eligible for relief under more than one provision and that the choice will usually rest with the taxpayer. It should be noted that certain of the reliefs must be set against the taxpayer's earned before unearned income. [**7.91**]

2   Relief under TA 1988 s 385: carry-forward

A loss which is sustained in carrying on a trade, profession or vocation can be carried forward under s 385 and set off against the first available profits of the same trade, profession or vocation without time limit. The loss must be deducted as far as possible from the earliest subsequent profits with the result that the taxpayer may lose his personal allowance.

EXAMPLE 7.13 *(See diagram below)*

Scrooge's accounts are as follows:

Accounting period

Year to 31 December 1987	£2,000 profit
Year to 31 December 1988	(£6,000) loss
Year to 31 December 1989	£1,600 profit
Year to 31 December 1990	£3,600 profit
Year to 31 December 1991	£4,000 profit

The income tax assessments are:

Tax year	*Taxable profit (loss)*
1988–89:	£2,000
1989–90:	Nil (£6,000 loss carried forward)
1990–91: (£1,600—£1,600)	Nil (s 385: £4,400 loss carried forward)
1991–92: (£3,600—£3,600)	Nil (s 385: £800 loss carried forward)
1992–93: (£4,000—£800)	£3,200 (s 385)

Scrooge would lose the benefit of his personal allowance in 1989–90, 1990–91 and 1991–92 if he has no other income against which to set it.

When a business receives income which has already been taxed at source (eg dividends) any loss brought forward under s 385 can be used against that taxed income and a repayment claim made (TA 1988 s 385(4)).

In calculating the loss to be carried forward under s 385, certain items may be treated as losses. For instance, by s 387 an annual payment which is made wholly and exclusively for the purpose of the business and assessed under TA 1988 s 349 (because the taxpayer has no income) and which cannot be relieved because there are no profits against which to set it, may be treated as a loss for s 385. The same principle applies to unrelieved interest payments (TA 1988 s 390).

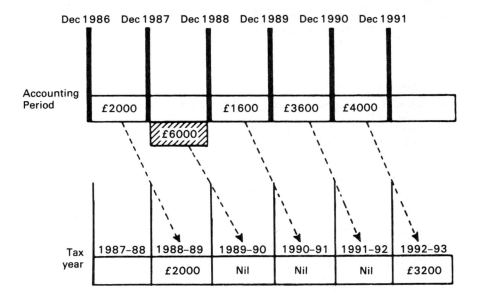

EXAMPLE 7.14

Oliver makes a loss of £10,000 in his accounting year ended 31 July 1991. He makes an annual payment each year on 1 June of £1,000. In 1992–93 there will be a nil assessment on his business profits, but under TA 1988 s 349 the Revenue require Oliver to pay basic rate income tax on £1,000 at 25% (£250). As he made a loss of £10,000 and has paid out £1,000 in total, Oliver's loss to be carried forward under s 385 is £11,000.

Losses can only be carried forward under s 385 against future profits from the same business. Thus, if the nature of the business changes in a future year, there can be no carry-forward of losses. In *Gordon and Blair Ltd v IRC* (1962) brewing losses could not be carried forward against bottling profits. Similarly, if the business ceases, there can be no carry-forward, although special rules operate on a change of partners (see Chapter 29).

There are two major drawbacks to loss relief under s 385. First, it is only available against profits from the same business and not against any other income of the taxpayer. Secondly, the relief is not immediate. Even assuming that the business makes profits in the future, loss relief may not be obtained for some years (see *Example 7.13*). In inflationary times, this delay renders the loss relief less valuable in real terms (cp TA 1988 s 380).   **[7.92]**

3   Relief under TA 1988 s 380: carry-across

Section 380 enables loss relief to be claimed in the year of assessment in which the loss is actually sustained. In theory, the relief should be apportioned when an accounting period straddles two tax years but, in practice, the Revenue give relief for the tax year in which the accounting period showing a loss ends. Relief under s 380 is given against the taxpayer's total income for the relevant year of assessment, earned before unearned income. In so far as any loss remains unrelieved in that year, it can be carried forward and set against his total income for one further year provided that the business is still being carried on for at least part of that year (TA 1988 s 380(2)).

EXAMPLE 7.15

Bertrand makes up his accounts to 30 September each year as follows:
Accounting period
Year to 30 September 1989   £5,000 profit
Year to 30 September 1990   £10,000 loss
Year to 30 September 1991   £2,000 profit

In each of the tax years 1990–91 and 1991–92 Bertrand also has other income which is assessed on a current year basis: viz £2,000 Schedule E (employment) income and £1,000 Schedule A (rental) income.

Under s 380 the loss of £10,000 can be relieved in the tax year 1990–91, in which it is made, and in the following tax year as follows, but with a loss of Bertrand's personal allowance in 1990–91.

Tax year	*Total income*	*Losses*
1990–91:	£	£
Schedule D Case I		
(Preceding Year Basis (PYB))	5,000	
Schedule E	2,000	
Schedule A	1,000	
	8,000	

Loss made in 1990–91		(10,000)
Section 380(1) relief	(8,000)	8,000
	Nil	(2,000)
1991–92:		
Schedule D Case I loss (PYB)	—	
Schedule E	2,000	
Section 380(2) relief	(2,000)	2,000
Schedule A	£1,000	

With the introduction of independent taxation for husband and wife it is no longer possible for unrelieved losses and unused capital allowances to set against the income of the taxpayer's spouse.

The taxpayer must make a specific written election for s 380 relief for each of the two years and must do so within two years of the end of the relevant year of assessment. Election may be made for the first and not for the second year or vice versa or for both years. When the election is made for both years and the business suffers a further loss in the next accounting period, the loss carried forward from the earlier year is set off first.

Certain restrictions are placed on the availability of s 380 relief in order to prevent a taxpayer indulging in a 'hobby' trade. TA 1988 s 384 denies the relief unless the taxpayer can show that the loss-making business was run on a commercial basis with a view to profit (although a reasonable expectation of profit is deemed conclusive evidence of this). By TA 1988 s 397, a farmer or market gardener will automatically lose the relief if he incurs a loss in each of the preceding five years unless he can show that any competent farmer or market gardener would have made the same losses. The moral here is 'let your losses be those of the reasonable man or make a profit every sixth year!' (See ESC B5 for the permitted deduction of maintenance expenses in the case of owner-occupied farms not farmed on a commercial basis.)   [**7.93**]

4 Extension of TA 1988 s 380 relief to a taxpayer's capital gains (FA 1991 s 72)

The fusion of the rates of income tax and CGT in 1988 did not involve a joining together of the taxes themselves. As a general principle, therefore, the two remain distinct so that income losses cannot generally be offset agains chargeable gains and nor can capital losses be offset against income. To some extent these divisions are blurred so far as company taxation is concerned: trading losses can be set against a company's 'profits' of the same accounting period and, to the extent unrelieved, against profits of a previous accounting period and for corporation tax purposes 'profits' includes the company's chargeable gains (TA 1988 s 393(2) and see [**28.53**]). FA 1991 has now brought the rules for the unincorporated business into line by permitting trading losses to be offset against the capital gains of the taxpayer in the tax year when the loss arises and in one following tax year. The following matters are particularly worthy of note about this new relief.

(1) The relief depends upon an election being made by the taxpayer and this claim for relief may only be made if a claim is also submitted under TA 1988 s 380 (ie to set the loss against the taxpayer's other income). Capital gains may only be used to the extent that the trading loss cannot be made good against the taxpayer's other income for the year.

(2) Relief is obtained by setting the trading loss against the amount which would otherwise be subject to a CGT charge *disregarding for this purpose the taxpayer's annual exemption*. This rule exactly mirrors that for CGT losses which must also be set against gains for the year when the loss is incurred even if the effect is that the taxpayer loses any benefit from his annual exemption (see [**14.81**]). For these purposes the trading losses are treated as an allowable capital loss made in that year.

(3) To the extent that full relief is not available in the year when the trading loss is incurred, any unrelieved balance may then be carried forward and set against gains in the following tax year in accordance with the s 380 procedure: note that this relief will not be available if that following year of assessment begins **after** the taxpayer has ceased to carry on the relevant trade etc.   [**7.94**]

EXAMPLE 7.16

Edwina makes up her accounts as a bricklayer to 31 December. The following table indicates her profit (losses) for 1990, 1991 and 1992 as well as her other income and capital gains (losses) for those years.

Accounts	DI (£)	Tax year	Other income (£)	Capital gains (£)
1990	3,500	1990–91	4,500	(20,000)
1991	(15,000)	1991–92	4,500	8,500
1992	(20,000)	1992–93	4,500	11,500

(1) *In tax year 1990–91* Edwina will be taxed on an income of £4,500 plus her DI income from 1989 (pyb—not given). Her capital loss must be carried forward for relief in the future.

(2) *In tax year 1991–92* Edwina's income will be £4,500 + £3,500 (DI, pyb) = £8,000. She may claim:
   (i) to offset £8,000 of the 1991 trading loss against her income. This will result in a loss of her personal relief (£3,295) so that income tax relief will be £4,705 × 25% = £1,176.25;
   (ii) if she makes the above claim she may also claim to set the remaining loss (£7,000) against her capital gain of £8,500. Note that the effect would be:
      (a) the 1990 capital loss of £20,000 would be further carried forward to 1992;
      (b) her CGT annual exemption of £5,500 for 1991 will be reduced to £1,500 which will reduce the remaining gain of £1,500 to nil. *£4,000 of that exemption will therefore be wasted*;
      (c) as a result of (b) the saving in CGT resulting from the claim will be £3,000 × 25% = £750.
   (iii) if both claims are submitted Edwina will exhaust her trading loss of £15,000 and total tax relief of £1,926.25 has been given (% rate of relief is 12.84%).

(3) *In tax year 1992–93* the position is relatively straightforward:
   (i) Edwina can claim to offset the £2,000 loss against her £4,500 income thereby losing (at current levels) £795 of her personal allowance.
   (ii) The carried-forward capital loss of £20,000 will reduce her £1,500 gain to zero but only after the annual exemption (currently £5,500) has been deducted. Unused loss carried to 1993–94 will therefore be £14,000.

(iii) Note that if Edwina had carried forward her trading loss from 1991 which exceeded her 1992-93 income the excess could be relieved against her £11,500 gain for that year by treating it as a loss of that year (ie it would be deducted—as in 1991-92—in priority to the annual exemption).

5 Relationship between TA 1988 ss 380 and 385

Section 380 requires a specific election, otherwise there is automatic carry-forward under s 385. To the extent that s 380 is chosen, it is only the balance of the loss remaining unrelieved under that section that can be carried forward under s 385.

The two advantages possessed by s 380 are that the relief is given immediately and against all income of the taxpayer. It follows that an unprofitable trade can be 'nursed' by a wealthy taxpayer. Section 380 may also be advantageous when it is likely that the business will close with the result that s 385 will cease to be available. However, s 380 should not be chosen if it would result in the loss of personal allowances or when profits or rates of tax are likely to rise and the taxpayer can afford to wait for his relief. **[7.95]-[7.110]**

VI RELIEF FOR LOSSES IN THE EARLY YEARS OF BUSINESS

1 TA 1988 s 381: initial loss relief

A business will often make losses in its early years and TA 1988 s 381 provides relief where a loss is sustained in the year of assessment in which the business is first carried on, or in any of the next three years of assessment, as an alternative to relief under TA 1988 ss 380 and 385.

Losses must be calculated on an actual basis in each year and the relief is obtained by a set-off against the taxpayer's total income of the three years of assessment preceding the year of loss. The set-off is against earlier years before later years and in each year is against the taxpayer's earned before unearned income. The effect of the relief is to revise earlier income tax assessments and to obtain a tax refund. Section 381 is available to individuals (including partners) for a maximum of four years only and is not available to a limited company. Therefore, where early losses are envisaged, it may be worth starting as a sole trader (or partnership) and at a later stage incorporating the business (see Chapter 32).

As with TA 1988 s 380, s 381 relief requires a specific election within two years from the end of the year of assessment in which the loss is sustained. In an attempt to prevent hobby trades the relief is denied unless it can be shown that the business was carried on on a commercial basis with a view to profit (TA 1988 s 381(4)). Further the relief cannot be extended to eight years by the taxpayer transferring the business to his spouse after the first four years (TA 1988 s 381(5)). **[7.111]**

EXAMPLE 7.17 *(see diagram following)*

Fergus began business as a sole practitioner on 1 July 1991. His results for the first two years of assessment were:

1991-92: loss £14,000 (ie 1 July 1991-5 April 1992)

1992–93: loss £3,000 (calculated on the actual basis: ie 6 April 1992–5 April 1993).

Before beginning his own business, Fergus was employed as an assistant solicitor. He also has income from dividends. This other income comprised:

	Salary (Schedule E)	Dividend (Schedule F)
1988–89	£9,600	£6,000
1989–90	£10,000	£6,400
1990–91	£12,000	£7,000
1991–92	—	£4,000
1992–93	—	£5,000

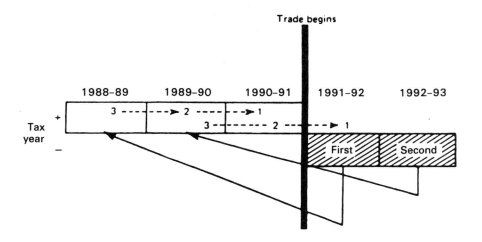

Fergus makes two separate elections for relief under TA 1988 s 381: first, for the £14,000 loss and subsequently for the £3,000 loss. The position is as follows:

	£
1988–89	
Schedule E income	9,600
Less part of 1991–92 loss carried back (under s 381)	(9,600)
	Nil
Schedule F income	6,000
Less balance of 1991–92 loss (s 381)	(4,400)
Revised assessment	£1,600
1989–90	
Schedule E income	10,000
Less 1992–93 loss carried back	(3,000)
	7,000
Schedule F income	6,400
Revised assessment	£13,400
1990–91	
Schedule E income	12,000
Schedule F income	7,000
No revision of assessment of	£19,000

1991-92

Schedule E income (Schedule D)	Nil
Schedule F income	4,000
No revision of assessment of	£4,000

1992-93

Schedule D income	Nil
Schedule F income	5,000
No revision of assessment of	£5,000

2 Relationship of s 381 with ss 380 and 385

As with s 380, relief under s 381 requires a specific election. The election need only be made for one year of loss, but, once made, that loss must be carried back against the taxpayer's income in the earlier years without limit, which may result in a loss of personal allowances.

Sections 381 and 380 are alternatives so that the same portion of any loss cannot be relieved under both sections (ie twice). Where, however, relief has been given as far as possible under one section, any surplus loss remaining can be relieved by a specific election under the other section (see *Butt v Haxby* (1983)). Any surplus loss still unrelieved will then be carried forward under s 385.

EXAMPLE 7.18

Angus begins trading on 1 August 1991 and in the period to 5 April 1992 makes a loss of £15,000. His income in the preceding three years (1988-89 onwards) amounted to £10,000. If Angus elects for s 381 relief he will have wasted his personal allowances in the preceding years. He will be left with an unrelieved loss of £5,000 which can be relieved under s 380 against any other income which he may have in 1991-92 and (by a further election) in 1992-93. To the extent that relief is not given under s 380, the surplus loss will be carried forward under s 385.

Which relief the taxpayer chooses will depend upon the facts. Section 381 relief is highly advantageous when the taxpayer has a large pre-trading income, since it will ensure a cash refund. Alternatively, if his other income in the year(s) of loss is large, relief under TA 1988 s 380 may be more attractive. Changes in income tax rates are an important factor to bear in mind. **[7.112]**

3 Losses and the opening year rules

The opening year rules of TA 1988 ss 61 and 62 are concerned only with the taxation of profits and do not affect the treatment of losses which are relieved in accordance with the above provisions.

In the case of a new business, as a result of the opening year rules, a period of loss may form the basis period of three years of assessment. However, the loss available for relief is limited to the actual loss sustained as reduced by any amount used to reduce profits in those basis periods. Compare two examples:

EXAMPLE 7.19

(1) Tartan began trading on 6 June 1991 with the following results:

6 June 1991–5 December 1991	£10,000 loss
6 December 1991–5 December 1992	£6,000 profit

Assessments (ignoring s 62 election)
1991–92: (actual)

6 June 1991–5 December 1991	£10,000 loss
6 December 1991–5 April 1992: $\frac{4}{12} \times$ £6,000	£2,000 profit
Schedule D Case I assessment	Nil

Note that a portion of the £10,000 loss is in effect used to offset the £2,000 profit (therefore £8,000 loss unused).

1992–93: (first 12 months)

6 June 1991–5 December 1991	£10,000 loss
6 December 1991–5 June 1992: $\frac{6}{12} \times$ £6,000	£3,000 profit
Schedule D Case I assessment	Nil

Note that £3,000 of the £8,000 surplus loss is used to offset the profit (leaving £5,000 loss).

1993–94: (PYB)

Profit of the year ending 5 December 1992	£6,000
Less s 385 loss (unused)	£5,000
Schedule D Case I assessment	£1,000

(2) Now assume that Tartan had the following results:

6 June 1991–5 December 1991	£3,000 loss
Year ending 5 December 1992	£6,000 profit

Assessments (ignoring s 62 election)
1991–92: (actual)

6 June 1991–5 December 1991	£3,000 loss
6 December 1991–5 April 1992	£2,000 profit
Schedule D Case I assessment	Nil

1992–93: (first 12 months)

6 June 1991–5 December 1991	£3,000 loss
6 December 1991–5 June 1992	£3,000 profit
Schedule D Case I assessment	Nil

1993–94: (PYB)

Year ending 5 December 1992	£6,000 profit

Notice in *Example 7.19(2)* that although no loss relief has been given under any of the specific loss provisions, the 'notional' losses (ie £5,000) used in arriving at assessments come to more than the actual loss of £3,000. This notional use of losses is permissible (*Westward Television Ltd v Hart* (1968)). It is only when the loss is to be carried forward under s 385 (or used for s 380 or s 381 relief) that relief is restricted to the actual loss.   **[7.113]–[7.130]**

VII RELIEFS FOR LOSSES IN THE FINAL YEARS

1 TA 1988 s 386: transfer of a business to a company

The general rule is that loss relief is personal to the taxpayer who sustains the loss; it cannot be 'sold' with the business or otherwise transferred. Thus, if a business is incorporated, any unabsorbed loss of the old business which ceases to trade cannot be carried forward under s 385 by the company. However, TA 1988 s 386 provides that where the business of a sole trader or a partnership is transferred to a company and the whole or main consideration for the transfer is the allotment of shares to the former proprietor, he can set his unabsorbed losses against income which he receives from the company for any year throughout which he owns the shares allotted to him and during which the company continues to trade. He will normally be able to set the losses against either dividends on the shares or salary if he is a director or employee of the company in the order of earned before unearned income.

EXAMPLE 7.20

Evans sells his business to a company in return for an allotment of shares on 30 September 1991. His unused losses from the trade amount to £4,200.

In the period from 1 October 1991 to 5 April 1992, he receives a salary of £3,000 and dividends (gross) of £400 from the company. In 1992–93 he receives a salary of £5,000 and dividends of £600. Evans obtains relief under s 386 as follows:

	Total income £	Losses £
1991–92		
Unabsorbed Schedule D Case I loss		(4,200)
Salary	3,000	
Dividends	400	
Less s 386 relief	3,400	
	(3,400)	3,400
	Nil	(800)
1992–93:		
Salary	5,000	
Less s 386 relief	(800)	800
	4,200	
Dividends	600	
	£4,800	

Relief under s 386 is given automatically (as an extension of s 385) as if the original business had not ceased and as if the income derived from the company were profits of that business. However, for all other purposes the business has discontinued and, if the taxpayer wants relief for his business loss in the year of discontinuance under s 380(1), or terminal relief under s 388 (see below), he must make a specific election to that effect. Notice that s 386 relief is given to the taxpayer who sustains the loss and affords no relief for losses made by the newly formed company. **[7.131]**

2   TA 1988 s 388: terminal loss relief

If a loss is sustained in the last 12 months of a business, the unabsorbed loss of that period, so far as not otherwise relieved (eg under TA 1988 s 380, in the year of discontinuance) may be relieved by set-off against the business profits of the three years of assessment preceding the one in which the business terminates. Relief is given as far as possible against later rather than earlier years.

The loss is calculated on an actual basis and includes (i) unrelieved capital allowances within that 12 month period, (ii) any annual payments charged under TA 1988 s 349, (iii) any unrelieved interest payments so long as they are incurred wholly and exclusively for the purposes of the business.

If profits of a preceding year are insufficient to absorb the loss, dividends and other income taxed at source in that year (and which are received in the course of carrying on the business) are treated as profits for the purposes of obtaining a repayment of income tax (TA 1988 s 385(4)).

Relief may be claimed under TA 1988 s 388 as an alternative to relief under TA 1988 s 386 (transfer to a company) and any unused loss can be relieved under s 386.   **[7.132]–[7.150]**

EXAMPLE 7.21 *(see diagram following)*

Dolly closes down her hairdressing business on 5 June 1991. Her results for the four years ending 5 December 1990 and for her final six months of business were:

Accounting period	Profit/loss	Tax years	Original assessments
Year to 5 December 1987	£11,000 profit		
Year to 5 December 1988	£7,000 profit	1987–88	£11,000
Year to 5 December 1989	£3,000 profit	1988–89	£7,000
Year to 5 December 1990	£1,000 profit	1989–90	£3,000
Six months to 5 June 1991	£12,000 loss	1990–91	£1,000

The 1991–92 assessment will be revised to nil under TA 1988 s 63 (the actual profits of the period 6 April 1991–6 June 1991 (none)). As the Revenue would not make a s 63 election in respect of 1989–90 and 1990–91 the assessment for these years remains unaltered. The 'terminal loss' is calculated as:

1991–92

6 April 1991–5 June 1991 ie $\frac{2}{6} \times$ £12,000 loss   £4,000 loss

1990–91

6 June 1990–5 December 1990 ie $\frac{6}{12} \times$ £1,000 profit   £500

6 December 1990–5 April 1991 ie $\frac{4}{6} \times$ £12,000 loss   £8,000 loss

£11,500 loss

This terminal loss can be relieved first in 1990–91 then in 1989–90 and finally in 1988–89 resulting in the following revised assessments (and repayments of tax):

Final assessments

1988–89	£9,500	(£11,000—£1,500)
1989–90	Nil	(£7,000—£7,000)
1990–91	Nil	(£3,000—£3,000)
1991–92	Nil	(£11,500)

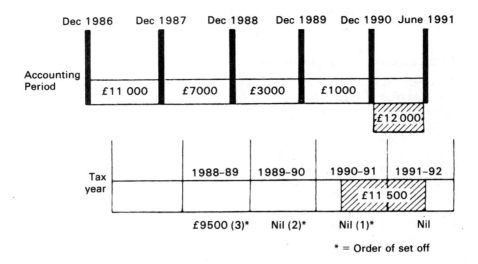

* = Order of set off

VIII   PROBLEMS AND SPECIAL CASES

1   Capital allowances and losses

Capital allowances are deductible from profits. They may be used to create or increase a loss under TA 1988 s 380 or s 381 in the year that the expenditure is incurred (TA 1988 s 383). Alternatively, any unused capital allowances may be carried forward and deducted from the profits of the next and subsequent accounting periods.

EXAMPLE 7.22

In the year ended 31 December 1990 Albert made a profit of £3,000 and in the year ended 31 December 1991 a loss of £2,000. In addition, on 1 December 1991 he bought a machine for which he is entitled to capital allowances of £200.

Ignoring the availability of loss relief, Albert's Schedule D Case I assessments will be:

1991–92 (year ending 31 December 1990):	£3,000 profit
1992–93 (year ending 31 December 1991):	Nil

In the accounting year 1991 Albert has made a loss of £2,000. If he elects for s 380 relief, he can treat his unused capital allowances of £200 as an additional loss to be relieved against his profits of 1991–92 resulting in a revised assessment for 1991–92 on an £800 profit (ie £3,000—[s 380 relief of £2,000 + capital allowances of £200]).

In so far as capital allowances are carried forward they may not be used to increase or create a s 380 or s 381 loss. However, as they may be deducted from profits in preference to the current capital allowances this restriction is usually of reduced importance.   **[7.151]**

2   Partnerships

The above reliefs apply to a member of a partnership in respect of his share of any loss in a year of assessment. Difficulties may arise, however, in deciding which reliefs are available on a deemed discontinuance under TA 1988 s

113, whether or not the partners make an election under TA 1988 s 113 to be taxed on the preceding year basis (for details see Chapter 29). **[7.152]**

3   **Investment in corporate trades** (TA 1988 s 574)

As a general rule, a person who subscribes for shares in a company and later disposes of them at a loss can only claim CGT relief for his loss. In an attempt to stimulate investment in corporate trades, however, s 574 enables the taxpayer to obtain income tax relief for his loss in certain circumstances. Broadly, the section allows an individual who has made a loss on the disposal of shares in a 'qualifying trading company' to deduct the loss from his total income in the year of assessment in which the loss is incurred. This relief is hedged about with restrictions:

(1)   It is available only to an individual who subscribes for shares in a company for money or money's worth, including one who acquires the shares from a subscribing spouse; it is not available to a subsequent purchaser of the shares.

(2)   The disposal giving rise to the loss must be a sale at arm's length for full consideration; or a distribution from the company on a dissolution or a winding up; or a deemed disposal under CGTA 1979 s 22(2) where the shares have become of negligible value.

(3)   The company must satisfy the complex requirements of s 576(4) and (5). Basically, it must be an unquoted trading company, resident in the UK, which does not trade in certain prohibited items such as land or shares and which is not a building society, or a registered industrial and provident society.

If these conditions are satisfied, the allowable loss is calculated on CGT principles and is deducted in priority to relief under TA 1988 ss 380 or 381 from the individual's earned, before unearned, income.

The deduction is given in the year of assessment in which the loss arises and in one following year. The taxpayer must make an election in each case within two years of the end of the relevant year of assessment.

Where the taxpayer has elected for s 574 relief for year 1 (when the loss occurs) any surplus loss can be set off against capital gains in year 1. If he subsequently elects to relieve that surplus loss under s 574 in year 2 instead, his CGT assessment for year 1 must be revised to prevent him from relieving the same loss twice. Any loss still unrelieved after the s 574 election in year 2 can be set off against capital gains (only) of that and subsequent years.

To prevent the taxpayer from obtaining double tax relief on his investment, any income tax relief he received on the acquisition of the shares under the Business Expansion Scheme (TA 1988 s 289; **[4.83]**) must be deducted from the base value of the shares when calculating an allowable loss for CGT and therefore, for s 574 (see *Example 4.21(2)*; **[4.87]**).   **[7.153]**

8 Schedule A—land

'Land, it has been said, is the perfect subject for taxation. This is undoubtedly
true.' (C Clark Taxmanship Hobart Paper (1964).)   [**8.1**]

I SCHEDULE A

1 Ambit

TA 1988 s 15 charges to tax the 'annual profits or gains arising in respect
of rents and certain other receipts from land'. The charge is, therefore, on:
(1) Rents under leases of land in the UK. Rent is not defined, but is given
    its ordinary meaning of a payment by an occupier of land to his landlord
    for the use of the land. 'Lease' includes an agreement for a lease but
    not a mortgage by way of lease. Rents are the most common form of
    receipt under Schedule A.
(2) Rentcharges and other forms of recurrent payment derived from land.
    A rentcharge is an annual sum which can last for ever and is payable
    otherwise than by a tenant to his landlord, eg by one freeholder to
    another.
(3) Most other kinds of income that a person receives by virtue of his
    ownership of land, eg, fees for easements and profits aprendre. (See for
    instance *Lowe v J W Ashmore Ltd* (1971) which held that payments received
    for the sale of turves fell within this provision and contrast *McClure
    v Petre* (1988) in which a 'one-off' payment in return for a licence to
    tip was held to be capital and therefore outside the provision.)
It should be noted that tax is charged under TA 1988 s 15 on annual
profits and gains: ie only on so much of the receipt as is left after making
certain deductions. 'Annual' means that the receipt must be income as opposed
to capital, although in certain circumstances premiums (capital payments
made on the grant of a lease) are deemed to be income (see below). This
crucial distinction between capital and income formed the basis of the
judgment in the *Petre* case where Browne-Wilkinson VC concluded that:

> 'the substance of the present matter is that the payments were received by the
> taxpayer as consideration for a once and for all disposal of a right or advantage
> appurtenant to the land; namely the right or advantage of using it for dumping.
> Immediately before the licence was granted the value of the land itself included
> the value of the right to turn it to advantage by using it for dumping. After
> the licence that right or advantage had gone forever in return for a lump sum.
> True the acreage of the land and the taxpayer's interest remain the same, but
> it was shorn of this valuable advantage. It was in truth a realisation of part
> of the value of the freehold. That strikes me as a disposal of a capital
> nature . . .'   [**8.2**]

Although the ambit of TA 1988 s 15 is very wide, the following types of income are not taxed under Schedule A:

Income expressly excluded from Schedule A (TA 1988 s 15(1) para 3)   This includes yearly interest; profits and gains arising from mines, quarries and certain other concerns such as markets, tolls, bridges and ferries which by TA 1988 s 55 are taxed under Schedule D Case I; mineral rents and royalties (which are taxed half as income under Schedule D and half as capital) and miscellaneous receipts of income from, eg, wayleaves or tolls, in all of which cases the income is received after basic rate tax has been deducted at source by the payer under TA 1988 s 119.   [**8.3**]

Furnished lettings   Where a landlord receives rent from furnished lettings that sum will include a payment for the use of the furniture. The whole rent is charged under Schedule D Case VI (see section 2 below) *unless* the landlord elects within two years from the end of the year of assessment to be assessed under Schedule A *for the portion attributable to the rental of the land*. The use of the furniture continues to be taxed under Schedule D Case (TA 1988 s 18(2)).   [**8.4**]

Receipts from trading on land   Only income which arises from the ownership of land is assessed under Schedule A. Thus, income received from a trade carried out on land is charged under Schedule D Case I as earned income (*Lowe v J W Ashmore Ltd* (1971)). This distinction will not always be obvious; eg, theatre or cinema receipts and profits from an hotel are receipts of a trade, but money received by a car park proprietor is arguably a receipt arising from the ownership of land.

If a landlord lets premises and provides services for the tenants he is *prima facie* assessable under Schedule A (or Schedule D Case VI if the premises are furnished) unless the receipts for services are receipts of a trade and assessable under Schedule D Case I. If the services amount to activities which are more than a mere exploitation of proprietary rights in the land, the receipts are trading receipts. In the case of let premises this is a question of fact and degree; it was thought that services over and above those provided by an ordinary landlord would be trading receipts (see *Fry v Salisbury House Estate Ltd* (1930)). A line of cases in the early 1980s suggests, however, that it will be very difficult for a landlord who provides services to succeed in establishing that they are anything more than a mere exploitation of proprietary rights. In *Webb v Conelee Properties Ltd* (1982), the court held that there was no such trade as 'the letting of properties producing a rent' since that is precisely what is charged to tax under Schedule A and the taxpayer had conducted no other activities which could have amounted to a trade. In *Griffiths v Jackson* (1983), income from letting furnished flats or bed-sitting rooms to students was held to be income from land assessable under Schedule D Case VI and not the earned income of a trade with its attendant benefits of capital allowances, generous loss relief provisions and the capital tax reliefs (see also *Gittos v Barclay* (1982)).

Although the letting of property will rarely, if ever, amount to a trade, the income from 'furnished holiday lettings' in the UK is subject to special treatment and is considered below while, in exceptional cases, lettings may amount to a 'business' for the purpose of IHT business property relief (see Chapter 23).   [**8.5**]

2 **Furnished lettings**

a) *Method of charge*

Profits made from letting furnished accommodation are primarily assessable under Schedule D Case VI (*see Ryall v Hoare* (1923)), although the taxpayer may elect for the profit from letting the accommodation only to be assessed under Schedule A (see above). The assessment under Schedule D Case VI is in respect of 'profits and gains' (TA 1988 s 69) with no express statutory provision allowing deductions from gross income. However, this expression implies a surplus of income after deducting expenses and, therefore, the rental profit is calculated in the same way as for Schedule (see sections 4 and 5 below). In addition, capital allowances are, in practice, available to the landlord for the depreciation and replacement of such non-deductible items as furniture and fittings. This allowance may be given in one of two ways, either by means of the renewals basis or by an allowance for depreciation. Under the renewals basis the entire cost of replacing the asset may be deducted in arriving at the profits from the lettings in the year when that expense is incurred. The alternative method, the allowance for depreciation basis, permits the deduction of (usually) 10% of the gross rent less water rates in each tax year that the premises are let. Once a taxpayer has claimed allowances on one of these two bases, Revenue practice is for that basis then to continue for that taxpayer.   [**8.6**]

EXAMPLE 8.1

Rakeman is the landlord of furnished premises the rent from which (assessed under Schedule D Case VI) is £10,000 in 1991–92. During that tax year, his total expenses comprising the costs of managing, maintaining and repairing the premises (including the decoration of two rooms and water rates of £800) amount to £6,000. His profit is, therefore, £4,000 (£10,000 minus £6,000). In addition, however, Rakeman spent £6,500 on refurbishments (buying new carpets and new kitchen and bathroom units). If Rakeman claims the renewals basis he has further deductible expenditure in 1991–92 of £6,500 leaving him with no Schedule D Case VI taxable income, but instead a loss of £2,500 (£10,000 minus (£6,000 plus £6,500)) which he can set against other Schedule D Case VI income in that tax year or in future tax years. Alternatively, under the depreciation basis, Rakeman can claim a 10% deduction of £920 calculated on gross rent less water rates (ie 10% × (£10,000 minus £800)) which he can treat as a further deductible expense to leave him with a Case VI taxable profit for 1991–92 of £3,080 (£10,000 minus (£6,000 plus £920)). Under this basis, he will continue to claim a 10% deduction in each tax year during which the premises are let.

b) *Basis of assessment (see also* [**9.21**]*)*

Under Schedule D Case VI tax is calculated either on a current or previous year basis on profits received. In practice, the Revenue adopt a current year basis unless the taxpayer requests otherwise. Thus in *Example 8.1*, tax on the 1991–92 profits will be due on 1 January 1992 unless Rakeman elects for the previous year's profits to be taxed on that date in which case the 1991–92 profits will be taxed on 1 January 1993.   [**8.7**]

c) *Schedule D Case VI or Schedule A?*

Whether a landlord should choose to be assessed under Schedule D Case VI or elect for Schedule A will largely depend upon his other income and losses and which Schedule offers him the greater allowable expenditure. Under Schedule D Case VI, losses can be offset against other Case VI profits for the same year or carried forward to set against profits in future years. Likewise, under Schedule A, losses can be offset against Schedule A profits of the same year, but there are restrictions on carrying forward Schedule A losses against profits of future years and against profits on the lettings of other property (see below). In practice, deductions for the landlord under Schedule A and Schedule D Case VI are similar, although, as there are no specific statutory rules governing deductible expenditure for Case VI the landlord has greater freedom in arguing for the deductibility of specific items. When several furnished properties are let by the same landlord it is likely that he will want them all to be assessed under the same Schedule whether that be Schedule A or Schedule D Case VI.   **[8.8]**

3 Furnished holiday lettings

TA 1988 ss 503–504 provide for income from furnished holiday lettings in the UK to be treated as trading income and for the CGT business reliefs to be available for such properties. The provisions apply to lettings by individuals and by companies.   **[8.9]**

Definition   The accommodation must be available for letting to the public commercially as furnished holiday accommodation for at least 140 days in the tax year and must be actually let for at least 70 days. These periods need not be continuous and accordingly both winter and summer holiday accommodation may qualify. To ensure a 'genuine' holiday letting, it must not 'normally' (undefined) be let to the same person continuously in any seven months of the year (but including the 70 day period above) for more than 31 days. In the remaining five months of the tax year, therefore, the landlord may do what he wishes with the property, eg let it continuously; keep it empty; go into occupation himself. The above requirements will however normally exclude student accommodation. The letting of caravans is included, in so far as it is not taxed as a trade under Schedule D Case I, but not the letting of sites (taxed under Schedule A) nor residential caravans for long term occupation (IR Press Release 1984 STI 386).

The term 'holiday' accommodation is undefined; presumably, if the above conditions are satisfied, it will be deemed to be a holiday letting (see eg *Gittos v Barclay* (1982) where these requirements are satisfied). Letting means occupation by a person other than the landlord and includes granting a licence to occupy.

Whether the accommodation qualifies as a holiday let in any tax year is judged on the facts of that year (for company landlords, the financial year). However, where the letting begins in a tax year (eg on 1 August 1991), it may qualify as a holiday let for that year if it satisfies the above requirements within the following 12 months (ie between 1 August 1991 and 31 July 1992). Likewise, a letting which ends in a tax year, must satisfy the necessary conditions during the previous 12 months.   **[8.10]**

Tax treatment   The income profits for the whole year will be assessed under Schedule D Case VI, but treated as trading profits for the purposes specified in TA 1988 s 503(1) and, therefore, receive most of the benefits of an assessment under Schedule D Case I. Thus, the income is earned income and the deductible expenses, loss relief and capital allowance rules of Case I apply. However, the basis of assessment remains Case VI so that profits are assessed on income received not receivable in the current year (see below) and neither the preceding year basis nor the opening and closing year rules of Case I apply. The tax is, however, payable in two equal instalments in January and July as under Case I.

For CGT purposes the letting is treated as a trade in any year when it satisfies the above conditions or would do so but for the fact that the property is under construction or repair. Thus, roll-over (replacement of business assets) relief (CGTA 1979 s 115); hold-over relief on a gift of business assets (CGTA 1979 s 126); and retirement relief (FA 1985 s 69) may be available on a disposal (see generally Chapter 16). However, a landlord who claims roll-over relief and occupies the property himself may not claim the main residence exemption against the entire gain on a subsequent disposal. In such a case the rolled-over gain is chargeable and the exemption applies only to any remaining gain. No special relief is given from IHT although it is thought that business property relief will be available (see [**23.45**]).

EXAMPLE 8.2

'Seaview' is purchased for £40,000 in 1985 and let as furnished holiday accommodation until 1991. It is then sold for £60,000 and the proceeds used in the purchase of 'Belvedere' for £85,000 which is also let. In 1993 the landlord takes possession and lives there until 1997 when he sells it for £145,000.

In 1991, the gain on 'Seaview' is rolled over into the purchase of 'Belvedere' giving it a base cost for CGT of £65,000. On the sale of 'Belvedere' in 1997 the gain is £80,000 of which £20,000 (rolled over from 'Seaview') is chargeable. The remaining gain is apportioned between the period of occupation which is exempt (ie 4/6 = £40,000) and the let period (ie 2/6 = £20,000) which is chargeable, unless eliminated under FA 1980 s 80 (see [**16.69**]).

If, instead, 'Belvedere' is sold in 1993 at the end of the season for £115,000, the gain of £50,000 might be eliminated by any retirement relief available to the landlord (he must show that the disposal is of a business or part of a business).

Where the same landlord lets several 'qualifying' properties, they are taxed as one trade. Should one or more properties qualify as furnished holiday lettings in the tax year and others not, because they fail to satisfy the 70 day requirement, the landlord can claim, within two years of the end of the relevant tax year, for the days of letting to be averaged between all or any of the properties thereby enabling all the properties to qualify. Thus, if property A is let in 1991–92 for 90 days and properties B and C for 50 days each respectively, A and B or A and C can be averaged so that two properties qualify; there are insufficient letting days for all three to qualify. [**8.11**]

4 Basis of assessment and collection of tax

Tax is charged under Schedule A on the profits of the current year of assessment and is due on or before 1 January of the tax year. As a result, the Revenue raise a provisional assessment on the taxpayer based on the previous year's rent which is later corrected when the true rent for the year is known. A landlord is, therefore, taxed on rent owing as well as rent received. He can, however, claim relief for any rent that he never receives so long as either he took reasonable steps to recover that rent or deliberately waived it to avoid hardship to a tenant (TA 1988 s 41).

Tax should be paid by the landlord. If –the fails to pay, it may be collected from any tenant in occupation, who can reimburse himself by deduction from subsequent payments of rent to the landlord. If the tenant is left out of pocket he can reclaim that sum from the Revenue (TA 1988 s 23). Alternatively, unpaid tax can be collected from any agent of the person in default who has received rent or receipts from any land on behalf of that person (TA 1988 s 23(7)). If a tenant pays rent direct to a non-UK resident landlord, he must deduct basic rate income tax from the rent and account for it to the Revenue (TA 1988 s 43). Similarly, where part of any premium paid to a non-resident landlord is treated as income in the landlord's hands (see below), the tenant must deduct basic rate income tax from that part and account for it to the Revenue.

When a UK letting agent receives rent on behalf of a non-resident he is chargeable thereon under TMA 1970 s 78. In such a case, the non-resident landlord is assessed and charged to income tax in the name of his agent in the same manner as the non-resident would have been taxed had he been UK resident. Accordingly, the agent has to submit appropriate tax returns and should deduct from the rent which he pays the appropriate amount of tax (if any, since it may be that the deductions available to the landlord—such as relief for the payment of interest—result in a nil tax assessment). Crucially liability is not limited (as above when a tenant pays directly to his non-resident landlord) to tax at the basic rate: rather it is the amount which would have been payable had the landlord been UK resident. Despite a statutory right of indemnity under TMA 1970 s 83(1) and the right to retain sufficient funds out of the rent to cover this liability, these provisions may pose problems for the UK agent (see further, Taxation 15 January 1988).   [**8.12**]

5   Deductions from rent

Income tax under Schedule A is charged on receipts less certain deductions. Allowable expenditure can only be deducted when it has been paid; the mere incurring of the liability is insufficient. The major deductions available against rental income, under TA 1988 s 25, are as follows: [**8.13**]

Payments in respect of maintenance, repairs, insurance or management   Maintenance and repairs must be distinguished from improvements which are capital expenditure and, therefore, not deductible from rent, except where the improvement is an inherent part of the maintenance, for example, the cost of replacing a rotten window with a new one is deductible despite involving an element of improvement; or where the improvement is made to pre-empt the need for certain future maintenance, for example, on replacing a wall that is partly damaged by dry rot, part of the total cost of rebuilding that relates to the treatment of dry rot is deductible. Otherwise, repairs are deductible only if they would be deductible under Schedule D Case I. Thus the cost of repairs is, for instance, usually disallowed (and treated as a capital expense) where the disrepair arose before the period of the relevant lease (see *Law Shipping Co Ltd v IRC* (1924) and *Odeon Associated Theatres Ltd v Jones* (1972) [**6.117**]). A landlord must, therefore, have regard to the state of repair of premises when bought for letting. (Note that the cost of making good prior dilapidations may be deductible where property passes between spouses on death: ESC A21.)

Insurance expenses, to be deductible, must relate to the cost of insuring the building and not its contents (unless the premises are furnished when the latter is deductible from such part of the total rent that relates to the letting of the furniture assessed under Schedule D Case VI (see 2 above)).

Management expenses include the expenses of managing the property (eg, advertising for tenants and collecting rent but not the cost of travelling to and from the property). For property companies the expenses of managing the land are deductible in arriving at Schedule A profits whereas the cost of managing the company is subject to the special corporation tax rules for management expenses (Chapter 28). **[8.14]**

Services The cost of providing services, where payment for the services is included in the rent, is deductible (TA 1988 s 25(2)(b)). Strictly, the services must be provided under the lease, but in practice, the Revenue allow a landlord to deduct all his commercial expenses of a revenue nature in providing services or amenities for tenants: eg the provision of central heating and the cleaning and lighting of the common parts. **[8.15]**

Rates Payments for water rates by the landlord are deductible expenses. **[8.16]**

Superior rent Payments of rent to a superior landlord, and rentcharges for which the landlord is responsible, are deductible. **[8.17]**

Interest relief Interest on a loan to purchase or improve the property is deductible from rent under TA 1988 s 355(1)(b) provided that the property is let at a commercial rent for at least 26 out of the 52 weeks in the tax year; or when the property is not let, it is available for letting, under repair or occupied as the only or main residence of the borrower, his divorced or separated spouse or a dependent relative.

Provided that these conditions are all satisfied, interest on a loan of any amount is deductible; there is no £30,000 ceiling as for a qualifying loan in connection with a private residence. Further, the interest is deductible from rent that the landlord receives from any property although it may not be deducted against any other income of the landlord. Surplus interest can be carried forward and deducted from rent in future years so long as the above conditions remain satisfied in those years. **[8.18]**

Capital allowances Capital allowances are available to the Schedule A taxpayer for expenditure on machinery and plant used in the management, repair, or maintenance of a building (TA 1988 s 32(1)) provided that he claims the allowances in accordance with s 32(5). The Schedule A taxpayer is then treated as if he were carrying on the trade of letting plant and machinery (CAA 1990 ss 61(1), 28) and must agree with the Revenue what proportion of the rent is attributable to the letting against which the allowances may be used (see *Example 8.3* below). Allowances may not be claimed however when the building is let as a dwelling house (CAA 1990 s 61(2)). They will therefore be available when the plant and machinery is provided for the use of more than one dwelling unit as, for example, in a block of flats. **[8.19]**

EXAMPLE 8.3

Minster owns a house converted into three self-contained flats each of which he has let to a tenant as from 1 January 1991 at an annual rent of £15,000 payable monthly in advance on the first day of each month. Minster has agreed with the Revenue that 25% of the total rent of £15,000 (ie £3,750) is attributable to the notional trade of letting plant and machinery which he provides for the use of all three flats. He incurs the following expenses:

				£
15 December	1990	Advertising for tenants		500
10 April	1991	Repair to burst pipe		110
11 April	1991	Water rates on house		800
9 May	1991	Installation of central heating		4,000
12 July	1991	Lighting of common parts		100
14 August	1991	Cleaning of common parts		600

His 1991–92 Schedule A assessment will be:
Rent receivable   £15,000
(May 1991–April 1992 inclusive):
apportioned for capital allowances as to:

	(a) *The building*	(b) *Plant etc.*
	£	£
	11,250(¾)	3,750(¼)

Less
(a) Expenses relating to the building:

	£	
Repairs	110	
Water rates	800	
Lighting	100	
Cleaning	600	1,610

(b) Capital allowances relating to the
letting of plant and machinery ie:
Central heating:
WDA at 25% × £4,000   1,000

Taxable profit for Schedule A: £9,640   +   £2,750 = £12,390

Notes:
(1) April 1991 rent is not included because it is receivable on 1 April 1991, ie in the tax year 1990–91.
(2) Tax under Schedule A for the tax year 1991–92 will be based on a provisional assessment taken from the previous tax year's figures (ie 1990–91) and will be due on 1 January 1992. When the figures for the year are known by Minster he will correct this assessment.
(3) Expenditure on central heating is an improvement relating to more than one dwelling unit for which capital allowances are, therefore, available against one quarter of the total rent.

6   **Deductions from other receipts** (TA 1988 s 28)
The expense rules in TA 1988 s 28 are more generous than those for rent in that they allow the taxpayer to deduct any expense of an income nature which is directly connected with the source of the income.   **[8.20]**

EXAMPLE 8.4

(1)   A owns a piece of land which he acquired in order to preserve the amenities of his home. The land is subject to a rentcharge of £2 pa. He derives no income from it. He contracts with B, in return for an annual payment of £5 pa, to allow B a right of way across the land, and to keep the path clear. It costs him £3 pa to keep the path clear. The £3 is an allowable

expense. The rentcharge is not allowable, because it is not an expense of the transaction under which B has a right of way. The income chargeable under Schedule A will, therefore, be £5 — £3 = £2.

(2)   C owns a field which is subject to a rentcharge of £10 pa. He uses it exclusively for profit by charging holiday-makers for the right to put tents there for short periods. The rentcharge is allowable as an expense of these transactions.

(From the Inland Revenue booklet 'Notes on the taxation of income from real property': IR 27 (1980)—now discontinued.)

7   Rules for excess expenditure; loss relief (TA 1988 s 25(3)–(9))

Schedule A losses can only be set off against Schedule A income and there is no carry-back of losses against Schedule A profits of a previous year. The extent to which Schedule A losses can be carried forward or set against profits on other premises depends upon the type of lease involved.

A *lease at a full rent* is one where the rent, on average, is sufficient to cover the landlord's expenses under the lease but need not be a full commercial rent.

A *tenant's repairing lease* is one under which the tenant is responsible for maintaining or repairing the whole or substantially the whole of the premises. Such a lease may or may not be at a full rent.

A lease which is not a tenant's repairing lease is one where the landlord is obliged to do some or all of the repairs (landlord's repairing lease). This lease also may or may not be at a full rent.

The theory underlying the following rules seems to be that a lease at a full rent is not acquired as a loss-making asset so that the loss relieving provisions are relatively generous. By contrast, a lease which is not at a full rent qualifies for a much restricted relief.

Carry-forward of losses   Losses arising under any kind of lease may always be carried forward and set off against rents from the same lease of the same premises in a subsequent year (TA 1988 s 25(3)).

Losses arising from a previous lease of the premises or from a 'void period' (a period when the property was not let) can be carried forward against rent from the same premises under a subsequent lease, provided that both leases are at a full rent; that the property was available for letting during any void period; and was not owner-occupied. Expenses in this case include making good any dilapidations incurred during a previous lease or void period. **[8.21]**

EXAMPLE 8.5

Property is let subject to a lease at a full rent running from 1983–1993 (lease 1). Expenses are incurred in repairing the premises in 1992–93 which are not fully relieved against the rent of that year. The property is empty from 1993 to 1995 whilst the landlord looks for suitable tenants. During this time he incurs expenditure in insuring and repairing the property. In 1995 he lets it (lease 2) under a tenant's repairing lease at a full rent.

Leases 1 and 2 are both leases at a full rent albeit lease 2 is a tenant's repairing lease. Accordingly, the unrelieved expenses of lease 1 in 1992–93 and of the void period can be carried forward and set against the first available rent received from lease 2 without time limit.

Pooling of losses (TA 1988 s 25(7))   If the same landlord has granted leases of different premises, excess expenditure incurred in one lease can be set against profits arising from a lease on another property in the same tax year, provided that both leases are at a full rent and that the lease showing the profit is not a tenant's repairing lease.   [**8.22**]

8   **The taxation of premiums under Schedule A** (TA 1988 ss 34–39)

A premium is a capital sum paid by a tenant to a landlord in connection with the grant of a lease. To understand the taxation of premiums, it should be noted that Schedule A was introduced before CGT so that a landlord could have avoided paying any tax by extracting a capital sum from the tenant instead of rent. Accordingly, certain premiums are deemed to be income and so chargeable to income tax. In so far as a premium is not chargeable as income it may be subject to CGT. As CGT is now charged at income tax rates, the importance of the distinction between the taxes has been reduced although not wholly removed in this area. For instance, when a landlord is entitled to substantial interest relief or has incurred deductible expenditure, he may desire any premium to be taxed as rent. Formerly, a system of top slicing afforded some relief against a higher rate income tax charge on these premiums. With the introduction of a single higher rate (40%), however, this relief was withdrawn from 6 April 1988.   [**8.23**]

a)   *The charge* (TA 1988 s 34)

If a lease is granted for a period not exceeding 50 years and the consideration includes a premium, a proportion of that premium is treated as additional rent taxable under Schedule A. This proportion is the amount that is left after deducting 2% of the premium for each complete year of the lease other than the first. The effect of the 2% discount is that the amount of premium charged to income tax falls with the length of the lease. For a one year lease all the premium is taxed and for a 50 year lease 2%.

EXAMPLE 8.6

Lease 16 years; premium £3,000.

Discount 2% of £3,000 over 15 years = £3,000 $\times \frac{2}{100}$ $\times$ 15 = £900

Chargeble slice: £3,000 — £900 = £2,100

The grant of a sub-lease of 50 years or less will, as a general rule, be taxed in the same way as the grant of a head lease. If, however, a premium on the grant of the head lease was taxed under Schedule A, this is taken into account when taxing any premium on the grant of the sub-lease (TA 1988 s 37).   [**8.24**]

b)   *Anti-avoidance provisions*

There are elaborate provisions designed to prevent the charge to income tax on premiums from being circumvented. First, a landlord cannot avoid the TA 1988 s 34 charge by disguising the length of the lease. If its length can be extended by an option to renew or shortened by an option to surrender or to terminate, those options will be taken into account only insofar as they are likely to be exercised (TA 1988 s 38).

EXAMPLE 8.7

L grants a lease to T for 60 years at a premium of £20,000 and a rent of £1,000 pa for the first ten years and thereafter at an annual rent of ten times the then market rent. T has an option to surrender the lease after ten years. For the purposes of Schedule A this is treated as a ten year lease since the tenant is likely to exercise the option to surrender in view of the penal increase in the rent after ten years.

Secondly, where a landlord, instead of taking a premium on the grant of a lease for 50 years or less, requires the tenant to make improvements to the premises, the amount by which the value of the landlord's reversion is increased as a result of those improvements is treated as a premium (TA 1988 s 34(2)). This provision does not, however, apply if the tenant is required to make improvements to another property of the landlord; if the obligation is not imposed by the lease; or if the expenditure would have been a deductible expense of the landlord.

EXAMPLE 8.8

Property is let from 1 June 1991, for 7 years. Under the terms of the lease the tenant is required to carry out certain structural alterations as a result of which the value of the landlord's interest in the premises is increased by £2,000.

Increase:	£2,000
Less discount: $\frac{2}{100} \times £2,000 \times 6$:	£240
Included in 1991–92 Schedule A profits:	£1,760

Thirdly, TA 1988 s 34(4) and (5) charge 'delayed premiums' as income. If a premium becomes payable at some date during the currency of the lease or the tenant has to pay a sum for the waiver or variation of any terms of the lease, the sum is treated as a premium and in both cases the premium is taxed in the year of receipt as a premium for the then unexpired period of the lease. If a tenant has to pay a sum for the surrender of a lease it is taxed as a premium on a lease running from the date of commencement to the date of surrender.

Fourthly, the assignment of a lease, which has been granted at an undervalue is charged under TA 1988 s 35. The charge under s 34 could be circumvented by a landlord granting a lease to, say, his spouse or to a company which he owns. No premium would be charged on the grant but the lease could then be assigned to the intended tenant and a premium taken. Section 34 only applies to a premium paid on the grant of a lease not on its assignment. However, s 35 provides that, when a lease is granted for less than its market premium, tax is charged under Schedule D Case VI on assignors of the lease up to the amount of premium foregone by the landlord and to the extent that such assignors have made a profit on that assignment.

EXAMPLE 8.9

A grants B a 21 year lease at a premium of £2,000 although he could have charged £3,000. Therefore, the 'amount foregone' is £1,000. A is chargeable under Schedule A on the premium that he actually receives.

Two years later B assigns the lease to C charging a premium of £2,800. B receives £800 more than he paid; that is within the 'amount foregone'.

B is, therefore, chargeable under Schedule D Case VI on:

$$£800 - \left(\frac{2}{100} \times 20 \times £800\right) = £480$$

Notice that the 'amount foregone' still outstanding is £200 and that the period of the lease remains at the original length (viz 21 years) for the purpose of discounting. Two years later C assigns the lease to D charging a premium of £3,200. He has received £400 more than he paid but only £200 of that is caught under TA 1988 s 35 since that exhausts the 'amount foregone' by A. C is chargeable, therefore, under Schedule D Case VI on:

$$£200 - \left(\frac{2}{100} \times 20 \times £200\right) = £120$$

An assignee should, therefore, ensure (so far as possible) that the lease was not granted at an undervalue, and if necessary should take advantage of the clearance procedure under TA 1988 s 35(3).

The final anti-avoidance provision prevents the grant of a lease from being disguised as a sale (TA 1988 s 36(1)). If D sells land (freehold or leasehold) to E with a right to have the property reconveyed to him in the future, any difference between the price paid by E and the reconveyance price payable by D is treated as a premium on a lease for the period between the sale and the reconveyance and is taxed under Schedule D Case VI.

TA 1988 s 36(3) extends TA 1988 s 36(1) so that if D sells land to E with a right for him (or a person connected with him) to take a leaseback of the property in the future, any difference between the price paid by E and the aggregate of the premium (if any) payable on the grant of a lease by E, together with the value of the reversion in E's hands, is treated as a premium on a lease for the period between the sale and leaseback and is taxed under Schedule D Case VI. So as not to prejudice a commercial sale and leaseback, this provision does not apply where the leaseback is within one month of the sale.   [**8.25**]

EXAMPLE 8.10

D sells land to E for £40,000 with a right to take a 20 year lease of the property after 11 years for a premium of £8,000. The value of E's reversionary interest subject to the lease is £2,000. There is a deemed premium under TA 1988 s 36(3) of £30,000 (£40,000 — £8,000 + £2,000) on a lease of 11 years. D is chargeable under Schedule D Case VI on:

$$£30,000 - \left(\frac{2}{100} \times £30,000 \times 20\right) = £24,000$$

c) Premium payable in instalments

If the premium is payable in instalments, tax is charged on the total of the instalments in the tax year when the first instalment is payable. Exceptionally the tax may be paid by instalments over the shorter of the period of the instalments of the premium and eight years if the taxpayer can satisfy the Revenue that to pay the tax in one lump sum would cause him 'undue hardship' (undue hardship is not defined; TA 1988 s 34(8)). This claim must be made within the tax year following the one when the first instalment of the premium became payable.   [**8.26**]

d) *Relief for traders paying a premium on trading premises* (TA 1988 s 87)

Rent is an allowable deduction from the trading income of a trader (TA 1988 s 74). If a trader is granted a lease of business premises for 50 years or less at a premium, he can treat a portion of the premium as an annual rent and deduct it from his trading income. This portion is the amount of the premium that is charged to income tax in the landlord's hands under Schedule A divided by the unexpired term of the lease. The rest of the premium is a capital expense.

A premium paid by a trader who takes an assignment of a lease is not allowable as a deduction from trading income unless the premium is caught by s 35. **[8.27]–[8.40]**

EXAMPLE 8.11

L grants T a lease of business premises for ten years at an annual rent of £100 and a premium of £10,000.

L is chargeable under Schedule A on £8,200 of the premium (see TA 1988 s 34). The yearly equivalent of this sum, £820 (£8,200 ÷ 10), can be treated by T as additional rent so that each year he can deduct rent of £920 (£820 + £100) from his trading receipts.

II   TA 1988 s 776 AND THE DEVELOPMENT OF LAND

1   **Transactions in land and s 776**

The section was formerly headed 'Artificial Transactions in Land' and s 776(1) states that it was enacted to prevent the avoidance of tax by persons concerned with land or its development. It seems clear, however, that the relevant transaction need not be *artificial* and, if *Page v Lowther* (see 8 below) is correct, a tax avoidance motive is not an essential pre-condition for liability. Capital sums falling within the terms of the section are brought within the income tax charge. **[8.41]**

2   **Trading under Schedule D Case 1**

Section 776 will not apply if the taxpayer engages in a trading transaction subject to an income tax charge under Schedule D Case I (see Chapter 6). In such cases land will be trading stock and all sums derived therefore will be subject to income tax. The definition of a trade has recently been restrictively interpreted in *Marson v Morton* (1986) in which the judge stated that:

'the mere fact that land is not income producing should not be decisive or even virtually decisive on the question whether it was bought as an investment' (see further **[6.23]**).

However, land originally acquired for a non-trading purpose (eg investment) may subsequently be appropriated to trading stock. At this point a capital gains tax charge may arise under CGTA 1979 s 122 although this can be avoided by the election to transfer the land at no-gain no-loss (see **[14.106]**). Whether such appropriation occurs will depend on the facts of each case. In *Taylor v Good* (1974), discussed at **[6.23]**, the house in question did not become trading stock merely because the taxpayer had applied for planning permission before the sale:

'If you find a trade in the purchase and sale of land, it may not be difficult to find that properties originally owned (for example) by inheritance, or bought for investment only, have been brought into the stock in trade of that trade. But where, as here, there is no question at all of absorption into a trade of dealing in land or lands previously acquired with no thought of dealing, there is no ground at all for holding that activities such as those in the present case, designed only to enhance the value of the land in the market, are to be taken as pointing to, still less as establishing, an adventure in the nature of trade.' (Russell LJ)

By contrast, in *Pilkington v Randall* (1966) land was held in a will trust for a brother and sister absolutely. It was sold at different times and roads and drains were constructed prior to the sales. Furthermore, the brother bought parcels of the land from his sister. He was held to be trading. At first instance, Cross J stated:

'I do not think that one can lay down hard and fast rules, such as that the construction of roads and sewers and the installation of services can never be enough to make the case one of embarking upon a trade. One has to look at the whole picture and say whether the amount of money spent on the development before sale and the objects for which and the circumstances in which the money was spent are such as to make it reasonable to say that what was inherited has changed its character and become part of the raw material or stock in trade of a business.'

In the Court of Appeal, Danckwerts LJ likewise stated that there was no general proposition of law to the effect that whenever a property owner develops his land by making roads and laying sewers and selling plots he can never be carrying on a trade:

'This would be opening the door very wide to modern property developers. I think the highest it can be put is that usually in such circumstances the property owner is not carrying on a trade, but whether in the particular case he is or is not doing so must depend on the facts of the particular case. It is essentially a question of fact and degree.'

It is apparent from the foregoing cases that how the land was originally acquired by the taxpayer is an important factor in determining whether he is trading. If by *inheritance* or *gift* the Revenue will have to show that it has at some point been appropriated to trading stock. On the other hand, if acquired by purchase the taxpayer's motive at that time will be relevant. If it is clear that it was acquired as an investment, again the burden will be on the Revenue to show that at a subsequent stage it was appropriated to trading stock. Furthermore, if land was originally acquired as an investment, the mere act of obtaining planning permission prior to a sale will not by itself result in an appropriation of the land to trading stock. Generally the taxpayer is entitled to get the best possible price for the land (*Taylor v Good*, above).

Care needs to be exercised if, as a prelude to sale to a developer, the taxpayer decides to acquire adjacent parcels of land. Such extra parcels will have been acquired purely for resale and there is a risk therefore that the taxpayer will be treated as a trader (and not just in relation to those portions but also in relation to the previously owned land). It is thought that the purchase of small areas of land will not create problems: the taxpayer will be seen as merely taking steps to obtain the best possible price for his existing land as in *Taylor v Good*. *Pilkington v Randall* may be distinguished in that the amount of land acquired was large and the taxpayer also undertook various preparatory works. Having said this, it will undoubtedly be advisable, whenever practicable, to arrange for the developer to acquire any extra land that will be needed for the development. **[8.42]**

3   The effect of falling within s 776

The section converts a gain which would otherwise be of a capital nature (and therefore in the case of an individual subject to CGT) into an income profit subject to tax under Schedule D Case VI for the chargeable period in which that gain is realised (s 776(3)). The gain is to be computed by such method as is 'just and reasonable' in all the circumstances (s 776(6)) so that CGT computational rules will not necessarily apply.

The effect of taxing the gain as income is that for an *individual* the maximum rate of charge is 40%. In the case of a *company* the rate of tax is either 35% or 25%: accordingly it may be advantageous to shelter the gain in a company. If the gain is realised by *trustees*, income tax will be charged at basic rate (25%). If there is an interest in possession, as a matter of trust law the capital sum will not belong to the life tenant and it is not thought that there is any provision in the Taxes Act which would enable the s 776 income to be taxed as that of the beneficiary. In general, therefore, gains realised through the medium of a trust will escape income tax at the top rate of 40% (subject to an exception where the trust income is deemed under the tax legislation to be that of the settlor: see further Chapter 11)..There remains a danger that trusts falling within TA 1988 s 686 will be subject to the additional rate charge and hence taxed at 35%. That section applies in two situations. First, to 'income which is to be accumulated'. These words are not thought appropriate to catch a sum which remains, for trust purposes, capital. Secondly, the section applies to income 'which is payable at the discretion of the trustees' and it is arguable that a sum treated as income by s 776 will fall within these words if the trustees of a settlement have a power to pay or advance capital to beneficiaries. Accordingly, there is a danger of an income tax charge in such cases at the 35% rate on s 776 gains. As against this construction of s 686, it is arguable that the word 'income' is used throughout the provision in a purely trust sense and will not apply to capital sums deemed to be income under the tax legislation. Furthermore, the Revenue are not known to have taken the point that payments caught by s 776 may fall within the provisions of s 686.

Because the gain is taxed as income under Schedule D Case VI it is unearned income and although it may be reduced by Case VI losses it cannot be reduced by pension contributions nor by Case I losses. **[8.43]**

4   When does s 776 apply?

The following requirements must all be satisfied:

Requirement I—

Either
(a) the land or property deriving its value from land is acquired with the sole or main object of realising a gain from disposing of the land etc (s 776(2)(a)); *or*
(b) land is held as trading stock (s 776(2)(b)); *or*
(c) the land held is developed with the sole or main object of realising a gain from disposing of the land when developed (s 776(21)(c)).

Requirement II—

A gain of a *capital* nature is obtained.

Requirement III—

The gain is obtained from a *disposal of the land.*

Requirement IV—

That gain must be obtained *either*
(a) by the person who acquired, held or developed the land or any connected person(s); *or*
(b) as a result of a scheme or arrangement which has allowed a gain to be realised by an indirect method by any person who is a party to or concerned in the arrangements or the scheme.   **[8.44]**

5   Comments on Requirement I

If land is held as trading stock or obtained with the main purpose of selling at a profit, that profit will be subject to tax under Case I in the majority of cases (see 2 above). However, a disposal of land is widened in s 776(4) to include transactions, arrangements, and schemes concerning the land or property deriving its value from the land as a result of which there is a disposal of the land or control over the land. Hence, it is likely that s 776(2)(a) will apply in cases where the land (or more likely property deriving its value from the land) is acquired with the intent of transferring control over the land by some indirect means.

An owner-occupier who decides to develop his land will naturally fall within s 776(2)(c). It is provided in s 776(7) that the relevant gain is that arising after the intention to develop is formed. Apart from the difficulties of determining when this occurs, the formation of this intention may result in the land becoming trading stock within 2 above with the result that any charge will arise under Case I (see also s 777(11)). The owner-occupier who sells his land for development by a third party will not normally fall within this provision unless he stipulates for some future payment linked to the value of the land after it has been developed (see 8, below).   **[8.45]**

6   Comments on Requirement II

As the gain must be of a capital nature, the section does not catch trading gains nor other gains of an income nature. Hence, if land is let (a disposal) there will be no charge under s 776 if rent only (assessable under Schedule A) is payable. Thus s 777(13) provides that a 'capital amount' means a sum which (apart from these provisions) does not fall to be included in the calculation of a person's income for the purposes of the Taxes Acts. A trading gain made by an overseas trust or company and not subject to UK tax under the Taxes Acts may, therefore, amount to a gain of a capital nature for these purposes (see *Yuill v Wilson*, 10, below).   **[8.46]**

7   Comments on Requirement III

For a charge under s 776 to arise there must be a disposal of land. 'Disposal' is not defined but it is clear that it may include the disposal of shares in a land company and an interest in a company, partnership, or trust which is wound up.

Land is also deemed to be disposed of if, as a result of arrangements and schemes falling within s 776(4), there is an effective' disposal of the land itself or control over the land. It is a moot point whether the letting of land at a rack rent is a disposal. Given that the value of the property in the hands of the taxpayer is unchanged, it may be argued that such a lease does not involve any disposal of land. As against that view, such a letting does confer rights in land on the tenant.

For tax to be imposed it is also necessary for a gain to be *realised*. Under s 777(13) this will only occur when a person can effectively enjoy or dispose of money or monies worth. In the case of the right to future sums the question is, therefore, whether such sums can be valued and treated as part of the disposal proceeds (see *Yuill v Wilson* (1980)). A further disposal for the purposes of s 776 will occur when sums become quantifiable (see *Yuill v Fletcher* (1984)).   **[8.47]**

8   **Comments on Requirement IV**

Obviously the person who holds or develops the land may be caught as may a person connected with him (for connected person see TA 1988 s 839). In addition, a gain realised through a scheme or arrangement by an indirect method, or as a result of a series of transactions, will lead to a s 776 charge on any person concerned in that scheme or arrangement. In such cases, tax is imposed to the extent of the gain realised by the particular individual as can be seen by the case of *Winterton v Edwards* (1980). In that case L was the prime mover in a complicated tax avoidance scheme and owned all the shares in the relevant property company except for two small holdings owned by W and B. He acquired two sites outside the company for development and when W and B protested at this he arranged to give them a share in any sale proceeds from the land. Section 776 assessments on W and B were upheld because, although they were not parties to L's various transactions, they were *concerned in* the transactions as a result of their small interests in the proceeds of sale. Hence, if one person intends to realise a gain within s 776 (in this case both acquiring and developing land with the intention of realising a gain on its disposal) other persons may then be caught, even though they lack that intention, if they participate in the arrangement (see also *Page v Lowther*, below).

The phrase 'scheme or arrangement' is wide enough to catch a vendor or land owner who retains a share of the ultimate development profits. In *Page v Lowther* (1983), trustees owned four houses forming a site suitable for redevelopment. They granted a 99-year lease to the developers who in turn granted underleases of new dwellings when constructed at premiums payable partly to the trustees and partly to the developers. In all, the trustees received premiums totalling £1.2 million. On these facts, the Court of Appeal held that the expression 'an arrangement or scheme' had no sinister overtones so that the grant of the lease by the trustees to the developers was such an arrangement. Further, the grant of the under-lease was a disposal (albeit not by the trustees) in return for a capital sum so that the trustees were held liable on their share under s 776. The Court of Appeal did not accept that the duty of the trustees to obtain the best possible price afforded any defence to them. The case is authority for the proposition that the section is not limited to artificial transactions nor need tax avoidance be a proven motive on the part of the taxpayer (see 1, above). For the rate of tax charged on the trustees see 3 above (it is not entirely clear, given these rates, why the case was pursued by the Revenue!).   **[8.48]**

9   Shares in landholding companies

There is a disposal of land if a controlling interest over it is disposed of (s 776(4)). Hence the disposal of a controlling shareholding in a land owning company is treated as a disposal of the land.

The further requirement, that a gain of a capital nature must be obtained from the disposal by a person owning that land *or by any connected person* may be satisfied when shares in a land owning company are sold if the vendor controls that company. In such a case he will then be a connected person (s 839(6)). If two or more shareholders act together their interests may be aggregated in order to determine whether they have control for these purposes: the agreement of a number of minority shareholders to sell their shares may amount to an 'arrangement' under s 776(4).

There is an exemption from charge under s 776(10) when land is held as trading stock by a company and there is a disposal of the shares in that company *provided* that the land is subsequently disposed of by the company in the normal course of its trade in order to ensure that all opportunity of profit in respect of that land arises to the company. To take advantage of this exemption it is normal when selling a property dealing company to obtain from the purchaser a warranty that the trading stock (ie the land) will be sold in the normal course of the trade. However, it is obviously difficult to draft such warranties and the vendor remains very much in the hands of the purchaser. It should also be noted that this exemption does not furnish any defence when a scheme or arrangement has been entered into.   **[8.49]**

10   Providing an opportunity

A gain may be obtained for another person (eg under s 776(7) trusts are treated as distinct entities from the beneficiaries). In general, a gain is obtained in such circumstances if the opportunity of making that gain is transmitted by premature sale or otherwise (s 776(5)): eg if B allows value to pass out of his land into A's land whereupon A makes a gain falling within the section, all or part of that gain may be attributed to B (s 776(8)). In such cases B is given a right of recovery against A for the tax that he suffers (under s 777(8)(a)) although this may prove to be worthless if A is a non-resident.

The opportunity of making a gain is not presumably transmitted merely because land is sold even when it is possible that a gain will be made in the future. As the following case illustrates, however, it is no defence to claim under this section that the land was transferred for full consideration.

In *Yuill v Wilson* (1980), Mr Yuill, who controlled various UK companies, arranged for land to be sold to Guernsey companies who thereupon obtained planning consent for redevelopment and sold the land back to a Yuill UK company at a substantial profit. This profit constituted a gain of a capital nature (see 6, above) and Mr Yuill was treated as a person who indirectly furnished the opportunity for the making of that gain. Notice that it was Yuill personally who was subject to charge not the companies which he controlled and which actually transferred the land to the Guernsey company. Note also that all these transactions were at market value. It is somewhat surprising that sales at full value can be regarded as a transfer of an opportunity to make a gain simply because at some later date the market value of the land increases.

Does an outright sale of land with the benefit of planning permission constitute the transmission of an opportunity? It is generally thought that the answer to this question is no so long as the sale is a genuine transaction (ie not to a connected person) for which full consideration is paid. The wording of the Act does not state this in terms although it may be argued that 'premature sale or otherwise' must imply some element of under-value. [8.50]

11 Typical situations

First, a landowner may sell his land for a capital sum at a time when there is obviously development potential. That sale will not usually be a trading transaction (assuming that there are no other trading factors present) and s 776 will also be inapplicable assuming that it is on arm's length terms to an unconnected person (see 10, above).

Secondly, the landowner may obtain planning permission and then sell the land. This is not usually trading (see *Taylor v Good*, 2 above) and s 776 will not apply if the sale is at arm's length etc (see 10, above).

Thirdly, the landowner may develop his own land. On an eventual disposal of the land or an interest therein he will be subject to an income tax charge either as a trader or under s 776. In both cases his gain will be computed from the time when the intention to develop was formed. If a landowner buys extra land with a view to developing the enlarged site he may then become a trader (*Pilkington v Randall*, see 2, above). Similarly, there is a risk of trading if agreements are entered into with an adjacent landowner (such agreements may even result in the formation of a trading partnership) although a mere agreement to find a single purchaser for two parcels of land should not have this result.

Finally, a vendor or landowner who intends to sell but who wishes to obtain a slice of any future development profits runs the risk of falling within *Page v Lowther* (see 8, above). In this case the courts proposed a fairly general test for the applicability of s 776: for instance 'has a gain of a capital nature been derived from the relevant disposal?' (which will usually be the leasing of the developed site) and 'did the (original landowner) obtain any gain from the disposals effected by the under-leases?' [8.51]

12 Possible ways of avoiding s 776 but still obtaining 'a slice of the action'

A vendor could insert a covenant against development into the contract of sale and subsequently agree to release this in return for a capital sum. Although this arrangement may offer advantages when there is no immediate prospect of the purchaser wishing to develop the land it is obviously impractical if that is his immediate intention. Furthermore, such restrictions may not be commercially acceptable to the purchaser.

Alternatively, provision could be made in the original sale agreement for a further sum to be payable based on a proportion of the market value of the land after it has been developed. Arguably this does not constitute a gain of a capital nature derived from a disposal of land falling within s 776(2)(c) and the other sub-sections ((a) and (b)) are inapplicable. Further, even if this sum is calculated by reference to rents achieved, it is thought that the capital sum is still not derived from a *particular disposal*.

There are two major objections to this arrangement. First, the developer may find it unacceptable since it imposes an obligation on him to pay a capital sum unrelated to monies received for letting the developed site. (Thus it will be payable even if he fails to let or sell that site.) Secondly, it has been suggested that the arrangement involves the landowner in trading. This view may be doubted: if it is correct it is difficult to see why *Page v Lowther* was argued under s 776 since the arrangements in that case would be trading transactions.

A further possibility is to shelter the gain by transferring the land to a trading company. This operation should be carried out before any development is undertaken and the result will then be that the land is held as trading stock so that any profit from the development will be an income receipt of that company (but taxed, at most, at 35%) and therefore a gain of a capital nature will not have been obtained. This arrangement depends upon the existence of a suitable company and there is obviously a risk of a s 776 charge if the shares in that company are subsequently sold for a capital sum (see 9 above).

As an alternative sheltering device, ensure that any gain is realised by trustees. Only the basic rate of tax (25%) will be payable unless s 686 can be invoked by the Revenue (see 3, above).

Finally, ensure that a capital sum is not received from a disposal of the developed land. Assume, for instance, that the purchaser/developer agrees that he would only take a rack rent (not premiums) on lettings of the developed site. For s 776 to apply in this case, a capital sum received by the taxpayer would have to fall within subsection (2)(c). Under that provision it is necessary for land to be developed 'with the sole or main object of realising a gain from disposing of the land when developed'. It is arguable that the grant of leases at a rack rent is not a disposal (see 7, above) and furthermore, that the receipt of rents will not amount to the realisation of a *gain* for the purpose of the subsection. The difficulties with this arrangement are, first, will the purchaser agree to accept only a rental return? And secondly, the original vendor remains entitled on the properties being let to a capital sum based upon a multiple of the rental value. Thus, it is arguable that *Page v Lowther* may apply since he will then have obtained a capital sum from a disposal of the developed land, albeit that that sum was paid by the original purchaser not the sub-lessee.   [**8.52**]

13   Other matters

Although there is a clearance procedure under s 776(11), opinions vary as to whether it should be used. In *Page v Lowther*, for instance, clearance was refused, the scheme went ahead and was then challenged. There are those who feel that applying for clearance merely puts the Revenue on notice. Unlike the other clearance procedures (eg under TA 1988 s 707 and CGTA 1979 s 88) the application must be made to the local tax office: ie the matter is considered at a much lower level where there is obviously a temptation simply to issue a blanket refusal giving no reasons.

Section 776 applies to non-UK residents if all or any part of the land is situated in the UK (s 776(13)). When the person entitled to the consideration is not resident in the UK the Revenue can require the payer to deduct income tax at the basic rate from the consideration and pay it over to them (s 777(9)). This can apply even if the recipient is not the taxable person but the Revenue obviously need to know about the transaction in advance and this will not normally be the case unless the consideration is payable by instalments. It is not entirely clear whether s 776 can apply to land situated outside the UK since the declaration in s 776(13) is ambiguous on this point. Section 776 does not apply to a gain arising to an individual on the disposal of his principal private residence which is exempt from CGT (CGTA 1979 ss 101–105), or (generously) which would be exempt from CGT were it not that the property was acquired with the intention of making a gain on its disposal (CGTA 1979 s 103(3)).   [**8.53**]

14   The importance of s 776 after FA 1988

Before FA 1988, it was frequently essential for a development to be structured outside s 776 in order that income tax at a top rate of 60% was avoided. Now that CGT is charged at income tax rates and the top rate has been reduced to 40%, the importance of the section is undoubtedly reduced. There remain, however, good reasons for seeking to ensure, in many cases, that the profit remains subject to CGT (for the continuing attractions of CGT, see [**37.13**]) but there will now be circumstances when it is to the taxpayer's advantage to fall within the section: eg when he has substantial unused personal allowances; unused loss relief; or can shelter any profit by BES relief. In some circumstances a lower income tax rate may be applicable. Take, for instance, the case of a settlement in which part of the property is held on discretionary or accumulation trusts falling within s 686. Capital gains made by such a settlement are taxed at 35% whereas if a s 776 gain is realised by the trustees the rate is (probably—see 3, above) 25%.   [**8.54**]

9 Schedule D Case VI—residual

I   Scope   [**9.1**]
II Basis of assessment   [**9.21**]
III Territorial scope   [**9.41**]

I SCOPE

Schedule D Case VI is a residual or sweeping-up Case. The charging provision of Case VI is TA 1988 s 18(3), which provides for tax to be charged on 'any annual profits or gains not falling under any other case of Schedule D and not charged by virtue of Schedules A C or E'. Apart from this general charge, certain categories of income are specifically charged under Schedule D Case VI.   [**9.1**]

1   The general charge (TA 1988 s 18(3))

Although potentially wide, catching any profits not otherwise charged to income tax, the ambit of Schedule D Case VI has been limited by the courts in a series of cases which are not always consistent. In common with Schedule D Cases I and II, the word 'annual' in s 18(3) means of an income nature rather than recurring each year. Capital receipts are not, therefore, caught. In *Scott v Ricketts* (1967) £39,000 was paid voluntarily to an estate agent (in addition to his fee) to persuade him to withdraw from participating in a property development scheme. It was held that the payment was a capital receipt and so not taxable under Schedule D Case VI.

The expression 'annual profits and gains' is construed *ejusdem generis* with other profits and gains under Schedule D. Accordingly, gifts, gambling winnings and findings do not constitute profits under Case VI. Furthermore an isolated purchase and sale of property as in *Jones v Leeming* (1930) where rubber estates were acquired for re-sale at a profit is either 'an adventure in the nature of a trade', in which case the profit is a trading receipt taxable under Schedule D Case I, or a capital transaction. But in neither case is Schedule D Case VI relevant.

The major example of profits falling within Case VI is those received from the performance of casual services, which are neither derived from an office or employment, nor from a profession or vocation under Schedule D Case II because the element of regularity is missing (see [**6.61**]). However, the profit must be substantially derived from the performance of services rather than from the sale of property although this distinction is sometimes difficult to draw. In *Hobbs v Hussey* (1942) a solicitor's clerk (who was not an author by vocation) contracted with a newspaper to write his memoirs and then to assign the copyright; the payment that he received was taxable under Schedule D Case VI since it was substantially in return for the performance of services. The fact that there was a subsidiary sale of property (the copyright) was irrelevant and did not make the payment a receipt of capital (see also

Housden v Marshall (1958) and *Alloway v Phillips* (1980)). By contrast, in *Earl Haig's Trustees v IRC* (1939), trustees who owned the copyright in the Earl's diaries allowed an author to use the diaries to write a biography in return for a half share of the profits from the book. This payment was not taxable under Schedule D Case VI since it was not a payment for services, but a capital receipt from the part-disposal of an asset (the diaries).

A payment that is partly in return for services and partly for the sale of property, will, it appears, be wholly taxable under Schedule D Case VI unless it can be apportioned. In *Hale v Shea* (1964), a payment to a retiring partner for future services (income) and for his share of the partnership assets (capital) was all taxed under Schedule D Case VI.

The payment must be made under an enforceable contract for ascertainable services, otherwise it is a gift and escapes income tax. Thus, in *Dickinson v Abel* (1969) a farm was owned by a trust and the taxpayer was a relation of a beneficiary. Because of this family connection, prospective purchasers offered him £10,000 if they managed to buy the farm for £100,000 or less. The taxpayer never agreed to provide services, but merely 'made the introduction' and eventually received £10,000. This payment was held to be a gift and escaped tax under Schedule D Case VI (see also *Scott v Ricketts* (above)). Notice, however, that once there is a contract for services, any receipt under it will be taxable even though it is not received for the particular services contracted for (see *Brocklesby v Merricks* (1934)). For other examples of payments for isolated services which are outside the normal business of the taxpayer and caught by Schedule D Case VI see *Ryall v Hoare* (1923) (payment of commission by a company to one of its directors for guaranteeing the company's overdraft) and *Lyons v Cowcher* (1916) (commission received from an isolated act of underwriting an issue of shares).

Casual profits received from activities which are analogous to a trade but which lack a fundamental characteristic may be caught by Schedule D Case VI. In *Cooper v Stubbs* (1925) profits received by a cotton broker from dealings in 'futures' were taxable under Schedule D Case VI as the profits of speculation rather than of trade. Today dealings in commodity and financial futures, traded options and financial options which are not part of a trade taxed under Schedule D Case I, will be charged to CGT rather than to income tax under Schedule D Case VI (TA 1988 s 128). There are also cases where the profits from stud fees have been taxed under Schedule D Case VI rather than Schedule D Case I (see for instance *Leader v Counsell* (1942)). It is difficult to see why these cases were not assessed under Case I, which catches single speculations as well as regular trading operations. **[9.2]**

2 Specific charges

The categories of income specifically charged under Case VI include:
(1) Income from furnished lettings (TA 1988 15(4); see Chapter 8).
(2) Income from furnished holiday lettings (TA 1988 s 503; see Chapter 8).
(3) Premiums on leases received by an assignor of the lease and not by a landlord (TA 1988 s 35; see Chapter 8).
(4) Sale and reconveyance of property (TA 1988 s 36(1); see Chapter 8).
(5) Sale and lease-back of property (TA 1988 s 36(3); see Chapter 8).
(6) Payments received for 'know-how' if not taxed as a trade receipt or as a capital gain (TA 1988 s 531(4); see Chapter 6).
(7) Certain balancing charges (CAA 1990 s 9(6); see Chapter 7).

(8)   Certain receipts after a change of accounting basis (TA 1988 s 104; see Chapter 6).

(9)   Post-cessation receipts (TA 1988 s 103; see Chapter 6).

(10) Income from certain settlements which is taxed as that of the settlor (for example, under TA 1988 s 674; see Chapter 11).

(11) Transactions in securities (TA 1988 ss 703–709; see Chapter 31).

(12) Transfer of assets abroad (TA 1988 s 739; see Chapter 13).

(13) Certain transactions in land (TA 1988 s 776; see Chapter 8).

(14) Gain on disposal by UK investor of a material interest in an offshore fund (TA 1988 ss 757–763; see below).   **[9.3]**

3   **Investment in 'roll-up' funds** (TA 1988 ss 757–763)

These sections seek to prevent UK residents from avoiding a charge to income or corporation tax by an investment in offshore 'roll-up' funds. Typically, the investment is in non-UK resident companies and unit trusts which do not distribute their income, so that the eventual return to the investor would only be charged to CGT (before FA 1988 at a rate significantly below the top rate of income tax).

TA 1988 s 761 ensures that, subject to three conditions being satisfied, there will be a charge to income tax under Schedule D Case VI or to corporation tax on any such gain accruing to a UK resident (including a trustee). The requirements are, first, that he must dispose of a material interest (ie one realisable within seven years after investment; see s 759); secondly, in an 'offshore fund' (see s 759); and, thirdly, on or after 1 January 1984, *except* where the fund has obtained Revenue clearance for each accounting period as a 'distributor' of its income (ie it distributes at least 85% of its income before permitted allowances: see TA 1988 Sch 27). Death is treated as a disposal; there is no indexation allowance; and hold-over relief has never been available. Finally, s 759 ensures that normal trading ventures or consortia are not caught by any of the above provisions. The Revenue's views on the interpretation of this legislation are set out in SP 2/86.   **[9.4]–[9.20]**

II   BASIS OF ASSESSMENT

Tax is calculated under Schedule D Case VI on all profits or gains actually received (not receivable) in the current year of assessment or (depending on the circumstances) according to the average profits of a period not greater than one year (TA 1988 s 69). There are no express rules for deductible expenses, but the words 'profits or gains' imply a surplus of income after deducting expenses. A loss that is made on one Schedule D Case VI transaction can only be used, however, against profits from other Case VI transactions in the same tax year and any surplus carried forward against profits from Case VI transactions in future years (TA 1988 s 392). There is no set-off against income from other sources (cp the loss rules under Schedule D Cases I and II and for furnished holiday lettings).

Whether Schedule D Case VI income is treated as earned or unearned income depends on its source. Casual profits from services for instance, are earned income, whereas rent from furnished lettings (other than furnished holiday lettings) is, generally, unearned.   **[9.21]–[9.40]**

III TERRITORIAL SCOPE

The usual principles apply (see TA 1988 s 18 and Chapter 13). Thus, in *Alloway v Phillips* (1980) a Canadian resident contracted with an English newspaper to provide information about her husband Charles Wilson, the Great Train Robber. She was taxed under Schedule D Case VI on the £39,000 that she received, since the source of her income was her rights under the contract (a chose in action) which was enforceable and situated in the UK. **[9.41]**

10 Schedule D Case III— annual payments

I   INTRODUCTORY

Schedule D Case III charges income tax in respect of:

> '(a)   any interest of money, whether yearly or otherwise, or any annuity or other annual payment, whether such payment is payable within or out of the United Kingdom, either as a charge on any property of the person paying the same by virtue of any deed or will or otherwise, or as a reservation out of it, or as a personal debt or obligation by virtue of any contract, or whether the same is received and payable half-yearly or at any shorter or more distant periods, but not including any payment chargeable under Schedule A, and
> (b)   all discounts, and
> (c)   income, except income charged under Schedule C, from securities bearing interest payable out of the public revenue.' (TA 1988 s 18(3).)

Income under Schedule D Case III is often termed 'pure income' because it will never be reduced by any deductible expenses; it is pure profit. Annuities and annual payments are sometimes referred to as settlements of income since they can operate to reduce the income of the payer and increase that of the payee. Hence, the payer may be seen as settling an income sum on the payee.

Income tax is charged under Case III on the person receiving or entitled to receive the income in question (in the case of payment by cheque the sum is received when it is credited to the account of the recipient; see *Parkside Leasing Ltd v Smith* (1985)). If the payment is not made at all there is no liability to tax (*Woodhouse v IRC* (1936)), but, if it is paid late, the rate of tax deducted and the time limits for a repayment claim are determined in the case of a payment falling under TA 1988 s 348 by reference to the year when the payment fell due (*IRC v Crawley* (1987), [**10.47**]).

In *MacPherson v Bond* (1985) a bank held a charge on the taxpayer's deposit account as security for a loan to a company. The taxpayer had not personally guaranteed this loan and accordingly interest earned on the deposit account and which was credited to it could not be said to reduce his personal liability. In the event, the company debt finally absorbed the whole of the deposit account plus interest but as Vinelott J explained:

> 'Even before the liability of the company to the bank had been finally determined ... the taxpayer's only prospect was that he would in time become entitled

to repayment of so much of the deposit as was not required to meet the company's liability to the bank and to interest on that part of the deposit. The crediting of interest on the whole of the deposit could therefore be aptly described as a mere book entry: a matter of convenience of accounting for the bank.'

On the facts of this case, because the taxpayer was not entitled to the interest, he was not subject to any tax charge thereon. By contrast, if the security is backed up by a personal guarantee, interest credited to the account is not then a mere book entry but can be seen as reducing the sum payable by the taxpayer under the guarantee. It will therefore be subject to income tax in the hands of the taxpayer as it arises even though he does not actually receive it! (*Dunmore v McGowan* (1978); *Peracha v Miley* (1990).)

The tax is assessed on the basis of the preceding tax year and special rules, therefore, apply for the years when a new source of income is acquired and impose tax on the actual income for the first two tax years (the current year basis). The preceding year basis then operates for the third tax year, but the taxpayer is given the option to be assessed on a current year basis. In the final tax year when the income is paid tax is charged on a current year basis. The Revenue have an option to assess the taxpayer on the current year basis for the penultimate tax year if that would result in a larger assessment to tax than on the preceding year basis.   **[10.1]-[10.20]**

EXAMPLE 10.1

Judy covenants to pay £200 on 1 January and 1 July each year to Happy so long as Happy is registered as unemployed. The first payment is made on 1 January 1985 and payments continue until September 1992 when Happy obtains employment as a social worker. The final payment is accordingly made on 1 July 1992.

Happy's income under Schedule D Case III is as follows:

1984–85	£200	(1 January 1985)
1985–86	£400	(1 July 1985; 1 January 1986)
1986–87	£400	(PYB; no difference if current year basis is chosen)
1987–88/1990–91	(PYB)	
1991–92	£400	(PYB; no difference if current year basis is chosen and, therefore, the Revenue need not exercise their election)
1992–93	£200	(1 July 1992)

II TERMINOLOGY

1 Interest

'Interest' is not statutorily defined, but was described as 'payment by time for the use of money' (per Rowlatt J in *Bennett v Ogston* (1930)). More precisely interest

'may be regarded either as representing the profit the lender might have made if he had had the use of the money, or conversely, the loss he suffered because he had not that use. The general idea is that he is entitled to compensation for the deprivation' (per Lord Wright in *Riches v Westminster Bank Ltd* (1947) 28 TC at 189).

Interest generally presupposes the idea of a debt to be repaid. The *Riches* case established that interest awarded by the court under the Law Reform (Miscellaneous Provisions) Act 1934 fell within the Schedule D Case III charge (today the award is under either the Supreme Court Act 1981 or the County Courts Act 1984).

EXAMPLE 10.2

Bigco Ltd executes a debenture deed in favour of Mr Big who has made a secured loan to the company of £10,000. The deed provides for repayment of the loan together with a 'premium' of £2,000 by the end of 1991 and interest at 10% pa on the full redemption figure (£12,000) until 1991. The interest falls within Schedule D Case III and the repayment of £10,000 is a capital sum. The so-called 'premium' may be seen as deferred interest or, alternatively, as a capital sum paid as compensation for the capital risk taken by Mr Big.

Generally, the true nature of the payment is a matter of fact and the terms used by the parties are not conclusive (see *Lomax v Peter Dixon & Son Ltd* (1943) and *Davies v Premier Investment Co Ltd* (1945)). So long as the rate of interest charged is commercial, it is likely that the sum on which the interest is calculated will be treated as capital and will escape both income tax and CGT unless the debt is a 'debt on a security' within the meaning of CGTA 1979 s 134 (see Chapter 16). For the taxation of deep discount stock see TA 1988 s 57 and Sch 4 and [**28.52**] and for the taxation of investment in certain offshore funds see TA 1988 s 757ff, and Chapter 9.

Finally, it should be noted that if the principal debtor defaults so that the moneys are paid under a contract of indemnity the sum will still be taxed as interest; if paid by a guarantor, the position is unclear (see *Re Hawkins, Hawkins v Hawkins* (1972) on indemnities and contrast *Holder v IRC* (1932) on guarantors). [**10.21**]

2   Annuities

Annuities fall into two broad categories. First, a purchased annuity usually arising from a contract with an insurance company under which a capital sum is paid in return for a right to income (an annuity) for a stated period of time. Secondly, annuities payable under an instrument; for instance, an annuity that is bequeathed in a will. The changes made by FA 1988 in the treatment of annual payments (considered below) do not affect annuities. [**10.22**]

3   Other annual payments

'Other annual payments' comprise a residual category, although the term is wide enough to include an annuity. Hence, all annuities may be described as annual payments but not all annual payments as annuities. The main features of an annual payment within Schedule D Case III were laid down by Jenkins LJ in *IRC v Whitworth Park Coal Co Ltd* (1958):

'(1)   To come within the rule as an "other annual payment" the payment in question must be *ejusdem generis* with the specific instances given in the shape of interest of money and annuities . . .

(2)   The payment in question must fall to be made under some binding legal obligation as distinct from being a mere voluntary payment . . .

(3)   The fact that the obligation to pay is imposed by an order of the court and does not arise by virtue of a contract does not exclude the payment . . .

(4) The payment in question must possess the essential quality of recurrence implied by the description "annual" . . .
(5) The payment in question must be in the nature of a "pure income" profit in the hands of the recipient.' **[10.23]**

The following matters should be borne in mind when applying the above propositions:

A legal obligation (propositions (2) and (3)) The legal obligation must arise from a contract, a court order, or a deed of covenant. Gifts, therefore, are not annual payments. However, it does not matter that the payments are not of the same amount each year nor that the payments are contingent (*Moss Empires Ltd v IRC* (1937); contrast *British Commonwealth International Newsfilm Agency Ltd v Mahany* (1963)).

EXAMPLE 10.3

(1) Willie has two rich uncles, Feisal and Kemal, and they each wish to give him £1,000 every Christmas. Feisal is a very precise man and executes a deed of covenant to pay Willie £1,000 every year on 25 December. Kemal merely hands over a cheque each year.
    The £1,000 paid under covenant by Feisal is an annual payment which if entered into before 15 March 1988 is within Schedule D Case III, whereas the gift from Kemal is not (and is not Willie's income despite its recurrent quality).
(2) Aunt Lucy covenants to make Paddington's income up to £3,000 pa for the rest of his life. In some years she has to pay him money, in other years not. The sums are still annual payments although the amount paid each year varies.

Income sums paid to a beneficiary by the trustees of a discretionary trust fund are annual payments falling within Case III. **[10.24]**

The payment must be 'annual' (proposition (4)) A payment is 'annual' if it is recurrent or is capable of recurrence. Payments made at intervals of less than a year will still be 'annual' provided that they may continue beyond a year. Periodic payments on divorce or separation are typical annual payments but note, however, that interim maintenance awarded by magistrates can only be ordered for three months so that sums paid under such orders apparently fall outside the definition of an annual payment.

Only payments which are income in the hands of the recipient are included (see for instance *Martin v Lowry* (1927) for the meaning of 'annual profits' under Schedule D Case I). Payments may, therefore, be annual income payments; or they may represent instalments of a capital sum; or they may represent part income and part capital (in the latter case the income element will usually be interest on a debt which is being repaid in instalments). The interest element of any payment will be subject to charge under Schedule D Case III.

In considering whether payments constitute capital and/or income, the form of the document drawn up by the parties is not conclusive and a payment may represent a capital expenditure of the payer, but an income receipt for the payee and (presumably) vice versa. **[10.25]**

EXAMPLE 10.4

Denis wants to sell his dental practice (which is worth £30,000) to Flossie and retire. The contract could be drawn up in a variety of different forms, eg:

(1) Flossie is to pay the purchase price of £30,000 over five years, at £6,000 pa. Each payment is a capital sum (see generally *IRC v Ramsay* (1935)).

(2) Flossie is to pay by instalments as in (1) above, but is to pay five instalments of £6,250 (so that the total sum to be paid will be £31,250). Each payment probably represents a capital and an income element and must accordingly be dissected. £6,000 is an instalment of capital and £250 interest on the unpaid balance (see *Secretary of State in Council of India v Scoble* (1903)).

(3) Denis agrees to be paid by Flossie either 15% of the profits of the business each year for the rest of his life or £1,000 pa whichever is the higher. Denis is in effect purchasing a life annuity so that the payments each year will be income in his hands (see *IRC v Church Comrs for England* (1977)); Flossie's payments are probably instalments of capital (see *IRC v Land Securities Investment Trust Ltd* (1969)).

The payment must be pure income profit in the hands of the recipient (proposition (5)) If the income is to be pure profit to the recipient, he must not have incurred allowable income expenditure in return for the payment. This proposition prevents any attempt to disguise trading receipts as annual payments (see Scrutton LJ in *Howe v IRC* (1919)).

The rule is relatively easy to apply in the case of payments to traders. Far more difficult is the position when the payments are to a charity (consider for instance *IRC v National Book League* (1957) and *Campbell v IRC* (1970)). It would appear that a payment will still fall within Schedule D Case III in cases where the recipient promises something in return so long as that promise does not relate to the provision of goods or services, ie does not involve expense (see eg Lord Upjohn in the *Campbell* case: 'pure profit' had no relation to 'pure bounty').

EXAMPLE 10.5

Jason enters into a covenant with his old public school to pay £4,000 pa for seven years in return for the school agreeing to take Jason's son who is a dunce. It is further agreed that Jason will pay the full fees for his son's education (see the discussion in *Campbell v IRC* (1968) 45 TC at 427). The payment represents pure income profit to the school since the counter-stipulation costs it nothing. The position would be different if fees were not paid by Jason, when the annual payment would be treated as a payment in return for the son's education.

Because a mere counter-stipulation is not enough to deprive payments of the quality of pure income profit, priority booking given by theatre or opera companies and private viewing days by art galleries to friends will not prevent covenanted payments from satisfying the pure income profit test. By contrast, the provision of reduced priced tickets for performances may well have this effect (see *Taw and Torridge Festival Society v IRC* (1959) which decided that benefits worth almost 25% of a membership subscription could not be ignored as insubstantial). As a result of this decision Revenue practice has been to ignore benefits worth *less than* 25% but to treat payments as not satisfying the 'pure income profit test' where the benefits are worth 25% *or more*. These rules were relaxed to a limited extent by FA 1989 s 59 which provided that in the case of deeds of covenant made in favour of heritage and conservation charities, the benefit of free entry to view the charities' property will not disqualify the payment from being pure income profit. It should be noted that this change is limited to specific charities and that the only benefit which is ignored is the right of free entry to the charities' property. **[10.26]-[10.40]**

III THE MACHINERY OF TAX COLLECTION (TA 1988 ss 348-350)

One of the characteristic features of Schedule D Case III is the provision under TA 1988 ss 348, 349 (and s 3) for the deduction and collection of tax at source from the payer. Both s 348 and s 349 are designed to achieve the same objective: under both, the Revenue collects basic rate income tax from the payer on the annual payment and the payer is permitted to deduct that sum from the amount paid to the payee. Generally, therefore, the payee will receive a net sum together with a credit for the basic rate income tax which has been deducted at source and paid to the Revenue on his behalf and will be assessed directly to higher rate tax, if appropriate; he is not entitled to claim that he has been underpaid because of the deduction at source by the payer (TA 1988 ss 348(1)(d), 349(1)). These provisions do not apply to the payment of interest –nor to annual payments taken outside the tax net by FA 1988 (see IV below). **[10.41]**

1 The operation of TA 1988 s 348 for the payer

Section 348 will apply 'where any annuity or other annual payment subject to the changes made by FA 1988: see IV below charged with tax under Case III of Schedule D, not being interest, is payable wholly out of profits or gains brought into charge to income tax...'. It is, therefore, confined to the payer who has income ('profits and gains') on which he is subject to income tax. Accordingly, it cannot apply to companies as they do not pay income tax. When the payer satisfies these requirements, it is presumed (in the absence of contrary evidence) that the payment is made out of his income.

EXAMPLE 10.6

Wilbur, with an income of £10,000 pa from investments, covenants before 15 March 1988 to pay his impecunious nephew Watson £1,000 pa for the next ten years.

Step 1: Wilbur is permitted under s 348(1)(c) to deduct fro m the £1,000 a sum equal to the basic rate tax thereon. Hence, at present rates, Wilbur can deduct £250 (25% × £1,000). He will, therefore, give Watson £750 together with a certificate showing that tax has been deducted (TA 1988 s 352; the appropriate form is IR 185).

Step 2: Wilbur's income is reduced from £10,000 to £9,000 because the covenanted sum operates as a charge on his income (he is settling £1,000 pa on Watson). It, therefore, follows that his 'total income' is £9,000 (TA 1988 s 835) and that he can set his personal allowances only against that sum (TA 1988 s 276). Wilbur's own tax will, therefore, be calculated on the taxable income that is left.

Step 3: In addition, Wilbur is also charged on the covenanted sum at the basic rate of income tax (see TA 1988 s 3).

The result is that the total cost of the covenant to Wilbur is £1,000 since he handed £750 to Watson at *Step 1* and £250 to the Revenue at *Step 3*.

As Viscount Simon explained in *Allchin v Coulthard* 1943 AC at 619, by deducting the tax from the covenant at source (*Step 1*) 'the payer recoups himself for the tax which he has paid or will pay on the annual payment'. It is, therefore, in the interests of the payer to make the deduction of tax and does not directly concern the Revenue since they will collect the basic rate tax under TA 1988 s 3 at *Step 3* in any event. Hence, s 348(1)(c) *permits* the payer to make the deduction, but does not compel deduction. The whole process in *Example 10.6* may be represented diagrammatically thus:

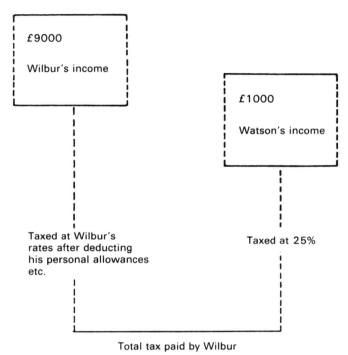

Total tax paid by Wilbur

[10.42]

2   The operation of TA 1988 s 349 for the payer

TA 1988 s 349 provides as follows:

> 'Where:—
> (a) any annuity or other annual payment charged with tax under Case III of Schedule D, not being interest, . . . is not payable, or not wholly payable, out of profits or gains brought into charge to income tax, the person by or through whom any payment thereof is made shall, on making the payment, deduct out of it a sum representing the amount of income tax thereon . . .'

Section 349 will apply when the payer has no income or insufficient income to cover the amount of the annual payment and when he is not subject to income tax. Annual payments made by companies are, therefore, payable subject to the deduction of income tax under s 349. Unlike under TA 1988 s 348, deduction from the covenanted sum is compulsory.

As soon as a relevant annual payment is made there is an obligation on the payer to notify the Revenue who will then assess him to basic rate income tax on the annual payment. The annual payment net of basic rate income tax is made to the recipient who receives a certificate of tax deducted on form IR 185.

Under s 349 tax may be collected from agents of the payer (on the dangers of being held liable as an agent see *Rye and Eyre v IRC* (1935)). This difference in collection machinery from that under s 348 is necessary because the payer will not normally be subject to income tax when a s 349 payment is made. It will not, therefore, be possible to collect the basic rate tax on the annual payment at the same time as the rest of his income tax. **[10.43]**

EXAMPLE 10.7

Wilbur (see *Example 10.6*) falls on hard times and receives no income. He remains bound by his covenant to pay Watson £1,000 pa. When he makes the next annual payment:
Step 1: Wilbur should deduct the basic rate tax (£250) on that annual sum and pay Watson £750 only.
Step 2: In accordance with s 350(1) Wilbur should notify the Revenue that the payment has been made. He will, therefore, receive an assessment to income tax for £250.
    The total cost of the covenant is, therefore, £1,000, made up of £750 paid to Watson and £250 to the Revenue.

3 The position of the recipient

The position of the recipient of an annual payment falling under Case III is broadly the same whether that payment is made under TA 1988 s 348 or s 349. He will have income under Schedule D Case III equivalent to the gross value of the payment (not just of the sum that he actually receives) and will be given a tax credit equal to the basic rate income tax deducted at source by the payer. Accordingly, he may be entitled to reclaim that tax (if he has unused personal allowances, for instance); or, the tax may exactly discharge his tax liability; or, he may be liable to extra income tax at the higher rate. This third possibility (more tax owed by the recipient) is comparatively rare since annual payments are seldom made to higher rate taxpayers and, in any event, anti-avoidance provisions (see **[10.62]**) will, in the majority of cases, deem the annual payment to be the income of the payer for the purpose of higher rate income tax. **[10.44]**

EXAMPLE 10.8

Watson received £750 from Wilbur in payment of a covenant for £1,000. He is also given an IR 185 certificate of tax deducted.
    Watson's income under Schedule D Case III is £1,000 and he has a credit for income tax paid of £250. Therefore, his tax position will be as follows:
(1) If he is subject to tax at the basic rate (ie if he has no unused allowances or charges), there is no further liability to tax and no question of a refund.
(2) If he has no other income and so has available personal allowances he can reclaim the £250 tax paid on his behalf by Wilbur. If he had (say) £200 of unused allowances he would have taxable income of £800 (£1,000− £200) on which tax at 25% would be £200. As the tax credit of £250 exceeds his tax liability by £50, he can obtain a refund of £50 of the tax deducted at source.
(3) If he has other income so that he is paying income tax at the top rate (currently 40%) even before the changes made in FA 1988 the £1,000 remains taxed as Wilbur's income for higher rate tax (TA 1988 s 683). No further tax was therefore payable by Watson.

4 **Principal problems arising in connection with the deduction of tax at source**

a) *The effect of failure to deduct tax at source*

The payer of an annual payment falling within Case III is allowed to deduct tax from the payment under s 348 and bound to do so under s 349. Failure to do so will not lead to any penalty. It will not generally concern the Revenue when the payment is made under s 348 since they will assess the payer to tax on the whole of his income without distinguishing the annual payment and if they fail to recover tax from the payer in a case where s 348 applies, the payee may be assessed.

Where there is a failure to pay the tax under s 349, however, the Revenue will seek to recover the sum either from the payer or by direct assessment from the payee. When an assessment is made upon the recipient the burden is on him to show that he was only paid a net sum. If he discharges that burden he cannot be assessed to tax (see eg *Hume v Asquith* (1969)).

Failure to deduct tax will of course affect the parties *inter se*. In general, if the payee has been overpaid, that overpayment cannot be reclaimed or corrected from later payments; it is a payment made under a mistake of law and the excess is treated as a perfected gift which cannot be undone (*Re Hatch* (1919)). There are a few exceptions to this general principle: if the mistake is one of fact recovery is possible (*Turvey v Dentons(1923) Ltd* (1953)); if the basic rate of tax increases after the payment, the excess can be recovered (TA 1988 s 821), but it appears that underdeductions cannot be recouped from later payments made in that tax year (*Johnson v Johnson* (1946) explaining *Taylor v Taylor* (1938)). There is of course nothing to stop a recipient who has been overpaid from reimbursing the payer!   **[10.45]**

> **EXAMPLE 10.9**
>
> Wilton has trading profits of £5,000 (on the preceding year basis) for the tax year 1991–92. He makes an annual payment to Watmore of £1,000 under an obligation entered into in 1987 from which he fails to deduct basic rate income tax.
> (1)   The Revenue may assess Wilton under the s 348 machinery.
> (2)   If Wilton fails to pay, the Revenue may assess Watmore. Note that in the event of Wilton paying the tax, Watmore's income is £1,000 with a credit for £250 tax paid. The extra £250 that he has received is ignored; it is a tax-free gift.

b) *The use of formulae*

TMA 1970 s 106(2) provides that 'every agreement for payment of interest ... or other annual payment in full without allowing any such deduction shall be void'. The parties may not, therefore, agree not to operate s 348 and s 349. If s 106(2) is infringed, the instrument is void only as to the provision seeking to oust the deduction machinery. The section is also limited in that it only applies to 'agreements', so that payments under court orders and wills are outside its terms (see Chapter 12).

Despite s 106, the parties will often wish to ensure that a fixed sum is paid each year to the recipient regardless of fluctuations in the basic rate of income tax. Say, for instance, that Felix is making annual payments to his aged mother, Felicity, and wants to ensure that she receives £750 each year. Whilst the basic rate is 25% a covenant to pay £1,000 pa would achieve this result. Were the basic rate to rise to 35%, however, Felicity would only receive £650. As it is not possible to agree to pay £750 and not to deduct tax, the only way of achieving what Felix wants is to use a formula in the covenant. The standard formula would be that 'Felix agrees to pay Felicity such sum as will after deduction of income tax at the basic rate for the time being in force leave £750'. This takes effect as an undertaking to pay the gross sum which after deducting the appropriate income tax leaves Felicity with £750. What she receives is, therefore, constant; what will vary with the rate of tax is the sum paid to the Revenue and, therefore, the total cost of the covenant to Felix.

An alternative formula would be to promise Felicity £750 'free of tax', which takes effect as an undertaking to pay such sum as after deduction of income tax leaves £750 (*Ferguson v IRC* (1969); a similar rule applies to court orders that are so worded). One danger if such a formula is employed is that it is arguable that a promise to pay £750 free of tax means that the recipient should in any event end up with neither more nor less than £750. It follows that if the recipient is liable to higher rate income tax on the annual payment the payer must reimburse him for that tax, whilst conversely, any repayment of tax should be returned to the payer (the rule in *Re Pettit* (1922); see Chapter 12). In view of these difficulties great care should be taken in drafting formulae. **[10.46]**

c) *Which section applies: TA 1988 s 348 or s 349?*

Difficulties will arise, for instance, if an annual payment falls due in a year when the payer has no income, but is finally paid in a year when he does have taxable income and vice versa (see generally *Luipaard's Vlei Estate and Gold Mining Co Ltd v IRC* (1930) and ESC A16). Which section applies is of considerable significance; it will, for instance, determine the ownership of the sum deducted from the annual payment since, under s 348, it belongs to the payer whereas under s 349 it should be handed to the Revenue. In general, if the payer has taxable income for the appropriate year, it is presumed that the payment is made out of that income. This provision is normally advantageous to the taxpayer as the following example illustrates.

EXAMPLE 10.10

Hank has taxable income of £10,000 for 1991–92 and pays Hiram £1,000 pa for ten years under a deed of covenant which he entered into in 1987.

(1) *If s 348 operates* Hank will be assessed to income tax on £10,000 at 25% = £2,500. (£9,000 is Hank's income and £1,000 is Hiram's).

(2) *If s 349 operates* Hank will be assessed on £10,000 at 25% (£2,500) together with £1,000 at 25% (£250). The total sum payable to the Revenue will be £2,750.

The presumption that s 348 applies if income is available is displaced when the payer has secured some fiscal or other advantage from charging the payment to capital (as in *Birmingham Corpn v IRC* (1930)), or where he has made a deliberate decision to charge the sum to capital (see, for instance, *Chancery Lane Safe Deposit and Offices Co Ltd v IRC* (1966)). In such cases, despite the availability of income profits, s 349 will be applied. (Special rules for interest payments made by companies and charged to a capital account are considered at **[28.45]**.)

In making an annual payment under TA 1988 s 348 the payer should deduct tax at the rate in force when the payment fell due and not at the rate when it was actually paid. Accordingly, in calculating the income of the payee, the covenanted sum will be treated as his income of the tax year in which it fell due and not of that in which the payment was made (if the two are different). In *IRC v Crawley* (1987) payments under a charitable covenant were made in arrears and, although the charity made a claim for repayment of tax deducted under TA 1988 s 348 within six years of the payment being made, the claim was refused because it was made more than six years after the date when the payments had fallen due. Vinelott J agreed with the Revenue's argument in the case that:

> 'the payer on making an annual payment deducts tax at the rate in force at the date when the payment became due or at the date of payment according to whether the payment is or is not made out of profits or gains brought into charge to tax. In estimating the total income of the payee the income is deemed to be the income of the year by reference to which the tax was deducted.'   **[10.47]–[10.60]**

IV   ANNUAL PAYMENTS AFTER FA 1988

1   Annual payments in tax planning

Annual payments have been used over the years for tax avoidance. Quite simply, a taxpayer subject to the higher rates of tax alienated a part of his income to a taxpayer with lower rates of tax (or, better still, to someone who paid no income tax). In *IRC v Duke of Westminster* (1936) gardeners were paid by means of a deed of covenant in lieu of wages with advantageous tax results.   **[10.61]**

EXAMPLE 10.11

Taking the tax year 1987–88 for illustration purposes, assume that Homer was then subject to income tax at the highest rate: 60%. He paid his son Hiram an allowance of £400 pa. Hiram had no other income. At Homer's marginal rates the total cost in gross terms of that allowance was £1,000 (since £1,000 — [60% × £1,000] = £400).

As an alternative, Homer could have covenanted to pay Hiram £1,000 pa. As an annual payment the result would have been:

(1)   Homer's income is reduced by £1,000 (ie he does not pay 60% tax on that sum).

(2)   Homer pays basic rate tax at source under (now) TA 1988 s 348.

(3)   Hiram receives a net sum and reclaims (because of his unused allowances) the tax paid at source by Homer.

The total cost to Homer is the same (£1,000), but Hiram receives an extra £600 and the Revenue loses £600 of tax.

2   TA 1988 Part XV (anti-avoidance)

Not surprisingly, legislation was introduced over the years to nullify many of the avoidance possibilities. It is now found in TA 1988 Pt XV, but originated in piecemeal enactments. As a result, the provisions overlap with each other and contain minor inconsistencies. It must also be borne in mind that the legislation is concerned with capital as well as income settlements. This breadth of coverage is inevitable since, if it is desired to stop a particular income settle-ment from attracting fiscal benefits, it is necessary to cover a settlement of income-producing assets (ie capital) which might otherwise achieve the same result. These provisions in the context of capital settlements are considered in Chapter 11.

In the context of annual payments the anti-avoidance provisions are only of limited relevance today because of the 1988 changes which (as discussed below) removed most annual payments from the income tax net. There are exceptional cases, however, where the payment remains effective (see [**10.64**], [**10.66**] and [**10.67**]) and in these three cases the following anti-avoidance rules remain important:

(1) *TA 1988 s 660:* short-term covenants not capable of lasting for more than six—or in the case of charities three—years;
(2) *TA 1988 s 671:* revocable covenants: see, in the context of capital settlements, [**11.63**];
(3) *TA 1988 s 663:* covenants to settlor's minor children—see [**11.65**];
(4) *TA 1988 s 664(2)(c) and s 676:* covenants to trustees who do not distribute income.   [**10.62**]

3 TA 1988 s 347A: taking annual payments outside the tax net

The logical culmination of this process came with FA 1988 s 36 (now TA 1988 s 347A) which in somewhat dramatic terms provided that:

'(1) A payment to which this section applies ie any annual payment made by an individual with only limited exceptions shall not be a charge on the income of the person liable to make it, and accordingly—
(a) his income shall be computed without any deduction being made on account of the payment, and
(b) the payment shall not form part of the income of the person to whom it is made or of any other person.'

The result is that the majority of annual payments now fall wholly outside the tax system: the results are illustrated in the following example.

EXAMPLE 10.12

On 20 June 1991 Toby, with an income of £50,000, entered into a deed of covenant to pay £1,000 per annum to his wastrel son, Jaques. Jaques has no income. As an annual payment entered into after 14 March 1988 the sum paid falls outside Case III with the following results:

(1) Toby is taxed on £50,000 without any deduction for the annual payment. As the payment has to be discharged out of taxed income, the gross cost to Toby (in 1991–92) is therefore £1,666.67. = 1000 + (1000 × 40/60) 2s higher rate taxpayer.
(2) The sum of £1,000 is paid over to Jaques.
(3) Jaques has no income so that his personal allowances remain unused.

The general principle which takes annual payments outside the tax net is subject to the following exceptions: [**10.63**]

a) *Existing obligations*

Payments made under existing obligations continue to be taxed under Schedule D Case III (FA 1988 s 36(3)). For these purposes an existing obligation means a binding obligation arising under a deed executed or written agreement made before 15 March 1988 and received by an Inspector of Taxes before the end of June 1988. Hence, in *Examples 10.6–8* above, it has been assumed that Wilbur entered into his deed of covenant before 15 March 1988. In addition to providing that 'old' deeds of covenant are still fully effective, existing maintenance obligations likewise continue to be taxed under Case III: these are analysed in detail in Chapter 36. It is not generally possible to amend an existing obligation (eg by increasing the sum to be paid) since any such alteration would amount to a new obligation and therefore would fall outside the tax system.   **[10.64]**

b) *The annual payment must be made by an individual*

TA 1988 s 347A is limited to annual payments made by individuals. Annuities, whether purchased or payable out of a deceased's estate, are therefore unaffected and similarly, the beneficiary of a discretionary trust who receives income payments from the trustees will continue to be assessed under Case III.   **[10.65]**

c) *Covenanted payments to charity*

These payments are expressly excluded from the section. Accordingly, Case III will continue to apply to such payments so that, provided that the relevant deed of covenant is drafted to avoid TA 1988 s 660 (so that it must be capable of lasting for more than three years) and s 671 (the covenant must not be revocable by the settlor) the sum paid will be a charge on the income of the payer; will be paid subject to deduction of basic rate income tax under s 348; and will be taxed as the income of the charity which may therefore reclaim the basic rate tax deducted at source.   **[10.66]**

d) *Bona fide commercial payments*

Annual payments made for *bona fide* commercial reasons in connection with a trade, profession or vocation continue to fall within Case III. The main example of such payments is annuities payable under partnership agreements to out-going partners: see further Chapter 29.   **[10.67]**

e) *The payment of interest*

These major changes, as already mentioned, only apply to annual payments: accordingly the tax treatment of interest continues unchanged and is considered below.   **[10.68]**–**[10.80]**

V   TAXATION OF INTEREST PAYMENTS

So far as interest payments are concerned two problems arise: first, should the payment be made gross (ie without any deduction of tax at source) or net (after such deduction): and secondly, can the payer deduct interest payments from his income?

TA 1988 ss 348 and 349 do not apply to interest payments, with the result that *they should generally be paid gross* and the recipient directly assessed to income tax under Schedule D Case III. In a number of cases, however, basic rate tax must be deducted at source and only a net amount paid. The main examples are: first, mortgage interest that is within the MIRAS scheme (see Chapter 4); and secondly, yearly interest chargeable to tax under Schedule D Case III and which is paid either:
(1) by a company or local authority otherwise than in a fiduciary or representative capacity, *eg debenture interest*; or
(2) by or on behalf of a partnership of which a company is a member; or

(3) by any person to another person whose usual place of abode is outside the UK (see TA 1988 s 349(2)).

In cases (1)–(3) above, the payer must deduct a sum equal to the basic rate of income tax from the payment and the provisions of TA 1988 s 349(1) apply so that the payer is under a duty to notify the Revenue that the payment has been made. Generally, interest must be 'yearly' if these provisions are to operate. The distinction between 'yearly' and 'short' interest depends upon the degree of permanence of the loan. The crucial question is whether it is stated, or expected, that the loan will last, or is capable of lasting, for 12 months or longer.

Even if the payment falls within one of the three categories of interest payments listed in s 349(2), it must still be paid gross if it is interest payable in the UK on an advance from a bank carrying on a *bona fide* banking business in the UK (on the meaning of '*bona fide* banking business' see *United Dominions Trust Ltd v Kirkwood* (1965)). Interest paid by such a bank (and certain other institutions) in the ordinary course of its business is subject to the deduction of basic rate income tax at source (with only limited exceptions: see [**4.23**]).

Finally, interest payments only operate as charges on the payer's income when the interest is 'protected' under TA 1988 ss 353–368 (see Chapter 4). Interest paid by a business will normally be a deductible expense of that business (see Chapter 6).   [**10.81**]–[**10.100**]

VI MISCELLANEOUS MATTERS

1 **Purchased life annuities** (TA 1988 s 656)

Purchased life annuities were formerly taxed as income with no allowance being given for their capital cost. TA 1988 s 656 now permits the amount of any annuity payment which falls within its scope to be dissected into an income and a capital amount. The capital amount in each payment is found by dividing the cost of the annuity by the life expectancy of the annuitant at that time, calculated according to government mortality tables. The balance is treated as income taxable under the rules of Schedule D Case III.

Generally, s 656 does not apply if the annuity is already given tax relief (as is the case with purchased annuities for a fixed term of years which have always been dissected in a similar fashion); or, if the annuity was not purchased by the annuitant but by a third party (eg if it was purchased as the result of a direction in a will); or, if the premiums qualified for tax relief under TA 1988 ss 266, 273 or 619 when they were paid or if the annuity is payable under approved personal pension arrangements.   [**10.101**]

2 **Patents and copyrights**

Patent royalties are payable subject to the deduction provisions of TA 1988 ss 348 and 349. Such payments may be annual payments, but will usually fall within Schedule D Cases I and II as receipts of a trade or profession. There are 'spreading provisions' in certain cases where lump sums are received (TA 1988 ss 524; 527, see [**6.152**]).

Copyright royalties do not fall within ss 348 and 349 and are payable without deduction of tax. The recipient will be taxed under either Schedule D

Case II (if a professional author) or otherwise under Schedule D Case VI. Again, spreading provisions are available for certain of these lump sum payments (TA 1988 ss 534–5; see [**6.151**]).   [**10.102**]

11 Trusts and settlements

I   General principles   [**11.1**]
II Trusts where the trustees are liable to a 10% surcharge (TA 1988 ss 686–687)   [**11.21**]
III The taxation of beneficiaries   [**11.41**]
IV The anti-avoidance provisions   [**11.61**]

Possible reforms in this area are canvassed in an Inland Revenue Consultative Document on the income and capital gains tax treatment of UK resident trusts which was published in March 1991. The main proposals are discussed in Appendix V: any amending legislation will not be introduced before FA 1992 *at the earliest*.   [**11.1**]

I GENERAL PRINCIPLES

The general principles that apply to trustees resemble those applying to PRs. During the life of a trust the trustees will be subject to basic rate income tax under the appropriate Schedule on all the income produced by the fund. They are not allowed to deduct their personal allowances (the trust income is, after all, not their property) nor those of any beneficiary. Furthermore, expenses incurred in administering the fund may not be deducted and are, therefore, paid out of taxed income.

EXAMPLE 11.1

(1) The trustees of the Jenkinson family trust run a bakery. The profits of that business will be calculated in accordance with the normal rules of Schedule D Case I and be subject to basic rate income tax in the trustees' hands. A change of trustees will not result in the discontinuance rules applying (TA 1988 s 113(7)).

(2) A and B, trustees of the Joel family settlement, farm trust land in partnership with Sir Joel (head of the family) who owns adjacent land. Normal rules of partnership taxation apply (see Chapter 29) and as the trustees have entered the partnership agreement *qua* trustees any change in their composition will not lead to a cessation for the purposes of the Schedule D deemed discontinuance rules. In the event of losses arising the relevant proportion may be set against other trust income.

Trustees will not be assessed in cases where the trust income accrues directly to a beneficiary who is not liable to pay income tax. The scope of this exception is limited and would appear to apply only where there is no liability to tax (for instance, because of non-residence or charitable status) and not where the income is untaxed merely because of the personal allowances of the beneficiary.

The theory behind this system of taxing trustees is that they are entitled to the income (because they can sue for it) and they will receive it in their fiduciary capacity. Furthermore, as a policy matter, it is essential to levy income tax on the trustees since otherwise, were income to be accumulated (turned into capital) as it arises, rather than distributed, it would escape income tax altogether.   [11.2]-[11.20]

II   TRUSTS WHERE THE TRUSTEES ARE LIABLE TO A 10% SURCHARGE (TA 1988 ss 686–687)

1   The charge imposed by TA 1988 s 686

Trustees are not liable to income tax at the higher rate because they are not individuals. There is, however, a special surcharge of 10% which applies to the income arising in certain trusts after deducting administrative expenses. (This 'additional rate' is currently 10%: see TA 1988 s 832(1) as amended by FA 1988 and note that a 35% CGT rate also applies to these trusts.)
   TA 1988 s 686(2) provides as follows:

> 'This section applies to income arising to trustees in any year of assessment so far as it—
> (a) is income which is to be accumulated or which is payable at the discretion of the trustees or any other person (whether or not the trustees have power to accumulate it); and
> (b) is neither (before being distributed) the income of any person other than the trustees nor treated for any of the purposes of the Income Tax Acts as the income of a settlor; and
> (c) is not income arising under a trust established for charitable purposes only; and
> (d) exceeds the income applied in defraying the expenses of the trustees in that year which are properly chargeable to income (or would be so chargeable but for any express provisions of the trust).'

   Broadly, trusts which contain a power for trustees to accumulate income, and trusts which give the trustees a discretion over the distribution of the income are caught. The purpose of the surcharge is to increase the cost of accumulating income in trusts.

EXAMPLE 11.2

(1) Magnus is a wealthy individual who pays income tax at the highest rate (currently 40%). He creates a settlement of income-producing assets on discretionary trusts for his children giving the trustees power to accumulate the income for 21 years. Under the general principles discussed above, the income which was accumulated would suffer tax at only 25% (instead of 40% in Magnus' hands) and would subsequently be paid out as capital and so be free from any further income tax. As a result of s 686, however, the trustees have to pay an extra 10% rate of tax (making a 35% rate in all) so that the attractions of the settlement to Magnus are reduced (although not wholly removed).

(2) Trustees of a discretionary trust have income of £10,000 and incur administrative expenses of £1,000. Their income tax assessment will be—

	£
Basic rate on £10,000 (25% of £10,000)	2,500
Section 686 surcharge on £9,000 (10% of £9,000)	900
Total tax liability	£3,400

Section 686(2)(a) was considered in *IRC v Berrill* (1982) where the settlor's son was entitled to the income from the fund unless the trustees exercised a power to accumulate it. Vinelott J held that s 686 applied since the income was 'income . . . which is payable at the discretion of the trustees'. 'Discretion' is apparently wide enough to cover a discretion or power to withhold income. The phrase 'income which is to be accumulated' in para (a) presumably refers to income which the trustees are under a positive duty to accumulate. A mere power to accumulate is not sufficient, although it will usually mean that the income 'is payable at the discretion of the trustees' within para (a).

In *Carver v Duncan* (1985) trustees paid premiums on policies of life assurance out of the income of the fund as they were permitted to do under the trust deed. The House of Lords held that the payments did not fall to be deducted under s 686(2)(d) which was limited to expenses which were properly chargeable to income under the general law. As the life assurance premiums were for the benefit of capital they should, as a matter of principle, be borne by capital and accordingly, the express authority in the instrument did not bring the sums within the section.

The surcharge will not apply to income which is treated as that of any person other than the trustees; for instance, to trusts where a beneficiary has a vested interest in the income (eg a life tenant) and also to trusts where the anti-avoidance provisions of TA 1988 Pt XV operate to deem the income to be that of the settlor (see [**11.61**]). Presumably the *Pilkington* settlement (see Chapter 24), in which the income of a life tenant could be taken from him after it had arisen by the exercise of a power to accumulate it, would be subject to the surcharge as the income still 'belongs' to the trustees.

Five other points should be noted: first, s 686 does not apply to the income of an estate of a deceased person during administration (though it may, of course, apply to a subsequent will trust). Secondly, the tax is due from the trustees on 1 December following the appropriate year of assessment. Thirdly, the deduction of basic rate income tax at source will not normally apply to accumulation and discretionary trusts which invest all or part of the fund in a bank deposit (see [**4.23**]). Fourthly, non-resident discretionary trustees are liable to the additional 10% rate on the UK income of the trust: in the case of dividends paid by a UK company they are not liable for basic rate income tax (TA 1988 s 233(1)(a)) and the additional rate is charged on the actual amount of the dividends (*IRC v Regent Trust Co Ltd* (1980)). Finally, a surcharge is imposed on 'income' and because this term is not defined it is limited to income in a trust sense: hence the various provisions in the legislation deeming capital sums to be income do not apply. For instance, if a company buys back its own shares from trustees in circumstances where the payment is taxed as a distribution, the sum received by the trustees will be capital and not subject to the surcharge. [**11.21**]

2 The charge imposed by TA 1988 s 687

The purpose of s 687 is to impose a further charge to income tax on income payments made at the trustees' discretion where the rates have increased between the time of the income arising (and trustees being taxed on it), and its distribution to beneficiaries. Section 687(2) provides that:

'The payment shall be treated as a net amount corresponding to a gross amount from which tax has been deducted at a rate equal to the sum of the basic rate and the additional rate in force for the year in which the payment is made;

and the sum treated as so deducted shall be treated, so far as not set off under the following provisions of this section, as income tax assessable on the trustees.'

The set-off referred to allows the trustees to deduct from the tax now payable the tax that was charged at basic rate under s 686 on that income when it arose.

EXAMPLE 11.3

In 1991–92 the trust produces £2,000 income. The income tax assessment (at 35%) will be for £700. In 1992–93 the trustees in the exercise of their discretion pay a net sum (£1,300) to a beneficiary. In that year the basic rate remains at 25% but the surcharge is 25%. The net payment must be grossed up in accordance with s 687(2) as follows:

$$£1,300 \times \frac{100}{100-50^*} = £2,600$$

*The grossing up formula deducts the rate of tax in force in 1992–93 from 100 — that rate is 25 + 25 = 50.

Hence, the tax liability is £1,300 which can be reduced by setting off the £700 paid in 1991–92. £600, therefore, remains payable.

It is thought that s 687 does not apply to income payments made by non-UK resident trustees to UK beneficiaries. Although the section is not on its face limited to UK trustees, it is expressed to apply instead of the sections imposing a charge to tax at source under Schedule D Case III, and income from overseas trusts falls not under this Case of Schedule D but under Case V. Further, the phrasing of ESC B18 proceeds upon the assumption thats 687 does not apply to confer a tax benefit on a UK beneficiary who receives such income.   **[11.22]–[11.40]**

III   THE TAXATION OF BENEFICIARIES

1   Taxing a beneficiary who is entitled to trust income

A beneficiary who is entitled to the income of a trust as it arises (or is entitled to have it applied for his benefit) is subject to income tax for the year of assessment in which that income arises, even if none of the money is paid to him during that year (*Baker v Archer-Shee* (1927)). The sum to which the beneficiary is entitled is that which is left in the trustees' hands after they have paid administration expenses and discharged their income tax liability. The beneficiary is, as a result, entitled to a net sum which must be grossed up by the basic rate of income tax in order to find the sum which enters his total income computation and to a credit for some of the income tax paid by the trustees; not, it should be noted, for the full amount in cases where management expenses have been deducted (*Macfarlane v IRC* (1929)).

Depending upon his other income and allowances, a beneficiary may be entitled to reclaim all or some of the tax paid by the trustees. Alternatively, he may be liable for tax at the higher rate. The income that he receives from the trust will be unearned even if it arises from a trade run by the trustees (see *Fry v Shiels' Trustees* (1915) and TA 1988 s 833(4) but note also *Baker v Archer-Shee* (1927) which indicates that if a beneficiary is entitled to the income as it arises, he will be taxed according to the rules of the Schedule appropriate to that source of income).

EXAMPLE 11.4

Zac is entitled to the income produced by a trust fund. In 1991-92 £6,000 is produced and the trustees incur administrative expenses of £1,000. The trustees will be subject to tax at 25% on the income of £6,000. The balance of the income available for Zac will be:

	£	£
Gross income		6,000
Less: tax	1,500	
expenses	1,000	2,500
		£3,500

Zac, is, therefore, taxed on £3,500 grossed up by tax at 25% ie:

$$\frac{£3,500 \times 100}{75} = £4,666.67$$

He will be given a credit for that portion of the basic rate tax paid by the trustees which is attributable to £4,666.67—this is £1,166.67.

Zac does not receive a credit for the rest of the tax paid by the trustees (£1,500—£1,166.67 = £333.33) and the result is that management expenses have been paid out of taxed income so that the total cost of these expenses is £1,333.33. (An alternative way of dealing with management expenses is considered at [**11.46**].)

'Income' for these purposes will not include items which are capital profits under trust law although income tax may have been charged upon them in the hands of the trustees: eg premiums treated as rent under TA 1988 s 34 and capital sums received on a disposal of land under TA 1988 s 776.   [**11.41**]

2 Taxing an annuitant

An annuitant under a trust is not entitled to income of the trust as it arises; he is taxed under Schedule D Case III on the income that he receives. As income tax will be deducted from the annuity by the trustees under TA 1988 s 348, an assessment for basic rate tax on the beneficiary will be precluded. He has a tax credit for the basic rate tax deducted at source in the usual way.   [**11.42**]

3 Taxing a discretionary beneficiary

A discretionary beneficiary has no right to a specific amount of income but is merely entitled to be considered. Any payments that he receives will be charged as his income under Schedule D Case III (they are annual payments since they may recur) and he will receive a credit for the tax paid by the trustees and attributable to that payment. As the trust is discretionary, that tax will be at a rate of 35% (TA 1988 s 686). The effect of s 686 is, therefore, to encourage trustees to distribute income to beneficiaries who are subject to income tax at less than 35% so that all or a part of the surcharge can be repaid.

Once an irrevocable decision has been taken by the trustees to retain income as a part of the capital of the fund, the sum accumulated loses its character as income and is treated in the same way as the original fund, ie as capital. It follows, therefore, that the income tax suffered by that income (at 35%) is irrecoverable and that no further income tax will be charged on the accumulations when they are eventually paid out to the beneficiaries as capital (although such distributions will have CGT and IHT consequences). In deciding whether it is more advantageous to accumulate income or to pay it out to beneficiaries under their discretionary powers, trustees need to consider, inter alia, the tax position of the individual beneficiaries.   [**11.43**]

EXAMPLE 11.5

Trustees receive trust income of £10,000. There are three discretionary beneficiaries (all unmarried), Ding, Dang and Dong. Ding has no other income and has an unused personal allowance; Dang is a basic rate taxpayer; and Dong is subject to tax at a marginal rate of 40%. The trustees are deciding whether to pay income to any one or more of the beneficiaries or whether to accumulate it. The following tax consequences will ensue:
(1) The trustees are subject to 35% tax on the trust income (ie £3,500 tax).
(2) If the trustees decide to pay all the income to Ding (who has no other income) he will be entitled to a partial repayment of tax as follows:

	£
Income (Schedule D Case III)	10,000
Less: personal allowance	3,295
Total income	£ 6,705
Inocme tax	
£6,705 at 25%	1,676.25
Less: tax credit	3,500.00
Tax refund	£(1,823.75)

(3) If the trustees pay the income to Dang (the basic rate tax payer), he will not be entitled to a refund of any basic rate tax, but, depending upon the amount of his other income, he may obtain a refund of part of the 10% surcharge.
(4) If the trustees pay the income to Dong (the higher rate tax payer), extra tax will be levied as follows:

	£
Income	£10,000
Tax at 40%	4,000
Less: tax credit	3,500
Tax owing	£ 500

(5) If the trustees accumulate the income, the £3,500 tax paid will be irrecoverable and the net income of £6,500 will be converted into capital. Ideally, the trustees will avoid payments to Dong, will consider appointing all or part of the income to Ding and Dang and accumulate any balance.

4 The dangers of supplementing income out of capital

Capital payments will not generally be subject to income tax. If a beneficiary is given a fixed amount of income each year and is entitled to have that sum made up out of capital should the trust fail to produce the requisite amount of income, however, such -('topping up' payments will be taxed as income in the hands of the beneficiary (see *Brodie's Will Trustees v IRC* (1933) and *Cunard's Trustees v IRC* (1946)).

> **EXAMPLE 11.6**
>
> (1) The settlor's widow is given an annuity of £4,000 pa; the trustees have a discretion to pay it out of the capital of the fund if the income is insufficient. The widow will be assessed to income tax on the payments that she receives whether paid out of income or capital since they will be annual payments (TA 1988 s 349 will apply to the extent that there is insufficient income in the trust and they are paid out of capital).
>
> (2) The settlor's widow is given an annuity of £4,000 pa and, in addition, the trustees have the power 'to apply capital for the benefit of the widow in such manner as they shall in their absolute discretion think fit'. Any supplements out of capital will now escape income tax since the widow has an interest in both income and capital, and payments out of capital will, therefore, be treated as advances of capital rather than as income payments.

In recent years the Revenue have sought to argue that payments made out of trust capital can still be taxed as income in the hands of the recipient beneficiary even when the payments are not paid in augmentation of an income interest. This argument is based on the Revenue's view that the income nature of the payment in the hands of the recipient can be discovered by looking at the size, recurrence, and purpose of the payments. *Stevenson v Wishart* (1987) provided a test case for this view since the discretionary trust income was there paid out in full each year to a charity and capital sums were then paid to one of the beneficiaries who had suffered a heart attack. The purpose of the payments was to cover medical expenses and the cost of living in a nursing home. The Revenue argument that these sums were paid out for an income purpose and were therefore subject to income tax was rejected both at first instance and by the Court of Appeal. Fox LJ stated that:

> 'There is nothing in the present case which indicates that the payments were of an income nature except their recurrence. I do not think that is sufficient. The trustees were disposing of capital in exercise of a power over capital. They did not create a recurring interest in property. If, in exercise of a power over capital, they chose to make at their discretion regular payments of capital to deal with the specific problems of the beneficiary's last years rather than release a single sum to her of a large amount, that does not seem to me to create an income interest. Their power was to appoint capital. What they appointed remained capital.'

The Court of Appeal did stress the exceptional nature of nursing home payments. Fox LJ, for instance, stated that such expenditure, although involving day to day maintenance, was emergency expenditure of very substantial amounts which would usually fall outside normal income resources. It may be, therefore, that if the expenditure was not of an emergency nature the Court would consider the payments to be income. A typical example is the payment of school fees out of a trust fund where the Revenue have argued for a number of years that lump sum payments can be taxed as the income of the recipient beneficiary in the year when that payment is made (see (1982) LS Gaz 692 and (1984) 3382).

It is understood that the Revenue currently treat advances or appointments out of trust capital as capital in the hands of the recipient beneficiary unless the payments in question fall within one of the following three categories. *First*, when they are designed to augment income as in the *Brodie* case; *secondly*, if the trust instrument contained a provision authorising the use of capital to maintain a beneficiary in the same degree of comfort as had been the case in the past (the *Cunard* case); and, finally, if the capital payment in question really amounts to an annuity (see *Jackson's Trustees v IRC* (1942)).   [**11.44**]

5   The divesting effects of Trustee Act 1925 s 31

The effects of s 31 (which may be excluded by the trust instrument) can be dealt with in two propositions: first, if an infant has a vested interest in the capital of a fund and the income is accumulated with the capital, the income belongs to the infant. Hence, the surcharge under s 686 is inapplicable since the income is that of a person other than the trustees ([**11.21**]); were the infant to die, both capital and income accumulations would belong to his estate. Secondly, if an infant has a vested interest in income only, eg to Albert for life where Albert is seven, the trustees will accumulate that income with the capital of the fund. Were the infant to die the accumulations would not pass to his estate. In this case s 31 has a divesting effect and for income tax purposes the accumulating income is subject to the TA 1988 s 686 surcharge because it does not belong to any particular beneficiary as it arises. In *Stanley v IRC* (1944) it was stated that 's 31 has effected a radical change in the law. The beneficiary is, in fact, for all practical purposes in precisely the same position as if his interest in surplus income were contingent.'   [**11.45**]

EXAMPLE 11.7

(1) Shares are settled for Amanda absolutely. She is aged six. Income produced by the shares (dividends) will be taxed as Amanda's income and grossed up at 25% with a credit for the basic rate tax deducted at source.

   If, instead, the fund was held for Amanda contingent upon her attaining the age of 21, the surcharge would apply to the income, as it is not Amanda's, and only sums paid out to her by the trustees in the exercise of their powers of maintenance would be taxed as her income (in which case she would, of course, have a credit for the 35% tax paid by the trustees). When Amanda becomes 18 she will be entitled to the income by virtue of s 31 (despite her interest remaining contingent until 21).

(2) Shares in a settlement are held on trust for Barbara (aged six) for life with remainder to her Uncle Silus. As Barbara, the life tenant, has only a vested interest in income the trustees will be liable for tax at 35% (in fact the dividends will have already suffered basic rate deduction at source). Barbara will not be subject to tax on the income and will not, therefore, be able to reclaim any of the tax paid by the trustees, except to the extent that income is applied for her maintenance.

Note: it may be possible to obtain income tax advantages without succession disadvantages by giving an infant a vested interest in income and a contingent interest in capital. If IHT could pose a problem on the death of that infant a 'bucket trust' could be set up (see (1984) LS Gaz 2938).   [**11.45**]

6 The taxation of management expenses

Management expenses, as already discussed, are deductible in calculating the 10% surcharge but not for basic rate purposes and the beneficiary is only entitled to the income that is left after deducting those expenses. Where a beneficiary has unused allowances (and, hence, will obtain a refund for any income tax paid by the trustees) the treatment of trustees' expenses results in a partial loss of that refund. A settlor should, therefore, give trustees a power to charge all expenses to capital or, in the absence of such a clause, trustees should consider paying the whole income to the beneficiary in return for an undertaking by him to reimburse the trustees for their expenditure. If the beneficiary entitled to the income is a higher rate taxpayer, however, the effect of the management expense rules is that he will be treated as entitled to less income, so that less tax will be paid and it will, therefore, be cheaper if the expenses are paid out of the trust income. [**11.46**]–[**11.60**]

EXAMPLE 11.8

Assure that the beneficiary has no other income and unused allowances.
(1) Expenses borne by the trustees

	£
Gross income of trust	1,000
Less: tax at 25%	250
	750
Less: expenses paid by trustees	100
Net income of beneficiary	650
Gross income of beneficiary $\left(£650 \times \frac{100}{75} \right) = £866.67$	
Tax refund (25% × £866.67)	216.67
Income retained by beneficiary	£866.67

(2) Contrast (1) with the case where the whole income is given to the beneficiary:

	£
Net income of beneficiary ((a) above)	750
Tax refund	250
Income received by beneficiary	1,000
Less: management expenses	100
Income retained by beneficiary	£900

IV   THE ANTI-AVOIDANCE PROVISIONS

1   Introductory

Prior to 15 March 1988, a wealthy individual paying income tax at a top rate of 60% who wished to transfer a part of his income, eg to a grandchild, could have done so in one of two ways. First, by entering into a deed of covenant (ie an income settlement); or, secondly, by transferring capital assets that produce the required amount of income to trustees to hold for the benefit of the chosen grandchild for a stated period. Inevitably, therefore, the legislation which sought to restrict the efficacy of covenants was also drafted so as to deal with capital settlements. Income settlements were generally rendered tax ineffective by TA 1988 s 347A so that the choice open to the wealthy taxpayer is whether or not to create a capital settlement. Not surprisingly, FA 1989 contained further provisions aimed at preventing what were essentially covenant arrangements being dressed up as capital settlements.

When the anti-avoidance rules operate, the provisions generally deem the income of a capital settlement to be that of the settlor and provide for him to recover from the trustees any tax that he suffers on that income in excess of the basic rate.

As recognised in the Consultative Document on Trusts (see generally Appendix V) there is a general need for simplification in this area where rules have developed in a piecemeal fashion since 1922 (so that considerable overlap exists) and where many of the rules have become obsolete. In broad terms, the various statutory provisions can be divided into three areas:
(1) rules which apply where the settlor's minor children benefit from his settlement ([**11.62**]);
(2) rules which apply where the settlor or his spouse have retained an interest in the settlement—whether or not actual benefits have been conferred ([**11.63**]);
(3) rules which apply where the settlor or his spouse or minor child have received a capital payment or benefit from the settlement ([**11.69**]).   [**11.61**]

2 Parental settlements in favour of infant unmarried children
(TA 1988 ss 663–664)

The income produced by settlements in favour of the settlor's own infant unmarried child will normally be treated as the income of the settlor during his lifetime. If income is accumulated, however, under an irrevocable capital settlement in favour of such beneficiaries, the income is not treated as that of the settlor (TA 1988 s 664(2)), but payments out of the fund will be treated as the settlor's income up to the amount of the accumulations (TA 1988 s 664(2)(b)).

EXAMPLE 11.9

Darien settles shares for the benefit of his three children: Amien, Darien Jr and Arres in equal shares contingent upon them attaining the age of 21. They are all infants and unmarried. If the income of the fund is £10,000 pa the income tax position is as follows:
(1) The trustees will be liable for income tax at a rate of 35% on that income (TA 1988 s 686).
(2) If the balance of the income (after the payment of tax) is accumulated, as the settlement is an irrevocable settlement of capital it will not be treated as the income of the settlor. Hence, so long as the income is retained in the trust no further income tax is payable. (Note: an irrevocable settlement depends upon both the general law and the provisions of TA 1988 s 665.)
(3) If any of the income is paid to a child, it is treated as income of Darien. Say, for instance, that £1,300 is paid to, or for the benefit of, Amien. The result will be that Darien's income is increased by £2,000 (£1,300 grossed up at 35%). He has a tax credit for the £700 tax paid by the trustees. If he is charged to further income tax on that sum, TA 1988 s 667 contains tax recovery provisions that will enable him to claim a refund from the trustees or from any other person to whom the income is payable (in this case Amien, Darien Jr and Arres, although recourse would only be had

to the beneficiaries to the extent that they had received income). If Darien is subject to a marginal rate of income tax of 40% the result is:

	£
Deemed income	2,000
Darien's tax (highest rate) at 40%	800
Less: tax credit (tax paid by trustees)	700
Tax owing	£ 100

(4) If all the net income (£6,500) is distributed amongst the three beneficiaries (and, therefore, treated as Darien's income), any further distributions to the beneficiaries will be capital advancements.

(5) This settlement will be an accumulation and maintenance trust for IHT purposes (see Chapter 26); but this does not bestow any income tax advantages.

(6) It should be noted that it is *sums* paid to or for the benefit of a child which are treated as the income of the settlor/parent and it may therefore be argued that a non-cash distribution *in specie* would not be caught.

Three other general matters should be noted. *First,* that income covenants by the settlor/parent in favour of trustees will be ineffective annual payments in accordance with the rules discussed in Chapter 10. *Secondly,* 'child' is widely defined to include 'a stepchild, an adopted child, and an illegitimate child' (TA 1988 s 670), but does not, presumably, include a foster child. *Finally,* the definition of settlement includes a transfer of assets (*Thomas v Marshall* (1953).)

If the settlor is not the parent of the infant beneficiary, TA 1988 s 663 is not applicable; grandparental settlements are, therefore, advantageous from an income tax point of view. Even if the settlor is the parent, so long as the income is accumulated, there will still be an income tax saving if the parent is subject to income tax at the higher rate of 40%. In particular, notice the income tax saving where capital is settled for an infant absolutely as illustrated in the following example:

EXAMPLE 11.10

Dad's marginal rate of income tax is 40%. He settles shares, which produce an income of £1,000, upon trust for his infant daughter absolutely. The income is accumulated.

(1) If Dad had received the income, the income tax payable would have been £400, so that he would have been left with £600.

(2) As the income is settled upon trust for his daughter absolutely, the income will be treated as belonging to her so long as it is accumulated. As a result, she will be able to set her allowances against the income which will result in no income tax being charged. (The 10% surcharge does not apply because the income belongs to a beneficiary.) The sum of £1,000 is, therefore, retained in the settlement. However, there must be no payments out of the fund until the daughter attains 18 (or marries under that age), otherwise the sums paid out will be taxed as Dad's income.

To avoid the application of TA 1988 s 663, the settlement must be irrevocable. There must, therefore, be no power to terminate the trust, whether that power is given to the settlor or to a stranger. Furthermore, TA 1988 s 665 requires that income or assets from the fund must not be payable, according to the terms of the settlement, to or for the benefit of the settlor or his spouse except for such payments made after the death of the child beneficiary or on the bankruptcy of the child, or on a purported charge or assignment of assets by the child. Thus a settlement will be irrevocable if the child is given a protected life interest under the standard trusts (found in Trustee Act 1925 s 33); and if the settlement is to revert to the settlor on the death of the infant beneficiary. Finally, under s 665, a settlement will not be irrevocable if it can be determined by act or default of any person. For example, a settlement that will terminate if the settlor ceases to be employed as Chief Executive of British Rail is not irrevocable.   [11.62]

3   Settlements in which the settlor retains an interest

There are currently six different charging rules: these may tax the settlor on the whole of the settlement income (TA 1988 ss 672, 674 and 674A); *or* only on undistributed settlement income (TA 1988 s 673); *or* on all income but only at rates in excess of the basic rate (TA 1988 ss 683, 684). For settlements created on or after 14 March 1989, however, TA 1988 s 674A has in practice superseded all the other provisions since it is drafted in wide enough terms to embrace them all.   [11.63]

a)   *Settlements in which the settlor retains an interest* (TA 1988 s 674A)

This provision was inserted by FA 1989 and was specifically aimed at preventing settlements being used in place of deeds of covenant. It effectively supersedes the other provisions catching a settlor who has retained an interest in the case of settlements created on or after 14 March 1989.

EXAMPLE 11.11

Jasper wishes to make provision for his son, Jonas, who is going up to Cambridge to read law. A covenant to pay Jonas £1,000 pa so long as he is studying law is, since FA 1988, ineffective for tax purposes. Accordingly, Jasper proposes to settle ICI shares on trust for Jonas for so long as he is reading law at Cambridge with a provision that thereafter the shares will revert to him.

Section 674A provides that if a settlor creates a settlement on or after 14 March 1989 *and does not divest himself absolutely of the property therein, the income from that property is taxed as his for all income tax purposes.* Accordingly, in the above example, because the property will revert to the settlor on the ending of Jonas' university career, Jasper will be taxed on the income. The section does not apply in cases where there has been an absolute divesting: hence were the property to pass on Jonas finishing his law studies to, eg, Jasper's daughter, the income would then fall outside the provision and be taxed as that of Jonas so long as he was studying law.

As from 6 April 1990 (ie from the introduction of independent taxation of husband and wife) s 674A has also applied to settlements when created *before* 14 March 1989 if the income is payable to the settlor's spouse. In the case of settlements created thereafter the section will also apply to income payable to a spouse *provided that* the settlor has not divested himself absolutely of the property. The circumstances in which a settlor is not to be treated as having divested himself of property are identical to those set out in s 683 and therefore, whenever any property is applicable for the benefit of the settlor's spouse under settlements on or after 14 March 1989, the section will apply unless that benefit derives from an outright gift made to the spouse (see TA 1988 ss 685(1) and 674A). **[11.64]**

EXAMPLE 11.12

(1) In April 1988 Popeye settled property on trust for his wife, Olive, for life with remainder to his children. Prior to 6 April 1990 the income from the settlement was taxed as that of Popeye under the general rule which aggregated income of husband and wife. From 6 April 1990 s 674A has applied (because this is a pre-March 1989 settlement in which the income (only) is paid to the settlor's wife) to deem the income to be that of Popeye.

(2) If a similar trust was set up in January 1990 the same results will follow. Before the introduction of independent taxation aggregation will operate as before: from 6 April 1990 because a benefit from the settlement is being received by the spouse of the settlor (and of course there is no outright gift to that person) the income will continue to be taxed as Popeye's under s 674A.

b) *Revocable settlements where the fund will revert* (TA 1988 s 672)

If there is a power to revoke the trusts (whoever possesses that power) and as a result the fund may revert to the settlor or his spouse, the income of the fund is treated as belonging to the settlor. It is all the income from the start of the trust which is so treated regardless of whether or not the power of revocation is exercised. However, if the power cannot be exercised for at least six years the income is not deemed to be the settlor's until the power becomes exercisable. If the power to revoke extends to only a portion of the fund, it is only the appropriate proportion of the income which is attributable to the amount of capital subject to the power of revocation which is treated as the settlor's. For these purposes, an ex-spouse is not a spouse and neither is the widow or widower of a deceased settlor (*Lord Vestey's Executors v IRC* (1949)).

If s 672 applies, the entire income of the settlement will be taxed as the settlor's unearned income under Schedule D Case VI despite the fact that he has received no income from the fund. It is treated as the top slice of his income but he can recover any higher rate tax charged, either from the trustees or from any person who has received income from the settlement (TA 1988 s 675). **[11.65]**

c) *Settlements in which the settlor is a discretionary beneficiary*
(TA 1988 s 674)

All the income arising under a settlement is treated as that of the settlor if, under the terms of that settlement, any person has, or may have, the power to pay that income or property to the settlor or his spouse. This provision does not apply if the discretionary power does not arise for at least six years from the creation of the settlement (but it will apply when the power becomes operative) and interests which are excluded under TA 1988 s 673 are excluded under this provision as well (they are listed below).

Tax paid by the settlor as a result of s 674 may be recovered from the trustees or from any beneficiary who receives income from the fund. **[11.66]**

d)   *Settlements with undistributed income* (TA 1988 s 673)

'Undistributed income' is defined as the total income of the trust less income payments to beneficiaries and expenses properly charged to income (TA 1988 s 682).

If the settlor is a discretionary beneficiary, the income is taxed as his income when it arises, in accordance with TA 1988 s 674 (above). TA 1988 s 673 provides that when the settlor (or his spouse) retains an interest in the settlement the undistributed income of the fund is taxed as the settlor's to the extent of his retained interest. An interest is retained if income or property in the fund will, or may, become payable to, or for the benefit of the settlor or his spouse. Presumably, therefore, if the settlor retains a reversionary interest in the whole of the capital of the fund, all the undistributed income is taxed as his under Schedule D Case VI. The settlor may recover any tax paid as a result of s 673 from the trustees or the beneficiaries.

EXAMPLE 11.13

Tim creates a settlement in favour of his two adult daughters Tina and Tanya, as concurrent life tenants, and he gives the trustees an overriding power to accumulate the income. Because he has not disposed of the remainder interest, Tim has retained an interest in the fund with the result that any accumulated income is taxed as his.

The nature of the interest which the settlor must retain, in order for TA 1988 s 673 to apply, has given rise to some discussion. A power to participate in the management of the trust is not, for instance, a sufficient interest (see *Lord Vestey's Executors v IRC* (1949)); likewise, the possibility that a beneficiary might make a gift back to the settlor is to be ignored; and the Revenue accept that if the trustees agree to pay the IHT bill that arises on the creation of the settlement, this will not amount to the reservation of an interest (SP 1/ 82 and see Chapter 24). Section 673(3) further provides that if any interest of the settlor is dependent upon the happening of certain events, income will not be deemed to be that of the settlor. The events are:

'(a)   if and so long as that income or property cannot become payable or applicable as aforesaid except in the event of:
  (i)   the bankruptcy of some person who is, or may become, beneficially entitled to that income or property; or
  (ii)   any assignment of, or charge on, that i) Income or property being made or given by some such person; or
  (iii)   in the case of a marriage settlement, the death of both the parties to the marriage and of all or any of the children of the marriage; or
  (iv)   the death under the age of twenty-five or some lower age of some person who would be beneficially entitled to that income or property on attaining that age; or
 (b)   fif and so long as some person is alive and under the age of twenty-five during whose life that income or property cannot become payable or applicable as aforesaid except in the event of that person becoming bankrupt or assigning or charging his interest in that income or property.'

Events (i) to (iv) in (a) above are alternatives but all the conditions in (b) must be satisfied if the settlor is not to retain an interest.   **[11.67]**

EXAMPLE 11.14

Harry settles property on trust for his godson Charles as protected life tenant (so that his interest will determine, inter alia, upon bankruptcy) contingent upon his attaining the age of 40. In the event of Charles' life interest being forfeited the fund is to pass to Harry's wife, Ruth. Charles is currently aged 19 and the settlement contains a power to accumulate the income for 21 years.

Although the settlor's wife, Ruth, is the beneficiary entitled in default, Harry, the settlor, is not treated as reserving an interest because of (b) above. Once Charles becomes 25, however, the accumulated income will be taxed as Harry's.

e) *Charging the settlor to excess liability* (TA 1988 s 683)

This section has been superseded by s 674A in the case of settlements created on or after 14 March 1989 (ante, [**11.64**]). In the case of settlements created before that date income which arises from property of which the settlor has not divested himself absolutely, is taxed as his for the purpose of excess liability. It is irrelevant that the income is distributed to another person. The section will only apply if the income is not caught by any of the anti-avoidance provisions discussed above and does not apply to divorce settlements (see [**36.6**]). A settlor will be treated as not having divested himself of the property (ie as continuing to have an interest in the property) in a wide range of circumstances (see, for instance, *Vandervell v IRC* (1967) and contrast *Watson v Holland* (1984)), although the four exceptions under TA 1988 s 673(3)(a) (see [**11.67**]) apply equally to s 683. [**11.68**]

4 **Receipt of capital benefits** (TA 1966 ss 677–678)

The purpose of this provision is to prevent the settlor obtaining any benefit from a settlement in which the income may be taxed at a lower rate than that which would have applied had the settlor retained the income. In effect, capital payments to the settlor (or his spouse) from the fund are matched with undistributed income of the fund and taxed as the settlor's income under Schedule D Case VI. The sum is grossed up at basic and the 10% additional rates but the settlor is entitled to a credit for tax paid by the trustees—although not to any repayment! There are no provisions enabling the settlor to recover any tax that he may have to pay.

A 'capital sum' covers any sum paid by way of loan or a repayment of a loan and any sum paid otherwise than as income and which is not paid for full consideration in money or money's worth (TA 1988 s 677(9)). A capital sum is treated as paid to the settlor if it is paid at his direction or, as a result of his assignment, to a third party (TA 1988 s 677(10)).

The capital sum will only be caught by s 677 to the extent that it is less than, or equals, the income available in the settlement; this means the undistributed income of the fund from any relevant year: ie any year of assessment after 1937–38. Any excess will not be charged in the year of receipt but it may be charged later if income becomes available in any of the next 11 years (TA 1988 s 677(1)(b)).

EXAMPLE 11.15

The undistributed net income of a settlement is as follows:

Year 1 £10,000
Year 2 £ 2,500
Year 3 £15,000
Year 4 £ 6,000
Year 5 £ 7,000

In year 3, the trustees lend the settlor £45,000. That loan is a capital sum and, therefore, the settlor is charged to income tax in year 3 on that sum to the extent that it represents available income. As the available income is £27,500 (years 1-3) he will be taxed on £27,500 grossed up at 35%—ie on £42,308. He will not be subject to basic or additional rate tax on that income so that if his marginal rate is 40% he will be taxed at 5% (40% — 35%).

The remaining £17,500 is carried forward to be taxed in succeeding years when income becomes available; in year 4, for instance, £6,000 is available. If the loan is repaid, there will be no further charge on available income in subsequent years, but any tax paid during the loan period cannot be recovered (s 677(4)).

Section 677 also applies to a capital sum received by the settlor from a body corporate connected with the settlement. Generally, a company will be connected with a settlement if it is a close company and the participators include the trustees of the settlement (TA 1988 s 681(5)). The width of s 677 and its somewhat capricious nature (see for instance *De Vigier v IRC* (1964)) means that settlements will often contain a clause prohibiting the payment of capital sums to the settlor or his spouse.   [**11.69**]

5   **General conclusions**

With the demise of the income settlement, the transfer of income producing capital assets has assumed greater importance. So long as the settlor is prepared to sever all interest in the property settled, the anti-avoidance provisions considered above need not cause problems in the majority of cases. Particularly attractive settlements include those made by grandparents on their infant grandchildren under which use is made of the grandchild's personal allowance to ensure that income in the settlement is effectively tax free. By contrast, parental settlements in favour of the settlor's own infant unmarried children are less attractive since (unless the settlement falls within *Example 11.10*) the income must be accumulated if it is not to attract tax at the settlor's rate. Hence, the settlement income will suffer an irrecoverable 35% charge. Given a top rate of income tax of only 40%, a saving of 5% may not justify the expenses involved in creating and running the relevant trust.   [**11.70**]

12 Estates in the course of administration

Personal Representatives ('PRs', meaning both executors and administrators) are under a duty to administer a deceased's estate. From the point of view of taxation this involves:

(1) A duty to settle the deceased's outstanding income tax to the date of death. Although this chapter is concerned primarily with income tax, notice that there may also be an outstanding CGT liability (see Chapter 15) and that the PRs cannot obtain a grant of probate until any IHT, payable on their application for a grant, has been accounted for (see Chapter 22).

(2) Liability to income tax during the administration period. In addition, the PRs may incur a CGT liability (see Chapter 15) and the original IHT bill may require adjustment as a result of events happening after the death (see Chapter 22).

In considering the taxation of an estate in the course of administration, it is also necessary to consider the liability of beneficiaries to tax on any income distributed to them from the estate.   [**12.1**]

I THE DECEASED'S INCOME

The PRs are liable for any income tax owed by the deceased (TMA 1970 s 74(1)). They should report the death to the appropriate inspector of taxes and complete an ordinary income tax return (Form 11) on behalf of the deceased for the period from 6 April preceding his death to the date of death, and for earlier tax years (if necessary!). In computing the income tax of the deceased, normal principles operate and full personal allowances are available for the year of death.

Any outstanding income tax is a debt of the estate thereby reducing the chargeable value for IHT. Conversely, any repayment of income tax will swell the assets of the estate and may increase the IHT bill on death. Failure to make the appropriate returns means that the Revenue can assess the PRs, at any time within three tax years from the end of the tax year of death, for any tax that is owing for a period that is within six years of the date of that assessment (not the date of death). An assessment is made for these purposes when the inspector authorised to make assessments signs the certificate contained in the assessment books kept at the relevant district (*Honig v Sarsfield* (1986)).   [**12.2**]

EXAMPLE 12.1

A died on 28 September 1991 (tax year 1991–92). If the Revenue assess his PRs on 2 January 1993 (tax year 1992–93) they can relate it back to the tax year 1986–87.

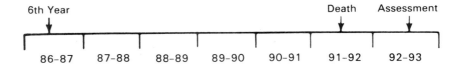

1   **Dividends**

Dividends received before the deceased's death form part of the deceased's income. For IHT purposes the quoted securities in the deceased's estate must be valued at death; if that quotation was '*ex div*' (ie it did not include the value of a declared dividend) the dividend that is to be paid must be added to the value of the security. This problem does not arise when the shares were valued at death 'cum div' since the quotation includes any accruing dividend to date.

If the dividend is paid after the death but relates to a period partly before and partly after death, it may have to be apportioned (Apportionment Act 1870 s 2) for succession purposes.

However, whether or not the dividend is apportioned for succession purposes any dividend paid after the deceased's death is treated as the income of the *estate and not of the deceased* and must not be included in the deceased's tax return (*IRC v Henderson's Executors* (1931)). This rule follows from the fact that as the dividends were never owed to the deceased they never became a part of his income. Only in cases where a dividend is declared due before death, but paid after that death will it be taxed as the deceased's income (see, for instance, *Re Sebright* (1944) and contrast *Potel v IRC* (1971)). Similarly, certain other investment income paid after death but relating to the period before death (for instance bank deposit interest) should be apportioned for succession purposes, but included as estate income for tax purposes. This rule may lead to some double taxation in that the income which is deemed for succession purposes to accrue before death is charged both to IHT (as part of the deceased's estate on death) and also to income tax in the hands of the PRs and beneficiaries. TA 1988 s 699 affords some relief against such double taxation but only to an absolutely entitled residuary beneficiary who is a higher rate taxpayer (see [**12.47**]).   [**12.3**]

EXAMPLE 12.2

T died on 30 May 1991 leaving his residuary estate (including 1,000 shares in B Ltd) to his brother B absolutely. On 15 June 1991 B Ltd declared a dividend on those shares of £450 (£600 gross) in respect of the year ending on 30 June. The dividend was paid on 28 July 1991.

Of this dividend 11/12 (£412.50) is deemed to have accrued before T's death and will be reflected in the value of the shares in T's estate which will have been valued 'cum div'. It will, thus, be taxed as part of the capital in T's estate.

However, for income tax purposes the whole dividend is taxed as the income of the estate, albeit with some relief for double taxation against any higher rate liability of B under TA 1988 s 699.

2 Trust income

Where the deceased was a life tenant under a trust, any income which was received by the trustees before his death is treated as his income and must be included in the PRs' tax return to the date of death. If income was paid to the trustees after the death but is attributable in part to the period before death tax is payable according to the actual apportionment. Any income that is apportioned to the deceased life tenant is taxed as the income of the estate—and not of the deceased (*Wood v Owen* (1941)).

Income that is apportioned to the deceased life tenant forms an asset of his estate, thereby increasing his IHT liability. This may result in an element of double IHT because the apportioned income will affect the value of the trust assets on which the trustees pay IHT on the life tenant's death. This double taxation is avoided by deducting the apportioned income from the value of the settled assets.

EXAMPLE 12.3

T who died on 30 June 1991 was life tenant of a trust. Included in the settled assets was debenture stock in Blank Ltd. On 31 December 1991 B Ltd paid to the trustees the annual interest of £75 (£100 gross). This interest was apportioned by the trustees as to half (£37.50) to T and half (£37.50) to the remainderman X. The £37.50 apportioned to the deceased is estate income. Notice, also, that the £37.50 besides forming an additional asset of T's estate for IHT purposes also swells the value of the trust fund on which the trustees pay IHT at T's rates (see Chapter 22). To avoid the £37.50 being charged twice to IHT, it is deducted from the value of the settled assets. (If T's free estate passed to a residuary beneficiary absolutely, the latter may be entitled to relief under TA 1988 s 699 above.)

If the Apportionment Act 1870 is excluded so that all the income is paid to either a subsequent life tenant or a remainderman, income tax follows the actual apportionment made. That income, therefore, is not taxed as part of the deceased's estate.   **[12.4]**

3 Sole traders and partners

As a general rule the death of a sole trader involves a discontinuance of the business so that the closing year rules must be applied (see TA 1988 s 63 and Chapter 6). If the business passes on death to a spouse, however, the discontinuance provisions are not applied, unless they are claimed (ESC A7). Therefore, for the year of his death, PRs must (unless ESC A7 applies) include in the deceased's tax return the actual profits of the business from the preceding 6 April to the date of death. They are liable for any extra tax arising from the exercise of the Revenue's election under TA 1988 s 63. Terminal loss relief under TA 1988 s 388 (see Chapter 7) may be available.

The death of a partner effects a discontinuance of the partnership so that the closing year rules must be applied, unless the PRs join in an election under TA 1988 s 113(2) (see generally Chapter 29).   **[12.5]-[12.20]**

II THE ADMINISTRATION PERIOD

The administration period is the period from the date of death until the date when the residue is ascertained and ready for distribution. Until that date no beneficiary is entitled to the income or to any property comprised in the estate and, accordingly, is not liable to income tax unless income is actually distributed to him. During the administration period, the PRs are liable, in a representative capacity, to income tax on all the income of the estate computed in the usual way. Their liability is only for basic rate income tax, never to higher rate. As they are not individuals, they have no personal reliefs. Tax relief is available, for one year from the making of the loan, for interest on a loan raised to pay the IHT payable on delivery of the PRs' account, which is attributable to personal property owned beneficially by the deceased and which vests in his PRs, provided that the loan is on a loan account not merely by way of overdraft (TA 1988 s 364). Relief is given against the income of the estate for the year in which the interest is paid but where that income is insufficient relief may be given against income of the preceding year and then against the future income of the estate.

If the PRs receive income from which basic rate tax has been deducted at source (such as dividends) they need not include such income in their tax return as they are subject to no further tax liability on it. Hence, they need only return details of income that they receive gross, such as National Savings Bank interest (on IR Form 1).

Dividends and certain other income received by the PRs after the death in respect of a period wholly or partly before death is taxed as the income of the estate whether or not it is apportioned for succession purposes. Similarly, trust income received by the trustees after the deceased life tenant's death and apportioned to him is taxed as the income of the estate (see [**12.4**]).

When the PRs carry on a business after the death of a sole trader in order to sell it as a going concern or to transfer it to a beneficiary, they must pay basic rate tax on any profits calculated in the usual way. Hence, they can deduct business expenses (TA 1988 s 74) and claim loss relief (normally under TA 1988 s 380 or s 385; s 381 does not apply). If the death effected a discontinuance of the business, the opening year rules apply as from the date of death (TA 1988 ss 61, 62 and see Chapter 6).

When property which produces no income is left to persons in succession (eg, to A for life, remainder to B) part of the capital sum realised on the sale of that property may be treated as income under the rule in *Re Earl of Chesterfield's Trusts* (1883) since, otherwise, the life tenant would receive nothing. Such equitable apportionment involves no income tax liability for the PRs (or the beneficiaries) because the apportionment is of a capital sum.   [**12.21**]-[**12.40**]

III TAXATION OF DISTRIBUTIONS TO BENEFICIARIES

All income received by the PRs suffers basic rate tax either by deduction at source or by direct assessment in their hands. From this taxed income the PRs deduct administration expenses chargeable against income, leaving a net sum available for distribution to beneficiaries entitled to the income from the estate.

If the PRs have a discretion whether to deduct administration expenses from income or capital they should carefully consider the tax position of the beneficiary (if any) entitled to the income. When that beneficiary has a large income, they should deduct their expenses from income so as to reduce his income and, therefore, his tax bill. Conversely, if the beneficiary has only a small income, they should deduct expenses from capital so as not to prejudice any claim that he may have for a repayment of basic rate tax. **[12.41]**

1 General legatees

A general legatee is a person who is entitled to a sum of money (a pecuniary legacy) not charged on any particular fund. This sum is capital and the legatee is generally not entitled to any income unless:
(1) the will directs the PRs to pay him interest; or
(2) the legacy remains unpaid at the end of the executor's year, in which case he is entitled to interest at 5% pa in the absence of a contrary direction; or
(3) the legacy is a 'statutory legacy' arising on intestacy (eg, to a surviving spouse) in which case he is entitled to interest at 6% pa from the date of death to the date of payment.
  Interest is paid gross by the PRs and the legatee is assessed directly to tax under Schedule D Case III on the interest in the year of receipt. If that interest is neither claimed nor paid, there is no income to be assessed in the beneficiary's hands (*Dewar v IRC* (1935)). Once a sum has been set aside to pay the legacy it may, however, be too late to disclaim the income (*Spens v IRC* (1970)). **[12.42]**

2 Specific legatees

A specific legatee is entitled to a particular item of property and to any income produced by it as from the date of death. Therefore, once the PRs vest the legacy in the beneficiary, any income from it which arose during the administration period is related back and taxed as the legatee's income for the tax year(s) when it arose. It will have suffered basic rate tax either through deduction at source or as a result of direct assessment on the PRs. Accordingly, the net income will be passed to the beneficiary together with a tax deduction certificate completed by the PRs. **[12.43]**

EXAMPLE 12.4

A died in September 1990 leaving his 1,000 shares in B Ltd to his nephew T. A dividend of £75 is paid in respect of the shares in January 1991. The administration is completed and the shares vested in T in May 1991 together with the dividend and tax credit for the £25 basic rate tax which has been deducted. T must include the £100 in his income tax return for the tax year 1990-91 (when the dividend was paid) and not 1991-92 (when T received it).

3 Annuitants

An annuity is a pecuniary legacy payable by instalments. The payments are income from which the PRs must deduct basic rate income tax. The net sum will be paid to the annuitant who will be given a certificate of tax deducted.
  A testator usually wants the annuitant to receive a constant sum despite

fluctuations in the tax rates. The two methods most commonly employed are:

(1) The testator provides for the payment of 'such sum as will after deduction of income tax at the basic rate for the time being in force leave (say) £75 pa'.

   The PRs must pay £75 grossed-up at the current basic rate, but they are not liable to indemnify the annuitant against any higher rate income tax for which he may be liable. Conversely, if the annuitant can reclaim all or any of the basic rate tax paid, he need not account for it to the PRs.

(2) If the testator provides for the payment of '£75 pa free from income tax' this imposes an obligation on the PRs to pay such sum as after deducting basic rate income tax leaves £75. However, it also means that the annuitant can recover from the PRs any higher rate tax that he may have to pay on the annuity and any basic rate tax that he can reclaim must be repaid to the PRs. In effect, he will never be left with more nor with less than £75 (see *Re Pettit, Le Fevre v Pettit* (1922), and Chapter 10).

An annuitant can insist on a capital sum being set aside to provide for his annuity (thereby creating an interest in possession trust for IHT purposes: see Chapter 24). If the capital in the estate is insufficient he can demand that the actuarial value of the annuity be paid to him, abated if necessary (*IRC v Lady Castlemaine* (1943)). This capitalised annuity is not subject to income tax either in the PRs' or in the annuitant's hands.

If the will directs the PRs to purchase an annuity for the beneficiary, he will be charged to income tax on the full amount of each annual payment and cannot claim relief under TA 1988 s 656 whereby only the income element is subject to income tax (see Chapter 10). The beneficiary should therefore demand that the PRs give him the appropriate capital sum so that he can buy the annuity himself and claim s 656 relief.

Where there is insufficient income in the estate to pay the annuity in full, the will may direct the PRs to make up the income from capital. If they do so, that capital is treated as income from which basic rate tax must be deducted (*Brodie's WT v IRC* (1933)). The unfortunate result of such 'top-up' provisions is to convert capital into income and it is, therefore, better to give the PRs a discretion to make good any shortfall in the annuity by capital advances.   [**12.44**]

4 Residuary beneficiaries

A beneficiary may have a limited or an absolute interest in residue. A limited interest exists where he is entitled to the income only, eg if the will leaves residue to 'my wife for life, remainder to my children', the wife is entitled only to income from the estate. An absolute interest exists when the beneficiary is entitled to both the income and capital of the residue, as where the residue is left to 'my wife absolutely'. PRs normally have to provide the Revenue with details of the residuary beneficiaries and the nature of their interests.   [**12.45**]

a) *Beneficiary with a limited interest in residue*

The total income produced by the residue during the administration period cannot be calculated accurately until the residue is finally ascertained and the administration completed. Any income paid to the beneficiary during that period will be paid net of basic rate income tax deducted by the PRs. The beneficiary must gross up these sums as part of his total income in the year of receipt for the purposes of his excess liability or to obtain a repayment of basic rate tax (as appropriate).

When the administration is completed, the total net income payments of the period are aggregated and are deemed to have been paid out to the beneficiary at a uniform rate over the administration period. This may necessitate adjustments to his original income tax liability. Such adjustments must be made within three years of the end of the tax year in which the administration is completed. **[12.46]**

EXAMPLE 12.5

Mildred dies on 6 April 1986 leaving the residue of her estate to her son, Sonny, for life, remainder to her daughter, Dotty, absolutely.

The PRs make payments to Sonny net of basic rate tax at 29% in 1986–87; 27% in 1987–88 and 25% in 1988–89. The administration is completed on 5 October 1988 when Sonny receives a final payment of £964. Sonny receives the following sums:

Year	*Net income received* £	*Grossed-up amount*
1986–87	71	£100 (inc tax credit £29)
1987–88	365	£500 (inc tax credit £135)
1988–89	964	£1,285 (inc tax credit £321)
	£1,400	

Sonny's total receipts are £1,400 (net) which sum is deemed to have been paid on a day-to-day basis over the administration period. Hence, Sonny's total income for the administration period is adjusted as follows:

Year	*Net income received* £	*Grossed-up amount*
1986–87	560	£789 (inc tax credit £229)
1987–88	560	£767 (inc tax credit £207)
1988–89 (6 months)	280	£373 (inc tax credit £93)
	£1,400	

Notice (1) That the income paid to Sonny will be the total income of the estate after deducting basic rate tax, any interest on legacies and interest on late payments of IHT, and any administration expenses properly charged to income.

(2) Although Sonny's total net income receipts (£1,400) will equal the net income of the estate his grossed-up income will differ from the total gross income of the estate for a number of reasons, but, in particular, because of changes in the basic rate of income tax and because of the payment of administration expenses by the PRs out of income net of basic rate tax.

b) *Beneficiary with an absolute interest in residue*

Such a beneficiary is entitled to receive both income and capital from the estate. He can, of course, only be charged to income tax insofar as any payments that he receives represent income. For the purpose of calculating to what extent the payments constitute income the following rules are applied (see TA 1988 ss 696(3) and (4), 699, 700).

First, sums paid to the beneficiary in any one year are deemed to be income (net of basic rate income tax) up to the amount of 'net residuary income' available and must be grossed up in order to calculate his total income for the year. 'Residuary income' is the total gross income received by the PRs in the relevant tax year less interest on legacies and on loans to pay IHT and less management expenses properly chargeable against income. 'Net residuary income' is the residuary income of the estate less basic rate tax for that year.

Secondly, any payment in excess of net residuary income is deemed to be capital.

Finally, within three years of the end of the tax year when the administration is completed, the initial assessments are revised as necessary so that the beneficiary is deemed to have received the full net residuary income for each tax year. Any balance that he has received is capital.

EXAMPLE 12.6

Carlos dies on 6 April 1987 leaving his residuary estate to his son, Carl.

The administration is completed on 5 April 1990 when Carl receives a final payment of £1,000.

During the course of the administration, Carl receives the following payments:

Year	Basic rate of income tax	Net residuary income	Carl's receipts
1987–88	27%	£700	£365
1988–89	25%	£700	£1,300
1989–90	25%	£700	£1,200

The income tax calculation proceeds as follows:

(1) *1987–88:* £365 is income in Carl's hands which he must gross up to £500. It will be taxed as part of his total income for that year. £335 of the net residuary income for 1987–88 is unapplied.

(2) *1988–89:* £700 is treated as income up to the net residuary income of that year (1988–89) which gives Carl total income of £933 (gross) for inclusion in his income tax return. The remaining £600 (£1,300 − £700) is capital.

(3) *1989–90:* £700 of the £1,200 paid to Carl is income (and is, therefore, £933 gross). The remaining £500 (£1,200 − £700) is capital.

(4) *5 April 1990:* Adjustments have to be made so that Carl is deemed to have received all the net residuary income produced by the estate over the administration period. Thus, in 1987–88 his income will be adjusted from £500 (£365 grossed up) to £959 (the £700 net residuary income grossed up). In both 1988–89 and 1989–90 adjustments are unnecessary since the income was distributed in full during those years.

Income which accrued before death, but is received by the PRs after death, is included in the value of the deceased's estate for IHT purposes and is also taxed as the income of the estate (see [**12.3**]). Some relief against this double taxation is provided by TA 1988 s 699 which allows a reduction in the residuary income for the purposes of any liability to higher rate tax of a residuary beneficiary absolutely entitled to residue. The reduction is of an amount equal to the IHT chargeable on that income at the estate rate and the resultant sum is then grossed up at the basic rate of income tax.   [**12.47**]

EXAMPLE 12.7

X died on 30 April 1991. He left his residuary estate including 1,000 debentures in B Ltd to his daughter D. His PRs received interest of £150 (£200 gross) from B Ltd in November 1991 in respect of that company's accounting year ending 31 October 1991. The whole interest is taxed as the income of the estate but, as half the interest accrued before death, that portion is included in X's estate for IHT purposes. Under TA 1988 s 699 if D is a higher rate taxpayer one-half of the interest is eligible for relief. Assume that the estate rate of IHT is 20%.

	£
Interest (gross)	£200
Sum accrued before death	100
Less income tax for year of death	25
	£75

	£
The relief is calculated as:	
£75 × 20% (IHT estate rate)	15
Add income tax	5
Grossed-up amount that can be deducted from the residuary income to reduce D's liability to higher rate income tax only	£20

13   The overseas dimension

The territorial scope of any tax raises both theoretical and practical questions. The UK system, for instance, proceeds on the basis that if an individual is closely connected with the UK he will be subject to UK tax on his property (both income and capital) worldwide. By contrast, an individual who has only a tenuous connection will be taxed on property (income and capital) situated in or arising from the UK and not on other, worldwide, assets. A strong element of practical reality inevitably permeates this area: theoretically the UK could impose a tax on the income of a Chinaman resident in Peking but little revenue would be raised from that source! (The practical constraints upon tax collection and enforcement are well illustrated in the House of Lords speeches in *Clark v Oceanic Contractors Inc* (1983): see [**13.41**]).

The 'connecting factors' which determine whether the individual should be subject to income tax are residence and ordinary residence and the meaning of these terms will be considered in this chapter. Notice, however, that this discussion will also be relevant when the territorial scope of CGT is considered (in Chapter 20); IHT (in Chapter 27); and corporation tax (in Chapter 28). Domicile, which is relevant for income tax but of prime concern for IHT, will be considered in Chapter 27.

Liability to UK income tax is determined by the source of the income and the residence of the recipient. As a general rule, a UK resident is subject to UK income tax on all his income wherever its source, including income arising abroad reign income'), whereas a non-UK resident is only liable to UK income tax on income arising to him in the UK (the 'foreign taxpayer'). However, a non-UK domiciled individual will only be taxed on foreign income if remitted to the UK.   [**13.1**]

I   RESIDENCE AND ORDINARY RESIDENCE

1   **Residence**

Neither 'residence' nor 'ordinary residence' is statutorily defined and therefore the meaning of these terms has to be sought in decisions of the courts and in the useful guidance booklet published by the Inland Revenue ('Residents and Non-Residents – liability to tax in the UK': IR 20 (1986)). The general dictionary definition of these words has usually been adopted but for taxation purposes questions of residence do not depend upon any mental element

*" 'An inivividual is resident and ordinarily resident in the
United Kingdom if he is living in the ordinary course
of his life, or for an extended period; also though normally
he lives here, if he is abroad for occasional residence
only; of if he visits the United Kingdom, year by year,
even though his main home is abroad' . . . who on earth
wrote this, Harold Pinter?"*

(unlike domicile). Hence, the American who finds himself stuck in the UK because of illness may become resident here although his intention is to return to America as soon as he is fit to travel.

A person can be resident in more than one country so that the UK citizen who spends the winter months in Manchester and the summer in the Costa del Sol is probably resident both in the UK and in Spain. Alternatively, an individual may have no residence as in the case of the travel writer who spends two years exploring North and South America by bus and is therefore continually on the move (or waiting to be on the move!). In this sense, residence contrasts with domicile since a person must always have a country of domicile and the abandonment of a domicile of choice therefore results in the revival of the domicile of origin.

A permanent abode is not necessary for residence in a country so that the individual who moves from UK hotel to UK hotel will be resident here. This proposition was graphically illustrated in the courts by reference to the example of that well known tax avoider, the homeless tramp:

> 'Take the case of a homeless tramp, who shelters tonight under a bridge, tomorrow in the greenwood and as the unwelcome occupant of a farm outhouse the night after. He wanders in this way all over the United Kingdom. But will anyone say that he does not live in the United Kingdom? – and will anyone regard it as a misuse of language to say he resides in the United Kingdom?' (Lord President Clyde in *Reid v IRC* (1926).)

Residence and ordinary residence are not decided in a vacuum but in relation to particular tax years and in general, the individual who is resident for any part of a tax year is treated as being resident for the whole of that year. This proposition, that it is generally not possible to split tax years into periods of residence and non-residence is made explicit in the capital gains tax legislation where it is provided in CGTA 1979 s 2 that CGT is levied if the individual is resident in the UK during *any part* of the tax year.

EXAMPLE 13.1

Alan, resident and ordinarily resident in the UK, goes to live abroad from June 1990 to March 1992. He will be treated as retaining his UK residence in 1990-91 and 1991-92.

As a matter of practice, however, but only in limited cases, the tax year may be split into a period of residence and non-residence. This is permitted, for instance, when an individual leaves the UK for permanent residence abroad and likewise when an individual comes to the UK for permanent residence purposes. In the former case, UK residence ceases on the day following the day of departure from the UK: in the latter, UK residence is acquired from the day of arrival. A similar splitting of the tax year occurs when an individual takes up full-time employment abroad.   [**13.2**]

2   Who is a UK resident?

In three situations an individual is treated as resident in the UK.

First, if he spends more than six months here in any one tax year. This absolute rule is derived from TA 1988 s 336 and six months is interpreted by the Revenue to mean 183 days (even in 1992 – a leap year!) It is normal practice to ignore days of arrival and departure (IR 20 para 8) although this will presumably not apply to the case of the EEC national who commutes to the UK to work each day!

Secondly, a person who has left the UK for permanent residence abroad is regarded as continuing to be resident here if he returns to the UK for periods which equal three months or more per tax year. It should be noted that the Revenue booklet refers to a test in terms of months (not 90 days) but in the case of short visits this three months period will inevitably have to be computed on a daily basis.

Thirdly, the individual who has UK accommodation available for his use and who merely sets foot in this country (even if he does not visit that accommodation) is treated as UK resident. In *Cooper v Cadwalader* (1904), for instance, an American barrister took a lease on a shooting box in Scotland where he lived for two months each year. He was held to be resident in the UK as was the taxpayer in *Loewenstein v de Salis* (1926) who had the use of a residence belonging to the company which he controlled and which he visited for hunting.

EXAMPLE 13.2

(1)   Barry comes to England from America to study law at London University. The course is to last three years. As Barry will be present in the UK for more than six months in each of those tax years he is UK resident from the date of his arrival.

(2)   Ellie comes to the UK on holiday from America. Usually her visit is for one month per annum. She will not be treated as UK resident (contrast the position if she bought a cottage in Dorset which she stayed in during her holiday).

This available accommodation test may operate harshly and as a trap for the unwary and only limited exceptions are recognised in the Revenue booklet (see para 28). A major exception is, however, found in TA 1988 s 335 which provides for the accommodation to be ignored in the case of an individual who works full time in a trade, profession, vocation, office or employment all the duties of which are performed outside the UK. Full time for these purposes is normally considered to mean a full working day five days a week and duties performed within the UK may only be ignored if their performance is merely incidental to the performance of other duties outside the UK. Precisely what is meant by incidental duties is somewhat unclear: in *Dixon v Robson* (1972), a KLM airline pilot who maintained an English residence was held not to perform merely incidental duties when he landed in the UK (in all, some 38 times out of a total of 811 flights over a period of six years). Undoubtedly where similar duties are performed in the UK to those abroad they cannot be incidental but the overseas employee who returns to the UK for, eg, fresh instructions or fresh stock would be considered to be performing merely incidental duties during that period.

EXAMPLE 13.3

Pedro, a pilot with Mexico Airlines, keeps a flat in London for stopovers in the UK. He otherwise resides in Mexico City but, if he visits the UK in any tax year, will be treated as UK resident in that year. Apart from scheduled stopovers (which fall within *Dixon v Robson* above) bringing an aircraft in for a major overhaul will result in the acquisition of resident status although an emergency landing will not! The UK does not have a double tax treaty with Mexico although Pedro's salary from Mexico Airlines should escape UK taxation under TA 1988 s 193 (long absence relief).

SP 2/91 is concerned with the 'three month rule' (the second situation above) and provides that 'any days spent in the UK because of *exceptional circumstances beyond an individual's control* (such as illness) are excluded from the calculation'. It should be noted that this SP does not apply for the purpose of computing the six month (or 183 days) period.   [13.3]

3 Acquiring and losing resident status

An individual who comes to the UK with the intention of taking up permanent residence here will be regarded as both resident and ordinarily resident from the date of arrival (so that the tax year is split). By contrast, a visitor will not become UK resident unless he falls within the tests set out in 2 above. A person who comes to the UK intending to spend three years or more here will be regarded as resident and ordinarily resident from the date of his arrival: if when he comes it is not clear whether he will spend three years here he will become ordinarily resident as from the beginning of the tax year in which he decides to stay or, if earlier, in which the third anniversary of his arrival falls.

The casual UK resident (eg one who spends an isolated six months here) will lose that resident status simply by returning abroad. Similarly, the individual who is UK resident by reason only of the accommodation test will cease to be resident if he sells that accommodation or if it ceases to be available for his use (eg if it is let commercially). If a person goes abroad for full-time service under a contract of employment which requires all the duties of his employment to be performed abroad (with any UK duties being merely incidental) and his absence from the UK extends over a period covering a complete tax year with interim visits to the UK not exceeding six months in any tax year or an average of three months per tax year, then he is normally regarded as neither resident nor ordinarily resident in the UK

from the day following the date of his departure. Available accommodation
is ignored in such cases.   **[13.4]**

4   **Ordinary residence**

Ordinary residence has been held to mean habitual residence: ie a regular
choice of abode which is a settled purpose and forms part of the regular
order of an individual's life (see, in particular, *R v Barnet London Borough
Council, ex p Nilish Shah* (1983)). A person may therefore be resident without
being ordinarily resident in the UK and vice versa.

> **EXAMPLE 13.4**
>
> (1) Bonzo has lived in Hackney for many years. He sells his terraced house
>   and goes on a world cruise for 18 months. He ceases to be UK resident
>   but remains ordinarily resident.
> (2) Claude, a French journalist, visits the UK for six months in the 1991–
>   92 tax year to study the eating habits of the natives. He becomes UK
>   resident but is not ordinarily resident.

In a number of cases liability to UK tax is *only* imposed on individuals
who are ordinarily resident in the UK (for instance under TA 1988 ss 739–
740) whilst, in other cases, liability arises if the individual is either resident
or ordinarily resident, eg CGT liability under CGTA 1979 s 2(1).

By TA 1988 s 334, a British citizen who has been ordinarily resident
in the UK and who leaves for occasional residence abroad will be treated
during his absence as remaining resident in the UK unless he can prove
to the contrary. In the case of *Reed v Clark* (1985), it was held that s 334
was a charging provision and was not, therefore, limited to persons who
were out of the UK for part only of a tax year but could equally apply
to persons living abroad throughout such a year of assessment. In that case,
however, the taxpayer (the pop star Dave Clark) left the UK with the
deliberate intention of living and working abroad for a limited period in
excess of one tax year and then returning to the UK. On these facts the
judge held that his absence could not be described as for the purpose of
merely occasional residence abroad so that he was not treated as still UK
resident under s 334. Occasional residence under this section, the judge
concluded, was to be contrasted with ordinary or settled residence.

> 'The presence of a tax avoidance intention may help to show, for instance,
> why a person went abroad at all or at the particular time he did, how long
> he intended to remain away, or where his home in fact was in the year of
> assessment. But residence abroad for a carefully chosen limited period of work
> there . . . is no less residence abroad for that period because the major reason
> for it was the avoidance of tax. Likewise with ordinary residence.' (Nicholls
> J, at 346.)   **[13.5]**

5   **Corporations, partnerships and trusts**

Corporations

Prior to 15 March 1988, a company was only regarded as resident in the
UK (and therefore subject to corporation tax on its world-wide profits) if
its central management and control was located in the UK. Central
management and control was considered to reside at the place where board

meetings were held and not necessarily where the company was incorporated or registered (see *De Beers Consolidated Mines v Howe* (1906) and SP 6/83).

EXAMPLE 13.5

The directors of a Kenyan subsidiary company always held meetings in Kenya but in fact the company was managed, in breach of its articles, by its UK parent company. The company was therefore held to be resident in England since the question was where the actual control and management was located (see *Unit Construction Co Ltd v Bullock* (1959)).

From 15 March 1988 this control and management test was supplemented by a further test based on the place of company incorporation (FA 1988 s 66). As a result, companies incorporated in the UK will always remain UK resident even if control and management is exercised abroad (hence, the non-resident UK company will become a thing of the past). Foreign incorporated companies may become resident, as before, if their central management and control is exercised in the UK. Transitional rules deal with the position of UK incorporated companies which were non-resident before 15 March and under these rules such companies will be deemed UK resident no later than 15 March 1993 (see further Chapter 28).   [13.6]

Partnerships

A similar central management and control test applies for partnerships. If the management and control of the business is exercised abroad, the firm is deemed to be non-resident even though individual partners may be resident in the UK and conversely a firm established abroad will be treated as resident in the UK if managed and controlled here. Given that a partnership is not normally taxed as a separate entity, even more important than the residence of the firm is the residence of the individual partners. The UK Revenue authorities will look through a UK partnership to the residence of its individual members for the purpose of deciding what, if any, is the liability of that person to taxation. So far as UK source income is concerned, individual members of a partnership will be subject to income tax at basic and higher rates whether UK resident or not. So far as non-UK source income is concerned, however, UK residents will be subject to tax on this income whereas partners who are non-UK resident will escape UK tax and will suffer tax either in the country where the profits are earned or, alternatively, in the country of their residence. In the case of a trading partnership which is itself managed and controlled in the United Kingdom, it is highly unlikely that a trade carried on, for instance, in France would be treated as being carried on wholly outside the UK and therefore the profits will attract tax under Case I of Schedule D and non-resident partners will suffer UK income tax.   [13.7]

Trustees and personal representatives

The residence of a trust is determined by reference to the trustees and the Revenue always considered that a trust was resident for income tax purposes in the UK if any *one* of them was so resident (cp residence rules for CGT). In *Dawson v IRC* (1989), however, three discretionary settlements (governed by English law) were established between 1946 and 1965 by a family then domiciled and resident in England. In 1969 the family became permanently resident in Switzerland and by 1975-6 of the three trustees only one was

UK resident. The assets then consisted primarily of securities in non-UK companies: the certificates were in the name of a Swiss bank and the income was paid into an account at that bank. In line with the practice already mentioned, the Revenue assessed the sole UK trustee to income tax on the whole income of the settlements. All trustee meetings were held in Switzerland and none of the income was remitted to the United Kingdom. The House of Lords concluded that the relevant provision in TA 1988 s 18(1)(a)(i) did not result in a tax charge arising since that provision required *all* persons entitled to the income to reside in the United Kingdom. Accordingly, it was limited to the case where all the trustees were UK resident. Lord Keith accepted that whichever way the decision had gone anomalies would result:

> 'Counsel for the Crown for his part observed that if the taxpayer's argument were correct the foreign income of an accumulation trust administered in England and governed by English law could be made to avoid taxation by the simple expedient of appointing one co-trustee resident abroad. He further maintained that the anti-avoidance provisions of TA 1988 ss 739–745 relating to the transfer of assets abroad could in the case of trusts be side-stepped by a similar expedient. The issue cannot be resolved by a balancing of the anomalies which would arise on either view ... It can be perceived that there will be much to be said for making the liability to tax depend on the centre of administration of the trust and the place of residence of the majority of the trustees as is the position with Capital Gains Tax ... but Parliament has not so far chosen to do that.'

Not surprisingly, FA 1989 ss 110–111 and 151 amended the law in line with the former Revenue practice. Accordingly, when the trustees of a settlement include one UK resident and one non-UK resident (a 'mixed' trust), the trustees will be treated as UK resident *unless* the settlor was neither resident, ordinarily resident, nor domiciled in the UK when he set up the trust or at a later time when he provided funds for the trust. Furthermore, assessments may now be made in the name of any one or more of the trustees. Thus, in the *Dawson* case the sole UK trustee could now be made liable to pay UK income tax on the entire overseas income which had not been remitted to the UK. Subject to transitional provisions for existing mixed trusts, these rules apply to income arising from 6 April 1989.

EXAMPLE 13.6

(1) The de Vere family trust was set up in 1980 when the settlor had no connection with the UK. All the trustees are non-UK resident and therefore the trust will be liable to UK income tax on UK source income *only*. This position will be unaltered provided that there is at least one non-UK resident trustee: FA 1989 s 110 cannot apply because the settlor had no connection with the UK and the House of Lords' ruling in *Dawson* requires all trustees to be UK resident if the trust's worldwide income is to be subject to UK tax.

(2) The Walpole trust was set up by UK residents. It has since been exported and currently all the trustees are non-UK resident and there is no UK source income. There is no liability to UK income tax.

(3) As in (2) except that there is now one UK resident trustee. The trust's world-wide income is subject to UK income tax which can be assessed on the UK resident trustee.

FA 1989 s 111 extended the residence rules for trustees to personal representatives and in so doing created an apparent injustice. Assume, for instance, that Dan Dare is an American domiciliary who comes to the UK to work or to start up a business. As it is envisaged that he will stay in this country for a number of years he acquires a house and other assets here and, accordingly, is advised to make a UK will (with UK personal representatives) disposing of this property. The bulk of his assets remain in America and a separate American will disposing of this property is also made. Assume then that Dan dies without having altered these arrangements. Under s 111 UK tax will be imposed on *all the income produced by his estate* passing under *both* wills since under his English will UK resident personal representatives have been appointed. As Dan is resident in the UK the conditions laid down for the operation of the section are satisfied given that the definition of personal representatives includes not just the UK appointees but also (in relation to another country) 'the persons having under its law any functions corresponding to the functions for administration purposes of personal representatives'. The end result appears unjust: surely UK tax should only be charged on UK source income arising under his UK estate? In practice, although no formal statement has been made, it is understood that the Revenue will apply the legislation in this way.   **[13.8]**

6   Double tax treaties

The standard double tax treaty contains a provision which will determine in which country a person is to be treated as resident. Such treaties proceed upon the assumption that a person will only be resident in one of the two treaty jurisdictions. It is important to realise that although the treaty may therefore lead to the person in question being treated as resident in only one of the two countries, this will only apply for the purposes of the taxes and types of income and gains covered by the relevant treaty. Accordingly, for other purposes, the individual may still be treated as resident in the other country.   **[13.9]**

7   Reform of the residence rules

On 28 July 1988 the Revenue issued a Consultative Document on reform of the residence rules for individuals. One of the main recommendations involved a redefinition of residence for tax purposes: in essence an individual present in the UK for 183 days or more in a year would be resident whereas a person present for 30 days or less in a tax year would not be resident. In cases where the individual was present for some period between 30 and 183 days in the year, his position would then be determined by including a proportion of days spent in the UK in the two preceding years. Available accommodation would cease to be relevant. So far as the basis of liability is concerned, a three tier system was envisaged: first, liability to tax on UK income only would apply to non-UK residents; secondly, an intermediate basis of taxation would apply to individuals resident in the UK for at least seven out of the previous 14 years subject to a further test such as domicile; and, finally, world-wide income and gains would be taxed in the case of all other UK residents. So far as the basis of tax is concerned, the document considered the rival merits and demerits of the remittance basis as against taxing a percentage of world-wide income and gains.

The attempts made by the document to relate liability for UK tax more closely to the degree of an individual's connection with this country did not attract favourable comments. Accordingly, during the 1989 Budget Debate, a government spokesman stated that:

'The UK derives considerable benefit from people who come here from overseas to carry on business and other activities. We have no wish to see them leave ... Considerable concern was expressed about the implications of moving to a world income basis of liability for certain categories of people not domiciled here. We decided that the world income approach would not provide a satisfactory basis of taxation for non-UK domiciled foreigners who are resident in this country. Therefore we do not intend pursuing it, and in those circumstances it is not our intention to bring forward any proposals at this time.'   **[13.10]-[13.20]**

II   TAXATION OF FOREIGN INCOME

1   **Profits of a trade, profession or vocation (Schedule D)**

a) *General*

A UK resident is assessed under Schedule D Cases I or II on all his profits arising from a trade, profession or vocation ('trade') carried on by him in the UK, despite some of the profits being attributable to overseas business: TA 1988 s 18(3).   **[13.21]**

b) *Trade carried on wholly abroad (Schedule D Case V)*

Non-resident trade   For a trader to be assessed under Schedule D Case V, he must be resident in the UK, but the trade must be carried on wholly abroad. This is a question of fact, and for the sole trader who is resident in the UK and who has the sole right to manage and control the business it will be difficult to argue that the trade is wholly carried on abroad (*Ogilvie v Kitton* (1908)).

A UK resident company may, however, be able to show that it is trading wholly abroad (*Mitchell v Egyptian Hotels Ltd* (1915)). Where the company establishes a foreign subsidiary (as opposed to a branch) it is a question of fact whether that subsidiary is carrying on its own trade or acting merely as agent for the parent company. The answer depends upon where the head and brains of the trade are to be found and not on who owns the shares. To avoid the risk of the subsidiary being treated as UK resident it is, therefore, prudent to ensure that UK resident directors are not in a majority on the subsidiary's board; that the non-resident directors of the subsidiary are men of substance who are capable of independent thought and judgment; and that board meetings (where 'real' decisions and not just 'rubber stampings' occur) should be held outside the UK. (Note, however, the rules taxing controlled foreign companies under TA 1988 ss 747–755; see **[28.164]**.)

If a non-resident partnership trades in the UK, any UK resident partner will be assessed under Case I on all the UK profits and under Case V on his share of any foreign profits. The crucial distinction is between trading *with* the UK and trading *within* the UK.

EXAMPLE 13.7

Wino and Co, a French partnership, have one partner resident in London who arranges for sales of their wine in the UK. In deciding whether the firm is trading in the UK (so that a Schedule D Case I assessment is appropriate) the precise mechanics of the wine sales are important. If contracts are made in the UK it is likely that a business in the UK is being carried on, whereas, if the orders are merely obtained here and the actual contracts are made in

France the firm is merely trading with the UK so that any assessment to UK tax will be under Case V (see generally the problem of when non-UK residents trade within the UK discussed at [**13.62**]).

Although 'trade' is used here to include professions and vocations, in practice, profits arising from a profession will rarely be taxed under Case V because the individual exercising his profession wholly abroad is unlikely to be a UK resident and hence will escape UK income tax completely (see *Davies v Braithwaite* (1931)). [**13.22**]

Computation of profits Tax under Case V is assessed on income arising in the preceding tax year whether or not it is remitted to the UK ('the arising basis'). If, however, the taxpayer is not domiciled or not ordinarily resident in the UK he is taxed under Case V on the remittance basis only: ie on actual sums received in the UK in the preceding tax year . . . 'from remittances payable in the UK or from property imported or from money or value arising from property not imported . . .' (TA 1988 s 65(5)).

The opening and closing year rules of Case I (TA 1988 ss 60–63) do not apply to income taxed under Case V. Instead, in the tax year when the source of the income first arises and for the following tax year, the taxpayer is taxed on the actual profits (or remittances if applicable) of the first tax year which puts him into the preceding tax year basis by the third year.

When the source ceases, the taxpayer is taxed in the final year on the actual profits of that year and in the penultimate year on actual profits or the preceding year basis whichever shows the greater profit. The rules are the same for a partnership except that TA 1988 s 113 does not apply so that there is no deemed discontinuance on a change of partners (s 113 is discussed in Chapter 29).

Deductible expenses (including travelling expenses if, broadly, the same conditions are met as in the case of an employee working abroad: see below), capital allowances and losses are calculated as under Case I, but loss relief is only given against other foreign (and not UK) income.

Where, despite the endeavours of the taxpayer, income which is taxed on the arising basis cannot be remitted to the UK because of foreign laws, executive action abroad, or the non-availability of foreign currency, the payment of tax is postponed until the problem passes. [**13.23**]

The remittance basis There is no definition of 'remittance' for income tax. Tax is levied under Case V on actual sums received or treated as received in the UK by the taxpayer on the preceding year basis and includes the proceeds from property representing a remittance, but does not include investments of the income which are brought into this country so long as they are not realised in the UK by the taxpayer (TA 1988 s 65 and see *Scottish Provident Institution v Allan* (1903)). The sum must be received as the income of the trader and not, eg, as a gift, nor as the income of someone else, nor as capital. This is a question of fact.

TA 1988 s 65 also contains anti-avoidance provisions designed to catch disguised remittances of a person ordinarily resident in the UK, eg, where the taxpayer arranges for his UK debt to be repaid out of profits earned abroad.

If the income is not remitted in the year when it arises, the trader cannot be taxed until the sums are remitted whereupon he is taxed by reference to the year of remission. As this could result in an increased tax bill, he can elect to be taxed by reference to the year when the particular remittances arose.

The remittance basis provides a valuable element in tax planning for non-domiciled UK residents.   **[13.24]**

EXAMPLE 13.8

(1) Carlos, domiciled and ordinarily resident in Spain, but resident in England carries on his business in France. Out of the profits of his business he buys a Picasso painting in France which he brings to England. This is property in kind and not a remittance under Case V. Were he to sell the Picasso in the UK, he would be taxable under TA 1988 s 65. (Note, however, that the remittance rules for emoluments (see **[13.37]**) are drafted in wider terms and catch some remittances of property in kind.)

(2) Diego, resident but not domiciled in the UK, arranges for his share of the profits in an overseas firm to be invested abroad. There is no remittance and therefore no UK tax charge. Should he need to remit foreign monies he will still avoid UK tax if the remitted sum is capital. He may be able to arrange this by operating two overseas bank accounts, one for capital and one for income. Assume, for instance, that he receives rents from letting land abroad which are paid into one account and that receipts from occasional land sales are paid into a separate account. Remittances from the latter are capital (and not subject to UK income tax though a CGT charge may arise: see Chapter 20) and Diego can compensate for the reduction in this account by arranging for sums in the other (income) account to be invested, for example, in the purchase of replacement land abroad.

2   Other categories of income

Income other than from a trade or employment which accrues to a UK resident from a foreign source will be taxed under Schedule C or under Schedule D Case IV or V.   **[13.25]**

a) *Schedule C*

Schedule C taxes dividends received from investments in UK and foreign public funds and foreign public authorities or institutions which are payable in the UK and dividends payable in the Republic of Ireland in respect of UK government securities registered with the Bank of Ireland. Under Schedule C, basic rate tax is deducted at source from the dividends by the person entrusted with making the payment in the UK (the paying agent) and the taxpayer is assessed to any higher rate tax on a current year basis.

Certain payments out of public funds are specifically not charged under Schedule C (eg interest from trustee savings banks and War Loan is directly assessed in the recipient's hands under Schedule D Case III).   **[13.26]**

b) *Schedule D Cases IV and V*

Today the operation of Schedule D Cases IV and V is identical and it is merely an historical anachronism that certain income is chargeable under one Case rather than the other. Strictly, Case IV taxes income arising to a UK resident from foreign securities, other than those charged under Schedule C, and Case V charges income from possessions outside the UK.

Tax is charged under both Cases on income arising in the preceding tax year but such income is taxed only on the remittance basis when the recipient is not domiciled in the UK, or resident but not ordinarily resident in the

UK (TA 1988 s 65(1)). The following categories of income are taxed under Cases IV or V: [**13.27**]

Distributions from companies Distributions are charged under Case V unless they relate to a secured debt: eg a debenture (Case IV). The distribution will only be taxable under either Case if it is of income. This is decided by applying the local law to see whether or not the *corpus* of the asset is left intact after the distribution: if it is, the payment will be taxed as income; if not, it is capital (*IRC v Reid's Trustees* (1949)). [**13.28**]

Income from land and unsecured loans Such income is taxable under Case V. [**13.29**]

Income from a foreign trust If a UK resident beneficiary has an absolute right to all or part of the income of the foreign trust (one where the trustees are non-UK resident and the assets are abroad), he is taxed under Case V on the income as it arises and whether or not he receives it (*Williams v Singer* (1921)). Similar principles apply to a discretionary beneficiary in whose favour the trustees have exercised their discretion to appoint income. [**13.30**]

Income from a foreign partnership In *Padmore v IRC* (1987) it was held that a UK resident partner was not subject to income tax under Schedule D Case V on his share of the profits of an overseas partnership because of the wording of the Jersey double tax treaty. The decision was reversed retrospectively and the present position therefore is that such treaties do not affect the taxation of a partner's share of overseas profits or gains (see TA 1988 s 112(4), (5)). [**13.30**]

Miscellany Certain pensions (see [**13.40**]) and alimony ordered by a foreign court are taxed under Case V. [**13.32**]

3 Employment income (Schedule E)

The three Cases of Schedule E aim to tax the emoluments wherever earned of a person resident or ordinarily resident in the UK.

The expression '*foreign emoluments*' used in all three Cases means the emoluments of a person not domiciled in the UK whose employer is not a UK resident. The employee may be resident or ordinarily resident in the UK (such as a French domiciled journalist employed by a French newspaper in England as their foreign correspondent). When an individual is in receipt of foreign emoluments and the duties of the relevant employment are performed wholly outside the UK, those emoluments are taxed on a remittance not a receipts basis. To ensure that taxation is charged on the remittance basis, it is therefore necessary to establish first, that the duties of the office are performed wholly outside the UK; secondly, under a contract of employment with a non-resident employer; and, thirdly, that the individual is not domiciled in the UK. Accordingly, in the case of a new arrival in the UK who will perform duties both abroad and in the UK, it is essential that the overseas duties should be carried out under a separate contract of employment. Obviously considerable care needs to be taken in drafting the terms of any such contract since the Revenue have the power to ensure that the emoluments are not artificially weighted in favour of the overseas contract. [**13.33**]

a) *Individual resident and ordinarily resident: Case I*

Where a person is resident and ordinarily resident in the UK, but is required by his employment to perform duties wholly or partly outside the UK, he is charged on all his emoluments under the usual principles of Schedule E (see Chapter 5) with the following limited relief.   [**13.34**]

Long absence (TA 1988 s 193; Sch 12)   Where the duties are performed wholly or partly abroad during a qualifying period of absence of at least 365 days the employee can deduct 100% of the emoluments earned during that period. This 365 day period is unlikely to fall all within one tax year—if it did the employee would probably be regarded as non-resident so that Case I would not apply and he would not be liable to UK tax on his foreign earnings. Accordingly, when it straddles tax years, the 100% deduction is given against so much of the total emoluments of that year as were earned during the part of the qualifying period falling within that year (see *Example 13.9*).

A qualifying period of 365 days means that the employee must be abroad for a *continuous* period of 365 days although a period abroad will be continuous for these purposes unless visits back to the UK exceed 62 consecutive days for any single period, or 1/6th of the total days in the period from leaving the UK to returning to the UK for the next visit (see *Example 13.9*). The period of permitted intervening days is increased from 62 to 183 and the permitted fraction from one-sixth to one-half in the case of seafarers (TA 1988 Sch 12 para 3(2A): increased further in FA 1991).

Terminal leave spent abroad will count as a qualifying period; if spent in the UK it will not (see *Robins v Durkin* (1988): days spent in the UK during the employment but after the period of absence from the UK had ended cannot be included in the 365 day qualifying period). Some duties (such as reporting back to base in the UK) can be regarded as incidental to overseas duties but the days so spent in the UK nevertheless count as 'days in the UK' in calculating the 1/6 and 62 day rules.

TA 1988 Sch 12 para 2 contains anti-avoidance provisions which apply whenever the duties of that employment or any other 'associated employment' held by the employee are not performed wholly abroad as would be the case if the intervals between periods of absence were spent performing duties in the UK. This is to prevent an abuse of the relief by the loading of emoluments onto the foreign duties. Employments are 'associated' if they are with the same employer or with different companies in the same group (see para 2(3) and *Platten v Brown* (1986)). It may, therefore, be advantageous for the employee to have a separate service contract for his duties abroad.

In applying this relief, TA 1988 Sch 12 para 6 provides that, if overseas duties are merely incidental to a main UK employment, they are deemed to be performed in the UK. Even where the duties are performed substantially abroad, any duties in the UK will be taken into account in calculating the relief (TA 1988 s 132(2), (3)).   [**13.35**]

EXAMPLE 13.9

(1) A spends 300 days abroad before returning to the UK for 65 days. He then goes abroad for a further 300 days. A does not have a qualifying period of 365 days absence because, although his period in the UK does not exceed 1/6th of the total, it exceeds 62 days.

(2) A has the following periods of absence from, and presence in, the UK.

Period	Days
1 Absent from UK	70
2 Present in UK	8
3 Absent from UK	105
4 Present in UK	26
5 Absent until final return	160
Total days	369

A has a qualifying period of 365 days which is not broken by the two periods in the UK. Period 2 can be amalgamated with 1 and 3 because 8 days is less than 1/6th of that total period of 183 days (from leaving the UK to the next visit). Presence in the UK on 34 days (2 and 4) is less than 1/6th of the final total period of 369 days.

EXAMPLE 13.10

Wanderer is employed as the export sales manager of Worldwide Enterprises PLC. He is absent from the UK on a sales promotion campaign in the Far East from 1 October 1990 to 31 December 1991 (458 days). During this period he returned to the UK to visit his mother for 21 days in 1990–91 and 30 days in 1991–92. His salary in 1990–91 was £16,000 and in 1991–92 £18,000. His duties are performed wholly abroad:

The whole period qualifies for the 100% deduction.

	1990–91 £	1991–92 £
Salary	16,000	18,000
Less: relief for overseas duties		
1990–91 100% × $\left(£16,000 \times \dfrac{188}{365}\right)$	8,241	
1991–92 100% × $\left(£18,000 \times \dfrac{270}{365}\right)$		13,315
Schedule E assessment	£7,759	£4,685

b) *Individual resident but not ordinarily resident: Case II*

Where a person is resident, but not ordinarily resident in the UK, he is assessed under Case II on emoluments for duties performed in the UK only.   **[13.36]**

c) *The remittance basis of Schedule E: Case III*

Case III applies to an employee who is resident (whether or not ordinarily resident) in the UK to tax emoluments which would otherwise escape tax under Cases I or II, but only if the emoluments are remitted to the UK.

Hence, Case III applies in two instances. First where the emoluments received in the UK are foreign emoluments and the duties of the employment are performed wholly abroad (so that neither Case I nor Case II can apply). Secondly, where the emoluments received in the UK are for duties performed abroad (so that Case II cannot apply) and the employee, although resident, is not ordinarily resident in the UK (so that Case I cannot apply).

Remittances, for Schedule E, are governed by TA 1988 s 132(5) and, basically, bear the same meaning as for Schedule D Case V (see **[13.24]** and TA 1988 s 65). Remittances under Schedule E are, however, assessed on a current year basis and may include the transmission to the UK of property in kind.

Where an employee, resident but not ordinarily resident, in the UK is potentially liable under both Cases II and III in respect of emoluments paid partly in the UK and partly abroad from a single employment performed inside and outside the UK, any emoluments paid in, enjoyed in, or remitted to the UK will only be taxed under Case III to the extent that they exceed the Case II emoluments for the year (SP 5/84). The emoluments assessable under Case II must be computed 'in a reasonable manner', ie on a time basis by reference to working days.   [**13.37**]

d) *Place of work*

In deciding whether the duties of an employment are in substance performed wholly abroad, merely incidental duties performed in the UK are ignored (TA 1988 s 132(2)). This is a question of fact, and the rule is restrictively construed (see *Robson v Dixon* (1972)). However, such incidental duties are included in calculating whether the employee is entitled to the deduction for long absence in Case I (TA 1988 s 132(3)).

By TA 1988 s 132(4) specific duties are always deemed to be performed in the UK; in particular Crown employments and certain duties of seamen and aircrew. The rules regarding the latter are, however, relaxed in applying the Case I long absence deduction. Generally, crews of ships and aircraft will be treated as performing their duties abroad in respect of any part of a voyage that does not begin *and* end in the UK.

For the purposes of income tax generally, areas designated under the Continental Shelf Act 1964 are regarded as part of the UK (eg workers on oil rigs in the UK sector of the North Sea are deemed to work in the UK).   [**13.38**]

e) *Deductible expenses*

Expenses (typically travel and subsistence) may be incurred by the employee, in which case the question of their deductibility arises, or, alternatively, they may be borne by the employer when they may be treated as an emolument of the employee. After two consultative documents the rules were relaxed and the following matters should be noted.

First, in cases where the employment is performed partly in the UK and partly abroad by a UK resident the expenditure incurred on all business journeys (including travel outside the UK is a deductible expense under the normal rules of Schedule E (a similar rule applies to the self-employed taxpayer who can deduct these expenses under the rules of Schedule D).

Secondly, the non-UK resident (eg the individual who works abroad throughout the tax year) and the taxpayer entitled to the long absence deduction will not suffer UK tax on reimbursements by their employer for travelling etc expenses incurred during those periods. For the Case I taxpayer who is wholly employed abroad, however, such expenses (and reimbursements) will not be excluded from tax under the usual rules of Schedule E (because they will not be 'necessarily incurred in the performance of' the employment duties). TA 1988 ss 193–4 therefore provide that he can deduct his costs of travelling to and from the UK to take up or leave the employment. If the expenses of board and lodging incurred in carrying out the duties abroad are paid or reimbursed by the employer, the employee will be entitled to a deduction so that those payments will not be emoluments.

In addition, where he spends 60 or more continuous days outside the UK, the expenses of travel of his spouse and children under 18 are not taxable if met by his employer (limited to two trips in each year of assessment). Any number of other journeys made by the employee between the place of work and the UK can be paid for by the employer without such payments being taxed as emoluments (though notice that the employee cannot deduct the costs of such journeys where he pays for them).

Finally, the travelling expenses that are available to expatriate (ie non-UK domiciled) employees working in the UK broadly mirror the provisions discussed above for UK residents who work abroad. Accordingly, so long as the employer bears the cost of (any number of) journeys undertaken between the employee's usual place of abode and the UK such sums will not be taxed as emoluments and there are similar provisions to those already discussed for visits by spouses and children. Notice however that the reliefs for expatriates are limited to a period of five years from the date of the employee's arrival in the UK (TA 1988 s 195). [**13.39**]

f) *Foreign pensions and annuities*

Foreign pensions and annuities are taxed under Schedule D Case V on 90% of the income arising in the preceding year. However, such income will be taxable under Schedule E if it is payable in the UK through a department or agent of a Commonwealth government. The overseas employee may therefore be better advised to take a tax-free golden handshake. [**13.40**]

g) *Collection of tax*

Tax on an employee's Schedule E emoluments is generally collected at source from the employer under the PAYE system (TA 1988 s 203 and see Chapter 5).

Where an employer is resident in the UK he must as a general rule operate PAYE in respect of all his employees assessable under Schedule E, except for those entitled to a 100% deduction when emoluments can be paid gross.

The application of TA 1988 s 203 to a non-resident employer, whose employees were assessable under Schedule E, was considered in *Clark v Oceanic Contractors Inc* (1983). In that case a non-resident company made payments abroad to employees engaged in performing duties in the UK sector of the North Sea and so within the UK for the purpose of liability under Schedule E (s 830(5)). The House of Lords held that s 203 applied to the employer company so that it should have operated PAYE in respect of the payments. When employees are assessable under Schedule E, the only limit on the territorial scope of s 203 is whether it can effectively be enforced. It will, therefore, apply to the non-resident employer who maintains a 'trading presence' in the UK. This was so in the *Oceanic* case: the company carried on activities in the UK and in the UK sector of the North Sea; was liable to corporation tax on its profits (TA 1988 s 11); and had an address for service in the UK.

If Schedule E emoluments are paid overseas by a non-UK resident employer with no trading presence in the UK, it appears therefore that the employer cannot be made to deduct tax under s 203 on making the payments. In these circumstances, the Revenue are empowered to collect the tax from the relevant employees, in four equal instalments, by direct assessment under the 'direct collection' method (TA 1988 s 205 and 1973 Regulations). [**13.41**]-[**13.60**]

III   THE TAXATION OF THE FOREIGN TAXPAYER

When, in any given tax year, an individual is not a UK resident, he will be liable to UK income tax on income which has its source in the UK, unless that income is exempt from income tax (eg UK Government securities exempted under TA 1988 s 47).

Income arising in the UK to the foreign taxpayer is generally taxed at basic and higher rate with no personal reliefs or allowances. Full personal allowances are, however, available to a foreign taxpayer who is a British subject or citizen of the Irish Republic; or is or has been a British Crown employee; or is employed in the service of a missionary society; or is employed in the service of any state under Her Majesty's protection; or is a resident of the Isle of Man or Channel Islands; or comes within a double taxation agreement providing for such relief; or has previously resided in the UK and is resident abroad for health reasons (of self or family); or is a widow whose late husband (or widower whose late wife) was a British Crown employee (TA 1988 s 278(2)).   [**13.61**]

1   **Profits of a trade, profession or vocation**

As an application of the source doctrine, the foreign taxpayer will be taxable under Schedule D Case I on the profits of any trade carried on *within* as opposed to *with* the UK. For these purposes, however, maintaining an administrative or representative office as opposed to a branch in the UK will not *per se* constitute trading within the UK. The same principle applies to the exercise of a profession or vocation although the exercise of either in the UK would normally render the taxpayer UK resident (TA 1988 s 18(1)(a)(iii)).

The majority of cases have been concerned with the sale of goods by a non-resident to a person in the UK. The courts have tended to say that the trade is carried on in the place where, under English law, the contract is made. This is the place where acceptance of the offer is communicated. In general terms, acceptance by post occurs at the place of posting, whereas acceptance by any other form (eg by telex) occurs at the place where acceptance is received. Accordingly, the non-resident who telexes his acceptance of an order to a UK customer is in danger of trading within the UK, whereas the non-resident who posts his acceptance to such a customer from outside the UK would appear to be merely trading with the UK. However, the place where contracts are made is only one (albeit important) factor to be considered. The better test is probably whether the trade which gives rise to the profits takes place in the UK (*Firestone Tyre and Rubber Co Ltd v Lewellin* (1957): see further [**13.22**]).

When a trade is carried on within the UK, the profits are computed under the normal rules for Schedule D Case I. If it proves difficult to determine the profits attributable to that trade, the Revenue tax the proportion of the profits that the UK turnover bears to the trader's total turnover.

Some relief is afforded by TMA 1970 s 81 to the foreign manufacturer who sells goods in the UK through a branch or agency to ensure that tax is charged on only the merchanting profit. When a foreign taxpayer is assessed to tax under Schedule D Case I, the tax can be levied on the branch and agency within the UK although certain agents, eg independent brokers, are excepted from this provision (TMA 1970 ss 78–79, 82).

So far as non-resident companies are concerned, ven if they are trading within the UK, there will be no liability to UK corporation tax unless that trade is carried on through a branch or agency. When that is not the case the liability will be to income tax not corporation tax (TA 1988 s 6(2)(b)). Obviously, in the latter case, as the company will not have any UK presence the UK Revenue may well be presented with insurmountable problems of tax collection. **[13.62]**

2 Employment income

The foreign taxpayer is assessed under Schedule E Case II on emoluments he receives for duties performed in the UK. Case II, in effect, treats the UK duties as a source of income which would otherwise escape tax completely. If the emoluments are foreign emoluments, some relief from tax may be available in appropriate cases (see **[13.37]**). **[13.63]**

3 Non-resident entertainers and sportsmen

The UK has encountered difficulties (also experienced by other countries) in securing tax payments from non-resident entertainers and sportsmen (eg tennis players, golfers, actors and pop stars) who only pay short visits to the country and who have often left before tax can be assessed and collected. Accordingly, a withholding tax was introduced from 1 May 1987 (TA 1988 ss 555-558; SI 1987/530). In general, the payer of the moneys is obliged to make returns to the Revenue at quarterly intervals and to account for basic rate income tax which he should deduct from the payment made to the entertainer. There is a *de minimis* provision which ensures that these rules do not operate if the total payments made in the tax year to an entertainer do not exceed £1,000. **[13.64]-[13.80]**

IV DOUBLE TAXATION RELIEF

Overseas income may be taxed in its country of origin and if UK tax is also chargeable on the same income, the taxpayer is entitled to relief in one of three ways. First, the UK has a number of double taxation agreements (treaties) with foreign countries. They differ in details, but generally provide that certain categories of income will be taxed in only one of the countries concerned (usually where the taxpayer is resident). Other income will be taxable in both countries, but with a credit for one amount of tax against the other.

Secondly, if there is no treaty in force, 'unilateral relief' is given under TA 1988 s 790. This takes the form of a credit against the UK tax equal to the foreign tax paid.

Thirdly, if neither of the above applies, unilateral relief may be given under TA 1988 s 811 by way of deduction (from the foreign income which is assessable to UK tax) of the amount of foreign tax paid. Relief by deduction is less advantageous to the taxpayer than relief by credit. **[13.81]-[13.100]**

V ANTI-AVOIDANCE LEGISLATION: TRANSFER OF ASSETS ABROAD (TA 1988 ss 739-746)

1 General

A person who is neither resident nor ordinarily resident in the UK cannot be assessed to UK income tax on income which arises from a source outside the UK. Accordingly, an individual resident in the UK could seek to avoid UK income tax by transferring income-producing assets to a non-UK resident who is not subject to UK income tax.

EXAMPLE 13.11

(1) Toby, a UK resident, owns land in Barbados which produces a substantial income. He transfers it to a non-UK resident company in return for an allotment of shares and is subsequently loaned money by the directors of that company.

(2) Toby also owns shares in a German company which he transfers to a non-UK resident trust. As one of the beneficiaries he is then advanced capital by the trustees.

To prevent such arrangements, TA 1988 s 739 provides that if an individual who is ordinarily resident in the UK transfers assets so that as a result of that transfer, or of associated operations, income becomes payable to any person resident or domiciled outside the UK and the transferor has either power to enjoy that income (TA 1988 s 739(2)) or receives a capital sum (TA 1988 s 739(3)), the income of the non-UK resident is taxed as that of the transferor under Schedule D Case VI. The scope of the original legislation (formerly TA 1970 s 478) was limited, in the case of *Vestey v IRC* (1980), to the original transferor of the assets or his spouse. As a result, fresh legislation (now s 740) was introduced to 'fill the gaps'.

An individual will avoid liability under these sections if he can prove that the transfer or associated operation was not made for the purpose of avoiding any tax or that it was a *bona fide* commercial transaction the purpose of which was not to avoid tax. However, there is no clearance procedure for either section and the onus of proof is on the taxpayer.   [**13.101**]

2 **Liability of the transferor** (TA 1988 s 739)

a) *General*

Two factors are essential to the operation of s 739. First, there must be a transfer of assets by an individual. This means a transfer of property or rights of any kind but also includes the creation of those rights so that the incorporation of a company or formation of a partnership may be caught. In *IRC v Brackett* (1986), the taxpayer, by entering into a contract of employment with a Jersey company, fell within the section since rights created under that contract were assets and, as 'transfer' included the creation of rights, those assets were transferred to a non-UK resident person for these purposes. The assets need not be situated in the UK.

Secondly, as a result of the transfer, either alone or together with associated operations, income must become payable to a non-UK resident or non-UK domiciled person. The person to whom the income becomes payable need not be non-resident at the time of transfer (*Congreve v IRC* (1948)). 'Person' includes a corporation and, for these purposes, a corporation incorporated outside the UK is always considered non-resident (TA 1988 s 742(8); the UK does not include the Channel Islands or Isle of Man).

'Associated operations' is widely defined in s 742(1) and case law. Basically, any operation (except death) which is carried out by any person (not necessarily the transferor) is capable of being an associated operation, provided only that, together with the transfer, it results in income becoming payable in accordance with the section (for a case where this did not happen see *Fynn v IRC* (1958)). Whether the operation has this result is judged objectively without regard to the intention of the person effecting the operation.

EXAMPLE 13.12

(1) Sam settles overseas property on a UK trust. Subsequently overseas trustees are appointed so that the trust becomes non-UK resident. Income produced in the trust may be taxed as Sam's under s 739.

(2) A transfers assets to a company resident in the UK. Subsequently it becomes non-UK resident and receives income from the assets which A has the power to enjoy. The removal of the company overseas is an associated operation which triggers s 739 (*Congreve v IRC* (1948)). Thus, an otherwise innocent transaction may be brought within the section.

(3) A transfers assets to a UK resident company, B Ltd, in consideration for an allotment of shares. Some years later B Ltd sells the assets to a non-resident company, C Ltd, in return for shares in C Ltd. The transfer by B Ltd to C Ltd is associated with the transfer of assets from A to B Ltd although the operations were not contemplated as part of a single scheme at the time of the transfer (*Corbett's Executrices v IRC* (1943)).

(4) A sells foreign investments to an overseas company in return for shares in that company. He makes a will leaving his residuary estate (which includes the shares) to his daughter. The making of the will, although not the death, is an operation associated with the transfer of the assets abroad. Hence, on the death of A the daughter becomes entitled to dividends on those shares and falls (today) within s 740 (cp *Bambridge v IRC* (1955)).

If there has been a transfer of assets resulting in income becoming payable to a non-UK resident, s 739 will then apply if the transferor has the power to enjoy *either* the income (s 739(2)) *or* the capital (s 739(3)) of that property.   **[13.102]**

b) *Section 739(2)*

Section 739(2) will only apply if, given that the above two conditions are satisfied, an individual ordinarily resident in the UK has 'power to enjoy the income of a person resident or domiciled outside the UK'. The income caught by the section need not be derived directly from the assets transferred, but the power of enjoyment must be held by the transferor or his spouse (*Vestey v IRC* (1980); TA 1988 s 742(9)(a)). An individual has the power to enjoy income if any of the five circumstances in s 742(2) are satisfied. Generally, they apply to any situation whereby the transferor receives, or is entitled to receive, any benefit in any form from the income:

(1) Where he receives a benefit (including a payment in kind) from the use of the income by any person.

EXAMPLE 13.13

A non-resident company uses its income profits to redeem the debentures of a UK resident individual. The capital received is a benefit within (1) because it results from a use of the income (*Latilla v IRC* (1943)).

(2) Where assets that he holds, or which are held for him, increase in value as a result of the income becoming payable to the non-UK resident.

EXAMPLE 13.14

(a) X Ltd, a non-resident company, is in debt to A, a UK resident. When income becomes payable to X Ltd, A's *chose in action* (the debt) increases in value (unless X Ltd had sufficient funds to repay the debt) because X Ltd is more likely to be able to honour its obligations (*Lord Howard de Walden v IRC* (1942)).

(b) As in (a) save that A also owned shares in X Ltd which he transferred to a discretionary trust for the benefit of himself and his family. The section applies because the value of the shares is increased and they are assets held for his benefit.

(3) Where he directly receives, or is entitled to receive, a benefit from the income or the assets representing the income.

EXAMPLE 13.15

(a) C, a UK resident transferor, holds 90% of the issued shares of a non-UK resident company, B Ltd, which gives him the right to a dividend when declared. C is entitled to receive a benefit within (3) (*Lee v IRC* (1941)). Similarly, if, after he has transferred his shares, the directors make a gift to him, C has then received a benefit and it does not matter that the directors were acting *ultra vires*.

(b) Trustees of a non-UK resident trust exercise their discretion to pay income to a UK resident settlor B. B has received a benefit within (3) above.

(4) Where he is a member of a class of discretionary beneficiaries who may become entitled to some of the income as a result of the exercise of a power by any person. Even if the power is never exercised so that the transferor never benefits, he is within (4). Thus, in *Example 13.14(b)*, B has power to enjoy the income whether or not he receives a benefit. This paragraph also catches the revocable settlement and settlements where trustees have power to appoint absolute or income interests back to the settlor.

(5) Where he can control the application of the income in any way, not necessarily for his own benefit. This does not include a right to direct the investments nor a power of appointment which is concerned with capital rather than income payments (*Lord Vestey's Executors v IRC* (1949)). Thus in *Example 13.15(a)* C has power to enjoy B Ltd's income through his ability to replace the existing directors by virtue of his 90% shareholding (contrast the power to appoint trustees; *IRC v Schroder* (1983)).

When applying these tests regard must be had to the overall effect of the transfer and anything to do with it (TA 1988 s 742(3)). **[13.103]**

c) *Section 739(3)*

Section 739(3) applies where, in connection with a transfer of assets abroad, the transferor or his spouse receives or is entitled to receive a capital sum, whether before or after the relevant transfer. 'Capital sum' is defined as a sum paid or payable by way of loan; or any sum (not being income) which is paid or payable otherwise than for full consideration in money or money's worth. **[13.104]**

EXAMPLE 13.16

B, a UK resident, who has transferred income-producing assets to a non-UK resident trust, has power to direct the investments of the trust. He authorises a loan to be made to his son. B falls within s 739(3).

d) *Computation of the income chargeable under TA 1988 s 739(2) and (3)*

When a transferor is caught by s 739(2), he can be assessed to income tax under Schedule D Case VI on the whole of the non-resident income from any source, not just the income which he has the power to enjoy or the income arising from the assets which he transferred (this aspect of *Congreve v IRC* (1948) was not apparently overruled by the House of Lords in *Vestey v IRC* (1980)).

If s 739(3) applies the transferor can only be assessed on the income arising as a result of the transfer of assets. The assessment is not limited to the amount of the capital sum, however, and includes income arising before the capital sum was paid or payable and all such income arising thereafter.

Should the Revenue assess both the transferor and his spouse under either subsection, they cannot tax the same income twice (TA 1988 s 744(1)), but must charge it in such proportions as they consider 'just and reasonable'.

In computing the income of the non-resident which is chargeable under s 739(2) or (3), the transferor is only entitled to such deductions and reliefs as he would have been allowed had he, and not the non-resident, actually received the income (see *Lord Chetwode v IRC* (1977); management charges of a non-resident company were not deductible by a UK resident individual, and see TA 1970 s 480(2)). If, however, the income has already suffered basic rate tax, this will not be collected again from the UK resident (TA 1988 s 743). [13.105]

3 **Liability of non-transferors: s 740**

This provision was designed to fill the gaps in the original legislation revealed by the *Vestey* case. Hence, it operates when the same conditions are satisfied as for s 739, whereupon it catches any individual ordinarily resident in the UK (other than the transferor or his spouse who are already caught by s 739) who receives a benefit from the assets transferred. The important limitation in s 740 is that such an individual is only assessed to income tax under Schedule D Case VI to the extent of any benefit that he receives. It should be realised therefore that the section leaves open planning opportunities. An overseas settlement (from which the settlor and any spouse are excluded) and in which the income is accumulated will be free from UK income tax unless and until benefits are conferred under s 740 (at the very least therefore there will be a deferment in UK tax).

The benefit is taxed under Schedule D Case VI as the income of the UK resident in the year of receipt to the extent that it does not exceed the 'relevant income' of the non-resident in the tax years up to and including the year when the benefit is paid. In so far as it exceeds the relevant income of those years, any excess is carried forward and set against the first available relevant income of future years until it is finally absorbed.

'Relevant income' means, in relation to an individual, income arising in any year of assessment to the non-resident and which, as a result of the transfer of assets, can be used to provide a benefit to that individual (s 740(3)).

The same income cannot be charged to tax twice (s 744). Therefore, where several beneficiaries receive benefits, the relevant income is allocated amongst them by the Revenue in such proportions as may be just and reasonable. The taxpayer may appeal against the apportionment to the Special Commissioners.

EXAMPLE 13.17

A non-resident discretionary trust has relevant income in three consecutive years of £6,000, £6,000 and £12,000 respectively. It makes payments to two UK resident beneficiaries in *Year* 2. It is assumed that the apportionment provisions would be applied pro rata and not according to the order in which the payments are made.

The benefits are taxed as follows:

		A £	B £
Year 1			
Benefits paid		Nil	Nil
Relevant income £6,000 (unapportioned)			

		A £	B £
Year 2			
Benefits		6,000	12,000
Relevant income	£6,000		
Plus income brought forward	£6,000		
	£12,000 apportioned	4,000	8,000
Untaxed benefit carried forward		2,000	4,000
Year 3			
Benefits paid		Nil	Nil
Relevant income	£12,000		
	£6,000 apportioned	2,000	4,000
Relevant income carried forward	£6,000	Nil	Nil

In *Year* 2 A and B are assessed to income tax under Case VI on £4,000 and £8,000 of their respective benefits. The balance is assessed in *Year 3*.

If the benefit is of a capital nature and results from a capital gain made by the non-resident, the same sum is not charged to both income tax under s 740 and CGT under FA 1981 s 80. To the extent that the benefit exceeds relevant income it is charged to CGT, in which case, it cannot be treated as income in a subsequent year under s 740 (TA 1988 s 740(6); see **[20.45]**). **[13.106]**

4 **Powers of the Revenue to obtain information** (TA 1988 s 745)

The Revenue have wide investigatory powers for the purposes of these sections which are exercisable against a taxpayer, and also against his advisers. They can demand, at 28 days notice, such particulars as they deem necessary.

A solicitor is exempted from these powers in that he can only be compelled to state that he was acting on his client's behalf and to give the client's name and address. However, he is presumably only exempt to the extent that he is acting qua solicitor. Thus, where he acts, eg as a tax consultant, he may not be able to claim the exemption.

A bank is also exempted from providing details of ordinary banking transactions (s 745(5)), except to the extent that it has acted for a customer in connection with either the formation and management of a non-resident company which would be close if resident in the UK and is not a trading company, or the creation or execution of a trust which may be used for schemes under these provisions. The banks' exemption has been narrowly construed in *Royal Bank of Canada v IRC* (1972) and in *Clinch v IRC* (1973) where a 'fishing expedition' was upheld in the courts. Other advisers, eg barristers and accountants, have no exemption from s 745. **[13.107]**

Section 3 Capital gains tax

Chapters

14 CGT—basic principles

'It is impossible to draw an unambiguous distinction between "capital" gains and "income" gains and the attempt to do so necessarily results in great uncertainty for the taxpayer because a particular transaction may or may not be found by the courts to fall on one side of the line or the other' (Carter Commission, Canada, 1966).   [**14.1**]

I INTRODUCTION

1 Background

Capital gains tax (CGT) was introduced in the Finance Act 1965 and was consolidated in the Capital Gains Tax Act 1979 (CGTA 1979). It was largely introduced to tax profits left untaxed by income tax. Income tax, in the much quoted dictum of Lord Macnaghten, was and is a tax on income. Thus, it does not tax the profit made on a disposal of a capital asset. However, since 1965, the taxpayer will be charged to CGT on his gain after deducting any available exemptions and reliefs.

As the then Chancellor of the Exchequer Mr James Callaghan, in his 1965 Budget speech introducing CGT, explained:

'Yield is not my main purpose ... The failure to tax capital gains is ... the greatest blot on our system of direct taxation. There is little dispute nowadays that capital gains confer much the same kind of benefit on the recipient as taxed earnings more hardly won. Yet earnings pay tax in full while capital gains go free ... This new tax will provide a background of equity and fair play...'   [**14.2**]

a) Overlap with income tax

CGT aims to tax only what is untaxed by income tax and, normally, there will be no CGT on a transaction that is chargeable to income tax. Hence, in the case of certain transactions which might attract both taxes, CGT is chargeable on only so much of the transaction as is not charged to income tax as for instance on the purchase and sale of assets which qualify for capital allowances (see [**7.27**] and [**14.53**]) and the grant of leases at a premium where part of the premium is assessable to income tax under Schedule A (see Chapter 8). There is, however, no general rule against double taxation that prevents the same sum from being subject to two different taxes and in Bye v Coren (1986) Scott J (whose judgment was upheld in the Court of Appeal) held that 'whether it is so subject is a matter of construction of the statute or statutes which have imposed the taxes'. CGTA 1979 s 31 will provide relief in most cases since it states that once an income tax assessment has become final in respect of a sum of money the same person cannot be subject to a CGT assessment on that same sum. Notice that there is nothing to prevent the Revenue from raising alternative assessments (eg to income tax and CGT) on the same sum of money (*Bye v Coren,* above).   [**14.3**]

b) *The changing face of CGT*

The scope of the tax has fluctuated since its introduction in 1965. The charge on death was removed in 1971 and criticism that the tax was levied on inflationary gains was largely removed by the introduction of an indexation allowance in 1982 and by the rebasing of the tax to 1982 (introduced in FA 1988). This trend towards limiting the scope of the tax was, however, reversed by changes made in FA 1989. These concerned lifetime gifts where the position from 1980 had been that in most cases tax could be postponed by the exercise of a hold-over election (provided for in FA 1980 s 79 as subsequently amended). From 14 March 1989 such a general election has no longer been available and it is now only possible to postpone tax in a limited number of cases (see Chapter 17). As a result, the present position is that CGT may be charged on a sale of assets which have increased in value by more than the rate of inflation and on a gift of assets where hold-over relief is not available (subject again to the value of the asset having increased in the hands of the donor by more than the rate of inflation over his period of ownership). The curious position is therefore that a tax aimed at catching profits may now apply to gifts (deemed profits) whereas the tax intended to catch all gifts (CTT now IHT) will only apply to lifetime gifts which are not potentially exempt or which are made in the period of seven years before the death of the donor!

The yield from CGT represents a mere 1.3% of the total revenue raised in direct taxes. In his 1984 Budget Speech the Rt Hon Nigel Lawson MP acknowledged the 'unfairness and complexity' of the CGT legislation. In his 1985 Budget Speech he declared that the right way to reform the tax was to improve the indexation allowance thereby ensuring that a charge was levied only on real and not inflationary gains. As a result of a number of improvements which he then introduced he felt able to conclude that 'the tax is now on a broadly acceptable and sustainable basis'. Three years later, his views had altered, however, and a further reform (rebasing the tax from 1982 instead of 1965) was introduced in FA 1988 to remedy the 'manifest injustice' of taxing 'paper profits resulting from the rampant inflation of the 1970s'. It is unfortunate that this apparently elusive quest for justice and fairness always seems to involve further complications to this already over complex tax.   [**14.4**]

2 **Basic principles**

CGT is charged on any gain resulting when a chargeable person makes a chargeable disposal of a chargeable asset. This gain is taxed on a current year basis on so much of the gain as is left after taking into account any exemptions or reliefs and after deducting any allowable losses. The tax is payable on 1 December following the year of assessment. It is, therefore, sensible to make disposals early in the tax year in order to achieve the greatest delay in the payment of tax.

The tax was introduced in 1965 and was not retrospective. Accordingly, it has only taxed gains arising after 6 April in that year. Thus, where an individual acquired an asset in 1960 for £10,000 and sold it in 1970 for £20,000, thereby making a gain of £10,000, only such part of the gain as accrued since 6 April 1965 was charged (see [**14.31**]). For assets owned on 31 March 1982 which are disposed of after 5 April 1988, the chargeable gain may be computed on the basis that the asset in question had been acquired in March 1982 at its then market value. This rebasing of the tax is discussed in detail and at [**14.32**] means that gains from 1965 to 1982 have now been removed from the tax charge.   [**14.5**]

a) *Who is a chargeable person?* (CGTA 1979 s 2)

Chargeable persons include individuals who are resident or ordinarily resident in the UK; trustees, personal representatives and partners. In the case of partners, each partner is charged separately in respect of his share of the partnership gains (CGTA 1979 s 60, see Chapter 29). Although companies are not chargeable persons for CGT purposes, the corporation tax to which they are subject is levied on corporate profits which include chargeable gains (see [**28.22**]).   [**14.6**]

b) *What is a chargeable asset?* (CGTA 1979 s 19(1))

A number of assets are not chargeable to CGT and the gain on the disposal of certain other assets is exempt from charge (for details see Chapter 16). Apart from these exclusions, however, all forms of property are assets for CGT purposes including options, debts, incorporeal property, any currency (other than sterling) and property that is created by the person disposing of it (eg goodwill which is built up from nothing by a trader). An asset which cannot be transferred by sale or gift may be within the definition. In *O'Brien v Benson's Hosiery (Holdings) Ltd* (1979), for instance, a director under a seven year service contract paid his employer £50,000 to be released from his obligations under the contract. The employer was charged to CGT on the basis that the contract, despite being non-assignable, was an asset under s 19(1) so that the release of those rights resulted in 'a capital sum being received in return for the forfeiture or surrender of rights' (CGTA 1979 s 20(1)(c); see further [**14.102**]).

In *Marren v Ingles* (1980) shares in a private company were sold for £750 per share, payable at the time of the sale, plus a further sum if the company obtained a Stock Exchange quotation and the market value of the shares at that time was in excess of £750 per share. Two years later a quotation was obtained and a further £2,825 per share was paid. The House of Lords held that the taxpayers were liable to CGT on the original sale price of £750 per share plus the value of the contingent right to receive a further sum (their Lordships did not attempt to put a value on it; was it nominal?). That right was a *chose in action* (a separate asset) which was disposed of for £2,825 per share two years later, leading to a further CGT liability.

A 'right' may be used in both a colloquial and a legal sense. It is quite clear that in its wider colloquial sense a right is not an asset for capital gains tax purposes: it must be legally enforceable and capable of being turned into money. In *Kirby v Thorn EMI plc* (1988), for instance, the Revenue argued at first instance that the right to engage in commercial activity was an asset for CGT purposes with the result that if the taxpayers agreed to restrict their commercial activities in return for a capital payment, that sum would be brought into charge to tax. This argument was rejected on the basis that freedom to indulge in commercial activity was not a legal right constituting an asset for capital gains tax purposes. On appeal, the Revenue produced an alternative argument that by restricting such activity the taxpayers had made a part disposal of the firm's goodwill and that therefore the payment in question was chargeable to capital gains tax. In this argument they were successful.   [14.7]

c) *Compensation, damages and Zim Properties*

Zim Properties v Proctor (1985) concerned a firm of solicitors acting for the taxpayer in a conveyancing transaction who were allegedly negligent, with the result that a sale of three properties owned by the taxpayer fell through. An action in negligence against the solicitors was eventually compromised and compensation of £69,000 was paid to the taxpayer. Undoubtedly, this was a capital sum, but was it derived from the disposal of an asset? Warner J held that it arose from the right of action against the solicitors which, as it could be turned into a capital sum by negotiating a compromise, was an asset for CGT purposes. Although the ownership of the properties put the taxpayer in the position to enjoy that right of action, the sum was not derived from the properties themselves, because, after receipt of that sum, the taxpayer still owned the properties.

This decision raises a number of difficult problems.

First, not all rights to payment or compensation are themselves 'assets' for CGT purposes. Warner J cited as an obvious example the right of a seller of property to payment of the price. The relevant asset in such a case must be the property itself (contrast, however, *Marren v Ingles*, discussed above). A further example is shown by *Drummond v Austin Brown* (1984) where a tenant's right to statutory compensation on the termination of his lease under the Landlord and Tenant Act 1954 was not subject to CGT; it was neither compensation for loss of the lease, nor was it derived from that lease (contrast *Davenport v Chilver* (1983) where the right to statutory compensation for confiscated property was held to be an asset). There are also a number of statutory exemptions: eg for damages following personal injury.

Secondly, Warner J held that the asset was acquired at the time when the taxpayer acted upon the allegedly negligent advice, although this matter is not free from doubt (see the House of Lords judgments in *Pirelli v Oscar Faber* (1983)).

Finally, the question of how to calculate the acquisition costs of this asset, namely, the taxpayer's right to sue was left unclear (see also *Marren v Ingles* and *O'Brien v Benson's Hosiery*). Arguably, it was acquired otherwise than by bargain at arm's length, so that the market value (if any) of the right should be taken at the moment of its acquisition (see CGTA 1979 s 29A(1), discussed at [14.22]: it may be doubted, however, whether the taxpayer is able to satisfy the requirements in s 29A(2)(b) and failure to do so would result in a nil acquisition cost). As the purpose of damages is to compensate the plaintiff, the award in such cases needs to be grossed-up if the damages themselves will be reduced by taxation.   [14.8]

d) *ESC 19 December 1988*

Some of the confusions resulting from the *Zim* case were solved by an ESC dated 19 December 1988. This concession affords relief from CGT in two ways. *First*, 'where the right of action arises by reason of the total or partial loss or destruction of or damage to a form of property which is an asset for CGT purposes, or because the claimant suffered some loss or disadvantage in connection with such a form of property, any gain or loss on the disposal of the right of action may by concession be computed as if the compensation derived from that asset and not from the right of action'.

EXAMPLE 14.1

(1) Because of the negligence of his land agent, Lord Q's sale of a plot of land to Out of Town Supermarkets Ltd falls through. The agent is forced to pay £70,000 in compensation to Lord Q. Instead of treating this sum as consideration on the disposal of a separate *chose in action* it may be treated as arising on a part disposal of the land itself (see **[14.37]** for the part disposal rules). Accordingly, part of the deductible expenditure attributable to that land may be deducted in arriving at Lord Q's chargeable gain.
(2) Zara, because of the negligence of her solicitor, ends up with less money from the sale of her main residence than would otherwise have been the case. Because the underlying asset (her main residence) is exempt from CGT (see **[16.61]**) any compensation paid by the solicitor will likewise escape tax.

The second situation where the concession affords relief is if there is no underlying asset. In this case, any gain accruing on the disposal of the right of action will be free from CGT.

EXAMPLE 14.2

Zappy, a wealthy taxpayer, suffers a massive income tax liability because his professional adviser negligently fails to shelter that income from tax by arranging for Zappy to invest in BES and in an industrial building in an enterprise zone. Substantial compensation is therefore paid to Zappy and because there is no underlying form of property which is an asset for CGT purposes, the sum is not subject to charge.

The logic behind this is that as the compensation merely puts the taxpayer into the position he would have been in but for the negligence, there should be no tax charge since the benefit which he was entitled to (a lesser income tax liability) is not itself subject to charge. It should be noted that the *Zim* case has no application to compensation payments which attract an income tax charge (see, for instance, *London and Thames Haven Oil Wharves Ltd v Attwooll* (1967):**[6.83]**) whilst its application in the context of warranties and indemnities on a company take-over is discussed in Chapter 33.
[14.9]–[14.20]

II CALCULATION OF THE GAIN

The gain on which CGT is chargeable is found by taking the disposal consideration of the asset and deducting from that figure any allowable expenditure (often called the 'base cost'). The disponer's acquisition cost is usually the main item of expenditure. If the allowable expenditure exceeds the disposal consideration, the disponer has made a loss for CGT purposes which may be used to reduce the gains that he has made on disposals of other assets (see **[14.51]**).

EXAMPLE 14.3

A sells a painting for £20,000 (the disposal consideration). He bought it six months ago for £14,000 (the acquisition cost) and has incurred no other deductible expenses. His chargeable gain is £6,000. If A sold the picture for £10,000 he would have an allowable loss of £4,000.

Inevitably, the calculation of disposal consideration and allowable expenditure is not always as simple as in the above example and the onus is on the taxpayer to establish what (if any) part of the disposal consideration is not within the charge to CGT (see *Neely v Rourke* (1987)).   **[14.21]**

1   What is the consideration for the disposal?

a) *General*

The term 'disposal' is not defined but covers a number of transactions. Where the disposal is by way of a sale at arm's length, the consideration for the disposal will be the proceeds of sale. For disposals between husband and wife the disposal consideration is deemed to be of such a sum that neither gain nor loss results (CGTA 1979 s 44), irrespective of whether actual consideration is given.

Where the disposal is not at arm's length, however, the consideration for the disposal is taken to be the market value of the asset at that date. This applies to gifts, to disposals between 'connected persons' (where the disposal is always deemed to be otherwise than by bargain at arm's length), to transfers of assets by a settlor into a settlement and to certain distributions by a company in respect of shares (CGTA 1979 s 29A(1)(a)). Also, in the case of disposals by excluded persons who are exempt from CGT (including charities, friendly societies, approved pension funds, and non-residents) the recipient is taken to acquire the asset at market value.

EXAMPLE 14.4

(1)   A gives a Ming vase worth £40,000 to the milkman. The consideration for the disposal is taken to be £40,000. If, instead, A sold the vase to his son B for £10,000, B is a 'connected person' and the consideration for the disposal is taken to be £40,000.

(2)   In 1990, A, a resident of Peru, gives a house in Mayfair worth £150,000 and which he had acquired in 1983 for £20,000 to his son B who is a UK resident. A is not chargeable to CGT on his gain of £130,000 because he is an excluded person and B acquires the property at a base value of £150,000.

Furthermore, the market value of the asset is taken to be the disposal consideration whenever the actual consideration cannot be valued or the consideration is services (CGTA 1979 s 29A(1)(b)).

EXAMPLE 14.5

A, an antiques dealer, gives B, a fellow dealer, his country cottage worth £40,000 in consideration of B entering into a restrictive covenant with A, whereby he (B) agrees not to open an antique shop in competition with A. The consideration for the disposal is taken to be £40,000.

This market value rule can work to a taxpayer's advantage by giving the recipient a high acquisition cost for any future disposal in a transaction where the disponer is not charged to CGT on the gain (known as 'reverse Nairn Williamson arrangements'). To some extent this is prevented from happening by CGTA 1979 s 29A(2) which provides that, where there is an acquisition without a disposal (eg the issue of shares by a company) and either no consideration is given for the asset, or the consideration is less than its market value, the actual consideration (if any) given prevails. [**14.22**]

EXAMPLE 14.6

A Ltd issues 1,000 £1 ordinary shares to B at par when their market value is £2 per share. The issue of shares by a company is not a disposal. This is, therefore, an acquisition of a chargeable asset by B without a disposal. Were it not for s 29A(2), B's acquisition cost of the shares would be £2,000. As it is, the transaction is caught so that B's acquisition cost is what he actually paid for the shares: ie £1,000.

b) *Connected persons*

'Connected persons' for CGT purposes fall into four categories (CGTA 1979 s 63).
(1) An individual is connected with his spouse, his or her relatives and their spouses. Relatives include siblings, direct ancestors (parents, grand parents), and lineal descendants (children, grandchildren) but not lateral relatives (uncles, aunts, nephews and nieces). Marriage continues for the purpose of this provision until final divorce (see *Aspden v Hildesley* (1982)).
(2) A company is connected with another company if both are under common control. A company is connected with another person if he (either alone or with other persons connected with him) controls that company.
(3) A partner is connected with a fellow partner and his spouse and their relatives except in relation to acquisitions and disposals of partnership assets under bona fide commercial arrangements (for example, where a new partner is given a share of the assets).
(4) A trustee is connected with the settlor, any person connected with the settlor and any close company in which the trustee or any beneficiary under the settlement is a participator (for the definition of close company and participator see Chapter 28). He is not connected with a beneficiary. [**14.23**]

c) *The market value of assets*

Where assets fall to be valued at market value, that is taken as the price for which those assets could be sold on the open market with no reduction for the fact that this may involve assuming that several assets are to be sold at the same time (CGTA 1979 s 150).

The market value of shares and securities listed in The Stock Exchange Daily Official List (CGTA 1979 s 150(3)) is taken as the lesser of:
(a) the lower of the two prices quoted for that security in the Daily Official List, plus 1/4 of the difference between the two prices ('quarter-up');
(b) half way between the highest and lowest prices at which bargains were recorded in that security on the relevant date excluding bargains at special prices ('mid price').

Unquoted shares and securities are valued on a number of criteria including the size of the holding and, therefore, the degree of control of the company.

Where the asset transferred is subject to a restriction, for example, land which is mortgaged, the value of the asset is reduced to take account of the restriction (CGTA 1979 s 62(6)). However, as an anti-avoidance measure, artificial and non-commercial restrictions in favour of connected persons are ignored (CGTA 1979 s 62(5)).

CGTA 1979 s 151 modified the market value rule in cases where a person acquired assets by a series of transactions from one or more connected persons. It imposed a charge upon the transferor(s) in cases where the value of all the assets transferred was greater when aggregated than when considered separately. This provision proved unsatisfactory (see [1985] STI 3) and was replaced by FA 1985 s 71 which applies when assets are fragmented (ie when one transferor makes two or more transfers to connected persons and the transfers occur within six years of each other).

EXAMPLE 14.7

Alf owned a pair of Ming vases which as a pair were worth £100,000 but separately each was worth only £40,000. In January 1991 he gave one to his daughter and in the following July the other to his son.
(i)   The disposal to his daughter was for an original market value of £40,000. However, as it is linked to the later disposal to his son, under FA 1985 Sch 21 the assets disposed of by the two disposals are valued as if they were disposed of by one disposal and the value attributed to each disposal is the appropriate proportion of that value. The market value of both vases is £100,000 and the appropriate proportion is £50,000. (Notice that this revaluation of an earlier transaction will lead to an adjusted CGT assessment.)
(ii) The later disposal, occurring within six years, is a linked transaction. Again the original market value (£40,000) is replaced by the appropriate proportion (£50,000).
(iii) Compare the CGT rules on a disposal of sets of chattels (see [**16.21**]) and the IHT associated operations provisions (see [**21.81**]).
(iv) With the removal of general hold-over relief in the case of disposals by way of gift these rules will be of increased importance. Presumably hold-over relief will continue to apply in the case of earlier disposals where the consideration has to be revalued because of a subsequent linked transaction.

Disposals to a spouse are treated as giving rise to neither gain nor loss (CGTA 1979 s 44: [**14.22**]) but may form part of a series in order to determine the value of any of the other transactions in that series.   [**14.24**]

d) *Deferred consideration* (CGTA 1979 s 40)

Where the consideration for the disposal is known at the date of the disposal but is payable in instalments or is subject to a contingency, the disponer is taxed on a gain calculated by reference to the full amount of the consideration receivable with no discount for the fact that payment is postponed. If, in fact, he never receives the full consideration his original CGT assessment is adjusted.

EXAMPLE 14.8

A bought land 5 years ago for £50,000. He sells it today for £100,000 payable in 2 years' time. A is taxed now on a gain of £50,000 despite the fact that he has received nothing and with no discount for the fact that the right to

£100,000 in 2 years' time is not worth £100,000 today. (For the CGT position when the purchase price is paid in instalments see [**14.83**].)

It may be that the deferred consideration cannot be valued because it is dependent on some future contingency. In Marren v Ingles (1980) part of the payment for the disposal of shares was to be calculated by reference to the price of the shares if and when the company obtained a Stock Exchange quotation. The taxpayer's gain on the disposal of the shares could not be calculated by reference to such an unquantifiable consideration. Accordingly he was treated as making two separate disposals. The first was the disposal of the shares. The consideration for this was the payment that the taxpayer actually received plus the value (if any) of the right to receive the future deferred sum (*a chose in action*). The value of the *chose in action* then formed the acquisition cost of that asset. Hence, once the deferred consideration became payable, the taxpayer was treated as making a second disposal, this time of the *chose in action*. He was, therefore, chargeable on the difference between the consideration received and whatever was the acquisition cost of that asset.

In *Marren v Ingles* the House of Lords did not attempt to value the chose in action. In all probability its value would have been nominal, with the result that on the first disposal (of the shares) the gain would have been calculated by reference only to the cash received, whilst on the second disposal (of the *chose in action*) the entire consideration received would constitute a gain. There is no element of double taxation involved in the *Marren v Ingles* situation. Instead, the CGT is collected (in effect) in two instalments with the result that the taxpayer may be better off than A, in *Example 14.8*, above, who is taxed on money years before receiving it. (Where the taxpayer is entitled to retirement relief on the disposal of the shares, however, the relief may not be exhausted on the share disposal, in which case the balance cannot be used against the gain on the disposal of the *chose in action*.) [**14.25**]

2 **What expenditure is deductible?**

Once the disposal consideration is known, the gain (or loss) can be calculated by deducting allowable expenditure. This is defined in CGTA 1979 s 32 as 'expenditure incurred wholly and exclusively' in: [**14.26**]

Acquiring the asset   The purchase price or market value, including any allowed incidental costs (such as stamp duty), or where the asset was created rather than acquired (for example, a painting) the cost of its creation may be deducted (CGTA 1979 s 32(1)(a)). In certain circumstances a deemed acquisition cost will be deducted. This is the case, for instance, when an asset is acquired by inheritance (probate value is the basic acquisition cost) and when the 1982 rebasing rules apply (market value in 1982 being the acquisition cost). [**14.27**]

Enhancing the value of the asset   Expenditure on improvements must be reflected in the state or nature of the asset at the time of its disposal. Thus, in the case of land, the costs of an application for planning permission which is never granted are not deductible, whereas the costs of building an extension are. Also deductible under this head are the costs of establishing, preserving or defending title to the asset (for example, the costs of a boundary dispute and, in the case of PRs, a proportion of probate expenses) (CGTA 1979 s 32(1)(b)).

In *Chaney v Watkis* (1986) the taxpayer agreed to pay his mother-in-law a cash sum (£9,400) if she gave vacant possession of his house which he wished to sell. Between exchange of contracts on the property and completion this agreement was varied by mutual consent. Instead of the cash sum, the taxpayer agreed to build an extension onto his own home and allow her to occupy it rent free for life. It was held that the cash sum would have been deductible in arriving at his gain on sale of the house if he had paid it (since vacant possession enhanced the value of the house). The same principle applied to a consideration in money's worth (the rent-free accommodation) and the case was remitted to the Commissioners for them to determine the value of this consideration. Two matters are especially worthy of note: first, that expenditure incurred post-contract but pre-completion was taken into account and the phrase 'at the time of the disposal' in s 32(1)(b) must be construed accordingly; and, secondly, that the taxpayer's mother-in-law was a protected tenant of the property (and had been before he purchased the house) and hence the agreement with her was a commercial arrangement.   **[14.28]**

Disposing of the asset   The incidental costs of disposal which are deductible include professional fees paid to a surveyor, valuer, auctioneer, accountant, agent or legal adviser; costs of the transfer or conveyance; costs of advertising to find a buyer and any costs incurred in making a valuation or apportionment necessary for CGT (CGTA 1979 s 32(1)(c)). Other taxes, such as IHT on a gift, are not deductible and neither is the cost of appealing against any CGT assessment!

The requirement in CGTA 1979 s 32 that expenditure must be 'wholly and exclusively' incurred makes use of the same test for allowable expenditure as that found for income tax under Schedule D Cases I and II. For CGT purposes, however, these words have been interpreted relatively liberally. In the case of *IRC v Richards' Executors* (1971), PRs who sold shares at a profit claimed to deduct from the sale proceeds the cost of valuing the relevant part of the deceased's estate for probate. The House of Lords held that they could do so even though the valuation was for the purposes of estate duty as well as for establishing title (ie even though the costs were 'dual purpose expenditure').

'Expenditure' within CGTA 1979 s 32 must be something that reduces the taxpayer's estate in some quantifiable way. Thus in *Oram v Johnson* (1980) the taxpayer who bought a second home for £2,500, renovated it himself and later sold it for £11,500 could not deduct the notional cost of his own labour.

On a deemed disposal and reacquisition (see **[18.41]**) notional expenses are not deductible (CGTA 1979 s 32(4)), but actual expenses are. Thus, in *IRC v Chubb's Settlement Trustees* (1971), where the life tenant and the remainderman ended a settlement by dividing the capital between them so that there was a deemed disposal under (now) CGTA 1979 s 54(1), the costs of preparing the deed of variation of the settlement were deductible (the result of this case is to leave s 32(4) as a prohibition on the deduction of imaginary expenses!).

The deduction of certain items of expenditure is specifically prohibited. For instance, interest on a loan to acquire the asset (CGTA 1979 s 32(3)); premiums paid under a policy of insurance against risks of loss of, or damage to, an asset; and, most important, any sums which a person can deduct in calculating his income for income tax. Additionally, no sum is deductible for CGT purposes which would be deductible for income tax, if the disponer were in fact using the relevant asset in a trade; in effect therefore, no items of an income, as opposed to a capital, nature will ever be deductible. For example, the cost of repair (as opposed to improvement) or of insurance of a chargeable asset, both of which are of an income nature, are disallowed as deductions for CGT. [**14.29**]

EXAMPLE 14.9

A buys a country cottage in 1985 for £11,000 to rent to Arab sheiks. He spends £6,000 in installing a gold plated bathroom and £4,000 on mending the leaking roof. Over the following 5 years he spends a further £500 on repairing leaking radiators and £400 on general maintenance. He pays a total of £3,000 on property insurance. He sells it in 1991 for £25,000.

His chargeable gain is:

	£	£
Sale proceeds		25,000
Less:		
Acquisition cost	11,000	
Cost of improvements	6,000	17,000
		£ 8,000

The cost of repairs, maintenance and insurance are not deductible for CGT because they are deductible in computing his income under Schedule A. The insurance premiums are specifically disallowed under CGTA 1979 s 141.

If A had bought the cottage as a second home, his gain on sale would still be £8,000; the other items are disallowed as deductions for CGT because they are of an income nature.

3 The indexation of allowable expenditure

Before 1982 capital gains tax made no allowance for the effects of inflation on the value of chargeable assets and, accordingly, it taxed both real and paper profits. FA 1982 afforded a measure of relief by introducing an indexation allowance for disposals of assets on or after 6 April 1982 (1 April in the case of companies) and FA 1985 made major improvements to that allowance in respect of disposals on or after 6 April 1985 (or 1 April). Generally items of allowable expenditure are now index-linked (to rises in the RPI), so that the eventual gain on disposal should represent only 'real' profits.

The indexation allowance is calculated by comparing the RPI for the month in which the allowable expenditure was incurred (ie due and payable) with the index for the month in which the disposal of the asset occurs. Assuming that the RPI has increased, the allowable expenditure is multiplied by the fraction

$$\frac{RD-RI}{RI}$$

where RD is the index for the month of disposal and RI is the index for the month in which the item of expenditure was incurred (this fraction, calculated to three decimal places, produces the 'indexed rise' decimal which is published by the Revenue each month). The resultant figure (known as the 'indexation allowance') is a further allowable deduction in arriving at the chargeable gain on disposal of the asset.

As the allowance is linked to allowable expenditure, it follows that, where an asset has a nil base cost (for instance, goodwill built up by the taxpayer) there can be no indexation allowance.   **[14.30]**

EXAMPLE 14.10

A painting was bought for £20,000 on 10 April 1986 and sold for £100,000 on 30 June 1991. RPI for April 1986 is 300; RPI for June 1991 is 500. The indexed rise is $\frac{(500-300)}{300}$: ie 0.667 (correct to three decimal places). Indexation allowance is: £20,000 × 0.667 = £13,332.

Therefore, the chargeable gain is:

	£	£
Sale proceeds		100,000
Less:		
Acquisition cost	20,000	
Indexation allowance	13,332	33,332
Chargeable gain		£66,668

Assume that the painting was restored on 12 November 1989 for £2,000. RPI for November 1989 is 400. Indexation allowance is £13,332, as above, plus: £2,000 × $\frac{(500-400)}{400}$ = £500

Therefore, the chargeable gain is £64,168 (£66,668—£2,000—£500)

4 Calculation of gains for assets acquired before 6 April 1965

Only gains after 6 April 1965 are chargeable (CGTA 1979 s 28(3)). Thus, for assets acquired before 6 April 1965, the legislation contains rules determining how much gain is deemed to have accrued since that date. Generally, the gain is deemed to accrue evenly over the whole period of ownership (the so-called straight line method: CGTA 1979 Sch 5 para 11(3)). The chargeable gain is, therefore, a proportion of the gross gain calculated by the formula:

$$\text{Gross gain} \times \frac{\text{years of ownership since 6 April 1965}}{\text{total years of ownership}} = \text{chargeable gain}$$

(*Note:* The indexation allowance must be deducted in arriving at the gross gain which is then time apportioned: see Smith v Schofield (1990).)

EXAMPLE 14.11

(The indexation allowance and 1982 rebasing have been ignored.)

	£
A bought a picture on 6 April 1964 for	5,000
He sells it on 6 April 1991 for	19,000
His gain is	£14,000

His chargeable gain is: £14,000 × $\frac{26}{27}$ = £13,481

In applying this formula, the ownership of the asset can never be treated as beginning earlier than 6 April 1945 (CGTA 1979 Sch 5 para 11(6)) so that if it was acquired before that date it is deemed to have been acquired on that date. These rules are now of small importance in view of the rebasing provisions which are considered in the next section.   **[14.31]**

5 Calculation of gains on assets owned on 31 March 1982 ('Rebasing')

New rules were introduced for assets owned on 31 March 1988 in FA 1988 and apply to disposals of such assets occurring after 5 April 1988. Broadly, these changes (commonly referred to as 'rebasing') substitute 31 March 1982 for 6 April 1965 in computing the chargeable gain: accordingly, that part of any capital gain which arose before 31 March 1982 is taken outside the tax net. **[14.32]**

Basic rule Assets which the taxpayer owned on 31 March 1982 are deemed to have been sold by that person and immediately 2reacquired by him at market value on that date. This rebasing inevitably requires the taxpayer to incur expenses in agreeing with the Revenue a valuation figure for the relevant asset in March 1982. **[14.33]**

EXAMPLE 14.12

Jacques' valuable collection of porcelain cost £12,000 in 1970; it is estimated to have been worth £100,000 on 31 March 1982 and has just been sold for £175,000. In computing Jacques' capital gain arising from his disposal, rebasing to March 1982 will result in a reduction in the gain from £163,000 to £75,000.

Qualifications In cases where a computation based on the actual costs and ignoring 1982 values would produce a smaller gain or loss, rebasing will not generally apply so that it is that smaller gain or loss which will be relevant. In those cases where one computation would produce a gain and the other a loss, there is deemed to be neither. **[14.34]**

EXAMPLE 14.13

(1) Assume that under rebasing the disposal of an asset would show a loss of £60,000 whereas ignoring 1982 values the loss would be only £35,000. In this case the £35,000 loss will be taken.
(2) Alternatively, assume that the disposal would show a gain of £25,000 if rebasing applied but only £15,000 if it did not. The smaller gain (£15,000) will be taxed.
(3) Under the rebasing calculation there is a gain of £50,000 on the disposal of a chargeable asset: on the alternative calculation ignoring 1982 values, however, there is a loss of £2,000. In this case there is deemed to be neither gain nor loss. (Similarly if the loss had been produced by rebasing and the gain under the alternative calculation.)
(4) Assume that there is a loss of £6,000 if the asset is rebased to 1982 but, on the alternative calculation, a loss of £20,000. In this case mandatory rebasing will occur with the result that the loss is restricted to £6,000.

The election Because the qualifications discussed above require the taxpayer to keep pre-1982 records and will usually involve alternative calculations, the taxpayer is given an election for rebasing to apply to all disposals of assets which he held on 31 March 1982. This election may be made at any time before 6 April 1990 or (if no election has been made by that time) within two years from the end of the tax year in which the first relevant disposal (ie of assets owned at 31 March 1982) occurs. The election is irrevocable and will apply to all disposals of assets owned on 31 March 1982 by the particular taxpayer. In SP 2/89 the Revenue indicated that they will always exercise their discretion to extend the election time limit to (at least) the date on which the statutory time limit would expire (ie six years) if the first relevant disposal was one on which the gain would not be chargeable (eg a disposal of private cars; chattels which are wasting assets; gilt-edged securities). **[14.35]**

Technical matters   The indexation allowance has been, in the majority of cases, computed on the basis of March 1982 values since FA 1985. Accordingly, the rebasing process will merely bring the rules for deductible expenditure into line with the indexation allowance. Obviously a crucial feature of these new rebasing rules is the determination of when an asset was acquired by the taxpayer. In exceptional cases, the ownership period of another person can be included in deciding whether the asset was owned on 31 March 1982. These are situations where the disponer has acquired the asset as a result of a no gain no loss disposal which took place after 31 March 1982 and was made by a transferor who had owned the asset before that date.

EXAMPLE 14.14

Doris inherited a gold snuff box on the death of her father in 1977. Its probate value was £10,000. In 1983 she gave it to her husband, Sid, on their wedding anniversary. In March 1982, the box was worth £25,000 and in 1983 £28,000. Sid has just sold the box for £35,000.
(i)   The 1983 transfer between spouses was made at no gain no loss so that Sid is treated as having acquired the box for £10,000.
(ii) In calculating the gain on sale, Sid is treated as having held the asset on 31 March 1982 so that the market value at that date (£25,000) will be his allowable base cost.

In certain other situations ownership of an asset may be related back to an earlier date: generally these are cases where the asset is treated as forming part of or replacing an earlier asset. This, for instance, is the case where new shares are acquired on a company takeover under CGTA ss 85–87 (see Chapter 19).

Where a capital gain is realised on a disposal but tax is postponed, eg under a hold-over election or when roll-over relief is available, there is still a relevant disposal at that time and hence, if that disposal occurred after 1982 but before 6 April 1988 and was of assets held by the disponor on 31 March 1982, simple rebasing is not available. Under FA 1988 Sch 9, however, when a gain was deferred on a disposal made between 1982 and 1988 and that gain was attributable (at least in part) to the disposal of an asset acquired before 31 March 1982, that deferred gain will be halved on the eventual disposal of that asset. **[14.36]**

EXAMPLE 14.15

Simpkin, who has been a partner in an estate agency business, sells his interest in goodwill in 1983. The acquisition cost of the goodwill was nil: its value in 1982 was estimated at £85,000. When he sold the goodwill in 1983 he obtained £100,000 which he then rolled over into the purchase of a farm purchased in 1985 at a total cost of £210,000. Accordingly, as a result of roll-over relief (see **[16.92]**), the base cost of the farm in Simpkin's hands was reduced to £110,000. As the farm was acquired in 1985 there is no question of rebasing. However, on the eventual sale, one-half of the deferred gain will be ignored so that Simpkin's base cost will be £110,000 + £50,000 (one-half of the deferred gain) = £160,000.

6 Part disposals

The term disposal includes a part disposal, so that whenever part of an asset or an interest in an asset is disposed of it is necessary to calculate the original cost of the part sold before any gain on it can be computed. This applies, for instance, to a sale of part of a land-holding or of part of a shareholding, or to the grant of a lease (for leases see [**14.39**]).

The formula used for calculating the deductible cost of the part sold is:

$$C \times \frac{A}{A = B}$$

Where   C = all the deductible expenditure on the whole asset
A = sale proceeds of the part of the asset sold
B = market value of part retained (at the time when the part is sold).

The indexation provisions are applied in the same way for part disposals as for disposals of the whole, except that only the apportioned expenditure is index-linked.

EXAMPLE 14.16

10 acres of land were bought for £10,000 on 1 January 1983. 4 acres of land were sold for £12,000 on 1 October 1991 (the remaining 6 acres are then worth £24,000). RPI for January 1983 is 250. RPI for October 1991 is 340.
Acquisition cost of the 4 acres sold is:

$$£10,000 \times \frac{£12,000}{£36,000} = £3,333$$

Indexation allowance is: £3,333 × 0.360 = £1,200

Therefore, the chargeable gain is:

	£	£
Sale proceeds		12,000
Less:		
Acquisition cost	4,000	
Indexation allowance	1,200	5,200
		£6,800

The part disposal formula need not be used (thereby removing the need to value the part of the asset not disposed of), when the cost of the part disposed of can be easily calculated. In particular, on a part disposal of shares of the same class in the same company the cost of each individual share can be worked out as a fraction of the total number owned by the taxpayer.

Further the rules will not be applied to small part disposals of land (CGTA 1979 ss 107–108) if the taxpayer so elects. Where the consideration received is 20% or less of the value of the entire holding and does not exceed £20,000 (or without limit for a disposal to an authority with compulsory powers of acquisition) the transaction need not be treated as a disposal. Instead, the taxpayer can elect to deduct the consideration received from the allowable expenditure applicable to the whole of the land. Similar principles apply to small capital distributions made by companies (see Chapter 19); and, by extra-statutory concession, to an exchange of interests in land which is in the joint beneficial ownership of two or more persons (see ESC D26:

the relief is given along the lines of CGTA 1979 s 111A and 111B—roll-over relief on compulsory acquisition of land and note *Jenkins v Brown* (1989): see [**18.2**]).   [**14.37**]

7   **Wasting assets** (CGTA 1979 ss 37–39)

A wasting asset is one with a predictable useful life not exceeding 50 years. If the asset is a wasting chattel (ie an item of tangible moveable property such as a television or washing machine), there is a general exemption from CGT. In the case of plant and machinery qualifying for capital allowances there are special rules (see [**14.53**]). Short leases of land are likewise subject to their own rules; freehold land, needless to say, can never be a wasting asset. Accordingly the main types of asset subject to the wasting asset rules are:

(a)   commodities dealt with on a terminal market (CGTA 1979 s 127(4));
(b)   foptions with the exception of quoted options to subscribe for shares in a company; traded options quoted on a recognised stock exchange or on the London Financial Futures Exchange (FA 1984 s 65); financial options (CGTA 1979 ss 137(9), 138) and options to acquire assets for use in a business (CGTA 1979 s 138);
(c)   purchased life interests in settled property where the predictable life expectation of the life tenant is 50 years or less (CGTA 1979 s 37);
(d)   fpatent rights;
(e)   fcopyrights in certain circumstances; and
(f)   leases for 50 years or less (other than of land: see below).

On disposal of any of the above assets any gain is calculated on the basis that the allowable expenditure on the asset is written down at a uniform rate over its expected useful life so that any claim for loss relief will be limited. Consistent with the general principles which apply to such assets, it is only the written down expenditure which is entitled to the indexation allowance.   [**14.38**]

EXAMPLE 14.17

Copyright (21 years unexpired) of a novel is bought for £3,000 on 1 April 1979. The copyright is sold for £2,600 on 1 April 1991. The market value of the copyright in March 1982 (18 years unexpired) is £2,800. RPI for March 1982 is 250; RPI for April 1991 is 350. The gain on disposal is calculated as follows:
Calculate written down acquisition cost:

$$£2,800 \times \frac{9 \text{ years}}{18 \text{ years}} = £1,400$$

The indexation allowance is:

$$£1,400 \times 0.4 = £560$$

Therefore, the chargeable gain is:

	£	£
Sale proceeds		2,600
Less:		
acquisition cost	1,400	
indexation allowance	560	1,960
Chargeable gain		£ 640

Note: If rebasing had not applied the gain would be:

Written down acquisition cost:

$$£3,000 \times \frac{9 \text{ years}}{21 \text{ years}} = \qquad £1,286$$

indexation allowance: $£1,286 \times 0.4 = \qquad \underline{£515}$

Total chargeable gain = $\qquad \underline{£771}$

8 Rules for leases of land

The grant of a lease out of a freehold or superior lease is a part disposal. The gain is, therefore, computed by deducting from the disposal consideration (ie the premium) the cost of the part disposed of, calculated as for any part disposal (see 6, above). Included in the denominator of the formula as a part of the market value of the land undisposed of is the value of any right to receive rent under the lease. In *Clarke v United Real (Moorgate) Ltd* (1988), the court held that a premium included any sum paid by a tenant to his landlord in consideration for the grant of a lease and therefore caught payments to the landlord covering past and future development costs.

A lease which has 50 or less years to run is a wasting asset. It does not depreciate evenly over time, however, so that on any assignment of it, its cost is written down, not as described in 6 above, but according to a special table in CGTA 1979 Sch 3 para 1.

Where a sub-lease is granted out of a lease which is a wasting asset, the ordinary part disposal formula is not applied. Instead, any gain is calculated by deducting from the consideration received for the sub-lease, that part of the allowable expenditure on the head lease which will waste away over the period of the sub-lease.

EXAMPLE 14.18

A acquires a lease of premises for 40 years for £5,000 (that lease is, therefore, a wasting asset). After 10 years he grants a sub-lease to B for 10 years at a premium of £1,000.

A's gain is calculated by deducting from the consideration on the part disposal (ie £1,000), such part of £5,000 as will waste away (in accordance with CGTA 1979 Sch 3 para 1) on a lease dropping from 30 years to 20 years.

Any part of a premium that is chargeable to income tax under Schedule A (see Chapter 8) is not charged to CGT. Thus, on the grant of a short lease out of an interest that is not a wasting asset (for example, the freehold) there must be deducted from the premium received such part of it as is taxed under Schedule A. The part disposal formula is then applied and in the numerator the sum representing the consideration received on the part disposal is the premium received less that part taxed under Schedule A. **[14.39]–[14.50]**

EXAMPLE 14.19

A buys freehold premises for £200,000. He grants a lease of the premises for 21 years at a premium of £100,000 and a rent. The value of the freehold subject to the lease and including the right to receive rent is now £150,000.

Of the premium of £100,000 20/50ths is discounted (ie £100,000×20×2/100) and the balance (ie £100,000×30/50) is taxed under Schedule A=£60,000.

A's chargeable gain is, therefore:	£
Consideration received	100,000
Less: amount taxed under Schedule A	60,000
	40,000

Less: cost of the part disposed of

$$£200,000 \times \frac{£40,000}{£100,000 + £150,000} = \qquad 32,000$$

Chargeable gain (ignoring indexation) £ 8,000

III   LOSSES FOR CGT

1   When does a loss arise?

A loss arises for CGT whenever the consideration for the disposal of a chargeable asset is less than the allowable expenditure incurred by the taxpayer (including any indexation allowance).

EXAMPLE 14.20

If an antique desk was bought for £12,000, restored for £1,000 and then sold for £11,000, a loss of £2,000 would result.

Where a loss arises the indexation allowance may further increase that loss and in cases where no loss would otherwise result, the indexation allowance may create such a loss.

EXAMPLE 14.21

A painting was bought for £50,000 on 1 November 1982 and sold for £60,000 on 4 May 1991. RPI for November 1982 is 320; RPI for May 1991 is 400. Indexation allowance:

$$£50,000 \times 0.250 = £12,500$$

Without any indexation allowance the gain is £10,000 (£60,000—£50,000) but the indexation allowance produces a loss of £2,500.

Had the picture been sold for £40,000 the loss of £10,000 would be increased by the indexation allowance to £22,500.

Although the disposal of a debt (other than a debt on a security) is usually exempt from CGT, a loss that is made on a qualifying loan to a trader may be treated as a capital loss (see [16.42]).

If an asset is destroyed or extinguished; abandoned, in the case of options that are not wasting assets ([14.105]); or if its value has become negligible (see [14.104]), the taxpayer may claim to have incurred an allowable loss.   [14.51]

2   Use of losses

Losses must be relieved primarily against gains of the taxpayer in the same year, but any surplus loss can be carried forward and set against his first available gain in future years without time limit.

Losses cannot be carried back and set against gains of previous years except for the net losses incurred by an individual in the year of his death (CGTA

1979 s 49(2)). Capital losses cannot generally be set against the taxpayer's income for tax purposes despite the 1988 changes which linked capital gains rates to the taxpayer's income tax position (see [**14.71**]). The only exception is for losses arising under the provisions dealing with investment in corporate trades in TA 1988 s 574 (see [**7.153**]). Similarly, income losses cannot generally be set against an individual's capital gains: although this rule is also subject to one exception — introduced in FA 1991 — whereby trading losses which cannot be relieved against the taxpayer's income may be set against his chargeable gains for both the year when the loss was incurred and one following tax year (see [**7.94**]).

A loss that is incurred on a disposal to a connected person can only be set against any gains on subsequent disposals to the same person (CGTA 1979 s 62(3)). [**14.52**]

3 Restriction of losses: capital allowances

Generally, chattels which are wasting assets are exempt from CGT (see [**16.21**]). Plant and machinery which are tangible moveable property are always classified as wasting assets, but will not be exempt from CGT if they are used in a trade and qualify for capital allowances (accordingly if capital allowances are withdrawn, eg because the asset is never brought into use in the business, the exemption will apply: see *Burman v Westminster Press Ltd* (1987)). Other assets which qualify for capital allowances, such as industrial buildings, will be chargeable assets because they are not wasting.

As CGT does not generally overlap with income tax, a gain which is charged to income tax will not be charged to CGT; and a loss will not be allowable for CGT if it is deductible for income tax. Thus, the gain or loss on a disposal of plant and machinery and other assets qualifying for capital allowances is calculated in the usual way (and not written down in the case of wasting assets) and any gain is charged to CGT to the extent that it exceeds the original cost of the asset.

[handwritten margin note:
10000
2500
———
7500
Sale   10000
B C   2500

If disposal > cost
cost used and
disposal diff
charged to CGT.*]*

EXAMPLE 14.22

	£
Year 1: Machine bought for	10,000
WDA at 25%	2,500
Year 2: Machine sold for	12,000

There is a balancing charge for income tax of £2,500 (ie to the extent of the capital allowance given—see further Chapter 7). The excess of the sale price over the acquisition cost (£2,000) is chargeable to CGT.

However, it is rare for plant and machinery to be sold at a gain; it is more likely to be sold at a loss, in which case the loss is not allowable for CGT to the extent that it is covered by capital allowances. Capital allowances may reduce a loss to nil, but they cannot produce a gain. [**14.53**]–[**14.70**]

EXAMPLE 14.23

	£
Machine bought for	4,000
Sold later for	2,000
Capital allowance given of	2,000

Loss for CGT is:

Disposal proceeds	2,000
Less: acquisition cost	4,000
Capital loss	(2,000)
Credit for capital allowances	2,000
Allowable loss	£ Nil

IV   RATE OF CGT

1 **Rates**

CGT was formerly charged at a flat rate of 30%. Changes in FA 1988, however, resulted in the abandonment of this single rate so that the position for disposals on or after 6 April 1988 is that the appropriate rate will depend upon the identity and circumstances of the disponor. In his 1988 Budget Speech, the Chancellor (Nigel Lawson) explained these changes as follows:

> 'Rebasing the tax so as to produce a fully indexed system makes it possible to bring the taxation of gains closer to that of income. In principle, there is little economic difference between income and capital gains, and many people effectively have the option of choosing to a significant extent which to receive. And, insofar as there is a difference, it is by no means clear why one should be taxed more heavily than the other. Taxing them at different rates distorts investment decisions and inevitably creates a major tax avoidance industry ... I therefore propose a fundamental reform ... I propose in future to apply the same rate of tax to income and capital gains alike ... Taxing capital gains at income tax rates makes for greater neutrality in the tax system. It is what we now do for companies. And it is also the practice in the United States, with the big difference that there they have neither indexation relief nor a separate capital gains tax threshold.'   [**14.71**]

Individuals   The rate of CGT is the same as the basic rate of income tax (for 1991–92, 25%), subject to the proviso that if in the year of assessment the taxpayer is liable to higher rate income tax, his capital gains will be charged at that higher rate: in effect CGT is therefore charged at the taxpayer's marginal income tax rate (FA 1988 s 98). Accordingly, capital gains realised in a particular tax year may push the individual into a higher rate which will apply to that gain. For many taxpayers linking the rates of income tax and CGT resulted in an increase in the rate of tax applicable to capital gains from 30% (in 1987–88) to 40%.   [**14.72**]

EXAMPLE 14.24

(i) Bill has no income in the tax year 1991–92 but realises chargeable capital gains of £10,000. His rate of tax on those gains is 25%: note that he cannot reduce the gain by deducting his unused personal allowance.

(ii) Had Bill's gain been £25,000, CGT would have been charged as follows:
first £23,700 at 25%
remaining £1,300 at 40%

(iii) Freda realised a gain of £10,000 in 1991 when her total income (after deducting charges and her personal allowance) was £15,000. She had paid £1,000 under a pre 1988 deed of covenant to her daughter, a student at Reading University. In calculating her capital gains tax charge, Freda's income will be treated as including the £1,000 annual payment even though

for income tax purposes it only forms part of her income for higher rate computations (see TA 1988 s 483). Hence, CGT will be charged as follows:
first £7,700 at 25%
remaining £2,300 at 40%

Companies Companies are subject to corporation tax, not CGT, but that tax is charged on corporate profits including chargeable gains. The rate of tax charged on such gains is therefore either 25% (small company rate) or 33% (see further Chapter 28). **[14.73]**

Personal representatives PRs are subject to tax at 25%. Accordingly, it may be advantageous for assets to be sold by the personal representatives rather than by the relevant beneficiary (see further Chapter 15). **[14.74]**

Trustees Trustees are subject to CGT at 25% subject to two main exceptions. *First*, if the trust is an accumulation or discretionary settlement, gains realised by trustees are taxed at 35% (FA 1988 s 100). For these purposes a trust is treated as accumulation or discretionary where all *or any part* of the income arising to the trustee in a year of assessment is liable to additional rate income tax under TA 1988 s 686 ([**11.21**]). The settlement is also accumulation and discretionary where all the income of the trustees is treated as that of the settlor but would otherwise have suffered additional rate tax.

The *second* exceptional case is designed to prevent the relatively low rate of charge on settlements from being employed by settlors who would otherwise be subject to capital gains tax at 40%. Accordingly, in cases where the settlor or his spouse has an interest in the settlement the rate of CGT will be determined according to the rates of the settlor (FA 1988 Sch 10).

A settlor retains an interest for these purposes if:

'(a) any property which may at any time be comprised in the settlement or any income which may arise under the settlement is, or will or may become, applicable for the benefit of or payable to the settlor or the spouse of the settlor in any circumstances whatsoever, or
(b) the settlor, or the spouse of the settlor, enjoys a benefit deriving directly or indirectly from any property which is comprised in the settlement or any income arising under the settlement.'

As can be appreciated these provisions are widely drawn so that they would catch, for instance, a situation where money was lent by the settlor to his trustees. **[14.75]**

EXAMPLE 14.25

(i) Trustees of the Blandings marriage settlement, set up by Lord Blanding in 1986, under which Fiona Blanding is the life tenant, realised chargeable gains of £150,000 in 1991–92. The rate of CGT is 25%.

(ii) Trustees of a trust set up by Fiona Blanding for her infant twins, Maxie and Minnie, realised chargeable gains of £150,000 in 1991–92. The rate of tax is 35% since the income will be accumulated by the trustees insofar as it is not paid for the maintenance or education of the twins.

(iii) The Blandings family trust now includes interests in possession in 95% of the fund with the remaining 5% being held on the original discretionary trusts. The rate of tax on capital gains realised by the trust is 35% whether such gains can be attributed to the 95% of the fund which is settled on fixed interest trusts or the 5% discretionary rump. Only if separate settlements existed would different rates apply (in which case the fixed interest portion would be subject to a 25% rate whilst gains in the rump would be taxed at 35%). For a contrary view, suggesting that separate funds of a single settlement can be taxed separately, see (1989) *Capital Taxes* p 7.

(iv) On 6 April 1988, Solomon settles his portfolio of shares on trust for himself for life giving the trustees a power to advance capital to him. CGT is postponed at that time by the hold-over election and therefore the chargeable gain will be realised in the future by the trustees. The appropriate rate of CGT that will then apply will be calculated by reference to Solomon's rates so that it is not possible to obtain a CGT advantage by ensuring that any gain is realised through a trust under which the settlor (or his spouse) remains a beneficiary or from which either may obtain a benefit. *Note:* The ending of general hold-over relief for disposals on and after 14 March 1989 presents further problems in any such scheme.

2   The annual exemption

The amount of the annual exemption depends on the capacity in which the person made a gain. The amount is index-linked and as the indexation allowance is also available as soon as expenditure is incurred the result is double relief for the taxpayer!   [**14.76**]

Individuals   The first £5,500 (for 1991–92) of the total gains in a tax year are exempt from CGT.

EXAMPLE 14.26

	£	£
A sells a painting for		17,000
Original cost of painting	8,700	
Indexation allowance (say)	1,000	9,700
Chargeable gain		7,300
Less: annual exemption for 1991–92		5,500
Gain charged to CGT		£1,800

If the exemption is unused in a tax year it is lost since there is no provision to carry it forward (contrast the IHT annual exemption).   [**14.77**]

Personal representatives   In the tax year of the deceased's death and the two following tax years, PRs have the same annual exemption as an individual. In the third and following tax years they have no annual exemption and so are charged to CGT on all chargeable gains they make (see [**15.61**]).   [**14.78**]

Trustees   Trustees have half the annual exemption available to an individual, ie £2,750 (for 1991–92). Where the same settlor has created more than one settlement the annual exemption is divided equally between them. Four settlements for instance would each have an exemption of £687.50. This is subject to a minimum exemption per trust of one-tenth of the individual's annual exemption, ie £550. Thus, if a settlor creates 10 settlements they will each have an exemption of £550.

Where the settlement is for the mentally or physically disabled, the trustees have the same exemption as an individual, ie £5,500 (subject to the same rules for groups of settlements).   [**14.79**]

Husband and wife   Husband and wife are both entitled to a full exemption (see further Chapter 35). Any unused annual exemption cannot be transferred to the other spouse. **[14.80]**

3 Order of set-off of capital losses

Current year losses must be deducted from current year gains in full.

EXAMPLE 14.27

A makes chargeable gains of £4,000 and incurs allowable losses of £3,000 in the tax year. His gain is reduced to £1,000 and is further reduced to zero by £1,000 of his annual exemption. He is forced to set his loss against gains for the year which would in any event have escaped tax because of the annual exemption.

Unrelieved losses in any tax year can be carried forward to future tax years without time limit though they must be deducted from the first available gains. However, the loss need only be used to reduce later gains to £5,500 (the amount covered by the annual exemption) and not to zero. Losses of one spouse can only be used to reduce the gains of that spouse—they cannot be set against gains of the other spouse.

EXAMPLE 14.28

A makes the following gains and losses:

Tax year	Gain	Loss
	£	£
Year 1	4,000	9,000
Year 2	7,500	3,000
Year 3	12,400	Nil

In Year 1 A pays no CGT and carries forward an unused loss of £5,000. His annual exemption for that year is wasted. In Year 2 A's gain is reduced to £4,500 and he pays no CGT as this is covered by his annual exemption. The £5,000 loss from year 1 does not reduce his gain to zero. It is carried forward to year 3. In Year 3 A can use the £5,000 loss that he is carrying forward from year 1 to reduce his gain to £7,400. After deducting his annual exemption he pays CGT on £1,900.

The relief afforded for trading losses against capital gains by TA 1988 s 380A is considered at **[7.94]**. **[14.81]**

4 When is CGT payable?

General rule

CGT is assessed on a current year basis and is generally payable in full on 1 December following the year of assessment or thirty days after assessment, if that is later. Interest is charged on tax remaining unpaid after the due date. **[14.82]**

Payment by instalments

CGT may be paid in instalments in two cases. *First*, when the consideration for the disposal is paid in instalments over a period exceeding 18 months running from the date of the disposal or later and the Revenue are satisfied that payment of tax in one lump sum would cause undue hardship. The instalments of tax can be spread over a maximum of eight years provided that the final instalment of tax is not payable after the final instalment of the disposal consideration has been received. Undue hardship is not defined—in practice, the Revenue consider whether the taxpayer could be expected to pay the full tax bill at once in the light of resources made available to him *as a result of that transaction.* Accordingly where payment is by instalments it will be relevant to show that the arrangement was a normal commercial one and resulted in a genuine deferment of the consideration (CGTA 1979 s 40; and see *Capital Taxes*, 1985, p 31).

Secondly, with the ending of general hold-over relief for gifts made on or after 14 March 1989, CGT may be paid by ten annual instalments when the gifted property is land; a controlling shareholding in any company; or a minority holding in an unquoted company provided that hold-over relief is not available on the disposal (CGTA 1979 s 7A). The outstanding instalments carry interest and become payable in full if the gifted asset is sold unless the original gift was made by an individual to an unconnected donee.

Finally, in a *Marren v Ingles* situation (see [**14.7**]) one incidental result of two disposals having occurred is that tax on the overall gain of the disponor will be paid in two stages.   [**14.83**]–[**14.100**]

V   MEANING OF 'DISPOSAL'

1   General

A 'disposal' is not defined for CGT. Giving the word its natural meaning, there will be a disposal of an asset whenever its ownership changes or whenever an owner divests himself of rights in, or interests over, an asset (for example, by sale, gift or exchange). Additionally, the term is extended by the legislation to cover certain transactions which would not fall within its commonsense meaning. Thus, in certain circumstances, trustees of a settlement are treated as disposing of and immediately reacquiring settlement assets at their market value ('deemed disposals': see [**18.43**]).

A part disposal of an asset is charged as a disposal according to the rules considered earlier ([**14.37**]). Death is not a disposal for CGT purposes (see Chapter 15).   [**14.101**]

2   Capital sums derived from assets (CGTA 1979 s 20)

Whenever a capital sum is derived from an asset there is a disposal for CGT. This is so whether or not the person who pays the capital sum receives anything in return for his payment (see *Marren v Ingles* (1980)).

It appears that all legal rights which can be turned to account by the extraction of a capital sum are assets for CGT purposes. The test is whether such rights can be converted into money or money's worth and the mere fact that they are non-assignable does not matter so long as consideration can be obtained in some other way (for instance, by surrendering the right). This is apparent from the case of *O'Brien v Benson's Hosiery (Holdings) Ltd* (1979) (see [**14.7**]). In *Marren v Ingles* (1980: see [**14.7**]) the right to receive an un-quantifiable sum in the future was considered to be an asset, a *chose in action*, from which a capital sum was derived when the right matured.

The rights must, however, be legally enforceable. Thus, a sum derived from a personal agreement, for example, by a person to restrict his future activities, is not a disposal because it is not a disposal of an asset (the right to work is not a legal right, although it may be a right of man!). Where a restrictive agreement is entered into by a trader or by a taxpayer exercising a profession it may be argued that there is a disposal of his goodwill for CGT purposes (see *Kirby v Thorn EMI plc* (1988)).

Four specific instances of disposals are given in s 20:

(1) where a capital sum is received by way of compensation for the loss of, or damage to, an asset (for instance, the receipt of damages for the wrongful destruction of an asset). It should be noted that there is only a disposal where a capital sum is received and so if the receipt is of an income nature, it is charged to income tax and not to CGT (an example is compensation received by a trader for loss of trading profits— see, for instance, *London and Thames Haven Oil Wharves Ltd v Attwooll* (1967) and *Lang v Rice* (1984));

(2) where a capital sum is received under an insurance policy for loss of or damage to an asset;

(3) where a capital sum is received in return for the forfeiture or surrender of rights. This category includes payments received in return for releasing another person from a contract (*O'Brien v Benson's Hosiery (Holdings) Ltd* (1979)); from a restrictive covenant; but not a statutory payment on the termination of a business tenancy since that sum is not derived from the lease (*Drummond v Austin Brown* (1984));

(4) where a capital sum is received for the use or exploitation of assets, for example, for the right to exploit a copyright or for the right to use goodwill created by another person.

The receipt of a capital sum from an asset under categories (1) and (2) above need not be treated as a disposal or part disposal provided that the asset has not been totally lost or destroyed. Instead, the taxpayer can elect to deduct compensation money from the acquisition cost of the asset thereby postponing a charge to CGT (CGTA 1979 s 21). However, this relief, which does not apply to wasting assets, is only available if one of three conditions is satisfied. *First*, the sum must be wholly used to restore the asset. *Secondly*, if the full amount of the capital sum is not used to restore the asset, the amount unused must not exceed 5% of the sum received. Where the sum unused exceeds 5%, the asset is treated as being partly disposed of for a consideration equivalent to the unused sum. *Thirdly*, the capital sum must be small (5% or less) compared with the value of the asset.   **[14.102]**

EXAMPLE 14.29

A buys a picture for £20,000 which is now worth £30,000. It is damaged by rain from a leaking roof and A receives £8,000 compensation with which he restores the picture. The £8,000 is deducted from the cost of the asset (£20,000), but it also qualifies as allowable expenditure on a future disposal so that for CGT the cost of the asset remains £20,000 and A is in the same position as if the damage had never occurred.

Assume, however, that A restores the picture for £7,600. The £400 unused does not exceed 5% of £8,000. It is, therefore, deducted from the total allowable expenditure which is reduced to £19,000.

Alternatively, if A received compensation of £1,500 which he does not use to restore the picture, A need not treat this receipt as a part disposal as it does not exceed 5% of the value of the picture (£30,000). Instead, he can elect to deduct £1,500 from his acquisition cost, so that the picture has a base value of £18,500 on a subsequent disposal.

3 **Total loss or destruction of an asset** (CGTA 1979 s 22(1))

Total loss or destruction of an asset is a disposal for CGT purposes and, where the owner of the asset receives no compensation, it may give rise to an allowable loss equal to the base costs of the taxpayer. Where the asset is tangible moveable property, however, the owner is deemed to dispose of it for £6,000 thereby restricting his loss relief. This limitation derives from the fact that gains on such assets are exempt from CGT in so far as the consideration does not exceed £6,000 (see [**16.21**]). As a corollary, therefore, loss relief on the disposal of these assets is not available where the consideration received is less than £6,000.

> **EXAMPLE 14.30**
>
> A buys a picture for £10,000 which is destroyed by fire; A is uninsured. Although the picture is now worthless, A's allowable loss is restricted to £4,000.

Land and the buildings on it are treated as separate assets for these purposes. Where the building is totally destroyed both assets are separately deemed to have been disposed of and reacquired, and it is the overall gain or loss which is taken into account.

Where the taxpayer later receives compensation or insurance moneys for an asset which is totally lost or destroyed, this would appear to be a further disposal for CGT purposes under CGTA 1979 s 20(1) since it is a capital sum derived from an asset (the right under the insurance contract). In practice, however, the Revenue treat both disposals (ie the entire loss of the asset and the receipt of capital moneys) as one transaction (see also the discussion of this problem by Hoffmann J in *Powlson v Welbeck Securities Ltd* (1986)). If the taxpayer uses the capital sum within one year of receipt to acquire a replacement asset, he may claim to roll over any gain made on the disposal of the destroyed asset against the cost of the replacement asset; this relief does not apply to wasting assets. If only part of the capital sum is used in replacement, only partial roll-over is available (CGTA 1979 s 21(4), (5)).

> **EXAMPLE 14.31**
>
> A buys a picture for £6,000 which is destroyed when its value is £10,000. He receives insurance money of £10,000 and uses it towards the purchase of a similar picture for £12,000. A has made a gain of £4,000 on the original picture (£10,000 — £6,000) on which he need not pay CGT. He may deduct the gain from the cost of the new picture so that his base cost becomes £8,000 (£12,000 — £4,000).
>
> Assume that A buys the new picture for only £7,000 and claims roll-over relief.
>
> Amount of insurance money not applied in replacement = £3,000 (£10,000 — £7,000).
>
> His chargeable gain is, therefore, £3,000 and £1,000 is rolled over so that A's base value for the new picture is £8,000 — £1,000 = £7,000.

The same relief applies where the asset destroyed is a building. The gain on the old building can be rolled over against the cost of the new building. Any gain deemed to have been made on the land cannot, however, be so treated and will, therefore, be chargeable. [**14.103**]

4 Assets becoming of negligible value (CGTA 1979 s 22(2))

Where an asset becomes of negligible value (for example, shares and securities in an insolvent company) the taxpayer is deemed to have disposed of and immediately reacquired the asset at its market value (nil) thus enabling him to claim loss relief. This disposal is deemed to occur in the tax year in which the Revenue accept the claim which may not be the same as the year in which the asset became of negligible value. In practice, a claim will be accepted for a tax year which ended within two years of the date of the claim, provided that the loss occurred before or in that earlier year (ESC D28). The timing of the claim is, therefore, important (*Williams v Bullivant* (1983) and see *Larner v Warrington* (1985)).

Should the value of the asset subsequently increase, the result of claiming relief under s 22(2) will be that on a later disposal the base value will be nil so that all the consideration received will be treated as a gain and there will be no question of claiming any indexation allowance.   [**14.104**]

5 Options (CGTA 1979 ss 137–139)

The grant of an option (whether to buy or to sell an asset) is a disposal, not of a part of the asset which is subject to the option, but of a separate asset, namely, the option itself at the date of the grant. The gain will be the consideration paid for the grant of the option less any incidental expenses (see *Strange v Openshaw* (1983)).

EXAMPLE 14.32

(1) A grants to B for £3,000 an option to buy A's country cottage in 2 years' time for £30,000 which is its current market value. A has made a gain of £3,000 from which he can deduct any incidental expenses involved in granting the option. (This is an option to buy.)

(2) A pays B £3,000 in return for an option to sell that country cottage to B in 2 years' time for £30,000. (This is an option to sell.) B has made a gain of £3,000 less any incidental expenses.

If the option is exercised, the grant and the exercise are treated as a single transaction for both grantor and grantee. It is understood that the Revenue will normally apply this treatment provided that the option is of short duration and/or for a relatively small consideration compared to the eventual sum payable on exercise. In other cases they may insist on imposing a tax charge on the grant of the option and then making suitable adjustments if and when it is eventually exercised.

EXAMPLE 14.33

As in *Example 14.32*, assuming that A had deductible expenses of £15,000.
(i) when B exercises the option and pays A £30,000 for the house, A's gain is:

	£
Proceeds from sale of house	30,000
Consideration for option	3,000
	33,000
Less: deductible expenses	15,000
Chargeable gain	£18,000

B's acquisition cost is £30,000 plus the cost of the option, ie £33,000 (both items will be index-linked from the dates when the expenditure was incurred).

(ii) where A exercises the option and sells the house to B for £30,000, A's gain is:

	£	£
Proceeds of sale		30,000
Less: cost of option	3,000	
deductible expenses	15,000	18,000
Chargeable gain		£12,000

B's acquisition cost of the cottage is only £27,000 (ie £30,000 reduced by the amount that he received for the option).

An option is a chargeable asset so that, if disposed of, there may be a chargeable gain or allowable loss. It will be a wasting asset unless it is an option to subscribe for shares which is quoted on The Stock Exchange; a traded option; a financial option; or it is an option to acquire assets to be used in a trade. The abandonment of an option which is a wasting asset is not a disposal (but notice that if a capital sum is received for relinquishing an option CGT will be chargeable on that sum under CGTA s 20(3): see *Golding v Kaufman* (1985) and BTR, 1985, p 124). Hence if an option is not to be exercised, mere abandonment will not give rise to any loss whereas the release of the option for a nominal consideration should give rise to an allowable CGT loss.   **[14.105]**

6   **Appropriations to and from a trader's stock-in-trade** (CGTA 1979 s 122)

There are two cases to consider. First, where a trader acquires an asset for private use and later appropriates it to his trade. As a general rule, this is a disposal and CGT is payable on the difference between the market value of the asset at the date of appropriation and its original cost.

EXAMPLE 14.34

A owns a picture gallery. He buys a picture for private use for £5,000 and transfers it to the gallery when it is worth £15,000. He has made a chargeable gain of £10,000. Later he sells the picture to a customer for £30,000. The profit on sale of £15,000 (£30,000—£15,000) is chargeable to income tax under Schedule D Case I.

However, the trader can elect to avoid paying CGT at the date of appropriation by transferring the asset into his business at a no gain/no loss value. When the asset is eventually sold, the total profit will be charged to income tax under Schedule D as a trading receipt. So, in the above example, were A to make the election he would pay no CGT, but instead he would be liable to income tax on a profit of £25,000 (£30,000—£5,000).

Whether the election should be exercised or not must depend upon the particular facts of each case. CGT may be more attractive as a choice of evils with its annual exemption but income tax, on the other hand, will be paid later (on eventual sale) and the profit so made may be offset against personal allowances or unused capital allowances.

Secondly, where an asset originally acquired as trading stock is taken out for the trader's private use. In this case, there is no election and the transfer is treated as a sale at market value for income tax purposes (see *Sharkey v Wernher* (1956) at [**6.95**]). The taxpayer will have market value as his CGT base cost. [**14.106**]

EXAMPLE 14.35

One of the pictures in A's gallery cost him £6,000. He removes it to hang it in his dining room when its market value is £16,000. He later sells it privately for £30,000.

On the appropriation out of trading stock, A is treated as selling the picture for its market value (£16,000) and the profit (£10,000) is assessed to income tax. The gain on the subsequent sale (£30,000 − £16,000 = £14,000) is chargeable to CGT.

7 Miscellaneous cases

Hire purchase agreements Although the purchaser! does not own the asset until he pays all the instalments, the vendor is treated as having disposed of the asset at the date when the purchaser is first able to use it (usually the date of the contract). The consideration for the disposal is the cash price payable under the contract. These transactions rarely give rise to a CGT charge, however, either because the asset is exempt (eg, a private car or a chattel worth less than £6,000) or because it is a wasting asset. Further, the contract will normally be a trading transaction falling within the income tax charge (for an illustration where these provisions were held to apply to the sale of a taxi-driver's licences see *Lyon v Pettigrew* (1985)).

In the rare case where there is a CGT charge and the contract is subsequently rescinded there will be repayment of CGT. [**14.107**]

Mortgages and charges (CGTA 1979 s 23) Neither the grant nor the redemption of a mortgage is a disposal. Where the property is sold by a mortgagee or his receiver, the sale is treated as a disposal by the mortgagor. [**14.108**]

Settled property On the happening of certain events the trustees are deemed to have disposed of the trust assets and immediately reacquired them (see Chapter 18). [**14.109**]

Value-shifting (CGTA 1979 s 25) There are anti-avoidance provisions intended to charge a person who passes value to another without actually making a disposal (see Chapter 19). [**14.110**]

8 Time of disposal

A disposal under a contract of sale takes place for CGT purposes at the date of the contract, not completion, with an adjustment of tax if completion never occurs (CGTA 1979 s 27(1): contrast s 32(1)(b)—see [**14.28**]). If the contract is conditional, the disposal takes place when the condition is fulfilled (s 27(2)). The subsection also provides that when a contract is conditional on the exercise of an option (presumably either a put or call option) the relevant disposal occurs when that option is exercised. In order to decide whether a contract is conditional for these purposes the contract in question has to be construed in order to determine whether any conditions stipulated therein are truly conditions precedent to any legal liability or whether they are merely conditions precedent to completion. In the former case there is a conditional contract for CGT purposes: in the latter, the contract is unconditional (*Eastham v Leigh London & Provincial Properties Ltd* (1971)).

EXAMPLE 14.36

Lord W agrees to grant a lease to Concrete (Development Company) Ltd if they obtain satisfactory planning permission to develop the relevant land as a business park. The contract to grant the lease is conditional on satisfactory permission being obtained and so the relevant part disposal will occur only if and when that happens.

Where a local authority compulsorily acquires land (other than under a contract), the disposal occurs when the compensation is agreed or when the authority enters the land (if earlier). In the case of gifts, disposal occurs when the ownership of the asset passes to the donee (usually the date of the gift). Where a capital sum is derived from an asset, the disposal occurs when the sum is received.   **[14.111]–[14.130]**

VI   CAPITAL GAIN OR INCOME PROFIT?

With the linking of the rates of CGT to the income tax rates of the taxpayer, much conventional tax planning designed to ensure that capital profits rather than income were received by a taxpayer, was rendered redundant. A number of anti-avoidance sections, notably TA 1988 s 639 and s 776, became of reduced importance. The distinction between capital and income receipts remains important, however, and the following are some of the factors to bear in mind. As will be apparent the facts of each individual case will largely determine whether the taxpayer is better off receiving a sum as capital or income.   **[14.131]**

1   Consequences of realising a capital gain

Tax on the gain will not be due until 1 December of the following tax year and in computing the chargeable gain not only will an indexation allowance be available, but in addition the £5,500 annual exemption may be deducted. Income profits are commonly taxed in the year of receipt without any allowance for indexation or an annual exemption. It is also important to remember that CGT is only levied when a disposal has occurred and therefore it may be possible to arrange disposals in the most advantageous tax year.   **[14.132]**

2   Taxation of income profits

Receiving a profit as income may be advantageous for the taxpayer in that the sum may be reduced by personal allowances; charges on income, unused losses and any sum remaining may then be sheltered from income tax, eg by investment in BES. To escape from the income tax net, it is often necessary to impose unattractive restrictions on the commercial arrangements, eg in the case of approved share option and incentive schemes. Accordingly, given the fusion of the rates of tax, the decision may now be taken that instead of striving to fall within an approved scheme it is more sensible to set up an unapproved scheme albeit that the individual employees are then subject to income tax on the profits that they make (see further **[34.25]**).   **[14.133]**

15 CGT—death

I GENERAL

On death the assets of the deceased are deemed to be acquired by the personal representatives (PRs) at their market value at death. There is an acquisition without a disposal: an uplift in the value of the assets but no charge to CGT (CGTA 1979 s 49(1)). Hence, death wipes out capital gains.

[**15.1**]-[**15.20**]

EXAMPLE 15.1

Included in T's estate on his death in October 1991 is a rare first edition of 'Ulysses' which T acquired in 1983 for £10,000. It is worth £100,000 at death. The gain of £90,000 is not chargeable on T's death. Instead his PRs acquire the asset at a new base value of £100,000.

II VALUATION OF CHARGEABLE ASSETS AT DEATH

The assets of the deceased are valued at their open market value at the date of death. The IHT valuation applies for this purpose (CGTA 1979 s 153) even though property may have been valued at an artificially high level under the special IHT related property provisions (see Chapter 22 but note that the Revenue are believed to take the view that these provisions only apply when the property is subject to IHT and hence do not apply if it is left to a surviving spouse). The market value for CGT is not, however, reduced by any IHT business or agricultural property relief.

Where land or property valued on death as 'related property' (see [**21.67**]) is sold within three years after the death, or quoted securities within one year, for less than the death valuation, the PRs may substitute a lower figure for the death valuation and so obtain a reduction in the IHT paid on death. Not surprisingly, this lower figure will also form the death value for CGT so that the PRs cannot claim CGT loss relief. As an alternative to reducing the estate valuation, the PRs may simply claim a CGT loss on the disposal. This would be advantageous where they have made chargeable gains on disposals of other assets in the estate and where no repayment of IHT would result from amending the value of the death estate.

Ideally, for CGT, the PRs want a high value for the assets on death because of the tax-free uplift, whereas for IHT they want as low a value as possible. Generally, of course, IHT will take precedence with the result that low valuation is usually the goal.   **[15.21]–[15.40]**

III   CGT LOSSES OF THE DECEASED

Any losses of the deceased in the tax year of his death must be set against gains of that year. Unused losses can then be set against the chargeable gains of the widow or widower for the whole of that tax year subject to an election by that person for this set-off not to apply. Any surplus loss at the end of the year of death can be carried back and set against chargeable gains of the deceased in the three tax years preceding the year of death, taking the most recent year first (CGTA 1979 s 49(2)). Any tax thus reclaimed will, of course, fall into the deceased's estate for IHT purposes!
[15.41]–[15.60]

IV   SALE OF DECEASED'S ASSETS BY PRs

A sale of the deceased's chargeable assets by his PRs is a disposal for CGT purposes and will be subject to CGT on the difference between the sale consideration and the market value at death. PRs pay tax at a rate of 25%. The normal deductions for the incidental expenses of sale are available and PRs can deduct an appropriate proportion of the cost of valuation of the estate for probate purposes (*IRC v Richards' Executors* (1971)). Although the Revenue publish a scale of allowable expenses for the cost of establishing title (see SP 7/81), PRs may claim to deduct more than the 'scale' figure in cases when higher expenses have been incurred. For deaths after March 1982, the PRs have the benefit of the indexation allowance. PRs have an annual exemption from CGT of £5,500 in the tax year of death and in each of the two following tax years. Thereafter they have no exemption, so that if it is intended thereafter to sell property in the estate and that sale will result in a chargeable gain, it may be advantageous to vest the asset in the appropriate beneficiary for him to sell. This will ensure that the beneficiary's annual exemption will be available to reduce the chargeable gain. On the other hand, it may be that any remaining gain will then be taxed at the 40% rate rather than at 25% as would have been the case if the trustees had sold the asset. Accordingly, the decision must depend upon the facts of each particular case.

EXAMPLE 15.2

(1) Dougall died in May 1985. In June 1991 a valuable Ming vase then worth £100,000 (probate value in 1985 £40,000) is to be sold. Administration of the estate has not been completed. The proceeds of sale will be split equally between Dougall's four children. The following possibilities should be considered:

   (i) The PRs could first appropriate the vase to the four children who could then sell it taking advantage of four CGT annual exemptions (£22,000 in all). The resultant gain (say £38,000) will then be divided equally (£9,500 per child) and taxed at the appropriate rate which may be 40%. *Accordingly, maximum tax will be £15,200*: or

(ii) The PRs could themselves sell the vase and realise gains of £60,000. No annual exemption will be available but the rate of CGT will be limited to 25%. *Accordingly, the maximum tax bill will be £15,000.*

Note: in appropriate cases PRs may prolong the administration of an estate so that they can eventually sell appreciating assets (typically land with development value) paying tax at only 25%.

(2) Continuing *Example 15.1*, if the PRs sell the book in March 1992 for £130,000, they have made a gross gain of £30,000 from which they can deduct their annual exemption of £5,000 (if unused); the incidental expenses of sale; a proportionate part of the cost of valuing the estate for probate in November 1991; and an indexation allowance, calculated on £100,000 as from October 1991, and on the relevant part of the cost of valuation as from November 1991.

Where the PRs dispose of a private dwelling house which, both before and after the death, was occupied by a person who is entitled on death to the whole, or substantially the whole, of the proceeds of sale from the house, either absolutely or for life, by concesssion PRs have the benefit of the private residence exemption from CGT (ESC D5).   **[15.61]–[15.80]**

EXAMPLE 15.3

Bill and his brother Ben live in Bill's house. On his death Bill leaves the house to Ben who goes on living in it. The property has to be sold by the PRs to pay for Bill's funeral. Any gain will be exempt.

V LOSSES OF THE PRs

Losses made by the PRs on disposals of chargeable assets during administration can be set off against chargeable gains on other sales made by them. Any surplus losses at the end of the administration period cannot be transferred to beneficiaries (*contrast* losses made by trustees which can be passed to a beneficiary when the trust ends: **[18.42]**). Accordingly, where PRs anticipate that a loss will not be relieved, they may prefer to transfer the loss-making asset to the relevant beneficiary so that he can sell it and obtain the loss relief.   **[15.81]–[15.100]**

VI DISPOSALS TO LEGATEES (CGTA 1979 s 49(4))

On the disposal of an asset to a legatee, the PRs make neither gain nor loss for CGT purposes and the legatee acquires the asset at the PRs' base value together with the expenses of transferring the asset to him.

EXAMPLE 15.4

The PRs transfer the book (see *Example 15.1*) to the legatee (L) under the will in March 1992 when it is worth £130,000. The cost of valuing the book as a part of the whole estate in November 1991 was £1,000 and the PRs incurred incidental expenses involved in the transfer of the book in March 1992 of £150. L sells the book in July 1993 for £140,000. On the disposal by the PRs to L, no chargeable gain accrues to the PRs and L's base value is:

	£
Market value at death	100,000
Valuation cost	1,000
Indexation allowance:	
On £100,000 from October 1991 to March 1992 (say)	300
and on £1,000 from November 1991 to March 1992 (say)	10
Expenses of transfer	150
Base cost of L	£101,460

When L sells the book in July 1993 for £140,000 he is charged to CGT on his gain which is £38,540 (£140,000—£101,460) as reduced by any allowable expenditure that he has incurred, including an indexation allowance on £101,460 from March 1992 to July 1993.

A legatee is defined in CGTA cccc1979 s 47(2) as any person taking under a testamentary disposition or on intestacy or partial intestacy, whether beneficially or as a trustee. This definition covers only property passing under the will or intestacy to a beneficiary and to the extent that a beneficiary contracts with the PRs to purchase a particular asset or to obtain a greater share in an asset he is not taking that asset *qua* legatee (*Passant v Jackson* (1986)). A '*donatio mortis causa*' is treated for these purposes as a testamentary disposition and not as a gift, so that the donee acquires the asset at its market value on the donor's death and the donor is not treated as having made a chargeable gain.

It is not always clear from the legislation whether a person who receives assets under a trust created by will or under the intestacy rules receives them as a legatee (in which case there is no charge to CGT) or as a beneficiary absolutely entitled as against the trustee, in which case there is a deemed disposal under CGTA 1979 s 54 which may be chargeable (see Chapter 18). In practice, this question was of limited importance prior to 14 March 1989 since any gain under s 54 could be held over under FA 1980 s 79 (as amended). With the removal of general hold-over relief, however, the problem is bound to arise. The answer to the question depends upon the status of the executors and the terms of the will (see *Cochrane's Executors v IRC* (1974) and *IRC v Matthew's Executors* (1984)). During the course of administration they are the sole owners of the deceased's assets, albeit in a fiduciary capacity (*Stamp Duties Comr (Queensland) v Livingston* (1965)) so that at that time the trust has not come into being for CGT purposes. Accordingly, if, before the completion of administration or the vesting of assets in the trustees (whichever first occurs), the property ceases to be settled for CGT purposes, it would appear that when it is eventually transferred to the relevant beneficiary he will take *qua* legatee (see *Example 15.5(2)* below).

EXAMPLE 15.5

(1) T dies leaving his house to executors on trust for sale for his three children all of whom are over 18, in equal shares absolutely. Whether the children receive the assets before the administration is completed or after the executors have assented to themselves as trustees does not matter since they take as legatees. For CGT purposes joint ownership does not result in the property being settled (CGTA 1979 s 46: see further Chapter 18).

(2) T dies leaving his property to executors on trust for sale for his widow for life and then for his three children absolutely, all of whom are over 18. If the widow dies *before the executors become trustees*, any distributions to

the children will be received as legatees since, for CGT purposes, the settlement ended on the widow's death. If, however, the widow dies *after* the executors have become trustees, the property was settled, so that the children receive assets as persons absolutely entitled as against the trustees with a consequent deemed disposal under CGTA 1979 s 54 (there will be no charge in this case because the event leading to their entitlement was the death of the life tenant: contrast the position if the interest had terminated *inter vivos*—see Chapter 18).

When the former matrimonial home of the deceased passes to his surviving spouse there is an uplift in the base value of the property on death in the usual way. On a subsequent disposal by that spouse, any gain since death will be exempt from CGT if the house has been occupied as that spouse's main residence. Even if it has not, by CGTA 1979 s 101(7), the deceased's period of ownership is deemed to be that of the surviving spouse in deciding what proportion of the gain (if any) is chargeable (see [**16.71**]).

[**15.101**]–[**15.120**]

EXAMPLE 15.6

T bought a house in 1983 for £50,000. It was his main residence until his death in 1987 when it was worth £150,000. His wife (W) never lived there with him, but became entitled to the house on his intestacy. T's administrators transferred the house to W in 1988. She thereupon occupied it as her main residence for one year and then went abroad until 1993 when she returned and sold the house for £250,000.

For the purpose of the main residence exemption, W can claim that she has occupied the house as her main residence for eight out of the ten years that it has been in the ownership of herself or T, ie:

1983–87 (4 years)	Occupied by T as his main residence
1987–88* (1 year)	Occupation by administrators treated as that of W and occupied by W
1990–93* (3 years)	Last three years of ownership disregarded (CGTA 1979 s 102)

W is, therefore, charged on a proportion of the gain:
(1) Sale consideration (£250,000) — base cost (£150,000) = £100,000 (assuming no other allowable expenses).
(2) Fraction chargeable: £100,000 × $^2/_{10}$ = £20,000

Were it not for s 101(7), she would be charged on a larger proportion of the gain, ie: £100,000 × $\frac{2 \text{ (sec*)}}{6 \text{ (length of her ownership)}}$ = £33,333

VII   DISCLAIMERS AND VARIATIONS (CGTA 1979 s 49(6))

Subject to certain conditions, which are the same as for IHT (see [**22.128**]), any variation of the deceased's will or of the intestacy rules, or any disclaimer, made in both cases within two years of the deceased's death can be treated for CGT (as for IHT) as if it were made by the deceased and is consequently not a chargeable disposal.

EXAMPLE 15.7

Facts as in *Example 15.1*. L is entitled under T's will to the book worth £100,000. Within two years of T's death L varies the will so that the book (now worth £140,000) passes to his brother B. This need not be a disposal for CGT. Instead, it can be treated as if T's will had so provided. Accordingly, B acquires the asset at its market value at death (£100,000) plus any additional expenses of the PRs.

The election that is available for CGT is identical to that available for IHT purposes. In most cases, it is likely that both the elections will be exercised so that the variation will be read back into the original will for both CGT and IHT purposes. This is not necessary, however, since the elections are independent of each other with the result that the IHT election can be exercised without the CGT election and *vice versa*. Careful thought should be given to this problem: consider the following: **[15.121]**

EXAMPLE 15.8

(1) A will leaves shares worth £100,000 to the testator's daughter. She transfers the shares within the permitted period to her mother (the testator's surviving spouse). The shares are then worth £105,000.

For IHT the election will be desirable as the result will be to reduce the testator's chargeable estate at death by £100,000 since the shares are now an exempt transfer to a surviving spouse.

For CGT the election to read the disposal back should not be made since, if the daughter makes a chargeable transfer, her gain will be £105,000 — £100,000 = £5,000 which will be covered by her annual CGT exemption. Her mother will then acquire the shares at the higher base cost of £105,000.

(2) A will leaves shares worth £100,000 to the testator's surviving spouse. After they have risen in value to £140,000 she decides (within the permitted time limit) to vary the will in favour of her daughter.

For IHT it is by no means obvious that the election should be made. If it is, £100,000 will constitute a chargeable death transfer. If it is not, the widow will make a lifetime gift of £140,000 which, if she survives by seven years, will be free of all tax. On the other hand, if it is likely that she will only survive her husband by a few weeks, then it will be necessary to consider whether it is better for £100,000 to be taxed as part of her dead husband's estate or for £140,000 to be taxed on her death.

For CGT the disposal should be read back into the will since otherwise there will be a chargeable gain of £140,000 — £100,000 = £40,000.

(3) Boris, domiciled in France, leaves his villa in Tuscany and monies in his Swiss bank account to his son Gaspard, a UK resident. By a variation of the terms of his will made within two years of Boris' death, the property is settled on discretionary Liechtenstein trusts for the benefit of Gaspard's family. For IHT purposes, reading back ensures that the settlement is excluded property. CGTA 1979 s 49(6)(b), however, provides that *for the purposes of that section* the variation shall be treated as effected by the deceased. Whether this means that for the purposes of FA 1981 s 80 an overseas settlement has been created by Boris (a non-UK domiciliary) or by Gaspard, is therefore far from clear. If the former, no CGT charges will arise on beneficiaries who receive capital payments from the trustees (see further the discussion of s 80 in Chapter 20). It is understood that the Revenue take the view that 'reading-back' is effective for the purpose of s 49 *only* but that the Special Commissioners, in a case to be appealed, have decided the opposite (see **[22.130]**).

16 CGT—exemptions and reliefs

In many cases a gain on the disposal of an asset will not be chargeable either because the gain itself is exempt or because the asset is not chargeable. Even if a gain is chargeable, there are various reliefs whereby the tax can be minimised or deferred indefinitely. As already noted at [**14.76**], there is an annual exemption for an individual whose gains do not exceed £5,500 in the tax year. [**16.1**]

I MISCELLANEOUS EXEMPTIONS

Exempt assets Certain assets are not chargeable to CGT. The taxpayer, therefore, realises no chargeable gain or, often more significantly, no allowable loss on their disposal. Non-chargeable assets include sterling (CGTA 1979 s 19(1)), National Savings Certificates, Premium Bonds and Save As You Earn deposits (CGTA 1979 s 71), private motor vehicles (CGTA 1979 s 130) and betting winnings (CGTA 1979 s 19(4)). Gains and losses arising on the disposal of investments in a Personal Equity Plan (PEP: see [**37.7**]) are disregarded. [**16.2**]

Exempt gains The following gains are exempt from CGT:
(a) damages for personal injuries (CGTA 1979 s 19(5));
(b) gains on the disposal of decorations for valour unless the decoration was acquired for money or money's worth (CGTA 1979 s 131);
(c) gains on the disposal of foreign currency obtained for private use (CGTA 1979 s 133). A foreign currency bank account is a chargeable asset (a debt) unless the sum in that account was obtained for the personal expenditure of an individual or his family outside the UK (CGTA 1979 s 135). Where several accounts in a particular foreign currency are owned by the same taxpayer he may treat them as one account so that direct transfers between the accounts will not be chargeable disposals (SP 10/84);
(d) gains on the disposal of gilt-edged securities (CGTA 1979 s 67): the exemption also applies to futures and options in these instruments;
(e) shares issued under the business expansion scheme are exempt from CGT on their first disposal (see [**4.87**]);
(f) the disposal of pension rights, annuity rights and annual payments will not generally give rise to a chargeable gain (CGTA 1979 s 144);
(g) any gain on the disposal of a life policy, a deferred annuity policy, or any rights under such policies, unless the disposal is by someone other

than the original beneficial owner and that person acquired the interest or right for money or money's worth (CGTA 1979 s 143(1)); and
(h) gains are exempt if made by such bodies as authorised unit trusts and investment trusts (FA 1980 s 81); and charities, provided that the gain is applied for charitable purposes (CGTA 1979 s 145(1)).   [16.3]

Charities   Disposals to charities and to certain national institutions are treated as made on a no gain/no loss basis (CGTA 1979 s 146 and IHTA 1984 Sch 3).   [16.4]

Heritage property and woodlands   The exemptions for heritage property are basically the same as for IHT (see Chapter 23). First, where property of national interest is given (or sold by private treaty) to a non-profit making body (including a charity or other national institution mentioned in CGTA 1979 s 146) any gain will be exempt from CGT provided that the Treasury so directs (see IHTA 1984 s 26(1)). Secondly, any gain on a disposal of such property may be conditionally exempt from CGT in the same way as for IHT (CGTA 1979 s 147; see IHTA 1984 ss 30, 31). Thirdly, the gain on any property that is accepted by the Treasury in satisfaction of IHT is exempt from CGT (CGTA 1979 s 147(2)(b)).   [16.5]–[16.20]

II   CHATTELS

A gain on the disposal of a chattel that is a wasting asset is generally exempt from CGT. A wasting asset is one with a predictable useful life of 50 years or less and includes yachts, caravans, washing machines, animals and all plant and machinery (see Chapter 14).

In the case of non-wasting chattels, if the disposal consideration is £6,000 or less, any gain is exempt (CGTA 1979 s 128(1)). CGT is as a result easier to administer as there is no need to calculate gains and losses on assets of minimal value since in practice the tax is limited to disposals of such chattels as valuable works of art, furniture, antiques, silver etc. Insofar as the disposal consideration exceeds £6,000, the chargeable gain is limited to 5/3 of the excess of that consideration over £6,000.

Where a loss is made on the disposal of a chattel and the disposal consideration is less than £6,000, the sum of £6,000 is substituted for that consideration so as to limit a claim for loss relief.

EXAMPLE 16.1

(1) A bought a necklace for £4,600 and later sold it for £7,200 so making a total gain of £2,600. The chargeable gain is reduced to 5/3 × £1,200 (£7,200—£6,000) = £2,000.
(2) A bought a brooch for £8,000 and sold it for £4,600 so making an actual loss of £3,400. He is deemed to have sold it for £6,000 so that his allowable loss is restricted to £2,000 (£8,000—£6,000).
    Note: For the purpose of this Example incidental costs of disposal and the indexation allowance have been ignored: they should, of course, be taken into account in computing the chargeable gain which is then subject to reduction.

The taxpayer cannot dispose of a set of articles by a series of separate transactions so as to take advantage of the £6,000 exemption on each disposal. Whether the disposals are to the same person or to connected persons (albeit

on different occasions) they are regarded as a single transaction (see also
FA 1985 s 71, [**14.24**]).   [**16.21**]–[**16.40**]

EXAMPLE 16.2

A owns three Rousseau paintings which, as a set, have a market value of £20,000.
He paid £4,000 for each of the paintings which individually are worth £6,000.
He sells all three paintings at different times to his sister B for £6,000 each.
He thereby appears to fall within the chattel exemption on each disposal. The
Revenue can, however, treat the three disposals as a single disposal of an asset
worth £20,000 with a base value of £12,000 so that A has made a chargeable
gain of £8,000. (The meaning of 'a set' is not always obvious: a valuable collection
of old lead soldiers, for instance, is arguably not a set and the wording of s 128(4)
suggests that at least three articles are required for a set.)

III   DEBTS

1   What is a debt?

A debt is a chargeable asset (CGTA 1979 s 19(1)). It is not defined, so
that it bears the common law meaning of 'a sum payable in respect of
a liquidated money demand recoverable by action' (*Rawley v Rawley* (1876)).
It can include a right to receive a sum of money that is not yet ascertained
(*O'Driscoll v Manchester Insurance Committee* (1915)) or a contingent right to
receive a definite sum (*Mortimore v IRC* (1864)). However, for the purposes
of CGT, it cannot include a right to receive an uncertain sum at an
unascertained date; there must be a liability, either present or contingent,
to pay a sum which is ascertained or capable of being ascertained at the
time of disposal (*Marren v Ingles* (1980)).   [**16.41**]

EXAMPLE 16.3

Barry agrees to sell his Ming vase to Bruce for £15,000 plus one half of any
profits that Bruce realises if he resells the vase in the next ten years. The disposal
consideration received for the vase is £15,000 plus the value of a *chose in action*.
As that *chose* is both contingent (on resale occurring) and for an unascertained
sum (half of any profits) it is not a debt.

2   The general principle

A disposal of a debt by the original creditor, his personal representatives
or legatee is exempt from CGT unless it is a debt on a security (below).
'Disposal' includes repayment of the debt (CGTA 1979 s 134(1),(2)). Since
a contractual debt will normally give a creditor merely the right to repayment
of the sum lent, together with interest, the disposal of a debt will rarely
generate a gain and the aim of CGTA 1979 s 134(1) is to exclude the more
likely claim for loss relief, particularly where the debt is never repaid. This
provision only applies to the original creditor so that an assignee of a debt
can claim an allowable loss if the debtor defaults, unless the assignee and
the creditor are connected persons (CGTA 1979 s 134(4)).

If the debt is satisfied by a transfer of property, that property is acquired
by the creditor at its market value. Since this could operate harshly for
an original creditor who can claim no allowable loss, s 134(3) provides that
on a subsequent disposal of the property, its base value shall be taken as
the value of the debt.

EXAMPLE 16.4

A owes B £30,000 and in full satisfaction of the debt he gives B a painting worth £22,000. B does not have an allowable loss of £8,000. However, if B later sells the painting for £40,000 he is taxed on a gain of £10,000 only (£40,000—£30,000).

The harshness of CGTA 1979 s 134(1) is mitigated by CGTA 1979 s 136, allowing original creditors to claim loss relief in respect of a 'qualifying loan'. The debt must have become irrecoverable and the creditor must not have assigned his rights. Creditor and debtor must not be married to each other nor be companies in the same group. A 'qualifying loan' must be used by a UK resident borrower *wholly for the purpose of a trade* (not being moneylending) carried on by him and the debt must not be 'on a security' (CGTA 1979 s 136; for time limits for claims see SP 3/83).   **[16.42]**

3   Debts on a security

The legislation distinguishes between debts which can normally only decrease in value and those with such characteristics that they may be disposed of at a profit. It, therefore, provides that a 'debt on a security' is chargeable to CGT even in the hands of the original creditor (CGTA 1979 s 134(1)).

Unfortunately, the term 'debt on a security' lacks both statutory and satisfactory judicial interpretation despite three cases (see *Cleveleys Investment Trust Co v IRC* (1971); *Aberdeen Construction Group Ltd v IRC* (1978); *W T Ramsay Ltd v IRC* (1981)). Apparently, the phrase 'debt on a security' has a limited and technical meaning and '[it] is not a synonym for a secured debt' per Lord Wilberforce in *Aberdeen Construction Group Ltd v IRC*. Thus, a mortgage which is a debt secured by an estate in land is not a debt on a security for the purposes of CGT. The word 'security' is defined in CGTA 1979 s 82(3) as including 'any loan stock or similar security whether of the government of the UK or elsewhere, or of any company, and whether secured or unsecured'. Despite the word 'including' the Revenue have stated that they regard the definition as exhaustive (SP 3/70) and their view has been generally accepted by the courts.

There are various requirements that a debt must fulfil in order to qualify as a debt on a security. As a minimum, the security should be marketable or capable of being dealt in, embodied at the very least in a contract and preferably in a document or certificate which must be either loan stock or similar to the loan stock of a government, local authority or company. It should have ordinary terms for repayment, with or without a premium and contain a provision for the payment of interest (*W T Ramsay Ltd v IRC*). If a debt satisfies these very narrow requirements, any disposal of it, whether or not by the original creditor, will result in a chargeable gain or allowable loss.   **[16.43]**

4   Qualifying corporate bonds

Gains on the disposal of a qualifying corporate bond (which will include most company (debentures) are exempt from CGT under FA 1984 s 64. Losses realised by the original investor may, however, attract relief under CGTA 1979 s 136A (inserted by FA 1990). This matter is considered further in Chapter 28.   **[16.44]-[16.60]**

IV THE MAIN RESIDENCE (CGTA 1979 ss 101-105)

Perhaps the most important exemption for the individual taxpayer is from any gain that he makes on the disposal of his principal private residence. This exemption, combined with mortgage interest relief, provides government encouragement for the investment of private capital in home ownership.   [**16.61**]

1 When is the exemption available?

The exemption is available for any gain arising on the disposal by gift or sale by a taxpayer of his only or main residence, including grounds of up to half a hectare (or such larger area as is required for the reasonable enjoyment of the dwelling house).

The question of whether a particular property is a taxpayer's 'only or main residence' is sometimes a difficult one to answer. If only one property is occupied by him as a residence the exemption *prima facie* applies. Where the taxpayer has two residences, only the residence which is his main residence can qualify for relief.

EXAMPLE 16.5

A owns one property in the country and he rents a flat in London. Any gain that A makes on the country property is not automatically exempt just because A owns only that property; A must be able to show that it is his 'main' residence.

Which of two residences is the main residence is a question of fact which is not decided simply by the periods of time spent in each. For a discussion of the courts' approach, see the income tax case of *Frost v Feltham* (1981) (see [**4.56**]).

When the taxpayer has two residences, he can elect for one to be treated as his main residence (CGTA 1979 s 101(5)). This election should be made even though one of the residences is not owned by the taxpayer (it may, for instance, be tied accommodation or a rented flat as in *Example 16.5*, above). The election can be backdated for up to two years and should be made within two years of acquiring a second residence. Failure to do so means that the inspector of taxes can decide which is the main residence, subject to the right of appeal by the taxpayer. The election can be varied.   [**16.62**]

2 How many residences can qualify for exemption?

Prior to 6 April 1988, a maximum of two houses qualified for exemption; the only or main residence and a property owned by the taxpayer but used as a residence by a dependent relative, rent-free and for no other consideration (CGTA 1979 s 105; but see ESC D20 which permitted, *inter alia*, the payment of rates and the cost of repairs to the dwelling house attributable to normal wear and tear).

FA 1988 s 111(1) provided that the dependent relative exemption would not apply to disposals on or after 6 April 1988 (note that mortgage interest relief was similarly withdrawn from dependent relative accommodation: see [**4.65**]). Limited transitional relief continues to be available so long as the dependent relative conditions are satisfied either on 5 April 1988 or at any earlier time. However, if qualifying occupation ceased before 6 April 1988 or ceases thereafter, the subsequent reoccupation of the property by a dependent relative will not be included in calculating the amount of any gain which, when the property is sold, is exempt from CGT.

EXAMPLE 16.6

Thoughtful's widowed mother-in-law has lived since 1980 rent free in a bijou cottage owned by Thoughtful. He does not provide similar accommodation for any other dependent relative.

(i) As an existing arrangement Thoughtful will continue to be entitled to the CGT exemption on any disposal of the cottage so long as his mother-in-law continues to live there on the same terms.

(ii) If the cottage is sold after 6 April 1988 and a small flat purchased as a replacement, no CGT will be charged on the sale but the flat will not qualify for any CGT relief.

(iii) If, instead, Thoughtful's mother-in-law ceases to occupy the cottage as her main residence either before or after 6 April 1988 but at some stage thereafter resumes occupation, no CGT exemption will be available to Thoughtful in respect of the gain attributable to his mother-in-law's later period of reoccupation.

Husband and wife can have only one main residence between them.   **[16.63]**

3   **Miscellaneous problems**

Land used with the house   The exemption for land of up to one acre only applies if it is used in connection with the residence. Thus, a gain made on a disposal of the land will not be exempt if the residence is sold before the land. In *Varty v Lynes* (1976) the taxpayer sold the house and part of the garden. Later he sold the remaining part of the garden with the benefit of planning permission. It was held that this second disposal was chargeable. Had the taxpayer sold the garden before or at the same time as the house, any gain would have been exempt. Brightman J accepted that his construction of CGTA 1979 s 101(1)(b) created an anomaly in that 'if the taxpayer goes out of occupation of the dwellinghouse a month before he sells it, the exemption will be lost in respect of the garden'. To deal with this narrow point the Revenue have stated that they would not seek to raise tax in such a case 'unless the garden had deve. 'pment value' (see CCAB, June 1976). This statement does not cover the normal problem where the house and land are sold separately as in the *Varty v Lynes* case itself.   **[16.64]**

What is a dwelling house?   This is a question of fact. In Makins v Elson (1977) the taxpayer bought land intending to build a house on it. In the meantime, he lived there in a caravan which was connected to the mains services. He never built the house and later sold both land and caravan at a profit. The caravan was held on the facts to be a dwelling house (contrast *Moore v Thompson* (1986)).   **[16.65]**

What is a residence?   This is also a question of fact and degree. In *Batey v Wakefield* (1982) a separate bungalow which was used by a caretaker within the grounds of the taxpayer's house was exempt from CGT on sale, on the basis that a residence can comprise several dwellings which need not necessarily be physically joined. The problem is whether the dwelling in question forms part of the residence and in *Markey v Sanders* (1987) Walton J held that this will only be the case if a building is separate from the main house when two conditions are satisfied. First, it must increase the enjoyment of the main house and, secondly, must be situated very close or adjacent to that house. He concluded that it was necessary to look at the group of buildings as a whole (including their size) in order to decide if they could be treated as a single main residence. Accordingly, he decided that in that particular case a staff bungalow some 130 metres from the main residence and standing in its own grounds could not be treated as part of a single residence with the result that on its disposal CGT was chargeable. It is far from easy to reconcile these two cases and arguable that Walton J paid insufficient attention to the meaning of the word 'residence'. In the later case of *Williams v Merrylees* (1987), for instance, Vinelott J stressed that the proximity of the two buildings was only one factor to be considered and refused to disturb a finding of the commissioners that a gardener's lodge 200 metres from the main house qualified for the exemption (see also *Lewis v Lady Rook* (1990)). **[16.66]**

Sale by trustees Where trustees dispose of a house which is the residence of a beneficiary who is entitled to occupy it by the terms of the settlement (CGTA 1979 s 104) or under a discretion exercised by the trustees, any gain is exempt. The latter point was decided in *Sansom v Peay* (1976) and has repercussions for IHT since the Revenue argue that the beneficiary in whose favour the discretion has been exercised thereby acquires an interest in possession in the settlement (see SP 10/79 and Chapter 24). **[16.67]**

Use of a house for a business If part of the house is used exclusively for business purposes, a proportionate part of the gain on a disposal of the property becomes chargeable (CGTA 19 s 103). However, as long as no part is used *exclusively* for business purposes no exemption will be lost. Doctors and dentists who have a surgery in their house are advised to hold a party in that surgery at least once a year (and to invite the local tax inspector!). **[16.68]**

Letting part of the property Where the whole or part of the property has been let as residential accommodation this may result in a partial loss of exemption. However, the gain attributable to the letting (calculated according to how much was let and for how long) will be exempt from CGT up to the lesser of £40,000 and the exemption attributable to the owner's occupation. This relief does not apply if the let portion forms a separate dwelling (FA 1980 s 80 and SP 14/80). The Revenue have stated that the taking of lodgers will not result in a loss of any of the exemption provided that the lodger lives as part of the family and shares living accommodation (SP 14/80).

In *Owen v Elliott* (1990) the taxpayer carried on the business of a private hotel or boarding house on premises which he also occupied as his main residence and argued that he was entitled to relief under s 80 since taking in hotel guests amounted to 'residential accommodation'. Reversing the Judge at First Instance, the Court of Appeal accepted this argument and rejected the contention that under s 80 the occupation had to be by persons making their home in the premises let as opposed to paying guests staying over night or on holiday. Leggatt LJ stated that:

> 'The expression "residential accommodation" does not directly or by association mean premises likely to be occupied as a home. It means living accommodation, by contrast, for example, with office accommodation. I regard as wholly artificial attempts to distinguish between a letting by the owner and a letting to the occupant; and between letting to a lodger and letting to a guest in a boarding

house; and between a letting that is likely to be used by the occupant as his
home and one that is not.' **[16.69]**

EXAMPLE 16.7

A sells his house which he has owned for 20 years realising a gain of £120,000.
He occupied the entire house during the first ten years. For the next six years
he let ¹/₃ of it and for the final four years the entire property.

	£	£
Total gain		120,000
Less exemptions		
(i) 10 years occupation	60,000	
(ii) 6 years occupation of ²/₃ (£60,000 × ²/₃ × ⁶/₁₀)	24,000	
(iii) final 3 years ownership (£60,000 × ³/₁₀)	18,000	
		102,000
Gain attributable to letting		18,000
Less exemption (part) [lower of £40000 and (iii) above]		18,000
Chargeable portion		£ Nil

Disposal by PRs   Concessionary relief may be available to PRs (see ESC
D5 discussed at **[15.61]**).   **[16.70]**

4   Effect of periods of absence

To qualify for the exemption, the taxpayer must occupy the property as
his only or main residence throughout the period of his ownership. As a
general rule, therefore, the effect of periods of absence is that on the disposal
of the residence a proportion of any gain will be charged. That proportion
is calculated by the formula:

$$\text{Total gain} \times \frac{\text{period of absence}}{\text{period of ownership}}$$

Special rules operate for husband and wife since in deciding whether a
house has been occupied as a main residence throughout the period of
ownership one spouse can take advantage of a period of ownership of the
other (CGTA 1979 s 101(7)(a): see **[15.101]** for an illustration of this rule).

Despite the general rule that absences render part of the gain chargeable,
certain absences are ignored. These include, by concession, the first 12 months
of ownership in cases where occupation was delayed because the house was
being built or altered (SP D4). The last three years of ownership are likewise
ignored and this often proves highly beneficial on a matrimonial breakdown
(see generally Chapter 36). It also means that a taxpayer owning two houses
can by careful use of his election obtain a tax advantage.

EXAMPLE 16.8

Judith has owned for many years a flat in London and a cottage in Wales.
She has elected for the flat to be her main residence. In 1991 she sells the
flat. She should, therefore, elect retrospectively for her Welsh cottage to be her
main residence from 1988 onwards.

CGTA 1979 s 102 allows other periods of absence to be ignored provided
that the owner had no other residence available for the exemption during

these periods and that he resided in the house before and after the absence in question. These periods are:

(a) any period or periods of absence not exceeding three years altogether;

(b) any period when the taxpayer was employed abroad; and

(c) a maximum period of four years where the owner could not occupy the property because he was employed elsewhere.

ESC D3 gives relief when the absence results from a non-owning spouse's employment and the Revenue also accept that, if the absence exceeds the permitted period in (a) and (c), it is only the excess which does not qualify for the exemption. The requirement that the taxpayer should reside after the period of absence will not apply in (b) and (c) if it is prevented by the terms of his employment (ESC D4). If he is required either by the nature of his employment or as the result of his trade or profession to live in other accommodation ('job-related accommodation'—see [4.56]) he will obtain the exemption if he buys a house intending to use it in the future as a main residence. It does not matter that he never occupies it and that it is let throughout, provided that he can show that he intended to live there. He should, of course, make the main residence election since he is occupying other (job-related) property. . [**16.71**]

5 Expenditure with profit-making motive

The exemption does not apply if the house was acquired wholly or partly for the purpose of realising a gain, nor to a gain attributable to any expenditure which was incurred wholly or partly for the purpose of realising a gain (CGTA 1979 s 103(3)). Presumably, the acquisition of a freehold reversion by a tenant with a view to selling an absolute title to the property would fall within this provision. If so, the portion of the gain attributable to the reversion would be assessable. The requirement of motive makes this provision difficult to apply. [**16.72**]–[**16.90**]

V BUSINESS RELIEFS

1 The problems and the taxes

A number of CGT reliefs relate to businesses both incorporated and unincorporated. Their aim is to enable businesses to be carried on and transferred without being threatened by taxation. Although this chapter is concerned only with CGT reliefs, a disposal of a business will normally involve other taxes. It may be by way of gift (including death) or by sale. If by way of gift, the relevant taxes will be CGT, income tax and IHT. For CGT, hold-over relief under CGTA 1979 s 126 will usually be available on a lifetime gift; on a death, there will be no CGT. Where the transfer is a sale, income tax and CGT may apply.

The CGT business reliefs may apply to a disposal of:

(a) a sole trade/profession;

(b) a part of a trade/profession (eg a partnership share);

(c) shares in a company; and

(d) assets used by a company or partnership in which the owner of the assets either owns shares or is a partner.

In a number of cases relief is given by a deferment of the capital gains tax charge and this is usually done by deducting the otherwise chargeable gain from the acquisition cost of a new or replacement asset (roll-over or hold-over relief[1]c). In such cases, although the benefits of 1982 rebasing (see

[**14.32**]) will not be available to the taxpayer, one-half of that deferred gain will be excluded from charge on a later disposal of the asset. Thus, in a typical case, if there has been a disposal of an asset owned on 31 March 1982 before 6 April 1988, a new asset will have been acquired at that date but for the purpose of computing the gain on a disposal after 5 April 1988 only one-half of the deferred gain will be brought into charge (FA 1988 Sch 9). [**16.91**]

2 Roll-over (replacement of business assets) (CGTA 1979 s 115)

Where certain assets of a business are sold and the proceeds of sale wholly re-invested in acquiring a new asset to be used in a business, the taxpayer can elect to roll over the gain and deduct it from the acquisition cost of the new asset. Tax is, therefore, postponed until the asset is sold and no new asset purchased.

EXAMPLE 16.9

A makes a gain of £50,000 on the sale of factory 1, but he immediately buys factory 2 for £120,000. He can roll the gain of £50,000 into the purchase price of factory 2 thereby reducing it to £70,000 (actual cost £120,000 minus rolled over gain of £50,000).

The old and the new asset must be comprised in the list of business assets in CGTA 1979 s 118. These are land and buildings; fixed plant and machinery; ships; aircraft; hovercraft; goodwill; satellites, space stations and spacecraft; milk and potato quotas. The old and new assets need not be of the same type however; eg, a gain on the sale of an aircraft can be rolled over into the purchase of a hovercraft. Further, although the old asset must have been used in the taxpayer's trade during the whole time that he owned it (otherwise only partial roll-over is allowed), it could have been used in successive trades provided that the gap between them did not exceed three years.

EXAMPLE 16.10

A inherited a freehold shop in 1979 when its value was £25,000. The shop was kept empty until 1985 when he decided to start a fish and chip shop. He sold the shop in 1991 for £60,000 and purchased new premises for £75,000. The value of the shop in 1982 was £36,000.
As a result of rebasing, his total gain (excluding indexation) is £24,000 and (counting only periods after March 1982) the premises have been used for business purposes during six-eighths of the ownership period. Hence £18,000 of the gain is rolled-over but the balance (£6,000) is taxed.

Land and buildings that are sold must be occupied as well as used for the purposes of the taxpayer's business. If the property is occupied by his partner or employee, he must be able to show that their occupation is representative (ie attributed to him) to obtain the relief. For occupation to be representative it must *either* (i) be essential for the partner or employee to occupy the property to perform his duties; *or* (ii) be an express term of the employment contract (or partnership agreement) that he should do so, and the occupation must enable him to perform his duties better. If either of these conditions is proved, the Revenue accept that the property is used for the purpose of the owner's trade (see *Anderton v Lamb* (1981)).

The new asset must be bought within one *year before* or three years *after* the disposal of the old one. The new asset need not be used in the same trade as the old but can be used in another trade carried on by the taxpayer simultaneously or successively, provided in the latter case that there is not more than a three year gap between the ceasing of one trade and the start of another (see SP 8/81). There is nothing to prevent the taxpayer from rolling his gain into the purchase of more than one asset or to require him to continue to use the new asset in a trade throughout his period of ownership (see further ESC D 22–25 which extend the relief, *inter alia*, to cover improvements to existing assets; the acquisition of a further interest in an asset already used for the purposes of the trade; and the partition of land on the dissolution of a partnership). Relief is not available to a non-UK resident who sells a chargeable asset and then purchases a new asset which is not chargeable because it is situated outside the UK (FA 1989 s 129).

This relief is also available to partnerships and to companies and it can be claimed for an asset which is owned by an individual and used by his partnership or family company (for the definition of such a company see [16.96]). In such cases the relief is only available to the individual and the replacement asset cannot be purchased by the partnership or company. Employees may claim the relief for assets owned by them so long as the assets are used (or, in the case of land and buildings, occupied) only for the purposes of the employment. (Note, however, that it is not necessary for the asset to be used *exclusively* by the employee in the course of his employment so that relief may apply even if the asset is provided for the general use of the employer: see SP 5/86.)

There are certain restrictions on the relief.

First, if the new asset is a depreciating asset (defined as a 'wasting asset' or one which will become a wasting asset within ten years such as a lease with 60 years unexpired) the gain on the old asset cannot be deducted from the cost of the new. Instead, tax on the gain is postponed until the earliest of the three following events:

(a) ten years elapse from the date of the purchase of the new asset; or
(b) the taxpayer disposes of the new asset; or
(c) the taxpayer ceases to use the new asset for the purposes of a trade.

If, before the deferred gain becomes chargeable, a new asset is acquired (whether the depreciating asset is sold or not), the deferred gain may be rolled into the new asset (see CGTA 1979 s 117).

EXAMPLE 16.11

Sam sells his freehold fish and chip shop for £25,000 thereby making a gain of £12,000. One year later he buys a 55 year lease on new premises for £27,000 and seven years after that acquires a further freehold shop for £35,000.

(1) Purchase of 55 year lease: this lease is a depreciating asset. The gain of £12,000 on the sale of the original shop is, therefore, held in suspense for ten years.

(2) Purchase of the freehold shop: as the purchase occurs within ten years of the gain, roll-over relief is available so that the purchase price is reduced to £23,000.

Secondly, if the whole of the proceeds of sale are not re-invested in acquiring the new asset there is a chargeable gain equivalent to the amount not re-invested and it is only the balance that is rolled over. Accordingly, if the purchase price of the new asset does not exceed the acquisition cost of the old, all the gain is chargeable and there is nothing to roll over. The new asset must, of course, be purchased for use in a business so that if there is an element of non-business user relief will be restricted accordingly.

EXAMPLE 16.12

A buys factory 1 for £50,000 and sells it for £100,000 thereby making a gain of £50,000. A buys factory 2 for £80,000. The amount not reinvested (£20,000, ie £100,000—£80,000) is chargeable. The balance of the gain (£30,000) is rolled over so that the acquisition cost of factory 2 is £50,000. If factory 2 had only cost £50,000 the amount not reinvested would equal the gain (ie £50,000) and be chargeable.

In *Tod v Mudd* (1987) the taxpayer sold his accountancy practice and with his wife bought premises in which they intended to carry on business as hoteliers in partnership. The premises were bought as tenants in common with a 75% interest being held by Mr Mudd and 25% by his wife and it was agreed that they would be used as to 75% for business purposes and 25% for private purposes. The partnership agreement stated that the business of the partnership should be conducted on that portion of the premises attributable to Mr Mudd's share. The court held that roll-over relief should be given to Mr Mudd but only on 75% of 75% of the purchase price because his interest as a tenant in common constituted a share in the whole property and not in a distinct 75% portion thereof. Accordingly, because of the way in which this arrangement had been structured, roll-over relief was restricted. There are a number of ways in which matters could have been organised so that full relief would have been given to Mr Mudd. First, he could have bought the whole of the new premises for business use and then given 25% to his wife. Secondly, he could have purchased an identified and separate portion of the premises (75% thereof) in his sole name and for business use leaving his wife to purchase the remaining portion for private purposes. Finally, the defective arrangement could have been cured had Mr Mudd bought out Mrs Mudd's 25% share within three years of the disposal of his accountancy practice.

If the taxpayer knows that the price of the new asset will be too low to enable him to claim roll-over (or full roll-over) relief and he is married, it may be advantageous to transfer a share in the old asset to his wife before it is sold although this ruse could be challenged under the *Ramsay* principle (Chapter 31).

EXAMPLE 16.13

H buys factory 1 for £50,000 and transfers 2/5 of it to his wife W. The factory is sold for £100,000. H's gain is £30,000 ([3/5 × £100,000]—[3/5 × £50,000]). W's gain is £20,000 ([2/5 × £100,000]—[2/5 × £50,000]).

H's share of the proceeds of sale is £60,000. H then buys factory 2 for £50,000. The proceeds of sale are not wholly re-invested in factory 2 and, therefore, H is charged to CGT on £10,000 (£60,000—£50,000). The balance of his gain £20,000 (£30,000—£10,000) can be rolled over, leaving him with a base value for factory 2 of £30,000. H and W between them are taxed on a gain of £30,000 instead of (as in *Example 16.12*) H being taxed on a gain of £50,000.

Finally, roll-over relief should not be claimed where the taxpayer makes an allowable loss on the sale of the old asset since he cannot add this loss to the base value of the new asset. Nor should he claim the relief where the gain does not exceed his annual exemption. Even if his gain does exceed the exempt limit, it may not be worth claiming the relief, as the claim cannot be to hold over only a part of the gain and the effect of reducing the base cost of an asset is to depress any indexation allowance. **[16.92]**

3 **Retirement relief** (FA 1985 ss 69–70; Sch 20)

The following conditions must be satisfied:
(a) the disponer must satisfy either an age or ill-health requirement and have owned the property for a minimum period of one year prior to the disposal;
(b) he must make a 'material disposal' or 'other qualifying disposal'; and
(c) the disposal must be of chargeable business assets.
    Various aspects of these conditions are considered below. **[16.93]**

The disponer Relief is given on all disposals of chargeable business assets (see below) by individuals, and in certain circumstances, by trustees. To be eligible for relief an individual must *either* be at least 55 years of age at the date of the disposal (although he need not retire from business); *or* he must have been forced to retire before that age on grounds of ill-health (see FA 1985 Sch 20 para 3 for detailed requirements that must be satisfied if ill-health is to be established and notice that the Revenue's decision on the matter is non-appealable).

If either of these conditions is satisfied retirement relief will be available but to obtain the *full* relief, the individual must have owned the appropriate asset for ten years prior to its disposal. If this ten year ownership condition is not satisfied in full the relief is scaled down so that a proportion will be available, provided that the asset has been owned for at least one year. Relief may be given on more than one occasion but is limited to the overall maximum.

EXAMPLE 16.14

(1) A retires aged 57 and disposes of his business owned for the previous 12 years. Full relief is available.
(2) As in (1) except that A is aged 53. No relief is available unless the retirement is on the grounds of ill-health; if it is, full relief will be given.
(3) A retires at 90 having owned a business for nine months. No relief is available because the minimum one year ownership period is not satisfied.

The relief may also be given in the case of settlements with an interest in possession (other than for a fixed term) provided that the beneficiary (not the trustees) satisfies the appropriate conditions. **[16.94]**

EXAMPLE 16.15

(1) A newsagent's shop was settled in favour of Benny for life. At the age of 61 and after running the business for 25 years Benny retires and the business is sold by the trustees. Maximum retirement relief will be available.
(2) As in (1) above except that the business was run by the two trustees. The business is sold when they are both over the age of 55, but no relief is available.

The amount of relief   Retirement relief exempts from charge gains of up to £150,000 and 50% of gains between £150,000 and £600,000. Hence, as the following example illustrates, the maximum relief now available is for gains of up to £375,000. $600000 - 150000 \times 50\% = 225000$ **[16.95]**
$$\frac{150000}{375000}$$

EXAMPLE 16.16

At the age of 60, Thad, who has been a partner in an estate agency business since 1960, sells his interest in that business realising capital gains of £900,000. He is entitled to maximum retirement relief calculated as follows:

£150,000 + [50% × (£600,000–£150,000)] = £150,000 + £225,000 = £375,000

In situations where the ten-year-ownership requirement has not been met, the relief must be reduced proportionately by the following method:
Stage 1:
Calculate the relevant chargeable gains which may attract relief. For this purpose no scaling down is involved.
Stage 2:
Calculate the appropriate percentage of relief to which the taxpayer is entitled. This involves considering the ownership period of the taxpayer as a percentage of ten years. Assume, for instance, that a particular taxpayer has owned the business for three years in which case the relevant percentage is 30%. (Had his ownership period been four years, the percentage would have been 40% and so on: the calculation will usually be in months and days.)
Stage 3:
Calculate the available amount of 'full relief'. The full relief is available on gains of up to £150,000 and therefore in the example considered the taxpayer will be entitled to a maximum of 30% of that figure, ie £45,000.
Stage 4:
Calculate the appropriate percentage of the upper limit of the half rate relief band. The half rate relief band applies to gains between £150,000 and £600,000 and it is necessary to calculate what percentage of the upper limit figure (£600,000) is available. In the example being considered this will be 30%: ie £180,000. $30\% \times 60000$
Stage 5:
The relief available to the taxpayer in the example under consideration is therefore:
(i)   gains within the full rate band: £45,000; plus
(ii) 50% of the gains within a half rate band running from £45,000 to £180,000. Hence, maximum relief in this band will be for gains of £67,500;
(iii) accordingly, the total gains available for retirement relief in the case of a taxpayer who has owned his business for three years only will be £112,500.
To illustrate how these limits operate, assume that the total gains of the taxpayer (arrived at as indicated in *Stage 1* above) are £600,000. Retirement relief calculated as above on a three-year-ownership period will exempt from charge £112,500 of those gains. Contrast, however, the position if the total gains were only £130,000. Now the available relief would be reduced as follows:
(i)   on the relevant portion of the full relief band £45,000 is available (*Stage 3* above); *plus*
(ii) one half of the gains between £45,000 and £130,000. Notice that the scaled down upper limit (£180,000) is ignored since this figure exceeds the actual gain realised.
  Hence, the relief available in this case is limited to £87,500 (ie £45,000 + £42,500).

A material disposal   The relief is given on a material disposal of business assets as defined in FA 1985 s 69(3)–(5).
  This includes first, a disposal of a business or part of a business; hence,

a sole trader who sells his business may qualify for the relief, as may a partner who sells his share in the partnership assets (see FA 1985 s 69(8)).

Secondly, the definition includes a disposal of assets which, at the time when the business ceased to be carried on, were in use for the purposes of that business. Generally, the business must have been owned by the individual; or by a partnership of which he was a member; or by his family company (see below).

The conditions for relief must be satisfied at the date when the business ceased (ie on or before that date the individual must have satisfied the age/ ill-health requirements and owned the business for a minimum of one year), but the disposal of the asset may occur within a 'permitted period' after that cessation. This period is one year, unless the Revenue by notice in writing allow a longer period in a particular case.

EXAMPLE 16.17

Jock had run a newsagent's business for many years, but on 1 July 1991 he ceased trading because of ill-health. He owned a lease on the shop which he was unable to assign until 1 January 1992. Retirement relief on the disposal of the lease will be available to Jock provided that on 1 July 1991 he is at least 55 or can prove ill-health and that he has owned the business for at least 12 months.

Unless the business ceases, relief is not given for a mere disposal of assets. Accordingly, on a disposal by an individual who is continuing in business, it may be necessary to decide whether that disposal is of part of a business (which qualifies for relief) or of assets used in the business (which does not). In *McGregor v Adcock* (1977) a farmer sold about one-sixth of his farming land with planning permission and continued farming the remainder. His claim for retirement relief failed because it was held that he had sold only a business asset and not a part of the business which continued unchanged after the disposal.

For relief to be available, Fox J considered that there must be 'such an interference with the whole complex of activities and assets as can be said to amount to . . . a part disposal of the business'. Subsequently, in *Mannion v Johnston* (1988) a taxpayer who farmed 78 acres sold 17 acres in April 1984 and a further 18 acres in the following December whilst in *Atkinson v Dancer* (1988) the taxpayer owned and farmed 28 acres, farmed a further 67 acres as tenant, and then sold 9 acres in all. Despite doubting whether the above test of Fox J was 'particularly helpful or illuminating', the *McGregor* case was followed and retirement relief refused in both cases. Giving judgment Peter Gibson J concluded that:

> 'In my judgment it must be implicit in [Fox J's] remarks that changes in activities and assets caused by something other than the sale are irrelevant. It is no doubt often the case that a farmer over [55] will decide to cut down on his farming activities. He may do so in a number of ways. He may decide to stop a particular activity completely; he may reduce the scale of the activity; he may do it simply by stopping to do that which he has done before; or he may sell the assets or undertaking. But unless the change in his activities is attributable to the disposal by way of sale it is simply not material that prior to the sale there had been a connection between the activity that has ceased or been reduced and that which is sold.'

It may be that relief will be available in cases where the taxpayer sells not just the land but assets appropriate to the business which he had carried on on that land. In his comments on the *Dancer* case the judge referred to 'a mere sale of 9 out of 89 acres with *no livestock or equipment or other stock or goodwill or anything else included in the sale*'. It may therefore follow that the cases would have been decided differently if the land had been sold along with (say) a tractor, a plough, a combine harvester, or cattle as appropriate.

Thirdly, relief may be available on a disposal of shares or securities in a family trading company or a family holding company. In this case the business must be owned by a trading company which is either the individual's family company or a member of a trading group of which the holding company is the individual's family company: and the individual must be a full-time working director of either that company or of another company in the group. The provisions do, however, recognise that a director may go into a period of semi-retirement before finally selling his shares. In such a case the ownership period is calculated by reference to the date when the taxpayer ceased to be a full-time director and, so long as he continues to work at least ten hours a week for the company in a managerial or technical capacity and retains his directorship, entitlement to the relief is preserved.   [**16.96**]

EXAMPLE 16.18

(1) A trading business is incorporated and all the shares in the company are owned by the sole director Rich. On a disposal of those shares relief may be available.

(2) Rich owns all the shares and is the sole director of Head Co Ltd. That company owns all the shares in two trading subsidiaries, Alpha Ltd and Beta Ltd. On a disposal of his shares in Head Co Ltd, Rich may be entitled to retirement relief.

(3) Andrew has been employed by his family company since leaving college at the age of 25. At the age of 45 he inherited 35% of the shares from his mother and was appointed to the Board of Directors. At 51 he decided to take it easy and ceased to work full time in the business although he retained a seat on the Board and continued to work three mornings a week. Four years later (aged 55) he disposed of his shares. He will be entitled to retirement relief which has in effect been 'frozen' from his semi-retirement (at the age of 51). Hence as he was a full-time working director in his family company for six years (from 45 to 51) his maximum relief will be limited (the appropriate percentage will be 60%).

Family Company   A family company is defined as one in which the transferor owns a minimum of 25% of the shares conferring voting rights or, alternatively, as one in which he owns at least 5% and he and his family together own more than 50% (FA 1985 Sch 20 para 1(2)). 'Family' comprises the transferor's spouse, parent or ancestor, child or descendant, brother or sister and the same relatives of his spouse but not more remote relatives such as uncles, aunts, nephews and nieces nor former husbands or wives although trustees' votes will be included if the settlement is in favour of the taxpayer and/ or his family.   [**16.97**]

EXAMPLE 16.19

Four friends, A, B, C and D, form a trading company ABCD Ltd. Each takes 25% of the ordinary share capital and is a full-time working director. For the purposes of retirement relief ABCD Ltd is the 'family' company of each of them (hence, the term is something of a misnomer!).

Other qualifying disposal By FA 1985 s 70(1), relief may be available on the disposal of an asset which was held for the purposes of an office or employment (other than as director of a family company) exercised by the disponer. Generally, the necessary conditions have to be satisfied with regard to the office or employment. Hence, the office or employment must have been held for at least 12 months before the disposal of the asset; if it terminates before the disposal of the asset the taxpayer must satisfy the age/ill-health requirement at the date of that termination and dispose of the asset within the 'permitted period' (as above, this will normally be 12 months) of that termination.

Relief is also given on the disposal of a business asset by an individual which had been used by a partnership (in which the disponer was a partner) or by his family company (an 'associated disposal'). To qualify for relief the disposal must take place as part of the withdrawal of the individual from participation in the business (ie it must be linked to the disposal of part at least of the taxpayer's share in his family company or partnership). The qualifying conditions (one year ownership and age/ill-health) must be satisfied in relation to that disposal, but it should be noted that relief on the associated disposal of the asset may be restricted if it was used in the appropriate business for part only of the taxpayer's period of ownership, or if a rent was charged for its use. In such cases relief shall be given against such part of the gain as appears to the Revenue to be 'just and reasonable' (FA 1985 Sch 20 para 10; note that, in certain circumstances, interest payments paid on behalf of the disponer may be treated as rent: see SP 4/85; p 36). **[16.98]**

EXAMPLE 16.20

A is aged 62 and acquired 60% of the shares in A Ltd at a cost of £40,000 ten years ago. He has been a full-time working director of A Ltd throughout this time. Five years ago A bought land for £100,000 which the company has since used rent-free. A gives the shares (now worth £100,000) and the land worth £180,000 to his son.

A is entitled to full relief (he is aged 62 and has owned the shares for ten years) which he can set against his gain on the shares (£60,000) and land (£80,000).

Notes
(1) Although the disposal of the land should be 'associated' with A's withdrawal from A Ltd, that disposal need not be to the person who obtains A's shares.
(2) If there is a delay in disposing of the land (eg when it is difficult to find a purchaser), relief will still be available so long as it can be shown that the intention throughout was to dispose of both shares and land.

Duration of ownership As stressed above, the relief depends upon the business assets being owned for a minimum of one year prior to disposal and, to obtain full relief, a ten year ownership period must be satisfied. When full relief is not available on a disposal, but in the preceding ten years a separate (and earlier) business had been carried on by the taxpayer, it may be regarded as the same business as that disposed of, provided that the earlier business did not terminate more than two years before the start of the later business (FA 1985 Sch 20 para 14). Provision is made for calculating relief on the later disposal in cases where the earlier disposal qualified for retirement relief (FA 1985 Sch 20 para 15).

EXAMPLE 16.21

(1) Sal, having owned a fish and chip shop for four years, transfers the business to Sal Ltd, in which he owns all the shares. After a further six years Sal retires aged 60 and sells the shares. Full relief is available since the periods of ownership are aggregated.

(2) Mal, having owned a fish and chip shop for four years, sells the business and goes cruising round the world. One year later he opens a vegetarian restaurant and six years later retires, aged 55, selling that business. Mal can aggregate the ownership periods of the different businesses, subject to the proviso that the extended period cannot begin earlier than ten years before the disposal of the vegetarian restaurant. Accordingly, although aggregation produces a ten year ownership period Mal can take advantage of only nine years' aggregation.

Aggregation of ownership is also possible where the business assets are transferred between spouses at a time when they are living together. The inter-spouse transfer, if effected inter vivos, will be at no gain, no loss (see [16.22]), but on a subsequent disposal of the assets the ownership period of the husband and wife may be aggregated. For aggregation to apply an election in writing by the transferee spouse is required and relief is generally limited by FA 1985 Sch 20 para 16(4) in cases where the inter-spouse disposal occurred inter vivos.   [16.99]

EXAMPLE 16.22

Jack transfers his ironmonger's business to his wife Jill after he has owned it for five years. After a further three years she disposes of it on attaining the age of 55. Jill may elect to aggregate Jack's five years' ownership with her three years' thereby giving relief calculated on the basis of an ownership period of eight years.

Note As the disposal occurred *inter vivos*, retirement relief on the disposal by Jill is the lower of (i) relief calculated on the basis of eight years ownership less the amount of any retirement relief claimed by Jack on disposals up to his disposal to Jill; and (ii) the relief available had the later transfer been by Jack; had the earlier transfer to Jill not occurred; and assuming that anything done by Jill in relation to the business had been done by Jack. Assuming that Jack received no retirement relief up to the date of disposal by Jill, the relief available will, as stated above, be arrived at taking the relevant percentage to be 80%.

Chargeable business assets   Relief is given only against gains occurring on the disposal of chargeable business assets. Accordingly, gains on other assets (eg private investments) may not benefit from the relief. The appropriate gains are aggregated and relief is then deducted; any remaining gains may be subject to charge.

When the disposal is of shares in a company, relief is given only against so much of the gain as is related to the chargeable business assets of the company. Such assets will include land, goodwill and plant and machinery which qualifies for capital allowances (see Chapter 7). Cash, debts and stock are not chargeable assets, whilst shares held in another company, although chargeable, are investment not business assets. In order to calculate the gain that is eligible for retirement relief, first, calculate the total gain on shares and then multiply by the fraction of chargeable business assets (CBA) divided by total chargeable assets (TCA):

$$\text{ie total gain on shares} \times \frac{\text{CBA}}{\text{TCA}} = \text{gain eligible for relief.}$$

EXAMPLE 16.23

A makes a gain of £140,000 on a disposal of shares in his family company and is entitled to retirement relief of £50,000. If the chargeable business assets of the company are valued at £200,000 and chargeable investment assets at £600,000, the amount of the gain against which retirement relief can be set is:

$$£140,000 \times \frac{\text{CBA}}{\text{TCA}} = £140,000 \times \frac{£200,000}{£800,000} = £35,000$$

Thus, the balance of the gain of £105,000 (£140,000– £35,000) is chargeable and A has unused retirement relief of £15,000 (£50,000–£35,000).

If the disposal is of shares in a holding company of a trading group the apportionment is by reference to the chargeable business assets and chargeable assets of every member of the trading group (ie of all the subsidiaries). **[16.100]**

Application to trusts

As mentioned above, the relief may be available when there is a material disposal by trustees of assets used for the purpose of a business, or of shares in a family company. Only trusts with an interest in possession may qualify (hence, discretionary trusts are excluded) and the relief is given by reference to the life tenant entitled in possession to the entire fund or to that part of the fund comprising the business assets (FA 1985 s 70(3)). There must be a disposal by the trustees of either shares or securities of a company or of assets used, or previously used, for the purposes of a business; and, in the former case, the beneficiary must cease to be a full-time working director on that disposal: whilst in the latter, the business must cease on the disposal. Accordingly, relief is not available for a part disposal of a business which thereafter continues nor for a part disposal of shares where the beneficiary remains a full-time working director of the company concerned.

In calculating the amount available for relief, the disposal is treated as being by the beneficiary and in cases where on the same day there is a disposal of business assets by the trustees and by the beneficiary himself the relief available is applied to the beneficiary's own disposal in priority to the trustees' disposal (FA 1985 Sch 20 para 13(3)). **[16.101]**

Claiming the relief

The relief is automatically given, except when the taxpayer has retired because of ill-health (when a claim must be made not later than two years after the relevant disposal) or when the disposal is by trustees (when a joint claim by the trustees and beneficiary is necessary). **[16.102]**

4   Postponement of CGT on gifts and undervalue sales (CGTA 1979 s 126 as amended by FA 1989 Sch 14 and s 124)

This provision is considered in detail in the next chapter.   [16.103]

5   Hold-over relief on the incorporation of a business (CGTA 1979 s 123)

This relief takes the form of a postponement of, rather than an exemption from, CGT. It applies when there is a disposal of an unincorporated business (whether by a sole trader, a partnership, or trustees) to a company and that disposal is wholly or partly in return for shares in that company. Any gains made on the disposal of chargeable business assets will be deducted from the value of the shares received (the gain is 'rolled into' the shares).

The business must be transferred as a going concern; a mere transfer of assets is insufficient. Further, all the assets of the business (excluding only cash) must be transferred to the company. As only a gain on business assets can be held over, it will be advisable to take investment assets out of the business before incorporation.

EXAMPLE 16.24

On the incorporation of a business for shares, there is a gain on business assets of £50,000. The market value of the shares is £150,000. The gain is rolled over by deducting it from the value of the shares so that the acquisition cost of the shares is £100,000 (£150,000-£50,000).

Where only a part of the total consideration given by the company is in shares (the rest being in cash or debentures), only a corresponding part of the chargeable gain can be rolled forward and deducted from the value of the shares. That part is found by applying the formula:

$$\text{Gain rolled forward} = \text{total gain} \times \frac{\text{market value of shares}}{\text{total consideration for transfer}}$$

In practice the assumption of liabilities by the company is not treated as consideration for this purpose.

EXAMPLE 16.25

A transfers his hotel business to Strong Ltd in return for £160,000, consisting of 10,000 shares (market value £120,000) and £40,000 cash. The chargeable business assets transferred are the premises (market value £130,000) the goodwill (market value £10,000) and furniture, fixtures etc (market value £20,000). On the premises and the goodwill A makes chargeable gains of £35,000 and £5,000 respectively.

Thus A's chargeable gain is:

$$£40,000 - \left(£40,000 \times \frac{£120,000}{£160,000} \right) = £40,000 - £30,000 = £10,000$$

and the acquisition cost of the shares is £120,000—£30,000 = £90,000 (ie £9 per share).

Although s 123 is a mandatory provision and generally results in the entire gain being held over, the Revenue accept that, if the relevant conditions are satisfied, retirement relief may first be deducted so that only the gain remaining is held over under s 123. So long as the company is the taxpayer's family company, retirement relief may be available on a disposal of the shares.

If it is desired to sell an unincorporated business it may be possible to use s 123 to defer any CGT liability on the sale. The business is first sold to a company and s 123 ensures that the vendors will not be subject to CGT until they dispose of their shares in that company. As the company acquires the business assets at market value, however (under CGTA 1979 s 29A: see [**14.22**]), the trade can immediately be resold to the intended purchaser without any CGT charge. [**16.104**]

6 Relief on company reconstructions and amalgamations

The relief afforded by CGTA 1979 ss 85–87 in respect of 'paper for paper exchanges' is considered in Chapter 33. [**16.105**]

17 CGT—gifts and sales at under-value

'Mr Turner has really argued his case on broader lines than I have so far indicated, and has used language, though moderate and reasonably temperate, as to the ways of Parliament in misusing language and in effect "deeming" him into a position which on any ordinary use of the words "capital gains" was impossible to assert. He in effect says "Here is a discreditable manipulation of words. The Statute is not truthful. Words ought to mean what they say".' (Russell LJ in *Turner v Follett* (1973) 48 TC at 621.)   [**17.1**]

I INTRODUCTORY

A disposal of an asset, otherwise than by way of a bargain at arm's length, is treated as a disposal at the open market value (CGTA 1979 s 29A). A donor is, therefore, deemed to receive the market value of the property that he has given away even though he has received nothing (*Turner v Follett* (1973)). A transaction between connected persons is always treated as a disposal at market value (CGTA 1979 s 62(2); for the definition of connected persons see [**14.23**]).

EXAMPLE 17.1

Jackson sells a valuable Ming vase to his son Pollock for £10,000 which is the price that he had paid for it ten years before. The market value of the vase at the date of sale is £45,000. This disposal between connected persons is deemed to be made otherwise than by way of bargain at arm's length so that market value is substituted for the price actually paid and Jackson is deemed to have received £45,000. Pollock is treated as acquiring the vase for a cost price of £45,000.

In addition to being treated as a disposal at market value for CGT purposes, a gift of assets may be chargeable (or potentially chargeable) to IHT. Only limited relief is available against this double charge.

First, in calculating the fall in value of the transferor's estate for IHT purposes, his CGT liability is ignored. IHT is not therefore charged on CGT paid by a donor (see [**21.61**]).

Secondly, if the CGT is paid not by the transferor but by the transferee, the amount of that tax will reduce the value transferred for IHT purposes (IHTA 1984 s 165(1)). Normally CGT is paid by the transferor but there is nothing to stop the parties from agreeing that the burden shall be discharged by the transferee.

EXAMPLE 17.2

Mr Big transfers a freehold office block to his daughter Martha Big. Assume that the value of the freehold (ignoring IHT business relief) is £750,000 and that the CGT amounts to £250,000.
(1) If the CGT is paid by Big the diminution in his estate for IHT purposes is £750,000 (ie it is *not* £750,000 + £250,000).
(2) If the CGT is paid by Martha the diminution in Big's estate is reduced to £500,000 (ie £750,000 —£250,000).

In certain situations CGT on a lifetime gift may be postponed if a hold-over election is made and these are considered in Sections III and IV, below. First, however, it is necessary to mention briefly the provision which allowed a general postponement of CGT but which was repealed by FA 1989.   **[17.2]–[17.20]**

II   HOLD-OVER RELIEF ON GIFTS UNDER FA 1980 s 79 (as amended)

1   General

From 1980–1989 it was possible to postpone the payment of CGT on the majority of lifetime gifts. Provided that a joint election was made by donor and donee, the donor was treated as disposing and the donee as acquiring the asset for its market value at the date of the gift *minus* the chargeable gain which was, there, held over. This postponement of tax continued until the asset was sold since, should the donee in turn make a gift of the asset, a further hold-over election was available. In the event of the donee dying still owning the asset, the entire gain was wiped out by the death uplift in value. This relief given by FA 1980 s 79 was extended in 1981 and 1982 to include the gains arising on the crea-tion and termination of settlements. The operation of s 79 is illustrated in *Example 17.3*.

EXAMPLE 17.3

(1) Dustin gave Portia a valuable diamond. Subsequently she in turn gave it to her lover Allonzo who immediately (and somewhat ungraciously) sold it. Assuming that suitable CGT elections were made tax was not paid on either gift but the entire held over gain was taxed on the eventual sale by Allonzo.
(2) Boy Sam settled his valuable jewellery collection on trusts for his companion Justin for life, remainder to his mother, Iris. Under a power in the settlement the trustees advanced the collection to Justin. No CGT arose on the creation of the settlement provided that Boy Sam so elected (in this case an election by the settlor alone sufficed) nor on the deemed disposal under CGTA 1979 s 54(1) resulting from the termination of the settlement when the property was advanced *in specie* to Justin. As in the case of outright gifts therefore CGT was postponed until the assets were sold.

In his 1989 Budget Speech Nigel Lawson announced the repeal of s 79 for disposals made on or after Budget Day (14 March 1989) citing as justification the fact that:

'[s 79] was introduced by my predecessor in 1980, when there was still capital transfer tax on lifetime gifts, in order to avoid a form of double taxation. But the tax on lifetime giving has since been abolished, and the relief is increasingly used as a simple form of tax avoidance.'

As a reasoned statement the above does not bear close scrutiny since there is still a potential IHT charge on all lifetime gifts (see Chapter 21 for a discussion of the potentially exempt transfer or 'PET'). The repeal of s 79 also produces the somewhat bizarre situation whereby the profit which a donor is deemed to have made may now attract a CGT charge (a tax primarily aimed at disposals by way of sale) but not a charge to the tax aimed specifically at gratuitous transfers of value (IHT formerly CTT)!

The detailed rules governing the operation of s 79 are not considered further but the 1989 changes leave a number of transitional problems which will now be discussed.   [17.21]

2 Transitional matters

First, disposals made before 14 March 1989 may still benefit from a hold-over election under s 79. The crucial matter is that the disposal must have been completed before 14 March. The timing of a disposal for the purposes of CGT has been discussed in Chapter 14; in the case of gifts this will normally be when the ownership of the property passes to the donee. This is dependent upon the nature of the property (eg chattels pass by delivery) and the donor must perfect his gift since there is no general power in the court to perfect an incomplete gift. In exceptional cases, however, beneficial title in the property will be transferred to the donee so that the gift is deemed to be complete once the donor has done everything in his power to transfer the relevant property (see, eg, *Re Rose* (1949) where the transfer of private company shares which required the approval of the Board of Directors was completed for these purposes once the donor had lodged the completed transfer forms with the company: at that stage he had done everything in *his* power to effect the transfer).

No time period for making hold-over elections was specified in s 79 and therefore the general six year period applicable to all claims in TMA 1970 s 43 applied. Elections may still therefore be made up until 14 March 1995 in respect of pre-Budget Day transfers.

When property was acquired before 14 March 1989 by a gift (or sale at undervalue) and an election to hold over under s 79 was made, the postponed charge to CGT will be triggered in certain circumstances. For instance, a gain held-over on creation of a settlement will become chargeable on the death of the life tenant (this matter, which involves a partial revival of the death charge, is discussed at [**18.46**]). Obviously, a subsequent sale of the property by the donee will also result in the held-over gain becoming taxable and it should be noted that the 50% reduction in the amount of the held-over gain in cases where the relevant gift was made between 1982 and 1988 may be relevant as illustrated in the following example.

EXAMPLE 17.4

Diane acquired a Matthew Smith oil painting for £10,000 in 1980. By 31 March 1982 its value had increased to £25,000. In June 1985 she gave the picture to her niece when its value was £40,000 and both entered into a s 79 hold-over election. In July 1991 the niece sold the picture for £50,000. Ignoring the indexation allowance and any incidental expenditure, the CGT position is as follows:

(1) *In 1985* the niece acquired the picture at a base cost of £10,000 (ie £40,000 minus the held-over gain of £30,000).

(2) In 1991 her gain on disposal is £40,000 but one half of the gain held over in 1985 (ie £15,000) is not subject to charge so that the chargeable gain is £25,000 (£40,000—£15,000).

Note: As a result of FA 1988 Sch 9 the niece's acquisition cost in 1985 is increased to £25,000 thereby affecting the calculation of the indexation allowance.

The s 79 election was only available if the transferee was resident or ordinarily resident in the UK. Further, if after an election had been made the transferee ceased to be so resident, the gain that had been held-over became immediately chargeable at the transferee's rate of tax at that time (FA 1981 s 79). These results still occur if the emigration occurs after 14 March 1989.

EXAMPLE 17.5

In 1987 Imelda's father gives her a Fabergé easter egg. A gain of £8,000 is held-over so that she has an acquisition cost of £10,000. In 1991 she takes up permanent residence in Spain. The held-over gain of £8,000 becomes chargeable 'immediately before' she ceases to be UK resident and will be assessed to tax at her rates in force in the tax year of emigration.

Even if the asset has increased in value to £30,000 by 1991, there is no question of charging that increase which is attributable to her period of ownership; any loss would likewise be ignored.

The CGT in such cases is payable primarily by the transferee, but if tax remains unpaid twelve months after the due date it can be recovered from the transferor (FA 1981 s 79(7)). In such an event the transferor is given a right to recover a corresponding sum from the transferee (FA 1981 s 79(9)) although, if the Revenue have not obtained payment from the transferee, the transferor is unlikely to succeed! The emigration charge will only operate if the original disposal on which the gain was held over occurred after 5 April 1981 and the emigration occurred within six years of that disposal (FA 1981 s 79(4)). Further, the charge will not apply if the transferee has left the UK because of work connected with his office or employment and performs all the duties of that office or employment outside the UK. He must not dispose of the asset whilst outside the UK (if so the gain is taxed unless the disposal is to a spouse) and must resume UK residence within three years of his initial departure otherwise the gain is taxed (FA 1981 s 79(5)).

It will obviously be unnecessary to invoke this emigration charge if, before becoming non-resident, the transferee had made a disposal of the asset (FA 1981 s 79(2)). That disposal will either have triggered the held-over gain or, if it was by way of gift and a s 79 election had been made, the asset pregnant with gain will now be owned by another UK resident, so that the Revenue are not threatened with a loss of tax. If that prior disposal is merely a part disposal, so triggering only a part of the held-over gain, the balance will be chargeable on emigration.

An exception to the provision that the transferor who emigrates after the disposal of the asset will not be subject to a charge is when that prior disposal is to the emigrating transferor's spouse. If that spouse had further disposed of the asset, however, that further disposal will be treated as if it had been by the transferor so that the emigration charge will not apply (FA 1981 s 79(3)).   **[17.22]**-**[17.40]**

III   GIFTS OF BUSINESS ASSETS (CGTA 1979 s 126 as amended)

When general hold-over relief under s 79 was available, s 126 was limited to the situation where business assets were given to a company. For disposals on or after 14 March 1989, however, the section has been substantially widened and amended.   **[17.41]**

1   When does s 126 apply?

There must be a disposal by *an individual* although this includes the deemed disposal made by trustees under CGTA 1979 s 54(1) on the termination of a trust (see Chapter 18). The disposal itself must be 'otherwise than under a bargain at arms length' and therefore includes both gifts and undervalue sales. The recipient can be any 'person', a term which embraces not just individuals but also trustees and companies.   **[17.42]**

2   What property is included?

The section is limited to gifts of business assets, defined as follows (s 126(1A)):
'an asset is within this sub-section if—

(a) it is, or is an interest in, an asset used for the purposes of a trade, profession or vocation carried on by—
(i) the transferor, or
(ii) his family company, or
(iii) a member of a trading group of which the holding company is his family company, or
(b) it consists of shares or securities of a trading company, or of the holding company of a trading group, where—
(1)   the shares or securities are neither quoted on a recognised stock exchange nor dealt in on the Unlisted Securities Market, or
(2)   the trading company or holding company is the transferor's family company.'

It should be noted that *any* asset is included provided only that it is used for the purposes of a trade, profession or vocation (contrast, for instance, roll-over reinvestment relief (see [**16.92**]) which is limited to certain categories of asset). Non-business assets do not attract relief and that part of the gain on a disposal of shares in a company which owns such assets is therefore excluded from relief (the appropriate calculation is similar although not identical to that used for retirement relief: see CGTA 1979 Sch 4 and [**16.99**]). Unlike retirement relief, a mere disposal of assets suffices: it is not necessary for the disposal to be of part of a business.

Whether an asset is used for the purposes of a trade may sometimes be a moot point: for instance, would the relief be available on a gift of a valuable Munch oil painting ('The Sick Corpse') which has adorned the offices of a funeral parlour for many years and is now given away by the proprietor?

Land qualifying (or which would qualify on a chargeable transfer being made) for 50% or 30% IHT agricultural property relief is specifically included as a business asset for these purposes (CGTA 1979 Sch 4).

An individual's 'family company' has the same meaning as for retirement relief (see [**16.96**]).

These definitions and requirements are modified in the case of business assets owned by trustees. Broadly, the relevant business must either be that of the trustee or of a beneficiary with an interest in possession in the settled property and in the case of a disposal of shares in a trading company either that company must not be quoted on the Stock Exchange or dealt in on the USM or, alternatively, at least 25% of the voting rights at the company's General Meeting must be exercisable by the trustees.   [**17.43**]

3 The election

Hold-over relief under the section will only be given on a claim being made by both transferor and transferee (save where the transferee is a trustee when only the transferor need elect: CGTA 1979 s 126(1)). These provisions are identical to those which applied under s 79 and, as no specific time limit for elections is prescribed, the usual six year period will apply. There is no prescribed form for this election and a simple letter signed by the relevant person(s) will therefore suffice. Note, however, that since the election is to hold over a gain which would otherwise be chargeable, it will be necessary to agree the amount of that gain with the Revenue. Accordingly, the election should be accompanied by relevant valuations.

EXAMPLE 17.6

(1) Sim gives his ironmongers business to his daughter Sammy in 1991. For CGT purposes any gain resulting from this gift of chargeable business assets may be held over on the joint election of Sim and Sammy.

(2) Jim settles his ironmongers business on trusts for his son who runs the business. As in (1) above, s 126 will apply: however in this case only Jim need elect. When the trust ends, eg on Jim's son, Jack, becoming absolutely entitled to the business, a further hold-over election may then be made by the trustees and Jack to postpone payment of tax which would otherwise arise under CGTA 1979 s 54(1).

(3) Oliver is the sole shareholder and director of a computer company (ACC Ltd) and owns the freehold site used by the company. He now gives away his shares to his four daughters equally and the freehold to his son. S 126 relief is available to postpone tax on all five gifts since ACC is both Oliver's family company and a private trading company.

When the election is made:

'(a) the amount of any chargeable gain which, apart from this section, would accrue to the transferor on the disposal, and
(b) the amount of the consideration for which, apart from this section, the transferee would be regarded for the purposes of capital gains tax as having acquired the asset or, as the case may be, the shares or securities, shall each be reduced by an amount equal to the held-over gain on the disposal.'

This is illustrated in the following *Example*:   **[17.44]**

EXAMPLE 17.7

Smiley gives Karla shares in his family company worth £35,000. Smiley's allowable expenditure for CGT purposes is £10,000. They make a joint election under s 126 so that the disposal consideration deemed to have been received by Smiley is reduced by the held-over gain: ie £35,000 — £25,000 = £10,000. Hence, Smiley is treated as disposing of the shares for £10,000 and, as his expenses are £10,000, he has made neither gain nor loss. Karla is treated as acquiring the shares for the same consideration, £10,000.

Assume that within twelve months of the gift Karla sells the shares for £41,000 incurring deductible expenses of £2,000. He will be assessed to CGT on a gain calculated as follows:

	£	£
Sale proceeds		41,000
Less:		
Acquisition cost	10,000	
Deductible expenses	2,000	
		12,000
Chargeable gain		£29,000

Notes:
(1) Of this gain, £4,000 is attributable to Karla's period of ownership (£29,000— £25,000) and £25,000 represents the gain held over on the gift from Smiley.
(2) Carla's deemed acquisition costs will include the value of Smiley's indexation allowance. Carla therefore obtains an indexation allowance on an indexation allowance. This result is less striking when it is realised that the RPI itself gives indexation on indexation.

4   The annual exemption and retirement relief

Section 126 operates by postponing the tax charge on 'the chargeable gains which would otherwise accrue to the transferor on the disposal'. The CGT *annual exemption* (see **[14.76]**) is deducted from individual's 'taxable amount' (CGTA 1979 s 5(1)) which is defined as the total chargeable gains for the year after deducting losses: s 4(1). Accordingly, as the annual exemption is deducted from chargeable gains, it is not possible to combine it with an election under s 126. Either the whole chargeable gain must be held over or it will be subject to CGT but with the benefit of the annual exemption. It follows that in the case of gifts of business assets where any gain will not exceed the annual exemption, the s 126 election should not be made: even if the gain just exceeds the exemption it may be preferable to pay a small CGT charge. In appropriate cases it will be possible to obtain the best of both worlds: ie to make two disposals, the first of an asset where the gain is covered by the annual exemption and the second of other business assets where hold-over relief under s 126 is claimed.

Unlike the annual exemption, *retirement relief* operates by reducing the gross gain made by a taxpayer on the disposal of a business or part of a business so that only the balance (if any) remaining is chargeable gain (FA 1985 Sch 20 para 6; and see Chapter 16). This relief can therefore be combined with s 126 so that the gain is first reduced by retirement relief and any remaining chargeable gain is then held over.   **[17.45]**

EXAMPLE 17.8

Magnus gives his greengrocers business to his daughter, Minima. There is a gain of £90,000 on the value of the chargeable assets transferred. If Magnus is entitled to retirement relief of £40,000, his gain will be reduced to £50,000 (£90,000—£40,000) and this can be held over if Magnus and Minima make a joint election under s 126.

5 Sales at undervalue

Although s 126 applies both to gifts and sales at undervalue, if the actual consideration paid on a disposal exceeds the allowable CGT deductions of the transferor, that excess is subject to charge. It is only the balance of any gain (ie the amount by which the consideration is less than the full value of the business asset) which may be held over under s 126.

EXAMPLE 17.9

Julius sells shares in his family company worth £25,000 to his brother Jason for £16,500. Julius has allowable deductions for CGT purposes of £11,500. The CGT position is:
(1)   Total gain on disposal: £25,000 — £11,500 = £13,500.
(2)   Excess of actual consideration over allowable deductions:
      £16,500 — £11,500 = £5,000.
(3)   Gain subject to CGT ((2) above) is £5,000 so that after deducting Julius' annual exemption tax payable is nil.
(4)   Balance of gain, £8,500 (ie (1)—(2)) can be held over under s 126.

If the partial consideration is less than the allowable deductions it is ignored so that a CGT loss cannot be created.

If retirement relief is available it is deducted first from any chargeable gain actually realised. Any unused relief is then deducted from the notional gain which arises as a result of treating the disposal as being at market value and any remaining gain may then be held over. **[17.46]**

EXAMPLE 17.10

Moira transfers her newsagent business to her son Michael. The base costs of the chargeable business assets total £50,000; their market value is £225,000. Michael is to pay his mother £100,000. Moira is entitled to retirement relief of £60,000. The CGT position is as follows:
(1)   Total gain on disposal: £225,000 — £50,000 = £175,000.
(2)   Excess of actual consideration over base cost: £100,000 — £50,000 = £50,000.
(3)   Deduct retirement relief from (2). The actual gain is therefore wiped out.
(4)   Balance of gain, £125,000 ((1) minus (2)) will be reduced by the remaining £10,000 of retirement relief and so £115,000 will then be held over if a s 126 election is made.

6 The interrelation of hold-over relief and IHT

The overlap between CGT and IHT in the area of lifetime gifts and gratuitous undervalue transfers has already been noted.

When chargeable gains are held over under s 126 the transferee can add to his CGT acquisition costs all or part of the IHT paid on the value of the gift. This principle applies whoever pays the IHT.

EXAMPLE 17.11

Wendy gives shares in her family cookery company ('Cook-Inn & Co') to her daughter, Kim. The chargeable gain arising of £100,000 is held-over under s 126 and Kim therefore acquires the shares at a value of £75,000. For IHT purposes the gift by Wendy is a potentially exempt transfer when made and therefore no tax is payable at that stage. Assume, however, that Wendy dies within seven years so that the gift then becomes chargeable and that IHT of £20,000 is paid. Kim can add that sum to her base cost for CGT purposes which therefore becomes £95,000 (£75,000 + £20,000).

Note:

(1) A similar principle applies in the case of lifetime gifts which are subject to an immediate inheritance tax charge;

(2) Although the inheritance tax paid is added to Kim's base cost in order to reduce her gain on a subsequent disposal of the shares, this sum is not an item of deductible expenditure for CGT purposes *and therefore does not benefit from the indexation allowance.*

(3) It may be that Kim has already disposed of the shares before the death of her mother. Nevertheless she is entitled to have her allowable expenditure increased by the IHT resulting from Wendy's death and therefore an adjustment will be made to any CGT paid on the disposal of the shares.

There are two limits on the amount of IHT that can be added to the donee's CGT base cost.

First, the maximum amount permissible is the IHT *attributable to the gift*. This means that if IHT had been paid by the transferor on a chargeable lifetime gift so that 'grossing-up' applied, it is only the IHT charged on the value of the gift received by the donee which can be used (grossing up is discussed in Chapter 21: with the introduction of the potentially exempt transfer it will now rarely occur).

Secondly, IHT which is added to the transferee's base cost cannot be used to create a CGT loss on a later disposal by the transferee. Accordingly, in *Example 17.11*, above, if Kim were to sell the shares after the death of Wendy for £90,000 she would only be able to use £15,000 of the IHT payable on Wendy's death since this could have the effect of wiping out any chargeable gain and she cannot use the remaining £5,000 to create a CGT loss.   **[17.47]**

7   Non-UK residents

Section 126 hold-over relief is not available if the transferee is neither resident nor ordinarily resident in the UK (CGTA 1979 s 126A). This limitation is necessary since disposals by such a person are outside the CGT net! In addition, any held-over gain will be triggered on the subsequent emigration (within six years) of the transferee. The rules which apply in such cases are identical to those already discussed in connection with the triggering of gains held over under s 79 (see FA 1981 s 79 as amended: **[17.22]**).   **[17.48]–[17.60]**

IV   GIFTS OF ASSETS ATTRACTING AN IMMEDIATE IHT CHARGE (CGTA 1979 s 147A)

The second situation where hold-over is available on a gift or undervalue sale, is if the relevant disposal 'is a chargeable transfer within the meaning of the IHTA 1984' or would be such a transfer but for the availability of the annual exemption. [**17.61**]

1 When is there an immediate IHT charge on inter vivos gifts?

Most lifetime transfers are now PETs which do not attract an immediate IHT charge: in such cases hold-over relief under this section is not available even if the PET subsequently becomes chargeable because of the death of the transferor within seven years. Consequently relief under s 147A is only available in the following cases:

(1) On a gift between individuals or on the creation of an accumulation and maintenance or disabled trust where such gifts fall outside the definition of a potentially exempt transfer. Such cases are rare: see [**21.42**].

(2) On a gift to or by trustees *which is not a PET*. This category embraces the creation and termination of no interest in possession trusts (typically, the discretionary trust).

Because s 147A(1) specifies that to come within its terms the disposal must be to and by either an individual or the trustees of a settlement, gifts to and by companies (which cannot be PETs) do not attract hold-over relief. (Unless, of course, the gift to a company is of a business asset when relief may be available under s 126 as discussed in III, above.) [**17.62**]

2 The relief

The hold-over relief afforded by s 147A is broadly the same as that given under s 126. Relief under s 147A does, however, take precedence over the s 126 relief (see CGTA 1979 s 126(2)(d)) and this may have attractions when what is contemplated is a transfer of shares in a family company which owns non-business assets since there is no apportionment requirement under s 147A (contrast [**17.43**] and see *Capital Taxes*, 1990, p 52).

An election is required in the same terms as under s 126; the effect of holding over the gain is the same (ie the asset is disposed of and acquired at market value less held-over gain); the transferee must be either UK resident or ordinarily resident and subsequent emigration may trigger the charge. Unlike s 126 there is, however, no restriction on the type of asset for which relief may be claimed. [**17.63**]

3 Practical uses of s 147A

The main situation where this provision will be employed is when a discretionary trust is either created or ended. In both cases an immediate IHT charge may arise so that the gain on any chargeable asset entering or leaving the trust may be held over. The following example illustrates the various permutations: [**17.64**]-[**17.80**]

EXAMPLE 17.12

(1) Jake transfers his portfolio of stocks and shares (worth £500,000) into a discretionary trust for his family; the transfer results in an immediate IHT charge and therefore any gain on the investments can be held-over if Jake (alone) elects under s 147A. Note that any IHT paid by Jake (ignoring grossing up) can be deducted by the trustees on a subsequent disposal of the shares (and this sum will be increased should an extra tax charge result from the death of Jake within seven years of establishing his trust).

(2)   Joseph establishes his discretionary trust by transferring land worth £140,000 to the trustees. As his first chargeable transfer, IHT will not be payable since it falls within Joseph's nil rate band. Despite this, hold-over relief under s 147A is available since the transfer by Joseph is (strictly) chargeable to IHT albeit at a nil rate. This gives the best of all worlds: no IHT but CGT hold-over (Note that s 147A also applies if a transfer of value which would otherwise attract an immediate IHT charge is covered by the transferor's annual exemption.)

(3)   Thal and Thad, trustees of the Mallard discretionary trust, appoint chargeable assets to Billy Beneficiary. For IHT, an 'exit' charge will arise (see [**26.23**]) and therefore any chargeable gain can be held-over on the joint election of Thal, Thad and Billy. Note that an appointment out of such a trust *within three months of its creation* does not give rise to any IHT charge (see [**26.25**]) and therefore CGT hold-over is not available in such a case.

(4)   Trustees Tom and Ted in exercise of powers conferred on them by the settlement, resettle the property on new trusts. This is a deemed disposal under s 54(1) for CGT purposes but any resulting gain may only be held-over if it is also a chargeable event for IHT. In many cases this will not be the case since the property will be treated as remaining comprised in the original settlement (IHTA 1984 s 81: see [**26.32**]). In particular, this will be the case where trustees of one discretionary trust reappoint the property upon new discretionary trusts. By contrast, the termination of a life interest whereupon property becomes held on discretionary trusts, although chargeable for IHT, is not a deemed disposal for CGT purposes unless a new settlement results.

(5)   Mr Wealthy wishes to give his seaside cottage (current value £100,000) to his son but is concerned to postpone the payment of any CGT on that disposal. If he settles the property on discretionary trusts there will be no IHT to pay provided that the transfer falls within his available nil rate band but CGT hold-over relief will be available. Were the trustees subsequently (eg six months later) to appoint the cottage to the son outright, there should still be no inheritance tax charge but again CGT hold-over relief will be available.

V   THE ACCUMULATION AND MAINTENANCE TRUST

Accumulation and maintenance trusts are the creature of the IHT legislation where they are accorded privileged treatment (see [**26.92**] ff).

In general terms, the *inter vivos* creation of such trusts is a PET so that, unless the assets settled are business property, hold-over relief is not available. The termination of such trusts generally occurs in one of two ways.

First (and the most common), termination is the result of a beneficiary becoming entitled to an interest in possession in the trust fund. Typically this will occur at 18 or 21 with capital vesting at a later age (often 25).

Secondly, the accumulation and maintenance trust may end with the trust assets becoming the absolute property of the beneficiary so that the settlement itself comes to an end.

So far as hold-over relief is concerned an election is permissible in the second case — irrespective of the nature of the settlement assets — under CGTA 1979 s 147A(2)(d). Relief is not, however, available in the more common first case where the beneficiary only becomes absolutely entitled to the property on the termination of a prior interest in possession.   [**17.81**]–[**17.100**]

EXAMPLE 17.13

(1) Property is settled on accumulation and maintenance trust for Floyd on attaining 18. At 18, Floyd becomes absolutely entitled to the assets; the accumulation and maintenance trust ends, a hold-over election is possible (whatever the nature of the settled property).

(2) Property is settled on accumulation and maintenance trusts for Sid contingent on his attaining the age of 25.

(a) *At 18:* Sid obtains an interest in possession under the Trustee Act 1925 s 31. For CGT purposes this does not occasion a deemed disposal and therefore there is no question of any tax charge arising. For IHT purposes the accumulation and maintenance trust has ended, being replaced by an interest in possession settlement.

(b) *At 25:* When Sid becomes absolutely entitled there is a deemed disposal for CGT purposes under CGTA 1979 s 54(1) but hold-over relief will only be available if (or to the extent that) the settled property comprises business assets.

(c) *Is it possible to vary the trusts so that hold-over relief will be available when Sid becomes 25?* Consider the consequences if Sid assigns his life interest to the trustees providing for it to be held on the trusts of the settlement with the income being accumulated until a beneficiary becomes absolutely entitled (does this turn the settlement back into an accumulation and maintenance trust thereby permitting hold-over when Sid becomes 25?). And, alternatively, consider the position if Sid were to settle his capital entitlement (before 25) on discretionary trusts (at 25 does his interest in possession come to an end in favour of a discretionary settlement which, being an immediately chargeable transfer, permits hold-over relief?).

VI   MISCELLANEOUS CASES

Hold-over relief under s 147A is also available in the following situations where the relevant transfer is exempt from any IHT charge:

(1) transfers to political parties under IHTA 1984 s 24;
(2) transfers for public benefit under IHTA 1984 s 26;
(3) transfers to maintenance funds for historic buildings under IHTA 1984 s 27 and for disposals out of settlement to such funds;
(4) transfers of designated property under IHTA 1984 s 30;
(5) transfers of works of art under IHTA 1984 s 78.

Finally, it may also be noted that there are other provisions in the CGT legislation which result in a postponement of tax. Share exchanges under CGTA 1979 ss 85–87 (considered in Chapter 19) and relief on the incorporation of a business under s 123 (discussed in Chapter 14) are examples whilst disposals between husband and wife are always taxed on a no gain no loss basis irrespective of any actual consideration paid ([**14.22**]).

[**17.101**]–[**17.120**]

VII   PAYMENT OF TAX BY INSTALMENTS

CGT must generally be paid on 1 December following the tax year when the disposal occurs and, even if the disponer receives payment in instalments, there is no general right to pay the tax by instalments (see [**14.83**]).

CGTA 1979 s 7A qualifies this general principle but only in the case of gifts of certain property (and not, apparently, sales at undervalue) and for deemed disposals of settled property. Broadly, the ability to pay by instalments will only, even in these cases, be available if the relevant chargeable gain could not have been held over under either s 126 or s 147A (notice therefore that failure to make the election will not give the right to pay tax by instalments).

The relevant property on which tax may be paid by instalments is land (including any estate or interest in land); a controlling shareholding; and a minority shareholding in a company neither quoted on the Stock Exchange or dealt in on the Unlisted Securities Market. The latter category will include all private companies which do not trade.

The person paying the CGT must give notice if he wishes to pay by instalments: tax is then paid by ten equal yearly instalments starting on the usual payment date (ie 1 December following the tax year of the disposal). Interest is charged on the unpaid CGT and is added to each instalment. The outstanding tax can be paid off any time and must be paid off if the gift was to a connected person or was a deemed disposal of settled property and the relevant assets are subsequently sold for valuable consideration.   [**17.121**]

EXAMPLE 17.14

In July 1991 Bob gives his seaside cottage to his daughter Thelma. The resulting capital gains tax of £50,000 may be paid by ten equal annual instalments on the appropriate notice being given by Bob (who is to pay that tax). The first instalment of £5,000 falls due on 1 December 1992 and subsequent instalments will carry interest on the unpaid balance of the CGT.

18 CGT—settlements

The CGT provisions seek to tax the settled fund and not the value of the individual interests of the beneficiaries. Actual disposals by the trustees and certain deemed disposals may trigger a charge, but disposals of beneficial interests will normally be exempt. With the repeal of FA 1980 s 79 ('hold-over relief') in the case of disposals made on or after 14 March 1989, the creation and termination of a settlement may now lead to a CGT charge.   [**18.1**]

I   WHAT IS A SETTLEMENT FOR THE PURPOSES OF CGT?

1   'Settled property': the provisions of CGTA 1979 s 46

'Settlement' is not defined but 'settled property' is 'any property held in trust' (CGTA 1979 s 51) with the exception of certain trusts mentioned in CGTA 1979 s 46. In the following three situations s 46 provides that, although there is a trust of property, the property is *not* 'settled property' and is treated as belonging to the beneficiary.

First, property is not settled where 'assets are held by a person as nominee for another person, or as trustee for another person absolutely entitled as against the trustee'. The provision covers nomineeships and bare or simple trusts.

EXAMPLE 18.1

Tim and Tom hold 1,000 shares in DNC Ltd on trust for Bertram, aged 26, absolutely. This is a bare trust since Bertram is solely entitled to the shares and can at any time bring the trust to an end (see *Saunders v Vautier* (1841)). The shares are treated as belonging to Bertram so that a disposal of those shares by the trustees is treated as being by Bertram and any transfer from the trustees to Bertram is ignored.

Secondly, where the property is held on trust 'for any person who would be [absolutely] entitled but for being an infant or other person under a disability' it is not settled.

EXAMPLE 18.2

(1) Topsy and Tim hold property for Alex absolutely, aged 9. Because of his age Alex cannot demand the property from the trustees and the trust is not, therefore, simple or bare. For CGT purposes, however, Alex is a person who would be absolutely entitled but for his infancy and he is treated as owning the assets in the fund.

(2) Teddy and Tiger hold property on trust for Noddy, aged 9, contingent upon his attaining the age of 18. At first sight it would seem that there is no material difference between this settlement and that considered in (1) above since, in both, the beneficiary would be absolutely entitled were it not for his infancy. Noddy, however, is not entitled to claim the fund from the trustees because of the provisions of the settlement. Unlike (1) above, Noddy's entitlement is contingent upon living to a certain age, so that, were he to ask the trustees to give him the property, they would refuse because he has not satisfied the contingency. This distinction would be more obvious if the settlement provided that the contingency to be satisfied by Noddy was the attaining of (say) 21 (see *Tomlinson v Glyns Executor and Trustee Co* (1970)). The fund in this example is, therefore, settled property for the purposes of CGT.

The *third* case mentioned in s 46 is where the fund is held for 'two or more persons who are or would be jointly [absolutely] entitled'. The word 'jointly' is not limited to the interests of joint tenants, but applies to concurrent ownership generally. It does not apply to interests which are successive, but only covers more than one beneficiary concurrently entitled 'in the same interest' (see *Kidson v MacDonald* (1974); *Booth v Ellard* (1980); and *IRC v Matthew's Executors* (1984)).

EXAMPLE 18.3

(1) Bill and Ben purchase Blackacre as tenants in common. The land is held on trust for sale pursuant to the Law of Property Act 1925 ss 34–36, but for the purposes of CGT the property is not settled and is treated as belonging to Bill and Ben equally (*Kidson v MacDonald* (1974)).

(2) Mr T and his family hold 72% of the issued share capital in T Ltd (their family company). In 1989 they enter into a written agreement as a result of which the shares are transferred to trustees and detailed restrictions, akin to pre-emption provisions in private company articles, are imposed. The beneficial interests of Mr T and his family are not however affected. Subsequently the shares are transferred out again to the various settlors. In such a 'pooling arrangement' the shares will be treated as nominee property with the result that there is no disposal for CGT purposes on the creation of the trust nor on its termination (cp *Booth v Ellard* (1980) and see *Jenkins v Brown* and *Warrington v Sterland* (1989) in which a similar result was arrived at (surprisingly?) in the case of a pooling of family farms).

(3) Thal and Tal hold property on trust for Simon for life, remainder to Karl absolutely. Although Simon and Karl are, in common parlance, jointly entitled to claim the fund from the trustees, they are not 'jointly absolutely entitled' within the meaning of s 46. The property is settled for CGT purposes.

It is the concept of being 'absolutely entitled as against the trustee' which lies at the root of the three cases mentioned in s 46. Section 46(2) provides that:

'It is hereby declared that references in this Act to any asset held by a person as trustee for another person absolutely entitled as against the trustee are references to a case where that other person has the exclusive right, subject only to satisfying any outstanding charge, lien or other right of the trustees to resort to the asset for payment of duty, taxes, costs or other outgoings, to direct how that asset shall be dealt with.'

The various rights against the property possessed by trustees and mentioned in s 46(2) refer to personal rights of indemnity; they do not cover other beneficial interests under the settlement.

EXAMPLE 18.4

Jackson is entitled to an annuity of £1,000 pa payable out of a settled fund held in trust for Xerxes absolutely. The property is settled for CGT purposes (*Stephenson v Barclays Bank Trust Co Ltd* (1975)).

Section 46(2) does not offer any guidance on the question of when a beneficiary has 'the exclusive right ... to direct how [the] asset in [the settlement] shall be dealt with'. Under general trust law beneficiaries will not be able to issue such directions unless they have the right to end the trust by demanding their share of the property (see eg *Re Brockbank* (1948)). Difficulties arise where one of a number of beneficiaries is entitled to a portion of the fund.

EXAMPLE 18.5

A fund is held for the three daughters of the settlor (Jane, June and Joy) contingent upon attaining 21 and, if more than one, in equal shares. Jane, the eldest is 21 and is, therefore, entitled to 1/3 of the assets. Whether she is absolutely entitled as against the trustees to that share depends upon the type of property held by the trustees. The general principle is that she will be entitled to claim her 1/3 share, but not if the effect of distributing that slice of the fund would be to damage the interests of the other beneficiaries. When the settled assets are land or a substantial private company shareholding this would normally be the result since, in the case of land, the asset will often have to be sold to raise the necessary moneys, and, in the case of shares, the trustees may lose a controlling interest in the company (see *Crowe v Appleby* (1975)).
(a) If Jane is absolutely entitled to her share that portion of the fund ceases to be settled (even though Jane leaves her share in the hands of the trustees).
(b) If the fund consists of land, Jane will not be absolutely entitled; hence, the settlement will continue until all three daughters either satisfy the contingency or die before 21. Only then will the fund cease to be settled since one or more persons will, at that point, become jointly absolutely entitled. (For problems that can arise on a division of a controlling shareholding see *Lloyds Bank plc v Duker* (1987).)

Finally, note that a person can become absolutely entitled to assets without being 'beneficially' entitled (see **[18.61]**).   **[18.2]-[18.20]**

II THE CREATION OF A SETTLEMENT

The creation of a settlement is a disposal of assets by the settlor whether the settlement is revocable or irrevocable, and whether or not the settlor or his spouse is a beneficiary (CGTA 1979 s 53). If chargeable assets are settled, a chargeable gain or allowable loss will result. As the settlor and his trustees are connected persons (CGTA 1979 s 62(3)), any loss resulting from the transfer will only be deductible from a subsequent disposal to those trustees at a gain. Hold-over relief under FA 1980 s 79 was repealed for disposals made on or after 14 March 1989. Only if the settled assets comprise business property or if the creation of the trust involves a chargeable transfer for IHT purposes will it now be possible to postpone the payment of the tax (see further Chapter 17). **[18.21]-[18.40]**

EXAMPLE 18.6

Roger settles his Van Gogh sketch 'Peasant with Pig' worth £200,000. His allowable expenditure totals £50,000. He also settles his main residence. The beneficiaries are his wife Rena for life with remainder to their two children Robina and Rybina. For CGT purposes, the following rules apply:
(1) *Main residence*   This is exempt from CGT.
(2) *The Van Gogh*   This is treated as disposed of for its market value (£200,000) and, hence, Roger has made a gain of £150,000.

III   ACTUAL AND DEEMED DISPOSALS BY TRUSTEES

A charge to CGT may arise as a result of either actual or deemed disposals of that property by the trustees. Notice, however, that where trust property is transferred, on a change of trustees, from old to new trustees, there is no charge to CGT since they are treated as a single and continuing body (CGTA 1979 s 52(1)).

The relevant rate of CGT depends upon the type of trust and whether or not the settlor has reserved an interest in his trust. In general, a 25% rate will apply but if the trust falls within TA 1988 s 686 (a discretionary or accumulation trust) the rate is increased to 35% whilst if the settlor has retained an interest tax is charged at his rate (ie at 25% or, more likely, 40%).

Trustees are generally only entitled to one half of the full annual exemption (ie to £2,750 in 1991-92: see **[14.79]**). **[18.41]**

1   Actual disposals by trustees

When chargeable assets are sold by trustees normal principles apply in calculating the gain (or loss) of the trustees. If the disposal generates a loss it may be set off against gains of the same year or of future years made by the trustees. If the loss is still unrelieved at the end of the trust period, it may be transferred to the beneficiary who becomes absolutely entitled to the fund. If more than one beneficiary becomes so entitled, the loss is apportioned between them (CGTA 1979 s 54(2)). (Note that a trust loss is more favourably treated than losses made by PRs; see **[15.81]**.)   **[18.42]**

2   The exit charge: CGTA 1979 s 54(1)

a) *The general rule*

CGTA 1979 s 54(1) provides for a deemed disposal of the chargeable assets in the fund, whenever a person becomes absolutely entitled to any portion of the settled property ('exit charge'). The trust ends with respect to that portion since there will either be an appointment of assets to a beneficiary, or, if the fund is still held by the trustees, a bare trust will result (see CGTA 1979 s 46(1)). The section is a 'deeming' provision and treats the assets of the fund as being sold by the trustees (so that it is trustee rates of CGT which are relevant) for their market value at that date and immediately reacquired for the same value, thereby ensuring that any increase in value in the chargeable assets is charged (except in the situation discussed below). The deemed reacquisition by the trustees is treated as the act of the person who is absolutely entitled to the fund as against the trustees (see CGTA 1979 s 46(1)). **[18.43]**

EXAMPLE 18.7

Shares in Dovecot Ltd are held by trustees for Simone absolutely, contingent upon attaining the age of 25. She has just become 25 and the shares are worth £100,000. The trustees' base costs (including any indexation allowance) are £25,000. She is now absolutely entitled to the fund and the trustees are deemed to sell the shares (for £100,000) and to re-acquire them (for £100,000). On the sale they have realised a chargeable gain of £75,000 (£100,000 − £25,000). The shares are deemed to be Simone's property so that if she directs their sale and, say, £107,000 is raised she will have a chargeable gain of £7,000 (£107,000 − £100,000).

b) *Disposals triggered by the death of a life tenant*

The termination of a life interest in possession because of the death of the life tenant may result in a deemed disposal by the trustees under s 54(1). Although there is still a deemed disposal and re-acquisition, no CGT (or loss relief) is charged (or allowed) on any resultant gain (loss) (CGTA 1979 s 56). This corresponds to the normal CGT principle that on death there is an uplift but no charge (see Chapter 15; and for the IHT consequences Chapter 25).

EXAMPLE 18.8

Property consisting of shares in Zac Ltd is held on trust for Irene for life, or until remarriage and thereafter to Dominic absolutely.
(1) *If Irene dies* There will be a deemed disposal and re-acquisition of the shares by the trustees (CGTA 1979 s 54(1)), but CGT will not be charged. The property henceforth belongs to Dominic.
(2) *If Irene remarries* The life interest will cease with the same consequences as in (1), save that CGT may be chargeable.

If a life interest is in a part only of the fund, the death of the life tenant will result in an uplift on the appropriate portion of each asset in the fund without any CGT charge thereon (CGTA 1979 s 56(1A)).
If the death of the life tenant causes the property to revert to the settlor the 'reverter to disponer' exception, which will be considered in more detail for IHT, applies (see **[25.35]**). The death of the life tenant in these circumstances does not lead to a charge to IHT and, hence, the normal uplift but no charge provisions of CGT must be modified to ensure that there is no double benefit. For CGT therefore the death will cause a deemed disposal and re-acquisition, but for such a sum as will ensure that neither gain nor loss accrues to the trustees (a no gain/no loss disposal). **[18.44]**

EXAMPLE 18.9

In 1985 Sue settled property (worth £14,000) on trust for Samantha for life. In 1991 Samantha dies and the acquisition value and allowable expenses of the trustees are then £15,000. There is a deemed disposal and re-acquisition by the trustees under s 54(1) for £15,000 (to ensure neither gain nor loss).

c) *The hold-over election and FA 1989*

Prior to 14 March 1989 it was possible to hold over a chargeable gain arising on the termination of a settlement provided that a suitable election was made. In the case of deemed disposals occurring on or after that date, however, hold-over relief is generally only permitted if the settled assets comprise business property or if the termination was a chargeable transfer for IHT purposes (a similar position now operates on the creation of the trust: see Chapter 17).   [**18.45**]

d) *Hold-over relief and the tax-free death uplift*

Normally, a tax-free uplift occurs when the death of the life tenant gives rise to a s 54(1) disposal. This general rule is, however, subject to one limitation. If the settlor had made an election to hold over his gain when he created the settlement (for instance where this occurred before 14 March 1989), that held-over gain may not be wiped out on the subsequent death of the life tenant. Instead, the held-over gain will be chargeable at that time (CGTA 1979 s 56A).

EXAMPLE 18.10

Property was settled on trust for Frank for life with remainder to Brian absolutely in 1987. The settlor elected to hold over the gain of £12,000 when he created the settlement. When Frank dies, the total gain on the deemed disposal made by the trustees is £40,000. The CGT position is:
(1) There will be a tax-free uplift on the death of Frank, but only for gains arising since the creation of the settlement. Of the total gain of £40,000, £28,000 is, therefore, free of CGT.
(2) The remaining £12,000 gain (the gain held over by the settlor) will be subject to tax on Frank's death.

The result of s 56A is a partial revival of the charge to CGT on death and can be explained as an anti-avoidance measure. Assume that in 1987 Bertha wished to give her daughter Brenda an asset on which there is a large unrealised capital gain. They could at that time both have elected for hold-over relief, but that would have resulted in Brenda taking over the gain. Alternatively, Bertha could have settled the asset on an aged life tenant, who was expected to die imminently, and given the remainder interest to Brenda. No CGT would have arisen on the creation of that settlement if Bertha elected for hold-over relief and, were it not for the anti-avoidance provision, the death of the life tenant would then have wiped out all gains leaving Brenda with the asset valued at its then market value.   [**18.46**]

e) *Allowable expenditure on a deemed disposal*

By its very nature a deemed disposal will rarely lead to any expenditure. CGTA 1979 s 32(4) (which prohibits notional expenditure) seems somewhat redundant, especially in the light of *IRC v Chubb's Settlement Trustees* (1971) which permits the deduction of actual expenses incurred upon the partition of a fund (see [**14.29**]). The normal indexation allowance is available to trustees and, once the settlement ends, to the beneficiary. [**18.47**]

3 The termination of a life interest on the death of the life tenant (CGTA 1979 s 55(1))

The death of a life tenant in possession, in cases where the settlement continues thereafter (ie where CGTA 1979 s 54(1) does not operate), results in a deemed disposal and re-acquisition of the assets in the fund by the trustees at their then market value (CGTA 1979 s 55(1)). CGT will not normally be imposed, and the purpose of s 55(1) is the familiar one of ensuring a tax-free uplift.

The termination of a life interest in a part of the fund, where the settlement continues thereafter, results in a proportionate uplift in the value of all the assets (but see SP 11/73).

A life interest is defined in s 55(4) as follows:

'(a) includes a right under the settlement to the income of, or the use or occupation of, settled property for the life of a person other than the person entitled to the right, or for lives,

(b) does not include any right which is contingent on the exercise of the discretion of the trustee or the discretion of some other person, and

(c) subject to subsection (5) below, does not include an annuity, notwithstanding that the anruity is payable out of or charged on settled property or the income of settled property.

(5) In this section the expression "life interest" shall include entitlement to an annuity created by the settlement if—

(a) some or all of the settled property is appropriated by the trustees as a fund out of which the annuity is payable, and

(b) there is no right of recourse to settled property not so appropriated, or to the income of settled property not so appropriated, and ... the settled property so appropriated shall, while the annuity is payable, and on the occasion of the death of the annuitant, be treated for the purposes of this section as being settled property under a separate settlement.'

EXAMPLE 18.11

Property is held on trust for Walter for life and thereafter for his son Vivian contingently on attaining 25. Walter dies when Vivian is 24. The CGT consequences are:

(1) *Death of Walter:* There is a deemed disposal of the property under CGTA 1979 s 55(1); there is a tax-free uplift. The settlement continues because Vivian is not yet 25.

(2) *Vivian becomes 25:* There is a further deemed disposal under s 54(1) and CGT may be charged on any increase in value of the assets since Walter's death.

As with deemed disposals under s 54(1) on the death of a life tenant, the full tax-free uplift on death does not apply to a gain held over on the creation of a settlement which will, therefore, become chargeable. [**18.48**]

4 Conclusions on deemed disposals under CGTA 1979 ss 54 and 55

The ending of general hold-over relief has had a dramatic effect on the CGT treatment of settlements. In particular, when it is no longer possible to postpone payment of the tax, it may prove prohibitively expensive to end a settlement. This may be the case with a life interest settlement so that it may be preferable to wait for the death: in the case of discretionary trusts, because there remains a chargeable transfer for IHT purposes, it remains possible to hold over any capital gains.

Resettlements of property (considered in the next Section) which were employed in order to obtain a lower rate of CGT must now be avoided if the act of resettlement will itself trigger a capital gains tax charge. Note, however, that not every change in beneficial interests results in a deemed disposal: for instance, if a life interest terminates, for a reason other than the death of the beneficiary and the settlement continues, there is no deemed disposal for CGT purposes and this is also the case when a beneficiary merely acquires a right to the income of the trust.   **[18.49]-[18.60]**

EXAMPLE 18.12

Property is settled upon trust for Belinda for life or until remarriage, and thereafter for Roger contingent upon his attaining 25. If Belinda remarries when Roger is 10, the CGT position is:

(1) *The remarriage of Belinda*: Belinda's remarriage terminates her life interest, but there is no deemed disposal as Roger is not at that time absolutely entitled to the fund. Hence, there are no CGT consequences.

(2) *When Roger attains 18*: He will become entitled to the income from the fund as a result of Trustee Act 1925 s 31. There is no CGT consequence.

(3) *When Roger attains 25*: There is a deemed disposal under s 54(1), and (unless the chargeable property comprises business assets) hold-over relief will not be available.

IV   RESETTLEMENTS

When property is transferred from one settlement into another, different, settlement a CGT charge may arise under CGTA 1979 s 54(1) because the trustees of the second settlement (who may be the same persons as the trustees of the original settlement) will become absolutely entitled to that property as against the original trustees (see *Hoare Trustees v Gardner* (1978)). Exactly when a resettlement occurs is still a matter of some uncertainty (see especially *Roome v Edwards* (1981); *Bond v Pickford* (1983); and, most recently, *Swires v Renton* (1991)). In *Roome v Edwards*, Lord Wilberforce stressed that the question should be approached 'in a practical and common sense manner' and suggested that relevant indicia included separate and defined property, separate trusts and separate trustees although he emphasised that such factors are helpful but not decisive and that the matter ultimately depends upon the particular facts of each case. Finally, he contrasted special powers of appointment which, when exercised, will usually not result in a resettlement of property, with wider powers (eg of advancement) which permit property to be wholly removed from the original settlement.

The Revenue's Statement of Practice, SP 7/84, gives some guidance on when the exercise of a power of advancement or appointment will not be treated as creating a new settlement.   **[18.61]-[18.80]**

EXAMPLE 18.13

The Bladcomb family trust was created in discretionary form in 1965 since when 90% of the assets have been irrevocably appointed on various interest in possession trusts with the remaining 10% being appointed on accumulation and maintenance trusts for infant beneficiaries. The various funds are administered by the original trustees of the 1965 discretionary trust. On these facts the property has remained comprised in the original settlement for CGT purposes. Accordingly:

(i) Even if separate trustees are appointed for, eg, part of the assets held on interest in possession trusts, the trustees of the original 1965 trust will remain liable for any CGT attributable to that portion of the assets.

(ii) Only one annual exemption is available for gains realised in any part of the settled fund (see [1987] *Taxation*, 2 October, for how this exemption should be divided between the various portions of the fund).

(iii) As 10% of the fund is held on discretionary and accumulation trusts, any capital gains realised by the trustees (in any portion of the fund) are subject to CGT at 35% not 25% (see further [**14.73**]). Although a reduction in the CGT rate applicable to the interest in possession part of the fund would occur if a separate settlement of the two parts occurred, the deemed disposal of the part of the fund passing to new trustees would attract a capital gains tax charge without the benefit of hold-over relief (unless the settled assets transferred were business property).

V DISPOSAL OF BENEFICIAL INTERESTS

There is no charge to CGT when a beneficiary disposes of his interest so long as that interest has not at any time been acquired for a consideration in money or money's worth other than another interest under that settlement (CGTA 1979 s 58(1): contrast the disposal of an interest in an unadministered estate and note that a disposal may *subsequently* become chargeable if the trustees cease to be UK resident).

Once a beneficial interest has been purchased for money or money's worth, however, a future disposal of that interest will be chargeable to CGT. (Note that the consideration does not have to be 'full' or 'adequate': ie any consideration however small will turn the interest into a chargeable asset.)

When a life interest has been sold, the wasting asset rules (see [**14.38**]) may apply on a subsequent disposal of that interest by the purchaser.

EXAMPLE 18.14

Ron is the remainderman under a settlement created by his father. He sells his interest to his friend Algy for £25,000. No CGT is charged. If Algy resells the remainder interest to Ginger for £31,000, Algy has made a chargeable gain of £6,000 (£31,000 — £25,000).

The termination of the settlement may result in the property passing to a purchaser of the remainder interest. As a result, that purchaser will dispose of his interest in consideration for receiving the property in the settlement (CGTA 1979 s 58(2)). This charge does not affect the deemed disposal by the trustees (and the possible CGT charge) under s 54(1).

EXAMPLE 18.15

Assume, in *Example 18.14*, that Ginger becomes entitled to the settled fund which is worth £80,000. He has realised a chargeable gain of £49,000 (£80,000 — £31,000). In addition, the usual deemed disposal rules under s 54(1) operate.

An exchange of interests by beneficiaries under a settlement is not treated as a purchase so that a later disposal of either interest will not be chargeable.   **[18.81]–[18.100]**

VI   MIGRATION OF SETTLEMENTS AND BENEFICIARIES

The CGT rules that apply to non-resident trusts are dealt with in Chapter 20 where the new provisions, introduced in FA 1991, are fully analysed. If part only of the fund is appointed to non-resident trustees who realise a chargeable gain and that part is still treated as comprised in the original settlement (see IV above), the original trustees can be made accountable for any CGT.   **[18.101]**

1   Disposal of beneficial interests in non-resident trusts

FA 1981 s 88 modifies the basic exemption from CGT for disposals of beneficial interests. With the introduction of an 'exit charge' when a settlement ceases to be UK resident the section has, in part, been repealed in relation to disposals occurring on or after 19 March 1991.   **[18.102]**

a) *Disposals prior to 19 March 1991*

Two rules applied.
First, if the disposal occurred *after* the trust had become non-resident, the disposal was chargeable to CGT (s 88(1)). This rule continues to apply.
Secondly, if the trust became non-resident after the disposal (so that the exemption under CGTA 1979 s 58(1) applied at the time of the disposal) the effect of the emigration was to *trigger a charge which was payable by the emigrating trustees.* (If the emigration was the result of new foreign trustees being appointed, the resultant chargeable gain was that of the retiring UK trustees.) In a sense, therefore, the exempt gain under s 58(1) was held in suspense (s 88(2)). FA 1981 s 88(2) did not apply to the trustees if, before becoming non-resident, they had disposed of all the assets which were subject to the trusts at the time when the disposal of the beneficial interest occurred. If some only of those assets were retained, the chargeable gain for which they could be held liable was limited to the value of those assets (FA 1981 s 88(3)(4)). If the trustees failed to pay tax under s 88(2) within 12 months of the due date, this could be charged at any time in the next five years on the former beneficiary who made a disposal of his interest, although he was given a right of recovery against the trustees (FA 1981 s 88(5)(6)).

EXAMPLE 18.16

Bloggs, the remainderman in a family trust, disposed of his interest for £50,000. Two years later in 1990 non-resident trustees were appointed. For CGT purposes:
(1)   The original sale by Bloggs was exempt (s 58(1)).
(2)   Immediately before the trust became non-resident the UK resident trustees were treated as making a chargeable gain equal to that which had accrued to Bloggs.

So far as the calculation of the tax charge on the disposal is concerned, in the majority of cases there would have been no acquisition cost given that the disponor was an original beneficiary of the settlement which had itself been created after March 1982.   **[18.103]**

b) *Disposals on or after 19 March 1991*

With the introduction of the exit charge on the emigration of a trust, maintaining s 88 intact would have led to the prospect of a double tax charge and hence FA 1991 s 88 makes suitable modifications. This section applies to the s 88(1) situation, ie where the beneficial interest arose *before* the emigration of the trust and its disposal *after* emigration. The charge to tax is preserved but it is provided that:

> 'in calculating any chargeable gain accruing on the disposal of the interest the person disposing of it shall be treated as having:
> (a) disposed of it immediately before the relevant time, and
> (b) immediately re-acquired it, at its market value at that time.'

Although not happily drafted, the purpose of the subsection is to fix the acquisition cost of the disponor at the date when the trustees emigrated (ie his acquisition cost will take into account the gains then realised and subject to UK tax). On first reading, the provision might be thought to impose a second charge at that time but this is not thought to be the case.

A further infelicity in the drafting is that the provision is said to be relevant for the purpose of calculating the chargeable gain of the disponor: surely it should also be relevant in arriving at any allowable loss which he may have suffered!

The quite separate charge that arose (levied on former UK trustees) if at the time when a trust was exported a beneficiary had already disposed of his interest in circumstances where s 58(1) prevented any charge from arising (see FA 1981 s 88(2) and *Example 18.16*) was rendered obsolete and repealed in relation to disposals on or after 19 March 1991.   **[18.104]**

EXAMPLE 18.17

The Halibut trust was set up in 1984 with Jason Halibut being entitled to the residue of the trust on the death of his sister, Rose. The trustees became non-resident on 20 March 1991 and Jason sold his remainder interest shortly afterwards for £150,000.

Analysis:
(i) Jason's disposal is a chargeable disposal under FA 1981 s 88(1);
(ii) In order to compute his chargeable gain (if any) the market value of that interest when the trust became non-resident on 20 March needs to be ascertained.

2 The migration of the settlement

FA 1981 s 81 ensured that, if a settlement became non-resident and then realised chargeable gains and capital payments had been made in a year when it was resident, any capital payment, so long as it was paid in anticipation of the subsequent disposal of assets, would be brought into charge under FA 1981 s 80 (see Chapter 20). With the introduction of the exit charge on the migration of UK settlements this provision, although remaining on the statute book, is largely redundant.   **[18.105]**

3 Hold-over relief and migration

Prior to the 1991 changes if a gain was held over on the making of a settlement that gain was triggered when the trustees became non-resident (either by ceasing to be resident or on the appointment of overseas trustees or by becoming dual resident). As with the deferred s 58 charge discussed above, the chargeable gain was deemed to accrue immediately before the trustees ceased to be resident, so that the old (UK) trustees were liable (FA 1981 s 79). This triggering of the charge at a rate (in interest in possession trusts) of 25% was unnecessary if chargeable disposals had already occurred after the creation of the settlement (FA 1981 s 79(2)) and with the introduction of a general exit charge on the migration of a trust this provision (insofar as it affected trustees) was redundant and it was repealed for migrations occurring after 18 March 1991.   **[18.106]–[18.120]**

VII RELIEF FROM AND PAYMENT OF CGT

1 **Payment**

CGT attributable to both actual and deemed disposals of settled property is assessed on the trustees. The rate of tax will, depending on the type of settlement, be charged at either 25% or 35% (see **[14.75]** and note that in exceptional cases the settlor's rate will apply). If the tax is not paid within six months of the due date for payment, it may be recovered from a beneficiary who has become absolutely entitled to the asset (or proceeds of sale therefrom) in respect of which the tax is chargeable. The beneficiary may be assessed in the trustees' name for a period of two years after the date when the tax became payable (CGTA 1979 s 52(4)).   **[18.121]**

2 **Exemptions and reliefs**

Exemptions and reliefs from CGT have been discussed in Chapter 16, but note the following matters in the context of settled property:

Main residence exemption May be available in the case of a house settled on both discretionary and on interest in possession trusts (see *Sansom v Peay* (1976)).   **[18.122]**

The annual exemption Trustees are generally allowed half of the exemption appropriate to an individual (for 1991–92, half of £5,500 = £2,750).   **[18.123]**

Death exemption The tax-free uplift will be available for trusts with a life interest, but not for discretionary trusts.   **[18.124]**

Retirement relief Retirement relief may be available for trusts with a life interest: it is not available for discretionary trusts.   **[18.125]**

Roll-over (reinvestment) relief Available only if the trustees are carrying on an unincorporated business.   **[18.126]**

19 CGT—companies and shareholders

I CGT PROBLEMS INVOLVING COMPANIES

1 CGT and corporation tax

Companies and unincorporated associations are not subject to CGT; chargeable gains are assessed to corporation tax. Broadly, the principles involved in computing the chargeable gain (or allowable loss) are the same as for individuals but the effective rate of corporation tax charged on the gain is either 25% or 33% (see Chapter 28).

Disposals within a group of companies (as defined) will generally be free of corporation tax. Any charge is held over until either the asset is sold outside the group or until the company which owns the asset leaves the group; see [**28.145**].   [**19.1**]

2 Company takeovers and mergers

If the takeover is by means of an issue of shares by the purchasing company (a 'paper exchange'), CGT on the gain made by the disposing shareholder may generally be postponed until the consideration shares are sold (CGTA 1979 ss 85–87). Where the assets of the target company are acquired for a cash consideration, a chargeable gain will result for the target company unless it obtains roll-over relief under CGTA 1979 ss 115–121 (see [**16.92**]). From the point of view of the target's shareholders, failure to obtain this relief would not only lead to a corporation tax charge on the gains raised by the sale of the assets, it would also leave them the problem of what to do with a 'cash shell' company (see further Chapter 33).

FA 1980 s 117 and Sch 18 contain provisions aimed at facilitating arrangements whereby trading activities of a single company or group are split up in order to be carried on either by two or more companies or by separate groups of companies ('demergers'; see [**33.41**]).   [**19.2**]

3 Incorporation of an existing business

CGTA 1979 s 123 affords relief in cases where a business is transferred to a company as a going concern in return for the issue of shares in the company (see [**16.103**]).   [**19.3**]-[**19.20**]

II CAPITAL DISTRIBUTIONS PAID TO SHAREHOLDERS

A capital distribution (whether in cash or assets) is treated as a disposal or part disposal of the shares in respect of which the distribution is received (CGTA 1979 s 72(1)). 'Capital distribution' is restrictively defined to exclude any distribution which is subject to income tax in the hands of the recipient (CGTA 1979 s 72(5)(b)). As the definition of a distribution for the purposes of Schedule F is extremely wide (see [**28.81**]) the CGT charge is confined to repayments of share capital and to distributions in the course of winding up.

EXAMPLE 19.1

(1) Prunella buys shares in Zaba Ltd for £40,000. Some years later the company repays to her £12,000 on a reduction of share capital. The value of Prunella's shares immediately after that reduction is £84,000.

The company has made a capital distribution for CGT purposes and Prunella has disposed of an interest in her shares in return for that payment. The part disposal rules must, therefore, be applied as follows:

(i) consideration for part disposal: £12,000
(ii) allocation of base cost of shares:

$$£40,000 \times \frac{A}{A + B} = £40,000 \times \frac{£12,000}{£12,000 + £84,000} = £5,000$$

(iii) gain on part disposal: £12,000 — £5,000 = £7,000.

(2) Stanley buys shares in Monley Ltd for £60,000. The company is wound up and Stanley is paid £75,000 in the liquidation. Stanley has disposed of his shares in return for the payment by the liquidator and, therefore, has a chargeable gain of £15,000 (£75,000 — £60,000).

If the company had been insolvent so that the shareholders received nothing Stanley should claim loss relief because his shares would have become of negligible value (see CGTA 1979 s 22(2); *Williams v Bullivant* (1983); and [**14.104**].) He has an allowable loss of £60,000.

These rules are also applied when a shareholder disposes of a right to acquire further shares in the company (CGTA 1979 s 73). The consideration received on the disposal is treated as if it were a capital distribution received from the company in respect of the shares held.

Under s 72(2), if the inspector is satisfied that the amount distributed is relatively small, the part disposal rules are not applied but the capital distribution is deducted from the allowable expenditure on the shares. The result is to increase a subsequent gain on the sale of the shares (in effect the provision operates as a postponement of CGT). On that later disposal the indexation allowance will presumably be calculated on the reduced allowable expenditure. For these purposes, a capital distribution is treated as small if it amounts to no more than 5% of the value of the shares in respect of which it is made (see Revenue booklet CGT 8 para 125). In practice, the Revenue will allow the taxpayer to be assessed on a part disposal (even when the distribution is small) if he so desires.

Under s 72(4) where the allowable expenditure is *less than* the amount distributed the taxpayer may elect that the part disposal rules shall not apply and that the expenditure shall be deducted from the amount distributed. *O'Rourke v Binks* (1991) decided, somewhat surprisingly, that under this subsection the amount distributed did not have to be small: indeed the judge held that the sum distributed (£246,699) was **not small**—nevertheless the total expenditure of £214,602 was deductible from that sum.

On a liquidation there will often be a number of payments made prior to the final winding-up and each is a part disposal of shares (subject to the relief for small distributions) so that the shares will need to be valued each time a distribution is made (see SP 1/72).

EXAMPLE 19.2

Mark purchased 5,000 shares in Rothko Ltd for £5,000. The company has now made a 1:5 rights issue at £1.25 per share. Mark is, therefore, entitled to a further 1,000 shares but, having no spare money, sells his rights to David for £250. At that time his 5,000 shares were worth £7,500. As the capital distribution (£250) is less than 5% of £7,500 the part disposal rules will not apply. Therefore, £250 will be deducted from Mark's £5,000 base cost (NB Mark may prefer the part disposal rules to apply since (i) any gain resulting may be covered by his annual exemption; and (ii) expenditure of £5,000 (rather than £4,750), will then be index-linked for the purpose of the indexation allowance).

When a company ceases trading, retirement relief may be available to the shareholder provided that the capital distribution by the liquidator does not consist of chargeable business assets. Further, that distribution must be made within one year of the cessation of trading (or such longer period as the Revenue may allow) and any gain on the deemed disposal of the shares under CGTA 1979 s 72 is only eligible for relief in the proportion which the company's chargeable business assets bear to its total chargeable assets.   **[19.21]–[19.40]**

III   THE DISPOSAL OF SHARES

1   Introduction

a) Pre FA 1982 system

A disposal of shares is a chargeable event. Before FA 1982, the CGT rules were relatively straightforward and involved treating identical shares as a single asset. This 'pooling' system involved a cumulative total of shares with sales being treated as part disposals from the pool and not as a disposal of a particular parcel of shares. Special rules applied where all or part of a shareholding was acquired before 6 April 1965.   **[19.41]**

EXAMPLE 19.3 (Pre FA 1982 pooling)

Low acquires ordinary shares in XYZ Ltd as follows:

Date	Shares	Cost (£)
1966	100	100
1970	60	250
1976	500	400
1978 (1:1 bonus)	660	—
1980 (1:10 rights)	132	132
Total	1452	£882

In 1980 Low was treated as owning a single asset (1,452 shares) which cost him £882. In 1981 he sold 726 shares for £726, a part disposal of one half of the holding. His chargeable gain was £726 — £441 (one half of the total cost of the asset) = £285.

b) *FA 1982 regime—operative from 6 April 1982 to 6 April 1985*

Shares of the same class acquired after 5 April 1982 and before 6 April 1985 were not pooled. Instead, each acquisition was treated as the acquisition of a separate asset (FA 1982 s 88(1)). A disposal of shares was then matched with a particular acquisition in accordance with detailed identification rules which applied even where the shares were distinguishable from each other by, for instance, being individually numbered. Shares were therefore treated as a 'fungible' asset. These rules were introduced because of the indexation allowance which made it necessary to know whether the shares disposed of had been acquired within 12 months (when no allowance was available) or, in other cases, to calculate the indexation allowance by reference to the original expenditure. The rules also sought to prohibit avoidance and saving schemes and seriously damaged bed and breakfasting arrangements. For companies the rules were operative from 1 April 1982.

Major changes in the indexation allowance made by FA 1985 enabled a form of share pooling to be reintroduced for shares. Although this change is of benefit to both taxpayers and their professional advisers, there are now four different sets of rules that may be applicable on a disposal of shares or securities:

(1)   The new pooling regime (see 2, below).
(2)   Rules that apply to shares acquired after 5 April 1965 and before 6 April 1982 (see 3, below).
(3)   Rules that apply to shares acquired before 6 April 1965 (pre CGT holdings); see 4, below.
(4)   Special rules that apply to certain types of security only. First, certain gilt edged securities and qualifying corporate bonds are exempt from CGT (see [**28.48**]). Secondly, other securities subject to the bond washing provisions (see [**31.61**]) together with deep discount securities, and certain offshore funds, are excluded from the new pooling provisions introduced by FA 1985. Accordingly, they remain governed by the system in FA 1982 ss 88–89.

Identification rules in FA 1985 determine the order of disposal of shares and securities (other than securities falling within (4) above) and these are discussed at 5 below. These complex provisions have not been altered by 1982 rebasing introduced in FA 1988.   [**19.42**]

2   **The new pooling rules** (FA 1985 s 68 and Sch 19)

Shares of the same class acquired after 5 April 1982 and still owned by the taxpayer on 6 April 1985 are treated as one asset and further acquisitions of the shares after that date form part of this single holding. There is an indexed pool of expenditure for each class of share and, if shares in the pool were acquired between 1982 and 1985, the initial value of this pool on 6 April 1985 comprises the acquisition costs of the relevant shares together with the indexation allowance (including an allowance for the first 12 months of ownership) that would have been given had the shares been sold on 5 April 1985.

EXAMPLE 19.4

Silver acquires 10,000 ordinary shares in Mines Ltd for £10,000 in August 1982 and a further 5,000 shares (cost £7,500) in November 1984. Assume 'indexed rise' from August 1982 to April 1985 was 0.25 and from November 1984 to April 1985 was 0.01.

The value of the pool of indexed expenditure on 5 April 1985 is accordingly:

	£
Cost of 10,000 shares	10,000
plus indexation allowance from August 1982 (£10,000 × 0.25)	2,500
Cost of 5,000 shares	7,500
plus indexation allowance from November 1984 (£7,500 × 0.01)	75
Indexed pool of expenditure	£20,075

If identical shares are acquired after 6 April 1985 they are added to the share pool with the cost of their acquisition increasing the indexed pool of expenditure (a similar result occurs if a rights issue is taken up). When there is a disposal (including a part disposal) of shares in the pool, any gain is calculated by deducting from the disposal consideration the appropriate proportion of the indexed pool of expenditure (which will include any indexation allowance for the period from the last operative event to the date of disposal).

EXAMPLE 19.5

Continuing with the facts of *Example 19.4* assume that in November 1985 Silver acquired a further 2,000 shares in Mines Ltd for £3,750 and that in January 1987 he sold 8,500 of his shareholding for £27,500 (incurring incidental costs on disposal of £1,500). Assume indexed rise from April–November 1985 of 0.006 and from November 1985 to January 1987 of 0.105.

(i) the acquisition of the further 2,000 shares: the new shares are pooled with the existing 15,000 shares to form a single holding and the indexed pool of qualifying expenditure is recalculated as follows:

	£
Indexed pool in April 1985	20,075
Plus indexed rise April–November 1985 £20,075 × 0.006	120.45
Plus cost of 2,000 shares (November 1985)	3,750
Indexed pool of expenditure	£23,945.45

(ii) the part disposal of 8,500 shares

(1) Calculate indexed pool of expenditure in January 1987:

	£
Indexed pool in November 1985	23,945.45
Plus indexed rise from November 1985 to January 1987 £23,945.45 × 0.105	2,514.27
Indexed pool in January 1987	£26,459.72

(2) Calculate proportion of pool attributable to shares sold:

ie $\dfrac{\text{shares sold}}{\text{total holding}} \times \text{pool}$

$$\frac{8,500}{17,000} \times \pounds 26,459.72 \qquad\qquad \underline{\underline{\pounds 13,229.86}}$$

(3) Gain on shares disposed of:	$\pounds$	$\pounds$
Consideration for sale		27,500
Less allowable expenses	13,229.86	
disposal cost	1,500.00	
		14,729.86
Gain on disposal		$\underline{\underline{\pounds 12,770.14}}$

(4) Reduced indexed pool of expenditure attributable to remaining 8,500 shares is £13,229.86.

(*Note:* The legislation requires both an indexed and an unindexed pool to be maintained: in practice, the procedure used in this *Example* will produce the correct chargeable gain.)   [**19.43**]

3   Shares acquired after 5 April 1965 and before 6 April 1982

Shares and securities of the same class acquired after 5 April 1965 and before 6 April 1982 are treated as a single asset with a single pool of expenditure (hence, they must not be aggregated with identical shares subsequently acquired). For the purpose of the indexation allowance and the rebasing rules the market value of the shares on 31 March 1982 will generally be treated as the taxpayer's acquisition cost.   [**19.44**]

4   Shares acquired before 6 April 1965

For unquoted shares any gain is deemed to accrue evenly (the 'straight-line method') and it is only the portion of the gain since 6 April 1965 which is chargeable (see [**14.31**]). The disponer may elect to have the gain computed by reference to the value of the shares on 6 April 1965. This election may only reduce a gain; it cannot increase a loss or replace a gain by a loss. Where different shares are disposed of on different dates the general rule of identification is first in, first out (CGTA 1979 Sch 5 paras 13–14).

For quoted shares and securities the general principle is that a gain is calculated by reference to their market value on 6 April 1965 (the rules for ascertaining the market value are laid down in CGTA 1979 Sch 6 paras 2(3), 3(2)). If, however, a computation based upon the original cost of the shares produces a smaller gain or loss, it is the smaller gain or loss which is taken. If one calculation produces a gain, and one a loss, there is deemed to be neither. Shares are identified on the first in, first out basis.

EXAMPLE 19.6

Norman bought ordinary shares in Woof PLC (a quoted company), as follows:

Date	Shares	Cost ($\pounds$)
1962	100	2,000
1963	100	6,000
1964	100	3,500

On 6 April 1965 each share is worth £30. *On 24 December 1965* 250 shares are sold for £10,000 (ie £40 per share). As only some of the shares are sold, identification is on the basis of FIFO: therefore, the 1962 and 1963 shares are sold together with 50 of the 1964 shares.

(i) *The 1962 shares:*   cost price £2,000
                          market value on 6 April 1965 £3,000
                          sold for £4,000
If market value on 6 April 1965 is taken, there is a gain of £1,000.

(ii) *The 1963 shares:*   cost price £6,000
                           market value on 6 April 1965 £3,000
                           sold for £4,000
A calculation based on the market value on 6 April 1965 produces a gain; that based on the original cost price produces a loss. Therefore, there is deemed to be neither.

(iii) *50 of the 1964 shares:* cost price £1,750
                               market value on 6 April 1965 £1,500
                               sold for £2,000
The gain is £250 arrived at by taking the original cost price of £1,750 (a larger gain of £500 would be produced using the market value on 6 April 1965).

(iv) Norman's total gain is, therefore, £1,250.

As an alternative to the above procedure, the taxpayer may elect to be charged by reference to the market value of either all his shares or all his securities or both on 6 April 1965 (ie pooling on 6 April 1965). The original cost becomes wholly irrelevant and can neither reduce a gain; reduce a loss; nor result in neither gain nor loss (CGTA 1979 Sch 5 para 4(1)). If, in *Example 19.6*, Norman made such an election his gain would be

$$£10,000 - £7,500 \ (5/6 \times £9,000) = £2,500.$$

FA 1985 Sch 19 para 6(3) permits this election to be made within two years after the end of the year in which the first disposal of such securities occurs after 5 April 1985 (31 March for companies). If the election is made, pre 1965 shares are treated either as part of the taxpayer's 1965-1982 pool or as forming a separate 1965-1982 pool (ie 3, above).   **[19.45]**

5 Identification rules on a disposal of shares

On a disposal of shares the following identification rules operate (FA 1985 Sch 19 Part IV). First, shares are identified with shares acquired on the same day (CGTA 1979 s 66). Secondly, if within a period of ten days securities are acquired, which either constitute a new holding or are added to a new holding (ie 2, above), and subsequently there is a disposal of identical shares, then so far as possible the acquisition and disposal are matched (FA 1985 Sch 19 para 18). Finally disposals are identified with identical shares owned by the taxpayer at the date of disposal on a last in first out (LIFO) basis. Accordingly, new pools (2, above) are exhausted first, then shares in the frozen, 1965-1982, pool (3, above) and finally, in cases where the appropriate election has not been made, shares acquired before 1965. As a result shares with the largest potential gain (those owned for the longest time) are deemed to be disposed of last. The identification rules must apply even if the disposal shares can be separately identified.   **[19.46]**

6 Effect of the identification rules on bear transactions and bed and breakfasting

Normally, shares will be acquired before they are sold. So far as transactions on The Stock Exchange are concerned, however, the delivery of shares which have been sold need not take place until the end of a Stock Exchange account (usually a fortnightly period). Shares may, therefore, be disposed of and later acquired within the same account. This is a 'bear transaction': the aim is to buy at a lower price to fulfil the earlier sale bargain.

A 'bed and breakfasting' arrangement is employed to enable the taxpayer to extract either a gain or loss from his shares without permanently disposing of those shares as the following example shows:

EXAMPLE 19.7

Alberich has unused CGT losses. He owns shares which have an unrealised gain and which he wishes to retain. He sells the shares at close of business one day and repurchases them at the start of business the next. Shares have been 'parked' overnight and the gain extracted. (Notice that 'b & b' transactions might equally be used to extract an allowable loss to set against realised gains).

As the ten day provision (discussed above) only matches disposals with acquisitions in the preceding ten day period it does not affect traditional 'bed and breakfasting' arrangements nor bear transactions. In correspondence with the Institute of Chartered Accountants (see [1985] STI 568) the Revenue considered the possible impact of the *Ramsay* principle (see Chapter 31) upon bed and breakfasting. After noting that the share identification rules in FA 1985 had removed some of the restrictions on this operation they stated 'it will remain necessary to make sure that the transactions involved are effective in (for instance) transferring beneficial ownership of the shares. Assets other than shares and securities may need special consideration in this context'.   **[19.47]-[19.60]**

IV   VALUE SHIFTING

Complex provisions designed to prevent 'value shifting' are found in CGTA 1979 ss 25-26D. Although the sections are not limited to shares, the commonest examples of value shifting involve shares.

Under CGTA 1979 s 25 three types of transaction are treated as disposals of an asset for CGT purposes, despite the absence of any consideration, so long as the person making the disposal could have obtained consideration. The disposal is deemed not to be at arm's length and the market value of the asset is the consideration actually received plus the value of the 'consideration forgone'. Instances of value shifting are: **[19.61]**

Controlling shareholdings Section 25(2) applies when a person having control (defined in TA 1970 s 302) of a company exercises that control so that value passes out of shares (or out of rights over the company) in a company owned by him, or by a person connected with him, into other shares in the company or into other rights over the company. In *Floor v Davis* (1979) the House of Lords decided that the provision could apply where more than one person exercised collective control over the company, and that it covered inertia as well as positive acts. **[19.62]**

EXAMPLE 19.8

Ron owns 9,900 ordinary £1 shares in Wronk Ltd and his son, Ray, owns 100. Each share is worth £40. At the instigation of Ron a further 10,000 shares are offered to the existing shareholders at their par value (a 1:1 rights issue). Ron declines to take up his quota and all the shares are subscribed by Ray. The value of Ron's shares has been substantially reduced as he now holds a minority of the issued shares. CGT will be charged under s 25(2).

Leases Section 25(4) provides as follows:

'If, after a transaction which results in the owner of land or of any other description of property becoming the lessee of the property, there is any adjustment of the rights and liabilities under the lease, whether or not involving the grant of a new lease, which is as a whole favourable to the lessor, there shall be a disposal by the lessee of an interest in the property.' **[19.63]**

EXAMPLE 19.9

Andrew conveys property to Edward by way of gift, but reserves to himself in the conveyance a long lease at a low rent. As the lease is valuable, the part disposal will give rise to a relatively small gain. Andrew later agrees to pay a rack rent so that the value of Edward's freehold is increased. When the rent is increased tax is charged on the consideration that could have been obtained for Andrew agreeing to pay that increased sum.

Extinction of rights The extinction or abrogation, in whole or in part, of a right or restriction over an asset is treated as a disposal by the person entitled to enforce that right (CGTA 1979 s 26): eg the release of a restrictive covenant or easement over land.

In contrast to s 25, s 26 applies only if there is an actual disposal of an asset. It strikes at schemes or arrangements, whether made before or after that disposal, as a result of which 'a tax-free benefit has been or will be conferred on the person making the disposal or a person with whom he is connected; or on any other person'. When it applies, the inspector is given power to adjust, as may be just and reasonable, the amount of gain or loss shown by the disposal (s 26(4)). This widely drafted provision will not operate if the taxpayer shows that the avoidance of tax was not the main purpose, or one of the main purposes, of the arrangement or scheme. Further, it does not catch disposals between husband and wife (within CGTA

1979 s 44); disposals between PRs and legatees; or disposals between companies which are members of a group. It applies to disposals after 29 March 1977 and has not yet been subjected to judicial scrutiny.   **[19.64]**

Groups of companies

FA 1989 s 136 introduced new sections 26A, 26B, 26C and 26D into CGTA 1979. These provisions are intended to prevent groups of companies from reducing or eliminating the capital gains tax charge that would otherwise arise on the sale of a subsidiary company.

They are aimed at devices whereby the value of a subsidiary company is reduced before its sale by, for instance, distributing unrealised capital gains to other group members. The benefit of the gain is thereby retained within the group and the value of the subsidiary reduced but the distribution itself is untaxed. This arrangement is now prevented by an appropriate addition being made to the sale consideration. The provision is not intended to catch distributions out of normal profits and reserves.   **[19.65]**

20 CGT—the foreign element

I GENERAL

1 Territorial scope: residence as the connecting factor

An individual who is resident or ordinarily resident in the UK in any year of assessment is taxed on his worldwide chargeable gains made during that year (CGTA 1979 s 2(1)). There are two qualifications to this general proposition.

First, where the gain is on overseas assets and cannot be remitted to the UK because of local legal restrictions, executive action by the foreign government or the unavailability of the local currency, CGT will only be charged when those difficulties cease.

Secondly, an individual who is resident, but not domiciled, in the UK is liable only to CGT on such gains on overseas assets as are remitted to the UK. For the location of assets, see [27.4] and note that a non-sterling bank account belonging to a non-UK domiciliary is located overseas (FA 1984 s 69).

A person who is neither resident nor ordinarily resident in the UK is generally not liable to CGT on gains wherever made. The special rules that apply in the case of overseas corporations are considered at [28.161]. A trust is not UK resident if a majority of the trustees are non-resident *and* the trust is administered outside the UK.   [20.1]

2 'Going non-resident' and concession D2

In the light of these provisions CGT may be avoided by an individual 'going non-resident': ie acquiring a residence abroad and then disposing of the asset in question. Residence and ordinary residence are not defined in the Taxes Acts and will be interpreted as for income tax (see further Chapter 13 and the Inland Revenue leaflet IR20 (1986)). A taxpayer is, for instance, always UK resident if present in the UK for 183 days or more in a the tax year, whilst absence from the UK for a complete tax year will not necessarily prevent the taxpayer from being both resident and ordinarily resident in the UK.

As with income tax, residence will usually be determined for a complete tax year and, indeed, CGTA 1979 s 2 provides that tax is levied if the individual is resident in the UK *during any part* of the tax year. It is only by concession that the tax year may be split into a period of residence and non-residence and the relevant provision (ESC D2) provides that:

'When a person leaves the United Kingdom and is treated on his departure as not resident and not ordinarily resident in the United Kingdom he is not charged to CGT on gains accruing to him from disposals made after the date of his departure.'

A taxpayer is treated as non-resident from his departure when he leaves the UK for permanent residence or to take up full-time employment abroad (see further Chapter 13). In *R v IRC, ex p Fulford-Dobson* (1987) a taxpayer obtained permanent employment in Germany and shortly before his departure his wife transferred a chargeable asset into his name (that disposal attracted no CGT because of the no gain no loss rule: see [**14.22**]). Within four days of leaving the UK the asset was sold and the taxpayer sought to avoid an assessment to CGT of £59,000 by claiming that he fell within the terms of the above concession. The court held, however, that the Revenue could restrict the giving of concessions and, in particular, could refuse to operate the concession 'in any case where an attempt is made to use it for tax avoidance'. If the taxpayer had retained the asset until the following tax year, and then had made the disposal, reliance upon the concession would have been unnecessary since tax would not be chargeable by virtue of CGTA 1979 s 2. (In a blatant case, however, could the Revenue successfully invoke *Furniss v Dawson* to argue that the disposal to the non-resident was a fiscal nullity and that the asset remained in the ownership of the resident spouse?).

Two other matters should be noticed. First, any CGT losses should be realised prior to departure; and, secondly, care should be taken to ensure that arrangements with a potential purchaser, made before going non-resident, do not amount to a disposal at that time. Accordingly, careful thought is required before a conditional contract is concluded or put and call options granted.

Concession D2 does not apply to trustees nor to gains realised on the disposal of assets of a business carried on in the UK through a branch or agency.

Gains may be taxed both in the UK and in a foreign country. Where the UK has a double taxation treaty with the relevant country, the matter is dealt with under the terms of the treaty. Otherwise, a person may claim unilateral relief from double taxation usually by receiving a tax credit against CGT for the foreign tax paid.   [**20.2**]–[**20.20**]

II   REMITTANCE OF GAINS BY A NON-UK DOMICILIARY

An individual who is resident or ordinarily resident, but not domiciled, in the UK is chargeable to CGT only on the remitted gains from overseas assets, with no relief for any overseas losses. The definition of remittance is wide and catches a sum resulting from the gains, which is paid, used or enjoyed in the UK or brought or sent to the UK in any form (CGTA 1979 s 14(2)) and a transfer to the UK of the proceeds of sale of assets purchased from the gain. Anti-avoidance provisions in TA 1988 s 65 designed to catch disguised remittances are extended to CGT. The section applies for example, where a loan (whether or not made in the UK so long as the moneys are remitted to the UK) is repaid out of the overseas gain.   [**20.21**]–[**20.40**]

III CGT LIABILITY OF NON-RESIDENTS

1 **Individuals**

A non-resident individual escapes tax even on disposals of assets situated in the UK *except* where he carries on a trade, profession or vocation in the UK through a branch or agency (CGTA 1979 s 12(1)). In such cases he is taxed on any gain that arises on a disposal of assets used or previously used for the business or held or acquired for that branch or agency (eg a lease of premises). Anti-avoidance measures introduced by FA 1989 prevent the charge under s 12 being avoided by removing assets from the UK or by ceasing to trade in the UK. In both cases a deemed disposal at market value will occur (compare the deemed disposal which results from the migration of a foreign company: see Chapter 28). Further, ESC D2 does not apply when disposals of assets used by a branch or agency are made during the year of emigration (see 1989 STI 306). Such disposals will therefore continue to be made by a UK resident and to attract a tax charge: in the following tax year disposals will fall under the s 12 charge with a deemed disposal arising on the final cessation of the trade.   **[20.41]**

2 **Companies**

A non-resident company is excluded from liability to CGT except where it trades in the UK through a branch or an agency (see Chapter 28). Thus, a non-resident investment company is never liable to CGT. However, UK *domiciled* individuals cannot form non-resident companies to avoid CGT on (*inter alia*) overseas gains. If a non-resident company would be a close company if it were resident in the UK, its chargeable gains are apportioned amongst UK resident shareholders in proportion to their entitlement to assets on a winding-up. There is no apportionment to a shareholder who is entitled to less than 5% of the assets or to a shareholder who is not domiciled in the UK. If the gains are already taxed in a foreign country with which the UK has a double taxation treaty, there is no apportionment. Otherwise the shareholder is charged on the apportioned gain with a claim for relief against double taxation (CGTA 1979 s 15).

The apportionment rule is not as great a disincentive to the formation of a non-resident company as it may appear since gains made on the disposal of most assets of a trading company that are used in the trade are not apportioned (CGTA 1979 s 15(5)). Thus, problems really arise only for the shareholder of a non-resident investment or holding company and in such cases apportionment may be avoided by interposing an overseas trust between the individual and the company (in which case gains are apportioned to the trusts and will then be subject to the FA 1981 s 80 charging regime: see FA 1981 s 85).

Losses made by the non-resident company cannot be used to reduce its gain before apportionment, nor can the losses as such be apportioned except to the extent that a shareholder has had a gain apportioned to him in that tax year and the apportioned loss would eliminate or reduce the gain. A shareholder can be reimbursed by the company for tax he has paid on apportioned gains without a further charge. Otherwise, he can deduct the tax paid from any gain made on a subsequent disposal of the shares.

Example 20.1

In the early 1980s the Wonka family set up a Jersey trust which owned all the shares in a Netherlands Antilles ('NA') company which in turn owned all the issued share capital of a Californian corporation ('CC'). Assume that the latter company owned substantial property interests around Los Angeles which have just been sold showing a substantial gain.

(i)   That gain realised by CC may be apportioned to NA: see CGTA 1979 s 15(9).

(ii) In turn, the apportioned gain may be further apportioned to the Jersey trust (FA 1981 s 85) and to the extent that the trust makes capital payments to UK beneficiaries, those apportioned gains may attract a UK tax charge.

Notice that the provisions whereby the profits of a 'controlled foreign company' including an investment company may be apportioned to its UK resident corporate members do not apply to its chargeable gains (see; TA 1988 s 747(6)).   **[20.42]**

3   **Trusts**

a)   *Background*

The CGT treatment of offshore trusts has undergone a number of changes of which the following is a brief summary.   **[20.43]**

From 1965–81: FA 1965 s 42 imposed a charging system for non-UK resident trusts which led to major difficulties and was ultimately abandoned in 1981.   **[20.44]**

From 1981: FA 1981 s 80 introduced a replacement charging system based on capital distributions being received by UK domiciled and resident beneficiaries. One consequence was that offshore trusts could be used to defer indefinitely the payment of CGT and, in addition, there was no exit charge when a UK trust migrated. Section 80 was supplemented as a result of changes introduced in FA 1991.   **[20.45]**

An exit charge: Since 19 March 1991 an exit charge has been levied on UK trusts which migrate: see FA 1991 ss 83–87.   **[20.46]**

Settlor reserving an interest: In cases where the settlor reserves an interest in his settlement (an 'interest' is widely defined) gains realised by non-UK resident trustees will result in a capital gains tax charge on the settlor: FA 1991 s 89 and Sch 16.   **[20.47]**

The 'interest' charge: An interest charge will supplement the s 80 charge in cases where capital distributions are not made out of a non-resident trust in which the trustees have realised gains (FA 1991 s 90 and Sch 17). **[20.48]**

b)   *Exporting an existing UK trust*

Moving a trust offshore has usually been undertaken in order to obtain all or some of the following benefits: protection from a reintroduction of exchange control; deferment of CGT; and deferment of income tax. So long as the settlor (and any spouse) are excluded from benefit UK income tax will be avoided unless beneficiaries ordinarily resident in the UK receive a benefit and the trust produces 'relevant income' (TA 1988 ss 739–740 and see **[13.111]**). For CGT, provided that the settlor does not retain any interest in his trust, FA 1981 s 80 will not lead to any UK tax charge so long as capital payments are not made to UK domiciled and resident beneficiaries.

In exporting trusts the following matters should be carefully noted.

First, a trust is only non-resident for CGT purposes when a majority of the trustees are neither resident nor ordinarily resident in the UK *and* the general administration of that trust is ordinarily carried on outside the UK.

Secondly, in blatant cases, where a trust is exported and gains are then immediately realised it is open to the Revenue to argue that under *Furniss v Dawson* principles the appointment of non-resident trustees is an artificial step which can be excised so that the gain is thereby made by the (former) UK trustees and is subject to tax. In this connection it is also important to remember that concession D2 (see [**20.2**]) does not apply to trustees and hence the tax year is not split so that the UK trustees may be taxed on gains realised later in the tax year after foreign resident trustees had been appointed.

Thirdly, it will be important to ensure, so far as possible, that all beneficiaries agree to the moving of the trust. The equitable rules on the appointment of overseas trustees were set out by Pennycuick VC in *Re Whitehead's Will Trusts* (1971) as follows:

> 'The law has been quite well established for upwards of a century that there is no absolute bar to the appointment of persons resident abroad as trustees of an English trust. I say "no absolute bar" in the sense that such an appointment would be prohibited by law and would consequently be invalid. On the other hand, apart from exceptional circumstances, it is not proper to make such an appointment, that is to say, the court would not, apart from exceptional circumstances, make such an appointment; nor would it be right for the donees of such a power to make an appointment out of court. If they did, presumably the court would be likely to interfere at the instance of beneficiaries. There do, however, exist exceptional circumstances in which such an appointment can properly be made. The most obvious are those in which the beneficiaries have settled permanently in some country outside the UK and what is proposed to be done is to appoint new trustees in that country.'

It should be noted that the Revenue themselves may not object to the appointment since they do not have *locus standi* but any UK trustee should consider taking indemnities from the new overseas trustees in case beneficiaries at some future date allege that breaches of trust have been committed and seek to set aside the appointment. It is also sensible to include in any trust instrument an express power for the existing trustees to retire in favour of non-resident trustees.

Finally, and even before the 1991 changes, the export of a trust triggered any gain held over when it was created (see Chapter 18) and there was also a trap for the retiring trustees if a disposal of a beneficial interest under the trust had already taken place (albeit that the disposal was wholly unconnected with the later export). Under CGTA 1979 s 58(1) the disposal will not normally have been chargeable when made (see [**18.81**]) but under FA 1981 s 88(2) the trustees were deemed immediately before becoming non-resident (so that it is the old UK trustees who were liable) to have realised the gain in fact made by the beneficiary. Once a trust is non-resident disposals of beneficial interests are not exempted from charge under s 58(1). It is not clear whether this rule will apply if the interest of a beneficiary terminates not as a result of any voluntary action on his part but by act of the trustees: eg where a life interest is terminated by the trustees under a power reserved to them in the settlement in a year when the trust is UK resident. In this case it is thought that the termination will not amount to a disposal for CGT purposes since whilst it is true that under the legislation certain involuntary disposals (eg a sale under a compulsory purchase order) are subject to charge (so that a voluntary act on the part of the donor is not always required) even in these cases there is a transfer of assets as opposed to a mere forfeiture of rights. So far as a forfeiture of rights is concerned there is no disposal unless a capital sum is paid or deemed to be paid on that forfeiting event (CGTA 1979 ss 20-22).

FA 1991 introduced an exit charge when a UK trust is exported. The basic principle is relatively straightforward. When trustees of a UK settlement become neither resident nor ordinarily resident in the UK, they are deemed to have disposed of assets in that settlement and immediately reacquired those same assets. This deemed disposal is closely modelled on that which has always applied when a person becomes absolutely entitled to settled property so that a settlement ends (see CGTA 1979 s 54) and on the exit charge which is levied when a non-UK incorporated company ceases to be UK resident (FA 1988 ss 105-106).

Imposing the exit charge gives rise to a number of problems. When, for instance, does the charge come into effect? Section 83(1) defines the phrase 'relevant time' as meaning any occasion when trustees become non-UK resident but sub-s (9) then makes it clear that the section itself is only to have effect *if the relevant time falls on or after 19 March 1991*.

A second problem is when do trustees become non-UK resident? A simple view would be that this would occur whenever UK trustees (Alan and Ben) are replaced by, say, two Jersey trustees (Cedric and Desmond). Certainly, if s 83 stood alone, such a simple change in the trusteeship would be 'the relevant time'. However, the section must be read in the light of the rest of the CGT legislation and under CGTA 1979 s 52(1) it is provided that:

> 'The trustees of the settlement shall for the purposes of this Act be treated as being a single and continuing body of persons . . . and that body shall be treated as being resident and ordinarily resident in the United Kingdom *unless the general administration of the trusts is ordinarily carried on outside the United Kingdom and the trustees or a majority of them for the time being are not resident or not ordinarily resident in the United Kingdom.*'

Replacing A and B with C and D will satisfy part of s 52(1) but there is a 'frequently overlooked' second limb in that provision: namely that the administration of the trust must be conducted outside the UK. Until that occurs, the trustees remain UK resident. In recent years, the Revenue have shown interest in this limb and have been known to enquire where the administration of any trust is conducted. With the advent of the exit charge, they may be expected to look with some care at UK settlements which have—so it is claimed—recently been exported. Assume, for instance, that C and D replaced A and B on 18 March 1991. If it transpired that on 19 March the general administration of that trust was not being carried on outside the UK but if it then became so carried on (say, for instance, there is a trustee meeting on 21 March 1991 and relevant bank accounts, share transfers etc are then completed) will it not be the case that an exit charge will arise since it is only on 21 March 1991 that the trustees have become non-UK resident? It may also be the case that in the light of the other FA 1991 changes a settlor may wish that he had never exported his trust: in that event it may be possible for him to argue that because the general administration of the trust has never been carried on outside the UK, the trust remains a UK trust.

So far as timing is concerned, the deemed disposal is said to take place 'immediately before' the relevant time: accordingly the disponors are the retiring UK trustees although, given that the CGT year cannot generally be split (see CGTA 1979 s 2), little seems to turn on this point. More significant is the question of who is liable to pay the tax and this is dealt with in s 85. That section begins with a reference to 'the migrating trustees' which is presumably a reference to the newly appointed foreign trustees. It then provides that if tax is not paid by those trustees within six months of the due date, any former trustees of that settlement who held office during the 'relevant period' can be made accountable. The relevant period (broadly) means the 12-month period which ends with the emigration (although not backdated before 19 March 1991). Assume, for instance, that A and B, two professional trustees, retire on 1 January 1992 in favour of two members of the relevant family. Those family trustees, however, subsequently (on 1 July 1992) retire in favour of two non-UK resident trustees, C and D, such retirement being without the prior knowledge of A and B. On these facts, the appointment of C and D constitutes the 'relevant time' for s 83 purposes and any gain arising as a result of the deemed disposal will therefore be payable on 1 December in the following tax year (ie on 1 December 1993). If not paid within six months of that date (by 1 July 1994) the Revenue may demand that tax from all or any of A, B and the family trustees. There is no obligation on the Revenue to seek to recover against *all* former trustees: instead, they can 'pick and choose' and the selected victim is not given any right of contribution against his fellow retired trustees. However, a former trustee can escape liability if he shows that 'when he ceased to be a trustee of the settlement there was no proposal that the trustees might become neither resident nor ordinarily resident in the UK'. Any trustee made liable is given a (worthless!) right of reimbursement against the migrating trustees.

The deemed disposal is of 'defined assets' which (predictably) includes all the assets which constitute the settled property at the relevant time with only two exceptions.

First, the term does not include UK assets used for the purpose of a trade carried on by the trustees through a UK branch or agency. This is because such assets remain within the UK tax net even after the trustees become non-resident: hence there is no need to subject them to the deemed disposal (see CGTA 1979 s 12).

The *second* exception is aimed at ensuring that the provisions of double tax treaties are not overridden. Broadly, if trustees are resident both in the UK and in a treaty country, and under the terms of the relevant treaty they would escape UK tax on a disposal of certain assets then, on emigrating, those assets are excluded from the category of 'defined assets'. All of which leads to the question, what will happen if UK trustees become dual resident after 19 March 1991? The answer (not a surprising answer!) is provided in s 86 where it is stated that the acquisition of dual resident status will result in a deemed disposal. This disposal is, however, limited to 'relevant assets', being those assets which by virtue of the relevant treaty will henceforth fall outside the UK tax net.

Finally, on the deemed disposal, s 83(6) and (7) and s 87 are worthy of mention. When trustees, before emigrating, sell chargeable assets used for the purpose of a trade and, within three years of that disposal but after becoming non-UK resident acquire replacement assets, then roll-over relief under CGTA 1979 ss 115-121 is not available *unless* the replacement assets remain in the tax net under s 12 (discussed above). Similar rules apply where trustees become dual resident if, in this case, the replacement asset would then fall outside the UK tax net under the relevant treaty.

Section 84 deals with what might be termed involuntary exports and imports. Assume that the trustees of a settlement are Adam (UK resident) and Cedric (a Jersey resident accountant) who does all the paperwork and performs the administrative tasks for the trustees. Adam dies with the result that the conditions laid down in CGTA 1979 s 52(1) are satisfied and the trust ceases to be UK resident. On these facts, there was no intention to export the trust and, indeed, the appointment of a new resident UK trustee will have the effect of reversing the process. Imposing an exit charge in such a case would be unjust and hence s 84 prevents the general charge arising under s 83 *provided that* within six months of Adam's death the trustees of the settlement become again UK resident. Perhaps inevitably there are two anti-avoidance measures: *first,* the exit charge remains for those defined assets which are disposed of during the period of non-UK residency (ie between the death and the resumption of residence) and, *secondly,* there is a similar charge if on the resumption of UK residence the trustees are dual resident with a result that certain of the assets will now fall outside the UK tax net under the terms of the relevant double tax treaty. Finally, the converse situation (a non-resident settlement becoming UK resident because of the death of a trustee) is provided for in sub-s (5) to (7). Reverting to non-resident status within six months of the death will not generally trigger the s 83 exit charge subject only to an exception where the period of UK residence has been used to add assets to the settlement claiming hold-over relief on that transfer. Resuming non-resident status will result in a deemed disposal at market value of such assets.   [**20.49**]

c)   *The FA 1981 s 80 charging structure*

Subject to the special rules which apply if the settlor has reserved an interest in his settlement (see e) below), FA 1981 s 80 applies to non-resident trusts in respect of gains made from 1981–82 onwards where the trustees are not resident or ordinarily resident in the UK during the tax year, but the settlor is domiciled and either resident or ordinarily resident in the UK at some time during the tax year or when the settlement was made. Hence, if the settlor was UK domiciled and resident at the date of its creation the apportionment rules of s 80 *always* apply, but if a settlement was originally created by a non-domiciled settlor, who subsequently becomes a UK domiciliary, it will be caught by these rules only for those years when the settlor is UK resident. 'Settlement' and 'settlor' are defined as for income tax (see TA 1988 s 681(4)) and settlor includes the testator or intestate where the settlement arises under a will or intestacy (FA 1981 s 83(7)).

EXAMPLE 20.2

Sergei, domiciled and resident in France, has settled his holiday home in Nice on an overseas trust for his daughter, Nina, who is domiciled and resident in England. He has created an overseas settlement which is not subject to UK capital gains tax. Assume, however, that Sergei intends to come and live in England with his daughter. If he is to acquire a UK domicile the settlement will then fall within s 80. Accordingly, if it is intended the Nice flat shall be sold that sale should occur before Sergei changes his domicile and residence.

When s 80 applies, the trustees calculate trust gains and losses in the usual way (but without any annual exemption) and the net gains are apportioned amongst beneficiaries who have received capital payments in that year. If a beneficiary is not domiciled in the UK during that year (even though resident or ordinarily resident), he is not charged on his portion of the gain so that although the gains are apportioned in accordance with capital payments made to *all* beneficiaries, it is only the gains apportioned to UK beneficiaries (ie beneficiaries who are domiciled and either resident or ordinarily resident in the UK) which are subject to charge. Unused losses of the trust cannot be apportioned but are carried forward by the trust. **[20.50]**

Method of apportionment: The net trust gains are apportioned to the beneficiaries rateably up to the amount of any capital payment made to them in that tax year. In so far as gains cannot be apportioned in one year (because of insufficient capital payments) they are carried forward and added to the gains of the next and following years. In so far as capital payments of previous years were not taken into account in apportioning gains (for example, because there were no gains in that year), they are carried forward and added to capital payments of a year when gains were made. A beneficiary to whom a trust gain is apportioned can set against it allowable losses and his annual exemption.

A 'capital payment' is any payment received by a beneficiary otherwise than as income and a payment may be direct or indirect (for instance, where trustees discharge an obligation of a beneficiary that will be a capital payment) and includes references to the transfer of an asset and the conferring of any other benefit (FA 1981 s 83(1),(2)). In cases where a beneficiary entitled to an interest in possession in the trusts is provided with an interest free loan or allowed to occupy a trust property rent-free, it is arguable that he has received no 'benefit' under s 83 since, had interest or rent been charged, it would have returned to him as life tenant.

EXAMPLE 20.3

A non-resident discretionary settlement has four beneficiaries, two of whom (A and B) are UK domiciled. Over 3 years the fund has no income and makes the following net gains and capital payments. No capital payments have been made to the non-UK domiciled beneficiaries.

	£	A £	B £
Year 1			
Capital payments		10,000	5,000
Net gains £6,000 apportioned		4,000	2,000
Capital payments c/f		6,000	3,000
Year 2			
Capital payments		3,000	6,000
Including payments b/f		9,000	9,000
Trust gains	20,000		
Amount apportioned	18,000	9,000	9,000
Gains c/f	£2,000	—	—

	£	A £	B £
Year 3		15,000	5,000
Capital payments			
Trust gains	10,000		
Gains b/f	2,000		
Amount apportioned	£12,000	9,000	3,000
Capital payments c/f		£6,000	£2,000

Where a beneficiary becomes absolutely entitled to an asset of the settlement he is treated as receiving a capital payment equivalent to the value of the asset so that the amount of trust gains apportioned to him is not limited to the gain (if any) shown by that asset. However, the beneficiary will receive the asset at its (market value under CGTA 1979 s 54(1). **[20.51]**

Relationship with income tax: What appears to be a capital payment by trustees may be treated as income in the hands of the beneficiary under the anti-avoidance provisions of TA 1988 ss 739–745 (see Chapter 13). Such payments are charged to income tax up to the trust income for that year; income from previous years is included to the extent that such income has not already been charged to a beneficiary. Any excess is treated as a capital payment for the purpose of the apportionment of trust gains. **[20.52]**

EXAMPLE 20.4

The same settlement as in *Example 20.3*, except that the following payments made to A and B over three years are first treated as income under TA 1988 ss 739–745.

	£	A £	B £
Year 1			
Trust payments		20,000	10,000
Trust income	£12,000		
Charged to income tax on A and B		8,000	4,000
		12,000	6,000
Trust gains	£15,000		
Apportioned for CGT		10,000	5,000
Payments c/f		£2,000	£1,000
Year 2			
Payments b/f		2,000	1,000
Payments made		10,000	11,000
		12,000	12,000
Trust income	30,000		
Charged to income tax on A and B	24,000	12,000	12,000
Income c/f	£6,000	—	—
Trust gains c/f	£12,000		

	£	A £	B £
Year 3		10,000	10,000
Trust payments			
Trust income	8,000		
Trust income b/f from year 2	6,000		
Charged to income tax on A and B	£14,000	7,000	7,000
		3,000	3,000
Trust gains	4,000		
Trust gains b/f from year 2	12,000		
	16,000		
Apportioned for CGT	6,000	3,000	3,000
Trust gains c/f	£10,000		

d) *The supplementary (interest) charge*

The supplementary charge may apply to beneficiaries who receive capital distributions on or after 6 April 1992. Because it is intended to be supplementary to the s 80 charge, it will only apply if those beneficiaries are UK domiciled and resident. Accordingly (as with the s 80 charge) this extra levy will *not* apply if *either* the settlor was and has remained non-domiciled or non-resident *or* the recipient beneficiary is non-resident or non-domiciled.

The charge itself is intended to operate as an interest charge on the delayed payment of CGT following a disposal of chargeable assets by non-resident trustees. The charge is, however, limited to a six-year period and therefore the time covered by the charge begins on the *later* of (*a*) 1 December in the tax year following the year in which the disposal occurred, and (*b*) 1 December six years before 1 December in the year of assessment following that in which the capital payment was made. The rate of charge is 10% per annum of the tax payable on the capital payment (this percentage may be amended by Statutory Instrument).

EXAMPLE 20.5

The Moisie Liechtenstein Trust realises capital gains in the tax year 1990-91 and a capital payment is made to a UK domiciled and resident Moisie beneficiary on 1 July 1996.
(i) That beneficiary will be assessed to CGT on the capital payment received (at current rates at, say, 40%).
(ii) The interest charge will begin to run on 1 December 1992 at 4% per annum (ie 10% of the ultimate tax charge). The charge itself will apply for the period from 1 December 1992 to 30 November in the year of assessment following that in which the capital payment is made (ie 30 November 1997 so that the interest charge continues to run after the capital payment has been made). In all five years will be subject to the charge (20%) thereby giving a total tax bill of 60% (at present rates the maximum interest charge is six years at 4% pa = 24% and so the maximum CGT levy is 64%).

The precise mechanics governing the supplementary charge are, perhaps inevitably, complex, with capital payments being matched first with total trust gains at 6 April 1991 and then on a first-in first-out basis. By way of concession, however, trustees are given at least 12 months in which to distribute gains since the interest charge does *not* apply to gains realised in the same or immediately preceding year of assessment.

EXAMPLE 20.6

(i) In 1990-91 the Cohen Offshore Settlement has accumulated trust gains of £100,000. Although the interest charge may begin to run on 1 December 1991 no charge will be levied on capital distributions made before 6 April 1992.
(ii) Assume that capital gains are realised in the Geary Cayman Islands Trust in March 1992. Although the interest charge may begin to run from December 1992 no charge will be imposed provided that the gain is distributed before 6 April 1993.

To what extent will the new charge encourage the break-up of existing offshore trusts? In cases where it is intended that property will be distributed to a UK beneficiary there is obviously some attraction in acting before 6 April

1992 in order to avoid the supplementary charge. In other cases, it should be remembered that one way of avoiding the s 80 charge—distributing to non-residents—remains available to 'wash-out' all the potential tax including this interest charge. Finally, for the wealthy family, who view their trust as a roll-up fund which they do not need to dip into, a 10% charge may be seen as a relatively small impost given that the deferred tax may be an insignificant percentage of the total offshore fund.   [20.53]

e)   *Taxing a settlor who has retained an interest in his trust (FA 1991 s 89 and Sch 16)*

The provisions of this Schedule parallel those in FA 1988 Sch 10 which deals with UK resident trusts (see [**14.75**]). When the Schedule applies, gains realised by the trustees, which would have attracted a UK CGT charge had the trustees been resident, are taxed as gains of the settlor and form the top slice of his taxable gains for that year. As in the Sch 10 rules, the gains are not reduced by a trustee annual exemption whilst losses realised by the trustees (although available to set against future gains which they may make) are not treated as losses of the settlor. The settlor is given a statutory right to recover any tax which he suffers from his trustees: the extent to which this right may be enforced in a foreign jurisdiction is, however, debatable.

In considering the provisions of this Schedule, two key questions need to be answered. *First*, which settlements are caught and, *secondly*, when does a settlor retain an interest for these purposes?

So far as the first question is concerned, the rules apply to 'qualifying settlements' which are defined in para 11 as settlements created 'on or after 19 March 1991'. Old settlements—existing at Budget Day 1991—are therefore generally outside the scope of the rules *but* para 11(2) provides that in four situations such settlements may *become* qualifying settlements.

EXAMPLE 20.7

(1)   The Jonas Family UK Trust was set up in 1982. In 1994 the trustees become non-UK resident. Not only will that event trigger an exit charge but, in addition, because the settlement was exported after 18 March 1991 it will become a 'qualifying settlement'.

(2)   The Popeye Settlement has been resident in Liechtenstein since 1989. In 1992:

   (a)   A court order is obtained in Vaduz whereby the beneficial class is widened to include the settlor. This has the effect of turning the trust into 'a qualifying settlement'. By contrast, in settlements where the trustees have always had the power to *add* beneficiaries and exercise that power to add the settlor after March 1991 (or indeed, to add other persons on the list in para 4(3), below) it is not thought that the terms of the trust have been varied so that it becomes 'qualifying settlement'.

   (b)   The trustees distributed funds to the settlor's spouse who is not a beneficiary. The effect of what is a breach of trust is to convert the trust into 'a qualifying settlement' since she is now a person who has enjoyed a benefit (and is on the list in para 4(3)) and she was not a person who might be expected to have enjoyed such a benefit from the settlement after 18 March 1991.

   (c)   On 1 March 1992 Julian Popeye added property to his father's trust. Such an addition, whether by the settlor or another, has the effect of turning the trust into a 'qualifying settlement'. This provision must be carefully watched: it does not apply in cases where there is an accretion to settlement funds (eg where the trust receives dividends or bonus shares from a company in which it has investments) and, as a result of a Report Stage amendment, it does not apply if the settlor adds property by discharging the fees of his trustees (to the extent that such fees cannot be discharged out of trust income). Bear in mind, however, that other additions—*however small*—have the effect of converting the *entire trust* into a 'qualifying settlement'.

Apart from the settlement needing to 'qualify', the Schedule only applies in years when the settlor is *both* domiciled and either resident or ordinarily resident in the UK. Gains realised in other years are not taxed as the settlor's and the Schedule ceases to apply from the year of assessment in which the settlor dies.

Turning to the second question, a settlor has an 'interest' if a 'defined person' benefits or will or may become entitled to a benefit in either the income or the capital of the settlement. Para 4(3) identifies a 'defined person' as follows:

'(a) the settlor;
(b) the settlor's spouse;
(c) any child of the settlor or of the settlor's spouse [no age limit];
(d) the spouse of any such child;
(e) a company controlled by a person or persons falling within paragraphs (a) to (d) above;
(f) a company associated with a company falling within paragraph (e) above.'

The list is formidable (contrast the provisions of FA 1988 Sch 10) and it is particularly worthy of note that children (including step-children) of whatever age are included. The only exclusions of real consequence are the settlor's cohabitee and his grandchildren! A deliberate policy decision was taken not to apply the provisions of Sch 10 to offshore trusts because it was intended to widen the class of defined persons. Note the trap which exists for settlors in cases where a UK trust has been created in favour of his children which is then exported. Although the settlor is otherwise excluded from all benefit under the rules of the trust, the effect of the export is to create a qualifying settlement with the result that gains will be taxed as the settlor's since defined persons (his children—even if they are geriatric adults) will or may benefit. **[20.54]**

f) *Leedale v Lewis (1982) and FA 1965 s 42 (CGTA 1979 s 17)*

From 6 April 1965 to 5 April 1981 FA 1965 s 42 (later CGTA 1979 s 17) provided that the gains were to be apportioned amongst the beneficiaries on a just and reasonable basis and taxed as if the beneficiaries had made the gains. The House of Lords in *Leedale v Lewis* (1982) considered the position of beneficiaries who had received nothing from a discretionary trust. They were originally assessed to CGT by reference to their ultimate fixed interests, but it was held that CGT could also be assessed by reference to their discretionary interests. This decision is obviously significant for trusts where the discretionary and fixed interests are in different hands (see eg *Bayley v Garrod* (1983)). Net gains may be apportioned after deduction of losses realised by the trustees (see *Ritchie v McKay* (1984)).

As a result of the widespread criticism of the *Leedale v Lewis* decision (see eg (1983) LS Gaz 461), FA 1984 s 70 and Sch 14 modified the 1965 provisions so that where tax has not already been paid on pre 1981 gains a beneficiary, who has not benefited from the trust, may claim that any payment of CGT be postponed until he does benefit (see further (1984) LS Gaz 3147). **[20.55]**

Section 4 Inheritance tax

Chapters

❛Poor Cyril – now he's not rich enough to moan about inheritance tax❜

Introduction—from estate duty to inheritance tax

Most countries impose some kind of wealth tax. It usually takes the form of a death duty either levied on property inherited or on the value of a deceased's estate on death. In the UK estate duty was introduced in 1894 as a tax on a deceased's property whether passing under a will or on intestacy. Over its long life the tax was extended from its originally narrow fiscal base (property passing on death) to catch certain gifts made in the period before death and at the time of its replacement by capital transfer tax it extended to gifts made in the seven years before death. By the 1970s estate duty was, however, widely condemned as an unsatisfactory tax. 'A voluntary tax'; 'a tax on vice: the vice of clinging to one's property until the last possible moment'—were typical descriptions.

In 1972 the Conservative government considered replacing estate duty with an inheritance tax (Cmnd 4930). The idea was that a beneficiary would keep a cumulative account of all gifts that he received on death and pay tax accordingly. Nothing came of this proposal, largely because such a tax would have been too costly to administer and because the Conservative government fell from office.

The Labour government, which came to power in 1974, was committed to achieving a major redistribution of wealth. As a first stage (without any prior consultation) it introduced CTT in the 1974 Budget. This tax had '... as its main purpose to make the estate duty not a voluntary tax, but a compulsory tax, as it was always intended to be' (Mr Healey, the then Chancellor of the Exchequer). A proposed wealth tax (Cmnd 5074) was never introduced. In reality CTT, substantially altered during its passage through Parliament in 1974–75, never achieved its espoused redistributive purpose. There was no doubt, however, that in concept it was a brilliantly simple tax which removed the arbitrariness of the old estate duty. All gifts of property, whether made inter vivos or on death, were cumulated with earlier gifts and progressive rates of tax applied to that cumulative total.

The advent of Conservative governments in 1979 has seen a steady erosion of the principles underlying CTT. The old idea of a fully comprehensive cradle to grave gifts tax was abandoned in 1981 in favour of ten year cumulation, thresholds were raised, and a new relief introduced for agricultural landlords. By 1986, as a percentage of GNP, CTT yielded less than one third of the revenue formerly produced by estate duty.

To some extent, the changes made by FA 1986 merely completed this process. Ten year cumulation was reduced to seven years and the majority of lifetime gifts made more than seven years before death were removed from charge. As in the days of estate duty, therefore, tax is now levied on death gifts and gifts made within seven years of death. In an attempt to prevent schemes whereby taxpayers could 'have their cake and eat it' (ie give property away but continue to enjoy the benefits from it) there was a further echo from estate duty in the reintroduction of rules taxing gifts with a reservation of benefit. These changes do not, however, amount to a replacement of CTT by estate duty but did represent a welding of certain estate duty rules onto the already battered corpse of CTT. The end result is simply a mess and to call this amalgam an inheritance tax is to further confuse matters since the tax is not levied on beneficiaries in proportion to what they receive from an estate and neither is it a true tax on inheritances since certain lifetime transfers are subject to charge. 'There has been no attempt at reform. The Chancellor has merely given us some reasons for making a shabby handout to the very rich. Not only has he reverted to the old estate duty, he has falsified the label' (Cedric Sandford, *Financial Times*, 26 March 1986).

Capital transfer tax was rechristened inheritance tax as from 25 July 1986 and the former legislation (the Capital Transfer Tax Act 1984) *may* be cited as the Inheritance Tax Act 1984 from that date (FA 1986 s 100). Despite the permissive nature of this section the new title for this Act will be used in this book and inheritance tax abbreviated to IHT. All references to CTT take effect as references to IHT and, as all references to estate duty became references to CTT in 1975, they now become references to IHT.

As a final curiosity it may be noted that the removal of a general hold-over election for CGT in the 1989 Budget was justified by the then Chancellor (Nigel Lawson) on a somewhat inaccurate view of the current scope of inheritance tax. In his Budget Speech, he stated that:

> 'the general hold-over relief for gifts was introduced by my predecessor in 1980, when there was still Capital Transfer Tax on lifetime gifts, in order to avoid a form of double taxation. But the tax on lifetime giving has since been abolished, and the relief is increasingly used as a simple form of tax avoidance.'

The bizarre position has now been reached whereby what was intended as a general tax on gifts has been limited (in the main) to gifts on or within seven years of death whilst a tax intended to catch capital profits may now operate to impose a tax charge on the profit deemed to be realised when a lifetime gift is made!

21 IHT—lifetime transfers

For a charge to IHT to arise, either immediately or at a future time, there must be a chargeable transfer. Whether and, if so, when tax is levied on that transfer then depends upon whether it is:

(1) *potentially exempt* in which case IHT will only be charged if the donor dies within seven years of that transfer: otherwise it is exempt.

(2) *chargeable immediately* because it does not fall within the definition of a potentially exempt transfer. In the event of the transferor dying within seven years of this chargeable transfer a supplementary charge to IHT may arise.

It is proposed to discuss first what is meant by a chargeable transfer and then to consider under what circumstances such a transfer is subject to IHT. [**21.1**]

I DEFINITION OF A 'CHARGEABLE TRANSFER'

The principal IHT charging provision is IHTA 1984 s 1 which states that 'IHT shall be charged on the value transferred by a chargeable transfer'. A chargeable transfer is then defined in IHTA 1984 s 2(1) as having three elements: there must be a transfer of value; made by an individual; which is not exempt. A transfer of value is defined in IHTA 1984 s 3(1) as any disposition which reduces the value of the transferor's estate and includes certain deemed transfers of value ('events on the happening of which tax is chargeable *as if* a transfer of value had been made'): see IHTA 1984 s 3(4). Examples of deemed transfers of value include the termination of an interest in possession in settled property (see Chapter 25) and transfers of value made by a close company which are apportioned amongst its participators [**21.121**].

'Disposition' is not defined, but the ordinary meaning is wide and includes any transfer of property whether by sale or gift; the creation of a settlement; and the release, discharge or surrender of a debt. Further, by IHTA 1984 s 3(3), it includes an omission to exercise a right. The right must presumably be a legal right and the omission must satisfy three requirements:

(1)   The estate of the person who fails to exercise the right must be reduced in value.

(2)   Someone else's estate (or a discretionary trust) must be increased in value (ie contrary to the usual principle, there must be a positive benefit to another).

(3)   The omission must be deliberate which is presumed to be the case in the absence of contrary evidence.

Examples of such omissions include failure to sue on a debt until after the limitation period has expired; failure to exercise an option either to sell or purchase property on favourable terms; and failure by a landlord to exercise his right to increase rent under a rent review clause. The omission will constitute a transfer of value at the latest time when it was possible to exercise the right, unless the taxpayer can show (1) that the omission was not deliberate but was a mistake of fact (eg he forgot) or of law (eg failure to realise that the debt had become statute barred) or (2) that it was the result of a reasonable commercial decision involving no element of bounty (eg failure to sue a debtor who was bankrupt).

The Revenue have recently intimated that s 3(3) of IHTA 1984 may apply in cases where an individual has reached pensionable age but has (for whatever reason) continued to work and not therefore drawn his pension. He has, however, settled on trust the lump sum which is payable if he dies before retiring (typically the trusts will be discretionary in form and for the benefit of his family). The attraction of such a declaration of trust is that should the lump sum be payable on his death then it will not form part of his estate and will therefore fall outside the tax net. The gist of the argument (and it should be stressed that at the time of writing the Revenue have not gone into print on this matter) is that the effect of not drawing a pension *at the earliest possible age* is that the individual has omitted to exercise his right as a result of which the trust which he has established has been increased in value. Accordingly at his death this omission to exercise the right will itself attract a tax charge. Precisely how this charge is to be computed has nowhere been stated and it may be that the attempt to invoke the section is wholly misplaced. After all, there are normally excellent commercial reasons for not taking a pension at the earliest pensionable age: most taxpayers cannot afford it! Faced with this uncertainty, however, it is likely that individuals will not for the time being create trusts of the death benefits payable under their pension policies until matters have been clarified.

Examples of dispositions which reduce the value of the transferor's estate include:

(1)   A gives his house worth £60,000 to his son B.

(2)   A sells his car worth £4,000 to his daughter C for £2,000.

(3)   A grants a lease of his factory to his nephew D at a peppercorn rent. The factory was worth £100,000; the reversion is worth only £60,000.

(4)   A is owed £1,000 by a colleague E. A releases the debt so that his estate falls in value.   [21.2]–[21.20]

II   WHAT DISPOSITIONS ARE NOT CHARGEABLE TRANSFERS?

1   **Commercial transactions** (IHTA 1984 s 10(1))

A disposition is not a transfer of value and, therefore, is not chargeable if the taxpayer can show that he did not intend to confer a gratuitous benefit on another. This provision excludes from charge commercial transactions which turn out to be bad bargains.

The onus is on the taxpayer to prove that he had no gratuitous intent. Therefore, a disposition reducing the value of the transferor's estate may trigger a liability to IHT (by analogy to a crime the disposition may be seen as the '*actus reus*' unless the taxpayer can show that he did not have the necessary '*mens rea*' for the liability to arise, ie that he had no gratuitous intent.

Notice that the transferor must not have intended to confer a gratuitous benefit on *any* person.

EXAMPLE 21.1

A purchases a holiday in the Bahamas in the name of C. A must show that he had no intention to confer a gratuitous benefit on C.

The burden of proving non-gratuitous intention differs according to whether the transaction is with a connected or unconnected person. A 'connected person' is defined as for CGT (IHTA 1984 s 270: for details see CGTA 1979 s 63 and [**14.23**]) and includes:

(1) relatives, extended for IHT to include uncle, aunt, nephew and niece;
(2) trustees, where the terms 'settlement', 'settlor' and 'trustees' have their IHT meaning (IHTA 1984 ss 43–45, see Chapter 24);
(3) partners (for certain purposes only); and
(4) certain close companies.

In order for a disposition between two *unconnected* persons not to be chargeable, the transferor must show that he had no gratuitous intent and that the transaction was made at arm's length. In the case of a disposition to a *connected* person, however, in addition to proving no gratuitous intent, the taxpayer must show that the transaction was a commercial one such as strangers might make.

EXAMPLE 21.2

T sells his house worth £70,000 to his daughter for £60,000. T will not escape a potential liability to IHT unless he can show that he never intended to confer a gratuitous benefit on his daughter and that the sale at an undervalue was the sort of transaction that he might have made with a stranger (eg that he needed money urgently and, therefore, sold at a reduced price).

The uncertainties thrown out by s 10 have long been a source of concern and accordingly the recent decision in *IRC v Spencer-Nairn* (1991) is welcome as the first authoritative guidance on the meaning of the section in the context of transfers between connected persons.

The taxpayer owned a large estate in Scotland. He had little experience on farming and estate management and therefore relied heavily on the family's adviser, a chartered accountant and actuary. In 1975 one of the farms was leased to a Jersey resident company at a rent which was largely absorbed in the costs of repairs and maintenance. Furthermore the Jersey company almost immediately demanded that the piggery buildings on the farm should be replaced at the taxpayer's expense. The adviser obtained a professional report which estimated the cost at in the region of £80,000. As the taxpayer could not afford this the adviser recommended that the farm should be sold.

He handled all matters connected with the sale and eventually it was sold for £101,350 to a second Jersey company. The farm was never advertised and the taxpayer therefore accepted this offer on the recommendation of his adviser: interestingly, neither the taxpayer nor the adviser were aware at the time that the company was a 'connected person'.

For CGT purposes the Lands Tribunal for Scotland determined the market value of the farm at £199,000 on the basis that, contrary to the adviser's view, the taxpayer was not liable to pay for the improvements demanded by the tenant. In due course (not entirely surprisingly!) the Revenue raised a CTT assessment on the basis of a transfer of value of £94,000. It was generally accepted that the taxpayer did not have a gratuitous intention: but the Revenue argued that the transfer was not such as the taxpayer would have made in an arm's length transaction with an unconnected person.

For s 10 to be relevant the transferor must have made a transfer of value (that is, he must have entered into a disposition as a result of which his estate has been diminished) and, once that is shown, the taxpayer is then forced into the position of having to show that he did not intend to make any gift *and* that what he did would satisfy the test of an objective commercial arrangement. It is understood that in recent years the Revenue have taken a restricted view (some would say a minimalistic view!) of the section. In effect they have argued that if there is a substantial fall in the transferor's estate that is the end of the matter. In *Spencer-Nairn* the Lord President dismissed arguments of this nature in a summary fashion:

> 'The fact that the transaction was for less than the open market value cannot be conclusive of the issues at this stage, otherwise the section would be deprived of its content. The gratuitous element in the transaction becomes therefore no more than a factor, which must be weighed in the balance with all the other facts and circumstances to see whether the onus which is on the transferor has been discharged.'

The case is, of course, a curiosity in that a substantially higher value had been determined by the Lands Tribunal, largely because of the view it took of the relevant Scottish agricultural holdings legislation. It had concluded that under that legislation the landlord was not obliged to erect the new piggery buildings. Clearly, had this burden rested on the landlord the actual sale price which he received would not have been unreasonable.

In applying the test in s 10 it was accepted by the Revenue that the vendor had no intention of conferring a gratuitous benefit on anyone so that the sole question for the court was whether the sale achieved was such as would have been made with a third party at arm's length. When the court came to apply this test, although it is basically drafted in objective terms, they found it necessary to incorporate subjective ingredients. The hypothetical vendor must be assumed to have held the belief of the landlord that the value of the property was diminished by his obligation to rebuild the piggeries. A wholly reasonable (and in the event mistaken) belief will not presumably be relevant. The *Spencer-Nairn* case is unusual in that the parties did not know that they were connected: in a sense therefore they were negotiating *as if* they were third parties on the open market.

> 'A good way of testing the question whether the sale was such as might be expected to be made in a transaction between persons not connected with each other is to see what persons who were unaware that they were connected with each other actually did' (Lord President Hope).

The following general conclusions are suggested on the decision:
(1) the question whether the transfer has a gratuitous intent is entirely subjective;
(2) there can be a sale at arm's length for the purposes of the second limb of s 10 even though the price realised is not approximately the same as the 'market value';
(3) in considering what amounts to an 'arm's length' sale features of the actual sale (such as the reasonably held beliefs of the vendor) must be taken into account—accordingly this limb is not a wholly objective test;
(4) the difficulty of ascertaining any sort of market value for an asset, such as the lease in this case, is all too apparent in a situation where the farm was really only of interest to the sitting tenant and he, on being approached on behalf of the landlord, has expressed no interest in acquiring the freehold. **[21.21]**

For certain property there are special rules:

a) *Reversionary interests*

A beneficiary under a settlement who purchases for value any reversionary interest in the same settlement may be charged to IHT on the price that he pays for the interest (IHTA 1984 s 55(2): for the rationale of this rule see p **[25.29]**. **[21.22]**

EXAMPLE 21.3

Property is settled on A for life, remainder to B absolutely. B has a reversionary interest. A buys B's interest for its commercial value of £50,000. A has made a chargeable transfer so that IHT may be charged on £50,000.

b) *Transfer of unquoted shares and debentures*

A transferor of unquoted shares and securities must show, in addition to lack of gratuitous intent, either that the sale was at a price freely negotiated at that time, or at such a price as might have been freely negotiated at that time (IHTA 1984 s 10(2)). In practice, such shares are rarely sold on an open market. Instead the company's articles will give shareholders a right of pre-emption if any shareholder wishes to sell. Provided that the right does not fix a price at which the shares must be offered to the remaining shareholders, but leaves it open to negotiation or professional valuation at the time of sale, the Revenue will usually accept that the sale is a *bona fide* commercial transaction satisfying the requirements of IHTA 1984 s 10(1). **[21.23]**

EXAMPLE 21.4

The articles of two private companies make the following provisions for share transfers:
(1) *ABC Ltd:* the shares shall be offered *pro rata* to the other shareholders who have an option to purchase at a price either freely negotiated or, in the event of any dispute, as fixed by an expert valuer.
(2) *DEF Ltd:* the shares shall be purchased at par value by the other shareholders. *Position of shareholders in ABC Ltd:* they will be able to take advantage of IHTA 1984 s 10(1) since the price is open to negotiation at the time of sale.

Position of shareholders in DEF Ltd: s 10(1) will not be available with the result that if the estate of a transferor falls in value (if, for instance, £1 shares have a market value of £1.50 at the time of transfer) IHT may be charged *even in the absence of gratuitous intent.* (Note that articles like those of DEF Ltd also cause problems for business property relief—see [**23.45**].

c) *Partnerships*

Partners are not connected persons for the purpose of transferring partnership assets from one to another.   [**21.24**]

EXAMPLE 21.5

A and B are partners sharing profits and owning assets in the ratio 50:50. They agree to alter their asset sharing ratio to 25:75 because A intends to devote less time to the business in the future. Although A's estate falls (he has transferred half of his partnership share to B), he will escape any possible liability to IHT under IHTA 1984 s 10(1) if he proves a lack of gratuitous intent. Assuming that A and B are not connected otherwise than as partners, lack of gratuitous intent will be presumed, since such transactions are part of the commercial arrangements between partners.

2   **Other non-chargeable dispositions**

Excluded property (IHTA 1984 s 6)   No IHT is charged on excluded property (see Chapter 27). The most important categories are property outside the UK owned by someone domiciled outside the UK and reversionary interests under a trust.   [**21.25**]

Exempt transfers (IHTA 1984 Part II)   Exempt transfers are not chargeable transfers and hence are not subject to charge (see Chapter 23). The most common exemptions are:
(1)   transfers between spouses, whether inter vivos or on death;
(2)   transfers up to £3,000 each tax year;
(3)   outright gifts of up to £250 pa to any number of different persons.   [**21.26**]

Waiver of remuneration and dividends (IHTA 1984 ss 14, 15)   A waiver or repayment of salaries and other remuneration assessable under Schedule E by a director or employee is not a chargeable transfer provided that the Schedule E assessment has not become final; the remuneration is formally waived (eg by deed) or if paid, repaid to the employer; and the employer adjusts his profits or losses to take account of the waiver or repayment.
    Similarly, a person may, in the 12 months before the right accrued (which time is identified in accordance with usual company law rules), waive a dividend on shares without liability to IHT. A general waiver of all future dividends is only effective for dividends payable for up to 12 months after the waiver and must, therefore, be renewed each year (see Chapter 32, *Example 32.6*, for an illustration of when a waiver of dividends will prove advantageous).   [**21.27**]

Voidable transfers (IHTA 1984 s 150)   Where a transfer is voidable (eg for duress or undue influence) and is set aside, it is treated for IHT purposes as if it had never been made, provided that a claim is made by the taxpayer. As a result any IHT paid on the transfer may be reclaimed. Tax on chargeable transfers made after the voidable transfer, but before it was avoided, must be recalculated and IHT refunded, if necessary. **[21.28]-[21.40]**

III WHEN ARE LIFETIME TRANSFERS SUBJECT TO IHT? THE POTENTIALLY EXEMPT TRANSFER (PET)

If the taxpayer makes a chargeable inter vivos transfer IHT may be charged at once: alternatively the transfer may be potentially exempt (a PET). In the latter case, IHT is only levied if the taxpayer dies within seven years of the transfer: otherwise the transfer is exempt. During the 'limbo' period (viz the period of seven years following the transfer or, if shorter, the period ending with the transferor's death) the PET is treated as if it were exempt (IHTA 1984 s 3A(5)) so that despite the legislation calling the transfer potentially exempt it would be more accurate to refer to it as potentially chargeable. With the exception of transfers involving discretionary trusts and transfers to companies the majority of lifetime transfers today fall within the definition of a PET. **[21.41]**

1 What is a PET?

A PET is by defined in IHTA 1984 s 3A(1) (inserted by FA 1986 and widened by F(No 2)A 1987). It must satisfy two preliminary requirements: first, it must be made by an individual on or after 18 March 1986; and secondly, the transfer must apart from this section be a chargeable transfer. If these requirements are satisfied the following three transfers then fall within the definition: **[21.42]**

a) *Outright gifts to individuals*

A transfer which is a gift to another individual is a PET so long as either the property transferred becomes comprised in the donee's estate or, by virtue of that transfer, the estate of the donee is increased (s 3A(2)). **[21.43]**

> **EXAMPLE 21.6**
> (1) Adam gives Bertham a gold hunter watch worth £5,000: this is a PET.
> (2) Claude pays Debussy's wine bill of £10,000. Although property is not transferred into the estate of Debussy, the result of Claude's transfer of value is to increase Debussy's estate by paying off his debt. Accordingly this also is a PET.
> (3) Edgar who owned 51% of the shares in Frome Ltd transfers 2% of the company's shares to Grace who had previously owned no shares in the company. Edgar suffers a substantial drop in the value of his estate (since he loses control of Frome Ltd) which exceeds the benefit received by Grace. It would appear, however, that the whole transfer is a PET (this view is accepted by the Revenue: see the booklet IHT 1 at p 8 (Eg 5)).

b) *Creation of accumulation and maintenance trusts or trusts for the disabled*

These trusts are fully discussed in Chapter 26. In both cases, the transfer which establishes the trust is only treated as a PET to the extent that the value transferred is attributable to property which by virtue of the transfer becomes settled. **[21.44]**

EXAMPLE 21.7

(1) A settles £100,000 in favour of his infant grandchildren on accumulation and maintenance trusts. This transfer is a PET.

(2) B settles an insurance policy, taken out on his own life, on accumulation and maintenance trusts. (This transfer is a PET.) He subsequently pays premiums on that policy and, although the payments are transfer of value, they do not increase the property in the settlement and are not, therefore, PETs. B should, therefore, consider making a gift of that sum each year to the trustees to enable them to pay the premiums on the policy.

c) *Interest in possession settlements*

Originally the *inter vivos* creation of fixed interest trusts (eg life interest trusts) and chargeable events connected with such trusts were excluded from the definition of a PET. From 17 March 1987, however, the PET definition was widened to include certain of these events.

As will be seen in Chapter 25, a beneficiary entitled to an interest in possession is treated as owning (for IHT purposes) the capital of the trust in which that interest subsists. Hence, the *inter vivos* creation of such a trust is treated as a gift to that person and the *inter vivos* termination of his interest as a gift by him to the person or persons next entitled. In *Example 21.8(1)* below, for instance, Willie is treated as if he had made a gift to Wilma (the next life tenant). Taking different facts, if on the termination of the relevant interest in possession the settled property is then held on discretionary trusts, the lifetime termination of that interest cannot be a PET, since the PET definition excludes the creation of trusts without interests in possession (see d) below).   [21.45]

EXAMPLE 21.8

Wilbur Wacker settles £100,000 on trust for his brother Willie for life, thereafter to his sister Wilma for life, with remainder to his godson Wilberforce. Wilbur's transfer is a PET. Subsequently he settles a life insurance policy on the same trusts and continues to pay the premiums to the insurance company (as in *Example 21.7(2)* above). The premiums will be PETs since the more restrictive definition of a PET in the context of the accumulation and maintenance trust does not apply to fixed trusts. Assume also that the following events occur:

(1) Willie surrenders his life interest on his fiftieth birthday: this deemed transfer of the property in the trust is a PET made by Willie.

(2) Wilma purchases Wilberforce's remainder interest for £60,000 (see *Example 21.3* above); this transfer by Wilma is a PET.

d) *The limits of PETs*

Although the majority of lifetime transfers fall within the PET definition, there remain two main categories which are immediately chargeable and, because of the wording of s 3A, there are a number of traps which may catch other transfers.

(1) *The creation of no interest in possession trusts:* A charge may be levied on the creation of, eg, discretionary trusts and, in addition, the anniversary and exit charges may occur during the life of the trust (see Chapter 26).

(2) 'Where, under any provision of this Act other than s 52, tax is in any circumstances to be charged as if a transfer of value had been made, that transfer shall be taken to be a transfer which is not a PET.'

This provision ensures that PETs are limited to lifetime gifts because it excludes the transfer deemed to take place immediately before death and it also means that tax charges will still arise when close companies are used to obtain an IHT advantage (see [**21.121**]).

(3) In the case of accumulation and maintenance and disabled trusts property must be transferred directly into the settlement if the PET definition is to be satisfied (see *Example 21.7(2)*).

(4) Jack pays the school fees of his infant grandson Jude or Simon buys a holiday for his uncle Albert. In neither case does property become comprised in the estate of another by virtue of the transfer, and neither Jude's nor Albert's estate is increased as a result of the transfer. Accordingly, both Jack and Simon have made immediately chargeable transfers of value (by contrast, a direct gift to each donee would ensure that the transfers were PETs).

(5) The reservation of benefit provisions are analysed in Chapter 22 but it should be noted that, when they apply, property which has been given away is brought back into the donor's estate at death. The original gift will normally have been a PET and, therefore, there is a possibility of a double charge to IHT should the donor die within seven years of that gift at a time when property is still subject to a reservation. (This double charge may be relieved by regulations discussed in Appendix VII.) [**21.46**]

e) *CGT tie-in*

CGT hold-over relief continues to be available in cases where a gift falls outside the PET definition provided that it is made *by* an individual or trustees to an individual or trustees. Both the creation and termination of a discretionary trust satisfy this wording so that the CGT that would otherwise be levied on the chargeable assets involved may be held over. By contrast, gifts to close companies do not involve gifts between individuals and trustees so that, unless the property given away is business property within the definition in CGTA 1979 s 126, hold-over relief will not be available (for the CGT position on gifts generally, see Chapter 17). [**21.47**]

f) *The taxation of PETs*

As already noted there is no charge to tax at the time when the PET is made and for all purposes that transfer is assumed to be exempt unless the transferor dies within the following seven years. There is, therefore, no duty to inform the Revenue that a PET has been made and for cumulation purposes it is ignored. All of this, however, changes if the donor dies within the following seven years: the former PET then becomes chargeable; must be reported; and the transfer must be entered into the taxpayer's cumulative total at the time when it was made. As a result, IHT on chargeable lifetime transfers may need to be recalculated (and may in any event attract a supplementary charge to tax). These consequences are illustrated in *Example 21.9* and fully explained in Chapter 22. [**21.48**]–[**21.60**]

EXAMPLE 21.9

(1) On 1 May 1987 Ian gave £3,000 to Joyce.
(2) On 1 May 1988 he settled £500,000 on discretionary trusts in favour of his family.
(3) On 1 May 1989 he gave £60,000 to his daughter.

(4)   On 1 May 1991 he died.

Ian, therefore, dies within seven years of all three transfers. The transfer in 1987 ((1) above) is, however, exempt since it is covered by his annual exemption (see [**23.2**]).

Transfer (2) was a chargeable lifetime transfer and attracted an IHT charge when made. Because of Ian's death within seven years a supplementary IHT charge will arise (the calculation of this additional IHT caused by death is explained in Chapter 22).

Transfer (3) was a PET. Because of Ian's death it is rendered chargeable and is subject to IHT. Further, Ian's cumulative total of chargeable transfers made in the seven years before death becomes (assuming the non-availability of the £3,000 annual exemption in both the years) £560,000. Had Ian lived until 1 May 1996 this PET would have become an exempt transfer (ie free from all IHT).

IV   ON WHAT VALUE IS IHT CALCULATED?

1   General: what is the cost of the gift?

Where an individual makes a chargeable disposition (including a PET rendered chargeable by death within seven years) IHT is charged on the amount by which his estate has fallen in value as a result of the transfer. For these purposes, a person's estate is the aggregate of all the property to which he is beneficially entitled (IHTA 1984 s 5(1)); it includes property over which he has a general power of appointment (IHTA 1984 s 5(2), because he could appoint the property to himself), but not property owned in a fiduciary or representative capacity: eg as trustee or PR.

In theory, therefore, the transferor's estate must be valued both before and after the transfer and the difference taxed. In practice, it is normally unnecessary to do this since the transferor's estate will only fall by the value of the gift. However, the cost to the transferor of the gift may be more than the value of the property handed over.

EXAMPLE 21.10

A gives £50,000 to a discretionary trust. His estate falls in value by £50,000 *plus* the IHT that he has to pay, ie £50,000 must be grossed up at the appropriate rate of IHT to discover the full cost of the gift to A (see Section VI).

Were he to give the trust land worth £50,000 his estate falls in value by the value of the property (£50,000) and by any CGT, and costs of transfer (such as conveyancing fees) that A pays. It also will fall by the IHT payable.

However, IHTA 1984 s 5(4) provides that, for the purpose of calculating the cost of the gift, the transferor's estate is deemed to drop by the value of the property plus the IHT paid by the transferor but *not* by any other tax nor by any incidental costs of transfer. Thus, in *Example 21.10*, A's estate drops in value by the value of the land and by the IHT that A pays.

Where the donees (the trustees in the above example) agree to pay the IHT, the overall cost of the gift is reduced since A's estate will fall only by the value of the property transferred. The trustees will be taxed on that fall in value.

EXAMPLE 21.11

A gives property worth £50,000 to the trustees. If A pays the IHT, the £50,000 is a net gift and if A is charged to IHT at 20% then that rate of tax is chargeable on the larger (gross) figure (here £62,500) which after payment of IHT at 20% leaves £50,000 in the trustees' hands.

50000 ÷ 0.8 =   62500 - gross figure

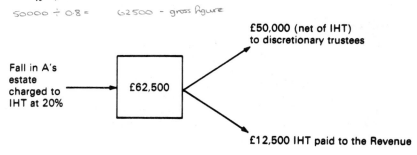

If, in this example, the trustees had paid the IHT the result would be:

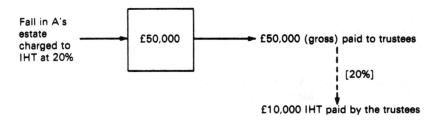

IHT is generally calculated on the fall in value of the transferor's estate not on the increase in value in the transferee's estate. This can work to the taxpayer's advantage, or disadvantage. **[21.61]**

EXAMPLE 21.12

Compare

(1) A gives B a single Picasso plate which is worth £20,000; B pays any IHT. In fact, B owns the remaining plates in the set (currently worth £150,000) and the acquisition of this final plate will give B's set a market value of £200,000. Although B's estate has increased in value by £50,000, IHT will only be charged on the fall in value in A's estate (£20,000).

(2) A owns 51% of the shares in A Ltd. This controlling interest is worth £100,000. He gives 2% of the shares to B who holds no other shares. 2% of the shares are worth (say) £2 but A, having lost control, will find that his estate has fallen by far more than £2—say to £80,000. It will be the loss to A (£20,000) not the gain to B (£2) which is taxed.

2 Problems in valuing an estate

Any calculation of IHT on a transfer will require a valuation of the property transferred (see generally IHTA 1984 Pt VI). As a general rule it is valued at the price that it would fetch on the open market. No reduction is made for the fact that the sale of a large quantity of a particular asset might cause the price to fall (IHTA 1984 s 160). **[21.62]**

a) *Examples of the value transferred*

Liabilities Incumbrances affecting property (to the extent that they were incurred for money or money's worth) reduce the value of the property (IHTA 1984 s 5(5)).   **[21.63]**

> **EXAMPLE 21.13**
>
> A gives his house to his son B. The market value of the house is £80,000, but it is subject to a mortgage to the Halifax Building Society of £25,000 which B agrees to discharge. Hence, the property is valued for IHT purposes at £55,000. (This position will commonly arise when a death gift of a house is made since, in the absence of a contrary intention stated in the will, the Administration of Estates Act 1925 s 35 provides that debts charged on property by the deceased must be borne by the legatee or donee of that property.)

Co-ownership of land If land worth £100,000 is owned equally by A and B, it might be assumed that the value of both half shares is £50,000. In fact the shares will be worth less than £50,000 since it will be difficult to sell such an interest on the open market (see the Lands Tribunal case of *Wight v IRC* (1984)). Whoever purchases will have to share the property with the other co-owner and in practice a discount of 10–15% is reasonable. (Note that because of the related property rules—discussed below—there will be no discount when the co-owners are husband and wife.)   **[21.64]**

Shares and securities When quoted shares and securities are transferred, their value is taken (as for CGT; see Chapter 14) as the smaller of the 'quarter up' and 'mid price' calculation.

Valuation of unquoted shares and securities is a large and complex topic beyond the scope of this book. A number of factors are taken into account, eg the company's profit record, its prospects, its assets and its liabilities. The percentage of shares which is being valued is a major factor. A majority shareholding of ordinary voting shares carries certain powers to control the affairs of the company (it will, for instance, give the owner the power to pass an ordinary resolution). A shareholding representing more than 75% confers greater powers, eg the power to pass special resolutions. Correspondingly, a shareholder who owns 50% or less of the voting power (and, even more so, a shareholding of 25% or less) has far fewer powers (he is a minority shareholder). In valuing majority and substantial minority holdings it appears that the Revenue accept a net asset valuation as the starting point and then apply a discount (between 10–15%) in the case of minority holdings.

In the case of shares and securities which are dealt in on the Unlisted Securities Market, although recent bargains through that market will be taken as a starting point, other factors may lead to a different value being finally adopted (see SP 18/80). When the shares are subject to a restriction upon their transfer (eg pre-emption rights) they are valued on the basis of a sale on the open market with the purchaser being permitted to purchase the shares, but then being subject to the restrictions (*IRC v Crossman* (1937) and see **[21.69]**).   **[21.65]**

b) *Special rules*

IHTA 1984 Part VI Chapter 1 contains special valuation rules designed to counter tax avoidance.   **[21.66]**

Related property (IHTA 1984 s 161) IHT savings could be engineered by splitting the ownership of certain assets (typically shares, sets of chattels, and interests in land) amongst two or more taxpayers. The saving would occur when the total value of the individual assets resulting from the split was less than the value of the original (undivided) asset. A pair of Ming vases, for instance, would be worth more as a pair than the combined values of the two individual vases. When it is desired to split the ownership of such assets, however, it should be remembered that the transfer needed to achieve this result will normally be potentially chargeable and, as any tax will be charged on the entire fall in value of the transferor's estate, no tax saving will result. Inter-spouse transfers are, however, free of IHT and hence, were it not for the related property provisions, could be used to achieve substantial savings by asset splitting. To frustrate such schemes the related property rules provide that, in appropriate circumstances, an asset must be valued together with other related property and a proportion of that total value is then attributed to the asset (compare the CGT provisions on asset splitting: [**14.24**].

EXAMPLE 21.14

X Ltd is a private company which has a share capital of £100 divided into 100 £1 shares. Assume that shares giving control (ie more than 50%) are worth £100 each and minority shareholdings £20 per share. If Alf owns 51% of the shares the value of his holding is £5,100 (£100 per share) but, if that 51% holding were split so that Alf has 25% and Bess 26% the value of those holdings (at £20 per share) would be £500 and £520 respectively.

Suppose that Alf and Bess are married. Alf transfers 26% of the company's shares to Bess. Alf becomes a minority shareholder with shares worth £500 but pays no IHT because transfers between spouses are exempt. Bess also has a minority holding worth £520. If Alf and Bess then each transfer their respective holdings to their son Fred, they may be liable to pay IHT on a value of £1,020, whereas if Alf had transferred his 51% holding to Fred directly he would be potentially liable to tax on £5,100. To prevent this IHT saving Alf and Bess's holdings are valued together as a majority holding worth £5,100. Accordingly, when Alf transfers his 25% holding to Fred this is 25/51 of the combined holding and is valued, therefore, at £2,500 (ie 25/51 of £5,100). Once Alf has disposed of his holding, Bess's 26% holding is then valued in the normal way on a subsequent transfer: ie as a minority holding worth £520 (in certain cases the associated operations rule or the '*Ramsay* principle' might be invoked; see [**21.81**]).

Inter-spouse transfers are the main instance of transfers which may attract the related property provisions. However, they also catch the other exempt transfers (eg to a charity or political party) in circumstances where, without such provisions, the transferor could obtain a similar tax advantage.

EXAMPLE 21.15

As *Example 21.14*, Alf owns 51% of the shares in X Ltd. He transfers 2% to a charity paying no IHT because the transfer is exempt. He then transfers the remaining 49% to Fred. Alf is a minority shareholder and the loss to his estate is only £980 compared with £5,100 if he had transferred the entire 51% holding directly to Fred. Some time later Fred might purchase the 2% holding from the charity for its market value of £40. Unless the two transfers (ie to the charity and to Fred) are more than five years apart, the charity's holding is related to Alf's so that his 49% holding is valued at £4,900 on the transfer to Fred.

The related property rules also apply to the deemed transfer on death subject to the proviso that if the property is sold within three years after the death for a price lower than the related property valuation, the property may be revalued on death ignoring the related property rules (see Chapter 22).   **[21.67]**

Property subject to an option (IHTA 1984 s 163)   When property is transferred as a result of the exercise of an option or other similar right created for full consideration, there should be no liability to IHT.

Where an option is granted for less than full consideration, however, there will be a chargeable transfer or a PET at that time and there may be a further charge when the option is exercised. A credit will be given against the value of the property transferred, when the option is exercised, for any consideration actually received and for any value that was charged to IHT on the grant of the option.   **[21.68]**

EXAMPLE 21.16

(1) Harold grants Daisy an option to purchase his house in three years' time for its present value of £12,000. Daisy pays £3,000 for the option. When Daisy exercises the option three years later the house is worth £25,000.

Harold has not made a transfer of value and is not liable to IHT since (as the option was granted for full consideration) the house is only worth £12,000 to him.

(2) Assume that Daisy gives no consideration for the option which is worth £3,000. IHT may, therefore, be chargeable on that sum. On the exercise of the option IHT may be payable on £13,000 (£25,000—£12,000) minus the sum that was chargeable on the grant of the option (£3,000). Hence, any charge will be on £10,000.

Property subject to a liability   The so-called *Crossman principle* (see **[21.65]**), which applies in valuing shares subject to transfer restrictions, has recently been applied in valuing a leasehold flat subject to a contingent liability. In *Alexander v IRC* (1991) a Barbican flat was purchased under the 'right to buy' provisions of the Housing Act 1980. All or part of the discount under that legislation had to be repaid in the event of the flat being sold within five years of its purchase. The taxpayer, however, died in the first year. The Court of Appeal—following *Crossman*—held that for valuation purposes the open market value must be taken even though the particular property could not be sold on the open market. In this case, the flat was to be valued on the basis of what a purchaser would pay to stand in the deceased's shoes: ie taking over the liability to repay the discount should he sell the proeprty within the prescribed period.   **[21.69]**

Non-assignable agricultural tenancies   The vexed question of whether a non-assignable agricultural tenancy has any value was decided in the affirmative by the Lands Tribunal for Scotland on *Crossman* principles (see generally **[23.56]** and *Capital Taxes*, 1985, p 13). Once it is accepted that *Crossman* applies to require an assumed sale then the question is merely one of fixing the correct value. In this Scottish case, *Baird's Executors v IRC* (1991), this matter was not argued and therefore the 'robust approach' of the District Valuer in taking 25% of the open market value was accepted (for a discussion of considerations which should be relevant, see *Capital Taxes News*, 1991, p 211: it is understood that a test case is to be brought in England).   **[21.70]**.

Life assurance policies Life assurance policies normally involve the payment of annual premiums in return for an eventual lump sum payable either on retirement or on death. Special valuation rules which do not apply on death (see [22.8]) are laid down by IHTA 1984 s 167 to prevent a tax saving when the benefit of such a policy is assigned.   **[21.71]–[21.80]**

EXAMPLE 21.17

A gives the benefit of a policy effected on his own life to B when its open market value is £10,000. A has paid five annual premiums of £5,000, so that the cost of providing the policy is £25,000 to date. For IHT purposes the policy is valued at the higher of its market value or the cost of providing the policy. As a result tax may be charged on £25,000.

V 'ASSOCIATED OPERATIONS' (IHTA 1984 s 268)

The legislation contains complicated provisions which apply to any type of property, to prevent a taxpayer from reducing the value of a gift or the IHT chargeable by a series of associated operations.
'Associated operations' are defined in IHTA 1984 s 268 as:

'(1) ... any two or more operations of any kind, being—
   (a) operations which affect the same property, or one of which affects some property and the other or others of which affect property which represents, whether directly or indirectly, that property, or income arising from that property, or any property representing accumulations of any such income; or (b) any two operations of which one is effected with reference to the other, or with a view to enabling the other to be effected or facilitating its being effected, and any further operation having a like relation to any of those two, and so on; whether those operations are effected by the same person or different persons, and whether or not they are simultaneous; and "operation" includes an omission.
(2) The granting of a lease for full consideration in money or money's worth shall not be taken to be associated with any operation effected more than three years after the grant, and no operation effected on or after 27 March 1974 shall be taken to be associated with an operation effected before that date.
(3) Where a transfer of value is made by associated operations carried out at different times it shall be treated as made at the time of the last of them; but where any one or more of the earlier operations also constitute a transfer of value made by the same transferor, the value transferred by the earlier operations shall be treated as reducing the value transferred by all the operations taken together, except to the extent that the transfer constituted by the earlier operations but not that made by all the operations taken together is exempt under s 18 (spouse exemption).'

The definition is extremely wide, and the Revenue have issued no general guidelines as to when they intend to invoke it. (Compare similar difficulties caused by the Ramsay principle which creates a judicial associated operations rule: see Chapter 31.) In *IRC v Macpherson* (1989) trustees entered into an agreement which reduced the value of the settled property and subsequently appointed that property in favour of a beneficiary. The House of Lords held that the two transactions were associated operations and that they formed part of an arrangement designed to confer a gratuitous benefit, this benefit being conferred by the appointment (see further [25.30]). The case affords some guidance on what events can be treated as part of a series of operations affecting the same property. Lord Jauncey (in a speech with which the other

Law Lords concurred) identified the boundaries of the associated operations provisions as follows:

> 'If an individual took steps which devalued his property on a Monday with a view to making a gift thereof on Tuesday, he would fail to satisfy the requirements of s 20(4) (now s 10(1)) because the act of devaluation and the gift would be considered together ... The definition in s 44 (now s 268) is extremely wide and is capable of covering a multitude of events affecting the same property which might have little or no apparent connection between them. It might be tempting to assume that any event which fell within this wide definition should be taken into account in determining what constituted a transaction for the purposes of s 20(4). However, counsel for the Crown accepted, rightly in my view, that some limitation must be imposed. Counsel for the trustees informed your Lordships that there was no authority on the meaning of the words "associated operations" in the context of capital transfer tax legislation but he referred to a decision of the Court of Appeal in Northern Ireland, *Herdman v IRC* (1967) in which the tax avoidance provisions of ss 412 and 413 of the Income Tax Act 1952 had been considered. Read short, s 412(1) provided that a charge to income tax arose where the individual had by means of a transfer of assets either alone or in conjunction with associated operations acquired rights whereby he could enjoy a particular description of income. Lord MacDermott CJ upheld a submission by the taxpayer that the only associated operations which were relevant to the subsection were those by means of which, in conjunction with the transfer, a taxpayer could enjoy the income and did not include associated operations taking place after the transfer had conferred upon the taxpayer the power to enjoy income. If the extended meaning of "transaction" is read into the opening words of s 20(4) the wording becomes:
>
> > "A disposition is not a transfer of value if it is shown that it was not intended, and was not made in a transaction includi:g a series of transactions and any associated operations intended, to confer any gratuitous benefit ..."
>
> So read it is clear that the intention to confer gratuitous benefit qualifies both transactions and associated operations. If an associated operation is not intended to confer such a benefit it is not relevant for the purpose of the subsection. That is not to say that it must necessarily *per se* confer a benefit but it must form a part of and contribute to a scheme which does confer such a benefit.'

As in *Craven v White* the House of Lords in *Macpherson* can be seen to be imposing limits on apparently wide-ranging provisions: in the case of s 268 the limitations are in thbbblbe form of only considering relevant transactions—ie transactions undertaken in relation to the property which are in some way linked together. It is worth noting that under s 268 there is no requirement that the series of transactions must have been pre-planned.

When the section applies, it enables the Revenue to tax as one transaction any number of separate transactions (including omissions) which, when looked at together, reduce the value of the taxpayer's estate. The transactions need not be carried out by the same person nor need they be simultaneous. Apparently the lifetime act of making a will can amount to an associated operation although the subsequent death will not be such an operation! (*Bambridge v IRC* (1955)). Intestacy would appear to be covered by the reference to an omission.

Section 268(1)(a) is concerned with the channelling of gifts, in particular between spouses (where the transfers are exempt).

In such dispositions the transferor is deemed to have made a transfer equivalent to the value of all the operations at the time when the last of them is made. If one of the operations involved a transfer of value by the same transferor, he is entitled to a credit for that value against the aggregate value of the whole operation unless the transfer was anyway exempt because it was made to a spouse (IHTA 1984 s 268(3)).

EXAMPLE 21.18

It is certain that H will die shortly whereas his wife is in good health. Any transfer H makes to his son (S), although a PET, will, therefore, be made chargeable by his death. Accordingly, he transfers £20,000 to his wife (W). W then passes the £20,000 to the son. Under IHTA 1984 s 268(1)(a) the Revenue can claim that the transfers (H to W and W to S) are 'associated'. H is deemed to have made a transfer of value equivalent to the value transferred by all the associated operations, ie £40,000, £20,000 (H to W) and £20,000 (W to S). However, on his death, IHT is only chargeable on £20,000 as his transfer of £20,000 to W is exempt as an inter-spouse transfer. It is unclear whether under s 268(3) IHT could also be charged on her gift of £20,000 to S. The preferable view is no since the one charge on H should cover all the relevant transfers; but assume that H also gives £3,000 to his son which is exempt by his annual exemption. All three transfers (H to S, H to W and W to S) are associated at the time of the last of them (W to S). Under IHTA 1984 s 268(3) on H's death IHT is not charged on the aggregate value of all three transfers (ie £43,000) but on £20,000 only because he has a credit for any previous (associated) transfers of value (the £3,000 transfer to S) and the inter-spouse transfer of £20,000.

Commenting upon the associated operation provisions, Mr Joel Barnett (then Chief Secretary to the Treasury) stated that they would only be used to attack inter-spouse transfers in blatant tax avoidance cases

'where the transfer by a husband to a wife was made on condition that the wife should at once use the money to make gifts to others, a charge on a gift by the husband might arise under s 268.' (Official Report, Standing Committee A; 13 February 1975 col 1596.)

The same approach is taken by the Revenue in relation to the possible application of the *Ramsay* principle (see Chapter 31).

Thus, spouses may channel gifts in order to utilise the poorer spouse's exemptions, eg the £3,000 annual exemption and the exemption for gifts on marriage of up to £5,000, and to obtain income tax and CGT benefits resulting from the independent taxation of spouses.

EXAMPLE 21.19

H is wealthy, his wife, W, is poor. Both wish to use up their full IHT exemptions and to provide for their son who is getting married. It would be sensible for the following scheme to be adopted:
Stage 1   H transfers £11,000 to W which is exempt as an inter-spouse transfer. This will enable W to utilise two years' annual exemption of £3,000 plus the £5,000 marriage exemption.
Stage 2   Both spouses then each give £11,000 to the son.

Apparently s 268 will not be invoked so long as the gift to W was not made on condition that she pass the property to S.

IHTA 1984 s 268 also enables the Revenue to put two separate transactions together.

EXAMPLE 21.20

(1) A owns two paintings which together are worth £60,000, but individually they are worth £20,000. A sells one picture for £20,000. This is a commercial transaction (s 10(1)) and, therefore, not subject to IHT. A then sells the second picture, also for £20,000, to the same purchaser.

As a result of the two transactions, the purchaser has paid only £40,000 but received value of £60,000 and A's estate has fallen in value by £20,000. The effect of s 268(1)(b) is that the Revenue can put the two transactions together and in appropriate cases tax the loss to his estate (ie £20,000) provided there is a gratuitous intent. Where the transactions are with a connected person the presumption of gratuitous intent will be hard to rebut. If both sales were to a commercial art gallery, however, it is likely that, despite s 268, no tax would be chargeable.

Contrast: assume as above that A owns two paintings but wishes to give one to his son. Accordingly he settles that picture on trust for himself for life, remainder to his son. No IHT is charged on creation of that settlement since A is treated as owning the picture (see Chapter 25). A then surrenders his life interest and as a result tax appears to be chargeable on the value of the picture in the settlement: ie on £20,000 only (IHTA 1984 s 52(1)). Could it be argued by an application of s 268 that A has directly disposed of the picture to his son so that £40,000 is subject to IHT? (Alternatively might *Furniss v Dawson* apply to produce that result?)

(2) A owns freehold premises worth £200,000. A gives the property to his nephew (N) in two stages. He grants a tenancy of the premises to N at a full market rent thereby incurring no potential liability to IHT. Two years later, he gives the freehold to N which being subject to a lease is worth only £100,000. Hence, there is a potential liability for IHT on £100,000 only, although A has given away property worth £200,000.

Under IHTA 1984 s 268(1)(b) the Revenue can tax the overall loss to his estate. IHTA 1984 s 268(2), however, provides an exemption where more than three years have elapsed between the grant of the lease for full consideration and the gift or sale of the reversion.

(3) A wants to give his annual exemption of £3,000 to B each year. Although he has no spare cash, he owns a house worth £30,000. Accordingly, A sells the house to B for £30,000 which is left outstanding as a loan repayable on demand. Each year A releases as much of the outstanding loan as is covered by his annual exemption. After ten years the loan is written off. The house is then worth £40,000 (the scheme is generally known as a 'sale and mortgage back'). A loan which is repayable on demand is not chargeable to IHT (see [**21.108**]) and the release of part of the loan each year, although a transfer of value, is covered by A's annual exemption.

These may be associated operations under IHTA 1984 s 268(1)(b). The Revenue have intimated that they would regard the overall transaction as a transfer of value by A of the asset at its market value (£40,000) at the date when the loan is written off. A would have a credit for his previous transfers of value, ie £30,000 (s 268(3)) and there would, therefore, be a potential charge to IHT on the capital appreciation element only, ie £10,000.

For the Revenue's view in *Example 21.20(3)* to be upheld they would have to show that the donor retained ownership of the house throughout the period of ten years. In support, it could be argued that the transferor's estate must be valued immediately after the disposition and that in the case of a disposition effected by associated operations that means at the time of the last of those operations (see IHTA 1984 ss 3(1), 268(3)). The counter-argument is that the value transferred is the difference between the value of the house immediately before the first stage in the operation (ie £30,000) and the value of the debt after the last operation (nil) so that the loss to the transferor is £30,000 all of which is covered by the annual exemptions.

In such a controversial area the practical advice must be to tread warily especially as the *Ramsay* principle may be used to attack any 'scheme' (see further Chapter 31). **[21.81]–[21.100]**

VI   HOW IS IHT CALCULATED?

1   **The principle of cumulation**

Each individual must keep a cumulative account of all the chargeable transfers made by him because IHT is levied not at a flat rate but at progressively higher rates according to that total. It is the cumulative amount which fixes the rate of IHT for each subsequent chargeable transfer. For transfers on and after 6 April 1991, IHT is charged at a rate of 0% for transfers up to a total of £140,000 and at a single rate of 40% thereafter. Lifetime transfers are, however, taxed at half rates so that the charge in such cases is at either 0% or 20%.

From 18 March 1986 cumulation has only been required over a seven year period. This restricted period contrasts strikingly with the original CTT legislation (in 1975) which had provided for unlimited cumulation (a ten year period was introduced in 1981).

EXAMPLE 21.21

(Ignoring exemptions, reliefs and assuming that current IHT rates apply throughout.)

A makes the following chargeable transfers (ie none of the transfers is a PET):

(1) *June 1988*   £100,000
Applying the half rates of IHT the £100,000 falls within the nil rate band.

(2) *June 1991*   £50,000
The starting point in using the table is £100,000 which was the point reached by the gift in 1988 and IHT is charged at rates applicable to transfers from £100,000 to £150,000:
ie first £40,000 at nil%
the final £10,000 at 20%.

(3) *July 1996*   £100,000
The 1988 gift of £100,000 drops out of the account as it was made more than seven years before. IHT is, therefore, charged at rates applicable to transfers from £50,000 to £150,000.

The change in cumulation resulting from the switch to inheritance tax may be illustrated as follows:

EXAMPLE 21.22

(1) A makes the following chargeable transfers:
on 17 March 1978 = £100,000
on 17 March 1986 = £50,000
Under the CTT regime tax on the £50,000 transfer is cumulated with the earlier £100,000 (made within 10 years).

(2) As above, save that the second transfer occurs on 18 March 1986. Seven year cumulation was introduced from 18 March so that the earlier transfer drops out of the taxpayer's cumulative total and hence the £50,000 is covered by A's nil rate band.

It must be stressed that the above discussion has been concerned solely with the cumulation of chargeable lifetime transfers since PETs are presumed to be exempt unless and until the transferor dies within seven years of the transfer. The effect of that death is to render the PET a chargeable transfer (thereby necessitating the payment of IHT) and, in addition, a supplementary charge may be levied on any chargeable transfers made in the seven years before death.

Finally, in cases where the deceased taxpayer had made a mixture of chargeable transfers and PETs in the seven years before death, tax paid on the chargeable transfers may have to be recalculated because the PETs are converted into chargeable transfers from the date when they were made.

EXAMPLE 21.23

T makes the following transfers of value:
Year 1 PET of £75,000
Year 2 chargeable transfer of £150,000
Year 4 T dies.

IHT charged on the chargeable transfer in *Year 2* will have been calculated ignoring the PET made in *Year 1*. Accordingly it will have proceeded on the basis that T had made no prior chargeable transfers. As a result of his death in Year 4, however, the PET of £75,000 is made chargeable in *Year 1* so that IHT on the *Year 2* transfer must be recalculated on the basis that when it was made T had made a prior chargeable transfer of £75,000. Hence it is recalculated on the IHT rates applicable from £75,000 to £225,000.

The impact of death on chargeable lifetime transfers and PETs is considered fully in Chapter 22.   **[21.101]**

2 Grossing-up

As already stated IHT is charged on the fall in value in the transferor's estate. Accordingly, tax is charged on the value of the gift *and* on the IHT on that gift, when the tax is paid by the transferor. To understand this principle, take the example of A, who has made no previous chargeable transfers and who settles £155,000 on discretionary trusts. IHT payable by A can be calculated as follows:

Step 1 Deduct from the transfer any part of it that is exempt. A has an available annual exemption of £3,000 (see further Chapter 23): there is, therefore, a chargeable transfer of £152,000.

Step 2 Calculate the rate(s) of IHT applicable to the chargeable transfer. The first £140,000 falls within the nil rate band and, therefore, IHT is payable only on the balance of £12,000 at 20%.

Step 3 If A pays the IHT on the gift, his estate falls in value by £152,000 plus the IHT payable on the £12,000, ie A is charged on the cost of the gift by treating the £152,000 as a gift net of tax.

Therefore, the part of the gift on which IHT is payable (here £12,000) must be 'grossed up' to reflect the amount of tax payable on the gift by using the formula:

$$\frac{100}{100-R}$$

where R is the rate of IHT applicable to the sum in question. In A's case the calculation is:

$$£12,000 \times \frac{100}{80} = £15,000 \text{ gross.}$$

(handwritten annotation:) Only £12000 chargeable due to exempt band
12000 ÷ 0·8 = 15000 is chargeable at 20% ie £3000

Thus, the cost of the gift to A is £155,000 of which the trust receives £152,000. The Revenue receive £3,000 in IHT. (Note that the trust also receives £3,000 free of IHT by virtue of A's annual exemption.)

As a result of the reduction in the number of tax rates to only two, 0% and 20%, the old problems of lifetime grossing up considered in earlier editions of this book have now disappeared. The present position is that once the taxpayer's cumulative total exceeds the nil rate band (currently £140,000) tax is levied (because of the grossing-up computation) at 25% on the excess. Thus, if A gives £50,000 to his close company (an immediately chargeable lifetime transfer) at a time when his cumulative total exceeds £140,000, tax on that transfer, if paid by A, will be 25% × £50,000 = £12,500.   [21.102]

3   Effect of the tax being paid by a person other than the transferor

Grossing-up is necessary to establish the cost to a donor of making a gift where the donor is paying the IHT. There is no grossing-up, however, if the tax is paid by any other person. Accordingly, as most lifetime transfers will be PETs, any IHT that is eventually charged will be due after the transferor's death and it will not, therefore, be necessary to gross up. Assume, for instance, that tax is paid by the transferee. He will be charged on the gift that he receives (strictly, on the fall in value of the transferor's estate) and the tax will be calculated according to the previous chargeable transfers of the donor.   [21.103]

EXAMPLE 21.24

(1)   A has made no previous chargeable transfers but has used up his annual exemption. He gives £150,000 to discretionary trustees who agree to pay the IHT due on the chargeable transfer. A has made a chargeable transfer of £150,000, on £10,000 of which IHT is payable at the rate of 20%. If the trustees pay, A's estate falls in value by only £150,000. The trustees are charged to IHT at A's rates. The trustees, therefore, pay IHT at 20% on £10,000 (ie £2,000) so that £500 less tax is paid than if A had paid (he would have paid tax at a rate of 25% on £10,000 = £2,500). However, the trust ends up with less property than if A had paid the IHT: £148,000, instead of £150,000. A further result of the trustees paying the tax is that A's cumulative total of gross chargeable transfers is lower for the purposes of future chargeable transfers, ie £150,000, rather than £152,500.

Compare

(2)   If the trustees are to pay the IHT on A's gift to them and A wants them to retain a net sum of £150,000 after paying the tax, A must give a larger sum (£152,500) to enable them to pay the tax of £2,500. The result is that whether donor or donee pays the IHT, the Revenue will receive £2,500 tax and the total cost to A will be the same.

4   Transferring non-cash assets the cheapest way

Where the gift is of a non-cash asset such as land, the IHT is calculated as before, but the question of who pays the tax and how much has to be paid will be of critical importance since neither party may have sufficient cash to pay the IHT without selling the asset. If the donor pays the IHT, the value of the gift must be grossed up. In addition, the tax must be paid

in one lump sum. If, however, the donee (normally trustees on a chargeable lifetime transfer) pays the tax, there is no grossing-up so that the transfer attracts less IHT. Additionally, in the case of certain assets the tax can be paid by the donee in ten yearly instalments (IHTA 1984 s 227). A further advantage of paying by instalments is that, if the asset is itself income producing, the donee may have income out of which to pay, or contribute towards, the instalments. Alternatively, the donor can fund the instalments paid by the donee by gifts out of his annual exemption. The assets on which IHT may be paid by instalments are:
(1) land, whether freehold or leasehold;
(2) a controlling shareholding of either quoted or unquoted shares;
(3) a minority shareholding of unquoted shares in certain circumstances (see [**22.57**]);
(4) a business or part of a business, eg a share in a partnership.

However, in the case of a transfer of land ((1) above), interest on the outstanding tax is charged when payment is made by instalments. [**21.104**]

EXAMPLE 21.25

A wants to settle his business which is valued at £410,000 on discretionary trusts. A has made no previous chargeable transfers. If A pays the tax (ignoring exemptions and reliefs) the gift (£410,000) must be grossed up so that the total cost to A is £477,500 and the IHT payable is £67,500; A must pay this in one lump sum. If the trust pays the tax, the £410,000 is a gross gift on which the IHT at A's rates is £54,000. Thus, there is a tax saving of £13,500. Further, the trust can pay the tax in instalments out of income from the business.

5   Problem areas

a) *Transfers of value by instalments* (IHTA 1984 s 262)

Where a person buys property at a price greater than its market value, the excess paid will be a transfer of value (assuming that donative intent is present). If the price is payable by instalments, part of each is deemed to be a transfer of value. That part is the proportion that the overall gift element bears to the price paid. [**21.105**]

EXAMPLE 21.26

A transfers property worth £40,000 to B for £80,000 payable by B in eight equal yearly instalments of £10,000. Hence, after eight years there will be a transfer of value of £40,000. The part of each instalment that is a chargeable transfer is:

$$\text{Annual instalment} \times \frac{\text{value of gift}}{\text{price payable}} = £10,000 \times \frac{£40,000}{£80,000} = £5,000.$$

b) *Transfers made on the same day* (IHTA 1984 s 266)

If a person makes more than one chargeable transfer on the same day and the order in which the transfers are made affects the overall amount of IHT payable, they are treated as made in the order which results in the least amount of IHT being payable (IHTA 1984 s 266(2)). This will be relevant where the transfers taken together straddle different rate bands and the donor does not pay the tax on all the transfers. Where this is the case the overall IHT will be less if the grossed-up gift is made first. In other cases an average rate of tax is calculated and applied to both transfers. When a PET made on the same day as a chargeable transfer is rendered chargeable by the donor's death within seven years these rules apply. **[21.106]**

c) *Transfers reported late* (IHTA 1984 s 264)

When a transfer is reported late (for the due date for reporting transfers see **[22.51]**) after IHT has been paid on a subsequent transfer, tax must be paid on the earlier transfer and an adjustment may have to be made to the tax bill on the later transfer. The tax payable on the earlier transfer is calculated as at the date of that transfer and interest is payable on the outstanding tax as from the date that it was due. If there is more than seven years between the earlier and the later transfers, no adjustment need be made in respect of the later transfer since the seven year limit on cumulation means that the later transfer is unaffected by the earlier transfer. When there is less than seven years between the two transfers the extra tax charged on the later transfer is levied on the earlier transfer in addition to the tax already due on that transfer. The recalculation problems that arise when PETs are chargeable are considered in Chapter 22. **[21.107]**

d) *Non-commercial loans*

There are no special charging provisions for loans of property and accordingly (subject only to IHTA 1984 s 29 which ensures that the usual exemptions and reliefs are available) tax will be charged, if at all, under general principles (notably has the loan resulted in a fall in value of the lender's estate?). In the case of money loans it is necessary to distinguish between interest-free loans repayable after a fixed term and loans repayable on demand. If A lends B £20,000 repayable in five years' time at no interest, A's estate is reduced in value because of the delay in repayment and A has made a transfer of value (assuming gratuitous intent). Accordingly A has made a PET equal to the difference between £20,000 and the value of the present right to receive £20,000 in five years' time.

If, instead, A lent B £20,000 repayable on demand with no interest charged, A's estate does not fall in value because it includes the immediate right to £20,000. Accordingly, A has not made a transfer of value and there is no question of any charge to IHT.

If a commercial rate of interest is charged on a loan, the transaction is not a chargeable transfer since the estate of the lender will not have fallen in value. Further, any interest may (normally) be waived without any charge to IHT by virtue of the exemption for regular payments out of income (see Chapter 23).

Loans repayable on demand are not generally subject to IHT, therefore, and may be employed so that the use of property, and any future increase in its value, is transferred free from IHT to another. **[21.108]**

EXAMPLE 21.27

Jasmine benefits her children without attracting a potential liability to IHT as follows:

(1) She lends her daughter £100,000 repayable on demand. The money is invested in a small terraced house in Fulham which quickly trebles in value. That increase in value belongs to the daughter who is merely obliged to repay the original sum loaned if and when Jasmine demands.

(2) She allows her son to occupy her London flat rent free. The son enjoys

the benefit of living there during the winter and lets the property to wealthy summer visitors. As there is no loss to Jasmine's estate the son's benefits are not subject to IHT.

e) *Relief against a double charge to IHT*

In a number of situations there is the possibility of a double charge to IHT:

EXAMPLE 21.28

Gustavus gives Adolphus his rare Swedish bible (a potentially exempt transfer). Two years later the bible is given back to Gustavus who dies shortly afterwards. As a result of his death within seven years the original gift of the bible is chargeable and, in addition, Gustavus' estate on death, which is subject to IHT, includes the bible.

Regulations made under FA 1986 s 104 provide a measure of relief in such cases and are discussed in Appendix VII. (Note that the CTT provisions dealing with mutual transfers were abolished in the case of donee gifts after 17 March 1986.)   **[21.109]–[21.120]**

VII   SPECIAL RULES FOR CLOSE COMPANIES

Only transfers of value made by individuals are chargeable to IHT (IHTA 1984 s 2(1)). An individual could, therefore, avoid IHT by forming a close company and using that company to make a gift to the intended donee, or a controlling shareholder in a close company could transfer his ownership of the company's assets indirectly by altering the capital structure of the company or the rights attached to his shares, so as to reduce the value of his shareholding in favour of the intended donee.

EXAMPLE 21.29

(1) A transfers assets worth £100,000 to A Ltd in return for shares worth £100,000. A's estate does not fall in value so that there is no liability to IHT. The company then gives one of the assets (worth £50,000) to A's son B. The company and not A has made a transfer of value.

(2) A Ltd has an issued share capital of £100 all in ordinary £1 shares owned by A. The company is worth £100,000. The company resolves:
(a) To convert A's shares into non-voting preference shares carrying only the right to a repayment of nominal value on a winding-up.
(b) To issue to B a further 100 £1 ordinary shares at par value.
The result is that the value has passed out of A's shares without any disposition by A. As a consequence IHT would not, *prima facie*, apply.

IHTA 1984 Part IV contains (inter alia) provisions designed to prevent an individual from using a close company to obtain a tax advantage in either of these ways. For the purposes of IHTA 1984 Part IV 'close company' and 'participator' have their corporation tax meaning (see Chapter 28) except that a close company includes a non-UK resident company which would be close if it was resident in the UK and participator does not include a loan creditor (IHTA 1984 s 102).   **[21.121]**

1 **Transfers of value by close companies** (IHTA 1984 s 94)

Where a close company makes a transfer of value, it is apportioned amongst the participators in proportion to their interests in the company, so that they are treated as having made the transfer ('lifting the veil') (IHTA 1984 s 94(1)). Thus, in *Example 21.29(1)* above, A is treated as having made a transfer of value of £50,000. For s 94(1) to apply the company must have made a transfer of value, ie its assets must fall in value by virtue of a non-commercial transaction (IHTA 1984 s 10(1)). The value apportioned to each participator is treated as a net amount which must be grossed up at the participator's appropriate rate of IHT. Any participator whose estate has increased in value as a result of that transfer can deduct the increase from the net amount (ignoring the effect that the transfer may have had on his rights in the company). The transfer in these circumstances is a deemed transfer of value and accordingly is not within the definition of a PET (see [**21.41**]). IHT is therefore chargeable.

EXAMPLE 21.30

A Ltd is owned as to 75% of the shares by A and 25% by B. It transfers land worth £100,000 to A. By IHTA 1984 s 94, A and B are treated as having made net transfers of value of £75,000 and £25,000 respectively. B will be charged to IHT on £25,000 grossed up at his rate of IHT. A, however, can deduct the increase in his estate (£100,000) from the net amount of the apportionment (£75,000), so that he pays no IHT. If A's shares (and B's) have diminished in value, the decrease is ignored.

Apportionment is not always as obvious as it may seem. For instance, in calculating a participator's interest in the company, the ownership of preference shares is usually disregarded (IHTA 1984 s 96). Further, where trustees are participators and the interest in the company is held in an interest-in-possession settlement (see Chapter 25) the apportioned amount is taxed as a reduction in the value of the life tenant's estate (IHTA 1984 s 99(2)(a)). In no-interest-in-possession trusts the apportioned amount is taxed as a payment out of the settled property by the trustees (IHTA 1984 s 99(2)(b)). Finally, where a close company is itself a participator in another close company any apportionment is then sub-apportioned to its own participators (IHTA 1984 s 95).

In two cases no apportionment occurs. First, if the transfer is charged to income tax or corporation tax in the donee's hands, there is no IHT liability (IHTA 1984 s 94(2)(a)). Secondly, where a participator is domiciled abroad, any apportionment made to him as a result of a transfer by a close company of property situated abroad is not charged to IHT (IHTA 1984 s 94(2)(b)).

EXAMPLE 21.31

(1) A Ltd (whose shares are owned 50% by A and 50% by B) pays a dividend. The dividend is not chargeable to IHT in A or B's hands because income tax is charged on that sum under Schedule F.

(2) A Ltd in (1) above provides A with free living accommodation and pays all the outgoings on the property. If A is a director or employee of A Ltd, these items are benefits in kind on which A pays income tax under Schedule E (see Chapter 5). If A is merely a shareholder in the company these payments are treated as a distribution by A Ltd and are charged to income tax in

A's hands under Schedule F. However, if A was not a member of A Ltd, there would be no income tax liability, so that the participator, B, would be treated for IHT purposes as having made a chargeable transfer of value under IHTA 1984 s 94(1).

(3) An English company, A Ltd, in which B and C each own 50% of the shares, gives a factory in France worth £100,000 to B, who is domiciled in the UK. C is domiciled in France and, therefore, the amount apportioned to him (£50,000) is not chargeable under IHTA 1984 s 94(1).

Participators can reduce their IHT on sums apportioned by the usual lifetime exemptions with the exception of the small gifts exemption and the exemption for gifts on marriage. Insofar as the transfer by the company is to a charity or political party it is exempt. The company is also entitled to 50% business relief if it transfers part of its business or shares in a trading subsidiary.

The company is primarily liable for the tax. If it fails to pay, secondary liability rests concurrently with the participators and beneficiaries of the transfer. A participator's liability is limited to tax on the amount apportioned to him; for a non-participator beneficiary it is limited to the increase in value of his estate.   **[21.122]**

2   **Deemed dispositions by participators** (IHTA 1984 s 98)

Whenever value is drained out of shares in a close company by an alteration (including extinguishment) of the share capital or by an alteration in the rights attached to shares, this is treated as a deemed disposition by the participators although the section does not deem a transfer of value to have been made. When such a transfer does occur liability for IHT under IHTA 1984 s 98 rests purely on the participators and not on the company. As there is no deemed transfer of value under s 98, such transfers are expressly prevented from being PETs by IHTA 1984 s 98(3) (see *Example 21.32(3)* below).   **[21.123]-[21.140]**

EXAMPLE 21.32

(1) Taking the facts of *Example 21.29(2)* above there is no actual transfer of value by A or A Ltd. However, under IHTA 1984 s 98 there is a deemed disposition by A equivalent to the fall in value of his shareholding. From owning all the shares and effectively all the assets he is left with a holding of 100 shares worth (probably) only their face value.

(2) A owns 60% and B 40% of the shares in A Ltd. Each share carries one vote. The articles of association of the company are altered so that A's shares continue to carry one vote, but B's shares are to carry three votes each. There is a deemed disposition by A to B equivalent to the drop in value in A's estate resulting from his loss of control of A Ltd.

(3) Zebadee, the sole shareholder in Zebadee Ltd, arranges for a bonus issue of fully paid preference shares which carry the right to a fixed dividend. He retains the shares but gives his valuable ordinary shares to his daughter. This familiar tax planning rearrangement depends in part upon the gift of the ordinary shares being a potentially exempt transfer. Under s 98(1) the alteration in the share structure is treated as a disposition by Zebadee but as the bonus shares are at that stage issued to him, he does not then make any transfer of value. Accordingly, the subsequent gift of the ordinary shares will be a PET. It is thought that the Revenue will not normally seek to argue that the bonus issue and later gift are associated operations falling within s 98(1) as an extended reorganisation (so that the gift of the shares is not prevented from being a PET by s 98(3)).

VIII   LIABILITY, ACCOUNTABILITY AND BURDEN

1   **Liability for IHT** (IHTA 1984 Part VII)

The person primarily liable for IHT on a chargeable lifetime transfer of
unsettled property is the transferor (IHTA 1984 s 199), although in certain
cases, his spouse may be held liable as a transferor to prevent him from
divesting himself of property to that spouse so that he is then unable to
meet an IHT bill (IHTA 1984 s 203).

EXAMPLE 21.33

H makes a gross chargeable transfer to a discretionary trust of £100,000 and
fails to pay IHT. He later transfers property worth £50,000 to his wife W which
is exempt (inter-spouse). W can be held liable for IHT not exceeding £50,000.

If the Revenue cannot collect the tax from the transferor (or his spouse)
they can then claim it, subject to specified limits, from one of the following:
(1)   The transferee, ie any person whose estate has increased in value as
      a result of the transfer. Liability is restricted to tax (at the transferor's
      rates) on the value of the gross transfer after deducting any unpaid
      tax.

EXAMPLE 21.34

A makes a *gross* chargeable transfer to discretionary trustees of £40,000 on which
IHT at A's rate of 20% is £8,000. A emigrates without paying the tax. The
Revenue can only claim £6,400 in tax from the trustees, ie

	£
Gross chargeable transfer by A	40,000
Less unpaid tax	8,000
Revised value transferred	£32,000
Trustees are liable for IHT at 20%	£6,400

---

(2)   Any person in whom the property has become vested after the transfer.
      This category includes a person to whom the transferee has in turn
      transferred the property; or, if the property has been settled, the trustees
      of the settlement and any beneficiary with an interest in possession in
      it; or a purchaser of the property unless he is a *bona fide* purchaser
      for money or money's worth and the property is not subject to an Inland
      Revenue charge. The liability of these persons is limited to tax on the
      net transfer only and liability is further limited, in the case of trustees
      and beneficiaries, to the value of the settled property and, in the case
      of a purchaser, to the value of the property. Also included within this
      category is any person who meddles with property so as to constitute
      himself a '*trustee de son tort*' and any person who manages the property
      on behalf of a person under a disability.
(3)   A beneficiary under a discretionary trust of the property to the extent
      that he receives income or any benefit from the trust. Liability is limited
      to the amount of his benefit after payment of any income tax.
The liability to pay additional IHT on a gift because of the transferor's

death within seven years, and liability to IHT on a PET which becomes a chargeable transfer is considered in Chapter 22.

Quite apart from those persons from whom they can claim tax, the Revenue have a charge for unpaid tax on the property transferred and on settled property where the liability arose on the making of the settlement or on a chargeable transfer of it (IHTA 1984 s 237). The charge takes effect in the same way as on death (see Chapter 22) except that for lifetime transfers it extends to personal property also. It will not bind a purchaser of land unless the charge is registered and in the case of personal property unless the purchaser has notice of the facts giving rise to the charge (IHTA 1984 s 238).

Once IHT on a chargeable transfer has been paid and accepted by the Revenue, liability for any further tax ceases six years after the later of the date when the tax was paid or the date when it became due (IHTA 1984 s 240(2)). However, if the Revenue can prove fraud, wilful default or neglect by a person liable for the tax (or by the settlor which results in an underpayment of tax by discretionary trustees), this six year period only starts to run once the Revenue know of the fraud, wilful default or neglect, as the case may be (IHTA 1984 s 240(3)). When the Revenue are satisfied that tax has been or will be paid, they may, at the request of a person liable for the tax, issue a certificate discharging persons and/or property from further liability (IHTA 1984 s 239).   [**21.141**]

2   **Accountability and payment**

a) *Duty to account*

An account need only be delivered in respect of a chargeable transfer which is not a PET: in the case of PETs an account is only required if the transferor dies within seven years (IHTA 1984 s 216). Thus, the Revenue need not be notified of a transfer of excluded property or of a transfer that is wholly exempt (eg within the annual exemption or inter-spouse), with the exception of an exempt transfer of settled property which must normally be notified. In addition, in two situations chargeable transfers are 'excepted' from the duty to account (SI 1981/1440). First, where the gift is by an individual and, together with other chargeable transfers in the same tax year, it does not exceed £10,000 so long as the gift and other chargeable transfers in the previous seven years do not exceed £40,000 in total; and secondly where the value transferred on the termination of an interest in possession in settled property is extinguished by the beneficiary's annual or marriage gifts exemption. As a general rule, the person who is primarily liable for the IHT must deliver the account. When the transfer is by a close company, nobody is under a duty to account, but in practice the company should do so in order to avoid a charge to interest on unpaid tax.

The account must be delivered within 12 months from the end of the month when the transfer was made or within three months from the date when that person first became liable to pay IHT (if later). In practice the account should be delivered earlier, since the tax is due before this date. Form IHT 100 is used for all lifetime transfers including transfers of settled property on life or death with an interest in possession. Anyone who fails to deliver an account, make a return, or provide information when required may be subject to penalties and the Revenue have a wide general power to obtain information from 'any' person (IHTA 1984 s 219) by means of a notice. They cannot use this power to compel a solicitor or barrister to disclose privileged information concerning a client, but they can use it to obtain the name and address of a client. **[21.142]**

b) *Payment of tax*

For all lifetime chargeable transfers of settled or unsettled property made between 6 April and 30 September, the tax is due on 30 April following and for transfers made between 1 October and 5 April it is due six months from the end of the month when the transfer was made (IHTA 1984 s 226). The optimum date to make a chargeable transfer is therefore 6 April which gives a 12 months delay before tax is due. **[21.143]**

Payment by instalments Generally IHT must be paid in one lump sum. IHTA 1984 s 212 provides that any person liable for the tax (except the transferor and his spouse) can sell, mortgage or charge the property even if it is not vested in him, so that if, for instance, A gives property to B who settles it on C for life, either B, the trustees, or C (if called upon to pay the tax) can sell, mortgage or charge the property in order to do so.

Despite the general rule, if the transferee pays the IHT he can elect in the case of certain assets only to pay the tax in ten yearly instalments; the first instalment becoming due when the tax is due (IHTA 1984 s 227). This lifetime instalment option is available for the same assets as on death (see **[22.57]**), except for the transfer of a minority holding of unquoted shares or securities within category (4) (relief when the IHT on instalment property amounts to 20% of the total bill). Trustees or beneficiaries who are liable for the tax on transfers of settled property can elect to pay in instalments provided that the property falls within one of the specified classes. Despite this election, the outstanding tax (and any interest due) may be paid at any time. Furthermore, if the relevant property is sold or transferred by a chargeable transfer the tax must be paid at once (IHTA 1984 s 227(4)). **[21.144]**

Interest Interest is charged on any tax which is not paid by the due date (IHTA 1984 s 233). Where the tax is to be paid by instalments, interest is charged on overdue instalments only, except in the case of land where interest is charged on all the outstanding tax. **[2.145]**

Satisfaction of tax The Revenue have a discretion to accept in satisfaction of tax (but not interest) any object that is pre-eminent for its national, scientific, historic or artistic interest (see IHTA 1984 s 231 and Chapter 23). **[21.146]**

Adjustments to the tax bill Subject to the six year limitation rule (see **[21.162]**) if the Revenue prove that too little tax was paid in respect of a chargeable transfer, tax underpaid is payable together with interest. Conversely, if too much tax was paid, the Revenue must refund the excess together with interest, which is free of income tax in the recipient's hands (IHTA 1984 s 235). **[21.147]**

3 Burden of tax

The question of who, as between the transferor and the transferee, should bear the tax on a lifetime transfer is a matter for the parties to decide as discussed above. The decision will affect the amount of tax payable (see **[21.103]**). The parties can agree at any time before the tax becomes due and the Revenue will accept their decision so long as the tax is paid. However, the agreement does not affect the liability of the parties, so that if the tax remains unpaid, the Revenue can collect it from persons liable under Part VII of the legislation (see **[21.141]**.   **[21.148]-[21.160]**

IX ADMINISTRATION AND APPEALS

1 Calculation of liability

IHT is not assessed by reference to the tax year. Instead, when the Revenue are informed of a chargeable transfer of value they raise an assessment called a determination (IHTA 1984 s 221). If they are not satisfied with an account or if none is delivered when they suspect that a chargeable transfer has occurred, they can raise a 'best of judgment' or estimated determination of the tax due. A determination of IHT liability is conclusive against the transferor and for all subsequent transfers, failing a written agreement with the Revenue to the contrary or an appeal.

If the taxpayer disputes the determination he can appeal to the Special Commissioners within 30 days of it (IHTA 1984 s 222). The appeal procedure is basically the same as under TMA 1970 for income tax, corporation tax and CGT, except that an appeal can be made direct to the High Court, thereby bypassing the commissioners, either by agreement with the Revenue or on application to the High Court. In this case, the appeal is not limited to points of law. Appeal then lies in the usual way to the Court of Appeal and, with leave, to the House of Lords (or by the 'leap frog' procedure direct to the House of Lords). The disputed tax is not payable at the first stage of the appeal (IHTA 1984 s 242). However, if there is a further appeal, the tax becomes payable; if this appeal is then successful, the tax must be repaid with interest.

Proceedings for the recovery of IHT can be taken by the Crown under the Crown Proceedings Act 1947 in the High Court. Straightforward cases may be taken in the County Court by Inland Revenue staff other than barristers or solicitors (IHTA 1984 s 244).   **[21.161]**

2 Back duty

IHT penalties have not yet been amended in line with the Keith Committee recommendations which have now been implemented for the other taxes. A Consultative Document on IHT is therefore anticipated in 1991. The present position is that if a person is fraudulent (including wilful default) in producing accounts and other information, the penalty is £50 plus twice the difference between the liability calculated on the true and false bases. For negligence, the penalty is £50 plus that difference (IHTA 1984 s 247). Solicitors and other agents who fraudulently produce incorrect information are liable to a maximum penalty of £500 reduced to £250 in cases of neglect (IHTA 1984 s 247(3)(4)).

Proceedings for these penalties may be taken before the Special Commissioners or the High Court within three years of the determination of the correct tax due (IHTA 1984 s 250).

Assessments to recover IHT lost through fraud, wilful default and neglect of a person liable for the tax (which for these purposes includes the settlor in the case of discretionary trusts) may be made up to six years from the discovery of the offence (IHTA 1984 s 240 ante).   **[21.162]-[21.180]**

X   LIFETIME GIVING UNDER INHERITANCE TAX— COMMENTS AND CONCLUSIONS

The switch from CTT to IHT necessitated a major reconsideration of estate planning techniques. Together with the CGT hold-over election the position was then highly favourable for the wealthy individual prepared to give away property during his life. By removing general hold-over relief, FA 1989 has introduced further complications! It is now obviously less satisfactory for a taxpayer to avoid the 40% IHT charge on property (by giving it away seven years before his death) if the gift itself will attract an immediate CGT charge at 40% on (in the case of assets with minimal allowable expenditure) the entire value of the asset. The somewhat complicated choices now available to the estate planner are discussed in detail in Chapter 37.

This chapter has concentrated on lifetime transfers which are immediately chargeable although, in the majority of cases, such transfers will be potentially exempt (a PET). For the chargeable transfer, however, the reduction in the cumulation period to seven years needs to be carefully considered. A wealthy individual can, for instance, settle his nil rate band (currently £140,000) on discretionary trusts at seven yearly intervals without attracting an IHT charge.

Most interest has, of course, been generated by the potentially exempt transfer since no charge to tax will arise if the transferor survivers by seven years. The prudent donee is advised to insure against the IHT chargeable in the event of death within that period (see Chapter 37) but it should be noted that, even if the PET does become chargeable, its value is frozen at the date of the transfer whilst the tax rate applicable is that in operation either at the date of the transfer or at the transferor's death *whichever is the lower* (see further Chapter 22). Finally, despite the generally favourable changes flowing from the introduction

of IHT, the rules have been substantially tightened up in cases where an individual makes a lifetime gift of property but reserves some benefit for himself. 'Gifts with reservation' are considered in the next chapter but it should be stressed that if any benefit has been reserved the *whole* of the property in question is treated as passing in the individual's estate at death so that the lifetime gift is, in effect, nullified.   **[21.181]**

22 IHT—death

I GENERAL

IHTA 1984 s 4(1) provides that

> 'on the death of any person (after 12 March 1975) tax shall be charged as if immediately before his death he had made a transfer of value and the value transferred by it had been equal to the value of his estate immediately before his death . . .'.

For IHT purposes, therefore, there is a deemed transfer of value which occurs immediately before the death and which must be cumulated with chargeable transfers made by the deceased in the preceding seven years. In addition to causing a charge on his estate at death, the death of an individual also has the effect of making chargeable potentially exempt transfers made in the seven years before death and it may lead to a supplementary IHT charge on chargeable transfers made in that same period. The complex tax computations that may occur on a death are illustrated in Section II after a consideration of what property is included in an estate at death and how that estate is to be valued.   [**22.1**]

1 Meaning of 'estate'

The definition of 'estate' for IHT purposes has already been considered in connection with lifetime transfers (IHTA 1984 s 5(1); see [**21.62**]). On death, however, the estate does not include excluded property (see Chapter 27 for the meaning of excluded property) although it does include property, given away by the deceased, where he reserved a benefit up to the time of his death (see [**22.3**]). As the transfer is deemed to occur immediately before the death, the estate includes any equitable joint tenancies of the deceased which pass by operation of law (*jus accrescendi*) at the moment of death.

EXAMPLE 22.1

Bill and his sister Bertha jointly own their home. The documents of title indicate that they are joint tenants so that on the death of either that share will pass automatically to the survivor and will not be transferred by will. For IHT purposes, however, the half share in the house will be included in their respective death estates and will be subject to charge (for the valuation of the half share see [**21.64**]).

The estate at death also includes a gift made before death in anticipation of death and conditional upon it occurring (a *donatio mortis causa*). Hence, although dominion over the property will have been handed over, it is still taxed as part of the deceased's estate at death.   [**22.2**]

2   Property subject to a reservation

It was possible, under the CTT regime, for taxpayers to give away property but at the same time to retain the benefit and control of it. Typical arrangements are illustrated in the following example.

EXAMPLE 22.2

(1) Joe creates a discretionary trust and includes himself amongst the beneficiaries.
(2) Arty owns a fine Constable landscape. He transfers legal ownership to his daughter by deed of gift but the picture remains firmly hanging up in his house until his death.
(3) Sam gives his Norfolk farm to his son and continues to live in the farmhouse.

These arrangements were obviously ideal for the moderately wealthy since, although the original transfer might attract tax (to the extent that it was not covered by the annual exemption and the nil rate band) future increases in value of the gifted property occurred outside the transferor's estate whilst, should the need arise (and especially in the schemes illustrated in *Example 22.2(1)*), the property could be recovered by the transferor. The widespread use of such arrangements made it likely that they would be attacked by legislation and the switch from CTT to IHT, which included the introduction of the potentially exempt transfer, made this inevitable. Accordingly, provisions were introduced to deal with property subject to a reservation (see FA 1986 s 102 and Sch 20) which apply to lifetime gifts made on or after 18 March 1986.

It is proposed to discuss the basic principles of the legislation in this part of the book: Chapter 37 discusses matters of detail and the tax planning implications of these rules. The legislation is closely based on earlier estate duty sections and the relevant estate duty authorities are, to some extent, relevant. A cautionary note should, however, be sounded since there are differences of wording in the new legislation (it has, for instance, been modernised) and a court might therefore be able to distinguish some of the earlier authorities.   [**22.3**]

a) *IHT consequences if property is subject to a reservation*

The gift of property subject to a reservation is treated, so far as the donor is concerned, as a partial nullity for IHT purposes. This is because he is deemed to remain beneficially entitled to the gifted property immediately before his death. It is clear from the wording of s 102(3) that the property only returns to the donor at this precise moment although, if the benefit reserved ceases during the lifetime of the donor, he is treated as making a potentially exempt transfer of the property at that time (a deemed PET).

No advantage therefore flows from releasing any reserved benefit just before death. Possible double charges to IHT in this area are dealt with in the regulations discussed in Appendix VII.

EXAMPLE 22.3

(1) In 1988 A gives his daughter his country cottage (then worth £50,000) in return for an annuity of £500 pa payable for the next 5 years. The annuity ends in 1992 and A dies in 1993. By stipulating for the payment of an annuity A is reserving a benefit.

(a) *the original transfer:* in 1988 is a PET. The value transferred will be reduced because of A's annuity entitlement.

(b) *on the ending of the annuity in 1992:*   A makes a potentially exempt transfer equal to the then value of the cottage.

(c) *with his death in 1993* both the earlier transfers are made chargeable.

(2) Had A died in 1991 the reservation would be operative at his death so that, in addition to the 1988 PET being made chargeable, the value of the cottage in 1991 forms part of his death estate.

For relief against a double IHT charge, see Appendix VII.

As a result of including the property in the deceased's estate immediately before death, it is necessary to value it at that time (and not at the time of the gift). Hence, where a transferor makes a gift with reservation there is no 'asset freezing' advantage. It also follows, of course, that as the value of the property swells the size of the estate, it may increase the estate rate of IHT (see [**22.36**] for 'estate rate') which is charged on the rest of the estate. Primary liability to pay the IHT attributable to reservation property lies with the donee (who should submit an account within twelve months of the death) although the donor's PRs are secondarily liable if tax remains unpaid at the end of twelve months from the death. PRs who have made a final distribution of the assets in the estate may therefore be faced with a wholly unexpected claim for more IHT and this matter is considered in detail at [**22.57**].   [**22.4**]

b) *When do the reservation rules apply?*

First, there must be disposal of property by way of gift. To base liability to IHT on the making of a gift does not fit in with the general scheme of the IHTA 1984 which fixes the tax charge upon chargeable transfers of value (see [**21.2**]). The resultant difficulties perfectly illustrate the problems of attempting to weld legislation from estate duty onto the CTT structure. Obviously, the gift must have been completed (and it should be remembered that the courts have no general power to perfect an uncompleted gift: see *Milroy v Lord* (1862)) but it may be assumed that the reservation provisions apply not just to pure gifts but also to the situation where, although partial consideration is furnished, there is still an element of bounty (see *A-G v Johnson* (1903)). A bad bargain, on the other hand, lacks any element of gift. The distinction between a gift (the basis of the reservation rules) and a transfer of value (the general basis for IHT liability) is illustrated in the following example:

EXAMPLE 22.4

(1) Adam owns a pair of Constable watercolours and sells one to his daughter, Jemima. He retains possession of the picture. Each picture is worth £10,000: as a pair they are worth £35,000. Jemima pays Adam £10,000 for the picture.
  (i) there is a *transfer of value* of £15,000 (drop in value of Adam's estate). This transfer is a PET (see [**21.43**]).
  (ii) is there a *gift* of property so that the reservation rules apply? As Jemima has paid full value for the picture that she has acquired there is presumably no element of gift so that the rules are inapplicable.

(2) Sam settles property on trust for himself for life remainder on discretionary trusts for his family (including Sam). Assume that the trustees have the power to terminate Sam's life interest which they exercise six months after the creation of the trust.
  (i) There is no *transfer of value* when Sam creates the settlement since he is the life tenant (IHTA 1984 s 49(1)).
  (ii) At that time Sam makes a *gift* of the remainder interest and, as a member of the discretionary class, will be treated by the Revenue as reserving a benefit in the gifted property.
  (iii) When his life interest terminates Sam makes a *transfer of value* (which is potentially exempt) but does not make a *gift* (contrast the position if he had voluntarily surrendered his interest). With the cessation of the life interest the fund is now held on discretionary trusts and (see (ii) above) is property subject to a reservation (FA 1986 Sch 20 para 5(1)).

Secondly, the reservation rules apply if full possession and enjoyment of the gifted property is not enjoyed by the donee either at or before the beginning of the *relevant period*. For this purpose the relevant period is the period ending with the donor's death and beginning either seven years before that date or (if later) the date of the gift.

EXAMPLE 22.5

(1) By deed of gift A gives B the family silver but he retains it locked in a cupboard till death.

(2) A gives full possession and enjoyment of the family silver to B and dies two years later.

(3) Assume in (1) above that the deed of gift was made in 1988 but that A handed over the silver in 1989 and dies in 1997.

(4) A gives the family silver to B in 1988 but borrows it back just before his death in 1995.

in (1) possession of the silver is never enjoyed by B so that there is a gift with reservation and the silver forms part of A's estate on death.

in (2) full possession and enjoyment is obtained at the beginning of the relevant period. (Hence no reservation although there is, of course, a failed PET.)

in (3) full possession and enjoyment is obtained more than seven years before death. (No reservation.)

in (4) although full possession and enjoyment was given to B, the return of the silver to A is important so far as the next requirement is concerned.

Thirdly, the reservation rules apply if the donor has not been excluded from benefit *at any time* during the relevant period. In *Example 22.5(4)* the return of the silver shortly before the donor's death results in the property being subject to a reservation at A's death and, accordingly, it is subject to IHT.

EXAMPLE 22.6

In 1924 the taxpayer created a settlement for his infant daughter contingent upon her attaining 30. He was wholly excluded from benefit. In 1938 (just before she became 30) he arranged with her to borrow the income from the trust fund in order to reduce his overdraft. Until 1943 he borrowed virtually all the income: he finally died in 1946 (see *Stamp Duties Commissioner of New South Wales v Permanent Trustee Co* (1956)). On these facts the Privy Council held that a benefit had been reserved for estate duty purposes and the same would be true for IHT. Notice that the settlor had no enforceable right to the income: he merely made an arrangement with his daughter which she could have revoked at any time.

The requirement that the donor must be excluded from all benefit during the relevant period is comprised in two alternative limbs. Limb I requires his exclusion from the gifted property, whilst Limb II stipulates that he should not have received any benefit 'by contract or otherwise'. The two limbs must be considered separately.

So far as Limb I is concerned, in order to determine whether the donor has been entirely excluded from the gifted property, it is necessary to decide what that property comprises. Estate duty cases point to a distinction of some subtlety between keeping back rights in the property (ie making only a partial gift) and giving the entire property but receiving a subsequent benefit therein from the donee (see [**37.31**] for a full discussion of this topic). Once the gift is correctly identified, the donor must be entirely excluded both in law and in fact (see *Example 22.6*).

EXAMPLE 22.7

A father owned two properties on which an informal farming partnership was carried on with his son. Profits were split two-thirds to the father, one-third to the son. The father gave one of the properties to his son, free of all conditions, so that the son could have farmed it independently. In fact both continued to farm the property sharing the profits equally. It was held that the father had not been entirely excluded from the gifted property (*Stamp Duties Commissioner of New South Wales v Owens* (1953)).

Certain benefits to the donor are specifically ignored. FA 1986 s 102(1) requires the entire exclusion or *virtually* the entire exclusion of the donor from the gifted property. 'Virtually the entire exclusion' had no predecessor in the estate duty legislation and is apparently designed to cover, for instance, occasional visits by the donor to a house which he had earlier given away (including short holidays!). A second exclusion is available where the donor furnishes full consideration for the benefit enjoyed (FA 1986 Sch 20 para 6(1)(a)). The gifted property, however, must be an interest in land or a chattel and to come within the exclusion actual occupation, enjoyment or possession of that property must have been resumed by the donor.

EXAMPLE 22.8

(1) Gift of land but donor is subsequently given shooting/fishing rights or rights to take timber. So long as full (not partial) consideration is furnished there is *no retention* of benefit.

(2) Gift of Ming vase—returned to donor in return for payment of full rent. *No reservation.*

(3) As in (1) save that donor sub-lets his rights. *Outside para 6(1)(a)* since actual enjoyment is not resumed and therefore there is a reservation of benefit.

(4) Gift of shares: donor continues to enjoy dividends and pays full value for that right. *Outside para 6(1)(a)* since the property in question is neither land nor chattels. Hence a benefit is reserved.

Finally a benefit may be ignored on hardship grounds but this provision is extremely restrictive and is concerned solely with the occupation of land by a donor of that land whose circumstances have changed since the original gift and who has become unable to maintain himself for reasons of old age or infirmity. Further, the donee must be related to the donor (or his spouse) and the provision of occupation must represent reasonable provision for the care and maintenance of the donor.

Limb II, that the donor must be excluded from any benefit by contract or otherwise, is sufficiently widely drafted to catch collateral benefits which do not take effect out of the gifted property:

EXAMPLE 22.9

(1) Charlie gives land in Sussex to his son Jasper who covenants, at the same time, to pay Charlie an annuity of £500 pa for the rest of his life. The land is property subject to a reservation (cp *A-G v Worrall* (1895): '. . . it is not necessary that the benefit to the donor should be by way of reservation' per Lopes LJ).

(2) Adam sells his farm to Bertram for £100,000 when its true value is £500,000. As a sale at undervalue there is an element of gift. However, it is not easy to see how the payment of £100,000 can amount to a benefit reserved. The estate duty cases do not go this far and even if it is accepted that there is a reserved benefit, it presumably ceases at the moment when the £100,000 is paid to Adam with the result that there may be a deemed PET on that date. Accordingly, the somewhat absurd result is that on the same day there would be a PET of £400,000 (value of farm less consideration received) and a further PET of £500,000 (value of property in which the reservation has ceased). It is understood that the Revenue will *not* argue that the £100,000 is a benefit reserved.

(3) Claude wishes to give his farm to his son Dada subject to Dada taking over the existing mortgage thereon. If the arrangement is structured in this manner the provision for the discharge of his mortgage may result in Claude reserving a benefit. Were he to sell the farm for the amount of the outstanding mortgage, however, that sale for partial consideration is not thought to involve a reservation (see (2) above); Dada could raise a mortgage on the security of the land; Claude would pay off his existing mortgage and any capital gain resulting from the consideration received (the gift element is subject to the hold-over election under CGTA 1979 s 126) would in many cases be covered by retirement relief (FA 1985 ss 69 and 70).

Although the benefit need not come from the gifted property itself, it must be reserved as part of a linked transaction: a purely accidental benefit, for instance, in no way connected with an earlier gift is ignored. In determining whether there is such a connection account must be taken of any associated operations (see FA 1986 Sch 20 para 6(1)(c) incorporating for these purposes IHTA 1984 s 268: see [**21.81**]). Finally, it should be noted that the second limb is concerned with benefits reserved 'by contract *or otherwise*'. According to estate duty authority these final words should be construed *eiusdem generis* with contract and, therefore, as requiring a legally enforceable obligation (see the unsatisfactory case of *A-G v Seccombe* (1911)). It seems most unlikely that courts today—in the era of *Ramsay*—would permit obligations binding in honour only to slip through this net, however, and the statutory associated operations rule (discussed above) is couched in terms of conduct (ie what actually happened) not of legal obligation. **[22.5]**

c) *Identifying property subject to a reservation*

FA 1986 Sch 20 paras 1–5 contains complex rules for identifying property subject to a reservation and makes provision, in particular, for what happens if the donee ceases to have possession and enjoyment of the property whether by sale or gift; for the effect of changes in the structure of bodies corporate when the original gift was of shares or securities; for the position if the donee predeceases the donor; and finally for the effect of changes in the nature of the property when the original gift was settled.

When property subject to the reservation qualified for agricultural or business relief at the date of the gift (see Chapter 23 for the requirements to be satisfied that relief may also be available if IHT is subsequently charged because of the retained benefit. **[22.6]**

d) *Conclusions*

The practical consequences of the reservation of benefit rules and the problems that they create are analysed in detail at **[37.30]**. As the effect of reserving a benefit is that the gifted property is taxed as part of the donor's estate on death it is obviously crucial to know when benefits have been retained. It is not just the value of the reserved benefit that is taxed but the whole property valued as at the date of death. For the donee the result may be a substantial (and unexpected) IHT bill: for the donor's PRs the danger of a liability to pay any tax not recovered from the donee and a higher estate rate on the property of the deceased. Considerable care should be taken, therefore, to ensure that the reservation rules are avoided and, as it will not be worthwhile deliberately reserving a benefit within s 102, the rules operate as a trap for the ignorant or the unfortunate. **[22.7]**

3   Valuation

In general assets must be valued at 'the price which the property might reasonably be expected to fetch if sold in the open market at that time'. No reduction is allowed for the fact that all the property is put on the market at the same time (IHTA 1984 s 160). This hypothetical sale occurs immediately before the death and (in general) the value arrived at for IHT purposes becomes the value at death for CGT purposes and, hence, the legatee's base cost (CGTA 1979 s 153). Where reliefs reduce the IHT value (notably business property relief) that relief is ignored for CGT purposes. Accordingly, for IHT, low values ensure the least tax payable but will give the legatee a low base cost and so a higher capital gain when he disposes of the asset.

Although the general rule is that assets should be valued immediately before death, IHTA 1984 Part VI permits values to be amended in certain circumstances, eg reasonable funeral expenses can be deducted (including a reasonable sum for mourning for family and servants and the cost of a tombstone or gravestone: see SP 7/87) and, in certain cases, a change in the value of assets caused by the death is taken into account.

EXAMPLE 22.10

(1) A took out a life insurance policy for £100,000 on his own life. Its value immediately before death would be equal to the surrender figure. As a result of A's death £100,000 will accrue to A's estate and hence the value of the policy for IHT purposes is treated as that figure (IHTA 1984 s 167(2)).

(2) A and B were joint tenants in equity of a freehold house worth £100,000. Immediately before A's death his joint interest would be worth in the region of £50,000. As a result of death that asset passes to B by survivorship (ie its value is nil to A's estate). In this case it is not possible to alter the pre-death valuation (IHTA 1984 s 171(2)).

In three cases the death valuation can be altered if the asset is sold within a short period of death for less than that valuation. Relief is not given merely because the asset falls in value after death; only if it is sold by bargain at arm's length is the relief available. Normally the sale proceeds will be substituted as the death valuation figure if an election is made by the person liable for the IHT on that asset (in practice this will be the PRs who should elect if IHT would thereby be reduced). Where such revaluations occur, not only must the IHT bill (and estate rate) on death be recalculated but also, for CGT purposes, the death valuation is correspondingly reduced so as to prevent any claim for loss relief. The three cases when this relief is available are: **[22.8]**

Related property sold within three years of death (IHTA 1984 s 176)   The meaning of related property has already been discussed (see Chapter 21). So long as a 'qualifying sale' (as defined) occurs, the property on death can be revalued ignoring the related property rules (ie as an asset on its own). Although the sale proceeds need not be the same as the death value, if the sale occurs within a short time of death the proceeds received will offer some evidence of that value. **[22.9]**

EXAMPLE 22.11

Sebastian's estate on death includes one of a pair of Constable watercolours of Suffolk sunsets. He leaves it to his son; the other is owned by his widow, Jemima. As a pair, the pictures are worth £200,000. Hence, applying the related property provisions, the watercolour is valued at £100,000 on Sebastian's death. If it were to be sold at Sotheby's some eight months after his death for £65,000, the death value could be recalculated ignoring the related property rules. It would be necessary to arrive at the value of the picture immediately before the death.

Quoted shares and securities sold within 12 months of death (IHTA 1984 s 178ff)   If sold for less than the death valuation the sale proceeds can be substituted for that figure. It should be noted that if this relief is claimed it will affect *all* such investments sold within the 12 month period; hence, the aggregate of the consideration received on such sales is substituted for the death values. Special rules operate if investments of the same description are repurchased. The shares or securities must be listed on the Stock Exchange or dealt in on the Unlisted Securities Market (the USM) so that the provisions do not apply to private company shares. **[22.10]**

Land sold within three years of death (IHTA 1984 s 190ff)   The relief extends to all interests in land and is similar to that available for quoted securities. Hence, all sales within the three year period are included in any election.   **[22.11]**

The 'appropriate person' In the case of both quoted shares and land, the election to substitute the sale proceeds must be made by the appropriate person who is defined in the legislation as 'the person liable for inheritance tax attributable to (the property)'. Obviously the election in such cases will commonly be made if the property is sold for less than its probate value but the sections are not so limited and therefore the election may appear attractive in the sort of case illustrated in *Example 22.12* where substituting a higher probate value would wipe out a capital gains tax liability: **[22.12]**

EXAMPLE 22.12

MacLeod left his entire estate to his wife Tammy on his death in 1989; it included land valued at death at £100,000. As a result of new regional development plans, the land now has hope value and is worth in the region of £500,000. Accordingly, it is now to be sold. An election to substitute the sale proceeds for the probate value would obviously be beneficial in CGT terms. However, because there is no appropriate person (since IHT is not payable on MacLeod's death), that election cannot be made.

4   Liabilities

In general, liabilities will reduce the value of an estate only if incurred for consideration in money or money's worth, eg an outstanding building society mortgage and the deceased's outstanding tax liability (IHTA 1984 s 5(5)). In addition to this general requirement, FA 1986 s 103 introduced new restrictions on the deductibility from his estate at death of debts and incumbrances created by the deceased. These provisions supplement s 5(5) but only apply to debts or incumbrances created after 17 March 1986. Broadly, their aim is to prevent the deduction of 'artificial' debts, ie those where the creditor had received gifts from the deceased as in the following example:

EXAMPLE 22.13

Berta gives a picture to her daughter Bertina in 1986. In 1987 she buys it back, leaving the purchase price outstanding until the date of her death.
(1)   The gift is a potentially exempt transfer and escapes IHT if Berta survives seven years.
(2)   The debt owed to Bertina is incurred for full consideration and would be deductible under IHTA 1984 s 5(5). Deduction is, however, prevented by FA 1986 s 103.

Section 103(1) provides that debts must be abated in whole or in part if any portion of the consideration for the debt was either derived from the deceased or was given by *any* person to whose resources the deceased had contributed. In the latter case contributions of the deceased are ignored, however, if it is shown (ie on behalf of the taxpayer) that the contribution was not made with reference to or to enable or facilitate the giving of that consideration.

Accordingly, unless property derived from the deceased furnished the consideration for the debt, a causal link is necessary between the contribution of the deceased and the subsequent debt transaction.

EXAMPLE 22.14

(1) In *Example 22.13* the consideration for the debt is property derived from the deceased and therefore the debt may not be deducted in arriving at the value of his estate. (NB it does not matter that the disposition of the deceased occurred before 17 March 1986 so long as *the debt* was incurred after that date.)

(2) In 1974 Jake give a diamond brooch to his daughter (Liz). In 1984 she in turn gave the brooch to her sister Sam. In 1988 Sam lends £50,000 to Jake who subsequently dies leaving that debt still outstanding.

The consideration for the debt was not derived from the deceased and Sam would (presumably) be able to show that, although she received property derived from the deceased the disposition of that property by the deceased was not linked to the subsequent transaction. Had Jake bought the brooch back from Liz in 1988 (leaving the price outstanding as a debt) the consideration for the debt would then be property derived from him so that the debt would not be deductible.

When a debt, which would otherwise not be deductible on death because of s 103(1), is repaid *inter vivos* the repayment is treated as a potentially exempt transfer (a deemed PET). This provision is essential since otherwise such debts could be repaid immediately before death without any IHT penalty. However, the application of this rule when a taxpayer repurchases property which he had earlier given away is a matter of some uncertainty. Take, for instance, the not uncommon case where A, having made a gift of a valuable chattel, subsequently decides that he cannot live without it. Accordingly, he repurchases that chattel paying full market value to the donee. Has A made a notional PET under s 103(5) at the time when he pays over the purchase price or, if the money is paid as part and parcel of the repurchase agreement, did A never incur any debt or incumbrance falling within the section? It is thought that the latter view is correct since if the purchase price is paid at once a debt will never arise.

It is also important to realise that an element of multiple charging will arise from the artificial debt rule (in *Example 22.13*, for instance, the PET is made chargeable if Berta dies before 1993; the debt is non-deductible and the picture is part of Berta's estate). However the regulations discussed in Appendix VII prevent the multiple imposition of IHT in this case. Finally, although a debt may not be deducted in order to arrive at the deceased's estate for IHT purposes, it must still be paid by the PRs and it is therefore treated as a specific gift by the deceased (see further [**22.81**]). [**22.13–22.30**]

EXAMPLE 22.15

(1) S settled property on discretionary trusts in 1980. In 1990 the trustees lend him £6,000. This debt is non-deductible. NB: it does not matter when the trust was created.

(2) Terry-Testator borrows £50,000 from the Midshire Bank which he gives to his son. The debt that he owes to the Bank is deductible on his death: in no sense is this an 'artificial debt'.

(3) Terry-Testator lends £50,000 to his daughter (interest free; repayable on demand). She buys a house with the money which increases in value. There is no transfer of value by Terry; the debt provisions are irrelevant, and Terry has not reserved any benefit in the property purchased with the loan.

II HOW TO CALCULATE THE IHT BILL ON DEATH

Tax is calculated according to the rates set out in the following table.

Gross cumulative transfer (£)	Rate (%) – Death	Rate (%) – Life
0 –140,000	0	0
Above 140,000	40	20

These rates (which came into force on 6 April 1991) will be applied to the estate at death and, in addition, where that death occurs within seven years of a chargeable lifetime transfer or PET made by the deceased the following results occur:

(1) In the case of a *chargeable transfer*, IHT must be recalculated in accordance with the rates of tax in force at the donor's death provided that these are less than the rates at the time of the transfer. Subject to taper relief, extra tax may then be payable.

(2) In the case of a PET, the transfer is treated as a chargeable transfer so that first, IHT must be calculated (subject to taper relief) at the rates current at the donor's death (again provided that these rates are less than those in force at the time when the transfer occurred: otherwise the latter apply), and secondly, as the PET must now be included in the total transfers of the taxpayer for cumulation purposes, this may necessitate a recalculation of the tax charged on other chargeable transfers made by the donor and, where a discretionary trust is involved, the recalculation of any exit charge. It is proposed to deal with these problems in order, looking first at the effect of death upon the chargeable lifetime transfers of the deceased and then at the taxation of the death estate. The consequences for discretionary trusts are considered in Chapter 26.   [22.31]

1 Chargeable transfers of the deceased made within seven years of his death

As already explained (see [21.101]) IHT will have been charged, at half the then death rate, at the time when the transfer was made. In computing that tax, transfers in the seven preceding years will have been included in the cumulative total of the transferor. As a result of his death within the following seven years IHT must be recalculated on the original value transferred at the full rate of IHT in force at the date of death. After deducting the tax originally paid, extra tax may be payable. Three qualifications must be made to this basic principle; first, if death occurs more than three years after the gift, taper relief ensures that only a percentage of the death rate is charged. The tapering percentages are as follows:

(a) where the transfer is made more than three but not more than four years before the death, 80%;

(b) where the transfer is made more than four but not more than five years before the death, 60%;

(c) where the transfer is made more than five but not more than six years before the death, 40%; and

(d) where the transfer is made more than six but not more than seven years before the death, 20%.

EXAMPLE 22.16

Danaos settles £200,000 on discretionary trusts in July 1991 (IHT is paid by the trustees). He dies:

(i) on 1 January 1993

or (ii) on 1 January 1997

or (iii) on 1 January 1999.

The *original transfer* in 1991 was subject to IHT at one half of rates in force for 1991–92 (see Table, [**22.31**]).

In (i) he dies within three years of the gift: accordingly, a charge at the full tax rates for 1992–93 must be calculated, tax paid in 1991 deducted, and any balance is then payable.

In (ii) he dies more than five but less than six years after the gift: therefore only 40% of the full amount of tax on death is to be calculated, the tax paid in 1991 deducted, and the balance (if any) is then payable.

In (iii) death occurs more than seven years after the transfer and therefore no supplementary tax is payable.

If it is assumed that the current rates of IHT apply throughout this period, the actual tax computations are as follows (assuming that the 1991 transfer was the first chargeable transfer of Danaos):

(a) *IHT on the 1991 chargeable transfer is as follows:*

first £140,000   —   nil

remaining £60,000 at 20%   —   £12,000

total IHT payable by the trustees is therefore £12,000.

(b) *If death occurs within three years:* tax on a transfer of £200,000 at the then death rates is:

first £140,000   —   nil

remaining £60,000 at 40%   —   £24,000

total IHT is therefore £24,000 which after deducting the sum paid in 1991 (£12,000) leaves a further £12,000 to be paid.

(c) *If death occurs in 1997* the calculation is as follows:

(i) full IHT at death rates £24,000 (as in (b) above)

(ii) take 40% (taper relief) of that tax: £24,000 × 40% = £9,600

(iii) As that sum is less than the tax actually paid in 1991 *there is no extra IHT to pay.*

It should be noted in *Example 22.16* that even though the result of taper relief may be to ensure that extra IHT is not payable because of the death, it does not lead to any refund of the original IHT paid when the chargeable transfer was made: in such cases the taper relief is inapplicable, see IHTA 1984 s 7(5). (The assumption in *Example 22.16* that rates of tax remain unchanged is, of course, unrealistic since the IHT rate bands are linked to rises in the RPI.)

A second qualification to the basic principle that death results in a recalculation of IHT on chargeable transfers made within seven years is that if the property given (other than tangible moveables which are wasting assets) falls in value by the date of death, the extra IHT is calculated on that reduced value.

EXAMPLE 22.17

In 1991 Dougal gave a Matisse figure drawing worth £200,000 to his discretionary trustees (who paid the IHT). He died in 1992 when the Matisse was worth only £175,000.
(1)   Assuming it was Dougal's first chargeable transfer IHT paid on the 1991 gift was £12,000.   60000 × 20%
(2)   Extra IHT on death (assume rates unchanged) is calculated on £175,000 = £14,000.
Hence extra IHT payable is £2,000.

Had the property been sold by the trustees before Dougal's death for £25,000 less than its value when given away by Dougal the extra (death) IHT would be charged on the sale proceeds with the same result as above. If, however, the property had been given away by the trustees before Dougal's death, even though its value might at that time have fallen by £25,000 since Dougal's original gift, no relief is given, with the result that the extra charge caused by Dougal's death will be levied on the full £200,000.

The final qualification to the basic rule concerns the transition from CTT to IHT. Under the CTT regime it was only chargeable transfers made within three years of death that suffered a supplementary charge to tax because of that death. FA 1986 Sch 19 para 40 therefore provides that for transfers made before 18 March 1986 the change to IHT shall not result in extra tax being levied.

EXAMPLE 22.18

Wary makes the following chargeable transfers:
(1)   in 1979 £100,000
(2)   in 1981 £25,000
(3)   in 1985 £50,000
(4)   on 17 March 1986 £40,000
(5)   he dies on 19 March 1987
The four transfers occurred during the CTT regime and suffered CTT at the then lifetime rates of tax. As ten year cumulation applied, the 1979 transfer was still in Wary's cumulative total when he made his gift on 17 March 1986. His death (after the introduction of IHT) has the following consequences:
(1)   his cumulative total at death (calculated according to the IHT cumulation period of seven years) is £115,000 (transfers (2)-(4));
(2)   the 1985 transfer, made within three years of death, is subject to a supplementary charge calculated on the rates of IHT in March 1987;
(3)   the 1981 transfer would not have attracted any supplementary CTT assessment since it was made more than three years before death. Accordingly there is no reassessment for IHT.

It will be realised that as a result of these rules the *value* of a chargeable lifetime transfer is not reduced in the seven year period since taper relief is given in terms of the rate of IHT to be charged on that transfer. Hence the full value of the life transfer remains in the cumulative total of the transferor and there is no reduction in the tax charged on his death estate. In cases where that transfer fell within the transferor's nil rate band taper relief does not therefore apply.   [**22.32**]

2   PETs made within seven years of death

The PET becomes a chargeable transfer and is subject to IHT) in accordance with the taxpayer's cumulative total at the date when it was made (ie taking into account chargeable transfers in the preceding seven years). The value transferred is frozen at the date of transfer unless the property has fallen in value by the date of death in which case the lower value is charged (the rules concerning the fall in value of assets are the same as those considered in 1 above). Despite these provisions, which look back to the actual date of the transfer of value, the IHT is calculated by reference to the rates in force at the date of death unless those rates have increased in which case the rates at the time of the transfer are taken (subject to taper relief, as in 1 above). **[22.33]**

EXAMPLE 22.19

In October 1988 Zanda gave a valuable doll (then worth £200,000) to her grand-daughter Cressida. She died in July 1992 when the value of the doll was £180,000. Assuming that Zanda had made no other transfers of value during her life, ignoring exemptions and reliefs, the IHT consequences are:
(1) The 1988 transfer was potentially exempt. However as Zanda dies within seven years it is made chargeable.
(2) As the asset has fallen in value by the date of death IHT is charged on the reduced value, ie on £180,000.
(3) IHT at the rates current when Zanda died is:
   first £140,000   —   nil
   next £40,000 at 40%   =   £16,000
Total IHT = £16,000.
(4) Taper relief is however available since Zanda died more than three years after the gift. Therefore:
   £16,000 × 80% (taper relief) = £12,800.
Note: although IHT is calculated by reference to the reduced value of the asset, for cumulation purposes the original value transferred (£200,000) is retained.

3 Position where a combination of PETs and chargeable transfers have been made within seven years of death

PETs are presumed to be exempt transfers unless the transferor dies within the seven year period. Accordingly, they are not cumulated in calculating IHT on subsequent chargeable transfers. Consider the following illustration:

EXAMPLE 22.20

In July 1988 Planer gives shares worth £160,000 to his son.
In March 1992 he settles land worth £150,000 on discretionary trusts and pays the IHT himself (so that grossing-up applies: see **[21.102]**).
He dies in February 1993. (Assume no other transfers of value were made by Planer; ignore exemptions and reliefs; current IHT rates apply throughout).
(1) The transfer in 1988 is a PET.
(2) In calculating the IHT on the chargeable transfer in 1992 the PET is ignored and IHT is £2,500.
   The chargeable transfer in 1992 is therefore £152,500 (£150,000 + £2,500).
(3) As a result of his death within seven years the PET is made chargeable and the IHT calculation is as follows:
   (a) *on the 1988 transfer* IHT at the rates when Planer died is subject to 60% taper relief (gifts more than four, less than five years before death). Hence IHT at death rates is:
      first £140,000 — nil
      next, £20,000 at 40% = £8,000
   Taper relief at 60%:
      £8,000 × 60% = £4,800 (tax on 1988 transfer)

NB primary liability for this tax falls upon the donee (see [**22.35**]). Grossing-up does not apply when IHT is charged, or additional tax is payable, because of death.

(b) *on the 1992 transfer*   IHT must be recalculated on this transfer since the transferor has died within seven years, and the former PET must be included in the cumulative total of Planer at the time when this transfer was made. Hence:
   (i) cumulative transfers of Planer in 1992 = £160,000
   (ii) value transferred in 1992 = £152,500
   (iii) IHT at death rates on transfers between £160,000 and £312,500 is £152,500 × 40% = £61,000
Taper relief is not available on this transfer since Planer dies within three years.
Therefore:
deduct IHT paid in 1992:
£61,000 — £2,500 = £58,500
Additional IHT payable on the 1992 transfer is £58,500
NB the cumulative total of transfers made by Planer at his death (which will affect the IHT payable on his death estate) is £312,500.

The following diagram illustrates how seven year cumulation operates for PETs and chargeable transfers (CTs) made within seven years of death:

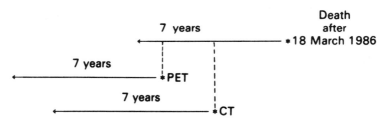

When a PET is made after an earlier chargeable transfer and the transferor dies in the following seven years tax on that PET will be calculated by including the earlier transfer in his cumulative total. In this sense the making of the PET means that there is no reduction in his cumulative total for a further seven years and the result is that IHT could eventually turn out to be higher than if the PET had never been made ('the PET trap'!).   [**22.34**]

EXAMPLE 22.21

Yvonne made a chargeable transfer of £140,000 on 1 May 1984 (under the CTT régime) and on 1 May 1989 made a gift of £200,000 to take advantage of the PET régime. Unfortunately, she dies after 1 May 1991 (when the 1984 transfer drops out of cumulation) but before 1 May 1992 (when taper relief begins to operate on the PET).
(a) IHT on the former PET (at current rates) is £80,000 since the 1984 transfer forms part of Yvonne's cumulative total in 1989. Tax on the death estate will then be calculated by including the 1989 transfer (the former PET) in Yvonne's cumulative total.
(b) Had Yvonne not made the 1989 PET so that £200,000 formed part of her death estate, tax thereon (ignoring the 1984 transfer which has dropped out of cumulation) is £24,000.
Extra IHT resulting from the making of the PET is therefore £80,000 – £24,000 = £56,000.

4 Accountability and liability for IHT on lifetime transfers made within seven years of death

The donee of a potentially exempt transfer which becomes chargeable by virtue of the subsequent death of the transferor must deliver an account to the Revenue within twelve months of the end of the month of death (IHTA 1984 s 216(1)(bb)). Tax itself is payable six months after the end of the month of death and interest on unpaid IHT runs from that date. There is no question of interest being charged from the date of the PET. Primary liability for the tax is placed upon the transferee although the Revenue may also claim the IHT from any person in whom the property is vested, whether beneficially or not, excluding however a purchaser of that property (unless it was subject to an Inland Revenue charge for the tax owing: see generally [**21.141**]).

To the extent that the above persons are not liable for the IHT *or* to the extent that any tax remains unpaid for twelve months after the death, the deceased's PRs may be held liable (IHTA 1984 s 199(2)). An application for a certificate of discharge in respect of IHT that may be payable on a PET may not be made before the expiration of two years from the death of the transferor (except where the Board exercise their discretion to receive an earlier application). If the property transferred qualified for the instalment option (see [**21.144**]) the tax resulting from death within seven years may be paid in instalments if the donee so elects and provided that he still owns qualifying property at the date of death (IHTA 1984 s 227(1A)).

So far as additional tax on chargeable lifetime transfers is concerned the same liability rules apply. Primary liability rests upon the donee although the deceased's PRs can be forced to pay the tax in the circumstances discussed above.

The problems posed for PRs by this contingent liability for IHT on PETs and *inter vivos* chargeable transfers are considered at [**22.57**].   [**22.35**]

5 Calculating IHT on the death estate

Having considered the treatment of PETs and the additional IHT on lifetime transfers that may result from the death of the transferor, it is now necessary to consider the taxation of the death estate (which includes property subject to a reservation and settled property in which the deceased was the life tenant). To calculate the IHT the following procedure should be adopted:

Step 1 Calculate total chargeable death estate; ignore, therefore, exempt transfers (eg to a spouse) and apply any available reliefs (eg reduce the value of relevant business property by the appropriate percentage).

Step 2 Join the table at the point reached by the transferor as a result of chargeable transfers made in the seven years before death. This cumulative total must include both transfers that were charged *ab initio* and PETs brought into charge as a result of the death.

Step 3 Calculate death IHT bill.

Step 4 Convert the tax to an average or estate rate—ie divide IHT *(Step 3)* by total chargeable estate (arrived at in *Step 1*) and multiply by 100 to obtain a percentage rate. It is then possible to say how much IHT each asset bears. This is necessary in cases where the IHT is not a testamentary expense but is borne by the legatee or by trustees of a settlement or by the donee of property subject to a reservation (see [**22.59**]). If the deceased had exhausted his nil rate band as a result of lifetime transfers made in the seven years before death, his death estate will be subject to tax at a rate of 40% which will be the estate rate.

EXAMPLE 22.22

Dougal has just died leaving an estate valued after payment of all debts etc at £80,000. A picture worth £10,000 is left to his daughter Diana (the will states that it is to bear its own IHT) and the rest of the estate is left to his son Dalgleish. Dougal made chargeable transfers in the seven years preceding his death of £100,000. To calculate the IHT on death:
(1)   Join the death table at £100,000 (lifetime cumulative total).
(2)   Calculate IHT on an estate of £80,000:

$$
\begin{array}{lr}
 & £ \\
£40{,}000 \times 0\% & 0 \\
£40{,}000 \times 40\% & \underline{16{,}000} \\
 & \underline{\underline{£16{,}000}}
\end{array}
$$

(3)   Calculate the estate rate

$$\frac{£16{,}000 \ (\text{IHT})}{£80{,}000 \ (\text{Estate})} \times 100 = 20\%$$

(4)   Apply estate rate to picture (ie 20% × £10,000) = £2,000. This sum will be payable by Diana.
(5)   Residue (£70,000) is taxed at 20% = £14,000. The balance will be paid to Dalgleish.

Property subject to a reservation and settled property in which the deceased had held an interest in possession at the date of death is included in the estate in order to calculate the estate rate of tax. The appropriate tax is, however, primarily the responsibility of either the donee or the trustees. The IHT position on death can be represented as follows:

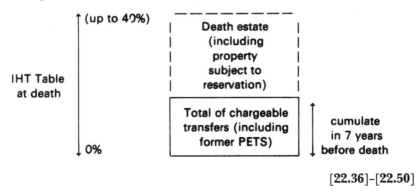

[22.36]–[22.50]

III   PAYMENT OF IHT—INCIDENCE AND BURDEN

If the deceased was domiciled in the UK at the time of his death, IHT is chargeable on all the property comprised in his estate whether situated in the UK or abroad. If, however, he was domiciled elsewhere, IHT is only chargeable on his property situated in the UK.   [22.51]

1 Who pays the IHT on death?

a) *Duty to account*

The deceased's PRs are generally under a duty to deliver to the Revenue within 12 months of the end of the month of the death an account specifying all the property that formed part of the deceased's estate immediately before his death and including property:
(1) in which the deceased had a beneficial interest in possession (eg where the deceased was the life tenant under a settlement); and
(2) property over which he had a general power of appointment (this property is included since such a power enabled the deceased to appoint himself the owner so that in effect the property is indistinguishable from property owned by him absolutely).

In practice, the PRs will deliver their account as soon as possible because first, they cannot obtain probate and, therefore, administer the estate until an account has been delivered and the IHT paid; and, secondly, they must pay interest on any IHT payable on death and which is unpaid by the end of the sixth month after the end of the month in which the deceased died (for instance, a death in January would mean that IHT is due before 1 August and, thereafter, interest would be payable). **[22.52]**

b) *'Excepted estates'* (SI 1981/880 amended by SI 1991/1248)

No account need be delivered in the case of an 'excepted estate'. The taxpayer must die domiciled in the UK; must have made no chargeable lifetime transfers; must not have been a life tenant under a settlement; his death estate must not include property subject to a reservation and he must not have owned at death foreign property amounting to more than £15,000. Subject thereto the estate will be excepted if the *gross* value at death does not exceed £125,000. This figure takes account of all property passing under the will or intestacy; of nominated property; and, in cases where the deceased had been a joint tenant of property, the value of the deceased's share in that property.

The Revenue reserve the right to call for an account (on Form 204) within 35 days of the issue of a grant of probate, but if they do not do so, the PRs are then automatically discharged from further liability. **[22.53]**

c) *IHT forms*

In cases other than b) above, to obtain a grant the PRs must submit an Inland Revenue account (an IHT Form). IHT Form 202 is a simplified form which proceeds on the assumption that there will be no IHT liability. The deceased must die domiciled in the UK; have made no chargeable lifetime transfers in the seven years before death; and have been neither entitled in an interest in possession trust nor have settled property in that seven year period. The estate must be made up of property situated in the UK only. If these conditions are satisfied IHT Form 202 is then the appropriate form so long as the *net* estate at death does not exceed the current IHT threshold (£140,000). Liabilities (including exemptions and reliefs from IHT) are deducted in arriving at the net figure. Accordingly, if a millionaire leaves his entire estate to his surviving spouse, IHT Form 202 will (assuming that the other requirements are met) be the appropriate form. Where the deceased had been a joint tenant at death it is only the value of his share of the property that is included.

If IHT Form 202 cannot be used, either IHT Form 200 or 201 (if the deceased died domiciled outside the UK) must be completed (see Appendix III for a completed IHT Form 200). **[22.54]**

d) *Liability for IHT* (IHTA 1984 Part VII)

Personal representatives   PRs must pay the IHT on assets owned beneficially by the deceased at the time of death and on land comprised in a settlement which vests in them as PRs. Their liability is personal, but limited to assets which they received as PRs or might have received but for their own neglect or default (IHTA 1984 s 204 and see *IRC v Stannard* (1984) which establishes that overseas PRs or trustees may find that their personal UK assets are seized to meet that liability). If the PRs fail to pay the IHT other persons are concurrently liable, namely:

(1) Executors *de son tort*, ie persons who interfere with the deceased's property so as to constitute themselves executors. Their liability is limited to the assets in their hands (see *IRC v Stype Investments (Jersey) Ltd* (1982)).

(2) Beneficiaries entitled under the will or on intestacy in whom the property becomes vested after death. Their liability is limited to the property that they receive.

(3) A purchaser of real property if an Inland Revenue charge is registered against that property. His liability is limited to the value of the charge.

(4) Any beneficiary entitled to an interest in possession in the property after the death. Liability is generally limited to the value of that property. **[22.55]**

Trustees   Where the deceased had an interest in possession in settled property at the date of his death, it is the trustees of the settlement who are liable for any IHT on the settled property to the extent that they received or could have received assets as trustees. Should the trustees not pay the tax, the persons set out in (3) and (4) above are concurrently liable. **[22.56]**

Contingent liability of PRs   In three cases PRs may incur liability to IHT if the persons primarily liable (the donees of the property) have reached the limits of their liability to pay or if the tax remains unpaid for twelve months after the death. These occasions are, first, when a lifetime chargeable transfer is subject to additional IHT because of the death; secondly, if a PET is brought into charge because of the death; and finally if the estate includes property subject to a reservation. The following Example illustrates the type of problem that may arise:

EXAMPLE 22.23

Mort dies leaving an estate (fully taxed) of £500,000. The PRs are unaware of any lifetime gifts and therefore pay IHT of £144,000 and distribute the remainder of the estate. Consider the following alternatives:

(1) After some years a lifetime gift by Mort of £140,000 which had been made six years before his death and was potentially exempt when made is discovered. Although no IHT is chargeable on that gift the PR's are accountable for extra IHT on the death estate of £56,000; or

(2) A gift of £1,000,000 made one year before Mort's death is discovered. In this case not only will the PR's be accountable for extra IHT of £56,000 as above but in addition if the donee fails to pay IHT on the £1,000,000 gift the PR's will be liable to pay that IHT (limited to the net assets in the estate which have passed through their hands).

Contingent liabilities present major problems for PRs and the following matters should be noted:

(1) Their liability may arise long after the estate has been fully administered and distributed (eg a PET may be discovered which is not only itself taxable but also affects the charge on subsequent lifetime chargeable transfers and on the death estate). It may therefore be important for PRs to obtain suitable indemnities from the residuary beneficiary before distributing the estate although such personal indemnities are of course always vulnerable (eg in the event of the bankruptcy of that beneficiary).

(2) The liability of PRs is always limited to the value of the estate (as discussed above). However, even if IHT has been paid on the estate and a certificate of discharge obtained they are still liable to pay the further tax that may arise in these three situations.

(3) If PRs pay IHT in these cases no right of recovery is given in IHTA 1984 against donees who were primarily liable except in the case of reservation of benefit property (in this situation s 211(3) affords a right of recovery). It is extremely doubtful whether such a right exists under general law. There is, of course, nothing to stop a donor taking an indemnity from his donee to pay any future IHT as a condition of making the PET. Such an arrangement would be expressed as an indemnity in favour of his estate and does not involve any reservation of benefit in the gifted property. As already mentioned, however, such personal indemnities are vulnerable in the event of the bankruptcy or emigration of the donee.

(4) It will not be satisfactory for PRs to retain estate assets to cover the danger of a future tax liability. Apart from being unpopular with beneficiaries there is no guarantee that PRs will retain an adequate sum to cover tax liability on a PET which they did not know had been made: only by retaining all the assets in the estate will they be wholly protected!

(5) Insurance would seem to be the obvious answer to all these problems. PRs should give full information on matters within their knowledge and then seek cover (up to the limit of their liability) in respect of an unforeseen IHT liability arising. It would seem reasonable for testators to give expressly a power to insure against these risks. It is understood that cover can be arranged on an individual basis in such cases with the premium payable ranging from 0.2% up to 2% of the amount of indemnity required. Accordingly in *Example 22.23* the cost would be (at most) 2% × £356,000 = £7,120.

Limited comfort to PRs is afforded by a letter from the Inland Revenue to the Law Society dated 11 February 1991 which states:

'The Capital Taxes Offices will not usually pursue for inheritance tax personal representatives who
— after making the fullest enquiries that are reasonably practicable in the circumstances to discover lifetime transfers, and so
— having done all in their power to make full disclosure of them to the Board of Inland Revenue
— have obtained a certificate of discharge and distributed the estate before a chargeable lifetime transfer comes to light.
This statement . . . is made without prejudice to the application in an appropriate case of s 199(2) Inheritance Tax Act 1984.'

In addition to persons who are liable for IHT on death, real property is automatically subject to an Inland Revenue charge from the date of death until the date when the IHT is paid (IHTA 1984 s 237(1)(a)).   **[22.57]**

e) *Payment of tax: the instalment option*

To obtain a grant of representation, PRs must pay all the IHT for which they are liable (on non-instalment option property: see below) when they deliver their account (IHT Form) to the Revenue. Additionally, they *may* pay the IHT for which they are not liable (eg IHT on settled property in which the deceased had an interest in possession) if they are asked to do so by the persons liable. (They will then of course be entitled to reimbursement.) If they refuse to pay such IHT, however, they are still entitled to a grant of probate since they have paid all the tax for which they are liable.

In the case of certain property the tax may, at the option of the PRs, be paid in ten yearly instalments with the first instalment falling due six months after the end of the month of death. The object of this facility is to prevent the particular assets from having to be sold by the PRs in order to raise the necessary IHT.

The instalment option is available on the following assets:

(1) land, freehold or leasehold, wherever situate;
(2) shares or securities in a company which gave the deceased control of that company ('control' is defined as voting control on all questions affecting the company as a whole);
(3) a non-controlling holding of shares or securities in an unquoted company (ie a company which is neither quoted on a recognised Stock Exchange nor dealt in on the Unlisted Securities Market)where the Revenue are satisfied that payment of the tax in one lump sum would cause 'undue hardship';
(4) a non-controlling holding as in (3) above where the tax on the shares or securities and on other property carrying the instalment option comprises at least 20% of the tax due from that particular person (in the same capacity);
(5) other non-controlling shareholdings in unquoted companies, where the value of the shares exceeds £20,000 and either their nominal value is at least 10% of the nominal value of all the issued shares in the company, or the shares are ordinary shares whose nominal value is at least 10% of the nominal value of all ordinary shares in the company; and
(6) a business or a share in a business, eg a partnership share.

An additional attraction of paying by instalments is that, generally, no interest is charged so long as each instalment is paid on the due date. In the event of late payment the interest charge is merely on the outstanding instalment. Interest is, however, charged on the total outstanding IHT liability (even if the instalments are paid on time) in the case of land which is not a business asset and shares in investment companies. If the asset subject to the instalment option is sold, the outstanding instalments of IHT become payable at once. Finally, it should be stressed that in the case of businesses the instalment option complements business property relief under IHTA 1984 ss 103–114 (see Chapter 23).

If the instalment option is exercised the first instalment is, as already mentioned, payable six months after the month of death. Hence, PRs will normally exercise the option *in order to pay as little IHT as possible before obtaining the grant.* Once the grant has been obtained they may then decide to discharge the IHT on the instalment property in one lump sum. PRs should, however, bear in mind that some IHT will usually be payable before the grant. The necessary cash may be obtained from the deceased's account at either a bank or a building society; from the sale of property for which a grant is not necessary; or by means of a personal loan from a beneficiary. If a loan has to be raised commercially, the interest thereon will qualify for income tax relief for 12 months from the making of the loan so long as it is on a loan account (not by way of overdraft) and is used to pay the tax attributable to personal property (including leaseholds and land held on trust for sale). The Keith Committee rejected suggestions that IHT should generally be made payable *after* a grant has been obtained (see Cmnd 9120 Chapter 33).

PRs will be advised therefore to exercise the instalment option to defer IHT until after obtaining the grant. Where the IHT is a testamentary expense, the tax can then be paid off in one lump sum. If the residuary legatee objects (it may, for instance, be necessary to sell an asset to pay the IHT), PRs could arrange to vest the residue in that beneficiary and for him to discharge the future instalments. Adequate security should, however, be taken in such cases because if the beneficiary defaults, the PRs remain liable for the outstanding IHT. In the case of a specific gift which bears its own IHT and which qualifies for the instalment option, the decision whether to discharge the entire IHT bill once probate has been obtained should be left to the legatee. PRs should not make a unilateral decision (see further [**22.59**]).

Once PRs have paid all the outstanding IHT they are entitled to a certificate of discharge under IHTA 1984 s 239(2).

As already discussed, the instalment option may also be available when a chargeable *inter vivos* transfer is made (see [**21.144**]) and when IHT becomes payable on a PET or additional IHT on a chargeable transfer. In these situations, however, further requirements must be satisfied before the option can be claimed. The donee must have retained the original property or, if it has been sold, have used the proceeds to purchase qualifying replacement property (for a discussion of these requirements in the context of business relief see [**23.50**]). Further, when the property consisted of unquoted shares or securities those assets must remain unquoted from the date of transfer to the date of death (IHTA 1984 s 227(1A)).   [**22.58**]

2 Allocating the burden of IHT

The Revenue are satisfied once the IHT due on the estate has been paid. However, as far as the PRs and beneficiaries under the will are concerned, the further question arises as to how the tax should be borne as between the beneficiaries: eg should the tax attributable to a specific legacy be paid out of the residue as a testamentary expense or is it charged on the property (the specific legacy)? The answer to this question is particularly important whenever specific legacies are combined with exempt or partially exempt residue, since, if the IHT is to be paid out of that residue, the grossing-up calculation under IHTA 1984 s 38 (see [**22.81**]) will be necessary and will result in more IHT being payable.

As a general rule, a testator can, and should, stipulate expressly in his will where the IHT on a specific bequest is to fall. The one exception is that any direction in the will to pay the IHT attributable to a chargeable share of residue out of exempt residue will be void. Chargeable residue must bear its own tax (see [**22.89**]).

If the will makes no provision for the burden of tax, the general principle is that IHT on UK unsettled property is a testamentary expense payable from residue. Under the estate duty regime land had, in such cases, borne its own duty, but the Scottish case of *Re Dougal* (1981) decided that the IHT legislation drew no distinction between realty and personalty and the matter was put beyond doubt by IHTA 1984 s 211.

EXAMPLE 22.24

In Lyslie's will his landed estate is left to his son and his stocks and shares to his daughter. The residue is left to his surviving spouse. In addition he owned a country cottage jointly with his brother, Ernie.
(1) IHT on the specific gifts of the land and securities is borne by the residue in the absence of any provision to the contrary in Lyslie's will. Note that the spouse exemption therefore only applies to exempt from charge what is left after the payment of IHT on the specific gifts.
(2) IHT on the joint property is paid by the PRs but ultimately borne by brother Ernie.

In drafting wills and administering estates the following matters should, therefore, be borne in mind:
(1) When drafting a new will, expressly state whether bequests are tax-bearing or are free of tax.
(2) Old wills which have been drawn up but are not yet in force should be checked to ensure that provision has been made for the payment of IHT on gifts of realty. The will may have been drafted on the assumption that such gifts bear their own tax in which case amendments will be necessary.
(3) IHT on foreign property and joint property will always be borne by the beneficiary unless the will provides to the contrary.
Assuming that the will contains a specific tax-bearing legacy, how will the IHT, in practice, be paid on it? As the PRs are primarily liable to the Revenue for the IHT, they will usually pay that tax in order to obtain probate and either deduct it from the legacy (eg if it is a pecuniary legacy) or recover it from the legatee. Where the PRs pay IHT which is not a testamentary expense (ie on all tax-bearing gifts), they have a right to recover that sum from the person in whom the property is vested (IHTA 1984 s 211(3)). As mentioned, the recovery of IHT in the case of pecuniary legacies presents no problems since the PRs can deduct the IHT from the legacy before handing over the balance to the legatee. For specific legacies of other property (ie land or chattels), the PRs have the power to sell, mortgage or charge the property in order to recover the tax. If they instead (usually at the legatee's request) propose to transfer the asset to him, they should ensure that they are given sufficient guarantees that the tax will be refunded to them.

Problems can arise for PRs who pay the IHT on specific tax-bearing legacies to which the instalment option applies. If they choose to pay the IHT on such legacies in one lump sum, when they seek to recover that tax from the legatee he can elect to repay them in instalments (IHTA 1984 s 213). Hence, the PRs should, after consulting the legatee, elect to pay the IHT on that property by instalments; if they do so, however, and if the legatee defaults in paying the instalments, the PRs remain concurrently liable for the outstanding IHT.

To avoid any dispute, when the PRs have paid IHT which they are entitled to recover from the legatee, they can obtain a certificate from the Revenue which is conclusive as to the amount of tax which they are entitled to recover (IHTA 1984 s 214).

In the three cases mentioned at [**22.57**] PRs are liable to pay IHT if the tax is not paid by the person primarily responsible. As this contingent liability will usually only arise more than twelve months after death, PRs should exercise caution whenever there is a risk of liability. When the tax liability is known, they should retain sufficient assets out of the estate to cover that bill (ie they should not make a final distribution of residue until all IHT resulting from the death has been paid). In other cases, as discussed earlier, PRs may be placed in an invidious position. [**22.59**]

3 Cases where the IHT has to be recalculated

There are a number of instances where the IHT paid on a deceased's estate will need to be recalculated. In general this will be necessary when the value of that estate is altered for some reason, or where the destination of a bequest is varied. The principal instances where recalculation is necessary are: [**22.60**]

Cases where sale proceeds are substituted for the death valuation (see [**22.8**]). [**22.61**]

The effect of variations and disclaimers Such instruments, if made within two years of the death, may be read back into the original will (see [**22.129**]). [**22.62**]

Discretionary trusts under IHTA 1984 s 144 If broken up within two years of death, tax is calculated as if the testator had provided in his will for the dispositions of the trustees (see [**22.125**]). [**22.63**]

Orders under the Inheritance (Provisions for Family and Dependants) Act 1975 When the court exercises its powers under s 2 of the 1975 Act to order financial provision out of the deceased's estate for his family and dependants, the order is treated as made by the deceased on death and may result in there having been an under- or over-payment of IHT on death. Any application under this Act should normally be made within six months of the testator's death, so that the PRs will have some warning that adjustments to the IHT bill may have to be made. Further adjustments to the tax bill may have to be made if the court makes an order under s 10 of the Act reclaiming property given away by the deceased in the six years prior to his death with the intention of defeating a claim for financial provision under the Act. In this case, the deceased's cumulative total of chargeable lifetime transfers in the previous seven years is reduced by the gift reclaimed. This, of itself, may affect the rate at which tax is charged on the deceased's estate on death. Also the value of the reclaimed property and any tax repaid on it falls into the deceased's estate thus necessitating a recalculation of the IHT payable on death.

The rules governing *post-mortem* rearrangements—considered at [**22.128**] ff —are bolstered up by a somewhat obscure anti-avoidance provision in IHTA 1984 s 29A (inserted by FA 1989). It is relevant when there is an exempt transfer on death (eg to the surviving spouse) and that beneficiary then, in satisfaction of a claim against the estate of the deceased, disposes of property 'not derived from the death transfer'.

EXAMPLE 22.25

A dies leaving everything to Mrs A. Dependant B has a claim against A's estate but is 'bought off' by Mrs A making a payment (out of her own resources) of £150,000.

(1) *In the absence of specific legislation:* the arrangement would probably be a PET by Mrs A to B and so free from IHT provided that Mrs A survived by seven years. Alternatively it could even be argued that there was no transfer of value since the compromise was a commercial arrangement under IHTA 1984 s 10. No IHT was, of course, charged on A's death.

(2) *Position under s 29A:* A's will is deemed amended to include a specific gift of £150,000 to B with the remainder (only) passing to Mrs A. Accordingly a recalculation will be necessary and an immediate IHT charge will arise. **[22.64]-[22.80]**

IV PROBLEMS CREATED BY THE PARTIALLY EXEMPT TRANSFER (IHTA 1984 ss 36–42)

1 When do ss 36–42 apply?

In many cases the calculation of the IHT bill on death will be relatively straightforward. Difficulties may, however, arise when a particular combination of dispositions is made in a will. IHTA 1984 ss 36–42 provide machinery for resolving these problems with a method of calculating the gross value of the gifts involved and, accordingly, the IHT payable. Consider, first, a number of instances where the calculation of the IHT on death poses no special difficulties: **[22.81]**

Where all the gifts are taxable: eg A leaves all his property to be divided equally amongst his four children. In this case the whole of A's estate is charged to IHT. **[22.82]**

Where all the gifts are exempt: eg A leaves all his property to a spouse and/ or a charity. In this case the whole estate is untaxed. **[22.83]**

Where specific gifts are exempt and the residue is chargeable: eg A leaves £100,000 to his spouse and the residue of £500,000 to his children. Here the gift to the spouse is exempt, but IHT is charged on the residue of £500,000 so that only the balance will be paid to the children. **[22.84]**

Where specific gifts are chargeable but bear their own tax under the terms of the will and the residue is exempt: eg A leaves a specific tax-bearing gift of £200,000 to his niece and the residue to his spouse. The spouse receives the residue after deduction of the £200,000 gift; IHT is calculated on the £200,000 and is borne by the niece. **[22.85]**

Where there are no specific gifts and part of the residue is exempt, part chargeable: eg A leaves his estate to be divided equally between his son and his spouse. The widow receives half the residue which is, therefore, exempt. The son receives the other half of the residue after the IHT charged on that half has been deducted. It should be noted that the chargeable portion of residue must always bear its own tax; any provision in the will to the contrary is void (IHTA 1984 s 41). A will which provides for half the testator's estate to pass to his surviving spouse and the other half to his daughter will not therefore (assuming that IHT is payable) result in the widow and daughter receiving half the estate each. Instead the daughter will receive less since any tax that is payable must come out of her share.

There are bequests where the calculation of the IHT is not so obvious however, and it becomes necessary to apply the rules in ss 36–42. Taking the simplest illustration, consider a will containing a specific gift which is chargeable but does not bear its own IHT and residue which is exempt, eg A's estate on death is valued at £300,000 and he leaves £200,000 to his daughter with remainder to his surviving spouse. In many ways this represents the structure of the typical family will and, as previously explained, the specific gift of £200,000 will be tax-free unless the will provides to the contrary. The problem which arises, therefore, is to decide how much IHT should be charged on the specific gift and this involves grossing up that gift. With the simplified IHT rate structure, grossing up has become relatively straightforward and, in the tax year 1991–92, the IHT payable will be two-thirds of the amount by which the chargeable legacies exceed the available nil rate band. Hence, assuming that A has an unused nil rate band of £140,000, tax payable on the daughter's legacy will be two-thirds of £200,000 – £140,000: ie £40,000. As a result:

(1) The gross value of the legacy becomes £240,000 and the daughter receives the correct net sum of £200,000 after deducting IHT at 40% on the amount by which the gross legacy exceeds the available nil rate band.
(2) The £40,000 tax is paid out of the residue leaving the surviving spouse with £60,000.

Where the partly exempt transfer contained business or agricultural property eligible for 50% relief and the death occurred before 18 March 1986, the correct combination of gifts achieved a substantial tax saving. For subsequent deaths these anomalous results have been prevented. Where the business property is specifically given to a beneficiary that person will, of course, benefit from the appropriate relief but in other cases the benefit of the relief is apportioned between the exempt and chargeable parts of the estate (IHTA 1984 s 39A). [22.86]

EXAMPLE 22.26

Deceased's estate is valued at £1,000,000 and includes business property (qualifying for 50% relief) worth £600,000. He left a £600,000 legacy to his widow and the residue to his daughter.

	£
Estate	1,000,000
less 50% relief on business property	300,000
value transferred	£700,000

(1) Legacy of £600,000 to widow is multiplied by

$$\frac{R \text{ (value transferred)}}{U \text{ (estate before relief)}} = \frac{£700,000}{£1,000,000} = £420,000$$

(2) Accordingly the value attributed to the residue (given to the daughter) is:

$$400,000 \times \frac{R \;(£700,000)}{U \;(£1,000,000)} = £280,000$$

(3) IHT is therefore charged on £280,000.

NB: the lowest tax bill therefore results if the agricultural or business property is specifically given to a non-exempt beneficiary. "Specific gift" is inadequately defined in IHTA 1984 s 42(1) and the following points may be noted:

(1)   an appropriation of business property in satisfaction of a pecuniary legacy does not count as a specific gift;

(2)   a direction to pay a pecuniary legacy 'out of' business property is likewise not a specific gift of business property (IHTA 1984 s 39A(6));

(3)   it is possible to employ a formula to leave business property equal in value to the testator's nil rate band *after* relief at 50%;

(4)   a defectively drafted will may be cured by an instrument of variation whereby a specific gift of business property is 'read back' into the will.

2   Effect of previous chargeable transfers on the ss 36–42 calculation

In considering the application of ss 36–42, it has so far been assumed that the deceased had made no previous chargeable lifetime transfers in the seven years before his death. If he has, the specific gift on death can only be grossed up after taking account of those cumulative lifetime transfers because they may affect the rate at which tax is charged on the estate on death.   [22.87]

EXAMPLE 22.27

A's estate on death is valued at £250,000 and he leaves £90,000 tax-free to his son and the residue to a charity. A had made gross lifetime transfers in the previous seven years of £140,000.

The lifetime gifts have wiped out A's nil rate band and therefore IHT on the specific legacy of £90,000 is two-thirds of £90,000 = £60,000. Accordingly, the gross legacy is £150,000 so that the charity is left with £100,000.

3   Double grossing-up

IHTA 1984 ss 36–42 also deal with the more complex problems that arise if specific tax-free gifts are combined with chargeable gifts bearing their own tax, and an exempt residue.

Assume that B makes a specific bequest of £170,000 tax-free to his son, and leaves a gift of £80,000 bearing its own tax to his daughter with residue of £400,000 (before deducting any IHT chargeable to residue) going to his spouse. To gross up the specific tax-free gift of £170,000 as if it were the only chargeable estate would produce insufficient IHT bearing in mind that there is an additional chargeable legacy of £80,000. On the other hand, if the £170,000 were grossed up at the estate rate applicable to £250,000 (ie the two gifts of £170,000 and £80,000) the resulting tax would be too high because the £80,000 gift should not be grossed up. Further, to gross up £170,000 at the estate rate applicable to the whole estate including the exempt residue would produce too much tax because this assumes, wrongly, that the residue is also taxable.

The solution provided in ss 36–42 is to gross up the specific tax-free gift at the estate rate applicable to a hypothetical chargeable estate consisting of the grossed-up specific tax-free gift and the gifts bearing their own tax. The procedure, known as double grossing-up, is as follows:

Step 1   Gross up the specific tax-free gift of £170,000 by multiplying excess over nil rate band by $^5/_3$: £30,000 × $^5/_3$ = £50,000.

$$£50,000 + £140,000 = £190,000$$

Step 2   Add to this figure the tax-bearing gift of £80,000 making a hypothetical chargeable estate of £270,000.

Step 3 Calculate IHT on £270,000 using the death table = £52,000. Then convert to an estate rate: viz

$$\frac{£52,000}{£270,000} \times 100 = 19.259$$

Step 4 Gross up the specific tax-free gift a second time at this rate of 19.259%:

$$£170,000 \times \frac{100}{100 - 19.250} = £210,549.78$$

Step 5 The chargeable part of the estate now consists of the grossed-up specific gift (£210,549.78) and the gift bearing its own tax (£80,000) = £290,549.78.

Step 6 On the figure of £290,549.78, IHT is re-calculated at £60,219.91 and the final estate rate is found:

$$\frac{£60,219.91}{£290,549.78} \times 100 = 20.726\%$$

Step 7 The grossed-up specific tax-free gift (£210,549.78) is then charged at this rate (20.726%) = tax of £43,638.55.

It should be noted that the IHT on specific tax-free gifts must always be paid from the residue and it is only the balance that is exempt so that the surviving spouse will receive £400,000–£43,638.55 = £356,361.45. The tax-bearing gift of £80,000 will of course be taxed at 20.726%, but the tax (ie £16,580.80) will be borne by the daughter.

To conclude, ss 36–42 are relevant whenever a tax-free specific gift is mixed with an exempt residue, and, if tax-bearing gifts are also included in the will, then a double grossing-up calculation is required. Logically, to gross up only twice is indefensible since the estate rate established at Step 6 should then be used to gross up further the £170,000 (ie repeat Step 4) and so on and so on! Thankfully, the statute only requires the grossing-up calculation to be done twice with the consequence that a small saving in IHT results! **[22.88]**

4 Problems where part of residue is exempt, part chargeable

So far we have been concerned with a wholly exempt residue. What, however, happens if part of the residue is chargeable? For example, A, whose estate is worth £500,000, leaves (as above) a specific tax-free gift of £170,000 to his son; a tax-bearing gift of £80,000 to his daughter; and the residue equally to his widow and his nephew. **[22.89–22.100]**

The method of calculating the IHT is basically the same as in the double grossing-up example above in that the chargeable portion of the residue (half to nephew) must be added to the hypothetical chargeable estate in *Step 2* to calculate the assumed estate rate. The difficulty is caused because, although IHT on grossed-up gifts is payable before the division of residue into chargeable and non-chargeable portions, the IHT on the nephew's portion of the residue must be deducted from his share of residue after it has been divided. This must be done despite any stipulation to the contrary in the will. To take account of this, the method for calculating the IHT payable in such cases is amended as follows:

Step 1 Gross up the specific tax-free gift of £170,000 to £190,000.

Step 2   Calculate the hypothetical chargeable estate by adding to the grossed-up gift of £190,000: (1) the tax-bearing gift of £80,000 and (2) the chargeable residue:

	£	£
Estate		500,000
Less: grossed-up gift	190,000	
tax-bearing gift	80,000	270,000
		£230,000

The nephew's share (the chargeable residue) is half of £230,000 = £115,000.
   This results in a hypothetical chargeable estate of
£190,000 + £80,000 + £115,000 = £385,000.

Step 3   Calculate the 'assumed estate rate' on £385,000:

$$\text{IHT on £385,000} = £98,000$$

$$\text{Estate rate is } \frac{£98,000}{£385,000} \times 100 = 25.455\%$$

Step 4   Gross up the specific tax-free gift at this rate of 25.455%

$$£170,000 \times \frac{100}{100 - 25.455} = £228,050.17$$

Step 5   The chargeable part of the estate now consists of:

	£	£
Estate		500,000
Less: grossed-up gift	228,050.17	
tax-bearing gift	80,000	308,050.17
		£191,949.83

Nephew's share is ¹/₂ × £191,949.83 = £95,974.91

Therefore, chargeable estate is
   £95,974.91 + £80,000 + £228,050.17 = £404,025.08

Step 6   Calculate the estate rate on the chargeable estate of £404.025.08

$$\text{IHT on £404,025.08} = £105,610.03$$

$$\text{Estate rate is } \frac{£105,610.03}{£404,025.08} \times 100 = 26.139\%$$

Step 7   The grossed-up specific tax-free gift of £228,050.17 is taxed at the rate of 26.139% = £59,610.03.

Step 8   The tax-bearing gift of £80,000 is taxed at 26.139% = £20,911.2. This tax is paid by the daughter.

Step 9   The residue remaining is £500,000 — (£170,000 + £59,610.03 + £80,000) = £190,389.97. This is then divided:
   Half residue to spouse = £95,194.98
   Half residue to nephew = £95,194.98 less IHT calculated at a rate of 26.139% on £95,974.91 (ie the nephew's share of the residue at *Step 5* above). Therefore, the tax on the nephew's share is £25,086.88 so that the nephew receives £70,108.1.   **[22.89]–[22.100]**

V ABATEMENT

Although ss 36–42 are mainly concerned with calculating the chargeable estate in cases where there is an exempt residue, they also deal with certain related matters:

Allocating relief where gifts exceed an exempt limit A transfer may be partly exempt only because it includes gifts which together exceed an exempt limit, eg a transfer to a non-UK domiciled spouse which exceeds £55,000. To deal with such cases IHTA 1984 s 38(2) provides for the exemption to be allocated between the various gifts as follows:
(1) Specific tax-bearing gifts take precedence over other gifts.
(2) Specific tax-free gifts receive relief in the proportion that their values bear to each other.
(3) All specific gifts take precedence over gifts of residue.   **[22.101]**

Abatement of gifts If a transferor makes gifts in his will which exceed the value of his estate, those gifts must be abated in accordance with IHTA 1984 s 37. There are two cases to consider:
(1) Where the gifts exceed the transferor's estate without regard to any tax payable, the gifts abate according to the rules contained in the Administration of Estates Act 1925 and tax is charged on the abated gifts.

EXAMPLE 22.28

A testator's net estate is worth £150,000. He left his house worth £50,000 to his nephew, the gift to bear its own tax, and a general tax-free legacy of £150,000 to a charity. Under IHTA 1984 s 37(1) the legacy must abate to £100,000 to be paid to the charity free of tax. The house will bear its own tax.

(2) Where the transferor's estate is only insufficient to meet the gifts as grossed-up under the rules in ss 36–42, abatement is governed by IHTA 1984 s 37(2). The order in which the gifts are abated depends on the general law.   **[22.102]–[22.120]**

VI SPECIFIC PROBLEMS ON DEATH

This section is concerned with a number of specific problems that should be considered when drafting wills. Points 1 to 3 are devoted to the difficulties that may arise when property is left to a beneficiary who dies either at the same time as the testator, or soon afterwards. In points 4 and 5 drafting flexible wills and amending the will after the testator's death are considered. Will planning involving the use of the spouse exemption is considered in Chapter 35.   **[22.121]**

1 Commorientes

Where A and B leave their property to each other and are both killed in a common catastrophe or otherwise die in circumstances such that it is not clear in what order they died, the Law of Property Act 1925 s 184 stipulates that the younger is deemed to have survived the elder. Hence, if A was the elder, he is presumed to have died first so that his property passes to

B (assuming no survivorship clause—see below) and IHT will be chargeable. B's will leaving everything to A will not take effect because of the prior death of A so that his assets (including his inheritance from A) will pass on intestacy. IHT would prima facie be chargeable. The result is that property bequeathed by the elder would (subject to quick succession relief) be charged to IHT twice. To prevent this double charge, IHTA 1984 s 4(2) provides that when tax is imposed on a deceased's estate under that section A and B 'shall be assumed to have died at the same instant'. Hence, A's estate is charged only once—on his death; it is not taxed a second time on B's death since the gift is treated as lapsing. LPA 1925 s 184 is, therefore, ousted in order to avoid a double charge to IHT, but it still governs the actual destination of the property bequeathed by A and the question of whether the transfer on A's death is chargeable. This may produce apparently bizarre results: [**22.122**]

EXAMPLE 22.29

(1) Fred (aged 60) and his wife Wilma (aged 55) are both killed in a car crash. Fred had left all his property to Wilma, Wilma had left all her property to their son Barnie. According to LPA 1925 s 184, the order of deaths is Fred then Wilma and Fred's property, therefore, passes to Wilma and thence to Barnie. However, the effect of IHTA 1984 s 4(2) is to impose IHT on Fred's death only; ie on the transfer to Wilma which is exempt from IHT, so that Barnie acquires Fred's property free from IHT.

Compare:

(2) Assume that Fred and Barnie are killed in the same crash and that Fred had left his property to Barnie who in turn had left his estate to charity. Although the property passes on Fred's death through Barnie's estate to the charity (which is exempt from IHT), there is a chargeable transfer on Fred's death to Barnie (see further 1987, *Capital Taxes*, p 61).

2 Survivorship clauses

To inherit property on a death it is necessary only to survive the testator so that if the beneficiary dies immediately after inheriting the property, the two deaths could mean two IHT charges. Some relief is provided by quick succession relief (see 3, below), but the prudent testator may seek to avoid this risk by providing in his will for the property to pass to the desired beneficiary only if that person survives him for a stated period. Such provisions are referred to as survivorship clauses and IHTA 1984 s 92 provides that so long as the clause does not exceed six months there will be (at most) only a single IHT charge.

EXAMPLE 22.30

T leaves £100,000 to A 'if he survives me by six months. If he does not the money is to go to B'.

The effect of IHTA 1984 s 92 is to leave matters in suspense for six months and then to read the will in the light of what has happened. Hence, if A does survive for six months it is as if the will had provided '£100,000 to A'; if he dies before the end of that period, it is as if the will had provided for £100,000 to go to B. The result is that two charges to IHT are avoided; there will merely be the one chargeable occasion when the testator dies.

In principle, it is good will drafting to include survivorship clauses. The danger of choosing a period in excess of six months is that IHTA 1984 s 92 will not apply so that the bequest will be settled property to which ordinary charging principles will apply. If a longer period is essential, insert a two year discretionary trust into the will (see 4, below).　　　**[22.123]**

3 **Quick succession relief** (IHTA 1984 s 141)

Quick succession relief offers a measure of relief against two charges to IHT when two chargeable events occur within five years of each other.

For unsettled property quick succession relief is only given on a death where the value of the deceased's estate had been increased by a chargeable transfer (*inter vivos* or on death) to the deceased made within the previous five years. It is not necessary for the property then transferred still to be part of the deceased's estate when he dies.

In the case of settled property the relief is only available (and necessary) for interest in possession trusts. It is given whenever an interest in possession terminates and hence can be deliberately activated by the life tenant assigning or surrendering his interest. The earlier transfer in the case of settled property will be either the creation of the settlement or a termination of some prior life interest.

EXAMPLE 22.31

In 1987 S settles property by will on A for life, B for life, C absolutely. In 1988 A dies and in 1989 B surrenders his life interest.

1987　IHT will be chargeable.

1988　Quick succession relief is available on A's death. The chargeable transfer in the previous five years was the creation of the settlement in 1987.

1989　Quick succession relief is available on the surrender of B's life interest. The chargeable transfer in the previous five years was the termination of A's life interest.

The relief reduces the IHT on the second chargeable occasion. IHT is calculated in the usual way and then reduced by a sum dependent upon two factors. First, how long has elapsed since the first chargeable transfer was made. The percentage of relief is available as follows:

100%　if previous transfer one year or less before death
　80%　if previous transfer one–two years before death
　60%　if previous transfer two–three years before death
　40%　if previous transfer three–four years before death
　20%　if previous transfer four–five years before death

The second factor is the amount of IHT paid on the first transfer. IHTA 1984 s 141(3) states that the relief is 'a percentage determined as above of the tax charged on so much of the value transferred by the first transfer as is attributable to the increase in the estate of the second transferor'. Hence, if A had left £55,000 to B who died within one year of that gift the appropriate percentage will be 100% of the tax charged on the transfer from A to B, but if the transfer by A had been his only chargeable transfer and, therefore, had fallen into the nil rate band the relief is 100% × 0!　　　**[22.124]**

EXAMPLE 22.32 (assuming current rates of IHT throughout)

(1)   *Tax-free legacy/death:* A, who has made no previous chargeable transfers, dies leaving an estate of £280,000 out of which he leaves a tax-free legacy of £140,000 to B. B dies 18 months later leaving an estate of £340,000.

(a)	IHT on A's estate	= £56,000
	Proportion paid in respect of tax-free legacy (50%)	= £28,000
(b)	Quick succession relief 80% × £28,000	= £22,400

		£
(c)	IHT on B's estate	80,000
	Less: Quick succession relief	22,400
	IHT payable	£57,600

(2)   Diego gives £25,000 to Madonna in October 1986 (a PET). Madonna dies in July 1988 and Diego in January 1989. As a result of Diego's death, the PET is chargeable and IHT of (say) £5,000 is paid by Madonna's estate.
   (a)   QSR at 80% is available—on the tax attributable to the increase in the donee's estate.
   (b)   The increase in Madonna's estate is £25,000 − £5,000 = £20,000. IHT attributable to that increase is:

$$\frac{20,000}{25,000} \times 5,000 = £4,000$$

   (c)   QSR available on Madonna's death is 80% × £4,000 = £3,200.

4   The two year discretionary trust on death (IHTA 1984 s 144)

If a testator creates, by his will, a trust without an interest in possession, so long as that trust is ended *within two years* of his death, the IHT that would normally arise under the discretionary trust charging rules 'shall not be charged but the Act shall have effect as if the will had provided that on the testator's death the property should be held as it is held after the event' (s 144(2)). In other words the dispositions of the trustees are 'read back' into the will. Such a trust enables wills to be drafted with some flexibility and is advantageous where, eg the testator is dying and desires his estate to be divided between his four children, but it not sure of the proper proportions. By inserting the two year trust a final decision about the exact distribution of the estate can be postponed for a further two years.

A typical flexible will involves the testator in settling all his property on discretionary trusts which may be expressly limited to a two year (or 24 months) period or which may be for the entire perpetuity period. Default provisions will then normally provide (in most cases) for property to be divided equally amongst the beneficiaries in the discretionary class should the trustees fail to exercise their dispositive powers within the permitted period. Obviously, if the trust is ended within two years of death the provisions of s 144 will apply: in other cases if the trust continues beyond that date the usual discretionary trust regime will apply.   [22.125]

a) *IHT consequences*

IHT will be charged at the estate rate on the property settled at death but if the ultimate distributions made by the trustees are 'read back' into the will that IHT may need to be recalculated. In *Example 22.33(1)*, for instance, a discretionary trust is ended in favour of the testator's surviving spouse and the reading back provisions result in a repayment of all the IHT charged on the death estate. *Example 22.33(2)* reveals an important restriction in the operation of s 144 in that it will only apply if the transfer out of the discretionary trust would otherwise attract a tax charge.   **[22.126]**

EXAMPLE 22.33

A creates a flexible trust in his will and the trustees:
(1)   Six months after death appoint the property to A's widow. This appointment is read back to A's death: ie it takes effect as an exempt spouse gift so that there is a resulting IHT repayment.
(2)   As in (1) but the appointment is made two months after death. Now there is no question of reading back since there is no charge imposed on events occurring within three months of the creation of a discretionay trust (IHTA 1984 s 64(4), see **[26.25]**). As a result, the original will remains intact, IHT is charged on the entire estate and the spouse exemption is unused.

b) *Theoretical problems and practical uses*

If it were obvious at the outset that the entire fund should be paid to the spouse, the trustees could execute an irrevocable appointment (even before any grant of probate although only after three months have elapsed from death in order to avoid the trap discussed in *Example 22.33(2)* and thereby avoid paying IHT on the fund. Note, however, that the 'reading back' provisions do not operate for CGT, so that, unless it can be said that the beneficiaries who receive the fund take as legatees under the will, there will be a deemed disposal of settled property under CGTA s 54(1) (see **[18.43]**: the hold-over election may be available to postpone any charge to tax). There have been suggestions that the immediate appointment of assets may be challenged by the Revenue on the basis that, unless property is *at that time* vested in the trustees, the trust is not completely constituted so that any appointment is ineffective. It is suggested that this argument fails to recognise that from the moment of death the trustees own property (the right to have the estate duly administered: a *chose in action*) which ensures that the trust is completely constituted so that the appointment can be validly made. (This question is more fully discussed in *Capital Taxes News*, November 1986, p 147. The Revenue did not raise this problem in the *Fitzwilliam* case and now appear to have abandoned this technical objection: see Chapter 31 and *Capital Taxes News*, July 1990, p 98.)

This trust can be used as an alternative to a survivorship clause. Say, for instance, that the testator wants Eric to get the property if he survives him by 18 months failing which Ernie is to receive it. This cannot be achieved by a conventional survivorship clause (which must be limited to six months; see **[22.123]**). If Eric and Ernie are made beneficiaries of a discretionary trust however, and the trustees know the testator's wishes concerning the distribution of the fund, there is no risk of a double IHT charge in carrying out his wishes.

Such a trust is obviously attractive as compared to variations and disclaimers. If there is any doubt about who should be given the deceased's estate, it is better to use a trust than to rely upon an appointed legatee voluntarily renouncing a benefit under the will. All the most convincing fiscal arguments will often fail to persuade people to give up property and they cannot be compelled to vary or to disclaim!   **[22.127]**

c) *The alternative way*

In cases where the testator is survived by his spouse there is now a more attractive way of drafting a flexible will. In simple terms the will should be drafted so as to leave the surviving spouse with a life interest in the deceased's estate. No IHT will be charged on death since the property will fall under the spouse exemption.

Under the terms of that will trust it is, however, provided, first, that the trustees have power to advance capital to the surviving spouse and, secondly, that they have the power to terminate the life interest in favour of a wide discretionary class of beneficiaries. The end result is that (in much the same way as under two year discretionary trusts) there is now flexibility in the testator's will. If the trustees decide that the spouse's interest should be terminated, in whole or in part, in favour of a particular beneficiary then that termination will result in the surviving spouse making a potentially exempt transfer. IHT will therefore be avoided unless the spouse dies within seven years.

As compared to the two year trust this form of will drafting has the merit of avoiding any tax charge on the death of the testator and may further avoid a tax charge on the termination of the interest in possession provided that the surviving spouse lives for the requisite seven year period.   [**22.128**]

5   Disclaimers and variations (post mortem tax planning)

It will often be desirable to effect changes in a will after the death of the testator, for instance, to rearrange the dispositions with a view to saving tax (and especially IHT). In practice, however, it is non-tax factors that are usually most significant—typically the need to provide for someone who is omitted from the will or who is inadequately provided for. It may even be that a beneficiary under the will decides that he does not want the bequest. In all these cases, persons named in the original will reject a portion of their inheritance; hence, they will (usually) be making a gratuitous transfer of value which will either constitute a chargeable lifetime transfer or a potentially exempt transfer. Other taxes too could be important—notably CGT and income tax.

These problems also arise on an intestacy—indeed the statutory intestacy provisions will often prove even less satisfactory than a will.

So far as both IHT and CGT are concerned certain changes to a will, or to the intestacy rules, are permitted, if made within two years of death, to take effect as if they had been provided for in the original will (for IHT see IHTA 1984 s 142; for CGT, CGTA 1979 s 49(6)-(9)). The effect of 'reading back' these changes into the will or amending the intestacy rules is to avoid the possibility of a second charge to IHT and any charge to CGT.

EXAMPLE 22.34

T by will leaves property to his three daughters equally. He omits his son with whom he had quarrelled bitterly. The daughters might agree to vary the will by providing that the four children take equally and, for the capital taxes, T's original will can be varied to make the desired provision. Hence, no daughter was taxed on the gift of a part of her share to her brother.

To take advantage of these provisions there must be a voluntary alteration of the testamentary provisions; in the case of enforced alterations: eg as a result of applications under the Inheritance (Provision for Family and Dependants) Act 1975, different provisions apply, see [**22.64**].   [**22.129**]

a) *Permitted ways of altering the will or intestacy*

There are two methods of altering the dispositions of a will or intestacy; by a disclaimer and by a variation. A *disclaimer* operates as a refusal to accept property and, hence, to be valid, should be made before any act of acceptance has occurred (such as receiving any benefit). When a disclaimer is effected the property passes according to fixed rules of law. It is not possible to disclaim in favour of a particular person. Hence, if a specific bequest is disclaimed the property falls into the residue of the will; if it is the residue itself which is disclaimed the property will pass as on an intestacy. Property can also be disclaimed on intestacy. A disclaimer is, therefore, an all or nothing event; it is not possible to retain part and disclaim the rest of a single gift. If, however, both a specific bequest and a share of residue are left to the same person, the benefit of one could be accepted and the other disclaimed.

In a *variation*, the deceased's provisions are altered at the choice of the person effecting the alteration so that the gift is redirected and the fact that some benefit had already accrued before the change (and that the estate had been fully administered) is irrelevant. Any part of a gift can be redirected. Unlike a beneficiary who disclaims, the person who makes the variation has owned an interest in the property of the deceased from the death up to the variation.   [**22.130**]

b) *The IHT rules on variations and disclaimers*

If the following conditions are satisfied the variation or disclaimer is not itself a transfer of value but instead takes effect as if the original will or intestacy had so provided:

(1) The variation or disclaimer must occur within two years of death. In the case of disclaimers it is likely that action will need to be taken soon after the death otherwise the benefit will have been accepted.

(2) The variation or disclaimer must be effected by an instrument in writing (in practice a deed should be used), executed by the person who would otherwise benefit.

(3) In the case of variations, where it is desired to 'read them back' into the original will, an election in writing to that effect must be made to the Revenue (normally within six months of the variation). This election should refer to the appropriate statutory provisions and must be made by the person making the variation and, where the effect of that election would be to increase the IHT chargeable on the death, also by the PRs. PRs can only refuse to join in such an election, however, if they have insufficient assets in their hands to discharge the extra IHT bill (for instance, where administration of the estate had been completed and the assets distributed). No election is necessary in the case of a disclaimer which, assuming that the other requirements are satisfied is automatically 'read back' into the will.

(4) A variation or disclaimer cannot be for money or money's worth, except where there are reciprocal disclaimers or other beneficiaries are also disclaiming for the ultimate benefit of a third person.

(5) All property comprised in the deceased's estate immediately before death can be redirected under these provisions except for property which the deceased was treated as owning by virtue of an interest in possession

in a settlement (although in this case relief may be afforded by IHTA 1984 s 93) and property included in the estate at death because of the reservation of benefit rules.

EXAMPLE 22.35

(1) A and T were joint tenants. On the death of T, A can redirect the half share of the property that he acquired by right of survivorship taking advantage of IHTA 1984 s 142. (There are obvious theoretical difficulties in this case and it is likely that A should effect a severance of the joint tenancy before making the variation.)

(2) T by will created a settlement giving C a life interest. C can redirect that interest under IHTA 1984 s 142.

(3) T was the life tenant of a fund—the property now vests in D absolutely. D cannot take advantage of IHTA 1984 s 142 if he varies the terms of the settlement by disposing of his interest. (Notice, however, that IHTA 1984 s 93 permits a beneficiary to disclaim an interest in settled property without that disclaimer being subject to IHT.)

(4) Mort had been life tenant of a trust fund and on his death the assets passed to his sister Mildred absolutely. He left his free estate equally to his widow and daughter. By a post-death variation the widow gave her half share to the daughter. Assuming that this variation is read back for IHT purposes the extra tax charged on Mort's death will affect the trustees who are not required to consent to the election and are not protected by a deed of discharge (IHTA 1984 s 239(4)).

(5) Father leaves 100,000 shares in J. Sainsbury plc to his daughter. She gives those shares to her son, within two years of his death, and reserves a collateral benefit. She elects to read the gift back into the will of her father and as her gift thereupon takes effect *for all IHT purposes* as if it had been made by the deceased the reservation rules are inapplicable.

(6) Boris, domiciled in France, leaves his villa in Tuscany and moneys in his Swiss bank account to his son Gaspard, a UK resident. By a variation of the terms of his will made within two years of Boris' death, the property is settled on discretionary Liechtenstein trusts for the benefit of Gaspard's family. *For IHT*, reading back ensures that the settlement is excluded property. *For CGT*, however, s 49(6)(b) provides that *for the purposes of that section* the variation shall be treated as effected by the deceased. Whether this means that for the purposes of FA 1981 s 80 an overseas settlement has been created by Boris (a non-UK domiciliary) or by Gaspard, is therefore far from clear. If the former, no CGT charges will arise on UK beneficiaries who received capital payments from the trustees. The Revenue consider Gaspard to be the settlor for CGT purposes but a recent Special Commissioners' case (to be appealed) suggests the contrary (see *Capital Taxes*, 1990, p 4).

In the case of variations, the choice to elect or not to elect is with the taxpayer. A similar election operates for CGT but it is not necessary to exercise both IHT and CGT elections; they can be used separately (see [**15.121**]).

PRs of deceased beneficiaries can enter into variations and disclaimers which can be read back into the original will. Further, the estate of a beneficiary alive at the testator's death can be increased by such a variation or disclaimer (see *Capital Taxes* vol 1, p 22).   [**22.131**]

EXAMPLE 22.36

(1) T leaves property to his wealthy brother. The brother wishes to redirect it to grandchildren. An election for IHT purposes is advisable since (a) it will not increase the IHT charged on T's death and (b) it will avoid a second charge at the brother's rates if the brother were to die within seven years of the gift (for which quick succession relief would not be available—see [**22.124**]).

(2) T leaves residue to his widow. She wishes to redirect a portion to her daughter. If the election is made, the IHT on T's death may be increased because an exempt bequest is being replaced with one that is chargeable. If the election is not made, on T's death the residue remains exempt but the widow will make a potentially exempt transfer. If she survives by seven years no IHT will be payable: if she survives by three years tapering relief will apply. Even if the PET becomes chargeable, any IHT may be reduced by the widow's annual exemption (in the year when the transfer is made) and the chargeable transfer may fall within her nil rate band. In cases like this, it will be advantageous to ensure that T's nil rate band is fully used up by a reading back election but, once that has been done, given a single rate of tax (40%), there is no advantage in reading back the variation since the rate of tax on the death of the widow will be the same and, moreover, tax will not be charged at once.

(3) In examples like (2) above a variation may be employed to redirect a posthumous increase in the value of the estate without any IHT charge. Assume for instance that the death estate of £100,000 has increased in value to £225,000. T's widow could vary the will (electing to read the change back) to provide for a specific legacy of £100,000 to herself with the residue to her daughter. Under the provisions of IHTA 1984 ss 36–42 the chargeable estate (£100,000) is attributed to the exempt legacy (see *Capital Taxes*, vol 1, p 82).

(4) H leaves £1m to his only daughter, D. His widow, W, dies soon afterwards leaving a small estate to D. D should consider varying H's will so that (say) £100,000 (to use up the nil rate band) is left to W. D will then receive that sum from W's estate.

Note: in (4) above the variation is artificial since it is designed solely to reduce the total IHT bill. D is left with all the property. Accordingly the arrangement could be attacked under the *Ramsay* principle although were D to redirect the benefit to her own children the variation could not then be attacked as wholly artificial since it would alter the ownership of the property.

c) *Other taxes*

So far as *stamp duty* is concerned changes in FA 1985 ensured that variations in writing made within two years after the death were not subject to *ad valorem* duty but instead required adjudication and a fixed duty stamp of 50p (see s 82 which removed *ad valorem* duty on voluntary dispositions and s 84 which provided a specific exemption from *ad valorem* sale duty in the case of other variations: ie where there is consideration involving an exchange of interests). No duty is payable on disclaimers which are treated as a refusal to accept, not a disposition of, property (FA 1985 repealed the fixed 50p duty on deeds which had formerly included deeds of disclaimer). This process of simplification was completed by the Stamp Duty (Exempt Instruments) Regulations 1987 (SI 1987/516) which removed the need for adjudication and the 50p stamp on instruments of variation containing the appropriately worded certificate (see further [**30.58**]).

As regards *income tax* there are no specific relieving provisions for variations and disclaimers. Accordingly, income arising between the date of death and the date of a variation will be taxed in accordance with the terms of the will. The Revenue consider that the deed cannot operate retrospectively and that it is irrelevant whether the original beneficiary actually received any income.

So far as a disclaimer is concerned the Revenue apparently consider that the basic income tax position is the same as for a variation, since the beneficiary's interest under the will remains intact up to the date of the disclaimer (see further *CTT News*, vol 5, p 142: it may be doubted whether this view is consistent with the idea of a disclaimer operating as a refusal to accept property).

A variation made by a beneficiary in favour of his own infant unmarried child creates a settlement for income tax purposes within TA 1988 Pt XV (see Chapter 11). Hence, income arising from the redirected property will be assessed as that of the parent (unless accumulated in a capital settlement). A disclaimer will escape these problems, if it is accepted that the property has never been owned by the disclaiming beneficiary.   **[22.132]**

d) *Technical difficulties*

Two technical problems have arisen in connection with instruments of variation. First, it was argued by the Revenue that for a variation to fall within the IHT relieving provision (IHTA 1984 s 142), the operative clause in the instrument of variation had to state that the transfer of property was taking effect as a variation to the provisions of a will or intestacy to avoid it being construed as a lifetime gift. Accordingly it was suggested that any variation should follow the wording of that section and provide as follows:

> 'The dispositions of property comprised in the estate of the testator (intestate) immediately before his death, shall be varied as follows . . .'

After further advice, however, the Revenue apparently abandoned this view (see 1985 LS Gaz 1454), but will, nevertheless, require the variation to indicate clearly the dispositions that are subject to it and vary their destination from that provided in the will or under the intestacy rules. Furthermore, the notice of election must refer to the appropriate statutory provisions. This change of position does not indicate that all technical objections to instruments of variation have been dropped, however, and as the Revenue consider that the instrument *itself* must vary the dispositions the use of a deed would appear to be necessary (although a written instrument is sufficient to transfer an existing equitable interest under LPA 1925 s 53(1)(c)).

The second difficulty concerned multiple variations which had been employed (before 1985) in an attempt to avoid *ad valorem* stamp duty. Although this device is no longer necessary it resulted in the Revenue interpreting IHTA 1984 s 142 as permitting only one variation per beneficiary. Again this is a position from which they have retreated, at least in part (see 1985 LS Gaz 1454); they now argue that an election, once made, is irrevocable and that s 142 will not apply to an instrument redirecting any item or part of any item that had already been redirected under an earlier instrument. Variations covering a number of items should ideally be made in one instrument 'to avoid any uncertainty', although the Revenue accept that multiple variations by a single beneficiary are not, as such, prohibited.

EXAMPLE 22.37

Under Eric's will £50,000 is left to his brother Wally and £100,000 to his surviving spouse Berta. The following events then occur within two years of Eric's death:
  (i) Wally executes a deed of variation in favour of his own children.
  (ii) Berta executes a deed varying £2,500 in favour of her sister Jennie and later a second variation for £47,500.
  (iii) Jennie executes a deed of variation for £25,000 in favour of her boyfriend Jonnie.

  The variations in (i) and (ii) apparently satisfy the requirements of IHTA 1984 s 142 as interpreted by the Revenue and so may be read back into Eric's will, whereas the variation in (iii) may not be so treated and, accordingly, will be a potentially exempt transfer.

The decision of *Russell v IRC* (1988) confirms the Revenue's interpretation of the legislation in deciding that a redirection of property already varied will not fall within s 142. The deceased had died in 1983 survived by his wife and four daughters. His estate included business assets (Lloyd's Underwriting interests) which qualified for business property relief from the then capital transfer tax. Under his will, most of the estate passed to his widow and was not therefore subject to a tax charge. As a corollary, however, business property relief was therefore wasted as was the nil rate band. Not surprisingly, therefore, the family decided to vary the dispositions of his will by providing for each daughter to receive a pecuniary legacy of £25,000 to be raised out of the business property. They hoped that by giving away the business property worth £100,000 which would qualify for a reduction in value of 50%, some £50,000 of the testator's nil rate band would thereby be utilised. The Revenue, however, took the view that these legacies were gifts of cash not of qualifying business assets with the result that as no 50% relief was available a tax charge would arise since part of each legacy would then fall outside the nil rate band. Although the family did not accept this, they tried again in 1985 by executing a fresh deed of variation whereby each daughter was to receive instead of a cash legacy a proportionate share of the business assets worth £25,000.

Mr Justice Knox had to decide whether this second deed was effective to carry out the family's intentions and if not whether the Revenue were correct in their interpretation of the 1983 deed. He decided that under the relevant statutory provision a benefit which had already been redirected once could not be further redirected and read back into the testator's will.

'My principal reason for accepting the Crown's submission that the hypothesis contained in s 142(1) should not be applied to that subsection itself is that this involves taking the hypothesis further than is necessary. No authority was cited to me of a statutory hypothesis being applied to the very provision which enacts the hypothesis. Such a tortuous process would merit a specific reference in the enactment to itself ...' (Knox J at 204).

Accordingly, on the facts of this case, as there had already been a valid variation in 1983, the further amendment in 1985 could not be read back. Having so decided he then concluded, however, that the Revenue's arguments that the 1983 variation did not have the effect of varying interests in business property was misconceived. He pointed out that the relevant cash gifts could only be satisfied (in this particular case) by resorting to business assets and therefore he was of the opinion that a division of that property by reference to a cash sum should be treated in the same way as a division by reference to a fraction of the assets.

In *Lake v Lake* (1989) Mervyn Davis J held that a deed of variation can be rectified by the court if words mistakenly used mean that it does not give effect to the parties' joint intention. It does not matter that the rectification achieves a tax advantage nor that it is made more than two years after the death. The courts must, however, be satisfied that the deed as executed contains errors: in this case the variation was designed to give legacies to children of the deceased but as the result of a clerical error such gifts were expressed to be 'free of tax'. As residue passed to an exempt beneficiary (the surviving spouse) grossing up was therefore necessary. The order for rectification substituted 'such gifts to bear their own tax' for 'free of tax' (see also *Matthews v Martin* (1991)).   **[22.133]**

6   IHT and estate duty

Up to 13 March 1975 the estate duty regime continued to operate. The various transitional provisions for estate duty and CTT/IHT are beyond the scope of this book although mention should be made of IHTA 1984 Sch 6 para 2 which preserves for IHT the old surviving spouse exemption. This exemption provided that, for estate duty purposes, where property was left to a surviving spouse in such circumstances that the spouse was not competent to dispose of it (for instance was given a life interest therein) estate duty would be charged on the first death but not again on the death of the survivor. This estate duty exemption was continued into the CTT (and now IHT) era by IHTA 1984 Sch 6 para 2 which excludes such property from charge whether the limited interest is terminated *inter vivos* or by the death of the surviving spouse. All too often this valuable exemption may be overlooked and an over emphasis on the attractions of making PETs may have unfortunate results.   **[22.134]**

EXAMPLE 22.38

(1)   On his death in 1973, Samson left his wife Delilah a life interest in his share portfolio. She is still alive and in robust health and the trustees have a power to advance capital to her. Estate duty was charged on Samson's death but because of para 2 there will be no charge to IHT when Delilah's interest comes to an end. At first sight, there appear to be advantages if the trustees advance capital to Delilah which she then transfers by means of a PET. However, this arrangement carries with it the risk of that capital being subject to an IHT charge if Delilah dies within seven years of her gift. Accordingly, an interest which is tax free is being replaced by a potentially chargeable transfer.

(2)   Terminating Delilah's interest during her life may, however, have other attractions. In particular, the exemption from charge in para 2 is limited to the value of the property in which the limited interest subsists but that property may, by forming part of Delilah's estate, affect the value of other assets in that estate. Assume, for instance, that Delilah owns 30% of the shares in a private company (Galilee Limited) in her own name and that a further 30% are subject to the life interest trust. When she dies she will be treated as owning 60% of the shares: a controlling holding which will be valued as such. Although one half of the value of that holding will be free from charge under para 2, the remaining portion will be taxed. Accordingly, it may be better in such cases for her life interest to be surrendered *inter vivos* even if that operation is only carried out on her death bed.

23 IHT—exemptions and reliefs

I   Lifetime exemptions and reliefs   [**23.2**]
II   Death exemptions and reliefs   [**23.21**]
III Exemptions for lifetime and death transfers   [**23.41**]

IHT does not exempt whole categories of property from charge, as does CGT. Instead, the definition of a chargeable transfer excludes exempt transfers (IHTA 1984 s 2(1)). Exemptions and reliefs apply therefore to a limited number of transfers of value: some for lifetime transfers only (including PETs rendered chargeable by death within seven years); some for death only; and some for all transfers, whether in lifetime or on death.

The exemptions may be justified on the grounds of necessity—some gifts must be permitted (eg Christmas and wedding presents); or, in the case of reliefs applicable to particular property, because it is desirable that the property should be preserved and not sold to pay the tax bill (eg business and agricultural reliefs).

The nil rate band (currently £140,000) is not an exempt transfer since transfers within this band are chargeable transfers, albeit taxed at 0%. Accordingly, exemptions and reliefs should be exhausted first so that the taxpayer's nil rate band is retained intact as long as possible.   [**23.1**]

I LIFETIME EXEMPTIONS AND RELIEFS

1 Transfers not exceeding £3,000 pa (IHTA 1984 s 19)

Up to £3,000 can be transferred free from IHT each tax year (6 April to 5 April). To the extent that this relief is unused in any one year it can be rolled forward for one tax year only. There is no general roll-forward since it is provided that it is only where the value transferred in any year falls short of £3,000 that the shortfall shall be added to next year's £3,000.

EXAMPLE 23.1

A makes chargeable transfers of £2,500 in 1988–89; £2,800 in 1989–90; and £3,700 in 1990–91.
For 1988–89: no IHT (£3,000 exemption) and £500 is carried forward.
For 1989–90: no IHT (£3,000 exemption) and £200 only is carried forward. The £500 from 1988–89 could only have been used to the extent that the transfer in 1989–90 exceeded £3,000.
For 1990–91: IHT on £500 (£3,200 is exempt).

The relief can operate by deducting £3,000 from a larger gift. Where several chargeable gifts are made in the same tax year, earlier gifts will be given the relief first; if several such gifts are made on the same day there is a *pro rata* apportionment of the relief irrespective of the actual order of gifts. The relief applies also to settlements with interests in possession although in this case it will only be given if the life tenant so elects (see [**23.36**]).

The relationship between the annual exemption and the PET is far from clearcut. The definition of a PET in IHTA 1984 s 3A is:

> 'a transfer of value ... which, apart from this section, would be a chargeable transfer (or to the extent which, apart from this section, it would be such a transfer) ...'.

The position can therefore be stated in two propositions:
(1) a transfer of value which is wholly covered by the annual exemption is not a PET but *an exempt transfer in its own right*;
(2) a transfer of value which exceeds the annual exempt amount is *to that extent a PET*.

These propositions represent the view of the CTO: they have the effect of depriving s 19(3A) of all meaning: that subsection provides that:

> 'A transfer of value which is a potentially exempt transfer—
> (a)   shall in the first instance be left out of account for the purposes of subsection (1) to (3) above; and
> (b)   if it proves to be a chargeable transfer, shall for the purposes of those subsections be taken into account as if, in the year it was made, it was made later than any transfer of value which was not a potentially exempt transfer.'

EXAMPLE 23.2

(1)   In 1991–92 Peta gives her father £2,500. This gift is an exempt transfer.
(2)   In the same tax year Beta gives her mother £6,500. Two annual exemptions mean that £6,000 is exempt: £500 is a PET.
(3)   Cheeta intends to set up a discretionary trust for his family and to make an outright gift to his sister. He should make the discretionary trust first thereby using up his annual exemption and on a subsequent day make a potentially exempt transfer to his sister.

What should a would-be donor do who does not wish to transfer assets/ money to the value of £3,000, but at the same time is reluctant to see the exemption lost? One solution is to vest an interest in property in the donee whilst retaining control of the asset (although great care must be taken to ensure that a benefit is not retained in the portion given since a transfer falling within the annual exemption is still a gift for the reservation of benefit rules: see [**22.5**]), but the device of selling the asset with the purchase price outstanding and releasing part of the debt each year equal to the annual exemption may fall foul of the associated operations rules (Chapter 21).   [23.2]

2   **Normal expenditure out of income** (IHTA 1984 s 21)

To qualify for relief the relevant transfer must be part of the normal and regular expenditure of the transferor; taking one year with the next it must be payable out of income, and, after allowing for all such transfers, the transferor must be left with sufficient income to maintain his usual standard of living. The legislation does not define 'usual standard of living', whilst the requirement that there must be regular payments out of income makes it impossible to apply to gifts of chattels. A further problem may be caused by the requirement that the payments be normal and regular. A pattern of payments is most easily shown where the taxpayer is committed to making the payment *ab initio* as, for instance, where he enters into a deed of covenant. In other cases a couple of payments might have to be made before there is sufficient evidence of regularity. As with the annual exemption, this exemption does not prevent a gift from being caught by the reservation of benefit rules.

EXAMPLE 23.3

A takes out a life insurance policy on his own life for £60,000 with the benefit of that policy being held on a trust for his grandchildren. A pays the premiums on the policy of £3,500 pa. He makes a transfer of value of £3,500 pa but he can make use of the normal expenditure exemption to avoid IHT so long as all the requirements for that exemption are satisfied. Alternatively, the £3,000 annual exemption would relieve most of the annual premium.

Anti-avoidance rules provide that:
(1) The normal expenditure exemption will not cover a life insurance premium unless the transferor can show that the life cover was not facilitated by and associated with an annuity purchased on his own life (IHTA 1984 s 21(2)).
(2) Under IHTA 1984 s 263 (unless the transferor can disprove the presumption of associated transactions, as above) an IHT charge can arise when the benefit of the life policy is vested in the donee. In general, if a charge arises, the sum assured by the life policy is treated as a transfer of value.

These special rules exist to prevent tax saving by the use of back-to-back insurance policies, as in the following example: **[23.3]**

EXAMPLE 23.4

Tony pays an insurance company £50,000 in return for an annuity of £7,000 pa for the rest of his life. At the same time he enters into a life insurance contract on his own life for £50,000 written in favour of his brother Ted. The potential advantages are that on the death of Tony the sum of £50,000 is no longer part of his estate and the annuity has no value when he died but can be used during his life to pay the premiums on the life insurance contract. The insurance proceeds will not attract IHT because they do not form part of his estate and Tony could claim that the premiums amounted to regular payments out of his income and so were free of IHT. The Revenue appear to accept that such arrangements are effective so long as the policies are not linked and, ideally, are taken out with different companies.

3 **Small gifts** (IHTA 1984 s 20)

Any number of £250 gifts can be made in any tax year by a donor provided that the gifts are to different donees. It must be an outright gift (not a gift into settlement) and the sum cannot be severed from a larger gift. The section provides that the transfers of value made to any one person in any one year must not exceed £250: accordingly, it is not generally possible to combine this small gifts exemption with the annual £3,000 exemption. A gift of £3,250 would, therefore, be exempt as to £3,000 (assuming that exemption was available) but the excess of £250 would not fall under s 20 even if the gift had been structured by means of two separate cheques. **[23.4]**

4   Gifts in consideration of marriage (IHTA 1984 s 22)

The gift must be made before or contemporaneously with marriage and only after marriage if in satisfaction of a prior legal obligation. It must be conditional upon the marriage taking place so that should the marriage not occur the donor must have the right to recover the gift (if this right is not exercised, there may be an IHT charge on the failure to exercise that right under IHTA 1984 s 3(3)). A particular marriage must be in contemplation; it will not suffice, for instance, for a father to make a gift to his two year old daughter expressed to be conditional upon her marriage on the fatalistic assumption that she is bound to get married eventually!

The exemption can be used to settle property, but only if the beneficiaries are limited to (generally) the couple, any issue, and spouses of such issue (see IHTA 1984 s 22(4)). Hence, a marriage cannot be used to effect a general settlement of assets within the family.

The sum exempt from IHT is:
(1) £5,000, if the donor is a parent of either party to the marriage. Thus, each of four parents can give £5,000 to the couple.
(2) £2,500, if the transferor is a remoter ancestor of either party to the marriage (eg a grandparent or great-grandparent) or if the transferor is a party to the marriage. The latter is designed to cover ante nuptial gifts since after marriage transfers between spouses are normally exempt without limit (see [23.41]).
(3) £1,000, in the case of any other transferors (eg a wedding guest).

When a gift of property is an exempt transfer because it was made in consideration of marriage, the reservation of benefit provisions do not apply.   [23.5]

EXAMPLE 23.5

(1) Father gives son a Matisse sculpture on the occasion of the son's marriage. It is worth £5,000. Possession of the piece is retained by the father but as the transfer is covered by the marriage exemption his continued possession does not fall within the reservation rules.
(2) Mum gives daughter an interest in her house equal to £5,000 when the daughter marries. Although Mum continues to live in the house the reservation rules do not apply.

5   Dispositions for maintenance etc (IHTA 1984 s 11)

Dispositions listed in IHTA 1984 s 11 are not transfers of value so that they are ignored for IHT purposes. The Revenue take the view that this exemption only applies to *inter vivos* dispositions, presumably because 'disposition' is not adequate to cover the deemed disposition on death.   [23.6]

Maintenance of a former spouse (IHTA 1984 s 11(1)(a))   Even without this provision such payments would in many cases escape IHT. If made before decree absolute, the exemption for gifts between spouses (see [23.41]) would operate and even after divorce they might escape IHT as regular payments out of income; or fall within the annual exemption; or be non-gratuitous transfers. What s 11 does is to put the matter beyond all doubt.

Two problems may be mentioned. First, maintenance is not defined, so that whether it could cover the transfer of capital assets (eg the former matrimonial home) is unclear. Secondly, if the payer dies but payment is to continue for the lifetime of the recipient, the position is unclear in the light of the Revenue's view that this exemption is limited to *inter vivos* dispositions. [23.7]

Maintenance of children Provision for the maintenance, education or training of a child of either party to a marriage (including stepchildren and adopted children) is not a transfer of value (IHTA 1984 s 11(2)). The maintenance can continue beyond the age of 18 if the child is in full-time education. Thus, school fees paid by parents escape IHT. Similar principles operate where the disposition is for the maintenance of a parent's illegitimate child (IHTA 1984 s 11(4)). A similar relief is given for the maintenance of other people's children if the child is an infant and not in the care of either parent; once the child is 18, not only must he be undergoing full-time education, but also the disponer must (in effect) have been *in loco parentis* to the child during his minority (IHTA 1984 s 11(2)). Hence, payment of school and college fees by grandparents will seldom escape IHT under this provision. [23.8]

Care or maintenance of a dependent relative The provision of maintenance whether direct or indirect must be reasonable and the relative (as defined in IHTA 1984 s 11(6)) must be incapacitated by old age or infirmity from maintaining himself (although mothers and mothers-in-law who are widowed or separated are always dependent relatives). [23.9]–[23.20]

II DEATH EXEMPTIONS AND RELIEFS

1 **Woodlands** (IHTA 1984 ss 125–130)

This relief takes effect by deferring IHT on growing trees and underwood forming part of the deceased's estate. Their value is left out of account on the death. An election must be made for the relief by written notice given (normally) within two years after the death. It is not available where the woodlands qualify for agricultural relief (see [23.54]). To prevent deathbed IHT saving schemes the land must not have been purchased by the deceased in the five years before his death (note, however, that the relief is available if the woodlands were obtained by gift or inheritance within the five year period). The relief does not apply to the land itself, but any IHT charged as a result of death can be paid in instalments. The deferred tax on the timber may become chargeable as follows: [23.21]

Sale of the timber with or without the land IHT will be charged on the net proceeds of sale, but deductions can be made for costs of selling the timber and also for the costs of replanting. The net proceeds are taxed according to full IHT rates at the date of the disposal and the tax is calculated by treating those proceeds as forming the highest part of the deceased's estate. The 50% business property relief may be available where the trees or underwood formed a business asset at the date of death and, but for the deferment election, would have qualified for that relief at that time. In such cases the relief is given against the net proceeds of sale. [23.22]

A gift of the timber Not only is the deferred charge triggered by a gift of the timber, but also the gift itself may be subject to IHT and, if it is merely a disposal of business assets (the timber) and not of the whole or a part of the business, business relief may not be available. In calculating the tax payable on the lifetime gift the value transferred is reduced by the triggered IHT charged on the death and the tax can be paid by interest-free instalments (whoever pays the IHT) spread over ten years (IHTA 1984 s 229). [23.23]

EXAMPLE 23.6

(1) Wally Wood dies in 1986 with a death estate of £200,000. In addition, he owns at death a woodlands business with the growing timber valued at £40,000 and the land etc valued at £30,000. The woodlands exemption is claimed by his daughter Wilma. In 1991 she sells the timber; the net proceeds of sale are £50,000.

   (a) *Position on Wally's death:* The timber is left out of account. The value of the rest of the business (£30,000) attracts 50% business relief, so that only £15,000 will be added to the £200,000 chargeable estate.

   (b) *Position on Wilma's sale:* The IHT charge is triggered. The net proceeds are reduced by 50% business relief to £25,000 which will be taxed according to the rates of IHT in force in 1991 for transfers between £215,000 (ie Wally's total chargeable death estate) and £240,000.

(2) As in (1) above except that Wilma settles the timber on her brother Woad in 1991 when its net value is £50,000. The deferred charge will be triggered as in paragraph (b) of (1) above. IHT on Wilma's gift will be calculated according to half the IHT rates in force for 1991. She can deduct from the net value of the timber the deferred tax ((1) above) and any IHT can be paid by instalments whether it is paid by her or by Woad.

PETs and estate duty   Under the estate duty régime, duty was not charged on the value of timber, trees, wood or underwood growing on land comprised in an estate at death. Instead, tax was deferred until such time as the woodlands were sold and was then levied at the death estate rate on the net proceeds of sale (subject to the proviso that duty could not exceed tax on the value of the timber at the date of the death). Pending sale, duty was therefore held in suspense and this deferral period only ceased on the happening of a later death when the woodlands again became subject to duty. The introduction of a charge on lifetime gifts with the advent of Capital Transfer Tax resulted in this deferral period terminating immediately after the first transfer of value occurring after 12 March 1975 in which the value transferred was determined by reference to the land in question (subject only to an exclusion if that transfer was to the transferor's spouse and therefore exempt from CTT: see FA 1975 s 49(4)). In such cases, the deferred estate duty charge was superseded by a charge to CTT on the transfer value.

With the introduction of the PET it was realised, during the passage of the Finance Act 1986 through Parliament, that a transfer of value of woodlands subject to estate duty deferral to another individual would, *prima facie*, be a PET but that the transfer would have the effect of ending the deferral period thereby cancelling any charge to duty without a compensating charge to IHT. Hence, Sch 19 para 46 was inserted into FA 1986 and provides that transfers of value made on or after 1 July 1986 which fall within FA 1975 s 49(4) and thereby bring to an end the estate duty deferral period *shall not be PETs*. Accordingly, such transfers remain immediately chargeable to IHT at the transferor's rates (with the possibility of a supplementary charge should he die within the following seven years).   **[23.24]**

EXAMPLE 23.7

On his death in May 1973 Claude left his landed estate to his son Charles. That estate included woodlands valued, in 1973, at £6,000. Consider the tax position in the following three situations:

(1) *If Charles sells the timber in 1990 for £16,000:* The net proceeds of sale will be subject to an estate duty charge levied at Claude's estate rate but duty

will be limited by reference to the value of the timber in 1973 (ie it will be charged on £6,000).

(2) *If Charles retains the timber until his death in 1990 when it passes to his daughter:* This transfer of value will end the estate duty deferral period so that the potential charge to duty will be removed. However, the transfer to his daughter will be subject to an IHT charge unless the woodlands deferral election under IHTA 1984 s 125 ff is claimed.

(3) *If Charles makes an* inter vivos *gift of his estate (including the woodlands) in August 1990 to his daughter:* Such a gift will not be potentially exempt because of para 46. Accordingly, it will terminate the estate duty suspense period, and will result in an immediate IHT charge levied according to Charles' rates. From the wording of para 46 it is not clear whether any part of this transfer can be potentially exempt or whether the entire value transferred is subject to an immediate charge. Undoubtedly the value of the timber will attract such a charge and likewise it would seem that the value of the land on which the timber is growing will fall outside the definition of a PET (see the wording of FA 1975 s 49(4)). What, however, if the transfer of value made by Charles includes other property, eg other parts of a landed estate which are not afforested? There was a real danger that none of the value transferred would be a PET since para 46 is not limited to that part of any transfer of value comprising the woodlands. The injustice was recognised by an Extra Statutory Concession published on 5 December 1990 which states that 'the scope of [para 46] will henceforth be restricted solely to that part of the value transferred which is attributable to the woodlands which are the subject of the deferred charge'.

2 **Death on active service** (IHTA 1984 s 154)

IHTA 1984 s 154 ensures that the estates of persons dying on active service, including members of the UDR and RUC killed by terrorists in Northern Ireland, are exempt from IHT. This provision has been generously interpreted to cover a death arising many years after a wound inflicted whilst on active service, so long as that wound was one of the causes of death; it need not have been the only, or even the direct cause (*Barty-King v Ministry of Defence* (1979)). A *donatio mortis causa* is covered by the exemption but not lifetime transfers, whilst transfers within seven years before death are still subject to the supplementary assessment. **[23.25]–[23.40]**

III EXEMPTIONS FOR LIFETIME AND DEATH TRANSFERS

1 **The inter-spouse exemption** (IHTA 1984 s 18)

This most valuable exemption from IHT for transfers between spouses is unlimited in amount except where the donee spouse is not domiciled in the UK when the amount excluded from IHT is £55,000. The use of this exemption is considered in different parts of this book and the following points represent a summary of those sections:

(1) For tax planning purposes the lowest total IHT bill is produced if the spouses ensure that they both use up their nil rate bands (see Chapter 35).

(2) Both should take advantage of the lifetime exemptions. The Revenue will normally not invoke the associated operations provisions to challenge a transfer between spouses even if it enables this to occur (Chapter 21).

(3) The rules for related property are designed to counter tax saving by splitting assets between spouses (see Chapter 21).

(4) IHT on a chargeable transfer by one spouse to a third party may be collected from the other spouse in certain circumstances (see Chapter 21).   **[23.41]**

2 **Business property relief** (IHTA 1984 ss 103–114)

The stated purpose of this relief (and of agricultural relief (below)) is to prevent a business from having to be sold in order to pay the IHT bill. Any IHT that is payable after allowing this relief may often be paid by interest-free instalments (see Chapter 21). The relief is given automatically.   **[23.42]**

a) *Meaning of 'relevant business property'*

Business property relief is given in respect of transfers of 'relevant business property' which is defined as any of the following:

(1) *A business*   Eg that of a sole trader or sole practitioner; or

(2) *An interest in a business*   Eg the share of a partner in either a trading or professional partnership. The relief is available irrespective of the size of the transferor's interest in that enterprise. A sole trader who transfers a part of his trade falls within this category and this may include a transfer of assets used in the business (*Fetherstonehaugh v IRC* (1984): contrast CGT retirement relief where a distinction is drawn between a disposal of part of a trade and of assets used in that trade: [**16.96**]).

(3) *Shares or securities which give the transferor control of the company*   Control does not have to be transferred; the requirement is simply that *at the time of transfer* the transferor should have such control (see [**23.49**]).

(4) *Shares in an unquoted company which gave the transferor more than 25% of the votes (a substantial minority share holding)*   As a result of (3) and (4) together an unquoted shareholding of above 25% of the total votes capable of being cast on all questions affecting the company as a whole may qualify for relief.

(5) *Shares in an unquoted company not falling within the above categories (3) and (4)*   Hence, all shareholdings in private companies can qualify for relief. (Shares are quoted when they are listed on a recognised stock exchange or dealt in on the Unlisted Securities Market (USM): IHTA 1984 s 272.)

(6) *Any land or building, plant or machinery which immediately before the transfer was used by a partnership in which the transferor was a partner or by a company of which he had control*   Control for these purposes requires a majority of votes (50%+) on all questions affecting the company as a whole. Hence, an unjust result is produced if the appropriate asset is used by a company in which the transferor owned 35% of the ordinary shares when no relief will be available. Had the asset been used by a partnership, however, in which he was entitled to 35% of all profits and surpluses, relief would be available. Relief is also available if the asset is held in a trust but is used by a life tenant for his own business or by a company which he controls.

Notice that the relief is given irrespective of whether a rent is charged for the use of the asset; in practice, however, a nominal rent only should be reserved to preserve any CGT retirement relief (see [**16.97**]).   **[23.43]**

b) *Amount of relief*

Relief is given by percentage reduction in the value of the business property transferred: ie on the value of assets used for business purposes less liabilities incurred for business purposes (IHTA 1984 s 110(b) and note that the value cannot be increased by charging business debts on non-business property: *contrast* agricultural relief). The chargeable transfer will be of that reduced sum, grossed-up if the transferor is to bear the IHT on a chargeable lifetime transfer. Business property relief is applied before other reliefs (for instance, the £3,000 *inter vivos* relief). The appropriate percentage depends upon which item of business property is transferred.

50% relief is available for businesses, interests in such business, controlling shareholdings and substantial minority shareholdings (ie categories (1), (2), (3) and (4) above).

30% relief is available for minority unquoted shareholdings (category (5) above) and for assets used by a business (category (6) above). **[23.44]**

EXAMPLE 23.8

Topsy is a partner in the firm of Topsy & Tim (builders). He owns the site of the firm's offices and goods yard. He settles the following property on his daughter Teasy for life: (1) his share of the business (value £500,000) and (2) the site (value £50,000). Business property relief will be available on the business at 50% so that the value transferred is reduced to £250,000 and on the site at 30% so that the value transferred is £35,000.

Notes:
  (i) Topsy's total transfers amount to £285,000 which may be further reduced if other exemptions are available.
  (ii) The effect of business property relief on the death of a transferor is to reduce the value of his estate and, hence, the estate rate. The full benefit of the relief is not therefore given to the business.
  (iii) IHT may remain payable on business property after deducting all available reliefs. Whether the chargeable transfer is made during lifetime or on death, it will usually be possible to pay the tax by interest-free instalments (see below for a discussion of the position when IHT or additional IHT is charged because of death within seven years of a chargeable transfer).

c) *Conditions if relief is to be available*

In general, relevant business property which has been owned for less than two years attracts no relief (IHTA 1984 s 106). However, technical provisions deal with the problems caused by a succession of businesses and ensure no loss of relief. Furthermore, the incorporation of a business will not affect the running of the two year period (IHTA 1984 s 107). Where a transfer of a business is made between spouses on death, the recipient can include the ownership period of the deceased spouse. This is not, however, the case with an *inter vivos* transfer (IHTA 1984 s 108). If the spouse takes the property as the result of a written variation read back into the will under IHTA 1984 s 142 the recipient is entitled to property on the death of the other spouse. When entitlement results from an appropriation of assets by the PRs this provision would not, however, apply.

EXAMPLE 23.9

(1)   Solomon incorporated his leather business by forming Solomon Ltd in which he holds 100% of the issued shares. For business property relief the two year ownership period begins with the commencement of Solomon's original leather business.

(2)   Solomon set up his family company one year before his death and left the shares to his wife in his will. She can include his one year ownership period towards satisfying the two year requirement. Had he made a lifetime gift to her such aggregation is not possible.

(3)   If Mrs Solomon had died within two years of the gift from her husband (whether that gift had been made *inter vivos* or on death) business relief will be available on her death so long as the conditions for relief were satisfied at the time of the earlier transfer by her husband (IHTA 1984, s 109). A similar result follows if the gift from her husband had been by will and she had made a lifetime chargeable transfer of the property within two years of his death (in this case relief could be afforded under s 109 and, if Mr Solomon had not satisfied the two year requirement, his period of ownership could be aggregated with that of Mrs Solomon under s 108).

Other provisions exclude from relief certain businesses (eg those designed to hold investments or to deal in securities or land), whilst private assets cannot be disguised as a part of the business in an attempt to take advantage of the relief (IHTA 1984 s 112: see the same problem in CGT [**16.100**]).

For income tax purposes there cannot be a *trade* of 'letting land' (see Chapter 8) but for IHT business relief the activities of a commercial landlord may amount to a *business* (see *Taxation*, 3 May 1990, p 126). It would appear that, provided the letting involves more than merely 'holding investments' (IHTA 1984 s 105(3)), business relief should be available. It is understood that the Special Commissioners have so decided in a case involving a commercial landlord who maintained a high quality of service to his professional tenants (embracing primarily cleaning operations and maintenance and decoration). The taxpayer was considered to be acting as a managing agent: his daily activities and his obligations far exceeded those normally placed on the holder of an investment. (Compare also the position of an hotelier who lives on his own premises and manages his own hotel: he is not the holder of a mere investment.) 'Business' is therefore a wider concept than 'trade'.

As it is designed for businesses, relief is obviously not available for transfers of the sale proceeds from a business and the relief does not extend to a business subject to a 'buy and sell' agreement. Such arrangements are common in partnership agreements and amongst shareholder/directors of companies and provide that if one of the partners or shareholder/directors dies then his PRs are obliged to sell the share(s) and the survivors are obliged to purchase them. As this is a binding contract, the beneficial ownership in the business or shares has passed to the purchaser so that business relief is not available (SP 12/80 see also 1984 STI 651 and for criticism of the Revenue's views *Capital Taxes*, 1985, p 4).   [**23.45**]

EXAMPLE 23.10

The shares of Zerzes Ltd are owned equally by the four directors. The articles of association provide that on the death of a shareholder his shares *shall* be sold to the remaining shareholder/directors who *must* purchase them. Business relief is not available on that death. If the other shareholders had merely possessed pre-emption rights, as no binding contract of sale exists, the relief would apply.

d) *Businesses held in settlements*

For interest in possession trusts the relief is given, as one would expect, by reference to the life tenant. So long as he satisfies the two year ownership test, relief will be given at the following rates:

50% relief for shares in companies controlled by the life tenant and for substantial minority shareholdings (taking into account both trust shares and any shares which he owns) and for businesses belonging to the trust;

30% relief for unquoted shares (not qualifying for 50% relief) held in the trust; and

30% relief for the assets listed in a) (6) above (see p 418) which are held in the trust and which are either used by the life tenant for his own business or by a company controlled by him. The case of *Fetherstonehaugh v IRC* (1984) concerned the availability of relief when land held under a strict settlement was used by the life tenant as part of his farming business (he was a sole trader absolutely entitled to the other business assets). The Court of Appeal held that 50% relief was available under section 105(1)(a) on the land in the settlement with the result that the subsequent introduction of 30% relief is apparently redundant in such cases. The Revenue now accept that in cases similar to *Fetherstonehaugh* the maximum 50% relief will be available since the land will be treated as an 'asset used in the business' and, as its value is included in the transfer of value, the land will be taxed on the basis that the deceased was the absolute owner of it.

For trusts without interests in possession the relief is given to the trust so long as the conditions are satisfied by the trustees, so that the beneficiaries are ignored. The relief will be given when the trust is subject to the anniversary charge and any resultant tax can be paid by instalments. When the business ceases to be relevant property (ie when it leaves the trust) business relief will again be available on fulfilment of the normal conditions.   [**23.46**]

e) *Relief for a controlling shareholding*

The maximum 50% relief is available when a person has control of a company. Under s 105(1)(b) this will be the case when he owns shares or securities which gave him control of the company immediately before the relevant transfer and for this purpose control is defined in IHTA 1984 s 269(1) as follows:

> 'a person has control of a company at any time if he then has the control of powers of voting on *all questions* affecting the company as a whole which if exercised would yield a majority of the votes capable of being exercised thereon . . .' (IHTA 1984 s 269(1)).

Hence, control of more than 50% of the votes exercisable in general meeting will ensure that the transferor has 'control' for the purposes of business property relief. A transfer of his shares will therefore attract 50% relief and a transfer of qualifying assets used by that company, 30% relief. In calculating whether he has control, a life tenant can aggregate shares held by the settlement with shares in his free estate, whilst the shares of husband and wife will be treated as one holding. In no other cases, however, can shares of different persons or bodies be added together in order to discover whether an individual has control or not. Notice that under s 105(1)(b) relief is available for all controlling shares in both quoted and unquoted companies.   [**23.47**]

f) Relief for substantial minority shareholdings

Under s 105(1)(bb) 50% relief is also available on a transfer of unquoted shares (not falling within s 105(1)(b)) which immediately before the transfer satisfied the following requirements:

> 'The shares (either by themselves or together with other shares or securities owned by the transferor) gave the transferor control of powers of voting on all questions affecting the company as a whole which if exercised would have yielded more than 25% of the votes capable of being exercised on them; and shares shall be taken to satisfy this condition if . . . they would have been sufficient to give the transferor such control.'

Accordingly, the test is satisfied in this case when the transferor owns more than 25% of the company's shares in an unquoted company: once he owns more than 50%, the s 269(1) definition of control is satisfied. In the case of quoted shares (including shares dealt in on the USM) business relief is of course only available if the stricter control requirements of s 269(1) are satisfied.   [**23.48**]

g) Problem areas

Care should be taken in reducing a controlling holding and where it is intended to make more than one transfer of the shares the transferor should keep control as long as possible.

EXAMPLE 23.11

(1) Albert owns 80% of the issued ordinary shares in Albert plc whose shares are dealt in on the USM. He makes a chargeable transfer of 30% of the company's shares in 1990 and of the remaining 50% in 1991. Business property relief at 50% is available on the transfer of the 30% holding in 1990 since Albert has control of Albert plc as defined in s 269(1). Note that it is not necessary actually to transfer control. On the transfer in 1991 no business relief is available since the 50% holding is not a controlling interest under s 269(1) and a transfer of quoted shares does not attract relief under s 105(1)(bb).

> If he had transferred 29% of the shares in 1990 with the remaining 51% passing in 1991, 50% relief as above would be available on the transfer in 1990, and on the 1991 transfer, since Albert still has control.

(2) Assume that Albert's shareholding (80%) was in a private company, Albert Ltd. A transfer of 30% of the shares in 1990 would qualify for relief at 50% under s 105(1)(b) and the remaining transfer in 1991 also qualifies for 50% relief under s 105(1)(bb).

> If Albert disposed of his holding in three instalments: 30% in 1990; 30% in 1991 and the final 20% in 1992 business relief would be available on all three transfers at 50% on the first (s 105(1)(b)); 50% on the second (s 105(1)(bb)) and 30% on the third (s 105(1)(c)—a minority unquoted shareholding).

It might be assumed that because of the two year ownership requirement, both the business property (eg the shares) and control must have been owned throughout this period. This, however, does not appear to be the case for relief under s 105(1)(b) since it is only the shares transferred which must have been owned for two years and control is only required immediately before the relevant transfer. Thus the taxpayer may discover—for instance as the result of a buy-back—that he obtains control of the company (with a resultant revaluation of his shares) and were he then to transfer those shares within two years of the event maximum business relief would be available.

EXAMPLE 23.12

Of the 100 issued ordinary shares in Buy-Back Ltd Zack owns 40, Jed 40 and the remaining 20 are split amongst miscellaneous charities. Assume that in July 1991 Buy-Back buys Zack's holding. As those shares are cancelled the issued capital falls to 60 shares of which Jed owns 40. Were he to die in September 1991, his shareholding would be subject to 50% relief.

In addition to control passing to a shareholder as a result of such extraneous events as a buy-back it may be possible for the partners in a quasi-partnership company to ensure that each obtains control for a short period (eg one month) to enable them to transfer their shareholding with the maximum business relief.

EXAMPLE 23.13

The shares in ABCD Limited are owned as to 25% each by A, B, C and D. The shares are divided into four classes in December 1990 which will carry control in January, February, March and April 1991 respectively. In January 1991 A transfers his shares.
(1)   As A has control (under s 269(1)) in January 1991 he is entitled to 50% relief.
(2)   If, at the same time, he transferred land, which had been used by his company, 30% relief would be available on that transfer.
(3)   Might temporary shifts of control be nullified under the *Ramsay* principle? Without being able to give a definite answer, it is arguable that, as the legislation expressly requires control at one moment only (viz immediately before the transfer), that is an end to the matter. It is, however, desirable that A should at the time of transfer actually possess control of the business: ie the other shareholders must accept that A could, if he wished, exercise his voting control over the affairs of the company.

The 50% relief given under s 105(1)(bb) (for substantial minority shareholdings) is subject to the conditions of s 109A being satisfied and that section requires the control requirement to be satisfied throughout the two years immediately preceding the transfer. Curiously, therefore, temporary control suffices for relief under s 105(1)(b) (as in *Example 23.12)* but not for relief under s 105(1)(bb)!

A shareholding in excess of 50% is worth significantly more than a minority (less than 25%) holding. This, to some extent, explains the different percentages of business relief. What is obviously disastrous is to own a controlling interest (valued as such) and yet be deprived of 50% relief because of a technicality. Formerly this could occur if a company's articles contained a *Bushell v Faith* clause designed to prevent a director from being removed by ordinary resolution (hence, circumventing the Companies Act 1985 s 303). For IHT purposes, such clauses may mean that no shareholder can have control of that company since no one will control '*all questions* affecting the company as a whole' (for the purpose of relief under s 105(1)(b)). With the introduction of 50% relief for substantial minority shareholdings this problem has largely disappeared.   [**23.49**]

EXAMPLE 23.14

A private company has two directors and shareholders, A and B, holding 80% and 20% of the shares respectively. B's directorship is protected by a '*Bushell v Faith* clause' giving him five votes per share on any resolution to dismiss him, whilst A has only one vote per share. Hence, for IHT purposes, despite his 80% stake, A does not have control on all questions affecting the company as a whole (since he does not possess more than 50% of the votes as required by s 105(1)(b)) but he will always control more than 25% of the votes (even on a resolution to dismiss B) and hence his business relief is at 50%.

h) *Business relief and the instalment option*

After deducting business property relief at the appropriate percentage, the reduced value of the business may attract IHT although it must be stressed that this value may be further reduced. Thus the normal IHT exemptions and reliefs are deducted *after* business relief so that a lifetime gift, for instance, may be reduced by the £3,000 annual exemption. Further, any tax that must be paid may normally be spread over ten years and paid by annual interest-free instalments (see [**22.58**]). This instalment election is only available, in the case of lifetime gifts, if the IHT is borne by the donee: on death the election should be made by the personal representatives. It should be noted that, although there is a striking similarity between assets which attract business relief and assets qualifying for the instalment option, there are limitations on the availability of instalment relief in the case of a transfer of unquoted shares not giving control (as defined in s 269, [**23.47**]), as the following table indicates:

Relevant business property (IHTA 1984, Pt V, Ch 1)	*Instalment assets* (IHTA 1984, Pt VIII)
s 105 (1)(a): a business or an interest in a business	*s 227*: a business or an interest in a business
s 105(1)(b): shares etc, giving control	*s 228(1)(a)*: shares etc, giving control
s 105(1)(bb) and (c): unquoted shares	*s 228(1)(c)*: unquoted shares with hardship; *s 228(1)(b)*: on death, unquoted shares being at least 20%, of the total transfer; *s 228(1)(d) and 228(3)*: unquoted shares within the 10% and £20,000 rule; *s 229*: woodlands; and *s 227(2)*: land

These limitations on the instalment option have been defended by the Inland Revenue on the grounds that 'it has been considered inappropriate for the instalment facility to apply in cases involving less than substantial interests in unquoted companies' (see further 1985 6 *CTT News* 284).   [**23.50**]

i) *PETs and additional IHT—when is relief available?*

When a transferor makes a lifetime chargeable transfer or a PET and dies within seven years, the IHT or extra IHT payable is calculated on the basis that business relief is not available unless the original (or substituted) property remains owned by the transferee at the death of the transferor (or at the death of the transferee if earlier) and would qualify for business relief immediately before the transferor's death (ignoring, however, the two year ownership requirement). The instalment option is similarly restricted since it is only available if the original or substituted business property is owned by the transferee at death. Relief is given for substituted property when the entire (net) proceeds of sale of the original property are reinvested within twelve months in the replacement qualifying property. **[23.51]**

EXAMPLE 23.15

(1) Sim gives his ironmongers business to his daughter, Sammy, in 1990 (a PET) and dies in 1991. Sammy has continued to run the business.
The PET becomes chargeable because of Sim's death within seven years: 50% relief is available (qualifying property retained by donee) and any IHT can be paid by ten instalments (the first being due six months from the end of the month of Sim's death).

(2) As in (1) save that Sammy immediately sold the business in 1990.
No business relief is available on Sim's death. The entire value of the business in 1990 is charged and forms part of Sim's cumulative total on death (unless Sammy buys replacement property within twelve months of the sale).

(3) As in (1) save that Sammy had incorporated the business late in 1990 and had continued to run it as the sole shareholder/director.
Business relief is available on Sim's death (substituted qualifying property).

(4) Assume that Sim had given Sammy 20% of the shares in his trading company and had retained the other 80% until his death.
The appropriate percentage of relief on the 1990 transfer (50%: see **[23.47]**) is determined by reference to the events in 1990 (ie by reference to the fact that Sim controls the company) and remains available on his death if Sammy still owns the shares.

(5) Sim settles business property on accumulation and maintenance trusts (a PET) but at the date of his death within seven years of that transfer, the property has vested in the trust beneficiaries absolutely. No business relief will be available since the original donees of the property (the trustees) have not retained it. Accordingly, the result is as in (2) above. It is thought that had Sim created an interest in possession trust and if the trustees had then exercised an express power in the trust to advance the business assets to the life tenant, relief would not be withdrawn since the original gift in settlement would have been treated as a gift to the life tenant.

EXAMPLE 23.16

Jock settles his business (then worth £500,000) on discretionary trusts in 1990 (a chargeable lifetime transfer). He dies in 1991 when the business has been sold by the trustees.

(1) *on the 1990 transfer*: 50% relief is available so that the value transferred is £250,000.

(2) *on the 1991 transfer*: no relief is available so that extra IHT is calculated upon a value transferred of £500,000. Note that the result of a withdrawal of relief is that the additional tax is charged on the entire value of the business but not so as to alter Jock's cumulative total (*contrast* the effect of loss of relief when the original transfer was a PET: see *Example 23.15(2)*).

j) Business property subject to a reservation

Business property subject to a reservation is treated as comprised in the donor's estate at death (if the reservation is still then subsisting) or, if the reservation ceases *inter vivos*, as forming the subject matter of a deemed PET made at that time (see generally [**22.4**]). In both cases business relief may be available to reduce the value of the property subject to charge. Whether the relief is available or not is generally decided by treating the transfer as made by the *donee* who must therefore satisfy the business property relief requirements (FA 1986 Sch 20 para 8). However, for these purposes, the period of ownership of the donor can be included with that of the donee in order to satisfy the two year requirement.

1   Any question of whether shares or securities fall within s 105(1)(b) or (bb) and thereby qualify for 50% business property relief must be decided as if the shares or securities were owned by the *donor* and had been owned by him since the date of the gift. Accordingly, other shares of the donor (or related property of the donor) will be relevant in deciding if these requirements are satisfied.   **[23.52]**

EXAMPLE 23.17

(1)   Wainwright gives his ironmonger's business to his daughter Tina and it is agreed that he shall be paid one half of the net profits from the business each year. He retains this benefit until the date of his death.

(a)   At the time of the original gift (a PET) the property satisfied the requirements for business relief. If the PET becomes chargeable as the result of Wainwright's death within the following seven years, relief continues to be available if Tina has retained the original property or acquired replacement property.

(b)   The business is also treated as forming part of Wainwright's estate on his death under FA 1986 s 102, but business relief may be available to reduce its value under FA 1986 Sch 20 para 8. Whether relief is available (and if so at what percentage) is decided by treating the transfer of value as made by the *donee*. Accordingly, Tina must satisfy the conditions for relief although she can include the period of ownership/occupation of Wainwright before the gift. (A similar provision applies if the reservation ceases during Wainwright's lifetime so that he is treated as making a PET.)

(2)   Assume that Wainwright owns 100% of the shares in Widgett's Ltd and gives 20% of those shares to Tina subject to a reserved benefit. Assuming that he dies within seven years:

(a)   Relief at 50% was originally available under s 105(1)(b) when the gift was made and continues to apply to that chargeable PET if Tina has retained the shares.

(b)   The shares are treated as forming part of Wainwright's estate because of the reserved benefit. Whether business relief is available depends upon two factors. First, Tina must satisfy the basic requirements: ie she must have retained the original shares which must still qualify as business property. Secondly, in order to arrive at the percentage of business relief it is assumed that the shares had been retained by Wainwright from the date of the gift until the date of his death. In this case 50% relief will therefore be available under s 105(1)(b), assuming that he has retained the remaining 80% of the shares in Widgett's Ltd. So long as he has retained more than 30% of those shares this requirement will continue to be satisfied because, aggregating the shares retained by him together with the 20% given to Tina, he will be treated as owning more than 50% of the shares at death. Even if he had retained only 6% of the **Widgett** shares, 50% relief will be given under s 105(1)(bb) both in respect of Tina's shares and, presumably, in respect of the small holding retained by Wainwright in his estate.

3 **Agricultural property relief** (IHTA 1984 ss 115–124)

IHTA 1984 ss 115–124 contain the rules, introduced originally in FA 1981, for giving relief in the case of transfers of agricultural property. As for business relief, this relief is given automatically. The old (pre 1981) regime will not be considered save for a brief mention of the transitional provisions. **[23.53]**

a) *Meaning of 'agricultural property' and 'agricultural value'*

Relief is given for transfers of value of agricultural property, defined as agricultural land or pasture including cottages, farm buildings and farmhouses together with land used with them so long as they are 'of a character appropriate to the property'. It is the 'agricultural value' of such property which is subject to the relief; this is defined as the value which the property would have if subject to a perpetual covenant prohibiting its use otherwise than as agricultural property. Enhanced value attributable to development potential is not subject to the relief (although business property relief can apply to this excess value). Otherwise, the normal valuation rules of IHTA 1984 Pt VI, eg on the basis of vacant possession, are applied. It should be noted that the value of agricultural property may be artificially enhanced for the purposes of the relief by charging agricultural debts on non-qualifying property (see *Example 23.18* below; IHTA 1984 ss 5(5), 162(4) and cf business property relief, **[23.44]**). Further, it is not necessary to transfer a farming business or part thereof in order to obtain relief; it can be given on a mere transfer of assets. When a milk quota is transferred with land, the value of that quota will normally enhance the value of the land: consequently, relief for agricultural property will be given for the value of the quota as reflected in the agricultural value of the land itself. **[23.54]**

EXAMPLE 23.18

A farmer owns a farm qualifying for 50% agricultural relief worth £1m and subject to a mortgage of £500,000. His other main assets are investments worth £500,000. Were he to die, the value of his estate on death would be £1m made up of the investments plus the farm after deducting the mortgage thereon. Agricultural relief at 50% would then be available on the *net* value of the farm (ie on £500,000) which would reduce that to £250,000 leaving a chargeable death estate of £750,000.

Suppose, however, that before his death the farmer arranged with the appropriate creditor to switch the mortgage from the agricultural land to the investments. The result then would be that on death the value of his estate would, as above, be £1m made up of the value of the farm (£1m) since the investments now, after deducting the mortgage, are valueless. Accordingly, agricultural relief is now available on the entire value of the farm and amounts to £500,000 leaving a chargeable death estate of £500,000.

b) *The amount of relief*

As with business relief, agricultural relief is given by a percentage reduction of the transferred value. Other exemptions (eg the £3,000 lifetime exemption) can be set against the reduced figure. Where the transferor is to pay the

IHT, this reduced figure must be grossed up. Any resultant tax may be paid by instalments. There are two levels of agricultural relief:

50% relief for the occupier of agricultural property subject to a two year ownership requirement. Into this category fall owner occupiers and tenant farmers in possession. Exceptionally, the 50% relief is also available where the transferor is a landlord out of possession. He must have owned the property for the seven years before the transfer and that property must have been occupied (by himself or another) for the purposes of agriculture throughout that period. Furthermore, he must have the right to obtain vacant possession within 12 months of the transfer. The existing tenant must not, therefore, enjoy the protection of the Agricultural Holdings Acts (see *Henderson v Karmel's Executors* (1984) for a consideration of the circumstances when an existing tenancy can be terminated).

30% relief is available in other cases and, therefore, covers a landlord owning a freehold reversion. The qualifying period of ownership is seven years immediately preceding the transfer and during this period the land must throughout have been occupied either by the transferor or by others for the purposes of agriculture. Although it was intended that the same amount of tax would be produced on the tenanted agricultural value after 30% relief as on the vacant possession agricultural value after 50% relief, it is probably advantageous to reduce the value of the land (eg by granting a lease of the entire property to a family partnership) and opting for 30% relief

EXAMPLE 23.19

(1) Adam lets agricultural property to a partnership consisting of himself, Bertram, and Claud. So far as Adam is concerned: (1) the 30% relief will be available for his freehold reversion; and (2) the 50% relief will apply to his leasehold interest in the land in his capacity as a partner.

(2) Assume Tom owns 800 acres of freehold land worth two million pounds.
   (i)   A gift to his son will, if he dies within seven years, lead to an IHT charge on one million pounds (after 50% relief).
   (ii) If his son were granted a tenancy for full consideration, that grant will not lead to any IHT charge and, assuming a 45% discount, the freehold reversion retained by Tom is worth £1,100,000. A subsequent gift of that reversion more than three years later (to avoid the associated operations provisions in IHTA 1984 s 268) will qualify for 30% relief so that the value transferred becomes £770,000.

(3) On retirement Dad leases his agricultural property to a partnership consisting of his four children, but retains the farmhouse as his main residence. If Dad subsequently wishes to transfer this valuable asset to his children it will not qualify for any relief: (a) the 30% relief will not be available as the property was not occupied by another for agricultural purposes; (b) the 50% relief will not be available as the property was not used for the purposes of agriculture in the two years before transfer (see 1984 LS Gaz 1274). It will also be important to ensure that Dad has not reserved any benefit in the gifted property (see[**22.3**]).

The relief (at 50% or 30% as appropriate) is available in three further cases: first, where agricultural property is held on discretionary trusts (50% relief, if the trustees have been farming the land themselves); secondly, where 'agricultural property' is held on trust for a life tenant under an interest in possession trust; and finally, where agricultural property is held by a company in which the transferor of shares has control. 'Control' has the same meaning as for business property relief. To claim the relief the appropriate two or seven year period of ownership must be satisfied by the company (vis-à-vis the agricultural property) and by the shareholder/ transferor (vis-à-vis the shares transferred). **[23.55]**

c) *Technical provisions*

As with business property relief there are technical provisions relating to replacement property, transfers between spouses, and succession from a donor. Similarly, a binding contract for the sale of the property results in agricultural relief not being available. Furthermore, the grant of a tenancy of agricultural property will not be a transfer of value provided that the grant is for full consideration in money or money's worth (IHTA 1984 s 16). Hence, it will no longer be necessary for the lessor to show (particularly in the case of transfers within the family) that he had no gratuitous intent and that the transaction was such as might be made with a stranger. The change (surprisingly made retrospective) is explicable because of the end of double discounting under the present system (for difficulties that may arise in ascertaining the market value of agricultural tenancies see 1984 LS Gaz 2749, 1985 LS Gaz 420 and 484 and *Baird's Executors v IRC* (1991) considered at [**21.70**]). The availability of the relief when extra IHT is payable, or a PET becomes chargeable, because of a death within seven years is subject to the same restrictions that apply for business property relief in these cases (see [**23.51**]). **[23.56]**

d) *Transitional relief; double discounting*

Under the rules which prevailed up to 1981 agricultural property relief was available where L let Whiteacre to a partnership consisting of himself and his children M and N. On a transfer of the freehold reversion (valued on a tenanted, not a vacant possession, basis) 50% relief was available. The ingredient of 'double discounting' consisted of first reducing the value of the property by granting the lease and then applying the full (50%) relief to that discounted value. As a *quid pro quo* the Revenue argued that the grant of the lease could be a transfer of value even if for a full commercial rent.

Double discount is not available under the new system of agricultural relief and the grant of the tenancy will not be a chargeable transfer of value if for full consideration (IHTA 1984 s 16). On a transitional basis, however, where land was let, as in the above example, on 10 March 1981 so that any transfer by L immediately before that date would have qualified for the 50% allowance, on the next transfer of value, that old relief will still apply. (Note that the old relief was limited to £250,000 of agricultural value before giving relief or to 1,000 acres, at the option of the taxpayer.) It is only the first actual transfer of that reversion after 10 March 1981 that will obtain the benefit of double discounting, so that it is important to ensure that that transfer is not exempt (eg to a spouse). Also, the transitional relief will not apply in cases where the pre-10 March 1981 tenancy has been surrendered and regranted. Similar transitional relief applies where before 10 March 1981 the land was let to a company which the transferor controlled. **[23.57]**

e) *Inter-relation of agricultural and business property reliefs*

The two reliefs are similar and overlap. The following distinctions are worthy of note:

(1) Agricultural relief must be given in priority to business relief (IHTA 1984 s 114(1)).

(2) Differences exist in the treatment of woodlands, crops, livestock, deadstock, plant and machinery, and farmhouses etc. Generally, in these areas business relief is more widely available.

(3) Agricultural relief is only available on property situated in the UK, Channel Islands and Isle of Man whereas business relief is not so restricted.   [23.58]

4   Relief for heritage property (IHTA 1984 ss 30-35 as amended)

In certain circumstances an application can be made to postpone the payment of IHT on transfers of value of heritage property. As tax can be postponed on any number of such transfers, the result is that a liability to IHT can be deferred indefinitely (similar deferral provisions operate for CGT: CGTA 1979 s 147(3)). Tax postponed under these provisions may subsequently become chargeable under s 32 on the happening of a 'chargeable event'. If the transfer is potentially exempt, an application for conditional exemption can only be made (and is only necessary) if the PET is rendered chargeable by the donor's death within seven years.   [23.59]

a) Conditions to be satisfied if IHT is to be deferred

In order to obtain this relief, first, the property must fall into one of two main categories designated by the Treasury:

Category 1   works of art (including pictures, prints and books) which are of 'national, scientific, historic, or artistic interest'.

Category 2   land and buildings which are (generally) of outstanding scenic, historic, or architectural interest. There is no requirement that the land must adjoin a qualifying building in order to qualify for the exemption (IHTA 1984 s 31 as amended by FA 1985 s 94).

Secondly, undertakings have to be given with respect to that property to take reasonable steps for its preservation; to secure reasonable access to the public (see *Works of Art: A Basic Guide* published by the Central Office of Information); and (in the case of Category 1 property) to keep the property in the UK. In appropriate cases of Category 1 property, it is sufficient for details of the object and its location to be entered on an official list of such assets. In the case of Category 2 property, additional undertakings are required in relation to land which does not adjoin a qualifying building (see FA 1985 s 94; Sch 26).

The undertaking must be given by 'such person as the Treasury think appropriate in the circumstances of the case'. In practice, this will mean a PR, trustee, legatee or donee.

A third requirement exists in the case of lifetime transfers of value. The transferor must have owned the asset for the six years immediately preceding the transfer if relief is to be given. Notice, however, that the six year requirement can be satisfied by aggregating periods of ownership of a husband and wife and that it does not apply in cases where the property has been inherited on a death and the exemption has then been successfully claimed. As an anti-avoidance provision it is surprising that the six year requirement is limited to inter vivos transfers since the result is that death bed schemes are permitted.   [23.60]

b) *Effect of deferring IHT*

Where relief is given the transfer is a 'conditionally exempt transfer'. So long as the undertakings are observed and the property is not further transferred IHT liability can be postponed. If there is a subsequent transfer, the exemption may be claimed a second time. Three 'chargeable events' cause the deferred IHT charge to become payable: first, a breach of the undertakings; secondly, a sale of the asset; and thirdly, a further transfer (*inter vivos* or on death) without a new undertaking. If a further transfer satisfies the requirements for a conditionally exempt transfer, not only will that transfer itself not be chargeable but it will not lead to any triggering of the deferred charge.

In the case where a fresh undertaking is given, but the transfer does not satisfy the other requirements for a transfer of heritage property (eg it is to a spouse or is made before the six year ownership requirement has been satisfied), no 'chargeable event' occurs (see IHTA 1984 s 32(5)). Thus, any deferred charge is not triggered, but the transfer itself may be chargeable (or potentially chargeable), if not to a spouse. [**23.61**]

c) *Calculation of the deferred IHT charge*

Calculation of the deferred IHT charge will depend upon what triggers the charge. If there is a breach of undertakings, the tax is charged upon the person who would be entitled to the proceeds of sale were the asset then sold. The value of the property at that date will be taxed according to the transferor's rates of IHT. Where he is alive, this is by reference to his cumulative total at the time of the triggering event (any PETs that he has made are ignored for these purposes even if they subsequently become chargeable); where he is dead, the property is added to his death estate and charged at the highest rate applicable to that estate but at half the Table rates unless the conditionally exempt transfer was made on his death.

EXAMPLE 23.20

In 1989 Aloysius settles a Rousseau painting (valued at £500,000) on discretionary trusts. The transfer is conditionally exempt, but, two years later (when the picture is worth £650,000), the trustee breaks the undertakings by refusing to allow the painting to be exhibited in the Primitive Exhibition in London. If Aloysius is still alive in 1991, IHT is calculated on £650,000 at Aloysius' rates according to his cumulative total of chargeable transfers in 1991. Had Aloysius died in 1990 with a death estate of £1,000,000, £650,000 would be charged at half the rates appropriate to the highest part of an estate of £1,650,000. As can be seen from this example, considerable care should be exercised in deciding whether the election should be made. If the relevant asset is likely to increase in value, it may be better to pay off the inheritance tax earlier assuming that sufficient funds are available.

If the deferred charge is triggered by a sale of the heritage property, the above principles operate, save that it is the net sale proceeds that will be subject to the deferred charge. Expenses of sale, including CGT, are deductible.

Calculation of the deferred charge is more complex where it is triggered by a gift of the heritage property since two chargeable transfers could occur; the first on the gift and the second by the triggering of the deferred charge. If the gift is a chargeable event (excluding PETs) the tax payable on that gift is credited against the triggered deferred charge. Where the gift is a chargeable transfer, but not a chargeable event, as the triggering charge does not arise the credit will be available against the next chargeable event affecting that property.

EXAMPLE 23.21

Eric makes a conditionally exempt transfer to Ernie on his death in 1988. Ernie in turn settles the asset on discretionary trusts in 1991 and the trustees do not give any undertaking.
The creation of the settlement is a chargeable transfer by Ernie. IHT will be calculated at half rates in 1991.
The triggered charge: the value of the asset in 1991 will be subject to IHT at Eric's death rates. A tax credit for IHT paid on the 1991 gift which is attributable to the value of the asset is available.
   If the trustees had given an appropriate undertaking in 1991, the trust would be taxed as above (the six year requirement is not satisfied by Ernie). The transfer is not a chargeable event so that no triggering of the conditionally exempt transfer occurs. The tax credit is available if this charge is triggered, eg by the trustees selling the asset.

If a conditionally exempt transfer is followed by a PET which is a chargeable event with regard to the property, IHT triggered is allowed as a credit against IHT payable if the PET becomes chargeable.
   Where there has been more than one conditionally exempt transfer of the same property, and a chargeable event occurs, the Revenue have the right to choose which of the earlier transferors (within 30 years before the chargeable event) shall be used for calculating the sum payable.   [**23.62**]

EXAMPLE 23.22

Z gives a picture to Y who gives it to X who sells it. There have been two conditionally exempt transfers ('by Z and Y) and the Revenue can choose (subject to the 30 year time limit) whether to levy the deferred IHT charge according to Z or Y's rates.

d) *Settled property*

The exemption may be available for heritage property held in a discretionary trust (IHTA 1984 ss 78, 79). Where it is held in an interest in possession trust, it is treated as belonging to the life tenant and the above rules are applied.   [**23.63**]

e) *Maintenance funds*

IHTA 1984 ss 27, 57(5) and Sch 4 paras 1-7 provide for no IHT to be charged when property (whether or not heritage property) is settled on trusts to secure the maintenance, repair etc of historic buildings. Such trusts also receive special income tax treatment (TA 1988 s 690ff) and, for CGT, the hold-over election under CGTA 1979 s 147A is available.
   These funds can be set up with a small sum of money so long as there is an intention to put in further sums later. The introduction of the PET in 1986 has, however, produced a dilemma for an estate owner. He could give away property to his successor as a PET and rely upon living for seven years in order to avoid IHT. Alternatively, he could transfer that property

by a conditionally exempt transfer into a maintenance fund. It is not, however, possible to make a gift of the property and then, if the donor dies within seven years, for the donee at that point to avoid the IHT charge by transferring the property into a maintenance fund.

Settled property will be free of IHT on the death of the life tenant if within two years after his death (three years if an application to court is necessary) the terms of the settlement are altered so that the property goes into a heritage maintenance fund (IHTA 1984 s 57A). **[23.64]**

f) Private treaty sales and acceptance in lieu

Heritage property can be given for national purposes or for the public benefit without any IHT or CGT charge arising. Alternatively, the property can be sold by private treaty (not at an auction) to heritage bodies listed in IHTA 1984 s 25(1) and Sch 3. Such a sale can offer substantial financial advantages for the owner. For instance, if conditionally exempt property is sold on the open market, conditional exemption is lost and furthermore a CGT charge may arise. By contrast, a sale by private treaty does not lead to a withdrawal of the exemption or IHT charge, nor is there a liability to CGT. Not surprisingly, because of these fiscal benefits the vendor will have to accept a lower price than if he sold on the open market. The relevant arrangement involves a 'douceur': broadly, the price that he will receive is the net value of the asset (ie market price less prospective tax liability) *plus* 25% of the tax saved. The following example is taken from 'Capital Taxation and The National Heritage' (IR 67) published by the Inland Revenue.

EXAMPLE 23.23

Calculation of the price, with 'douceur' (usually 25% but subject to negotiation), at which a previously conditionally exempted object can be sold to a public body by private treaty.

Agreed current market value (say)		£100,000
Tax applicable thereto:		
CGT @ (say) 30% on gain element, assumed to be £40,000	£12,000	
ED, CTT or IHT exemption granted on a previous conditionally exempt transfer now recoverable @ say 60% on £88,000 (ie market value less CGT)	£52,800	
Total tax	£64,800	£ 64,800
Net after full tax		£ 35,200
Add back 25% of tax (the 'douceur')		£ 16,200
Price payable by a purchaser, all retained by vendor		£ 51,400

The Revenue writes off the total tax of £64,800 (£12,000 + £52,800).

The vendor has £16,200 more than if he had sold the object for £100,000 in the open market and paid the tax. The public body acquires the object for £48,600 less than its open market value.

Under these arrangements the offeror obtains the benefit of any rise in the value of property between the date of the offer and its acceptance by the Inland Revenue, but he has to pay interest on the unpaid IHT until his offer is accepted. From 18 March 1987, taxpayers have been able to continue on this basis *or* to elect for the value of the property to be taken at the date of the offer (thereby avoiding the payment of any interest but forgoing the benefit of any subsequent rise in the value of the property: F(No 2) A 1987 s 97)).

An asset can be offered to the Revenue in lieu of tax (see IHTA 1984 s 230(1)). Acceptance in lieu of tax has similar financial advantages for the vendor to a private treaty sale. The Secretary of State has to agree to accept such assets and it should be noted that the standard of objects which can be so accepted is very much higher than that required for the conditional exemption. [**23.65**]

5   Gifts to political parties (IHTA 1984 s 24)

Such gifts are exempt from IHT, whether made during life or on death (the former limitation of £100,000 in the case of gifts made on death or within one year of death was removed by FA 1988). There are detailed provisions which deny relief where the gift is delayed, conditional, made for a limited period, or could be used for other purposes (IHTA 1984 s 24(3), (4)). Any capital gain that would otherwise arise can be held-over under CGTA 1979 s 147A. [**23.66**]

6   Gifts to charities (IHTA 1984 s 23)

Gifts to charities are exempt without limit. As with gifts to political parties detailed provisions deny the exemption if the vesting of the gift is postponed; if it is conditional; if it is made for a limited period; or if it could be used for non-charitable purposes (on charitable gifts see generally Appendix IX and the recent case of *Guild v IRC* (1991)). [**23.67**]

24 IHT—settlements: definition and classification

I   Introductory and definitions   **[24.1]**
II   Classification of settlements   **[24.21]**
III   Creation of settlements   **[24.41]**
IV   Payment of IHT   **[24.61]**
V   Reservation of benefit   **[24.81]**

I INTRODUCTORY AND DEFINITIONS

The objective when taxing settled property is to ensure that it is the capital of the settlement which is subject to tax and not just the value of the various beneficial interests. Successive governments have also affirmed that the object of the IHT provisions is to ensure that settled property is taxed no more or less heavily than unsettled property.   **[24.1]**

1   What is a settlement?

'Settlement' is defined in IHTA 1984 s 43:
'(2) "Settlement" means any disposition or dispositions of property, whether effected by instrument, by parole or by operation of law, or partly in one way and partly in another, whereby the property is for the time being—
(a) held in trust for persons in succession or for any person subject to a contingency; or
(b) held by trustees on trust to accumulate the whole or part of any income of the property or with power to make payments out of that income at the discretion of the trustees or some other person, with or without power to accumulate surplus income; or
(c) charged or burdened (otherwise than for full consideration in money or money's worth paid for his own use or benefit to the person making the disposition), with the payment of any annuity or other periodical payment payable for a life or any other limited or terminable period; . . .
(3) A lease of property which is for life or lives, or for a period ascertainable only by reference to a death, or which is terminable on, or at a date ascertainable only by reference to, a death, shall be treated as a settlement and the property as settled property, unless the lease was granted for full consideration in money or money's worth, and where a lease not granted as a lease at a rack rent is at any time to become a lease at an increased rent it shall be treated as terminable at that time.'

EXAMPLE 24.1

(1) Property is settled on X for life remainder to Y and Z absolutely (a fixed trust; see (2)(a) above).
(2) Property is held on trust for 'such of A, B, C, D, E and F as my trustees in their absolute discretion may select' (a discretionary trust; see (2)(b) above).
(3) Property is held on trust 'for A contingent on attaining 18' (a contingency settlement; see (2)(a) above).

(4) Property is held on trust by A and B as trustees for Z absolutely (a bare trust, although for IHT purposes there is no settlement and the property is treated as belonging to Z).

(5) A and B jointly purchase Blackacre. Under LPA 1925 ss 34-36 there is a statutory trust for sale with A and B holding the land on trust (as joint tenants) for themselves as either joint tenants or tenants in common in equity. For IHT purposes there is no settlement and the property belongs to A and B equally.

(6) A grants B a lease of Blackacre for his (B's) life at a peppercorn rent. This is a settlement for IHT purposes and A is the trustee of the property (IHTA 1984 s 45). Under LPA 1925 s 149 the lease is treated as being for a term of 90 years which is determinable on the death of B.

(7) A owns Blackacre. He reserves a lease on the property for his life and sells the freehold reversion for full value. It would appear that the lease is granted for full consideration (in money or money's worth) with the result that there is no settlement for IHT purposes (see SP E10).

As discussed at [18.6] difficulties have arisen in identifying, for CGT purposes, when property has been resettled (ie when a new settlement has been created out of an existing settlement). Difficulties may also occur when it is necessary to determine whether the settlor has created one or more settlements. It is likely that similar problems will arise in IHT and the definition of 'settlement', set out above, is unlikely to prove of assistance in resolving these problems. In *Minden Trust (Cayman) Ltd v IRC* (1984) an appointment of settled property in favour of overseas beneficiaries was held to amend the terms of the original settlement so that the terms of that appointment read with the original settlement were dispositions of property and therefore a settlement. It appears to follow that whenever trustees exercise dispositive powers which result in property being held in trust that exercise must be treated as a settlement.   [24.2]

EXAMPLE 24.2

Each year Sam creates a discretionary trust of £3,000 (thereby utilising his annual exemption) and his wife does likewise. Accordingly at the end of five years there are ten mini discretionary trusts. As a matter of trust law, and assuming that each settlement is correctly documented, there is no reason why this series should be treated as one settlement. So far as the IHT legislation is concerned the settlements are not made on the same day (see IHTA 1984 s 62); the associated operations provisions (IHTA 1984 s 268) would seem inapplicable; and the *Ramsay* principle, although of uncertain ambit, could only be applied with difficulty to a series of gifts. Obviously the separate trusts should be kept apart (there should be no pooling of property) and each settlement should be fully documented.

2   Settlors and trustees

In the majority of cases it is not difficult to identify the settlor, since there will usually be one settlor who will create a settlement by a 'disposition' of property (which may include a series of associated operations; see IHTA 1984 s 272). If that settlor adds further property, this creates no problems in the interest in possession settlement, but difficulties arise if the settlement is discretionary (see [26.33]) with further complications if the original property was excluded property and the additional property was not, or *vice versa* (see Chapter 27). A settlement may have more than one settlor:

EXAMPLE 24.3

(1) Bill and Ben create a settlement in favour of their neighbour Barum.
(2) Bill adds property to a settlement that had been created two years ago by Ben in favour of neighbour Barum.

IHTA 1984 s 44(2) states that: 'Where more than one person is a settlor in relation to a settlement and the circumstances so require, this Part of this Act (except sections 48(4)-(6)) shall have effect in relation to it as if the settled property were comprised in separate settlements'. *Thomas v IRC* (1981) indicates that this provision only applies where an identifiable capital fund has been provided by each settlor. The fund will be treated as two separate settlements in the case of discretionary trusts where both the incidence of the periodic charge and the amount of IHT chargeable may be affected. IHTA 1984 s 44(1) defines settlor (in terms similar to those for income tax purposes—see Chapter 11) thus:

> 'In this Act "settlor", in relation to a settlement, includes any person by whom the settlement was made directly or indirectly, and ... includes any person who has provided funds directly or indirectly for the purpose of or in connection with the settlements or has made with any other person a reciprocal arrangement for that other person to make the settlement.'

A further problem arises where there is only one settlor who adds property to his settlement; is this for IHT purposes one settlement or two? This question is significant in relation to discretionary trusts (especially with regard to timing and rate of the periodic and inter-periodic charges) and where excluded property is involved in a settlement. As a matter of trust law, there will be a single settlement where funds are held and managed by one set of trustees for one set of beneficiaries, so that such additions will usually not lead to the creation of separate settlements. When it would be advantageous for there to be two settlements, a separate settlement deed with (ideally) separate trustees should be employed.

The ordinary meaning is given to the term 'a trustee', although by IHTA 1984 s 45 it includes any person in whom the settled property or its management is for the time being vested. In cases where a lease for lives is treated as a settlement the lessor is the trustee.   **[24.3]-[24.20]**

II CLASSIFICATION OF SETTLEMENTS

1 **The three categories**

Settlements for IHT purposes must be divided into three categories.

Category 1 A settlement with an interest in possession, eg where the property is held for an adult tenant for life who, by virtue of his interest, is entitled to the income and has an interest in possession'.

Category 2 A settlement lacking an interest in possession, eg where trustees are given a discretion over the distribution of the income so that no beneficiary has an interest in possession. At most, beneficiaries have the right to be considered when the discretion is exercised by the trustees; the right to ensure that the fund is properly administered; and the right to join with all the other beneficiaries to bring the settlement to an end.

This category also includes settlements where the property is held on trust for a minor contingent on his attaining a specified age. As long as the beneficiary is a minor there will be no interest in possession and the settlement will fall into Category 2, unless the trust satisfies the requirements for a Category 3 accumulation and maintenance settlement.

Category 3   Into this category fall special or privileged trusts. They lack an interest in possession, but are not subject to the Category 2 regime. The main example to be considered in this book is the accumulation and maintenance trust for children.

To place a particular trust into its correct category is important for two reasons. First, because the IHT treatment of each is totally different both as to incidence of tax and as to the amount of tax charged; and secondly, because a change from one category to another will normally give rise to an IHT charge. For example, if a life interest ceases, whereupon the fund is held on discretionary trusts, the settlement moves from Category 1 to Category 2, and a chargeable occasion (the ending of a life interest) has occurred.   [**24.21**]

2   The meaning of an 'interest in possession'

Normally trusts can easily be slotted into their correct category. Trusts falling within Category 3 are carefully defined so that any trust not specifically falling into one of those special cases must fall into Category 2. Problems are principally caused by the borderline between Categories 1 and 2 where the division is drawn according to whether the settlement has an interest in possession or not. In the majority of cases no problems will arise: at one extreme stands the life interest settlement; at the other the discretionary trust. However, what of a settlement which provides for the income to be paid to Albert, unless the trustees decide to pay it to Bertram, or to accumulate it; or where the property in the trust is enjoyed *in specie* by one beneficiary as the result of the exercise of a discretion (eg a beneficiary living in a dwelling house which was part of a discretionary fund)? To resolve these difficulties, the phrase an 'interest in possession' needs definition. The legislation does not assist; instead, its meaning must be gleaned from a Press Notice of the Revenue and *Re Pilkington (Pearson v IRC)* (1980) which largely endorses the statements in that Press Notice.   [**24.22**]

The Inland Revenue Press Notice (12 February 1976) provides as follows:

> '. . . an interest in settled property exists where the person having the interest has the *immediate entitlement* (subject to any prior claims by the trustees for expenses or other outgoings properly payable out of income) *to any income* produced by that property as the income arises; but . . . a discretion or power, in whatever form, which can be exercised *after income arises* so as to withhold it from that person negatives the existence of an interest in possession. For this purpose a power to accumulate income is regarded as a power to withhold it, unless any accumulation must be held solely for the person having the interest or his personal representatives.
>   On the other hand the existence of a mere power of revocation or appointment, the exercise of which would determine the interest wholly or in part (but which, so long as it remains unexercised, does not affect the beneficiary's immediate entitlement to income) does not . . . prevent the interest from being an interest in possession.'

The first paragraph is concerned with the existence of discretions or powers which might affect the destination of the income after it has arisen and which prevent the existence of any interest in possession (eg a provision enabling the trustees to accumulate income or to divert it for the benefit of other beneficiaries). The second paragraph concerns overriding powers which, if exercised, would terminate the entire interest of the beneficiary, but which do not prevent the existence of an interest in possession (eg the statutory power of advancement). Administrative expenses charged on the income can be ignored in deciding whether there is an interest in possession, so long as such payments are for 'outgoings properly payable out of income'. A clause in the settlement permitting expenses of a capital nature to be so charged is, therefore, not covered and the Revenue consider that the mere presence of such a clause is fatal to the existence of any interest in possession. [24.23]

Re Pilkington (Pearson v IRC) (1980) In essence, the facts of the case are simple. Both capital and income of the fund were held for the settlor's three adult daughters in equal shares subject to three overriding powers exercisable by the trustees: (1) to appoint capital and income amongst the daughters, their spouses and issue; (2) to accumulate so much of the income as they should think fit; and (3) to apply any income towards the payment or discharge of any taxes, costs or other outgoings which would otherwise be payable out of capital. The trustees had regularly exercised their powers to accumulate the income. What caused the disputed IHT assessment (for a mere £444.73) was the irrevocable appointment of some £16,000 from the fund to one of the daughters. There was no doubt that, as a result of the appointment, she obtained an interest in possession in that appointed sum; but did she already have an interest in possession in the fund? If so, no IHT would be chargeable on the appointment (see [**25.28**]); if not, there would be a charge because the appointed funds had passed from a 'no interest in possession' to an 'interest in possession' settlement (Category 2 to Category 1).

The Revenue contended that the existence of the overriding power to accumulate and the provision enabling all expenses to be charged to income deprived the settlement of any interest in possession. It was common ground that whether such powers had been exercised or not was irrelevant in deciding the case. The overriding power of appointment over capital and income was not seen as endangering the existence of any interest in possession (see paragraph 2 of the Press Notice).

For the bare majority of the House of Lords the presence of the overriding discretion to accumulate the income was fatal to the existence of any interest in possession. 'A present right to present enjoyment' was how an interest in possession was defined and the beneficiary did not have a present right. 'Their enjoyment of any income from the trust fund depended on the trustees' decision as to accumulation of income' (per Viscount Dilhorne). No distinction is to be drawn between a trust to pay income to a beneficiary, but with an overriding power to accumulate and a trust to accumulate, but with a power to pay. Hence, in the following examples there is no interest in possession:

(1) to A for life but trustees may accumulate the income; and
(2) the income shall be accumulated but trustees may make payments to
    A. [24.24]

3   **Problems remaining after Pilkington**

The test laid down by the majority in the House of Lords established some certainty in a difficult area of law and it is possible to say that the borderline between trusts with and without an interest in possession is reasonably easy to draw; where there is uncertainty about the entitlement of a beneficiary to income, it is likely that the settlement will fall into the 'no interest in possession' regime. In the light of the favourable changes made to the IHT treatment of discretionary trusts in FA 1982 that may be no bad thing for taxpayers!   **[24.25]**

The following are some of the difficulties left in the wake of *Pilkington*:

Dispositive and administrative powers   For there to be an interest in possession the beneficiary must be entitled to the income as it arises. Were this test to be applied strictly, however, even a trust with a life tenant receiving the income might fail to satisfy the requirement because trustees may deduct management expenses from that income, so that few beneficiaries are entitled to all the income as it arises. This problem was considered by Viscount Dilhorne as follows:

> '... Parliament distinguished between the administration of a trust and the dispositive powers of trustees ... A life tenant has an interest in possession but his interest only extends to the net income of the property, that is to say, after deduction from the gross income of expenses etc properly incurred in the management of the trust by the trustees in the exercise of their powers. A dispositive power is a power to dispose of the net income. Sometimes the line between an administrative and a dispositive power may be difficult to draw but that does not mean that there is not a valid distinction.'

In *Pilkington* the trustees had an overriding discretion to apply income towards the payment of any taxes, costs, or other outgoings which would otherwise be payable out of capital and the Revenue took the view that the existence of this overriding power was a further reason for the settlement lacking an interest in possession. Was this power administrative (in which case its presence did not affect the existence of any interest in possession) or dispositive (fatal to the existence of such an interest)? Viscount Dilhorne decided that the power was administrative. Acceptable though this argument may be for management expenses, is it convincing when applied to other expenses and taxes (eg CGT and IHT) which would normally be payable out of the capital of the fund? (In *Miller v IRC* (1987) the Court of Session held that a power to employ income to make good depreciation in the capital value of assets in the fund was administrative.) It must be stressed that the House of Lords did not have to decide whether the Revenue's contention was correct or not; Viscount Dilhorne's observations are *obiter dicta* and the Revenue still adhere to their Press Notice ([**24.24**]). Would-be settlors should be advised not to insert such clauses.   **[24.26]**

Power to allow beneficiaries to occupy a dwelling house   This power may exist both in settlements which otherwise have an interest in possession and in those without. The mere existence of such a power is to be ignored; problems will only arise if and when it is exercised. SP 10/79 indicates that if such a power was exercised so as to allow, for a definite or indefinite period, someone other than the life tenant to have exclusive or joint right of residence in a dwelling house as a permanent home, there would be an IHT charge on the partial ending of a life interest. In the case of a fund otherwise lacking an interest in possession, the exercise of the power would result in the creation of such an interest and therefore, an IHT charge would arise. Whether this view is correct is arguable; in *Swales v IRC* (1984), for instance, the taxpayer's argument that the mandating of trust income to a beneficiary was equivalent to providing a residence for permanent occupation (and accordingly created an interest in possession) was rejected by the court. In practice, any challenge could prove costly to the taxpayer, and trustees who possess such powers should think carefully before exercising them.

Interest-free loans to beneficiaries The Revenue's view is that a free loan to a beneficiary creates an interest in possession in the fund. As the beneficiary becomes a debtor (to the extent of the loan), one wonders in what assets his interest subsists; the moneys loaned would appear to belong absolutely to him. Again, trustees should avoid making such loans and, if need be, the trust should guarantee a bank loan to the beneficiary.   [**24.27**]

EXAMPLE 24.4

The trustees of a discretionary trust lend £10,000 to beneficiary A in 1989. In 1991 he repays that sum in full. If the Revenue's view is correct, the result is that:
(1) In 1989: A has an interest in possession in £10,000. IHT is chargeable.
(2) In 1991: A's interest in possession ceases. IHT is chargeable.

Position of the last surviving member of a discretionary class If the class of beneficiaries has closed, the sole survivor is entitled to the income as it arises so that there is an interest in possession. When the class has not closed, however, trustees have a reasonable time to decide how the accrued income is to be distributed and, if a further beneficiary could come into existence before that period has elapsed, the current beneficiary is not automatically entitled to the income as it arises so that there is no interest in possession (*Moore and Osborne v IRC* (1984)). Likewise, if the class has not closed and the trustees have a power to accumulate income.   [**24.28**]-[**24.40**]

III CREATION OF SETTLEMENTS

The creation of a settlement may constitute a chargeable transfer of value by the settlor. If the burden of paying the IHT is put upon the trustees of the settlement, the Revenue accept that the settlor will not thereby retain an interest in the settlement under the income tax provisions in TA 1988 Pt XV (SP 1/82).

When an interest in possession trust is created no IHT is charged in the following examples.

EXAMPLE 24.5

(1) S settles £100,000 on trust for himself for life with remainder to his children. As S, the life tenant, is deemed to own the entire fund (and not simply a life interest in it) his estate has not fallen in value.
(2) S settles £100,000 on trust for his wife for life, remainder to his children. S's wife is treated as owning the fund so that S's transfer is an exempt transfer to a spouse.

The *inter vivos* creation of a settlement will be a potentially exempt transfer in the following cases:

(1) If the otherwise chargeable transfer creates an interest in possession trust.

(2) If the trust satisfies the definition of an accumulation and maintenance settlement or disabled trust.

In other cases (and notably therefore when a discretionary trust is created), there will be an immediate chargeable transfer. Even if the settlement as created contains an interest in possession, the termination of that interest during the lifetime of the settlor and within seven years of the setting up of the trust will trigger the anti-avoidance rules in IHTA 1984 s 54A if a discretionary trust then arises (see [**25.31**]). [**24.41**]-[**24.60**]

IV   PAYMENT OF IHT

Primary liability for IHT arising during the course of the settlement rests upon the settlement's trustees. Their liability is limited to the property which they have received or disposed of or become liable to account for to a beneficiary and such other property which they would have received but for their own neglect or default.

If trustees fail to pay, the Revenue can collect tax from any of the following (IHTA 1984 s 201(1)):

(1) Any person entitled to an interest in possession in the settled property. His liability is limited to the value of the trust property, out of which he can claim an indemnity for the tax he has paid.

(2) Any beneficiary under a discretionary trust up to the value of the property that he receives (after paying income tax on it) and with no right to an indemnity for the tax he is called upon to pay.

(3) The settlor, where the trustees are resident outside the UK, since, should the trustees not pay, the Revenue cannot enforce payment abroad. If the settlor pays he has a right to recover the tax from the trust.

If IHT payable on creation of the trust is paid by the trustees (eg in the case of a discretionary trust) the settlor does not as a result retain an interest in the settlement for income tax purposes (SP 1/82). [**24.61**]-[**24.80**]

V   RESERVATION OF BENEFIT

The creation of *inter vivos* settlements cause particular problems in the reservation of benefit area and the following matters are especially worthy of note:

(1) If the settlor appoints himself a trustee of the settlement, that appointment will not by itself amount to a reserved benefit, thereby permitting a settlor to retain control over the settled property. If the terms of the settlement provide for his remuneration, however, there will then be a reservation in the settled property (*Oakes v Stamp Duties Comr* (1954)). One way round this decision is for the settlor/trustee to be paid by an annuity, since such an arrangement will not constitute a reserved benefit and the ending of that annuity will not lead to any IHT charge (IHTA 1984 s 90). Particular difficulties are caused if the settlor/trustee is a director of a company whose shares are held in the trust fund. The general rule of equity is that a trustee may not profit from his position and this means that he will generally have to account for any director's fees that he may receive. It is standard practice, however, for the trust deed to provide that a trustee need not in such cases account for those fees. When the settlor/trustee is allowed to retain fees under the deed it is arguable that he has reserved a benefit in the trust

assets within the ruling in the *Oakes* case. The Revenue have, however, recently indicated that they will not take this point so long as the director's remuneration is on reasonable commercial terms. Unless the settlor is particularly determined to remain as a trustee, there is no doubt that it is safer in all cases to appoint independent persons as trustees.

(2) If the settlor reserves an interest for himself under his settlement, whether he does so expressly or whether his interest arises by operation of law, there is no reservation of benefit and he is treated as making a partial gift (see further Chapter 37).

EXAMPLE 24.6

S created a settlement for his infant son, absolutely on attaining 21. No provision was made for what should happen if the son were to die before that age, and therefore there was a resulting trust to the settlor. The settlor died whilst the son was still an infant and was held to have reserved no benefit. Instead, he was treated as making a partial gift: ie a gift of the settled property less the retained remainder interest therein. (*Stamp Duties Commissioner v Perpetual Trustee Co* (1943); and see *Re Cochrane* (1906) where the settlor expressly reserved surplus income.)

The position with regard to discretionary trusts is more problematic. It appears that if the settlor is one of the beneficiaries, he is not entirely excluded from the property with the result that the entire fund will be included as part of his estate. In view of the limited nature of a discretionary beneficiary's rights (see *Gartside v IRC* (1968)) it is unlikely that he can be treated as making a partial gift. The Revenue's position, therefore, is that in all cases where a settlor is a discretionary beneficiary he will be treated as having reserved a benefit in the entire settled fund despite the fact that he may receive no payments as such a beneficiary. Although there is some doubt about the correctness of this view, taxpayers face the familiar dilemma in that they would probably have to appeal to the House of Lords to overturn this argument. The insertion of the settlor's spouse as a discretionary beneficiary does not by itself result in a reserved benefit. Were that spouse to receive property from the settlement, however, which was then shared with or used for the benefit of the settlor, the Revenue will then argue that there is a reserved benefit in the property. Finally, the reservation rules do not apply to an exempt gift to a spouse. Accordingly, and subject to the associated operation rules and the *Ramsay* principle, a reserved benefit may escape s 102 by being channelled through a spouse. **[24.81]**

EXAMPLE 24.7

Bill settles property on his wife Berta for life and subject thereto on discretionary trusts for a class of beneficiaries which includes Bill. Berta's life interest terminates after six months. It is thought that Bill has not reserved any benefit although he is one of the objects of the discretionary trust.

25 IHT—settlements with an interest in possession

I BASIC PRINCIPLES

1 General

The beneficiary entitled to the income of a fund (usually the life tenant) is treated as owning that portion of the capital of the fund. This rule is a fiction since in no sense is the life tenant the owner of the capital in the fund.

As all the capital is treated as being owned by the life tenant, for IHT purposes it forms part of his estate, so that on a chargeable occasion IHT is charged at his rates. The settlement itself is not a taxable entity (contrast the rules for discretionary trusts), although primary liability for IHT falls upon the trustees.

As the life tenant is treated as owning all the capital in the fund, other beneficiaries with 'reversionary interests' own nothing. IHTA 1984 s 47 defines reversionary interests widely to cover

> 'a future interest under a settlement, whether it is vested or contingent (including an interest expectant on the termination of an interest in possession which, by virtue of section 50 . . . , is treated as subsisting in part of any property)'.

Generally, reversionary interests are excluded property and can be transferred without a charge to IHT (see III below). Despite the breadth of this definition, the term would not appear to catch the interests of discretionary beneficiaries since such rights as they possess (to compel due administration; to be considered; and jointly to wind up the fund) are present rights. Their interests are neither in possession nor in reversion.

The interest in possession trust is unique in having a special charging system based upon the fiction that the fund belongs to the person with the interest in possession. The IHT levy on other settlements operates by treating the settlement as a separate chargeable entity and by (generally) imposing a tax charge at regular intervals. There appears to be no reason why this method, if it achieves its stated object of 'neutrality', should not be applied across the board.   **[25.1]**

2 Who is treated as owning the fund?

Life interests The beneficiary entitled to an interest in possession is treated as being beneficially entitled to the property, or to an appropriate part of that property; if there is more than one, it is necessary to apportion the capital in the fund (IHTA 1984 s 49(1)).

A beneficiary who has the right to the income of the fund for a period shorter than his lifetime (however short the period may be) is still treated for IHT as owning the entire settled fund. If the settlement does not produce any income, but instead the beneficiary is entitled to use the capital assets in the fund, IHTA 1984 s 49(1) suggests that he is treated as owning those assets. If the use is enjoyed by more than one beneficiary, the value of the fund is apportioned under IHTA 1984 s 50(5) in accordance with the 'annual value' of their respective interests. Annual value is not defined.   **[25.2]**

EXAMPLE 25.1

Bill and Ben, beneficiaries under a strict settlement, jointly occupy 'Snodlands', the ancestral home, which is worth £150,000. This capital value must be apportioned to Bill and Ben in proportion to the annual value of their respective interests. As their interests are equal the apportionment will be as to £75,000 each.

A beneficiary entitled to a fixed amount of income   Difficulties arise where one beneficiary is entitled to a fixed amount of income each year (eg an annuity) and any balance is paid to another beneficiary. If the amounts of income paid to the two were compared in the year when a chargeable event occurred, a tax saving could be engineered. Assume, for instance, that the annuity interest terminates so that IHT is charged on its value. The proportion of capital attributable to that interest and, therefore, the IHT would be reduced if the trustees switched investments into assets producing a high income in that year. As a result a relatively small proportion of the total income would be payable to the annuitant who would be treated as owning an equivalently small portion of the capital. When a chargeable event affects the interest in the residue of the income (eg, through termination) the trustees could switch the assets into low income producers, thereby achieving a similar reduction in IHT.

IHTA 1984 s 50(3) is designed to counter such schemes by providing that the Treasury may prescribe higher and lower income yields which take effect as limits beyond which any fluctuations in the actual income of the fund are ignored (see SI 1980/1000).

EXAMPLE 25.2

The value of the settlement is £100,000; income per annum £25,000. A is entitled to an annuity of £5,000 pa; B to the balance of the income. If there is a chargeable transfer affecting the annuity, A is not treated as owning £20,000 of the capital ([£5,000 ÷ £25,000] × £100,000) but instead a proportion of the Treasury 'higher rate' yield. Assume that the shigher rate is 15% on the relevant day; the calculation is, therefore:

Notional income = 15% of £100,000 = £15,000.
A's annuity is £5,000; as a proportion of income it is £5,000 ÷ £15,000; A's share of capital is, therefore, [£5,000 ÷ £15,000] × £100,000 = £33,333.

This calculation is used whenever the actual income yield exceeds the prescribed higher rate. The calculation cannot lead to a charge in excess of the total value of the fund!

When a chargeable transfer affecting the interest in the balance of the income occurs, if the actual income produced falls below the prescribed lower rate, the calculation proceeds as if the fund yielded that rate. If both interests in the settlement are chargeable on the same occasion, the prescribed rates do not apply because the entire fund is chargeable.   **[25.3]**

A lease treated as a settlement   When a lease is treated as a settlement (eg a lease for life or lives), the lessee is treated as owning the whole of the leased property save for any part treated as belonging to the lessor. To calculate the lessor's portion it is necessary to compare what he received when the lease was granted with what would have been a full consideration for the lease at that time (IHTA 1984 ss 50(6), 170).   **[25.4]–[25.20]**

> **EXAMPLE 25.3**
>
> (1)   Land worth £100,000 is let to A for his life. The lessor receives no consideration so that A is treated as owning the whole of the leased property (ie £100,000). The granting of the lease is a potentially exempt transfer by the lessor of £100,000.
>
> (2)   As above, save that full consideration is furnished. The lease is not treated as a settlement (see Chapter 24). No IHT will be charged on its creation as the lessor's estate does not fall in value.
>
> (3)   Partial consideration (equivalent to 40% of a full consideration) is furnished so that the value of the lessor's interest is 40% of £100,000 = £40,000. The value of the lessee's interest is £60,000 and the granting of the lease is a chargeable transfer of £60,000.

II   WHEN IS IHT CHARGED?

IHT may be charged on the creation of the settlement and whenever an interest in possession terminates. These events may occur *inter vivos* or on death: in the former case FA 1986 limited the definition of the potentially exempt transfer to *exclude* the creation of interest in possession settlements and chargeable occasions occurring during their lifetime. This limitation, which cut across the principles of neutrality in the taxation of settlements and the fiction that the life tenant owned the fund, was inserted because of concern that the interest in possession trust would otherwise be used in a scheme of tax avoidance. It was feared that an interest in possession trust would be set up by a PET (thereby avoiding an immediate tax charge); quickly terminated (thereby triggering an IHT charge but calculated according to the rates of the chosen life tenant who would be a 'man of straw'); and replaced by a discretionary trust. In this fashion the settlor would, in effect, create a discretionary trust by means of a PET. Although F(No 2)A 1987 removed this limitation on the scope of PETs, continuing fears that interest in possession trusts would be abused led to the introduction of complex anti-avoidance rules which are considered below.   **[25.21]**

1   Creation of interest in possession trusts

If the trust is set up on death the usual IHT charging regime operates (see Chapter 22). If created *inter vivos*, the extended definition of a PET means that no immediate charge to IHT will result. Under general rules, such a charge will only occur if the settlor dies within seven years; anti-avoidance rules, may however, trigger a charge by reference to the settlor's circumstances when he created the trust if the life interest ends within seven years, at a time when the settlor is still alive and the property then becomes held on trusts without an interest in possession (see [**25.31**] for a discussion of these rules). [**25.22**]

EXAMPLE 25.4

(1) Sam settles property on his daughter Sally for life, remainder to Oxfam. The creation of the trust is a PET and there is no question of the anti-avoidance rules applying because the trust ends on Sally's death.

(2) Sid settles property on a stranger, Jake Straw, for life or until such time as the trustees determine and thereafter the property is to be held on discretionary trusts for Sid's family and relatives. The creation of the trust is a PET; a later termination of Jake's life interest will be a chargeable transfer and may trigger the anti-avoidance rules.

(3) Sam settles property on Susan, his daughter, for life, remainder to her twins at 21. Susan surrenders her life interest when the twins are (i) 17, (ii) 18, (iii) 21.

The creation of the trust is a PET as is the surrender of Susan's life interest. If it is surrendered at (i), the fund is then held for accumulation and maintenance trusts (a PET); if surrendered at (ii), the transfer is to the twins as interest in possession beneficiaries (a PET); while finally, if surrendered at (iii), the twins are absolutely entitled and so it will be an outright gift and therefore a PET.

2 The charge on death

As the assets in the settlement are treated as part of the property of the deceased at the time of his death, IHT is charged on the settled fund at the estate rate appropriate to his estate. The tax attributable to the settled property should be paid by the trustees. Notice that although the trustees pay this tax, the inclusion of the value of the fund in the deceased's estate may increase the estate rate, thereby causing a higher percentage charge on his free estate. [**25.23**]

EXAMPLE 25.5

The settlement consists of securities worth £100,000 and is held for Albinoni for life with remainder to Busoni. Albinoni has just died and the value of his free estate is £75,000; he made chargeable lifetime transfers of £50,000. IHT will be calculated as follows:

(1) Chargeable death estate: £75,000 + £100,000 (the settlement) = £175,000.
(2) Join table at £50,000 (point reached by lifetime transfers).
(3) Calculate death IHT (£34,000).
(4) Convert to estate rate

$$\frac{\text{tax}}{\text{estate}} \times 100: \text{ie} \frac{£34,000}{£175,000} \times 100 = 19.43\%.$$

(5) IHT attributable to settled property is 19.43% of £100,000 = £19,430.

3 Inter-vivos terminations

An actual or deemed termination of an interest in possession which occurs during the life of the relevant beneficiary will be a PET provided that the property is, after that event, held for one or more beneficiaries absolutely (so that the settlement is at an end), or for a further interest in possession or on accumulation and maintenance or disabled trusts. Accordingly, IHT will only be payable in such cases if the former life tenant dies within seven years of the termination. If the above requirements are not satisfied (eg where after the termination the fund is held on discretionary trusts) there is an immediate charge to tax on the termination of the interest in possession and the anti-avoidance rules may be triggered (see [**25.31**]).   [**25.24**]

Actual terminations   A charge to IHT may arise if the interest of the life tenant ceases and is calculated on the basis that the life tenant had made a transfer of value at that time.   [**25.25**]

EXAMPLE 25.6

(1) £100,000 is held on trust for Albinoni for life or until remarriage and thereafter for Busoni. If Albinoni remarries his life interest terminates and he makes a PET. Accordingly, should he die within seven years, thereafter, IHT will be charged on the value of the fund at the time when his interest ended.

If Albinoni never remarried, but consented to an advancement of £50,000 to Busoni, his interest ends in that portion of the fund and he makes a PET. In the event of that PET becoming chargeable, IHT may be charged on £50,000. Three years later Albinoni surrenders his life interest in the fund, now worth £120,000. This is a further PET; IHT may therefore be charged (if he dies in the following seven years) on £120,000. Notice that in all cases any tax charge is levied on a value transferred which is 'equal to the value of the property in which his interest subsisted' (see s 52(1)). The principle of calculating loss to donor's estate (see [**21.61**]) is therefore inapplicable in such cases.

(2) Claude owns 49% of the shares in his family trading company, Money Box Ltd, and is the life tenant under a settlement which owns a further 12% of those shares. The remainder beneficiary under the trust is Claude's daughter. No dividends are paid by the company. The tax position if Claude were to surrender his interest in possession is as follows:

(a) The surrender of a beneficial interest in a settlement is generally free from CGT (CGTA 1979, s 58(1)). Assuming that the settlement ends, any gain arising on the deemed disposal under CGTA 1979 s 54(1) may be held-over.

(b) For IHT purposes, Claude will make a potentially exempt transfer but the value transferred is limited to the value of the shares in the settlement (IHTA 1984, s 52(1)). Thus only the value of a 12% minority holding will be subject to tax in the event of Claude's death within seven years, 50% business property relief may be available.

(c) On Claude's death his estate will then comprise only a 49% minority shareholding attracting 50% business property relief.

(d) The merit of this arrangement is that the substantial loss to Claude's estate resulting from his loss of control of the company has not attracted a tax charge: instead, both shareholdings have been valued separately. Surrender of the life interest can occur on Claude's death-bed but the advantages will not, of course, be obtained if the life interest is retained and the 49% holding given away!

Deemed terminations   IHTA 1984 s 51(1) provides that if the beneficiary disposes of his beneficial interest in possession, that disposal 'shall not be a transfer of value but shall be treated as the coming to an end of the interest'. The absence of gratuitous intent does not prevent an IHT charge on the termination of beneficial interests in possession. As with actual terminations, the life tenant will normally make a PET so that tax will only be charged if he dies within seven years thereafter.   [**25.26**]

EXAMPLE 25.7

(1) Albinoni assigns by way of gift his life interest to Cortot. IHT will be charged as if that life interest had terminated. Cortot becomes a tenant *pur autre vie* and when Albinoni dies Cortot's interest in possession terminates so raising the possibility of a further IHT charge. Both Albinoni and Cortot have made PETs.

(2) If, instead of gifting his interest, Albinoni sells it to Cortot for £20,000 (full value) and the fund was then worth £100,000, Albinoni's interest terminates so that he has made a transfer of value of £100,000. However, as he has received £20,000, he has made a PET equal to the fall in his estate of £80,000 (£100,000—£20,000: IHTA 1984 s 52(2)).

Partition of the fund A partition of the fund between life tenant and remainderman causes the interest in possession to terminate and IHT may be charged (if the life tenant dies within seven years) on that portion of the fund passing to the remainderman (IHTA 1984 s 53(2)).   **[25.27]**

EXAMPLE 25.8

Albinoni and Busoni partition the £100,000 fund in the proportions 40:60. Albinoni is treated as making a PET of £100,000, but IHT may be charged on only £60,000 (£100,000—£40,000). It should be remembered that any IHT will be payable out of the fund to be divided.

Advancements to life tenant/satisfaction of a contingency If all or part of the capital of the fund is paid to the life tenant, or if he becomes absolutely entitled to the capital, his interest in possession will determine pro tanto, but no IHT will be charged since there will be no fall in the value of his estate (IHTA 1984 s 53(2)).   **[25.28]**

EXAMPLE 25.9

Property is settled upon Delibes contingent on his attaining the age of 30. At 18, he will be entitled to the income of the settlement (Trustee Act 1925 s 31); an interest in possession will, therefore, arise. At 30, that interest terminates, but, as he is now absolutely entitled to the capital, no IHT is chargeable.

Purchase of a reversionary interest by the life tenant (IHTA 1984 ss 10, 55(1)) As the life tenant owns the fund it follows that his potential tax bill could be reduced were he to purchase a reversionary interest in that settlement. Assume, for instance, that B has £60,000 in his bank account and is the life tenant of a fund with a capital value of £100,000. For IHT purposes he owns £160,000. If B were to purchase the reversionary interest in the same settlement, however, for its market value of £60,000, the result would be as follows: first, B's estate has not fallen in value. Originally it included £60,000; after the purchase it includes a reversionary interest worth £60,000 since, although excluded property, the reversionary interest must still be valued. Secondly, B's estate now consists of the settlement fund valued at £100,000 and has been depleted by the £60,000 paid for the reversionary interest so that a possible charge to IHT on £60,000 has been avoided.

To prevent such a loss of IHT, IHTA 1984 s 55(1) provides that the reversionary interest is not to be valued as a part of B's estate at the time of its purchase (thereby ensuring that his estate has fallen in value) whilst

IHTA 1984 s 10 is excluded from applying in this case thereby ensuring that the fall in value may be subject to charge even though there is no donative intent. Hence, by paying £60,000 for the reversionary interest B has made a PET of £60,000 which will be taxed if he dies in the following seven years.   [25.29]

Transactions reducing the value of the property   When the value of the fund is diminished by a depreciatory transaction entered into between the trustees and a beneficiary (or persons connected with him) tax is charged as if the fall in value were a partial termination of the interest in possession (IHTA 1984 s 52(3)). A commercial transaction lacking gratuitous intent is not caught by this provision.

   Macpherson v IRC (1988) illustrates the operation of these provisions. In that case the value of pictures held in a trust fund was diminished by an arrangement with a person connected with a beneficiary as a result of which, in return for taking over care, custody and insurance of the pictures, that person was entitled to keep the pictures for his personal enjoyment for some fourteen years. Although this arrangement was a commercial transaction, lacking gratuitous intent when looked at in isolation, it was associated with a subsequent operation (the appointment of a protected life interest) which did confer a gratuitous benefit so that the exception did not apply and the reduction in value of the fund was subject to charge.   [25.30]

EXAMPLE 25.10

Trustees grant a 50 year lease of a property worth £100,000 at a peppercorn rent to the brother of a reversionary beneficiary. As a result the property left in the settlement is the freehold reversion worth only £20,000. The granting of the lease is a depreciatory transaction which causes the value of the fund to fall by £80,000 and as it is made with a person connected with a beneficiary, IHTA 1984 s 52(3) will apply and IHT may be levied as if the life interest in £80,000 had ended. (Contrast the position if the lease had been granted to the brother in return for a commercial rent.)

4   **Anti-avoidance** (IHTA 1984 s 54A and s 54B)

The non-interest in possession trust (typically the discretionary trust) may not be created by a PET and these provisions are designed to ensure that this prohibition cannot be circumvented by channelling property into such a trust via an interest in possession settlement.   [25.31]

a) *When do the rules apply?*

The three prerequisites are that an interest in possession trust is set up by means of a PET; it terminates either as a result of the life tenant dying or by his interest ceasing *inter vivos*; and at that time a no-interest in possession trust (other than an accumulation and maintenance settlement) arises. If the termination occurs within seven years of the creation of the original interest in possession trust and at a time when the settlor is still alive, the anti-avoidance rules then apply.   [25.32]

b) *Operation of the rules*

The IHT charge on the property at the time when the interest in possession ends is taken to be the higher of two alternative calculations. First, the IHT that would arise under normal charging principles: ie by taxing the fund as if the transfer had been made by the life tenant at the time of termination. The rates of charge will be either half rates (when there is an *inter vivos* termination) or full death rates when termination occurs as a result of the death of the life tenant. The alternative calculation involves deeming the settled property to have been transferred at the time of termination by a hypothetical transferor who in the preceding seven years had made chargeable transfers equal in value to those made by the settlor in the seven years before he created the settlement. For the purpose of this second calculation half rates are used. **[25.33]**

EXAMPLE 25.11

In 1989 Sam settles £90,000 on trust for Pam for life or until remarriage and thereafter on discretionary trusts for Sam's relatives and friends. His cumulative total at that time is £100,000 and he has made PETs of £85,000. Pam remarries one year later at a time when she has made chargeable transfers of £50,000; PETs of £45,000; and when the settled property is worth £110,000.

(1) The anti-avoidance provisions are relevant since the conditions for their operation are satisfied.

(2) IHT, ignoring these provisions, would be calculated at Pam's rates: ie on a chargeable transfer from £50,000 to £160,000. Alternatively, the tax may be calculated by taking a hypothetical transferor who has Sam's cumulative total at the time when he created the trust; hence on this calculation the £110,000 will be taxed as a chargeable transfer from £100,000 to £210,000. In this example the second calculation will be adopted since a greater amount of IHT results. This tax must be paid by the trustees.

(3) Assume that either Sam or Pam died after the termination of the interest in possession trust. This may result in a recalculation of the IHT liability (in this example PETs made by that person in the seven years before death would become chargeable). So far as the anti-avoidance rules are concerned, however, there is no question of disturbing the basis on which the IHT calculation was made in the first place. Hence, as was shown in (2) above, the greater tax was produced by taking the hypothetical transferor and, therefore, the subsequent death of Pam is irrelevant since it cannot be used to switch the basis of computation to Pam's cumulative total. By contrast, the death of Sam may involve additional IHT liability since his PETs of £85,000 may now become chargeable and thus included in the hypothetical transferor's total when the settlement was created.

c) *How to avoid the anti-avoidance rules*

First, if the interest in possession continues for seven years these rules do not apply. Secondly, they are not in point if the settlement was created without an immediate interest in possession (eg if the settlor started with an accumulation and maintenance trust which subsequently turned into an interest in possession trust), or if the settlement was created by means of an exempt transfer (eg if a life interest was given to the settlor's spouse and that interest was subsequently terminated in favour of a discretionary trust). Thirdly, trustees can prevent the anti-avoidance rules from applying if, *within six months* of the ending of the interest in possession, they terminate the discretionary trust either by an absolute appointment or by creating a further life interest. Finally, it is always possible to channel property into a discretionary trust by a PET, if an outright gift is made to another individual (a PET) who then settles the gifted property on the appropriate discretionary trusts (a chargeable transfer but taxed at *his* rates). The obvious drawback is that the transferor in this case has no legal right to force the donee to settle the outright gift; too great a degree of trust has to be reposed in that person! **[25.34]**

5   Exemptions and reliefs

Reverter to settlor/spouse (IHTA 1984 s 53(3)–(5))   If, on the termination of an interest in possession, property reverts to the settlor, there is no charge to IHT unless the settlor (or his spouse) had acquired that interest for money or money's worth. This exemption also applies when the property passes to the settlor's spouse or (if the settlor is dead) to his widow or widower so long as that reverter occurs within two years of his death.   **[25.35]**

EXAMPLE 25.12

Janacek creates a settlement of £100,000 in favour of K for life. When K dies and the property reverts to the settlor no IHT will be charged.
Contrast the position, if the settlement provided that the fund was to pass to L on the death of the life tenant, but the settlor's wife had purchased that remainder interest and given it to her husband as a Christmas present. On the death of the life tenant, although the property will revert to the settlor, the normal charge to IHT will apply.

Use of the life tenant's exemptions   The spouse exemption is available on the termination of the interest in possession if the person who then becomes entitled, whether absolutely or to another interest in possession, is the spouse of the former life tenant. IHTA 1984 s 57 permits the use of the life tenant's annual (£3,000 pa) exemption and the exemption for gifts in consideration of marriage on the *inter* vivos termination of an interest in possession if the life tenant so elects (see IHTA 1984 s 57(3), (4)). The exemptions for small gifts (£250) and normal expenditure out of income cannot be used.

EXAMPLE 25.13

Orff is the life tenant of the fund. His wife and son are entitled equally in remainder. If he surrenders the life interest, there will be no tax on the half-share passing to his wife (spouse exemption). The chargeable half-share passing to his son is a PET and, should it become chargeable because of his death within seven years, the annual exemption and, if surrender coincides with the marriage of the son, the £5,000 marriage gift relief will be available.

Although there is no duty to report the making of a PET, the appropriate notice should be given to the trustees by the life tenant indicating that he wishes the transfer to be covered by his relevant exemption so that it can then be submitted to the Revenue as required by s 57(4). If this procedure is carried out, should the PET become chargeable the appropriate exemption will then be available.   **[25.36]**

The surviving spouse exemption   The carry-over of this estate duty relief is discussed at **[22.134]**. The first spouse must have died before 13 November 1974 and the relief ensures that IHT is not charged on the termination of the surviving spouse's interest in the property whether that occurs *inter vivos* or on death (IHTA 1984 Sch 6 para 2).   **[25.37]**

Excluded property   If the settlement contains excluded property, IHT is not charged on that portion of the fund (IHTA 1984 ss 5(1), 53(1)).   **[25.38]**

IHTA 1984 s 11 dispositions If the interest in possession is disposed of for the purpose of maintaining the disponer's child or supporting a dependent relative, IHT is not charged (see Chapter 23). **[25.39]**

Charities Tax is not charged if on the termination of the interest in possession the property is held on trust for charitable purposes. **[25.40]**

Protective trusts The forfeiture of a protected life interest is normally not chargeable (see Chapter 26). **[25.41]**

Variations and disclaimers Dispositions of the deceased may be altered after his death by means of either an instrument of variation or disclaimer without incurring a second IHT charge. Disclaimers are possible in the case both of settlements created by the deceased (IHTA 1984 s 142) and pre-existing settlements in which the death has resulted in a person becoming entitled to an interest in settled property (IHTA 1984 s 93). Variations are only permitted for settlements created on death, not for settlements in which the deceased had been the beneficiary. **[25.42]**

EXAMPLE 25.14

Poulenc, the life tenant of the settlement created by his father, has just died. His brother Quercus is now the life tenant in possession and if he assigns his interest within two years of Poulenc's death, the normal charging provisions will apply. (Note (i) he could disclaim his interest without any IHT charge (IHTA 1984 s 93); (ii) see **[22.131]** for problems caused to trustees when other property of the deceased is varied or disclaimed).

Quick succession relief (IHTA 1984 s 141) This relief is similar to that for unsettled property. The first chargeable transfer may be either the creation of the settlement or any subsequent termination of an interest in possession (whether that termination occurs *inter vivos* or on death). Hence, it can be voluntarily used (by the life tenant surrendering or assigning his interest) whereas in the case of unsettled property it is only available on a death. The calculation of the relief in cases where there is more than one later transfer is dealt with in IHTA 1984 s 141(4). **[25.43]**

EXAMPLE 25.15

(1) A settlement is created in January 1987; (2) the life interest ends in half of the fund in March 1989; (3) the life interest ends in the rest of the fund in February 1990. Assume that both PETs become chargeable because of the death of the life tenant within seven years.

Quick succession relief is available at a rate of 60% on event (2); and again at a rate of 40% on event (3). Generally, relief is given in respect of the earlier transfer first ((2) above). To the extent that the relief given represents less than the whole of the tax charged on the original net transfer ((1) above), further relief can then be given in respect of subsequent transfers ((3) above) until relief equal to the whole of the tax (in (1) above) has been given.

Business reliefs In a settlement containing business property that property is treated as belonging to the life tenant who must fulfil the conditions for relief (IHTA 1984 ss 103–114).

EXAMPLE 25.16

Satie is the life tenant of the settlement. He holds 30% of the shares in the trading company Teleman Ltd, and the trust holds a further 25%. Further, the trust owns the factory premises which are leased to the company. On death of Satie, IHT business relief is available as follows:

(1) *On the shares*: the relief (assuming that the two-year ownership condition is satisfied) is at 50% on Satie's shares and on those of the fund. The life tenant is treated as having controlled the company (within s 105(1)(b)) since he held 30% (his own) and is treated as owning a further 25% of the shares.

(2) *On the land*: the relief is at 30% since the asset is used by a company controlled by the life tenant. (But see *Fetherstonhaugh v IRC* (1984).)

Similar principles operate for agricultural relief: ie the life tenant must satisfy the conditions of two years' occupation or seven years' ownership (ownership by the settlement being attributed to the life tenant).   **[25.44]–[25.60]**

III   THE TAXATION OF REVERSIONARY INTERESTS

As reversionary interests are generally excluded property their disposition does not lead to an IHT charge.

EXAMPLE 25.17

A fund is settled on trust for A for life (A is currently aged 88); B for life (B is 78); and C absolutely (C (A's son) is 70).

This settlement is likely to be subjected to three IHT charges within a fairly short period. The position would be much improved if B and C disposed of their reversionary interests:

(1) B should surrender his interest. Taking into account his age it has little value and is merely an IHT trap.

(2) C should assign his interest to (ideally) a younger person. He might for instance have minor grandchildren and an accumulation and maintenance trust in their favour would be an attractive possibility.

The result of this reorganisation is that the fund is now threatened by only one IHT charge (on A's death) in the immediate future.

In four cases reversionary interests are not excluded property. This is to prevent their use as a tax avoidance device.

First, a sale of a reversionary interest to a beneficiary under the same trust, who is entitled to a prior interest, is a chargeable transfer (see **[25.29]**).

Secondly, a disposition of a reversionary interest which has at any time, and by any person, been acquired for a consideration in money or money's worth is chargeable to IHT. (For special rules where that interest is situated outside the UK see Chapter 27.)

EXAMPLE 25.18

Umberto sells his reversionary interest to Vidor (a stranger to the trust) for its market value, £20,000. If the general rules operated the position would be that:

(1) Vidor will not be charged to IHT, and as Umberto is disposing of excluded property no IHT is chargeable.

(2)   Vidor has replaced chargeable assets (£20,000) with excluded property so that were he to die or make an *inter vivos* gift IHT would be avoided.

IHTA 1984 s 48(1)(a) and s 48(3) prevent this result. The reversion ceases to be excluded property once it has been purchased (even for a small consideration) with the result that a disposition by Vidor will lead to an IHT charge.

Thirdly, a disposition of a reversionary interest is chargeable if it is one to which either the settlor or his spouse is, or has been, beneficially entitled (IHTA 1984 s 48(1)(b)).

EXAMPLE 25.19

Viv settles property worth £100,000 on trust for his father Will for life (Will is 92). Viv retains the reversionary interest which he then gives to his daughter Ursula. If the general rules were not modified the position would be that:
(1)   The creation of the settlement would be a PET by Viv but the diminution in his estate would be very small (the difference between £100,000 and the value of a reversionary interest in £100,000 subject only to the termination of the interest of a 92 year old life tenant!).
(2)   The transfer of the reversion by Viv would escape IHT since it is excluded property.

IHTA 1984 s 48(1)(b) ensures that the reversion is chargeable so that Viv achieves no tax saving (and, indeed, is left with the danger of a higher IHT bill than if he had never created the settlement since the death of Will is a chargeable event).

Fourthly, the disposition of a reversionary interest is chargeable where that interest is expectant upon the termination of a lease which is treated as a settlement (typically one for life or lives; IHTA 1984 s 48(1)(c)). The result is that the lessor's reversion is treated in the same way as a reversionary interest purchased for money or money's worth so that on any disposition of it, IHT will be charged.   **[25.61]**

26 IHT—settlements without an interest in possession

I INTRODUCTION AND TERMINOLOGY

The method of charging settlements lacking an interest in possession is totally different from that for settlements with such an interest. Instead of attributing the fund to one of the beneficiaries, it is the settlement itself which is the taxable entity for IHT. Like an individual, it must keep a record of chargeable transfers made, although, unlike the individual, it will never die and so will only be taxed at half rates. The method of charge was radically altered by FA 1982 in relation to events occurring after 8 March 1982. For convenience this chapter will discuss the taxing provisions of FA 1982 (now IHTA 1984 Part III, Chapter III) by reference to the discretionary trust which is the most significant of the 'no interest in possession' settlements. In fact the category of 'no interest in possession settlement' is wider than discretionary trusts catching for instance, the type of settlement in the *Pilkington* case (Chapter 24) and funds where the beneficiaries' interests are contingent.

EXAMPLE 26.1

(1) A fund of £100,000 is held upon trust for such of A, B, C, D, E and F as the trustees may in their absolute discretion (which extends over both income and capital) think appropriate. The trust is one without an interest in possession.

(2) Dad settles property on trust for son contingent on his attaining 30. Son is aged 21 at the date of the settlement and the income is to be accumulated until son attains 30. There is no interest in possession.

IHT is charged on 'relevant property' (IHTA 1984 s 58(1)) defined as settled property (other than excluded property) in which there is no qualifying interest in possession, with the exception of property settled on the 'special trusts' considered in Sections V and VI below.

A 'qualifying interest in possession' is one owned beneficially by an individual or, in restricted circumstances, by a company. If within one settlement there exists an interest in possession in a part only of the settled property, the charge to IHT under Part III, Chapter III is on the portion which lacks such an interest.   [**26.1**]-[**26.20**]

II THE METHOD OF CHARGE

The central feature is the periodic or anniversary charge imposed upon discretionary trusts at ten-yearly intervals. The anniversary is calculated from the date on which the trust was created (IHTA 1984 s 61(1)) subject to special rules when the trust follows a life interest in favour of the settlor's spouse (see *Example 26.3*).

EXAMPLE 26.2

Silus creates a discretionary trust on 1 January 1989. The first anniversary charge will fall on 1 January 1999; the next on 1 January 2009 and so on. If the trust had been created by will and he had died on 31 December 1988, that date marks the creation of the settlement (IHTA 1984 s 83).

EXAMPLE 26.3

Silus creates (in 1988) a settlement in favour of his wife Selina for life; thereafter for such of his three daughters as the trustees may in their absolute discretion select. Selina dies in 1989. For IHT purposes the discretionary trust is created by Selina on her death (IHTA 1984 s 80). The ten year anniversary, however, runs from the creation of the original settlement in 1988 (IHTA 1984 s 61(2)).

Apart from the anniversary charge, IHT will also be levied (the 'exit charge') on the happening of certain events. In general, the IHT then charged is a proportion of the last periodic charge. Special charging provisions operate for chargeable events which occur before the first ten year anniversary when the first periodic charge is levied.   [26.21]

1 The creation of the settlement

This will, generally, be a chargeable transfer of value by the settlor for IHT purposes (the creation of a discretionary settlement is not a potentially exempt transfer: see [21.46]). The following matters should be noted: *first*, if the settlement is created *inter vivos*, grossing-up applies unless IHT is paid out of the fund.

Secondly, the cumulative total of chargeable transfers made by the settlor is crucial since it enters the cumulative total of the settlement on all future chargeable occasions (ie his transfers do not drop out of the cumulative total after seven years). Therefore, in order to calculate the correct IHT charge it is essential that the trustees are told the settlor's cumulative total at the date when he created the trust. When as a result of the settlor's fraud, wilful default or neglect there is an underpayment of IHT, the Revenue may recover that sum from the trustees outside the normal six-year time limit. In such cases the time limit is six years from the date when the impropriety comes to the notice of the Revenue (IHTA 1984 s 240(3)). Obviously a problem would arise for trustees if at the time when the underpayment came to light they held insufficient assets to discharge the extra IHT bill since they could be made personally liable for the tax unpaid. The Revenue have, however, stated that where the trustees have acted in good faith and hold insufficient settlement assets they will not seek to recover any unpaid tax from them personally (1984 LS Gaz 3517).

Thirdly, a 'related settlement' is one created by the same settlor on the same day as the discretionary trust (other than a charitable trust). Generally such settlements should be avoided (see below). The possible advantages of 'pilot' trusts are considered in Chapter 37.

Fourthly, additions of property by the original settlor to his settlement should also be avoided (see [**26.33**]). If property is added by a person other than the original settlor, the addition will be treated as a separate settlement.

Particular problems may arise for the trustees if the settlor dies within seven years of creating the trust. If this happens PETs made before the settlement was created and within seven years of his death become chargeable so that tax on creation of the settlement and the computation of any exit charge made during this period may need to be recalculated. If extra tax becomes payable this is primarily the responsibility of the settlement trustees and their liability is not limited to settlement property in their hands *at that time*. Given this danger it will obviously be prudent for trustees who are distributing property from the discretionary trust within the first seven years to retain sufficient funds or take suitable indemnities to cover their contingent IHT liability.   [**26.22**]

EXAMPLE 26.4

Sumar makes the following transfers of value:
May 1988   £150,000 to his sister Sufi (a PET).
May 1989   £71,000 to a family discretionary trust.
In May 1990 the trustees distribute the entire fund to the beneficiaries and in May 1991 Sumar dies.

As a result of his death, the 1988 PET is chargeable (the resultant IHT is primarily the responsibility of Sufi) and in addition tax on the creation of the settlement must be recalculated.

When it was set up the PET was ignored so that the transfer fell within Sumar's nil rate band. With his death however, IHT must be calculated, at the rates in force in May 1991, on transfers from £150,000 to £221,000 (tax is £28,400). In addition it is likely that no IHT will have been charged on the distribution of the fund and therefore a recomputation is again necessary with the trustees being liable for the resulting bill.

2   Exit charges before the first ten year anniversary

a) *When will an exit charge arise?*

A charge is imposed whenever property in the settlement ceases to be 'relevant property' (IHTA 1984 s 65). Hence, if the trustees appoint property to a beneficiary or if an interest in possession arises in any portion of the fund, there will be an IHT charge to the extent of the property ceasing to be held on discretionary trusts. If the resultant IHT is paid out of the property that is left in the discretionary trust, grossing-up will apply. A charge is also imposed if the trustees make a disposition as a result of which the value of relevant property comprised in the settlement falls (a 'depreciatory transaction'; see [**25.30**], but notice that there is no requirement that the transaction be made with a beneficiary or with a person connected with him).

The exit charge does not apply to a payment of costs or expenses (so long as it is 'fairly attributable' to the relevant property), nor does it catch a payment which is income of any person for the purposes of income tax (IHTA 1984 s 65(5)).   [**26.23**]

b) *Calculation of the settlement rate*

The calculation of the rate of IHT is based upon half the full IHT rates, even if the trust was set up under the will of the settlor. The rate of tax actually payable is then 30% of those rates applicable to a hypothetical chargeable transfer.

Step 1   This postulated transfer is made up of the sum of the following:
(1) the value of the property in the settlement immediately after it commenced;
(2) the value (at the date of the addition) of any added property; and
(3) the value of property in a related settlement (valued immediately after it commenced (IHTA 1984 s 68(5)).

No account is taken of any rise or fall in the value of the settled fund and the value comprised in the settlement and in any related settlement can include property subject to an interest in possession.

Step 2   Tax at half rates on this hypothetical transfer is calculated by joining the table at the point reached by the cumulative total of previous chargeable transfers made by the settlor in the seven years before he created the settlement. Other chargeable transfers made on the same day as the settlement are ignored and, therefore, if the settlement was created on death, other gifts made in the will or on intestacy are ignored (IHTA 1984 s 68(4)(b)).

Step 3   The resultant tax is converted to an average rate (the equivalent of an estate rate) and 30% of that rate is then taken. The resultant rate (the 'settlement rate') is used as the basis for calculating the exit charge.   [26.24]

EXAMPLE 26.5

Justinian settles £100,000 on discretionary trusts on 1 April 1991. His total chargeable transfers immediately before that date stood at £60,000. He pays the IHT. If an exit charge arises before the first ten year anniversary of the fund (1 April 2001) the settlement rate would be calculated as follows:

Step 1   Calculate the hypothetical chargeable transfer. As there is no added property and no related settlement it comprises only the value of the property in the settlement immediately after its creation (ie £100,000).

Step 2   Cumulate the £100,000 with the previous chargeable transfers of Justinian (ie £60,000). Taking the current IHT rates, tax on transfers between £60,000 and £160,000 is £4,000.

Step 3   The tax converted to a percentage rate is 4%; 30% of that rate produces a 'settlement rate' of 1.2%.

c) *The tax charged*

The charge is on the fall in value of the fund. To establish the rate of charge, a further proportion of the settlement rate must be calculated equal to 1/40th of the settlement rate for each complete successive quarter that has elapsed from the creation of the settlement to the date of the exit charge. That proportion of the settlement rate is applied to the chargeable transfer (the 'effective rate').

EXAMPLE 26.6

Assume in *Example 26.5* that on 25 March 1993 there was an exit charge on £20,000 ceasing to be relevant property. The 'effective rate' of IHT is calculated as follows:

Step 1   Take completed quarters since the settlement was created, ie seven.

Step 2   Take 7/40ths of the 'settlement rate' (1.2%) to discover the 'effective rate' = 0.21%.

Step 3   The effective rate is applied to the fall in value of the relevant property. The IHT will, therefore, be £42 if the tax is borne by the beneficiary; or £42.09 if borne by the remaining fund.

There is no charge on events that occur in the first three months of the settlement (IHTA 1984 s 65(4)) nor, where the trust was set up by the settlor on his death, on events occurring within two years of that death (see [**22.125**]).   [**26.25**]

3   The charge on the first ten year anniversary

a) *What property is charged?*

The charge is levied on the value of the relevant property comprised in the settlement immediately before the anniversary (IHTA 1984 s 64).

The charge is levied on relevant property and at first sight no distinction appears to be drawn between income and capital in the fund. The Revenue now accept, however, that income only becomes relevant property, and thus subject to charge, when it has been accumulated (see SP 8/86). Pending accumulation the income is not subject to the anniversary charge and can, of course, be distributed free from any exit charge (see [**26.23**]). The crucial question is, therefore, at what moment is income accumulated? Obviously accumulation occurs once an irrevocable decision to that effect has been taken by trustees, it may also occur after a reasonable time for distribution has passed (but see *Re Locker* (1977) where income which arose between 1965 and 1968 was still available for distribution in 1977). The legislation gives no guidance on what property is treated as being distributed first: ie if an appointment is made by the trustees out of property comprised in the settlement, does it come out of the original capital or out of accumulations of income? As a reduced charge may apply to property which has been added to the trust (such as accumulated income: see [**26.32**]) this is an important omission (for the approach adopted in practice by the CTO see *Capital Taxes News*, vol 8, May 1989).

The assets in the fund are valued according to general principles and, if they include business or agricultural property, the reliefs appropriate to that property will apply, subject to satisfaction of the relevant conditions. Any IHT charged on such property will be payable in instalments.   [**26.26**]

b) *Calculation of the rate of IHT*

Half rates will be used and, as with the exit charge, the calculation depends upon a hypothetical chargeable transfer.

Step 1   Calculate the hypothetical chargeable transfer which is made up of the sum of the following:
(1)   the value of relevant property comprised in the settlement immediately before the anniversary;

(2) the value, immediately after it was created, of property comprised in a 'related settlement'; and

(3) the value, at the date when the settlement was created, of any non-relevant property then in the settlement which has not subsequently become relevant property.

Normally the hypothetical chargeable transfer will be made up exclusively of property falling within category (1). Categories (2) and (3), which affect the rate of IHT to be charged without themselves being taxed, are anti-avoidance measures. Related settlements are included because transfers made on the same day as the creation of the settlement are normally ignored and, therefore, an IHT advantage could be achieved if the settlor were to set up a series of small funds rather than one large fund. Non-relevant property in the settlement is included because the trustees could switch the values between the two portions of the fund.

Step 2 Calculate tax at half rates on the hypothetical chargeable transfer by joining the table at the point reached by:

(1) the chargeable transfers of the settlor made in the *seven* years before he created the settlement; and

(2) chargeable transfers made by the settlement in the first *ten* years. Where a settlement was created after 26 March 1974 and before 9 March 1982, distribution payments (as defined by the IHT charging regime in force between those dates) must also be cumulated (IHTA 1984 s 66(6)).

Discretionary settlements will, therefore, have their own total of chargeable transfers with transfers over a ten-year period being cumulated (the seven-year period used for individuals is not employed for discretionary trusts). The unique feature of a settlement's cumulation lies in the inclusion (and it never drops out[1]) of chargeable transfers of the settlor in the seven years before the settlement is created.

Step 3 The IHT is converted to a percentage and 30% of that rate is then taken and charged upon the relevant property in the settlement.

The highest rate of IHT is 20% (half of 40%). The highest effective rate (anniversary rate) is, therefore, 30% of 20%, ie 6%. Where the settlement comprises business property qualifying for 50% relief, this effective rate falls to 3% and assuming that the option to pay in instalments is exercised, the annual charge over the ten-year period becomes a mere 0.3%. **[26.27]**

EXAMPLE 26.7

Take the facts of *Example 26.6* (viz, original fund £100,000, exit charge on £20,000; previous transfers of settlor £60,000). In addition, assume Justinian had created a second settlement of £15,000 on 1 April 1991.

The fund is worth £105,000 at the first ten year anniversary.

(1) Relevant property to be taxed is £105,000

(2) Calculate hypothetical chargeable transfer

	£
Relevant property, as above	105,000
Property in related settlement	15,000
	£120,000

(3) Settlement's cumulative IHT total:

	£
Settlor's earlier transfers	60,000
Chargeable transfers of trustees in preceeding ten years	20,000
	£80,000

(4) Tax from the table (at half rates) on transfers from £80,000 to £200,000 (£120,000 + £80,000) = £12,000 so that, as a percentage rate IHT is 10%.
(5) The 'effective rate' is 30% of 10% = 3%.
     Tax payable is £105,000 × 3% = £3,150.

4 Exit charges after the first anniversary charge and between anniversaries

The same events will trigger an exit charge after the first ten year anniversary as before it. The IHT charge will be levied on the fall in value of the fund with grossing-up, if necessary. The rate of charge is a proportion of the effective rate charged at the first ten year anniversary. That proportion is 1/40th for each complete quarter from the date of the first anniversary charge to the date of the exit charge (IHTA 1984 s 69).

EXAMPLE 26.8

Continuing *Example 26.7*, exactly 15 months later the trustees appoint £25,000 to a beneficiary. The IHT (assuming no grossing-up) will be:
£25,000 × 3% × 5/40 (5 quarters since last ten year anniversary) = £93.75.

If the rates of IHT have been reduced (including the raising of the rate bands) between the anniversary and exit charges, the lower rates will apply to the exit charge and, therefore, the rate of charge on the first anniversary will have to be recalculated at those rates (IHTA 1984 Sch 2 para 3). So long as the IHT rate bands remain linked to rises in the retail prices index (IHTA 1984 s 8) recalculation is likely to be the norm.

No exit charge is levied if the chargeable event occurs within the first quarter following the anniversary charge (see [**26.25**]).   [**26.28**]

5 Later periodic charges

The principles that applied on the first ten year anniversary operate on subsequent ten year anniversaries. So far as the hypothetical chargeable transfer is concerned the same items will be included (so that the value of property in a related settlement and of non-relevant property in the settlement is always included). The cumulative total of the fund will, as before, include the chargeable transfers of the settlor made in the seven years before he created the settlement and the transfers out of the settlement in the ten years immediately preceding the anniversary (earlier transfers by the settlement fall out of the cumulative total). The remaining stages of the calculation are unaltered.   [**26.29**]

6 Technical problems

The basic structure of the charging provisions in IHTA 1984 ss 58–69 is relatively straightforward. The charge to IHT is built upon a series of periodic charges with interim charges (where appropriate) which are levied at a fraction of the full periodic charge. A number of technical matters should be noted.   [**26.30**]

Reduction in the rate of the anniversary charge   If property has not been in the settlement for the entire preceding ten years (as will be the case when income is accumulated during that period) there is a proportionate reduction in the charge (IHTA 1984 s 66(2)). The reduction in the periodic rate is calculated by reference to the number of completed quarters which expired before the property became relevant property in the settlement.

EXAMPLE 26.9

Assume in *Example 26.7* that £15,000 had become relevant property on 30 April 1997.

The IHT charge on the first ten year anniversary (on 1 April 2001) would now be calculated as follows:

(1)   £90,000 (£105,000 — £15,000) at 3% = £2,700.

(2)   The £15,000 will be charged at a proportion of the periodic charge rate: viz— 3% reduced by 24/40 since 24 complete quarters elapsed from the creation of the settlement (on 1 April 1991) to the date when the £15,000 became relevant property. As a result the IHT charged is £15,000 × 1.2% = £180.

This proportionate reduction in the effective rate of the periodic charge will not affect the calculation of IHT on events occurring after the anniversary, ie any exit charge is at the full effective rate.

The legislation does not contain provisions which enable specific property to be identified. Thus, the reduction mentioned above applies to the value of the relevant property in the fund at the ten year anniversary 'attributable' to property which was not relevant property throughout the preceding ten years. Presumably, therefore, some sort of proportionate calculation will be necessary where the value of the fund has shown an increase. Furthermore, if accumulated income is caught by the anniversary charge, a separate calculation will have to be made with regard to each separate accumulation, as being property which has not been in the settlement for the whole of the previous decade (see SP 8/86: [**26.26**]). [**26.31**]

Transfers between settlements   IHTA 1984 s 81 prevents a tax advantage from switching property between discretionary settlements, by providing that such property remains comprised in the first settlement. It would seem to follow that property cannot be moved out of a discretionary trust to avoid an anniversary charge; that property cannot be switched from a fund with a high cumulative total to one with a lower total; and that the transfer of property from one discretionary fund to another will not be chargeable (for a discussion of this provision, see 1989 *Capital Taxes News*, vol 8, p 219). [**26.32**]

Added property   Special rules operate if, after the settlement commenced (and after 8 March 1982), the settlor made a chargeable transfer as a result of which the value of the property comprised in the settlement was increased (IHTA 1984 s 67(1)). Note that it is only additions by the settlor that trigger these provisions and that it is the value of the fund which must be increased and not necessarily the amount of property in that fund. Transfers which have the effect of increasing the value of the fund are ignored if they are not primarily intended to have that effect and do not in fact increase the value by more than 5%.

EXAMPLE 26.10

Sam, the settlor, creates in 1989 a discretionary trust of stocks and shares in Sham Ltd and the benefit of a life insurance policy on Sam's life.
(1) Each year Sam adds property to the settlement, equal to his annual IHT exemption.
(2) Sam continues to pay the premiums on the life policy each year.
(3) Sam transfers further shares in Sham Ltd.
  The special rules for added property will not apply in either cases (1) or (2), since Sam is not making a chargeable transfer; the first transfer is covered by his annual exemption and the second by the exemption for normal expenditure out of income. The transfer of further shares to the fund, however, is caught by the provisions of IHTA 1984 s 67, relating to added property.

If the added property provisions apply, the calculation of the periodic charge which immediately follows the addition will be modified. For the purposes of the hypothetical chargeable transfer, the cumulative total of the settlor's chargeable transfers will be the higher of the totals (1) immediately before creating the settlement plus transfers made by the settlement before the addition; and (2) immediately before transferring the added property, deducting from this latter total the transfer made on creation of the settlement and a transfer to any related settlement. Thus the settlor should avoid additions, since they may cause more IHT to be charged at the next anniversary and it will, therefore, be preferable to create a separate settlement. **[26.33]**

The timing of the exit charge Assume that a discretionary trust has been in existence for nearly ten years and that the trustees now wish to distribute all or part of the fund to the beneficiaries. Are they better off doing so just before the ten year anniversary or should they wait until just after that anniversary? Generally, it will be advantageous to distribute *before* an anniversary because IHT payable will be calculated at rates then in force but on historic values: ie on the value of the fund when it was settled or at the last ten year anniversary. By contrast, if the trustees delay until after the anniversary, IHT (still at current rates) will then be assessed on the present value of the fund. To this general proposition one major exception exists which may well be the result of defective drafting in the legislation. It relates to a fund consisting of property qualifying for either business relief or agricultural relief. In this situation trustees *should not* break up the fund immediately before the first anniversary. This is illustrated in the following example: **[26.34]-[26.50]**

EXAMPLE 26.11

A discretionary settlement was created on 1 January 1987. At all times it has consisted of business property which will qualify for 50% relief. Assume no earlier transfers by settlor and that the value of the property is £500,000 throughout. Consider the effect of business relief if:
  (i) *the trustees distribute the entire fund on 25 December 1996*. The distribution occurs before the first ten year anniversary. The entire value of the property in the settlement immediately after it commenced must be included in the hypothetical transfer of value since there is no business relief reduction. Therefore £500,000 must be included (IHTA 1984 s 111(5)(a)). The rate thus calculated is then applied to the fund as reduced by business relief. Hence, although the amount subject to the charge is only £250,000 (£500,000 minus 50% relief), a higher rate of IHT will apply.

(ii) *the trustees distribute the entire fund on 3 January 1997*. As the first ten year anniversary fell on 1 January there will be no exit charge because the distribution is within three months of that anniversary. So far as the anniversary charge is concerned the property subject to the charge will be reduced by 50% relief to £250,000; and for the purpose of calculating the hypothetical chargeable transfer the value of the property is similarly reduced by the relief.

III EXEMPTIONS AND RELIEFS

Many of the exemptions from IHT will not apply to property in discretionary trusts, eg the annual exemption, the marriage exemption, and the exemption for normal expenditure out of income. There is also no exemption if the settled fund reverts to either the settlor or his spouse (and note that if the settlor is a beneficiary, or even merely a paid trustee, the reservation of benefit provisions apply). Business and agricultural property relief may, however, be available, provided that the necessary conditions for the relief are met by the trustees. There is no question of any aggregation with similar property owned by a discretionary beneficiary.

Exit charges are not levied in certain cases when property leaves the settlement, eg:

(1) Property ceasing to be relevant property within three months of the creation of the trust or of an anniversary charge or within two years of creation (if the trust was set up on death) is not subject to an exit charge ([**22.125**] and [**26.25**]).

(2) Property may pass, without attracting an exit charge, to such privileged trusts as employee trusts (IHTA 1984 s 75); maintenance funds for historic buildings (IHTA 1984 Sch 4 para 16); permanent charities (IHTA 1984 s 76(1)); political parties in accordance with the exemption in IHTA 1984 s 24 (IHTA 1984 s 76(1)(b); and see Chapter 23); national heritage bodies (IHTA 1984 s 76(1)(c)); and non-profit making bodies approved by the Treasury and holding heritage property (IHTA 1984 s 76(1)(d), (2)). There is no exemption in the case of property passing into an accumulation and maintenance trust.

If a discretionary fund includes excluded property the periodic and exit charges will not apply to that portion of the fund.   [**26.51**]–[**26.70**]

IV DISCRETIONARY TRUSTS CREATED BEFORE 27 MARCH 1974

Discretionary settlements created before 27 March 1974 are subject to special rules for the calculation of tax which will generally result in less tax being charged (see generally IHTA 1984 ss 66–68).   [**26.71**]

1 Chargeable events occurring before the first ten year anniversary

The rate of IHT to be charged is set out in IHTA 1984 s 68(6). As the settlement is treated as a separate taxable entity only transfers made by the settlement are cumulated. Such chargeable transfers will either be distribution payments (if made under the regime in force from 1974 to 1982) or chargeable events under IHTA 1984 s 65. Once the cumulative total is known, the rate of tax will be calculated at half rate and the charge will be at 30% of that rate.   [**26.72**]

2   The first anniversary charge

No anniversary charge can apply before 1 April 1983. Thus, the first discretionary trust to suffer this charge is one created on 1 April 1973 (or 1963; 1953; 1943 and so on).

The amount subject to the charge is calculated in the normal way. In calculating the rate of charge, however, it is only chargeable transfers of the settlement in the preceding ten years that are cumulated (as the settlement predates CTT/IHT the settlor obviously has no chargeable transfers to cumulate). Property in a related settlement and non-relevant property in the settlement are ignored. As before, the rate of charge is reduced if property has not been relevant property throughout the decade preceding the first anniversary. The danger of increasing an IHT bill by an addition of property by the settlor (see [**26.33**]) is even greater with these old trusts. If such an addition has been made, the settlor's chargeable transfers in the seven-year period before the addition must be cumulated in calculating the rate of tax on the anniversary charge (IHTA 1984 s 67(4)). The effective rate of charge for the anniversary charge is (as for new trusts) 30% of the rate calculated according to half the table rates.   [**26.73**]

3   Chargeable events after the first anniversary charge

The position is the same as for new trusts. The charge is based upon the rate charged at the last anniversary.   [**26.74**]–[**26.90**]

> **EXAMPLE 26.12**
>
> In November 1971 Maggie settled £400,000 on discretionary trusts for her family. The following events have since occurred:
> *In May 1982*: a distribution payment of £100,000.
> *In May 1991*: trustees distribute a further sum of £85,000 (tax borne by beneficiary).
> *In November 1991*: the first ten year anniversary. The value of relevant property then in the fund is £300,000.
> IHT will be charged as follows:
> (1)   *May 1991*: The distribution will be a chargeable event occurring before the first ten year anniversary. IHT will be calculated on the table by cumulating the chargeable transfer of £85,000 with the earlier transfer made by the settlement (the distribution payment of £100,000). The rate of IHT is, therefore, 10.59% and the effective rate 3.176%. IHT is £2,700.
> (Notice that there is no proportionate reduction in the effective rate for exit charges levied on old discretionary trusts before the first anniversary.)
> (2)   *November 1991*: The anniversary charge will be calculated on the relevant property in the settlement (£100,000). The cumulative total of transfers made by the settlement is £185,000 (£100,000 plus £85,000) so that the rate of IHT according to the table is 20%. The effective rate is, therefore, 6%. IHT payable will be £6,000 (6% of £100,000).

V   ACCUMULATION AND MAINTENANCE TRUSTS
(IHTA 1984 s 71)

1   Tax treatment

Inheritance tax   Rather than make outright gifts to minor children, funds will frequently be settled in trust for their benefit. If special treatment were not accorded to such settlements the IHT charges would discriminate between gifts to adults and settled gifts to infants.

EXAMPLE 26.13

Simon makes two gifts: to his brother, Enrico, and to his two month old granddaughter, Frederica.

(1) *The gift to Enrico:* The gift is a potentially exempt transfer and therefore only subject to IHT if Simon dies within seven years.

(2) *The gift to Frederica:* In view of her age, it is necessary to settle the property on trusts which give the trustees the power to maintain Frederica, but which give her no interest in possession. Under general principles, the creation of that settlement will be a chargeable transfer of value and the discretionary trust charging regime will thereupon operate. As a result there would be anniversary charges and, when Frederica obtains either an interest in possession or an absolute interest in the settled fund, an 'exit' charge.

The objective of the special provisions that apply to accumulation and maintenance trusts is to prevent this double charge. The *inter vivos* creation of an accumulation and maintenance settlement is accordingly a potentially exempt transfer (a PET) and thereafter, so long as the property continues to be held on accumulation and maintenance trusts, the ten year anniversary charge will not apply and there will be no proportionate periodic charge when the property leaves the trust. As a result, the taxation of gifts to children is treated in the same way as gifts to adults. **[26.91]**

Other taxes The privileged status of the accumulation and maintenance trust only applies for the purposes of IHT with the result that, so far as the other taxes are concerned, general principles operate. This will usually mean that so far as capital gains tax is concerned hold-over relief is not generally available on the *inter vivos* creation of the trust and will only be available on its termination in the limited circumstances set out in Chapter 17: notably if a beneficiary becomes absolutely entitled to the assets on the ending of the accumulation period. Capital gains realised by the trustees will be subject to tax at a 35% rate. For income tax, the creation of an A & M trust by a parent on behalf of his own infant unmarried children will result in any income which is distributed being taxed as his under TA 1988 s 683. Given the nature of an accumulation and maintenance trust, the trustees will suffer income tax at the rate of 35% (TA 1988 s 686).

The IHT attractions of these trusts have to some extent been eroded by their income tax and CGT treatment. Especially as a result of the CGT changes in FA 1988 and FA 1989 it should no longer be assumed that the A & M trust is always the 'best buy'. **[26.92]**

2 The requirements of IHTA 1984 s 71

To qualify for the privileged IHT treatment, an accumulation and maintenance trust has to satisfy the three requirements considered below. Failure to do so means that the normal charging system applies. When the requirements cease to be satisfied IHT will not usually be charged save in exceptional cases (see **[26.98]**). **[26.93]**

3 Requirement 1

'One or more persons (. . . beneficiaries) will, on or before attaining a specified age not exceeding 25, become entitled to, or to an interest in possession in, the settled property or part of it' (IHTA 1984 s 71).

Requirement 1 is concerned with the age at which a beneficiary becomes entitled either to the income from the fund or to the fund itself. The age of 25 is specified as a maximum age limit and this is a generously late age when one considers that the purpose of these rules is to deal with settlements for infant children.

EXAMPLE 26.14

(1) Property is settled upon trust 'for A absolutely, contingent on attaining the age of 18'. A will become entitled to both income and capital at that age so that Requirement 1 is satisfied.

(2) Property is settled upon trust 'for B absolutely, contingent upon attaining the age of 30'. At first sight Requirement 1 is broken since B will not acquire the capital in the fund until after the age of 25. However, the requirement will be **satisfied** if the beneficiary acquires an interest in possession before 25; B will do so, because the Trustee Act 1925 s 31 (if not expressly excluded) provides that when a **beneficiary** with a contingent interest attains 18, that beneficiary shall thereupon be entitled to the income produced by the fund even though he has not yet **satisfied** the contingency.

The requirement that a beneficiary *'will'* become entitled does not require absolute certainty; death, for instance, can always prevent entitlement. The word causes particular problems when trustees possess overriding powers of advancement and appointment (dispositive powers) which, if exercised, could result in entitlement being postponed beyond 25. So long as the dispositive power can only be exercised **amongst** the existing beneficiaries and cannot postpone entitlement beyond the age of 25, Requirement 1 is satisfied. Accordingly, a power to vary or determine the respective shares of members of the class, even to the extent of excluding some members altogether, is permissible.

EXAMPLE 26.15

Property is held on trust for the three children of A contingent upon their attaining the age of 25 and, if more than one, in equal shares. The trustees are given overriding powers of appointment, exercisable until a beneficiary attains 25, to appoint the fund to one or more of the beneficiaries as they see fit. Requirement 1 is satisfied since the property will vest absolutely in the beneficiaries no later than the age of 25. The existence of the overriding power of appointment is irrelevant since it cannot be exercised other than in favour of the class of beneficiaries and cannot be used to postpone the vesting of the fund until after a beneficiary has attained 25.

The mere existence of a common form power of advancement will not prevent Requirement 1 from being satisfied (see *Lord Inglewood v IRC* (1983)). It should be noted, however, that such powers can be exercised so as to postpone the vesting of property in a beneficiary beyond the age stated in the trust document and, hence, beyond the age of 25 (see *Pilkington v IRC* (1962)) and they can, in exceptional cases, result in property being paid to a non-beneficiary (as in *Re Clore's Settlement Trust* (1966) where the payment was to the beneficiary's favourite charity). Obviously, if the power is so exercised a charge to IHT will result.

The effect of powers of appointment which, if exercised, would break Requirement 1, was considered in a Revenue Press Release of 19 January 1975 and is illustrated by the following example:

EXAMPLE 26.16

Property is settled 'for the children of E contingent on their attaining 25'. The trustees are given the following (alternative) overriding powers of appointment.

(1) *To appoint income and capital to E's sister F:* The mere existence of this power causes the settlement to break Requirement 1. There is no certainty that the fund will pass to E's children since the power might be exercised in favour of F.

(2) *To appoint income to E's brother G:* The same consequence will follow since the mere existence of this power means that the income could be used for the benefit of G and, hence, break Requirement 2 (for details of this Requirement see below).

(3) *To appoint capital and income to E's relatives so long as those relatives are no older than 25:* This power does not break Requirement 1 since whoever receives the settled fund, whether E's children or his relatives, will be no older than 25.

It may be difficult to decide whether or not the settlement contains a power of revocation or appointment which will break Requirement 1. In *Lord Inglewood v IRC* (1981), Vinelott J distinguished between events provided for in the trust instrument and events wholly outside the settlor's control:

'. . . the terms of the settlement must be such that one or more of the beneficiaries, if they or one of them survive to the specified age, will be bound to take a vested interest on or before attaining that age . . . Of course, a beneficiary may assign his interest, or be deprived of it, by an arrangement, or by bankruptcy, before he attains a vested interest. But he is not then deprived of it under the terms of the settlement, so these possible events, unlike the exercise of a power of revocation or appointment, must be disregarded.' 1981 STC at 318 (see also Fox LJ, in the Court of Appeal, 1983 STC at 138).

EXAMPLE 26.17

Sebag creates a settlement in favour of his second daughter, Juno, under which she will obtain the property if she attains the age of 18. If she marries before that age, however, the property is to pass to Sebag's brother, Sebastian.

This provision in the settlement could operate to deprive Juno of the property in circumstances when, as a matter of general law, she would not be so deprived. The settlement does not satisfy Requirement 1 and so does not qualify for privileged treatment.

Two other matters should be noted in relation to Requirement 1. First, even if a trust instrument fails to specify an age at which the beneficiary will become entitled to either the income or capital, the Revenue accept that so long as it is clear from the terms of that instrument and the known ages of the beneficiaries that one or more persons will in fact become entitled before the age of 25, Requirement 1 will be satisfied (ESC F8).

Secondly, for an accumulation and maintenance trust to be created there must be a living beneficiary at that time. It is possible to set up a trust for a class of persons including some who are unborn ('the grandchildren of the settlor' for instance), but there must be at least one member of the class in existence at the date of creation (IHTA 1984 s 71(7)). If the single living beneficiary dies, the fund (assuming that it was set up for a class of beneficiaries) will remain in existence as an accumulation and maintenance trust until a further member of that class is born. If a further class member

is never born, the fund will eventually pass elsewhere and at that stage
an IHT charge may arise.   **[26.94]**

4 Requirement 2

'No interest in possession subsists in the settled property (or part) and the income
from it is to be accumulated so far as it is not applied for the maintenance,
education or benefit of such a person' (IHTA 1984 s 71).

There must be no interest in possession and once such an interest arises,
the settlement breaks Requirement 2 and ceases to be an accumulation and
maintenance trust.

If there is to be no interest in possession in the income, what is to be
done with it? Two possibilities are envisaged by Requirement 2; it can either
be used for the benefit of a beneficiary (eg under a power of maintenance),
or it can be accumulated. There must be a valid power to accumulate:
accordingly once the accumulation period ends Requirement 2 will cease
to be satisfied and the settlement will no longer be an A&M trust.

EXAMPLE 26.18

A trust is set up for Loeb, the child of the settlor, contingent on his attaining
the age of 25. So long as he is a minor the trustees will have a power to maintain
him out of the income of the fund and a power to accumulate any surplus
income (Trustee Act 1925 s 31). When Loeb becomes 18 he will be entitled
to the income of the fund so that an interest in possession will arise and the
settlement will cease to be an accumulation and maintenance trust. The ending
of the trust will not lead to any IHT charge.

Care should be taken in choosing the appropriate period if the intention
is to accumulate income beyond the minorities of the beneficiaries. Various
periods are permitted under the LPA 1925 ss 164 and 165 and under the
Trustee Act 1925 s 31, but some of them may cause the trust to fall outside
the definition of an accumulation and maintenance settlement. In the case
of an *inter vivos* trust, for instance, a direction to accumulate 'during the
lifetime of the settlor' would mean that an interest in possession might not
arise until after the beneficiaries had attained the age of 25; likewise, a
provision to accumulate for 21 years when the beneficiaries are over the
age of four would be fatal.   **[26.95]**

5 Requirement 3

'Either
  (i) not more than 25 years have elapsed since the day on which the settlement
      was made or (if later) since the time when the settled property (or part)
      began to satisfy Requirements 1 and 2, or
 (ii) all the persons who are, or have been beneficiaries are, or were, either
      grandchildren of a common grandparent, or children, widows or widowers
      of such grandchildren who were themselves beneficiaries but died before
      becoming entitled as mentioned in Requirement 1' (IHTA 1984 s 71).

Requirement 3 was first introduced in FA 1976 to stop the accumulation
and maintenance trust from being used to benefit more than one generation.
There are two ways in which it can be satisfied. First, the trust must not

last for more than 25 years from the date when the fund became settled on accumulation and maintenance trusts. The second (alternative) limb of Requirement 3 is satisfied if all the beneficiaries have a common grandparent.

EXAMPLE 26.19

(1) Property is settled for the children and grandchildren of the settlor. As there is no grandparent common to all the beneficiaries, the trust must not last for longer than 25 years if an exit charge to IHT is to be avoided.

(2) Property is settled for the children of brothers Bill and Ben. As there is a common grandparent the duration of the settlement does not need to be limited to 25 years.

There is one case in which two generations can be benefited under an accumulation and maintenance trust since substitution *per stirpes* is permitted where the original beneficiaries had a common grandparent and one of those beneficiaries has died. **[26.96]**

6 Advantages of accumulation and maintenance trusts

No IHT is charged when property from an accumulation and maintenance trust becomes subject to an interest in possession in favour of one or more of the beneficiaries, or when any part of the fund is appointed absolutely to such a beneficiary (IHTA 1984 s 71(3),(4)). This exemption, together with the exclusion of the anniversary charge (IHTA 1984 s 58(1)(b)), means that once the property is settled on these trusts there should be no IHT liability. Furthermore the inter vivos creation of the trust is a potentially exempt transfer.

EXAMPLE 26.20

'... to A absolutely contingent on attaining 25'. This straightforward trust will satisfy the Requirements so long as A is an infant. Consider, however, the position:

(1) *When A attains 18:* he will be entitled to the income from the fund (Trustee Act 1925 s 31) and, therefore, Requirement 2 is broken. No IHT is charged on the arising of the interest in possession.

(2) *When A attains 25:* ordinary principles for interest in possession settlements apply; A's life interest comes to an end, but no IHT is payable since the life tenant is entitled to all the property (see IHTA 1984 s 53(2)).

(3) *If A dies aged 19:* IHT will be assessed on the termination of an interest in possession (IHTA 1984 s 51(1)).

As already discussed, there is nothing to prevent an accumulation and maintenance trust from being created for an open class of beneficiaries, eg 'for all my grandchildren both born and yet to be born'. If such a trust is to be created, it is important to ensure that the class of beneficiaries will close when the eldest obtains a vested interest in either the income or capital. Failure to do so will result in a partial divesting of the beneficiary with the vested interest when a further beneficiary is born, and, as a result, an IHT charge. Class-closing rules may be implied at common law (see *Andrews v Partington* (1791)), but it is safer to insert an express provision to that effect.

IHTA 1984 s 71(4)(b) provides that 'tax shall not be charged ... on the death of a beneficiary before attaining the specified age'. It follows that, if the entire class of beneficiaries is wiped out, an accumulation and maintenance trust will cease on the death of the final member, but, whoever then becomes entitled to the fund, no IHT will be payable. When it is necessary to wait and see if a further beneficiary is born, however this provision will not operate, since it is not the death of the beneficiary which ends the accumulation and maintenance trust in such a case, but the failure of a further beneficiary to be born within the trust period.

EXAMPLE 26.21

(1) Property is settled upon trust for Zed's grandchild, Yvonne, contingent upon her attaining 18. If she were to die aged 16, the property would (in the absence of any provision to the contrary) revert to Zed and no IHT would be payable.

(2) Property is settled upon trust for Victor's children contingent upon their attaining 21 and, if more than one, in equal shares. Victor's one child, Daphne, died in 1984 aged 12 and Victor himself has just died.

No charge to IHT arose on Daphne's death and the property continued to be held on accumulation and maintenance trusts until Victor died when the trust ended with a charge to IHT.

The accumulation and maintenance trust can be drafted to achieve a considerable degree of flexibility. It is common for such a trust to contain the following provisions:

(1) Primary beneficiaries are present and future grandchildren with a class-closing provision.

(2) The trustees are given a revocable power of appointment among the beneficiaries (inapplicable once a beneficiary has attained 25).

(3) The A & M trust will end with beneficiaries being entitled to interests in possession (not absolute interests) and thereafter such a beneficiary is given power to appoint a life interest to his surviving spouse and divide up the capital as he sees fit between his children. However:

(4) The trustees retain an overriding power to determine the life interest of any beneficiary who has attained (say) 26 and appoint the property in favour of one or more secondary beneficiaries, often called discretionary beneficiaries.

As a result, this kind of settlement includes more than one generation of beneficiaries; has great flexibility; but still qualifies as an accumulation and maintenance trust on its creation.   [26.97]

7   Occasions when an 'exit charge' will arise

It will be rare for property to leave an accumulation and maintenance trust otherwise than by appointment to a beneficiary and so long as this happens no IHT is chargeable. Provision is, however, made for calculating an 'exit charge' in the following four circumstances (IHTA 1984 ss 70(6),71(5)):

(1) When depreciatory transactions entered into by the trustees reduce the value of the fund (IHTA 1984 s 71(3)(b)).

(2) When the 25-year period provided for in Requirement 3 is exceeded and the beneficiaries do not have a common grandparent.

(3) When property is advanced to a non-beneficiary or resettled on trusts which do not comply with the three Requirements.

(4) If the trust ends some time after the final surviving beneficiary has died (see *Example 26.21(2)*).

IHT is calculated in these cases on the value of the fund according to how long the property has been held on the accumulation and maintenance trusts:

0.25% for each of the first 40 complete successive quarters in the relevant period;

0.20% for each of the next 40;

0.15% for each of the next 40;

0.10% for each of the next 40; and

0.05% for each of the next 40.

Hence, on expiry of the permitted 25 years IHT at a rate of 21% will apply to the fund. Thereafter, normal discretionary trust rules will apply, so that five years later there will be an anniversary charge. [**26.98**]–[**26.110**]

VI OTHER SPECIAL TRUSTS

1 Charitable trusts

If a trust is perpetually dedicated to charitable purposes, there is no charge to IHT and the fund is not 'relevant property' (IHTA 1984 s 58). Transfers to charities are exempt, whether made by individuals or by trustees of discretionary trusts (IHTA 1984 s 76).

IHTA 1984 s 70 is concerned with temporary charitable trusts which that section defines as 'settled property held for charitable purposes only until the end of a period (whether defined by a date or in some other way)' and ensures that when the fund ceases to be held for such purposes an exit charge will arise. That charge (which is calculated in the same way as for accumulation and maintenance trusts; see above) will never exceed a 30% rate which is reached after 50 years. [**26.111**]

2 Trusts for the benefit of mentally disabled persons and persons in receipt of an attendance allowance (IHTA 1984 s 89)

These rules were recast in 1981. As from 10 March 1981, a qualifying trust for a disabled person is treated as giving that person an interest in possession. As a result the IHT regime for no interest in possession trusts does not apply. The *inter vivos* creation of this trust by a person other than the relevant beneficiary is a potentially exempt transfer. There are no restrictions on the application of income which can therefore be used for the benefit of other members of the class of beneficiaries. This can be particularly useful where the application of income to the 'principal' disabled beneficiary could jeopardise his entitlement to state benefits. Obviously a charge to IHT will arise on the death of the disabled person whose deemed interest in possession will aggregate with his free estate in the normal way. Although disabled trusts can also obtain CGT advantages (eg a full annual exemption for the trustees), to qualify the disabled beneficiary must be entitled to at least one half of the income which would mean that inheritance tax relief would be lost since no interest in possession can subsist under s 89 (see generally 1989 *Capital Taxes News*, vol 8, p 174). [**26.112**]

3 Pension funds (IHTA 1984 s 151)

A superannuation scheme or fund approved by the Revenue for income tax purposes is not subject to the rules for no interest in possession trusts.

A benefit payable out of that fund which becomes comprised in a discretionary trust is, however, subject to the normal charging rules; the person entitled to that benefit being treated as the settlor.   **[26.113]**

4   Employee trusts (IHTA 1984 s 86)

These trusts will not in law be charitable unless they are directed to the relief of poverty amongst employees (see *Oppenheim v Tobacco Securities Trust Co Ltd* (1951)). They may, however, enjoy considerable IHT privileges. Their creation will not involve a transfer of value, whether made by an individual (IHTA 1984 s 28) or by a discretionary trust (IHTA 1984 s 75). Once created, the fund is largely exempted from the IHT provisions governing discretionary trusts, especially from the anniversary charge. To qualify for this treatment, the fund must be held for the benefit of persons employed in a particular trade or profession together with their dependants.   **[26.114]**

5   Compensation funds (IHTA 1984 ss 58, 63)

Trusts set up by professional bodies and trade associations for the purpose of indemnifying clients and customers against loss incurred through the default of their members are exempt from the rules for no interest in possession trusts.   **[26.115]**

6   Newspaper trusts

The provisions relating to employee trusts (above) are extended to cover newspaper trusts such as the Scott Trust (which owned the Guardian) and the Telegraph Newspaper Trust (which owned the *Daily Telegraph*).   **[26.116]**

7   Maintenance funds for historic buildings (IHTA 1984 s 77, Sch 4)

IHT exemptions are available for maintenance funds where property is settled and the Treasury give a direction under IHTA 1984 Sch 4 para 1. Once the trust ceases, for any reason, to carry out its specialised function, an exit charge, calculated in the same way as for accumulation and maintenance trusts, occurs.   **[26.117]**

8   Protective trusts (IHTA 1984 ss 73, 88)

A protective trust is set up either by using the statutory model provided for by the Trustee Act 1925 s 33, or by express provisions which closely resemble that provision.

These trusts have always been subject to special IHT rules and, as originally enacted, the rules offered considerable scope for tax avoidance (see IHTA 1984 s 73 and *Thomas v IRC* (1981)). Accordingly the rules were changed with effect from 11 April 1978 by providing that the life tenant is deemed to continue to have an interest in possession for IHT purposes despite the forfeiture of his interest (IHTA 1984 s 88). It, therefore, follows that the discretionary trust regime is not applicable to the trust that arises upon such forfeiture. Should the capital be advanced to a person other than the life tenant, a charge to IHT will arise and on the death of the beneficiary the fund will be treated as part of his estate for IHT purposes (*Cholmondeley v IRC* (1986) and see 1987, BTR, p 55). As a result of these rules there is the curious anomaly that, after a forfeiture of the life interest, the interest in possession rules apply to a discretionary trust.

One cautionary note should be added; this system of charging only applies to protective trusts set up under Trustee Act 1925 s 33 or to trusts 'to the like effect'. Minor variations to the statutory norm are, therefore, allowed; but not perhaps the inclusion of different beneficiaries under the discretionary trust, nor a provision which enables a forfeited life interest to revive after the lapse of a period of time. In such cases, the normal rules applicable to interest in possession and discretionary trusts apply.   **[26.118]**

27 IHT—excluded property and the foreign element

As a general rule, IHT is chargeable on all property within the UK regardless of its owner's domicile and on property, wheresoever situate, which is beneficially owned by an individual domiciled in the UK.

Any transfer of 'excluded property', however, is not chargeable to IHT (IHTA 1984 ss 3(2) and 5(1)). The main example of excluded property is 'property situated outside the UK . . . if the person beneficially entitled to it is

an individual domiciled outside the UK' (IHTA 1984 s 6(1)). In determining whether property is excluded property the relevant factors include not only the domicile of the transferor who is the beneficial owner of the property and the situation of the property (situs), but also the nature of the transferred property, since certain property is excluded regardless of its situs or the domicile of its owner.   [**27.1**]

I DOMICILE AND SITUS

1 **Domicile** (and see Appendix IV)

a) *General rules*

Whether property is excluded property depends in the first place on the domicile (rather than the residence or nationality) of the transferor. An individual cannot, under English law, be without a domicile which connotes a legal relationship between an individual and a territory. There are three kinds of domicile: domicile of origin, domicile of choice and domicile of dependence.

A person acquires a *domicile of origin* at the moment when he is born. He will usually take the domicile of his father unless he is illegitimate or born after his father's death in which case he takes the domicile of his mother. A domicile of origin is never completely lost, but may be superseded by a domicile of dependence or choice; it will revive if the other type of domicile lapses.

A person cannot acquire a *domicile of choice* until he is 16 or marries under that age. Whether someone has replaced his domicile of origin (or dependence) by a domicile of choice is a question of fact which involves physical presence in the country concerned and evidence of a settled intention to remain there permanently or indefinitely (*'animus manendi'*).

Two categories of individual may acquire a *domicile by dependence*: unmarried infants under the age of 16 acquire their father's domicile by dependence and women who married before 1 January 1974 acquire their husband's domicile by dependence. **[27.2]**

b) *Deemed domicile*

If a person's domicile under the general law is outside the UK, he may be deemed to be domiciled in the UK, for IHT purposes only, in one of two circumstances (IHTA 1984 s 267).

First, if a person was domiciled in the UK on or after 10 December 1974 and within the three years immediately preceding the transfer in question, he will be deemed to be domiciled in the UK at the time of making the transfer (IHTA 1984 s 267(1)(a)). This provision is aimed at the taxpayer who moves his property out of the UK and then emigrates to avoid future IHT liability on transfers of that property. In such a case he will have to wait a further three years from the date of emigration for his property to become excluded property under IHTA 1984 s 6(1).

Secondly, a person will be deemed domiciled in the UK if he was resident for income tax purposes in the UK on or after 10 December 1974 and in not less than 17 out of the 20 income tax years ending with the income tax year in which he made the relevant transfer (IHTA 1984 s 267(1)(b)). This provision aims to catch the person who has lived in the UK for a long time even though he never became domiciled here under the general law. Residence is used in the income tax sense (see Chapter 13), but without applying the accommodation test and it is important to realise that it does not require residence for a complete period of 17 years. This is because the Act is concerned with a person who is resident in a tax year and such residence may be acquired if the individual concerned comes to the UK at the very end of that year (eg on 1 April) with the intention of remaining indefinitely in the United Kingdom. In such a case, the individual will be resident for the tax year which is about to end and that will count as the first year of residence for the purpose of the 17-year test. Similarly, were he to leave the United Kingdom immediately after the commencement of a tax year, then he would be treated as resident in the United Kingdom in that final tax year. Accordingly, in an extreme case, an individual could arrive in the United Kingdom on 1 April in one year, remain for the next 15 years and then leave on 10 April in year 17 and yet be caught by the 17-year test, even though only being resident in the United Kingdom for a little over 15 years.

EXAMPLE 27.1

(1) Jack who was domiciled in England moved to New Zealand on 1 July 1989 intending to settle there permanently. He died on 1 January 1991 when according to the general law he had acquired a domicile of choice in New Zealand. However, because Jack had a UK domicile and died within three years of losing it, he is deemed under s 267(1)(a) to have died domiciled in the UK. Accordingly, all his property wherever situated (excluding gilts; see below) is potentially chargeable to IHT. Jack would have had to survive until 1 July 1992 to avoid being caught by this provision.

(2) On 5 June 1990, Jim who is domiciled under the general law in Ruritania and who is a director of BB Ltd (the UK subsidiary of a Ruritanian company) gives a house that he owns in Ruritania to his son. By virtue of his job Jim has been resident for income tax purposes in England since 1 January 1968, but he intends to return to Ruritania when he retires. For IHT purposes

Jim is deemed to be domiciled in England under s 267(1)(b); the gift will, therefore, be subject to IHT if Jim dies within seven years.

(3)   Boer, resident in the UK but domiciled in South Africa, forms an overseas company to which he transfers the ownership of all his UK property. Accordingly he appears to have exchanged chargeable assets (UK property) for excluded property (shares in the overseas company). As a blatant tax avoidance scheme will this arrangement fall within the *Ramsay* principle? (see, for instance, *Young v Phillips* (1984) and *Capital Taxes*, 1984, p 33).

The case of *Re Clore (deceased) (No 2)* (1984) should be carefully studied by those who propose to change their domicile for tax reasons.   **[27.3]**

2   Situs

Subject to contrary provisions in double taxation treaties (and special rules for certain property) the situs of property depends on common law rules and on the type of property involved. For instance:

(1)   An interest in land (including a leasehold estate or rentcharge) is situated where the land is physically located.

(2)   Chattels (other than ships and aircraft) are situated at the place where they are kept at the relevant time.

(3)   Registered shares and securities are situated where they are registered or, if transferable upon more than one register, where they would normally be dealt with in the ordinary course of business.

(4)   Bearer shares and securities, transferable by delivery, are situated where the certificate or other document of title is kept.

(5)   A bank account (ie the debt owed by the bank) is situated at the branch which maintains the account. (Special rules deal with non-residents' foreign currency bank accounts; IHTA 1984 s 157.)   **[27.4]–[27.20]**

"Im not complaining. Henry, it's just that I always think of sunshine, palm-fringed beaches and villas whenever I think of taxhavens . . ."

II WHAT IS EXCLUDED PROPERTY?

1 Property situated outside the UK and owned beneficially by a non-UK domiciliary (IHTA 1984 s 6(1))

All property falling into this category is excluded regardless of its nature. Settled property situated abroad will be excluded property if the settlor was domiciled outside the UK at the time when he made the settlement (IHTA 1984 s 48(3)). In deciding whether the transferor is a UK domiciliary at the time of the transfer the deeming provisions of IHTA 1984 s 267 will generally operate. If the settlor retains an interest in possession either for himself or his spouse, an additional test is imposed in determining whether property is excluded property. This test looks at where the settlor or the spouse (if the interest was reserved for him) was domiciled when that interest in possession ended (IHTA 1984 s 82). As this provision only applies where the property is *initially* settled with a life interest on the settlor or his spouse, it may be circumvented if the trust commences in discretionary form and is then converted into a life interest.   **[27.21]**

EXAMPLE 27.2

(1) Franc, domiciled in Belgium, intends to buy a house in East Anglia. If he buys it in his own name it will be subject to IHT on his death. If he buys it through an overseas company, however, he will then own overseas assets (the company shares) which fall outside the IHT net. Note that if he occupies the house and is a director of the overseas company, the Revenue will probably seek to tax him on an emolument equal to the value of the property each year under the provisions of TA 1988 s 145 (see *Example 5.11*).

(2) Erik, domiciled in Sweden, settles Swedish property on discretionary trusts for himself and his family. He subsequently acquires an English domicile of choice. The settlement is excluded property for IHT purposes (IHTA 1984 s 48(3)), although the assets form part of the settlor's estate when he dies because of the reservation of benefit rules in FA 1986 s 102(3). The Revenue accept in this case that the property remains excluded so that it will not be subject to any charge. The position is, however, less clear if Erik is excluded from all benefit during his life when a deemed PET occurs under s 102(4).

(3) Boris, domiciled in France, died in February 1989 and left his villa in Tuscany and moneys in his Swiss bank account to his son Gaspard, a UK resident. By a variation of the terms of his will made within two years of Boris' death the property is settled on discretionary Liechtenstein trusts for the benefit of Gaspard's family. *For IHT,* reading back ensures that the settlement is excluded property. *For CGT,* however, s 49(6)(b) provides that *for the purposes of that section* the variation shall be treated as effected by the deceased. Whether this means that for the purposes of FA 1981 s 80 an overseas settlement has been created by Boris (a non-UK domiciliary) or by Gaspard, is therefore far from clear. If the former, no CGT charges will arise on UK beneficiaries who receive capital payments from the trustees. Revenue practice is to treat the settlement as created by Gaspard but a recent decision of the Special Commissioners—which is to be appealed—suggests that this is not correct.

2 Property which is exempt despite being situated in the UK

Government securities Certain government securities (gilts) issued before 18 March 1977 and beneficially owned by a person neither domiciled nor ordinarily resident in the UK are exempt from IHT (IHTA 1984 s 6(2)). The deeming provisions of IHTA 1984 s 267 do not apply to such transferors. Such gilts also receive privileged treatment for CGT (CGTA 1979 s 67 and Sch 2; FA 1985 s 67) and for income tax (TA 1988 s 47). If these securities are settled they will be excluded property if either the person beneficially entitled to an interest in possession (eg a life tenant) is neither domiciled nor ordinarily resident in the UK, or, in the case of a discretionary trust, if none of the beneficiaries are domiciled or ordinarily resident in the UK (IHTA 1984 s 48(4)).

IHTA 1984 s 48(5) introduced anti-avoidance provisions:
(1) If gilts are transferred from one settlement to another they will only be excluded property if the beneficiaries of *both* settlements are non-UK resident or domiciled. This prevents gilts from being channelled from a discretionary trust where they were not excluded property (because some of the beneficiaries were UK domiciled and/or resident) to a new settlement with non-domiciled beneficiaries only, where they would be excluded property (as was done in *Minden Trust (Cayman) Ltd v IRC* (1984)).
(2) Where a close company is a beneficiary of a trust, any gilts owned by the trust will be excluded property only if all participators in the company are non-UK domiciled and resident, irrespective of the company's domicile. This aims to prevent individuals from using a company to avoid IHT.

This privileged tax treatment only applies to gilts issued before 18 March 1977. All transfers of value of gilts issued thereafter are chargeable to IHT even if in the beneficial ownership of individuals domiciled and resident outside the UK.   **[27.22]**

Certain property owned by persons domiciled in the Channel Islands or Isle of Man
Certain savings (eg national savings certificates) are excluded property if they are in the beneficial ownership of a person domiciled and resident in the Channel Islands or the Isle of Man (IHTA 1984 ss 6(3), 267(4)).   **[27.23]**

Visiting forces   Certain property owned in the UK by visiting forces and staff of allied headquarters is excluded property (IHTA 1984 s 155). **[27.24]**

Overseas pensions   Certain overseas pensions (usually payable by ex-colonial governments) are exempt from IHT on the pensioner's death regardless of his domicile (IHTA 1984 s 153).   **[27.25]–[27.40]**

For the inter-relationship of excluded property and settlements see below.

III   DOUBLE TAXATION RELIEF FOR NON-EXCLUDED PROPERTY

Non-excluded property may be (exposed to a double charge to tax (especially on the death of the owner); once to IHT in the UK and again to a similar tax imposed by a foreign country. Relief against such double charge may be afforded in one of two ways.

First, the UK may have a double taxation treaty with the relevant country when the position is governed by IHTA 1984 s 158. The provisions of the treaty will override all the relevant IHT legislation and common law rules regarding the situs of property (for the individual provisions of each such treaty see Foster *Capital Taxes Encyclopaedia, foreign element, F4*).

Under these treaties, the country in which the transferor is domiciled is generally entitled to tax all property of which he was the beneficial owner. The other country involved usually has the right to tax some of that property, eg land situated there. In such cases the country of domicile will give relief against the resulting double taxation. Most of these treaties also contain provisions to catch the individual who changes his domicile shortly before death to avoid tax.

Secondly, where no double taxation treaty exists, unilateral relief is given in the form of a credit for the foreign tax liability against IHT payable in the UK (IHTA 1984 s 159). The amount of the credit depends on where the relevant property is situated; in some cases no credit is available if the overseas tax is not similar to IHT, although some relief is, effectively, given since, in calculating the reduction in the transferor's estate for calculating IHT, the amount of overseas tax paid will be disregarded (IHTA 1984 s 5(3)). This relief is naturally less beneficial than a tax credit because the transferor must still bear the double tax. **[27.41]-[27.60]**

IV MISCELLANEOUS POINTS

1 Valuation of the estate—allowable deductions

Certain liabilities of a transferor are deductible when calculating the value of his estate for IHT purposes (see **[22.13]**). However, any liability to a non-UK resident is deductible as far as possible from a transferor's foreign before his UK estate. As a result, a foreign domiciliary who is chargeable to IHT on his UK assets cannot usually deduct his foreign liabilities from his UK estate. There are two exceptions to this rule. First, if a liability of a non-UK resident has to be discharged in the UK, it is deductible from the UK estate; secondly, any liability which encumbers property in the UK, reduces the value of that property. **[27.61]**

EXAMPLE 27.3

Adolphus dies domiciled in Ethiopia. His estate includes cash in a London bank account, shares in UK companies and a stud farm in Weybridge which is mortgaged to an Ethiopian glue factory. He owes a UK travel company £500 for a ticket bought to enable his daughter to travel around Texas and £200,000 to a Dallas horse dealer. IHT is chargeable on his UK assets. However, the loan is deductible from the value of his stud farm and £500 is deductible from the UK estate generally. There is no reduction for the debt of £200,000 assuming he has sufficient foreign property.

2 Expenses of administering property abroad

Administration expenses are not generally deductible from the value of the deceased's estate. However, the expense of administering or realising property situated abroad on death is deductible from the value of the relevant property up to a limit of 5% of its value. **[27.62]**

3 Enforcement of tax abroad

On the death of a foreign domiciliary with UK assets, the deceased's PRs cannot administer his property until they have paid any IHT and obtained a grant of probate. However, the collection of IHT on lifetime transfers by a foreign domiciliary presents a problem if both the transferor and transferee are resident outside the UK and there is no available property in the UK which can be impounded.   **[27.63]**

4 Foreign assets

If a foreign government imposes restrictions as a result of which UK executors cannot immediately transfer to this country sufficient of the deceased's foreign assets for the payment of inheritance tax attributable to them, they are given the option of deferring payment until that transfer can be made. If the amount that is finally brought into the UK is less than the IHT, any balance will be waived (see ESC F6).   **[27.64]-[27.80]**

V FOREIGN SETTLEMENTS, REVERSIONARY INTERESTS AND EXCLUDED PROPERTY

1 Foreign settlements

As a general rule settled property which is situated abroad is excluded property if the settlor was domiciled outside the UK when the settlement was made (IHTA 1984 s 48(3)). The domicile deeming provisions of IHTA 1984 s 267 only apply to a settlor who settled property after 10 December 1974. Therefore, the domicile of the individual beneficiaries under a foreign settlement is irrelevant, so that even if a beneficiary is domiciled in the UK, there will be no charge to IHT on the termination of his interest in possession nor on any payment made to him from a discretionary trust.   **[27.81]**

EXAMPLE 27.4

Generous, domiciled in the USA, settles shares in US companies on his nephew, Tom, for life. Tom is domiciled and resident in the UK. The property is excluded property, being property situated abroad settled by a settlor domiciled at that time outside the UK, so that there will be no charge to IHT on the ending of Tom's life interest.

If, however, those shares were exchanged for shares in UK companies, the property would no longer be excluded and there would be a charge to IHT on the termination of Tom's life interest.

If Generous had settled those same US shares on discretionary trusts for his nephews, all of whom were UK domiciled, the property would be, for the same reason, excluded property, so that the normal discretionary trust charges to IHT will not apply.

2 Reversionary interests

a) Definition

For IHT purposes any future interest in settled property is classified as a reversionary interest. The term, therefore, includes an interest dependent on the termination of an interest in possession, whether that interest is vested or contingent. A contingent interest where the settlement does not have an interest in possession is also a reversionary interest for IHT purposes.

EXAMPLE 27.5

Property is settled on the following trusts:
(1) A for life, remainder to B for life, remainder to C. B and C both have reversionary interests for IHT purposes.
(2) A for life, remainder to B for life, remainder to C if he survives B. C's contingent remainder is a reversionary interest for IHT purposes.
(3) To A absolutely contingent upon his attaining the age of 21. A is currently aged six and has a reversionary interest for IHT purposes.

The interest of a discretionary beneficiary is not, however, a 'reversionary interest', being in no sense a future interest. Such a beneficiary has certain present rights, particularly the right to be considered by the trustees when they exercise their discretion and the right to compel due administration of the fund. The value of such an interest is likely to be nil, however, since the beneficiary has no right to any of the income or capital of the settlement. He has merely a hope (*'spes'*). **[27.82]**

b) *'Situs' of a reversionary interest*

A reversionary interest under a trust for sale is a chose in action rather than an interest in the specific settled assets be they land or personalty (*Re Smyth, Leach v Leach* (1898)). In other cases the position is unclear; but by analogy with estate duty principles it will be a chose in action if the settled assets are personalty; but an interest in the settled assets themselves if they are land. Since a chose in action is normally situated in the country in which it is recoverable (*New York Life Insurance Co v Public Trustee* (1924)), in some cases the reversionary interest will not be situated in the same place as the settled assets. **[27.83]**

c) *Reversionary interests—the general rule*

A reversionary interest is excluded property for IHT (IHTA 1984 s 48(1); see **[25.61]**) with three exceptions designed to counter tax avoidance:
(1) Where it was purchased for money or money's worth. **[27.84]**

EXAMPLE 27.6

There is a settlement on A for life, remainder to B. B sells his interest to X who gives it to his brother Y. X has made a transfer of value (a PET) of a reversionary interest (which can be valued by taking into account the value of the settled fund and the life expectancy of A).

(2) Where it is an interest to which the settlor or his spouse is beneficially entitled.
(3) Where a lease for life or lives is granted for no or partial consideration, there is a settlement for IHT (IHTA 1984 s 43(3)) and the lessor's interest is a reversionary interest (IHTA 1984 s 47). Such a reversionary interest is only excluded property to the extent that the lessor did not receive full consideration on the grant (see IHTA 1984 s 48(1)(c) for valuation of the lessee's interest in possession and IHTA 1984 s 170 for the valuation of the lessor's interest).

EXAMPLE 27.7

L grants a lease of property worth £30,000 to T for £10,000 for T's life. T is treated for IHT purposes, as having an interest in possession and, therefore, as absolute owner of two-thirds of the property (£30,000—£10,000). L is treated as the owner of one-third of the property (because he received £10,000). Therefore, one-third of his reversionary interest is not excluded property.

d) *Reversionary interests—the foreign element*

Under IHTA 1984 s 48(1) a reversionary interest (with the three exceptions above) is excluded property regardless of the domicile of the settlor or reversioner or the situs of the interest. Where the settled property is in the UK, but the reversionary interest is situated abroad (see b) above) and beneficially owned by a foreign domiciliary, the interest probably is excluded property in all cases under the general rule of IHTA 1984 s 6(1).

However, the status of a reversionary interest in settled property situated outside the UK is cast into some doubt by virtue of IHTA 1984 s 48(3) to which s 6(1) is expressly made subject (IHTA 1984 s 48(3)(b)). Section 48(3) states:

'where property comprised in a settlement is situated outside the UK
(a)   the property (but not a reversionary interest in the property) is excluded property unless the settlor was domiciled in the UK at the time the settlement was made; and
(b)   section 6(1) above applies to a reversionary interest in the property, but does not otherwise apply in relation to the property.'

This provision appears to exclude the operation of s 48(1) by saying that a reversionary interest in settled property situated abroad is only excluded property (under the general rule in s 6(1)) if it is itself situated abroad and owned by a foreign domiciliary.

However, it has been suggested that s 48(3) only prevails over s 48(1) in cases of conflict and that there is no conflict here since the words 'but not a reversionary interest' in s 48(3)(a) simply mean that whether a reversionary interest is excluded property depends not on the *situs* of the settled property nor on the settlor's domicile, but on the general rule in s 48(1).

In summary, therefore, a reversionary interest is always excluded property regardless of *situs* or domicile with three exceptions (see [**25.61**]). Even if the interest falls within one of the exceptions, it will still be excluded property if the interest (regardless of the whereabouts of the settled property) is situated outside the UK and beneficially owned by a foreign domiciliary (IHTA 1984 s 6(1)); or if the reversionary interest is itself settled property, is situated abroad and was settled by a foreign domiciliary (IHTA 1984 s 6(1) and s 48(3)).

For a discussion of the tax planning opportunities afforded by reversionary interests see [**37.24**].   [**27.85**]

Section 5 Business enterprise and stamp duty

Chapters

28 Corporation tax

'The major reform of business taxation, which I introduced in 1984, and which was completed in 1986, has given us one of the lowest corporation tax rates in the world. This has encouraged overseas companies to invest in Britain and, most important of all, has greatly improved the quality of investment by British firms. It is a crucial part of an environment in which company profitability has recovered to its highest level for some twenty years. It has succeeded in its objectives.'
(Chancellor of the Exchequer, the Rt Hon Nigel Lawson MP, Budget Statement 15 March 1988.)   **[28.1]**

I INTRODUCTION

Corporation tax was introduced by FA 1965 and applies to all bodies corporate including authorised unit trusts and unincorporated associations (see, for instance, *Blackpool Marton v Martin* (1990) in which an unincorporated members' club was liable to corporation tax) but not partnerships or local authorities. It is levied on the profits of a company which are made up of both income profits, computed according to income tax principles, and capital profits which will be assessed in accordance with CGT rules. The 1965 legislation was substantially amended by FA 1972 (with effect from 1 April 1973); it is common to refer to the system in force from 1966 to 1973 as the *classical* system and that introduced in 1973 (and still in force today) as the *imputation* system.

The classical system had two main features. First, dividends, and company distributions generally, were not allowed as deductions in arriving at profits; instead they were payable out of net profits and were further subject to income tax (and, if relevant, to surtax) in the hands of the recipient. Secondly, a special category of company, the close company, was created which was to be subject to special rules largely designed to frustrate the use of small companies in tax planning schemes.

The Conservative government (1970-74) introduced changes in the operation of corporation tax. The special penalties suffered by close companies were gradually reduced but, most significantly, the imputation system fundamentally altered the rules dealing with the taxation of distributions. In general, the new system was designed to achieve parity in the taxation of a company's profits whether those profits were retained or distributed to shareholders, since the classical system had resulted in the double taxation of distributions, first as profits of the company and then as dividends in the hands of the shareholder. The cornerstone of the new system was advance corporation tax (ACT) which is generally payable on all company distributions. ACT serves a dual purpose since it represents a payment of both corporation tax for the company and basic rate income tax for the recipient shareholder.

Although the imputation system has been retained in its essential features, changes made to corporation tax by subsequent Finance Acts have substantially altered its impact. The major reduction in the rates of corporation tax combined with the phased abolition of the 100% first year capital allowance (see Chapter 7) resulted in Inland Revenue statistics showing a dramatically increased tax yield from companies as compared with earlier years. The FA 1984 reduction in rates also marked a shift away from the old classical system since, for small companies, the reduction has rendered dividends (in effect) tax deductible and for other companies has virtually eradicated the element of double charge.

One major criticism of the imputation system remains. It produces inequality of treatment as between the company and the unincorporated business: in particular, the small company is able to avoid any substantial levy to corporation tax by, for instance, paying out its 'profits' as salaries to its director-shareholders. A Green Paper (Cmnd 8456, January 1982) which discussed alternatives to the present system has never been implemented.   **[28.2]–[28.20]**

II   GENERAL PRINCIPLES—RATES OF TAX

The tax is charged by reference to financial years (FY) which run from 1 April to 31 March and are referred to by the calendar year in which they commence. Hence, FY 1991 means the financial year running from 1 April 1991 to 31 March 1992. The rate at which corporation tax is charged was formerly fixed in arrears; however, FA 1984 fixed the rate for 1983 at 50% but also provided that for FYs 1984, 1985, and 1986 the rate should be 45%, 40%, and 35% respectively. The rate remained 35% in FYs 1987, 1988 and 1989. FA 1991 reduced the rate for FY 1990 to 34% and introduced a rate of 33% for 1991 (the special rate for small companies is discussed at **[28.23]**). Where companies are wound up, the rate charged during their final financial year will be that fixed for the preceding financial year (TA 1988 s 342(2)).

In tabular form the rates are as follows:

Financial year	Rate (%)
1983	50
1984	45
1985	40
1986	35
1987	35
1988	35
1989	35
1990	34
1991	33

Corporation tax is charged on a current year basis on the company's profits of the financial year. Therefore, where a company's accounting period straddles two financial years the profits must be apportioned on a time basis (TA 1988 s 8(3)).

EXAMPLE 28.1

Grr Ltd makes up its accounts to 31 December. For the years ended 1990 and 1991 its trading profits were £2,000,000 and £1,600,000 respectively. The rate of corporation tax for FY 1989 is 35%; for 1990 is 34% and for 1991 33%.

The tax will be calculated as follows:

(i) *Profits of £2,000,000 apportioned:*
January 1990–April 1990:
3/12 of £2,000,000 = £500,000 taxed at 35% (FY 1989)
April 1990–December 1990:
9/12 of £2,000,000 = £1,500,000 taxed at 34% (FY 1990)
(ii) *Profits of £1,600,000 apportioned:*
January 1991–April 1991:
3/12 of £1,600,000 = £400,000 taxed at 34% (FY 1990)
April 1991–December 1991:
9/12 of £1,600,000 = £1,200,000 taxed at 33% (FY 1991)

The tax is payable within nine months after the end of the accounting period on which it was assessed or (if later) within one month from the making of the assessment. Hence, in *Example 28.1* the tax will normally be due by 30 September in each year.

An important exception applied to trading companies incorporated before the introduction of corporation tax in 1966 which retained their interval of payment from the earlier income tax system, thereby enabling them to delay payment of tax by a maximum of 21 months after the end of their accounting period (TA 1970 s 244). In order to prevent abuses of this benefit (and in particular the sale of such companies), TA 1988 Sch 30 provided for TA 1970 s 244 to cease to apply for accounting periods beginning after 16 March 1987. Instead, for that accounting period and the following two periods, the payment of tax was accelerated in three equal stages in order to reach the normal nine month payment date by the end of the third accounting period. **[28.21]**

1 Capital gains

The capital gains of a company are included in its profits and charged to corporation tax at the rate in force for the relevant financial year. For accounting periods ending before 17 March 1987, relief from the full tax rate was obtained by ensuring that such gains were charged to corporation tax at the same rate as for the gains of an individual.

For accounting periods beginning after 16 March 1987, however, chargeable gains were made subject to the full corporation tax rate in force in the financial year in which the gain is made. As a result the corporation tax rate on a gain realised in FY 1991 will be 33% (unless the 25% small company rate applies: see below). Unlike individuals, companies are not entitled to an annual exemption. **[28.22]**

2 The small company rate

A measure of relief from the full corporation tax rate is provided by the small company rate which, for FY 1991, is 25%, the same as the basic rate of income tax (TA 1988 s 13). This rate applies to any company (other than a close investment-holding company—see [**28.129**]) whose profits, both income and capital, do not exceed £250,000 in the accounting period. The 25% rate may offer an advantage to the small company since it is significantly less than the 40% higher rate which may apply to an individual's income and capital gains.

Where a company's profits exceed £250,000 but not £1,250,000 tapering relief is available, the effect of which is (for FY 1991) to impose corporation tax at the rate of 35% on profits above £250,000 but below £1,250,000. This avoids a sudden leap to the full rate of corporation tax. The corporation tax definition of a small company is purely related to its profits for any particular financial year and for this purpose profits include franked investment income (see [**28.42**]).

If a company wishes to take advantage of TA 1988 s 13 it must submit an appropriate claim. In practice, this will require a clear indication in the company's return that the profit should be charged at the small companies rate or that marginal relief is appropriate. Any such statement should also indicate whether or not there are associated companies (see SP 1/91).

Changes in the small company rate and in the definition of the small company itself may be tabulated as follows:

Financial year	Small company rate (%)	Profit limit (£)	Higher limit (£)	Taper (%)
1988	25	100,000	500,000	37.5
1989	25	150,000	750,000	37.5
1990	25	200,000	1,000,000	36.25
1991	25	250,000	1,250,000	35

EXAMPLE 28.2

(1) Zee Ltd makes up its accounts to 31 March each year. For the year ending 31 March 1992 the company had trading profits of £80,000 and had made chargeable gains of £42,000.

The profits of Zee Ltd for corporation tax purposes are:

	£
Trading (ie income) profits	80,000
Chargeable gains	42,000
Chargeable profits	£122,000

Zee Ltd will, therefore, qualify for the small companies rate so that corporation tax will be charged as follows:

Chargeable profits (£122,000) at 25% = £30,500

(2) Were the income profits of Zee Ltd to be £280,000 then, with the addition of chargeable gains (£42,000), the small companies threshold of £250,000 would be exceeded by £72,000 so that a form of tapering relief would apply as follows:

(i) Corporation tax payable:
£322,000 (ie £280,000 + £42,000) × 33%   £106,260

(ii) Less tapering relief (TA 1988 s 13(2)):
(upper relevant amount — profits) × statutory fraction

ie $(£1,250,000 - £322,000) \times \dfrac{1}{50}$ (ie 2%)

$£18,560$

(iii) Total tax ((i) — (ii)) $£87,700$

Two points should be stressed in connection with the small companies rate. *First*, anti-avoidance provisions exist to prevent the fragmentation of a business amongst subsidiaries in an attempt to create a whole series of small companies. *Secondly*, although tapering relief (also known as the marginal rate) applies where profits fall into the range £250,000 to £1,250,000, this does not mean that the tax on profits in excess of £250,000 is at a rate below 33%. This is because the purpose of tapering relief is to increase gradually the average rate of corporation tax from the 25% payable by a company with profits of £250,000 to the 33% payable by a company with profits of £1,250,000. To achieve this result the rate applicable to the slice of profits between £250,000 and £1,250,000 has to *exceed* 33%. At present this marginal rate is 35% calculated as follows:

Tax on £250,000 at 25%	=	£62,500
Tax on £1,250,000 at 33%	=	£412,500
Difference (£412,500 — £62,500)	=	£350,000

Therefore, £350,000 corporation tax has to be raised on profits falling between £250,000 and £1,250,000 (ie on £1,000,000).
Hence, as a percentage, tax on £1,000,000 will be

$$\frac{350,000}{1,000,000} \times 100 = 35\%$$

Thus, continuing *Example 28.3(2)* (above)
Corporation tax of £87,700 on profits of £322,000 can be analysed as:

		£
First £250,000 of profits at 25%	=	62,500
Final £72,000 of profit at 35%	=	£25,200
		£87,700

In determining whether tapering relief is available, franked investment income ('FII') is taken into account (see **[28.42]** for the meaning of FII). Broadly, tapering relief is not available on the profits of a company insofar as those profits include FII, other than FII received from a member of the same group of companies. Accordingly, if the profits of a company include FII the tapering relief calculation set out in *Example 28.2(2)* must be adjusted.

EXAMPLE 28.3

HN Limited makes up accounts to 31 March each year. For this year ended 31 March 1992 the company has trading profits of £300,000 and receives FII of £200,000 from another (non-group) UK company (ie £150,000 + £50,000 tax credit).

The corporation tax calculation is as follows:

(1) Tax at 33% on £300,000 £99,000
(the dividend income is ignored at this stage)

(ii) Less tapering relief:

$$(\text{upper relevant amount} - \text{profits}) \times \text{statutory fraction} \times \frac{\text{basic profits}}{\text{profits}}$$

'*basic profits*' means profits subject to corporation tax
'*profits*' means basic profits plus FII

$$\text{ie } (1,250,000 - 300,000) \times \frac{1}{50} \times \frac{300,000}{500,000} = £11,400$$

(iii) Total tax ((i) — (ii)) = £87,600

The fact that a company's profits may just exceed £250,000 thereby attracting this relatively high marginal rate of 35% on the excess over £250,000 is of practical significance when considering how much money the directors of family companies should take by way of remuneration (or how much should be paid into the company's pension scheme). The marginal corporation tax rate exceeds the basic rate of income tax so that it will be advantageous to pay out such moneys in the form of salaries in cases where the directors are not liable to income tax at rates exceeding 25% or by making increased contributions to the company pension scheme. Thus, in *Example 28.2(2)* above, the directors of Zee Ltd should consider paying themselves increased salaries or bonuses of £72,000 before 31 March 1992. In this way, the company's taxable profits for that accounting period will be reduced to £250,000 which (taxed at 25%) results in a tax saving of £25,200 (£87,700 — £62,500) (see further Chapter 32). **[28.23]–[28.40]**

III HOW TO CALCULATE THE PROFITS OF A COMPANY

Profits of a company are defined as including both income profits and capital gains (TA 1988 s 6(4)(a)). **[28.41]**

1 Income profits

a) *General principles*

Generally, income profits have to be computed in accordance with the income tax rules that apply in the year of assessment in which the company's accounting period ends (TA 1988 s 9). Each class of income will, therefore, be calculated under the same Schedules that apply for income tax. Thus, a trading company having no other income will compute its profits in accordance with the rules of Schedule D Case I so that the rules for what expenditure is deductible (discussed in Chapter 6) apply to companies. Accordingly, the salaries and fees paid to its directors and employees will be allowable expenses under TA 1988 s 74 but note that TA 1988 s 337(2)(b) prohibits the deduction, as an expense, of annual payments, annuities, and yearly- interest unless paid on a loan from a bank carrying on business in the UK. Such payments must be relieved, if at all, as charges on income (see **[28.44]**). **[28.42]**

b) *Foreign exchange gains and losses*

In *Beauchamp v F W Woolworth plc* (1989) the Law Lords disallowed a claim to deduct exchange losses because the loans were capital in nature and so any loss could not give rise to an income deduction. In general terms, when a taxpayer borrows money for a fixed period (eg five years) he obtains an asset or advantage which endures for that period. The loan will only be a Revenue transaction if it is part of the day-to-day incidents of carrying on the business and if it is both temporary and fluctuating. The current position is far from satisfactory and it is hoped that the Consultation Document ('Foreign Exchange Gains and Losses') published on 19 March 1991 will lead to reforms. **[28.43]**

c) *Employee trusts*

Payments into employee trusts may constitute deductible expenditure if they are of an income nature (see *Heather v P E Consulting Group* (1978), discussed at [**6.112**]). If the trust qualifies as a statutory 'ESOP', however, deduction will always be given even if the payments are strictly of a capital sum (ESOPs are discussed in Chapter 34). **[28.44]**

d) *Franked investment income*

In calculating income profits no account is taken of dividends and other distributions received by one UK company from another (*franked investment income:* TA 1988 s 208). The utilisation of such income is considered at [**28.98**]. Notice, however, that franked investment income (FII) is included in the profits of a company for the purpose of discovering whether the small companies rate is applicable and calculating how much tapering relief is available, although this income is not then taxed (TA 1988 s 13(7) and see *Example 28.3*). Where income is received by a company net of income tax deducted at source (eg building society interest, debenture interest and annuities received by companies), the gross income is included in the profits of the company and a credit is given against the corporation tax payable for the tax deducted at source.

EXAMPLE 28.4

Lexo Ltd makes up its accounts to 31 March each year. The accounts for the period ending 31 March 1992 show the following:

		£
Trading profit		210,000
Profit from lettings		40,000
Building society interest received:		
net	£37,500	
plus tax credit	£12,500	
Gross		50,000
Total profits		£300,000

	£
Corporation tax payable:	
£250,000 at 25% + £50,000 at 35%	80,000
Less building society tax credit	12,500
	£67,500

Notes
(1) The trading profit is calculated according to the rules of Schedule D Case I, for 1991/92, and the profit from lettings according to Schedule A.
(2) Building society interest is not franked investment income, but is treated in the same way as other sums received subject to deduction of income

tax at source. If the tax credit exceeded the corporation tax payable, the excess would be repaid to the company.

The income tax principles are relevant only in determining the amount of the company's income profits—other enactments of that legislation are not relevant. Thus the preceding year rules and the opening and closing year provisions of Schedule D have no application to companies and there is no question of any personal reliefs or allowances applying. The system of capital allowances applies to companies with suitable modifications (see Chapter 7). The specific difficulties that may arise when an existing business or partnership is converted into a company are dealt with separately in Chapter 33.   **[28.45]**

2   Capital gains

A company's chargeable gains are computed in the same way as for an individual. Hence, the definition of chargeable assets and the occasions when a disposal occurs are common to both individuals and companies. The annual exemption (currently £5,500) is not available for disposals by companies. In the case of disposals between companies in the same group the disposal is treated as giving rise to neither gain nor loss until either the asset is disposed of outside the group or until the recipient company leaves the group (see **[28.145]**). A disadvantage suffered by a company and its shareholders is that on any capital gain realised by the company there is an element of double taxation since not only will the company suffer corporation tax on the gain, but also the shareholder whose shares may have increased in value as a result of the capital profit (albeit, after tax) will suffer capital gains tax when he disposes of those shares.

> **EXAMPLE 28.5**
>
> Saloman Ltd (a small company wholly owned by John Saloman) makes a chargeable gain of £100,000. It will suffer corporation tax of £25,000 (25%) on that gain. Saloman's shares will have increased in value by, say, £75,000 so that were he to sell them he would suffer capital gains tax at (say) 40% of (ignoring exemptions and reliefs) £30,000. Effectively, therefore, the corporate gain has been subject to tax at 55% (25% paid by the company and 30% by Saloman). If Saloman Ltd were not a small company this percentage would be 59.8% (33% paid by the company and 26.8% by Saloman). Consider extracting the profit by the payment of a dividend: **[32.51]**.

Vesting appreciating assets in private companies may, therefore, be tax inefficient and it may be better for the shareholder to retain those assets and lease them to the company (see **[32.57]**).   **[28.46]**

3   Deducting charges on income

TA 1988 s 338(1) provides that:

> '... any charges on income paid by the company in the accounting period, so far as paid out of the company's profits brought into charge to corporation tax shall be allowed as deductions against the total profits for the period as reduced by any other relief from tax other than group relief'.

It follows that such charges may be set against all the company's profits, including chargeable gains. As the charges reduce profits any deductions arrived at in calculating those profits cannot be deducted a second time as a charge (TA 1988 s 338(2)). Interest payments, for instance, which are deducted as a business expense in arriving at trading profits under the Schedule D Case I rules cannot be deducted a second time as a charge. As s 338(1) refers to sums actually paid, it is important for a company to organise, so far as possible, its payments which constitute charges on income to be made at the end of one accounting period rather than at the beginning of the next in order to obtain the earliest possible tax relief. Where charges exceed the total profits for the year, the excess will still qualify for a measure of tax relief (see [28.46]; contrast the position of individual taxpayers who obtain no relief). [28.47]

a) *Meaning of 'charges on income'*

The following are the main charges on income:
(a) annual interest, annuities or any other annual payment;
(b) any other interest payable on a loan from a bank carrying on a bona fide banking business in the UK (see *Hafton Properties Ltd v McHugh* (1987)); and
(c) royalties and sums paid in respect of user of a patent and certain mining rents and royalties.

Hence, debenture interest falls under (a) above, whilst short term interest falls within (b), although the standard example, the bank overdraft, would usually be deducted as a business expense in arriving at profits. These permitted charges can only be deducted if:
(1) The payment is to be borne by the company. Thus, no deduction is allowed where a right to reimbursement exists.
(2) The payment must be charged to income in the company's accounts, except that deduction will be permitted for interest payments even though the payment appears in the company's books as a capital expense (TA 1988 s 338(3)).
(3) The payment, except for certain payments to charity, must be made under a liability incurred for valuable and sufficient consideration.

EXAMPLE 28.6

Zeus Ltd makes the following covenanted payments:
(i) £5,000 pa to the Society to Promote Antiquarian Studies (a registered charity).
(ii) £8,000 pa to the trustees of a trust fund set up by the company to educate the children of its employees and to provide evening classes in arts and crafts for its employees.

The payment of £5,000 pa: will be a charge on income so long as it is capable of lasting for more than three years (TA 1988 s 339(8)). The charity will obtain a full tax rebate so that basic rate income tax (deducted at source by the company under TA 1988 s 349 (see Chapter 10)) will be refunded.
The payment of £8,000 pa: is not a charitable payment (see *Oppenheim v Tobacco Securities Trust Co Ltd* (1951)) and will only be an allowable charge if incurred for suitable consideration. In *Ball v National & Grindlay's Bank Ltd* (1971) the Court of Appeal concluded that at the time when the covenant was made it must be possible to show that the company was receiving adequate consideration for the payments. Such consideration could be in the form of money or money's worth including an obligation to the company. Hence, it is likely that the £8,000

would *not* be deductible as a charge since it will not suffice to show that there was some business advantage in making the payment, and no consideration in money or money's worth is being received by the company. Such payments do not offer tax advantages, therefore, and the company might be advised to avoid the use of annual payments altogether and to argue that the costs of establishing and maintaining the trust are allowable business expenses and, therefore, deductible under TA 1988 s 74 in arriving at profits (see TA 1988 s 337(2)(b)).

FA 1986 created a new form of charge on income for 'qualifying donations' to charity made by non-close resident companies. The sum must *not* have been payable under a deed of covenant nor deductible in arriving at the company's profits: hence the relief was for 'one-off' payments. In respect of payments made before 19 March 1991 a single donation equal to no more than 3% of the dividends paid on the company's ordinary shares could be paid as a qualifying donation. There is no such limit on payments made on or after that date (see generally on 'Gift Aid' Appendix IX). As in the case of covenanted payments, income tax at the basic rate must be deducted by the paying company and may be recovered by the recipient charity. In the hands of the charity the payment is treated as if it were made under covenant so that the basic rate income tax can be reclaimed.

(4) Interest payments must be paid by a company which exists wholly or mainly for the purpose of carrying on a trade (or alternatively the payment must be wholly and exclusively laid out for trading purposes); or the company must be an investment company (including an authorised unit trust); or the relevant loan must be to purchase land occupied by the company. These requirements are not particularly demanding since virtually all companies will be trading or investment companies (note, however, difficulties for an unincorporated association which does not trade; although it pays corporation tax, it cannot deduct interest payments).　　　　　　　　　　　　　　　　　　　　　　**[28.48]**

b) *Interest payments: charges or deductible expenses?*

As discussed above, interest payments may be treated as a deductible expense (thereby reducing trading profits) or as a charge on income (reducing total profits from whatever source the company may choose). There may be tax advantages in ensuring that the interest is treated as either a charge or deduction depending on the circumstances.

EXAMPLE 28.7

(1) Depressed Ltd has unrelieved trading losses carried forward (see **[28.52]**) of £5,000; trading profits in the current year of £6,000; Schedule A income of £4,000; and has made interest payments of £5,000. If the interest payments are deducted as an expense of the trade, Depressed Ltd will pay corporation tax as follows:

　(i) trading profits (£6,000) less interest (£5,000) = £1,000. Then deduct losses carried forward (£1,000) so that trading profit is reduced to nil leaving £4,000 unrelieved losses.

　(ii) Schedule A income (£4,000) subject to corporation tax.

By contrast, if the interest had been treated as a charge on income, the position would have been:

(i) Schedule A income (£4,000), deduct interest (a charge) so that it is reduced to nil.

(ii) trading profits (£6,000), deduct unrelieved interest charge (£1,000) and all carried forward losses so that profit reduced to nil.

(2) Loss Maker Ltd has no income profits and has made interest payments. It had made trading profits in its previous accounting period. If the interest payments are treated as charges the only relief available will be to carry them forward as a trading expense (see [**28.52**]). By contrast, if the interest were a deductible trading expense, tax relief could be given immediately by set-off against the previous year's profits (see [**28.53**]).

It will often be possible to ensure that interest is treated in the most advantageous fashion. For instance, yearly interest paid to any person other than a bank cannot be deducted as a trading expense (TA 1988 s 337(2)(b)): hence, in appropriate circumstances, it will be advantageous for the company to borrow from a subsidiary rather than a bank. The recent case of *Minsham Properties Ltd v Price* (1990) illustrates the difficulties that can arise if interest payments are not carefully structured.   [**28.49**]

c) *Raising finance: shares, debentures and deep discount securities*

There are two major sources of corporate finance. Money can either be raised by an allotment of *shares* so that the contributors become members of the company and will generally expect to receive dividends on those shares. Alternatively, money can be borrowed with the company creating *debentures* and paying interest to the debenture holders. Such interest will qualify as a charge on a company's profits and so obtain tax relief at the full rate. Dividends, however, are not deductible from a company's profits since they are not charges on income. As a result of the imputation system a full double charge to tax is avoided and relief is given at 25%. Therefore, whilst the corporation tax rate exceeds the 25% level of relief, there remains a discrimination in favour of debentures and against raising funds by a share issue. For small companies, the corporation tax rate is now 25% so that there is no element of double taxation; for other companies, the rate is 33% so that the discrimination against dividends although still present is relatively small.   [**28.50**]

Qualifying corporate bonds   As has been discussed in Chapter 16, certain loans to traders which prove to be irrecoverable qualify for capital gains loss relief (see CGTA 1979 s 136). The majority of company loans, however, do not fall within this provision since they are 'debts on security' and hence excluded from that section. Up until 14 March 1989 this did not matter since relief was separately available for losses incurred by such investors under CGTA 1979 s 134 (relief for debts on security).

Since March 1989 the law in this area has suffered a bewildering series of changes and the following is an outline statement of those changes and of the current position.

First, qualifying corporate bonds ('QCB') have since 1986 been wholly exempt from CGT (FA 1984 s 64). Gains are therefore tax free and no relief is available for losses. The original definition of a QCB involved a sterling denominated bond, debenture or loan stock whether secured or unsecured. Further, the definition was restricted to securities which were *either* themselves quoted on the UK Stock Exchange *or* dealt in on the USM *or*, alternatively, which were issued by a body with other securities so quoted (or dealt in).

Secondly, FA 1989 s 139 widened the definition of a QCB to embrace such securities *whether or not issued by a quoted body*. The consequence was to extend the definition to include virtually all company securities. As a result, the disposal of such securities was wholly exempt from CGT with the result that losses incurred on that disposal were not tax allowable. Not surprisingly, considerable attention was focused on the definition of a QCB in order to draw up an agreement which fell *outside* that definition but which still amounted to a debt on security thereby enabling loss relief to be available under CGTA 1979 s 134. Two devices were commonly employed. First, a QCB must be 'expressed in sterling and in respect of which no provision is made for conversion into or redemption in a currency other than sterling' (FA 1984 s 64(2)(c) and (3)). Accordingly, provisions for redemption in another currency or by reference to another currency could be included to take the bond outside the QCB definition. An alternative lay in the requirement that to be a QCB the debt in question must 'represent and have at all times represented a normal commercial loan' (see FA s 64(2)(b) and, for the definition of a normal commercial loan, TA 1988 Sch 18 para 1 as amended by FA 1991). Providing a right of conversion into shares would ensure that the test was *not* met so that the security was not a QCB.

Thirdly, the next stage in the drama (tragedy?) was the introduction, effected by FA 1990, of new ss 136A and 136B into CGTA 1979. Whilst leaving QCBs free from any capital gains charge these sections provide that a capital loss arising on the disposal of such bonds will attract tax relief in certain restricted circumstances:

(a)   the bonds themselves must be held or issued after 14 March 1989;
(b)   the allowable loss is restricted to the taxpayer's actual loss with no account being taken of any indexation allowance;
(c)   relief is only available to the original investor who must show that he has not assigned any right to recover any outstanding amount of the principal of the loan;
(d)   a claim has to be made that the value of the bond has become negligible;
(e)   were the debt not a debt on security it would qualify for relief under s 136 (loan to trader). Accordingly, the money lent must be used by the borrower wholly for the purposes of a trade carried on by him.

Fourthly, special rules exist to deal with the situation where a gain is 'rolled into' a qualifying corporate bond. Assume, for instance, that Toby sells his company to Vulture Ltd in consideration for an issue of securities in Vulture which fall within the definition of a QCB. Toby's gains on the disposal of his shares can be rolled into the replacement securities by virtue of CGTA 1979 ss 85–87 (see [**19.2**]). Because the replacement securities are QCBs, special rules in FA 1984 Sch 13 apply as a result of which the postponed gain will be triggered on a subsequent disposal of the QCB. In effect the gain is held in suspense and will arise *even if* the QCB is sold at a loss or is written off. Toby may therefore realise nothing on his QCB and yet be left with a tax liability. To add insult to injury, relief under CGTA 1979 s 136A will not be available even if the security has become of negligible value because the loan in question will not have been used wholly for trading purposes (rather it enabled Vulture Ltd to acquire Toby's company). If Toby dies still owning the QCB the suspended gain will pass to his personal representatives and so fall into charge when they dispose of the bond.   [**28.51**]

Deep discount and deep gain securities   A deep discount security is defined as a redeemable security, excluding shares, issued at a price which is substantially below its redemption price and carrying little or no interest (TA 1988 s 57 and Sch 4). The discount must generally be more than 15% of the total amount payable on redemption or $1/2$% per annum of that amount for each year between the date of issue and redemption. The discount is treated as deemed annual income accruing on a compound interest basis. The issuing company will deduct this deemed income each year as a charge on income despite the fact that it will not actually pay the discount until redemption. The holder of the security will be taxed under Case III of Schedule D when he disposes of the security or when it is redeemed. Disposal has its usual CGT meaning, but if the holder dies, he is treated as receiving the accrued income immediately before death (so that it must be entered in his final income tax return). As the discount is subject to income tax in a single year, holders should dispose of deep discount securities in their most advantageous tax year. If the disposal results in an overall profit in excess of the accrued income, CGT may be charged on the excess; if a loss results, CGT loss relief will be available.

A deep gain security is defined, broadly, as a security which has all the characteristics of a deep discount security but has a variable redemption price, or some other variable feature, which takes it outside the definition of a deep discount security (FA 1989 s 94 and Sch 11).

If a deep gain security is transferred or redeemed for an amount in excess of the acquisition price, the excess is subject to tax under Case III of Schedule D. If the holder of the deep gain security dies, he is treated as transferring the security at market value and thus may be deemed to have received a taxable sum. A deep gain security will be either a gilt edged security or a qualifying corporate bond and thus exempt from CGT in most cases.

Certain convertible securities issued after 9 June 1990 were removed from the normal rules governing deep gain securities. If the holder has an option to redeem the security at his own discretion before the redemption date and the security is convertible into ordinary shares, the security is a 'qualifying convertible security'.

If such a security is sold before the right of the holder to redeem it has expired, or if he actually exercises that option, he will be liable to income tax under Case III of Schedule D on an element of his profit (see FA 1990 Sch 10).

Any residual gain or loss will be subject to normal CGT provisions and so an allowable loss may result. If the security is converted into shares, CGT rules will apply and the gain realised on conversion can be rolled over. Similarly, if the holder does not exercise his right to redeem his security or to convert it into shares, but instead disposes of it, he will make a disposal for CGT purposes. **[28.52]**

Coupon stripping There are anti-avoidance provisions designed to prevent the deferral of tax by 'coupon stripping'. This device involves a company acquiring interest-bearing securities and itself issuing deep discount stocks so that the interest received on the securities acquired may be offset by deductions in respect of deemed income payable on the deep discount stocks. In the case of deep discount stock issued in these circumstances a charge to tax, which roughly corresponds to the deductions allowed to the issuing company (see the detailed requirements in TA 1988 Sch 4 para 2), is imposed upon the holder of that stock. The amounts taxed as the income of the holder during his period of ownership are deducted from the sum on disposal or redemption of the security.

On a note of caution, when considering the financing of a UK subsidiary of a non-resident parent TA 1988 s 209(2)(e)(iv) should not be overlooked. This provides that interest paid on a security (eg loan stock) to a non-resident parent which owns 75% or more of the paying company will be treated as a distribution (see [**28.88**]).   [**28.53**]

4   Loss relief

Different relieving provisions apply depending upon the type of loss which the company has made. In all cases, however, it is only the company (or exceptionally another company in the same group: see [**28.142**]) which is entitled to the relief and never the members of the company. The loss is thus 'locked into' the company and this is a matter of some significance in deciding whether to commence business as a company or partnership (see further Chapter 32).

Losses are deducted from the appropriate profits of the company in priority to charges on income.   [**28.54**]

a) *Relief for trading losses: 'carry-forward'* (TA 1988 s 393(1))

A trading loss can be carried forward and set against trading profits from the *same* trade in the future. (The equivalent relief for the unincorporated trader is found in TA 1988 s 385(1).) A claim for relief must be made within six years of the end of the accounting period in which the loss was incurred. The relief is given by reducing the trading income of the succeeding accounting period or periods. In cases where such trading income is insufficient to absorb the full loss, interest and dividends received by the company may be treated as trading income for the purpose of loss relief (TA 1988 s 393(8)) provided that such income would have been taxed as trading income if tax had not been assessed under other provisions. Dividends received by a company whose trade involves dealing in shares fall into this category.

Unrelieved charges on income may be carried forward as a trading expense but only to the extent that the charge was made 'wholly and exclusively for the purposes of the trade' (TA 1988 s 393(9)). Thus, any charges not so made should be relieved against current year profits in priority, leaving only those payments to be carried forward which satisfy the 'wholly and exclusively' test.   [**28.55**]

EXAMPLE 28.8

Hee Ltd had the following corporation tax computation:

	£
Schedule D Case I profit	6,000
Chargeable gains	1,500
	7,500
Less charges on income (total £8,500) limited to	7,500
Taxable profits	£ Nil
Unrelieved charges	£1,000

If all the charges had been laid out wholly and exclusively for Hee Ltd's trade then £1,000 can be carried forward as a loss under s 393(1). But if only £500 had been so expended, the remaining £500 is unrelieved.

b) *Relief for trading losses against current and previous profits* (TA 1988 s 393(A) inserted by FA 1991 s 73)

A company may set its trading loss against profits of the same accounting period. (The nearest equivalent for the individual is the relief afforded by TA 1988 s 380.) Notice that as the relief is to set the loss against other profits it follows that all current profits can be used, including capital gains.

EXAMPLE 28.9

Haw Ltd's accounts for the financial year show the following: a trading loss of £6,000; rental income of £5,000; chargeable gains of £3,000; and charges on income of £1,000. The corporation tax computation would be:

	£
Schedule A	5,000
Chargeable gains	3,000
	8,000
Less trading loss	6,000
	2,000
Less charges on income	1,000
Profits for corporation tax	£1,000

Where a loss cannot be relieved, or cannot be fully relieved, against profits of the same accounting period a claim may be made to carry that loss back against profits of a previous accounting period. If the loss was incurred in an accounting period ending *on or before* 31 March 1991, the loss may only be carried back against profits of the previous accounting period (TA 1988 s 393(2)). If the loss was incurred in an accounting period ending *after* 31 March 1991, the loss may be carried back against profits of the previous *three* years. The company must have been carrying on the same trade in the earlier period and the claim has to be made within two years of the end of the accounting period in which the loss was incurred (TA 1988 s 393(A)(10) subject to the Board's discretion to extend that period). Any claim for loss relief will take effect before any charges on income are deducted but *after* any loss made in that earlier year. **[28.56]**

EXAMPLE 28.10

How Ltd prepares its accounts to the year ended 31 May. Its accounts show the following:

	Trading profits (losses) £	*Charges on income* £
Year to 31 May 1991	(12,000)	Nil
Year to 31 May 1990	(6,000)	1,000
Year to 31 May 1989	5,000	1,000
Year to 31 May 1988	25,000	Nil
Year to 31 May 1987	30,000	Nil

In respect of the year ended 31 May 1990 a claim for section 393(2) relief would result in the following corporation tax computation:

Profits of 1990	Nil
Profits of 1989	5,000
Less 1990 losses	5,000
Taxable profits for 1989	Nil

As a result of the claim:
(i) Any tax paid for the 1989 accounts will be recovered.
(ii) The 1990 loss has not been fully relieved since, in respect of periods ending on or before 31 March 1991, a loss may only be carried back one year.
(iii) The loss relief absorbs all of the profits for 1989. The charges on income will not obtain tax relief unless carried forward as trading losses under provisions already discussed (see [**28.46**]). Hence, from 1990, How Ltd has unrelieved losses of £1,000 and unrelieved charges on income of £2,000 to carry forward.

In respect of the year ended 31 May 1991 a claim for s 393(A) relief would result in the following corporation tax computation:

Profits of 1991	Nil
Profits of 1990	Nil
Profits of 1989	Nil
Profits of 1988	25,000
Less 1991 losses	12,000
Taxable profits for 1988	13,000

As a result of the claim:
(i) Part of the tax paid for 1988 will be recovered.
(ii) The company still has unrelieved losses of £1,000 for 1990 and unrelieved charges on income of £2,000 for 1989 and 1990 which it can carry forward.

A number of technical points should be made in connection with the new relief under s 393A.

First, that it has replaced the old relief which had been available for terminal losses under TA 1988 s 394. That relief had similarly allowed a three-year carry-back of trading losses but *only* against past income from the trade and only for a loss incurred in the final 12 months of that company's trade.

Secondly, on a claim being made the loss will be set against profits of preceding accounting periods falling in the previous three years. It is not possible to claim to offset the loss against a particular year in that three-year period: rather it must be offset against *later* periods first. A 1992 loss, for instance, will be offset against 1991; then 1990, and, finally, against the 1989 accounting period.

Thirdly, capital allowances may increase the loss to be relieved under s 393A although it should be noted that capital allowances carried forward from an earlier period do not qualify.   [**28.57**]

c) *General restrictions on the availability of trading loss relief*

There are a number of restrictions on the availability of trading loss relief.   [**28.58**]

A commercial purpose   First, the trade must be carried on commercially with a view to the realisation of a gain if s 393(2) relief is to be available. Carry-forward (s 393(1)) relief will, however, always apply.   [**28.59**]

Acquiring a tax loss company   Secondly, TA 1988 s 768 prevents the carry-forward of losses (s 393(1)) in certain circumstances where, after the loss has been incurred, there has been a substantial change in the ownership of the company's shares. *The purpose of these provisions was to stop the practice of purchasing companies in order to acquire their accumulated tax losses.* With the new rules introduced as from 1 April 1991 permitting the carry-back of a trading loss against profits for up to three years, amendments were made to s 768 to ensure that similar rules will apply to stop losses incurred *after* the change of ownership from being carried back, in certain circumstances, against profits before the change (TA 1988 s 768A inserted by FA 1991 Sch 15). There are two relevant factors:

(1) whether there has been a substantial change of ownership; and
(2) what has happened to the business of the company.

TA 1988 s 769 contains detailed rules providing for what constitutes a substantial change in ownership; basically it amounts to a change in the beneficial ownership of more than 50% of the ordinary share capital.

So far as the business of the company is concerned the rules in s 768 apply if either:

(a) there is a change in the ownership accompanied by a major change in the nature or conduct of the trade and both changes occur within a three-year period (for the interpretation of 'major' see *Willis v Peeters Picture Frames Ltd* (1983) and a case on the now repealed stock relief *Purchase v Tesco Stores Ltd* (1984)); or
(b) a change in ownership follows a period when the trade carried on by the company has become small or negligible and only after that change of ownership has there been any considerable revival.

In the latter case no time period is prescribed and the danger is that a new owner who merely improves the conduct and profitability of the company, as opposed to changing the nature of its trade, will find that accumulated losses are not available for relief. **[28.60]**

Corporate reconstructions When a company ceases to carry on a trade (eg when the trade is sold) that trade is treated as ceasing even though it may in fact continue by being carried on by another company (TA 1988 s 337(1)). So far as losses are concerned, the result will be that the carry-forward relief will cease to be available, although terminal loss relief may be claimed.

Of course, where a reconstruction has occurred as a result of which the trade passes from one company to another and both companies are under common control, these consequences would be economic nonsense and penalise the parties concerned. Thus, TA 1988 s 343 contains provisions which operate in such circumstances to permit losses and capital allowances to be carried forward from the predecessor to the successor company. The decision in *Falmer Jeans v Rodin* (1990) illustrates how these provisions operate when the successor company carries on the trade as part of its existing trading activities.

As a result of amendments made in 1986, however, there are restrictions on the amount of loss which can be carried forward *when the transferor company is insolvent at the time of the transfer*. Broadly, if the successor company fails to take over all the liabilities of the transferor (as when part only of the trade—the successful part!—is being hived-down into a new 'clean' company) and the transferor has insufficient assets to cover them, the losses which can be transferred are reduced by the amount by which the predecessor's 'relevant liabilities' exceeded its 'relevant assets'.

For s 343 to operate the same person or persons must, at any time within the period of two years after the change, directly or indirectly, own the trade (or not less than a three-quarter share in it) and must have owned that trade or the same interest therein within the period of one year before the change. Ownership is normally determined by reference to the ordinary share capital which is, however, given by TA 1988 s 832 a wider definition than its normal meaning and includes all issued share capital except shares which carry a fixed rate dividend and no other interest in the profits of the company.

The normal hiving-down operation satisfies these requirements although the FA 1986 restrictions on the amount of loss that can be carried forward have removed some of the attractions of the hive-down since when only a part of the transferor's trade is transferred (as in the typical hive-down) apportionments must be made to determine what fraction of the loss can be carried forward. The successor company can amalgamate the predecessor's trade with another enterprise already carried on, although, in this situation, the carried-forward loss relief will only be available against future profits arising from the old trade.   [**28.61**]

EXAMPLE 28.11

The ordinary share capital of Zee Ltd and Pee Ltd is owned as follows:

	Zee Ltd	*Pee Ltd*
Alan	10	8
Ben	6	12
Claud	30	40
Dennis	29	20
Others	25	20

A transfer of a trade from Zee Ltd to Pee Ltd would fall within s 343 since the 75% common ownership test is satisfied albeit that the relevant shares in Pee Ltd are owned by the same persons in different proportions.

d) *Relief for income losses other than trading losses*

Schedule D Case VI losses may be set against Schedule D Case VI income for either the current year or first available future accounting period (TA 1988 s 396). In the case of losses under Schedule A the normal relieving provisions provided for in that Schedule apply (see Chapter 8).   [**28.62**]

e) *Relief for capital losses*

Losses which would be deductible in computing liability to capital gains tax can be set against the first available chargeable gains made by the company. Such losses cannot be offset against income profits.   [**28.63**]

5   **Management expenses**

Investment companies can deduct sums paid out in management expenses (such as salaries and general office expenditure) from their total profits. If such expenditure is unrelieved, it can be carried forward and offset in future years, but not back to a previous accounting period. Unrelieved charges can likewise be carried forward and treated as management expenses in future years so long as such charges were incurred 'wholly and exclusively for the purpose of the company's business' (TA 1988 s 75(3)). The term 'investment company' is defined as including:

> 'any company whose business consists wholly or mainly in the making of investments and the principal part of whose income is derived therefrom...' (TA 1988 s 130).

Hence, authorised unit trusts and savings banks (with the specific exclusion of a trustee savings bank as defined under the Trustee Savings Bank Act 1981) are included. It follows that the relief will often be given by setting the expenses against the franked investment income of the company (see [**28.98**]). For companies whose business consists of managing land, expenses involved in administering that land will be deductible from the Schedule A profits, whereas the general running costs of the company will be management expenses. Trading companies do not, of course, require a provision dealing with management expenses since such sums will be deducted in arriving at the Schedule D profits. [**28.64**]–[**28.80**]

IV DISTRIBUTIONS

Distributions made by a company are not deductible in arriving at that company's profits for corporation tax, but will be paid out of taxed profits. [**28.81**]

1 **Meaning of a distribution** (TA 1988 ss 209–211)

Distribution is widely defined since the intention is to catch not just the most obvious methods of paying profits to shareholders (such as a dividend), but also all payments and transfers by a company to its members other than repayment of capital subscribed. The tax treatment of distributions depends upon whether they are 'qualifying' or 'non-qualifying'; this distinction will be considered later. The main instance of a distribution is a dividend (including a capital dividend); other examples are discussed below. [**28.82**]

Any distribution out of the assets of the company which is made in respect of shares except in so far as it is a repayment of capital or equal to any new consideration received Where sums are returned to shareholders on a reduction of capital, they will not be distributions so long as they do not exceed the original amount subscribed (including any premium paid on the allotment of the shares). Payments to members on a winding up are expressly excluded from the definition of a distribution (such sums will usually be liable to capital gains tax in the hands of the shareholders). The issue of bonus shares is not itself a distribution, but a repayment of share capital within the following ten years will be a distribution up to the amount paid up on the bonus issue. [**28.83**]

EXAMPLE 28.12

U Ltd has a share capital of 100 ordinary £1 shares. It makes a 1:1 bonus issue by capitalising £100 of reserves. Later it repays the shareholders 50p per share on a reduction of capital. Each shareholder is treated as receiving a distribution on the reduction in capital.

Position of a shareholder: Originally, he owned one £1 share. After the bonus issue, he owns two £1 shares. After the reduction in capital, he owns two 50p shares and has £1 in cash. The shareholder is in the same position as if he had received a £1 dividend and is taxed as such.

A reduction of share capital followed by a bonus issue Essentially, this is the same operation as above and has similar taxation consequences. These consequences will not follow if the gap between repayment and the bonus issue exceeds ten years, so long as the bonus issue is not of redeemable shares and so long as the company is not a closely controlled company within TA 1988 s 704. In addition, the bonus issue cannot be regarded as a distribution if the repaid share capital consisted of fully paid preference shares.   [28.84]

EXAMPLE 28.13

As in *Example 28.12*, U Ltd has a share capital of 100 £1 shares. It makes a reduction of share capital by repaying 50p per share. It then issues 100 50p bonus shares (ie a 1:1 issue).

Position of a shareholder: Initially, he held one £1 share. After the repayment of capital, he owns one 50p share and has 50p in cash. After the bonus issue, he owns two 50p shares and has received 50p in cash. Hence, he has shares of identical aggregate par value to the one share held at the start and has received a 50p payment from the company which will be treated as a distribution.

The issue of bonus redeemable shares and bonus securities A bonus issue of redeemable shares (ie shares which the company has express authority or an obligation to redeem in the future) and of securities is a distribution. Unlike the other examples of a distribution, however, this category is a 'non-qualifying' distribution. The taxation consequences of this are considered at [28.101], but it should be noted that this category is unique in being the one distribution where the company is not at the time of the distribution paying out moneys to shareholders, but is entering into a commitment so to do in the future. Hence, the issue represents a potential rather than an immediate charge on profits. The value of the distribution will, in the case of shares, be the nominal value together with any premium payable on redemption. In the case of other securities, it will be the amount secured together with any premium payable on redemption. When redeemable shares and securities are redeemed, the redemption will normally be a qualifying distribution.   [28.85]

A transfer by a company to its members of assets or liabilities which are worth more than any new consideration furnished by the member The excess of any assets or liabilities transferred by a company to its members over any new consideration furnished by the members will be a distribution.   [28.86]

The stock dividend option TA 1988 s 249 provides that where bonus shares are offered to shareholders instead of a cash dividend, the bonus shares will be treated as a distribution. The benefit for the issuing company is that no advance corporation tax is payable on the allotment of these shares.   [28.87]

Certain interest payments Interest payments geared to the profits of the company (irrespective of the reasonableness of the rate) or excessive interest (which exceeds a reasonable commercial return) may be treated as distributions by TA 1988 s 209(2)(d),(e)(iii). These rules cannot be used to achieve a tax advantage in the case of 'equity loans' and, accordingly, when the lender is a UK company subject to corporation tax interest geared to profits is not a distribution, but is taxed in the normal way (see [1982] STI 107). Interest payments on bonus securities and on securities which are convertible whether directly or indirectly into shares in the company (unless listed on The Stock Exchange) are distributions. Similarly, interest payments made to an overseas parent by a 75% subsidiary will be treated as a distribution under TA 1988 s 209(2)(e)(iv). **[28.88]**

EXAMPLE 28.14

Zec Ltd borrows £50,000 from Mr Con at a rate of interest of 20% pa. A reasonable commercial rate would be 12%. The company is paying £10,000 pa to Con of which £6,000 is deductible from profits for corporation tax purposes. That sum is also interest for TA 1988 s 349(2) so that basic rate tax should be deducted at source. So far as the excess (£4,000 pa) is concerned it will be a distribution on which ACT is payable and Con will be assessed on the gross amount under Schedule F.

2 Distributions and the purchase by the company of its own shares

The Companies Act 1985 ss 159–181 allows companies (so long as authorised by their articles of association) to purchase their own shares. Generally, such purchases must be paid for out of distributable profits, but private companies may be able to use capital. However, but for TA 1988 s 219, any payment to a shareholder in excess of the sum paid on the original allotment of the shares would be treated as a distribution, unless the repayment occurs on a winding up of the company. Therefore, s 219 provides that, in certain circumstances, when shares are bought back moneys received by a shareholder will not be treated as a distribution so that any profit made will be charged, if at all, to CGT. Accordingly, shares sold to the company will be treated no differently from sales to any other person. However, the provisions are restrictive, so that in some cases there will still be a distribution. The requirements, if buy-backs are not to involve a distribution, are complex and will be considered under three headings. **[28.89]**

The purchasing company The purchasing company must not be listed on the official list of a Stock Exchange but its shares may be dealt in on the Unlisted Securities Market. It must be either a trading company or the holding company of a trading group. **[28.90]**

The vendor of the shares The vendor may be an individual, a trustee, the PR of a deceased shareholder, or a company. He should be resident and, if an individual, ordinarily resident in the UK. Normally, the shares must have been owned for at least five years and it is not possible to aggregate different ownership periods (hence settlor/trustees and trustees/beneficiaries must each satisfy the five-year period). In the exceptional cases of husband/wife and of the deceased/his PRs and legatees aggregation is permissible and in the latter case the aggregated ownership period need only be three years.

The vendor should either dispose of all his shares in the company or at least 'substantially reduce' his shareholding. The Revenue take the view that a holding will only be substantially reduced if the shareholder reduces his fractional interest in the company's issued capital by at least 25% and is not left with a dominant (at least 30%) holding of the issued shares. In calculating these fractions, spouses and associates generally are treated as one person. As any transactions in the same shares within 12 months of the sale will form part of the same transaction, it follows that shares should not be repurchased from the company within a period of one year. When determining whether a substantial reduction has been achieved it should be remembered that shares bought back are cancelled. **[28.91]**

EXAMPLE 28.15

Buy-back Ltd has an issued share capital of 200 £1 shares. Adam owns 120 of the shares and sells 90 of them to Buy-back Ltd.

Adam's fraction before sale   120/200 = 0.6
Adam's fraction after sale   30/110 = 0.27
                                            75% × 0.6 = 0.45

Accordingly, Adam has substantially reduced his shareholding and is not left with a dominant holding of issued shares.

The reason for the sale   There are two permissible reasons. First, the purchase by the company must benefit its trade (or that of a 75% subsidiary) and not be part of a scheme designed to enable the shareholders to participate in the company's profits without receiving a dividend or otherwise to avoid tax. The requirement that the purchase must be a 'benefit to the trade' is not an easy test to apply. For instance, the buying out of dissident shareholders is certainly for the benefit of the company but that, presumably, is not the same unless it can be shown that the continued dissension was harming the management and, therefore, the trade of the company. In practice the Revenue have stated (see SP 2/82) that they will expect the requirement to be satisfied in such cases and indeed in cases where the vendor shareholder is 'genuinely' giving up his entire interest of all kinds in the company.

EXAMPLE 28.16

(1)   It is proposed that WW Ltd (an unquoted trading company) purchases the shares of Mr Wam, one of the original founders of the company in 1970. He is willing to sell a 60% holding but wishes to keep a small (5%) holding for sentimental reasons. Mr Wam is retiring in favour of a new management team. The transaction will be for the benefit of the trade of WW Ltd and, the other conditions being satisfied, the payment for the shares will not be a distribution.

(2)   Sal is the sole shareholder in Sal Ltd, an unquoted trading company. Profits amount to £100,000 for the present accounting period and Sal Ltd plans to use them to purchase 50% of Sal's shares. This scheme will not be within the provisions of TA 1988 s 219 because:

(a) it would appear to be a scheme designed to pass the profits to Sal without declaring a dividend;

(b) Sal is not substantially reducing her holding since she will still own all the shares in Sal Ltd;

(c) the purchase is not for the benefit of Sal Ltd's trade.

The second permitted reason for the sale of the shares is where the whole, or substantially the whole, of the proceeds of sale is to be used by the recipient in discharging his IHT liability charged on a death. The money must be so used within two years of the death and it has to be shown that the IHT cannot be paid without undue hardship unless the shares are sold back to the company. In this case the above requirements as to the vendor of the shares do not apply. The IHT need not be owing in respect of the shares.   **[28.92]**

EXAMPLE 28.17

(1)   Sam inherits the family residence on his father's death. Under the terms of the will it is to bear its own IHT which can be raised by the sale of Sam's shareholding in Sham Ltd (a trading company which is not listed).

The only alternative would involve the sale of the family house. If the shares are sold to Sham Ltd the purchase moneys will not be treated as a distribution.

(2) Sue inherits 30% of the share capital of Carruthers Ltd. She does not want the shares and arranges for the company to buy them back. Although this arrangement falls outside the relief for hardship on a death, it would appear that there will be no distribution since such a payment will be for the benefit of the trade (see SP 2/82 and above).

Position if the vendor is a UK company If the vendor of the shares is a UK company the position can be summarised as follows:

First, assuming that s 219 applies so that the payment is *not* taxed as a distribution it will be taxed as a chargeable gain in the ordinary way.

Secondly, if the payment does not satisfy the s 219 requirements it will then be treated as a distribution and hence, in the hands of the vendor company, as *franked investment income*. Accordingly, it would be attractive for buy-backs in such cases to fall *outside* s 219 since the vendor would not only escape corporation tax on the sale proceeds but would, in addition, be entitled to an ACT credit. It was not perhaps entirely surprising, therefore, that the Revenue issued SP 4/89 which provides as follows:

'If the purchase of its own shares by a company resident in the UK gives rise to a distribution, and a shareholder receiving such a distribution is itself a company, the distribution is included in the consideration for the disposal of the shares for the purposes of the charge to corporation tax on chargeable gains. In the Inland Revenue's view the effect of TA 1988 ss 208, 345(3) is that the distribution does not suffer a tax charge as income within the terms of CGTA 1979 s 31(1).'

If correct, the result is that corporation tax will be charged on a capital gain but the Statement has attracted a welter of criticism (see, for instance, Richard Bramwell writing in *Taxation*, 21 September 1989).

EXAMPLE 28.18

KP Ltd owns 500 shares in SJ Ltd which it acquired at par for £1 each in March 1983.

SJ Ltd buys the shares back for £5 each in June 1989.

(1) *If the purchase is within s 219*, KP Ltd's tax position will be as follows:

	£
Sale proceeds for CGT	5,000
less price paid by SJ Ltd	500
Capital gain (ignoring indexation)	£4,500

(2) *If the purchase is outside s 219* KP Ltd's tax position will be as follows:

	£
Consideration received	5,000
Net distribution (£5,000 − £500)	4,500
plus ACT paid thereon	1,500
Franked investment income	£6,000

Note: If SP 4/89 is correct KP Ltd will have realised the same chargeable gain as in (1) above.

It should be remembered that, when the distribution rules apply, it is only the excess of the purchase proceeds over the amount originally paid to the company for the shares that is treated as a distribution. As the sum treated as a distribution must then be ignored in calculating the vendor's CGT position, it is, therefore, possible for him to make a CGT loss whilst selling the shares at a profit.

EXAMPLE 28.19

Risker subscribed for 200 shares in BB Ltd paying the par value of £1 per share. He sold the shares two years ago to Tusker for £500 and BB Ltd has now bought the shares for £950. Assuming that the sale is outside the scope of TA 1988 s 219 Tusker's tax position is as follows:

	£
Total consideration received	£950
Net distribution (£950 – £200)	750
plus ACT thereon paid by BB Ltd	250
Gross dividend (subject to Schedule F income tax)	£1,000

	£
Sale proceeds for CGT purposes (£950 – £750)	200
Price paid by Tusker	500
CGT loss	£(300)

It has already been pointed out that when a purchase of own shares is being made from a company, the distribution rules may be more advantageous to that shareholder than the provisions of s 219. As a result of the harmonisation of rates of income tax and CGT, the position of the individual shareholder must also be considered carefully to see if there is a real benefit to be derived from the use of s 219. Furthermore, if the purchasing company is able to set all the ACT on a distribution against MCT, the company itself may be better served by keeping the buy-back outside s 219.

EXAMPLE 28.20

Alfie Ltd has an issued share capital of £20,000 comprised of 20,000 £1 ordinary shares allotted at par. Harry, a higher rate taxpayer, owns 10,000 shares. The company wishes to buy Harry's shares for £5 each in the accounting year ended 31 July 1991 during which it made profits of £200,000.

Company's tax position
(1)   If the purchase is within s 219:

	£
Profits	200,000
MCT	50,000
Net profits	£150,000

(2)   If the purchase is outside s 219:

		£
Profits		200,000
MCT at 25%	50,000	
Less ACT on buy-back	13,333	36,667
		163,333
ACT on buy-back		13,333
Net profits		£150,000

Harry's tax position	£
(1) If purchase is within s 219	
Sale proceeds for CGT	50,000
Less original issue price	10,000
Chargeable gain (ignoring indexation)	£40,000
CGT @ 40%	£16,000
	£
(2) If purchase is outside s 219	
Net distribution (50,000 — 10,000)	40,000
Plus ACT paid	13,333
Gross distribution	£53,333
Tax @ 40%	21,333
Less ACT credit	13,333
Tax payable	£8,000

Whenever the buy-back of shares is proposed, advance clearance can be obtained for the scheme and the same application (sent in duplicate) can be used for a clearance under TA 1988 s 707 (see Chapter 31). Similarly, if the arrangement is designed to fall outside TA 1988 s 219, negative clearance can be obtained. As no instrument of share transfer is necessary on a buy-back, stamp duty was formerly not charged. As from 27 October 1986, however, the return that must be made by the company to Companies House (form 169) is subject to duty 'as if it were an instrument transferring shares on sale' (FA 1986 s 66). Accordingly, *ad valorem* duty at $1/2$% is charged. (Note that the redemption of redeemable preference shares is outside the section and is free from duty.) **[28.93]**

3 The taxation of qualifying distributions

The taxation of distributions is governed by the imputation system. The central feature is ACT which represents for the company making the payment a partial (or, for small companies, a total) discharge of its corporation tax bill. The shareholder is given a credit for this ACT so that he will receive his dividend together with a credit equivalent to basic rate income tax. The rules to be considered in this section apply to all qualifying distributions. For convenience, however, examples will concentrate on the most common form of distribution, the cash dividend. **[28.94]**

a) *The payment of a dividend*

A company is obliged to pay ACT to the Revenue when it pays a dividend to its shareholders (an interim dividend is paid when actually made: a final dividend is paid on the date when it is declared due and payable). For the purpose of collecting ACT the calendar year is divided into quarters and at the end of each quarter (ie on 31 March, 30 June, 30 September and 31 December) the company must make a return indicating what dividends have been paid in the three month period just ended. If dividends have been paid, the appropriate ACT should be paid within 14 days of the end of the quarter except where the company has franked investment income available to cover the distribution that it makes. In such a case ACT need not be paid (see **[28.98]**).

The rate of ACT is determined in accordance with the following fraction:

$$\frac{I}{100 - I}$$

where I is the basic rate of income tax for the year of assessment beginning in the financial year for which the rate of ACT is to be fixed. For financial year 1991, therefore, the rate of ACT is:

$$\frac{25}{100 - 25} = \frac{25}{75}$$

[**28.95**]

EXAMPLE 28.21

On 1 February 1992 Zed Ltd pays total dividends of £75,000 to shareholders. This should appear in the quarterly return on 31 March 1992 and within 14 days thereof the sum of £25,000 ($^{25}/_{75}$ of £75,000) should be paid as ACT to the Revenue.

b) *The use of ACT by the company*

The corporation tax that companies pay nine months after the end of the accounting period (see [**28.21**]) is known as mainstream corporation tax (MCT). Formerly ACT on dividends paid during an accounting period could be deducted from the MCT bill on the *income* profits of that period only. However, in line with corporate gains being taxed at the normal corporation tax rate (either 33% or 25%), ACT paid on dividends can now be deducted from the MCT bill on *all* profits of that period, including, therefore, chargeable gains (TA 1988 s 239(1)). Notice therefore, that, where capital gains made by a company are distributed as dividends the ACT thereon can be deducted from the subsequent corporation tax charged on all profits not just income profits as was formerly the case. Profits for this purpose means the income and capital profits of the company less charges on income, allowable income and capital losses, and management expenses.

EXAMPLE 28.22

In *Example 28.21* Zed's accounts to 31 March 1992 show profits of £1,000,000 (income profits of £750,000 and capital profits of £250,000). The MCT bill is as follows:

	£
£1,000,000 at 33%	330,000
Less ACT paid during accounting year	25,000
Balance payable by 1 January 1993: ie	£305,000

   Zed's total corporation tax bill is £330,000 which will be paid in two instalments (the ACT portion and the MCT balance). Had no dividends been paid to shareholders during the accounting year, there would have been no ACT payable and the MCT bill would have been £330,000 payable by 1 January 1993: ie nine months after the end of the accounting period.

   Thus, the payment of a dividend will not, unless full ACT set-off cannot be claimed (see below), increase the total corporation tax charged. It merely, as its name suggests, results in an advanced payment of that tax.   [**28.96**]

c) *The problems of surplus ACT*

The obvious situation where there is surplus ACT is when the company pays dividends in a year when it has made no profits.

EXAMPLE 28.23

The accounts of Eve Ltd for the period ended 31 March 1992 show no profits, but during that year dividends of £75,000 were paid out of distributable profits, made by the company in the previous accounting period. The corporation tax position is:
(1) ACT of £25,000 (25/75 of £75,000) paid on the dividends.
(2) There is no MCT bill for the period to be reduced by the ACT paid.
(3) The company has surplus ACT of £25,000.

Surplus ACT also occurs where distributions exceed the 'permitted level' since there is a limit to the amount of MCT that can be cancelled by ACT. The maximum ACT set-off is the amount of ACT which would have been paid if the dividend declared together with ACT thereon equalled the profits for the year. In practical terms this is equivalént to the basic rate of income tax on the profits, so that for small companies (taxed at 25%) the MCT bill can be reduced to zero.

EXAMPLE 28.24

Xerxes Ltd pays dividends of £2,100,000 in 1992. During the same accounting period it has profits of £1,500,000. (This disparity between dividend and profits can be explained (as in *Example 28.23*, above) by assuming that the company paid out past accumulated profits.) For corporation tax purposes:
(1) ACT of £700,000 (25/75 of £2,100,000) is paid on the dividend.
(2) MCT at 33% on the £1,500,000 profits is £495,000. This cannot be wiped out by ACT of £700,000. The maximum ACT available will be £375,000 (25% of £1,500,000) since:
Dividends of £1,125,000 plus ACT thereon of £375,000 equals the profits (£1,500,000) for the year.
   Hence, Xerxes Ltd will have surplus ACT of £325,000 (£700,000 — £375,000) and the total corporation tax bill will be:

	£	
ACT	700,000	
+ MCT	120,000	(£495,000 — £375,000)
	£820,000	

An alternative way of explaining how much ACT can be set off against MCT on profits is to say that the rate of MCT can be reduced from 33% to 8% at the most, or, in the case of small companies, from 25% to 0%.   [28.97]

d) *The set-off of surplus ACT*

For accounting periods ending after 31 March 1984 and before 17 March 1987 a company can carry back surplus ACT and set it against MCT on *income* profits only of the six accounting periods immediately preceding the period showing the surplus, taking the more recent period first; for accounting periods beginning after 16 March 1987, a company can carry back surplus ACT to set it against MCT on *all* its profits (including, therefore, capital profits) of those preceding six years (TA 1988 s 239(3)). A refund of corporation tax will only result if the permitted level of set-off (against income or total profits as relevant) has not been reached in those years. If a surplus still remains it can then be carried forward without time limit and set off against MCT on future profits in the first year when the full quota of dividends has not been paid. (This extended carry-back period is particularly beneficial in view of the order of set-off of foreign taxation credits (see [**28.164**]).)

EXAMPLE 28.25

The following represents the dividends paid and profits made by a company during seven consecutive accounting periods (assuming a 33% rate of corporation tax throughout with an ACT fraction of $^{25}/_{75}$).

(a)	(b)	(c)	(d)	(e)	(f)	(g)
					Maximum	Amount
			ACT	MCT	set-off	unused
Post			(25/75 ×	(33% × (c))	(25% × (c))	in year
16.3.87	Dividend	Profit	(b))			((f)–(d))
	£	£	£	£	£	£
Year 1	Nil	200,000	Nil	66,000	50,000	50,000
Year 2	75,000	100,000	25,000	33,000	25,000	—
Year 3	75,000	100,000	25,000	33,000	25,000	—
Year 4	37,500	100,000	12,500	33,000	25,000	12,500
Year 5	Nil	50,000	Nil	16,500	12,500	12,500
Year 6	15,000	40,000	5,000	13,200	10,000	5,000
Year 7	375,000	100,000	125,000	33,000	25,000	—
Year 8	37,500	60,000	12,500	19,800	15,000	2,500

In Year 7 the ACT is £125,000 which can only be partially offset against the MCT bill for the year. MCT at £33,000 (33% × £100,000) can be reduced by the maximum set-off of £25,000 to £8,000, but no further, leaving surplus ACT of £100,000 (£125,000 − £25,000).

Uses of surplus ACT
(1) Carry back to years 6, 5, 4 and 1 relieving £5,000, £12,500, £12,500 and £50,000 respectively and leaving surplus ACT of £20,000 (£100,000 − £80,000).
(2) Carry forward £20,000 to future years without time limit using the first available profits but subject to the permitted level of set-off in each year. In year 8 the surplus can be further reduced to £17,500 (£20,000 − £2,500).

There is a two-year time limit for claiming the relief. This limit is relevant for the actual making of a claim: the settlement of the amount of that claim may, however, take a much longer time. To what extent therefore can claims be adjusted in the light of events occurring outside the two-year period? In part this question boils down to the difference between amending an existing claim (or fleshing out the details) and submitting a new, out-of-time (and therefore ineffective) claim. The matter arose in *Procter & Gamble v Taylerson* (1990) where the taxpayers, having claimed to carry back surplus ACT, subsequently incurred substantial trading losses. The original claim had been to carry back the surplus to the 1978 accounting period. Losses, however, arose in 1982 (after the amount of that claim had been agreed with the Revenue) and because these losses could also be carried back the taxpayers then sought to amend the ACT claim to include a carry back to 1977. The Court of Appeal held that such an adjustment amounted to a new claim which, being outside the two-year time limit, was **ineffective**.

The decision leaves open the extent to which events arising whilst the claim is unsettled can be taken into account.

It is notable that the amount of the claim had been agreed by the time the losses were incurred. Balcombe LJ commented:

'While I would be prepared to accept that the letter may be regarded as a claim to carry back ACT, ... subject to adjustments in matter of detail, ... the letter cannot be construed ... as a claim to carry back the whole surplus of ACT of whatever amount and whenever and however that surplus might arise.' [28.98]

e) Franked investment income

Dividends and other distributions received by one UK company from another are not generally subject to corporation tax in the recipient's hands. The sum paid, together with a tax credit for the ACT thereon, is known as franked investment income (FII:TA 1988 s 208). Generally, the recipient company will only be able to obtain a refund of the ACT paid on the distribution if either that distribution is expressly exempt from tax or if the recipient is wholly exempt from corporation tax or is exempt on all its income save for trading income (see TA 1988 s 231(2)—an instance of an exempt corporation would be a charitable company). For the majority of companies, therefore, there will be no question of a tax refund, and instead, the tax credit may be utilised in one of two ways. First, to 'frank' the receiving company's own distributions paid in the accounting period when the FII is received. Hence, ACT will not be payable on such distributions and, if already paid in an earlier quarter of the accounting period, will be refunded. If FII is not fully used in an accounting period, any surplus can be carried forward (without time limit) and used to frank future distributions.

EXAMPLE 28.26

During the accounting period ending 31 March 1992 Sellco Ltd has profits of £1,000,000. It receives dividends of £75,000 from Buyco Ltd (another UK company) and itself pays out dividends of £150,000 during the year.
(1) Sellco has FII of £75,000 + £25,000 = £100,000.
(2) On paying the £150,000 dividend it can offset the credit on the FII to reduce its ACT liability:

	£
Dividend	150,000
ACT payable	50,000
FII set-off	25,000
Balance ACT owing	£25,000

(3) Profits for the year are £1,000,000 (and do not include FII) so that the MCT liability will be:

	£
MCT at 33%	330,000
Less ACT	25,000
Balance owing	£305,000

(4) In effect Sellco passes its FII on to its own shareholders.

The second use to which an FII tax credit can be put is to obtain partial loss relief. If a company in any year has trading losses or charges on income or management expenses which exceed the profits of that year, any surplus FII received in that year may, if a claim is made by the company, be treated as if it were profits liable to corporation tax and the FII tax credit can be recovered directly from the Revenue. 'Surplus FII' excludes FII carried forward from an earlier year (TA 1988 s 242(9)).   **[28.99]**

EXAMPLE 28.27

Investaco Ltd has FII of £50,000 for the accounting year ended 31 March 1992. It has unrelieved management expenses of £20,000. It may treat £20,000 of FII as profits subject to corporation tax. Hence:

	£
FII 'profits'	20,000
Less management expenses	20,000
Corporation tax payable	£ Nil

The refund of tax paid is £5,000 (the ACT portion of £20,000 FII: ie 25% × £20,000).

Notes
(1) Some loss relief (£5,000) has been obtained at once.
(2) The relief is only partial, however, since, had the expenses of £20,000 been set against profits subject to corporation tax at 33%, the tax saving would be not £5,000 but 33% × £20,000 = £6,600. To ensure that full relief is available compensating adjustments are made in later accounting periods where the distributions exceed FII to ensure that the balance of the loss relief is then given (TA 1988 s 242(5)).

f) *The position of individual shareholders who receive dividends*

Dividends are assessed to income tax under Schedule F on the gross sum, ie the dividend actually paid together with the ACT paid on it. The individual receives a tax credit equal to the ACT paid by the company (or treated as discharged by any FII used by the paying company). The credit is equal to the basic rate of income tax so that only if the recipient is subject to the higher rate will there be a further income tax charge.   **[28.100]**

EXAMPLE 28.28

Cam, Mem and Bert are three shareholders in Fromage Ltd and each receives a dividend of £75 in the income tax year 1991–92. Cam has no other income and unused personal allowances; Mem is a basic rate taxpayer; and Bert is subject to income tax at the highest rate (40%). Each has an income of £100 under Schedule F and each receives a tax credit for £25.
Cam, who has unused personal allowances, will be able to reclaim the £25 tax credit.
Mem has had the correct amount of tax deducted at source, having used all her personal allowances.
Bert will be subject to extra tax of £15 (40% of £100 = £40, less his tax credit of £25).

g) *Conclusions on the taxation of dividends*

As already noted, ACT is the pivot of the imputation system. For the company, it is an advance payment of corporation tax. For the shareholder, it represents basic rate income tax. For small companies the system results in the payment of a dividend being fully deductible for corporation tax purposes (since the ACT wipes out the MCT liability). For other companies, however, an element of double charge remains since the shareholder is not given a credit for all the corporation tax paid by the company. The residual MCT liability of 8% cannot be offset against his higher rate income tax liability so that the effective rate of tax on dividends may amount to 46.4% (see *Example 28.29(1)*). Although the element of double charge has been reduced over the past years by the lowering of the corporation tax rate from 52% in FY 1982 to the current 33%, the advantages of raising money by debentures, where there is no double charge as the interest is tax deductible by the company, have been noted at [**28.47**] and are further considered in Chapter 32.

EXAMPLE 28.29

(1) *Maximum tax liability on distribution for the individual shareholder/company*

	£
Company's profit	100
Corporation tax (at 33%)	33
Net profit	£67
Distributed net profits	67
ACT (25/75 × £67)	22.33
Gross dividend	£89.33
Income tax (at 40% on £89.33)	35.73
Less basic rate tax credit	22.33
Income tax bill	£13.40

Total tax payable is: £10.67 (MCT)	
plus £22.33 (ACT)	
plus £13.40 (income tax)	£ 46.40
Net income after *all* tax deducted is:	£ 53.60
	£100.00

(2) Cash Company has accumulated profits over the years of £500,000. If this sum is now distributed as a dividend, ACT thereon may be carried back and set against past payments of MCT so at least a partial refund may be obtained. By contrast, the shareholders wind up the company in order to extract this profit, they may suffer a substantial CGT charge since their shares will have increased in value since originally acquired. With the harmonisation of the income tax and CGT rates, there will often be no significant advantage in realising a capital gain rather than an income profit.

Two tax planning matters for the company to bear in mind should be mentioned. *First*, dividends should be paid as late as possible in the accounting period so that ACT is paid as close as possible to MCT (ie accelerated payment is kept to the minimum period of eight and a half months). *Secondly*, it is desirable to pay a dividend *after* the receipt of FII; if dividends are paid first, ACT must be paid and then reclaimed. [**28.101**]

4　The taxation of non-qualifying distributions

An issue of bonus redeemable shares or securities is a non-qualifying distribution. The two main features of qualifying distributions (the payment of ACT by the company and a tax credit for the shareholder) do not apply to non-qualifying distributions. Instead, the distribution is taxed in two stages: *first*, the issue of the securities has no tax effect on the issuing company and, so far as the recipient is concerned, no assessment to basic rate income tax. It follows that the only tax consequence will be an assessment on the shareholder for any higher rate income tax calculated at his higher rate for that year less basic rate. Secondly, when the shares are redeemed, the redemption will be a qualifying distribution with the normal taxation consequences (see [**28.93**]), save that, if the shareholder is then liable for income tax at the higher rate, a deduction is made for any higher rate tax which he originally paid on the non-qualifying distribution.

[**28.102**]]–[[**28.120**]

EXAMPLE 28.30

Stage (1) Shareholder Sam has a taxable income of £23,700. He receives bonus redeemable shares whose redemption value is 50. His income tax liability will be calculated by adding £750 to his other income and calculating tax on that £750 as the highest portion of that total. His taxable income is £24,450 (£23,700 + £750). The tax rate applicable on the top £750 is 40%. Therefore:

	£
Higher rate tax (40%) on £750	300
Less basic rate tax (25% × £750)	187.50
Income tax owing	£112.50

Stage (2) When the shares are redeemed and Sam is paid £750 his taxable income is still £23,700 and the bands and rates of tax are unchanged. The tax position is as follows:

(1)　The company will pay ACT of £250 on the capital distribution.
(2)　Sam's income under Schedule F will be £1,000 and he will have a tax credit for £250.
(3)　Sam's income tax bill will be calculated thus:

	£
Tax on £1,000 at highest rate (40%)	400
Less tax credit	250
	150
deduct higher rate paid on non-qualifying distribution	112.50
Income tax owing	£37.50

V　CLOSE COMPANIES

Companies controlled by one person or by a small group of individuals could be operated so as to secure tax advantages that would be unavailable to the individual taxpayer or to the larger corporate taxpayer. As a result there have been special rules since 1922 aimed at preventing such schemes. FA 1965 introduced a relatively fierce regime for the closely controlled company but since that date a relaxation in the provisions has occurred: most recently, for instance, FA 1989 removed the statutory apportionment of income provisions providing instead for 'close investment companies' (as defined) to be subject to the full rate of corporation tax rate even if they would otherwise qualify as small companies. **[28.121]**

1 What is a close company?

The definition of a close company is:

'one which is under the control of five or fewer participators, or of participators who are directors' (TA 1988 s 414(1)).

Hence, it may be either director-controlled (irrespective of the number of directors involved) or controlled by five or fewer participators. **[28.122]**

a) *The meaning of 'control'*

A person (or two or more persons taken together) is deemed to have control of a company if:

(a) he can exercise control over the company's affairs, in particular by possessing or acquiring the greater part of the share capital or voting power; or

(b) he possesses or is entitled to acquire:

   (i) such part of the issued share capital as would give him a right to the greater part of the income of the company if it were all to be distributed, or

   (ii) the right to the greater part of the assets available for distribution among the participators on a winding up or in any other circumstances.

In deciding whether a person has control there must be attributed to him any rights vested in his nominees, his associates and companies controlled by him or his associates. A 'nominee' is a person holding assets for another. **[28.123]**

b) *The meaning of 'participator', 'associate' and 'director'* (TA 1988 s 417)

'*Participator*' is defined as a person having a share or interest in the capital or income of the company and includes a person who is entitled to acquire share capital or voting rights and loan creditors (but not a bank lending in the ordinary course of its business; TA 1988 s 417(1), (9)).

'*Associate*' of a participator includes: (a) any person related to him as spouse, parent, remoter forebear, sibling, child or remoter issue, and as partner; (b) the trustees of any settlement set up by him or by any person related to him; and (c) fellow beneficiaries under a trust of the company's shares or entitled to shares in the company under the will of a deceased shareholder (TA 1988 s 417(3)).

'*Director*' is defined as a person who occupies that post; any person in accordance with whose instructions the directors act; and a manager paid by the company who, with his associates, owns or controls 20% of the company's ordinary share capital (TA 1988 s 417(5)). **[28.124]**

c) *Companies which are not close*

The following companies which would otherwise fall within the above definition are treated as not being close companies:

(a) any non-resident company;

(b) fcompanies which are registered industrial and provident societies;

(c) companies controlled by or on behalf of the Crown;

(d) companies which would be close companies save for the fact that they are controlled through the beneficial ownership of their shares by one or more companies which are not close companies (therefore, the subsidiary of a non-close company is normally not a close company): note, however, s 414(6) which provides that the UK subsidiary of a foreign parent will be close if the parent would be close were it UK resident;

(e) companies whose shares have been quoted and dealt in on a recognised stock exchange during the preceding 12 months, provided shares carrying at least 35% of the voting power are beneficially held by the public. Shares are not held by the public if (inter alia) they are held by a director of the company or his associates and the exception does not apply when the principal members (ie the five members who hold the greatest voting power in the company, but excluding any who hold less than 5% of the voting power) possess more than 85% of the total voting power.   **[28.125]**

d) *Illustrations of the definition*

Most small private companies will be close. Where there are fewer than ten shareholders the company must be close since five or fewer shareholders must control it. In other situations the matter may require some thought!   **[28.126]**

EXAMPLE 28.31

Aviary Ltd has an authorised and issued share capital of 60,000 ordinary shares of £1 each. Each share carries one vote. The shares are held as follows:

	Ordinary shares
Mr A Robin, Chairman	5,000
Mr B Raven, Managing Director	2,800
Mr C Crow, Director	2,400
Mr D Hawk, Director	4,400
Mr E Thrush, Director	2,200
Mr F Robin, son of A Robin	1,800
Mr G Magpie, Sales Manager	3,600
Mr H Magpie, father of G Magpie	3,000
Mrs J Eagle, sister of G Magpie	3,000
Mrs K Wren, sister of G Magpie	2,400
Sundry small shareholders	29,400
	60,000

Is Aviary Ltd a close company? It will be necessary to consider voting control and to discover whether it is either a company controlled by five or fewer participators or a company controlled by directors who are participators.

Participator/holding		5 largest shareholdings	Shareholdings of all 'directors'
G Magpie—Sales Manager	3,600		
Add associate holdings:			
H Magpie—father	3,000		
Mrs J Eagle—sister	3,000		
Mrs K Wren—sister	2,400		
	12,000	12,000	12,000

A Robin—Chairman	5,000		
Add associate holding:			
F Robin—son	1,800		
	6,800	6,800	6,800
D Hawk—Director		4,400	4,400
B Raven—Managing Director		2,800	2,800
C Crow—Director		2,400	2,400
E Thrush—Director		—	2,200
Total shares		28,400	30,600

Although not controlled by five or fewer participators, Aviary Ltd is a close company because it is controlled by its directors. Notice that for this purpose, Mr G Magpie, the sales manager, is treated as a director because with his associates he holds 20% of the company's shares (TA 1988 s 417(5)).

2 Special rules that apply to close companies

a) *Extended meaning of 'distribution'* (TA 1988 s 418)

Close companies are treated as making distributions when they incur expenses in providing living accommodation or other benefits in kind for a participator or his associates. This rule does not apply in cases where the benefit is subject to taxation under the provisions of TA 1988 ss 153–168 (see Chapter 5), and is designed to catch benefits conferred upon shareholders and debenture holders who are neither directors nor higher-paid employees of that company. The normal rules which govern the taxation of distributions apply. [28.127]

EXAMPLE 28.32

DB Ltd, a close company, provides free holidays costing £1,500 each for Barry, a director, Barney, a shareholder and Betty, a debenture holder.
(1) *Barry's holiday* The cost will be a deductible business expense of DB Ltd. Barry will be assessed under the Schedule E rules on the benefit of £1,500 which he has received.
(2) *Barney's and Betty's holiday* In neither case will the expense be charged under Schedule E but, as both are participators, the expense will be treated as a distribution. Hence, DB Ltd will be required to pay ACT on the expense incurred (in each case this will amount to 25/75 of £1,500 = £500) and Barney and Betty will each have income under Schedule F of £2,000 with a credit for the £500 ACT paid.

b) *Loans to participators and their associates* (TA 1988 s 419)

A close company which makes a loan to a participator or his associate is obliged to pay to the Revenue tax on that loan at the rate of ACT then in force. However, the loan itself is not a distribution. The sum received by the Revenue is not ACT and the borrower is not entitled to any tax credit. The payment to the Revenue may best be described as a 'forced' loan so that, if the participator repays the sum lent, the Revenue will repay the sum that it received. If, however, the loan is either released or written off, the sum held by the Revenue is likewise forfeited and, in addition, the participator will be assessed to income tax at higher rates (if applicable) on the amount of the loan grossed-up at the basic rate for the year of release (for the meaning of a release in this context see *Collins v Addies* and *Greenfield v Bains* (1991)). He will not be liable to the basic rate charge but cannot reclaim any basic rate tax. It follows that loans can be used to defer higher rate tax but not ACT (basic rate). The company will receive no credit against its corporation tax bill for the sum paid to the Revenue. The company must notify the Revenue of the making of such a loan within twelve months from the end of the accounting period in which it is made (failure to do so results in interest on the tax liability being charged from 1 April following the making of the loan). Under the new system of corporation tax collection known as 'pay and file' (see [**28.181**]) which is due to be introduced in respect of accounting periods ending after 1 September 1993, tax payable under TA 1988 s 419 will be due within 14 days after the end of the accounting period in which the loan is made. Tax is assessable regardless of whether all or part of the loan has been repaid at the time of assessment.

EXAMPLE 28.33

In 1990 Simco Ltd lends £75,000 to Mr Needy, a shareholder. In 1991 it releases the debt of Needy.
(1)   *Tax position in 1990*   Simco Ltd will pay the Revenue £25,000 (25/75 of £75,000). This sum is not ACT. Mr Needy suffers no tax consequences.
(2)   *Tax position in 1991*   The Revenue will keep the £25,000. (The company will never get ACT relief for this sum.) Needy will be subject to income tax at higher rate on the loan (£75,000) grossed-up by the basic rate of income tax for 1991 (25%). Hence, he will be taxed on £100,000; and if it is assumed that he is subject to a 40% rate of tax, he will be required to pay further tax of £40,000 − £25,000 = £15,000.

These loan provisions also catch debts owed to the company, save for the situation where goods or services have been supplied in the ordinary course of the business of the company and the period of credit is either normal or does not exceed six months. Debts assigned to the company are likewise treated as loans but the misappropriation of a company's funds does not create a debt since the necessary consensus is lacking (*Stephens v Pittas* (1983)).

These rules do not apply to loans made in the ordinary course of a company's business of moneylending nor to loans not exceeding £15,000 to someone who works full-time for the company and who does not have a material interest in it (a material interest is normally 5% of the ordinary shares). Exceptionally, it may be advantageous to accept a charge under s 419 since the effective charge for the loan (33%) may be less than the income tax rate that would apply were the sum paid as remuneration or dividends.

Two other points must be mentioned. First, if the loan is to a director or higher paid employee, income tax may be charged, under TA 1988 s 160, on interest forgone; and secondly, loans to directors are, in general, prohibited under Companies Act 1985 s 330.   [**28.128**]

c) *Statutory apportionment and close investment holding companies*

One of the main reasons for the introduction of special rules for close companies was to prevent the hoarding of profits within a company in order to avoid high rates of income tax. For accounting periods beginning on or before 31 March 1989 this was achieved through the use of statutory apportionment. This deemed 'relevant income' (which included certain annual payments and interest expenses) to have been distributed to the shareholders so that income tax could be charged on this deemed income as if there had been a normal qualifying distribution. The most effective way to avoid apportionment was, therefore, to distribute profits.

In his 1989 Budget Speech the then Chancellor, Nigel Lawson, declared that:

> 'The rules for the so called apportionment of close companies' income are notoriously complex, taking up some 20 pages of impenetrable legislation. These rules are no longer needed and I propose to abolish them. I believe that family businesses in particular will welcome this substantial simplification.
>
> I do, however, have to guard against the avoidance of tax on investment income by channelling it through a closely controlled investment company.'

As a result, the Close Investment Holding Company ('CIC') was born. The original Finance Bill legislation was, after being greeted with universal disbelief (which arose both because of what was proposed and because of the ineptitude of the drafting), withdrawn and significantly watered down provisions eventually introduced in FA 1989 s 105. In essence, these rules only apply to close companies which are not trading companies or members of a trading group and for these purposes a company will be trading if it exists wholly or mainly for the purposes of trading so that it will not necessarily have to trade in every accounting period in order to satisfy the test. Companies which deal in land, shares or securities are trading companies for these purposes and a company carrying on property investment on a commercial basis will likewise be treated as a trading company and therefore will not be a CIC.

The consequence of being a CIC is that the small companies rate of corporation tax (currently 25%) will not be available: instead the company will suffer corporation tax at the main rate of 33%.   **[28.129]–[28.140]**

VI GROUPS OF COMPANIES

1 **What is a group?**

A group of companies as defined in TA 1970 s 272 comprises at least a parent company (a holding company) which controls another company known as a subsidiary. Groups may consist of any number of interlocking companies; a company for these purposes includes an industrial and provident society; a trustee savings bank; and a building society (TA 1970 s 272(2)). Commercially, a group may be regarded as a single entity; so far as the law is concerned, however, they are generally treated as separate legal entities. The tax legislation to some extent accords with commercial reality in conferring a number of useful reliefs upon companies in a group. These reliefs depend upon the structure of the group: some for instance are available to '51% groups'; some to '75% groups' and 'consortia'; some to '100% consortia', whilst provision is made for the case where a company is both a member of a group and either one of the joint owners of a consortium company or is jointly owned by a consortium.

A '51% group' exists where at least 51% of the ordinary share capital of one company is beneficially owned, directly or indirectly, by another company; and a '75% group' where at least 75% of the ordinary share capital of one company is so owned (TA 1988 s 838). Certain privileges may be available, even if the 75% or 51% group requirement is not satisfied, in cases where at least 75% of the shares of a trading company are owned by a consortium of UK corporate members.   **[28.141]**

2   Taxation privileges available to groups

a) *Group and consortium relief* (TA 1988 s 402)

Group relief applies to 75% groups and to consortia provided that at least 75% of its share capital is owned by UK resident corporate members who each own at least a 5% interest in the consortium company. Thus, individuals or non-resident companies can own up to a 25% interest in a consortium company although they will not qualify for group relief.

EXAMPLE 28.34

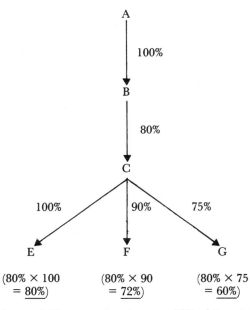

A, B, C and E form a 75% group. A only owns 72% of F and 60% of G. The latter two companies cannot, therefore, form part of a 75% group with A. However, C, E, F and G form a further group.

The relief enables any of the items deductible from total profits (generally charges on income, trading losses, and management expenses; see TA 1988 s 403) to be surrendered to another company in the group or consortium except that such items may not be surrendered by a dual resident investing company to another member of a UK group (TA 1988 s 404). Generally, however, these amounts can be used to reduce the taxable profits of the 'claimant' company on being given up by the 'surrendering' company. It is not necessary to make a payment for group relief but if one is made it is ignored in computing profits and losses of both companies for tax purposes. The relief is more restrictive in the case of consortia since the claimant is only entitled to the fraction of the item available (eg a trading loss) which is proportionate to that member's share in the consortium.

The claimant company must use the relief in the year of surrender; it cannot be carried back or forward and is deducted from total profits after any charges on the income of the claimant company. It need not be surrendered in full (contrast loss relief under TA 1988 s 393(2) where the full loss must be relieved if there are sufficient profits).

A claim for relief must be made within a two-year period. In *Gallic Leasing Ltd v Coburn* (1991), the Court of Appeal held that a valid claim involved the identification of the surrendering company and the amount of loss to be surrendered by each such company. The court stressed that each claim had to be considered separately and that the time period was tied to the surrendering company's accounting period. Hence, if companies A and B surrendered losses to group company C there are two separate claims for relief. Further, 'to constitute a claim, a sufficiently defined quantification of the sums to be surrendered is . . . a necessary requirement. That does not mean that it must be immediately quantifiable. It may have to await figures and calculations not yet available' (Fox LJ).

The problems of 'back-up' or 'top up' claims was considered in the earlier decision of *Farmer v Bankers Trust International Ltd* (1990) which illustrates some of the difficulties that the two-year time limitation can cause. The claim that was made in that case indicated that relief would be sought from various group companies in a particular order (broadly, against companies A and B with a possible back-up claim against C if necessary). The court decided that the taxpayers were tied to the set of priorities identified in that claim and could not subsequently decide that the entire claim be met by company C.

EXAMPLE 28.35

Little Ltd is the wholly-owned subsidiary of Large Ltd. Both companies make up accounts to 31 March and for the year ended 31 March 1991, Little Ltd has trading losses of £20,000 and Large Ltd profits of £400,000. All the loss could be surrendered to Large Ltd resulting in the profits being reduced to £380,000. Alternatively, Little Ltd might carry back all or a part of the loss under TA 1988 s 393(2) and merely surrender the balance. If Large Ltd were to pay £5,000 for the surrender, that sum would be ignored for tax purposes.

TA 1988 s 409 contains provisions to prevent tax avoidance through the use of group relief in an accounting period when a company joins or leaves a group or consortium (eg the setting of losses of existing members against profits made by an incoming member before entry). Generally, profits and losses of the company will continue to be time-apportioned between the two parts of that period, but if this works unreasonably or unjustly (eg where the profits are uneven) such other methods shall be used as may be just and reasonable.

Similarly, TA 1988 s 410 (formerly FA 1973 s 29) is designed to prevent artificial manipulation of the group relief provisions: in particular, the forming of groups on a temporary basis and in order to obtain the relief. Under the terms of this section a company will not be regarded as a member of a group if 'arrangements' are in existence for the transfer of that company to another group (for the meaning of 'arrangements' see SP 5/80 and on the general interpretation of this section *Pilkington v IRC* (1982)). Relief is not available during any period when such arrangements are in force. In *Shepherd v Law Land plc* (1990), for instance, arrangements (an option to purchase the shares of the subsidiary company) came into existence on 6 January 1983 and ceased five weeks later on 11 February 1983 (the option was never taken up). In the accounting period ending 31 March 1983 group relief was therefore not available for that five-week period.

In *J Sainsbury plc v O'Connor* (1991) a joint venture company (Homebase) was formed by Sainsbury's and a Belgium company in which Sainsbury's held 75% of the issued share capital and the Belgians the remaining 25%. There was in addition a cross-option agreement whereby 5% of that share capital could be acquired by the Belgians. The options were not exercisable for a five-year period and, in the event, were never exercised. Did their existence prevent Sainsbury's being entitled to group relief? The Court of Appeal decided that they were so entitled: *first*, because mere existence of the options did not deprive Sainsbury's of their beneficial ownership in the relevant shares: accordingly they satisfied the 75% test. *Secondly*, because the existence of the options did not amount to arrangements which affected the rights of the relevant shares within the test for such arrangements laid down in TA 1988 Sch 18. It is likely that the case will be appealed to the House of Lords and the decision of the lower courts on the second matter (the arrangements question) must be considered debatable.

The group relief provisions do not provide for the pooling of capital losses. Accordingly, it is common for chargeable assets to be transferred within the group (taking advantage of TA 1970 s 273 which prevents any chargeable gain arising: see below) to enable these losses to be utilised.   [**28.142**]

EXAMPLE 28.36

Subsidiary company Alpha intends to sell land to P, but will realise a capital gain of £80,000 on that sale. Assume that another subsidiary company (Beta) has unused capital losses of £100,000. The land could be sold to Beta for full value and then resold by Beta to P.

(i) *on the sale to Beta:* the disposal is on a no gain/no loss basis irrespective of the actual consideration paid (TA 1970 s 273: below). No gain is, therefore, realised by Alpha.

(ii) *on the sale to P:* the gain of £80,000 is realised by Beta, which can use its losses to avoid any corporation tax charge.

This operation is obviously a scheme; it contains an artificial step (the sale to and by Beta), and so at first sight would appear to fall within the *Ramsay* principle. In *News International v IRC* (1989), however, on similar facts Vinelott J held that the principle did not apply. The acquisition of a loss-making company to which the parent then transferred shares for sale on the Stock Market did not involve a composite transaction. Crucially, the terms of the actual sale had not been arranged before the intra group transfer. It does not appear to matter that the subsidiary was acquired for the express purpose of utilising its unrelieved losses.

---

b) *Surrender of ACT*

Within 51% groups a parent which has surplus ACT arising as a result of a dividend payment may surrender all or part of that surplus to a subsidiary (TA 1988 s 240). The recipient company may then use the surrendered ACT against its own corporation tax bill provided that the recipient was a subsidiary of the parent throughout the accounting period in which the ACT was paid.   [**28.143**]

c) *Dividends and charges* (TA 1988 s 247)

Charges on income (for instance interest payments) may be paid gross (without deducting basic rate income tax) between companies in a 51% group or 75% consortium (although in the case of consortia, interest may only be paid gross by the consortium company to a consortium member and not vice versa). As a general rule, the payee is taxed on the payment under Schedule D Case III on the date when that payment is credited to his account which is not necessarily the same date as the date of the payment (see *Parkside Leasing Ltd v Smith* (1985): [**10.1**]). There is an exception for payments made after 16 March 1987 between companies in a group or under common control when (as an anti-avoidance measure) the payment will be deemed to be made and received on the same date (TA 1988 s 341). Dividends (but not other distributions) can also be paid without ACT so long as both payer and recipient agree (the sum is called 'group income': see TA 1988 s 247). So far as the recipient company is concerned, it will not be entitled to a tax credit and the sum it receives will not be franked investment income. There is, of course, nothing to stop ACT being paid and a credit given in the normal way; this may be advantageous when the recipient company wishes to make a dividend payment outside the group and so will wish to receive franked investment income. [**28.144**]

d) *Capital reliefs—the transfer of assets and roll-over relief*

The transfer of an asset within a 75% group is treated as being for such consideration as ensures that neither gain nor loss results (TA 1970 s 273). The result is, therefore, to hold over any gain and any tax is postponed until the asset is disposed of outside the group or until the company owning the asset leaves the group (TA 1970 s 278). For stamp duty purposes *ad valorem* duty will be avoided if the transfer takes place in a 90% group between parent and subsidiary or between one subsidiary and another (FA 1930 s 42). A potential purchaser of a company should, therefore, check whether the company will be subject to such 'exit' charges in the event of its leaving its existing group, or whether any company in a group he acquires has any member company with such a potential 'exit' charge. However, the charge will not arise on a company leaving a group more than six years after the intra-group transfer.

The 'exit' disposal under TA 1970 s 278 may be deliberately triggered, usually in order to crystallise a capital loss as the following example illustrates.

EXAMPLE 28.37

Alpha Ltd transfers a chargeable asset showing a capital loss to subsidiary company Beta Ltd which has realised capital profits. TA 1970 s 273 ensures that the transfer is at no gain, no loss. Beta Ltd then issues shares to a non-group company (Omega Ltd) so that there is a deemed disposal of the asset under TA 1970 s 278 and the loss is thereby realised which can be used to offset Beta's capital gains. Omega then sells the shares to Alpha Ltd. (Whether *Furniss v Dawson* would deny tax relief to Beta Ltd in this example is uncertain; notice that the transaction has resulted in a permanent change in the capital structure of Beta Ltd.)

If the asset transferred had not formed part of the trading stock of the transferor but is appropriated to the trading stock of the transferee the transfer itself is covered by the no gain, no loss rule of s 273; but the transferee is then given an election when the asset is appropriated to his stock (see TA 1970 s 274: this election is similar to that discussed at [**14.106**]). *Either* that appropriation is taxed as a disposal at market value thereby triggering any capital gain (or loss) *or*, alternatively, the transferee may elect to convert that gain into a trading profit (or loss) by postponing any tax until the asset is sold. *Example 14.34* illustrates the operation of this election.

In *Coates v Arndale Properties Ltd* (1984) an attempt to take advantage of the election to obtain group relief for a loss on a capital asset was unsuccessful. The House of Lords concluded that the transferee never acquired the asset as trading stock because it was immediately resold to another member of the same group. Hence, the transaction was not covered by the election. This 'constructional' approach to a tax relieving provision may be contrasted with the House of Lords decision in *Furniss v Dawson:* see further [**31.26**]. In *Reed v Nova Securities Ltd* (1985) the House of Lords were again concerned with the question of when assets are acquired as trading stock and concluded that not only must those assets be of a kind which were sold in the ordinary course of the company's trade but also that they were acquired with a view to resale at a profit.

For roll-over or reinvestment relief, trades carried on by companies in a 75% group are treated as a single trade. Hence, a chargeable gain made by one group member on a disposal of an asset outside the group can be rolled over into an asset acquired from outside the group by another group member (TA 1970 s 276 and SP D19).

EXAMPLE 28.38

R Ltd, S Ltd and Q Ltd are members of a 75% group. The following transactions occur:
(1)   R Ltd disposes of an office block with a base cost of £100,000 to Q Ltd when its value is £150,000;
(2)   Q Ltd sells that asset to T Ltd for £150,000; and
(3)   S Ltd acquires a new office block for use in its business for £200,000.
The taxation consequences of these transactions are:
(1)   *The intra-group transfer from R Ltd to Q Ltd*   is treated as being for no gain/ no loss so that tax on the gain (£50,000) is postponed. Q's base cost is, therefore, £100,000.
(2)   *The sale by Q Ltd to T Ltd*   The asset leaves the group so that a chargeable gain of £50,000 arises to Q Ltd.
(3)   *The replacement asset purchased by S Ltd*   On a claim being made by both companies (Q Ltd and S Ltd) the gain of Q Ltd can be rolled over into the purchase by S Ltd. Hence, S Ltd's base cost of the new asset will be £150,000 (£200,000 – £50,000) and Q Ltd will not be assessed on a gain as a result of the disposal to T Ltd.

The CGT rules in FA 1985 s 71 and Sch 21 dealing with assets disposed of in a series of linked transactions (see [**14.24**]) do not apply to transactions between companies in the same (75%) group which, under TA 1970 s 273, give rise to neither gain nor loss. Thus such transactions do not count as part of any linked series (contrast the situation where there is a transfer between spouses). Special provision is however made for the following case.   [**28.145**]

EXAMPLE 28.39

Asset 1 is transferred by a series of intra group transfers from Slim Ltd to Short Ltd; then to Tall Ltd and finally from Tall Ltd to a connected outsider Wilbur. Asset 2 is transferred directly by Slim Ltd to Wilbur. So long as Wilbur is connected with both Tall Ltd and Slim Ltd the disposal of Asset 1 is treated as having been made by Slim Ltd to him and hence can be linked to the disposal of Asset 2. Any increase in the tax chargeable on the disposal of Asset 1 remains the liability of Tall Ltd (FA 1985 s 71(7)).

e) *Schemes of reconstruction*

Assume that Alpha Limited, with a wholly-owned subsidiary Beta Limited, now acquires all the issued share capital in a further UK company, Gamma Limited. It then desires to merge the businesses of Beta Limited and Gamma Limited by liquidating Gamma once its assets have been transferred to Beta. The simplest and most tax efficient way of achieving this result would be for a scheme of reconstruction falling within the Companies Act 1985 s 582 to be implemented. This would involve the transfer of Gamma Limited's business to Beta in return for an issue of shares by Beta to Alpha Limited followed by the liquidation of Gamma. The transfer of the undertaking will be governed by TA 1970 s 267 since it falls within a scheme of amalgamation or reconstruction. Under this provision no corporation tax will arise on the transfer of chargeable assets which are rolled over into the new company. Equally, the transfer should not attract an ad valorem stamp duty charge since the relevant instrument will fall either under FA 1930 s 42 (a transfer between associated companies) or FA 1986 s 75 (an amalgamation). The issue of the further shares by Beta to Alpha will be governed by CGTA 1979 s 86 which ensures that so far as Alpha is concerned the old shares are treated as merged with the new. Accordingly, no charge will arise at this point and the whole operation should be submitted in advance for clearance. **[28.146]**

3 **The advantages and disadvantages of forming a group**

Commercially, groups of companies have obvious attractions; different enterprises can be segregated into different corporate units each with its limited liability and separate identity. Each trade will, to a greater or lesser extent, have a separate management and in the event of a decision to sell any branch of the enterprise, the appropriate company can be sold to the purchaser. From a taxation point of view, however, and despite the various reliefs considered above, forming a group is often disadvantageous because the various grouping provisions do not cause all the companies to be treated as one for tax purposes and, accordingly, certain reliefs are restricted. One obvious, but nevertheless potentially significant, problem with using groups which is sometimes overlooked, is the effect on the application of the small companies rate of tax to the members of the group. Where companies are 'associated', the upper and lower limits for each associated company for calculating whether tapering relief is available are divided by the number of associated companies plus one. This can lead to the loss of tapering relief and hence a failure by the group as a whole to take full advantage of the small companies rate of corporation tax. Two companies are associated if they are under common control or if one has control of the other (TA 1988 s 13). **[28.147]–[28.160]**

VII   THE OVERSEAS DIMENSION

A company which is resident in the UK is liable to corporation tax on all its profits wherever arising (TA 1988 s 8(1)). A non-resident company is liable to corporation tax only if it trades in the UK through a branch or agency and liability will then be restricted to the chargeable profits from that branch or agency (TA 1988 s 11). A non-resident company trading in the UK but not through any branch or agency, cannot be assessed to corporation tax but will automatically be subject to UK income tax: in such cases, as the company will probably not have any UK presence, the UK Revenue may have problems of tax collection. Any charge under the CGT rules will only arise on the trade assets of non-resident persons who are deemed to be trading through a branch or agency in the United Kingdom (CGTA 1979 s 12).   **[28.161]**

1   **The meaning of 'residence'**

Traditionally, companies have been treated as UK resident and taxed accordingly if their central management and control was situated in the UK. The law developed in a series of cases and where precisely management and control is exercised is obviously a factual question of some difficulty. Generally, of course, such powers will be vested in the board of directors, so that the problem becomes one of identifying where the board exercises its powers. Two general points should be stressed. *First*, that the overseas country where the company was incorporated is usually of small significance when it is a question of establishing UK residence. *Secondly*, it is possible under English law for a company to be 'dual resident', namely resident in more than one country (for the Revenue's views on the meaning of residence see SP 6/83).

From 15 March 1988 this residence test has been supplemented by an additional test based upon the place of company incorporation. As a result, UK incorporated companies will always be taxed as UK residents irrespective of where central management and control is exercised. There is now therefore a dual test in operation as a result of which a company will be UK resident if *either* it was incorporated here *or*, in the case of companies incorporated abroad, its central management and control is located here (SP 1/90 sets out the Revenue's views on these new rules). UK incorporated companies which were non-resident immediately before 15 March 1988 and were then carrying on business will, under transitional rules, not be deemed to become UK resident until 15 March 1993. There is, however, nothing to stop such companies becoming UK resident at an earlier date if central management and control becomes exercised in the UK. It should also be remembered that a UK incorporated company whose place of effective management is in a country with which the UK has concluded a double tax treaty may, if the treaty contains the appropriate article, continue to be treated as a resident of that other country for the purposes of the treaty.   **[28.162]**

EXAMPLE 28.40

(1) Styx Ltd, a UK incorporated company, was trading on 15 March 1988 and, because its management was located in Liechtenstein, was then taxed as a non-UK resident. It will become UK resident at the latest on 15 March 1993 whereupon its world-wide profits will then fall into charge to UK

corporation tax. Accordingly, it may be desirable to run down the business of the company before that date.

(2) Aster Ltd is incorporated in the UK on 16 March 1988 and is managed and controlled from Liechtenstein. It is taxed as a UK resident corporation.

(3) Rambo Ltd is incorporated in Panama and controlled by directors resident in the UK. It is taxed as a UK resident company.

2 Tax consequences of ceasing to be UK resident

A UK incorporated company cannot lose its UK residence. In the case of overseas companies, however, if central management and control becomes located elsewhere, UK residence will cease and in that event a tax charge will arise on the unrealised gains of the company immediately prior to its change of residence. The charge to tax is introduced by provisions in FA 1988 which deem the company to have disposed of all its assets at market value immediately before it migrates and to have immediately reacquired them: any claim for roll-over reinvestment relief on the deemed proceeds of such assets is excluded.

EXAMPLE 28.41

On 1 August 1989 Rambo Ltd (see *Example 28.40*, above) ceases to be UK resident. At the relevant time it owns chargeable assets worth £200,000 on which its allowable expenditure is £50,000. Immediately before its change in residence it is deemed to sell the assets for £200,000, immediately reacquiring them, and thereby realising corporation tax profits of £150,000 in Financial Year 1989.

The company must inform the Revenue in advance of its intention to cease UK residence (see SP 2/90 for the procedure to be followed) and this should be done by notice in writing specifying the time when this change will occur and should include a statement of UK tax payable together with particulars of how that tax is to be paid. The tax in question may include any PAYE for which the company is liable. If such tax remains unpaid for more than six months, it may then be recovered from, inter alia, a controlling director or another company in the same group. Failure by the company to comply with the notification procedures before ceasing to be UK resident may lead to a penalty on both the company and certain other persons: the maximum amount payable being equal to the tax unpaid at the time when the company ceased to be resident. [28.163]

3 Taxing resident companies

All profits wherever made by a UK resident company will be charged to corporation tax subject to any available double taxation reliefs. Any credit for foreign tax may be set against corporation tax on the UK company's foreign income or gains in priority to ACT (TA 1988 s 797(4)). When a trade is to be carried out by a UK company in a foreign country there are three possible methods of operation available.

First, the trade may be with that country so that there is no trading presence within the country and foreign tax is avoided (typically a representative office is established in the foreign country).

Secondly, a branch may be opened overseas which, from a UK tax point of view, results in any profits being subject to corporation tax. It also means that loss relief will be available and that problems of leaving the UK are avoided. Double tax relief permits the set-off of foreign tax against UK corporation tax on the profits of the branch either by virtue of a double tax treaty with the relevant country (TA 1988 s 788) or by unilateral relief (TA 1988 s 790).

EXAMPLE 28.42

Accounting period to 31 March 1992

	£
UK profits	2,000,000
Overseas branch profit (income and gains)	100,000
(overseas tax paid £25,000)	
	£2,100,000
Corporation tax (33%)	693,000
less relief	25,000
UK tax payable	£668,000

Notes
(1) Double tax relief cannot exceed the amount of corporation tax attributable to the foreign income or gains; hence the maximum relief in this example is 33% of £80,000 = £28,000. *should it not be 33% x 100000 = £33000*
(2) Double tax relief is set against corporation tax on overseas income or gains in priority to ACT; relief is available for unused ACT (see [**28.97**]).

Thirdly, a subsidiary non-resident company may be formed with the result that corporation tax is generally avoided on profits until they are distributed to the UK by way of dividend. The attractions are obviously considerable when the tax rates in the overseas country are very low in comparison with those in the UK and TA 1988 ss 747–756 introduced provisions to prevent tax avoidance by the use of controlled foreign companies (CFC). The provisions enable the Board to apportion chargeable profits amongst all persons with an interest in the CFC and to assess a UK resident company holding such an interest, provided that at least 10% of the profits would be apportioned to it. These provisions only apply if the CFC is under UK control and is resident in a 'low tax' area, defined as one where the tax is less than one-half of what would have been charged in the UK (for FY 1991, therefore, at rates of less than $16^{1}/_{2}\%$), and which is not on the list of countries to which the provisions will not be applied. Even then, the CFC's chargeable profits must exceed £20,000. There are provisions to ensure that a charge will only arise where a CFC is used with the object of avoiding tax and to exclude CFCs which pursue an 'acceptable distribution policy', or carry on 'exempt activities'. The provisions do not catch chargeable gains which may be apportioned amongst UK shareholders under CGTA 1979 s 15 when the overseas company is 'close' (see Chapter 20).   [**28.164**]

4 Taxing non-UK resident companies

Companies not resident in the UK are subject to corporation tax on income arising from a trade carried on in the UK through a branch or agency. The crucial factor in establishing a liability to UK tax is, therefore, whether a trade is carried on within the United Kingdom or not. This question depends primarily upon where contracts are made: if within the United Kingdom then UK tax is attracted; if outside the United Kingdom then there will be no charge (see further Chapter 13). Other income arising from a UK source may be charged to income tax in the non-resident company's hands (TA 1988 s 6(2)). Hence, a property investment company with no branch or agency in the UK, but owning land in the UK, would be assessed to income tax on the profits arising from that land. Similarly, a trading company carrying out a UK contract without establishing any branch or agency would be subject to income tax and not corporation tax.

Capital gains will be chargeable only if they arise from property associated with the trade carried on by the branch or agency (TA 1988 s 11(2); CGTA 1979 s 12). In the case, therefore, of a non-resident property company owning land in the UK, no chargeable gain will arise on a disposal of its capital assets. A UK resident subsidiary of an overseas company will be a separate legal entity from the overseas company and will be subject to UK tax on its worldwide income. From 20 March 1990 if a UK branch or agency is transferred to a UK resident company in the same world-wide group as the transferor company, a tax charge can be postponed if a joint election is made by both companies (TA 1970 s 273A). **[28.165]**

5 Taxing non-resident shareholders of resident companies

The tax credit and franked investment income provisions only apply to a resident shareholder. Therefore a non-resident is generally not entitled to any tax credit (TA 1988 s 231) and neither is he liable to income tax at the basic rate. In the case of an individual, liability to income tax at the higher rates might arise, charged upon the amount of the distribution (not grossed-up) to the extent that those higher rates exceed the basic rate. The shareholder might be able to claim the benefit of double taxation relief. **[28.166]–[28.180]**

VIII PAY AND FILE

1 Introduction

Following recommendations made in the Keith Committee Report (Cmnd 8822, see [2.101]) designed to streamline the machinery for the assessment and collection of corporation tax, F(No 2)A 1987 ss 82–91 amended TMA 1970 by introducing a new system ('pay and file') for company returns. The system is designed to pave the way for an efficient machinery of self-assessment.

At present, the Revenue send out approximately 65,000 corporation tax returns each year of which only some 10% are completed. This is followed by the raising of an assessment, the majority of which are inevitably estimated and which are therefore appealed against by the taxpayer. Once a company has submitted its accounts, the figures then have to be agreed, whereupon a further assessment is made and the tax thereon must be paid within 30 days. This whole process is both costly and time-consuming and results in a considerable delay in the collection of corporation tax.

It is planned that pay and file will become operative on 30 September 1993 (although this date may be changed if the Revenue has not managed to put the necessary computer systems in place by this time). The pay and file rules will therefore apply to accounting periods ending on or after 1 October 1993. The legislation governing pay and file was introduced in 1987 to enable the Revenue to organise its operations and to give taxpayers and their advisers sufficient time to prepare for the introduction of the new system. Since the publication of the Keith Report, the Revenue have been involved in consultations with bodies representing business and the legal and accountancy professions. The most recent consultative document on the topic was published by the Revenue in February 1991 and contained the proposed forms to be used by companies when making returns under the new system. In the same month the Revenue also published a booklet entitled *A First Guide to Corporation Tax Pay and File* to introduce the taxpayers to the new system.   [**28.181**]

2   The operation of pay and file

a) *Payment of tax and filing returns*

Pay and file system is based on self-assessment. Under the system a company will be required to pay its corporation tax—or at least what the company calculates to be its liability—within nine months of the end of its accounting period. To assist in this process, the Revenue will issue a new form of corporation tax return (CT 200). Companies will be required to complete this return and deliver it to the Revenue within 12 months of the end of the period to which the return relates. The return will include a corporation tax computation which will enable the company to calculate its own liability. When filing its return a company must deliver computations showing how the figures in the return were calculated and a copy of its audited accounts for the period.

Under pay and file, claims for group relief, capital allowances and repayments of income tax will have to be made by way of a completed tax return. If a company wishes to alter any of these claims or to revise the corporation tax calculation, a new form of amended return (CT 201) must be used. Alterations to these details will not be accepted in any other form.

The requirement to make a return under pay and file is not automatic—a company is only required to make such a return if a form is sent to it. However, a company which is liable to pay corporation tax in respect of an accounting period must notify the Revenue of this fact within 12 months of the end of that accounting period. Furthermore, the company must pay its estimated corporation tax liability by the normal due date (ie nine months after the end of the accounting period).   [**28.182**]

b) *Interest*

Although tax returns under pay and file need not be filed until up to 12 months after the end of the relevant accounting period, it must be stressed that the normal due date for payment of corporation tax remains nine months after the end of the accounting period. Interest will run as from this date if the tax has not been paid. Interest on any overpayment or underpayment will also be calculated from the due date. Not surprisingly, the interest on overpayments will not be as high as the interest on underpayments, and in line with the Revenue's intended future practice, the rates of interest will be closely linked to market rates.   [**28.183**]

c) *Late and incorrect returns* (TMA 1970 s 94)

If a completed return is not delivered to the Revenue within the 12-month period, the following rapidly escalating penalties are automatically imposed:

Return filed within 12 months	:	no penalty
Return filed within 15 months	:	£100
Return filed within 18 months	:	£200
Return filed within 24 months	:	£200 + 10% of unpaid tax
Return filed outside 24 months	:	£200 + 10% of unpaid tax

Those companies which are guilty of persistent failure to make returns are subject to more severe penalties since if a penalty has been levied in respect of both of the two previous accounting periods, and the return for the third period is also late, the flat rate penalties become £500 (instead of £100) and £1,000 (instead of £200). **[28.184]**

EXAMPLE 28.43

A Ltd makes up its accounts to 31 October each year. Its corporation tax return for the year ended 31 October 1993 is submitted on:
(a) 15 November 1994; or
(b) 15 March 1995; or
(c) 15 January 1996: no tax was unpaid on 1 May 1995; or
(d) 15 January 1996: £1,000 tax was unpaid on 1 May 1995, but was paid by 10 June 1995.
The penalties levied under each of these alternatives are:
(a) £100 (£500 if the returns for the previous two accounting periods were also late);
(b) £200 (£1,000 if the returns for the previous two accounting periods were also late);
(c) £200 (or £1,000—notice no tax-related penalty is due);
(d) £400 (or £1,200—a tax-related penalty (20% × £1,000) is added to the flat rate penalty).
For the purposes of calculating penalties, 'unpaid tax' means the amount owing after 18 months, account being taken of credit for income tax withheld, but not for any surplus ACT carried back unless it is a surplus carried back for less than two years.

EXAMPLE 28.44

B Ltd did not file its corporation tax return for the accounting period ended 31 October 1993 until 15 June 1996. The final corporation tax due was £1m which was paid as follows:

(a)	ACT credit on dividend paid during 1993	£400,000
(b)	CT paid on the normal due date (1 August 1994)	£300,000
(c)	ACT carried back (on dividend paid in 1994)	£ 80,000
(d)	ACT carried back (on dividend paid in 1996)	£200,000
(e)	CT paid when accounts finally agreed in 1997	£ 20,000
		£1,000,000

Any tax-related penalty will be based on £220,000 being:		
(d)	ACT carried back for more than two years	£200,000
(e)	CT unpaid on 1 May 1994	£ 20,000
		£220,000

If a company negligently or fraudulently files a false return, penalties can be up to 100% of the tax lost.

d) *Assessments*

A final assessment will be issued by the Revenue once a company's liability has been agreed. Companies will be entitled to repayments of income tax deducted at source before its final liability is agreed. The use of estimated assessments will be limited under pay and file to situations where the Revenue believe that, for example, a return understates the true liability.

Special provision is made in pay and file for the collection of tax payable in respect of loans to participators in close companies under TA s 419 (see [**28.128**]). Once the system comes into operation, the amount of tax payable on such loans will be due 14 days after the end of the accounting period in which the loan is made.   [**28.185**]

29 The taxation of partnerships

Unlike companies and unincorporated associations, a partnership, whether trading or professional, is not subject to any special rules of taxation. To a limited extent it is treated as a separate entity, but, generally, the ordinary principles of income tax, CGT and IHT have to be applied to each partner individually. **[29.1]**

I INCOME TAX

For the purposes of assessing and collecting income tax a partnership is to some extent treated as a separate entity. A trading partnership will be taxed under the rules of Schedule D Case I, a professional partnership under Schedule D Case II. In both cases, the precedent partner (which means the senior partner or the partner whose name appears first in the partnership deed) must make a return of partnership income (TMA 1970 s 9). Each individual partner should make his own separate tax return in which he claims his personal allowances (TA 1988 s 277). The Revenue will then make a joint assessment to tax in the partnership name (TA 1988 s 111). This tax bill, which is simply the aggregate tax for which each partner is liable, is based upon each partner's share of profits for the current tax year and takes into account his personal reliefs, charges on income, and 50% of his Class 4 NIC paid in the tax year on his share of the profits which attracts relief as a charge on income (see [**4.66**]). The Revenue will supply information to the senior partner as to how the bill was calculated so that on receipt of the tax bill individual accountability can be established between the partners. The tax will be due in two equal instalments, on 1 January in the appropriate tax year, and on 1 July following the tax year. **[29.2]**

1 Liability for the tax

The tax can be paid either by each partner remitting his own share, or by the firm discharging the bill when arrangements will be made to charge individual partners with their proportion, normally by debiting their current account. Liability of the partners for the assessment is joint, but not several, so that if the bill is not paid the Revenue can proceed for the entire sum against any one of the partners who can join his fellow partners as co-defendants (RSC Ord 15 r6). On the death of a partner his estate is released from liability to the Revenue for any unpaid tax, except where the deceased was the last surviving partner when his estate will be liable for all the tax, with the right of contribution from his former partners' estates (see *Harrison v Willis Bros* (1965)). Thus, if one partner is bankrupt, the Revenue will not be affected since they can proceed against the other (solvent) partners for the full amount of tax; it is they who will suffer because of that bankruptcy.

The nature of the partnership tax bill was well illustrated in the case of *Stevens v Britten* (1954) where a retiring partner was to be indemnified by the continuing partners for all partnership liabilities outstanding at the date of his retirement. Since the partnership's liabilities included the income tax bill presented after his retirement, but in respect of a period before his retirement, the retiring partner was entitled to be indemnified against his share of that bill.   [29.3]

EXAMPLE 29.1

A and B have been in partnership for five years. Their net profits (for tax purposes) for the 12 month period ended 31 December 1990 are £80,000 assessable in 1991-92 (preceding-year basis; see below).

In 1991-92 A and B share profits equally and have no other income. They pay Class 4 NIC amounting to £900.90 each (6.3% × £14,300 (£20,200 − £5,900)), of which 50% (£450.45) constitutes a charge on income for both A and B. In addition A has other charges on income of £4,000 and personal reliefs of £5,015; B has other charges on income of £3,000 and a personal relief of £3,295.

The partnership income tax bill for 1990-91 is calculated as follows:

	A	B
	£	£
Income from all sources:		
ie share of profits (Sch DI/II)	40,000	40,000
Less: charges on income	4,450.45	3,450.45
Total income	35,549.55	36,594.55
Less: personal reliefs	5,015	3,295
Taxable income	£30,534.55	£33,254.55
Tax payable at basic (and higher) rate	£ 8,658.82	£ 9,746.82

In 1991-92 an assessment for tax of £18,405.64 (ie £8,658.82 + £9,746.82) is made on the partnership; each partner is jointly liable for the whole of the tax bill (ie £18,405.64).

---

2   How to calculate the profits of the partnership

a) *Contrast the sole trader/practitioner*

The procedure for calculating the profits of a partnership under Schedule D Cases I and II is basically the same as for the sole trader or practitioner (see Chapter 6).

In *MacKinlay v Arthur Young McClelland Moores & Co* (1989) the Court of Appeal allowed a partnership to deduct removal costs paid to encourage two partners to move house: in one case from London to Southampton, in the other from Newcastle to Bristol. In both cases the move was desirable from the point of view of the firm's business and neither partner would have agreed to move had his relocation expenses not been borne by the firm. Slade J explained the Court of Appeal decision and distinguised the *Mallalieu* case (see **[6.113]**) as follows:

'The analogy between the case of expenses incurred by a sole trader of which he is the beneficiary and the case of expenses incurred by a partnership, of which one partner is the beneficiary, is a misleading one. Section 74(a) . . . directs attention to the object of the *spender*, not the recipient. In the first of those two cases it is impossible to differentiate between the objects of the taxpayer *qua* spender and *qua* beneficiary; . . . in the second case, where the payer and the beneficiary are not the same, it is clearly possible to evaluate the objects of the payer in incurring the expenditure separately and distinctly from those of the beneficiary . . . The Revenue (must) ascertain the purpose of the expenditure at least primarily by what was referred to in argument as the ''collective purpose'' of the partnership in incurring it.'

Not surprisingly, the House of Lords reversed the Court of Appeal and, in so doing, restated the principles underlying the rules governing the deduction of business expenditure. The House of Lords held, first, that there was no difference for these purposes between a partnership—even a large professional body run by a management committee on corporate lines— and a sole practitioner. In both cases, to be deductible, expenditure must be 'wholly and exclusively laid out or expended for the purposes of the trade, profession or vocation'. Only in very limited situations is an English partnership a separate entity for tax purposes and the speeches of the Law Lords emphasise again that tax rules applicable to individuals must apply to unincorporated bodies. In some cases this is easier said than done: for instance, the application of CGT principles to partnerships is far from straightforward, as will be discussed later.

A second principle to emerge from the speeches is that (in the words of Lord Oliver) 'a partner working in the business or undertaking of the partnership is in a very different position from an employee'. Crucially, he is also a proprietor and accordingly any money which he withdraws from the business whether in the form of a share of profits, 'salary', or interest on partnership capital, must be treated as a share of profits. This matter will be discussed later. It remains, however, an over-simplification to assume that *no sums* paid out by the firm to a partner can amount to a deductible business expense for the firm. Rent, for instance, paid to a partner who leases premises to his firm (provided, of course, that the sum involved is not excessive) will attract an income tax charge in the hands of the recipient partner. The removal expenses considered by the House of Lords in *Arthur Young* did not fall into a similar category. **[29.4]**

b) *The basis of assessment*

Generally, and the matter is essentially one of Revenue practice, trading partnerships will be assessed on the earnings basis. Professional partnerships will be required to render accounts on the earnings basis for the first three years, but thereafter may be permitted to change to either the bills delivered basis (so long as they give an undertaking to bill clients regularly) or even to the cash basis. The cash basis is particularly advantageous for an expanding business because the increase in debtors (unpaid bills) will be ignored.

The preceding year basis of assessment applies to partnerships (see **[6.141]**). Thus, the optimum accounting date in order to obtain the greatest delay in paying the tax bill is 6 April (this gives a 21-month delay before the first instalment is due with a further six-month period before the second is payable). However, the firm should choose its accounting date carefully as the averaging procedure applied by the Revenue on a change of accounting date (see IR 26; **[6.144]**) may result in increased liability to tax.

Although tax will normally be charged on profits calculated on the preceding year basis, those profits will be allocated between the partners in accordance with the profit-sharing ratio in force for the tax year when the profits are assessed and *not* by reference to any arrangement in force for the accounting year when the profits were earned.

EXAMPLE 29.2

Zea and Co make up their accounts to 31 December. For the year ending 31 December 1990 profits were £60,000 divided equally between Z and E. On 6 April 1991 a new arrangement was entered into whereby Z agreed to take 60% and E 40% of the profit.

£60,000 will be the assessable profits for 1991–92 (preceding year basis). Tax will be assessed according to the profit-sharing ratio in force *for that tax year* (1991–92).

Hence:
Z's share = 60% × £60,000 = £36,000
E's share = 40% × £60,000 = £24,000

Notice that Z is, therefore, taxed on £6,000 profits which E had received in 1990. If the changed sharing ratio comes into force on a day other than the first day of the tax year it is necessary to divide the profits on a time basis and then to apply the different sharing ratios to those divided profits. Say, for instance, that the change occurred on 5 October 1991:

Profits from 6 April to 5 October 1991 = £30,000 (¹/₂ × £60,000) divided between Z and E in the ratio 50:50. Therefore, Z's share is £15,000 and E's share is £15,000.

Profits from 6 October 1991 to 5 April 1992 = £30,000 (¹/₂ × £60,000) divided between Z and E in the ratio 60:40. Therefore, Z's share is £18,000 and E's share is £12,000.

Thus, of the total taxable profits for 1991–92 of £60,000, Z's share is £33,000 (£15,000 + £18,000) and E's share is £27,000 (£15,000 + £12,000).

Although standard accounting practice as amended by the appropriate tax statutes is applied in arriving at the taxable profit (see Chapter 6), a number of specific matters merit comment: **[29.5]**

Salary paid to partners How a partner's salary is taxed depends on whether he is a partner or merely an employee of the firm. The terms employed by the parties themselves are not decisive of the matter; it is the substance of the relationship between them, as determined from the partnership agreement that needs to be considered (see *Stekel v Ellice* (1973) discussed at **[5.22]**). Notice, however, that the Revenue's usual practice is to assess salaried partners under Schedule E with the result that changes involving them will not cause a cessation of the business. In view of the relatively high level of National Insurance contributions payable by an employer in respect of his higher paid employees (see Chapter 32), the firm should consider carefully how it wishes new 'partners' to be taxed and draft the partnership agreement accordingly.

If the individual is merely an employee the salary paid is a deductible partnership expense on which he should be assessed under Schedule E with tax deducted at source under the PAYE machinery. If the individual is a partner, however, the salary is not an allowable expense of the firm but an agreed profit sharing method. Hence, the firm's accounts must show the profits as including salaries paid to partners which are then taken into account when apportioning those profits amongst the partners. Where salary entitlement changes between the accounting year and the tax year when those profits are assessed to income tax it follows that (i) any salary actually paid in the accounting year will be added back for the purpose of calculating the profits chargeable to tax, but (ii) when the profits are allocated for the tax year, it is the salaries then paid which are taken into account. **[29.6]**

EXAMPLE 29.3

Balthazar, Mountolive and Justine are in partnership sharing profits in the ratio 3:2:1 after deducting salaries agreed at £1,000, £2,000 and £3,000 respectively. In the year ended 31 December 1990 the business profits (after deducting salaries) were £12,000.

For 1991–92 the assessment on the firm will be on £18,000 (the Revenue treating the salaries as a profit-sharing method) attributed to the partners as follows:

Balthazar:	£1,000 (salary) plus £6,000	(3/6 × £12,000) =	£7,000
Mountolive:	£2,000 (salary) plus £4,000	(2/6 × £12,000) =	£6,000
Justine:	£3,000 (salary) plus £2,000	(1/6 × £12,000) =	£5,000
	£6,000 (salaries) + £12,000	(balance of profits) =	£18,000

If the partners are entitled to personal allowances and charges on income of £3,000, £2,500 and £2,000 respectively (£7,500 in total) for 1991–92, the tax liability of the firm and its division between the partners will be as follows (assuming that they have no other sources of income):

	Balthazar £	*Mountolive* £	*Justine* £
Total income	7,000	6,000	5,000
Less personal allowances	3,000	2,500	2,000
Taxable income	£4,000	£3,500	£3,000
Tax chargeable (at 25%)	£1,000	£ 875	£750

The total of the partners' liabilities is £2,625 (£1,000 + £875 + £750). Therefore, the firm is assessed on £18,000 less allowances of £7,500 ie £10,500 at 25% = £2,625.

The tax should be paid in two equal instalments on 1 January and 1 July 1992.

Interest paid to partners Partners may be paid interest on capital they contribute to the firm. As with salaries, the interest is not a deductible expense, but is treated as a profit-sharing method. Hence, the profits must be adjusted by adding back the interest and the share of each of the partners in the profits then calculated. **[29.7]**

Rent paid to a partner Where premises are owned by one partner and leased to the firm, any rent paid will be an allowable deduction from the firm's profits, unless it is exorbitant; the partner concerned will be taxed on that rent as unearned income under Schedule A. It may be more attractive for the premises to be let to the partnership at a nominal rent and for the partner to receive his payment in the form of an increased share of the profits. This will not of course be tax deductible by the firm, but the partner concerned will have the benefit of an assessment under Schedule D Cases

I or II (rather than Schedule A) and, potentially, full CGT retirement relief on an eventual disposal of the premises (see [**16.97**]).

When the partner has taken out a loan for the purchase or improvement of the premises the interest on which may qualify for income tax relief, care must be taken to obtain that relief and, at the same time, preserve full retirement relief on those premises (see SP 4/85 and *R v Inspector of Taxes, ex p Brumfield* (1989) discussed at [**4.51**]. Thus if he receives rent from the firm or if the firm discharges the interest payments ('deemed rent') income tax relief will be obtained by setting the interest due against the rent (or deemed rent) but retirement relief will be restricted. Notice, of course, that if the premises belong to all the partners they cannot let those premises to the firm sice a person cannot let property to himself (see *Rye v Rye* (1962)). [**29.8**]

Deposit interest on solicitor's clients' money (See LS Gaz 19 April 1978)   Where client's money is held in a general (ie undesignated) client bank deposit account the interest earned belongs to the partnership, but will not form a part of the firm's profits assessed under Schedule D Case II. Instead the interest will be apportioned between the partners and taxed under Schedule D Case III as unearned income.

Where the firm pays a client interest on money held in that account the Revenue apply the following principles: first, the sums paid are not an allowable deduction in calculating the firm's profits; secondly, the sum is paid gross (ie basic rate tax is not deducted); thirdly, the partners will only be assessed under Schedule D Case III on any balance remaining after such payments. [**29.9**]

Losses   Losses incurred by the partnership will be apportioned between the partners in the same way as any profits, each partner dealing with his share of the loss under the normal relieving provisions (see Chapter 7). The operation of these provisions on a change in the partners is discussed at [**29.16**]. In the case of a limited partner, however (whether an individual or a company), loss relief is restricted to the amount which that partner has at risk in the partnership (see TA 1988 s 117 reversing *Reed v Young* (1986)). [**29.10**]

3   Interest relief on loans to acquire a share in a partnership

Tax relief is available for interest on money which is borrowed to acquire a share in a partnership, or to be used by the firm, or to acquire machinery or plant to be used by the firm. The relief operates by enabling the borrower to deduct the interest as a charge on his income (TA 1988 ss 362, 359(1),(2); see Chapter 4). In contrast, where the firm borrows money, any interest paid can only be a deductible business expense (TA 1988 s 174; see Chapter 6). [**29.11**]

4   Changes in the partnership

a) *Basic income tax rule: a deemed discontinuance*

This section is concerned with a change in the partners not with an alteration in the profit-sharing ratios in cases where the partners of the firm remain the same. The following examples all represent changes in the partners of a firm:

old firm	the change	new firm
(1) AB	take in C	ABC
(2) ABC	C leaves	AB
(3) ABC	replace C with D	ABD
(4) ABC	death of C	AB
*(5) A	creates partnership	AB
*(6) AB	dissolution of partnership	A

(5) and (6) although not examples of changes in a continuing partnership are subject to similar rules.

Any change in the ownership of a business, eg the taking in of a new partner, results in a deemed discontinuance of the old business. Hence, in the above examples the old firm is treated as discontinued and a new firm as commencing the business (TA 1988 s 113). As a result, the old partners are subject to the closing year rules (which have been considered at [6.145]) and the new partners are assessed in accordance with opening year rules. So far as the opening year rules are concerned the position is as follows:

(1) Prior to 19 March 1985 the 'normal' opening year rules (ie those discussed at [6.143]) were applied to all partnership changes (thus they applied in the six illustrations listed above).

(2) For changes of partners *within a continuing partnership* new opening rules were, however, introduced for changes after 18 March 1985. Notice therefore that these new rules do not apply in *Illustrations* (5) and (6) above since the changes do not occur within a continuing partnership.

It is not proposed to discuss further the closing year rules nor the 'normal' opening rules but the new rules are considered in section b) below.

Although a deemed discontinuance is provided for in s 113(1), it is possible to prevent this from happening in cases where at least one person has continued to be engaged in the business before and after the change and *all* those engaged in the business before and after the change make the necessary election (TA 1988 s 113(2)). This election for a continuance, which ensures that the closing and opening rules do not apply, is considered below (see c)) and whether partners should exercise this election or not is discussed in section d). Finally (see e) below), the effect of changes in the partners when losses are being made by the firm is considered.   [29.12]

b) *Special opening year rules for continuing partnerships*

These opening year rules apply where there is at least one common partner in the old and the new partnership and the same business continues to be carried on (ie as in (1)-(4) above).

In contrast to the ordinary opening year rules which displace the normal (ie preceding year) basis for only two years with the result that the new firm's first 12 months of profit form the basis for its assessments to tax in its first 3 years, these special rules displace the normal basis for the year in which the change occurs and the *three* following years of assessment.

In the year of assessment in which the change occurs the firm is taxed on its actual profits from the date of the change to the end of the tax year. In the second, third and fourth years of assessment, the firm is assessed on its actual profits earned in those tax years. In the fifth and subsequent years of assessment, the normal (preceding year) basis of assessment applies, although the firm has an election (under TA 1988 s 62) in respect of the fifth and sixth years to be taxed on the actual profits of those years. The election must be made within seven years after the end of the fifth year of assessment for both the fifth and sixth years. The election can be withdrawn within that same period.   **[29.13]**

EXAMPLE 29.4

(1) Big, Medium and Little were in partnership as Big and Co drawing up accounts to 30 September each year. On 30 September 1991, Little retired from the partnership and the new firm of Big and Medium began on 1 October 1991. The firm has the following profits:

Accounting period	Profit (£)
Year ended 30 September 1992	3,000
Year ended 30 September 1993	10,000
Year ended 30 September 1994	12,000
Year ended 30 September 1995	14,000
Year ended 30 September 1996	6,000
Year ended 30 September 1997	16,000

Its taxable profits in the first 5 years of assessment (under the special opening year rules) are as follows (see also the diagram on the next page):

Tax year	Basis period		Profit (£)
1991–92 *First*	Actual: 1 October 1991–5 April 1992 ie $\frac{6}{12} \times £3,000$		1,500
1992–93 *Second*	Actual: 6 April 1992–5 April 1993 ie $\frac{6}{12} \times £3,000$	= £1,500	
plus	$\frac{6}{12} \times £10,000$	= £5,000	
			6,500
1993–94 *Third*	Actual: 6 April 1993–5 April 1994 ie $\frac{6}{12} \times £10,000$	= £5,000	
plus	$\frac{6}{12} \times £12,000$	= £6,000	
			11,000
1994–95 *Fourth*	Actual: 6 April 1994–5 April 1995 ie $\frac{6}{12} \times £12,000$	= £6,000	
plus	$\frac{6}{12} \times £14,000$	= £7,000	
			13,000
1995–96 Fifth	Preceding year: Year ended 30 September 1994		12,000
1996–97 *Sixth*	Preceding year: Year ended 30 September 1995		14,000
	Total profits		£58,000

Note: Big and Medium would make an election under TA 1988 s 62(4) to revise the amendments for 1995–96 and 1996–97 to an actual basis as this will produce profits of only £10,000 and £11,000 respectively thereby reducing the total profits over the first 6 years by £5,000 to £53,000.

(2) Take the same facts as in (1) except that on 30 September 1991 both Medium and Little retire from the partnership and the new sole trade of Big & Co commences on 1 October 1991 and is subject to the ordinary opening

year rules of TA 1988 s 61. Its taxable profits in the first 6 years of assessment are as below (see also diagram below):

Years of assessment		*Profits (£)*
1991–92 *First*	Actual: 1 October 1991–5 April 1992	1,500
1992–93 *Second*	First 12 months of trading ie 1 October 1991–30 September 1992	3,000
1993–94 *Third*	Preceding year ie year ending 30 September 1992	3,000
1994–95 *Fourth*	Preceding year ie year ending 30 September 1993	10,000
1995–96 *Fifth*	Preceding year ie year ending 30 September 1994	12,000
1996–97 *Sixth*	Preceding year ie year ending 30 September 1995	14,000
	Total profits for first five years	£43,500

Note: Big & Co would not make an election to revise its 1992–93 and 1993–94 assessments to an actual basis as this would produce extra taxable profit of £3,500 in 1992–93 and £8,000 in 1993–94 thereby increasing the overall profit to £55,000.

1991–92	1992–93	1993–94	1994–95	1995–96	1996–97
£1,500	£6,500	£11,000	£13,000	£12,000 (£10,000)	£14,000 (£11,000)

Oct 91/ Oct 92	Oct 92/ Oct 93	Oct 93/ Oct 94	Oct 94/ Oct 95	Oct 95/ Oct 96	Oct 96/ Oct 97
£3,000	£10,000	£12,000	£14,000	£6,000	£16,000

£1,500	£3,000 (£6,500)	£3,000 (£11,000)	£10,000	£12,000	£14,000
1991–92	1992–93	1993–94	1994–95	1995–96	1996–97

[1] New rules; [2] Accounting years; [3] Old rules.

c) *Electing for a continuance* (TA 1988 s 113(2))

The deemed discontinuance rules of TA 1988 s 113(1) will not apply if all the partners (or their PRs) before and after the change make a written election (within two years of that change) that the firm shall continue to be taxed on the preceding year basis. As a result the closing and opening year rules are excluded. The same trade must be carried on before and after the change.

The continuing partners should ensure that all necessary consents for an election can be obtained. Hence, new partners will usually only be admitted to the partnership if they agree (often in a recital to the partnership deed) to join in making a TA 1988 s 113 election if required to do so by the other partners. Provision should also be made in the partnership deed to ensure that a partner who leaves can be required to join in any election and for the PRs of a deceased partner to be likewise under a duty to sign the notice of election if required to do so by the continuing partners.

Where an election is made so that the firm continues to be taxed on the preceding year basis, the new partnership will be assessed on profits earned by the old partnership.

EXAMPLE 29.5

For the year ended 31 December 1990 Zea and Co's adjusted profits were £100,000 divided equally between Z and E. On 6 April 1991 A became a partner receiving 20% of the profits and joined in a s 113(2) election.

£100,000 will be the taxable profits for 1991-92 (preceding year basis). Profits are allocated on a *current year* basis—ie in accordance with the profit-sharing agreement of the partners in 1991-92. As A is then a partner the allocation will be:

Total profits	=	£100,000
A's 20%	=	£20,000
Balance	=	£80,000
Z and E (40% each)	=	£40,000 each

Although Z and E will have each received £50,000 of the profits earned in 1989, they will be taxed only on £40,000 of those profits. A, on the other hand, will be taxed on £20,000 but received none of the 1990 profits!

It is common for an incoming partner, the personal representatives of a deceased partner and outgoing partners to be given an indemnity in the partnership deed for any extra tax occasioned by their joining in the s 113 election. The wording of such an indemnity is important; it will not provide for an indemnity for *all* the tax suffered by the elector, but only for any extra tax resulting from the election. Hence, if tax paid would have been less had the election not been made (calculated according to opening year principles) than the tax actually paid as a result of the election, that difference will be recoverable under the indemnity. Where profits are rising the indemnity will be valueless since tax under the opening rules would be *more* than tax calculated according to the preceding year rules. Even in cases where the profits are static, no advantage results. In many cases a new partner will have been a former employee of the firm with the result that the profits are likely to rise to reflect the fact that his salary ceases to be payable and, therefore, to be a deductible expense. Only if profits are falling is there likely to be any payment made under the indemnity. Whether the same indemnities will continue to be given in the light of the special opening year rules for continuing partnerships is somewhat doubtful. Hitherto the indemnity has covered only the first three tax years of the new firm. Under the special provisions, however, it will operate for the first seven years so that it is far more likely that the existing partners will have to make reimbursement payments to the incoming partner.

One alternative to an indemnity is to provide that each new partner shall pay, as his share of the firm's tax bill, tax on what he actually receives.

This clause, however, is not easy to reconcile with the preceding year basis of assessment. In *Example 29.5*, for instance, should A only pay tax on 20% of the profits actually earned in 1991–92 when they are assessed in 1992–93 or (and preferably) should he pay tax on that sum in 1991–92 with the remaining tax apportioned between Z and E × Where profits are rising the incoming partner will pay more tax than on the preceding year basis: where they are falling he will pay less.

Where a partnership change occurs on a day other than the first day of the tax year, the tax assessment will be divided into two: one on the old partners, and one on the new with the profits being apportioned on a 'just' basis. In practice, time-apportionment is employed.

EXAMPLE 29.6

If in *Example 29.5* A had joined the firm on 5 October 1991, the income tax would be calculated thus:

Profits for tax year 1991–92 = £100,000 (preceding year basis)

Profits from 6 April–5 October = £50,000 (6 months)

Z's share (50%) = £25,000
E's share (50%) = £25,000

Profits from 6 October–5 April = £50,000 (6 months)

A's share (20%) = £10,000
Z's share (40%) = £20,000
E's share (40%) = £20,000

The total profits for 1991–92 of £100,000 will, therefore, be allocated as to £45,000 to each of Z and E and £10,000 to A.

There is nothing to prevent a whole series of elections being made at short intervals. Indeed the operation of large professional partnerships makes such elections commonplace. Special provision is, however, made for the case where two changes occur within two years of each other and the election for a continuance is made on the first, but not on the second of those changes (TA 1988 s 113(3)(b)). In this case, on the second change (the discontinuance), the closing rules will apply as if the first change had never occurred. Hence, although the earlier change is not treated as a discontinuance, the operation of the closing rules can increase the liability of a partner who left the firm at the time of the election for a continuance. **[29.14]**

d) *When should the election for a continuance be made?*

Whether the firm should make the election depends on the facts; in particular, whether a cessation will result in the application of the special or the old discontinuance rules to the new firm. Where the old rules apply the election will generally be advantageous if profits are rising. If profits are static or falling, it may not, since a cessation will result in the profits of the first 12 months of the new firm forming the basis of taxation for the first three years of assessment.

Profits can be kept low in the first year of the new firm by advancing revenue expenditure and borrowing into that period and by transferring work in progress from the old to the new firm for a value exceeding cost (under TA 1988 s 101, see **[6.90]**).

The main reason for the introduction of the special rules was to prevent firms from taking advantage of these rules by arranging a cessation approximately every five years before a year in which the profits would then be kept low by the above methods. For changes to which the special rules apply, a planned cessation confers a tax advantage only for the first year of assessment after the change and this may be outweighed by the potential disadvantages attendant on such a cessation. For instance, if the firm had drawn up its accounts on the cash basis, the cessation will result in a return to the earnings basis for three years, whilst assessment on the actual basis for four years after a cessation results in the loss of the income tax deferral facility implied in any assessment on the preceding year basis.

EXAMPLE 29.7

As in *Example 29.4(1)* above and in the tax year of change (1991–92) the Revenue will issue estimated assessments for the partnership tax due on 1 January 1992 and 1 July 1992 even though the partnership accounts and the partners' profit shares are not finalised until (say) 1 January 1993 (ie 6 months after the end of the accounting period). The same problem will arise in each of the 3 following tax years.

Note:
(1) If income tax is underpaid as a result of the assessments, Big & Co will be liable to interest on the underpayment from the date when the tax was due.
(2) The 1991–92 assessment will have to be agreed with the Inspector before the partners' retirement annuity relief can be calculated.

In view of these disadvantages it is likely that the election will be made in the majority of deemed discontinuances. It should be remembered, however, that the special opening rules do not apply to *actual* discontinuances: eg on a merger (or demerger) where there is a change in the nature of the business carried on by the two firms comprised in the merger (or demerger) (see *Humphries (George) Ltd v Cook* (1934) and, for the Revenue view, SP 9/ 86). Further, the fact that the new rules do not apply to the dissolution of a firm where one partner only is left to continue the business may lead to strategic partnership demergers and cessations to which the old opening rules continue to apply.   [**29.15**]

EXAMPLE 29.8

(1) Firm A and firm B, both estate agents, agree to a merger. Given that the new firm, AB, will carry on the same business (albeit on an expanded scale) the Revenue view is that AB has succeeded to the businesses of both the old firms. Accordingly, the choices facing the partners are; first, to elect under s 113(2) in respect of both businesses; secondly, to elect in respect of one only (the election might be that AB continues the business of A); or, thirdly, to accept a discontinuance under s 113 in which event the special opening rules will apply to AB. (SP 9/86 para 3.)
(2) Firm AB splits into its component parts, partnership A and partnership B. It is a question of fact whether A or B has succeeded to the trade of AB but this will often not be the case so that there will be discontinuance of the business of AB and two new businesses (subject to the normal opening rules) will have commenced. The Revenue accept that a succession may occur if 'one of the businesses carried on after the division was so large in relation to the rest as to be recognisably "the business" as previously carried on'. (SP 9/86 para 5.)

e) The deemed discontinuance and loss relief

The deemed discontinuance rules do not affect entitlement to loss relief. Instead, the loss provisions look to what actually happens to the individual partners. Hence,

(1) Relief under TA 1988 s 380 and FA 1991 s 72 (carry-across) and TA 1988 s 385 (carry-forward) is available so long as the taxpayer remains engaged in the same business as a partner before and after the change. In *Illustration (1)* at [**29.12**], for instance, A and B will be able to utilise these loss provisions.

(2) Relief under TA 1988 s 388 (terminal relief) is only available to an outgoing partner and only if the continuation election is not made. The continuing partners cannot take advantage of the deemed discontinuance to claim terminal relief. In *Illustration (2)*, therefore, C may be able to take advantage of s 388 (he will, of course, not be able to claim relief under TA 1988 s 380, FA 1991 s 72 or TA 1988 s 385), but A and B will be unable to do so.

(3) Relief under TA 1988 s 381 (new businesses and professions) will be available only to new partners. Thus, in *Illustration (1)*, C will be entitled to use s 381; and, in *Illustration (3)*. [**29.16**]

5 Income tax consequences of leaving the partnership

a) Consultancies

An outgoing partner may be retained as a consultant whereupon he will often be paid a substantial fee in return for relatively minor duties. For income tax purposes, the consultant is not a partner so that any sum paid to him by the firm will be a deductible business expense under Schedule D Case II assuming that it can be justified according to the 'wholly and exclusively' test (see Chapter 6 and note *Copeman v Flood* (1941)). The consultant will normally be occupying a Schedule E office or employment so that PAYE should be operated and he may benefit from joining the firm's pension scheme for a few years. In some cases he may be able to establish that he is exercising a profession or vocation and should, therefore, be assessed under Schedule D Case II. This argument is more likely to succeed where the individual holds consultancies with several different bodies, or where he is not paid a 'salary' but an *ad hoc* fee each time advice is given. In view of the heavy National Insurance contributions payable by a firm in respect of highly paid employees (see [**32.43**]) the firm should consider carefully whether it may be preferable to retain the individual as a partner with a reduced profit share rather than as a consultant and Schedule E employee. [**29.17**]

b) Payment of annuities by continuing partners

Professional partnership agreements often make provision for the payment of annuities to retiring partners in consideration for the outgoing partner surrendering his share of the firm's goodwill and of its capital assets (see [**29.44**] ff). It is largely a matter of commercial expediency whether such annuities are to be payable and if so for how long and for what amount. The recipient would probably prefer an annuity linked to the profits of the business (eg 10% of the net profits) rather than a fixed sum, as this should offer 'inflation proofing'. The following income tax provisions should be noted: [**29.18**]

Position of paying partners   It is usual for the cost of an annuity to be borne by the partners in the same proportion as they share the profits. They are treated as making fully effective annual payments which means that the payments are deductible from their income as a charge on income and should be paid net of basic rate income tax (see Chapter 10). Further, the annuity will not be caught by TA 1988 s 347A or s 674A and will therefore be a tax effective settlement of income so long as it is payable under a partnership agreement to a former member of that partnership, or his widow or other dependants (where the partner is dead the annuity must not be payable for more than ten years) and is payable under a liability incurred for full consideration.

Alternatively, the annuity will be a fully effective annual payment if it is paid in connection with the acquisition of a share in the business of the outgoing partner (TA 1988 s 683(1)(a) and (6)).

The partnership agreement will often provide for any incoming partner to take over the cost of an appropriate share of the annuity and that, should the firm cease to exist, the outstanding years of the annuity are to be valued and treated as a debt owed by the partnership at the date of its cessation.   **[29.19]**

Position of the recipient   The recipient will be taxed on the annuity under the rules of Schedule D Case III (see Chapter 10) with a credit for basic rate tax deducted at source. The annuity will be taxed in his hands as earned income to the extent that the amount payable does not exceed one-half of the average of that partner's best three years' profits out of the last seven; any excess is unearned income (TA 1988 s 628). Those profit figures are index-linked. Hence, where he is paid a fixed annuity the proportion treated as earned income may vary from year to year.

Notice that if the annuity is payable after the recipient's death to a widow(er) or dependants, they may have problems enforcing the payments should the continuing partners default (see *Beswick v Beswick* (1967)).   **[29.20]**

EXAMPLE 29.9

The partnership agreement of Falstaff and Co provides for retiring partners to be paid an annuity for ten years after retirement amounting to 10% of the annual net profits of the firm earned in the preceding accounting year.

Hal retires as a partner on 5 April 1991. His share of the profit (index-linked) in the last seven years before his retirement is as follows:

1990–91	£20,000*	1986–87	£11,000*
1989–90	£14,000*	1985–86	£ 8,000
1988–89	£ 8,000	1984–85	£ 9,000
1987–88	£ 7,000		

In the tax year 1991–92 Falstaff & Co's net profits (calculated on the preceding year basis) amount to £90,000. The continuing partners will pay Hal £6,750, ie 10% × £90,000 = £9,000 less basic rate income tax deducted at source under TA 1988 s 348. Hal must enter the gross amount of the payment (£9,000) in his income tax calculation for 1991–92 with a tax credit for £2,250 (basic rate tax deducted at source).

The £9,000 is treated as earned income in Hal's hands up to a limit of £7,500 (being half the average share of his taxable profits in the best three of the last seven years before retirement (ie 1990–91; 1989–90; 1986–87). The balance of £1,500 is treated as unearned income.

c) *Retirement annuities and personal pension schemes*

In addition to or instead of (b) above, partners as self-employed individuals should provide for their retirement by taking out insurance. Prior to 1 July 1988, such insurance had to take the form of a retirement annuity contract approved by the Inland Revenue under TA 1988 s 619. However, in order to bring retirement provision for the self-employed into line with that available to employees, TA 1988 ss 630–655 required both employees who contract out of occupational pension schemes on or after 1 July 1988 and partners who provide for their retirement after the same date to enter new personal pension scheme arrangements. Pensions are considered further in Appendix VIII. [**29.21**]

d) *The well timed departure!*

A well-timed departure (typically by the senior partner) may, as a result of the firm making a continuation election, result in a substantial tax holiday. Note, in the following example, the contrast between the share of profits taken by that partner (£156,000) and the sum on which he is actually taxed (£66,000)! [**29.22**]–[**29.40**]

EXAMPLE 29.10

The accounts of the firm are made up to 6 April each year and the senior partner retires on 6 April 1989. The election for a continuance is made.

Year ended	Adjusted profits	Senior partner's 30%	Year of assessment	Senior partner pays tax on
6.4.86	100,000	30,000	1987/88	30,000
6.4.87	120,000	36,000	1988/89	36,000
6.4.88	140,000	42,000	1989/90	Nil
6.4.89	160,000	48,000	1990/91	Nil
6.4.90	180,000	Nil	1991/92	Nil
		£156,000		£66,000

II CAPITAL GAINS TAX

1 General

The application of CGT principles to partnerships causes considerable difficulties which are exacerbated by the failure of the legislation to make express provision for the treatment of partnerships. It is, therefore, necessary to apply rules designed for individuals to firms and rely on the Revenue Statements of Practice SP D12; SP 1/79; and SP 1/89 which do not have the force of law and are a poor substitute for proper legislation in this field.

In applying the CGT legislation to partnerships the general principle is that CGT is triggered by a disposal of a chargeable asset which is treated as made by the individual partners. Although the tax return is made by the firm, the assessment is made on the individual partners (CGTA 1979 s 60; TMA 1970 s 12(4)) in the proportions in which they own the asset surpluses and is determined primarily by the partnership deed. In the absence of any specific agreement, such entitlement follows the profit-sharing arrangements. Often, however, the asset surplus entitlement will be different from the profit sharing ratio to reflect the partners' respective contributions to the capital of the business.   **[29.41]**

EXAMPLE 29.11

(1) Flip & Co, a trading partnership, has three partners, Flip, Flap and Flop, who share asset surpluses in the ratio 3:2:1. In 1987 the firm acquired a valuable Ming vase for a base cost of £60,000; they sell it subsequently for £180,000. The gain of the firm (ignoring any incidental costs of disposal and the indexation allowance) is £120,000. CGT will be calculated separately for each partner:

Flip owns 3/6 of the asset and, therefore, has a base cost of £30,000 and is entitled to 3/6 of the sale proceeds (£90,000); his gain is £60,000 (ie he is entitled to 3/6 of the partnership gain).

Flap's base cost is 2/6 of £60,000 (£20,000) and his share of the proceeds is 2/6 of £180,000 (£60,000) so that his gain is £40,000.

Flop's base cost is 1/6 of £60,000 (£10,000) and his share of the proceeds is 1/6 of £180,000 (£30,000) so that his gain is £20,000.

(2) Assume that the Ming vase is given to Flip in recognition of his 25 years' service with the firm. It is worth £180,000 at the date of the gift. The position of Flap and Flop is basically unchanged and they have made gains of £40,000 and £20,000 respectively. Tax may be postponed by an election under CGTA 1979 s 126 if the donors and Flip agree. In that event Flap will dispose of his 2/6 share for £20,000 and Flop his 1/6 share for £10,000.

The position of Flip is that since he is given the asset he is not treated as making a disposal of his original 3/6 share in the asset (see SP D12 para 3).

Hence, the only difficulty is to discover Flip's base cost. Under general principles it will be:

	£	
	30,000	(cost of original 3/6 share)
plus	60,000	(market value of Flap's 2/6 share at date of gift)
plus	30,000	(market value of Flop's 1/6 share at date of gift)
	£120,000	

The result is that Flip's own gain (£60,000) is held over until such time as he disposes of the vase.

If an election is made under CGTA 1979 s 126 Flip's base cost becomes:

	£	
	30,000	(as above)
plus	20,000	(balance after deducting held-over gain on Flap's share)
plus	10,000	(balance after deducting held-over gain on Flop's share)
	£60,000	

2 Changing the asset surplus sharing ratio

CGT may be triggered when the asset surplus sharing ratio is altered.

Old partners	New partners	Old asset surplus sharing ratio	New asset surplus sharing ratio
(1) AB	ABC	1:1	1:1:1
(2) AB	AB	1:1	2:1
(3) ABC	ABD	1:1:1	2:2:1

In all the above cases there has been a change in the entitlement to asset surpluses (and, therefore, to the beneficial ownership of the capital assets). No asset has been disposed of outside the firm, but there has been a disposal of a share of the assets between the partners. In (1) above A and B formerly owned the assets equally; C now joins the firm and is entitled to 1/3 of the asset surpluses. A and B have each made a disposal of 1/3 of their original share in the assets. A, for instance, is now entitled to 1/3 instead of 1/2 or, to put the matter another way, they have together made a disposal of 1/3 of the total assets to C. In (2), although the partners remain the same, the sharing ratio is altered so that B is making a disposal to A of 1/3 of his share of the assets. In (3), C is disposing of a 1/3 share in the assets amongst the continuing partners, A, B and D (A and B each acquire an extra 1/15 of the assets and D 3/15).

Such changes in the sharing ratio are likely to occur principally in three cases: (i) on the retirement or expulsion of a partner; (ii) on the introduction of a new partner; and (iii) on the amendment of the original agreement. It should be noted that the mere revaluation of an asset in the accounts of the firm has no CGT consequences since the revaluation is neither a disposal of an asset nor of a share in assets. (Compare the individual taxpayer who is not assessed to CGT merely because his Ming vase has risen in value from £50,000 to £75,000.)

Whether CGT will be assessed on the disponer depends upon whether he is paid for the share in the asset that he transfers, or whether an adjustment is made to his capital account in the firm by crediting it for that share so that no money is actually paid to him. The CGT position in the latter case will turn upon whether the relevant asset had been revalued in the firm's balance sheet. In some cases, however, the relevant assets may not have been revalued in the accounts. Therefore, on the disposal, the disponer's capital account will not be credited with any gain. For CGT purposes, there has been neither gain nor loss so that no CGT will be payable. This is an example of a no gain/no loss disposal (and is treated as such for the purposes of rebasing and indexation, see SP 1/89) and results in the postponement of payment of any CGT.

EXAMPLE 29.12

(1) Fleur and Camilla have been in partnership sharing profits and asset surpluses equally. The only substantial chargeable asset of the business is the freehold shop which cost £40,000 in 1983. Fleur now sells her share to Charlotte for £75,000.

Fleur has made a disposal of her half share in the asset and her gain (ignoring any incidental costs of disposal and the indexation allowance) will be:

	£
Consideration received	75,000
Less base cost (50% of £40,000)	20,000
Gain	£55,000

(2) Slick and Slack are in partnership owning asset surpluses in the ratio 2:1.

The main capital asset is the firm's premises which cost £30,000 in 1983 and have recently been revalued at £75,000. The two partners have the following interests in this capital asset:

	Slick £	Slack £
Original expenditure	20,000	10,000
Share of increased value	30,000	15,000
	£50,000	£25,000

Sloth joins the firm and Slick disposes of one half of his share to Sloth with the result that the sharing ratio becomes 1:1:1. The capital account of Slick will be credited with the value of the share transferred and ultimately he will be paid that sum of money. Slick has thus disposed of 1/3 of the asset (or 1/2 of his share) which has a value of £25,000. That sum will be credited to his capital account with the result that he will have made a gain (ignoring the indexation allowance) for CGT purposes of £25,000 (consideration for the share disposed of) less £10,000 (base cost of the share disposed of) = £15,000.

Slick will be assessed to CGT on this gain despite the fact that he may not be entitled to receive the £25,000 until the firm is dissolved or until he leaves it. So far as the incoming partner Sloth is concerned he will acquire a 1/3 share of the capital asset, of a value of £25,000, and that figure will be his base cost (it will often be the capital sum that he will pay into the firm on becoming a partner).

(3) If in (2) above Slick and Slack had never revalued the premises (which appear in the accounts at their original cost price of £30,000) on the disposal to Sloth, Slick will be treated as transferring half of his share for its book value (£10,000) with the result that he will have made no gain. Correspondingly, Sloth's base cost will be £10,000 so that he is acquiring an asset pregnant with gain.

A failure to revalue an asset, with a subsequent transfer of it at cost, might be viewed as a gift to the incoming partner so that market value should be substituted for the share transferred. In *Example 29.12 (3)* this would produce a gain for Slick of £15,000 (£25,000 — £10,000). However, although partners are generally connected persons, they are not so treated in respect of transfers of partnership assets. Hence, the presumption of gift will not apply unless the partners are connected in some other capacity, eg parent and child, and even in those circumstances the Revenue state that 'market value will not be substituted ... if nothing would have been paid had the parties been at arm's length' (SP D12 para 7). In all cases, therefore, there will be no question of market value being substituted *so long as the transaction can be shown to be one entered into at arm's length*. Normally, the commercial nature of the arrangement will be assumed. Where there are connected persons, however, the onus is on the taxpayer to show that identical transactions would have been made with a stranger. This onus will usually be discharged by showing that the incoming partner was assuming a large share of responsibility for the running of the business and, thus, furnishing consideration for his share of the assets.

If the bounty element is so great that the transfer must be treated as a gift, the Revenue have stated that 'the deemed disposal proceeds will fall to be treated in the same way as a payment outside the accounts'. In such a case any CGT can be postponed by the parties electing to hold-over the gain under CGTA 1979 s 126.   **[29.42]**

EXAMPLE 29.13

Jake and Jules are brothers and are in business together sharing profits equally. The chargeable assets of the firm cost a total of £20,000 and are now worth £200,000 although they have not been revalued in the firm's books. Jake now transfers his 50% share to his two sons, Jason and Jasper. For CGT Jake's base cost is £10,000 (1/2 of £20,000). As those assets have not been revalued, they will be passed at that value to his sons. CGT will not be payable.

Should the Revenue successfully claim (as is likely) that the arrangement did not amount to an arm's length bargain, Jake, Jason, and Jasper could make an election under CGTA 1979 s 126 to hold over Jake's gain.

3 Goodwill

Goodwill is a chargeable asset for CGT purposes. Thus, the disposal of the whole or part of a firm's goodwill may be an occasion of charge to CGT. Problems have arisen in recent years (especially with regard to professional partnerships) when the existing partners decided not to charge future incoming partners for any share of the firm's goodwill and, therefore, to write off the goodwill in the partnership's balance sheet. On the question as to whether those partners who originally paid for a share of that goodwill (usually on becoming partners in the firm) can then claim immediate CGT loss relief, the following principles may be suggested.

First, on an actual disposal of the goodwill, whether on retirement or to an incoming partner, provided that its value has been written off in the partnership's balance sheet, an allowable loss for CGT purposes may be claimed by the disposing partner.

EXAMPLE 29.14

Alfie is a partner in Cockney Films & Co. When he joined the firm in 1983 he paid £10,000 for a share in the goodwill. The firm has decided to write off goodwill since incoming partners will no longer be expected to pay for a share of it. When he retires and a new partner, Slicker, joins there will be no payment for Alfie's share of goodwill and Alfie will have made a loss for CGT purposes of £10,000 (being the difference between what he originally paid for the asset and the consideration received on its disposal; for the CGT treatment of losses see [**14.81**]).

Secondly, at the time when the goodwill is written off in the balance sheet, the partners may wish to claim immediate loss relief based on CGTA 1979 s 22(2) which allows a claim for loss relief when 'the inspector is satisfied that the value of an asset has become negligible'. The Revenue do not agree that the mere writing off of goodwill has this result but take the view that goodwill retains its value even though no longer paid for by incoming partners or shown in the firm's balance sheet, on the grounds that if the business were sold, the consideration would include a sum for goodwill. Whether this fact should influence the valuation of an individual partner's share in circumstances where he could not unilaterally receive consideration for it is most debatable. The law in this area is not settled, with a few inspectors apparently allowing loss claims. (On the time limit for making claims under s 22(2) see ESC D28.) **[29.43]**

4 **Payment of annuities**

When a partner leaves the firm any annuity payments that he receives from the continuing partners will be subject to income tax ([**29.20**]) and, in addition, their capitalised value may be treated as consideration for the disposal of a share of the partnership assets (CGTA 1979 s 31(3)) and CGT levied on any resultant gain. In SP D12 the Revenue have indicated when this will be the case:

'The capitalised value of the annuity will only be treated as consideration for the disposal of his share in the partnership assets, if it is more than can be regarded as a reasonable recognition of the past contribution of work and effort by the partner to the partnership. Provided that the former partner had been in the partnership for at least ten years an annuity will be regarded as reasonable for this purpose if it is no more than two-thirds of his average share of the profits in the best three of the last seven years in which he was required to devote substantially the whole of his time to acting as a partner.

For lesser periods the following fractions will be used instead of the two-thirds:

Complete years in partnership	Fraction
1–5	1/60 for each year
6	8/60
7	16/60
8	24/60
9	32/60'

Where the partner receives both an annuity and a lump sum, the Revenue's view is that:

'If the outgoing partner is paid a lump sum and an annuity, the Revenue will not charge CGT on the capitalised value of the annuity provided that the annuity and one-ninth of the lump sum together do not exceed the relevant fraction of the retired partner's average share of the profits' (SP 1/79).

The lump sum will, therefore, always be charged to CGT and it may cause the capitalised value of the annuity to be taxed.   [**29.44**]

EXAMPLE 29.15

(1) Charles and Claude agree to pay their partner, Clarence, who retires on 5 April 1992 after 18 years as a partner, an annuity of £3,000 pa for the next 10 years. His share of the profits in the last 7 years of the partnership was as follows:

Tax year	Profits £	Tax year	Profits £
1991–92	5,000	1987–88	2,000
1990–91	10,000*	1986–87	4,000
1989–90	14,000*	1985–86	5,000
1988–89	12,000*		

The annuity does not exceed two-thirds of Clarence's average share of profits in the best 3 years (those asterisked) of the last 7 years before retirement, ie $2/3 \times$ £36,000 divided by 3 = £8,000. Therefore, no CGT is paid on the capitalised value. (Note that for income tax purposes the annuity will be earned income in Clarence's hands up to £6,000; ie $1/2 \times$ £36,000 divided by 3.)

Contrast the position if Clarence had been paid an annuity of £9,000 pa. As the permitted £8,000 figure is exceeded the entire capitalised value of that annuity will be subject to CGT.

(2)   Assume that, in addition to the annuity (in (1)), it is agreed that Clarence is to receive a lump sum of £54,000. His CGT position is as follows:
  (i)   the annuity will be subject to income tax;
  (ii) the lump sum (£54,000) will be subject to CGT in so far as it represents consideration for a disposal of chargeable assets; and
  (iii) the capitalised value of the annuity will also be included for CGT purposes since the annuity (£3,000) plus 1/9 of the lump sum (£6,000) exceeds the 2/3 limit of £8,000.

5   Reliefs

These reliefs have been considered in detail earlier. Those of particular relevance to partnerships are: **[29.45]**

Hold-over relief under CGTA 1979 s 126.   **[29.46]**

Roll-over (reinvestment) relief (CGTA 1979 s 115). Of particular importance, notice the extension of the relief in two circumstances. *First*, it applies to assets which are owned by an individual partner and used by the firm, so long as the entire proceeds of disposal are reinvested in another business asset used by the firm or used in a new trade carried on by the partner (see [1974] BTR 409). *Secondly*, where land (or another qualifying asset) is partitioned between the partners it is treated as a new asset for the purpose of this relief provided that the firm is dissolved immediately afterwards (see ESC D23).

Retirement relief   The relief will apply when a partner disposes of his share of the business. By FA 1985 s 70, the relief is extended to cover the disposal of an asset owned by a partner provided that it is used by the firm at that time and that its disposal is associated with the disposal of his partnership share (see **[16.98]**, *Example 16.20*). For these purposes it is sufficient if the disposal represents merely a partial withdrawal from the business.

   Since the payment of an actual or deemed rent to the individual partner operates to deny full relief, a partner who wishes to keep an asset in his name, whilst allowing the firm to use it, should ensure that he is paid for its use by an increased share of the profits rather than by a payment of rent.   **[29.47]**

Hold-over relief (CGTA 1979 s 123). This relief is available on the incorporation of a partnership.   **[29.48]-[29.60]**

III   INHERITANCE TAX

As with CGT, there are few specific references in the IHT legislation to partnerships. General principles, therefore, operate and gratuitous transfers of partnership assets or interests therein may be treated as transfers of value by the individual partners (see *Example 29.16*).

   Normally, the share of a retiring partner in the firm will pass to the continuing partners. There is no risk of an IHT charge where full consideration is paid, and, even where that is not so, IHT will be avoided if (as is usually the case) the transfer is a commercial transaction within IHTA 1984 s 10(1) (see **[21.20]**).

EXAMPLE 29.16

Big & Co has twenty partners all equally entitled to profits. The following changes are to occur:

(1) Partner Zack is retiring and is to receive an annuity for his share of the assets. His share of goodwill is to pass automatically under the partnership deed to the continuing partners.

(2) Partner Uriah is to devote less time to the business and will receive a reduced share of the profits (including capital profits). At the same time, partner Victor is to be paid an increased profit share to reflect his central position within the firm.

(3) Partner Yvonne is retiring and her place is to be taken by her daughter Brenda. No payment is to be made by Brenda.

The IHT consequences of these transactions are as follows:

(1) *Zack*   There is no risk of an IHT charge since consideration is given for his assets (there may not even be a fall in value in his estate). Regarding the automatic accrual of goodwill, it is generally thought that the estate duty case of *A-G v Boden* (1912) is still good law for IHT. Thus, mutual covenants by the partners that goodwill shall pass to the surviving partners on death or retirement without any cash payment will make the transfer of goodwill non-gratuitous within IHTA 1984 s 10(1). This principle should apply even where the other parties are, or include, connected persons since it should be possible to show that identical arrangements would have been made with partners who were not so connected.

(2) *Uriah*   The loss to Uriah's estate is the result of a commercial bargain since he is being allowed to devote less time to the business; IHT is not, therefore, potentially chargeable. Likewise, increasing the profit-sharing ratio of Victor is merely a recognition by the other partners of his commercial necessity to the firm.

(3) *Yvonne*   The new partner is a connected person and it will be hard to justify this arrangement on commercial grounds as it would not have been entered into with a stranger. On that basis, IHT will be assessed on the fall in value of Yvonne's estate if she dies within seven years after the transaction.

The major IHT reliefs applicable to trading and professional partnerships will be business property relief, agricultural relief, and the instalment option (see Chapter 23). Two points of particular relevance to partnerships should be repeated: *first*, on a transfer of assets held outside the firm and consisting of land, buildings and machinery or plant, business property relief at 30% may be available. If the asset is owned by the partnership the full 50% relief may apply. *Secondly*, the IHT business reliefs are not available where a partner's share is subject to a binding contract of sale at the time of transfer. Therefore, if it is desired to ensure that on the death or retirement of a partner his share shall pass to the survivors whilst at the same time preserving IHT business property relief, the partnership deed should avoid either imposing an obligation on the remaining partners to purchase his share or even providing for his share to accrue automatically to them. Instead the deed should give the surviving partners an option to purchase that share (see [**23.45**] and [1984] STI 651).   [**29.61**]

30 Stamp duty

'The law upon the subject of stamps is altogether a matter positivi juris. It involves nothing of principle or reason but depends altogether upon the language of the legislature.' (Taunton J in Morley v Hall (1834).)   [**30.1**]

I   INTRODUCTION

The first stamp duties were introduced in 1694 during the reign of William and Mary and they have since remained a permanent feature of the fiscal landscape. The cardinal feature of stamp duty and one which distinguishes it from the other direct taxes is that it is strictly a charge on instruments and not on either transactions or on persons. This originally simple structure has, however, been eroded gradually over the years by the growth of numerous charges to and exemptions from duty.   [**30.2**]

1   Reform

In response to a government Consultative Document issued in 1983 ('The Scope for Reforming Stamp Duties'), FA 1985 removed much dead wood and effected a significant simplification of the tax. In addition to reducing the rate of *ad valorem* duty on sales of shares and marketable securities, FA 1986 broadened the base of the duty to include instruments (executed in connection with eg company takeovers) which had previously enjoyed an exemption. It also introduced the stamp duty reserve tax (SDRT) which levied duty on certain transactions where no stamped document exists. The SDRT, in reality, was a new tax since it is levied on transactions rather than instruments and is related to stamp duty only insofar as it can be avoided (or duty collected will be repaid) if a duly stamped instrument is produced within six years of the transaction. Further major reforms were envisaged in FA 1990. Duty was to be removed from all transactions in shares to coincide with the introduction of paperless dealing under the Stock Exchange's new share transfer system ('taurus').

In the event, the 1991 Finance Act has gone even further in providing for the abolition of stamp duty charges on *all* property *other than* land and buildings. These measures are intended to come into effect at the same time as the 1990 abolitions and it is now expected that this will be in May 1992. The following matters are worthy of note.

First, stamp duty at $1/2\%$ on shares, and $1^1/2\%$ on depository receipts, SDRT, duty on the transfer of units in a unit trust, 1% and fixed duty (usually 50p) charges on property such as patents, goodwill and debt are all to be abolished.

Secondly, the remaining duties will be the 1% sale duty on land and buildings together with associated fixed charges and the charge on the premium and rent of new leases.

Thirdly, the definition of land includes an interest in land and an interest in the proceeds of sale when land is held on trust for sale. A transfer of mineral rights would usually be subject to duty.

Fourthly, in cases where a transaction includes land and other property which is exempt from duty (for instance, where on the sale of a business the premises are transferred with other assets) the consideration paid must be apportioned as may be fair and just. Duty will then be charged only on the portion attributed to the non-exempt property.   **[30.3]**

2   **General structure of the duty**

The present system of stamp duties depends primarily upon the Stamp Act 1891 and the Stamp Duties Management Act 1891 as amended by subsequent Finance Acts.

Stamp duty (as mentioned above) is conceptually straightforward. It is levied upon any 'instrument' (the term includes 'every written document') which falls within one of the 'Heads of Charge' (analogous to the income tax Schedules) and is not covered by an exemption. Thus, if a transaction can be effected without a written instrument, duty will be avoided.

> **EXAMPLE 30.1**
>
> Alonzo agrees to sell his country estate to his cousin, Bonzo, for £100,000. Stamp duty at the *ad valorem* rate of 1% will be charged on any instrument of transfer but if the matter is 'left in contract' (ie if no such instrument is executed) duty is avoided.

The amount of stamp duty to be paid depends upon each individual head of charge, but the sum will be either a fixed duty of (usually) 50p or an *ad valorem* duty which will be calculated (usually) by reference to the value of the transaction recorded in the instrument.   **[30.4]-[30.20]**

The interaction of stamp duty with VAT is addressed in SP 6/91. For stamp duty purposes the consideration on sale is the gross amount inclusive of VAT. By contrast stamp duty never forms any part of the consideration for VAT.

II   ENFORCEMENT AND ADMINISTRATION

The legislation does not directly state who is accountable for the duty. The main sanction for non-payment is that, unless properly stamped, no document executed in the UK or relating to any property that is situated in the UK, will be admissible in evidence in any civil proceedings (SA 1891 s 14(1) and see *Fengl v Fengl* (1914)). Unstamped documents are admissible in criminal proceedings; failure to stamp does not involve any criminal liability; and an agreement between the parties not to stamp the instrument does not amount to a criminal conspiracy. In some cases fines are imposed for offences in relation to stamp duty.

Technically an instrument should be stamped before execution. In practice, however, the Revenue permit stamping within 30 days after execution without imposing any penalty. Late stamping is permitted subject to the payment of a penalty of £10 and, where the duty exceeds £10, interest at 5% pa from the date of execution up to a maximum of the unpaid duty. In certain cases, the legislation names the person who is liable for the penalty—in the case of a conveyance on sale for instance it is the transferee or purchaser (SA 1891 s 15(2)).

The administration of stamp duty is under the Commissioners of Inland Revenue but the day to day work of administration is carried out, in England and Wales, by the Controller of Stamps, and, in Scotland, by the Controller (Stamps) Scotland. In the event of a dispute there will normally be an adjudication followed by the stating of a case by the commissioners with a hearing in the Chancery Division of the High Court. There is a right of appeal to the Court of Appeal and, ultimately, to the House of Lords. Unlike other taxes the taxpayer has to pay the assessed duty before the appeal is heard.

If required to do so the commissioners must state whether, in their opinion, any executed instrument is subject to a stamp duty charge and if so must state the amount of duty chargeable (the *adjudication* process: SA 1891 s 12). Adjudication may be voluntary, in which case the individual will be asking the commissioners to confirm that no duty is payable on the instrument, or, alternatively it may be necessary to ascertain the correct duty to be paid. In certain cases, however, legislation makes adjudication compulsory to ensure that the correct amount of duty is paid or to ensure that an instrument is covered by an exemption from duty (eg where there is a company reconstruction and exemption from duty is sought: see [**30.82**]). Such instruments are deemed not to have been properly stamped unless adjudicated bearing a stamp to that effect. Orders made by the court under the Variation of Trusts Act 1958 also require adjudication (see Practice Note 1966 1 All ER 672 and [**30.54**]).

The process of adjudication is an essential step in the appeals procedure and it also provides the best means by which a third party can be satisfied as to the correctness of the stamp duty paid.

In three cases instruments must be produced to the commissioners. In general, production should be within 30 days of execution and the obligation lies upon the transferee or lessee. Such instruments will then be impressed with a produced stamp (a 'PD' stamp) which is quite independent of any stamp denoting duty or any adjudication stamp. Penalties for failure to produce are the same as those which apply on failure to stamp. Such instruments are:

(1) a transfer on sale of a fee simple of land;
(2) a lease (or agreement for a lease) of land for a term of seven years or more;
(3) a transfer on sale of a lease as in (2) (FA 1931 s 28 Sch 2).

Originally this information was necessary for the assessment of the land tax imposed by FA 1931. With the abolition of that tax in 1934 the provisions were left unrepealed since they are useful to valuers in assessing compensation claims in compulsory purchase cases. In an attempt to speed up domestic conveyancing transactions, however, FA 1985 s 89 enabled the commissioners to make regulations providing that transfers of registered land below the stamp duty threshold (currently £30,000) should be exempted from these requirements. These regulations, the Stamp Duty (Exempt Instruments) Regulations 1985 (1985/1688), came into effect on 1 January 1986. Accordingly, in these cases the appropriate instrument of transfer should be sent directly to the Land Registry along with the particulars delivered form (see [1986] LS Gaz 405). [**30.21**]-[**30.40**]

III   THE OCCASIONS OF CHARGE

For an instrument to be chargeable to stamp duty it must fall within one of the heads of charge. If it falls within more than one head, the Revenue, although only entitled to one of the duties, can choose the head that will produce the higher duty (*Speyer Bros v IRC* (1908)). Where several instruments are employed to carry out the same transaction, it is only the principal instrument of conveyance that is charged to *ad valorem* duty. The other instruments can only be charged with the 50p miscellaneous conveyance duty which cannot exceed the *ad valorem* duty payable in respect of the principal instrument (SA 1891 s 58(3)).   **[30.41]**

EXAMPLE 30.2

Phee exchanges his seaside cottage with Simple for a town flat in Chelsea and 'equality money' of £40,000.
(1)   The principal instrument (decided by the parties) will be subject to 1% ad valorem duty on the equality money (ie on £40,000).
(2)   Any other instrument is subject to a fixed 50p duty.
(3)   If the equality money did not exceed £30,000 so that ad valorem duty is at the nil rate on the principal instrument, any other instrument will likewise attract nil duty.

1   **Conveyance or transfer on sale** (SA 1891 Sch 1)

This head of charge covers the conveyance or transfer on sale of any property and the duty charged is *ad valorem* at a rate for shares and securities of 50p per £100 or part of £100 of the consideration: ie $^1/_2$%. For other property the rate is 1% unless the consideration does not exceed £30,000 and the instrument contains a certificate of value when the duty is nil. The certificate must state that the transaction effected by the instrument does not form part of a larger transaction or series of transactions in respect of which the amount or value or aggregate amount or value of the consideration exceeds £30,000. Little guidance is given as to the meaning of 'a series of transactions'. Take, for instance, the sale of four properties from A to B each for £30,000. Assuming that there are four separate transactions, none would attract duty. Treated as one transaction, however, duty at 1% is charged. If the transactions are simultaneous they must amount to a single operation; even if not, such a series of conveyances has all the hallmarks of an associated operation.

EXAMPLE 30.3

(i)   Jason agrees to buy a plot of land for £20,000 on which a house, costing £30,000, is to be built. No duty is paid because the land is below the £30,000 threshold.
(ii)   Foolish pays £50,000 for a plot of land together with a completed house thereon. He is subject to £500 duty (1% × £50,000).
Note   The Revenue's attitude to the purchase of new houses is set out in SP 10/ 87 which reproduces an earlier 1957 statement. In general, the charge to duty will depend upon whether there is one contract for a completed house (as in (ii) above) or two separate contracts (as in (i)). Whether one document is used or two is irrelevant and the Revenue consider that 'arrangements for the sale of land and for building work which are so inter-locked that the purchaser or lessee cannot obtain vacant possession of the land until he has paid both the land price and the full building price provide a strong indication that there is a single bargain for the sale of a completed house as a package deal'.

The nil rate is not operated on the 'slice system' so that once the consideration exceeds £30,000, it is all taxed at 1%. Furthermore the nil rate cannot be used on instruments which transfer shares and other marketable securities (FA 1963 s 55(2)), presumably because larger transactions could easily be split into £30,000 slices. **[30.42]**

Meaning of 'sale' Although 'sale' is not defined, there will need to be a vendor, a purchaser, and normally a money consideration (although there is no requirement that the consideration must be adequate). Duty is charged on the amount or value of the consideration and where it is in sterling, there will be no problem. If the consideration is in foreign currencies, duty is charged on the sterling equivalent at the rate of exchange applying on the date of execution of the instrument (FA 1985 s 88).

Special provisions operate where the consideration is to be paid over a number of years (SA 1891 s 56). *First*, where the payments are for a definite period not exceeding 20 years the charge is on the total of all those payments (SA 1891 s 56(1)). *Secondly*, if the payments are to last in perpetuity; or for a period exceeding 20 years; or for a period of indefinite length which is not terminable on death, the charge is on the amount payable during 20 years starting with the date of the sale (SA 1891 s 56(2)). For a discussion of the meaning of 'a payment for a period' see *Blendett Ltd v IRC* (1984) and *Quietlece Ltd v IRC* (1984). *Thirdly*, if the payments are to last during a life or lives, duty is charged on the total amount payable during the 12 years from the date of the instrument. The payer's age is irrelevant (SA 1891 s 56(3)).

EXAMPLE 30.4

(1) If the consideration is £10,000 pa payable for eight years, duty will be charged on £80,000 (SA 1891 s 56(1)).
(2) If the consideration is £10,000 pa payable so long as the recipient lives in London, duty will be charged on £10,000$\times$20 = £200,000 (SA 1891 s 56(2)).
(3) £10,000 pa is payable during the life of the payer. Duty is charged on £10,000 $\times$ 12 = £120,000 (SA 1891 s 56(3)).

These rules for instalment payments apply only to periodic payments which are new requirements and part of the bargain for sale; they do not apply to payments which are naturally a part of the property sold (as, for instance, a payment of rent on the creation of a lease). **[30.43]**

Meaning of 'consideration' Although the consideration for a sale will normally be money, for stamp duty purposes stock or marketable securities and debts and other liabilities are treated as sale consideration (SA 1891 s 55, s 57).

EXAMPLE 30.5

(1) Julie sells her house to Samantha for £20,000. In addition Samantha agrees to repay Julie's overdraft of £10,000 (a similar result would occur if Samantha took over the outstanding mortgage on the property). The consideration furnished for stamp duty will be £20,000 + £10,000 = £30,000.
(2) Julie sells her lease to Jane in consideration for the transfer of 100 £1 shares in F Ltd. The consideration for stamp duty will be the shares. Generally, the shares will be valued in accordance with the procedure adopted for CGT (see CGTA 1979 s 150 and SP 18/80). Although the shares constitute the consideration for the conveyance of the house, the converse is not the case so that the transfer of the shares themselves will attract only 50p duty.

If consideration other than money, stocks, shares or the assumption of liabilities is furnished, the transaction will not be treated as a sale for stamp duty purposes. In *Littlewoods Mail Order Stores Ltd v IRC* (1962), for instance, the exchange of a freehold reversion for a leasehold interest in the same property was not treated as the sale of the freehold in exchange for the rent reserved by the lease.   [**30.44**]

Transfers of property subject to a debt (SP 6/90)

Does the transfer of mortgaged property amount to a sale for the purposes of *ad valorem* duty? The SP draws a contrast between the following cases:

Case 1   The transferee of mortgaged property covenants (either in the transfer or separately) to discharge the debt or indemnify the transferor. The transfer is a sale with the consideration being the amount of the debt.

Case 2   As in *Case 1*, except that the transferor covenants to pay the debt so that no liability is assumed by the transferee. The transfer is a voluntary disposition and can be certified under Category L of the 1987 Regulations.

Case 3   If there is no express covenant or undertaking by either party the Revenue will imply a covenant by the transferee (except in Scotland). This implied covenant will arise even if the mortgaged property is in joint names and transferred to one of the joint holders and even if both parties were jointly liable on the mortgage.

Case 4   If chargeable consideration unrelated to the debt is given by the transferee for the mortgaged property the conveyance is then subject to *ad valorem* duty as a sale on the aggregate of that consideration and the debt whether or not liability for that debt has been assumed by the transferee.   [**30.45**]

Assents   Certain assents have been treated as sales: for instance, an assent by a deceased's PRs in favour of the person to whom the deceased, prior to his death, had contracted to sell property (*GHR Co v IRC* (1943)). Sale duty was also charged when property was appropriated in satisfaction of the surviving spouse's monetary claim on an intestacy and whenever a pecuniary legacy was satisfied by the appropriation of assets with the consent of the beneficiary under the Administration of Estates Act 1925 s 41 (see *Jopling v IRC* (1940)). FA 1985 s 84, however, excluded appropriations in or towards the satisfaction of a general pecuniary legacy and appropriations to a surviving spouse on an intestacy from sale duty. Accordingly, wills need no longer expressly provide that PRs may appropriate assets without the consent of the beneficiary in order to avoid a sale and, therefore, duty. From 1 May 1987 these assents are also free of the fixed 50p duty and the adjudication requirement (SI 1987/516). Other assents are free of all duty. Therefore property specifically left to a beneficiary under a will is not subject to *ad valorem* duty when it is transferred to that person, nor is property which is appropriated to a surviving spouse in accordance with the intestacy rules.   [**30.46**]

Partnership dissolutions   On the dissolution of a partnership, the division (or partition) of the assets between the partners will not be treated as a sale (*MacLeod v IRC* (1885)) but, if an outgoing partner is 'bought out', the instrument effecting that arrangement will be a sale (*Garnett v IRC* (1899)). A partition document is subject to a fixed 50p duty. The mere withdrawal of partnership capital does not attract any charge and neither does the introduction of cash by an in-coming partner. However, when an in-coming partner pays for an interest in the business, the relevant document may operate as a conveyance on sale. Given these permutations, considerable care should be exercised in structuring both the admission of new partners and the retirement of old partners. **[30.47]**

EXAMPLE 30.6

Dave joins the partnership of Bob, Mick & Tom. He contributes capital of £10,000. This by itself will not amount to a sale. If, however, he pays the money to the other partners or they make a simultaneous withdrawal of capital, the deed or instrument of partnership will be charged as a conveyance or transfer on sale of partnership property to Dave.

Exchanges It is important to distinguish sales from exchanges. There is a specific head of charge in the Stamp Act for exchanges which applies to exchanges of real or heritable property (SA 1891 s 73 Sch 1; see **[30.66]**). **[30.48]**

EXAMPLE 30.7

(1) A exchanges 10 shares in Zee Ltd for B's 10 shares in Aah Ltd. This is a sale (*Chesterfield Brewery Co v IRC* (1899)).
(2) A exchanges Blackacre for Whiteacre which was owned by B. This is an exchange not a sale and gives rise to fixed duty of 50p. If equality money exceeding £100 is paid by one party to the exchange to the other it is subject to 1% *ad valorem* duty as a sale.

Sub-sales A purchaser who resells land before it is transferred to him can avoid stamp duty by ensuring that it is transferred directly to a sub-purchaser. The duty is calculated on the sub-sale consideration (SA 1891 s 58(4)(5)). These provisions offer planning opportunities. For instance, the purchaser of land may delay completion relying upon his equitable title that is obtained on exchange of contracts and he may then sell the property to a third party who thus becomes a sub-purchaser. Accordingly, it is that person who is liable for *ad valorem* duty. Similar arrangements may be employed for transfers between companies when the *intra* group exemption of FA 1930 s 42 is unavailable.

EXAMPLE 30.8

Selina agrees to purchase Redmeadow from Angela for £40,000. She immediately agrees to resell Redmeadow to Anna for £50,000 and arranges for Angela to convey Redmeadow directly to Anna. Duty will be assessed on Anna on £50,000. No duty will be charged on Selina.
Instead of the sale of all of Redmeadow to Anna, assume that only one-quarter is resold to her for £12,500. The one-quarter sold to Anna is conveyed directly to her by Angela; the rest is conveyed to Selina. Duty would be charged:
(1) *On Anna* on £12,500 at nil rate.
(2) *On Selina* on three-quarters of her consideration (ie on £30,000). It forms part of a transaction for which the consideration exceeds £30,000 so that the nil rate does not apply.
Note that a partial resale to a connected person would not save any duty, as the operation would be treated as a series of transactions.

To counter a stamp duty avoidance scheme on the sale of land, s 58(4) and (5) do not apply in respect of sub-sale contracts where the sub-sale consideration is less than the value of the property immediately before the sub-sale. In such a case duty is charged on the price which the property might reasonably be expected to fetch at that time on a sale in the open market. Even before the introduction of this anti-avoidance legislation, the Revenue had begun to challenge the efficacy of this and similar schemes under the *Ramsay* principle (see [**30.63**] and Chapter 31).   [**30.49**]

'Leaving the matter in contract'   Stamp duty is often avoided by agreeing to transfer the asset and then failing to execute the formal transfer. The contract itself will not normally be subject to duty but if it is specifically enforceable (as in the case of land) the purchaser will become the equitable owner of the property by virtue of that agreement. The contract must contemplate that the transaction will be completed. Notice, however, that any attempt to transfer the full legal title (or to recite that the purchaser is the owner of the property) will be subject to duty at the full rate (see, eg, *Oughtred v IRC* (1960)). In the case of a purchase of shares after 26 October 1986, when the sale is not evinced by a duly stamped instrument, stamp duty reserve tax may be charged on the transaction (see [**30.101**]).

Documents specifically exempted from sale duty under FA 1985   The following dispositions are specifically exempted from ad valorem sale duty under SA 1891 Sch 1.
(1) A deed of variation of a deceased person's property made in consideration of the making of a variation in respect of another of the dispositions (see [**30.56**]).
(2) An assent whereby property is appropriated by a PR in or towards the satisfaction of a general pecuniary legacy or in satisfaction of the interest of a surviving spouse on an intestacy (see [**30.46**]).
(3) A transfer of property on matrimonial breakdown (see [**30.57**]).
(4) Company reconstructions not involving any real change in ownership (see [**30.85**]).   [**30.50**]

2   Conveyance or transfer not on sale

a) *General*

In the case of conveyances or transfers of any other kind (ie not on sale) the duty is fixed at 50p. This will include the dispositions considered below and decrees or orders of the court or commissioners whereby property is transferred or vested in any person (SA 1891 s 62). The 1987 Regulations (see e), below) provide an exemption from the 50p fixed duty in a number of the more common situations where property is transferred otherwise than on sale. There will still be cases, however, where duty remains payable: for instance:
(1) Transfer from a beneficial owner to his nominee (including a declaration of trust: see below).
(2) Transfer from a nominee to the beneficial owner.
(3) Transfer from one nominee to another nominee of the same beneficial owner.
(4) Transfer by way of security for a loan or re-transfer to the original transferor on repayment of a loan.
(5) Transfer from the trustees of a profit-sharing scheme to a participant in the scheme.   [**30.51**]

b) *Voluntary dispositions*

Prior to FA 1985, *ad valorem* duty was charged on the value of the property transferred by a voluntary disposition 'as if' it were a conveyance or transfer on sale under F(1909–10)A 1910 s 74. This was, therefore, not strictly a separate head of charge and the rate of charge was as for a conveyance on sale. FA 1985 s 82, however, abolished the charge to *ad valorem* duty under s 74 in relation to all voluntary dispositions executed after 25 March 1985. An adjudication stamp continued to be required together with the fixed 50p duty but those requirements were in turn removed by SI 1987/ 516. With the repeal of *ad valorem* duty on gifts, bad bargains and sales at under-value are charged as 'conveyances on sale' with duty being levied on the actual consideration furnished. **[30.52]**

EXAMPLE 30.9

(1) Junius conveys his house to his son Brutus for £40,000. There is evidence that the open market value of the property is £55,000. *Ad valorem* duty on a conveyance on sale of £40,000 will be charged.
(2) Titan gives his house worth £100,000 to his son Titus. Titus is to discharge the outstanding mortgage on the property of £55,000 in favour of the Rookyu Building Society. *Ad valorem* duty will be charged on a conveyance on sale of £55,000 (the value of the mortgage debt assumed by Titus).

A declaration of trust Trusts may be created by self-declaration or by transferring the property to trustees to hold for the intended beneficiaries. A declaration of trust in writing is subject to a fixed charge of 50p but the transfer of assets by the settlor to the trustees will not attract duty unless consideration is furnished (when it will be a sale). Deeds effecting changes of trustees are not subject to duty. **[30.53]**

Orders under the Variation of Trusts Act 1958 When a variation order is made by the courts, an undertaking is given to submit a duplicate of that order for adjudication (see Practice Note, 1966). Any duty payable thereon would be on the basis of a voluntary disposition, however, and therefore the continuing requirement of adjudication appears to be redundant. **[30.54]**

Release and renunciation Prior to FA 1985 *ad valorem* duty was charged on the release of a life interest in a settlement whereas a fixed duty of 50p only was charged on advancements of capital in favour of remaindermen. It was, accordingly, desirable to ensure that property was advanced to a remaindermen rather than passing to him on the surrender of a life interest. As releases are now subject to the fixed 50p duty only, it follows that the stamp duty attractions of advancements have been removed. **[30.55]**

c) *Variations of dispositions of a deceased person*

The CGT and IHT implications of varying or disclaiming dispositions of property of the deceased under his will or under the rules of intestacy are discussed in Chapters 15 and 22 respectively.

Before FA 1985, an instrument of variation was generally liable to ad valorem duty as a voluntary disposition and required adjudication, whereas a deed of disclaimer (being a refusal of property) was subject only to the fixed 50p duty applicable to deeds (*Re Stratton's Disclaimer* (1958)). In a very few cases the deed of variation would constitute a sale and be subject, therefore, to *ad valorem* sale duty. FA 1985 provided an exemption from *ad valorem* duty for all deeds of variation and the fixed 50p duty and adjudication requirement were removed by SI 1987/516. With the abolition of the fixed 50p duty on deeds the present position is that neither variations nor disclaimers attract duty although in the former case the certificate requirements of SI 1987/516 must be satisfied.   [30.56]

d) *Transfers of property on matrimonial breakdown*

Until FA 1985 there was no specific exemption from duty for transfers of property between spouses and former spouses. Thus, any such transfer made on the breakdown of marriage was subject to *ad valorem* sale duty, unless it was made pursuant to a court order or a separation deed when only the fixed 50p duty was charged.

FA 1985 s 83, however, provided that any instrument which transferred property from one party to the marriage to the other was specifically exempt from sale duty and subject to a fixed 50p duty only provided that the disposition was made pursuant to a court order on divorce, nullity or judicial separation; or to a court order made later, but in connection with the divorce or to an agreement made between the parties in connection with the breakdown of that marriage (see further Chapter 35). SI 1987/516 has completed the process by removing the 50p duty and adjudication requirement.   [30.57]

e) *The Stamp Duty (Exempt Instruments) Regulations 1987*

Instruments falling within the categories listed in the Schedule to these Regulations, which are correctly certified, are exempted from the fixed duty of 50p which would otherwise be chargeable and should not be presented at stamp offices for adjudication. The appropriate certificate should be included in, endorsed or attached to, the instrument and should refer to the category in the Schedule under which exemption is claimed. The following is a suggested form of wording for such certificates:

'I hereby certify that this instrument falls within category   in the Schedule to the Stamp Duty (Exempt Instruments) Regulations 1987.'

The following are the exempt categories:
Category A: The vesting of property subject to a trust in the trustees on the appointment of a new trustee or in the continuing trustees on the retirement of a trustee.
Category B: The conveyance or transfer of property subject of a specific devise or legacy to a beneficiary named in the will (contrast Category D below).
Category C: The conveyance or transfer of property which forms part of an intestate estate to the person entitled on intestacy.
Category D: The appropriation of property in satisfaction of a general legacy of money or in satisfaction of any interest of a surviving spouse in an intestate's estate.
Category E: The conveyance or transfer of property forming part of the residuary estate of a testator to a beneficiary entitled under the will.
Category F: The conveyance or transfer of property out of a settlement in or towards the satisfaction of a beneficiary's interest in accordance with the provisions of the settlement (the relevant interest must not have been acquired for money or money's worth).
Category G: The conveyance or transfer of property on and in consideration of marriage to a party or to trustees to be held on a marriage settlement.

Category H: The conveyance or transfer of property in connection with divorce etc (see above).

Category I: The conveyance or transfer by the liquidator of property which formed part of the assets of the company in a liquidation to a shareholder in satisfaction of his rights on the winding up.

Category J: The grant in fee simple of an easement in or over land for no consideration in money or money's worth.

Category K: The grant of a servitude for no consideration in money or money's worth.

Category L: The conveyance or transfer of property as a voluntary disposition inter vivos.

Category M: The conveyance or transfer of property under a post death variation. **[30.58]**

3 Leases and agreements for leases

Duty is levied in accordance with SA 1891 Sch 1 on the grant of a lease or tack (tack is the Scottish equivalent of lease). To be dutiable the lease must be of land, tenements or heritable subjects; leases of personalty are not included. Likewise, duty is not charged on licences because they do not confer a proprietary interest in the land.

Stamp duty is charged on both the rent and the premium reserved in a lease. The premium is charged in the same way as if it were the consideration for a sale. Duty is, therefore, *ad valorem* unless the nil rate band applies which it does not if any associated rent payable under the lease averages more than £300 pa. Duty on the rent depends upon the average rent and the term of the lease. In the case of a lease for an uncertain rent or no rent or premium there is a fixed duty of £2. An exchange of a leasehold property for a freehold property does not take effect as an exchange and neither is it a conveyance on sale: accordingly it attracts a fixed 50p duty as a conveyance or transfer not on sale (*IRC v Littlewoods Mail Order Stores Ltd* (1962)). Leases to charities are exempt from duty (FA 1982 s 129).

A lease or agreement for a lease for seven years or more must also be produced and stamped with a produced stamp (see **[30.21]**).

In general, fixed duties are charged on short term leases at low rents and *ad valorem* duty on leases for more than a year and on periodic tenancies. The duty on rent is as follows: **[30.59]**

Lease for a definite term of less than one year In the case of a furnished letting for a definite term of less than one year there is no duty if the rent is below £500 pa; if it exceeds £500 pa, duty of £1 is payable. In other cases duty is charged as if the lease were a lease for one year at the actual rent reserved. **[30.60]**

Leases for a definite term of at least one year or for an indefinite term

Term not exceeding 7 years or indefinite	
rent not exceeding £500 pa	nil
rent exceeding £500 pa	50p duty per £50 or part thereof (1%)
Term exceeding 7 years but not 35 years	£1 per £50 or part thereof (2%)
Term exceeding 35 years but not 100 years	£6 per £50 or part thereof (12%)
Term exceeding 100 years	£12 per £50 or part thereof (24%)

For leases exceeding seven years, the above level of duty on rent is charged at a sliding scale if the rent does not exceed £500 pa (for details see FA 1982 s 128(3)).

As mentioned above where all or a part of the consideration for a lease for a definite term in excess of one year, or for an indefinite term, is money or stock or security (a premium), duty is charged on the value of that consideration at the rates which apply to a conveyance or transfer on sale. *Ad valorem* duty will, therefore, be charged although the nil rate band will apply (if a certificate of value is included in the lease) unless the rent exceeds £300 pa.   [**30.61**]

EXAMPLE 30.10

(1) Bos grants Big a ten year lease at a rent of £250 pa and a premium of £29,000. As the term exceeds seven years, the normal charge on the rent will be at 1%, but since the rent is below £500 pa a sliding scale will apply (currently duty will be £5). So long as the lease contains a certificate of value, duty will be charged at nil% on the premium of £29,000.

(2) Rac Developers wish to take a 150 year lease on a development site. However, because stamp duty at a rate of 24% would be payable, it is agreed that they will take a 99 year lease with an option to renew for a further 51 years. Duty payable is therefore halved.

a) *Terminology*

There is no definition of *'rent'*. It is in essence a payment reserved out of the land, paid by the tenant to recompense the landlord for loss of exclusive possession. Any service charge reserved in addition to rent is assessed as rent. If that charge is unascertained, as where it is a proportion of the costs incurred from time to time, or is dependent upon services provided by the landlord, fixed duty of £2 is payable and the basic rent is subject to *ad valorem* duty.

If the amount of rent is unascertained but the lease stipulates for a maximum rent, that sum attracts duty. In the absence of a maximum figure, a specified minimum rent or a basic rent which is subject to adjustment could be charged (for this so-called 'contingency principle' see *Coventry City Council v IRC* (1978)). A progressive rent is averaged over the term of a lease.

EXAMPLE 30.11

Lord grants Serf a ten-year lease. For the first five years the rent is £1,000 pa; thereafter £1,500 pa. The average rent (on which duty is assessed) is £1,250 pa. (Duty will be at £1 per £50—ie £25.) Had the lease merely provided for a rent review at the end of five years, duty would be charged on the actual rent reserved (£1,000).

The term *'premium'* does not appear in the Act which imposes duty on 'consideration, moving either to the lessor or to any other person, consisting of money, stock or security'. It should be noted, therefore, that the premium, if paid to a person other than the landlord, still attracts duty. Where the tenant is obliged under the terms of the lease to carry out improvements either to the property let, or to any other property of the landlord, the value of such works is not subject to stamp duty.

As duty on rent is determined primarily by the duration of the lease, its length must be identified at the date of execution. In general, any part of a term commencing before the date of execution of the lease is ignored (which can have unfortunate results: see *Example 30.12(4)*, below). The following rules apply to ascertain the duration of a lease.

First, a lease for a term of years with an option to renew for a further specified period is subject to duty on the original term. *Secondly*, on a lease for a fixed term which can thereafter be determined by notice, the term is taken as the length of the fixed term plus the period that must elapse before determination (FA 1963 s 56(3)). *Thirdly*, a lease for a specified period which may be terminable on an earlier event occurring is treated as a lease for the specified period and not as a lease for an indefinite period. *Fourthly*, leases for life or lives or for a term of years determinable on the marriage of the lessee are treated as leases for 90 years in accordance with the LPA 1925 s 149(6). **[30.62]**

EXAMPLE 30.12

(1) A ten-year term with an option to renew for a further five years is charged as a ten-year lease.

(2) A seven-year term is granted which may thereafter be determined on giving six months' notice after the expiration of that term. Duty would be assessed on the basis of a lease for seven years six months.

(3) A lease granted for 99 years if A, B and C should live so long is treated as a lease exceeding 35 years and not exceeding 100 (*Earl Mount Edgcumbe v IRC* (1911)).

(4) A 99-year lease begins to run on 29 September 1989, but is only formally executed on 25 March 1990. If the rent charged is £50 pa for the first 33 years; £100 pa for the next 33 years, with £150 pa being charged for the final 33 years, duty will be charged on an average rent of £100.25 pa (ie the average rent taking the length of the lease to be 98 1/2 years). Duty is, therefore, £18 whereas on an average rent of £100 (ie if spread over the actual duration of the 99 year lease) it would have been only £12!

b) *Agreements for a lease*

An agreement for a lease for a term of less than 35 years or for an indefinite term has always been charged as a lease for the term and consideration specified in the agreement (SA 1891 s 75(1)). Accordingly, agreements for a lease for a fixed term in *excess of* 35 years were excluded from duty with the result that a widely used stamp duty avoidance scheme was devised whereby the purchaser of a freehold or long leasehold interest arranged for a nominee to agree to take a lease exceeding 35 years from the vendor. The purchaser then acquired the superior interest for a nominal consideration. In *Ingram v IRC* (1986) it was held that such schemes fell within the *Ramsay* principle and that the lease could therefore be ignored and duty on the entire purchase price charged upon the conveyance of the freehold reversion (the case is discussed in Chapter 31). Before this decision, FA 1984 s 111 amended the existing legislation by providing that an agreement for a lease for a term exceeding 35 years, and made after 19 March 1984 (and prior thereto not chargeable) will be charged under s 75. The duty paid thereon must be denoted on any conveyance of a freehold or leasehold interest in land against which the agreement is directly enforceable (eg when the agreement is for a sub lease it need not be denoted on a conveyance of the freehold reversion).

The penalty for not stamping any agreement for a lease made after 19 March

1984 falls on the 'lessee' (SA 1891 s 11). A lease later made to carry out (substantially) the terms of the agreement is chargeable on the difference between the duty paid on the agreement and any duty then payable (SA 1891 s 75(2)).   **[30.63]**

c) *Surrenders and variations*

When a lease is surrendered, the surrender is subject to duty as a conveyance or transfer on sale on any consideration paid by the landlord. If no consideration is paid, the fixed 50p duty is charged. Where a lease is surrendered and a new lease granted the surrendered lease will attract 50p duty whilst the new lease will be assessed in the usual way. Duty is not attracted when a lease expires at the end of its term.   **[30.64]**

4   The sale of a business

The practice of 'leaving matters in contract' has already been noted (see **[30.101]**). Duty may thereby be avoided on a conveyance of realty so long as the purchaser is prepared to take only an equitable title to the property transferred. In practice this will often be unacceptable so that a formal transfer will be executed and duty paid. When goodwill and equitable interests are sold, however, the contract will be specifically enforceable and, for practical purposes, there would be no need to execute a formal conveyance or transfer. Duty would, therefore, not be paid on such sales (see *IRC v G Angus & Co* (1889)). To ensure that duty is not so easily avoided SA 1891 s 59 provides that:

> 'Any contract or agreement for the sale of any equitable estate or interest in any property whatsoever, or for the sale of any estate or interest in any property except lands, tenements, hereditaments, or heritages, or property locally situate out of the United Kingdom, or goods, wares or merchandise, or stock, or marketable securities, or any ship or vessel, or part interest, share, or property of or in any ship or vessel, shall be charged with the same ad valorem duty, to be paid by the purchaser, as if it were an actual conveyance on sale of the estate, interest, or property contracted or agreed to be sold.'

The provision starts by imposing liability to *ad valorem* duty on all sale contracts but then excludes from its ambit the most common categories of property (eg land and shares) leaving only a residue of assets subject to the duty, principally debts, goodwill, and the benefit of contracts. The asset must be situated in the UK. An agreement for a lease falls outside the section, but an option to purchase a legal interest in land is an equitable interest and, thus, within the charge (*George Wimpey & Co Ltd v IRC* (1975)). If duty is charged under s 59, a subsequent conveyance or transfer of the property is not subject to further *ad valorem* duty and should be stamped with a denoting stamp (see s 59(3)). In many cases a number of assets are agreed to be sold for one consideration. For stamp duty purposes an apportionment of that consideration amongst the assets will need to be made on form Stamps 22. The most important transaction caught by SA 1891 s 59 is the sale of a business (see further Chapter 33).   **[30.65]**

5   **Exchange or partition** (SA 1891 s 73 and Sch 1)

For exchanges or partitions of real or heritable property fixed duty of 50p is charged unless consideration in excess of £100 is given for equality. If so, *ad valorem* duty is charged on that equality money unless the nil rate applies (SA 1891 s 73 and Sch 1).

For exchanges or partitions of any other property, fixed duty of 50p is charged on any document as a conveyance or transfer not on sale. If equality money is paid, the transaction may be seen as a sale and *ad valorem* duty will be payable on the equality money and other consideration within the meaning of SA 1891 ss 55–60 (see [**30.44**]).

It should be noted that an exchange of shares is two sales not an exchange (*Chesterfield Brewery Co v IRC* (1899)) and that two agreements for sale for cash effected by deed of exchange are treated as two separate sale contracts (*(Viscount) Portman v IRC* (1956)). The severance and partition of an equitable joint tenancy in land can be carried out by a notice to sever (LPA 1925 ss 28(3), 36(2)) which must be in writing but will not be subject to duty.   [**30.66**]

EXAMPLE 30.13

Bee exchanges Redmeadow (worth £40,000) with Boo for Blackacre (worth £25,000) and £15,000 in cash. The equality money is subject to duty but so long as the appropriate certificate of value is included ('not exceeding £30,000') the £15,000 will be charged at the nil rate of duty.

6 Depositary receipts (FA 1986 ss 67–69)

A 1½% charge is imposed when UK shares are converted into depositary receipts or transferred to a clearing house for transfer through a computerised settlement system which enables UK shares to be bought and sold without payment of stamp duty. The charge is levied on the consideration paid if the transfer falls under the conveyance or transfer on sale head of charge: otherwise, if shares are deposited by the owner in exchange for a depositary receipt, it is levied on the value of the shares at that time.   [**30.67**]

7 Other documents subject to stamp duty

In addition to the occasions of charge already considered, **ad valorem** duty is chargeable on life insurance policies at 50p per £1,000 of the sum insured; certain bearer instruments (see FA 1963 s 59) at varying rates from 1½ of the market value to 10p for every £50 or part thereof of the market value; and bonds, covenants or instruments increasing the rent reserved by another instrument is dutiable as a lease in consideration of the additional rent thereby made payable (see SA 1891 s 77(5)). FA 1985 s 85 abolished some 13 of the previous heads of fixed duty, including the residual 50p duty on deeds not chargeable under any other head. Accordingly, the fixed duties that, currently, remain are chargeable in respect of the following documents only:
(1) Conveyance or transfer of any other kind – 50p (see [**30.51**]).
(2) Duplicate or counterpart of any instrument chargeable with duty (eg a lease) – maximum 50p (see SA 1891 ss 72, 11).
(3) Exchange or partition relating to realty where the amount of the equalisation payments does not exceed £100 – 50p.
(4) Lease of a furnished letting for a definite term of less than one year where the rent for the whole term exceeds £500 – £1 (see [**30.60**]).
(5) Leases not stampable under any other head – £2.
(6) Release or renunciation of any property or interest in property and

which is not subject to sale duty (eg a partnership share) see [**30.55**]
- 50p.

(7) Surrender of any kind which is not chargeable to sale duty
(50p).   [**30.68**]-[**30.80**]

IV   EXEMPTIONS AND RELIEFS FROM STAMP DUTY

1   General

Exemption from duty is conferred upon a number of documents, in particular:

(1) Wills.

(2) Contracts of employment.

(3) Transfers to a charitable body, charitable trust or to the trustees of
the National Heritage Memorial Fund (FA 1982 s 129).

(4) Renounceable letters of allotment with a renunciation period not
exceeding six months (although if transferred for value they will attract
SDRT).

(5) Transfers of gilts and loan stock which cannot be converted into equities
(but including loan stock convertible into other, non-convertible, loan
stock; see FA 1976, s 126(2) and SP 3/284).

(6) The issue of bearer debentures.

(7) Mortgages.   [**30.81**]

2   Exemptions from stamp duty for companies

FA 1986 pursued a policy of reducing the rate of duty on sales of shares
and securities from 1% to $1/2$% and of extending the scope of duty in order
to preserve 'fiscal neutrality'. Hence a number of transactions which were
not subject to duty because they were exempt were brought into charge.
Thus, contracts by which a company agrees to buy back its own shares
now attract duty which is charged on the relevant return to the Registrar
of Companies (form 169). Similarly, the transfer of a renounceable letter
of allotment (save where it relates to stock which would itself be exempt
if transferred) has been brought into charge. Prior to the 1986 Budget there
were a number of reliefs from duty on company reconstructions and take-
overs but, from 25 March 1986, these reliefs were generally removed so that
duty at $1/2$% became payable. The reliefs in question are as follows:

(1) *FA 1927 s 55* relief on certain reconstructions and amalgamations.

(2) *FA 1985 s 78* relief on 'paper for paper' exchanges.

(3) *FA 1985 s 79* relief on a reconstruction under Companies Act 1985 s 582.

(4) *FA 1980 Sch 18 para 12* relief on certain demergers.

It should be noted however, that the substance of FA 1927 s 55 is preserved
by FA 1986 s 76 as a relief to ensure that the transfer of an undertaking
is subject to duty at $1/2$% and not the full 1% which is normally charged
on sales. This new relief differs from the old s 55 in that there is no requirement
that the transaction be a reconstruction or amalgamation and, as the shares
may be issued to any of the target company's shareholders, it is available
to demergers taking the form of a transfer of a trade to a new company.
Adjudication is required.   [**30.82**]

The following exemptions from duty remain.

a) *A demerger which is effected by a direct distribution of a subsidiary's shares since this is not a conveyance on sale* **[30.83]**

b) *Transfers between associated companies (FA 1930 s 42)*

Conveyance or transfer duty is not charged on an instrument by which one company transfers property to an associated company. The detailed require
ments are in FA 1930 s 42 which requires that one of the companies in question must beneficially own, directly or indirectly, at least 90% (by nominal value) of the issued share capital of the other, or a third company beneficially owns, directly or indirectly at least 90% of the issued share capital of each.

FA 1967 s 27(3) contains provisions to prevent abuse of the s 42 relief; of particular note is the requirement that the transaction in respect of which relief is sought must not form part of an arrangement whereby the transferor's interest in the transferee's share capital will be reduced below 90%. **[30.84]**

c) *Reconstructions where there is no real change of ownership* (FA 1986 s 75 and s 77)

Exemption from *ad valorem* duty is given when, pursuant to a scheme of reconstruction of the target company, the whole or part of its undertaking (s 75), or the whole of its issued share capital (s 77), is acquired by the acquiring company. The registered office of the acquirer must be in the UK and, apart from the assumption of liabilities, the consideration furnished must be shares in the acquirer. These consideration shares must be issued to all shareholders of the target company only (and not to that company itself) and the acquisition must be for *bona fide* commercial reasons and not have any tax avoidance as a main purpose. After the acquisition each shareholder in the target company must hold shares in the acquirer and vice versa and the proportion of the shares of one company held by any shareholder must be the same as the proportion of the shares in the other company held by that same shareholder (ie the shares must be issued on a *pro rata* basis). Any instrument employed to convey or transfer property under such a reconstruction requires adjudication. Given these requirements, which ensure that the undertaking is held by the same shareholders before and after the acquisition, this exemption is extremely limited. A reconstruction under Companies Act 1985 s 582 may fall within this relief as illustrated below:

Illustration 1

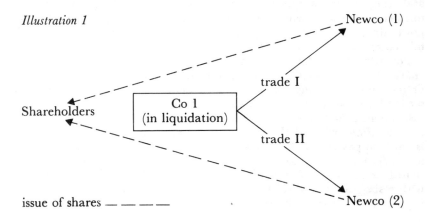

Company 1 is liquidated and its two component trades are split with the ownership being transferred to Newco (1) and Newco (2). Those companies then issue shares to the shareholders of Company 1. This reconstruction qualifies for relief: contrast, however, the following illustration which does not:

Illustration 2

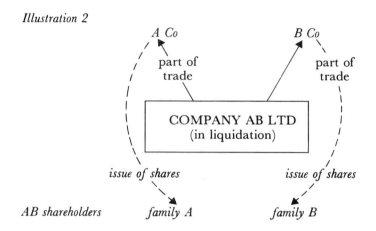

In *Illustration 2* there is a similar partition but, instead of the shares in the two new companies being divided amongst all the original shareholders, the shares in A Co now pass only to the original shareholders who comprised the A family and the B Co shares to the B family. (The amplex requirements to be met if s 77 is to apply are discussed in the Tax Journal, 8 February 1990 at p 20).   **[30.85]-[30.100]**

V   STAMP DUTY RESERVE TAX

SDRT was a new tax imposed on transactions affecting chargeable securities after 26 October 1986. The intention was to ensure that on any purchase of shares duty is payable at $1/2\%$ even if there was no relevant document to stamp. Hence SDRT applies to purchasers unless the sale is evidenced by a duly stamped instrument and, in particular, applies where the shares are registered in the name of a nominee who acts for both buyer and seller and when letters of allotment are transferred. The charge does not apply to stocks and shares which are exempt from duty (eg gilt-edged securities); nor to traded options within CGTA s 137(9); nor to stock or securities subject to charge under the bearer head.

For duty (at $1/2\%$) to be payable there must be an agreement to transfer chargeable securities (defined in FA 1986 s 99(3)) for a consideration in money or money's worth and either no instrument of transfer covering all those securities is executed within two months of the contract or the relevant instrument is not stamped within that period. The duty is levied on the consideration paid (so that it does not apply to gifts) and the transferee is liable to pay (unless he is a nominee when his principal is liable). Finally, if a duly stamped transfer is produced after the relevant two-month period, SDRT is cancelled (if not already paid) or refunded if a claim is made within six years of the contract. When tax of at least £25 is repaid interest is payable (FA 1986 ss 86-99).

EXAMPLE 30.14

(1) Adam receives a renounceable letter of allotment of shares in Zeta Ltd.
  (i) If he applies to be registered there will be no charge to duty since there has been no transfer of the rights comprised in the letter.
  (ii) If he renounces the rights and transfers the letter of allotment to Bertha who in turn transfers to Charles, SDRT may apply to those transfers.
(2) Bertram buys and sells securities within the same Stock Exchange account or there is a purchase of shares which are registered in the name of a nominee acting for both seller and purchaser.

In addition to the principal charge described above, SDRT also applies to shares converted into depositary receipts and to shares put into a clearance system. As it is designed to supplement the charge to duty on depositary receipts (see [**30.67**]), it is charged at a rate of $1^1/2$%. [**30.101**]

PART B PRACTICE AND PLANNING

Chapters

31 The 'Ramsay principle', tax planning and anti-avoidance legislation

I Introductory [31.1]
II Artificial schemes and the 'Ramsay principle' [31.21]
III Statutory provisions to counter tax avoidance [31.51]

I INTRODUCTORY

·MADDOCKS·

The desire to avoid the payment of tax need scarcely occasion surprise. In the average case it will amount to no more than a sensible use of the available exemptions and reliefs which are provided in all tax legislation. In other cases, where the sums involved are greater, the methods adopted by the 'tax planning industry' to escape the fiscal net may take on a complexity that is beyond the comprehension of most individuals and may involve schemes which are divorced from reality. The potential tax avoided (or saved) by these schemes is considerable and to combat their effectiveness the Revenue have two main weapons at their disposal. The first is legislative and takes the form of enactments directed against specific avoidance schemes. The provisions designed to prevent artificial transactions in land have been considered in Chapter 8; those aimed at combating the transfer of assets overseas in Chapter 13; and the various provisions aimed at transactions in securities, bond washing and dividend stripping are considered in this chapter. The general characteristic of such legislation is that it is designed to deal with a specific problem, normally after it has arisen, but does not purport to prevent new schemes in different areas. Given a sophisticated legal profession, loopholes in such provisions will be exploited and need constant plugging.

The second weapon in the Revenue's armoury is to challenge in the courts the legal efficacy of avoidance schemes. In the past they won few victories. In *IRC v Duke of Westminster* (1936) the object of the scheme was to make servants' wages deductible in arriving at the Duke's total income by paying them by deed of covenant. Hence, although there was no binding agreement to that effect, it was accepted that so long as payments were made under the covenant they would not claim their wages. The House of Lords upheld the scheme saying that, in deciding the consequence of a transaction, the courts will look at its legal nature and not take account of any supposed artificiality.

In recent years, however, the Revenue have achieved some successes especially in the House of Lords. The culmination of recent decisions are the House of Lords cases of *W T Ramsay Ltd v IRC, Eilbeck v Rawling* (1981), *IRC v Burmah Oil Co Ltd* (1982); *Furniss v Dawson* (1984) and *Craven v White* (1988). These decisions have sounded the death knell to artificial avoidance schemes and, coupled with the high level of hostility shown by the Revenue to such schemes (as evidenced by *IRC v Rossminster Ltd* (1980)), should deter potential customers from purchasing avoidance packages. The current status of Westminster's case is left unclear by these judgments which do, however, show that present judicial attitudes to tax avoidance are very different from those prevailing in the 1930s. In *Furniss v Dawson*, Lord Roskill considered that 'the ghost of the Duke of Westminster has haunted the administration of this branch of the law for too long.' [**31.1**]-[**31.20**]

II   ARTIFICIAL SCHEMES AND THE '*RAMSAY* PRINCIPLE'

1   **The decisions in Ramsay and Burmah Oil**

In both *Ramsay* and *Burmah Oil* the taxpayers sought to obtain the benefits of capital gains tax loss relief in order to wipe out large profits. To achieve this end both adopted schemes involving a series of steps to be carried out in rapid succession according to a prearranged timetable. Once started, it was intended that the schemes should be carried through to their conclusion which would be that a capital loss had been incurred. In reality, a comparison of the taxpayer's position at the start and finish showed that either no real loss was suffered, or, in *Ramsay's* case, that the only loss suffered was the professional fees paid for the implementation of the scheme! The House of Lords decided that such schemes should be viewed not as a series of separate transactions, none of which was a sham, but as a whole; the position of the taxpayer in real terms being compared at the start and at the finish. Thus, the scheme involved no real loss and was self-cancelling. In *Ramsay* Lord Wilberforce expounded this new approach to avoidance schemes and sought to explain the decision in *Westminster's* case:

> 'While obliging the court to accept documents or transactions, found to be genuine, as such, it does not compel the court to look at a document or a transaction in blinkers, isolated from any context to which it properly belongs. If it can be seen that a document or transaction was intended to have effect as part of a nexus or series of transactions, or as an ingredient of a wider transaction intended as a whole, there is nothing in the doctrine to prevent it being so regarded; to do so is not to prefer form to substance, or substance to form. It is the task of the court to ascertain the legal nature of any transaction to which it is sought to attach a tax, or a tax consequence, and if that emerges from a series, or combination of transactions, intended to operate as such, it is that series or combination which may be regarded' ([1981] STC at 180). [**31.21**]

2 **Extending** *Ramsay: Furniss v Dawson*

The *Ramsay* and *Burmah Oil* cases both involved circular schemes, the sole object of which was the avoidance of tax. *Furniss v Dawson*, on the other hand, was concerned with the deferment of capital gains tax by channelling the sale of chargeable assets through an intermediary company. The facts of the case are simple. The Dawsons decided to sell shares to Wood Bastow Holdings Ltd ('Wood Bastow') for £152,000. To defer the CGT that would otherwise have been payable, the shares were first sold to a newly incorporated Manx company ('Greenjacket') for the sum of £152,000 which was satisfied by an issue of shares in that company. The purchased shares were then immediately resold by Greenjacket to Wood Bastow for £152,000. The attraction of the scheme was that at no stage did any CGT liability arise: the sale to Greenjacket was specifically exempted from charge under FA 1965 Sch 7 para 6(2) (see now CGTA 1979 s 85(1)), whilst the resale by Greenjacket did not yield any profit to that company (the shares were purchased and sold for £152,000). As the price paid by Wood Bastow was received and retained by Greenjacket the scheme was not circular or self-cancelling: it involved a separate legal entity (Greenjacket) which ended up with the sale proceeds of the shares.

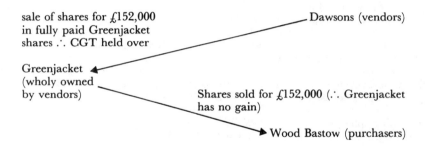

sale of shares for £152,000
in fully paid Greenjacket
shares ∴ CGT held over

Dawsons (vendors)

Greenjacket
(wholy owned
by vendors)

Shares sold for £152,000 (∴ Greenjacket
has no gain)

Wood Bastow (purchasers)

Before the Special Commissioners, Vinelott J, and a unanimous Court of Appeal, CGT was held not to be payable. The sale proceeds had been paid to Greenjacket and, in the phrase of Slade LJ in the Court of Appeal, the existence of Greenjacket had 'enduring legal consequences'. Before the House of Lords it was accepted that for a *scintilla temporis* legal and beneficial title to the shares passed to Greenjacket. Lord Brightman, however, in the only fully argued speech (which was concurred in by the other Lords) viewed the series of transactions as a pre-planned scheme:

> 'The whole process was planned and executed with faultless precision. The meetings began at 12.45 pm on 20 December, at which time the shareholdings of the operating companies were still owned by the Dawsons unaffected by any contract of sale. They ended with the shareholdings in the ownership of Wood Bastow. The minutes do not disclose when the meeting ended but perhaps it was all over in time for lunch.'

As its purpose was to obtain a deferral of CGT, he concluded that the scheme should be viewed as a whole and 'the court must then look at the end result. Precisely how the end result will be taxed will depend on the terms of the taxing statute sought to be applied.' Applying that test 'there was a disposal of the shares by the Dawsons in favour of Wood Bastow in consideration of a sum of money paid with the concurrence of the Dawsons to Greenjacket'. The gain on this disposal was subject to CGT. Lord

Brightman stressed that, so long as a pre-planned tax saving scheme existed no distinction should be drawn between the case where the steps were carried out in pursuance of a contract and one where, although the steps were preordained, separate binding contracts only arose at each stage. Although Greenjacket was not contractually bound to resell the shares to Wood Bastow, it was preordained (ie there was an informal arrangement) that this would occur. Hence, 'the day is not saved for the taxpayer because the arrangement is unsigned or contains the magic words "this is not a binding contract"'. In a similar vein, Lord Fraser of Tullybelton considered that 'the series of two transactions . . . were planned as a single scheme and . . . it should be viewed as a whole'.

The case remains of fundamental significance; above all it must be emphasised that the House of Lords restated the 'Ramsay principle' on a broad base and laid down no precise guidelines for its future operation. Lord Scarman, in particular, stressed the uncertain extent of the new approach:

> 'I am aware, and the legal profession (and others) must understand, that the law in this area is in an early stage of development. Speeches in your Lordships' House and judgments in the appellate courts are concerned more to chart a way forward between principles accepted and not to be rejected than to attempt anything so ambitious as to determine finally the limit beyond which the safe channel of acceptable tax avoidance shelves into the dangerous shallows of unacceptable tax evasion. The law will develop from case to case. Lord Wilberforce in *Ramsay's* case referred to "the emerging principle" of the law. What has been established with certainty by the House in *Ramsay's* case is that the determination of what does, and what does not, constitute unacceptable tax evasion is a subject suited to development by judicial process. Difficult though the task may be for judges, it is one which is beyond the power of the blunt instrument of legislation. Whatever a statute may provide, it has to be interpreted and applied by the courts and ultimately it will prove to be in this area of judge-made law that our elusive journey's end will be found.'

A ready acceptance that new law is being created and that this is the proper function of the judiciary is apparent and Lord Scarman in the passage quoted above, appears to be giving a new meaning to the terms 'tax avoidance' and 'tax evasion'. Such sentiments did not, however, commend themselves to the majority of the House of Lords in the most recent *Ramsay* cases (*Craven v White* and conjoined appeals which are considered in the next section). Lord Goff, for instance, expressed the basis of the *Ramsay* decision as follows:

> 'It would be naive in the extreme to imagine that the principle is not concerned with the outlawing of unacceptable tax avoidance. It plainly is. But it would be equally mistaken to regard the principle as in any sense a moral principle, or having any foundation in morality. It plainly is not. We can see this clearly from Lord Brightman's description of the scheme in *Furniss* as an honest scheme; and I would likewise so describe the schemes in the present three appeals. What the courts have established, however, is that certain tax avoidance schemes, although not shams in the sense of not being what they purport to be, are nevertheless unacceptable because they embrace transactions which are not "real" disposals and do not generate "real" losses (or gains) and so are held not to attract certain fiscal consequences which would normally be attached to disposals or losses (or gains) under the relevant statute. It is these unacceptable tax avoidance schemes which Lord Scarman described as "tax evasion" – a label which is perhaps better kept for those transactions which are traditionally so described because they are legal.'   **[31.22]**

3 The limits of the '*Ramsay* principle': *Craven v White*

As already mentioned one of the features of the judgments in *Furniss v Dawson*, was a reluctance to lay down precise boundaries to the *Ramsay* principle. Lord Brightman did, however, suggest that there are two basic requirements. *First*, there must be a preordained series of transactions (a 'scheme') although there need be no binding contract to carry the entire scheme through, and furthermore the scheme may include the attainment of a legitimate business end. In the *Dawson* case the scheme enabled shares to be sold from the Dawsons to Wood Bastow. *Secondly*, there must be steps in the scheme whose sole purpose is to avoid (or defer) a liability to tax. Such steps may have a 'business effect' but no 'business purpose'. The insertion of Greenjacket was such a step: in the words of Lord Brightman 'that inserted step had no business purpose apart from the deferment of tax, although it had a business effect. If the sale had taken place in 1964 before capital gains tax was introduced, there would have been no Greenjacket.'

The requirements are not, however, easy to apply. Two of their Lordships considered that *Westminster's* case could be distinguished as involving a single and not a composite transaction. Certainly the covenant was a single transaction, but its sole purpose was the avoidance of income tax and it was only entered into on the 'understanding' that the gardeners would not seek to claim their wages. Hence the making of the covenant was a step which had no commercial purpose save for the avoidance of tax. It is arguable, however, that unlike Greenjacket, which was an artificial person under the control of the Dawsons, the gardener's continuing right to sue for his wages serves to distinguish the case. Furthermore, as the covenant was to last for a period of seven years or the joint lives of the parties, it could have continued after the employment had terminated.

Any pre-arranged scheme which involves either tax avoidance, tax deferral or merely the preservation of an existing tax benefit is potentially within the *Ramsay* principle. A single tax-efficient transaction is presumably not within the *Ramsay* principle since the case does *not* state that persons must so organise their affairs that they pay the maximum amount of tax!

In three conjoined appeals (*Craven v White, Baylis v Gregory*), and IRC *v Bowater Property Developments Ltd*) the House of Lords was faced with the question when does a series of transactions form part of a pre-planned scheme (or alternatively, constitute a single composite transaction)? [**31.23**]

a) *Craven v White and Baylis v Gregory*

At first sight the facts of both cases closely resemble those of *Furniss v Dawson*. In *Craven v White* the taxpayers arranged for shares to be sold to J Ltd (see the diagram below) after those shares had first been transferred to M Ltd, an Isle of Man company which had been specially acquired for the purpose. The proceeds of sale were paid to M Ltd and were then loaned to the taxpayers. This loan back completed the transaction (contrast *Dawson* where it was assumed that the moneys were retained in the Isle of Man company) although the courts did not consider that this final step was of particular significance. Despite the similarities in the two cases, both Peter Gibson J and a unanimous Court of Appeal were not persuaded that the insertion of M Ltd was an artificial step capable of excision and were unable to agree that this case involved a pre-planned scheme. The crucial factor was that the taxpayers were throughout uncertain whether they would succeed in selling their shares to J Ltd, or indeed to any other purchaser (although this was what they desired) and they accepted that they might end up merging their company with the business of a third party, C Ltd. In *Baylis v Gregory*, the taxpayers were negotiating for the sale of their shares in a family company and envisaged that this would be carried out through an Isle of Man company as had been done in *Dawson*. However, the negotiations were broken off and then the Isle of Man company was incorporated and shares exchanged at a time when no other purchaser was on the horizon. This occurred in March 1974 and the shares were not eventually sold until January 1976. On these facts assessments to CGT raised on the basis that there had been a direct share sale by the original proprietors to the ultimate purchaser, were discharged both at first instance and by the Court of Appeal. **[31.24]**

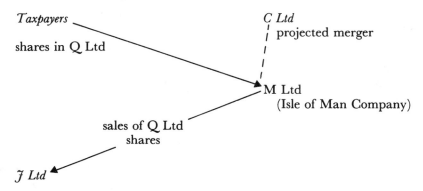

b) *IRC v Bowater Property Developments Ltd*

The case concerned a DLT fragmentation scheme that was widely employed before legislation in 1980 nullified *inter*-company fragmentations taking place after March 25 1980.

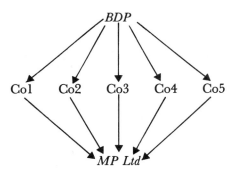

Bowater (BPD) divided the land in question into five slices among five other companies in the group. These companies were chosen because none had used any part of their annual exemption from DLT and the sole object of this transaction was to avoid DLT which would otherwise fall upon BPD if the land was sold, as intended, to MP Ltd. At the time of fragmentation there was a firm expectation that the sale to MP Ltd would proceed although there was no question of any contract being signed at that time and, indeed, some three months later, the projected sale was called off by MP Ltd. It was accepted that the fragmentation was effected without any commercial or business purpose apart from the hope of a tax advantage. In the following year, negotiations were, however, recommenced and the sale duly occurred. Warner J and the Court of Appeal refused to excise the fragmentation step and to treat the sale to MP Ltd as having been effected by BPD. They concluded that there was no pre-arranged scheme: 'in no sense was the second transaction (the sale to MP Ltd) pre-arranged or pre-ordained at the time when the fragmentation was carried out'. [31.25]

c) *The House of Lords speeches*

It is important to note that the Law Lords unanimously rejected the Revenue's appeals in two of the cases (*Baylis v Gregory and Bowater*) and it was only with regard to the *Craven v White* appeal that Lords Templeman and Goff dissented from their colleagues in finding in favour of the Revenue. Accordingly, a degree of unanimity can be discerned in the speeches and there is no doubt that they mark a significant limitation on the *Ramsay* principle. Having said this, however, the speeches also reveal a considerable level of disagreement on the ambit of that principle and the role of the courts in the area of tax avoidance. At one extreme stand the views of Lord Templeman:

'I have read the drafts of the speeches to be delivered in these present appeals. Three of those speeches accept the extreme argument of the taxpayer that *Furniss* is limited to its own facts or is limited to a transaction which has reached an advanced stage of negotiation (whatever that expression means) before the preceding tax avoidance transaction is carried out. These limitations would distort the effect of *Furniss*, are not based on principle, are not to be derived from the speeches in *Furniss*, and if followed, would only revive a surprised tax avoidance industry and cost the general body of taxpayers hundreds of millions of pounds by enabling artificial tax avoidance schemes to alter the incidence of taxation. In *Furniss*, Lord Brightman was not alone in delivering a magisterial rebuke to those judges who sought to place limitations on *Ramsay* ... In my opinion, a knife-edged majority has no power to limit this principle which has been responsible for four decisions of this House approved by a large number of our predecessors.'

By contrast, Lord Oliver (with whose speech Lords Keith and Jauncey concurred) expressed only limited support for the *Furniss v Dawson* approach:

'I confess to having been a less than enthusiastic convert to *Furniss v Dawson* because I found, initially at any rate, some difficulty in following the intellectual process by which in contra-distinction to the cases which preceded it, it reconstructed the transaction which had taken place in that case in a way which disapplied the specific statutory consequences which, on the face of them, attach to the intermediate transfer which had in fact taken place and which the Special Commissioners had found as a fact was a genuine transaction.'

So far as the actual issue in the cases was concerned (viz when a pre-planned series of transactions exists) the majority – Lords Keith, Oliver and Jauncey – adopted a far more restrictive view than Lords Templeman and Goff. Lord Jauncey, for instance, suggested the following definition of a 'composite transaction':

'A step in a linear transaction which has no business purpose apart from the avoidance or deferment of tax liability will be treated as forming part of a pre-ordained series of transactions or of a composite transaction if it was taken at a time when negotiations or arrangements for the carrying through as a continuous process of a subsequent transaction which actually takes place had reached a stage when there was no real likelihood that such subsequent transaction would not take place and if thereafter such negotiations or arrangements were carried through to completion without genuine interruption.'

The cases of *Baylis v Gregory* and *Bowater* obviously failed to satisfy such a test whilst in *Craven v White*, at the time of the share exchange, there was a real possibility that the subsequent sale would not occur since negotiations with the prospective purchaser were still continuing and had not been concluded. Accordingly, the majority held that the exchange of shares was a transaction independent from the sale which later occurred.

By contrast with the views of the majority, Lords Templeman and Goff adopted a more flexible approach to the question when a pre-planned scheme exists. Lord Templeman, for instance, expressed himself as follows:

'In *Furniss* . . . the transactions formed part of a scheme although the Dawsons had no control, direct or indirect over Wood Bastow and could at no stage oblige Wood Bastow to buy shares in the operating company. But both transactions were part of a scheme which was planned by Dawsons, which in the event was successful and which produced a taxable transaction. Two transactions can form part of a scheme even though it is wholly uncertain when the first transaction is carried out whether the taxpayer who is responsible for the scheme will succeed in procuring the second transaction to be carried out at all. . . . if the shadowy, undefined and indefinable expressions "practically certain", "practical likelihood", and "practical contemplation" possess any meanings, those expressions and those meanings are not to be derived from *Furniss*.'

Lord Goff appeared to adopt an even wider test:

'. . . it is not necessary that the details of the second step should be settled at the time when the first step was taken, nor that they should exactly correspond with those planned in advance.'

Even applying the wider tests advocated above, neither *Bowater* nor *Bayliss v Gregory* involved a pre-planned series of transactions: in the former, 'the scheme was frustrated when (the prospective purchasers) abandoned the negotiations' whilst, in the latter, 'the taxpayers placed themselves in a position to escape tax *in the future* but there was no scheme (Lord Templeman)'.

As the *ratio decidendi* of the case must be found in the more limited test laid down by the majority, it is now necessary to investigate what degree of certainty is necessary for a pre-planned scheme. How sure must the taxpayers be that the scheme which was eventually implemented was always going to be so implemented? Looking at the speeches of the majority, it is possible to extract a number of phrases which define this degree of certainty. They are set out below but it would follow, given the inevitable vagueness embraced in such phrases, that much room has been left for future disagreements:

'The taxpayers were by no means in a position for all practical purposes to ensure that the sale went through.' (Lord Keith in relation to *Craven v White*).

'. . . a single indivisible composite whole – a concept which may be summed up in homely terms by asking the question whether at the material time that whole is already "cut and dried". . . . so certain of fulfilment that it is intellectually and practically possible to conclude that there has indeed taken place one single and indivisible process. . . . a degree of certainty and control over the end result at the time when the intermediate steps are taken . . . it does seem to me to be essential at least that the principal terms should be agreed to the point at which it can be said that there is no practical likelihood that the transaction which actually takes place will not take place.' (Lord Oliver)

The majority speeches are striking in that they stress that the *Ramsay* principle is, at base, a rule of statutory construction. Lord Oliver, for instance, stated in relation to *Dawson* that 'the question is when is a disposal not a disposal within the terms of the statute'. Obviously such an approach has also been used in other tax cases in order to frustrate avoidance schemes: see for instance the decision in *Reed v Nova Securities Ltd* (1985) where on a construction of TA 1970 s 274 it was held that shares were not acquired as trading stock (for an analysis of this 'parallel attack' on trading transactions entered into, in whole or in part, for fiscal reasons, see (1990) BTR 52). It is, however, difficult to fit both the decisions in the earlier cases and certainly the speeches in *Dawson* into a constructional approach. As a simple matter of language, the share exchange carried out in the various cases undoubtedly occurred and involved a disposal of assets. Accordingly, to excise that disposal cannot be a simple exercise in statutory interpretation but must result from a wholly extraneous rule which is more akin to the striking out of a 'sham' transaction. **[31.26]**

4 Parliamentary Statement by the Chief Secretary to the Treasury

In commenting upon *Furniss v Dawson*, the Rt Hon Peter Rees QC, MP stated that:

> 'Taken with the decision in *Ramsay's* case, it is now clear that the widespread assumption based on the *Duke of Westminster's* case in the 1930s—that the courts will always look at the form rather than the substance of a transaction or various transactions—is no longer valid.
>
> The House of Lords made it clear that this is an evolving area of law, but the emerging principles do not in any way call into question the tax treatment of covenants, leasing transactions and other straightforward commercial transactions. Nor is there any question of the Inland Revenue challenging, for example, the tax treatment of straightforward transfers of assets between members of the same group of companies. I also assure the House that, in accordance with normal practice, the Inland Revenue will not seek to reopen cases when assessments were properly settled in accordance with prevailing practice and became final before that decision.
>
> The Board of Inland Revenue will also see whether clearance for types of case of special importance or general guidance for the benefit of taxpayers and their advisers can be given. The principle in *Furniss v Dawson* should lead, in future, to greater simplicity in our tax system and will, I hope, enable us in time to prune out provisions which owe their existence to the complexities of a high rate—some might say a confiscatory rate—tax system with a multiplicity of special reliefs.' (HC Deb, Vol 58, col 254.)

This statement was reiterated and, in some respects, added to in an exchange of correspondence between the Board of Inland Revenue and the Institute of Chartered Accountants (see [1985] STI 568 where the correspondence is set out in full). The following matters are particularly significant.

First, that the new approach will not be applied retrospectively to cases where assessments have been finalised. It may, of course, be applied to identical cases which arise in the future or are 'in the pipeline', as is evident from the attitude of the Stamp Office to certain pre-FA 1984 conveyancing schemes designed to avoid duty; they have taken the view that such schemes fall within the scope of *Ramsay* and have assessed the transaction accordingly, leaving it up to the taxpayer to challenge their assessment in the courts (see [**30.63**]). Thus, only in a limited sense is *Ramsay* not to be applied retrospectively.

Secondly, there is no intention to upset the treatment of covenants and 'straightforward commercial transactions'. So far as covenants are concerned, it is not entirely clear whether *Westminster* involved a scheme or a single transaction (a straightforward covenant), whilst capital covenants, which are usually executed in favour of charities, are surely not just simple covenants although expressly excepted from *Ramsay* in the correspondence. The phrase 'other straightforward commercial transactions' is not particularly helpful: presumably in *Furniss v Dawson*, although the entire transaction was commercial (the sale of shares to Wood Bastow), it was infected by an artificial step (the insertion of Greenjacket) so that it ceased to be 'straightforward'. Lord Brightman considered that the *Ramsay* approach could apply only if steps were inserted 'which have no commercial (business) purpose apart from the avoidance of a liability to tax' ([1984] STC at 166). Nevertheless, whether the insertion of some relatively insignificant business purpose will be sufficient to save a scheme, is uncertain: it remains possible that the law will develop to frustrate schemes where 'the main purpose, or one of the main purposes, is avoidance of liability to (tax) . . .' (as is the case if CGT relief is to be available on a share for share exchange).

Thirdly, it is clear that the Revenue assume that *Ramsay* applies generally to all taxes and the *Ingram* decision (see below) offers considerable support for this view. It was recently held in the High Court, for instance, that the doctrine is capable of applying to VAT although it was not invoked since the court decided that the relevant scheme amounted to a single genuine transaction. The particular arrangement was designed to avoid the VAT charge on building alterations which came into effect on 1 June 1984. Accordingly, the taxpayers arranged to be paid in full for the alterations before that date and this was achieved as part of an agreement under which the payment in question was lent back to the customer (under a commercial loan) and was then repaid by instalments equal to the amounts periodically certified as payable by the architects. In effect, therefore, payment for the work did occur after the deadline for the introduction of VAT but, because of the legal arrangements entered into, the taxpayers argued that the late instalments represented the repayment of a commercial loan. This abbreviated summary of the facts reveals the high level of artificiality involved in the case and accordingly the decision of the High Court that Ramsay did not apply is somewhat surprising. To categorise the scheme as a single transaction is in itself open to doubt and it was even accepted by the taxpayer that the sole reason for the arrangements was to avoid a VAT liability! (*Customs and Excise Comrs v Faith Construction Ltd* (1989): the Court of Appeal did not need to consider the possible application of *Ramsay*).

Fourthly, the statement envisages some simplification of tax legislation in the wake of the decision in *Furniss v Dawson*. Presumably, anti-avoidance legislation will be rendered unnecessary so long as the courts preserve the *Ramsay* principle on a broad basis. It will be surprising, however, if the existing provisions are removed from the statute book and one of the most puzzling problems left unanswered by *Furniss v Dawson* is how to marry the new approach with these statutory provisions.

Fifthly, the Chief Secretary expressly exempts from *Ramsay* straightforward transfers of assets between members of the same group of companies. For some taxation purposes, groups are looked at as a whole (see, for instance, the group relief and the group income provisions). There is, however, no provision enabling the pooling of *capital* losses and arrangements designed to remedy this gap in the legislation are to be permitted. The intra-group transfer must, however, be straightforward: *Shepherd v Lyntress Ltd; News International plc v Shepherd* (1989) provides a graphic illustration of the kind of arrangement which will be attacked. In that case a company which realised a capital loss was acquired as part of the News International Group with the express object of using its loss relief. Chargeable assets pregnant with gain were transferred to the new group member and immediately sold (some on the day of transfer!). That transfer of the assets intra-group did not attract any tax charge and so the eventual gain on sale was available for off-set against the losses. The Revenue, not surprisingly, argued that the whole transaction fell within the scope of *Ramsay*. Vinelott J was unimpressed:

> 'The Commissioners cannot characterise a series of steps as a single composite transaction unless they have first found facts sufficient to support that inference. In the instant case there is no finding by the Special Commissioners that any step had been taken to place the shares of LWT, News Corporation and Broken Hill [these were the assets pregnant with gain transferred intra-group] for sale through the Stock Exchange at the time when these shares were transferred to Lyntress and Salcombe [these were the "loss" companies]. It is not enough to say that they were transferred with a view to a sale and in order that the gain should be realised by Lyntress and Salcombe. That would be to make the fiscal motive alone a sufficient ground for imposing tax.'

Crucially therefore the judge, following the *Craven v White* decision, concluded that there was no reason to suspect that arrangements had been made for the sale of the shares on the Stock Exchange before their transfer to the loss making companies: he stressed that it was doubtful whether such sales would have occurred if the price had collapsed immediately after the transfer.   [31.27]

5   Stamp duty and the *Ingram* case

It has been argued that there is no room for the application of the *Ramsay* principle to stamp duty because, inter alia, it is a duty on documents not transactions. However, in *Ingram v IRC* (1985), Vinelott J held that a stamp duty scheme designed to avoid duty on the purchase of land by splitting the transaction into stages fell within *Furniss v Dawson* and was therefore ineffective. The scheme involved, first, the purchaser agreeing to take a 999-year lease of the property at a premium of £145,000 and small annual rent; secondly, the sale of the property subject to that lease to a company for £500; and finally the resale of the property by the company to the purchaser for £600. As a result of these transactions the taxpayer acquired full title to the land (by merger of the leasehold and freehold interests) but it was intended that the consideration paid for the long lease would escape duty (since agreements for leases exceeding thirty-five years were excluded from charge under Stamp Act 1891 s 75) so that only the small sum paid on the transfer of the freehold would be subject to duty.

The judge held that, were it not for the *Ramsay* principle, it was clear that the taxpayer's contentions were correct and that the transfer was what it purported to be—ie of a freehold interest subject to the agreement for the lease which had reduced its value. An application of the *Ramsay* principle, however, required the composite transaction to be 'recharacterised'. Accordingly, the leasehold agreement should be excised as an artificial transaction, leaving the instrument of transfer subject to duty as a transfer of the entire freehold interest at the agreed price (ie £145,600).

Three important matters emerge from this judgment.

First, Vinelott J stated that the principle that, if a document was genuine, the court could not go behind it to some supposed underlying substance (derived from *IRC v Duke of Westminster*) had no application to composite transactions entered into for the purpose of avoiding tax and the result of the new approach of the House of Lords was that many decisions (including some of the House of Lords) needed reappraisal.

Secondly, the view that *Ramsay* had no application in the field of stamp duty was rejected '*after considerable hesitation*'. Although the duty was levied on instruments not transactions, in order to determine the nature of a particular instrument, the court had to ascertain the substance of the transaction effected by it—a task which should be carried out by applying the Ramsay principle.

Finally, it is, of course, still necessary at the end of the recharacterisation of the transaction to find an instrument to stamp (in this case the final transfer to the purchaser). Had that document not been executed so that the freehold interest (subject to the long lease) was left outstanding in a company (eg one controlled by the taxpayers) would the same result have followed? Presumably, the agreement for the lease could not be stamped because of the express wording of s 75 whereas to impose duty on the transfer of the freehold would ignore the continuing separation of freehold and leasehold interests. Given the apparent willingness of the House of Lords to pierce the corporate veil in tax avoidance cases (as was done in *Furniss v Dawson*), however, such a result is at least possible!

As a postscript to this important decision it should be noted that the avoidance scheme employed in the *Ingram* case is now prevented by FA 1984 s 111 in the case of agreements for leases in excess of thirty-five years made after 19 March 1984 (see [**30.63**]).　　　　　　　　　　　　　　　　　　[**31.28**]

6　The Fitzwilliam case

The 10th Earl Fitzwilliam died on 21 September 1979 survived by his 81 year old wife. Under the terms of his 1977 will, and after leaving a number of pecuniary legacies, his residuary estate was settled on a 23 month discretionary trust for a class of beneficiaries including Lady Fitzwilliam and with a provision that in default of exercise and at the end of that period the estate was to be held for Lady Fitzwilliam for life with remainder to her daughter Lady Hastings. The value of the residuary estate was certified just over £12.4m and accordingly if the trustees exercised their powers to appoint that property away from Lady Fitzwilliam CTT at a rate of 75% would apply. By contrast, if the property passed to Lady Fitzwilliam no charge would then be imposed although, given her age and then state of health, there was obviously a considerable danger that she too would die in which case the property would on that occasion be taxed at 75%. In his judgment, Vinelott J referred to 'the crushing burden of CTT'.

On the death of the 10th Earl, CTT was paid on the pecuniary legacies but not on the property comprised in the residuary estate and therefore subject to the 23 month trust. It is usually thought, despite the fact that a surviving spouse is named as one of the beneficiaries, that tax must be paid in such cases albeit that recovery is then possible if the spouse is appointed the property or alternatively takes in default at the end of the 23 month period. In this case, however, CTT was paid only on the pecuniary legacies and, despite criticism from the Revenue, it appears that the Probate Office were consulted and were agreeable to this. Vinelott J did not comment other than to observe that because of the illiquid nature of the estate 'it would in fact have been very difficult for the executors to have delayed probate until a sum sufficient to pay the whole of the CTT had been raised'. It

FITZWILLIAM: 'THE SCHEME'

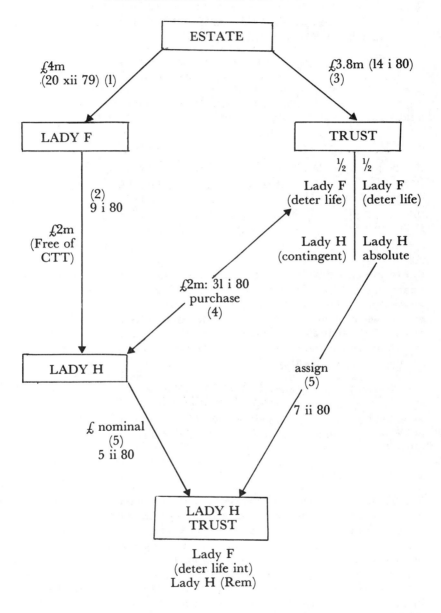

should be noted that the exemption for transfers between spouses contained in IHTA 1984 s 18 allows for a wait and see period of up to 12 months (see s 18(3)(b)). Whether this period can be doubled by employing a so-called 'two year discretionary' trust remains a moot point.

The will trustees and two beneficiaries (Lady Fitzwilliam and Lady Hastings) entered into a series of transactions, devised by professional advisers, and designed to mitigate the ultimate CTT bill. It should be noted that the transactions were to a large degree artificial and in some cases circular. The end result, however, was that some £7.8m had been distributed out of the residuary estate—£3.8m to Lady Hastings and £4m to Lady

Fitzwilliam—without, it appeared, any CTT liability arising. To assist in understanding how the schemes were structured reference should be made to the diagram below: it should also be realised that a part of the scheme rested on a 'plain blunder in the legislation'. **[31.29]**

Stage 1

On 20 December 1979 part of the residuary estate to a value of £4m was appointed out to Lady Fitzwilliam. The intention at that time was that land would be appropriated in satisfaction of the appointed sum. **[31.30]**

Stage 2

By cheque, back-dated to 9 January 1980, Lady Fitzwilliam then gave £2m (free of CTT) to Lady Hastings. At that time lifetime gifts attracted a CTT charge and, unless the tax was paid by the donee, were subject to grossing up. Accordingly, the total cost of this gift to Lady Fitzwilliam was in the region of £5m! **[31.31]**

Stage 3

On 14 January 1980 the trustees appointed a further portion of the residuary estate, to a value of £3.8m, on the following trusts. The income was to be paid to Lady Fitzwilliam until her death or until 15 February 1980 (if earlier) whereupon, as to one moiety, the capital was to pass to Lady Hastings absolutely (so that she had a vested remainder interest and this will be referred to as the 'vested moiety') but as to the other moiety the capital was only to pass to Lady Hastings if she was living on the termination of Lady Fitzwilliam's interest in possession (so that as regards this moiety Lady Hastings had a contingent remainder interest: the 'contingent moiety'). Note that the appointment to Lady Fitzwilliam on interest in possession trusts would not result in any capital transfer tax liability but that the termination of her interest (which must of course occur *at the latest* in the following month) would! **[31.32]**

Stage 4

On 31 January 1990, in consideration for the payment of £2m, Lady Fitzwilliam assigned to Lady Hastings her income interest in the contingent moiety. The CTT consequences of this transaction were that Lady Fitzwilliam thereby made an immediate transfer of value equal in value to one-half of the capital then in the settlement: ie one-half of £3.8m (see FA 1975 Sch 5 para 4(2), now IHTA 1984 s 52(1)). However, by para 4(4) of Sch 5 (now IHTA 1984 s 52(2)) – enacted as an anti-avoidance measure – if an interest in possession was assigned for value then CTT was only charged on the excess of the capital value of that interest (one-half of £3.8m) over the consideration paid. Accordingly, as the £2m paid by Lady Hastings exceeded the £1.9m capital value of the interest, no CTT was payable on the assignment by Lady Fitzwilliam.

As a result of the assignment Lady Hastings was now entitled both to an interest in possession in the contingent moiety and, of course, to the capital outright on the termination of that interest in February 1980 provided that she was then alive. Because of the governing fiction that for CTT/IHT purposes a beneficiary with an interest in possession is treated as owning the underlying capital, there is, of course, no tax liability if the interest in possession beneficiary becomes entitled to the underlying capital (IHTA 1984 s 53(2) formerly FA 1975 Sch 5 para 4(a)).

Stage 4 did not therefore involve any adverse CTT consequences and, indeed, because of the mutual transfer provisions which existed at this time (see FA 1976 ss 86-87) enabled substantial benefits to be obtained. In simple terms the mutual transfer rules enabled a gift to be 'nullified' provided that the value of the gifted property was returned to the donor. Not only was the return transfer free from CTT but the original gift itself was thereupon treated as cancelled. Applying these rules to the present facts it will be recalled that at *Stage 2* Lady Fitzwilliam had made a gift of £2m to Lady Hastings on which CTT was payable. At *Stage 4* Lady Hastings paid an equivalent sum to Lady Fitzwilliam in return for an assignment of her determinable life interest. Accordingly, and to the extent that the payment by Lady Hastings was a transfer of value, not only would that payment be free from *CTT but it would also have the effect of nullifying the earlier gift at Stage 1* which had been made by Lady Fitzwilliam. It is at this stage that the 'plain blunder' in the legislation becomes relevant. FA 1978 s 69(7) had been introduced in order to counter complex tax avoidance schemes and provided that when an interest in possession was purchased then in order to decide whether the purchaser had made any transfer of value the usual principle that the interest in possession was to be valued on the basis of underlying capital must be ignored. Instead, the interest itself must be valued. Applying that principle to these particular facts, Lady Fitzwilliam's interest had a purely nominal value so that the £2m paid by Lady Hastings was virtually all gift and could therefore be relieved under the mutual transfer rules.

The end result was that the sum of £2m had been returned to Lady Fitzwilliam (free from any CTT charge) and that some £1.9m had been extracted from the estate and paid to Lady Hastings without any CTT charge. It may be noted in passing that the mutual transfer provisions were repealed with the introduction of Inheritance Tax in 1986.   [**31.33**]

Stage 5

The final stage involved Lady Hastings settling a nominal sum on 5 February 1980. Under the terms of the trust Lady Fitzwilliam was entitled to a determinable life interest (in this case the interest determined on Lady Fitzwilliam's death or 15 March 1980, whichever occurred first) with a remainder to Lady Hastings herself. Two days after establishing the trust Lady Hastings assigned her absolute remainder interest (created at *Stage 3*, above) to the trustees to be held on the same trusts. The effect of the assignment was that Lady Fitzwilliam's interest in possession did not determine on 15 February 1980 (as would have been the case in the absence of the assignment) but instead continued for a further month. When it did eventually determine the property in Lady Hastings' settlement then passed to her. Accordingly, any CTT charge was avoided by the 'reverter to settlor' exemption (see FA 1975 Sch 5 para 4(5): now IHTA 1984 s 53(3)).

The Revenue's argument that Lady Hastings was not the only settlor of the property in her settlement so that this exemption was at the very least limited in its application, was rejected: Vinelott J pointed out that it was hard to discover who else could have been a settlor of these funds:

'I find it difficult to see how the Tenth Earl can be said to have provided funds "in connection with" a settlement which was not in contemplation when he died ... there must be some real connection linking the original provider of a fund and the settlement before the former person can be said to have been the settlor—some connection, that is, beyond the mere fact that historically the settled fund originated with him. Otherwise, in a case where, for instance, "A" gave a sum of money to his son which the son then settled entirely of his own volition, "A" would fall to be treated as a "settlor" or "the settlor" of the fund for the purposes of Schedule 5—a conclusion which seems to me self evidently absurd. It may be that if there was some understanding or arrangement even falling short of an enforceable agreement between "A" and his son, that "A" would settle the monies provided by "A", "A" would fall to be treated as the settlor; it may be that in this case if there had been such an arrangement or understanding between the trustees and Lady Hastings at the time when the £3.8m appointment was made, it could be said that they were or that the Tenth Earl was to be treated as the settlor. I express no opinion on that. On the evidence before the Commissioners the settlement made by Lady Hastings was made of her own volition; there was no such arrangement or understanding.'

With the termination of Lady Fitzwilliam's interest, the remaining £1.9m therefore passed to Lady Hastings without any CTT charge. It may be noted that the reverter to settlor exemption used to such advantage in this case has now been curtailed: IHTA 1984 s 53(5)(b) provides that the exemption will not apply if its application 'depends upon a reversionary interest having been transferred into a settlement on or after 10 March 1981'. (This amendment of the law was made by FA 1981 s 104(1)).   **[31.34]**

The importance of the Fitzwilliam case

It was accepted without argument that the Ramsay principle is capable of application in the area of CTT/IHT. Some commentators had felt that, because of the existence of a statutory associated operations provision (see IHTA 1984 s 268), there was no room for *Ramsay* to apply. Vinelott J swiftly dismissed the possible application of this section, however, noting that 'the associated operations provisions in the CTT legislation have a very limited scope'.

The other difficulty that some had foreseen in applying Ramsay to IHT arrangements is based on practical considerations: how easy is it to show that a series of gifts form part of a preordained transaction? In deciding that the various steps entered into by Lady Fitzwilliam, Lady Hastings, and the executors did not amount to a preordained series of transactions, Vinelott J added considerable fuel to these doubts. Quite clearly the steps carried out were highly artificial: establishing life interests determinable within weeks of their creation can hardly be justified on the basis of any serious donative intent vis-à-vis the beneficiary! The arrangements were, at least in part, circular: the £2m, for instance, passed from the executors to Lady Fitzwilliam on to Lady Hastings and finally back to Lady Fitzwilliam! Finally, the transactions, by successfully exploiting loopholes in the legislation, resulted in some £3.8m passing from the estate of the 10th Earl to Lady Hastings free from CTT. As the judge himself noted, it was on any view 'a very artificial scheme'.

Why therefore did *Ramsay* not apply? Understandably, the Revenue faced difficulties in formulating their case. Viewing steps 1–5 as part of a single operation and, by excising the various intermediary steps concluding that CTT should be levied on the basis that £3.8m had been distributed out of the estate directly to Lady Hastings, would appear to be the obvious argument. As against this, however, Vinelott J pointed out:

'it cannot be said that all the steps that were in fact taken were taken in pursuance

of a single composite scheme of which the first step was the appointment of
£4m to Lady Fitzwilliam and the end result of which would be that Lady
Fitzwilliam would be left with £4m and Lady Hastings with £3.8m, for it was
not in contemplation until after 3 January that under the arrangements that
were being made and were constantly evolving Lady Fitzwilliam would be left
with £4m. Moreover it was not until 3 January that the proposal that Lady
Fitzwilliam would make a settlement which would be used to take advantage
of the reverter to settlor exemption was dropped and an appointment of a further
fund of £1.9m in which Lady Fitzwilliam would take a short term interest later
enlarged by an assignment by Lady Hastings of her reversionary interest was
substituted.'

An alternative argument put forward by the Revenue was that all the
steps from and including the gift of £2m by Lady Fitzwilliam to Lady Hastings
were part of a single composite transaction. Again the judge concluded that
there were insuperable obstacles in the way of this argument:

'The difficulty is quite simply that given there was in the minds of [the professional
advisers] a scheme ... and which was in fact carried into effect albeit with
some modifications, the scheme could not be carried into effect without the
co-operation of Lady Fitzwilliam and Lady Hastings nor indeed could it succeed
unless Lady Fitzwilliam whose expectation of life was in doubt survived until
15 March. The details of the scheme were not known to either of them on
7 and 9 January respectively.'

Other recent cases have also explored the degree of certainty that must
be present at the commencement of a series of operations for that series
to amount to a preordained transaction. In *Craven v White* for instance, there
was no certainty that the sale of the shares would proceed; in *IRC v Bowater*
the ultimate purchaser was nowhere in sight; whilst in *Shepherd v Lyntress*
the mere fact that shares had been transferred to a company with a view
to re-sale on the Stock Exchange by that company *on the very next day* was
insufficient since at the time of transfer the shares had not been placed for
sale on the Exchange and, indeed, if the share price had collapsed the next
day it was doubtful whether the sales would have occurred.

Crucial to Vinelott's judgment is his view that neither Lady Hastings
nor Lady Fitzwilliam slavishly followed the dictates of their tax advisers:
so far as Lady Fitzwilliam was concerned:

'I do not see how it can be said that from the inception of the scheme Lady
Fitzwilliam gave *carte blanche* to Curry & Co to carry the whole scheme into
effect on her behalf and on behalf of Lady Hastings.'

Whilst, on Lady Hastings' role, he concluded that:

'she was not putty in the hands of her solicitors. The choice whether to adopt
the proposals was her choice.'

Although it is undeniably true that Lady Fitzwilliam and Lady Hastings
were kept fully informed of each step and freely consented at each stage
and although it is further the case that they were not presented with a
fully packaged scheme at the outset, it should be noted that neither insisted
upon changes being made to the proposals that were made to them. Lady
Fitzwilliam, for instance, apparently agreed not only to make a £2m gift
to Lady Hastings but also to bear CTT on that gift and the resulting sum
was 'on any view potentially a very heavy burden and in excess of Lady
Fitzwilliam's immediate resources'.

How relevant is it, therefore, that the consequences involved in making
this gift were fully explained to Lady Fitzwilliam? In truth, neither the

professional advisers nor Lady Fitzwilliam can seriously have contemplated that the gift would stand alone and that the full amount of tax would therefore be payable by Lady Fitzwilliam: at the very least the gift must have formed part of a package of measures designed to alleviate the CTT burden on the estate.

Undoubtedly, a distinction can be drawn between at the one extreme a tax avoidance scheme which is purchased as a whole and the individual steps of which are never fully explained to the client (as was the case in *Ramsay* itself) and at the other extreme the type of scheme which evolves during its implementation (as in the *Fitzwilliam* case). To apply *Ramsay* to the former but not to the latter, however, must open the door to relatively straightforward tax avoidance arrangements. Presenting the client with half the package on day one and the remainder on day two taking the risk of him dying in the interim is one obvious solution. Generally keeping the client in the dark about each step in a composite transaction would appear similarly efficacious! The one message that does appear from the *Fitzwilliam* case is that even though *Ramsay* is capable of applying to CTT/IHT planning arrangements, it is relatively straightforward for the professional adviser to ensure that, in practice, it will not!   [**31.35**]

7   Conclusions

The *Ramsay* line of cases are based on principles of common application. In *Cairns v MacDiarmid* (1983) the taxpayer's claim for income tax relief for interest payments was dismissed by the Court of Appeal on the grounds, inter alia, that the scheme fell within the '*Ramsay* principle'. Sir John Donaldson MR concluded that:

> 'The whole transaction was "out of this world". Although no sham, it lacked all reality. It did not even have the reality of *Ramsay's* case in that [the taxpayer] neither paid a fee nor incurred any expenses. But, as in that case, at the end of a series of connected and intended transactions, his financial position was precisely as it was at the beginning!' [1983] STC at 182 (he made similar comments in *Sherdley v Sherdley* but the House of Lords subsequently ruled that *Ramsay* had no application to orders made under the Matrimonial Causes Act).

There is no suggestion that the Revenue would seek to challenge the normal IHT arrangements between spouses designed to ensure that both make full use of the available exemptions and reliefs and nil rate band of tax. Similar arrangements may be entered into in order to take advantage of the independent taxation of spouses.

There is no inherent reason why the *Ramsay* doctrine should not be used by the taxpayer. Indeed, as it provides for the excision of artificial steps in order to discover what the real transaction is for taxation purposes, it must presumably apply for all purposes. Although some support for this view may be found in *Young v Phillips* (1984), in *Bird v IRC* (1985) Vinelott J at first instance, without expressing a concluded view on the matter, thought it unlikely that when a taxpayer embarked on a series of transactions designed to avoid tax he could later argue (when those transactions were challenged under anti-avoidance legislation such as TA 1970 s 460) that they should be treated as a fiscal nullity. Further he expressed the view that a party cannot blow 'hot and cold' so that the Revenue could not argue that a scheme fell within TA 1988 s 703 (thereby accepting that all the steps were effective but that the end result was nullified by statute) and, as an alternative, seek to excise certain of those steps under the *Ramsay* approach.

Wholly artificial schemes are obviously to be avoided and certain PETA plans, notably those which sought to avoid IHT altogether, are accordingly, liable to challenge (see further *Capital Taxes*, 1984, p 59). The reservation of benefit provisions introduced in 1986 have, in any event, killed off inheritance trusts and PETA plans entered into after 17 March 1986.

The use of options in tax planning needs careful thought in the wake of the *Furniss* decision. It has in recent years become common to spread the sale of land over a number of years by means of options and part of the attraction has been to mitigate the vendor's CGT and (until its abolition in FA 1985) DLT liability by taking advantage of more than one annual exemption. Assume, for instance, that A wishes to sell Blackacre to B and will realise a gain of £12,000 on that sale. Were he to divide Blackacre into two equal portions and agree to sell the first portion in the tax year 1991–92 and, at the same time, grant call option to purchase the second portion in the following tax year, it would appear that for CGT purposes the land has been disposed of in two different tax years and A will therefore have two annual exemptions available (notice that A could ensure that B is obliged to purchase the land by taking a 'put' option enabling him to require B to purchase the second parcel if he fails to exercise his call option).

There is no doubt that such schemes amount to a pre-ordained series of transactions and arguably the options represent steps which have been inserted purely for the avoidance of tax, since, in the absence of CGT considerations, A would have sold the whole of Blackacre to B in 1991–92. If the steps are excised it may be argued that there was effectively a sale of the land to B at the time when the contract of sale for the first parcel was made and the put and call options taken. Doubts have been expressed about the validity of this argument (see (1984) DLS Gaz 3478) and if the 'option-step' is excised it is by no means clear that the *Ramsay* doctrine permits the sale of all the land to be treated as occurring in 1991–92. It may be that the Revenue now accept the efficacy of cross-options—certainly there has still been no challenge raised to the various DLT option schemes—whilst it may be noted that in *J Sainsbury Ltd v O'Connor* (1990) (a case considered in detail in Chapter 28) Millett J commented at first instance:

> 'From a commercial point of view, of course, the simultaneous creation of both put and call options puts the parties in much the same position as an unconditional contract of sale would do; but in law the two situations are quite distinct.'

Commercial reasons may, in particular cases, justify the use of options and the *Ramsay* argument is obviously more difficult to sustain when cross-options are not employed but a call option alone is taken by the purchaser.

[31.36]–[31.50]

III STATUTORY PROVISIONS TO COUNTER TAX AVOIDANCE

1 **The legislation**

The major provisions that have been enacted in attempts to deal with specific instances of tax avoidance are set out below. In many cases they were designed to prevent the conversion of income profits into capital gains taxed at a lower rate. With the harmonisation in the rates of the two taxes, such provisions are of reduced importance. **[31.51]**

Transactions in securities TA 1988 ss 703]–[709 (originally enacted in FA 1960). **[31.52]**

Bond washing and dividend stripping   Various provisions deal with these problems, the oldest dating back to FA 1927 with the most recent being in TA 1988 ss 710–728.   [**31.53**]

Transfer of assets overseas   Originally enacted in FA 1936, these provisions were amended in 1981 as a result of Vestey v IRC (1980) (see Chapter 13).   [**31.54**]

Artificial transactions in land   For TA 1988 s 776 see Chapter 8. Statutory provisions also regulate sale and leaseback transactions (TA 1988 ss 779]–[784); see Chapter 6.   [**31.55**]

Sale of income derived from personal activities   TA 1988 s 775 (originally enacted in FA 1969) prevents the conversion of future taxable income into capital gains subject to CGT. The avoidance typically involved entertainers who sold their services to a company formed for that purpose and then sold the shares in that company.   [**31.56**]

The use of tax losses and transfer pricing   TA 1988 s 768 (originating in FA 1969) imposes restrictions upon the purchase of tax loss companies (see Chapter 28). Sales at under or overvalue may be subject to challenge under TA 1988 s 770, and under the *Sharkey v Wernher* principle (see Chapter 6).   [**31.57**]

2   Typical avoidance schemes involving securities

A company is a legal entity distinct from its shareholders and, therefore, provides fertile ground for such tax avoidance schemes as dividend stripping and bond washing.   [**31.58**]

Dividend stripping   The simplest illustration of dividend stripping is where A owns A Ltd which has profits available for distribution. A sells the shares to B who is a dealer in securities. A receives a capital sum which reflects the undistributed profits in the company. B will take out the profits from A Ltd (as a dividend) which will be taxed as income but the shares will now be worth less (reflecting the fact that they have been stripped of their dividend). B will, therefore, make a trading loss when he sells the shares which can be set off against the dividend income that B has received (usually under the provisions of TA 1988 s 380: see [**7.93**]). The result is that corporate profits have been extracted free of tax.

The courts were often invited to hold that the purchase and sale of the shares was not a trading transaction. In some cases they decided that it was trading; in others, not (contrast, eg, *Griffiths v J P Harrison (Watford) Ltd* (1962) with *FA and AB Ltd v Lupton* (1971) and see *Coates v Arndale Properties Ltd* (1984) and, for consideration of the effect of fiscal motives, *Ensign Tankers (Leasing) Ltd v Stokes* (1991)). The close company legislation sought to tackle one part of the problem by preventing the accumulation of profits in close companies (see [**28.129**]). In 1960 the problem was attacked with legislation aimed at transactions in securities generally.   [**31.59**]

Bond washing   Dividends only become a taxpayer's income when they are due and payable; when that happens the shareholder can claim the sum from the company as a debt. Usually there is a time gap between declaration and payment which provides an opportunity to wash the shares (or bonds) of their dividend. The washing process usually involves a taxpayer who is subject to no income tax or to lower rates only. Assume, for instance, that shares are owned by A who is subject to income tax at a high rate. When a dividend is declared on his shares he sells them to his cousin, a student with unused personal allowances. A is, therefore, receiving a capital sum for the shares on which CGT rather than income tax will be charged. The dividends are paid to the cousin who suffers little if any income tax thereon. Finally, the shares may be repurchased by A after payment of the dividend. Legislative provisions (notably TA 1988 s 729 and the accrued income scheme discussed below) prevent the most blatant examples of bond washing. **[31.60]**

3 The accrued income scheme

TA 1988 ss 710–728 are designed to prevent the bond washing of fixed interest securities.

The practice of bond washing involved the conversion of income into capital and resulted in that sum being taxed, if at all, to CGT (with the result that as most fixed interest securities were exempt from CGT if held for 12 months or more, tax was often avoided). Accordingly, these provisions treat interest on securities as accruing on a day to day basis between the interest payment dates. On a disposal, therefore, the vendor is subject to income tax under ScheduleD Case VI on the interest accruing from the immediately preceding interest payment date to the date of disposal and the purchaser is treated as owning the income from that date. It follows that when the sale is with accrued interest ('cum div') the vendor is treated as entitled to extra interest and the purchaser gets relief for a corresponding amount. Conversely, if the sale is without accrued interest ('ex div'), the vendor will obtain relief on an amount equal to the interest to which the purchaser is regarded as entitled. The apportioned sums are treated as received on the day when the interest period ends and are subject to tax under Schedule D Case VI for the chargeable period in which they are received. As a result of these provisions appropriate amendments are made in the computation of any capital gains on the disposal of the securities (although for disposals after 1 July 1986 gilt-edged securities and qualifying corporate bonds are generally exempt from CGT: FA 1985 s 67) and securities covered by the scheme are excluded from the anti-bond washing provisions which preceded this new legislation.

EXAMPLE 31.1

Elena owns £100,000 in nominal value of Government stock paying interest at 10% pa on 30 June and 31 December. She sells that stock 'cum div' to Henrietta on 30 September 1991 for £99,780.

(i) *Elena's tax position*: She is subject to income tax under Schedule D Case VI in 1991–92 on three months' accrued interest (£2,500) for the period from 30 June 1991 (the last payment date) to 30 September (disposal or settlement date).

(ii) *Henrietta's tax position*: Assuming that she retains the stock until 31 December 1991 she will then be subject to income tax on the interest paid as follows:

Interest payment to 31 December 1991	=	£5,000
Deduct accrued interest purchased (1 July to 30 September)	=	£2,500
Reduced amount taxable	=	£2,500

(iii) Had the sale been 'ex div' so that the interest payment of £5,000 to 31 December 1991 was retained by Elena, she would be taxed on £2,500 of that figure and the balance of £2,500 (ie interest from the date of disposal to the date of sale) would be taxed in Henrietta's hands.

The securities caught by these provisions are defined in s 710 and include bearer bonds, UK and foreign securities, and securities whether secured or unsecured issued by governments, companies, local authorities and other institutions. Excluded from the provisions are ordinary or preference shares, National Savings Certificates, certificates of deposit, bills of exchange, Treasury bills, local authority bills and similar instruments. All taxpayers (ie individuals, companies and trusts) resident or ordinarily resident in the UK are within the provisions, but there are specific exclusions for financial traders (whose profits on sale are taxed anyway as income under Schedule D Case I) and for individuals holding securities with a nominal value not exceeding £5,000. For a consideration of how the accrued income scheme affects PRs and trustees, see (1986) LS Gaz 3399 and (1987) LS Gaz 2022.   [31.61]

4   Transactions in securities (TA 1988 ss 703–709)

These provisions are amongst the most obscure and complex in the tax legislation. Their object is to cancel (for taxation purposes) a tax advantage gained as the result of a transaction in securities. This cancellation will be effected either by an assessment to income tax under Schedule D Case VI at a maximum rate of 40%; or by such other adjustments as may be prescribed by the Revenue, such as the refusal of a tax repayment (TA 1988 s 703(3)). The three conditions which must be satisfied before the provisions of s 703 can be invoked are considered below.   [31.62]

There must be a transaction in securities   'Transaction' and 'securities' are given a wide meaning. A transaction apart from covering purchases, sales and exchanges can include the combined effects of a series of operations . Securities include stocks and shares (TA 1988 s 709(2)) and also a secured debt (see *IRC v Parker* (1966)).   [31.63]

As a result of the transaction the taxpayer either obtains, or is in a position to obtain, a tax advantage   'Tax advantage' is defined in TA 1988 s 709(1). An advantage will arise if money is received in the non-taxable shape of a loan rather than in the (taxable) form of a capital dividend (*Bird v IRC* (1988)). One of the uncertainties raised by the definition is whether a capital gains tax advantage is included; the section was introduced before CGT and the widely held view is that CGT is not included. Where shares are sold, there is the possibility of both a CGT charge and an assessment under TA 1988 s 703. Revenue practice is to give a credit for CGT paid against a liability under s 703 (see *IRC v Garvin* (1981)). In the *Bird* case, assessments under s 703 were reduced because of the corporation tax suffered by the relevant company.

There will be no liability under s 703 if the taxpayer can show that the transaction was carried out for bona fide commercial reasons and that obtaining a tax advantage was not one of its main objects (TA 1988 s 703(1)). This is a matter of intention and, as it is a question of fact, the findings of the Special Commissioners on such matters can only be overturned by the court in exceptional cases (*IRC v Brebner* (1967)). In *Clark v IRC* (1978), it was held that this commercial test had to be applied not just to the actual sale of the securities, but in the light of all the relevant circumstances. On the particular facts, the sole purpose of the sale was to enable the taxpayer to raise money for the purchase of a farm and there were sound commercial reasons for that purchase. Fox J decided, therefore, that there was a good defence to an assessment under s 703. **[31.64]**

Any one of five circumstances specified in TA 1988 s 704 must be present Paragraph A of TA 1988 s 704 is concerned with the distribution of an abnormal dividend to a person entitled to tax relief thereon and catches the classical dividend stripping operation.

Paragraph B prevents the use of trading losses that may arise for a share dealer on a sale of shares and applies where the value of shares has fallen after the stripping of a dividend.

Paragraph C is aimed at the party to a dividend stripping transaction who receives a capital sum whilst the other party receives an abnormal dividend and catches the original owner of the shares.

Paragraph D is limited to closely controlled companies whose shares are not dealt in on a UK stock exchange. It applies where, in connection with the distribution of the profits of a company, a person receives a consideration which represents the assets of the company available for distribution, or the value of its stock in trade, or is received in respect of future receipts of the company. Unlike Paragraph C, it does not require an abnormal dividend to be paid, nor a resultant fall in value of the securities. The general purpose is to catch cases where the shareholders of a company obtain property which might have been used to pay dividends. It was considered by the House of Lords in *IRC v Parker* (1966), *Cleary v IRC* (1968), *Williams v IRC* (1980), and *IRC v Garvin* (1981).

Finally, Paragraph E overlaps to a large extent with the other paragraphs. It will be relevant when one Paragraph D company acquires another by means of a share exchange and in connection with that transfer a person receives non-taxable consideration in the form of share capital or other security. That consideration must either be, or represent, the value of assets available for distribution by a Paragraph D company.

Where there is a risk that a transaction falls within the scope of s 703, a clearance under TA 1988 s 707 may be obtained. The Revenue have 30 days from the date of the application, or receipt by them of any further information requested, to decide whether to serve a notice on the taxpayer stating that they believe the transaction(s) fall within s 703. If clearance is refused, although the Revenue are under no duty to give their reasons, they will do so in appropriate cases and occasionally grant the taxpayer an interview to clarify the position.

If a notice is served on the taxpayer to the effect that the Revenue believe that his transaction is caught by s 703 he is given by statutory declaration a right of reply within 30 days and if the Revenue decide to continue with the matter a Tribunal is set up under TA 1988 s 706 to determine whether there is a *prima facie* case for proceeding further (the taxpayer is not entitled to appear before this tribunal). If a case is found to exist, the Revenue will then serve a notice under s 703(3) indicating how they intend to counter the alleged tax advantage. The taxpayer has a right of appeal against their decision to the Special Commissioners. **[3.65]**

32 Choice of business medium

I INTRODUCTORY—THE AVAILABLE OPTIONS

When commencing a business the participators will normally have an unrestricted choice between operating through the medium of a company or partnership. The only major legal limitation is that partnerships cannot, save in the case of certain professions, such as accountants and solicitors, be formed with more than 20 partners (Companies Act 1985 s 716). Professions which because of professional regulations cannot operate through the medium of a limited company, may, however, set up a company to service the running of their premises and notably to provide staff, furniture and equipment.

The typical company will be the limited private company and the typical partnership will consist of a number of partners with unlimited personal liability.   [**32.1**]

There are, however, other possibilities such as:

The public company   Its attraction is the ability to raise funds from the public (contrast the restriction on private companies: Companies Act 1985 s 81). In practice, of course, it is unlikely that a new business would commence as a public company since the costs involved are considerable and only in very limited cases would a Stock Exchange listing or permission to deal in the company's shares on the Unlisted Securities Market be granted for a completely new enterprise.   [**32.2**]

The unlimited company   This suffers from the disadvantage that the liability of the shareholders is unlimited—hence, they are in the same position *vis-a-vis* creditors as partners (albeit with the convenience of corporate personality). However, the unlimited company need not file the statutory company accounts thus enabling it to preserve a greater degree of secrecy; and it can return share capital to members more easily than can a limited company. Nevertheless, the defect of unlimited liability will in most cases outweigh any advantages.   [**32.3**]

The limited partnership   In practice, these have been few in number. Their creation is regulated by formalities akin to those which have to be satisfied if a company is to be formed and although there can be partners whose liability for the debts of the firm is limited, there must also be at least one general (or unlimited) partner. Furthermore, if a limited partner takes any part in the management of the firm, he loses the protection of his limited liability and becomes a general partner. Thus, a limited partner who has put, say, £10,000 into the firm might be obliged to allow it to be lost by inept management since any attempt to interfere would put at risk the whole of his personal fortune.   **[32.4]**

Partnerships with companies This hybrid business medium involves an individual joining in partnership with a limited company. If the individual is also a director of the company concerned, making him a limited partner offers attractions since he can participate in the management of the business qua director of the company. The particular advantages afforded by the arrangement lie in the regulation of profit-sharing ratios to take account of different income and corporation tax rates and to maximise the use of business losses.   **[32.5]**

Any comparison between the major practical alternatives of a partnership or a limited company involves a consideration of both non-tax and tax factors.   **[32.6]–[32.20]**

II NON-TAX FACTORS

1 Limited liability

A limited company is a separate legal entity and is solely liable for its debts and obligations. The shareholders' liability is restricted to the sum that they agreed to put into the business and this liability cannot be increased without their consent (Companies Act 1985 s 16). The limited company offers the ideal vehicle for the individual who wishes to set up in business, but who is not prepared to risk his entire personal fortune in the venture.

EXAMPLE 32.1

Brian is the sole beneficial shareholder in Wretched Ltd. The company is in liquidation with total debts of £50,000 and assets of only £20,000. Brian has a personal wealth of £100,000, but the creditors of Wretched Ltd cannot look to Brian for payment of the shortfall other than in exceptional circumstances.

There are exceptions to the principle of limited liability and in certain circumstances the 'veil of incorporation' has been lifted by statute and by the judiciary. Although these instances are rare, the director of a private company should be aware that there are circumstances in which he might be liable for the debts of the company. Most notably, a director of a company which has entered insolvent liquidation who is found guilty of wrongful trading under the Insolvency Act 1986 s 214 can be ordered by a court to contribute to the assets of that company. (For an example of directors' liability under s 214 see *Re Produce Marketing Consortium Limited (No 2)* (1989).)

On a practical level, in order to obtain finance for his company a shareholder/director will often be required to give security for the liabilities of the company by way of a personal guarantee. To the extent that personal guarantees are given, limited liability will be illusory. However, who will demand such guarantees? Major lenders, lease finance companies and landlords, but rarely trade creditors and certainly not customers. Furthermore, it may be possible for a small company to take advantage of the Small Firms Loan Guarantee Scheme whereby the Government will provide guarantees for up to 70% of a loan (in some circumstances 85%) of up to £100,000 made by a clearing bank or another Government selected institution.   **[32.21]**

2   Corporate personality

A company will never die: it can only be liquidated. The death of a shareholder need not affect the business; the only result will be a transmission of some of the shares of the company. Sole traders and partners enjoy no such advantages, because the assets of the business will be vested in them so that death will disrupt the smooth running of the organisation. Further, from the point of view of simple estate planning, the company provides assets (shares) which are both easy to transfer and easy to divide into separate parcels. A large shareholding can be fragmented between different members of the shareholder's family whereas the ownership of an unincorporated business is not easily divisible.

The existence of a separate legal entity (the company) means that the shareholder/proprietor can enter into legally binding contracts with it (see *Lee v Lee's Air Farming Ltd* (1961)). Normally the shareholder in the small private company will be concerned in the management of the business as a director and will ensure that he enters into a lucrative long-term service contract with the company. Amongst a number of advantages that such contracts offer will be the protection of both statute and common law in the event of the employment being prematurely terminated and preferential treatment for arrears of wages in the event of the company's insolvency.

It is also possible to obtain a valuation advantage by incorporating a business. A 10% partner, for instance, is treated as owning 10% of the firm's assets but a 10% minority shareholder will obtain a substantial discount on the value of his shareholding (because of the very limited rights possessed by such shareholders). Hence incorporating a business may be a useful first step as a prelude to a gift of the property.   **[32.22]**

3   Obtaining finance

Companies have advantages when it comes to raising finance. Apart from issuing risk capital in the form of shares, money can also be raised by loans secured by fixed and floating charges. The fixed charge is common to both incorporated and unincorporated businesses (eg the land mortgage), but a floating charge is a unique advantage of companies. It operates as a charge over (usually) the entire undertaking and has the advantage of leaving the company free to deal with the assets of the business as it sees fit save to the extent that the terms of the charge provide otherwise. The floating charge will only crystallise on liquidation or when a default, as specified in the deed of charge, occurs.

How advantageous is the floating charge? This question can only be answered by considering whether creditors will be satisfied with the protection afforded by it and in many cases they will not be. Quite apart from the inherent defects of a non-crystallised charge, the steady addition by statute over the years to the list of preferential creditors on an insolvency has greatly weakened the attractions of such charges. Accordingly, the characteristic feature of company charging in recent years has been the practice of creditors to demand fixed security (see, eg *Siebe Gorman & Co Ltd v Barclays Bank Ltd* (1979) and the growth of *Romalpa* clauses).   **[32.23]**

4   Formality, rigidity and costs

By comparison with the unincorporated business, a company suffers from formality and rigidity and has greater operating costs. A partnership or sole trade can be established with an almost total lack of documentation and formality. A company can be bought 'off the peg' for as little as £140 but the costs of a tailor-made company are usually higher. The obligation to file forms is then a regular feature of a company's life, especially the obligation to file an annual return (with a fee of £32) and to submit annual audited accounts to the Registrar of Companies. Such requirements, however, are probably a small price for the benefits of limited liability and, in practice, the costs of a well-drafted partnership deed may be equal to the expenses involved in company formation.

As an artificial entity, companies must be formed for specific purposes set out in the objects clause of its memorandum of association. Actions in excess of these prescribed objects are ultra vires and, at common law, were void. This difficulty should not be exaggerated since, *first*, objects clauses will generally be drafted in such wide terms that they will embrace all conceivable activities and, *secondly*, as a result of the Companies Act 1989, a company's memorandum may state that the object of the company is to carry on business as a general commercial company (ie any trade or business whatsoever). **[32.24]**–**[32.40]**

III THE TAXATION FACTORS

The formation of a company presents the danger that the company will be taxed as an entity distinct from its members so that double taxation will result. In certain areas specific provisions take away this problem, but elsewhere it remains a major argument against incorporation. Any comparison cannot be just between the taxation of individuals and the taxation of companies, since there is also the need to consider the individual as a director/employee of that company. The topic must, therefore, include some discussion of the pros and cons of being employed as opposed to self-employed. **[32.41]**

1 **Taxation of income profits**

a) *Rates of tax*

Income tax on the profits of a partnership or sole trade will never exceed 40% and that level will only be reached when the individual's taxable income exceeds £23,700. Corporation tax will be charged on the profits of the company at either 33% or 25% depending upon whether the company is a small company (see Chapter 28). Unlike income tax, corporation tax is levied at a flat rate so that in the case of a company taxed at 33% all its profits will be charged at this rate. For an individual whose taxable income exceeds £23,700, the marginal rate will be 40%, but this will, of course, only apply to the slice of income above £23,700. For small companies whose profits exceed £250,000 but fall below £1,250,000 there is a system of tapering relief and tax on profits which fall within that zone is charged at the marginal rate of 35%. It will be advantageous to ensure that the company avoids making profits taxed at this marginal rate: keeping a company's profits below £250,000 can be achieved by a number of methods: eg paying out additional tax deductible sums to its directors in the form of salaries or bonuses; by making extra contributions to a pension scheme; or by setting up a share incentive scheme for its directors/employees.

EXAMPLE 32.2

AJ Ltd has taxable profits for the year ended 31 March 1992 of £260,000 after paying its two directors salaries of £21,000 each. To avoid paying corporation tax at 35% on profits above £250,000, AJ Ltd pays each of the two directors a further cash bonus of £5,000.

This has the following results (assuming that the directors have no other income and are entitled to the personal allowance).

			£
(1)	*Taxation of AJ Ltd*		
	Taxable profit to date		260,000
	Less bonuses to directors (£10,000)		
	NIC (@ 10.40% = £1,040)		11,040
	Revised profit for year		£248,960
	Corporation tax at 25%		£62,240
(2)	*Taxation of the directors*		
	Total income (£21,000 + £5,000)	26,000	
	Less personal relief	3,295	
	Taxable income	£22,705	
	Income tax payable by each:		
	£22,705 at 25%	£5,676	
	Total income tax paid		£11,352
(3)	Total tax paid (£62,240 + £11,352)		£73,592

Notes:
(a) Dividends cannot be used to reduce profits below £250,000.
(b) Had the bonus payments not been paid, the total tax bill would have been:

			£
(1)	*Taxation of AJ Ltd*		
	Taxable profits		260,000
	Corporation tax payable:		
	£250,000 at 25%		62,500
	£10,000 at 35%		3,500
			£66,000
(2)	*Taxation of directors*		
	Total income	21,000	
	Less personal relief	3,295	
	Taxable income	£17,705	
	Income tax payable by each:		
	£17,705 at 25%	4,426	
	Total income tax paid		£8,852
(3)	Total tax paid		£74,852

Hence, the extra tax paid is £74,852 — £73,592 = £1,260.

(c) The bonus payments will result in a NIC liability for the company of £1,040 (ie £10,000 at 10.4%) and the overall saving is therefore reduced to £260. (On ways to avoid NIC on bonus payments see [**32.56**].)

Example 32.3 shows the advantages of a small company when it is desired to retain profits for use in the business.

EXAMPLE 32.3

Business profits are estimated to be £40,000 in the year ended 31 January 1992 and the proprietor will take £15,000, but leave the remainder in the business to finance expansion.

(1) If an unincorporated business:

	£	
Total income	40,000	
Tax relief for NIC	450	
Taxable income (ignoring reliefs)		£39,550

Income tax on £39,550:

£23,700 @ 25%	5,925	
£15,850 @ 40%	6,340	
	£12,265	

NIC		
Class 2	268	
Class 4	901	
	£1,169	

		£
Total amount received after tax and NIC:		40,000
Less	12,265	
	1,169	13,434
		£26,566

(2) If a company with £15,000 paid out as emoluments and the balance retained:

Proprietor:	£	£
Taxable income (ignoring reliefs)		15,000
Tax on £15,000 @ 25%	3,750	
NIC on £15,000	1,160	4,910
Total amount received after tax and NIC		£10,090

Company:		£
Total profits:		40,000
Less remuneration	15,000	
NIC on remuneration	1,560	16,560
Taxable profits		23,440
Corporation tax on £23,440 at 25%		5,860
Retained profit		£17,580

The amount of profits that can be retained in a small company is 75%, ie after paying corporation tax at the rate of 25%. The tax saving in this example of £1,104 ((£10,090 + £17,580) − £26,566) is extra profits retained for the business.

If the company was not a small company, so that it was paying tax on income and capital profits at 33%, there would be no tax advantage in profit retention unless the proprietors were liable to income tax at a rate of 40%.

If the business is generating profits in excess of the needs of the proprietor(s), the ability to use the lower corporation tax rates to retain profits (as in *Example 32.3*) represents one of the attractions of incorporation. Further, it should be noted that with the disappearance of first year capital allowances (see [**7.2**]), the costs of acquiring plant, machinery and industrial buildings have to be borne out of taxed rather than pre-tax profits. Hence, the retention of profits is a factor of importance in most businesses. [**32.42**]

b) *The effect of paying all the profits out as remuneration*

Employees' remuneration is deductible as a business expense of the company (TA 1988 s 74), and will be subject to income tax under Schedule E. The amount paid to a full-time working director is unlikely to be challenged as excessive (contrast *Copeman v William J Flood & Sons Ltd* (1941)) so that, if all the profits are paid out as remuneration, the company will pay no corporation tax. The only tax charged on the profits will, therefore, be income tax so that the only difference between a shareholder/director who extracts all the profits as salary and the self-employed sole trader lies in the contrasts between Schedule E and Schedule D taxation. The main points of comparison are:

(1) Dates for paying the tax: this is discussed in more detail in c) below.
(2) Pension entitlements: the pensions available for employees and for the self-employed are discussed in Appendix VIII. It should be remembered that, although the pension choices are now similar in both cases, one advantage for employees is that tax deductible contributions to their pension schemes can also be made by their employer (ie by the company), thus boosting their eventual entitlement under the scheme.
(3) So far as the provision of perks and other benefits in kind is concerned, a combination of the rules taxing fringe benefits of directors (see p 63) and the deductible expense rules of ScheduleE puts the self-employed in a more favourable position.
(4) Social security aspects: the salary paid to employees, including directors, attracts Class 1 National Insurance contributions payable by both employer (the company) and the employee in accordance with the following Table. Rates payable by the self-employed (Class 2 and Class 4 contributions) are also set out.

National Insurance contributions (from 6 April 1991)

Contributions for employees (Class 1) – not contracted out

Earnings (per week)	less than £52.00	less than £85.00	less than £130.00	less than £185.00	less than £390.00	more than £390.00
Employee contribution	Nil	2% on first £52 plus 9% on remainder				£31.46 pw
Employer contribution	Nil	4.6%	6.6%	8.6%	10.4%	10.4%

Contributions for employees (Class 1) – contracted out

Earnings (per week)	less than £52.00	less than £85.00	less than £130.00	less than £185.00	up to £390.00	more than £390.00
Employee contribution	Nil	2% on first £52 plus 7% on remainder				£24.70
Employer contribution	Nil	4.6% on £52 1.2% on remainder	6.6% on £52 3.2% on remainder	8.6% on £52 5.2% on remainder	10.4% on £52 6.65% on remainder	£27.88 pw + 10.4% on excess over £390

2 *Contributions for the self-employed*

Class 2 (weekly rate)	£5.15
Class 4	6.30%
lower profits limit	£5,900
upper profits limit	£20,200

(maximum payable £900.90)

Half of the Class 4 contribution is deductible in calculating the individual's total income for the year of assessment.   **[32.43]**

EXAMPLE 32.4

(1) Alison is the beneficial owner of the entire share capital and sole director of Trendy Ltd. Assume that in the year ended 31 March 1992 the company makes profits of £44,160 and she pays herself a salary of £40,000 to avoid a charge to corporation tax (ie the salary plus the company's NIC, equals £44,160). The total tax and non-contracted out national insurance is as follows:

		£	£
(a)	National insurance		
	Payable by company	4,160.00	
	Payable by Alison	1,635.92	5,795.92
(b)	Corporation tax		Nil
(c)	Income tax under Schedule E		
	(ignoring allowances)		12,445.00
(d)	Total tax and NIC		£18,240.92
(e)	Total as % of profits		41.31%

(2) Kathy is a sole trader with profits for 1991–92 of £44,160. Her tax bill is as follows:

		£	£
(a)	National insurance		
	Class 2	267.80	
	Class 4	900.90	
			1,168.70
(b)	Income tax under Schedule D Case I		
	Income	£44,160.00	
	Less half Class 4 NIC	450.45	
		£43,709.55	
	Tax on £43,709.55		13,928.82
(c)	Total tax and NIC		£15,097.52
(d)	Total as % of profits		34.19%

c) *Dates for paying tax*

The sole trader can obtain a delay of up to 21 months in paying the first instalment of income tax with a further six months' delay before the final instalment is due. Even with an accounting period which ends on 5 April (the most disadvantageous day for income tax purposes) there will be a delay of nine months before the first instalment (see Chapter 6).

For companies, there is a maximum delay of nine months from the ending of the accounting period to the payment of corporation tax. This is equivalent to the shortest possible delay before the first instalment of income tax is payable by a sole trader and a company does not have the advantage of paying in two instalments. Where company profits are all paid out in directors' fees the tax charge will be under the PAYE system. If a company pays a dividend it will have to pay ACT, an advance payment of its MCT. It should, therefore, delay paying the dividend until as late as possible in its accounting period (see further [**28.100**]).   [**32.44**]

d) *Trading losses*

The advantages afforded by relief for trading losses generally lie with the unincorporated business. Company losses are 'locked in' so that they cannot be used by the owners to set against their income and instead, relief will only be given when the company makes profits (see [**28.51**]). Until FA 1991, the ability to set a trading loss against capital gains in the year in which the loss was incurred was the one real advantage that the company had over the unincorporated trader. However, in respect of losses sustained in the tax year 1991-92 and subsequent years, an unincorporated trader can set trading losses against capital gains in the same way as a company (see [**7.93**]). The unincorporated trader is also able to set his trading losses against his other income under the provisions of TA 1988 s 380 and, so far as early losses are concerned, against previous income as a result of TA 1988 s 381 (see Chapter 7). It is often argued that when a new business is likely to show early losses, the ideal is to start that business as an unincorporated trade and then, when profitable, to incorporate. However, if early losses exceed the wildest expectations of the trader the advantage of income tax loss relief will not compensate for the disaster of bankruptcy. Had the loss been realised by a company, of course, limited liability would have protected the proprietors from bankruptcy.   [**32.45**]

EXAMPLE 32.5

Having worked in the Civil Service for many years, Samantha has resigned to open a boutique. She anticipates trading losses in the early years. She has a substantial private income.
(1)   If she forms a company to run the business, trading losses can be relieved only against future corporate profits (including capital gains).
(2)   If she operates as a sole trader the losses can be set against her private income (and capital gains) for the year of the loss (TA 1988 s 380) or against her income, including that from the Civil Service, in previous years (TA 1988 s 381) or against both (*Butt v Haxby* (1983)).

e) *Interest relief*

Income tax relief is generally available on the interest paid on loans to acquire a share in either a partnership or a close company. To qualify, the taxpayer no longer has to work for the greater part of his time in the business (see generally Chapter 4). Relief is also available on loans raised for the benefit of the close company or partnership. Interest paid on loans to finance the business will usually be a deductible business expense, and in addition companies may deduct certain interest payments as a charge on income (TA 1988 s 338).   [**32.46**]

f) *Corporate investment reliefs*

Various reliefs have been introduced in an attempt to stimulate investment in trading companies. [**32.47**]

Venture capital (TA 1988 s 574) Section 574 is designed to encourage the purchase of shares in unquoted trading companies, and allows a loss on disposal of the shares (including failure of the venture) to be relieved against income (see further [**7.153**]). It is not available for moneys lost in an unincorporated enterprise, but the partner who lends money to the partnership may be able to claim a capital loss under CGTA 1979 s 22 if the partnership defaults and the debt is a debt on a security, or under CGTA 1979 s 136 where the debt is not on a security. [**32.48**]

Business expansion scheme (TA 1988 s 289) Subject to detailed provisions being satisfied, the scheme permits the sum invested in a company to be deducted from the investor's income at the highest rates (see further Chapter 4). [**32.49**]

g) *Taking surplus profits out of a company*

One of the drawbacks of a company may occur when the proprietor desires to extract surplus profits for his own benefit. Legal theory—the company is a separate legal entity—means that the extraction will be charged to tax and, as the profits extracted may have already been subject to charge in the company's hands, there is a risk of double taxation. The major methods of 'bleeding off[1]a' profits are: [**32.50**]

Paying dividends In the case of small companies there is no element of double taxation since ACT paid on the dividend discharges the MCT bill of the company and surplus ACT may be carried back for up to six years. For other companies, an element of double charge occurs since the ACT will not discharge the full MCT bill and the shareholder obtains no credit for this extra corporation tax (see Chapter 28 and see *Example 28.31(1)*).

It should be remembered that a shareholder may waive his entitlement to a dividend before it is declared and it will not then be treated as paid to him since it never becomes due and payable. Accordingly, ACT is not charged on that sum and neither does it enter the income of the shareholder for income tax purposes. Further by IHTA 1984 s 15, it will not be a transfer of value if it is made within one year before the dividend is declared. Hence, two advantageous uses of the waiver for purposes may be noted: first it may enable the company to declare a larger dividend on the other shares; secondly, it can be employed to enable profits to be extracted by shareholders who are not directors by the latter waiving their dividend and taking their share of the profits as remuneration. [**32.51**]

EXAMPLE 32.6

Magna is a higher rate taxpayer with a 75% shareholding in Magna Ltd. His daughter, Minima is the managing director with a 15% shareholding and his son Minimus owns 10% of the shares and is an unemployed sociologist with unused allowances and reliefs. Profits could be extracted from Magna Ltd as follows:

(a)   Magna could waive his entitlement to dividends; as a higher rate taxpayer he does not wish to increase his taxable income for the year.

(b)   Minima could likewise waive her entitlement to dividends and arrange to receive extra remuneration instead, preferably in the form of extra benefits in kind since these will not result in increased NIC for the company.

(c)   Minimus could receive a dividend; since he is not employed by the company it is not possible for his share of the profits to be paid as salary.

Interest payments   Normally interest will be a deductible charge on income for the company but excessive interest payments, and any attempt to link the interest to the profits of the company results in an application of the rules that apply for dividends (see [**28.88**]). Interest payments have to be in respect of *bona fide* loans.   [**32.52**]

Lending the profits   Apart from restrictions on the making of loans to directors in the Companies Act 1985, the company concerned will usually be close with the result that the provisions of TA 1988 s 419 will apply (see [**28.128**]), so that it is 'forced' to pay a sum of money to the Revenue which will only be refunded when the loan is repaid.   [**32.53**]

Extracting the profits by selling the shares   Profits made by the company will usually be reflected in the value of the shares. Hence, a sale of the shares should ensure that the profit is obtained by the shareholder. This method of extracting profits suffers from two defects. *First*, there will be double taxation since not only will the company's profit be subject to corporation tax, but also the share sale will be a taxable occasion.

Secondly, the sale of the shares may fall foul of TA 1988 s 703 (see Chapter 31) so that the gain made will be taxed as unearned income.   [**32.54**]

EXAMPLE 32.7

(1)   Hoco Ltd makes income profits of £100. Corporation tax at 25% is £25 so that £75 is retained by Hoco Ltd. If all the shares are owned by Mr Hoco they would be worth £75 more. Therefore, were he to sell his shares, he would make a gain of £75 subject to (say) 40% CGT = £30. The total tax attributable to the company's £100 profit is therefore £55 (£25 paid by Hoco Ltd and £30 paid by Hoco.) Were TA 1988 s 703 successfully invoked Hoco would be subject to income tax at a maximum rate of 40%.

As can be seen from this example the fusion of the rates of income tax and CGT may remove any advantage to the Revenue from involving s 703. Advantages in taking a profit as capital gain (rather than as income) do however remain: see [**38.13**]).

(2)   Doug is the sole shareholder of Doug Enterprises Ltd, a company which is a 'cash shell' having disposed of its business assets some months ago. It has paid a substantial amount of corporation tax on the gain thereby realised. Doug is willing to transfer some of the shares to his children and would like them to receive at least part of the cash in the company. Doug should consider the following arrangement:

Stage 1: Doug settles shares on discretionary trusts for the benefit, inter alia, of his children. CGT hold-over relief is available and IHT may be avoided if the value transferred falls within Doug's nil rate band.

Stage 2: The company then buys back its shares from the trustees. This will be a distribution by the company and the ACT payable may be offset against the corporation tax paid on the profits. So far as the trustees are concerned no further income tax charge at the additional rate will arise since the sum will be received by them as capital.

Stage 3: The trustees subsequently distribute capital to the children: no

CGT is payable and IHT will be avoided if the transfer falls within the nil band.

Extraction in the form of remuneration   As already discussed, this method avoids any double charge to tax since the sum paid will be deductible for corporation tax and, therefore, subject only to income tax. In the typical small private company, where all the shareholders are also full time working directors, profits are bled off in this fashion. (See *Ebrahimi v Westbourne Galleries Ltd* (1973) for a practical illustration of such a private company and for a salutary lesson in what can happen if things go wrong!) Increases in the amount of National Insurance contributions by the company (discussed above) should, however, be borne in mind when fixing levels of remuneration.   **[32.55]**

Dividends or remuneration?   The main choice facing proprietors of the private company is, therefore, between dividends and salary. Until recently the payment of salary had obvious attractions: it was fully deductible by the company and was taxed as the earned income of the recipient. The removal of the investment income surcharge and of the element of double taxation in the case of dividends paid by small private companies combined with the high level of National Insurance contributions has improved the position of the dividend, however, and removed some of the advantages of paying emoluments.

EXAMPLE 32.8

Take the facts of *Example 32.4(1)* above where it was shown that Alison, the sole director/shareholder of Trendy Ltd, would suffer combined tax and National Insurance of £18,240.92 on a salary of £40,000. If Trendy Ltd paid her a dividend of £33,120 instead of a salary the tax position would be as follows:

	£
Dividend	33,120
ACT	11,040
Total dividend	£44,160
Income tax on £44,160	14,109
Less ACT tax credit	11,040
Total tax payable by Alison	£3,069
Total tax on profits of £44,160: ACT	11,040
Income tax	3,069
	£14,109
Total tax as a % of profits	31.95%

Note: As the ACT paid by the company at 25% discharges both Alison's basic rate income tax on the dividend and the ACT due from the company on the £44,160 gross dividend, the £44,160 distributed profit is, in effect, free from corporation tax in the company's hands.

In considering profit extraction bear in mind the following factors:
(1) National Insurance contributions are calculated on salary (including any bonuses and commission) but excluding benefits in kind (other than the provision of a company car on which employers are liable for national insurance contributions calculated using the scale rates applicable for income tax purposes). Accordingly, instead of paying extra salary to

highly paid employees, the employer should consider providing increased benefits (including improved pension arrangements and share incentive schemes). There has recently been an increase in the popularity of the 'gilt bonus', whereby a company awards its employees a bonus not in the form of cash, but in the form of gilt-edged stock or units in a gilt-edged stock-based unit trust scheme. There are a number of unit trusts specifically marketed for this purpose offering a particularly narrow 'spread' (ie the difference between the purchase price and the sale price on any given day is very small). In common with most other benefits in kind, a gilt bonus escapes both employers' and employees' National Insurance contributions, even though the units can be immediately realised for cash by the employee.

(2) Depressing salaries to artificially low levels should be avoided. Pension contributions and entitlement will be affected whilst regular payments of dividends will increase the value of shares in the company which will, in turn, increase the dangers of a high CGT or IHT charge.

(3) Dividends can only be paid in years when the company has accumulated realised profits.   [32.56]

2 Capital taxes

Recent changes in the capital taxation of companies have placed the small company in an improved position vis-a¹T-vis the unincorporated business.

Sole traders and partners are subject to CGT at a rate of either 25% or 40% with an annual exemption (for 1991–92) of £5,500. For partnerships, the rules for calculating the CGT liability of the individual partners are applied in accord-ance with SP D/12 (see Chapter 29). So far as companies are concerned, capital gains are taxed at the normal corporation tax rate: ie at either 25% or 33%. Such gains are, of course, included in determining whether the small company rate is applicable. In terms of tax rates, therefore, companies may be at an advantage since the individual will usually find that a 40% rate of tax will apply to his gain whereas the company will, at worst, be subject only to a 33% rate.

In many cases both individuals and companies will be able to defer a charge by claiming roll-over reinvestment relief under CGTA 1979 s 115 (see [16.92]). In other cases, the company should consider disposing of the asset in a year when its trading profits are low so that it may come within the small company's 25% rate of charge (the same advice holds good for individuals but often the basic rate band will have been exceeded by taxable income). Capital profits can be taken out of the company by means of a dividend, the ACT on which can be set against the company's MCT on all its profits. In this way, a shareholder who wishes to realise the capital profit on his shares can avoid the double charge to tax that would otherwise result when he sells those shares (see *Example 32.9*).

EXAMPLE 32.9

In its accounting period ending 31 December 1992, Kafka Ltd, a small company, makes capital profits of £100. K, a basic rate taxpayer, is the sole shareholder/director and wishes to obtain the benefit of this profit.

(1) Sale of shares
Kafka Ltd incurs a corporation tax charge of £25 on the £100 of capital profit. Accordingly the net profit of £75 is retained in the company. If K were to sell his shares for a price reflecting this retained profit he would be subject

to CGT of £18.75 on the retained profit (ie 25% × £75). Hence, the total tax attributable to the company's £100 capital profit will be £43.75 (£25 corporation tax + £18.75 CGT).

(2) *Payment of dividend*
If, instead of selling his shares, K arranges for Kafka Ltd to distribute the profit by way of dividend the tax position is as follows:

	£
Dividend	75
ACT thereon	25
	£100
K's income (Schedule F)	100
Income tax at 25%	25
Less ACT credit	25
Total tax paid	£25

Kafka Ltd is not liable to pay MCT because of the ACT set-off. Hence, K saves tax of £18.75 (ie £43.75 in (1) −£25 in (2)).

Over the years the practice has grown up of keeping appreciating capital assets out of a company. In part, this is to avoid any risk of a double charge to capital gains tax: but undoubtedly the most compelling reason is very often the desire of the owner of the asset to retain all of any future profits made from the sale of that asset! In such a case, therefore, the relevant shareholder will allow the asset to be used by the company, but will retain its ownership.

On its disposal therefore, any gain will be subject to CGT only in the hands of the shareholder. The difficulty is that although a double charge may be avoided, other problems can be created, for instance:

(1) *Retirement relief* can apply to assets used by both partnerships and companies so long as the owner is either a partner or a full-time working director in a family trading company (see [**16.93**]).

(2) *IHT business property relief* Relief may be available if the asset is given away, but only at 30% and, in the case of an asset used by a company, only if the owner is a controlling shareholder (which limits the relief to those cases where the individual has more than 50% of the company's voting shares). For a partner the relief is available whatever the size of his share in the partnership (see [**23.43**]).

(3) *Payment for use of the asset* Apart from such payments being subject to income tax, they will either prevent retirement relief from applying or restrict the amount of gain which can be wiped out by the relief. Hence, it will be better for the taxpayer to take, instead, an increased share of the profits or, in the case of a company, a greater salary.

(4) *Section 123 relief* Hold-over relief for CGT will not be available if assets (except cash) are retained outside the company.

(5) *Paying IHT by instalments* This is generally not available in the case of assets held outside a company except for land (when interest will be charged on the unpaid IHT).

(6) *Value Added Tax* If a new commercial building is acquired, the purchaser will almost certainly have to pay VAT on the purchase price. If this VAT is to be recovered, the purchaser will need to register for VAT and to charge VAT on the rent which he receives. This adds to the

administrative burden on the owner and necessitates that he charge rent giving rise to the difficulties referred to in (3), above.

For IHT purposes, two comparisons between the company and the unincorporated business should be noted. First, the facility to pay the tax by instalments, which is generally available on a transfer of a business or part of a business, is only available on a transfer of shares if that transfer satisfies detailed requirements (see [**23.50**]). Secondly, the changes introduced in 1987 extended business property relief at the 50% level to a shareholder in an unquoted company who controlled more than 25% of that company's shares (see Chapter 23). This represented an attempt to equate the position of the shareholder with that of the partner in a partnership who qualified for the 50% relief whatever the size of his share. However, land and buildings, plant and machinery used by the partnership and owned by a partner attracts 30% relief, whereas, if used by a company in which the transferor controls 50% or less of the shares it attracts no business property relief.   [**32.57**]

3   Stamp duty

Sales of a business, a part of a business and of shares will at present lead to a stamp duty charge on the instrument of transfer. The nil rate band is not available on a share transfer and duty is accordingly always charged at an ad valorem rate of only $^1/2$% per £100 or part thereof. For businesses and shares in a partnership the nil rate may be available and assets that can be transferred by delivery need not be subject to duty (see Chapter 33). The former charge to capital duty on share capital raised by companies was abolished for transactions occurring on or after 16 March 1988 and the changes in duty which will take effect on the introduction of TAURUS are discussed at [**30.3**].   [**32.58**]–[**32.70**]

IV   GENERAL CONCLUSIONS

It was often pointed out that, although the non-taxation factors tend to favour incorporation (notably the bene
fit of limited liability), tax considerations probably favoured the unincorporated trader. Changes, however, to corporate tax rates and to the taxation of corporate gains, have arguably altered this conclusion and strengthened the arguments in favour of incorporation as a small company. Note in particular:

(1) The small companies rate of 25%, which is equivalent to the basic rate of income tax and which encourages the retention of profits (up to £250,000 pa) in the company (see *Example 32.3*).

(2) The top rate of corporation tax (33%) is less than the higher rate of income tax (40%) and applies to both income and capital profits.

(3) The removal of discrimination against dividends which are (in effect) fully tax deductible by small companies and largely deductible in the case of other companies. Further, the extended set-off for surplus ACT means that MCT on past profits (both income and capital) can be recovered.

(4) Interest on loan capital is deductible as a charge on companies' profits.

(5) As a result of FA 1985 retirement relief is more widely available on a disposal of shares held in a family company (including a holding company of a family trading group).

(6) The danger of an investor being 'locked-into' the private company has been reduced by the 'buy back' provisions (see [**28.89**]).

(7) Taxpayers are given incentives to invest in corporate trades; notably through the business expansion scheme which for higher rate taxpayers offers an ideal 'tax shelter' (see [**4.83**]).

Two final points may be mentioned. *First*, questions of commercial 'prestige' favour incorporation: perhaps the label 'company director' is more impressive than 'sole trader'! *Secondly*, and by way of a cautionary note, considerable tax reliefs are given to encourage firms to incorporate and new corporate businesses to commence, but the same is not true on disincorporation. It may well be the case that a company is easier to get into than to escape from and this is a factor to be remembered when the decision to incorporate is taken (see the Consultative Document on Disincorporation published on 2 July 1987). [**32.71**]

33 Takeovers and mergers

Some aspects of business takeovers will be considered in this chapter, although in view of the complexities and technicality of the subject all that is attempted is a general introduction to the problems involved.   **[33.1]**

I TRANSFER OF AN UNINCORPORATED BUSINESS TO A COMPANY

This section is concerned with the problems when an existing unincorporated business is transferred to a limited company. There are obviously a variety of ways in which this might happen, for instance:

(1) The transfer could be to a company formed or purchased 'off the shelf' by the proprietor of the business to take over the running of that business. Normally the transfer will be in consideration of the issue of shares in that new company (see *Salomon v Salomon & Co* (1897)).

(2) The business might be taken over by an existing company in return for shares in the company, cash, or a combination of both. Where cash is received the recipient might then use the moneys to start a new business or he might retire on the proceeds of the sale.   **[33.2]**

1 Income tax

Unincorporated trades are subject to income tax under Schedule D Case I and the result of a company takeover is that the closing year rules will apply so that the proprietor will be assessable (at the election of the inspector of taxes) to income tax on his actual profits of the final three tax years. The sum payable will be due 30 days after the date of the assessment so that the taxpayer should ensure that he has sufficient cash (from the sale of the business or elsewhere) to meet this bill. Where assets only are sold and the former proprietor continues trading, these results do not follow: he will continue to be taxed according to the preceding year rules.

Termination of a business results in terminal loss relief (TA 1988 s 388(1)). As an alternative, where the business is sold to a company wholly or mainly for shares, the taxpayer can elect for any year throughout which he retains beneficial ownership of the shares to set off unrelieved trading losses against income that he receives from the company. The set-off must first be used against salary if the proprietor is employed by the company but any balance can be used to reclaim tax on dividends paid by the company (TA 1988 s 386: see Chapter 7). The loss cannot, of course, be transferred to the company.

A discontinuance may result in a claw-back of capital allowances by a balancing charge. Where the transfer is to a company controlled by the transferor, however, an election can be made by both parties, in the case of machinery and plant, that the trade shall not be treated as discontinued so that the company will take over the tax position of that person. That election must be made within two years of the date of succession.   [**33.3**]

2   Capital gains tax

a) *The available reliefs*

Any takeover involves the transfer of chargeable assets to the company with a consequent risk of CGT. A number of reliefs may be available: [**33.4**]

Where the transfer is in return for shares   Hold-over relief under CGTA 1979 s 123 is available and operates to roll any gain on the business assets into the replacement shares. Capital gains tax will, therefore, be postponed until the shares are sold. For the relief to apply, all the business assets (except cash) must be transferred to the company. It follows that retention of appreciating business assets prevents s 123 from applying and any attempt to remove those assets from the business prior to its incorporation (eg by transferring them to a spouse) may result in the Revenue applying the *Ramsay* principle to deny s 123 relief. If the consideration is partly shares and partly cash an appropriate portion of the gain will be subject to charge and only the balance will be held over (see Chapter 16). Special rules operate if part of the consideration furnished is a qualifying coporate bond (see [**28.48**]). If the transferor qualifies for retirement relief in respect of the unincorporated business, the Revenue will permit him to deduct that relief from any gains arising on the incorporation and to hold over any remaining gain under s 123. Alternatively, if retirement relief is either not desired or is unavailable on the incorporation, it may be available on a subsequent disposal of the shares provided that the company is a 'family company'. For the purpose of the ten year ownership requirement, aggregation of the ownership of the business and the shares is permitted (see Chapter 16).   [**33.5**]

A transfer for cash   Roll-over reinvestment relief under CGTA 1979 s 115 may be available if the disponer reinvests the proceeds of sale of permitted assets within the prescribed period (see [**16.92**]). Where the disponer is over 55, retirement relief may be available.   [**33.6**]

A gift to the company   Under CGTA 1979 s 123 all the assets of the business must be transferred to the company. It is possible to avoid CGT when some assets are to be retained by the transferor and transferee making an election to hold over the gain on the assets transferred under CGTA 1979 s 126. The use of this hold-over election under s 126 should, however, be carefully considered since the effect is to transfer any capital gain in the assets to the company. Accordingly it can lead to a double charge when that gain is ultimately realised (see further Chapter 32 and *Example 33.1* below).

It may be more efficient in appropriate circumstances for no such election to be made. When retirement relief is available to relieve in whole or in part the gain, that relief is given first with any balance of chargeable gain then being held-over (see [**16.103**]).   [**33.7**]

The retention of appreciating assets outside the company   The double charge which may arise when capital gains are realised by a company means that where a business is incorporated, therefore, there may be attractions in retaining outside the corporation assets which are likely to appreciate substantially in value and to allow the company to use or lease those assets. Difficulties will, however, arise if this is done. For instance, CGTA 1979 s 123 will not apply to the incorporation so that, unless retirement relief or hold-over relief is available, gains on the incorporation will be subject to charge. The owner of the asset may, however, be entitled to retirement relief on the eventual disposal of the asset (subject to satisfying the conditions of FA 1985 s 70 and Sch 20 para 10) and if he were to sell the asset and reinvest the proceeds, roll-over relief may be available under CGTA 1979 s 120. A gift of the retained asset should attract hold-over relief under CGTA 1979 s 126 and business property relief for IHT at a rate of 30% so long as he controls (within the IHTA 1984 s 269 definition) the company.   [33.8]

b) *Incorporation under s 123 or s 126*

To obtain relief under s 123, all business assets (except cash) must be transferred to the company and therefore it may be more attractive to incorporate by using the s 126 route which may also result in stamp duty savings.   [33.9]

EXAMPLE 33.1

Slick intends to incorporate his existing business. Accordingly, Slick Ltd is formed with £100 share capital. Slick then sells to Slick Ltd goodwill (if any) for a nominal sum and other assets at their CGT base cost. The consideration may either be paid in cash or left outstanding as a loan to Slick Ltd. An election under CGTA 1979 s 126 is then made. The following matters should be noted –

(1) Slick is free to retain the ownership of whichever assets he desires (hence avoiding the problems of s 123).

(2) Stamp duty will be charged only on those assets transferred and hence will not apply to the value of debtors if Slick retains title in the debts (which he can then collect as agent for the company).

(3) Under s 126 the gain is rolled over against Slick Ltd's base cost of the assets whereas under s 123 it is the base cost of the shares held by the shareholder which is reduced. Again, s 126 may be attractive since it does not leave the proprietor holding shares pregnant with gain whilst, if the postponed gain is realised by Slick Ltd, roll-over (reinvestment) relief may be available. Note, however, that Slick Ltd will obtain the benefit of the CGT indexation allowance only on the base value of the assets transferred. A further problem which may arise if s 126 is used is that the postponed gain may be effectively taxed twice – once on disposal by the company of chargeable assets and the second time when the shares showing an increased value are sold.

3   Stamp duty

The sale of a business to a company may involve a charge to stamp duty (see Chapter 3) unless the contract contains a certificate of value (so that the nil rate applies). Duty will be charged on the land, goodwill, book debts (including VAT), cash in a deposit account, patents, copyright and know-how. It need not be charged on goods, wares and merchandise which can be transferred by delivery. Items such as stock-in-trade and cash in hand or in a current account must be included in the contract for sale of the business but need not be included in the certificate of value so long as they are not transferred by the instrument of transfer. An apportionment of consideration between the chargeable and non-chargeable assets is made on Stamps Form 22. Duty will, however, be charged on liabilities taken over by a purchaser. **[33.10]**

EXAMPLE 33.2

Yol agrees to sell his business to M Ltd for £39,000. M Ltd further agrees to take over Yol's outstanding liabilities to secured and trade creditors. The state of Yol's business is:

Liabilities	£	Assets	£
Secured creditors	8,000	Freehold	23,000
Trade creditors	12,000	Goodwill	6,000
		Stock	9,000
Excess of assets		Book debts	12,000
over liabilities	39,000	Deposit a/c	9,000
	£59,000		£59,000

M Ltd will purchase the business for a consideration for stamp duty purposes of £59,000, ie £39,000 (purchase price) + £20,000 (liabilities taken over).

Stamp duty will be reduced if the following measures are adopted:

(1) Cash is put into current account before contract.
(2) Yol retains the book debts (£12,000) to pay off trade creditors.
(3) Yol could retain the freehold premises and grant M Ltd a lease or licence to use them. This may not prove satisfactory where the company is not owned by Yol.
(4) The title to the stock does not pass under the conveyance but by delivery.

As a result of taking steps (1), (2) and (4) the consideration for stamp duty is reduced by £30,000 (£9,000 (cash) + £9,000 (stock) + £12,000 (book debts)) from £59,000 to £29,000. As a result no duty is charged provided a certificate of value is inserted into the contract and the appropriate entries made on Form 22. Retention of the book debts means that CGTA 1979 s 123 relief will not be available on the disposal of the chargeable assets.

Note: See **[30.3]** for the reform of stamp duty which is expected to be implemented in May 1992. The effect will be to limit the duty to land transactions.

4 Problems for a purchasing company

Where the business is not being incorporated by the existing owner but instead is being sold to an existing company other difficulties for that purchaser should be noted. For instance, if the business is acquired as a going concern it must be treated separately for corporation tax purposes from any existing trade already carried on. The price paid for items such as land, plant and machinery, and goodwill constitute the purchaser's base cost for the purpose of computing any future capital gains. So far as capital allowances are concerned, a conflict of interest is likely with the vendor being concerned to attribute as small a sum as possible to such assets in order to avoid a balancing charge whilst for the purchaser a high figure will give him a greater capital allowance. The agreed apportionment set out in Form 22 will normally be accepted by the Revenue but will probably only be reached after hard bargaining between the parties. **[33.11]**

5 **Other matters**

A number of ancillary matters should also be considered on incorporation or sale of a business. The following summarises the more important:

(1) If an existing trade is incorporated, contracts of employment automatically transfer with the business. Where assets alone are sold, however, claims for redundancy will occur if staff are reduced. (See especially the Employment Protection (Consolidation) Act 1978 and the Transfer of Undertakings (Protection of Employment) Regulations 1981.)

(2) If the vendor of the business is a director of the purchasing company (this will normally be the case when a business is being incorporated) under Companies Act 1985 s 320 a general meeting of the company will usually have to approve the agreement. If new shares are to be issued it will be necessary to ensure that the company has available shares (if necessary, share capital should be increased: see Companies Act 1985 s 121); that the directors have the power to allot such shares (see Companies Act 1985 s 80); and that any pre-emption provisions in the articles of association have either been satisfied or do not apply to shares issued in return for a non-cash consideration.

(3) So long as the company is registered for VAT before the transfer of the business as a going concern, there will be no charge on the transfer of items which are subject to VAT on the sale of the business (VAT Act 1983 s 33). VAT may be chargeable on a mere transfer of assets (see VAT (Special Provisions) Order 1981 (SI 1981/1471)).

(4) Ensure that all necessary consents are obtained and/or documents amended, eg a landlord's consent to the assignment of a lease.

(5) If the business is sold for cash, the vendor should remember that for IHT purposes, business property relief and the instalment option will not be available on any transfer of value of that cash. An asset which carries a partial exemption for IHT is, therefore, being exchanged for cash which has no such exemption.   **[33.12]–[33.20]**

II COMPANY TAKEOVERS

A sale of a company may take one of two different forms. Either the assets of the target company may be purchased; or the shares of that company may be acquired. In the former, the shareholders of the target will be left with a company whose sole asset is cash; in the latter, the shareholders themselves will be left with cash. Alternatively the take-over may be by a share exchange in which case the vendors will be left with shares in the purchaser. On a share acquisition, the purchaser will have acquired the entire enterprise as a going concern and, if a corporate purchaser, will have acquired a subsidiary company. In an assets takeover, the purchaser may simply amalgamate those assets with his existing business so that instead of acquiring a new enterprise he may simply be expanding the existing business.   **[33.21]**

1 **Considerations on an assets sale**

a) *The vendor*

If the vendor company intends to continue in business, an asset sale has the advantage that the vendor company will not be subject to corporation tax on any capital gains realised on prescribed assets if these are rolled over into the purchase of new assets within the permitted time. It is possible to reinvest in a completely different trade (see SP 8/81 and Chapter 16). A disposal of stock results in a corporation tax charge and a disposal of machinery and plant may lead to balancing charges.

If the company plans to discontinue trading permanently, the consequences are far from satisfactory. The company will be assessed on the capital profits made on the sale. The normal carry-back of losses over the three previous years will be available (see [**28.56**]), but carry-forward relief will of course be lost. Problems will arise if the shareholders wish to extract the cash from the company. The result will be either an income tax charge on a distribution, or a charge to capital gains tax on a liquidation in addition to the tax charge already borne by the company. Retirement relief may be available on a liquidation if the conditions of FA 1985 s 70(4) are satisfied. Generally, however, if the vendors plan to discontinue their business, they should not engage in a sale of assets; it is better for them to sell the shares.   [**33.22**]

b) *The purchaser*

The first and most obvious attraction is that the purchaser can select which assets he wants to acquire since he will not be acquiring the entire entity. Secondly, save in respect of employees (which the purchaser will take over if there is a transfer of a business of a going concern), the purchaser will not run the risk of acquiring liabilities which he does not want and/or of which he is not aware. Thirdly, the purchaser will be entitled to capital allowances (for instance, on the purchase of plant and machinery) and to roll-over relief on the purchase of prescribed assets.   [**33.23**]

2 **Considerations on a share sale**

a) *The vendor*

This will be the preferable solution if the vendors are intending to go out of business. The sale of shares will be a disposal for CGT purposes and, if the requirements are satisfied, retirement relief is available. Because the company is sold, there is no change of owner of the business so that continuity of employment is automatically preserved and all debts and liabilities effectively pass to the purchaser. Needless to say the vendors will normally be required to give certain undertakings and warranties to the purchaser so that there will be some continuing personal liability.

If the purchase moneys are to be paid in instalments, CGT will still be charged on the total sum at once unless the Revenue allow the tax to be paid by instalments (see CGTA 1979 s 40). Where the consideration is partly cash and partly a *chose in action* (eg a proportion of the share price if and when the company goes public as in *Marren v Ingles* (1980); see [**14.7**]) retirement relief will only be available against the cash received and the value of the *chose* (if any); it will not be available on the later disposal of the *chose in action*.

If the vendors intend to stay in business, a share sale is normally not recommended since, for CGT, gains on the sale of the shares cannot be rolled over into the purchase of new business assets.   [**33.24**]

b) *The purchaser*

The company is bought *in toto* so that there will be continuity in the business. There will be no tax relief for the purchase of the shares themselves. It is possible to carry forward trading losses suffered by the company prior to the sale of the shares but by TA 1988 s 393(1) these losses may only be set against profits *in the same trade*. If the trade has ceased at any time carry-forward is not possible even if an identical trade is later restarted. Further, TA 1988 s 768 prevents relief in the event (*inter alia*) of a 'major change in the nature or conduct of the trade' within a period of three years of the sale (see *Willis v Peeters Picture Frames Ltd* (1983); [**28.57**]). The prudent purchaser should, therefore, tread warily for three years before attempting any major revitalisation of the target company.

One headache for the purchaser is to ascertain what skeletons are hidden in the target company's cupboards. To this end, warranties and indemnities will normally be sought. In a typical share acquisition agreement the vendor will be asked to warrant at the time of sale that the company has no undisclosed tax liabilities. Since the function of tax warranties is not only to protect the purchaser against future liabilities but also to extract for the purchaser information about the company, tax warranties normally involve detailed points. For example, the vendor will be asked to warrant that the company has duly and punctually paid all taxes, has operated the PAYE system correctly and has not been involved in any anti-avoidance scheme. It is usual to back up these warranties with a deed of tax indemnity whereby the vendor indemnifies the purchaser against any tax liability of the company which comes to light after the sale but by reference to a pre-completion event and which was not disclosed to the purchaser. As a result of *Zim Properties Ltd v Proctor* (1985) (see [**14.8**]) payments made under such indemnities were thought to be taxable in the hands of the recipient as the proceeds of the disposal of a chose in action (ie the right to sue was considered a separate asset). This led to the practice of inserting a 'grossing-up' clause in the deed of indemnity to ensure that the amount payable in the event of a claim would equal the liability under the deed plus the tax payable by the purchaser thereon. However, the ESC dated 19 December 1988 made it clear that, *provided that payments under indemnities are made to the purchaser*, they will be regarded as a reduction in the purchase price and therefore not subject to tax (contrast the position if payments are made to the company).

When purchasing a subsidiary company special points arise. In particular, there may be a CGT claw-back charge under TA 1970 s 278(3) in respect of assets transferred to the subsidiary by another group company on a no loss/no gain basis under s 273 (see [**28.145**]).   [**33.25**]

c) *Pre-sale dividend strip*

The use of a pre-sale dividend to extract value from a subsidiary before its sale has always been a well-used tax saving device for such dividends can be paid under a group election without ACT. With the equalisation of rates of income tax and CGT, the pre-sale dividend strip has also become popular with individual vendors of private companies as a means of reducing the tax liability on sale.

EXAMPLE 33.3

SJ Ltd has £400,000 of undistributed profits. The owner, Mr Simon Wise, has been offered £2 million for his shares, producing a capital gain of £1.2 million which, taxed at 40%, would lead to a CGT liability of £480,000.

If, before the sale, a dividend of £300,000 is paid to Mr Wise and the sale price is reduced to £1.7 million, he will suffer a CGT liability of £360,000 plus higher rate income tax on his gross dividend of £400,000 (ie £400,000 at 40% = £160,000) less the basic rate tax credit of £100,000. Thus, Mr Wise will pay tax totalling £420,000, a saving of £60,000.

The target company will be required to account for the ACT payable on the dividend in the usual way within 14 days of the end of three month period in which it is paid (see [**28.94**]). However, the ACT can generally be set off against MCT liability for profits made during the accounting period in which the dividend was paid but the amount of set-off is not unlimited and there may be an ACT surplus as a result of a particularly large dividend. This can be carried back up to the six years under TA 1988 s 239 (see [**28.97**]) but a purchaser will be concerned to ensure that this is possible and should also be aware that the company's future dividend policy may be affected by a large pre-sale dividend strip.

There are no specific anti-avoidance provisions to prevent tax saving through a dividend strip because the existing legislation is all aimed at stopping the conversion of income profit into capital profit, not the other way round. It is unlikely that the principle of *Furniss v Dawson* could be applied to the standard dividend strip. [**33.26**]

d) *Stamp duty problems: the 'pref-trick'*

The transfer of shares will normally be assessable to ad valorem stamp duty at ¹/₂% (although this duty will shortly be abolished, see [**30.1**]). In the interests of a purchaser, the sale was often effected by the 'pref-trick' which was designed to minimise duty. The scheme relied on a stamp duty exemption for renounceable letters of allotment and there was no doubt that the 'pref-trick' was an artificial tax saving device. After a somewhat ill-conceived attempt to stop the trick by invoking the *Ramsay* principle (see further *Revenue Law—principles and practice* (3rd edn (1985), p 511)), FA 1985 s 81 imposed stamp duty on the renunciation of the right to share allotment in an attempt to prevent modified versions of the trick that had developed to circumvent the *Ramsay* threat. Even that section was thought by some to be ineffective (see, for instance, [1985] BTR 201) but matters were put beyond doubt with the extension of duty to bearer letters of allotment in FA 1986 (see further Chapter 30). [**33.27**]

3 **Takeover by means of a share issue**

Shares or assets in the target may be acquired in exchange for an issue of shares in the acquiring company. In such an event:
(1) On a share exchange CGT should not apply to the vendors since a roll-over deferral is available provided that the arrangement is a *bona fide* commercial one and, generally, that more than 25% of the target's shares are owned or acquired by the purchaser (CGTA 1979 s 85). Deferral is also available if the exchange is as a result of a general offer made to the shareholders of the target which is conditional upon the purchaser acquiring control of the target and is for *bona fide* commercial purposes. A clearance can be obtained from the Revenue that these

requirements are satisfied. For the vendors, there is a risk that although the old shares qualified for retirement relief the new shares do not.

(2) *Marren v Ingles* (see [**14.7**]) can present problems in share for share transactions where shares in the vendor are transferred to a purchaser in return for an immediate issue of shares in the purchaser together with a future right to further shares (an arrangement sometimes referred to as a 'earn-out' since the further share issue is often made dependent on a future profit target being met). These future shares (ie the deferred consideration) do not fall within CGTA 1979 s 85 and accordingly were not granted a clearance by the Revenue. A number of arrangements were employed to avoid the problems thus posed. Commonly these involved an issue of loan stock by the purchaser which was ultimately converted into shares (ie the deferred shares) in the purchaser. The immediate exchange of shares for convertible loan stock fell within CGTA 1979 s 85 whilst the subsequent conversion of the loan stock was free from capital gains tax under CGTA 1979 s 82. It is understood that clearances have been granted when such arrangements have been entered into.

In any event, the problems of earn outs were eased by an extra statutory concession, dated 26 April 1988, which provides that

> 'where an agreement for the sale of shares or debentures in a company creates a right to an unascertainable element (whether or not subject to a maximum) against the purchaser which is acquired by the vendor at the time of disposal and that right falls to be satisfied wholly by the issue of shares or debentures, then, notwithstanding a concurrent right to consideration other than in the form of shares or debentures, the Board are prepared to treat the right to shares or debentures in the hands of the vendor as a security within the meaning of CGTA 1979 s 82.'

Relief under s 85 is therefore available if the other conditions are satisfied. As can be seen from the above extract the concession is not happily worded but it is understood that the Revenue will apply it to the extent that the future consideration can only be satisfied by an issue of shares or debentures and will therefore ignore the existence of a concurrent or separate right to a cash payment (such right will, of course, not attract relief from capital gains tax).

(3) If assets of the target are transferred in return for shares by way of a *bona fide* commercial arrangement with the target going into liquidation, there will be no corporation tax on the transfer of assets by the target. Instead, the assets will be transferred at no gain/no loss, so that tax will be deferred until the purchaser sells (TA 1970 s 267). The shares in the purchaser company received by the vendor's shareholders are not subject to CGT until sold (CGTA 1979 s 86). Clearance is available under both these provisions.

(4) On a share-for-share exchange stamp duty at $1/2\%$ will be payable (although this duty will shortly be abolished, see [**30.1**]).

[**33.28**]–[**33.40**]

III   DEMERGERS AND RECONSTRUCTIONS

Splitting up groups of companies or splitting a company into separate parts under separate ownership had not attracted, until recently, special taxation provisions. FA 1980 Sch 18 (now TA 1988 ss 213–217), however, was designed to take distributions which are made to achieve a demerger outside the normal income tax treatment of distributions (under TA 1988 s 209) and also to give relief from other taxes such as CGT and originally from stamp duty although that relief was withdrawn in FA 1986. The conditions to be satisfied are highly technical and cannot be used to separate trades from investments (see generally SP 13/80 and note *Combined Technologies Corpn plc v IRC* (1985) in which relief from stamp duty was held not to extend to documents effected before the demerger, but without which that demerger could not have occurred). In general, three types of transaction constitute a demerger and qualify for advantageous tax treatment:

(1) A transfer to ordinary shareholders of shares in another company of which the transferor owns at least 75% of the ordinary share capital. This is the so-called 'direct demerger' in the sense that the shares pass directly to the shareholders of the demerged company.

(2) A transfer of a trade by company 1 to company 2 which issues shares in return to company 1's ordinary shareholders. This and (3) below are 'indirect demergers' since the trades or subsidiaries pass first to a company who then issues shares to the original shareholders in the demerged company.

(3) An amalgamation of (1) and (2): viz shares in company 1's 75% subsidiary are transferred to company 2 in return for shares in that company.

Even where a transaction would appear to fall within one of these transactions, further criteria have to be satisfied if relief is to be given. Only trading companies and groups are covered, and each entity resulting from any split must be a trading entity. Further, the reason for the split must be to benefit some or all of the trading activities which before the distribution were carried on by a single company and after the distribution by two or more companies. The purpose of the demerger must not be to save tax nor must it be intended as a means of transferring control of the company to a third party. A clearance procedure is available and the form of application is set out in SP 13/80.

EXAMPLE 33.4

Audivis Ltd carries on, inter alia, two separate trades as a result of a merger of two existing businesses. Its shareholders are family A and family B who are concerned in the running of the different trades. The merger has failed and so two new companies (Audi Ltd and Vis Ltd) are formed and the trades are split between these two companies by way of an indirect demerger. As a result, the A family receive shares in Audi Ltd and the B family shares in Vis Ltd. So long as the provisions in the demerger legislation are satisfied (eg the transfer must not occur on the liquidation of Audivis Ltd) the share allotments will be treated as 'exempt distributions'. Broadly, therefore, tax is postponed until the new shares are sold.

Unlike a demerger, a reconstruction occurs when the business undertaking continues in an altered form and remains owned by substantially the same persons (the classic definition of a reconstruction is by Buckley J in *Re South African Supply and Cold Storage Co* (1904)). The original company will be liquidated in this process. Thus, the requirement on a reconstruction that substantially the same persons must carry on the business distinguishes a demerger from a reconstruction. (In *Example 33.4* above, for instance, the demerger cannot also be a reconstruction since the Audi Ltd portion of the business is exclusively run by the A family after the demerger, but note the effect of SP 5/85 below.)

EXAMPLE 33.5

Crash Ltd is liquidated and the viable portion of the business transferred to a newly incorporated company (Ash Ltd) whose shares are issued directly to the shareholders of Crash Ltd.

Notes
(1)   This reconstruction may be carried out quickly and cheaply under Insolvency Act 1986 s 110.
(2)   Relief from any charge to capital gains tax (see TA 1970 s 267, CGTA 1979 s 86) may be available as described on [**28.146**]. Relief from stamp duty is available if the requirements of FA 1986 ss 75–77 are satisfied (see [**30.85**]).

Some relaxation of the restrictive definition of a reconstruction is, however, provided by SP 5/85 in which the Revenue accept that a division of a company (as in *Example 33.5* above) will be treated as reconstruction for capital gains tax purposes (so that relief will be afforded by TA 1970 s 267 and CGTA 1979 s 86). This Statement of Practice does not, however, give relief from stamp duty.

Confusingly, therefore, where a demerger is intended, relief may be afforded under either a statutory provision or an extra-statutory concession. Although the two overlap, there are important distinctions: if the original company is liquidated, for instance, the statutory provisions are inapplicable, whilst under SP 5/85 relief from stamp duty is not available.   [**33.41**]–[**33.60**]

IV   MANAGEMENT BUY-OUTS

There has been a noticeable increase in management buy-outs (MBOs) in recent years and, in the majority of cases, they have been commercially successful (see Economist Intelligence Unit Special Report No 164). The distinction between an MBO and an employee buy-out is that in the latter the business is purchased by all or a part of the work force not just by the managers. There are three typical situations when a buy-out may occur; first, when a subsidiary (or division) is purchased from a group of companies; secondly, when the owners sell the family company or its business; and thirdly when a receiver or liquidator sells all or a part of the failed undertaking often by means of a hive-down. As with any takeover the management may purchase either shares of the target company or the assets of the business and similar considerations to those discussed on at [**33.22**] apply in deciding which is the most advantageous method for vendor and purchaser.

When the company is purchased (ie a share purchase) the normal indemnities and warranties should be sought by the management team although the vendors will often take the view that if there are 'skeletons in the cupboard' this is a matter of which the managers will have knowledge.

The major difficulties involved in buy-outs relate to the financing of the purchase since the management team will lack sufficient funds to purchase the business out of their own resources. Accordingly the bulk of the finance must be supplied by institutional investors and the target company or business is generally purchased by a newly formed company ('Newco') in which the managers have voting control but in which the majority of the finance has been provided by the institutions (this will normally be in the form of unsecured loan stock and convertible preference shares).

It may be possible to use the assets of the target company to assist in the purchase of its own shares (see the Companies Act 1985, Pt V, Chapter VI). The target's assets may for instance be used as security for the institutions' loans after it has been purchased. Alternatively, dividends or loans may be paid to Newco to enable it to discharge interest payments to the institutions (care should be taken to ensure that when Newco is a holding company it has sufficient profits against which to obtain tax relief for the interest payments). Finally, the target could be liquidated after its purchase and its assets transferred up to Newco. This would have the attraction of ending the holding company/trading subsidiary structure but care should be taken to ensure that the transfer of assets does not trigger a CGT charge (see CGTA 1979 s 72). Accordingly, it might be more satisfactory to transfer the business of the target as a going concern at book value and to leave the consideration outstanding on an inter-company loan account. The target would then be left as a 'shell' company.

So far as the managers are concerned, apart from using their own personal wealth to purchase shares in Newco, it will often be necessary for them to raise additional funds by way of loans. Income tax relief may be available on the interest paid on such loans (see generally Chapter 4). Under TA 1988 s 360 relief is given if the taxpayer works for the greater part of his time in the actual management or conduct of the company. When the buy-out is arranged through Newco, it is essential to ensure that it satisfies the test for a close trading company if s 360 relief is to be available. In practice, this means ensuring that 75% or more of its income is derived from trading subsidiaries and the Revenue accept that, so long as it is in receipt of the appropriate amount of dividends or income from the target during its first accounting period, this requirement will be treated as satisfied at the time when the managers make their investment. Thus, if at some later date Newco ceases to satisfy the conditions of s 360 relief will not be withdrawn. Relief may alternatively be available under TA 1988 s 361. Newco must be employee-controlled (ie full-time employees should control more than 50% of the ordinary share capital and votes) and it must be an unquoted trading company or the holding company of a trading group. For the purpose of this requirement Newco may qualify even though it has only the one trading subsidiary. If the company ceases to be employee-controlled, however, tax relief is withdrawn. Reference has already been made to the potential income tax liability of managers under FA 1988 ss 77–89 resulting from an acquisition of shares in their capacity as employees (see Chapter 5). Further, if shares are offered at below market price an income tax liability under the general provisions taxing benefits in kind could arise. **[33.61]**

34 Employee participation: options, incentives, trusts and profit related pay

'Right – that takes care of the company reindeer,
Now, about the share option scheme for
the elves . . .'

I INTRODUCTION

1 **Background**

In recent years there has been a substantial growth in share option and share incentive schemes designed to reward company employees, especially senior management. A major attraction of such schemes is that they bring together the interests of the employee and the company since, so long as those shares are retained by the employee, that shareholding is likely to be his most valuable disposable asset after his main residence.

The present Government is an avid supporter of employee participation as an important part of its policy of promoting wider share ownership. This support has been expressed by the introduction of various 'Approved Schemes' to which significant tax benefits for the employee have been attached.

It is evident, however, that most approved employee share schemes have been directed by employers at senior management. The focus of the Government's attention over the last three years or so has therefore been directed at encouraging employers to provide schemes for the benefit of all employees. Hence, qualifying employee share ownership trusts (generally called 'ESOPs') were introduced in FA 1989 and subsequently refined to make them more attractive to employers in FA 1990. In the latest Finance

Act the Chancellor significantly increased the limits applicable to all employee savings related share options and provided that if an employer sets up all employee approved schemes, the option price on a selective approved share option scheme can be up to 15% below the market value of the shares at the date when the option is granted.

This chapter covers the complete range of employee participation and is not limited to schemes involving shares; a brief section is therefore devoted to Profit Related Pay. **[34.1]**

2 Taxation of share incentives

An individual, who is given shares by his employer as a result of that employment, receives a taxable emolument and will suffer income tax on the market value of those shares on the date when he receives them. Similarly, an employee who is sold shares by his employer at an undervalue receives an emolument equal to the difference between the price paid and the market value of the shares at the date of purchase (TA 1988 s 135). (These types of arrangement, where the employee receives shares, not share options, are referred to as 'share incentives'.)

As a result, various schemes, including the use of *share options*, were used in an attempt to circumvent the income tax net. Inevitably, anti-avoidance legislation was then passed in an attempt to widen that net! The present position is that if, by reason of his employment, an individual is granted options to purchase shares, he is not taxed on the value of the options *at that time* unless the options are capable of being exercised more than seven years after the grant. However, the whole gain made on the shares will be subject to income tax at the time *when the option is exercised* although credit will be given for any tax which is actually paid on the grant of an option lasting more than seven years (TA 1988 s 135).

The taxation of *share incentives* is more complex than the comments above might suggest. Under FA 1988 ss 77–89, income tax is charged on the growth in value of shares owned by employees in certain circumstances. There are two main heads of charge: first, that attaching to any growth in value arising from the lifting of restrictions and, secondly, that attaching to the growth value of shares in a 'dependent subsidiary'. Unfortunately, the legislation designed to impose these charges is somewhat vague and imprecise in its application.

There are, however, certain employee share schemes which are given favourable tax treatment. These are the 'approved schemes' and profits made by the employees under such schemes are treated as capital gains, therefore being subject to CGT rather than income tax. Although the unification of the rates of income tax and capital gains has reduced the tax advantages of approved schemes, attractions still remain. **[34.2]]–[[34.20]**

II TYPES OF EMPLOYEE PARTICIPATION

1 Approved share option and share incentive schemes generally

The so-called 'approved schemes' are those share option and share incentive schemes which satisfy the requirements originally contained in the FA 1978, FA 1980 and FA 1984. There are three types of approved schemes, being respectively, approved profit sharing schemes, savings related share option schemes and share option schemes. As stated above, the basic tax principle is that any profit made by the employees on the disposal of the shares acquired under an approved scheme *is subject to CGT and not income tax.*

The main characteristics of the three types of scheme are set out below. Many of the conditions which must be satisfied are common to all three types of approved scheme. For example:

(1) *The type of shares*   The shares must be ordinary, fully paid-up, non-redeemable shares in the employing company or its parent (or, if the employer is a consortium company, in a member of that consortium). Furthermore, the shares must be quoted on a recognised Stock Exchange or, if not quoted, must be in a company which is either controlled by a quoted company or not controlled by any other company.

(2) *Restrictions attached to the shares*   Two kinds of restriction are permitted. Firstly, restrictions which attach to *all* shares of the *same class* and, secondly, restrictions imposed by the Articles of Association requiring shares held by directors or employees to be disposed of *when the holders cease to be directors or employees.*

(3) *The exclusion of persons holding a material interest*   An individual who holds a material interest in *either* the company which issues the shares *or* a company which controls the issuing company, is not eligible to participate in an approved scheme. For these purposes, an individual holds a material interest if he either alone, or together with associates, beneficially owns or controls 25% of the ordinary share capital of the company or, in the case of FA 1984 schemes, 10% of the ordinary share capital (TA 1988 s 187(3)). 'Associate' means, broadly, a relative or partner or trustee of any settlement in which the employee has an interest. However, an individual who is a beneficiary under an employee trust which owns shares in the company will not have an interest in those shares for these purposes.   [34.21]

2   Approved profit sharing schemes (FA 1978 schemes; now TA 1988 s 186 and Sch 10)

These schemes are centred on a *trust fund* set up by the employer company. With contributions provided by the employer, trustees acquire shares in the company (either by subscription or purchase) and appropriate these to individual employees (ie shares are held by the trustees for a particular employee). The amount paid into the trust by the employer may vary according to the company's profitability so that a direct link between the performance of the company and the value of the benefit to the employees can be established at the outset and can be maintained throughout the life of the scheme.

The conditions for Revenue approval of a profit sharing scheme include the following:

(1) *All* full-time working directors and employees must be given the *right* to participate (although the scheme may specify a qualifying period of employment of up to five years before an employee becomes eligible). Hence, the allocation of shares is not at the trustee's discretion. However, the formula by which the employer calculates his contributions for each employee can take account of length of service and level of salary of the individual employee.

(2) The market value of shares appropriated to an employee in *any one year* must not *exceed* £3,000 or 10% of the employee's salary for that year, if greater, subject to an *upper limit* of £8,000. (If this limit is exceeded, the excess shares do not qualify for any relief.)

(3) The trust deed must oblige the trustees to notify an employee of the number of shares allocated to him, together with details of the market price, as soon as possible after shares have been appropriated to him.

(4) The shares appropriated must be retained by the trustees for *at least two years*. No tax charge arises on the appropriation or on any subsequent increase in the value of the shares. After appropriation, dividends belong to the employee.

Once the two year period has expired, the employee can direct the trustees to sell the shares, although to avoid all income tax liability the shares must not be disposed of until *at least five years* after the appropriation date. If sold *within five years*, income tax is payable on a percentage of the *original market value* of the shares (ie at the date of appropriation) as follows:

When sold	% taxed
Up to 4 years after appropriation	100%
4–5 years after appropriation	75%

The employee may, of course, be subject to CGT on his profit (even if free of income tax), taking his acquisition cost for this purpose as the market value of the shares *at the date of their appropriation*. If the employment ceases because of redundancy, premature retirement caused by ill-health or the attainment of normal retirement age, and the shares are sold within the five year period, the percentage of the original market value charged to income tax is reduced to 50%.

These schemes are tax efficient for *employers*, who can deduct sums paid to the trustees as a business expense (or an expense of management) for corporation tax, *provided that* the sums are spent by the trustees in acquiring shares within nine months or are used to pay the trustees' expenses. The employer can also deduct the cost of setting up the scheme provided that the trustees do not acquire shares before approval is obtained from the Revenue.

EXAMPLE 34.1

Eric, an employee, is a basic rate taxpayer to whom trustees under an approved profit sharing scheme appropriate shares when their market value is £1,000. His employer pays corporation tax at 35%. At Eric's direction, the trustees sell the shares after $4^{1}/_{2}$ years for £2,000.

(1) The company had transferred £1,000 to the trust and this sum is used by the trustees to subscribe for a new issue of shares by the company. The company obtains tax relief of £330 (33% of £1,000) so that the net cost is £670. *There is a net inflow of £330 into the company* since the company will have paid out £670, and received £1,000 attributable to its issued share capital account.

(2) When the shares are sold after $4^{1}/_{2}$ years for £2,000 Eric will be subject to income tax – calculated on 75% of the value of the shares when appropriated (£1,000). Assuming that he is a basic rate taxpayer his liability will be £187.50 (25% of £750). There is unlikely to be any CGT liability on the gain of £1,000 (£2,000—£1,000) because of Eric's annual exemption.

The company has, therefore, incurred a net cost of £670 and the employee has received £1,812.50 (£2,000—£187.50).

As explained below, the best way of providing employees with relatively large shareholdings is under an FA 1984 share option scheme. However, although the limits under a profit sharing scheme seem somewhat prohibitive, it should be noted that by operating a scheme over a five year period an employee can be appropriated shares with a base cost equal to 10% of his annual salary up to a total over five years of £40,000. It is therefore possible in a large company for a substantial block of shares to be placed in friendly hands. This may be a comfort to the 'bid conscious' quoted company although a scheme created *solely* to block potential predators might be invalid.

Non-quoted companies may, however, experience difficulties in using approved profit sharing schemes, since there is no ready market for shares once employees decide to sell. Accordingly, the only way in which a share option scheme can effectively be run by a non-quoted company is by giving the trustees power to purchase shares from the employees or, perhaps, creating a separate ESOP for that purpose (see Section 6 below).   **[34.22]**

3   Approved savings related share option schemes (FA 1980 schemes; now TA 1988 s 185 and Sch 9)

Savings related schemes, in contrast to profit sharing schemes, are funded by contributions from the employees themselves. These are accumulated in standard Save As You Earn contracts which are taken out at the time the options are granted. The proceeds (repayments, including five year bonus, plus interest) are used to provide funds for the exercise of the options to acquire Ordinary Shares in the employer company. The maximum permitted monthly contribution to SAYE contracts is currently *£250*.

The *price* of the shares must be fixed at the time *when the employee is granted* the option and must not be less than 80% of the market value of the shares at that time. Generally, the option must not be exercisable or must not be exercised within three years of its acquisition. (In practice, it will normally be exercised when the SAYE contract matures at the end of five or seven years.) The employee is *exempt from any charge to income tax* on the grant or exercise of the option. The only charge is to *CGT if and when the shares are sold*.

To gain approval, the scheme must be open to *all* employees and satisfy detailed conditions set out in TA 1988 Sch 9. For example:
(1) the option rights must be non-transferable;
(2) the scheme must provide that, if a participant dies before the expiration of five or seven years, his rights must be exercised, if at all, within 12 months of death; and
(3) if a participant ceases to be an employee by reason of injury, disability, redundancy, or retirement at pensionable age, his rights must be exercised within six months of leaving work.

The scheme may provide that, if the company is taken over, employees must be given the right to exchange their existing options for options in the acquiring company and, provided that this is done within six months of the take-over, there will be no tax consequences.

Unlike FA 1984 approved schemes (see Section 4 below), the employee is not required to produce a large sum of money to exercise his option, since sufficient funds will have accrued through the SAYE scheme. This encourages the employee to *retain* his shares, since he is not forced to sell to repay loans taken to acquire the shares.   **[34.23]**

4   Approved share option schemes (FA 1984: now TA 1988 s 185 and Sch 9)

FA 1984 introduced an approved share option scheme not linked to savings under SAYE. If the scheme (including an existing unapproved scheme which either satisfies the necessary conditions or incorporates them) is approved, then, as with savings related schemes under FA 1980, there is *no income tax charge on the exercise* of an option to acquire ordinary shares in the employer company. The only charge is to *CGT if and when the shares are sold.*

The detailed conditions for approval are set out in TA 1988 Sch 9. In particular, the following should be noted:

(1) although the price charged for the shares must generally not be less than their market value at the date when the option was granted, an employer who operates an approved all employee share scheme (ie an approved **profit-sharing** scheme as described in 2, above, or an approved savings related share option scheme as described in 3, above) will be able after 1 January 1992 to grant options at up to 15% below the market price at the time when the option is granted;

(2) the scheme must be restricted to employees and full-time working directors, save that employees who exercise the option after they have left full-time employment and their PRs (who exercise the option within one year of death) may be included;

(3) the option must be exercisable *after* three *but within* ten years of its grant; and

(4) the aggregate market value (generally at the time of the grant) of the total shares available per employee must not exceed *the greater of* £100,000 and four times the employee's current or previous year's salary (or, in the absence of a preceding year salary, his annual salary).

Unlike profit sharing and savings related share option schemes, *these schemes may be selective.* Further, part-time employees may be included provided that they work a minimum of 20 hours per week (or, for a director, 25 hours).

There is no reason why the exercise of the options should not be dependent upon the achievement of *performance targets.* The Revenue have refused approval to schemes which contain provisions for varying or inserting performance conditions after the option has been granted but the recent decision in *IRC v Burton Group plc* (1990) suggests that performance criteria can be amended *after* the grant of the options.

'... the employee will be given the right to acquire a number of shares specified in the option. The number may be reduced if performance conditions and key task conditions are not met. It is accepted by the Crown that to the extent that these conditions are set when the option is granted the employee has a right to acquire shares within s 185(1) notwithstanding that the number of shares which he may be entitled to acquire may be diminished by the operation of the conditions. I do not think that it makes any difference that the directors of the company reserve the right to impose new conditions but only in circumstances which are clearly stated and which must be "reasonably considered ... to be a fair measure of the performance of the holder of the relevant job" and which relate to specified matters, and to vary key tasks if and only if the directors consider that "a different key task would be fairer measure of the performance of the holder of the job" and one which "the Directors reasonably consider will result in any key task in relation to the job being less difficult to satisfy than it would have been without such amendment". Put shortly, in my judgment it can make no difference that the number of shares which the employee may be entitled to acquire on the exercise of the option may be governed not only by conditions set when the option is granted but by conditions subsequently imposed or varied but imposed or varied in good faith in order to ensure that the scheme operates fairly and effectively as an incentive scheme.'

The available evidence suggests that the schemes so far introduced have largely been in favour of top management. With the increase in employers' national insurance contributions and the consequent pressure to avoid paying large salary increases, it may be that schemes under the 1984 legislation will, in future, be made available to a greater range of employees. The evidence also suggests that many option holders exercise their rights and then immediately sell their shares. This is often because the employee needs to borrow the funds in order to exercise his options (for tax relief in respect of interest paid on loans taken out to acquire shares, see Chapter 4).   **[34.24]**

5   Unapproved schemes

As already discussed, the allotment of shares at an undervalue to an employee will normally result in an immediate charge to income tax. In addition, income tax may be charged on the grant of an option to acquire such shares; on any release or assignment of it; and on the exercise or omission to exercise the option (TA 1988 ss 135–136).

EXAMPLE 34.2

John is granted an option to acquire 10,000 shares in a company at 30p per share. The option can be exercised at any time in the next six years and the price is fixed at the current market value. John pays £10 for the option, which he exercises five years later when the shares are worth 75p. He sells the shares six months later for 85p per share.

(1)   There is no charge on the grant of the option since the option period does not exceed 7 years.

(2)   When the option is exercised, the sum taxed as an emolument is calculated as follows:

Market value of shares at exercise:		
10,000 × 75p		£7,500
Deduct		
Option price	£10	
Price paid 10,000 × 30p	£3,000	£3,010
Sum assessed to income tax under		
Schedule E		£4,490

Note: Tax is charged on the above sum *despite the fact that the shares have not been sold by the employee.*

(3)   On the subsequent sale of the shares any further gain is subject to CGT:

Sale proceeds: 10,000 × 85p		£8,500
Deduct		
Option price	£10	
Price paid	£3,000	
Sum assessed to income tax	£4,490	
		£7,500
Gain subject to CGT		£1,000

(*Note:* No account is taken of any indexation allowance or other allowable CGT expenses in this example.)

Apart from the rules on options, as has already been noted (see **[34.2]**), a subsequent increase in the value of shares held by an employee may be subject to income tax if the relevant shares were originally issued to the employee subject to restrictions which have been lifted.

Particular difficulties may arise when groups of companies wish to motivate employees of a subsidiary company by permitting them to acquire shares in that subsidiary rather than in the parent company. Given the comparative ease with which value can be shifted into a subsidiary (resulting in an increase in the value of the subsidiaries' shares), the legislation has to make special provision to cover such cases. Broadly, subsidiaries which do not satisfy the requirements laid down in FA 1988 s 86 are *'dependent subsidiaries'* and shares allotted therein will attract an income tax charge *either* when the employee sells the shares *or* seven years after he acquires them, *whichever is the earlier.*

EXAMPLE 34.3

Alan takes the opportunity in December 1988 to purchase 10,000 'B' ordinary shares in his employer Sad Ltd. The shares are subject to certain restrictions as a result of which their value is fixed at £5 per share, which Alan duly pays. After five years, in December 1993, the restrictions are lifted so that the shares rank for all purposes as ordinary shares in the company. As a result their value increases to £12. Some six months later, in July 1994, Alan sells the shares for £14 per share. The tax charges levied on Alan are as follows:

(1) *On the lifting of the restrictions in 1993* income tax will be charged (under Schedule E) on the amount by which the shares increased in value as a result of those restrictions being lifted. Accordingly, Alan will be taxed on £7 per share (ie on a total sum of £70,000).

(2) *On the disposal of the shares in 1994* his CGT charge will be computed allowing as a deductible expense both the sum originally paid for the shares (£5 per share) and the sum taxed in 1993 when the restrictions were lifted (a further £7 per share).

Therefore his gain (ignoring indexation and any other available deductions) is £2 per share (ie a total gain of £20,000).

Having described the complex income tax treatment of unapproved schemes (although these may result in a tax liability not greatly in excess of that under approved schemes—see [**34.51**]) what benefits do such schemes offer? *The key is flexibility.* Unapproved schemes can be selective in any way the employer wishes. They can relate to any type of share and can be made subject to adjustable performance targets.

So far, references to unapproved schemes have been to schemes which are not within the detailed requirements of approved schemes but still relate to actual share values. If the objective of the employer is to relate pay to performance of the company, then consideration should also be given to *phantom schemes.* These are basically bonuses paid to selected employees which are calculated by reference to the increase in value of the company's ordinary shares. The 'gain' (ie increase in value over the chosen period) is taxed as any other Schedule E emolument in the hands of the employee. From the company's point of view, the advantages include, first, the avoidance of the expense of creating a full-blown share option or incentive scheme; secondly, the fact that the bonus payments are deductible for corporation tax purposes; and, thirdly, the interests of other shareholders are not affected. [**34.25**]

6   **Employee trusts**

Unapproved employee trusts

The term 'employee trust' has no statutory definition but, in broad terms, an employee trust is a discretionary trust the actual and potential beneficiaries of which are defined by reference to employment. Such trusts may enjoy favoured treatment for inheritance tax, capital gain tax, income tax, corporation tax and stamp duty. Consequently, they may be used as a tax efficient means of providing not only incentives to employees but benefits for employees (eg those in difficult circumstances).

There are several other important functions of employee trusts. First, they offer non-quoted companies the opportunity of creating a market for the sale and purchase of their shares (without such a market, non-quoted companies cannot effectively embark upon any share incentive or share option scheme). Secondly, they can be used to build up a large shareholding in friendly hands so that the company will be protected against any unwanted take-overs and outside interferences. Thirdly, they promote relations between employer and employee since they can be viewed as a demonstration of an employer's concern for the welfare of his staff. Finally, and in the same way as approved 1978 schemes (see [**34.22**]), they offer the company further funds at low cost.

Payments by the establishing employer are deductible under normal principles if they are of a revenue (income) nature (see *Heather v P E Consulting Group* (1978): [**6.112**]). Such payments should not be made under a binding legal obligation nor expressed as instalments of a lump sum. The best policy is to make regular payments geared to a variable factor—eg a percentage of profits.

Payments by the trustees to employees will be emoluments taxable under Schedule E. The trustees will pay tax at 35% on any income which they receive and, if this is distributed, by ESC A68 the recipient employee will be entitled to a credit for this tax paid by the trustees.

The trust can be used simply to make cash payments to beneficiaries, or it can, for example, purchase shares and then sell them to the employees, the consideration being paid by instalments.

When dealing with trusts, IHT is an additional tax consideration. To qualify for favoured treatment, an employee trust must satisfy the conditions set out in IHTA 1984 s 86 and especially the requirement that *all or most* of the employees of the establishment employer *must be* within the class of potential beneficiaries. If the trust falls outside s 86, contributions to the trust may be transfers of value for IHT purposes (eg if the employer is a close company). Further, the trust will then be subject to an IHT charge on each ten-year anniversary and an exit charge when capital is distributed. (Further reference is made to this at p 453.)   [**34.26**]

Employee share ownership plans

An employer who makes contributions to and/or incurs costs in setting up a qualifying employee share ownership plan (an 'ESOP') can deduct those contributions (even if of a capital nature) and costs in full if, broadly, the following conditions are satisfied:
(1)   the beneficiaries of the ESOP include *all* full-time employees who have been working for the company for between one and five years. Part-time workers are therefore excluded. Former employees can be beneficiaries for up to 18 months after they have left the company;

(2) the ESOP trustees, within 9 months of receipt, apply the funds for a qualifying purpose: eg in the purchase of shares in the company establishing the trust; in the repayment and servicing of loans taken to purchase shares; in the making of payments to beneficiaries and in the payment of expenses (these are the same requirements as for approved profit sharing schemes);

(3) the ESOP trustees transfer any securities which they acquire to a beneficiary or to an approved profit sharing scheme (a '1978 scheme') within seven years of acquisition (ESOPs cannot be combined with savings related (SAYE) share option schemes); and

(4) the ESOP trustees are at least three in number and include one person who is a trust corporation, a solicitor or a member of another professional body approved by the Revenue. A majority of the trustees must be persons who are *not*, and have never been, directors of a company within the establishing company's group. However, a majority of the trustees *must be* persons who are employees of the group and who have been elected by the employees of the group.

ESOPs are able to borrow funds from the employing company or from third parties and, in the latter case, such loans may be repaid by means of tax deductible payments received from the company. An amendment to the financial assistance provisions in the 1985 Companies Act contained in Companies Act 1989 s 132 makes it clear that contributions to an ESOP made by a company in good faith in the interests of the company will not constitute illegal financial assistance.

Nevertheless, beyond the certainty that all contributions made by a company will be deductible, the qualifying ESOP introduced in 1989 offered no great benefit in comparison to the ordinary employee trust, since its tax position was precisely the same. Indeed, the stringent conditions to be satisfied if the trust was to qualify as an ESOP proved too much of a burden. Not surprisingly, therefore it appears that only one 'Statutory ESOP' has so far been set up! One particular point to note is that because an ESOP cannot benefit all employees (since those with less than one year's service must be excluded) it may attract the ten year anniversary IHT charge (currently at a maximum rate of 6%). It was widely predicted that the 1990 Finance Act would relax the statutory requirements. In fact, the only change was a provision enabling shareholders who sold their shares to a qualifying ESOP (which must hold a 10% stake in the company either at that time or within twelve months of the sale) to roll-over any capital gains tax that would otherwise be payable into the purchase of other chargeable assets acquired within six months of that sale. Not the least of the difficulties with the statutory ESOP is to ensure that the relevant trust documentation satisfies the detailed statutory requirements. An Inland Revenue Press Release of 9 May 1990 announced a clearance procedure which can be used by trustees of *an established trust* to obtain confirmation that a prospective vendor of shares will be entitled to hold-over relief if he sells his shares to them. Somewhat ludicrously this clearance procedure was not available in advance of the establishment of the trust but on 14 December 1990 it was announced that the Inland Revenue would be 'prepared to examine and comment on draft trust deeds submitted to them' (see (1991) STI 13).

There is scope for the involvement of ESOPs in management buy-outs. For practical purposes, the maximum percentages of a company's shares that could be placed in the hands of employees through an ESOP is probably 49%, with 51% owned by the managers. Banks dislike worker co-operatives—something which would arise if the ESOP took control.

Despite the considerable publicity surrounding the changes introduced in FA 1989, it is clear that if an employer is looking for tax efficient remuneration packages, employee trusts alone—whether ESOPs or unapproved trusts—are not particularly attractive.   **[34.27]**

7   **Profit Related Pay ('PRP')** (TA 1988 ss 169–184 Sch 8)

Income tax relief is available for payments made to employees under a registered PRP scheme. Under such a scheme part of an employee's pay fluctuates with the business profits of his employer. The Inland Revenue Press Release accompanying the introduction of PRP in 1987 pointed out that:

> 'Two considerable advantages flow from arrangements which relate pay to profits. First, the workforce have a more direct personal interest in the success of their business; and, second, there would be a greater degree of pay flexibility in the face of changing market conditions.'

PRP links payments to profits *not performance*: accordingly it will be payable even if profits remain static and each employee's entitlement is determined by the scheme rules—there is no discretionary element. Accordingly, the emphasis is not so much on providing incentives as to link in salary to profitability so that the employees as a group share in the good and bad times!

Subject to a maximum of 20% of his pay or £4,000 (whichever is the lower), an employee will receive the whole of his PRP tax free provided that it relates to profits made in an accounting period beginning on or after 1 April 1991. If the PRP relates to an accounting period before this date, only half of the PRP is tax free. PRP is not, however, free of National Insurance contributions. Note that the limits on tax free PRP do not restrict the amount of PRP which can be paid, merely the amount of tax relief.

In order to gain registration, a PRP scheme must satisfy the number of detailed conditions contained in TA 1988 Sch 8. For instance, the scheme must specify the *employment unit* to which it relates. This can be either the whole of a business or any part of a business which produces independently audited accounts. Following changes introduced by FA 1989, if there is an existing conventional PRP scheme, then a scheme covering employment units which have a central function (eg research or head office operations) but which do not themselves generate profits can also be registered. In that case, the amount of PRP must be calculated by reference to the profits of the business as a whole. Unlike the various share options and incentive schemes PRP is not limited to corporate employers: it can be established by any trading entity whether individual, partnership or corporation.

Other conditions for registration include the following:

(1) the scheme must include *at least 80%* of the employees within the employment unit. However, it may exclude part-time workers (ie up to 20 hours) and new recruits with less than three years service with the employer. Anyone with an interest in 25% or more of the ordinary share capital of the company must be excluded;

(2) the method of determining the 'profit pool', from which the PRP is paid must be set out out in the scheme and must be one of two methods:

Method A: a specified percentage of profits of the employment unit during the relevant period; or

Method B: by reference to the relationship between the profits for the relevant period and the profits of the preceding year:

(3) distribution of the pool must be complete and the scheme must specify when the payment to the employees is to take place. This does not mean that all participating employees must receive the same amount since the legislation specifically allows factors such as levels of remuneration and length of service to be taken into account. In addition the Revenue have indicated that attendance record and age are other factors which may be considered. It is, however, essential that the method of distribution is set out in the rules and based on objective factors rather than an exercise of discretion.

After an unenthusiastic reception, PRP has gathered popularity. By the end of March 1991, 1,277 schemes had been registered covering 350,100 employees. This represents an increase of 50% over the previous year in the number of employees covered by PRP. The increased tax benefits introduced by FA 1991 should encourage even more employers to adopt the scheme. **[34.28]]-[[34.40]**

III   CHOICE OF SCHEME

1   **Non-tax aspects**

Whenever any commercial transaction is considered it is vital to look at the tax implications from all angles. However, no transaction can or should be entirely tax driven. Thus, an employer should first decide what commercial objective he is seeking by his scheme of employee participation. Set out below is a list of the likely objectives, together with a note of the schemes (approved and non-approved) which may go at least some way towards achieving them. **[34.41]**

a) *Tax efficient bonus scheme*

Depending on considerations of size and selectivity, a PRP scheme can provide immediate tax efficient benefits; in the longer term, however, the share related approved schemes are the most efficient schemes to operate. The selectivity offered by FA 1984 schemes may be the deciding factor (see h) below). **[34.42]**

b) *Performance related incentives*

Unapproved schemes are better in this regard because targets can be changed and directly related to individual performance. With all approved schemes, targets must be fixed at the outset (although the decision in *IRC v Burton Group plc* (1990) affords some flexibility in approved schemes). If looking to profitability of the company, rather than individual employees, an FA 1978 scheme, or ESOP, may be preferred, since both enable the amount passing into the trust for the benefit of the employee to be directly related to the company's performance (subject in the former case to the usual limits). **[34.43]**

c) *Reward for growth in share value*

Share incentive schemes are preferable, probably share options, and again the selectivity of FA 1984 scheme makes them the more attractive of the approved schemes. However, if there are difficulties with Investment Protection Committees (see below), a phantom share option scheme or ESOP/ employee trust arrangement might be appropriate. **[34.44]**

d) *Retention of employees*

Long running schemes which cannot be shortened are required. An FA 1984 scheme or FA 1980 scheme are appropriate because they can be drawn over a long period and made subject to an employee remaining with the company. Unapproved schemes with restrictions on sale could also be used (but the implications of FA 1988 ss 77–89 (see [**34.25**]) may make these unattractive).   [**34.45**]

e) *Creation of 'friendly' share holdings*

With FA 1984 schemes, shares are often sold immediately after exercise of option and it is therefore better to use an employee trust or FA 1978 scheme to create a friendly block holding. This has the added benefit of the shares of the employees being 'co-ordinated' through trustees. Alternatively, use an FA 1978 scheme because these schemes tend not to result in an immediate sale because the employee does not need to borrow funds to exercise the option.   [**34.46**]

f) *Creation of market in non-quoted shares*

An ESOP or ordinary employee trust will be ideal.   [**34.47**]

g) *Generation of sense of identity between employees and the company*

Any form of share ownership should promote this and the normal procedure would be to tie this into a long-term commitment as suggested above. The employee trust is particularly useful in this respect.   [**34.48**]

h) *Selective employee participation*

One problem with all approved schemes (including ESOPs) is that they must apply to *all* employees (subject to qualifying periods of employment) with the exception of FA 1984 schemes. Should the FA 1984 scheme be unacceptable, consider an unapproved scheme which provides *total* flexibility on this matter.   [**34.49**]

2   **Tax aspects**

Having determined what type of scheme can best meet his commercial objectives, the employer will need to look at the relative tax benefits of the various schemes available. Two main questions need to be asked: first, do approved schemes offer real tax benefits in comparison with non-approved schemes and, second, if they do, which of the approved schemes are most beneficial?   [**34.50**]

Approved or unapproved?

So far as share based schemes are concerned, it has been explained that the benefits provided under *approved* schemes will be subject only to *CGT* in the employee's hands, and that any charge will arise only if and when the relevant shares are *sold*. By contrast, benefits provided for an employee under an *unapproved* scheme will always be taxed as *income* and charges can arise even *before sale*.

Prior to FA 1988, with a top rate of income tax of 60% as compared with a capital gains tax rate of only 30%, the attractions of approved schemes from an employee's taxation point of view were obvious. Since 1988–89, however, capital gains have been charged at either 25% (the basic rate of income tax) or (more likely) at the higher 40% rate. Accordingly, for many taxpayers, the rate of capital gains tax has been increased and, together with the reduction in the annual exemption to £5,500, *the taxation of such gains has to some extent been equated with the treatment of income profits.* To this extent, the distinction between approved and unapproved schemes has, therefore, become somewhat blurred.

However, a capital gain rather than an income profit will still be advantageous for the following reasons. First, the due date for payment of the two taxes differs: emoluments under Schedule E attract an immediate tax charge, whereas any capital gain realised will only fall into charge on 1 December following the tax year in which the disposal occurred. Secondly, in arriving at the chargeable gain, an individual will be entitled both to an indexation allowance and to an annual exemption of £5,500. Thirdly, the taxation of benefits received under approved schemes is only triggered off on the disposal of the shares: accordingly, so long as the employee or director intends to retain the shares over a period of years, no charge will arise. In due course, that individual may be able to arrange for disposals to occur in different tax years (thereby taking advantage of more than one annual exemption) and for disposals to be channelled through his family. **[34.51]**

Which approved scheme?

If the employer decides that his overall objectives fit within the structure of an approved scheme, which scheme should be chosen? This question should be answered by looking at the non-tax aspects of the matter, since it will be evident from these factors which is most appropriate.

The main difference between the various approved share incentive schemes lies in the amount of relief available, with FA 1984 share options generally providing the greatest tax benefit, and the attraction of selectivity.

The only wholly tax free benefits which can be obtained are those provided under PRP, but the limit imposed upon the amount of PRP reduces its attraction.

The employee trust offers no tax benefit to the employee at all and so, if such a scheme is adopted, it will not be for reasons of saving the employee tax.

From the *employer's* point of view, all contributions to whatever scheme, if wholly and exclusively for the purposes of the business, will be tax deductible. **[34.52]**

3 Other shareholders

The presence of institutional shareholders may be a further factor for a company considering setting up an employee participation scheme to consider. Any listed company must follow the rules of the investment protection committees ('IPCs') which impose limits as to the number of shares which can be subject to employee options and, broadly, set the ceiling at 10%. Further, IPCs generally do not accept the use of subsidiaries for share option schemes. For a company approaching this limit therefore, there will be a need to look to the schemes—approved or unapproved—which do not involve options. The obvious choice is the ESOP, over which, provided the trust purchases shares at market value, the IPCs will have no control. **[34.53]**

35 Taxation of the family unit

*"And what are you going to give me to make up
for all those wasted years on a joint assessment"*

'The present system for the taxation of married couples goes back 180 years. It taxes the income of a married woman as if it belonged to her husband. Quite simply, that is no longer acceptable. ... the time has come to take action. I therefore propose a major reform of personal taxation with two objectives. First, to give married women the same privacy and independence in their tax affairs as everyone else and second, to bring to an end the ways in which the tax system can penalise marriage. I have decided to introduce, at the earliest practical date, April 1990, a completely new system of independent taxation. ... The tax system will continue to recognise marriage as it should do. At the same time, from 1990 married women will pay their own tax, on the basis of their own income, and have their own tax return, when one is necessary. There will, of course, be nothing to stop married women from asking their husbands to handle their tax affairs, or vice versa, as before; and many will no doubt do so. But what matters is that, for the first time ever, married women will have the right to complete independence and privacy so far as tax is concerned.' (The Chancellor of the Exchequer, the Rt Hon Nigel Lawson MP, Budget Speech, 15 March 1988.) **[35.1]**

I INTRODUCTION

Until 6 April 1990 the income tax system proceeded on the basis that 'a woman's income chargeable to tax shall . . . be deemed for income tax purposes to be her husband's income and not to be her income' (see TA 1988 s 279—originally enacted in 1806). This system of **aggregation** attracted a growing volume of criticism in the 1980's. It had already been considered by two Royal Commissions earlier this century: the Royal Commission on Income Tax in 1920 and the Radcliffe Commission in 1954, both of which concluded in favour of a continuation of the present structure. In 1980 a Consultative Paper, *The Taxation of Husband and Wife* (Cmnd 8093), aired the problems but produced no obvious alternative to the present system. A further consultative Green Paper, *The Reform of Personal Taxation* (Cmnd 9756), was produced in March 1986 and, although it only elicited a 'disappointingly thin response', FA 1988 introduced a new system of independent taxation of husband and wife which came into force from 6 April 1990. This chapter concentrates on this new system: details of the tax treatment of spouses prior to this date may be found in earlier editions of this book.   [**35.2**]-[**35.20**]

II INCOME TAX

1 **Independent taxation of husband and wife** (see generally IR 83)

As explained in Chapter 4, from 6 April 1990 every taxpayer resident in the United Kingdon has been entitled to a personal allowance (£3,295 for 1991/92) that can be set against all types of income, both earned and unearned. The major advance this marks for the married woman is that she now has an allowance to set against her investment income. Under the previous system, whether she had elected to be taxed separately from her husband or had received the Wife's Earned Income Relief, such personal allowances as had been available could only be set against her earned income. Her investment income was always added to her husband's income and taxed at his rates.   [**35.21**]

2 **The married couple's allowance**

A man who is married and whose wife is living with him for any part of the tax year can claim the married couple's allowance for that year in addition to the personal allowance. For 1991/92 the married couple's allowance is £1,720 which represented the difference between the former Married Man's Allowance and the Single Person's Allowance. In the short term this allowance was retained to ensure that the position of the married couple did not worsen as a result of the introduction of independent taxation. This allowance was not, however, increased in 1991-92 and the apparent intention is to let it 'wither away'.

TA 1988 s 282 defines the phrase 'living with her husband' as follows:

'(1) A married woman shall be treated for income tax purposes as living with her husband unless—
  (a) They are separated under an Order of a Court of competent jurisdiction, or by Deed of Separation, or
  (b) They are in fact separated in such circumstances that the separation is likely to be permanent.

For income tax purposes, therefore, a marriage ends at the time of actual separation. Continuing to live in the same house will not normally amount to separation, although if the building is divided into two flats which are self-contained, it is likely that the couple will be living apart for income tax purposes (FA 1988 s 257A). In *Holmes v Mitchell* (1991) the husband and wife had ceased to be one household in 1972 and become two households even though they continued to live under the same roof and there was no physical division of the dwelling space. With the husband's subsequent declaration of intent to seek a divorce, some ten years later the circumstances of the separation were then such that it was likely to be permanent.

A husband may elect that all or part of the married couple's allowance be transferred to his wife in circumstances where his own income in a tax year is insufficient to make full use of the allowance. A wife on the other hand is not entitled to any part of that allowance *unless* her husband has asked his tax office to transfer it to her. By contrast, a husband and wife cannot transfer any part of the personal allowance to each other. If the married couple's allowance has been reduced in the year of marriage (see [**35.24**]) it is that reduced allowance which forms the maximum amount which can be transferred to the wife.

In calculating the amount of the married couple's allowance which is available for transfer to the wife a special calculation has to be made. The amount that can be transferred is the amount of the married couple's allowance which exceeds the husband's taxable income after his allowances and reliefs have been deducted. Mortgage interest payments under the MIRAS scheme, Business Expansion Scheme payments, and certain other payments on which basic rate tax relief is given at source are not deductible for the purpose of this transfer calculation, although non-MIRAS interest relief is deductible (TA 1988 s 257B).   [**35.22**]

EXAMPLE 35.1

Susan and Nicholas are a married couple living together throughout the tax year 1991–92. Nicholas has a part-time job bringing in £3,500 pa. In addition he has £500 of investment income and pays interest of £500 on their joint mortage under MIRAS Susan earns £20,000 pa.

Both Nicholas and Susan are entitled to the personal allowance for 1991–92 of £3,295. In addition Nicholas is entitled to the married couple's allowance of £1,720.

In order to calculate how much of the married couple's allowance can be transferred to Susan, Nicholas' total income is £4,000. No deduction is made for the interest paid under MIRAS for the purpose of this calculation.

	£	£
Nicholas' married couples' allowance		1,720
Deduct: total income	4,000	
minus his personal allowance	3,295	705
Married couples' allowance transferable to Susan		1,015

Nicholas and Susan's taxable income for 1991–92:

Nicholas			Susan		
	£	£		£	£
Income		4,000	Income		20,000
Allowances:			Allowances:		
Personal	3,295		Personal	3,295	
Married couple (part)	705	4,000	Married couple (part)	1,015	4,310
Taxable income		Nil	Taxable income		15,690

There are procedural requirements for a transfer of the married couple's allowance from husband to wife. The husband must give notice (on Form IR 575) to the relevant tax inspector that the relief is to be transferred. The notice must be given not later than six years after the end of the tax year to which it relates and once given is irrevocable (TA 1988 s 257B(3)).

3 Elderly couples

The increased allowances available in such cases are discussed in Chapter 4. [35.23]

4 Tax in year of marriage

The personal allowance is available to both husband and wife in the year of marriage in the normal way. However the married couple's allowance for the year of marriage is reduced by one-twelfth for each complete tax month before the date of marriage. For example, in the case of a couple marrying on 4 August, the man would lose three-twelfths of the married couple's allowance since there are three complete tax months in that tax year during which the couple are not married.

Where a man marries who is already entitled to the married couple's allowance (because of a previous marriage in the same tax year) the allowance in the year of marriage is not reduced.

If a married couple separate in one tax year but are reconciled in a later year, and were not divorced in the meantime, the husband will get the full married couple's allowance in the year of reconciliation. There is no *pro rata* reduction, as there is for the year of marriage. [35.24]

5 Death of either spouse

If the wife dies the husband will get the full married couple's allowance for that tax year, in addition to his personal allowance. For subsequent years he will receive only the personal allowance (assuming that he does not re-marry).

By contrast, if the husband dies, in addition to her personal allowance the wife will receive, first, any balance of the married couple's allowance which remains unused against her husband's income for that year; secondly, the additional personal allowance if she has a child living with her after her husband's death, and, thirdly, the Widow's Bereavement Allowance for the tax year in which the husband dies and for the following tax year, provided that she has not remarried by the start of that following year. The position of a surviving wife can be summarised diagrammatically as shown overleaf:

6 Reliefs, limits and exemptions

Mortgage interest relief From 6 April 1990 a husband and wife will share the mortgage interest relief allowance currently set at £30,000. If the loan is in their joint names, the £30,000 limit will be divided equally between them so that each will receive relief for payments of interest of up to £15,000. If, however, the loan is in the name of only one spouse then that person will get tax relief on the interest paid, up to the £30,000 limit.

However, it is possible for a married couple not wishing these rules to apply to make a joint election to the effect that the limit of the tax relief will be allocated between them *in any way they choose*. In the past this was

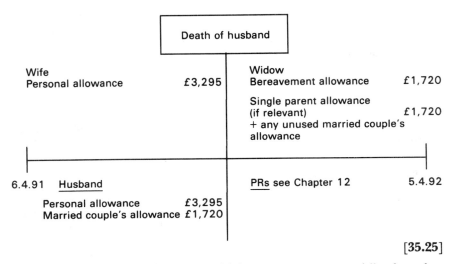

[35.25]

advisable where one spouse was a higher rate taxpayer, while the other was not, since the relief was more valuable for the spouse paying tax at higher rate. With the restriction of mortgage interest relief to basic rate income tax (see TA 1988 s 354(4) as amended by FA 1991 removing relief against assessments to excess liability) and since the majority of mortgages fall within the MIRAS scheme, the result is that as basic rate relief is given by deduction from the interest payments, *there is no longer any advantage in electing to transfer the benefit of the tax relief.* Only if the mortgage falls outside the MIRAS scheme will benefits remain where one spouse is a non-taxpayer (his share of interest should be transferred to the other spouse). The following account of the mechanics of making the joint election is, therefore, included largely for the purpose of explaining the mechanics of making (late!) elections for 1990–91.

Any election must be made within twelve months of the end of the tax year to which it applies or such longer period as the Board may allow (see the revised SP 9/89—the Board's discretion will normally be exercised if the delay has been caused by sickness, absence abroad, serious personal difficulties, or unavailability of the relevant information). Once made, that election will apply for subsequent years of assessment until it is amended or withdrawn.

Either husband or wife, having made an election, may for any subsequent year unilaterally withdraw the election and the election will then not have effect in relation to either of them for the year in which the notice of withdrawal is given or subsequent years. The parties then revert to the relief being allocated on an equal basis. The same time limits apply for revocation.

EXAMPLE 35.2

Andrew and Beverley have a joint mortgage of £40,000, £30,000 of which qualifies for mortgage interest relief. Andrew earns £35,000 pa while Beverley earns £10,000. Neither has any other income. The interest payments made in *1990–91* total £4,500.

Andrew and Beverley should elect that all the mortgage interest relief be allocated to Andrew, since he pays tax at the higher rate of 40%.

If interest relief split equally

	Andrew £	Beverley £
Salaries	35,000	10,000
Less: Mortgage interest	2,250	2,250
Personal allowance	3,005	3,005
Married couple's allowance	1,720	
	6,970	5,255
Taxable income	28,030	4,745
Tax payable:		
Tax at 25% (on first £20,700 for Andrew)	5,175	1,186.25
Excess at 40%	2,932	
	8,107	1,186.25

Total tax: £9,293.25

If interest relief all allocated to Andrew

	Andrew £	Beverley £
Salaries	35,000	10,000
Less: Mortage interest	4,500	
Personal allowance	3,005	3,005
Married couple's allowance	1,720	
	9,220	3,005
Taxable income	25,780	6,995
Tax payable:		
Tax at 25% (on first £20,700 for Andrew)	5,175	1,748.75
Excess at 40%	2,032	
	7,207	1,748.75

Total tax: £8,955.75 (tax saving = £337.50)

The appropriate form to submit to the tax office to make the necessary election is Form 15 (1990). Married couples with an existing allocation of interest election for 1989/90 should be sent a Form 15 (1990) to make the new election for 1990–91 and subsequent years (FA 1988 Sch 3 para 14). Their existing allocation election is not automatically carried forward. **[35.26]**

Business Expansion Scheme ('BES') Husband and wife each have their own minimum (£500) and maximum (£40,000) limits for BES relief on qualifying share subscriptions (see Chapter 4). **[35.27]**

Close company loans Close companies are exempt from a tax charge on loans to full-time employees without a material interest in their company, and their husbands or wives, if the sum of outstanding loans to the employee and the employee's husband or wife does not exceed £15,000. Under independent taxation there are separate £15,000 limits for husband and wife if both are employees of the company, and if a loan is made for the first time on or after 6 April 1990. **[35.28]**

Capital allowances and charges Capital allowances due by way of discharge or repayment are given against income of a specified class or, on election, against other income for the year or the following year. From 6 April 1990 such allowances can be set only against the income of the person who incurred the expenditure. Where charges on income are concerned, eg a donation to charity under a deed of covenant or the payment of an annuity, if a married couple are jointly liable to make a payment the amount each person *actually pays* is the amount of his or her charge for tax purposes. If it is unclear how much each person pays the tax office will adopt a 50:50 split.

Annual payments under a covenant made by a husband in favour of his wife, or *vice versa*, do not rank as a charge on the payer's income and the person who receives the payment does not pay tax on it. However, where a couple are separated, some relief on maintenance payments may be due (see Chapter 36).   [35.29]

7   Trading losses

From 1990/91 the trading loss of one spouse cannot be offset against the income of the other spouse. Instead, any unused loss may be carried forward to set against the income in the following year of the spouse who incurred the loss.   [35.30]

8   Jointly held property

The advent of independent taxation of husband and wife has necessitated the introduction of special rules to determine how income arising from property jointly owned by both spouses should be taxed. Previously, since such income was generally unearned income, it was taxed as the husband's regardless of the beneficial ownership of the property in question. The rules apply to 'income from assets held in the names of a husband and wife who are living together' (TA 1988 s 282A(1)).

The general rule is that income which arises from jointly held property will, for income tax purposes, be treated as income to which husband and wife are entitled equally (TA 1988 s 282A). Thus, if husband and wife have a joint building society account even if they have contributed to it in unequal proportions—each is treated as owning one-half of the interest arising, and taxed accordingly.

The 50:50 rule does not apply to income to which neither spouse is beneficially entitled; to partnership Case I and II Schedule D income; to the income of a married couple who are separated; to the situation where property is held in the name of one party only; or where some other legislation (eg that governing settlements) directs that the income should be taxed in a different way.

It is, however, possible for the general 50:50 rule to be displaced (eg in respect of income to which one spouse only is beneficially entitled or in respect of income to which they are beneficially entitled in unequal shares). For the rule to be displaced an appropriate declaration must be made specifying the shares in which the income is, in fact, beneficially enjoyed by one or both spouses. Any declaration must relate to both the income arising from the property and the property itself, and the income cannot be shared in different proportions to the capital. Any declaration will have effect in relation to income arising on or after the date of the declaration.

Notice of any declaration must be given to the appropriate tax inspector within the period of 60 days beginning with the date of the declaration and must be made on the prescribed Form 17.

EXAMPLE 35.3

John and Susan jointly own £1,000 10% loan stock in XYZ plc producing annual interest of £100. Each will be taxed on one-half of the income. They may enter into a declaration of trust giving John a 1% beneficial interest in the stock and Susan a 99% beneficial interest. If, following that trust, the appropriate declaration is made on form 17 and submitted to the Revenue within 60 days, as from the date of that declaration Susan will be taxed on 99% of the income and John on 1%.

Some spouses might prefer to rely on the 50:50 rule when, in fact, the asset is owned between them in different proportions. Say, for example, the husband owns an income-producing asset worth £1,000. He might transfer it into the joint names of himself and his wife but only give his wife a 1% beneficial interest in the asset. Nevertheless, if no unequal shares declaration is made, under the 50:50 rule the wife will be taxed on 50% of the income. The husband, however, will own 99% of the asset.   [35.31]

9 Planning opportunities

The new rules offer planning opportunities to many couples. In particular, if one spouse is a higher rate taxpayer and the other is subject to basic rate only, it will be advantageous for income tax purposes for the former to transfer income-producing assets to the other spouse to ensure that his or her personal allowance and basic rate of tax band is fully utilised. There may also be advantages (see [35.57]). Care must, however, be taken to ensure that any transfer is an outright gift of assets with 'no strings'. Certain gifts will not be treated as outright gifts, namely:
(1) a gift not carrying the right to the whole of the income from the property given, or
(2) a gift which is wholly or substantially a right to income (without being a gift of the underlying capital), or
(3) a gift subject to conditions, or
(4) a gift where the property given or any income or property derived from it is or might be paid to or for the benefit of the donor.
In such circumstances, the gift will be treated as a settlement and any income arising treated as the donor's for income tax purposes (TA 1988 ss 674A and 685). To be certain that the inter-spouse gift is effective for income tax purposes it is vital to ensure that the gift is outright, incapable of being revoked, unconditional and of matching proportions of income and capital.

The above rules do not catch a gift where the donee, of his or her own accord, chooses to apply the income or capital in some way which might benefit the donor and the Revenue have confirmed that property which might return to the donor following the death of the donee under the donee's will or under the intestacy rules will not, for that reason, fail to be treated as an outright gift.

As noted above, the one way of making an outright gift of unequal amounts of income and capital is to arrange for the capital to be owned jointly, albeit in unequal shares, and then to rely upon the presumption of equality to ensure that half of the income is taxed as that of the spouse with the small capital entitlement.   [35.32]–[35.50]

III   CAPITAL GAINS TAX

1   Separate taxation of gains

As from 6 April 1990 the gains of each spouse have been calculated separately and each is entitled to his or her own annual exemption (£5,500 for 1991–92). Previously the gains of a couple had been aggregated and, generally, added to the husband's income for the purpose of calculating the applicable rate of tax. Only one annual exemption had been available per couple.   [35.51]

2   Losses

The losses of a spouse can only be offset against his or her own chargeable gains and not the gains of the other spouse. Accordingly, if a spouse has unused losses in one tax year, they must be carried forward to subsequent tax years to set against the chargeable gains of that spouse.   [35.52]

3   Inter-spouse transfers (CGTA 1979 s 44)

The disposal of an asset by one spouse to another is treated as being for such consideration as gives rise to neither gain nor loss. This rule operates whether or not any consideration is furnished for the transfer and in spite of the couple being connected persons. Effectively, therefore, gains are held over and the asset will be acquired at the base cost of the disponer spouse together with any incidental costs involved in the disposal. The rule in s 44 applies only as long as the spouses are 'living together' *at any time* during the relevant tax year. The indexation allowance will be included in the deemed consideration.

EXAMPLE 35.4

Jim gives his wife Judy two birthday presents on 1 January 1991, a Ming vase which he acquired from Christie's on 1 April 1985 and a painting by William Roberts acquired on 10 April 1983.
    The disposal by Jim will be at no gain no loss and Judy's base costs will include an indexation allowance on the vase from April 1985 to January 1991 and on the picture from April 1983 to January 1991.

A little publicised legislative change occured at the time when independent taxation was introduced on to the statute book in 1988. That occasion was used to tidy up a number of the rules dealing with tax treatment of husband and wife and one such provision (TA 1988 s 282) concerned the question of when a married couple are 'separated' for income tax and CGT purposes. Apart from the well-known situation where they are 'living apart in such circumstances that the separation is likely to be permanent', a couple had also been deemed separated in the case where one was and the other was not resident in the UK during a year of assessment and also when, although both were UK resident, one was absent from the UK throughout the relevant tax year. FA 1988 Sch 3 para 11 repealed this deeming provision with effect from 1990–91. The result is that the couple now remain 'living together' (and therefore taxed as a married couple) in such circumstances. Hence CGTA 1979 s 44 will apply to inter-spouse transfers of chargeable assets.
    Assume, for instance, that the non-resident spouse were to transfer a plot of land in Herefordshire showing a substantial gain to the resident spouse.

By virtue of s 44 that land will now be acquired at no gain, no loss. *Contrast,* however, the position under the old deemed separation rules. Because the couple were not then living togther s 44 was inapplicable. Nonetheless they remained connected persons (because married: see CGTA 1979 s 63) and hence any transfer of chargeable assets would be at market value under CGTA 1979 s 29A (see s 62(2)). Hence a UK resident spouse would have acquired the land at current value so that the gain which had accrued during the ownership of the non-resident would be tax free. Alas, another loophole gone . . .! **[35.53]**

4 Retirement relief

Retirement relief is available to both spouses and may be used to ensure that gains of £750,000 in aggregate are exempt from charge (see Chapter 16). **[35.54]**

5 Cohabitees and children

General CGT principles operate for disposals between cohabitees and between parents and their children. In the case of disposals to children the connected persons rules operate with the result that any disposal will be deemed to be made at market value. **[35.55]**

6 Principal private residence

Only one principal private residence exemption is available where a married couple live together. **[35.56]**

7 Jointly held assets

Where assets are disposed of which were held in joint names of husband and wife, each spouse will be regarded as owning a half share of the asset and charged to CGT accordingly. This is subject to the couple having made a declaration that the asset is held in different shares: in such a case the gain is charged *pro rata* according to their respective shares in the property.

Any declaration that has been made for income tax purposes regarding jointly held property (see **[35.31]** above) will have a corresponding effect for CGT purposes. **[35.57]**

8 Planning opportunities

If one spouse's annual CGT exemption will not be utilised whilst the other spouse's is fully utilised, it may be worth the couple transferring assets (at no gain no loss under s 44 discussed above) to the 'poorer' spouse so that both exemptions are used. **[35.58]–[35.70]**

IV INHERITANCE TAX

1 General principles

There is no aggregation of spouses' chargeable transfers for IHT purposes so that they are treated as separate taxable entities and are each entitled to the full exemptions and reliefs. It is immaterial whether they are living together and a couple remain married for IHT until the decree absolute which terminates the marriage. If care is taken with the associated operations ([**21.81**]) and related property ([**21.67**]) rules, transfers between spouses offer an opportunity to mitigate IHT since they are exempt without limit (except where the donee spouse is domiciled abroad, when only £55,000 may be transferred free of IHT). This inter-spouse exemption means that full use may be taken of both spouses' exemptions and reliefs and benefits may be obtained by ensuring that both nil rate bands are fully used.   [**35.71**]

2 Equalisation between spouses

Before the changes in IHT rate bands made by FA 1988, the standard tax planning advice given to spouses was that each should make the same total of chargeable transfers: ie the chargeable transfers of the husband both during life and on death should be equal to those made by his wife. If this advice was followed then both would have taken full advantage of the lower rate bands of IHT. With the introduction of the simplified rate structure so that there is now merely two rates of tax (0% and 40%), this advice no longer holds good. Instead, ideal IHT planning for spouses should now be designed to ensure the following: [**35.72**]

1) *Full use is made of PETs*   Whenever practicable, PETs should be employed to transfer wealth *inter vivos* to future generations. The spouse with the greater life expectancy should make the bulk of such transfers in order to minimise the risk of the PET failing. If necessary, property can be transferred from the wealthy to the poorer spouse to enable the transfer to be made without the risk of the associated operations provisions applying (see [**21.81**]).   [**35.73**]

2) *Full use is made of the nil rate band*   In drafting family wills it is desirable to ensure that both spouses fully exhaust their nil rate bands: ie that both make chargeable gifts to, eg, children of £140,000. Above that level there is no IHT advantage in the first spouse to die making further chargeable transfers. Rather he should be advised to leave the balance to his surviving spouse who may then dispose of it to children either by means of PETs or by will. In such cases even if the transfer by the surviving spouse turns out to be chargeable no extra IHT will arise since all such transfers will fall within the 40% rate band.   [**35.74**]

EXAMPLE 35.5

Husband (H) has an estate of £500,000; wife (W) an estate of £85,000.

(1) *If H leaves all to W and dies first:*
      IHT on H's death   Nil (spouse exemption)
      IHT on W's death   £178,000 (on £585,000).

(2) *Contrast if H leaves £140,000 to his children with remainder only to W:*
      IHT on H's death   Nil (on £140,000)
      IHT on W's death   £122,000 (on £445,000).

Accordingly, IHT saved is £56,000 (ie 40% × £140,000).
(3) If W dies before H, full use could not be made of her nil rate band (because her estate only amounts to £85,000). It is therefore desirable on these facts for H to make an *inter vivos* transfer so that W has an estate large enough to cover the nil band.
(4) When drafting a family will designed to utilise the nil rate band it is possible

to leave a legacy equal to £140,000 (the current nil rate band) or, alternatively, if it is desired to take account of future increases in the threshold of that band, to employ a formula along the following lines:

> 'I GIVE such sum as at my death equals the maximum amount which could be given by this will without IHT becoming payable in respect of the gift.'

One risk thrown up by employing a formula is that should a future government dramatically increase the nil rate band (eg to £300,000) then the testator might find that his entire estate is going to the children so that inadequate provision is made for his spouse. When the combined estates for the husband and wife are relatively modest (below say £300,000), leaving £140,000 outright to the children on the death of the first spouse may be unacceptable since the couple will probably wish the bulk of the estate to pass to the survivor. The mini-discretionary trust (illustrated in *Example 35.6* below) provides a halfway house that may be employed in such cases.

EXAMPLE 35.6

Ma and Pa are relatively poor: joint assets below £275,000 including their dwelling house. It is likely that all or at least the bulk of the combined estate will be needed by the survivor and the scope for lifetime planning is non-existent. As discussed above it is obviously desirable that the nil rate band of the first to die is utilised. In this case, however, leaving £140,000 away from the surviving spouse is probably unacceptable since it will be desirable to ensure that the surviving spouse can obtain all the property should the need arise. At the same time, there are advantages of using up the nil rate band in favour of (say) children. One way of achieving both objectives is to set up a discretionary trust, often called a 'mini discretionary trust', of £140,000 in the following terms:

(a) *duration of trust:* the full perpetuity period—say, 80 years;
(b) *beneficiaries:* surviving spouse, children and grandchildren;
(c) *the discretion:* a wide discretion in the trustees to appoint both income and capital during the trust period;
(d) *provision in default:* should there still be unappointed assets at the end of the trust period the amount should be divided in equal shares amongst the living beneficiaries; and
(e) *protection of surviving spouse:* provision that the surviving spouse is to be the beneficiary with the greatest claim upon the trustees (if desired, the spouse could be appointed a trustee).

Such a trust has the attractions that there will be no IHT payable on creation through the use of the testator's nil rate band; assuming that the rates of IHT remain linked to inflation, subsequent anniversary and exit charges are likely to be nil or very small; and the paramount wish of the testator for flexibility is achieved since, if the need arises, the entire fund can be distributed to the surviving spouse; otherwise full use has been made of the testator's nil rate band.

3 How to leave property to a spouse: outright and limited gifts

A separate problem raised by gifts to spouses is whether such a gift should be absolute or for a limited (eg life) interest. So far as IHT is concerned, both types of gift fall within the spouse exemption so that it can generally be said that the tax is neutral. To some extent, therefore, the decision can be made on non-fiscal grounds.

The *outright gift* has the attraction of flexibility. The surviving spouse is free to use the property for any purpose and may therefore employ it to the best advantage of the family in the future. As an inevitable corollary, however, because the assets are given free from all conditions, an imprudent spouse may fritter away the inheritance and leave nothing for the children.

A *life interest* avoids the dangers inherent in the absolute gift by ensuring that the capital assets will eventually pass to persons entitled in remainder (usually children or grandchildren). Giving an interest in income may, however, be inadequate for the needs of the surviving spouse. A sudden emergency requiring a substantial capital outlay, for instance, may arise and if the absolute gift suffers from being too flexible the limited interest may well prove too inflexible! An alternative to the two major types of gifts considered above is for a limited interest to be conferred on the spouse, but for the trustees of the will to be given a power to advance capital sums to that beneficiary. Such a power can then be exercised should the need arise, bearing in mind that capital sums advanced to the interest in possession beneficiary are free from IHT (IHTA 1984 s 52(2)). Giving only a life interest to a surviving spouse may give rise to a further disadvantage in that it restricts the ability of that person to pass on the property by means of potentially exempt lifetime transfers. It is true that by including a power to advance capital as set out above, the problem can be partly solved: however, the end result is somewhat cumbrous with the trustee advancing assets to the life tenant in order for that person to make PETs of the same property.

A life interest may, however, be employed *to ensure that the surviving spouse makes a potentially exempt transfer.* Assume, for instance, that a husband wishes the bulk of his estate to pass on his death to his grandchildren on accumulation and maintenance trusts. His wife is much younger but he is concerned that, should he leave the property to her absolutely, it will never find its way to the grandchildren. On these facts the husband should be advised to settle property in his will with his spouse being given an immediate interest in possession. The trustees should then be given the power to terminate the interest (say six months after his death) whereupon the will should provide for the property to be held on the desired trusts for the grandchildren. There is no IHT charged on the husband's death because of the spouse exemption and the subsequent termination of the interest in possession will be a potentially exempt transfer by the surviving spouse (see **[22.127]** for a discussion of this flexible method of will drafting as compared to the traditional two year discretionary trust under IHTA 1984 s 144).   **[35.75]**

4 Cohabitees and children

The general principles of IHT apply to transfers between cohabitees (so that *inter vivos* transfers will be PETS: death transfers chargeable) and between parents and children. In the latter case the connected person provisions apply.   **[35.76]**

5 Post mortem adjustments

The rules governing *post mortem* rearrangements (see **[22.128]**) are bolstered up by an anti-avoidance provision in IHTA 1984 s 29A (inserted by FA 1989). It is relevant when there is an exempt transfer on death (eg to the surviving spouse) and the recipient then, in satisfaction of a claim against the estate of the deceased, disposes of property 'not derived from the death transfer'.   **[35.77]-[35.90]**

EXAMPLE 35.7

A dies leaving everything to Mrs A. Dependant B has a claim against A's estate but is 'bought-off' by Mrs A making a payment (out of her own resources) of £150,000.

(1) *In the absence of specific legislation* the arrangement would probably be a PET by Mrs A to B and so free from IHT provided Mrs A survived by seven years. Alternatively, it could be argued that there was no transfer of value since the compromise was a commercial arrangement under s 10 (see [**21.21**]). No IHT is charged on A's death.

(2) *Position under s 29A:* A's will is deemed amended to include a specific gift of £150,000 to B with the remainder (only) passing to Mrs A. Accordingly, an immediate IHT charge will arise.

V STAMP DUTY

A gift between spouses is (like all voluntary dispositions) exempt from *ad valorem* duty; a sale between spouses is subject to *ad valorem* duty only if it is made otherwise than in connection with the breakdown of the marriage (see FA 1985 s 83, and [**30.57**]). The residual 50p duty and adjudication requirement was removed for instruments executed after 1 May 1987 if the appropriate certificate is completed (Stamp Duty (Exempt Instruments) Regulations 1987 (SI 1987/516)—and see in particular categories H and L of the Schedule). [**35.91**]–[**35.110**]

VI ADMINISTRATION OF THE NEW SYSTEM

From 1990–91 each spouse's tax affairs will be dealt with separately, and not necessarily by the same tax office. It is each spouse's own responsibility to furnish, if required, a tax return in respect of his or her income and gains for the tax year in question.

The Revenue are not permitted to disclose information regarding one spouse's tax affairs to the other without the spouse in question's written permission. [**35.111**]–[**35.130**]

VII COMPARISONS IN THE TREATMENT OF SPOUSES AND COHABITEES

The later Thatcher/Lawson years witnessed little short of a revolution in the taxation of married couples and cohabitees. From the vantage point of 1991, it may be concluded that before 1988 cohabitees enjoyed certain important tax benefits denied to married couples: thereafter, the pendulum swung to the opposite extreme so that it is now married couples who enjoy benefits denied to cohabitees. It is not the purpose of this section to discuss the rival merits of cohabitation as against matrimony, nor indeed to consider what role taxation should play in influencing the conduct of individuals. It may, however, be suggested that to treat cohabitation on a par with marriage for taxation purposes must be impractical in cases where that relationship is likely to be transitory; in other cases (notably situations falling within the old idea of a 'common law marriage') a different argument may be thought persuasive, albeit that deciding when a temporary accommodation has become permanent may be far from easy! The recently published *Marriage and Divorce Statistics 1989* indicate that fewer single people are getting married and that those who have tried the experience are increasingly reluctant to repeat it: in both cases couples are opting to live with each other rather than go through the marriage ceremony. Finding a satisfactory tax regime for cohabitees is therefore a growing problem.

Apart from limited and piecemeal changes — such as the restriction of the so-called single person's allowance to ensure that only one such allowance was available to cohabitees — the major tax changes in recent years were brought about, first, by FA 1988 which severely curtailed the tax efficiency of maintenance payments and wholly removed the tax benefits associated with a deed of covenant and, secondly, by the introduction, from April 1990, of independent taxation for husband and wife. As some compensation for cohabitees it may be noted that various anti-avoidance rules based upon a test of 'connected persons' will not normally apply to them. In such cases transactions between the cohabiting couple will be taxed in the same way as transactions between strangers. Take, for instance, IHTA 1984 s 10, which is intended to ensure that IHT does not catch the bad bargain (see [**21.21**]). In the case of a transfer between cohabitees, in order to avoid any question of an IHT charge, it is only necessary to show an absence of gratuitous intent on the part of the transferor. It is not necessary to go further, as is the case when the transferee is a connected person, and to show that the transfer in question is one that would have been entered into with a third party. Admittedly this is small beer in the majority of cases where the crucial point in any case where property is transferred between a couple (whether married or otherwise) will be the exemption from charge for inter-spouse transfers.

Consider, however, as a second illustration the CGT rules which apply to tax the settlor on the gains realised by his trustees in cases where he has retained an interest in his trust. For UK trusts, FA 1988 Sch 10 limits the charge to situations where the settlor or his spouse (no mention of other members of the family, nor of cohabitation) can benefit directly or indirectly from property in the settlement (see [**14.75**]). The legislation on offshore trusts goes further: a settlor has an interest if a benefit may be enjoyed by a category of 'defined persons' which also includes children (plus their spouses) and companies controlled by such persons (including any company controlled by that company!) Still no mention of the cohabitee!

Turning to specific areas. So far as interest relief for mortgage payments is concerned, a married couple are restricted to one £30,000 mortgage ceiling so that it is not possible for both husband and wife to take out qualifying £30,000 loans. So far as the allocation of relief is concerned, although the presumption is that it will be divided equally between the couple it is possible for relief to be transferred, at the joint election of the parties, from one spouse to the other (but see [**35.26**]).

For loans taken out before 1 August 1988 to purchase a main residence, the £30,000 limit applied to each borrower although spouses were treated as one person and so entitled only to a single relief. Unmarried couples therefore could obtain twice as much relief as the married couple. For loans taken on or after that date this benefit has been removed and the £30,000 limit on relief is now given *per residence* irrespective of the number of borrowers. This restriction does not, of course, prevent cohabitees from each owning a property qualifying as their main residence. In such cases, not only will each have an available CGT exemption for that main residence, but in addition both may obtain income tax relief on qualifying loans of up to £30,000. In line with other provisions aimed at tax avoidance which have already been considered, resrictions on which loans qualify for the purpose of income tax relief (in TA 1988 s 355(5)) are aimed at artificial transactions and include situations where vendor and purchaser are husband and wife, or where the purchase involves a settlor (or his spouse) and the trustees of his settlement. Again there is no mention of the cohabitee!

A major area where cohabitees suffer tax disadvantages is that of tax allowances and reliefs. For income tax purposes, the restriction of the single parent allowance has already been noted and the introduction of a uniform personal allowance ('the' personal allowance) for all individuals irrespective of marital status was not accompanied by the immediate removal of all vestiges of the old married order. Accordingly a married couple are still given a special allowance — transferable from the husband to wife if he alone elects! — although it is envisaged that this hangover from the former tax treatment will disappear. Hence the level of the married couple's allowance (£1,720) has not been increased for the current tax year. For CGT purposes the annual exempt amount (up to £5,500 for 1991–92) is available to *all* taxpayers (and hence to both husband and wife) whilst for IHT the general exemptions (£3,000 per annum; gifts in consideration of marriage; and normal expenditure out of income) are, of course, available to all. Crucially, however, special reliefs are available to a married couple which enable assets to be transferred *inter se* without the risk of any tax charge. For IHT purposes this relief is unlimited in amount save for the situation where the donee spouse is a non-UK domiciliary (and therefore potentially outside the UK tax net). For CGT purposes, disposals between spouses are treated on a no-gain no-loss basis (see CGTA 1979 s 44).

It is the absence of any capital tax relief for transfers *inter se* which is the greatest disadvantage facing cohabitees. Elementary tax planning schemes are, as a result, fraught with difficulties. For income tax purposes, for instance, ensuring that a couple take full advantage of their individual allowances and basic rate tax band will frequently involve an outright transfer of an income-producing asset. In the case of cohabitees, care must be taken to ensure that if that transfer is a chargeable asset it falls within the transferor's annual CGT exemption whilst, for IHT purposes, if that transfer exceeds the £3,000 annual exemption it will constitute a potentially chargeable transfer. Will drafting for the cohabitor is likewise a problematic exercise: if everthing is left to his cohabitee, the estate will be subject to a 40% tax levy once the £140,000 nil rate band has been exhausted. There is no exempt transfer to shelter behind in such cases: no simple channelling operation which can be performed to make any tax liability disappear as in the case of married couples.

A common trap which arises in many cases is as follows. Assume that Terry and June cohabit in No 44 Railway Cuttings, a house which they own as joint tenants. Terry dies without having made a will (a negligent death) with the result that his free estate (ie his property other than his share of Railway Cuttings) passes to his parents. June is not, of course, entitled to any property on his intestacy although she could bring an action for reasonable financial provision under the Inheritance (Provision for Family and Dependants) Act 1975 provided she can show that she was financially dependent on Terry. In cases where both cohabitees have had full-time jobs this is unlikely to be the case. To return to the example, assume that the total value of Terry's estate exceeds the IHT nil rate threshold: say, for instance, that Terry's half-share in the house is worth £170,000 and that this free estate is likewise worth £170,000. (It may in passing be noticed that in valuing Terry's half-share in the house a discount on the basis of the joint occupation should be allowed. Such a discount is not, of course, available in the case of a half-share owned by husband and wife because of the related property rules in IHTA 1984 s 161: see [**21.67**].) The IHT bill (£80,000 assuming that Terry had an intact nil rate band) will be split equally and June will be accountable for the £40,000 attributable to Terry's share in the house since the burden of IHT charged on joint property falls on that property. She has received nothing under Terry's intestacy and given that his parents may be unwilling to make any contribution towards the IHT charge on Railway Cuttings, the end result is that unless she can afford to raise a mortgage or alternatively to pay the tax in instalments (with interest) she will end up being forced to sell the house.   [**35.131**]

36 Matrimonial breakdown

I   Income tax   [**36.2**]
II   Capital gains tax   [**36.21**]
III   Inheritance tax   [**36.41**]
IV   The matrimonial home   [**36.61**]

Matrimonial breakdown often has major tax repercussions. It is also an occasion when there is some scope for tax planning and where a number of pitfalls need to be avoided. Changes in the tax treatment of maintenance payments in FA 1988 meant that some of the traditional arrangements were no longer satisfactory. [**36.1**]

I INCOME TAX

1 General principles

On the breakdown of a marriage the parties revert to single status. For income tax purposes marriage ends when the parties separate 'in such circumstances that the separation is likely to be permanent'. With the introduction of independent taxation of spouses as from 6 April 1990, both parties will, in any event, have been taxed separately whilst married so that each will have been entitled to the personal allowance (£3,295 for 1991–92) with the husband—in most cases—also receiving the benefit of the married couple's allowance (£1,720 for 1991–92). This married couple's allowance will continue to be given to the man for the tax year of separation but thereafter each party will normally receive merely the personal allowance. If there are infant children the additional personal allowance may also be payable to the parent who has custody of those children (for further details see Chapter 4 where personal allowances and reliefs are dealt with). [**36.2**]

2 Effect of FA 1988 on maintenance payments

Under the guise of 'simplifying the tax treatment of maintenance payments' major changes in the treatment of such payments were made by FA 1988. As a result, new maintenance payments were largely removed from the tax system. In particular, payments in favour of children attract no tax relief whilst payments to a former spouse only qualify for tax relief up to a maximum of (in 1991–92) £1,720.

The importance of these changes went far beyond mere questions of simplification and, although poorer families remained largely unaffected, couples in the middle income bracket suffered because of the withdrawal of relief for payments in favour of children and the severe limitations on the relief in the case of payments to a former spouse. It seems inevitable that the changes must result in a reduction in the amounts paid under maintenance arrangements. For the wealthy, a switch to outright transfers of capital instead of income payments appears likely. Existing maintenance arrangements (as defined: see below) continue to benefit from tax relief whether in favour of an ex-spouse or children but the relief available is pegged at the level of the maintenance payment in 1988-89.

The position of 'new' maintenance payments will now be considered and the definition of 'an existing obligation' will be analysed. Finally, the tax treatment of payments made under obligations existing at the time the new rules were introduced will be explained.   **[36.3]**

3   Tax treatment of 'new' maintenance payments (TA 1988 s 374A inserted by FA 1988)

Payments of maintenance, whether to spouses or children, have largely been removed from the income tax system with the following three consequences. First, the payer is not entitled to deduct the sum paid as a charge on his income and is therefore forced to make the payment out of taxed income. Secondly, the sum is paid over gross to the recipient: there is no question of deducting income tax at source. Finally, the sum is received free from income tax: ie it no longer falls under Schedule D Case III as an annual payment (nor, in the case of payments arising outside the UK, under Schedule D Case V). Only limited compensation for the payer is offered by a special deduction from his taxable income equal to the married couple's allowance in 1991-92 this amounts to £1,720. It should be stressed that this extra allowance is only available in the case of payments to a former or separated spouse: it is not available in the case of maintenance payments made to children.   **[36.4]**

EXAMPLE 36.1

Under a court order made on 1 July 1990 Eric is obliged to make payments of £2,000 per annum to each of his infant children Robert and Rosie and payments of £3,500 per annum to his former wife Erica.

(1) Eric cannot deduct any of the payments from his income tax liability and therefore may have to meet the payments out of income which has suffered tax at the top rate of 40%.

(2) The sums are not treated as the income of the children nor as the income of Erica so that their personal allowances may be wasted.

(3) Only limited relief is provided by Eric being entitled to claim a deduction from his income in 1991-92 for up to £1,720 in respect of payments made to his former spouse (only).

4   'Existing obligations'

Maintenance payments made under existing obligations continue to attract income tax relief. Such obligations are defined as follows.

First, an obligation arising under a court order made before 15 March 1988 or before the end of June 1988 so long as the application to court was made on or before 15 March 1988.

Secondly, payments made under a deed executed or written agreement made before 15 March 1988 and received by the appropriate Tax Inspector before the end of June 1988.

Thirdly, payments under an oral agreement made before 15 March 1988 written particulars of which were received by the Tax Inspector before the end of June 1988.

Finally, payments made under a court order made on or after 15 March 1988 or under a written agreement made on or after that date where the order or agreement replaces, varies or supplements an order or agreement which falls within the foregoing definition of an existing obligation. Notice that the fourth category above does not contain any time limit: in other words, obligations in force on 15 March 1988 can be varied at any time in the future, although where such variation results in extra payments falling due, tax relief will only be available for extra payments made in the year 1988-89. It may be noted that FA 1988 s 38(3) refers to payments 'due and paid' for 1988-89 for the purpose of these pegging provisions. This appears to mean that where payments were in arrear at the end of 1988-89 those arrears neither qualify for relief from income tax in the year 1988-89 nor count towards the pegged limit for later years *until such time as they are actually paid*. Once they have been so paid they will then count towards the limit for the year in which they were due. On pegging see *Example 36.4*.   **[36.5]**

5 Tax treatment of payments made under existing obligations

The tax treatment of maintenance payments made before 15 March 1988 depended on whether they were made to a former spouse or to a child. In the former case, so long as the payment was made under a legal obligation (whether that obligation arose by written agreement; deed of covenant; or under a court order) the sum paid was fully deductible by the payer in arriving at his income tax computation and was taxed as the income of the recipient under Schedule D Case III. Technically, the payment constituted a charge on the payer's income with basic rate income tax being collected at source under the provisions of TA 1988 s 348 (see further Chapter 10).

In the case of payments to children, a similar result followed if a court order was obtained directing the payment to be made to the child direct, payments would then constitute a charge on the income of the payer; were made net of basic rate tax; and the recipient child was then entitled to recover income tax deducted at source to the extent of any unused personal allowance. Payments to infant unmarried children not made under a court order, however, did not attract this favourable tax relief since they were caught by TA 1988 s 663 (see Chapter 10) and were therefore taxed as the income of the payer.

EXAMPLE 36.2

By court order dated 1 July 1987, Jason (taxed in 1987-88 at 60% on the top slice of his income) is ordered to pay his former wife Griselda maintenance of £6,000 per annum and his infant son Steven £3,000 per annum.
(1) Jason can deduct £9,000 from his total income for 1987-88 so that the net cost of the payments to Jason is only 40%.
(2) He will deduct income tax at the basic rate from the payment, handing over only a net sum.
(3) Griselda and Steven are taxed on incomes of £6,000 and £3,000 per annum respectively with a credit for the basic rate income tax deducted at source by Jason.

Two other matters are worthy of note in connection with old maintenance payments. First, in exceptional circumstances such payments were made gross: for this to happen the payments in question had to satisfy the definition of a 'small maintenance payment' (see TA 1988 s 351). Secondly, the House of Lords in the case of *Sherdley v Sherdley* (1987) accepted that maintenance payments could be ordered by the court to cover a child's school fees and would then qualify for income tax relief. They further accepted that a custodial father could seek such orders against himself.

FA 1988 provided that payments made under existing obligations will continue to receive income tax relief as set out above whether the payments are made to a former or separated spouse or to a child. However, the following matters should be carefully noted. First, *in 1988-89* the payments continued to be made subject to deduction of basic rate income tax at source (unless the small maintenance provisions applied) and where the payments were to a former spouse that spouse could claim an extra personal allowance of £1,490. (Remarkably, therefore, the position of such a spouse was improved by a Finance Act designed to reduce tax relief on maintenance payments!)

For *1989-90 and following years*, however, payments under existing obligations ceased to be charges on the payer's income with the result that he only obtained tax relief on making a claim and made the payments gross (ie without deducting basic rate income tax at source). So far as the payee is concerned, he was directly taxed on the income received under Schedule D Case III. In the case of payments to a former spouse, the extra allowance of (£1,720 for 1991-92) continued to be available to the recipient.

EXAMPLE 36.3

Under a Court Order made in 1987 Julie is obliged to make payments to her former husband Hugo of £7,000 and to her infant child Katie of £2,000 per annum. Hugo has no other income and has custody of Katie. Under existing arrangements the tax treatment of these payments in 1991-92 is as follows:

(1)   Julie cannot deduct £9,000 in calculating her total income. She will need to submit a claim to obtain income tax relief.

(2)   The £2,000 received by Katie will be covered by her personal allowance and therefore tax free.

(3)   Of the £7,000 received by Hugo £5,015 will fall within his personal allowances (£3,295 being the personal allowance + £1,720 being the single parent allowance) and he can claim a deduction for a further sum of £1,720. Hence, he will only suffer income tax on the balance of £265.

It is possible for an election to be made by a person making maintenance payments under existing obligations for the new rules to apply to such payments. Such an election will rarely be of any benefit in the tax year 1991-92: one exception is where the payer of maintenance is non-UK resident and therefore obtains no tax relief on the payments whilst the recipient is subject to UK tax thereon – if the election is made the payments will be free of tax in the hands of the recipient. In future years an election may be beneficial if maintenance payments increase and the pegged limit for relief, discussed above, is less than the maximum amount of relief available under the new rules.

EXAMPLE 36.4

(1)   Under an existing obligation created by court order, Samson paid Delilah £15,000 pa and his child £3,000 pa by way of maintenance payments. In 1991-92 payments for the child ceased but the payments to Delilah were increased to £18,000 by an amendment order. The amendment will fall within FA 1988 s 36(5)(b) as being a variation in favour of an existing person and accordingly as the pegged sum for 1988-89 is £18,000 this amount

is available to cover the extra payment to Delilah. Accordingly the old rules will apply to this increased payment.

Note: This, at first sight, somewhat surprising result is confirmed in *Taxation*, 4 May 1989, p 117 where it is noted—in question 10—that the only limitation is that new recipients cannot be added. It remains, however, something of a moot point whether Delilah in this example would be taxed on the new amount (£18,000) or only on the sum received in 1988-89 (£15,000): see in particular FA 1988 s 38(4).)

(2) Under an existing obligation, Frank is ordered to pay his former wife, Sheila, £1,000 per annum. In 1991-92 that sum is increased to £2,500 per annum. As a result of pegging, under the old rules Frank can only deduct £1,000. However, under the new rules he will be entitled to a deduction of £1,720. Will an election be desirable in this case or will the total payment be split so that Frank will get a deduction for £1,720 under the new rules in any event?

Note that the election is irrevocable once made and will apply to all maintenance payments made by that payer. Accordingly, in *Example 36.4* if Frank was also obliged to make payments to his infant children it is unlikely that any election would be desirable since the new system affords no relief for such payments.

One problem which now arises is to decide what is to happen in the case of orders and agreements made under the old system involving the payment of a net sum after deduction of tax. Consider, for instance, the case where the payer is ordered to make payments to his former spouse of £20,000 pa 'free of tax'. In the current tax year will he be obliged to pay £20,000 or £20,000 grossed up by income tax at the current basic rate × If the latter, the sum of £26,666.67 will have to be handed over. As a second illustration, old maintenance arrangements were often in the form of a court order under which (say) a father was obliged to make payments to his infant child of 'such sum as will after deduction of income tax at the basic rate equal (specified) school fees'. Usually that sum was then paid to the school as agent for the child: a somewhat artificial device which seems to have prompted the 1988 changes! Again the problem which now arises is whether the father is obliged to hand over merely the school fees for the year or that amount grossed up at the 25% basic rate.

Essentially the answer to these questions involves an interpretation of the relevant agreement or court order. Matters are not quite that simple, however, since the sum handed over will be subject to income tax in the hands of the recipient so that the Revenue are of necessity involved. Having said that, the taxation of annual payments under Schedule D Case III depends upon income being received rather than mere receivability: income tax is therefore charged on the sum actually handed over (*Dewar v IRC* (1935); *Woodhouse v IRC* (1936)).

The Revenue accept that the matter turns on the interpretation of the relevant agreement or order and that they have no power to impose their own interpretation since the matter is one for the courts and the parties. In correspondence they have commented that they would accept any 'reasonable interpretation' of the agreement or order. It seems to the authors that they are in no real position to refuse to accept even an unreasonable interpretation!

All of which leaves open the question, what is the answer in the two examples above! In the first case, it is thought that the intention of the order is to provide the former spouse not just with £20,000 but also with the relevant tax credit. Accordingly, the sum to be handed over each year should be grossed up by the current basic rate of income tax. A similar view applies to the second case where the intention of the order is again not just to provide for the payment of the school fees but also to cover any income tax liability which might arise thereon or, alternatively, to provide for the enjoyment of the greater sum which would result from a repayment claim.

So much for existing orders: in the case of future orders and agreements, the crucial fact to remember is that what limited tax relief is now available (an allowance equal to the married couple's allowance which is given to the payer) is only available in the case of orders and payments in favour of a former spouse. *No tax advantage results from obtaining court orders in favour of children.* A second point to remember is that orders in the form of the examples discussed above should be avoided. What should now be ordered or agreed is that a gross sum be paid since tax thereon will now be collected from the recipient.   **[36.6]–[36.20]**

II   CAPITAL GAINS TAX

Disposals between spouses are not subject to CGT and are treated as made for a consideration which will produce neither gain nor loss (see CGTA 1979 s 44; Chapter 14). Once the spouses separate this provision ceases to apply and the ordinary rules of CGT operate (but note *Gubay v Kington* (1984)). Hence, a transfer of chargeable assets between spouses after their separation may be subject to CGT (see, for instance, *Aspden v Hildesley* (1982)). As a result of FA 1989 (which removed general hold-over relief) it is therefore crucial that the re-organisation of capital assets on the breakdown of a marriage should be arranged, so far as possible, to come within s 44. That section only applies in cases where the disposal is between spouses who 'in that year of assessment' were living togther. Accordingly, if assets are not transferred in the year of separation, the no gain no loss rule will be inapplicable. Although the exemption for inter-spouse transfers is lost in the tax year following separation, the couple remain connected persons until final divorce so that disposals between separation and divorce are deemed not to be bargains at arm's length, but are treated as for a consideration equal to the market value of the property (CGTA 1979 s 62).

For the year 1991–92 husband and wife are each entitled to their own annual CGT exemption (£5,500) and this entitlement will remain unaffected by separation.   **[36.21]–[36.40]**

III   INHERITANCE TAX

For IHT purposes marriage continues until the final divorce so that transfers between spouses after separation and before divorce continue to be exempt. After final divorce, the general rules operate, unless the dispositions are exempt under IHTA 1984 s 11 (see **[23.6]**). Maintenance payments fall within s 11 and are, therefore, exempt from IHT. However, s 11 is probably not wide enough to cover maintenance paid by way of a transfer of a capital sum or of a capital asset which may, therefore, be chargeable unless it does not reduce the transferor's estate (eg because it is in satisfaction of outstanding financial claims by the former spouse), or lacks gratuitous intent. In most cases the absence of gratuitous intent ensures no tax charge for transfers between former spouses which result from the breakdown of the marriage (see the statement of the Senior Registrar of the Family Division made with the agreement of the Revenue (1975) 119 SJ 396).   **[36.41]–[36.60]**

IV THE MATRIMONIAL HOME

1 The difficulties

The matrimonial home will often be the only valuable asset owned by a couple so that its destination on divorce poses a number of tax problems. Before considering these, however, it is important to discover who owns the home. One spouse may be the sole owner at law but the other spouse may have acquired an equitable interest in the property either expressly (eg by agreement between the parties in writing) or under a resulting or constructive trust arising from that spouse's substantial direct or indirect contributions to the purchase price of the property (see eg *Gissing v Gissing* (1971); *Hazell v Hazell* (1972); and contrast *Burns v Burns* (1984)). If the house is to be sold on divorce, or its ownership transferred in whole or in part from one (former) spouse to the other, problems of income tax, CGT and (exceptionally) IHT may arise.   **[36.61]**

2 Income tax

Usually the property will be subject to a mortgage in favour of either a building society or a bank. It is important to remember that to qualify for tax relief on the mortgage the borrower must own an interest in the property and must occupy it as his main residence. Relief for a house occupied by a former or separated spouse was removed by FA 1988. Accordingly, on a marriage breakdown, it is important to ensure that both an interest in the house and the mortgage thereon is transferred into the name of the occupying spouse (usually the estranged wife). Building societies and banks will normally be willing to agree to this arrangement as long as they are satisfied that the wife will have sufficient funds to pay the mortgage. In practice, proof that the husband is obliged to make adequate maintenance payments, or that the wife has sufficient alternative funds of her own, will suffice. For the husband this arrangement will be attractive because the wife is entitled to tax relief on the interest payments so that the sum that he is required to pay as maintenance is less than would have been the case had he directly discharged mortgage payments (which would not have qualified for tax relief).

If the MIRAS scheme applies to the mortgage the borrower is entitled to pay the interest net of basic rate tax even if he or she has little or no tax liability. Accordingly, to maximise family resources on a marriage breakdown it is important to ensure that interest paid by the occupying spouse is within this scheme. It is also important to ensure that the interest falls within the scheme before finalising the maintenance computations.   **[36.62]**

EXAMPLE 36.5

Jim and Judy have separated. Jim's income is £25,000. Judy has no income. The matrimonial home is in Jim's name alone and is to be occupied by Judy. It is charged with an outstanding mortgage of £20,000. The alternatives open to Jim and Judy are:

(1) Jim could go on paying the mortgage but would obtain no tax relief on the interest payments which he makes. Accordingly he should be advised to transfer an interest in the house to Judy together with an obligation to discharge the mortgage.

(2) Jim could therefore transfer the entire ownership of the house to Judy and arrange for the mortgage also to be transferred to her. She would then be entitled to the appropriate tax relief and Jim would pay her increased maintenance to cover the total cost of the payments. Care should be taken to ensure that the correct sum is paid: for instance, if the net repayments are £219 per month that is the sum which should be paid by way of extra maintenance. Jim will, of course, have the full £30,000 loan relief available should he decide (and should he be able to afford) to buy a further house.

(3) If Jim deserts Judy, she may have to take over the mortgage payments even though the house is registered in Jim's name. Strictly, she should obtain no relief on those payments, since she does not own any interest in the property. By concession, however, relief is allowed (see the pamphlet *Income Tax, Separation and Divorce:* IR 30).

3   Capital gains tax

Before separation any disposal of the matrimonial property will be exempt from CGT if it is the spouses' main residence. Once the parties separate, however, an absent spouse who has an interest in the property may incur a CGT liability on a disposal of it. Difficulties principally arise in two cases: assume in each case that the husband owns the house which he has left, and that the wife remains in occupation throughout.   **[36.63]**

Case 1   The house is to be transferred to the wife. This disposal by the husband will not fall within the no gain no loss rules of CGTA 1979 s 44 since the parties have been separated throughout the relevant tax year. Further, the husband has been absent from the house since the date of separation. So long as the disposal occurs within 3 years of that date, no charge will arise on any part of the gain (CGTA 1979 s 102(1) amended by FA 1991), but once that 3-year period expires, the proportion of the total gain that is deemed to have accrued from the end of that period may be chargeable (the appropriate calculation is described at **[16.71]**). Any charge is, however, avoided if concession D6 applies:

> 'Where a married couple separate or are divorced and one partner ceases to occupy the matrimonial home and subsequently as part of a financial settlement disposes of the home, or an interest in it, to the other partner, the home may be regarded for the purpose of sections 101 to 103 of the Capital Gains Tax Act 1979 as continuing to be a residence of the transferring partner from the date his or her occupation ceases until the date of transfer, provided that it has throughout this period been the other partner's only or main residence. Thus, where a husband leaves the matrimonial home while still owning it, the usual capital gains tax exemption or relief for a taxpayer's only or main residence would be given on the subsequent transfer to the wife, provided she has continued to live in the house and the husband has not elected that some other house should be treated for capital gains tax purposes as his main residence for this period.'

Provided that the wife has continuously occupied the house as her only or main residence and the husband has not elected for another house to be his main residence, the disposal of the house may, therefore, occur many years after the separation.   **[36.64]**

Case 2 The house is to be sold. If the sale occurs more than 3 years after the separation, ESC D6 (because the disposal is not to the wife) is not available, so that there will be a charge on a proportion of the total gain. [**36.65**]

4 IHT and stamp duty

Transactions involving the matrimonial home will not usually involve IHT. Either the inter-spouse exemption still applies or, after divorce, there is no gratuitous intent (see [**21.21**]). Instruments transferring property between spouses and former spouses executed after 25 March 1985 and as a result of the breakdown of marriage are not subject to *ad valorem* duty whether the transfer is made pursuant to a court order or by the agreement of the parties alone (see FA 1985 s 83). Furthermore, if the appropriate certificate is given there is no fixed 50p duty nor adjudication requirement (SI 1987/ 516). [**36.66**]

5 The taxation consequences of typical court orders

In order to consider the taxation implications of four typical court orders dealing with the matrimonial home on divorce, assume throughout that the spouse who has left (H) owns the matrimonial home. [**36.67**]

a) *The order for outright transfer (the 'clean-break')*

H is ordered to transfer the entire ownership of the house to W (see *Hanlon v Hanlon* (1978)). H may also be ordered to make maintenance payments covering, inter alia, any mortgage payments to be made by W. [**36.68**]

Income tax W will obtain relief on any mortgage interest payment if she makes them. [**36.69**]

CGT The disposal to W attracts no charge if it occurs within 3 years of separation; if it occurs later, there is no charge if ESC D6 applies. [**36.70**]

IHT No charge arises as a transfer pursuant to a court order lacks gratuitous intent. [**36.71**]

b) *H and W become joint owners of the house with sale postponed*

H is ordered to transfer an interest in the house to W. The couple will be tenants in common. W will be entitled to live in the house to the exclusion of H and the sale will be postponed until (for instance) the children reach 18 (see *Mesher v Mesher* (1980)). [**36.72**]

Income tax As W has an interest in the house she will be entitled to mortgage interest relief provided that she makes the payments. [**36.73**]

CGT When the half interest in the house is transferred to W the result is as in a) above. On the eventual sale of the house, a proportion of the gain on H's share will be chargeable (corresponding to his period of absence), unless it can be argued that the effect of the order is to create a settlement. Normally, jointly owned land is not settled (see CGTA 1979 s 46; *Kidson v MacDonald* (1974) and Chapter 18). It may, however, be argued that because W has an exclusive right to occupy under the terms of the order the parties are not 'jointly absolutely entitled' since they do not have identical interests in the property. Accordingly, if the property is settled, no CGT will be charged upon its disposal, because it will have been occupied by W 'under the terms of the settlement' (see CGTA 1979 s 104).   **[36.74]**

IHT   The property is not settled as there is no succession of interests (IHTA 1984 s 43). Hence if either party died their estate at death would include the half share of the house valued with a discount of 10–15%.   **[36.75]**

c) Settling the house

W is given the right to live in the house for her life, or until remarriage, or until voluntary departure, whichever happens first. Thereafter, the house is to be sold and the proceeds divided equally between H and W (see *Martin v Martin* (1977)).   **[36.76]**

Income tax   W has an interest in the property for the purpose of claiming tax relief on the mortgage payments.   **[36.77]**

CGT   The creation of the settlement will not be chargeable (as in a) above) and on the termination of the life interest although a deemed disposal under CGTA 1979 s 54(1) will occur (see **[18.43]**), no charge to CGT will arise because of either the main residence exemption (CGTA 1979 s 104) or because of the death exemption.   **[36.78]**

IHT   There will be no charge on the creation of the settlement (see a) above). W has an interest in possession and is, accordingly, deemed to own the house (IHTA 1984 s 50(5) and Chapter 25). On the ending of her life interest, a charge will not arise on the half share to which she or her estate then becomes entitled. If H is still alive, the other half share is excluded from charge under the reverter to settlor provisions (**[25.35]**). If H dies before W, his reversionary interest in the proceeds of sale is not excluded property, however, and is, therefore, chargeable (IHTA 1984 s 48(1); **[25.61]**) and a further charge will arise when the life interest ends in that half share on W's death since the revertor to settlor exemption does not apply.   **[36.79]**

d) Outright transfer subject to a charge over the property in favour of the transferor

H transfers the house to W, but is granted a charge over the property either for a specific sum (as in *Hector v Hector* (1973)), or for a proportion of the sale proceeds (as in *Browne v Pritchard* (1975)). Sale and payment may be postponed until the children attain 18 or until W dies or wishes to leave the house.   **[36.80]**

Income tax   To obtain mortgage interest relief W must make the mortgage payments.   **[36.81]**

IHT   The property is not settled, but belongs to W]–[no charge.   **[36.82]**

CGT   The transfer to W should not be chargeable on the principles in a) above. On the eventual sale, the position is not entirely clear. If H's charge is for a specific sum, this must be a debt due to H. Therefore, when the house is finally sold and the debt repaid there will be no charge to CGT on the repayment (CGTA 1979 s 134; see **[16.42]**). If the charge is for a proportionate share of the proceeds of sale, however, H's right is not a debt, but a *chose in action*, ie the right to a future uncertain sum; see *Marren v Ingles* (1980). As a result, when the house is eventually sold and a sum of money paid to H, there will be a chargeable disposal of that chose in action.   **[36.83]**

e) *Conclusions*

It must be stressed that the taxation factors are not the most important considerations to be borne in mind when considering financial adjustments upon a matrimonial breakdown. The outright transfer may be the ideal for tax purposes, but it leaves the husband with no interest in the former matrimonial home and so deprives him of any capital appreciation. Further, the court has no power to adjust property orders once made, so they must be correct at the start. Finally, a transfer of the house or an interest therein is quite different from a declaration (normally under the Married Women's Property Act 1882) that a woman owns, and has always owned, a share in the asset. No transfer is involved in such cases and all the taxation consequences of transfers discussed above are irrelevant.   **[36.84]**

37 Planning—gifts, wills and trusts

> '... every man is entitled if he can to order his affairs so as that the tax attaching under the appropriate Acts is less than it otherwise would be' (Lord Tomlin in *IRC v Duke of Westminster* (1936)).

The replacement of CTT by IHT necessitated a radical reappraisal of formerly accepted estate planning and will drafting techniques. In particular, the ability to make a wholly tax-free lifetime gift has opened a door through which wealth may be transferred to later generations. So far as personal tax planning is concerned, the trend of recent years has been for a reduction in tax rates accompanied by the abolition of traditional reliefs exemptions and shelters. This chapter is divided into two sections: in the first various aspects of personal tax planning are considered and in the second the problem of how to transfer wealth to a later generation is discussed.   [**37.1**]

I PERSONAL TAX PLANNING

After the restatement of the *Ramsay* principle in *Craven v White* (1988) sensible financial planning, as opposed to tax avoidance on a large and artificial scale, remains possible.

Composite transactions containing an artificial step designed to avoid or defer tax should obviously be avoided, but a single transaction which achieves a tax advantage remains permissible, eg there is no reason why an individual paying income tax at the highest rate should not invest in assets which will show only capital appreciation or 'shelter' his income by investment in the business expansion scheme. The following represents some of the basic tax saving methods that may be employed. [**37.2**]

1 Use of exemptions and reliefs

Full use of the available exemptions and reliefs is probably the single most advantageous planning advice that can be given. Realising capital gains annually so as to utilise the annual exemption and ensuring that the IHT lifetime exemptions and reliefs are used whenever circumstances permit are obvious examples. The various reliefs require careful study because of the detailed conditions precedent to their application, eg IHT business property relief will not apply if a contract to sell the property has been concluded before the date of its transfer (the transfer is then considered to be not of business property, but of the proceeds of sale; see Chapter 23). An asset sale by a company provides another example of a trap since it will leave the proprietors with the problems inherent in a 'cash-shell' company and may be disastrous if they wish to retire from the business (see Chapter 33). [**37.3**]

2 Life assurance: pension contributions

Life assurance has always been a valuable tool in the tax planner's armoury and has, if anything, increased in importance with the advent of IHT. Taking out insurance to cover the prospective tax bill on death is recommended although it must be remembered that the policy should be written in trust for the intended beneficiary (other than a spouse) thereby ensuring that the policy proceeds are not themselves taxed as part of the death estate. New problems were created by the introduction of IHT: the risk of a tax charge on a PET in the event of the donor dying within seven years may be insured against and as the value of the gift is fixed at the date of transfer, the maximum IHT liability (assuming that the rates of tax are not retrospectively increased) will be known so that some kind of decreasing seven-year term assurance will be appropriate (such insurance may, of course, be taken out by the donor as well as by the donee and it may be advantageous to settle such policies on discretionary trusts: this matter is further considered below).

For a taxpayer who can afford the payments, making the maximum permitted contributions into pension funds is a valuable way of reducing the income tax bill. Under the new pension regime both employed and self-employed may normally invest a substantial portion of net relevant earnings in approved schemes. In-house pension schemes will continue to offer significant advantages for the small business. [**37.4**]

3 Foreign domiciliaries and overseas tax planning

Such persons should avoid an IHT charge on UK property. Take, for instance, the individual domiciled and resident in France who wishes to buy a house in Liverpool for his son. If he buys the property himself it will be subject to IHT on his death (no income tax or CGT problems arise). He may avoid such a charge by purchasing the house through an overseas company owned by a foreign trust (see Chapter 7). The Revenue do, however, take the view that:

> 'someone who directly or indirectly controls the company (including control through some intermediary body such as a trust) which has provided him with living accommodation will generally be a director as defined in section 168 of ICTA 1988. He will therefore be chargeable to income tax on the annual value as calculated by reference to sections 145 and 146 ICTA 1988. This treatment would apply to any other Schedule E benefits similarly provided. It also applies whether or not the individual receives other emoluments from the company.'

So far as UK residents are concerned the transfer of assets and settlements abroad may result in income tax and CGT advantages: notably in a deferral of those taxes (see further Chapter 13 and Chapter 20).   [37.5]

4   Investment opportunities for higher rate taxpayers (and others?)

a) *Business expansion scheme ('BES')*

The attractions of the business expansion scheme have been discussed at [**4.83**]. Up to £40,000 can be invested in each tax year either directly or in an approved fund.   [37.6]

b) *Personal Equity Plans ('PEPs')*

FA 1986 introduced a new tax incentive aimed at encouraging saving through the purchase of shares and the scheme has been much improved by subsequent changes (now TA 1988 s 333). This personal equity plan (PEP) permits resident individuals to invest up to £6,000 pa with an authorised PEP manager. The resulting fund may be invested in equities listed on a UK stock exchange or dealt in on the USM, and up to £3,000 maximum can be placed in unit trusts. Although the initial investment attracts no tax relief (contrast the business expansion scheme), the following tax advantages are conferred.

First, no income tax is charged on income arising from the investment (ie dividends).

Secondly, no CGT is charged on the disposal of the investment nor on a switch of investments within the PEP. Given the relatively small sums that may be invested in the PEP, relief from CGT is presumably the major attraction for taxpayers although with a current annual exemption of £5,500 only individuals who have already exhausted that exemption will benefit. It should also be remembered that PEP fund managers will deduct a management charge (expected to be about 3% of the sum invested).

From 1 January 1992 it will be possible to invest up to £3,000 per annum in a single company PEP ('a corporate PEP') as well as investing £6,000 in one or more other companies ('the general PEP'). Accordingly, up to £9,000 per annum will be available for PEP investment. Since the PEP scheme began, a total 1.2 million plans have been taken out with over £3 billion invested.   [37.7]

c)   *Tax exempt special savings accounts ('TESSAs')*

The relative success of PEPs encouraged the introduction—from 1 January 1991—of tax exempt special savings accounts (TESSAs: FA 1990 s 28). The intention is to stimulate savings in (largely risk free) interest bearing accounts with banks and building societies. Adult individuals, and for this purpose husband and wife are, of course, separate individuals, can open one TESSA account with either a bank or building society in which interest earned on the sum deposited will be free from income tax *provided that* the savings are left in the account for five years. Maximum permitted savings over the five year period are £9,000 but this figure may be arrived at in a variety of ways since the scheme is intended to be flexible. For instance, the individual can make regular savings of up to £150 month or, alternatively, deposit up to £3,000 in the TESSA in year 1 with up to £1,800 in each of the following three years and then up to £600 in year 5.

It has to be said that the sums involved are hardly startling—for a basic rate taxpayer the saving will be less than £100 per annum. Once the five year time period has ended the account will then cease to qualify for tax relief with the result that interest subsequently earned will become subject to tax in the normal way.

An advantage of TESSA is that although the capital must remain frozen in the account during the five year period, interest earned in any one year (less a sum equivalent to the basic rate income tax for that year) may be withdrawn. Assume, for instance, that interest of £200 is credited to the account in June 1991—£150 may then be withdrawn without giving rise to any tax penalty. The saver is not therefore deprived of all benefit from his investment during the five year qualifying period. The retention of an amount equal to the basic rate tax on interest earned in each year is, in a sense, security in case the investment should cease to qualify for relief under TESSA. Of course, if the investment continues so to qualify for the full five year period, the retained amount of interest will then be handed to the taxpayer in full. By contrast, however, if the investment ceases to qualify (eg if capital is withdrawn or an excessive amount of interest withdrawn) the result will be an immediate cancellation of the tax advantages and the saver may then find himself in a worse position than would have been the case if he had made a non-TESSA investment since all the interest credited to the date of cancellation will immediately be subject to income tax *at the rates in force in the year of cancellation.* Not only is there a risk that rates may have risen since the interest was earned, but, in addition, taxing all the interest in a single year may result in the taxpayer becoming subject to higher rate liability. Should the taxpayer die during the five year qualifying period the TESSA will then end but without any tax charge arising.

The introduction of this new form of saving inevitably prompts comparisons with PEPs. An important difference is that unlike a PEP, a TESSA investment should not involve the investor in any management charges. There is of course nothing to stop an individual making both investments and, taking the limit of investments in PEPs at £9,000 per annum (both corporate and general PEP), the maximum tax free investment that can be made in both plans over the next five years is as follows:

Under the PEP — £9,000 × 5 = £45,000

Under TESSA — £9,000 over five years   **[37.8]**

d) *Save As You Earn ('SAYE')*

SAYE contracts were first introduced in 1969 and allow a fixed monthly saving of between (only!) £1 and £20 for five years (for SAYE share option schemes the monthly investment permitted is £250). As compared with TESSA investments, the sum invested (maximum £1,200 over five years) is therefore relatively derisory and no interest can be withdrawn during the five year period of the scheme. Instead the investor receives at the end a tax free bonus equivalent to the interest earned over the period and this bonus is doubled if the sum is not withdrawn for a further two years. The schemes can be offered by the Department for National Savings; unincorporated building societies and, as a result of (changes in FA 1990, banks.   **[37.9]**

e)   *Enterprise Zones*

Tax relief is available (suitable only for the higher rate taxpayer) on long-term investment in industrial buildings in a designated Enterprise Zone. Minimum investment is £5,000 and a full depreciation allowance, on the cost of the building, is available against taxable income. Loans taken out to fund the investment may likewise qualify for tax relief. Apart from the practical difficulties of selling the building, the depreciation allowance will, in any event, be clawed back if the sale occurs within 25 years.   **[37.10]**

5   **Transferring the family company**

Transferring ownership of the family company to members of the younger generation can be achieved without attracting a tax bill of any magnitude, although considerable advance planning is desirable since it is important that ownership of the business be transferred over as long a period as possible. The typical scheme proceeds as follows (assuming that the existing share capital is 100 £1 shares owned equally by A and B who each wish to transfer their holding to their children):

(1)   The existing share capital (100 £1 shares) is converted into 'A Ordinary Shares' and initially these shares attract 99% of the profits of the business and will entitle their owners to 99% of the assets on a winding up.

(2)   The sum of £100 is capitalised and 100 £1 shares are issued, fully paid, to the existing shareholders (ie a 1:1 bonus issue). These new shares are classified as 'B Ordinary Shares' and are transferred to the intended beneficiaries (ie A's and B's children).

(3)   At the end of a specified period (typically, twenty years) the B shares obtain those rights which formerly attached to the A shares—ie the attribution of 99% of the profits available for distribution and the right to 99% of the surplus assets on a winding up. At the same time the A shares become of nominal value. As a result of these steps the value of the company has, over a period of twenty years, been syphoned off into the B shares with the result that ownership of the business has shifted to the next generation.

The taxation consequences of this operation are as follows:

(1)   CGT: the issue of the bonus shares is a reorganisation which does not involve any disposal of assets by the existing shareholders. The transfer of the B ordinary shares is, therefore, a part disposal of assets, but the value of those shares is, at that time, low, and, in any event, any gain generated may be held over by a joint election under CGTA 1979 s 126. When the B shares acquire those rights which formerly attached to the A shares there should be no further tax charge and CGTA 1979 s 25 would not appear to be relevant at that time (any exercise of control will have occurred twenty years earlier, on the reorganisation).

(2)   Stamp duty: the transfer of the B Ordinary shares will, as a voluntary disposition, be free from duty and adjudication if the appropriate certificate is included.

(3)   IHT: the reorganisation and subsequent transfer would appear to form an associated operation within IHTA 1984 s 268 so that the fall in value

of the donor's estate as a result of both events will be relevant. This fall should, however, be relatively slight (reflecting the small value of the B shares) and any subsequent increase in the value of those shares results, not from any further disposition, but from the efflux of time.

Two other matters should be mentioned.

First, the time period that should elapse between the capital reorganisation and the value shifting into the B Ordinary Shares. Twenty years is the selected period in many precedents but the precise length of time must obviously depend upon the ages of the parties: the shorter the period the greater the fall in value of the donor's estate when the B shares are given away.

Secondly, there is the danger that the owner of the original A shares will die at a time when those shares still have a substantial value. This raises the problem of who they should be left to. Ideally, a spouse, so that IHT will not be charged, and they should probably *not* be left to the owners of the B shares in order to avoid any suggestion that such a legacy could be associated with the earlier reorganisation and transfer of the B shares. Presumably, a discretionary trust in which the B shareholders are beneficiaries would be a safer alternative; in any event, given the falling value of the A shares, the problem only arises in the short term.   **[37.11]**

6   Charitable gifts and the taxation of charities

The various tax incentives for charitable gifts are discussed in Appendix IX and include:

(1)   Higher rate income tax relief (without limit) for charitable covenants capable of exceeding three years. Available for both individuals and companies.

(2)   Deposit (or capital) covenants will not be attacked under the *Ramsay* principle.

(3)   FA 1986 introduced a payroll deduction scheme for employees (see now TA 1988, s 202).

(4)   Transfers to charities are exempt from IHT; are taxed on a no gain no loss basis for CGT; and there is a stamp duty exemption for instruments transferring property to a charity.

(5)   With effect from 1 October 1990 individuals and companies have been able to make 'one-off' payments to charity by way of 'Gift-Aid'.

(6)   Charities are generally exempt from corporation tax, income tax, and CGT provided that the income and gains are applied for charitable purposes only.

(7)   FA 1991 s 68 introduced tax relief for gifts by businesses (whether or not incorporated) of items of equipment—manufactured, sold or used in the course of the trade—to educational establishments (see now TA 1988 s 84).

The Finance Bill 1986 originally contained provisions to combat abuses of charitable relief (one particular abuse involved the return of 'gifts' to the donor after tax relief had been collected). The proposed anti-avoidance clauses drew a distinction between 'private indirect' charities and others and restricted the available tax reliefs in the former case. After fierce opposition the measures were withdrawn by the Government and revised provisions introduced (TA 1988 ss 505–6). Broadly, tax relief is restricted where a charity uses its funds for non-charitable expenditure or makes payments to overseas bodies without taking reasonable steps to ensure that the payments are then used for charitable purposes. Certain loans or investments which cannot be shown to be for the benefit of the charity will similarly lead to a withdrawal of relief. The distinction between private indirect and other charities was dropped.

Two other matters are worthy of note. First, covenanted payments made by a subsidiary company to its parent charity must be paid under deduction of tax if the payer is to obtain relief thereon (a refund of tax may be obtained by the recipient parent company in apropriate cases). Secondly, where a charity is only entitled to a partial tax exemption, higher rate tax relief for covenanted donations to that charity is similarly restricted.

Gift Aid may be employed to achieve a 'cake and eat it' result. It will be recalled that for the purposes of IHT there are certain situations where 'reading back fictions' are available. For instance, a deed of variation falling within IHTA 1984 s 142 may be read back into the will of the testator (and therefore taxed as if that testator had made the relevant disposition of property) and, similarly, a precatory gift, falling within IHTA 1984 s 143, attracts reading back. The fiction in both these cases holds good for IHT but not for income tax where the analysis remains that the original gift of the deceased became the property of the named beneficiary who then in turn transferred that property to another person.

Assume therefore that Berta, who has just died, has left £200,000 to her daughter Janice. Janice now wishes to make a substantial donation to Green (and therefore charitable) Causes. Accordingly, she employs the Gift Aid scheme to pay over £50,000 to the charity obtaining full income tax relief. As a quite separate operation she also enters into an instrument of variation whereby Berta's will is amended to provide for a gift of £50,000 to the charity (IHT free: if the tax has been paid a refund is therefore in order) with the remaining £150,000 being paid to Janice. Janice has combined Gift Aid with an instrument of variation and she may, if she so wishes, have a second slice of this particular cake in the next year since a will can, of course, be varied more than once within the relevant two year period.   [37.12]

7   Income and capital profits

Traditional tax planning advice has always been to ensure, so far as possible, that profits are realised in the form of capital gains rather than as income. Before 1965 this resulted in such profits being tax free: with the introduction of CGT it had the advantage that the profits were subject to a lower rate of charge (the flat 30% rate). Now that income tax rates have been extended to capital gains, the argument that capital profits can enjoy a lower tax rate is no longer relevant, and accordingly there will be circumstances when it may be desirable to realise the profits in the form of income (eg when the taxpayer has unused personal allowances; available loss relief; or can shelter the income by, for instance, investment in BES). In the majority of cases, however, it will still be advantageous for the profit to be subject to the capital gains tax regime since:

(i)   the chargeable gain may be reduced by an indexation allowance;
(ii) the taxpayer enjoys a £5,500 annual exemption;
(iii) no charge to CGT arises until a disposal takes place and this may be postponed until the most advantageous tax year;
(iv) CGT is not payable until 1 December in the following tax year;
(v)   gains on certain assets are exempt from CGT whilst certain other gains may not be subject to a tax charge (eg if they are covered by retirement relief) or may be rolled over so that the charge is postponed (eg if reinvestment relief is available).

Rebasing capital gains to 1982 coupled with the indexation allowance (currently running at over 65% in the case of 1982 assets) should now have the effect of unlocking certain assets. In many cases before rebasing the taxpayer will have felt that the built-in capital gains tax charge was prohibitive of any sale.   **[37.13]–[37.20]**

II   THE TRANSFER OF WEALTH

As mentioned earlier, the introduction of IHT has necessitated a thorough reconsideration of estate planning and will drafting. The following matters should be considered.   **[37.21]**

1   The attractions of lifetime gifts

Lifetime gifts, which satisfy the test for a potentially exempt transfer, are free of IHT so long as the donor survives the gift by seven years. So far as other taxes are concerned, any CGT liability may now be held-over only in limited cases (see Chapter 17) so that gifts of chargeable assets likely to produce a substantial chargeable gain must be avoided. Any instrument of transfer that is required to transfer the property is subject neither to stamp duty nor adjudication if the appropriate certificate is completed. When assets are retained until death IHT is then payable at rates of up to 40%.

The attractions of lifetime gifts are removed if the donor dies shortly after the gift. For CGT purposes, particularly unfortunate results may follow since the tax-free uplift on death will have been lost, CGT charged on the gain and no IHT advantage obtained (see Chapter 15).

Remember, however, that even a 'failed PET' (ie where the donor dies within seven years of his gift) may confer some tax advantages.

First, the value of the gift is generally frozen at the time when made (subject only to a reduction in value if the property has fallen in value by the date of death: see **[22.32]**). 'Asset freezing' therefore ensures that any increase in the value of gifted property slips through the tax net.

Secondly, tax is charged on the failed PET by reference to the rates of IHT current at either the time of the gift or the date of death *whichever is the lower* ('tax freezing').

Finally, taper relief may reduce the tax charge although not the donor's cumulative total once he survives his gift by three years: see **[22.32]**.

In most cases the significant advantages of lifetime giving will only be relevant to the very wealthy who can afford to part with substantial assets. For the moderately wealthy, the desirability of lifetime gifts will often be offset by the necessity to retain access to the property given, and the introduction of the reservation of benefit rules in FA 1986 have made this objective difficult to achieve (see further 9, below).   **[37.22]**

2   Seven-year cumulation and the use of exemptions and reliefs

As had always been the case with CTT, full use should be made of the exemptions and reliefs from IHT. The annual exemption (£3,000 pa) and exemption for normal expenditure out of income (especially useful for the payment of insurance premiums) should be fully utilised and, in the case of husband and wife, assets can be transferred between them, where necessary, to ensure full use of the exemptions.

The reduction of the cumulation period to seven years means that the IHT nil rate band (currently £140,000) can be given away every seven years.

In most cases lifetime gifts will constitute PETs and will therefore be presumed free of IHT. Should the taxpayer desire to make chargeable lifetime transfers, however, this ability to make transfers of value equal to the nil rate band every seven years may be crucial.

EXAMPLE 37.1

Zeus wishes to create a discretionary trust for his unruly family. He could settle £140,000 (thereby using up his nil rate band) and subsequently add to that settlement by transfers equal to his annual exemption. After seven years a second discretionary trust could be created and so on. (Note that capital gains held-over relief is available for transfers into—and out of—discretionary trusts.)

When a lifetime gift of business property is desired extra caution is required since even if business (or agricultural) relief is available at the time of the transfer it may not be available if the donor dies within seven years (see [23.51]).   [37.23]

3   What property should be given away

Assuming that the client is willing to make lifetime gifts and is in possession of substantial assets the next question to consider is what property should be given away *inter vivos*.

A number of obvious suggestions may be made: in principle, of course, assets which are currently at a low value but which may be expected substantially to increase in value offer the ideal solution.

(1) First *excluded property* which for inheritance tax purposes comprises all reversionary and future interests under settlements.

EXAMPLE 37.2

The beneficiaries under a settlement are A, the life tenant (aged 90); B, who will obtain a life interest on the death of A (he is aged 89); and C, entitled in remainder (aged 88).

As can be seen from these facts there is a risk of a triple tax charge: once on the death of A followed immediately by a second charge on the death of B and thereafter on the death of C. A is treated for inheritance tax purposes as owning the entire capital in the settlement: B and C therefore have excluded property (reversionary interests).

Ideal advice in this case would be for B to surrender up his life interest to the trustees (no tax charge since the property is excluded) and for C to assign his remainder interest to persons of the younger generation; typically to his own grandchildren (or even great-grandchildren[1]) on accumulation and maintenance trusts. By such devices the spectre of three tax charges is now replaced by the risk of a single charge levied as and when A dies.

So far as that charge is concerned if the view is taken that A at the age of 90 has a life expectancy of seven years (or alternatively if the beneficiaries are prepared to invest in a deep freeze) then he may now be encouraged to make a potentially exempt transfer of the property on to the accumulation and maintenance trusts established by C.

(2) The ideal property to transfer is *that which is likely to increase in value* in the future since, even if the transferor dies within seven years of his transfer,

it is that lower value which will fall into charge under the value freezing provisions considered earlier. Amongst typical items of property so qualifying are landlords' reversions where the lease is a wasting asset and private company shares where the business is new but is expected substantially to increase in value.

(3) So far as *insurance policies* are concerned, there will rarely be any attraction in allowing them to fall into the deceased's estate.

Far better for it to be held on trust even for a surviving spouse since although there will be no inheritance tax charge in any event, by settling the policy the moneys can be paid out to the surviving spouse immediately on production of the death certificate thereby providing an immediate provision of capital funds at the time when they are most likely to be badly needed.

In passing it may be noted that it is not just a straightforward insurance policy which can be settled in this fashion but also any *death in service* benefit under a standard retirement annuity scheme.

(4) On the death of an individual his estate is treated as including not just free estate but also settled property in which an *interest in possession* had been retained up until the date of death and this will have the result not just of swelling the value of assets at death but will also affect valuations of free estate.

EXAMPLE 37.3

Claude owns 49% of the shares in his family company, Money Box Ltd, and is the life tenant under a settlement which owns a further 12% of those shares. The remainder beneficiary is Claude's daughter. No dividend has ever been paid by the company. Consider the tax position if Claude were to surrender his interest in possession.

As matters stand at present Claude is treated as owning 61% of the shares and therefore will be assessed to inheritance tax on the value of a controlling shareholding (after business property relief of 50%). However he is deriving no benefit from the 12% of the shares held in trust (ignoring for these purposes the question of controlling the company) and therefore should consider giving up that interest before he dies. If he does so there will be a termination of his interest in possession (a potentially exempt transfer) and should tax be payable because of his death within seven years it will then be assessed in accordance with the rules set out in IHTA 1984 s 52. Under that provision it is stated that the tax charge shall be levied on the value of the property *in the settlement*. It is only the 12% of the shares which will therefore attract tax: in other words the provision excludes any question of valuing the fall in Claude's estate. The tax benefits deriving therefrom are therefore considerable since even if the surrender occurs immediately before Claude's death the IHT charge will merely be levied on a 12% shareholding and the charge on the following death on a 49% shareholding. Accordingly, a substantial valuation advantage will have been obtained and, furthermore, it will usually be the case that 50% business property relief remains available because Claude has retained a substantial minority shareholding. Can the benefit illustrated in *Example 37.3* be achieved in a situation where Claude owns 61% of the shares and transfers 12% to a trust in which he has an interest in possession? That interest is then surrendered as described above. **[37.24]**

4   Deathbed planning

The legislation is not full of loopholes which enable efficient deathbed tax planning. However there are certain matters which can be carried out even at the eleventh hour.

(1) First, the soon-to-die should be encouraged to exhaust all his *inter vivos exemptions and reliefs*—notably the £3,000 annual exemption which is, of course, not available for death transfers.

(2) In appropriate cases, and notably where farming clients are involved, scope exists to maximise the availability of agricultural property relief by *switching secured debts* from the agricultural property to the soon-to-die's free estate.

EXAMPLE 37.4

Farmer owns a farm qualifying for 50% relief, worth £1 million, subject to a mortgage of £500,000. He also owns investments worth £600,000.

(1) At present the value of agricultural property is £500,000 after deducting the mortgage and the value of the investments £600,000 so that the value of the death transfer will be £1,100,000. Agricultural property relief at 50% will reduce the net value of the farm to £250,000 leaving an IHT charge on £850,000.

(2) However, if the mortgage is switched to the investments, the value of agricultural property then becomes £1 million subject to 50% relief (reducing the chargeable value to £500,000) whilst the value of the investments is reduced to £100,000 (after deducting the £500,000 secured debt) thereby leaving a chargeable death estate of only £600,000. This switching of debts can occur *at any time*.

(3) One consequence of the introduction of inheritance tax and with it the gift with reservation was the possiblity of double charges arising. Typically this will be the case where a gift is made but because of the reservation rules the property is deemed to remain in the donor's estate at the date of his death.

To cope with this problem and other situations where double charges may arise the double charges regulations were eventually introduced in 1987. However a careful reading of the regulations suggests that loopholes exist which can be exploited by good old fashioned schemes!

EXAMPLE 37.5

Adam gives property worth £100,000 to his daughter Berta in 1988 and buys that property back for £75,000 (which represents less than full consideration) in 1990. He dies in 1991.

Regulation 4 affords relief where property has been given away within seven years of the death (so that it is brought into charge on death) but has come back into the donor's estate at the time of his death by a return gift from his donee. (In effect this regulation replaced the old mutual transfer relief which applied for CTT purposes.)

The crucial point to appreciate is that the regulation can apply when the property returns to the original donor's estate *otherwise than for full consideration*. Accordingly there is nothing to stop him buying back the property so long as he pays less than a full consideration.

If he does so the result will be that the regulation applies so that the sum paid to recover the property will pass out of his estate. This is what has happened in *Example 37.5* since if we assume that Adam dies without having bought back the property then the PET of £100,000 may be subject to inheritance tax. And if that property had been *given* back to him then *either* the original gift of £100,000 would attract a tax charge or the property in his estate at death would attract the tax charge and, under the regulations, the Revenue can choose whichever computation will yield the higher amount of tax.

What has happened in *Example 37.5* is, however, that Adam has *bought* the property back at *less than full consideration*. The general principle of giving relief against a double charge continues to apply so that only £100,000 will be taxed either as a lifetime gift or as part of his estate and, furthermore, the £75,000 paid for the property cannot be a chargeable transfer by Adam since it was not made with gratuitous intent *with the result that this sum slips out of Adam's estate*.

Obviously this loophole in the regulations can best be exploited in cases where a lifetime gift has already been made and is now, given the state of health of the donor, bound to be clawed into charge. In such cases buying back the property at an undervalue is attractive. In other cases it may be that the whole arrangement must be set up on the deathbed: in other words a property is given away and immediately bought back within a few hours of death. It seems unlikely that the Revenue would look kindly on such an obvious scheme but is there anything to lose . . .?   [37.25]

5 Discretionary trusts

The attractions of discretionary trusts (notably their flexibility) are well known and, in general, the IHT charging regime is not unfavourable to their existence. The tax is, for instance, always levied at half-rates and is charged on ten year anniversaries at 30% of those rates. Accordingly, the maximum IHT charge is 6% (30% × (¹/₂ of 40)). Where the property qualifies for agricultural or business relief and IHT is paid by instalments, the rate falls to a mere 0.3% pa.

The introduction of IHT affected discretionary trusts in two main ways. First, their position is improved in that it is only the previous chargeable transfers of the settlor in the seven years prior to creating the trust that must be cumulated in arriving at the anniversary charge. Secondly, in comparison with outright gifts and interest in possession trusts, their position is made less attractive since neither the creation of a discretionary trust nor any distribution from the trust fall within the definition of a potentially exempt transfer. Setting up a discretionary trust will usually amount to a chargeable lifetime transfer therefore, although the settlor may take advantage of his nil rate band as illustrated in *Example 37.1*. As some compensation, the changes in CGT hold-over relief introduced by FA 1989 mean that using a discretionary trust is one way in which this relief remains available. Discretionary trusts are likely to remain attractive in the following situations:

(a) Small inter vivos discretionary settlements (as in *Example 37.1* above). Notice also that two discretionary settlements can be used to create two nil band trusts when the transferor is transferring one and a half times his nil rate band: see *Example 37.6*.

EXAMPLE 37.6

A taxpayer transfers business property to two discretionary trusts as follows:

Into Discretionary Trust 1 property which reduces his estate by £70,000 after business property relief.

Into Discretionary Trust 2 property which reduces his estate by £35,000 after business property relief.

In both cases, assume that relief was given at 50% and that the business property is then sold by the trustees. The result is that the first discretionary trust is worth £140,000 and, in working out any inheritance tax charges, the settlor's cumulative total when the trust was created was nil. The second discretionary trust is worth £70,000 and was set up at a time when the cumulative total of the settlor was £70,000. Accordingly, the two trusts are nil rate band trusts, but remember that to avoid the related settlement rules, they should be created on separate days.

In appropriate cases a settlor can create a number of pilot settlements each with a full nil rate band.

EXAMPLE 37.7

S wishes to put £400,000 into discretionary trusts. He therefore creates four pilot trusts of £10 each on *different days* (so that they are not 'related settlements') and subsequently and *on the same day* pays £99,990 into each trust thus created. The trusts are not related since they are created on different days and each comprises £100,000. As transfers made on the same day are ignored in computing the settlor's cumulative total, that total is either £10 or £20 or £30 when the relevant addition is made. Notice that although each settlement will enjoy a full nil rate band, the transfer of £400,000 into settlement will of course attract an immediate IHT charge at half rates.

Also crucial to appreciate is the situation illustrated in *Example 37.1* where the original settlement fell within the nil rate band of the settlor since should this trust be broken up just before the first ten year anniversary then even though the property may substantially have increased in value no tax charge will result since the rate of charge is fixed by reference to the values originally settled.

EXAMPLE 37.8

A wishes to settle shares in A Ltd, current value £220,000, on wide discretionary trusts for his family including his wife (but excluding himself). In ten years time the shares will be worth £1 million. Consider whether a single settlement or, eg, four settlements each worth £55,000 would be best.

Assuming that the shares attract business property relief at 50% the inheritance tax consequences at the time of the first ten year charge are as follows:

(1) Assuming that a single settlement is employed, that charge will be levied on the value of property then in the settlement: ie £1,000,000 less 50% relief equals £500,000;

(2) Assuming, however, that four separate settlements each of £55,000 were created so that at the time of the anniversary charge each was worth £250,000. The IHT position would then depend upon whether the four settlements had originally been created on a single day (so that they are related settlements) or on four separate days.

(3) If the settlements are related settlements the periodic charge will be calculated

in the case of each settlement by assuming that the cumulative total of each was £82,500 (ie the value of the three settlements created on the same day—£55,000—less 50% business relief). Accordingly inheritance tax will be charged on a transfer from £82,500 to £207,500.

(4) By contrast if the settlements were created on four different days each settlement would be charged as follows:

Settlement 1: Inheritance tax will be charged on a transfer of £125,000 with no cumulative total.

Settlement 2: Inheritance tax will be charged on a transfer from £27,500 (cumulating *settlement 1*) to £152,500.

Settlement 3: Inheritance tax will be charged on a transfer from £55,000 (cumulating two earlier settlements) to £180,000.

Settlement 4: Inheritance tax will be charged on a transfer from £82,500 (the three earlier settlements) to £207,500.

Accordingly, if it is envisaged that the value of property in a settlement is likely to rise substantially (as may well be the case with private company shares), it will always be advantageous to create more than one settlement (subject of course to the probable increase in the cost of creation and administrative costs of running the settlements).

(b) In will drafting the use of the mini (£140,000) discretionary trust remains attractive for the smaller estate (see [**35.74**]).

(c) It may be possible to set up discretionary trusts by channelling property through an accumulation and maintenance trust (ie taking advantage of 'children of straw'). Furthermore, a creative use of the reservation of benefit rules may enable a discretionary trust to be created by a PET as in the following example. [**37.26**]

EXAMPLE 37.9

Devious wishes to create a discretionary trust in favour of his family (but excluding himself):

(1) He settles property on the appropriate discretionary trusts, but ensures that he reserves for himself a substantial benefit within FA 1986 s 102. Accordingly the diminution in his estate and the immediate IHT charge are very small.

(2) Later Devious releases his reserved benefit, so that there is a deemed PET of the settled property which is then held on discretionary trusts for his family. Accordingly, Devious has created that trust by a PET.

6 Interest in possession trusts

The definition of a PET includes the inter vivos creation and termination of interest in possession trusts. Accordingly, such trusts are treated in much the same way as outright gifts for IHT purposes. It is possible to build a degree of flexibility into these fixed interest trusts; trustees, for instance, may be given power to advance capital to the life tenant and to revoke the interest in possession without endangering the IHT status of the trust. Capital gains realised by trustees of interest in possession trusts are subject to charge at 25% (unless the settlor or his spouse is a beneficiary or has obtained a benefit from the trust). This will be attractive in cases where the life tenant would otherwise suffer a 40% charge. [**37.27**]

7 **Provision for infant children**

Any trust for a minor should be drafted to comply with the requirements for an accumulation and maintenance trust and contingent gifts to infants will normally fall within IHTA 1984 s 71. Absolute gifts have also proved attractive in recent years (see (1984) *Capital Taxes* p 66, see *Example 37.10*). [**37.28**]

> **EXAMPLE 37.10**
>
> Property is settled upon trust for Hubert, aged two, absolutely.
> *Income tax*: As Hubert owns the income, the 10% surcharge on trust income is not applicable. Hence, even if the income is accumulated (and it may have to be to avoid the deeming provisions of TA 1988 ss 663-4), the trustees only pay tax at the basic rate of 25% and Hubert can set his personal allowance against the income.
> *CGT*: The property is not settled (CGTA 1979 s 46), but is treated as belonging to Hubert. Chargeable gains made by the trustees can, therefore, be reduced by his annual exemption.
> *IHT*: Presumably the property is settled and Hubert has an interest in possession (see [**24.1**]), so that were he to die the capital of the fund would form part of his estate. Although the trust is not an accumulation and maintenance trust, its creation is a PET.

8 **Provision for a surviving spouse**

Transfers will not attract IHT because of the inter spouse exemption. The question of how much should be given to a spouse has already been considered at [**35.72**].

Apart from the question of how much to give, there is the separate problem of whether to give the surviving spouse a life or an absolute interest. IHT is now broadly neutral as between these two methods of giving and the decision can therefore be made on non-fiscal grounds. There is no doubt that the outright gift makes it easier for the surviving spouse to make future PETs and, if a life interest only is to be given, it will, therefore, be sensible for the trustees to be given a power to advance capital to that spouse. Giving the surviving spouse a revocable life interest enables life-time gifts to be channelled through that person (the 'compulsory PET'!). [**37.29**]

9 **Reserving benefits after FA 1986**

The avowed purpose behind the provisions of FA 1986 was to prevent the 'cake and eat it' arrangements that had flourished in the CTT era (see [**22.3**] for an analysis of these provisions). A major problem for the estate planner is the extent to which the rules achieve their purpose since, in addition to exceptions provided for in the legislation itself, there are a number of loopholes that may be exploited. Thus if care is taken in drafting the terms of the relevant gift, the retention rules may be inapplicable (see a) below). When it is necessary to identify the property given away for the purpose of imposing IHT, it may be that there is a defect in the rules of FA 1986 Sch 20 with regard to gifts of cash. Such gifts are expressly excluded from the rules and it is arguable that once the money is spent by the donee there is no property in which a benefit can be reserved (and a similar principle would apply if property originally given was turned into cash by the donee and that cash was then either dissipated or used to purchase a replacement asset). A further apparent loophole relates to inter-spouse transfers and is considered below (see d) below) whilst the new rules do not prevent the retention of control over the property given (see b), below). **[37.30]**

a) *Drafting: reservation or partial gift ('shearing')*

'[By retaining] something which he has never given, a donor does not bring himself within the mischief of the statutory provisions . . . In the simplest analysis, if A gives to B all his estates in Wiltshire except Blackacre, he does not except Blackacre out of what he has given; he just does not give Blackacre' (Lord Simonds in *St Aubyn v AG* (1952)). **[37.31]**

EXAMPLE 37.11

(1) A owned freehold land. A sheep farming business was carried on in partnership with his six children on it.
1913: he gave the land to his children. The partnership continued.
1929: A died.
What had he given away in 1913? Only his interest in the land subject to the rights of the partnership. Accordingly there was no property subject to a reservation of benefit (see *Munro v Stamp Duties Comr* (1934)).

(2) In 1934 a father made an absolute gift of grazing land to his son. In 1935 that land was bought into a partnership with, inter alia, the father. On the death of the father in 1952 it was held that he had reserved a benefit in the land because of his interest in the partnership. (See *Chick v Stamp Duties Comr* (1958): contrast (1) above in that interest of the father arose *after* the absolute gift.)

(3) A gift of freehold land was subject to an equitable obligation to grant an immediate lease back to the donor. There is dicta in the Court of Appeal that there must be a reservation of benefit in such cases, although in the particular case the donee had also entered into covenants (full repairing and to pay tithe redemption duty) which necessarily cut down what was given and so amounted to a reserved benefit (see *Nichols v IRC* (1975)).

(4) T owns Whiteacre. He grants a lease to a nominee, assigns the freehold reversion to his daughter, and continues to occupy the property. T has made a partial gift (of the reversion) and the retention of benefit rules do not apply (contrast *Nichols* ante).

There have been suggestions that the Revenue will not accept the efficacy of shearing operations unless the grant of the lease is a 'prior independent transaction'. Limited support for this view may be found in *obiter dicta* in the *Nichols* case and it should be noted that in *Munro* ((1), above) not only was there a substantial time gap between the grant of the lease and the gift of the freehold but, at the time when the lease was granted, the donor had no intention of making a gift of the freehold: ie it was both prior and demonstrably independent. Doubts about shearing operations have been increased as a result of *Kildrummy (Jersey) Ltd v IRC* (1990), a case decided in the Scottish Court of Session and concerning a stamp duty avoidance scheme.

Attempting to avoid duty, the taxpayers formed a Jersey company to which they granted a lease over property which they owned outright: the Kildrummy estate. That Jersey company executed a declaration that the lease was held 'in trust and as nominee for' the taxpayers. Just over one month later the freehold was disposed of to a second Jersey company. The Court of Session decided, unanimously, that the grant of the lease to the nominee company was null and void. Lord Sutherland commented as follows:

'There is no doubt that it is perfectly competent for a person to enter into a contract with his nominee but such a contract would normally be of an administrative nature to regulate the relationship between the parties and to describe the matters which the nominees are empowered to do by their principal. A contract of lease, however, is in my opinion of an entirely different nature. It involves the creation of mutual rights and obligations which can only be given any meaning if the contract is between two independent parties'.

The case has obvious relevance for the traditional shearing operation in both England and Scotland. Grounds exist for believing that the rules in Scotland may be different from those in England (see *Capital Taxes News*, March 1991, p 199) but, pending clarification on the point, any shearing operation should be approached with extreme caution and wherever practical the use of a nominee avoided. The grant of a lease by A into the joint names of himself and his wife (who is not his nominee) followed by a later gift of the freehold would be preferable.

b) *Settlements*

Although the basic principles have been discussed elsewhere, the following matters bear repeating. First, if the settlor reserves an interest for himself under his settlement, whether he does so expressly or whether his interest arises by operation of law, there is no reservation of benefit and he is treated as making a partial gift.

The position with regard to discretionary trusts is more problematic. It appears that if the settlor is one of the beneficiaries he is not entirely excluded from the property with the result that the entire fund will be included as part of his estate. In view of the limited nature of a discretionary beneficiary's rights (see *Gartside v IRC* (1968)), it is unlikely that he can be treated as making a partial gift.

Secondly, a danger arises if the settlor is one of the trustees and is entitled to remuneration as trustee. According to the estate duty case of *Oakes v Stamp Duties Comr* (1954) he has reserved a benefit. No danger arises, however, if the settlor/trustee is not entitled to remuneration and therefore it is possible for a donor to retain control over property given into settlement without infringing the reservation of benefit rules.   **[37.32]**

c) *Benefits which are permitted*

It is only necessary for the property to be enjoyed virtually to the entire exclusion of the donor thereby permitting the occasional visit or holiday (see **[22.5]**). More important is the exception where the donor provides full consideration for the benefit retained.   **[37.33]**

EXAMPLE 37.12

(1) Dad gives his farm to Phil but continues to reside in the farm house under a lease which requires him to pay a full rent. Dad's continued use of a part of the gifted property does not bring the reservation rules into play.

(2) Elderly parents make unconditional gifts of a share in their house to their children (so that the children become tenants in common with the parents). Assuming that they all reside in the house and each bears his share of the running cost, it appears that the parents' continued occupation or enjoyment of that part of the house which they have given away is in return for similar enjoyment by the children of the other part of the property. Accordingly, the parents' occupation is for full consideration (illustration given in Standing Committee G: Hansard 10 June 1986, col 425).

The restrictive nature of this illustration is all too obvious: it is assumed, for instance, that the children are occupying the house with their parents. If they lived elsewhere would their *right* to occupy be sufficient to lead to the same result? (Furthermore, if they never lived in the house after the making of the gift can they be said to have assumed 'full possession and enjoyment' of the gifted property?) It appears implicit in the statement that ownership of the house is divided equally between the various tenants in common since otherwise the full consideration argument would seem inapplicable.

Perhaps the major difficulty with the views expressed in the statement is that they appear to proceed upon the premise that the house is divided into 'parts' so that the parents use the children's 'part' in return for letting the children use their 'part'. In reality, of course, the interest of a tenant in common is in the whole property: *he is the owner of an undivided share.* Accordingly, the right of such a tenant to occupy the entire property is derived from the interest retained. As it does not amount to a reservation in the gifted share the full consideration argument becomes irrelevant. If this view is correct, it would follow that the precise interest of a tenant in common (eg does he have a 50% share or only 1%?) becomes irrelevant since whatever the size of the interest it confers a right to occupy the entirety.

d) *Reservation and spouses*

The reservation of benefit rules do not apply in the case of an inter spouse transfer nor do they prevent the donor from reserving a benefit in favour of his spouse. [37.34]

EXAMPLE 37.13

(1) S creates a discretionary trust. He is the unpaid trustee, his wife is one of the beneficiaries. S has not reserved any benefit although it appears that *if* his wife benefits under the trust and *if* he shares that benefit the Revenue will argue that he has not been excluded from enjoyment or benefit in the gifted property.

(2) H settles land on his wife, W, for life and reserves a benefit for himself. Her life interest is terminated after (say) six months by the trustees whereupon the land (burdened by H's reserved benefit) passes to his daughter. H does not fall within the reservation of benefit rules unless the revenue can successfully argue that there has been an associated operation so that H has made a direct gift with reservation to the daughter.

e) *Post death variations*

Instruments of variation and disclaimer provide an ideal way for transferring wealth without causing any tax charge to arise and even allow the disponor to reserve a benefit in the property.

EXAMPLE 37.14

Father leaves his country cottage to his daughter. She continues to use it for regular holidays and at all bank holidays but transfers it to her son by instrument of variation made within two years of father's death and read back into his will.

The crucial point to realise is that for inheritance tax purposes (although not capital gains!) the variation is treated as made by father for all IHT purposes so that his daughter has not made a gift of property capable of falling within the reservation of benefit provisions. [37.35]

10   **Conclusion**

Probably the best planning advice today is to avoid the wholly artificial pre-packaged scheme and to concentrate upon the opportunities specifically afforded in the legislation for tax saving. It should also be stressed that tax saving is not everything and that ultimately the whims and foibles of individuals will (and should) be paramount!   [**37.36**]

PART C APPENDICES

APPENDIX I: THE *GOURLEY* PRINCIPLE AND
GOLDEN HANDSHAKES

British Transport Commission v Gourley (1956) and subsequent cases are concerned
with the assessment of damages to be awarded by the courts in tort and
breach of contract. The cases are not concerned with the tax treatment
of the sum once it has been awarded. Damages in tort for personal injury
are not taxed, but damages for breach of contract, and, in tort, for financial
loss, may be subject to charge if they represent compensation for lost profits
(see *London and Thames Haven Oil Wharves Ltd v Attwooll* (1967)) and, especially,
when they are payable on the termination of an employment contract. (In
certain circumstances a disposal of contractual rights may attract CGT: see
[**14.7**]). The interrelation between *Gourley* and the golden handshake rules
will briefly be considered below. [**I.1**]

1 The assessment of damages by the court

Damages should compensate the innocent party in a breach of contract;
they should not normally penalise the contract breaker. Hence, if an
employment contract has been broken, the damages should reflect the fact
that, had the employee performed the contract, he would only have been
left with the benefit of a net sum after payment of tax. Therefore, the damages
awarded should be computed by reference to that net sum. Obviously this
will adequately compensate the plaintiff so long as the damages are not
themselves taxed; if they are, the net sum will be insufficient. [**I.2**]

2 The problem of TA 1988 s 148

Apart from the first £30,000 which is exempt, tax is imposed upon payments
made on a breach of an employment contract. It could be argued that once
a payment is subject to charge (as terminal payments are by virtue of TA 1988
s 148), there is no room for the application of the *Gourley* rule and a gross
sum should be paid. The courts, however, have distinguished between terminal
payments of less than £30,000 and those in excess of £30,000. A payment
below £30,000 is free of tax and, therefore, the amount awarded should
be calculated on Gourley principles (see *Parsons v BMN Laboratories* (1963)).
Lyndale Fashion Manufacturers v Rich (1973) shows that the calculation should
proceed as if the damages formed the highest slice of the recipient's income
for the year (see LS Gaz 1983 346). If the net damages exceed £30,000
(after making the appropriate Gourley deduction), those damages must be
increased by a sum equal to the estimated income tax that will be charged
on the award under TA 1988 s 148. This final net award will represent as
realistically as possible the actual loss suffered (*Shove v Downs Surgical plc*
(1984) and see (1984) MLR 471, where the conflicting decisions of the courts
are discussed). [**I.3**]

APPENDIX II: WOODLANDS AND SCHEDULE B

1   **Introduction**

The income taxation of commercial woodlands before 6 April 1988 fell under either Schedule B or, at the taxpayers election, under Schedule D Case I. As from 6 April 1988 the charge to tax under Schedule B was abolished and, subject to transitional provisions, the right of occupiers of commercial woodlands to elect for assessment under Schedule D Case I ceased on 15 March 1988. Thus, commercial woodlands have been wholly removed from the scope of income tax and corporation tax with the result that expenditure for the cost of planting and maintaining the trees will not be allowed as a tax deduction against other income and the proceeds from the sale of the trees will not be charged to tax.   **[II.1]**

2   **Taxation before 6 April 1988** (TA 1988 s 16)

Tax under Schedule B was levied on the occupier of woodlands managed on a commercial basis with a view to the realisation of profit. If the woodland was not so managed no liability to income tax arose. An 'occupier' for Schedule B did not include a person who had the use of woodlands for felling and removing timber in connection with his trade and who was taxed on his profits under Schedule D Case I.

Schedule B tax was unique in being levied on a notional income, equivalent to one-third of the 'annual value' of the land. This was calculated as the rent an occupier would receive if the land was to be let in its natural and unimproved state (ignoring any planted trees) under a lease whereby the tenant paid the rent and the landlord was responsible for the cost of repairs and insurance.

Although the annual value generally produced a low taxable income (the Revenue estimated it to be an average of about 15p per acre) it was still likely to exceed the occupier's actual income while the trees matured. No deduction for expenses nor capital allowances could be claimed under Schedule B.

Accordingly, the occupier was given an election to be taxed on his actual profits (if any) calculated under Schedule D Case I. This election was irreversible as regards that taxpayer's period of occupation and an occupier was not able to be selective in his election which had to apply to all woodlands on the same estate. Under Schedule D Case I, the profits from the occupation of the woodlands constituted a trade: felled timber was treated as stock in trade, but not the growing timber which was a fixed asset.

By contrast, if the taxpayer carried on a trade in products derived from the woodlands, this has always been (and continues to be) treated as a separate trade taxed under Schedule D Case I. In *Collins v Fraser* (1969), for instance, the occupier of woodlands who manufactured and sold crates made from the timber was held to be carrying on a separate trade.

Generally, taxpayers made an election under Schedule D Case I when the trees were immature and non-income producing so that they could claim capital allowances and loss relief. Once the trees reached maturity and became income producing they would transfer the woodland to a partnership or company which they controlled in order to revert to the Schedule B basis. There was no requirement that a new occupier should be unconnected with the previous one.

Announcing the ending of the old tax system in his 1988 Budget speech, the Chancellor commented that:

> 'the present system cannot be justified. It enables top rate taxpayers in particular to shelter other income from tax, by setting it against expenditure in forestry, while the proceeds from any eventual sale are effectively tax free. It is, perhaps, a measure of the absurdity of the present system that the exemption of commercial woodlands from tax will, in time, actually increase tax revenues by over £10,000,000 a year.'   [**II.2**]

3 **Transitional provisions** (FA 1988 Sch 6 para 4)

An occupier of commercial woodlands may still elect to be assessed under Schedule D Case I after 15 March 1988 (thereby obtaining the deductions noted above) if:

(a) he made arrangements for his occupation of the woodlands before that date; *or*

(b) he was occupying the woodlands on that date; *or*

(c) although not occupying them on that date he subsequently did occupy them, having entered into a contract for the afforestation of the land or applied for a grant from the Forestry Commission relating to the use of the land for forestry before 15 March.

If an occupier is able to make an election after 15 March 1988 he is effectively in the same position as he would have been before 6 April 1988. However, the transitional period will cease on 6 April 1993 when commercial woodland will be completely removed from the scope of income and corporation tax.

Election for taxation under Schedule D Case I must be made within two years after the end of the chargeable period to which it relates, and is irreversible. The election will extend to the whole of the woodlands on the estate but woodlands may be treated as a separate estate if the occupier so elects. As with the old regime, however, a change of occupier of the woodlands will terminate the Schedule D election regardless of any connection between the new and former occupier.   [**II.3**]

4 **Taxation after 5 April 1988** (FA 1988 Sch 6 para 2)

Unless an occupier has made a Schedule D Case I election before 15 March 1988 or is able to make such an election after that date under the transitional rules, his income from commercial woodlands falls outside the scope of income tax. His profits are therefore tax free, but his losses and expenses go unrelieved, and capital allowances are not available.   [**II.4**]

APPENDIX III: INHERITANCE TAX FORMS: COMPLETING THE IHT 200

1 General introduction

From 20 March 1989, eight new IHT forms for England and Wales became available. They replaced the old CTT forms which had continued in use after the demise of that tax in 1986. The full list of the new forms is as follows:

Subject	*Form*
(a) Death	
Account to lead to grant of representation of transferor who died domiciled in the United Kingdom on or after 18 March 1986	IHT 200
Alternative where deceased died domiciled out of the United Kingdom	IHT 201
Deceased died domiciled in the United Kingdom, but the estate does not exceed the inheritance tax threshold at the time of death and certain other conditions are met	IHT 202
[Instructions for completion of IHT 200 and IHT 201]	IHT 210
(b) *Lifetime transfers*	
Transfers of value made on or after 18 March 1986, including:	IHT 100
(i) potentially exempt transfers ('PETs') chargeable on death of the transferor within seven years;	
(ii) gifts of property with reservation;	
(iii) terminations of interests in possession in settled property; and	
(iv) other chargeable lifetime transfers.	
[Instructions for completion of IHT 100]	IHT 110
(c) *Discretionary trusts*	
Chargeable events on or after 25 July 1986 involving settlements without an interest in possession	IHT 101
[Instructions for completion of IHT 101]	IHT 111

[III.1]

2 Completing the IHT Account 200

General

IHT Form 200 is the appropriate form for PRs to use when applying for a grant of representation to the estate of a deceased person who dies domiciled in the UK where the estate is not an excepted estate and where IHT Form 202 is inapplicable. For a description of how to complete the form, see the booklet (Form 210). IHT Form 200 contains 12 pages. If tax is payable it must be accompanied, in appropriate circumstances, by Form 40 (schedule of shares and securities) and Form 37B (land owned by the deceased). The Account divides into the following parts:

(a) Pages 1 and 2 contain the personal details of the deceased and a declaration signed by the intended PRs that the form is correctly completed.

(b) Page 3 consists of questions designed to discover whether the deceased made chargeable lifetime transfers which might not otherwise be apparent from a list of his assets.

(c) Pages 4–9 comprise sections 1, 2, 3 and 4 of the Account:

Section 1 lists all the property of the deceased in the UK which he owned solely and beneficially before his death and which now vests in his PRs (excluding property over which he had a general power of appointment exercisable by will). It is divided into two parts.

Part A is for property on which tax cannot be paid by instalments (eg chattels) and on which PRs must pay IHT on delivery of the form.

Part B is for property subject to the instalment option (eg land). In both parts the gross value of the property must be entered, any liabilities which reduce that value being shown separately.

By FA 1986 s 103 certain 'artificial' debts created after 17 March 1986 (see [**22.13**] and page 9 of the Account) are not deductible.

Section 2 is for property beneficially owned by the deceased, which does not vest in his PRs on death, but for which they are liable to pay the IHT. It includes foreign and nominated property and jointly owned property which passes to a co-owner by right of survivorship. It is also divided into two parts; part A for property without the instalment option (less liabilities); part B for property with the instalment option (less liabilities).

Section 3 is for property in which the deceased had a limited interest under a trust (eg as life tenant) and property over which he had a general power of appointment exercisable by will.

The trustees of the settlement, not the PRs, are liable for IHT on this property but its value must be included to determine the deceased's estate rate of tax. Provision is made in this section for the tax to be paid on the settled fund when the form is delivered if the trustees so choose (in practice, this is unlikely to happen). The section also includes property subject to a reservation at the date of the donor's death (see [**22.3**]). Tax on such property is primarily the responsibility of the donee.

Section 4 requires details of any artificial debts created by the deceased. Such debts may not be deducted in arriving at the total chargeable transfers made by the deceased (see [**22.13**] for a discussion of what constitutes such a debt).

(d) On page 10 any IHT exemptions and reliefs (eg spouse exemption; business reliefs; charity exemptions) on property within Sections 1, 2 or 3 must be claimed. These are carried to page 11.

(e) Page 11 is the assessment page to which the totals from Sections 1, 2, 3 and page 10 are carried. It provides a format for calculating the total tax (if any) that is due and the tax (if any) that is payable on delivery of the Account.

(f) Page 12 is a summary of pages 1–11 for probate purposes. The IHT Form and any tax due must be sent to the Central Accounting Office in Worthing. The receipted IHT Form will be filed with the probate papers (see *Practice Direction* [1989] 3 All ER 938, issued on 30 November 1989 by the Senior Registrar of the Family Division: effective from 2 January 1990). [**III.2**]

3   **Completion of the form—case illustration**

<u>Siegfried George Lomax deceased</u>

The following information is taken from the file of Mallet & Co (solicitors) of 11 Ducks Lane, Cooknam, Northamptonshire—solicitors for the PRs of the deceased.

Full name of the deceased	Siegfried George Lomax
Last residential address	Church View, Resurrection Lane, Cooknam, Northamptonshire
Occupation	Company director
Date of birth	5 November 1910
Date of death	4 July 1991
Surviving relatives	Two children and brother
Will	Dated 1 January 1984
Executors	(1) George Siegfried Lomax (son), 15 Sun Street, Hardwick, Yorkshire
	(2) Elspeth Georgina Pollax (daughter), The Range, Horseshoe Close, Barrowmouth, Devon
Terms of the will	Pecuniary legacy of £5,000 to the RSPCA
	Specific legacy of shares in Buttons Ltd to son, George Lomax
	Residue to children equally

Assets

	£
Cash	100
Midshire Bank, Cooknam:	
Current account	740
Deposit account	420
Interest to date of death (net)	16
Personal chattels, household goods etc valued at	5,960
Director's fees to date of death	1,000
Policy of assurance payable to the estate by Moon Life Assurance Co	25,000
Thrifty Building Society account	17,900
Interest to date of death (net)	64
Minority holdings of quoted shares as valued (all 'cum div')	20,765
Freehold property	
(1) Church View (above) owned solely and beneficially by deceased, but subject to a mortgage to the Thrifty Building Society (below). House valued at	145,000
(2) Primrose Cottage, Rosetree Lane, Bangor, Wales owned by the deceased as a joint tenant with his brother Siegmund Earnest Lomax of the same address. The whole is valued at	70,000
Unquoted shares: 99% holding in Buttons Ltd, which manufactures buttons. The holding comprises 10,000 unquoted shares, the valuation of which has been agreed between the Revenue and the deceased's accountants, Prigmore & Co at £10 per share, ie	100,000

Liabilities

Electricity account outstanding	80
Housekeeper's wages (Annie Pringle)	100
British Telecom	32

Income tax (estimated)	1,225
Mark Cole & Sons (butchers)	12
Chinns up (victuallers)	120
Funeral expenses (excluding tombstone)	560
Mortgage on Church View	10,125

Other relevant information

(1)　On 25 December 1985 the deceased gave his daughter, Elspeth £20,000. He made no other gifts or settlements in the seven years prior to his death. This gift was a chargeable transfer when made during the CTT regime: it is included in the cumulative total of the deceased for the purpose of calculating the IHT bill on death.

(2)　The deceased was life tenant in the Lomax Will Trust established by the will of his father Tristan Lomax who died on 8 April 1960. The settled funds now pass to the deceased's son George. They consist of:

Investments valued at	48,640
Cash (uninvested)	400
Income accrued due	80
Income subsequently apportioned to deceased life tenant	60

(3)　In 1987 the deceased gave his country cottage ('Wye Knot') to his daughter, Elspeth. He has continued to occupy the cottage during the summer months and the PRs have been advised that the cottage falls within the gift with reservation rules. The value of the cottage in 1987 was £25,000: at death it was worth £40,000.　**[III.3]**

Method of payment

The PRs will take out a loan to pay the IHT due on delivery of the form. They will elect wherever possible to pay IHT by instalments so as to reduce the amount that they have to borrow. Once probate has been obtained, they propose to sell Church View to pay off the loan and the remaining IHT.　**[III.4]**

4　Page by page analysis

The IHT form will now be completed for this estate. Note that for the purpose of this exercise, it is assumed that the valuations of all the deceased's assets have been agreed with the Revenue. In practice, however, this is unlikely in the case of certain assets (eg land and unquoted shareholdings) and PRs submit the form on the basis of estimated valuations and complete a corrective account when the valuations are agreed.　**[III.5]**

Inland Revenue
Inheritance Tax *

Inland Revenue Account

- For use where the deceased died on or after 18 March 1986 domiciled in the United Kingdom
- Please see IHT 210 for instructions on how to complete this form

* *Capital Transfer Tax in the case of a death before 25 July 1986*

For Official Use

Your reference

LH

Your telephone number

Cooknam 451

Name and address of solicitors ∅

(1) Mallet & Co
11 Ducks Lane
Cooknam
Northamptonshire
Postcode NR2 4PQ

∅ All communications concerning Inheritance Tax will be sent to the Solicitors unless the executors or administrators request otherwise.

In the High Court of Justice Family Division (Probate)

(2)   The   District **Registry** at Carlshire

In the estate of

Date of Grant

Please use CAPITAL letters

Surname	Date of birth
(3) LOMAX	0 5 N O V 1 9 1 0

Title and Forenames	Date of death
MR SIEGFRIED GEORGE	0 4 J U L 1 9 9 0

Marital Status   *Please tick as appropriate*

Married [ ]   Single [ ]   Divorced [ ]   Widowed [✓]

Surviving Relatives

Husband [ ]   Wife [ ]   Child(ren) [✓]   Parent(s) [ ]

Domicile   (4)
England and Wales [✓]   Scotland [ ]   N.Ireland [ ]

Last usual address

CHURCH VIEW
RESURRECTION LANE
COOKNAM
NORTHAMPTONSHIRE
Postcode   NR2 1PQ

Occupation   COMPANY DIRECTOR

Please state the Tax District at which the tax affairs of the deceased were handled	SALFORD 16 DISTRICT	Tax District Reference TG/767/LOM

Please give the names and permanent addresses of the executors or intending administrators:

(5) GEORGE SIEGFRIED LOMAX
15 SUN STREET
HARDWICK
YORKSHIRE   Postcode YS3 1LP

ELSPETH GEORGINA POLLAX
THE RANGE
HORSESHOE CLOSE   BARROWMOUTH
DEVON   Postcode   DL1 2BS

Postcode

Postcode

IHT200

(1) Details of the PRs' solicitors with whom the Capital Taxes Office will communicate.

(2) Outside London it has been common practice for an Inland Revenue account to be sent to District Probate Registries with cheques for the payment of IHT. The relevant documents have then been forwarded to the Inland Revenue Finance Division for the accounts to be receipted and then returned to the Probate Registries. As the result of a Practice Direction issued on 30 November 1989 by the Senior Registrar of the Family Division this practice ceased with effect from 2 January 1990. Accounts must now be sent to the Inland Revenue, Finance Division (Cashier), Barrington Road, Worthing, West Sussex so that they can be properly receipted *before* presentation of the relevant papers to the Probate Registries.

(3) Personal details of the deceased.

(4) If the deceased had died domiciled outside the UK, IHT Form 201 would be the appropriate form to use.

(5) The deceased's executors complete the declaration on page 2.

Declaration

(6) 1 .x̶/̶We desire to obtain a grant of probate of the will

of the aforenamed deceased.

(7) 2. To the best of x̶m̶y̶/our knowledge and belief all the statements and particulars furnished in this account and its accompanying schedules are true and complete.

Delete paragraph if inappropriate (8) 3. I̶/̶We have made the fullest enquiries that are reasonably practicable in the circumstances but have not been able to ascertain the exact value of the property referred to in Exhibit   to section   . So far as the value can now be estimated, it is stated in section   x̶/̶We undertake, as soon as the value is ascertained, to deliver a further account, and to pay both any additional tax payable for which I̶/̶We may be liable, and any further tax payable, for which I/We may be liable on the other property mentioned in this account.

Delete what is inappropriate (9) 4. So far as the tax on the property disclosed in sections 1B, 2B and 3 may be paid by instalments, I̶/̶We elect to pay/N̶o̶t̶ ̶t̶o̶ ̶p̶a̶y̶ by instalments as indicated in these sections.

(10)

Signed by the above-named

GEORGE SIEGFRIED LOMAX

date

Signed by the above-named

ELSPETH GEORGINA POLLAX

date

Signed by the above-named

date

Signed by the above-named

date

Warning

An executor or intending administrator who fails to make the fullest enquiries that are reasonably practicable in the circumstances may be liable to penalties.

He or she may be liable to penalties or prosecution if he or she fails to disclose in Section 1A, 1B, 2A, 2B and 3 (as appropriate) and in his or her answers to the questions on page 3 and at the foot of page 9 all the property to the best of his or her knowledge and belief in respect of which tax may be payable on the death of the deceased.

(11)   Transfers of value which need not be reported are

a. gifts or other transfers of value made to the deceased's spouse unless at the time of transfer the deceased was domiciled in the United Kingdom and the spouse was not

b. gifts of money not exceeding £3,000 in any one year, where the executors or intending administrators are satisfied that they are wholly exempt as normal gifts out of income

c. outright gifts to one individual which are clearly exempt as not exceeding £250 in any one year (to 5 April): (for gifts before 6 April 1980 the exemption is restricted to £100 in any one year)

d. other gifts of money, or of shares or securities quoted on the Stock Exchange, where these, together with any other gifts not within (b) or (c) above, do not in total exceed the exemption for gifts of £3,000 in any one year (to 5 April)

(6) The executors want a grant of probate as opposed to a grant of letters of administration with or without will annexed.

(7) The declaration made by the PRs requires them to take all practicable steps to ensure that the form is correct.

(8) There are no items in this estate that the PRs have been unable to value. (Notice that any valuations referred to should accompany the form.)

(9) So far as possible the PRs elect to pay the tax by instalments.

(10) Declaration signed by the PRs. Before signing the declaration, the 'warning' in the right hand box should be brought to the PRs' attention to emphasise the seriousness of their task.

(11) Exempt lifetime gifts need not be reported by the PRs: note that item b. is the normal expenditure out of income exemption. The figure £3,000 lacks statutory authority: above that level gifts may still be exempt but the PRs are then under a duty to report them on page 3 of the form.

- Any property mentioned on this page which is subject to Inheritance Tax, whether or nor tax is actually payable, **must** also be included in sections 1A, 1B, 2A, 2B, or 3 of this account as appropriate. If it is claimed that the property is not subject to Inheritance Tax, reasons should be given.
- Even if a full report has been made or any other information relevant to the answers to any of the questions below has been given to an Inland Revenue Office, affirmative answers must nonetheless be given to the appropriate questions. Please also identify the office and quote any relevant official reference.
- Where necessary schedules may be attached.

1. Gifts etc.

For official use only

Did the deceased, within 7 years of his/her death

Please tick yes or no

	yes	no
(12) • make any gift, settlement or other transfer of value other than a transfer mentioned in the notes on page 2.	✓	
• make any disposition for the maintenance of a relative		✓
• pay any premium on a policy of life assurance not included in Section 1 of this form?		✓

Did the deceased at any time on or after 18 March 1986 dispose of any property by way of gift where either

	yes	no
(13) • possession and enjoyment of the property was not bona fide assumed by the donee, or		✓
• the property was not enjoyed to the entire exclusion of the donor and of any benefit to him/her by contract or otherwise?	✓	

(14) If the reply to any of the questions above is "yes", please give full particulars including dates, details of any property affected and the names and addresses of the other parties concerned, on a separate sheet of paper.

2. Settled property

	yes	no
(15) • Was the deceased, at the time of his/her death, entitled to a life interest, annuity or other interest in possession in settled property whether as beneficiary under the settlement or otherwise?	✓	
• Did the deceased cease to be entitled to any such interest in settled property within 7 years of his/her death?		✓

If the reply to either question is "yes", please give full particulars of the title (including, in the case of a Will/intestacy, the name and date of death of the testator/intestate and date and place of grant). Where the interest was under a settlement and no previous report has been made, kindly forward a copy of the settlement.

3. Nominations

	yes	no
(16) Did the deceased in his lifetime nominate any Savings Bank Account, Savings Certificates or other assets in favour of any person?		✓

If you have answered "yes", please give full particulars in section 2 on page 8.

4. Joint property

	yes	no
(17) Was the deceased joint owner of any property of any description or did he/she hold any money on a joint account (apart from property or money of which he/she was merely a trustee)?	✓	

If you have answered "yes" please give the following details on a separate sheet of paper

- the date when the joint ownership began (or the date of opening the joint account)
- The name(s) of the other joint owner(s)
- By whom and from what source the joint property was provided and, if it or its purchase price was contributed by one or more of the joint owners, the extent of the contribution made by each
- how the income (if any) was dealt with and enjoyed
- whether the deceased's interest passed under his/her will or intestacy or by survivorship.

(12) The gift of £20,000 to the deceased's daughter was made within seven years of the death. Accordingly, it must be cumulated for the purpose of calculating the rate at which the deceased's estate will be charged on death, although it does not form part of the deceased's taxable estate on death (see page 11 of Form).

(13) Property given away subject to a reservation is included in the donor's estate at death if the reserved benefit is still continuing: if the benefit came to an end during the donor's life a deemed PET will occur at that time (see [**22.3**]).

(14) Full details of the gift of 'Wye Knot' must be given. The Double Charges Regulations (see Appendix VII) ensure that *either* the value of the cottage in 1987 at the time of the gift or its value at death are charged and, because of the substantial increase in the value of the cottage, it is assumed that the latter applies.

(15) (See also (34)). The deceased was a life tenant in the Lomax Will Trust. His death triggers a charge to IHT on the entire value of the settled fund. The tax is borne by the trustees not the estate. The value of the fund forms part of the deceased's estate for the purposes of calculating the estate rate at which both the deceased's free estate and the settled fund is charged.

(16) A nomination in the prescribed form takes effect in the same way as a disposition by will and the property remains comprised in the estate at death. By contrast, a mere request to trustees of a company pension scheme is not a nomination and property in the pension fund is not therefore included in the death estate.

(17) (See also (33)). Although the deceased's joint tenancy in Primrose Cottage passes by right of survivorship to his brother and does not vest in his PRs, the value of his interest immediately before death forms part of his estate. Notice that all joint property is covered by this question not just beneficial joint tenancies passing by right of survivorship.

Section 1

A schedule of all the property of the deceased within the United Kingdom to which the deceased was beneficially entitled and in respect of which the grant is made, excluding property over which the deceased had and exercised by will a general power of appointment. The appointed property should be included in Section 3. Property gifted by the deceased subject to a reservation retained by the deceased should also be included in Section 3 rather than here.

		Gross value at date of death*	For official use only
	Section 1A Property without the Instalment Option		
(18)	**Stocks, shares, debentures and other securities** as set out in CAP 40:		
	• **Quoted** in the Stock Exchange daily official list except so far as included in Section 1B	20,765	
	• **Others**, except so far as included in Section 1B		
	National Savings Certificates and interest to the date of death		
	Uncashed dividents and interest received, dividends declared, and interest accrued due, in respect of the above investments, to the date of death, as statement annexed		
	Cash at the bank:		
	• On current account and interest (if any) to the date of death at		
(19)	MIDSHIRE BANK COOKNAM	740	
	• On deposit and interest to the date of death at		
	MIDSHIRE BANK COOKNAM	436	
	Cash (other than cash at banks)	100	
	Money at a National or Trustee Savings Bank and interest to the date of death, as statement annexed		
	Money out on Mortgage, and **interest** to the date of death, as statement annexed		
	Money with a building society, co-operative or friendly society, and **interest** to the date of death, as statement annexed		
	Money out on promissary notes, bonds and other securities, and **interest** to the date of death, as statement annexed THRIFTY B/S	17,964	
	Other debts due to the deceased and **interest** to the date of death, except book debts included in Section 1B, as statement annexed		
	Unpaid purchase money of real and leasehold property contracted in the lifetime of the deceased to be sold, as statement annexed		
	Rents of the deceased's own real and leasehold property to the date of death		
	Apportionment of the rents of the deceased's real and leasehold property to the date of death		
	Income accrued due, but not received before the death, arising from real and personal property, in which the deceased had a life or other limited interest, viz:-		
(20)	LOMAX WILL TRUST	80	
	Apportionment of Income from that source to the date of death	60	
	Any other income, apportioned where necessary, to which the deceased was entitled at his death (eg pensions, annuities, director's fees, etc) as statement annexed DIRECTOR'S FEES FROM BUTTONS LTD	1,000	
(21)	**Policies of insurance and bonuses** (if any) thereon, on the life of the deceased, as statement annexed MOON LIFE ASSURANCE CO (without profits)	25,000	
(22)	**Saleable value of policies of insurance and bonuses** (if any) not payable on the death of the deceased, as statement annexed		
	All claims for exemptions or reliefs should be made in the Summary on page 10 **To be carried forward**	66,145	

(18) The instalment option is not available for the deceased's quoted shares because none of the holdings constitutes a controlling shareholding (see IHTA 1984 s 228(1)(a) and Chapter 22). The holdings must be listed (with values) on Form 40. If shares are quoted 'ex div' at the date of death, the dividend must be added to this figure.

(19) Net interest on the deposit account which has accrued to the date of death is included in the deceased's estate for IHT purposes.

(20) Any income which accrued to the trustees of the Lomax Will Trust before the deceased's death forms part of his estate for IHT purposes, even though the trustees have not paid it over (ie £80). Also, income paid to the trustees after the deceased's death and apportioned to him forms part of his estate (ie £60).

(21) The fees to which the deceased was entitled form part of his estate.

(22) The value of the policy forms part of the deceased's estate on death. Notice that if the policy had been written in trust for a third party it would not be included in the estate; details would, however, be given on page 3, question 1(c) because the payment of the premiums might have been chargeable transfers of value. If the deceased had paid money into an approved superannuation scheme giving the trustees an absolute discretion as to whom the benefits were payable on his death, those benefits would not form part of his estate and need not, therefore, be included in the form. If, however, certain beneficiaries are given benefits by the deceased's will or intestacy or if the deceased had a general power to nominate beneficiaries, the benefits are included and must be valued under 'other personal property' on page 5.

			Gross value at date of death*	For official use only
(23)		Brought forward	66,145	

Household and personal goods, including pictures, china, linen, clothes, books plate, jewels, motor cars, boats, etc.

Sold, realised gross £

Unsold, estimated £ 5,960   5,960

(24) **The deceased's interest expectant upon death of**

aged   years, under the will/intestacy of

who died on the
or under a settlement dated the
and made between

(setting out the parties to the deed), in the property set out in the statement annexed, of which fund the present trustees are

Tick as appropriate

Was the interest at any time acquired for value whether by the deceased or a predecessor in title?   Yes ☐   No ☐

Income tax payable

Other personal property not comprised under the preceding heads
Please give details

Gross property not subject to the instalment option to be carried to page 6 and to the Probate Summary on page 12.   72,105

* All claims for exemptions or reliefs should be made in the Summary on page 10

Section 1A   Continued

(23) Self-explanatory. In practice, a valuation would have to accompany the IHT form (not shown here). Details and individual values of items valued at £500 and upwards should be given.

(24) For the treatment of reversionary interests, see [**25.61**].

Section 1A **continued**

Schedule of liabilities and funeral expenses. Particulars of the funeral expenses of the deceased and the liabilities due and owing from him at the time of his death to persons resident within the United Kingdom or to persons resident out of the United Kingdom but contracted to be paid in the United Kingdom, or charged on property situated within the United Kingdom (other than liabilities deducted in Section 1B or section 2 under footnote (b) on page 8).

Name and address of creditor	Description of liability	Amount	For official use only
(25) Electricity Board	Electricity Account	80	
British Telecom	Telephone Account	32	
Annie Pringle	Housekeeper's Wages	100	
Mark Cole & Sons	Butcher	12	
Chinns Up	Wine	120	
Inland Revenue	Income Tax (estimated)	1,225	

Funeral expenses

(26) S Toomay & Bros, Cooknam		560	

Total to be carried to the Summary below and to the Probate Summary on page 12		2,129

Summary

Gross property (from page 5) not subject to the instalment option	72,105
Less total of liabilities and funeral expenses from above	2,129
(27) Net property in the United Kingdom not subject to the instalment option to be carried to page 11 (Section 1A, net total before relief(s))	69,976

Section 4 on page 9 must be completed in respect of all liabilities listed above schedule.

(25) The deceased's debts which are not attributable to any particular property are included here.

(26) Funeral expenses are only deductible if reasonable.

(27) The value of the deceased's Section 1A property less debts (ie £69,976) is taken to page 11.

NB all the expenses deducted satisfy the requirements of FA 1986 s 103 since consideration for those debts was not property derived from the deceased (see further page 9 of the Account).

Section 1B	Property with the Instalment Option	For official use only

Tick as appropriate

(28)
- Is the tax on this property to be paid on delivery of this account?　Yes [ ]　No [✓]
- Is payment to be made in yearly instalments?　Yes [✓]　No [ ]

	Value at date of death
(29) **Land etc.** owned by the deceased in the United Kingdom (not being settled land) whether or not subject to a trust for sale as described on Cap 37 annexed.	145,000
Business interests	
• Net value of deceased's interest in the business(es), as statement or balance sheet annexed.	
• Net value of deceased's interest as partner in the firm of [blank] as statement or balance sheet annexed	
Stocks, shares, debentures and other securities, as set out on Cap 40.	
(30) • Shares or securities etc within Section 228(1) (a) Inheritance Tax Act 1984 which gave the deceased control of the company immediately before his death *see Section 269 Inheritance Tax Act 1984.* Shareholding in Buttons Ltd	100,000
• Other unquoted shares or securities etc. within Section 228(1) (b) or (c) or (d) Inheritance Tax Act 1984 (all other unquoted shares to be included in Section 1A).	
Value of property within the instalment option to be carried to the Probate Summary on Page 12.	245,000

Liabilities charged at the date of the deceased's death on the property included above other than those already taken into account above

Particulars of liability	Property on which charged	Amount
(31) Mortgage to Thrifty Building Society	Church View Resurrection Lane Cooknam Northamptonshire	10,125
Total liabilities to be carried to the Probate Summary on page 12.		10,125

(32) Value of property with the instalment option less liabilities to be carried to page 11 (Section 1B, net total before reliefs).	234,875

* All claims for exemptions and reliefs should be made in the Summary on page 10.

Section 4 on page 9 must be completed in respect of all liabilities listed above

(28) As far as possible, the PRs elect to pay IHT by ten yearly instalments. (They hope to discharge the IHT liability before the first instalment falls due on 1 February 1992 by realising assets in the estate once they have obtained the grant of probate.) Instalment option property owned solely and beneficially by the deceased comprises Church View and his controlling shareholding in Buttons Ltd.

(29) The gross value of Church View is shown here. Full details of the property must be set out on Form 37B (not reproduced).

(30) The holding and its value must be detailed with the deceased's quoted shares on Form 40 (not reproduced). Valuation has been made by an accountant and agreed with the Revenue (not reproduced). Business property relief on the value of the holding is claimed elsewhere (see (38)).

(31) The mortgage is a deductible liability.

(32) The deduction is given against the total value of the Section 1B property. As all the IHT is a testamentary expense this is irrelevant. If, however, Church View had been the subject of a specific tax-bearing devise, the devisee would only be liable for IHT on the value of Church View less the mortgage, ie on £134,875.

Section 2

All other property on which the personal representatives are liable to pay the tax (or would be liable if any tax were payable) including:-

- all nominated property and property passing by survivorship
- all property situated outside the UK

Section 2A - Property without the Instalment Option

For official use only

Particulars of the property, local situation and details of disposition if nominated or in joint names	Value at date of death
Gross Value	

Liabilities˙ in respect of the property above	Amount
Name and Address of Creditor	Description of liability	
	Total liabilities	

Net value to be carried to page 11 (Section 2A, net total before reliefs)

Section 2B - Property with the Instalment Option

Tick as appropriate

- Is the tax on this property to be paid on delivery of this account?   ☐ Yes   ☑ No
- Is payment to be made by yearly instalments?   ☑ Yes   ☐ No

Particulars of the property, local situation and details of disposition if nominated or in joint names	Value at date of death
(33) Freehold property Primrose Cotage, Rosetree Lane, Bangor, Wales held by deceased and his brother SIEGMUND EARNEST LOMAX as beneficial joint tenants	31,500
Gross Value	31,500

Liabilities˙ In respect of the property above	Amount
Name and Address of Creditor	Description of Liability	
	Total liabilities	

Net value to be carried to page 11 (Section 2B, net total before reliefs)   31,500

˙ All claims for exemptions or reliefs should be made in the Summary on page 10
+ Liabilities   (a) due from the deceased at the time of his death to persons resident outside the United Kingdom (other than liabilities contracted to be paid in the United Kingdom, or charged on property within the United Kingdom which have been deducted in Sections 1A and 1B) or
(b) (so far as not included in (a) charged upon incurred in connection with or otherwise affecting the property included in this Section

Section 4 on page 9 must be completed in respect of all liabilities listed above.

(33) The deceased had no foreign or nominated property. The only property which he owned jointly (and which passes to his brother by right of survivorship) is Primrose Cottage. The instalment option is available for tax attributable to the value of the deceased's half share. Although the land is worth £70,000 the value of the deceased's half share (£35,000) will be discounted (usually by about 10%) to (say) £31,500 to allow for the fact that it does not carry the right to exclusive occupation of any portion of the house.

Section 3

Any other property in the UK and elsewhere in which the deceased had or is treated as having had a beneficial interest in possession immediately before his death including:-

- property over which the deceased had and exercised by will a general power of appointment.
- property outside the UK comprised in a settlement made by a UK domiciled person.
- property gifted by the deceased subject to a reservation retained by the deceased.

Part 1 Property on which tax is elected to be paid on delivery of this account should be listed below and headed "Part 1"

- Is the tax on any property with the Instalment Option to be paid by yearly　*Tick as appropriate* instalments?

  ☐ Yes　　☐ No

- Separate net totals for Part 1 (property without the instalment option) and Part 1 (property with the instalment option) should be carried to page 11 (Sections 1a (non-instalment option property) and 1b (instalment option property) net totals before reliefs).

Part 2 Property on which tax is not to be paid on delivery of this account should be listed below and headed "Part 2" and its net value carried to page 11 (Section 1c, net total before reliefs).

Separate consecutive numbering for part 1 and part 2	Particulars of the property	Net value at date of death *		For official use only
		Property without the instalment option £	Property with the instalment option £	
(34) Part 2	(i)　LOMAX WILL TRUST CTO L4590. The deceased was the life tenant under the will of his father (died 8/4/1960).			
	Quoted stocks and shares as per Form 40 (annexed) Cash capital	48,640 400 £49,040		
(35) Part 2	(ii)　"WYE KNOT" Nr Tintern Gloucs Transferred to Elspeth Pollax by instrument of transfer dated 30 October 1987.		40,000	

* *All claims for exemptions or reliefs should be made in the Summary on page 10*

Section 4

Deductions of liabilities listed in this account

Tick as appropriate

(36)

　　　　　　　　　　　　　　　　　Yes　　　No

　　　　　　　　　　　　　　　　　☐　　　☑

In the case of any liability for which a decuction has been taken in either section 1A, 1B, 2A, 2B or 3 of this account did the consideration for any such debt or incumbrance incurred or created on or after 18 March 1986 consist of property derived from the deceased or was the consideration given by any person who was at any time entitled to, or amongst whose resources there was at any time included any property derived from the deceased?

If "Yes", please give full particulars, including the liabilities in question, the consideration given and the derivation of that consideration from the deceased.

Please attach schedules as necessary.

(34) For the reasons stated at (15) the value of the whole settled fund at the date of the deceased's death must be included. Either (as here) the trustee(s) will account separately for the tax attributable to the settled property (Part 2 property); or, if the trustee(s) provide the deceased's PRs with the necessary funds to do so, the PRs can elect to pay this tax on the delivery of the Form together with the tax on the deceased's free estate (Part 1 property). As the settled property does not consist of instalment option property, the tax will be payable by the trustee(s) in one lump sum six months after the date of the deceased's death (ie by 1 February 1992). Insofar as the settled fund comprises shares and securities, these must be set out on Form 40 (not reproduced). As there have been no advances or property taken out of settlement (which affect the calculation of the IHT bill) there must be a statement to this effect. The trustee and the trust's solicitors must be identified as the Revenue will need to communicate with them. The settlement has a CTO reference as a result of the admission of Tristan Lomax's will to probate.

(35) Property subject to a reservation of benefit ('Wye Knot') should be entered here.

(36) Artificial debts (see [**22.13**]) must be itemised here.

Summary of exemptions and reliefs against capital

- please see instruction booklet IHT 210 as to how this page should be completed

- Schedules should be attached as necessary

Property in respect of which exemption or relief is claimed. The description should not be more detailed than is necessary to identify the property	Nature of exemption or relief claimed	Net value of property £	Amounts exemption or relief claimed £	For official use only
Property included in Section 1A				
(37) Pecuniary legacy (RSPCA)	charity exemption	5,000	5,000	
Total of exemptions and reliefs Section 1A to be carried to page 11 (reliefs column)			5,000	
Property included in Section 1B				
(38) Shares in Buttons Ltd	Business property relief (50%)	100,000	50,000	
Total of exemptions and reliefs Section 1B to be carried to page 11 (reliefs column)			50,000	
Property included in other sections - state and show separately which section (sections 2A and B and 3 (Part 1) and 3 (Part 2) A separate total of exemptions and reliefs for each of these sections should be carried to page 11 (reliefs column)				

(37) The pecuniary legacy to charity is exempt from IHT. As the exemption does not relate to specific property it is claimed against Section 1A property.

(38) The value of the deceased's controlling shareholding in Buttons Ltd (£100,000) is eligible for 50% business property relief (ie £50,000). If the legacy were tax-bearing, the legatee, George Lomax, would be liable for tax at the estate rate on that reduced value.

Assessment of Inheritance Tax

Summary for determining chargeable rates (39)

Section of accounts	Net total £	Reliefs £	Value of property after reliefs £
1(a) Property without the instalment option			
1A	69,976	5,000	64,976
2A	-	-	-
3. Part 1	-	-	-
Total 1(a)	69,976	5,000	64,976
1(b) Property with the instalment option			
1B	234,875	50,000	184,875
2B	31,500	-	31,500
3. Part 1	Nil	-	-
Total 1(b)	266,375	50,000	216,375
1(c) Other property on which tax is not being paid on this account			
3. Part 2	89,040	-	89,040
Total 1(c)	89,040	-	89,040
Total 1 (a) to (c)	425,391	55,000	A 370,391
Cumulative total of chargeable transfers made prior to the deceased's death (40)		B	20,000
Aggregate chargeable transfers (A + B)		C	390,391

Calculation of tax

	£	p
Tax on C on first £ 128,000 plus on balance of £ 262,391@40%	Nil	
	104,956	00
(41) Total	104,956	00
Less tax on B at death rate on first £20,000 ~~☒☒☒☒☒ ☒☒☒☒☒~~ ~~☒☒☒☒☒☒☒☒☒☒☒ ☒☒☒~~	Nil	
(42) Total	Nil	
Less QSR (as attached schedule)	Nil	
Total tax chargeable on A (43)	D 104,956	00

Any capital figure multiplied by $\frac{D}{A}$ gives the proportion of tax assessable on that capital

Value on which tax is now being paid

	Value of property	
	non-instalment £	Instalment option £
Total value at 1(a)	64,976	
That part of 1(b) on which tax now to be paid		216,375

Amount payable on this account

Non instalment property (44)	£	p
Total value at 1(a) £ 64,976 × $\frac{D}{A}$ =	18,412	02
Less reliefs against tax other than QSR	-	
Net tax	18,412	02
*add interest on net tax from (45) 19 to 19 (years days at %)	-	-
Total tax and interest on non-instalment property (carried to page 12)	18,412	02
Additional tax and interest due under S7 IHTA 1984-as attached schedule (carried to page 12) (47)	-	-

Instalment option property (46)	£	p
That part of 1(b) on which tax now to be paid £ 216,375 × $\frac{D}{A}$ =	61,313	42
Less reliefs against tax other than QSR		
Net tax	61,313	42
*add interest on net tax from 19 to 19 (years days at %)	-	-
Instalments - tenths of net tax	6,131	34
add interest on instalments now assessed from 19 (date last instalment due) to 19 (days at %)	-	-
†add interest on whole of tax on instalment property from 19 to 19 (years days at %)	-	-
Total tax and interest on instalment option property (carried to page 12)	6,131	34

Interest
* Tax becomes due 6 months after the end of the month in which the death occurred. Unpaid tax carries interest from and including the day after the due date, irrespective of the reason for the late payment.
† Only if the due date for the second or subsequent instalment has now passed and interest relief (see IHT 210) is not in point, add here interest on the whole of the net tax on the instalment option property up to the due date of the last instalment.
Interest on overpaid tax; please note that, where tax or interest is paid in excess of the amount found to be due, interest is allowed on the amount overpaid.

(39) Page 11 is the assessment page. The purpose of the top half of the page is to calculate the rate of IHT at which the deceased's estate is chargeable and to calculate the tax payable. However, not all that tax is necessarily payable on delivery of the form or by the PRs. The purpose of the bottom half, therefore, is to calculate the amount of tax payable on delivery of the IHT Form.

(40) A, B and C together yield the value of the deceased's total gross cumulative transfers (£390,391) made up of the transfer on death (being the net value of property from Sections 1, 2 and 3 less any exemptions or reliefs), plus the value of any chargeable transfers made within seven years before death (ie £20,000 to daughter Elspeth).

(41) The tax on a chargeable transfer of £390,391 is calculated from the IHT table, ie £100,156.40.

(42) The £20,000 lifetime gift only forms part of the deceased's chargeable transfers for the purpose of calculating the rate at which tax is to be charged on death. Accordingly, a sum equal to the tax at table rates on a gift of £20,000 must be deducted from the tax bill. As the gift fell within the deceased's nil rate band, no tax is, or was, payable on this figure, so there is nothing to deduct. (Notice that the chargeable estate on death is £370,391, ie £390,391—£20,000.)

(43) The total tax payable on this estate (£370,391) is £100,156.40. This tax is attributable to the four types of property comprised in the estate:

(1) the value of the non-instalment option property, ie £64,976, on which the PRs are to pay tax at once;
(2) the value of the instalment option property, ie £216,375 made up of Church View (£134,875); the holding in Buttons Ltd (£100,000—£50,000£50,000); and Primrose Cottage (£31,500);
(3) the value of the settled fund (£49,040) on which the trustees are responsible for the tax;
(4) the value of the property subject to a reservation ('Wye Knot') which is £40,000: the donee, Elspeth, is liable for the tax.
The tax (£100,156.40) is allocated between these four groups of property *pro rata.*

(44) The tax attributable to the non-instalment option property is the proportion of the total tax (£100,156.40) that the value of that property (£64,976) bears to the total chargeable estate (£370,391). The tax payable on delivery of the form is £17,569.98. (Note that this property is charged at an effective estate rate of 27.041%, ie:

$$\frac{\text{Tax}}{\text{Chargeable estate}} = \frac{£100,156.40}{£370,391} \times 100.)$$

(45) Interest is charged only on tax that is outstanding six months after the end of the month of the deceased's death. As he died on 4 July 1991 and this account is delivered on 18 September 1991, no interest is payable.

(46)   The value of the instalment option property is £216,375. No tax is payable on the delivery of this account as the first instalment only becomes due six months after the end of the month of death. This sum is calculated as:

$$\frac{£216,375}{£370,391} \times 100,156.40 = \text{total tax of } £58,509.35$$

The first instalment due on 1 February 1992 will be £5,850.93 (£58,509.35 ÷ 10). It carries interest from the date the first instalment is due (1 February 1992) to the date of payment.

Subsequent instalments insofar as the tax payable is attributable to the value of land (ie Church View and Primrose Cottage) carry interest on the whole of the unpaid IHT (and on the whole of the current instalment, if it is overdue). There will be no interest charged on the unpaid IHT attributable to the value of the holding in Buttons Ltd so long as each instalment is paid on time.

If any of the property is sold, the balance of the outstanding tax attributable to that property (with interest if applicable) becomes payable immediately. Remember that in this case, the PRs hope to sell Church View and discharge all the outstanding tax, ie £58,509.35 before the first instalment becomes due.

The total tax payable on the deceased's free estate is £17,569.98+£58,509.35=£76,079.33. The balance of the tax attributable to the settled fund and 'Wye Knot' and payable by the Trustees and Elspeth is:

$$\frac{£89,040}{£370,391} \times 100,156.40 = £24,077.07$$

(47)   Any gift made during the CTT regime and within three years of the deceased's death must be re-assessed at death rates and any extra tax (ie the difference between the tax payable on that gift at the rates at the date of death and the tax paid on the gift at half rates) is due, not from the deceased's PRs, but from the donee (Elspeth Pollax). The gift of £20,000 fell within the deceased's nil rate band so that no IHT is payable.

Probate Summary

		£
Aggregate Gross Value which in law devolves on and vests in the personal representatives of the deceased, for and in respect of which the Grant is to be made	Section 1A	72,105
	Section 1B	245,000
	Section 3*	–

* absolute power property only

(48) **Total to be carried to the probate papers** 317,105

Deduct

Section 1A, total of liabilities and funeral expenses	2,129
Section 1B, total of liabilities	10,125

(49) **Net value for probate purposes** 304,851

For official use only	Total of Tax and Interest from page 11	£
	Total Tax and Interest - Non-Instalment Property	18,412.02
	Total Tax and Interest - Instalment Option Property	Nil
	Additional Tax and Interest due under S7 Inheritance Tax Act 1984	–
	Total tax and interest payable now on this account	18,412.02
EDP	On the basis of this Account the tax (and interest) payable now is	18,412.02

_____ Mallet & Co _____   19/9/ 1990

Solicitor(s) for the applicant(s)

This receipt and stamp do not imply that the assessment is not subject to rectification: the account will be fully examined after the issue of the grant.

Prints of this form and of the instructions (IHT 210) can be obtained from the Capital Taxes Office, Inland Revenue, Rockley Road, London W14 0DF and on personal application only at the Stamps Office, Room G3, South West Wing, Bush House, Strand, WC2B 4QN the London Chief Post Office, King Edward Street, EC1A 1AA, the Branch Post Offices at 24 Throgmorton Street, EC2N 2JE; 40 Fleet Street, EC4Y 1BT; 181 High Holborn, WC1 1AA; 2-4 Bishops Court, Chancery Lane, WC2A 1EA and from other large branch post offices in major towns and cities outside the Metropolitan Postal District as listed in form CAP 18 (which can be obtained from the Capital Taxes Office).

(48) This figure is entered in the executor's oath as the gross value of the estate which vests in the PRs and for which they are applying for a grant of probate. Section 2 and 3 property is excluded because it does not vest in the PRs; the fact that they may be liable for tax on it is irrelevant for probate purposes.

(49) Probate fees are calculated on this figure.

NB Under IHT chargeable lifetime gifts made in the seven years before death may suffer additional tax on death and PETs made during that same period become chargeable. In this case study the only gift made by the deceased had occurred before 18 March 1986 at a time when CTT was operative. For a discussion of how PETs and chargeable transfers are assessed to IHT on a death within seven years see [**22.32**].   [**III.6**]

APPENDIX IV: DOMICILE—REFORM

A non-UK domiciliary is normally only subject to UK taxation on overseas income and gains if remitted into the United Kingdom when resident here and is not subject to inheritance tax on property situated outside the United Kingdom. Every person must be domiciled in one particular country: domicile is therefore unlike residence since it is possible (as already noted) for an individual (eg a compulsive traveller) not to be resident in any particular state. There are a number of different types of domicile. First, a *domicile of origin* which is acquired at birth. Usually a child will take the domicile of his father unless he is either illegitimate or born after his father's death in which case he takes the domicile of his mother. This domicile of origin is never completely lost although it may be superseded by a domicile of dependence or choice: in particular, a domicile of origin will revive if the later domicile lapses.

The domicile of an unmarried child under the age of 16 (14 or 12 respectively for boys and girls under Scottish law) may only be changed if the parent on whom the domicile depends changes his or her domicile. In such cases the child in question acquires a *domicile of dependency*. On reaching the age of 16 or marrying thereunder a person remains domiciled in the country in which he was domiciled immediately before that event unless and until that domicile is abandoned and either a domicile of choice is acquired or a domicile of origin revives. A *domicile of choice* is only acquired by residence in the appropriate country coupled with an intention on the part of the individual to make his home in that country permanently or indefinitely. Residence in this context probably involves little more than physical presence in the country so that even a brief period of days may be sufficient. However, it must be accompanied by the requisite intention to remain and this intention to acquire a new domicile must amount to a fixed and settled purpose or represent a final and deliberate intention to abandon the former domicile. Hence there are cases which have decided that the hope of returning to the erstwhile domicile will prevent the acquisition of a domicile of choice although a merely speculative intention to return to a former domicile in the future will probably not be sufficient.

Perhaps the feature of the present law which has been most criticised is the concept of a domicile of origin. Very often this is wholly artificial since it may result in an individual being domiciled in a country with which he has never had any real connection. Take, for instance, the case of a child born to Pakistani parents who live in England but at the relevant time have retained their domicile of origin in Pakistan. The child automatically acquires a domicile of origin in Pakistan, a country which he may never visit in his life. This peculiarity of the domicile of origin may be particularly important under the present law since this type of domicile possesses adhesive qualities in that it will revive if a subsequent domicile is abandoned without a new domicile of choice being at that time acquired. In the case of the child considered above, for instance, he may acquire a domicile of dependence in England when his parents lose their Pakistan domicile. Should he in later life abandon that English domicile of dependence, however, and pursue a nomadic life his Pakistan domicile of origin will then revive to fill the gap thus created.

Such a revival of a domicile of origin is not an uncommon occurrence. It will happen, for instance, when a domicile of choice is abandoned before residence is taken up in the country which the individual intends to be his new domicile. Thus, when an individual born in the UK, but who has acquired a domicile of choice in Japan, leaves that country in order to take up a new domicile in Switzerland and takes several weeks in travelling between those two countries, he will in the interim see his domicile of origin revive to fill that gap. In federal jurisdictions (such as the United Kingdom and the United States) this may frequently occur. A UK emigrant to the United States who settles first in New England but who then moves across the continent in search of work may acquire a domicile of choice in an eastern state but with each move that domicile will cease and, pending the acquisition of a new domicile of choice, his old English domicile of origin will revive. It should, of course, be remembered that UK inheritance tax may then be payable on his worldwide property should he die within three years of such a UK domicile ceasing! (See further below.)

The Law Commission recommended that a number of changes be made in the existing law of domicile (Law Com No 168, Scot Law Com No 107). Probably most important from a taxation point of view would be the abolition of the domicile of origin. In its place a child under the age of 16 would acquire a domicile in the country with which he is most closely connected. When a child's parents are domiciled in the same country and he is living with them, there will be a rebuttable presumption that he is most closely connected with that country. It is likely that in the example of the Pakistani couple discussed earlier the child would not be treated as domiciled in Pakistan, however, but will be most closely connected with the UK (so that the presumption would be rebutted).

Following from this change, a former domicile will never automatically revive. Hence, when a domicile is abandoned without the acquisition of a new domicile of choice, the individual will be treated as retaining a domicile in the last jurisdiction in which he had a domicile. This proposal ensures that a person's domicile will always be in a jurisdiction with which he had, at least at some time, a significant connection and accordingly the domicile of choice will obtain some of the adhesive properties currently associated with a domicile of origin. In the earlier example of the individual who left Japan for Switzerland, the abolition of the domicile of origin will mean that his Japanese domicile of choice will continue until a Swiss domicile is acquired.

Inheritance tax is unique in employing domicile as the *sole* connecting factor. As already noted, a UK domiciliary is subject to tax on his worldwide assets, a non-UK domiciliary only on his UK assets. Apart from the ordinary rules for domicile, already considered, inheritance tax also includes the concept of a deemed domicile in the UK. Thus, even if a person's domicile under the general law is outside the UK, he may in two circumstances be deemed UK-domiciled (these situations are discussed in Chapter 27). Nothing in the Law Commission's proposals is intended to change the deeming provisions for inheritance tax.   **[IV.1]**

APPENDIX V: TRUSTS — A CONSULTATIVE DOCUMENT

1 **Introductory**

The Consultative Document produced on Budget Day 1991 is the result of a study that had been announced by Norman Lamont when Chief Secretary to the Treasury in 1988. The Document is limited in two important respects. First, it is concerned solely with UK resident trusts. This is unfortunate since many of the problems addressed are common to both resident and non-resident trusts: the question of when a settlor should be taxed on gains realised by his trustees is one such case which is considered below. Secondly, it considers only income tax and capital gains tax: other taxes, and notably inheritance tax, form no part of this study.

The paper envisages that representations should be received by the Inland Revenue no later than 30 September 1991. Thereafter the process has not been laid down: possibly draft clauses will be produced for consideration but it is quite clear that legislation will not occur before the 1992 Finance Act *at the earliest*. Given current political uncertainties there must be a strong possibility that the implementation of any changes will be delayed beyond 1992.

Apart from closing certain loopholes in the tax net the Document proceeds on the premise that the tax system, wherever possible, should be simplified and the considerable amount of dead wood removed. As always in taxation matters, however, simplification—if it is to be achieved—may be at the price of certain injustices.   **[V.1]**

2 **Governing principles and policy problems**

As a basic premise it is stated that the rules for income tax and capital gains tax should be harmonised whenever practical and the tax treatment of trusts should be neutral, in the sense that it should be in line with the taxation of individuals. Settled property should be taxed neither more nor less heavily. This, it may be recalled, was the espoused aim of an earlier Consultative Document on the Capital Transfer Tax treatment of discretionary trusts which leads to the 1982 reforms.

There are two major policy problems confronting the would-be reformer. *First*, it is possible to tax a trust as if it was a separate person, distinct both from its settlor and beneficiaries. However, it is unlikely that any such approach would commend itself to the Inland Revenue since it would enable settlors to create any number of separate taxable entities each with their own rates, exemptions and reliefs. Accordingly, it is likely that trusts will be linked *either* with the settlor on the one hand (provided that he is still alive) *or*, alternatively, with the appropriate beneficiaries. In the latter case, the discretionary trust has always been a source of difficulty: how can one identify the relevant beneficiary or beneficiaries? The current CTT/IHT regime has abandoned any attempt to do so and instead treats the trust as a separate taxable entity: the fact that there is a 'principal beneficiary' who receives the bulk of the income and substantial advances of capital is irrelevant.

Treating trust property as still belonging to the settlor for the purposes of taxation has been a growing tendency in recent years. If the settlor has retained an 'interest' in his settlement (and the key question is what constitutes such an interest) the tax regime will operate as if that settlement were the settlor's own property. In income tax, for instance, income is taxed as that of the settlor as it arises under the melange of rules in TA 1988 Part XV. Under the capital gains tax rules in FA 1988 Sch 10, trust gains are taxed as if they were those of the settlor, whilst for offshore trusts rules introduced in FA 1991 s 89 and Sch 16 provide for the same result in a significantly wider range of situations. In this respect UK law is moving in the direction of American fiscal legislation.

To a considerable extent, of course, rules deeming income and gains to belong to the settlor for taxation purposes are at variance with basic principles of trust law where the trust property belongs to the beneficiaries. Difficulties can therefore arise: for instance, the capital gains tax rules in Sch 10 require tax to be paid first by the settlor and only thereafter is he given a right of indemnity against his trustees. In the case of offshore trusts there must be some doubt as to whether tax paid by a UK settlor will be recovered from his offshore trustees despite a similar statutory 'right'. To some extent the Revenue are happy to treat the settlor as the owner of trust assets when it suits them but not otherwise. Under the CGT legislation in Sch 10, tax is charged on the settlor on gains realised by his offshore trustees but he is not enabled to take advantage of any settlement losses!

One area not satisfactorily addressed in the Consultative Document is the need for uniformity in deciding when a settlor retains an interest in his settlement. To what extent, for instance, should he be treated as the taxable person if it is only his spouse who is a beneficiary? Current legislation treats the spouse as an extension of the settlor for these purposes but this runs contrary to the whole spirit of independent taxation. In passing it may be noticed that there is no proposal in the Consultative Document to reform the unsatisfactory rules governing 'outright gifts' between spouses. The general principle is that it is only such transfers which result in an asset leaving the estate of the donor spouse: a gift of a limited interest (for instance a gift to the donor's wife for life remainder to his children) does not achieve this result and the settlor remains subject to both income and capital gains tax on that settlement's income and gains.

Apart from spouses, there remains the question of what other persons should be treated as an extension of the settlor. Beneficiaries who are his infant children, for instance, may result in an income tax levy against the settlor (see TA 1988 s 663) and, indeed, in the case of offshore trusts, even adult children will provoke this result. As a matter of consistency it is difficult to see why the definition of when a settlor remains interested in his settlement should be different for income tax and capital gains tax and, in the area of capital gains tax, between resident and offshore trusts. Nonetheless the introduction in 1991 of a new regime for offshore trusts deliberately extended the list of persons who, if beneficiaries, would result in the settlor being subject to capital gains tax on gains produced by his trustees.

One area where the plea for simplification must be justified lies in the income tax anti-avoidance rules (TA 1988 Part XV). The legislation abounds with references to covenants (since 1988 generally no longer tax effective) and, even in the context of capital settlements, the provisions overlap and many have been rendered redundant with the introduction (in FA 1989) of TA 1988 s 674A. Those sections in the Document recommending substantial pruning are worthy of support.   **[V.2]**

3 **Areas where no change is recommended**

(i) *Bare trusts:* There is no intention to change the rules in this area. In general, the tax system treats the beneficiary as being the owner of the trust assets. A similar result is arrived at as a matter of trust law with the trustees having no active duties to perform. Tucked away in para 23 of Schedule A, however, is one important change. At present a bare trust for the infant unmarried child of the settlor can have income tax advantages and the paragraph proposes to remove these by taxing the income in such cases as the settlor's (see *Example 37.10*).

(ii) *Interest in possession trusts:* No change is proposed in the income tax treatment. Basic rate tax is normally deducted at source; the beneficiary receives a credit for that tax and may then suffer a higher rate assessment. (In passing it will be recalled that for inheritance tax purposes the beneficiary with the interest in possession is, by a fiction, treated as the owner of the underlying capital assets.)

Changes are, however, envisaged in the capital gains tax treatment of such trusts: at present CGT is only charged at the 25% rate and hence there may be scope for channelling assets through an interest in possession trust (see 5 below).

(iii) *CGT annual exemption:* Most trusts only benefit from one half of the exemption available to individuals and there are further fragmentation rules in the event of a settlor creating more than one settlement. It is not envisaged that these provisions will be amended.

(iv) *CGT—creation of trusts:* There are no proposals to extend hold-over relief and, indeed, it is suggested that except for business assets such relief should *only be available in the event of an inheritance tax charge then arising.* Were this to be implemented the result would be that creating a nil rate band discretionary trust in order to obtain CGT hold-over relief would no longer be effective. Accordingly, if it seems likely that these proposals will be implemented in the tax year 1992-93 setting up such nil rate band trusts before 5 April 1992 is an important planning point.

The Consultative Document leaves the current position whereby hold-over relief is not available if a PET becomes chargeable because of the donor's death in the following seven-year period intact. It is hard to understand the logic of this if it is intended that when there is an inheritance tax charge there should be hold-over relief for capital gains tax.

(v) *CGT—trust termination:* The Consultative Document canvasses the possibility of a deferral relief being available when property comes out of a settlement. The preferred route would be by a no gain, no loss disposal rather than by hold-over relief (presumably so that it will not in all cases be necessary to obtain a market value of the assets at that time). Any such extension would, of course, enable tax to be postponed when what was once an accumulation and maintenance trust comes to an end at a time when an interest in possession has arisen (see *Example 17.13*).

The preferred form of relief is by means of a no gain, no loss disposal, so that unless there are amendments in the legislation it will not be possible to carry forward losses of the trust. (At present such losses pass through to a beneficiary who becomes absolutely entitled: contrast losses incurred by personal representatives which are not transferred to a legatee and see 6 below.) **[V.3]**

4 Areas of proposed change

(1) The rules for the residence of trusts for income tax and capital gains tax should be the same and the income tax rules laid down in the wake

of the *Dawson* decision should apply to both (see FA 1989 s 110 and *Example 13.6*).

(2) *Discretionary and accumulation and maintenance trusts—taxation of income:* It is proposed that the current 10% surcharge under TA 1988 s 686 should end and be replaced as follows:

(a) *Provided* that income is distributed basic rate tax should be paid by the trustees and a credit given to the beneficiaries. This is the system which already applies to interest in possession trusts.

(b) To the extent that income is *not distributed* there will be no extra tax charge on that income *provided that* it does not exceed an annual threshold. The Consultative Document envisages such a threshold being one half of the basic rate tax band but that it will be fragmented (in much the same way as the CGT annual exempt amount is fragmented) in the event of a settlor creating more than one settlement.

(c) Undistributed income above that threshold will be subject to the same higher rate liability (currently 15%) as that which applies to individuals.

Although there have been critics of the surcharge under TA 1988 s 686, the new proposals are themselves open to criticism on two main grounds.

First, there is the key question, when is income undistributed for these purposes? The test proposed in the Consultative Document is *not* whether the income has been accumulated. (It will be recalled that any decision on whether to distribute or accumulate income can be taken by trustees within *a reasonable time after the income has arisen* and that may be anything between one and five years.) The basic proposition in the Consultative Document is that income is undistributed if it is in the trustee's hands at the end of the tax year in which it arose (5 April) subject only to a late distributions relief which would enable income distributed in the period up until 30 June following the tax year to count as distributed income for these purposes. Many advisers and administrators feel that the 30 June deadline is unsatisfactory and suggested alternatives have varied from a six-month period running from the end of the tax year to a full year with the possibility of the excess liability being levied and then refunded to the trustees in the event of a payment out to a beneficiary during this period.

The second main criticism of the reform proposals concentrates upon the position of a beneficiary who receives trust income. To the extent that the income has suffered only basic rate tax (as will be the case with interest in possession trusts and with discretionary and accumulation trusts where the income is distributed during the tax year or up until 30 April following) the beneficiary is given a credit for the tax deducted at source and will himself be liable for any higher rate income tax. What, however, of the position if the distribution is made out of income which, in the trustee's hands, has suffered a higher rate charge? The Consultative Document envisages a beneficiary only being given credit for the basic rate tax paid by the trustees on the somewhat flimsy ground that 'it will be very confusing for beneficiaries if they receive tax credits at two different rates'. Were this proposal to be implemented the result would be a species of double taxation in such cases since income could be distributed which had already borne tax at 40% in the trustee's hands and the beneficiary would then be subject to a further levy at 15% on the income received grossed up at the basic rate band (at current rates that would lead to an effective rate of tax on the income of 52%).

It may also be noted that the proposals in this part of the Document (and indeed elsewhere) are based on the premise that tax rates will remain at 25% and 40%: substantial increases or the introduction of further rate bands would lead to a chaotic picture   [**V.4**].

5 Capital gains tax

Changes are proposed in the way in which capital gains tax is computed for both interest in possession and discretionary and accumulation trusts. In the former case the current 25% rate is thought to be too low (bearing in mind that the beneficiary may be subject to tax at 40%) whilst in the latter case it is hard to see any justification for a 35% rate.

The basic proposal is to align the treatment of such gains with that of individuals. The gains would, therefore, in the case of *all* settlements, be treated as the top slice of that settlement's undistributed income. In the case of interest in possession trusts the result will usually be that the trust gains will fall within the basic rate band of that settlement because the settlement will not have undistributed income. Where larger gains are involved, however, tax may be imposed at a 40% rate. If these proposals are to be introduced from 6 April next it may be advantageous for trustees of interest in possession trusts to make disposals in 1991/2 at the 25% rate.

In the case of accumulation and discretionary trusts the gains will also be treated as the top slice of the undistributed income: in this case it may be that the basic rate band has already been exhausted so that gains will be subject to charge at a 40% rate.

It is not thought that these changes will satisfactorily overcome the current difficulties that arise when part of a trust fund is held on interest in possession trusts and part on discretionary or accumulation trusts. At present CGT at a rate of 35% is charged on gains of the trust *even if* the majority of the fund is held on interest in possession trusts (see *Example 14.25*).

In considering the effect of the proposed changes, assume that Adam has attained an interest in possession in one half of the trust fund but that the other half is held on discretionary and accumulation trusts. To the extent that gains are realised in Adam's part of the trust the undistributed income in the other part will be relevant in determining the appropriate tax rate. Accordingly, although there may be no undistributed income in Adam's moiety a 40% rate may apply.

Finally, the anti-fragmentation rule may have unfortunate consequences.

Assume that the trustees of Adam's settlement appoint part of the trust fund (and it may be a relatively small amount) on to a new settlement. Under the fragmentation rules both settlements (because they derive from a common settlor) will enjoy a basic rate band equal to one-half of the full band. Presumably (the matter is not absolutely clear) if a further settlement is carved out of Adam's original settlement the basic rate band will then be divided into three and so on. The Consultative Document contains no provisions enabling a surrender to be made by any of the three trusts of the unused portion of its basic rate band to the other trusts.   [**V.5**]

6 Personal representatives

It is proposed that the present system whereby personal representatives suffer income tax at the 25% rate should continue to apply with a similar rule for capital gains tax for the year of death and next two years *only*. Thereafter the system for charging PRs to capital gains tax will be the same as that which will apply to trustees. One welcome reform proposal would enable the unused losses of personal representatives to be passed on to the legatees for offset against their chargeable gains.   **[V.6]**

APPENDIX VI: YEAR END TAX PLANNING

Significant tax savings may result from taking action before the end of a tax year. Thus it is always prudent to ensure that full advantage has been taken of exemptions and reliefs since once April 5 has passed it may be too late. Consider, for instance, the following five matters:

(1) *Inheritance tax:* ensure that use has been made of the annual £3,000 exemption. Remember that the exemption can be rolled forward for one year only: an individual may therefore be able to give away £6,000 in 1991/92 (the 1990-91 and 1991-92 exemptions) and a married couple £12,000. This annual exemption applies to dispositions of all forms of property: it is not necessary to transfer cash. The normal expenditure out of income and small gifts (£250 per donee per tax year) exemptions should also be utilised.

(2) *Capital gains tax:* gains of up to £5,500 fall within the CGT annual exemption for 1991-92. This exemption may not be carried forward for use in future years. Thought should be given therefore to making disposals or part disposals of assets when the resulting gain will be tax free (eg gains on shares and unit trusts could be 'washed' free of chargeable gains and the repurchased securities would then benefit from a higher base cost). Husband and wife should ensure that both take full advantage of this exemption. Personal representatives, it should be remembered, are also entitled to the annual exemption to set against gains realised in the year of death and in each of the two following tax years. Check, therefore, that this exemption is available before any disposals are made since in cases where it is not, it may be advantageous to vest the asset in the beneficiary and for him then to sell it and thereby use up his annual exemption. By way of qualification, the annual exemption is not, of course, the be all and end all and there may still be advantages in the PRs disposing of the asset—even when no exemption is available— in situations where their rate of CGT (25%) is lower than that of the relevant beneficiary. As a matter of general principle, CGT is charged on disposals made by individuals resident or ordinarily resident in the UK at any time during the tax year. Ensure, therefore, that all necessary steps have been taken prior to 6 April to sever those links with the UK which provide *indicia* of residence or ordinary residence if it is intended that a disposal will be made in the next tax year.

(3) *Retirement provision:* up to a fixed percentage of net relevant earnings can be invested each year in an approved retirement benefit or personal pension scheme. Such premiums generally qualify for full tax relief in the year when paid. In addition to paying the premiums for 1991-92 a taxpayer can make good underpayments of premiums in any of the previous six years (ie back to 1985-86). Further, if last year's permitted sum was not paid in full the taxpayer can elect (before April 5) that premiums paid in 1991-92 will be deemed to be paid in the last tax year (ie in 1990-91). Immediate tax relief will therefore be available if that election is made and it also enables underpayments from seven years ago (ie in 1984-85) to be topped up.

(4) *Income tax:* Finally to income tax where, apart from last minute pension top-ups and BES investments, the philanthropic may be attracted to the idea of making a charitable gift qualifying for full tax relief. Traditionally such gifts had to be by means of deed of covenant and would normally bind the taxpayer over a number of years. Since October

1990, however, Gift Aid has been avaiiable and affords relief for one-off cash payments to charity. The basic conditions are well known: each gift must be of at least £600 to attract the relief but there can be any number of such gifts and the old ceiling of £5 million has now been removed. The gifts must be of cash although gifts by credit card are permitted. Tax relief is at both basic and higher rates: basic rate being refunded to the charity, the higher rate to the taxpayer.

In parenthesis, it may be noted that Gift Aid *does not* provide any solution in the common situation where the non-charitable (typically trading) activities of a charity are carried on through the medium of a separate company. The intention is that that company will aim to pay up its profits without any tax charge to the charity. In this area the old method involving deeds of covenant and (for small companies), dividend payments, must still be employed.   **[VI.1]**

APPENDIX VII: RELIEF AGAINST DOUBLE CHARGES TO IHT

The risk of a double charge to IHT arises in a number of situations and FA 1986 s 104 enabled the Board to make regulations to give relief to taxpayers in certain cases. The Regulations were made on 30 June 1987 and came into force on 22 July 1987, although the relief is given for transfers of value made, and other events occurring on or after 18 March 1986 (the Inheritance Tax (Double Charges Relief) Regulations 1987: SI 1987/1130).   **[VII.1]**

Case 1—PETs and death

The first case is concerned with the area of mutual transfers, ie where property is transferred (by a PET which becomes chargeable) but at the death of the donor he has received back property from his donee (either the original property or property which represents it) which is included in the donor's death estate. The position is illustrated in the following example (note that in all the examples in this Appendix, which are based on illustrations given in the Regulations themselves, it is as assumed that 1987–88 IHT rates apply throughout and that no exemptions or reliefs are available).

EXAMPLE VII.1

July 1987	A makes a gift of a Matthew Smith oil painting (value £100,000) to B (a PET)	
July 1988	A makes a gift into a discretionary trust of £95,000	IHT paid £750
Jan 1989	A makes a further gift into the same trust of £45,000	IHT paid £6,750
Jan 1990	B dies and the Smith picture returns to A	
Apr 1991	A dies. His death estate of £300,000 includes the picture returned to him in 1990 which is still worth £100,000	

If no relief were available, A in *Example VII.1* would be subject to IHT on the value of the picture twice: once when it was given away in 1987 (the chargeable PET) and a second time on its value in 1991 (as part of his death estate). In addition A's cumulative total would be increased by the 1987 PET, thereby necessitating a recalculation of the tax charged on the 1988 and 1989 transfers and resulting in a higher charge on his death estate.

Regulation 4 affords relief in this situation and provides for two alternative IHT calculations to be made and for the lower amount of tax produced by those calculations to be payable. The alternative calculations may be illustrated as follows:

EXAMPLE VII.1 continued

First calculation:
Charge the picture as part of a death estate and ignore the 1987 PET.

July 1987	PET £100,000 ignored	Tax nil
July 1988	Gift £95,000—tax £1,500 less £750 already paid	Tax payable £ 750
Jan 1989	Gift £45,000: tax £13,500 less £6,750 already paid	Tax payable £ 6,750

Apr 1991   Death estate £300,000   Tax payable
                                                    £153,000

Total tax due as result of A's death   £160,500

(Note that because the 1987 PET is ignored A's cumulative total is unaltered and a recalculation of tax on the 1988 and 1989 transfers is unnecessary)

Second calculation:
Charge the 1987 PET and ignore the value of the picture on A's death
July 1987   PET £100,000: tax with taper relief   £ 2,400
July 1988   Gift £95,000: tax £34,000 less
            £750 already paid   £ 33.250
Jan 1989   Gift £45,000: tax £20,000 less
            £6,750 already paid   £ 13,250
Apr 1991   Death estate £200,000   £111,000

Total tax due as result of A's death   £159,900

Tax payable
The first calculation gives a higher amount of tax. Therefore the PET is reduced to nil and tax on the other transfers is as in the first calculation.

It may be that Regulation 4 is capable of being exploited to the benefit of the taxpayer as can be seen from the following illustration. Assume that Adam gives property worth £100,000 to his daughter Berta in 1989 and buys the property back for £75,000 (which represents less than full consideration) in 1990. He then dies in 1990. Under Regulation 4 the value of the property (£100,000) will remain subject to IHT but Adam's estate has been reduced by the £75,000 paid for the property (see especially regulation 4(3)(a)).   [**VII.2**]

Case 2—Gifts with a reservation and subsequent death

This case covers the situation where a gift with a reservation (either immediately chargeable or a chargeable PET) is followed by the death of the donor at a time when he still enjoys a reserved benefit or within seven years of that benefit ceasing (ie within seven years of the deemed PET: see [**22.3**]). The situation is illustrated in *Example VII.2*.

EXAMPLE VII.2

Jan 1988   A makes a PET of £150,000 to B
Mar 1992   A makes a gift of a house worth £200,000 into a   IHT paid
            discretionary trust but continues to live in the   £19,500
            property. The gift is of property subject to a
            reservation
Feb 1995   A dies still living in the house. His death estate is
            valued at £400,000 including the house which is
            then worth £300,000

Regulation 5 prevents double taxation of the house in this *Example* by providing for two separate IHT calculations to be made as follows: [**VII.3**]

EXAMPLE VII.2 continued

First calculation:
Charge the house as part of A's death estate and ignore the gift with reservation:

		Tax
Jan 1988	PET (exempt)	Nil
Mar 1992	Gift with reservation ignored	Nil
Feb 1995	Death estate £400,000: tax £144,000 minus £19,500 already paid	£124,500
Total tax due as a result of A's death		£124,500

(*Note:* credit for tax already paid on the gift with reservation cannot exceed the amount of death tax attributable to that property. In this example the tax so attributable is £108,000 (ie £144,000 × 300,000/400,000)—hence credit is given for the full amount of £19,500.)

Second calculation:
The gift with reservation is charged and the value of the gifted property is ignored in taxing the death estate:

		Tax
Jan 1988	PET now exempt	Nil
Mar 1992	Gift of house £200,000: tax £39,000 less £19,500 already paid	£19,500
Feb 1995	Death estate £100,000 (ignoring house)	£48,000
Total tax due as result of A's death:		£67,500

Tax payable: the first calculation yields a higher amount of tax. Therefore the gift of the house in 1992 is ignored and tax on death is charged as in the first calculation giving credit for IHT already paid.

Case 3—Artificial debts and death

Relief is afforded under Regulation 6 when a chargeable transfer (or chargeable PET) is followed by the transferor incurring a liability to his transferee which fall within FA 1986 s 103 (the artificial debt rules).

EXAMPLE VII.3

Nov 1987	X makes a PET of cash (£95,000) to Y
Dec 1987	Y makes a loan to X of £95,000
May 1988	X makes a gift into a discretionary trust of £20,000
Apr 1993	X dies. His death estate is worth £182,000 and the loan from Y remains outstanding

Under s 103 the deduction of £95,000 would be disallowed so that the 1987 PET and the disallowed debt would both attract an IHT charge. Relief is provided, however, under this Regulation on the basis of the following alternative calculations: **[VII.4]**

EXAMPLE VII.3 continued

First calculation:
Ignore the 1987 gift but do not allow the debt to be deducted in the death estate.

		Tax
Nov 1987	PET ignored	Nil
May 1988	£20,000	Nil
Apr 1993	Death estate £182,000	£39,800
Total tax due as result of X's death:		£39,800

Second calculation:
Charge the 1987 PET but allow the debt to be deducted from the estate at death.

		Tax
Nov 1987	PET £95,000 tax with taper relief	£ 600
May 1988	Gift £20,000: tax with taper relief	£ 3,600
Apr 1993	Death estate (£182,000—loan of £95,000)	£32,300
Total tax due as result of X's death:		£36,500

Tax payable: the first calculation gives a higher amount of tax. Therefore the debt is disallowed against the death estate but the PET of £95,000 is not charged.

Case 4—Chargeable transfers and death

Under FA 1986 s 104(1)(d) Regulations can be made to prevent a double charge to IHT in circumstances 'similar' to those dealt with in the first three cases above.

Regulation 7, made in pursuance of this power, applies when an individual makes a chargeable transfer of value to a *person* after 17 March 1986, and dies within 7 years of that transfer, at a time when he was beneficially entitled to property which either directly or indirectly represented the property which had been transferred by the original chargeable transfer.

For relief to be given under this Regulation it is important to realise that the lifetime transfer must have been chargeable when made. The majority of transfers to individuals will not therefore fall within its ambit since they will be PETs. Accordingly, the Regulation is only of importance in the following cases:

(1) When the chargeable transfer is to a discretionary trust which subsequently returns all or part of the property to settlor.
(2) When the chargeable transfer is to a company with, again, that property being returned to the transferor.
(3) Between 18 March 1986 and 17 March 1987 the creation of an interest in possession trust was immediately chargeable and therefore if such a trust was created during that period and property is later returned to the settlor the Regulation would, *prima facie*, be applicable.

It should be noted that the Regulation does not afford relief in cases where the chargeable transfer occurred before *18 March 1986* and the gift-back after that date. In such cases, the repeal of the CTT mutual transfer rules in 1986 means that the gift-back may be subject to charge without the possibility of any relief.

As with the other cases discussed above, relief under Regulation 7 is given on the basis of two alternative calculations. The first includes the returned property in the death estate but ignores the original chargeable transfer (although there is no question of any refund of tax paid at that time[1]).

The second calculation taxes the original chargeable transfer (ie it may be subject to a supplementary charge on death and remains in the taxpayer's cumulative total) but ignores the returned property in taxing the transferor's death estate. **[VII.5]**

APPENDIX VIII: PENSIONS

1 **Introduction**

The provision of financial security in old age is a major concern not only for an individual and his dependants, but also for the state. The state discharges its duty in this area by providing a statutory pension scheme which is available to all who make national insurance contributions. As this provides relatively small benefits, however, occupational pension schemes (private schemes provided by an employer for his employees) are crucially important and represent a significant (albeit hidden) part of an employee's remuneration. The self-employed and others who cannot benefit from an occupational scheme (nor from the earnings-related state scheme: SERPs) have always had to make their own arrangements and, with the advent of personal pensions, employees are now free to contract out of their employer's scheme and make their own arrangements if they so desire.

Until 1 July 1988 non-occupational schemes took the form of approved retirement annuity contracts under TA 1970 s 226 (now TA 1988 ss 619–620). Traditionally such schemes compared badly with occupational pensions because there were no employer's contributions and the benefits earned and hence payable were less generous because the level of permitted contributions was lower. In line with its desire to promote popular capitalism, Conservative governments under Margaret Thatcher have promoted wider home ownership, wider share ownership, and have introduced the necessary tax changes to allow expansion in the ownership of pensions. This has been achieved through 'personal pensions' (originally provided for in the Social Security Act 1986).

As from 1 July 1988 individuals have been able to leave their company pension scheme (membership of which therefore became voluntary), contract out of SERPs (the earnings related government scheme); and make their own pension arrangements through a personal pension purchased from a life company, unit trust group, bank or building society. Given that such a pension is 'personal' to the individual it is portable in the event of any change in his employment. For those who wish to remain in their company's scheme a free-standing AVC (Additional Voluntary Contribution) may be purchased to provide an additional pension on retirement.

A pension is treated as earned income in the hands of the recipient and is subject to income tax under Schedule E unless it is paid by a non-UK resident in which case it is taxed under Schedule D Case V (TA 1988 s 133). Pensions paid as a result of death on active service are exempt from income tax (TA 1988 s 318).   **[VIII.1]**

2 **The state scheme**

The state scheme is funded by national insurance contributions. It is in two parts: the first part, from which employers *cannot* contract out, is the flat rate pension the old age pension) payable from the age of 65 for men and 60 for women who have contributed to it for nine-tenths of their working lives. The second part is an earnings-related pension ('SERPs'), which is an additional pension related to individual employees' earnings and which employers and employees may 'contract out' of—in the former case by providing an appropriate occupational scheme.

The main disadvantages of the state scheme are that:

(1) the retirement age is not flexible, but is restricted to 65 for a man, 60 for a woman;

(2) although the employer's contributions are not taxed as emoluments of the employee (TA 1988 s 696), there is no income tax relief for the employee's own contributions;

(3) for the tax year 1991-92, earnings above £20,280 are unpensionable;

(4) there is no right to commute part of the pension for a tax-free lump sum;

(5) it is not funded on a current basis.

It is likely that the earnings related part of the state scheme will eventually be abolished, leaving individuals to make their own arrangements through occupational schemes or personal pensions. **[VIII.2]**

3 **Occupational pension schemes** (TA 1988 ss 590–612)

a) *Relationship to SERPs*

As already mentioned private schemes can be contracted out of the second tier of the state scheme (SERPs). In such cases the national insurance contributions of both employer and employee are reduced and payments are instead made to the private scheme. Contracting out is a complicated process, but, basically, the private scheme must be approved by the Occupational Pensions Board and, if it is to enjoy tax advantages, by the Inland Revenue Superannuation Fund Office (see IR 12 (1979) which contains SFO notes on approval of occupational pension schemes). **[VIII.3]**

b) *Contributory and non-contributory schemes*

Private schemes may be funded by contributions from both employer and employee. In the case of non-contributory schemes, however, all the contributions are by the employer and as those sums are not taxed as emoluments of the employee (TA 1988 s 596) and are deductible in arriving at the profits of the employer they represent a valuable tax-free fringe benefit. Further, because of the high level of employer's national insurance contributions in the case of higher paid employees (10.4% of salary in the case of employees earning more than £390 pw) increased contributions by the employer to such a scheme may prove more attractive than paying a higher wage or bonus. Although there is no fixed upper limit on an employer's contribution to an occupational scheme, the essential requirement is that contributions must be adequate to ensure the appropriate pension benefits. Accordingly, as from 6 April 1987 pension schemes must keep the surplus of assets over liabilities within a prescribed limit. If this limit is exceeded, the surplus must then be reduced in one of three ways: *either* by improving benefits; *or* by giving contribution holidays to employees and/or employers; *or* by a refund to the employer. Any such a refund is, however, subject to a 40% tax charge deducted at source (TA 1988 s 601). **[VIII.4]**

c) *Administration*

The company pension fund is generally administered by trustees who are responsible for making the investments and paying the pensions. Alternatively, responsibility for providing the pensions may be passed to an insurance company which receives premiums in the form of employer/employee contributions. **[VIII.5]**

Self-administered schemes provide flexibility and can be more cost-effective than insurance company schemes. Small self-administered schemes (broadly those with less than 12 members) are particularly suited to controlling shareholders of private companies (see SFO Memorandum No 58: February 1979). Directors of the relevant company may be appointed trustees of the pension fund together with one professional trustee and, as they will be given wide investment powers, may employ the fund for the benefit of the company itself. For instance, they can purchase the business premises and then lease it back to the company at a commercial rent. The rent will be tax deductible by the company and tax free in the hands of the pension fund trustees. Additionally, the trustees may be given the power to make loans (of up to 50% of the value of the fund) to the company and may invest in the company's shares. **[VIII.6]**

EXAMPLE VIII.1

A small family company trades profitably. Mr and Mrs A themselves own the property from which the business is conducted (current value £80,000) and all the shares in the company. The business is now run by their three daughters. A small self-administered pension scheme is established and the following events occur:

(1) A contribution of £40,000 is made by the company to the scheme. In practice, this sum will be deducted in arriving at the profits of the business (probably by spreading over a number of years).

(2) The fund is loaned £40,000 by a bank.

(3) The trustees of the scheme pay Mr and Mrs A £80,000 for the property.

(4) The trustees lease the property to the company charging a rent of £8,000 pa. This is an allowable expense for corporation tax purposes so far as the company is concerned and the rental income is tax-free so far as the fund is concerned.

Note: (a) In the future the bank loan can be repaid out of pension contributions and rental income; (b) the property has been taken out of the estates of Mr and Mrs A and will therefore be tax free when they die; (c) as and when pensions become payable the property may have to be sold to raise funds to purchase life annuities.

d) *Tax treatment of occupational pensions*

Retirement benefit schemes (schemes for the provision of 'relevant benefits') are governed for tax purposes by a code originally introduced in FA 1970.

The term 'relevant benefits' is widely defined to cover virtually any kind of payment to an employee or to his widow, children or dependants made as a result of his retirement or death (TA 1988 s 611). Most private schemes are governed by this code, but only if the scheme is 'exempt approved' within the meaning of the legislation (see section e) below), will it enjoy the following tax advantages:

(1) The employer's contributions will not be taxed as the employee's income. (The same is true for contributions to SERPs; for contributions made by a foreign government for its employees in the UK; and where the contributions are for a non-UK resident working wholly abroad.)

(2) The employer's contributions are a deductible business expense in arriving at his profits.

(3) The employee obtains income tax relief on his own contributions (through PAYE: see TA 1988 s 692(7)) subject to a limit of 15% of his gross emoluments (but see (4) below). In practice, employee contributions do not usually exceed 8% although an employee may increase his contributions by making additional voluntary contributions (AVCs) which, so long as they do not result in the 15% ceiling being exceeded, attract full income tax relief. AVCs can be paid either into the employer's pension scheme or,

alternatively, the employee may prefer to enter into a free-standing arrangement (ie to enter into a personal pension contract.

When free-standing AVCs were first introduced the provider was required to check with the company's pension scheme that the employee's contribution limits were not being exceeded. This involved a substantial amount of work especially since the checks had to continue until the retirement of the employee[1] Not surprisingly, FA 1989 relaxed these provisions so that only comparatively simple checks (not involving the employer's scheme) are now needed in the case of contributions up to £2,400 pa whilst for contributions over that amount there is a simplified procedure and normally no need to make continuous checks until retirement. As a necessary corollary, however, any excess funds at retirement, although paid out to the employee, will be subject to a tax charge which will broadly make up for the tax relief given on the contributions and for the contributions being free of tax in the pension fund. For the basic rate taxpayer this rate of charge (in 1991–92) is 35%: for higher rate taxpayers 48%.

(4) A major change introduced by FA 1989 was the introduction of *an earnings limit of £60,000* (raised to £64,800 for 1990–91 and to £71,400 for 1991–92). This ceiling applies for the purpose of calculating certain benefits paid and contribution levels in the case of tax approved pension schemes established on or after 14 March 1989 and also applies to new entrants to existing schemes who join on or after 1 June 1989. Although the ceiling is increased, this is by reference to movements in prices rather than earnings.

EXAMPLE VIII.2

Gerontius' salary is £150,000 pa and he is subject to the pension ceiling. The maximum pension that can be funded is two thirds of £71,400 (ie £47,600 see (5), below) and the maximum cash sum £107,100 (2.25 × £47,600) subject in the case of commutations to the completion of 20 years' service. Both figures are indexed in line with prices.

Benefits in excess of the £71,400 limit may be provided under top-up schemes *which are not tax approved*. Although an employer's contributions to such schemes are deductible in computing his taxable profit, that sum will be taxed as an emolument of the employee and the scheme's assets will be subject to normal tax charges (ie to CGT on a disposal of investments and income tax on income produced by the assets).

(5) After 10 years service the employee's pension may be equal to two thirds final salary (subject to indexation) and, subject to 20 years service, may be commuted in part for a capital sum. This can amount to one and a half times final remuneration (tax free) and, if paid, results in the payment of a reduced pension. AVCs may not be included in calculating this figure if the AVC arrangement was entered into after 7 April 1987 and, for members joining a scheme on or after 17 March 1987, the maximum tax free lump sum is limited to £150,000.

To further complicate matters, FA 1989 permitted a maximum pension of two thirds final earnings to be paid (subject to the £71,400 ceiling in (4) above) after 20 years service on early retirement between the ages of 50 and 70 and provided for the maximum allowable tax-free lump sum payable on retirement to be the greater of (a) 380ths of final earnings for each year of service, and (b) 2.25 times the pension at retirement prior to commutation.

The 1989 provisions generally apply to pension schemes established on

The 1989 provisions generally apply to pension schemes established on or after 14 March 1989 and to new entrants existing schemes who join on or after 1 June 1989. Although the more generous early retirement provisions can be applied to members of existing schemes who joined *before* 1 June, this will only be allowed if, as a *quid pro quo,* the scheme applies the £71,400 limit and the amended tax-free lump sum limit.

(6) Payments made to the employee's dependants on his death will not be charged to IHT provided that they are made at the trustees' discretion (in practice, an employee may make a 'declaration of wish' indicating who he would like to benefit on his death, and the trustees obviously pay particular attention to this when exercising their discretion).

(7) The pension fund is not subject to income tax on the investments (except for any income produced from commercial trading), nor to CGT on any disposal of investments.   **[VIII.7]**

e) Meaning of 'exempt approved'

If the retirement benefits scheme satisfies the requirements in TA 1988 s 590 it must be approved. These requirements are narrow but under TA 1988 s 591 the Revenue have a wide discretion to approve schemes which do not satisfy them all (see IR 12 'Practice Notes' and the model rules and guidance notes for simplified occupational pensions schemes). Detailed study of s 590 and IR 12 is advised, but the main conditions which the scheme must meet relate to who can benefit; who administers the scheme; the level of contributions; the minimum and maximum benefits payable; and specification of the retirement age.

Besides being approved, a private scheme must be exempt if it is to receive the above tax benefits. This requires the scheme to be established under 'irrevocable trusts', ie it must be of a permanent nature so that it cannot be interfered with by the employer. Most schemes will be formally set up with a trust deed and set of rules.   **[VIII.8]**

4   Retirement annuity contracts

Prior to 1 July 1988 the self-employed and employees in non-pensionable employment made provision for their retirement by entering into retirement annuity contracts approved by the Inland Revenue under TA 1988 s 619. From that date it has not been possible to take out new retirement annuity contracts since they were then superseded by personal pensions (see 5, below). As many individuals continue to make payments and receive benefits under retirement annuity contracts, and will continue to do so in the foreseeable future, their main features are briefly discussed in this section. As discussed in the following section retirement annuities are a money purchase arrangement so that although contributions are limited there is no ceiling on the eventual pension that is paid.

(1) Under an approved retirement annuity contract the premiums paid are allowable deductions for income tax purposes at the taxpayer's highest rates. To be approved the scheme must (generally) provide for the annuity to be paid to the insured between the ages of 60 and 75 and must prohibit surrender or assignment of the benefit of the annuity.

(2) Commutation of part of the benefit is permissible provided that the lump sum does not exceed three times the value of the annuity payable after commutation (see TA 1988 s 620(3). As from 17 March 1987 the maximum lump sum that may be paid is fixed at £150,000.

(3) The premiums must not exceed a percentage of the individual's 'net relevant earnings' in the tax year. Prior to 1987-88, this percentage depended upon the partner's date of birth. Thus, it was $17^1/2\%$ for those born after 1933 with a staged increase from 20% to $32^1/2\%$ for those born between 1933 and 1907. From 1987-88, however, this percentage has been calculated according to age in the relevant tax year as follows:

50 or under	$17\frac{1}{2}\%$
51 to 55	20%
56 to 60	$22\frac{1}{2}\%$
61 and over	$27\frac{1}{2}\%$

These contribution limits were not amended in FA 1989 and are now less generous than those available in the case of personal pensions. However, the ceiling of £71,400 which now applies both to occupational pensions and to personal pensions *does not affect retirement annuity contracts.*

In the event of excessive contributions being made the excess will not attract tax relief.

'Net relevant earnings' means an individual's earned income less capital allowances, allowable expenses and losses (if relevant).

(4) The Revenue may approve contracts which provide either for a lump sum consisting only of a return of contributions paid, plus reasonable interest and bonuses out of profits to be payable to prescribed individuals on the death of the insured before the age of 75, or for an annuity to be paid in such circumstances to a surviving spouse. In the latter case, premiums on that annuity must not exceed 5% of net relevant earnings and total premiums paid must not exceed the percentage ceiling.

(5) If an individual dies before retirement, the insurance company will pay a lump sum calculated in accordance with the terms of the scheme and it is possible for the insured to settle such death benefits on discretionary trusts for his family and dependants. The attraction of so doing is that the payment will then not form part of his estate on death and will be free from IHT. Further, the creation of the settlement will itself be free from IHT provided that the settlor was then in good health. In such a case, although the creation of the trust will be a chargeable transfer (since the insured's estate is diminished by the value of the death benefit), the value transferred will be nominal. In practice, the Revenue will presume that the settlor was in good health provided that he survives the creation of his trust by two years. Payments out of the trust, if made within two years of the settlor's death, will likewise be free from IHT.

The CTO have recently indicated that failure to take a pension at the earliest permissible retirement age may amount to an omission to exercise a right thereby giving rise to an IHT charge on death if the pension is never taken. This matter is discussed at [21.2] and for the present it may be sensible to wait for clarification of the position before establishing new trusts.

(6) Individuals, especially partners in their early years, may be unable to afford to pay the full permitted premiums each year, in which case any shortfall in one year can be carried forward for six years and relieved in addition to the normal relief in any of those tax years (see *Example VIII.3(1)*).

To a limited extent premiums paid in one tax year can, at the election of the taxpayer (which must be made before 6 July in the following tax year), be treated as paid in the previous tax year or, if he has no net relevant earnings in that year, in the tax year before that (see *Example VIII.3(2)*). The effect is to give tax relief as if the premium had been paid in that earlier year; such relief will, of course, only be available up to the appropriate percentage ceiling. This provision is likely to prove of greatest benefit in a partner's final tax year prior to retirement when he may not earn sufficient income to cover his premiums for that tax year.   **[VIII.9]**

EXAMPLE VIII.3

(1) Ray joins the firm of Wayne & Hank in May 1987 and entered into a retirement annuity contract (under TA 1988 s 619). The following table indicates his net relevant earnings (NRE) and premium contributions in subsequent tax years:

Tax year	NRE £	Premiums paid £	Shortfall £
1987–88	10,000	1,000	750
1988–89	15,000	1,000	1,625
1989–90	15,000	2,625 (17½%)	—
1990–91	20,000	3,500 (17½%)	—

In 1991–92 his NRE amount to £25,000 and in addition to the full contribution for that year (£4,375) he can pay off the entire shortfall (£750 + £1,625 = £2,375) and will, therefore, obtain tax relief in 1991–92 on total premiums of £6,750 (£4,375 + £2,375). If he wishes to pay off only a part of the shortfall then the £750 from 1987–88 will be used first.

(2) Hank retires from partnership with Wayne and Ray in June 1992. The following table indicates his net relevant earnings (NRE) and premium contributions during his final years with the partnership.

Tax year	NRE £	Premiums paid £	Overpayment £
1992–93	5,000	1,750	875
1991–92	15,000	2,500	(125)
1990–91	15,000	2,000	(500)

The overpayment of £875 in 1992–93 can be partially offset by claiming additional tax relief in 1991–92 on £125. If tax has already been paid in that year, Hank will be entitled to a rebate. The remaining £750 overpayment will not attract relief. This example illustrates the dangers involved in any overpayment of premiums; underpayments can be made good in later years, but overpayments will often receive no tax relief.

5   Personal pensions

As already discussed, personal pensions replaced retirement annuity contracts and are now available in the following circumstances:
(1) for the self-employed;
(2) for the employee in non-pensionable employment;
(3) for an employee who wishes to 'top-up' his occupational pension;
(4) for an employee who has 'contracted out' of his occupational pension scheme.

Many of the features of personal pensions are the same as those already discussed in the context of retirement annuity contracts. In particular, contributions up to the permitted level (see below) qualify for income tax relief at the individual's highest rate and those contributions are invested in a tax exempt fund. As this fund is not subject to investment controls, the individual may choose to pay his contributions into a high risk fund. Unlike the majority of occupational pension schemes, therefore, personal pensions are money purchase contracts: in other words it is the accumulated savings from the chosen fund which will eventually be used to buy an annuity (the pension) from a life insurance company. Accordingly, the eventual pension payable is not limited to a fraction of the individual's earnings at any particular time. Other features of personal pensions worthy of note include the following:

(1) As with retirement annuity contracts the maximum contributions are computed by reference to a percentage of the individual's 'net relevant earnings'. For 1991–92 the relevant percentage which can be contributed, dependent upon the taxpayer's age, is set out in the following table.

Age	Max contribution
36 to 45	20%
46 to 50	25%
51 to 55	30%
56 to 60	35%
61 or more	40%

Note that a higher level of contribution is permitted than in the case of retirement annuity contracts (but see (2) below).

(2) As with occupational pensions, the tax relief available will, however, be restricted to contributions on earnings of up to £70,400 pa (to be increased in line with prices). Assume, therefore, that Gerontius in *Example VIII.2* above was paying into a personal pension and was aged 57. The maximum contribution that will attract tax relief in 1991–92 is limited to 35% × £70,400.

(3) So far as lump sum payments are concerned, in the case of personal pension plans entered into on or after 27 July 1989, the £150,000 ceiling (which continues to apply to retirement annuity contracts) has been removed and, instead, the maximum tax free lump sum permitted at retirement is 25% of the total fund excluding 'protected rights' (as defined) but including the value of dependants' benefits.

(4) The rules for both carry-back of contributions and carry-forward of unused contributions mirror those for retirement annuity contracts except that there are provisions to deal with the situation where an individual is contributing both to an (old) retirement annuity contract and to a (new) personal pension scheme. In such cases, relief for contributions will be available under two sets of rules but limited to the overall maximum amount of relief. Furthermore, contributions under a personal pension scheme in any tax year when carry-forward of unused relief under a retirement annuity contract is available will reduce the available relief. An individual who elects to carry back contributions under a personal pension to 1987–88, 1986–87 or 1985–86 will be treated as contributing to a retirement annuity contract and the unused relief in the tax year to which the contributions are carried back will be calculated under the (old) rules in TA 1988 s 619. Similarly, if he elects to carry forward unused relief from a year before 1988–89 so as to contribute to a personal pension, the unused relief will be calculated under the (old) rules of TA 1988 s 619.

(5) The more generous percentage of contribution relief for personal pensions and the ceiling of £70,400 do not affect the amount of unused relief which may be carried forward from the last six years. In cases where a person contributes both to a retirement annuity contract and personal pension, contributions to the retirement annuity contract are relieved first and deducted from the maximum contribution which may be paid to the personal pension (TA 1988 s 655). **[VIII.10]**

APPENDIX IX: TAX TREATMENT OF CHARITIES

There is a useful Inland Revenue explanatory leaflet (IR 75) and, given the complexity in the definition of charity which is case-law based rather than statutory, reference should also be made to standard works on charities such as *Tudor* and *Picarda*.   [IX.1]

1 'Qualifying charities'

(i) Tax reliefs are only available for bodies which are registered as a charity with the Charity Commissioners or, in the case of charities not required to register, which satisfy the Inland Revenue that they are established for charitable purposes only. Educational and other institutions specified in Charities Act 1960 Sch 2; places of worship; charities without a permanent endowment; and charities in Scotland and Northern Ireland fall into the latter category.

(ii) The legal definition of charity is complex depending, as it does, on a voluminous body of case law. The roots of the definition may be traced to the preamble to the Charitable Uses Act 1601 which listed those purposes considered to be charitable *at that time*. Subsequent case law has extended that list by reference to the supposed 'spirit and intendment' of the preamble—albeit that judges have frequently confessed that the spirit and intendment of that measure has been stretched almost to breaking point! The end result is that:

> 'The words "charity" and "charitable" bear, for the purposes of English law and equity, meanings totally different from the senses in which they are used in ordinary educated speech, or, for instance, in the Authorised Version of the Bible.' (Lord Hailsham in *IRC v McMullen* (1981).)

(iii) Traditionally charities are classified as falling into four categories: for the relief of poverty; for educational purposes; for the promotion of religion; and for other purposes beneficial to the community, although the threadbare nature of this classification is apparent from the final catch-all category. The definition of religion has excited controversy in recent years as has the requirement that charitable trusts must be for the benefit of the public at large or a sufficient section of the public. As a result of this latter requirement a trust to educate the children of employees of a large public company and its subsidiaries was held not charitable (the beneficiaries not comprising a section of the public), nor was a trust for a Carmelite Convent containing 20 contemplative nuns whose activities were not considered by the House of Lords to confer any benefit on an outside world which they never visited. As may be appreciated the case law on the meaning of charity is rich in absurdities!

The charitable purposes do not have to be carried out exclusively in the United Kingdom: the Charity Commissioners accept charitable purposes abroad on the assumption that 'the relief of poverty and the advancement of education and religion are charitable in all parts of the world'; but in connection with trusts coming under the fourth head (other purposes beneficial to the community) they take a defensive position and say that there must be a benefit, albeit indirect, to the community of the United Kingdom and add that 'it is easier to establish this benefit in relation to Commonwealth than to foreign countries'. Why these distinctions should be drawn is far from clear but the practice of the

Charity Commissioners is, of course, crucial since acceptance by them as a charity (and entry on the register) will in turn lead to an acceptance by the Inland Revenue that the organisation will qualify for tax benefits. Theoretically a body may exist for charitable purposes without being registered, but it is highly unlikely that its charitable status will be accepted by the Revenue and, under the Charities Act 1960, the charitable trustees would be in breach of a duty to register and to supply appropriate documents to the Commissioners.

The Charity Commissioners are limited in their operations to England and Wales; in Scotland, a register of charities is maintained by the Inland Revenue. Further, the Commissioners' jurisdiction is restricted to charities which are defined in s 45 of the Act as 'any institution, corporate or not, which is established for charitable purposes and is subject to the control of the High Court in the exercise of the Court's jurisdiction with respect to charities'. Overseas charities will, in practice, only come within this definition if a majority of the trustees or the bulk of the funds are subject to the control of the High Court and therefore to supervision by the Attorney General.

As a result of these limitations, charitable purposes carried out through United Kingdom resident companies managed by non-resident trustees will—unless there are funds in the United Kingdom—fail to obtain registration by the Charity Commissioners. Given that the company itself is resident here for corporation tax purposes, the somewhat bizarre result may be that income and profits will attract a tax charge since the tax relief available to charities under Taxes Act 1988 s 505 has a similarly restricted ambit to that confining the Charity Commissioners' jurisdiction. Despite charity being defined in the Taxes Act as 'any body of persons established for charitable purposes only' the House of Lords decided in *Camille and Henry Dreyfus Foundation Inc v IRC* (1956) that these words had to be limited to a body of persons or trusts established for such purposes *in the United Kingdom*. In that case a foundation established in the State of New York and which carried on all its activities in the USA was not entitled to exemption (under the forerunner of s 505) for substantial royalties which it received from a company resident in the United Kingdom.

English law has generally refused to accept that non-charitable purpose trusts are valid. Amongst the reasons given for this attitude are that in a number of cases the purposes have been so imprecisely drafted that it would be difficult to control the trustees in the exercise of their functions; in other cases the purposes would continue forever and therefore breach the perpetuity rule; whilst certain purposes have been stigmatised as useless or capricious (see, for instance, *McCaig v University of Glasgow* 1907 SC 231 in which the court set aside a will trust that would have involved building statues of the deceased and other 'artistic towers' at prominent points on his estate). The unfortunate result of this approach has been that in general only charitable purpose trusts are valid and hence the courts have tended to extend the definition of charity to encompass dubious cases in the knowledge that failure to do so would lead to the trusts being held invalid.

(iv) The tax reliefs which will be noted below are available to all charities. Given that the definition now embraces purposes often of little benefit to the public, it is debatable whether this position is satisfactory. In 1975 the Expenditure Committee of the House of Commons made the following recommendation:

'Legislation should be introduced whereby all charities should be required to satisfy the test of purposes beneficial to the community. In the case of those charities formally admitted under one of the other heads, namely the relief of poverty, the advancement of education and the advancement of religion, they should continue to qualify only if they also satisfy the main criteria. We do not believe such a change would affect the great majority of charities in any way; but we do believe it would act as a check to abuse at the fringe.'

In a similar vein, Lord Cross of Chelsea in *Dingle v Turner* (1972) argued as follows:

'As Counsel for the Attorney General remarked in the course of argument, the law of charity is bedevilled by the fact that charitable trusts enjoy two quite different sorts of privilege. On the one hand, they enjoy immunity from the laws against perpetuity and uncertainty and though individual potential beneficiaries cannot sue to enforce them, the public interest arising is protected by the Attorney General. If this was all, there would be no reason for the courts not to look favourably on the claim of any "purpose" trust to be considered as a charity if it seemed calculated to confer some real benefit on those intended to benefit by it . . . But that is not all. Charities automatically enjoy fiscal privileges which with the increasing burden of taxation have become more and more important and in deciding that such and such a trust is a charitable trust, the court is endowing it with a substantial annual subsidy at the expense of the taxpayer. Indeed, claims for trusts to rank as charities are just as often challenged by the Revenue as by those who would take the fund if the trust was invalid. It is, of course, unfortunate that the recognition of any trust as a valid charitable trust should automatically attract fiscal privileges, for the question whether a trust to further some purpose is so little likely to benefit the public that it ought to be declared invalid and the question whether it is likely to confer such great benefits on the public that it should enjoy fiscal immunity are really two quite different questions. The logical solution would be to separate them and to say ... that only some charities should enjoy fiscal privileges.'   [**IX.2**]

2 Tax relief on charitable income and gains

(i) TA 1988 s 505 and CGTA 1979 s 145 confer relief from income tax; capital gains tax; and corporation tax in respect of:
—rent from land and property;
—interest and dividends;
—covenanted donations;
—single gifts by companies and individuals;
—grants from other charities;
—chargeable gains.
In cases where tax has been deducted at source, the recipient charity is entitled to a refund by application to the Inland Revenue Charities division (see generally SP 3/87).
(ii) In addition to the above, a trade carried on by a charity and which produces profits will be exempt from tax provided that *either* the trade carries out a primary purpose of the charity (eg an educational charity running a school) *or* the work is done mainly by beneficiaries of the charity; for example, a charity set up to provide work for the disabled. In those cases where the proposed trade will not satisfy these tests, the device commonly adopted by charities is to incorporate a company to

carry out the work and for the profits thereby produced to be covenanted-up to the charity. The result of so doing is that the profits of the company will be kept at zero and the sums received by the charity will not themselves attract tax. With the current rates of ACT and corporation tax for small companies an alternative (and arguably more satisfactory method) is for the profits to be paid up to the charity by means of a dividend. **[IX.3]**

3 Expenditure by a charitable body

To qualify for the tax benefits set out in 2, above, the charity must spend its money *only for charitable purposes*. Such expenditure will, of course, include the cost of its own charitable activities; buying assets to be used in activities; administrative and fund-raising costs; and the payment of money to bodies established to carry out the work of the charity. It is crucial to bear in mind, however, that spending money non-charitably will not only result in a withdrawal of tax relief so far as both the charity and (in certain cases) its donors are concerned, but may also involve the appropriate trustees in committing a breach of trust and in a criminal offence (see further 5, below). In *IRC v Educational Grants Association Ltd* (1967), the Educational Grants Association had been established for the advancement of education and had a close relationship with The Metal Box Company Ltd in that the bulk of its income came from a Deed of Covenant executed in its favour by that company. On a repayment claim for income tax deducted at source being made, it transpired that between 76% and 85% of the income of the charity had been applied for the education of children of persons connected with The Metal Box Company Ltd. Accordingly the claim for repayment failed since the court was not convinced that the income of the charity was being applied for 'charitable purposes only'. In deciding that the organisation had expended money for non-charitable purposes, the judge accepted that this involved concluding that the managers had acted *ultra vires* in spending the Association's income: he therefore concluded: 'it is of course open to a comparable body to frame its objects so as to make clear that its income may be applied for private as well as public purposes, but in that case it may not obtain tax relief. It does not seem to me that such a body can have it both ways.' **[IX.4]**

4 Effective charitable giving

(i) *Deeds of covenant:* Sums paid under deed of covenant are tax effective (ie they reduce the income of the payer) provided that the covenant is *capable of lasting for more than three years* (TA 1988 ss 660–662). This requirement can, therefore, be satisfied if *either* a fixed period in excess of three years is chosen (hence the popularity of the four-year covenant) *or*, alternatively, if a period of uncertain duration is chosen which *might* exceed three years. The duration of an annual payment must be considered in the light of circumstances prevailing at the start: so long as capable of lasting more than three years at that time, subsequent events are therefore ignored. If, however, a covenant reserves to the covenantor (or any other person) a power of revocation which could be exercised to bring it to an end before the expiration of three years, then the annual payment is caught by TA 1988 s 671 and rendered ineffective. For an example of the position of charitable covenants entered into by companies, see *Example 28.6* at **[28.45]**. Reference should be made to SP 4/90 for the Revenue's practice on charitable covenants. In particular, it should be noted that from 31 July 1990 it is no longer necessary for a covenant made in England, Wales or Northern Ireland to be sealed. It is sufficient if the covenant is signed and dated.

(ii) *Deposit covenants:* In recent years deposit covenants have proved popular: they are particularly beneficial to the taxpayer who wishes to give a lump sum to the relevant charity but who also wishes to obtain the normal income tax benefits associated with covenanted payments. In essence, the arrangement involves a covenant to pay annually one quarter of a stated capital sum over a four-year period. That entire capital sum, however, is handed over to the charity at once and is therefore said to be held by the charity 'on deposit'. Thereafter, each year, a fraction of that sum is released in satisfaction of the covenant (see further SP 4/90). Although these arrangements smack of artificiality and could conceivably fall within the *Ramsay* principle, the Revenue have expressly stated that they will not be challenged provided that they are made in favour of charity (see further Chapter 31).

(iii) *Payroll giving:* The so-called 'payroll deduction scheme' has been discussed at [**5.112**]. In broad terms it involves employers who wish to set up a scheme for their employees entering into a contract with an agency approved by the Inland Revenue. Employees who wish to join the scheme authorise their employer to deduct the relevant amount from their pay before calculating PAYE tax due and to pay over the relevant amount to the agency. The function of the agency is to act as a clearing house, distributing the appropriate sums to the individual charities which have been nominated by the employees.

(iv) *One-off gifts (FA 1990 ss 25–26):* An innovation of recent years has been the introduction of tax reliefs for one-off gifts to charity. Since 1986 companies (other than close companies) have been able to obtain corporation tax reliefs for single gifts to charities up to a limit equivalent to 3% of the dividends paid by the company in the same accounting period. 'Gift Aid' (single gifts by individuals and companies) came into effect on 1 October 1990 and extended this relief to single gifts of £600 or more subject to a maximum limit of £5m on total qualifying gifts by any company or individual in any relevant year. Even those limits have now been abolished and with effect from 19 March 1991 companies and individuals can now claim tax relief on gifts to charity with no upper limit provided, of course, that the gift does not exceed the total income or profits of the individual or company concerned in the relevant year. For non-close companies there is no £600 lower limit: in such cases single gifts of any amount therefore qualify for relief

Such gifts will be made subject to deduction of basic rate income tax at source which will be accounted for by the relevant individual or corporation to the Revenue and then refunded to the charity on an appropriate claim being made. For the payer (whether individual or company) full tax relief will be available for the gross sum paid. For example, if the donor is an individual who gives £1,200 to charity net of basic rate income tax, in the year 1991/92 the charity will be able to claim a tax repayment of £400 (25% of the gross equivalent of the sum paid: ie £1,600). If that individual is a higher rate tax payer his taxable income will be reduced by £1,600.

Abolishing the upper limit for all single charitable gifts will simplify arrangements for charitable giving, particularly for companies which have associated companies. Prior to 19 March the upper limit of £5m was shared between associated companies. The changes in the 1991 Finance Act are of less significance for individuals. It remains the case that gift aid is unlikely to replace the deed of covenant as the most popular method of charitable giving since although covenants bind the payer for a number of years, they enable smaller sums to be paid to charity.

(v) *Capital gifts:* CGTA 1979 s 146 provides that for capital gains tax purposes gifts to charity shall be at no gain no loss (compare the similar rule for inter-spouse gifts under CGTA 1979 s 44). For IHT purposes, such gifts are exempt transfers of value under IHTA 1984 s 23.

(vi) *Business gifts to educational establishments:* FA 1991 s 68 (inserting a new TA 1988 s 84) provides relief for gifts of equipment by businesses to schools and other educational establishments. The relief applies to gifts by companies and unincorporated businesses of items of equipment either manufactured, sold or used in the course of their trade. It applies where such equipment is given to educational establishments, whether schools or higher educational institutions.

The company or unincorporated business will be allowed a deduction for the cost of acquiring or manufacturing the item of plant machinery or in calculating its taxable profits. This means that the business will be given full relief for the cost of the item and there will be no charge on the profit foregone by reason of the gift. Further, items of equipment used in the course of the donor's trade, and on which capital allowances have been given, will be treated as having been disposed of at nil value, so that the balance of allowances due on the asset will be given to the business in the normal way.

This new relief brings the tax treatment of gifts of equipment into line with the treatment of gifts of cash used by the recipient to purchase equipment.   **[IX.5]**

5 Restriction on tax relief

In cases where a charity spends money on non-charitable purposes or invests or lends money in ways which are not for the benefit of the charitable objects, tax relief on the income or gains so employed may be withdrawn. The charity may therefore be taxed on the income or gains misused. In addition, under provisions introduced in 1986, larger charities are subject to more detailed rules in such circumstances which may result in tax relief given in earlier years being withdrawn.

So far as donors are concerned, in cases where that donation has not been applied for charitable purposes, tax relief at higher rate may be lost.   **[IX.6]**

APPENDIX X: EUROPEAN ECONOMIC INTEREST GROUPINGS

The introduction of European Economic Interest Groupings ('EEIGs') is a major development in international law, being the first really cross-border legal vehicle within the European Community. EEIGs are intended to promote economic co-operation between persons in the European Community (EC) by providing a vehicle with a structure which is common throughout the Community. The relevant Community Regulation concerning EEIGs (Council Regulation EEC No 2137/85 Article 40) is directly applicable throughout the Community and had retrospective effect from 1 July 1989. In order to make the Regulation fully effective in Member States, however, some additional domestic legislation is required. As the UK Consultative Document on the subject, which was issued in January 1990, comments, 'an EEIG is a new optional form of business entity for businesses looking to co-operate internationally, perhaps to pool common support activities such as research and development or marketing, or possibly to co-operate on individual projects.'   [**X.1**]

1   **Structure**

In order to establish an EEIG, all that is required is for the members to enter into a contract which is registered at the appropriate registry in a Member State of the EC. In the United Kingdom, registration is with the relevant Registrar of Companies. Any business, whether a company, a partnership or a sole trader, can join with others to set up an EEIG, provided they are based in the European Community and that there are members from at least two Member States. An EEIG may not consist entirely of members from one State only.

Although the intention is that an EEIG is to be a flexible structure capable of having an independent legal personality, it is not intended to replace the role of a company: the creation of a 'European company' remains a further objective of the Community. An EEIG may only be established to facilitate or develop the economic activities of its members and to improve or increase the results of those activities. The activities of the EEIG must, therefore, be ancillary to the economic activities of its members.

These provisions are not without difficulties. For example, while a US company may participate in an EEIG through a subsidiary which is incorporated in a Member State, the activities of the EEIG will be restricted unless the subsidiary is active. This is because there is no provision for 'looking through' to the activities of the parent company. The requirement that an EEIG must have members from at least two Member States means that the prospect of dissolution is a real issue: an EEIG formed by two members from France and one from the UK will face dissolution if the UK member decides to pull out unless another participator outside France can be found.

An EEIG cannot supplant its members and cannot manage or supervise them or any other undertaking. It cannot hold shares in its members or in another undertaking unless it is necessary for the achievement of its objects and is done on its members' behalf.   [**X.2**]

2 **Taxation**

a) *Fiscal transparency*

The basis for the tax treatment of an EEIG is set out in Article 40 of the European Council Regulation 2137/85 ('the Regulation') which provides:

> 'The profits or losses resulting from the activities of a grouping shall be taxable only in the hands of its members.'

This concept is known as 'fiscal transparency' and is intended to facilitate multi-national trading co-operation. The principle is, in theory, simple but, in its implementation, will be rather more complicated than at first appears not least because it has been left to the individual Member States to draft the necessary legislation in each country.

The European Community has given only outline indication of the way in which EEIGs are to be taxed. The provisions in Schedule 11 to the United Kingdom 1990 Finance Act seek to give effect to the guidelines set out by the Commission. They are relatively brief whilst trying to legislate in respect of one of the most complicated areas of taxation, namely international partnerships (see TA 1988 s 510 inserted by FA 1990).   [**X.3**]

b) *Taxation of trading and non-trading EEIGs*

A distinction is made in the UK legislation between trading and non-trading EEIGs.

Where an EEIG carries on a trade or profession, the legislation provides that the trade or profession is treated, for the purposes of charging tax in respect of income and gains, as carried on in partnership. This is helpful in that an existing body of law can be applied immediately to the taxation of the trade or profession but this area of law is unfortunately complex. It should be noted, however, that it is only the trade or profession that is treated as carried on in partnership. Thus if an EEIG holds assets which are *not* used for the purposes of the trade or profession, it is presumed that partnership tax treatment would not be applicable in relation to those assets.

The application of the CGT provisions concerning partnerships to EEIGs which are involved in a trading activity means that whenever a member joins or leaves a grouping, and whenever there is a change in asset-sharing (or profit-sharing) ratios, acquisitions and disposals will be treated as occurring. This may prove both expensive and time-consuming although the Inland Revenue has confirmed that they will apply the usual concessions for partnerships which will mitigate some of the worst problems by permitting deferral of tax on some internal changes within a grouping. The Inland Revenue has also said that gains arising on property held by groupings or in relation to groupings themselves may be subject to roll-over relief by a UK member in accordance with the normal rules. This will enable a UK corporate member to roll-over a gain arising on the disposal of property by a grouping into acquisitions made by the companies in the same CGT group. The roll-over position, will, however, be more restrictive for non-residents in accordance with the changes brought in by FA 1989 s 129.

Despite the helpful attitude being taken by the Inland Revenue the taxation of capital gains arising in a grouping is likely to remain a difficult area. There is considerable divergence in the taxation of capital gains internationally and a mixture of reliefs, ranging from reduced rates for long-term gains in some countries, to the ability to roll-over certain types of capital gain in other jurisdictions. For a grouping consisting of members from two or more different EC Member States, there may be difficulty in ensuring that mismatches are not created between different jurisdictions which give rise to potential double taxation.

One of the consequences of the limited nature of the fiscal transparency of an EEIG is that dealings between members of an EEIG and the EEIG itself cannot be disregarded for VAT and stamp duty purposes. It also means that an EEIG will, as is made clear in the Inland Revenue Press Release of 19 April 1990, be responsible for applying UK tax collection procedures, including operating PAYE in respect of its employees and deducting tax as appropriate from certain payments (such as annual payments, interest and royalties).

In the case of a *non-trading EEIG*, the Grouping is treated as the agent of its members for the purposes of charging tax on income or gains. Accordingly, the activities of the EEIG are treated as those of its members acting jointly; as if each member has a share of the Grouping's property rights and liabilities. The extent of the members' shares is determined in accordance with the provisions of the contract under which the EEIG is established. If that contract does not make any such provision, the members' shares will be equal to their share of the profits of the EEIG. If the contract makes no provision as to profit-sharing, all members of the EEIG will be treated as having equal shares.

The effect of the Finance Act provisions is to apply to non-trading EEIGs a tax regime similar to that applying to a non-trading partnership. For example, disposal of assets by the members of the non-trading EEIG will be treated as taking place for tax purposes not only where the EEIG itself disposes of assets but also where persons join or leave an EEIG or when asset-sharing ratios are altered. In the UK, capital gains tax for partnerships is largely governed by Inland Revenue Statement of Practice D12 (see Chapter 29). It is now clear that most of the provisions of this SP will apply in relation to trading or professional EEIGs (which are treated, as mentioned above, as partnerships under the rules) but it is not clear whether it will apply in the case of non-trading or professional EEIGs. The Inland Revenue Press Release of 19 April 1990 states that where no trade or profession is carried on 'the capital gains treatment will not follow that for partnerships' which suggests that it will not be applied.   [**X.4**]

c) *International taxation problems*

Further potential problems may arise because of the interim relationship between the structure of an EEIG and the operation of the OECD Model double tax treaty. As mentioned above, for tax purposes, an EEIG will not be seen as a taxable body but a collection of separate taxable members. Article 4 of the Model Treaty applies to taxable persons or bodies who are 'resident in a contractual State' so that the EEIG will never fall within the scope of the treaty. It was originally thought that this might give rise to significant problems concerning the payment of interest on loans by members of the EEIG or interest on royalty payments to group members.

The Inland Revenue has, however, made its position clear in relation to the treatment of payments made by or to a grouping with a UK member. It has indicated that it would look through the grouping and treat the appropriate part of the payment as made by or to the UK member. In this way, a UK member would be treated as having paid an appropriate part of the annual payments made by the grouping and, therefore, would be entitled to treat it as a charge to income. Tax deducted by the grouping will be considered as tax deducted by the member. Credit will similarly be given for tax withheld on receipts by a grouping as if the member had suffered that withholding.

Whilst the UK Inland Revenue has made its position clear, however, the provisions applying in each Member State will need to be checked in each case.   [**X.5**]

3 Conclusion

The concept of an EEIG is novel and potentially significant. A number of EEIGs have now been formed. Despite some enthusiasm, however, there remains a variety of inherent tax problems which is likely to deter the creation of large numbers of EEIGs despite the intended benefits of simplicity and flexibility. It is to be hoped that further consideration will be given to the taxation consequences both by the EEC itself and by all Member States so that this useful commercial vehicle for promoting cross-border co-operation in the Community does not remain stifled by fiscal problems.   [**X.6**]

Index